S0-AXV-862

nelsonbrain.com

NELSON
brain
.com

Save on textbooks and other resources
by visiting **www.nelsonbrain.com**!

Using SAM with *Principles of Information Systems* Is Easy!

SAM (Skills Assessment Manager) is the premier proficiency-based assessment and training environment for Microsoft® Office. Reliable web-based software, along with an inviting user interface, provides maximum learning flexibility. SAM builds skills and confidence with a variety of real-life simulations, and SAM Projects' assignments prepare students for today's workplace.

When used together, ***Principles of Information Systems*** and **SAM** offer the following, in one easy-to-use, robust platform:

- Hands-on simulations for Access® and Excel® in SAM Exams or Training so that you can learn or brush up on skills you may not feel comfortable with and then take exams to prove mastery of those skills.

- Real-world projects so you can confirm that you know how to truly apply your skills in Access® and Excel® to solve business problems.

Visit **www.cengage.com/samcentral** for more information!

**FIRST
CANADIAN
EDITION**

Principles of Information Systems
A Managerial Approach

Ralph M. Stair
Professor Emeritus, Florida State University

George W. Reynolds
Instructor, Strayer University

Jamison Aldcorn
Professor, Seneca College of Applied Arts and Technology

Derrick J. Neufeld
Associate Professor, University of Western Ontario

NELSON / EDUCATION

NELSON / EDUCATION

Principles of Information Systems: A Managerial Approach, First Canadian Edition

by Ralph M. Stair, George W. Reynolds, Jamison Aldcorn, and Derrick J. Neufeld

Vice President, Editorial Higher Education:
Anne Williams

Acquisitions Editor:
Alwynn Pinard

Executive Marketing Manager:
Dave Ward

Developmental Editor:
Rod Banister

Photo and Permissions Researcher:
Jessie Coffey

Senior Content Production Manager:
Natalia Denesiuk Harris

Production Service:
Integra Software Services Pvt. Ltd.

Copy Editor:
Wendy Thomas

Proofreader:
Integra Software Services Pvt. Ltd.

Indexer:
Integra Software Services Pvt. Ltd.

Manufacturing Manager:
Joanne McNeil

Design Director:
Ken Phipps

Managing Designer:
Franca Amore

Interior Design Modifications:
Peter Papayanakis

Box Images:
Ethical and Societal Issues:
Tatiana Popova/Shutterstock.com;
Information Systems @ Work:
iconspro/Shutterstock.com

Cover Design:
Eugene Lo

Cover Image:
© Masterfile

Compositor:
Integra Software Services Pvt. Ltd

Printer:
RR Donnelley

Copyright © 2012 by Nelson Education Ltd.

Adapted from *Principles of Information Systems,* Tenth Edition, by Ralph M. Stair and George W. Reynolds, published by Course Technology, a part of Cengage Learning. Copyright © 2012 by Course Technology, Cengage Learning.

Printed and bound in the United States of America
1 2 3 4   14 13 12 11

For more information contact Nelson Education Ltd., 1120 Birchmount Road, Toronto, Ontario, M1K 5G4. Or you can visit our Internet site at http://www.nelson.com

Statistics Canada information is used with the permission of Statistics Canada. Users are forbidden to copy this material and/or redisseminate the data, in an original or modified form, for commercial purposes, without the expressed permissions of Statistics Canada. Information on the availability of the wide range of data from Statistics Canada can be obtained from Statistics Canada's Regional Offices, its World Wide Web site at <http://www.statcan.gc.ca>, and its toll-free access number 1-800-263-1136.

ALL RIGHTS RESERVED. No part of this work covered by the copyright herein may be reproduced, transcribed, or used in any form or by any means—graphic, electronic, or mechanical, including photocopying, recording, taping, Web distribution, or information storage and retrieval systems—without the written permission of the publisher.

For permission to use material from this text or product, submit all requests online at www.cengage.com/permissions. Further questions about permissions can be emailed to permissionrequest@cengage.com

Every effort has been made to trace ownership of all copyrighted material and to secure permission from copyright holders. In the event of any question arising as to the use of any material, we will be pleased to make the necessary corrections in future printings.

Library and Archives Canada Cataloguing in Publication Data

Principles of information systems : a managerial approach / Ralph M. Stair ... [et al.]. — 1st Canadian ed.

Includes bibliographical reference and index.
ISBN 978-0-17-650394-9

1. Management information systems. I. Stair, Ralph M.

T58.6.P75 2011   658.4'038
C2011-906153-8

ISBN-13: 978-0-17-650394-9
ISBN-10: 0-17-650394-3

For Lila and Leslie
—RMS

To my grandchildren: Michael, Jacob, Jared, Fievel, Aubrey, Elijah, Abrielle, Sofia, Elliot
—GWR

For Sandra and Alex
—JA

For Colleen, Zanna, and Sydney
—DN

BRIEF CONTENTS

CONTENTS

Chapter 11   Knowledge Management and Specialized Information Systems   440

As organizations continue to operate in an increasingly competitive and global market-place, workers in all business areas, including accounting, customer service, finance, human resources, information systems (IS), logistics, marketing, manufacturing, and research and development, must be well prepared to make the significant contributions required for success. Regardless of your future role, even if you are an entrepreneur, you need to understand what information systems can and cannot do and be able to use them to help you accomplish your work. You will be expected to discover opportunities to use information systems and to participate in the design of solutions to business problems employing information systems. You will be challenged to identify and evaluate information systems options. To be successful, you must be able to view information systems from the perspective of business and organizational needs. For your solutions to be accepted, you must recognize and address their impact on co-workers, customers, suppliers, and other key business partners. For these reasons, a course in information systems is essential for students in today's high-tech world.

Principles of Information Systems, First Canadian Edition, continues the tradition and approach of the American textbook. Our primary objective is to provide the best information systems text and accompanying materials for the first information systems course required of all business students. We want you to learn to use information systems to ensure your personal success in your current or future job and to improve the success of your organization. Through surveys, questionnaires, focus groups, and feedback that we have received from past adopters, as well as others who teach in the field, we have been able to develop the highest-quality set of teaching materials available to help you achieve these goals.

Principles of Information Systems, First Canadian Edition, stands proudly at the beginning of the IS curriculum and remains unchallenged in its position as the only IS principles text offering the basic IS concepts that every business student must learn to be successful. In the past, instructors of the introductory course faced a dilemma. On one hand, experience in business organizations allows students to grasp the complexities underlying important IS concepts. For this reason, many schools delayed presenting these concepts until students completed a large portion of the core business requirements. On the other hand, delaying the presentation of IS concepts until students have matured within the business curriculum often forces the one or two required introductory IS courses to focus only on personal computing software tools and, at best, merely to introduce computer concepts.

This text has been written specifically for the introductory course in the IS curriculum. *Principles of Information Systems,* First Canadian Edition, treats the appropriate computer and IS concepts together with a strong managerial emphasis on meeting business and organizational needs within a Canadian context.

APPROACH OF THE TEXT

Principles of Information Systems, First Canadian Edition, offers the traditional coverage of computer concepts, but it places the material within the context of meeting business and organizational needs within Canada and globally. Placing information system concepts in this context and taking a general management perspective has always set the text apart from general computer books, thus making it appealing not only to management information systems (MIS) majors but also to students from other fields of study. The text isn't overly technical, but deals with the role that information systems play in an organization and the key principles a manager needs to grasp to be successful. These principles of IS are brought together and presented in a way that is both understandable and relevant. In addition, this book offers an overview of the entire IS discipline, while giving students a solid foundation for further study in advanced IS courses such as programming, systems analysis and design, project management, database management, data communications, website and systems development, electronic commerce and mobile commerce applications, and decision support. Thus, it serves the needs of both general business students and those who will become IS professionals.

The overall vision, framework, and pedagogy that made the American editions so popular have been retained in the Canadian edition, offering a number of benefits to students. We continue to present IS concepts with a managerial emphasis. While the fundamental vision of this market-leading text remains unchanged, the first Canadian edition highlights established principles and draws out new ones that have emerged as a result of business, organizational, and technological change.

IS Principles First, Where They Belong

Exposing students to fundamental IS principles is an advantage for students who do not later return to the discipline for advanced courses. Since most functional areas in business rely on information systems, an understanding of IS principles helps students in other course work. In addition, introducing students to the principles of information systems helps future business managers and entrepreneurs employ information systems successfully and avoid mishaps that often result in unfortunate consequences. Furthermore, presenting IS concepts at the introductory level creates interest among general business students who may later choose information systems as a field of concentration.

Author Team

Ralph Stair, George Reynolds, Jamison Aldcorn, and Derrick Neufeld have more than 70 years of academic and industrial experience. Ralph Stair brings years of writing, teaching, and academic experience to this text. He wrote numerous books and a large number of articles while at Florida State University. George Reynolds brings a wealth of computer and industrial experience to the project, with more than 30 years of experience working in government, institutional, and commercial IS organizations. He has written numerous college IS texts and has taught the introductory IS course at the University of Cincinnati, the College of Mount St. Joseph, and Strayer University. Jamison Aldcorn, professor and coordinator of the Bachelor of Commerce degree at Seneca College in Ontario, adapted the textbook for the Canadian market. He has written several textbooks and teaches IS courses at Seneca. Derrick Neufeld, a professor of Information Systems at the Richard Ivey School of Business, is an award-winning researcher with more than 50 articles published in top management journals, conference proceedings, and book chapters. Professor Neufeld teaches in Ivey's HBA, MBA, EMBA, and PhD programs, and he has published many field-based teaching case studies for the classroom over the past 20 years.

The Stair, Reynolds, Aldcorn, and Neufeld team brings a solid conceptual foundation and practical IS experience to students.

GOALS OF THIS TEXT

Because *Principles of Information Systems,* First Canadian Edition, is written for all business majors, we believe it is important not only to present a realistic perspective on IS in business but also to provide students with the skills they can use to be effective business leaders in their organization. To that end, *Principles of Information Systems,* First Canadian Edition, has four main goals:

1. To provide a core of IS principles with which every business student should be familiar
2. To offer a survey of the IS discipline that will enable all business students to understand the relationship of IS courses to their curriculum as a whole
3. To present the changing role of the IS professional
4. To show the value of the discipline as an attractive field of specialization

By achieving these goals, *Principles of Information Systems,* First Canadian Edition, will enable students, regardless of their major, to understand and use fundamental information systems principles so that they can function more efficiently and effectively as workers, managers, decision makers, and organizational leaders.

IS Principles

Principles of Information Systems, First Canadian Edition, although comprehensive, cannot cover every aspect of the rapidly changing IS discipline. The authors, having recognized this, provide students with an essential core of guiding IS principles to use as they face the career challenges ahead. Think of principles as basic truths or rules that remain constant regardless of the situation. As such, they provide strong guidance in the face of tough decisions. A set of IS principles is highlighted at the beginning of each chapter. The application of these principles to solve real-world problems is driven home from the opening vignettes to the end-of-chapter material. The ultimate goal of *Principles of Information Systems* is to develop effective, thinking, action-oriented employees by instilling them with principles to help guide their decision making and actions.

Survey of the IS Discipline

This text not only offers the traditional coverage of computer concepts but also provides a broad framework to impart to students a solid grounding in the business uses of technology. In addition to serving general business students, this book offers an overview of the entire IS discipline and solidly prepares future IS professionals for advanced IS courses and their careers in the rapidly changing IS discipline.

Changing Role of the IS Professional

As business and the IS discipline have changed, so too has the role of the IS professional. Once considered a technical specialist, today the IS professional operates as an internal consultant to all functional areas of the organization, being knowledgeable about their needs and competent in bringing the power of information systems to bear throughout the organization. The IS professional views issues through a global perspective that encompasses the entire organization and the broader industry and business environment in which it operates.

The scope of responsibilities of an IS professional today is not confined to just his or her employer but encompasses the entire interconnected network of employees, suppliers, customers, competitors, regulatory agencies, and other entities, no matter where they are located. This broad scope of responsibilities creates a new challenge: how to help an organization survive in a highly interconnected, highly competitive global environment. In accepting that challenge, the IS professional plays a pivotal role in shaping the business itself and ensuring its success. To survive, businesses must now strive for the highest level of customer satisfaction and loyalty through innovative products and services, competitive prices, and ever-improving product and service quality. The IS professional assumes the critical responsibility of determining the organization's approach to both overall cost and quality performance and therefore plays an important role in the ongoing survival of the organization. This new duality in the role of the IS employee—a professional who exercises a specialist's skills with a generalist's perspective—is reflected throughout the book.

IS as a Field for Further Study

Despite the poor economy and effects of outsourcing, a survey of Human Resources professionals still puts technology and health care as the top fields of study. And business administration and computer science remain among the most sought-after majors by employers. Indeed, the long-term job prospects for skilled and business-savvy information systems professionals is optimistic. Employment of such workers is expected to grow faster than the average for all occupations through the year 2018.

A career in IS can be exciting, challenging, and rewarding! It is important to show the value of the discipline as an appealing field of study and that the IS graduate is no longer a technical recluse. Today, perhaps more than ever before, the IS professional must be able to align IS and organizational goals and to ensure that IS investments are justified from a business perspective. The need to draw bright and interested students into the IS discipline is part of our ongoing responsibility. Upon graduation, IS graduates at many schools are among the highest paid of all business graduates. Throughout this text, the many challenges and opportunities available to IS professionals are highlighted and emphasized.

The first Canadian edition focuses on IS principles and strives to be the most current text on the market. Canadian and multinational company case studies and examples throughout the textbook provide a wealth of practical information for students and instructors.

Overall principle. This book continues to stress a single all-encompassing theme: the right information, if it is delivered to the right person, in the right fashion, and at the right time, can improve and ensure organizational effectiveness and efficiency.

Information systems principles. Information systems principles summarize key concepts that every student should know. These principles are highlighted at the start of each chapter and covered thoroughly in the text.

Global perspective. We stress the global aspects of information systems as a major theme.

Extensive changes and updates in each chapter. The authors worked hard to provide the most current information available in this first Canadian edition. Over 800 new references and examples of Canadian and international organizations using information systems are included in this new textbook.

Learning objectives linked to principles. Carefully crafted learning objectives are included with every chapter. The learning objectives are linked to the Information Systems Principles and reflect what a student should be able to accomplish after completing a chapter.

Opening vignettes emphasize international aspects. All of the chapter-opening vignettes raise actual issues from Canadian, foreign-based, and multinational companies.

Why Learn About? features. Each chapter has a "Why Learn About?" section at the beginning of the chapter to pique student interest. The section sets the stage for students by briefly describing the importance of the chapter's material to the students—whatever their chosen field.

Information Systems @ Work special interest boxes. Each chapter has an "Information Systems @ Work" box that shows how information systems are used in a variety of business career areas.

Ethical and Societal Issues special interest boxes. Each chapter includes an "Ethical and Societal Issues" box that presents a timely look at the ethical challenges and the societal impact of information systems.

Current examples, boxes, cases, and references. We take great pride in presenting the most recent examples, boxes, cases, and references throughout the text. Some of these were developed at the last possible moment, literally weeks before the book went into publication. Information on new hardware and software, the latest operating systems, mobile commerce, the Internet, electronic commerce, ethical and societal issues, and many other current developments can be found throughout the text. Our adopters have come to expect the best and most recent material. We have done everything we can to meet or exceed these expectations.

Summary linked to principles. Each chapter includes a detailed summary, with each section of the summary tied to an associated information systems principle.

Self-assessment tests. This popular feature helps students review and test their understanding of key chapter concepts.

Career exercises. End-of-chapter career exercises ask students to research how a topic discussed in the chapter relates to a business area of their choice. Students are encouraged to use the Internet, the library, or interviews to collect information about business careers.

End-of-chapter cases. Each case explores a chapter concept or problem that a real-world company or organization has faced and provides students with an opportunity to apply the principles covered to real-world problems from actual organizations. The cases can be assigned as individual homework exercises or serve as a basis for class discussion.

Ivey School of Business Case Studies. Four end-of-chapter cases and two integrative cases at the end of Parts 3 and 4 are included in the textbook. These cases enable students to apply the IS skills they have learned to well-known Canadian companies such as Royal Bank, Open Text Corporation, and the Canadian Automobile Association.

Integrated, comprehensive Web case. The Altitude Online case provides an integrated and comprehensive case that runs parallel to the text. Discussion questions and critical thinking questions for the Web case are found at the end of each chapter of the text. The case follows the activities of two individuals employed at the fictitious Altitude Online consulting firm as they are challenged to complete various IS-related projects. Discussion Questions and Critical Thinking Questions for the Web case are found at the end of each chapter of the text. The cases provide a realistic fictional work environment in which students may imagine themselves in the role of systems analyst. Information systems problems are addressed using the state-of-the-art techniques discussed in the chapters.

STUDENT RESOURCES

CourseMate

The more you study, the better the results. Make the most of your study time by accessing everything you need to succeed in one place. Read your textbook, make notes, review flashcards, and take practice quizzes—online with CourseMate. Adapted by Ashraf Hashmi of Mohawk College, CourseMate for *Principles of Information Systems,* First Canadian Edition, includes the following:

- An interactive eBook with highlighting, note taking, and an interactive glossary

- Interactive learning tools, including the following:

  - **PowerPoint® Slides:** The book's PowerPoint® presentations cover the key points from each chapter. Adapted by Norman Shaw of Ryerson University, these presentations are a useful study tool.

  - **Classic Cases:** A frequent request from adopters is that they'd like a broader selection of cases to choose from. To meet this need, a set of over 200 cases from the various American editions of the text are included here. These are the authors' choices of the "best cases" from these editions and span a broad range of companies and industries.

  - **Links to Useful Websites:** Chapters in *Principles of Information Systems,* First Canadian Edition, reference many interesting websites. Links in this resource take you directly to the home pages of those sites so that you can explore them. There are additional links to websites that the authors think you would be interested in checking out.

  - **Hands-On Activities:** Use these hands-on activities to test your comprehension of IS topics and enhance your skills using Microsoft® Office applications and the Internet. Using these links, you can access three critical-thinking exercises per chapter. Each activity asks you to work with an Office tool or do some research on the Internet.

- **Quizzes:** This tool allows you to access multiple-choice questions for each chapter; test yourself and then submit your answers. You will immediately find out what questions you got right and what you got wrong. For each question that you answer incorrectly, you are given the correct answer and the page in your text where that information is covered.

- **Glossary of Key Terms:** The glossary of key terms from the text is available to search.

- **Online Readings:** This feature provides you with access to a computer database that contains articles relating to hot topics in Information Systems.

Access CourseMate for *Principles of Information Systems,* First Canadian Edition, at www.NelsonBrain.com.

INSTRUCTOR RESOURCES

The teaching tools that accompany this text offer many options for enhancing a course. And, as always, we are committed to providing one of the best teaching resource packages available in this market.

About NETA

The **Nelson Education Teaching Advantage (NETA)** program delivers research-based instructor resources that promote student engagement and higher-order thinking to enable the success of Canadian students and educators.

Instructors today face many challenges. Resources are limited, time is scarce, and a new kind of student has emerged: one who is juggling school with work, has gaps in his or her basic knowledge, and is immersed in technology in a way that has led to a completely new style of learning. In response, Nelson Education has gathered a group of dedicated instructors to advise us on the creation of richer and more flexible ancillaries that respond to the needs of today's teaching environments. In consultation with the editorial advisory board, Nelson Education has completely rethought the structure, approaches, and formats of our key textbook ancillaries. We've also increased our investment in editorial support for our ancillary authors. The result is the Nelson Education Teaching Advantage.

One of NETA's key components is *NETA Assessment.* It relates to testing materials: not just Nelson's Test Banks and Computerized Test Banks, but also in-text self-tests, Study Guides and web quizzes, and homework programs like CNOW. Under *NETA Assessment,* Nelson's authors create multiple-choice questions that reflect research-based best practices for constructing effective questions and testing not just recall but also higher-order thinking. Our guidelines were developed by David DiBattista, a 3M National Teaching Fellow whose recent research as a professor of psychology at Brock University has focused on multiple-choice testing. All Test Bank authors receive training at workshops conducted by Prof. DiBattista, as do the copyeditors assigned to each Test Bank. A copy of *Multiple Choice Tests: Getting Beyond Remembering,* Prof. DiBattista's guide to writing effective tests, is included the Nelson Test Bank/Computerized Test Bank package for *Principles of Information Systems,* First Canadian Edition. The Test Bank for *Principles of Information Systems* was prepared under the NETA program (see below under Instructor's Resource CD for more information).

Instructor's Resource CD

Key instructor ancillaries are provided on the *Instructor's Resource CD* (ISBN 978-0-17-662762-1), giving instructors the ultimate tool for customizing lectures and presentations. The IRCD includes

- **NETA Assessment—Test Bank and Computerized Test Bank**: The Test Bank has been adapted by Claude Sam-Foh of Ryerson University. It includes over 300 multiple-choice questions written according to NETA guidelines for effective construction and development of higher-order questions. Also included are true/false, completion, and essay questions. Test Bank files are provided in Word format for easy editing and in PDF format for convenient printing, whatever your system.

    The Computerized Test Bank by ExamView® includes all the questions from the Test Bank. The easy-to-use ExamView® software is compatible with Microsoft Windows and Mac. ExamView® is a powerful objective-based test generator that enables instructors to create paper-, LAN-, or Web-based tests from test banks designed specifically for their Nelson Education texts. Instructors can utilize the ultra-efficient Test Wizard to create tests in less than five minutes by drawing from Nelson Education's question banks or customizing their own exams from scratch. Page references for all Nelson-developed questions are provided so you can cross-reference test results with the book. Tests can be exported to WebCT, Blackboard, and other formats.

- **Instructor's Manual**: The First Canadian Edition Instructor's Manual, adapted by Frank Fusca of Humber College, provides valuable chapter overviews; highlights key principles and learning objectives; and also provides teaching tips, quick quizzes, class discussion topics, additional projects and resources, and key terms. As always, we are committed to providing the best teaching resource packages available in this market.

- **Solutions**: Solutions to all end-of-chapter material are provided in a separate document for your convenience and were prepared by Canadian co-author Jamison Aldcorn of Seneca College.

- **PowerPoint® Presentations**: A set of impressive Microsoft® PowerPoint® slides, adapted by Norman Shaw of Ryerson University, is available for each chapter. These slides are included to serve as a teaching aid for classroom presentation, to make available to students on the network for chapter review, or to be printed for classroom distribution. Our presentations help students focus on the main topics of each chapter, take better notes, and prepare for examinations. Instructors can also add their own slides for additional topics they introduce to the class.

- **Figure Files**: Figure files in jpeg format allow instructors to create their own presentations using figures taken directly from the text.

CourseMate

Cengage Learning's CourseMate for *Principles of Information Systems,* First Canadian Edition, brings course concepts to life with interactive learning, study, and exam preparation tools that support the printed textbook. Watch student comprehension soar as your class works with the printed textbook and the textbook-specific website. CourseMate goes beyond the book to deliver what you need! Learn more at **www.stair1ce.nelson.com**.

- **Engagement Tracker**
    How do you assess your students' engagement in your course? How do you know your students have read the material or viewed the resources you've assigned? How can you tell if your students are struggling with a concept? With CourseMate, you can use the included Engagement Tracker to assess student preparation and

engagement. Use the tracking tools to see progress for the class as a whole or for individual students. Identify students at risk early in the course. Uncover which concepts are most difficult for your class. Monitor time on task. Keep your students engaged.

- **Interactive Teaching and Learning Tools**
  CourseMate includes interactive teaching and learning tools:

  - Quizzes

  - Flashcards

  - PowerPoint presentations

  - and more

  These assets enable students to review for tests and prepare for class, and address the needs of students' varied learning styles.

- **Interactive eBook**
  In addition to interactive teaching and learning tools, CourseMate includes an interactive eBook. Students can take notes, highlight, search, and interact with embedded media specific to their book. Use it as a supplement to the printed text, or as a substitute—the choice is your students' with CourseMate.

ACKNOWLEDGMENTS

A book of this scope and undertaking requires a strong team effort. We would like to thank all of our fellow teammates at Nelson Education for their dedication and hard work. Our appreciation goes out to all the many people who worked behind the scenes to bring this effort to fruition, including Jessie Coffey, our photo researcher. We would like to acknowledge and thank Rod Banister, our developmental editor, who deserves special recognition for his tireless effort and help in all stages of this project. Thanks also to Natalia Denesiuk Harris, our Sr. Content Project Manager, who shepherded the book through the production process.

We appreciate the feedback and suggestions of the reviewers of both the American Edition and manuscript for the First Canadian Edition who helped guide the direction of this textbook:

Edmund Baumann, Humber College
Fred Douglas, Sheridan College
Marina Erechtchoukova, York University
Al Ersser, Mohawk College
Frank Fusca, Humber College
Franca Giacomelli, Humber College
Debbie A. Gorval, Kwantlen Polytechnic University
Ashraf Hashmi, Mohawk College
Dennis Kira, Concordia University
Bharat Maheshwari, University of Windsor
Shauna Roch, Fanshawe College
Claude Sam-Foh, Ryerson University
Ibrahim Sumrain, Grant McEwan University
John H. Walker, Brock University

We are grateful to the sales force at Nelson Education whose efforts make this all possible. You helped to get valuable feedback from current and potential textbook adopters.

Ralph Stair would like to thank the Department of Management and its faculty members in the College of Business Administration at Florida State University for their support. He would also like to thank his family, Lila and Leslie, for their support. George Reynolds would like to thank his wife, Ginnie, for her patience and support in this major project. Jamison Aldcorn would like to thank his wife, Sandra, for her support and encouragement. Derrick Neufeld is grateful to the staff of Ivey Publishing at the Richard Ivey School of Business for their excellent assistance, and ever thankful for his wife and partner, Colleen.

To Previous American Textbook Adopters and Potential New Users

We sincerely appreciate our loyal adopters of the previous American editions and welcome new users of *Principles of Information Systems,* First Canadian Edition. We truly value your needs and feedback. We hope the First Canadian Edition continues to meet your high expectations.

OUR COMMITMENT

We are committed to listening to our adopters and readers and to developing creative solutions to meet their needs. The field of IS continually evolves, and we strongly encourage your participation in helping us provide the freshest, most relevant information possible.

We welcome your input and feedback. If you have any questions or comments regarding *Principles of Information Systems,* First Canadian Edition, please contact us through Nelson Education Ltd. or your local representative.

Jamison Aldcorn
Derrick Neufeld
July 2011

Information Systems in Organizations and Society

(Source: iDesign/Shutterstock.com)

CHAPTER · 1 ·

Introduction to Information Systems

(Source: iDesign/Shutterstock.com)

PRINCIPLES	LEARNING OBJECTIVES
▪ The value of information is directly linked to how it helps decision makers achieve the organization's goals.	▪ Discuss why it is important to study and understand information systems. ▪ Distinguish data from information and describe the characteristics used to evaluate the quality of data.
▪ Computers and information systems help make it possible for organizations to improve the way they conduct business. The use of information systems to add value to the organization is strongly influenced by organizational structure, culture, and change.	▪ Name the components of a computer-based information system and describe several system characteristics and benefits. ▪ Discuss how organizational structure, culture, and change affect the type of information systems that the organization implements. ▪ Identify the major steps of the systems development process and state the goal of each.
▪ Because information systems are so important, businesses need to be sure that improvements or completely new systems help lower costs, increase profits, improve service, or achieve a competitive advantage.	▪ Define the term "competitive advantage" and identify the factors that lead firms to seek competitive advantage. ▪ Discuss strategic planning for competitive advantage. ▪ Describe how the performance of an information system can be measured.
▪ Information systems must be applied thoughtfully and carefully so that society, businesses, and industries can reap their enormous benefits.	▪ Describe some of the threats that information systems and the Internet can pose to security and privacy. ▪ Discuss the expanding role and benefits of information systems in business and industry.

Information Systems in the Global Economy ⟩
Marriott International Inc.

The Power of Information and a Strong Corporate Culture

You've probably heard that "information is power." In fact, the power of information depends on how it serves a specific need at a certain time. Information is most powerful when it enables strategic decision making. It must be delivered to the right person at the right time with as little effort as possible. For businesses, correctly managing strategic information can mean the difference between success and failure. Consequently, today's businesses invest a large percentage of their budgets in systems designed to deliver the right information to the right people at the right time. Such is the case for Marriott International Inc.

Marriott International is a global corporation with a rich culture that dates back to 1927. At that time, a missionary named J. Willard Marriott decided to open a root beer stand so that people could find a reprieve from the sweltering summers. That small root beer stand grew into a chain of restaurants and hotels, which today totals over 3,200 properties operating under 19 brands in 67 countries.

J. Willard passed the business on to his son J. W. Marriott, Jr., who has since worked to maintain the corporate culture that his father created. In 1997, J. W. Marriott published a book titled *The Spirit to Serve*, which is required reading for Marriott new hires and emphasizes the tenets of the "Marriott way." Topics in the book range from corporate history and mission to procedures for the best ways to do everything necessary to run a hotel, including the famous 66-step process for cleaning a hotel room. A copy of *The Spirit to Serve* is such a strong part of Marriott culture that it is placed in every Marriott room.

Marriott's executive vice president and chief information officer (CIO), Carl Wilson, is also big on principles, policies, and procedures. In 1997, he published a document titled "Information Resources Operating Values," which provides principles that guide all corporate information systems (IS) decision making. They include "Never be satisfied with the way things are today; continue to improve them to make them better," "Even in the good times, you ought to behave like you're in the bad times," and "Stop doing things that aren't adding value." The document is given to every employee in a format suitable for framing. You'll find it mounted on most Marriott office walls. Wilson believes that policies and procedures free up managers to be creative and resourceful.

Continuous improvement is a tenet that drives IS development in most companies. Each new development effort seeks to improve old systems by designing more effective ways to meet an organization's overarching goals. As competition has become fiercer and the economy more challenging, information systems specialists are under pressure to be frugal and design systems that provide value to the company. In many companies, only projects that can guarantee a return on investment (ROI) are considered for financing. Recently Marriott took on an ambitious systems development project that not only assisted the corporation in meeting its mission but also provided an impressive ROI.

Part of Marriott's philosophy is to make every customer interaction meaningful. In order to do so, Marriott must better understand its customers' needs so that they can be better served. To maximize its customer relations, Marriott first needed to track all interactions between its customers and employees at its properties. Combined, the records of these interactions could reveal detailed customer habits, interests, and experiences. Unfortunately, the size of Marriott's business and the diversity of its brands around the world made it difficult to integrate customer records. Each Marriott brand, such as Courtyard, Fairfield, Residence Inn, Ritz-Carlton, BVLGARI, and Renaissance, maintains its own information systems and databases. Marriott properties around the world also deal in different languages and currencies, further complicating the integration of information.

To address the problem, a cross-functional team was established that included marketing leaders, brand leaders, and information systems specialists. The team began by defining its marketing goals. It established exactly what Marriott experiences were to be shared across all Marriott brands and regions, such as the reservation process, promotional campaigns, and customer service. Once established, the group precisely defined what information it needed to acquire about customers to improve and standardize those experiences. Database administrators designed a database to collect and combine data from all Marriott properties into one large database called a data warehouse. Network administrators developed systems to draw data from corporate databases around the world on a regular schedule. Information systems specialists designed software to mine the data for useful information that could be accessed through online reports. All of this work was directed by Marriott's CIO, Carl Wilson.

The resulting system provides a keen awareness of the histories and interactions of customers across all Marriott properties and brands. Marriott's marketing department uses statistical models to present special deals to customers based on their unique interests and travel habits. For example, Marriott used its new data warehouse and systems in a marketing campaign that sent out 2.9 million unique e-mail messages with offers targeting each recipient. The campaign exceeded its revenue goals by 35 percent. Additionally, Web-based self-service tools helped to reduce campaign development time from six weeks to just two days.

Overall, the data integration project is considered a huge success. Marriott provides customers with offers that are better tailored to their needs; customers appreciate getting fewer, but more meaningful, offers. The success of the project can be measured in ROI by calculating the value of the reduced amount of effort required by employees, and the higher level of business provided by marketing efforts, and dividing that by the amount invested in the new system. Besides producing a significant ROI, the project is also successful because customers are better served, which is Marriott's primary mission. This information systems development project provides Marriott with a competitive advantage over others in the industry who have not taken the effort to better understand their customers.

As you read this chapter, consider the following:

- How can information systems support the mission of a corporation like Marriott and assist it in gaining a competitive advantage?
- How does a company's culture affect the development and acceptance of new information systems?
- Why is communication among information system personnel and business managers across the organizational structure important to the design and implementation of new information systems?

Why Learn About Information Systems in Organizations?

Information systems are used in almost every imaginable profession and company. Entrepreneurs and small business owners use information systems to reach customers around the world. Sales representatives use information systems to advertise products, communicate with customers, and analyze sales trends. Managers use them to make multimillion-dollar decisions, such as whether to build a manufacturing plant or research a cancer drug. Organizations of all types use information systems to cut costs and increase profits. After graduating, a management major might be hired by a shipping company to help design a computerized system to improve employee productivity. A marketing major might work for a national retailer analyzing customer needs in different areas of the country. An accounting major might work for an accounting or consulting firm using an information system to audit other companies' financial records. A real estate major might use the Internet and work in an organizational structure with clients, builders, and a legal team located around the world. A biochemist might conduct research for a drug company and use a computer to evaluate the potential of a new cancer treatment. An entrepreneur might use information systems to advertise and sell products and bill customers.

Although your career might be different from your classmates', you will almost certainly work with computers and information systems to help you and your company or organization become more efficient, effective, productive, and competitive in its industry. In this chapter, you will see how information systems can help organizations produce higher-quality products and increase their return on investment. We begin by investigating organizations and information systems.

People and organizations use information every day. The components that are used are often called an information system. An **information system (IS)** is a set of interrelated components that collect, manipulate, store, and disseminate data and information and provide a feedback mechanism to meet an objective.[1] It is the feedback mechanism that helps organizations achieve their goals, such as increasing profits or improving customer service.[2] This book emphasizes the benefits of an information system, including speed, accuracy, increased revenues, and reduced costs.

We interact with information systems every day, both personally and professionally. We use automated teller machines at banks, access information over the Internet, select information from kiosks with touch screens, and scan the bar codes on our purchases at self-checkout lanes. Major *Fortune 500* companies can spend more than $1 billion per year on information systems. Knowing the potential of information systems and putting this knowledge to work can help individuals enjoy a successful career and help organizations reach their goals.

information system (IS)
A set of interrelated components that collect, manipulate, store, and disseminate data and information and provide a feedback mechanism to meet an objective.

Information systems are everywhere. An air traveller checks in for a flight using a kiosk, which sends the check-in information to a network to verify the traveller's reservation and flight information. The kiosk's system processes the information and prints a boarding pass, speeding airport check-in times.

(Source: Courtesy of Air Canada.)

Today we live in an information economy.[3] Information itself has value, and commerce often involves the exchange of information rather than tangible goods. Systems based on computers are increasingly being used to create, store, and transfer information. Using information systems, investors make multimillion-dollar decisions, financial institutions transfer billions of dollars around the world electronically, and manufacturers order supplies and distribute goods faster than ever before. Computers and information systems will continue to change businesses and the way we live. To prepare for these innovations, you need to be familiar with fundamental information concepts.

INFORMATION CONCEPTS

Information is a central concept of this book. The term is used in the title of the book, in this section, and in almost every chapter. To be an effective manager in any area of business, you need to understand that information is one of an organization's most valuable resources. This term, however, is often confused with *data*.

Data, Information, and Knowledge

data
Raw facts, such as an employee number, total hours worked in a week, inventory part numbers, or sales orders.

information
A collection of facts organized and processed so that they have additional value beyond the value of the individual facts.

Data consists of raw facts, such as an employee number, total hours worked in a week, inventory part numbers, or sales orders. As shown in Table 1.1, several types of data can represent these facts. When facts are arranged in a meaningful manner, they become information. **Information** is a collection of facts organized and processed so that they have additional value beyond the value of the individual facts. For example, sales managers might find that knowing the total monthly sales suits their purpose more (i.e., is more valuable) than knowing the number of sales for each sales representative. Providing information to customers can also help companies increase revenues and profits. FedEx, a worldwide leader in shipping packages and products around the world, believes that information about a package can be as important as the package itself for many of its customers.[4] Information generated by FedEx and other organizations is being placed on the Internet more now than ever.

Table 1.1

Types of Data

Data	Represented by
Alphanumeric data	Numbers, letters, and other characters
Image data	Graphic images and pictures
Audio data	Sound, noise, or tones
Video data	Moving images or pictures

Data represents real-world things. Hospitals, physicians' offices, and pharmacies, for example, maintain patient medical data, which represents actual patients with specific health situations. In many cases, these health-care providers are converting data to electronic form. Some have developed electronic records management (ERM) systems to store, organize, and control important data. However, data—raw facts—has little value beyond its existence. The Canadian government, for example, has provided $500 million to Canada Health Infoway to encourage the greater use of electronic health records and to help health-care providers develop medical records programs to store and use the vast amount of medical data that is generated each year.[5] Medical records systems can be used to generate critical health-related information, which in turn can save money and lives.

Here is another example of the difference between data and information. Consider data as pieces of railroad track in a model railroad kit. Each piece of track has limited inherent value as a single object. However, if you define a relationship among the pieces of the track, they gain value. By arranging the pieces in a certain way, a railroad layout begins to emerge (see Figure 1.1a). Data and information work the same way. Rules and relationships can be set up to organize data into useful, valuable information.

Figure 1.1

Defining and Organizing Relationships Among Data Creates Information

(a)

(b)

The type of information created depends on the relationships defined among existing data. For example, you could rearrange the pieces of track to form different layouts. Adding new or different data means you can redefine relationships and create new information. For instance, adding new pieces to the track can greatly increase the value—in this case, variety and fun—of the final product. You can now create a more elaborate railroad layout (see Figure 1.1b). Likewise, a sales manager could add specific product data to sales data to create monthly sales information organized by product line. The manager could use this information to determine which product lines are the most popular and profitable.

Turning data into information is a **process**, or a set of logically related tasks performed to achieve a defined outcome. The process of defining relationships among data to create useful information requires knowledge. **Knowledge** is the awareness and understanding of a set of information and the ways that information can be made useful to support a specific task or reach a decision. Having knowledge means understanding relationships in information. Part of the knowledge you need to build a railroad layout, for instance, is the understanding of how much space you have for the layout, how many trains will run on the track, and how fast they will travel. Selecting or rejecting facts according to their relevancy to particular tasks is based on the knowledge used in the process of converting data into information. Therefore, you can also think of information as data made more useful through the application of knowledge. *Knowledge workers (KWs)* are people who create, use, and disseminate knowledge and are usually professionals in science, engineering, business, and other areas.[6] A *knowledge management system (KMS)* is an organized collection of people, procedures, software, databases, and devices used to create, store, and use the organization's knowledge and experience.[7] Research has shown that the success of a KMS is linked to how easy it is to use and how satisfied users are with it.[8]

In some cases, people organize or process data mentally or manually. In other cases, they use a computer. Where the data comes from or how it is processed is less important than whether the data is transformed into results that are useful and valuable. This transformation process is shown in Figure 1.2.

process
A set of logically related tasks performed to achieve a defined outcome.

knowledge
The awareness and understanding of a set of information and ways that information can be made useful to support a specific task or reach a decision.

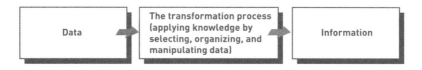

Figure 1.2

The Process of Transforming Data into Information

The Characteristics of Valuable Information

To be valuable to managers and decision makers, information should have the characteristics described in Table 1.2. These characteristics make the information more valuable to an organization. Many shipping companies, for example, can determine the exact location of inventory items and packages in their systems, and this information makes them responsive to their customers. In contrast, if an organization's information is not accurate or complete, people can make poor decisions, costing thousands or even millions of dollars. If information is not relevant, is not delivered to decision makers in a timely fashion, or is too complex to understand, it can be of little value to the organization.

Depending on the type of data you need, some of these attributes are more important than others. For example, with market-intelligence data, some inaccuracy and incompleteness is acceptable, but timeliness is essential. Infinium, a Toronto-based stock-trading company, requires the most timely market information possible so it can place profitable trades.[9] Infinium uses an approach called high-frequency trading, which requires powerful and very fast computers to make its trades. On some days, Infinium is often one of the largest traders, measured by volume of shares, of major companies listed on the Toronto Stock Exchange. Similarly, market intelligence might alert you that competitors are about to make

Characteristics	Definitions
Accessible	Information should be easily accessible by authorized users so they can obtain it in the right format and at the right time to meet their needs.
Accurate	Accurate information is error free. In some cases, inaccurate information is generated because inaccurate data is fed into the transformation process. This is commonly called garbage in, garbage out (GIGO).
Complete	Complete information contains all the important facts. For example, an investment report that does not include all important costs is not complete.
Economical	Information should also be relatively economical to produce. Decision makers must always balance the value of information with the cost of producing it.
Flexible	Flexible information can be used for a variety of purposes. For example, information on how much inventory is on hand for a particular part can be used by a sales representative in closing a sale, by a production manager to determine whether more inventory is needed, and by a financial executive to determine the total value the company has invested in inventory.
Relevant	Relevant information is important to the decision maker. Information showing that lumber prices might drop might not be relevant to a computer chip manufacturer.
Reliable	Reliable information can be trusted by users. In many cases, the reliability of the information depends on the reliability of the data-collection method. In other instances, reliability depends on the source of the information. A rumour from an unknown source that oil prices might go up might not be reliable.
Secure	Information should be secure from access by unauthorized users.
Simple	Information should be simple, not complex. Sophisticated and detailed information might not be needed. In fact, too much information can cause information overload, whereby a decision maker has too much information and is unable to determine what is really important.
Timely	Timely information is delivered when it is needed. Knowing last week's weather conditions will not help when trying to decide what coat to wear today.
Verifiable	Information should be verifiable. This means that you can check it to make sure it is correct, perhaps by checking many sources for the same information.

Table 1.2

Characteristics of Valuable
Information

a major price cut. The exact details and timing of the price cut might not be as important as being warned far enough in advance to plan how to react. On the other hand, accuracy, verifiability, and completeness are critical for data used in accounting to manage company assets such as cash, inventory, and equipment.

The Value of Information

The value of information is directly linked to how it helps decision makers achieve their organization's goals. Valuable information can help people in their organizations perform tasks more efficiently and effectively. Consider a market forecast that predicts a high demand for a new product. If you use this information to develop the new product and your company makes an additional profit of $10,000, the value of this information to the company is $10,000 minus the cost of the information. Valuable information can also help managers decide whether to invest in additional information systems and technology. A new computerized ordering system might cost $30,000 but generate an additional $50,000 in sales. The *value added* by the new system is the additional revenue from the increased sales of $20,000. Most corporations have cost reduction as a primary goal. Using information systems, some manufacturing companies have slashed inventory costs by millions of dollars. Other companies have increased inventory levels to increase profits. Walmart, for example, uses information about certain regions of the country and specific situations to increase needed inventory levels of certain products and improve overall profitability. In other cases, the value of information can be realized in cost savings.

SYSTEM CONCEPTS

Like information, another central concept of this book is that of a system. A **system** is a set of elements or components that interact to accomplish goals. The elements themselves and the relationships among them determine how the system works. Systems have inputs, processing mechanisms, outputs, and feedback (see Figure 1.3). For example, consider an automatic car wash. Tangible *inputs* for the process are a dirty car, water, and various cleaning ingredients. Time, energy, skill, and knowledge also serve as inputs to the system because they are needed to operate it. Skill is the ability to successfully operate the liquid sprayer, foaming brush, and air dryer devices. Knowledge is used to define the steps in the car wash operation and the order in which the steps are executed.

system
A set of elements or components that interact to accomplish goals.

Figure 1.3

Components of a System

A system's four components consist of input, processing, output, and feedback.

Input ⟶ Processing ⟶ Output

Feedback

The *processing mechanisms* consist of first selecting which cleaning option you want (wash only, wash with wax, wash with wax and hand dry, etc.) and communicating that to the operator of the car wash. A *feedback mechanism* is your assessment of how clean the car is. Liquid sprayers shoot clear water, liquid soap, or car wax depending on where your car is in the process and which options you selected. The *output* is a clean car. As in all systems, independent elements or components (the liquid sprayer, foaming brush, and air dryer) interact to create a clean car.

System Performance and Standards

System performance can be measured in various ways. **Efficiency** is a measure of what is produced divided by what is consumed. It can range from 0 to 100 percent. For example, the efficiency of a motor is the energy produced (in terms of work done) divided by the energy consumed (in terms of electricity or fuel). Some motors have an efficiency of 50 percent or less because of the energy lost to friction and heat generation.

Efficiency is a relative term used to compare systems. For example, a hybrid gasoline engine for an automobile or truck can be more efficient than a traditional gasoline engine because, for the equivalent amount of fuel consumed, the hybrid engine travels more miles and gets better gas mileage. Many organizations can reduce their energy usage by investing in more energy-efficient computer systems.[10]

Effectiveness is a measure of the extent to which a system achieves its goals. It can be computed by dividing the goals actually achieved by the total of the stated goals. For example, a company might want to achieve a net profit of $100 million for the year using a new information system. Actual profits, however, might only be $85 million for the year. In this case, the effectiveness is 85 percent (85/100 = 85%). Of course, companies measure

efficiency
A measure of what is produced divided by what is consumed.

effectiveness
A measure of the extent to which a system achieves its goals; it can be computed by dividing the goals actually achieved by the total of the stated goals.

effectiveness using different measures. According to the chief information officer (CIO) of Wipro, a large consulting and outsourcing company, "An important metric for us is when our people … deliver an improved bottom line. When there's a reduction in people travelling for collaborating on projects, that's an important measure of effectiveness."[11]

system performance standard
A specific objective of the system.

Evaluating system performance also calls for using performance standards. A **system performance standard** is a specific objective of the system. For example, a system performance standard for a marketing campaign might be to have each sales representative sell $100,000 of a certain type of product each year (see Figure 1.4a). A system performance standard for a manufacturing process might be to provide no more than 1 percent defective parts (see Figure 1.4b). After standards are established, system performance is measured and compared with the standard. Variances from the standard are determinants of system performance.

Figure 1.4

System Performance Standards

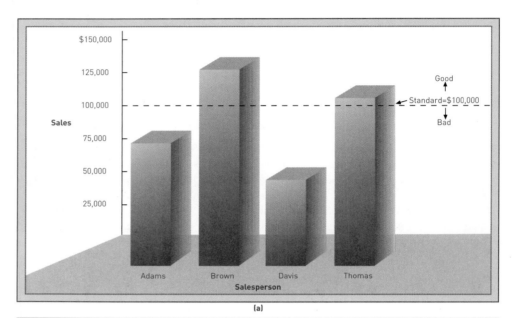

(a)

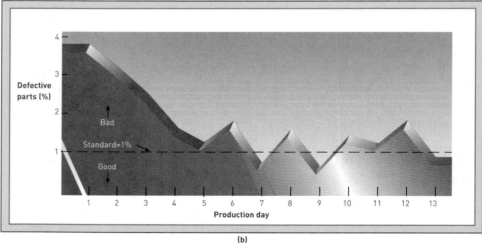

(b)

WHAT IS AN INFORMATION SYSTEM?

As mentioned previously, an information system (IS) is a set of interrelated elements or components that collect (input), manipulate (process), store, and disseminate (output) data and information, and provide a corrective reaction (feedback mechanism) to meet an objective (see Figure 1.5). The feedback mechanism is the component that helps organizations achieve their goals, such as increasing profits or improving customer service.

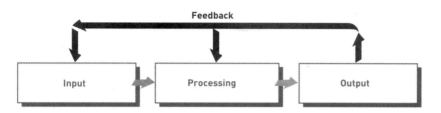

Figure 1.5

The Components of an Information System

Feedback is critical to the successful operation of a system.

Input, Processing, Output, Feedback

Input
In information systems, **input** is the activity of gathering and capturing raw data. In producing paycheques, for example, the number of hours every employee works must be collected before paycheques can be calculated or printed. In a university grading system, instructors must submit student grades before a summary of grades can be compiled and sent to students.

input
The activity of gathering and capturing raw data.

Processing
In information systems, **processing** means converting or transforming data into useful outputs. Processing can involve making calculations, comparing data and taking alternative actions, and storing data for future use.

processing
Converting or transforming data into useful outputs.

Processing can be done manually or with computer assistance. In a payroll application, the number of hours each employee worked must be converted into net, or take-home, pay. Other inputs often include employee ID number and department. The processing can first involve multiplying the number of hours worked by the employee's hourly pay rate to get gross pay. If weekly hours worked exceed 40, overtime pay might also be included. Then deductions—for example, federal and provincial taxes, contributions to insurance or savings plans—are subtracted from gross pay to get net pay.

After these calculations and comparisons are performed, the results are typically stored. *Storage* involves keeping data and information available for future use, including output, discussed next.

Output
In information systems, **output** involves producing useful information, usually in the form of documents and reports. Outputs can include paycheques for employees, reports for managers, and information supplied to stockholders, banks, government agencies, and other groups. In some cases, output from one system can become input for another. For example, output from a system that processes sales orders can be used as input to a customer billing system.

output
Production of useful information, usually in the form of documents and reports.

Feedback
In information systems, **feedback** is information from the system that is used to make changes to input or processing activities. For example, errors or problems might make it necessary to correct input data or change a process. Consider a payroll example. Perhaps the number of hours an employee worked was entered as 400 instead of 40. Fortunately, most information systems check to make sure that data falls within certain ranges. For number of hours worked, the range might be from 0 to 100 because it is unlikely that an employee would work more than 100 hours in a week. The information system would determine that 400 hours is out of range and provide feedback. The feedback is used to check and correct the input on the number of hours worked to 40. If undetected, this error would result in a very high net pay!

feedback
Output that is used to make changes to input or processing activities.

Feedback is also important for managers and decision makers. For example, a furniture maker could use a computerized feedback system to link its suppliers and plants. The output from an information system might indicate that inventory levels for mahogany and oak are getting low—a potential problem. A manager could use this feedback to decide to order more wood. These new inventory orders then become input to the system. In addition to this reactive approach, a computer system can also be proactive—predicting future events to avoid problems. This concept, often called **forecasting**, can be used to estimate future sales and order more inventory before a shortage occurs. Forecasting is also used to predict the strength and landfall sites of hurricanes, future stock market values, and who will win a political election. Disappointed with existing weather forecasting systems, Robert Baron developed a more sophisticated forecasting approach that used radar data along with other meteorological data to forecast storms and weather. Today, his weather forecasting software generates about $25 million in annual revenues.[12]

forecasting
Predicting future events to avoid problems.

Forecasting systems can help meteorologists predict the strength and landfall sites of tropical storms.

(Source: AP Photo/Bullit Marquez.)

Manual and Computerized Information Systems

As discussed earlier, an information system can be manual or computerized. For example, some investment analysts manually draw charts and trend lines to assist them in making investment decisions. Tracking data on stock prices (input) over the last few months or years, these analysts develop patterns on graph paper (processing) that help them determine what stock prices are likely to do in the next few days or weeks (output). Some investors have made millions of dollars using manual stock analysis information systems. Of course, today many excellent computerized information systems follow stock indexes and markets and suggest when large blocks of stocks should be purchased or sold (called "program trading") to take advantage of market discrepancies.

Computer-Based Information Systems

computer-based information system (CBIS)
A single set of hardware, software, databases, telecommunications, people, and procedures that are configured to collect, manipulate, store, and process data into information.

A **computer-based information system (CBIS)** is a single set of hardware, software, databases, telecommunications, people, and procedures that are configured to collect, manipulate, store, and process data into information. Lloyd's Insurance in London used a CBIS to reduce paper transactions and convert to an electronic insurance system. The CBIS allows Lloyd's to insure people and property more efficiently and effectively. Lloyd's often insures the unusual, including actress Betty Grable's legs, Rolling Stone Keith Richard's hands, and a possible appearance of the Loch Ness Monster (Nessie) in Scotland, which would result in a large payment for the person first seeing the monster.

technology infrastructure
All the hardware, software, databases, telecommunications, people, and procedures that are configured to collect, manipulate, store, and process data into information.

The components of a CBIS are illustrated in Figure 1.6. "Information technology (IT)" refers to hardware, software, databases, and telecommunications. A business's **technology infrastructure** includes all the hardware, software, databases, telecommunications, people, and procedures that are configured to collect, manipulate, store, and process data into information. The technology infrastructure is a set of shared IS resources that form the foundation of each computer-based information system.

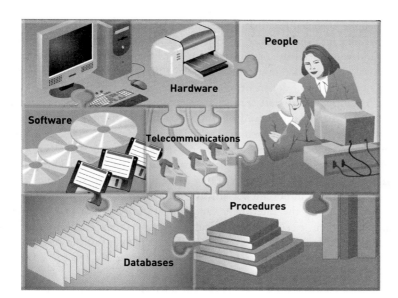

Figure 1.6

The Components of a Computer-Based Information System

Hardware consists of computer equipment used to perform input, processing, and output activities. Input devices include keyboards, mice and other pointing devices, automatic scanning devices, and equipment that can read magnetic ink characters. Processing devices include computer chips that contain the central processing unit and main memory.

Software consists of the computer programs that govern the operation of the computer. These programs allow a computer to process payroll, send bills to customers, and provide managers with information to increase profits, reduce costs, and provide better customer service. The two types of software are system software, such as Microsoft Windows Vista and Windows 7, which control basic computer operations including start-up and printing, and applications software, such as Microsoft Office 2010, which allows you to accomplish specific tasks, including word processing or tabulating numbers.[13]

A **database** is an organized collection of facts and information, typically consisting of two or more related data files. An organization's database can contain facts and information on customers, employees, inventory, competitors' sales, online purchases, and much more. **Telecommunications** is the electronic transmission of signals for communications, which enables organizations to carry out their processes and tasks through effective computer networks. Telecommunications can take place through wires or wireless and satellite transmissions.[14] In the 1920s, the Canadian Press was one of the first users of telecommunications, sending news over telegraph wires that linked the country from coast to coast. **Networks** connect computers and equipment in a building, around the country, or around the world to enable electronic communication. People are the most important element in most computer-based information systems. They make the difference between success and failure for most organizations. **Procedures** include the strategies, policies, methods, and rules for using the CBIS, including the operation, maintenance, and security of the computer system.

The **Internet** is the world's largest computer network, consisting of thousands of interconnected networks, all freely exchanging information. Increasingly, businesses and people are using the Internet to run and deliver important applications, such as accessing vast databases, performing sophisticated business analyses, and getting a variety of reports. This concept, called "cloud computing," allows people to get the information they need from the Internet (the cloud) instead of from desktop or corporate computers.[15] Some applications are available to everyone (public cloud computing), while other applications are available only to corporate employees and managers (private cloud computing.)[16] Internet sites like MySpace (*www.myspace.com*) and Facebook (*www.facebook.com*) have become popular places to connect with friends and colleagues. People can also send short messages up to 140 characters using Twitter (*www.twitter.com*) over the Internet.[17]

hardware
Computer equipment used to perform input, processing, and output activities.

software
The computer programs that govern the operation of the computer.

database
An organized collection of facts and information.

telecommunications
The electronic transmission of signals for communications; enables organizations to carry out their processes and tasks through effective computer networks.

networks
Computers and equipment that are connected in a building, around the country, or around the world to enable electronic communications.

procedures
The strategies, policies, methods, and rules for using a CBIS.

Internet
The world's largest computer network, consisting of thousands of interconnected networks, all freely exchanging information.

Some people, however, fear that this increased usage can lead to problems, including criminals hacking into the Internet and gaining access to sensitive personal information. The speed and widespread use of information systems opens users to a variety of threats from unethical people.[18] Computer criminals and terrorists, for example, have used the Internet to steal millions of dollars or promote terrorism and violence. Some studies report that 50 to 75 percent of corporate security attacks come from people inside the company.[19] Computer-related attacks can come from individuals, groups, companies, and even countries.[20] Although information systems can provide enormous benefits, they do have drawbacks. Some drawbacks are minor, such as receiving unwanted e-mail.[21] Other problems can be more severe, such as when people's personal data, including social insurance and credit card numbers, is lost or stolen, resulting in credit card fraud and ruined credit. Individual privacy is also an important social issue. People can inadvertently disclose personal information while using the Internet.[22] Once private information or photos have been placed on the Internet, it can be very difficult to remove them.[23] In response to possible abuses, a number of laws have been passed to protect people from invasion of their privacy; these laws include the *Privacy Act* and *Personal Information Protection and Electronic Documents Act* (PIPEDA).

Ethical issues concern what is generally considered right or wrong. Some IS professionals believe that computers can create new opportunities for unethical behaviour. Unethical investors have placed false rumours or incorrect information about a company on the Internet and tried to influence its stock price to make money.

The World Wide Web (WWW), or the Web, is a network of links on the Internet to documents containing text, graphics, video, and sound. Information about the documents and access to them are controlled and provided by tens of thousands of special computers called Web servers. The Web is one of many services available over the Internet and provides access to millions of documents. New Internet technologies and increased Internet communications and collaboration are collectively called Web 2.0.[24] The technology used to create the Internet is also being applied within companies and organizations to create **intranets**, which allow people in an organization to exchange information and work on projects. ING DIRECT Canada (*www.ingdirect.ca/en*), for example, used its intranet to get ideas from its employees. According to one corporate executive, "Many of the ideas we've been able to implement are from front-line staff who talk to our customers every day and know what they want."[25] Companies often use intranets to connect their employees around the globe. An **extranet** is a network based on Web technologies that allows selected outsiders, such as business partners and customers, to access authorized resources of a company's intranet. Many people use extranets every day without realizing it—to track shipped goods, order products from their suppliers, or access customer assistance from other companies. If you log on to the FedEx site (*www.fedex.com*) to check the status of a package, for example, you are using an extranet.

intranet
An internal network based on Web technologies that allows people within an organization to exchange information and work on projects.

extranet
A network based on Web technologies that allows selected outsiders, such as business partners and customers, to access authorized resources of a company's intranet.

Doctors use cloud computing and other types of websites to provide better patient care and reduce costs.

(Source: B Busco/Getty Images.)

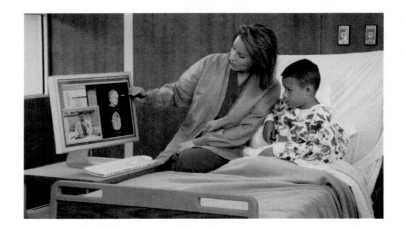

ETHICAL AND SOCIETAL ISSUES

Who Is Interested in Your Social Network Updates?

More than two-thirds of the world's online population uses social networks such as Facebook, MySpace, and Twitter to stay in touch with friends. It is likely that you are one of them. In 2008, social networks became more popular than e-mail, with 66.8 percent of Internet users accessing member communities. Most members of social networks use a posting feature that allows them to share their day-to-day thoughts and activities with their circle of friends. Facebook calls these postings "updates," while Twitter calls them "tweets." Most users do not realize the value of their comments, updates, or tweets to people outside their circle.

Businesses are flocking to social networks to harvest consumer sentiment for use in guiding product development. They are also watching social networks to confront negative publicity. The broad use of social networks and the careful analysis of billions of messages have made it possible to collect public sentiment and build customer relations in a manner never done before. But sifting through the babble to discover comments of interest is challenging.

A number of information system companies have sprung up to provide products designed to monitor social media. Companies such as Alterian, Radian6, Attensity, Visible Technologies, Conversion, and Nielsen Online provide social-media monitoring systems for businesses and organizations. Because social media monitoring is a young technology, there is no standard approach to it. Similar to a search engine, the systems typically traverse the continuous streams of comments in social networks looking for key terms related to specified products. Artificial intelligence (AI) techniques that automate the interpretation of user comments make it possible to quickly identify comments of particular interest. Ultimately, they generate analytic and performance reports for the human expert to evaluate. Systems that monitor social media enable useful information to be drawn from billions of seemingly mundane and unrelated messages.

Monitoring social media can focus on the management of brand reputation, public relations, or even market research. Companies such as Porter Airlines hire full-time social media experts who interact with customers online to address problems and complaints. For example, if you complain about the company's service on Twitter, you might be contacted by a Porter Airlines employee offering to help you.

The social network service owners are well aware of the value of the information that flows over their networks. Most of them intend to build their business through the comments and attention of their members. Whether through targeted ads or selling access to user data, social networks can become very lucrative businesses. Why else would Twitter, a service with apparently no business model, be worth over a billion dollars? Twitter's goal is to grow to one billion members and provide interested parties with the pulse of the planet.

How do users feel about their "personal" comments being harvested to make billions for Internet companies? Regardless of what users think, it is likely that businesses will increasingly analyze the continuous flow of data over social networks to generate insights they can use.

Discussion Questions

1. Do you think it is ethical for social networks to sell access to user information to businesses for market research and other uses? Why or why not?
2. What service does the monitoring of social media ultimately provide for consumers?

Critical Thinking Questions

1. What competitive advantage does the monitoring of social media provide to companies that invest in it?
2. Why is the monitoring of social media considered a CBIS?

SOURCES: Ostrow, Adam, "Social Networking More Popular than Email," *Mashable*, March 9, 2009, *http://mashable.com/2009/03/09/social-networking-more-popular-than-email*; Zabin, Jeff, "Finding Out What They're Saying About You Is Worth Every Penny," *E-Commerce Times*, November 12, 2009, *www.ecommercetimes.com/rsstory/68624.html*; Bensen, Connie, "Do You Know What People Are Saying About You?" *Reuters UK*, September 14, 2009, *http://blogs.reuters.com/great-debate-uk/2009/09/14/do-you-know-what-people-are-saying-about-you*; Schonfeld, Erick, "Twitter's Internal Strategy Laid Bare: To Be "The Pulse of the Planet," *TechCrunch*, July 16, 2009, *www.techcrunch.com/2009/07/16/twitters-internal-strategy-laid-bare-to-be-the-pulse-of-the-planet*; Reisner, Rebecca, "Comcast's Twitter Man," *Business Week*, January 13, 2009, *www.businessweek.com/managing/content/jan2009/ca20090113_373506.htm*; McCarthy, Carolina, "Nielsen: Twitter's Growing Really, Really, Really, Really Fast," CNET, March 2009, *http://news.cnet.com/8301-13577_3-10200161-36.html*; Nielsen Staff, "Social Networking's New Global Footprint," *NielsenWire*, March 9, 2009, *http://blog.nielsen.com/nielsenwire/global/social-networking-new-global-footprint/*.

BUSINESS INFORMATION SYSTEMS

The most common types of information systems used in business organizations are those designed for electronic and mobile commerce, transaction processing, management information, and decision support. The systems are often integrated in one product and delivered by the same software package. See Figure 1.7. For example, some business information systems process transactions, deliver information, and support decisions. Figure 1.8 shows a simple overview of the development of important transaction processing systems (TPS), management information systems (MIS), and decision support systems (DSS).

Figure 1.7

Business Information Systems

Business information systems are often integrated in one product and can be delivered by the same software package.

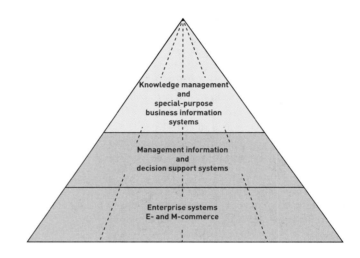

Figure 1.8

The Development of Important Business Information Systems

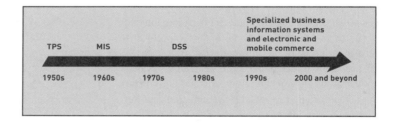

e-commerce
Any business transaction executed electronically between companies (business-to-business, or B2B), companies and consumers (business-to-consumer, or B2C), consumers and other consumers (consumer-to-consumer, or C2C), business and the public sector, and consumers and the public sector.

mobile commerce (m-commerce)
The use of mobile, wireless devices to place orders and conduct business.

electronic business (e-business)
Using information systems and the Internet to perform all business-related tasks and functions.

Electronic and Mobile Commerce

E-commerce involves any business transaction executed electronically between companies (business-to-business, or B2B), companies and consumers (business-to-consumer, or B2C), consumers and other consumers (consumer-to-consumer, or C2C), business and the public sector, and consumers and the public sector.[26] **Mobile commerce (m-commerce)** is the use of mobile, wireless devices to place orders and conduct business. **Electronic business (e-business)** goes beyond e-commerce and e-procurement by using information systems and the Internet to perform all business-related tasks and functions, such as accounting, finance, marketing, manufacturing, and human resource activities. E-business also includes working with customers, suppliers, strategic partners, and stakeholders. Compared to traditional business strategy, e-business strategy is flexible and adaptable. See Figure 1.9.

Enterprise Systems: Transaction Processing Systems and Enterprise Resource Planning

Enterprise systems that process daily transactions have evolved from **transaction processing systems (TPS)**, an organized collection of people, procedures, software, databases, and

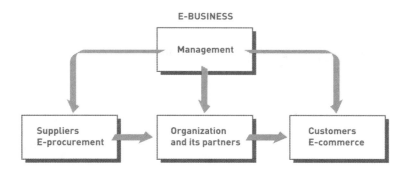

E-BUSINESS

Figure 1.9

Electronic Business

E-business goes beyond e-commerce to include using information systems and the Internet to perform all business-related tasks and functions, such as accounting, finance, marketing, manufacturing, and human resources activities.

devices used to record completed business transactions to **enterprise resource planning (ERP) system**, a set of integrated programs that manages the vital business operations for an entire organization. Canada Post uses an ERP system to reduce costs and improve services. According to the business transformation manager, "The ERP system enabled us to provide a rich, uniform experience across all channels and helped us differentiate service levels based on customers."[27]

Management Information and Decision Support Systems

Information from a transaction processing system or ERP is used in management information and decision support systems. A **management information system (MIS)** is an organized collection of people, procedures, software, databases, and devices that provides routine information to managers and decision makers. An MIS focuses on operational efficiency. Manufacturing, marketing, production, finance, and other functional areas are supported by MISs and are linked through a common database. People quickly recognized that computer systems could support additional decision-making activities. A **decision support system (DSS)** is an organized collection of people, procedures, software, databases, and devices that support problem-specific decision making. The focus of a DSS is on making effective decisions. Whereas an MIS helps an organization "do things right," a DSS helps a manager "do the right thing."[28] A DSS goes beyond a traditional MIS by providing immediate assistance in solving problems. Many of these problems are unique and complex, and key information is often difficult to obtain. The Royal Bank of Canada avoided $15 million in credit fraud losses by using a DSS.[29] Indigo Books and Music uses a DSS to identify its high-value customers and to predict when and what type of products their customers will purchase based on past purchases.[30]

Specialized Business Information Systems: Knowledge Management, Artificial Intelligence, Expert Systems, and Virtual Reality

In addition to TPSs, MISs, and DSSs, organizations often rely on specialized systems. Many use knowledge management systems (KMSs) to create, store, share, and use the organization's knowledge and experience.[31] Acquired Intelligence, a British Columbia company, developed a KMS for the University of Victoria to assess graduate school applicants. Some specialized systems are based on the notion of **artificial intelligence (AI)**, in which the computer system takes on the characteristics of human intelligence. The field of artificial intelligence includes several subfields (see Figure 1.10 on the next page). **Expert systems** give the computer the ability to make suggestions and function like an expert in a particular field, helping enhance the performance of the novice user. The unique value of expert systems is that they allow organizations to capture and use the wisdom of experts and specialists.[32] **Virtual reality** is the simulation of a real or imagined environment that can be experienced visually in three dimensions.[33] The Canadian government invested $1.5 million to develop a virtual reality rehabilitation system for injured Canadian Forces personnel.[34] Now, let's examine how information systems are created.

transaction processing system (TPS)
An organized collection of people, procedures, software, databases, and devices used to record completed business transactions.

enterprise resource planning (ERP) system
A set of integrated programs that manages the vital business operations for an entire organization.

management information system (MIS)
An organized collection of people, procedures, software, databases, and devices that provides routine information to managers and decision makers.

decision support system (DSS)
An organized collection of people, procedures, software, databases, and devices that support problem-specific decision making.

artificial intelligence (AI)
A field in which the computer system takes on the characteristics of human intelligence.

expert systems
A system that gives a computer the ability to make suggestions and function like an expert in a particular field.

virtual reality
The simulation of a real or imagined environment that can be experienced visually in three dimensions.

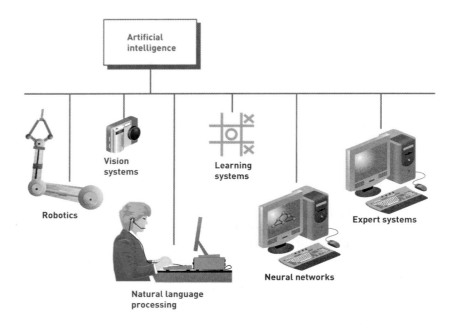

Figure 1.10

The Major Elements of Artificial Intelligence

ORGANIZATIONS AND INFORMATION SYSTEMS

Technology has changed the way organizations work in recent years. While technology once was used primarily to automate manual processes, information technology has transformed the nature of work and the shape of organizations themselves. In this chapter and throughout the book, you will explore the benefits and drawbacks of information technology in today's organizations around the globe.[35]

An **organization** is a formal collection of people and other resources established to accomplish a set of goals. The primary goal of a for-profit organization is to maximize shareholder value, often measured by the price of the company stock. Nonprofit organizations include social groups, religious groups, universities, and other organizations that do not have profit as their goal. As discussed in this chapter, the ability of an organization to achieve its goals is often a function of the organization's overall structure, culture, and ability to change.

An organization is a system, which means that it has inputs, processing mechanisms, outputs, and feedback. An organization constantly uses money, people, materials, machines and other equipment, data, and information. As shown in Figure 1.11, resources such as materials, people, and money serve as inputs to the organizational system from the environment; they go through a transformation mechanism; and then outputs are produced to the environment. The outputs from the transformation mechanism are usually goods or services, which are of higher relative value than the inputs alone. Through adding value or worth, organizations attempt to increase performance and achieve their goals. According to one chief information officer (CIO), "As business executives, other than the CEO, CIOs are best positioned to help drive business outcomes ... to increase top- and bottom-line performance."[36]

How does the organizational system increase the value of resources? In the transformation mechanism, subsystems contain processes that help turn inputs into goods or services of increased value. These processes increase the relative worth of the combined inputs on their way to becoming final outputs. Let's reconsider the simple car wash example (see Figure 1.3 on page 9). The first process is washing the car. The output of this system—a clean but wet car—is worth more than the mere collection of ingredients (soap and water), as evidenced by the popularity of automatic car washes. Consumers are willing to pay for the skill, knowledge, time, and energy required to wash their cars. The second process is drying—transforming the wet car into a dry one with no water spotting. Again, consumers are willing to pay for the additional skill, knowledge, time, and energy required to accomplish this transformation.

organization
A formal collection of people and other resources established to accomplish a set of goals.

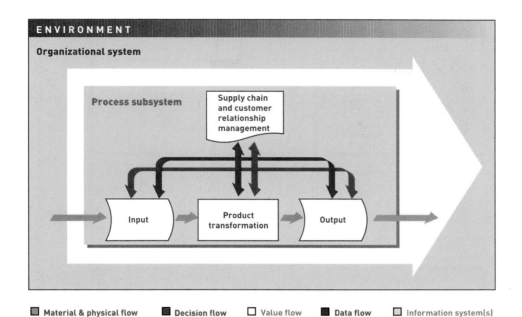

Figure 1.11

A General Model of an Organization

Information systems support and work within all parts of an organizational process. Although not shown in this simple model, input to the process subsystem can come from internal and external sources. Just prior to entering the subsystem, data is external. After it enters the subsystem, it becomes internal. Likewise, goods and services can be output to either internal or external systems.

Providing value to a stakeholder—customer, supplier, manager, shareholder, or employee—is the primary goal of any organization. The value chain, first described by Michael Porter in a 1985 *Harvard Business Review* article, reveals how organizations can add value to their products and services. The **value chain** is a series (chain) of activities that includes inbound logistics, warehouse and storage, production and manufacturing, finished product storage, outbound logistics, marketing and sales, and customer service. See Figure 1.12 on the next page. You investigate each activity in the chain to determine how to increase the value perceived by a customer. Depending on the customer, value might mean lower price, better service, higher quality, or uniqueness of a product. The value comes from the skill, knowledge, time, and energy that the company invests in the product or activity. The value chain is just as important to companies that don't manufacture products, such as tax preparers, retail stores, legal firms, and other service providers. By adding a significant amount of value to their products and services, companies ensure success.

value chain
A series (chain) of activities that includes inbound logistics, warehouse and storage, production, finished product storage, outbound logistics, marketing and sales, and customer service.

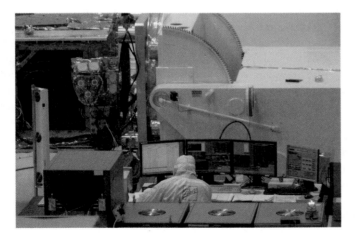

Combining a value chain with just-in-time (JIT) inventory means companies can deliver materials or parts when they are needed. Ball Aerospace uses JIT to help reduce inventory costs and enhance customer satisfaction.

(Source: AP Photo/Denver Post, R. J. Sangosti.)

Managing the supply chain and customer relationships are two key elements of managing the value chain. Supply chain management (SCM) helps determine what supplies are required for the value chain, what quantities are needed to meet customer demand, how the supplies should be processed (manufactured) into finished goods and services, and

Figure 1.12

The Value Chain of a
Manufacturing Company

Managing raw materials, inbound
logistics, and warehouse and storage
facilities is called *upstream management*. Managing finished product
storage, outbound logistics, marketing
and sales, and customer service is
called *downstream management*.

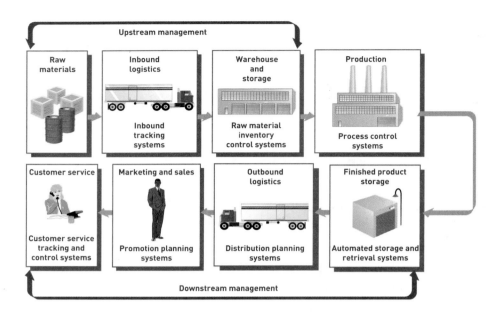

how the shipment of supplies and products to customers should be scheduled, monitored, and controlled.[37] Companies use a number of approaches to manage their supply chains. Some automotive companies, for example, require that their suppliers are located close to manufacturing plants. Sysco, a food distribution company, uses a sophisticated supply chain management system that incorporates software and databases to prepare and ship over 20 million tons of meats, produce, and other food items to restaurants and other outlets every year.[38] The company supplies one out of three cafeterias, sports stadiums, restaurants, and other food stores in North America.

More and more organizations are accomplishing SCM by using the Internet and electronic marketplaces (e-marketplaces). When an organization has many suppliers, it can use Internet exchanges to negotiate favourable prices and service. With more companies and nonprofit organizations having operations around the world, SCM has become a global practice.[39] According to the chief information officer of Wipro, "As a service company, driving an efficient supply chain is essential for our profitability."[40]

Customer relationship management (CRM) programs help companies of all sizes manage all aspects of customer encounters, including marketing and advertising, sales, customer service after the sale, and programs to retain loyal customers.[41] Often, CRM software uses a variety of information sources, including sales from retail stores, surveys, e-mail, and Internet browsing habits, to compile comprehensive customer profiles. CRM systems can also get customer feedback to help design new products and services. See Figure 1.13. To be of most benefit, CRM programs must be tailored for each company or organization. Best Buy Canada has developed its Rewards Zone loyalty program to improve its level of customer service and to deliver member-only benefits like product sales, concert events, and contests to customers who enroll in the program. Oracle, SalesForce, and other companies develop and sell CRM software.[42] CRM software can also be purchased as a service and delivered over the Internet instead of being installed on corporate computers.

What role does an information system play in these processes? A traditional view of information systems holds that organizations use them to control and monitor processes and ensure effectiveness and efficiency. An information system can turn feedback from the subsystems into more meaningful information for employees. This information might summarize the performance of the subsystems and be used to change how the system operates. Such changes could involve using different raw materials (inputs), designing new

Figure 1.13

SAP CRM

Companies in more than 25 industries use SAP's CRM software to reduce cost and increase decision-making ability in all aspects of their customer relationship management.

(Source: Courtesy of SAP.)

assembly-line procedures (product transformation), or developing new products and services (outputs). In this view, the information system is external to the process and serves to monitor or control it.

A more contemporary view, however, holds that information systems are often so intimately involved that they are *part of* the process itself. From this perspective, the information system plays an integral role in the process, whether providing input, aiding product transformation, or producing output. Consider a phone directory business that creates phone books for international corporations. A corporate customer requests a phone directory listing all steel suppliers in Canada. Using its information system, the directory business can sort files to find the suppliers' names and phone numbers and organize them into an alphabetical list. The information system itself is an integral part of this process. It does not just monitor the process externally but works as part of the process to transform raw data into a product. In this example, the information system turns input (names and phone numbers) into a salable output (a phone directory). The same system might also provide the input (data files) and output (printed pages for the directory).

The latter view provides a new perspective on how and why businesses can use information systems. Rather than attempting to understand information systems independent of the organization, businesses consider the potential role of information systems within the process itself, often leading to the discovery of new and better ways to accomplish business processes.

Organizational Structures

Organizational structure refers to organizational subunits and the way they relate to the overall organization. An organization's structure depends on its goals and its approach to management. Organization structure can affect how a company views and uses information systems. The types of organizational structures typically include traditional, project, team, and virtual.

Traditional Organizational Structure

A **traditional organizational structure**, also called a "hierarchical structure," is like a managerial pyramid where the hierarchy of decision making and authority flows from the strategic management at the top down to operational management and nonmanagement employees. Compared to lower levels, the strategic level, including the president of the

organizational structure
Organizational subunits and the way they relate to the overall organization.

traditional organizational structure
An organizational structure in which the hierarchy of decision making and authority flows from the strategic management at the top down to operational management and nonmanagement employees.

Aldra Manages Workflow to Support Customization

Aldra Fenster und Türen GmbH, or Aldra for short, is a leading door and window manufacturer with over 300 dealers in Germany and Scandinavia. Aldra is well known for its precision craftsmanship in manufacturing intricate, custom-designed windows. In the early 1970s, the company developed a unique method of manufacturing windows from plastic. Combined with its customization service, this cost-saving manufacturing innovation gave Aldra a leg up on the competition.

Aldra's custom window design and manufacturing has created challenges in its corporate workflow and information processing. Mass-producing windows and doors in standard sizes is far easier than creating custom designs, where production techniques change from one item to the next. At Aldra, most orders have unique requirements in size, shape, materials, function, and embedded technology. To support custom orders, Aldra must provide considerable flexibility in both its manufacturing processes and its information systems.

Providing customized manufacturing does not excuse Aldra from meeting the tight deadlines imposed by costly construction projects. Aggressive construction schedules rarely allow for the extra time required to produce custom products. Aldra found that the complexities of building its high-quality products were causing confusion in the order processing system and delays in manufacturing, leading to missed deadlines. Order specifications were sometimes incomplete or incorrect, and correcting orders is time consuming. Lack of coordination among departments resulted in additional errors that occasionally resulted in costly idle time on the production line. The lack of coordination also led to errors in calculating manufacturing costs, which reduced profits. Aldra set out to implement a new system that would assist the company in managing its value chain and corporate workflow.

Aldra purchased information systems from Infor Corporation that allowed the company to better coordinate efforts across departments. Using the software, Aldra now models its critical core processes (workflows) and then uses the models to improve communication across the value chain. The models define the specific employees involved in the various stages of the process. The system then generates daily activities for each employee displayed in a particular area on the computer desktop. As activities approach their deadline, they are moved to the top of the list. Employees also receive e-mail notices of new or pressing actions needing attention.

Aldra's new workflow management system depends on a corporate-wide system that stores and manipulates all order details. Top managers can view orders to see how they are progressing through the value chain, so they can intervene when necessary.

Aldra implemented the new system in an unusually short amount of time. The company spent three days installing the system, another three days training managers in how to model workflow processes, and two weeks to model processes and train users. The benefits of the new system were almost immediately apparent. Within weeks, the company's adherence to delivery dates was improved by over 95 percent. Cost estimates are now reliably calculated. Employees make more productive use of their time, and customers are happy. Aldra is looking to expand the use of its new systems to other areas of its business.

Discussion Questions

1. What problems did Aldra's new information systems address, and what was the root of those problems?
2. How did Aldra's new systems assist employees in being more productive?

Critical Thinking Questions

1. What lessons can be learned from this case about managing information in a value chain?
2. How does an organization determine when it is worthwhile to invest in a system such as Aldra's workflow management system?

SOURCES: Infor Staff, "Aldra Fenster und Türen GmbH," Aldra Customer Profile, accessed December 24, 2009, *www.infor.com/content/casestudies/296661*; Infor ERP systems website, accessed December 24, 2009; Aldra website (translated), accessed December 24, 2009, *www.aldra.de*.

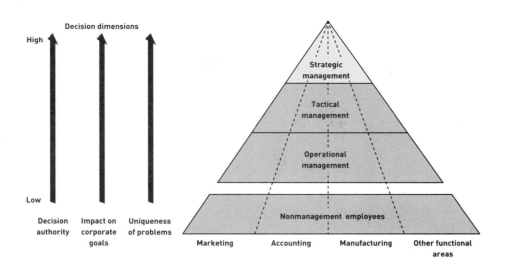

Figure 1.14

A simplified model of the organization, showing the managerial pyramid from top-level managers to nonmanagement employees.

company and vice presidents, has a higher degree of decision authority, more impact on corporate goals, and more unique problems to solve. See Figure 1.14. The major departments are usually divided according to function and can include marketing, production, information systems, finance and accounting, research and development, and so on. See Figure 1.15. The positions or departments that are directly associated with making, packing, or shipping goods are called line positions. A production supervisor who reports to a vice president of production is an example of a line position. Other positions might not be directly involved with the formal chain of command but instead assist a department or area. These are called staff positions, such as a legal counsel reporting to the president.

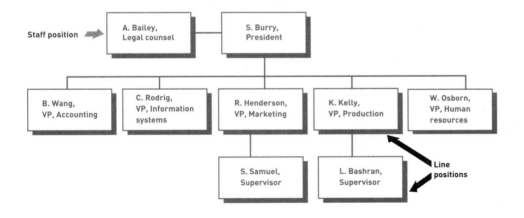

Figure 1.15

A Traditional Organizational Structure

Today, the trend is to reduce the number of management levels, or layers, in the traditional organizational structure. This type of structure, often called a **flat organizational structure**, empowers employees at lower levels to make decisions and solve problems without needing permission from midlevel managers. **Empowerment** gives employees and their managers more responsibility and authority to make decisions, take action, and have more control over their jobs.[43] For example, an empowered sales clerk could respond to certain customer requests or problems without needing permission from a supervisor.

Information systems can be a key element in empowering employees because they provide the information employees need to make decisions. The employees might also be empowered to develop or use their own personal information systems, such as a simple forecasting model or spreadsheet.

flat organizational structure
An organizational structure with a reduced number of management layers.

empowerment
Giving employees and their managers more responsibility and authority to make decisions, take certain actions, and have more control over their jobs.

project organizational structure
A structure centred on major products or services.

Project and Team Organizational Structures

A **project organizational structure** is centred on major products or services.[44] For example, in a manufacturing firm that produces baby food and other baby products, each line is produced by a separate unit. Traditional functions such as marketing, finance, and production are positioned within these major units. See Figure 1.16. Many project teams are temporary—when the project is complete, the members go on to new teams formed for another project.

Figure 1.16

A Project Organizational Structure

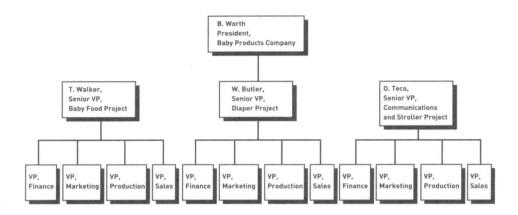

The **team organizational structure** is centred on work teams or groups. In some cases, these teams are small; in others, they are very large. Typically, each team has a leader who reports to an upper-level manager. Depending on its tasks, the team can be temporary or permanent. A hospital, for example, can form small teams to organize its physicians, nurses and other health-care professionals to work with individual patients.

team organizational structure
A structure centred on work teams or groups.

Virtual Organizational Structure and Collaborative Work

A **virtual organizational structure** uses individuals, groups, or complete business units in geographically dispersed areas. Work can be done anywhere, anytime.[45] Virtual teams help ensure the participation of the best available people to solve important organizational problems. A virtual organization structure can reduce costs for an organization. Using a virtual structure can also be good for employees, saving the time and costs of commuting. Improving performance and effectiveness is also important. According to the chief information officer of the outsourcing company Wipro, "The next big thing for my industry will be virtual delivery by global teams. This is an extension of the global delivery model for outsourcing, and it will allow virtual teams to work together more effectively."[46] Virtual teams are also being used in education.[47] According to a director of education, "It's a really good idea for a teacher to have some experience in virtual education. The future of education is going to push a lot more in that direction." The authors and publishing team for this book used a virtual team structure, consisting of people from across Canada who worked over a year to complete the project. They used the Internet to send chapter files and related documents to each other in developing the textbook and related materials you are using.

virtual organizational structure
A structure that uses individuals, groups, or complete business units in geographically dispersed areas.

Successful virtual organizational structures share key characteristics. One strategy is to have in-house employees concentrate on the firm's core businesses and use virtual employees, groups, or businesses to do other business tasks. Even with sophisticated IS tools, teams still benefit from face-to-face meetings, especially at the beginning of new projects. Some experts have proposed the following for virtual teams.

- When possible, use virtual team members who know each other or use technology that helps virtual team members quickly get to know each other.
- Use virtual team members who are already connected with other people and resources throughout the organization.
- Keep virtual team projects as independent as possible from other projects, so that a delay or problem with one team doesn't affect the progress or success of another virtual team.

Virtual teams let people consult with experts no matter their physical location; they are especially useful in health care.

(Source: AP Photo/Paul Sancya.)

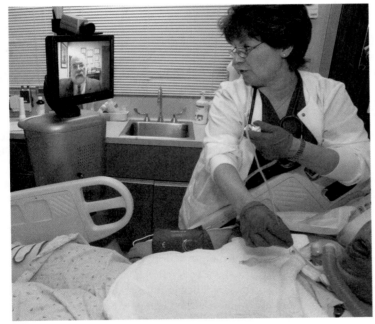

- Develop Internet resources, such as Teamspace (*www.teamspace.com*) and similar collaborative software, that help virtual teams communicate and collaborate on important projects.
- Make sure that virtual team projects are challenging, meaningful, and interesting.

A virtual organizational structure allows *collaborative* work, in which managers and employees can effectively work in groups, even those composed of members from around the world. To stay connected, some virtual teams use smartphones and mobile devices that connect to the Internet. In other cases, a social networking site such as Facebook (*www.facebook.com*) can be used to help virtual teams work together.[48]

Organizational Culture and Change

Culture is a set of major understandings and assumptions shared by a group, such as within an ethnic group or a country. **Organizational culture** consists of the major understandings and assumptions for a business, corporation, or other organization. The understandings, which can include common beliefs, values, and approaches to decision making, are often

culture
A set of major understandings and assumptions shared by a group.

organizational culture
The major understandings and assumptions for a business, corporation, or other organization.

A virtual organizational structure allows collaborative work, in which managers and employees can effectively work in groups, even those composed of members from around the world.

(Source: Jon Feingersh/Blend Images/ Getty Images.)

organizational change
How for-profit and nonprofit organizations plan for, implement, and handle change.

not stated or documented as goals or formal policies. For example, Procter & Gamble Canada has an organizational culture that places an extremely high value on understanding its customers and their needs. As another example, employees might be expected to be clean-cut, wear conservative outfits, and be courteous in dealing with all customers. Sometimes organizational culture is formed over years. In other cases, top-level managers can form it rapidly—for example, by starting a "casual Friday" dress policy. Organizational culture can also have a positive effect on the successful development of new information systems that support the organization's culture. Some health-care professionals believe that a good organizational culture can improve patient health and safety.[49]

Organizational change deals with how for-profit and nonprofit organizations plan for, implement, and handle change. Change can be caused by internal factors, such as those initiated by employees at all levels, or external factors, such as those wrought by competitors, stockholders, federal and provincial laws, community regulations, natural occurrences (such as floods), and general economic conditions. Organizational change also occurs when two or more organizations merge. When organizations merge, integrating their information systems can be critical to future success. When VeriSign, a division of Symantec, acquired and merged with a number of companies, it had to integrate various information systems.[50] According to the chief information officer of VeriSign, "By being decisive and making the goals and objectives clear, we were able to fuse multiple teams into a single unit, which in the end was smaller and far more productive." Unfortunately, many organizations consider the integration of their various information systems too late in the merger process.

Change can be sustaining or disruptive.[51] Sustaining change can help an organization improve the supply of raw materials, the production process, and the products and services it offers. Developing new manufacturing equipment to make disk drives is an example of a sustaining change for a computer manufacturer. The new equipment might reduce the costs of producing the disk drives and improve overall performance. Disruptive change, on the other hand, can completely transform an industry or create new ones, which can harm an organization's performance or even put it out of business. In general, disruptive technologies might not originally have good performance, low cost, or even strong demand. Over time, however, they often replace existing technologies. They can cause profitable, stable companies to fail when they don't change or adopt the new technology. On a positive note, disruptive change often results in new, successful companies and offers consumers the potential of new products and services at reduced costs and superior performance.

change model
A representation of change theories that identifies the phases of change and the best way to implement them.

The dynamics of change can be viewed in a change model. A **change model** represents change theories by identifying the phases of change and the best way to implement them. Kurt Lewin and Edgar Schein propose a three-stage approach for change;

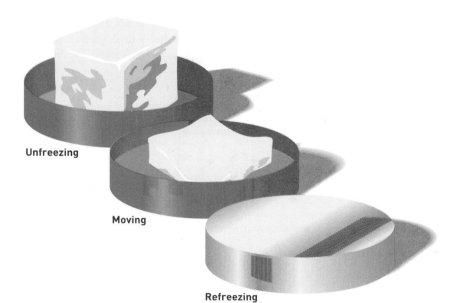

Figure 1.17

A Change Model

Unfreezing

Moving

Refreezing

see Figure 1.17. The first stage, "unfreezing", is ceasing old habits and creating a climate that is receptive to change. "Moving", the second stage, is learning new work methods, behaviours, and systems. The final stage, "refreezing", involves reinforcing changes to make the new process second nature, accepted, and part of the job.[52] When a company introduces a new information system, a few members of the organization must become agents of change to confront and overcome possible resistance to change. They are champions of the new system and its benefits. Understanding the dynamics of change can help them confront and overcome resistance from employees and others so that the new system can be used to maximum efficiency and effectiveness. In addition to the Lewin-Schein change model discussed above, there are other change models, publications, and courses that can help organizations manage change, including *Managing at the Speed of Change* and *Project Change Management* by Conner Partners (*www.connerpartners.com*), *Leading Change* and *The Heart Of Change* by John Kotter (*www.theheartofchange.com*), and many others.

Organizational learning is closely related to organizational change. All organizations adapt to new conditions or alter their practices over time—some better than others. Collectively, these adaptations and adjustments based on experience and ideas are called **organizational learning**. Assembly-line workers, secretaries, clerks, managers, and executives learn better ways of doing business and incorporate them into their day-to-day activities. This includes organizations that merge and acquire other companies.[53] According to one IBM analyst, "The key thing that IBM and other successful acquirers figured out in recent years is that while individuals count, it's process and organizational learning that matter most." Organizational learning can also lead to increased job satisfaction.[54] In some cases, the adjustments can be a radical redesign of business processes, often called reengineering. In other cases, these adjustments can be more incremental, a concept called continuous improvement. Both adjustments reflect an organization's strategy, the long-term plan of action for achieving their goals.

organizational learning
The adaptations to new conditions or alterations of organizational practices over time.

Reengineering and Continuous Improvement

To stay competitive, organizations must occasionally make fundamental changes in the way they do business. In other words, they must change the activities, tasks, or processes they use to achieve their goals. **Reengineering**, also called **process redesign** and business process reengineering (BPR), involves the radical redesign of business processes, organizational structures, information systems, and values of the organization to achieve a breakthrough in business results. BBVA, a large financial services firm with offices around the world, used reengineering

reengineering (process redesign)
The radical redesign of business processes, organizational structures, information systems, and values of the organization to achieve a breakthrough in business results.

to streamline its operations and save about $2 million in its office operations in Madrid and New York.[55] See Figure 1.18. Reengineering can reduce delivery time, increase product and service quality, enhance customer satisfaction, and increase revenues and profitability.

Figure 1.18

Reengineering

Reengineering involves the radical redesign of business processes, organizational structure, information systems, and values of the organization to achieve a breakthrough in business results.

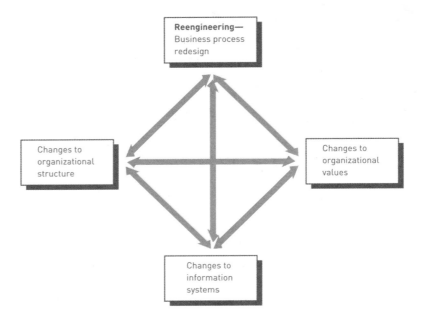

In contrast to simply automating the existing work process, reengineering challenges the fundamental assumptions governing their design. It requires finding and vigorously challenging old rules blocking major business process changes. These rules are like anchors weighing down a firm and keeping it from competing effectively. Table 1.3 provides some examples of such rules.

Table 1.3

Selected Business Rules That Affect Business Processes

Rule	Original Rationale	Potential Problem
Hold small orders until full-truckload shipments can be assembled.	Reduce delivery costs.	Customer delivery is slow—lost sales.
Do not accept an order until customer credit is approved.	Reduce potential for bad debt.	Customer service is poor—lost sales.
Let headquarters make all merchandising decisions.	Reduce number of items carried in inventory.	Customers perceive organization has limited product selection—lost sales.

continuous improvement
Constantly seeking ways to improve business processes to add value to products and services.

In contrast to reengineering, the idea of **continuous improvement** is to constantly seek ways to improve business processes and add value to products and services.[56] This continual change will increase customer satisfaction and loyalty and ensure long-term profitability. Manufacturing companies make continual product changes and improvements. Service organizations regularly find ways to provide faster and more effective assistance to customers. By doing so, these companies increase customer loyalty, minimize the chance of customer dissatisfaction, and diminish the opportunity for competitive inroads. Table 1.4 compares these two strategies.

User Satisfaction and Technology Acceptance

To be effective, reengineering and continuous improvement efforts must result in satisfied users and be accepted and used throughout the organization. Over the years, IS researchers have studied user satisfaction and technology acceptance as they relate to IS attitudes and usage.[57] Although user satisfaction and technology acceptance started as two separate theories, some believe that they are related concepts. [58]

Business Process Reengineering	Continuous Improvement
Strong action taken to solve serious problem	Routine action taken to make minor improvements
Top-down change driven by senior executives	Bottom-up change driven by workers
Broad in scope; cuts across departments	Narrow in scope; focus is on tasks in a given area
Goal is to achieve a major breakthrough	Goal is continuous, gradual improvements
Often led by outsiders	Usually led by workers close to the business
Information system integral to the solution	Information systems provide data to guide the improvement team

Table 1.4

Comparing Business Process Reengineering to Continuous Improvement

User satisfaction with a computer system and the information it generates often depend on the quality of the system and the value of the information it delivers to users.[59] A quality information system is usually flexible, efficient, accessible, and timely. Quality information is accurate, reliable, current, complete, and delivered in the proper format.[60]

The **technology acceptance model (TAM)** specifies the factors that can lead to better attitudes about the information system, along with higher acceptance and usage of it.[61] These factors include the perceived usefulness of the technology, the ease of its use, its quality, and the degree to which the organization supports its use.[62] Studies have shown that user satisfaction and technology acceptance are critical in health care.[63] Doctors and other health-care professionals need training and time to accept and use new technology and databases before they can help them reduce medical errors and save lives.

You can determine the actual usage of an information system by the amount of technology diffusion and infusion.[64] **Technology diffusion** is a measure of how widely technology is spread throughout an organization. An organization in which computers and information systems are located in most departments and areas has a high level of technology diffusion.[65] Some online merchants such as Amazon.ca have a high diffusion and use computer systems to perform most of their business functions, including marketing, purchasing, and billing. **Technology infusion**, on the other hand, is the extent to which technology permeates an area or department. In other words, it is a measure of how deeply embedded technology is in an area of the organization. Some architectural firms, for example, use computers in all aspects of designing a building, from drafting to final blueprints. See Figure 1.19. The design area, thus, has a high level of infusion. Of course, a firm can have a high level of

technology acceptance model (TAM)
A model that describes the factors leading to higher levels of acceptance and usage of technology.

technology diffusion
A measure of how widely technology is spread throughout the organization.

technology infusion
The extent to which technology is deeply integrated into an area or department.

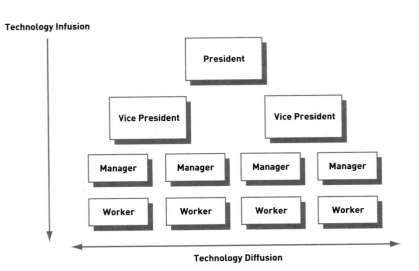

Figure 1.19

Technology Infusion and Diffusion

infusion in one part of its operations and a low level of diffusion overall. The architectural firm might use computers in all aspects of design (high infusion in the design area), but not to perform other business functions, including billing, purchasing, and marketing (low diffusion overall). Diffusion and infusion often depend on the technology available now and in the future, the size and type of the organization, and the environmental factors that include the competition, government regulations, suppliers, and so on. This is often called the technology, organization, and environment (TOE) framework.[66]

Although an organization might have a high level of diffusion and infusion, with computers throughout the organization, this does not necessarily mean that information systems are being used to their full potential. In fact, the assimilation and use of expensive computer technology throughout organizations varies greatly.[67] Providing training and support to employees usually increases the use of a new information system.[68] Companies also hope that a high level of diffusion, infusion, satisfaction, and acceptance will lead to greater performance and profitability.[69] How appropriate and useful the information system is to the tasks or activities being performed, often called Task-Technology Fit (TTF), can also lead to greater performance and profitability.[70]

Quality

quality
The ability of a product or service to meet or exceed customer expectations.

The definition of the term "quality" has evolved over the years. In the early years of quality control, firms were concerned with meeting design specifications—that is, conforming to standards. If a product performed as designed, it was considered a high-quality product. A product can perform its intended function, however, and still not satisfy customer needs. Today, **quality** means the ability of a product or service to meet or exceed customer expectations. For example, a computer that users say performs well and is easy to maintain and repair would be considered a high-quality product. This view of quality is completely customer oriented. In 2010, Toyota recalled 6.5 million cars to correct two problems that could cause the vehicles' gas pedals to stick. In response to the quality issues, Toyota established seven new product quality testing centres in Canada and the United States to become a more quality-focused and responsive organization.[71] Organizations now use techniques to ensure quality, including total quality management and Six Sigma. For example, Canada Post used Six Sigma techniques to save millions of dollars.[72] See Table 1.5.

Table 1.5

Total Quality Management and Six Sigma

Technique	Description	Examples
Total Quality Management (TQM)	Involves developing a keen awareness of customer needs, adopting a strategic vision for quality, empowering employees, and rewarding employees and managers for producing high-quality products.[73]	The Ghana Investment Promotion Center, an organization that promotes investment and businesses in Ghana, West Africa, won a world quality award based on TQM.[74] Manulife Financial's Individual Wealth Management division used TQM to improve the quality of all its business processes to achieve a 23% improvement in customer service.[75]
Six Sigma	A statistical term that means products and services will meet quality standards 99.9997% of the time. In a normal distribution curve used in statistics, six standard deviations (six sigma) is 99.9997% of the area under the curve. Six Sigma was developed at Motorola, Inc., in the mid-1980s.[76]	Maple Leaf Foods, a $6.5-billion food company, uses Six Sigma to improve quality by eliminating waste and unneeded steps. There are a number of training and certification programs for Six Sigma.[77]

Outsourcing, On-Demand Computing, and Downsizing

A significant portion of an organization's expenses are used to hire, train, and compensate employees. Naturally, organizations try to control costs by determining the number of employees they need to maintain high-quality goods and services. Strategies to contain these personnel costs include outsourcing, on-demand computing, and downsizing.

Outsourcing involves contracting with outside professional services to meet specific business needs. Often, companies outsource a business process, such as recruiting and hiring employees, developing advertising materials, promoting product sales, or setting up a global telecommunications network. Organizations often outsource a process to focus more closely on their core business—and target limited resources to meet strategic goals. Australian airline Virgin Blue, for example, outsourced many of its routine business applications to Verizon, a business communications company, to free up its IS staff for important strategic IS projects.[78]

Companies that are considering outsourcing to cut the cost of their IS operations need to make this decision carefully. A growing number of organizations are finding that outsourcing does not necessarily lead to reduced costs. One of the primary reasons for cost increases is poorly written contracts that allow vendors to tack on unexpected charges. Other potential drawbacks of outsourcing include loss of control and flexibility, overlooked opportunities to strengthen core competency, and low employee morale.

On-demand computing is an extension of the outsourcing approach, and many companies offer it to business clients and customers. **On-demand computing**, also called on-demand business and utility computing, involves rapidly responding to the organization's flow of work as the need for computer resources varies. It is often called utility computing because the organization pays for computing resources from a computer or consulting company, just as it pays for electricity from a utility company. This approach treats the information system—including hardware, software, databases, telecommunications, personnel, and other components—more as a service than as separate products. In other words, instead of purchasing hardware, software, and database systems, the organization pays a fee only for the systems it needs at peak times. This approach can save money because the organization does not pay for systems that it doesn't routinely need. It also allows the organization's IS staff to concentrate on more strategic issues. Related approaches include hardware as a service, software as a service, and database as a service. These approaches are discussed in more detail in the hardware, software, and database chapters.

Downsizing involves reducing the number of employees to cut costs. The term "rightsizing" is also used. Rather than pick a specific business process to downsize, companies usually look to downsize across the entire company. Downsizing clearly reduces total payroll costs, though the quality of products and services and employee morale can suffer.

outsourcing
Contracting with outside professional services to meet specific business needs.

on-demand computing
Contracting for computer resources to rapidly respond to an organization's varying workflow. Also called on-demand business and utility computing.

downsizing
Reducing the number of employees to cut costs.

COMPETITIVE ADVANTAGE

A **competitive advantage** is a significant and ideally long-term benefit to a company over its competition and can result in higher-quality products, better customer service, and lower costs. According to the chief information officer of a large consulting company, "An efficiently run IT organization can be a significant source of competitive advantage."[79] An organization often uses its information system to help achieve a competitive advantage. Shermag, a large Canadian furniture manufacturing company, for example, achieved a competitive advantage by reducing total operating costs by more than 20 percent using its information system to streamline its supply chain and reduce the cost of wood and other raw materials.[80] In his book *Good to Great,* Jim Collins outlines how technology can be used to accelerate companies to greatness.[81] Table 1.6 (on page 33) shows how a few companies accomplished this. Ultimately, it is not how much a company spends on information systems but how it makes and manages investments in technology. Companies can spend less and get more value.

competitive advantage
A significant and ideally long-term benefit to a company over its competition.

The New Corporate Mantra: Social and Environmental Responsibility

Green and socially responsible efforts are making their way into most businesses' mission statements. Efforts to address environmental impact looks good for a company on paper. As well, efforts to "go green" can actually save companies money and can assist them in running more efficiently. Such was the case recently at the North Coast Electric Company.

According to its website, North Coast Electric is one of the "largest and fastest growing electrical distributors in the [United States]." It has 34 service centres distributed across Alaska, Arizona, Idaho, Oregon, and Washington. North Coast provides a wide variety of electrical services, including electrical contracting, specialty lighting sales and installation, electrical automation sales and installation, commercial and national electrical contracting, data communication sales and installation, green solutions, supply solutions, and tool sales and distribution.

Recently, North Coast Electric chief operating officer (COO) Rick Bumpus won the appreciation and respect of employees and customers with an innovative information system designed to save tons of paper each year. Until recently, each day across its 34 service centres, North Coast Electric employees would print out and mail hundreds of customer invoices. With a recently installed enterprise resource planning (ERP) system, North Coast Electric was finally in a position to manage finances from across all service centres centrally. Bumpus realized that the new system opened the door to paperless invoicing and savings in many areas.

Bumpus adopted an electronic document, or e-document, delivery system that eliminated the need for paper invoices. The e-document system was provided by a third party that managed all the billing online. Each day, instead of printing hundreds of invoices, North Coast Electric uploads its invoices to Billtrust Corporation, which carries out North Coast's e-billing instructions. Some customers opt to have their e-bills e-mailed as a PDF attachment. Others prefer to log on to North Coast's "Invoice Gateway" and access invoices electronically on the Web. Customers can also import their invoices directly to their own accounting software such as QuickBooks.

Many companies are moving to e-documents for invoicing, especially small to midsize businesses (SMBs). E-billing allows companies to streamline the billing process, getting invoices to customers more quickly. It reduces the time required for manual billing, and it saves paper and postage, which is especially important because many businesses are looking for ways to reduce their use of paper. It's a move that is good for the environment and good for the corporate budget. Not only does eliminating the use of paper save trees, but it also reduces carbon emissions by eliminating the need to drive vehicles that deliver the paper.

Digital Insight, a division of Intuit Corporation that helps businesses and consumers manage money online, reduced its paper use by 40 percent in its first year of using electronic invoices. The reduction was a useful way to meet Intuit's aggressive corporate social responsibility goals. Digital Insight also saved half a million dollars and reduced the amount of time between sending invoices and receiving payments.

Analysts think that the time is ripe for the rise of e-documents. The new emphasis on being socially and environmentally responsible gives businesses a good excuse to suggest e-billing to customers. Although invoicing is a popular way to use e-documents, companies also create e-documents for financial statements, letters, and reports. Many e-document companies have started in recent years to provide convenient and robust e-document services. Companies that outsource their e-documents operations to third parties can sometimes enjoy additional benefits. Some of these e-document companies assist their customers in building support for electronic invoicing among their clients.

Moving to e-documents was listed as the highest priority for 48 percent of businesses polled in 2009. It is anticipated that in the near future, the number of electronic invoices delivered will exceed the number of paper invoices delivered among businesses.

Discussion Questions

1. What benefits do electronic invoices provide to businesses, customers, and the environment?
2. Why would a company decide to outsource its e-documents systems?

Critical Thinking Questions

1. Could paper become obsolete as a medium for communication? Or do some services require the use of paper and can therefore never be digitized?
2. Do you prefer to have paper records of your finances rather than electronic? What benefits does paper provide you? What benefits do electronic records provide?

SOURCES: Shein, Esther, "The ROI of e-Document dDelivery," Computerworld, April 6, 2009, www.computerworld.com; Digital Insight website, accessed December 24, 2009, www.digitalinsight.com; North Coast Electric website, accessed December 24, 2009, www.northcoastelectric.com; Billtrust website, accessed December 24, 2009, www.billtrust.com.

Company	Business	Competitive Use of Information Systems
Gillette	Consumer products	Developed advanced computerized manufacturing systems to produce high-quality products at low cost
Shoppers Drug Mart	Drugstore	Developed communications systems to link local stores to centralized computer systems
President's Choice Financial	Financial services	Developed online, no-fee 24-hour banking and increased customer service using information systems

Table 1.6

How Some Companies Used Technology to Improve Their Business

Taking advantage of the existing situation, including an economic downturn, can also help a firm achieve a competitive advantage. In 2010 and 2011, while some companies struggled with the economy and slumping sales, other companies were investing in information systems to give them a long-term advantage.[82] UPS, for example, planned on investing about $1 billion in new information systems. According to the company's CIO, "We firmly believe the strong companies will come out of this downturn stronger. This is an opportunity to get your company positioned to grow on the upturn."

Factors That Lead Firms to Seek Competitive Advantage

A number of factors can lead to attaining a competitive advantage. Michael Porter, a prominent management theorist, suggested a now widely accepted competitive forces model, also called the **five-forces model**. The five forces are (1) the rivalry among existing competitors, (2) the threat of new entrants, (3) the threat of substitute products and services, (4) the bargaining power of buyers, and (5) the bargaining power of suppliers. The more these forces combine in any instance, the more likely firms will seek competitive advantage and the more dramatic the results of such an advantage will be.

five-forces model
A widely accepted model that identifies five key factors that can lead to attainment of competitive advantage: (1) the rivalry among existing competitors, (2) the threat of new entrants, (3) the threat of substitute products and services, (4) the bargaining power of buyers, and (5) the bargaining power of suppliers.

Rivalry Among Existing Competitors

Typically, highly competitive industries are characterized by high fixed costs of entering or leaving the industry, low degrees of product differentiation, and many competitors. Although all firms are rivals with their competitors, industries with stronger rivalries tend to have more firms seeking competitive advantage. To gain an advantage over competitors, companies constantly analyze how they use their resources and assets. This resource-based view is an approach to acquiring and controlling assets or resources that can help the company achieve a competitive advantage. For example, a transportation company might decide to invest in radio-frequency technology to tag and trace products as they move from one location to another.

Threat of New Entrants

A threat appears when entry and exit costs to an industry are low and the technology needed to start and maintain a business is commonly available. For example, a small restaurant is threatened by new competitors. Owners of small restaurants do not require millions of dollars to start the business, food costs do not decline substantially for large volumes, and food processing and preparation equipment is easily available. When the threat of new market entrants is high, the desire to seek and maintain competitive advantage to dissuade new entrants is also usually high.

Threat of Substitute Products and Services

Companies that offer one type of goods or services are threatened by other companies that offer similar goods or services. The more consumers can obtain similar products and services that satisfy their needs, the more likely firms are to try to establish competitive advantage.

In the restaurant industry, competition is fierce because entry costs are low. Therefore, a small restaurant that enters the market can be a threat to existing restaurants.

(Source: Emin Kuliyev/Shutterstock.com.)

For example, consider the photographic industry. When digital cameras became popular, traditional film companies had to respond to stay competitive and profitable. Traditional film companies, such as Kodak and others, started to offer additional products and enhanced services, including digital cameras, the ability to produce digital images from traditional film cameras, and websites that could be used to store, view, print, and share pictures.

Bargaining Power of Customers and Suppliers

Large customers tend to influence a firm, and this influence can increase significantly if the customers can threaten to switch to rival companies. When customers have a lot of bargaining power, companies increase their competitive advantage to retain their customers. Similarly, when the bargaining power of suppliers is strong, companies need to improve their competitive advantage to maintain their bargaining position. Suppliers can also help an organization gain a competitive advantage. Some suppliers enter into strategic alliances with firms and eventually act as a part of the company. Suppliers and companies can use telecommunications to link their computers and personnel to react quickly and provide parts or supplies as necessary to satisfy customers.

Strategic Planning for Competitive Advantage

To be competitive, a company must be fast, nimble, flexible, innovative, productive, economical, and customer oriented. It must also align its IS strategy with general business strategies and objectives.[83] Given the five market forces previously mentioned, Porter and others have proposed a number of strategies to attain competitive advantage, including cost leadership, differentiation, niche strategy, altering the industry structure, creating new products and services, and improving existing product lines and services.[84] In some cases, one of these strategies becomes dominant. For example, with a cost leadership strategy, cost can be the key consideration—at the expense of other factors if need be.

- **Cost leadership.** Deliver the lowest possible cost for products and services. Walmart and other discount retailers have used this strategy for years. Cost leadership is often achieved by reducing the costs of raw materials through aggressive negotiations with suppliers, becoming more efficient with production and manufacturing processes, and reducing warehousing and shipping costs. Some companies use outsourcing to cut costs when making products or completing services.
- **Differentiation.** Deliver different products and services. This strategy can involve producing a variety of products, giving customers more choices, or delivering higher-quality products and services. Many car companies make different models that use the same basic parts and components, giving customers more options. Other car companies attempt to increase perceived quality and safety to differentiate their products and

Walmart and other discount retailers have used a cost leadership strategy to deliver the lowest possible price for products and services.

(Source: Jeff Zelevansky/Getty Images.)

appeal to consumers who are willing to pay higher prices for these features. Companies that try to differentiate their products often strive to uncover and eliminate counterfeit products produced and delivered by others.

- **Niche strategy.** Deliver to only a small, niche market. Porsche, for example, doesn't produce inexpensive economy cars. It makes high-performance sports cars and SUVs. Rolex makes only high-quality, expensive watches. It doesn't make inexpensive, plastic watches.

Porsche is an example of a company with a niche strategy, producing only high-performance sports cars and SUVs.

(Source: Max Earey/Shutterstock.com.)

- **Altering the industry structure.** Change the industry to become more favourable to the company or organization. The introduction of low-fare airline carriers, such as Porter Airlines and WestJet, has changed the Canadian airline industry, making it difficult for Air Canada to make high profit margins. To compete, Air Canada launched Jazz, its regional and destination airline, and introduced many economy and business class fares that offer clients different travel options. Creating strategic alliances can also alter the industry structure. A **strategic alliance**, also called a **strategic partnership**, is an agreement between two or more companies that involves the joint production and distribution of goods and services. As a member of the Star Alliance, a global airline network of international airlines, Air Canada can offer its customers improved convenience and efficiency when travelling around the world.

strategic alliance (or strategic partnership)
An agreement between two or more companies that involves the joint production and distribution of goods and services.

- **Creating new products and services.** Introduce new products and services periodically or frequently. This strategy always helps a firm gain a competitive advantage, especially for the computer industry and other high-tech businesses. If an organization does not introduce new products and services every few months, the company can quickly stagnate, lose market share, and decline. Companies that stay on top are constantly developing new products and services. CIBC, for example, was the first Canadian bank to offer an Internet-based mobile banking application for the iPhone.[85]

- **Improving existing product lines and services.** Make real or perceived improvements to existing product lines and services. Manufacturers of household products are always advertising new and improved products. In some cases, the improvements are more perceived than actual refinements; usually, only minor changes are made to the existing product, such as to reduce the amount of sugar in breakfast cereal.

- **Other strategies.** Some companies seek strong *growth in sales*, hoping that it can increase profits in the long run due to increased sales. Being the *first to market* is another competitive strategy. Apple Computer was one of the first companies to offer complete and easy-to-use personal computers. Some companies offer *customized* products and services to achieve a competitive advantage. Dell, for example, builds custom PCs for consumers. *Hire the best people* is another example of a competitive strategy. The assumption is that the best people will determine the best products and services to deliver to the market and the best approach to deliver these products and services. Having *agile* information systems that can rapidly change with changing conditions and environments can be a key to information systems success and a competitive advantage.[86] Achieving a high level of efficiency and effectiveness is an important challenge of developing an agile information system. Other challenges included satisfying various governmental regulations, meeting customer requirements, and maintaining a good growth level. *Innovation* is another competitive strategy.[87] Vodafone relied on outside help to provide innovative solutions in its wireless business.[88] According its chief executive, "The only way to create a fertile environment for innovation is to have open platforms and leverage them." Natural Selection, a San Diego company, originally developed a computer program that attempted to analyze past inventions and suggest future ones.[89] Although the original program was not an immediate success, the approach has been used by General Electric, the U.S. Air Force, and others to cut costs and streamline delivery routes of products. According to one expert, "Successful innovations are often built on the back of failed ones." A lack of innovation can lead to a loss in competitiveness and long-term profitability.[90] Some believe that less innovation has led to lower productivity, lower profits, and lower wages and salaries for managers and workers. Companies can also combine one or more of these strategies. In addition to customization, Dell attempts to offer low-cost computers (cost leadership) and top-notch service (differentiation).

PERFORMANCE-BASED INFORMATION SYSTEMS

Businesses have passed through at least three major stages in their use of information systems. In the first stage, organizations focused on using information systems to reduce costs and improve productivity. TransUnion, a large credit reporting company, reduced computer-related costs by about $2.5 million annually by investing $50,000 in a corporate social networking Internet site.[91] According to the chief technology officer, "The savings mostly come out of teams that would have historically said 'Buy me more hardware' or 'I need a new software tool' who figured out how to solve their problems without asking for those things." Companies can also use software tools, such as Apptio's IT Cost Optimization Solutions, to cut the costs of computer upgrades, reduce the number of computers, and help determine what to charge business units for providing computer services and equipment.[92]

The second stage was defined by Porter and others. It was oriented toward gaining a competitive advantage. In many cases, companies spent large amounts on information systems and downplayed the costs.

Today, companies are shifting from strategic management to performance-based management of their information systems. In this third stage, companies carefully consider both strategic advantage and costs. They use productivity, return on investment (ROI), net present value, and other measures of performance to evaluate the contributions their information systems make to their businesses. Figure 1.20 illustrates these stages. This balanced approach attempts to reduce costs and increase revenues.

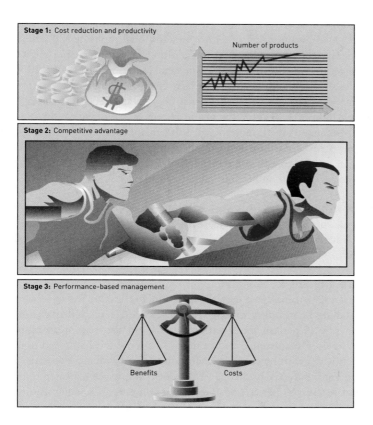

Figure 1.20

Three Stages in the Business Use of Information Systems

Productivity

Developing information systems that measure and control productivity is a key element for most organizations. **Productivity** is a measure of the output achieved divided by the input required. A higher level of output for a given level of input means greater productivity; a lower level of output for a given level of input means lower productivity. The numbers assigned to productivity levels are not always based on labour hours—productivity can be based on factors such as the amount of raw materials used, resulting quality, or time to produce the goods or service. The value of the productivity number is not as significant as how it compares with other time periods, settings, and organizations. Xerox has developed an information system called Lean Document Production (LDP) solutions, intended to increase printer productivity and reduce costs.[93] According to one researcher, "These solutions, which Xerox has implemented in approximately 100 sites to date, have provided dramatic productivity and cost improvements for both print shops and document-manufacturing facilities."

Productivity = (Output / Input) × 100%

After a basic level of productivity is measured, an information system can monitor and compare it over time to see whether productivity is increasing. Then a company can take corrective action if productivity drops below certain levels. An automotive

productivity
A measure of the output achieved divided by the input required.

company, for example, might use robots in assembling new cars to increase its labour productivity and reduce costs. In addition to measuring productivity, an information system can be used within a process to significantly increase productivity. Thus improved productivity can result in faster customer response, lower costs, and increased customer satisfaction.

Return on Investment and the Value of Information Systems

return on investment (ROI)
One measure of IS value that investigates the additional profits or benefits that are generated as a percentage of the investment in IS technology.

One measure of IS value is **return on investment** (**ROI**). This measure investigates the additional profits or benefits that are generated as a percentage of the investment in IS technology. A small business that generates an additional profit of $20,000 for the year as a result of an investment of $100,000 for additional computer equipment and software would have a return on investment of 20 percent ($20,000/$100,000). ROI calculations can be complex, including investment returns over several years and the impact of the time value of money. Some researchers believe that how an IS function is managed and run is one of the best indicators of the value of the system to the organization and its return on investment.[94] Because of the importance of ROI, many computer companies provide ROI calculators to potential customers. ROI calculators are typically provided on a vendor's website and can be used to estimate returns. Kodak, for example, has an ROI calculator for many of its products based on lifetime value to customers.[95]

Earnings Growth

Another measure of IS value is the increase in profit, or earnings growth, the system brings. For instance, a mail-order company might install an order-processing system that generates a 7 percent earnings growth compared with the previous year.

Market Share and Speed to Market

Market share is the percentage of sales that a product or service has in relation to the total market. If installing a new online catalogue increases sales, it might help a company increase its market share by 20 percent. Information systems can also help organizations bring new products and services to customers in less time. This is often called speed to market. Speed can also be a critical performance objective for many organizations. Alternative stock trading systems to the Toronto Stock Exchange (TSE), for example, are expected to grow from less than 3 percent to over 40 percent on the trading volume in Canadian equities within the next few years due to automation and increases in high-frequency equity trading.[96]

Customer Awareness and Satisfaction

Although customer satisfaction can be difficult to quantify, about half of today's best global companies measure the performance of their information systems based on feedback from internal and external users. Some companies and nonprofit organizations use surveys and questionnaires to determine whether the IS investment has increased customer awareness and satisfaction.

Total Cost of Ownership

total cost of ownership (TCO)
The sum of all costs over the life of an information system, including the costs to acquire components such as the technology, technical support, administrative costs, and end-user operations.

Another way to measure the value of information systems was developed by the Gartner Group and is called the **total cost of ownership** (**TCO**). TCO is the sum of all costs over the life of the information system, including the costs to acquire components such as the technology, technical support, administrative costs, and end-user operations. Hitachi uses TCO to promote its projectors to businesses and individuals.[97] TCO is also used by many other companies to rate and select hardware, software, databases, and other computer-related components.

Return on investment, earnings growth, market share, customer satisfaction, and TCO are only a few measures that companies use to plan for and maximize the value of their IS investments. Regardless of the difficulties, organizations must attempt to evaluate the contributions that information systems make to assess their progress and plan for the future. Information systems and personnel are too important to leave to chance.

Risk

In addition to the return-on-investment measures of a new or modified system discussed in this chapter, managers must also consider the risks of designing, developing, and implementing these systems. Information systems can sometimes be costly failures. Some systems development efforts fail to meet their cost or schedule goals. In Ontario, a $1-billion provincial electronic health record project failed to operate as intended.[98] The risks of designing, developing, and implementing new or modified systems are covered in more detail in Chapters 12 and 13, which discuss systems development.

SYSTEMS DEVELOPMENT

Systems development is the activity of creating or modifying information systems. Systems development projects can range from small to very large and are conducted in fields as diverse as stock analysis and video game development. Individuals from around the world are using the steps of systems development to create unique applications for the iPhone.[99] People inside a company can develop systems, or companies can use outsourcing, hiring an outside company to perform some or all of a systems development project. Outsourcing allows a company to focus on what it does best and delegate other functions to companies with expertise in systems development. Systems development failures can be a result of poor planning and scheduling, insufficient management of risk, poor requirements determination, and lack of user involvement. One strategy for improving the results of a systems development project is to divide it into several steps, each with a well-defined goal and set of tasks to accomplish (see Figure 1.21).

The first two steps of systems development are systems investigation and analysis. The goal of the systems investigation is to gain a clear understanding of the problem to be solved or opportunity to be addressed. After an organization understands the problem, the next question is "Is the problem worth solving?" If the decision is to continue with the solution, the next step, systems analysis, defines the problems and opportunities of the existing system. During systems investigation and analysis, as well as design maintenance and review, discussed next, the project must have the complete support of top-level managers and must focus on developing systems that achieve business goals.

Systems design determines how the new system should be developed to meet the business needs defined during systems analysis. For some companies, this involves environmental design that attempts to reduce impact on the environment while still making a profit. The GreenStar Network project, for example, could make Canada the largest Internet service provider with almost no carbon footprint. The project will use cloud computing and a virtual infrastructure of linked data centres across Canada. The data centres will run on renewable green energy.[100] Systems implementation involves creating or acquiring the various system components (hardware,

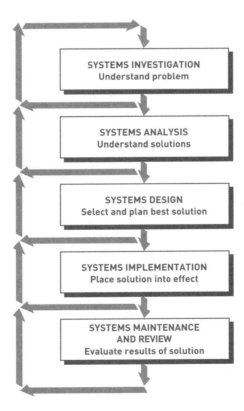

Figure 1.21

An Overview of Systems Development

software, databases, etc.) defined in the design step, assembling them, and putting the new system into operation. For many organizations, this includes purchasing software, hardware, databases, and other IS components. The purpose of systems maintenance and review is to check and modify the system so that it continues to meet changing business needs.

GLOBAL CHALLENGES IN INFORMATION SYSTEMS

Changes in society as a result of increased international trade and cultural exchange, often called globalization, have always had a significant impact on organizations and their information systems. Global markets have expanded. People and companies can get products and services from around the world, instead of around the corner or across town. These opportunities, however, introduce numerous obstacles and issues, including challenges involving culture and language.

- **Cultural challenges.** Countries and regional areas have their own cultures and customs that can significantly affect individuals and organizations involved in global trade.
- **Language challenges.** Language differences can make it difficult to translate exact meanings from one language to another.
- **Time and distance challenges.** Time and distance issues can be difficult to overcome for individuals and organizations involved with global trade in remote locations. Large time differences make it difficult to talk to people on the other side of the world. With long distances, it can take days to get a product or part from one location to another.
- **Infrastructure challenges.** High-quality electricity and water might not be available in certain parts of the world. Telephone services, Internet connections, and skilled employees might be expensive or not readily available.
- **Currency challenges.** The value of various currencies can vary significantly over time, making international trade more difficult and complex.
- **Product and service challenges.** Traditional products that are physical or tangible, such as an automobile or bicycle, can be difficult to deliver to the global market. However, electronic products (e-products) and electronic services (e-services) can be delivered to customers electronically, over the phone, via networks, through the Internet, or by other electronic means. Software, music, books, manuals, and advice can all be delivered globally and over the Internet.
- **Technology transfer issues.** Most governments don't allow certain military-related equipment and systems to be sold to some countries. Even so, some believe that foreign companies are stealing intellectual property, trade secrets, and copyrighted materials and that they are counterfeiting products and services.
- **Local, regional, and national laws.** Each region and country has a set of laws that must be obeyed by citizens and organizations operating in the country. These laws can deal with a variety of issues, including trade secrets, patents, copyrights, protection of personal or financial data, privacy, and much more. Laws restricting how data enters or exits a country are often called transborder data-flow laws. Keeping track of these laws and incorporating them into the procedures and computer systems of multinational and transnational organizations can be very difficult and time consuming, requiring expert legal advice.
- **Trade agreements.** Countries often enter into trade agreements with each other. The North American Free Trade Agreement (NAFTA) and the Central American Free Trade Agreement (CAFTA) are examples. The European Union (EU) is another example of a group of countries with an international trade agreement.[101] Free trade agreements have also been established between Canada and Costa Rica, Canada and Israel, Chile and Korea, Mexico and Japan, the United States and Jordan, and many others.[102]

SUMMARY

Principle:

The value of information is directly linked to how it helps decision makers achieve the organization's goals.

Information systems are used in almost every imaginable career area. Regardless of your college or university major or chosen career, you will find that information systems are indispensable tools to help you achieve your career goals. Learning about information systems can help you get your first job, earn promotions, and advance your career.

Data consists of raw facts; information is data transformed into a meaningful form. The process of defining relationships among data requires knowledge. Knowledge is an awareness and understanding of a set of information and the way that information can support a specific task. To be valuable, information must have several characteristics: it should be accurate, complete, economical to produce, flexible, reliable, relevant, simple to understand, timely, verifiable, accessible, and secure. The value of information is directly linked to how it helps people achieve their organizations' goals.

Principle:

Computers and information systems help make it possible for organizations to improve the way they conduct business. The use of information systems to add value to the organization is strongly influenced by organizational structure, culture, and change.

Organizations use information systems to support their goals. Because information systems typically are designed to improve productivity, organizations should devise methods for measuring the system's impact on productivity. System performance is measured by its efficiency and effectiveness. Efficiency is a measure of what is produced divided by what is consumed; effectiveness measures the extent to which a system achieves its goals. A systems performance standard is a specific objective.

An organization is a formal collection of people and other resources established to accomplish a set of goals. The primary goal of a for-profit organization is to maximize shareholder value. Nonprofit organizations include social groups, religious groups, universities, and other organizations that do not have profit as the primary goal.

Organizations are systems with inputs, transformation mechanisms, and outputs. Value-added processes increase the relative worth of the combined inputs on their way to becoming final outputs of the organization. The value chain is a series (chain) of activities that includes (1) inbound logistics, (2) warehouse and storage, (3) production, (4) finished product storage, (5) outbound logistics, (6) marketing and sales, and (7) customer service.

Organizational structure refers to how organizational subunits relate to the overall organization. Several basic organizational structures include traditional, project, team, and virtual. A virtual organizational structure employs individuals, groups, or complete business units in geographically dispersed areas. These can involve people in various countries operating in different time zones and different cultures from each other.

Organizational culture consists of the major understandings and assumptions for a business, corporation, or organization. Organizational change deals with how profit and nonprofit organizations plan for, implement, and handle change. Change can be caused by internal or external factors. The stages of the change model are unfreezing, moving, and refreezing. According to the concept of organizational learning, organizations adapt to new conditions or alter practices over time.

Principle:

Because information systems are so important, businesses need to be sure that improvements or completely new systems help lower costs, increase profits, improve service, or achieve a competitive advantage.

Business process reengineering involves the radical redesign of business processes, organizational structures, information systems, and values of the organization to achieve a breakthrough in results. Continuous improvement to business processes can add value to products and services.

The extent to which technology is used throughout an organization can be a function of technology diffusion, infusion, and acceptance. Technology diffusion is a measure of how widely technology is in place throughout an organization. Technology infusion is the extent to which technology permeates an area or department. User satisfaction with a computer system and the information it generates depends on the quality of the system and the resulting information. The technology acceptance model (TAM) investigates factors—such as the perceived usefulness of the technology, the ease of use of the technology, the quality of the information system, and the degree to which the organization supports the use of the information system—to predict IS usage and performance.

Total quality management consists of a collection of approaches, tools, and techniques that fosters a commitment to quality throughout the organization. Six Sigma is often used in quality control. It is based on a statistical term that means 99.9997 percent of the time, products and services will meet quality standards.

Outsourcing involves contracting with outside professional services to meet specific business needs. This approach allows the company to focus more closely on its core business and to target its limited resources to meet strategic goals. Downsizing involves reducing the number of employees to reduce payroll costs; however, it can lead to unwanted side effects.

Competitive advantage is usually embodied in either a product or service that has the most added value to consumers and that is unavailable from the competition or in an internal system that delivers benefits to a firm not enjoyed by its competition. Porter's five-forces model covers factors that lead firms to seek competitive advantage: the rivalry among existing competitors, the threat of new market entrants, the threat of substitute products and services, the bargaining power of buyers, and the bargaining power of suppliers. Strategies to address these factors and to attain competitive advantage include cost leadership, differentiation, niche strategy, altering the industry structure, creating new products and services, and improving existing product lines and services.

Developing information systems that measure and control productivity is a key element for most organizations. A useful measure of the value of an IS project is return on investment (ROI). This measure investigates the additional profits or benefits that are generated as a percentage of the investment in IS technology. Total cost of ownership (TCO) can also be a useful measure.

Principle:

Information systems must be applied thoughtfully and carefully so that society, businesses, and industries can reap their enormous benefits.

Systems development involves creating or modifying existing business systems. The major steps of this process and their goals are systems investigation (gain a clear understanding of what the problem is), systems analysis (define what the system must do to solve the problem), systems design (determine exactly how the system will work to meet the business needs), systems implementation (create or acquire the various system components defined in the design step), and systems maintenance and review (maintain and then modify the system so that it continues to meet changing business needs).

Information systems play a fundamental and ever-expanding role in society, business, and industry. But their use can also raise serious security, privacy, and ethical issues. Effective information systems can have a major impact on corporate strategy and organizational success. Businesses around the globe are enjoying better safety and service, greater efficiency and effectiveness, reduced expenses, and improved decision making and control because of information systems. Changes in society as a result of increased international trade and cultural exchange due to globalization have always had a significant impact on organizations and their information systems. These opportunities, however, introduce numerous obstacles and issues, including challenges involving culture and language.

CHAPTER 1: SELF-ASSESSMENT TEST

The value of information is directly linked to how it helps decision makers achieve the organization's goals.

1. A(n) _____ is a set of interrelated components that collect, manipulate, and disseminate data and information as well as provide a feedback mechanism to meet an objective.
2. A(n) _____ is a set of elements or components that interact to accomplish a goal.
3. Which of the following is best described as a measure of what is produced divided by what is consumed?
   a. efficiency
   b. effectiveness
   c. performance
   d. productivity
4. What system is an organized collection of people, procedures, software, databases, and devices used to create, store, share, and use the organization's experience and knowledge?
   a. a TPS (transaction processing system)
   b. a MIS (management information system)
   c. a DSS (decision support system)
   d. a KMS (knowledge management system)

The use of information systems to add value to the organization is strongly influenced by organizational structure, culture, and change.

5. User satisfaction with a computer system and the information it generates often depends on the quality of the system and the resulting information. True or False?

6. Which of the following employs individuals, groups, or complete business units in geographically dispersed areas, often requiring telecommunications or the Internet?
   a. learning structure
   b. virtual structure
   c. a continuous improvement plan
   d. a reengineering project

Because information systems are so important, businesses need to be sure that improvements or completely new systems help lower costs, increase profits, improve service, or achieve a competitive advantage.

7. _____ involves contracting with outside professional services to meet specific business needs.
8. Which of the following best describes quality as it is understood today?
   a. achieving production standards
   b. meeting or exceeding customer expectations
   c. maximizing total profits
   d. meeting or achieving design specifications
9. Technology satisfaction is a measure of how widely technology is spread throughout an organization. True or False?
10. Reengineering is also called _____.
11. _____ is a measure of the additional profits or benefits generated as a percentage of the investment in IS technology.

Information systems must be applied thoughtfully and carefully so that society, businesses, and industries can reap their enormous benefits.

12. What defines the problems and opportunities of an existing system?
    a. systems analysis
    b. systems review
    c. systems development
    d. systems design

CHAPTER 1: SELF-ASSESSMENT TEST ANSWERS

(1) information system (2) system (3) a (4) d (5) True (6) b (7) Outsourcing (8) b (9) False (10) process redesign (11) Return on investment (12) a

REVIEW QUESTIONS

1. How is data different from information? Information from knowledge?
2. What is the difference between efficiency and effectiveness?
3. How is system performance measured?
4. What is a computer-based information system? What are its components?
5. What is the difference between e-commerce and m-commerce?
6. What role does an information system play in today's organizations?
7. What is reengineering? What are the potential benefits of performing a process redesign?
8. What is the difference between reengineering and continuous improvement?
9. What is the difference between technology infusion and technology diffusion?
10. What is quality? What is total quality management (TQM)? What is Six Sigma?
11. What are organizational change and organizational learning?
12. List and define the basic organizational structures.
13. Briefly describe the three-stage organizational change model.
14. What are some general strategies employed by organizations to achieve competitive advantage?
15. Define the term "productivity." How can a company best use productivity measurements?
16. What is the total cost of ownership?
17. Identify the steps in the systems development process and state the goal of each.

DISCUSSION QUESTIONS

1. Describe the "ideal" automated class registration system for a college or university. Compare this "ideal" system with what is available at your college or university.
2. You have decided to open an Internet site to buy and sell used music CDs. Describe your approach to customer relationship management for your new business.
3. Discuss how information systems are linked to the business objectives of an organization.
4. What are the advantages of using a traditional organizational structure? What are the disadvantages?
5. How would you measure technology diffusion and infusion?
6. You have been asked to participate in preparing your company's strategic plan. Specifically, your task is to analyze the competitive marketplace using Porter's five-forces model. Prepare your analysis, using your knowledge of a business you have worked for or have an interest in working for.
7. Based on the analysis you performed in Discussion Question 6, what possible strategies could your organization adopt to address these challenges? What role could information systems play in these strategies? Use Porter's strategies as a guide.
8. There are many ways to evaluate the effectiveness of an information system. Discuss each method and describe when one method would be preferred over another method.

PROBLEM-SOLVING EXERCISES

1. Prepare a data disk and a backup disk for the problem-solving exercises and other computer-based assignments you will complete in this class. Create one folder for each chapter in the textbook (you should have 13 folders). As you work through the problem-solving exercises and complete other work using the computer, save your assignments for each chapter in the appropriate folder. On the label of each disk or USB flash drive, be sure to include your name, course, and section. On one disk write "Working Copy"; on the other write "Backup."

2. Search through several business magazines (*Business Week, Computerworld, PC Week,* etc.) or use an Internet search engine to find recent articles that describe potential social or ethical issues related to the use of an information system. Use word processing software to write a one-page report summarizing what you discovered.

3. Do some research to obtain estimates of the rate of growth of social networking sites like MySpace and Facebook. Use the plotting capabilities of your spreadsheet or graphics software to produce a bar chart of that growth over a number of years. Share your findings with the class.

4. Identify three companies that make the highest-quality products or services for an industry of your choice. Find the number of employees, total sales, total profits, and earnings growth rate for these three firms. Using a database program, enter this information for the last year. Use the database to generate a report of the three companies with the highest earnings growth rate. Use your word processor to create a document that describes these firms and why you believe they make the highest-quality products and services. What other measures would you use to determine which is the best company with regard to future profit potential? Does high quality always mean high profits?

5. A new IS project has been proposed that is expected to produce not only cost savings but also an increase in revenue. The initial costs to establish the system are estimated to be $500,000. The remaining cash flow data is presented in the following table.

	Year 1	Year 2	Year 3	Year 4	Year 5
Increased Revenue ($)	0	100	150	200	250
Cost Savings ($)	0	50	50	50	50
Depreciation ($)	0	75	75	75	75
Initial Expense ($)	500				

Note: All amounts are in hundreds of thousands.

a. Using a spreadsheet program, calculate the return on investment (ROI) for this project. Assume that the cost of capital is 7 percent.

b. How would the rate of return change if the project delivered $50,000 in additional revenue and generated cost savings of $25,000 in the first year?

TEAM ACTIVITIES

1. Before you can do a team activity, you need a team! With the other members of your group, use word processing software to write a one-page summary of what your team hopes to gain from this course and what you are willing to do to accomplish these goals. Send the report to your instructor via e-mail.

2. With your team, interview one or more instructors or professors at your college or university. Describe how they keep current with the latest teaching and research developments in their field.

3. Research a firm that has achieved a competitive advantage. Write a brief report that describes how the company was able to achieve its competitive advantage.

WEB EXERCISES

1. This book emphasizes the importance of information. You can get information from the Internet by going to a specific address, such as *www.ibm.com* or *www.gov.bc.ca.* This will give you access to the home pages of the IBM corporation and the British Columbia provincial government. Note that "com" is used for businesses or

commercial operations, "gov" is used for some governmental offices, and "ca" is used for Canadian websites. Another approach is to use a search engine, which is a website that allows you to enter key words or phrases to find information. Yahoo!, developed by two university students, was one of the first search engines on the Internet. You can also locate information through lists or menus. The search engine will return other websites (hits) that correspond to a search request. Using Yahoo! at *www.yahoo.ca* or Google at *www.google.ca*, search for information about a company discussed in this chapter. You might be asked to develop a report or send an e-mail message to your instructor about the company and its products and services.

2. Use the Internet to search for information about a company that has excellent or poor product quality in your estimation. You can use a search engine, such as Google, or a database at your college or university. Write a brief report describing what you found. What leads to higher-quality products? How can an information system help a company produce higher-quality products?
3. Using the Internet, search for information on the use of information systems in a company or organization that interests you. How does the organization use technology to help it accomplish its goals?

CAREER EXERCISES

1. Assume that you have decided to become an entrepreneur in a technology-related business. Describe the technology-related business, including its products and services. How would you organize your business? Write a brief business plan on how you would make your business a success.
2. Pick the five best companies for your career. Describe the quality of the products and services offered by each company. What employee benefits and opportunities are available from each company? How does each company use information systems to its benefit? Are the best companies always the ones with the highest-quality products and services?

CASE STUDIES

Case One
Creativity Moves Up the Value Chain

Creativity Inc. deals in beads, baubles, and stylized paper to "bring crafters' dreams to reality by providing the materials to give life to their ideas and imagination." Creativity owns six well-known brands in the craft industry: Autumn Leaves, Blue Moon Beads, Crop in Style, DND, Hip in a Hurry, and Westrim Crafts. The company is one of the top five wholesale suppliers to national craft chains in the United States with 500 employees at four office and warehouse locations in California and one in Hong Kong.

Creativity outsources the manufacturing of its designs to production facilities across Asia. Crates of assorted beads, scrapbooking supplies, and papercrafting materials flow through Creativity's port-side warehouses to craft stores and department stores across the United States. In this way, Creativity facilitates the value chain for craft retailers.

In 2007, Creativity found its business model challenged by growing globalization and economic hardships. To save money, some of its customers decided to "do away with the middleman" and purchase crafting materials directly from the Asian

manufacturers. Creativity needed to find new ways to provide value to its customers.

Creativity's challenges are not unique. Many businesses are facing growing competition from low-cost manufacturers and service providers in developing countries. To survive, they need to find a way to move up the value chain—that is, to provide valuable services beyond upstream management of the supply chain. Many are turning to information systems to assist in that move.

Creativity turned to IBM's Cognos 8 Business Intelligence suite to identify high-value products that could not be manufactured by its low-cost overseas competitors. The company acquired data about purchase transactions from retailers in craft-related markets and added that data to its data warehouse. Using the Cognos software and Smart Software's SmartForecast program, Creativity determined a need for more "design-oriented, fashion-oriented" products—especially ones associated with popular U.S. media, such as television shows and celebrities.

By shifting its focus to fashion-based craft products, Creativity made up for the business it lost in the low-cost crafting material market. In fact, fashion-oriented products are now the dominant portion of its business, making up more than 50 percent of its products and a much higher percentage of its profits.

Creativity also uses Cognos to determine which customer segments are most profitable. The company can then focus its efforts in those areas to boost profitability. In addition, Creativity created the "Analytical Center of Excellence," composed of representatives from all of its brands. By improving communication between its brands and sharing its research findings, Creativity elevated the corporate awareness of the entire company and created an environment where everyone is working toward common goals. To further communication, CIO Jim Mulholland used Cognos to develop a software dashboard that provides corporate news and information on the desktops of company managers across its brands. These communication improvements help safeguard against duplication of effort. Each brand is aware of what the other brands are experiencing and working on, allowing brands to learn from each other.

Creativity and other struggling businesses want to create valuable information from low-cost data to learn how to work more intelligently and efficiently. Integrating data from transactions, call centres, Web logs, sales reps, external sources, and elsewhere into data warehouses for analysis allows companies to discover what products are likely to sell, what products return the highest profits, where to cut costs, where to invest for the highest return, and other key information to fuel smart decision making. Many businesses are counting on information systems to provide the knowledge to survive tough economic times.

Discussion Questions

1. Describe the global economic forces that pushed Creativity to move up the value chain.
2. What information did Creativity use to boost its profits and remain solvent?

Critical Thinking Questions

1. What role does communication play in creating savings for a multi-brand company like Creative?
2. What lessons does Creative's story provide for other businesses? What does this forecast for the global marketplace in general?

SOURCES: Mitchell, Robert, "Smart and Cheap: Business Intelligence on a Budget," *Computerworld*, May 14, 2009, *www.computerworld.com*; Creativity Inc. website, accessed December 26, 2009, *www.creativityinc.com*; Cognos website, accessed December 26, 2009, *www-01.ibm.com/software/data/cognos*.

Case Two
Media Companies Centralize and Outsource to Survive

The transition of media from television and newspapers to the Internet has those industries scrambling to redefine their business models. A powerful force driving the change is advertisers' transition to digital media. Consider as evidence the decision by Pepsi to discontinue its famous Super Bowl commercials so it could invest more heavily in an online marketing campaign. Such transitions of advertising dollars from traditional media to the Internet are dramatically affecting media companies, especially news agencies. News agencies are changing the way they produce the news by centralizing and outsourcing operations to make up for lost revenue.

While outsourcing IT operations to India and other countries is hardly a new concept for businesses in general, media companies have been late to the game. Recently media companies have begun outsourcing information system services and are considering outsourcing many others.

News Corp UK announced that it outsourced its data centre management and IT infrastructure operations to HCL Technologies Ltd., a major Indian offshore company. India's offshore companies and others around the world are extending their reach into other media services above and beyond traditional information systems.

Pagemasters is an Australian company that provides copy-editing services for media companies. It recently partnered with the Canadian Press to set up a branch in Toronto to service North American news agencies. The *Toronto Star* laid off 78 employees who were responsible for copy editing and pagination, replacing them with outsourced services from Pagemasters. The move saved the newspaper an estimated 40 percent in the cost of these services. Pagemasters does not provide savings by using low-wage employees, as is the case with developing countries. Instead it provides savings by applying efficiencies and economies of scale. In other words, because editing and pagination is its only focus, Pagemasters is able to apply its expertise to reduce its costs and serve many newspapers more efficiently.

The 78 unemployed *Toronto Star* copy editors could seek employment from Pagemasters or another similar company. If they do, they will be participating in a different business model for the media industry. Centralizing business tasks is a trend in outsourcing with roots within the companies themselves. Rather than having many copy desks, one for each area of a publication, a media company could centralize the work into a single copy desk that serves all aspects of the publication. The natural next step is to outsource those centralized functions when they can cut expenses without losing quality.

After outsourcing information system infrastructure and data centre operations, the next opportunity for experiencing savings is to outsource content management. Bangalore-based Wipro Technologies Ltd. announced that it is working with a "major North American media company" to manage its online content. Media companies are now beginning to outsource editorial services and even some content creation as well. As they outsource increasing amounts of organizational operations, media companies must determine what unique service they provide that distinguishes them from their competitors.

Discussion Questions

1. What social and economic forces are causing the media industry to redefine its business model?
2. What changes are those in the media industry making to adapt to their financial challenges?

Critical Thinking Questions

1. What risks to quality, if any, do media companies face when outsourcing editing and content creation to overseas countries?
2. How does centralizing and outsourcing services in the media industry compare to centralizing and outsourcing in other businesses?

SOURCES: Thibodeau, Patrick, "Media Increasingly Outsources Tech, Copy Editing," *Computerworld*, December 9, 2009; Vranica, Suzanne, "Pepsi Benches Its Drinks," *Wall Street Journal online*, *online.wsj.com*, December 17, 2009; Pagemasters website, *www.pagemasters.com.au*, accessed December 26, 2009.

Questions for Web Case

See the website for this book to read about the Altitude Online case for this chapter. The following questions cover this Web case.

Altitude Online: Addressing the Needs of the Organization

Discussion Questions

1. What are the advantages of Altitude Online adopting a new ERP system compared to simply connecting existing corporate systems?

2. What information do you think Jon should collect from the branch offices to plan the new centralized information system?

3. Why isn't an out-of-the-box ERP system enough for Altitude Online? What additional needs does the company have? Is this the case for businesses in other industries as well?

Critical Thinking Questions

1. While Jon is visiting the branch offices, how might he prepare them for the inevitable upheaval caused by the upcoming overhaul to the information system? Why do you think Jon is taking weeks to directly communicate with stakeholders about the new system?

2. Why do you think Jon and the system administrators decided to outsource the software for this system to an ERP company rather than developing it from scratch themselves?

NOTES

Sources for the opening vignette: Swanborg, Rick, "CRM: How Marriott Broke Down Customer Data Siloes," *CIO*, November 11, 2009, *www.cio.com*; Overby, Stephanie, "The Keys to Marriott's Success," *CIO*, August 15, 2003, *www.cio.com*; Marriott website—Corporate Information, accessed December 23, 2009, *www.marriott.com/corporateinfo*.

1 Ramiller, N., et al, "Management Implications in Information Systems Research," *Journal of the Association for Information Systems*, Vol. 10, 2009, p. 474.
2 Lurie, N., & Swaminathan, J. M., "Is Timely Information Always Better? The Effect of Feedback Frequency on Decision Making," *Organizational Behavior and Human Decision Processes*, March 2009, p. 315.
3 Pinch, Trevor, "Selling Technology: The Changing Shape of Sales in an Information Economy," *Industrial & Labor Relations Review*, Vol. 23, October 2008, p. 331.
4 Marcial, Gene, "How Expeditors Move the Freight," *BusinessWeek*, November 16, 2009, p. 93.
5 Department of Finance, "Budget 2009—Budget in Brief," *www.budget.gc.ca/2009/glance-apercu/brief-bref-eng.html*, accessed October 21, 2010.
6 Moon, M., "Knowledge Worker Productivity," *Journal of Digital Asset Management*, August 2009, p. 178.
7 Hahn, J., et al., "Knowledge Management Systems and Organizational Knowledge Processing Systems," *Decision Support Systems*, November 2009, p. 332.
8 Lai, J., "How Reward, Computer Self-efficacy, and Perceived Power Security Affect Knowledge Management Systems Success," *Journal of the American Society for Information Science and Technology*, February 2009, p. 332.
9 Daly, John, "There's Millions in Those Milliseconds," *Globe and Mail*, *www.theglobeandmail.com/report-on-business/rob-magazine/theres-millions-in-those-milliseconds/article1443505/*, accessed October 21, 2010.
10 Gardner, David W., "IT Energy Efficiency Slips in Priority," *InformationWeek*, September 8, 2009.
11 "CIO Profiles: Laxman Kumar Badiga," *InformationWeek*, March 2, 2009, p. 16.
12 Farrell, Maureen, "Weatherman," *Forbes*, March 16, 2009, p. 58.
13 Burrows, Peter, "Will Windows 7 Reboot PC Sales?," *BusinessWeek*, September 14, 2009, p. 20.
14 Woolley, Scott, "Extraterrestrial Dreams," *Forbes*, April 13, 2009, p. 36.
15 Hamm, Steve, "Cloud Computing's Big Bang for Business," *BusinessWeek*, June 15, 2009, p. 42.
16 Foley, John, "10 Cloud Computing Predictions," *InformationWeek*, February 2, 2009, p. 20.
17 Angwin, Julia, "My New Twitter Flock," *Wall Street Journal*, March 14, 2009, p. W2.
18 Conlin, Michelle, "To Catch a Corporate Thief," *BusinessWeek*, February 16, 2009, p. 52.
19 D'Arcy, John, et al., "User Awareness of Security Countermeasures," *Information Systems Research*, March 2009, p. 79.
20 Worthen, Ben, "Wide Cyber Attack Is Linked to China," *Wall Street Journal*, March 30, 2009, p. A18.
21 "Ohm Economics," *Forbes*, February 2, 2009, p. 34.
22 "How Web Searches Can Destroy Your Privacy," *Parade*, February 8, 2009, p. 8.
23 Mayor, Tracy, "Erasing Your Tracks," *Computerworld*, November 17, 2009, p. 26.
24 Weier, Mary Hayes, "Collaboration Is Key to Increased Efficiency," *InformationWeek*, September 14, 2009, p. 90.
25 Grant, Tavia, "Workplace Democracy," *Globe and Mail*, May 30, 2009, p. B14.
26 Huang, M., "Marketing and Electronic Commerce," *Electronic Commerce Research and Applications*, October 16, 2009, p. 4.
27 SAP Customer Success Story, "Canada Post," *www.sap.com/canada/solutions/pdf/Canada_Post_BSuite.pdf*, accessed October 21, 2010.
28 Fagerholt, Kjetil, et al., "An Ocean of Opportunities," *OR/MS Today*, April 2009, p. 26.
29 "SAS Helps Royal Bank of Canada Avoid $15 Million in Credit Fraud Losses," *www.sas.com/offices/NA/canada/en/success/SAS-RBC.html*, accessed October 16, 2010.
30 "SAS Helps Indigo Get Personal with Reading Enthusiasts," *www.sas.com/offices/NA/canada/en/success/Indigo.html*, accessed October 16, 2010.
31 Conley, C., et al., "Factors Critical to Knowledge Management Success," *Advances in Developing Human Resources*, August 2009, p. 334.

32 Feng, W., Duan, Y., Fu, Z., & Mathews, B., "Understanding Expert Systems Applications from a Knowledge Transfer Perspective," *Knowledge Management Research & Practice*, June 2009, p. 131.

33 Walton, T., "Virtual Reality Is Reality," *Design Management Review*, Winter 2009, p. 6.

34 "Minister of National Defence Announces New Virtual Reality System at the Glenrose Rehabilitation Hospital," Canada News Centre, *www.news.gc.ca*, April 18, 2010.

35 "The Global CIO Fifth," *InformationWeek*, May 25, 2009, p. 25.

36 "CIO Profiles: Phil Fasano," *InformationWeek*, May 25, 2009, p. 14.

37 Dong, S., et al., "Information Technology in Supply Chains," *Information Systems Research*, March 2009, p. 18.

38 Yang, Jia Lynn, "Veggie Tales," *Fortune*, June 8, 2009, p. 25.

39 Sinha, K., et al., "Health Care Supply Chain Design," *Decision Sciences*, May 2009, p. 197.

40 "CIO Profiles: Laxman Kumar Badiga," *InformationWeek*, March 2, 2009, p. 16.

41 Huifen, Chen, "Courting the Small Enterprise," *Business Times Singapore*, September 22, 2009.

42 Weier, Mary Hayes, "CRM as a Service," *InformationWeek*, February 2, 2009, p. 16.

43 "Center for Empowerment and Economic Development," *Economics Weekly*, September 18, 2009, p. 79.

44 Gevers, J., "Team Self-Regulation and Meeting Deadlines with Project Teams," *European Journal of Work and Organizational Psychology*, September 2009, p. 295.

45 Pressley, C., & Williams, G., "Any Time, Any Place, Anywhere," *Utility Week*, March 27, 2009.

46 "CIO Profiles: Laxman Kumar Badiga," *InformationWeek*, March 2, 2009, p. 16.

47 Brown, Marilyn, "Teachers in Training Take Virtual Lessons," *Tampa Tribune*, January 19, 2009, p. 6.

48 Hempel, Jessi, "How Facebook Is Taking Over Our Lives," *Fortune*, March 2, 2009, p. 49.

49 Singer, S., et al., "Identifying Organizational Cultures That Promote Patient Safety," *Health Care Management Review*, October-December 2009, p. 300.

50 "CIO Profiles: Ken Silva," *InformationWeek*, September 7, 2009, p. 8.

51 Christensen, Clayton, *The Innovator's Dilemma*, Harvard Business School Press, 1997, p. 225, and *The Inventor's Solution*, Harvard Business School Press, 2003.

52 Schein, E. H., *Process Consultation: Its Role in Organizational Development*, Reading, MA: Addison-Wesley, 1969. See also Keen, Peter G. W., "Information Systems and Organizational Change," *Communications of the ACM*, Vol. 24, No. 1, January 1981, pp. 24–33.

53 Klee, Kenneth, "IBM Players Change, But Not M&A Playbook," *Daily Deal*, July 8, 2009.

54 Chiva, R., "Organizational Learning Capabilities and Job Satisfaction," *British Journal of Management*, September 2009, p. 323.

55 "BBVA Reengineers Operations, Saves $2 Million," *TechWeb*, June 4, 2009.

56 Keller, Ralph, "What's Continuous Improvement Worth?" *Industry Week*, August 2008, p. 12.

57 Conry-Murray, Andrew, "A Measure of Satisfaction," *InformationWeek*, January 26, 2009, p. 19.

58 Wixom, Barbara, & Todd, Peter, "A Theoretical Integration of User Satisfaction and Technology Acceptance," *Information Systems Research*, March 2005, p. 85.

59 Bailey, J., & Pearson, W., "Development of a Tool for Measuring and Analyzing Computer User Satisfaction," *Management Science*, 29(5), 1983, p. 530.

60 Chaparro, Barbara, et al., "Using the End-User Computing Satisfaction Instrument to Measure Satisfaction with a Web Site," *Decision Sciences*, May 2005, p. 341.

61 Schwarz, A., & Chin, W., "Toward an Understanding of the Nature and Definition of IT Acceptance," *Journal of the Association for Information Systems*, April 2007, p. 230.

62 Davis, F., "Perceived Usefulness, Perceived Ease of Use, and User Acceptance of Information Technology," *MIS Quarterly*, 13(3) 1989, p. 319. Kwon, H. S., & Chidambaram, L., "A Test of the Technology Acceptance Model," *Proceedings of the Hawaii International Conference on System Sciences*, January 4–7, 2000.

63 Ilie, V., et al., "Paper Versus Electronic Medical Records," *Decision Sciences*, May 2009, p. 213.

64 Barki, H., et al., "Information System Use-Related Activity," *Information Systems Research*, June 2007, p. 173.

65 Loch, Christoph, & Huberman, Bernardo, "A Punctuated-Equilibrium Model of Technology Diffusion," *Management Science*, February 1999, p. 160.

66 Tornatzky, L., & Fleischer, M., *The Process of Technological Innovation*, Lexington, MA: Lexington Books, 1990; Zhu, K., & Kraemer, K., "Post-Adoption Variations in Usage and Value of E-Business by Organizations," *Information Systems Research*, March 2005, p. 61.

67 Armstrong, C., & Sambamurthy, V., "Information Technology Assimilation in Firms," *Information Systems Research*, April 1999, p. 304.

68 Sykes, T., & Venkatesh, V., "Model of Acceptance with Peer Support," *MIS Quarterly*, June 2009, p. 371.

69 Agarwal, Ritu, & Prasad, Jayesh, "Are Individual Differences Germane to the Acceptance of New Information Technology?" *Decision Sciences*, Spring 1999, p. 361.

70 Fuller, R., & Denis, A., "Does Fit Matter?" *Information Systems Research*, March 2009, p. 2.

71 "Toyota to Expand Product Quality Field Offices Across United States and Canada," *http://pressroom.toyota.com/pr/tms/toyota/toyota-consumer-safety-advisory-102572.aspx*, accessed July 28, 2010.

72 "Battling Inefficiencies with Six Sigma," *www.sixsigmaonline.org/six-sigma-training-certification-information/articles/battling-inefficiencies-with-six-sigma.html*, accessed September 25, 2010.

73 Elbo, Reylito, "Total Quality Concepts in HR," *Business World*, August 14, 2009, p. S1.

74 "IPC Wins Gold Star Award," *Africa News*, October 19, 2009.

75 "25th Annual Canada Awards for Excellence, National Quality Institute," *www.nqi.ca/galadinner2009/2009CAEProfiles.aspx#8*, accessed September 25, 2010.

76 Richardson, Karen, "The Six Sigma Factor for Home Depot," *Wall Street Journal*, January 4, 2007, p. C3.

77 *www.sixsigma.com* and *www.6sigma.us*, accessed November 15, 2009.

78 "Virgin Blue Group Contracts Verizon," *Airline Industry Information*, September 22, 2009.

79 Gupta, Aseem, "CIO Profiles: Aseem Gupta," *InformationWeek*, April 20, 2009, p. 14.

80 D'Amours, M., et al., "Optimization Helps Shermag Gain Competitive Advantage," *Interfaces*, July-August, 2009, p. 329.

81 Collins, Jim, *Good to Great*, New York: Harper Collins Books, 2001, p. 300.

82 Murphy, Chris, "In for the Long Haul," *InformationWeek*, January 19, 2009, p. 38.

83 Porter, M. E., *Competitive Advantage: Creating and Sustaining Superior Performance*, New York: Free Press, 1985; *Competitive Strategy: Techniques for Analyzing Industries and Competitors*, New York: Free Press, 1980; and *Competitive Advantage of Nations*, New York: Free Press, 1990.

84 Porter, M. E., & Millar, V., "How Information Systems Give You Competitive Advantage," *Journal of Business Strategy*, Winter 1985. See also Porter, M. E., *Competitive Advantage*, New York: Free Press, 1985.

85 "CIBC Becomes First Major Canadian Bank to Offer a Mobile Banking App for iPhone," *CIBC.com*, accessed September 25, 2010.

86 Goodhue, D., et al., "Addressing Business Agility Challenges with Enterprise Systems," *MIS Quarterly Executive*, June 2009, p. 73.

87 Brynjolfsson, Erik, et al., "The New, Faster Face of Innovation," *Wall Street Journal*, August 17, 2009, p. R3.

88 Capell, Kerry, "Vodafone: Embracing Open Source with Open Arms," *BusinessWeek*, April 20, 2009, p. 52.

89 Reena, J., "Dusting Off a Big Idea in Hard Times," *BusinessWeek*, June 22, 2009, p. 44.

90 Mandel, Michael, "Innovation Interrupted," *BusinessWeek*, June 15, 2009, p. 35.

91 Murphy, Chris, "TransUnion Finds Cost Savings, Seeks More," *Information-Week*, March 23, 2009, p. 24.

92 Foley, John, "Cost Control," *InformationWeek,* March 2, 2009, p. 18.

93 Rai, S., et al., "LDP—O.R. Enhanced Productivity Improvements for the Printing Industry," *Interfaces*, January 2009, p. 69.

94 Tiwana, A., "Governance-Knowledge Fit in Systems Development Projects," *Information Systems Research*, June 2009, p. 180.

95 "Kodak Insite Campaign Manager," *Print Week,* July 10, 2009, p. 28.

96 Greenwood, John, "Alternative Trading Systems About to Get Their Day in the Sun," *Financial Post*, April 14, 2009, *nationalpost.com*, accessed September 25, 2010.

97 "Hitachi's Quintet of Projectors," *AV Magazine*, September 1, 2009, p. 28.

98 Staff, "Ehealth Scandal a $1B Waste: Auditor," CBC News, October 7, 2009, *www.cbc.ca/canada/toronto/story/2009/10/07/ehealth-auditor.html*, accessed October 17, 2010.

99 Kane, Yukare Iwatani, "Apple Woos Developers with New iPhone," *Wall Street Journal*, March 18, 2009, p. B6.

100 GreenStarnet website, *www.Greenstarnetwork.com*, accessed October 18, 2010.

101 European Commission website, *http://ec.europa.eu/trade/index_en.htm*, accessed December 10, 2009.

102 Foreign Trade Information website, *www.sice.oas.org/agreements_e.asp*, accessed December 10, 2009.

CHAPTER · 2 ·

The Personal and Social Impact of Computers

(Source: iDesign/Shutterstock.com)

PRINCIPLES	LEARNING OBJECTIVES
▪ **Policies and procedures must be established to avoid waste and mistakes associated with computer usage.**	▪ Describe some examples of waste and mistakes in an IS environment, their causes, and possible solutions. ▪ Identify policies and procedures useful in eliminating waste and mistakes. ▪ Discuss the principles and limits of an individual's right to privacy.
▪ **Computer crime is a serious and rapidly growing area of concern requiring management attention.**	▪ Explain the types of computer crime and their effects. ▪ Identify specific measures to prevent computer crime.
▪ **Jobs, equipment, and working conditions must be designed to avoid negative health effects from computers.**	▪ List the important negative effects of computers on the work environment. ▪ Identify specific actions that must be taken to ensure the health and safety of employees.
▪ **Practitioners in many professions subscribe to a code of ethics that states the principles and core values that are essential to their work.**	▪ Outline criteria for the ethical use of information systems.

Information Systems in the Global Economy
Facebook

Balancing Profits and Privacy

Facebook has grown to be one of the most popular and influential online businesses. The enormously successful online social network has roughly half a billion members and over a billion dollars in annual revenue, earned primarily from advertisements. Facebook's slogan is "Giving people the power to share and make the world more open and connected." Facebook's mission, combined with its popularity and influence, has often put the company in the hot seat when it comes to privacy and security concerns. Any lapses in ethical judgment on Facebook's part could negatively affect a great number of people and at the same time threaten the company's future.

Facebook walks a fine line between its mission—making the world more open and connected—and its obligation to protect the privacy of its members. Facebook's mission is largely influenced by the financial benefits it enjoys when it can share its users' information with the companies that advertise on its site. The more "open" Facebook users are with their information, the more money Facebook makes. The personal information that users store on Facebook is a gold mine for marketers and advertisers. Facebook users provide a detailed profile including their interests, likes and dislikes, opinions, day-to-day activities and thoughts, photos, lists of friends, and product purchase information. Combined, this information can provide businesses with valuable insight into the hearts and minds of Facebook members, which allows companies to pitch their products more effectively.

In 2010, Facebook rolled out new technology called Open Graph, which provides businesses with the ability to include Facebook "Like" links on Web pages of their products. When a Facebook user clicks the "Like" link on a product page, a message about the product is posted to the user's Facebook news feed, and the connection is stored in the user's Facebook profile. Open Graph provides Facebook users with the ability to conveniently express their interests and product loyalties online, share that information with friends, and build communities around products. However, privacy advocates view the technology as a serious threat to user privacy, because participating businesses can use the technology to more easily access user's profile information.

In early 2010, Facebook leaned too far toward sharing information at the risk of upsetting its users over privacy infringements. At the height of the Open Graph backlash, more than half of Facebook users polled indicated that they were considering deleting their Facebook accounts. Facebook responded by providing privacy controls that made it easier for users to indicate to Facebook to keep their information private. Still, privacy groups are not satisfied and have continuously appealed to Facebook to make all user information private unless the user "opts in" to sharing. Facebook has refused these appeals, arguing that agreeing would reduce the user data that it has access to and deeply cut into its profits. Thus Facebook continuously teeters between privacy and profits, working to keep members content and to keep its profits increasing.

Facebook is not alone in its balancing act. All online businesses that profit from advertising are in the same situation, including Google, Yahoo!, MySpace, and many others. In fact, all businesses that collect member or customer private information have ethical and legal responsibilities for keeping that information safe, secure, and private. For example, Facebook must have a user's consent to share information with third parties. This is granted when a user creates a Facebook account and agrees to the terms of service. Facebook must also take measures to ensure that the user information it stores is safe from hackers. Because it stores so much valuable information, Facebook has become a target for all types of hacker attacks and schemes. Microblogging has similar concerns and filters all URLs referenced by its users to make sure the referenced sites are safe.

Facebook serves as the ultimate example of the pressures that businesses experience regarding the information they collect. These pressures come from a variety of sources. There is pressure from users or customers when they threaten to leave due to dissatisfaction with business practices. There is also pressure from provincial and federal laws. For example, based on an investigation by the Privacy Commissioner of Canada, Facebook was forced to change its privacy policies to comply with Canada's privacy law, *Privacy Act* and *Personal Information Protection and Electronic Documents Act* (PIPEDA). The main concerns of the Office of the Privacy Commissioner (OPC) were the sharing of personal information with third-party developers and the use and retention of users' personal information.[1] For international businesses, this extends to the laws of all the countries in which they do business. There is also the pressure of ethical standards to which a business holds itself and the ethical demands of special interest groups such as privacy advocates. Some of these pressures could be greatly reduced through the application of ethical standards to which a business could subscribe. Movements such as the Data Portability Project (*www.portabilitypolicy.org*) are pushing for standards to embrace what a business can and cannot do with the information it collects from its customers.

The issues addressed in this chapter are of growing importance to businesses and individuals. The valuable information that businesses store in Internet-connected databases is continuously targeted by hackers and swindlers. Businesses must maintain high ethical standards in the way they treat that information and wisdom in the way they secure that information in order to gain the trust of their customers.

As you read this chapter, consider the following:

- What are the primary concerns of corporations regarding security, privacy, and ethics?
- What strategies can assist a company with issues of security and privacy, and at what cost?

Why Learn About the Personal and Social Impact of the Internet?

Both opportunities and threats surround a wide range of nontechnical issues associated with the use of information systems and the Internet. The issues span the full spectrum—from preventing computer waste and mistakes, to avoiding violations of privacy, to complying with laws on collecting data about customers, to monitoring employees. If you become a member of a human resources, information systems, or legal department within an organization, you will likely be charged with leading the organization in dealing with these and other issues covered in this chapter. Also, as a user of information systems and the Internet, it is in your own self-interest to become well versed on these issues. You need to know about the topics in this chapter to help avoid becoming a victim of crime, fraud, privacy invasion, and other potential problems. This chapter begins with a discussion of preventing computer waste and mistakes.

The first chapter discussed the significant benefits of computer-based information systems in business. Computers have become such valuable tools that today's businesspeople have difficulty imagining work without them. Yet the information age has also brought the following potential problems for workers, companies, and society in general:

- Computer waste and mistakes
- Computer crime
- Privacy issues
- Work environment problems
- Ethical issues

This chapter discusses some of the social and ethical issues as a reminder of these important considerations underlying the design, building, and use of computer-based information systems. No business organization, and, hence, no information system, operates in a vacuum. All IS professionals, business managers, and users have a responsibility to see that the potential consequences of IS use are fully considered. Even entrepreneurs, especially those who use computers and the Internet, must be aware of the potential personal and social impact of computers.

Managers and users at all levels play a major role in helping organizations achieve the positive benefits of IS. These people must also take the lead in helping to minimize or eliminate the negative consequences of poorly designed and improperly utilized information systems. For managers and users to have such an influence, they must be properly educated. Many of the issues presented in this chapter may have a significant impact on the systems design and control issues you will address in later chapters.

COMPUTER WASTE AND MISTAKES

Computer-related waste and mistakes are major causes of computer problems, contributing as they do to unnecessarily high costs and lost profits. Computer waste involves the inappropriate use of computer technology and resources. Computer-related mistakes refer to errors, failures, and other computer problems that make computer output incorrect or not useful; most of these are caused by human error. This section explores the damage that can be done as a result of computer waste and mistakes.

Computer Waste

The U.S. government is the largest single user of information systems in the world. It should come as no surprise, then, that the U.S. government also generates more waste than other organizations. For example, poorly designed information systems prevent the government from making sure recipients qualify before they receive a government payment; therefore, the government is creating a "do not pay list" to ensure that government cheques are no longer sent to people who do not qualify. During 2009, almost $110 billion in federal funds were paid to the wrong person or for the wrong reason, including payments to 20,000 deceased people. Federal agencies will check the new list to ensure that the payees are in "good standing" (and alive!) before issuing a cheque.[2] Most observers wonder, "Why haven't we been doing this all along?"[3]

The government is not unique in this regard—the same type of waste and misuse found in the public sector also exists in the private sector. Some companies discard old software and computer systems when they still have value. Others waste corporate resources to build and maintain complex systems that are never used to their fullest extent.

A less dramatic, yet still relevant, example of waste is the amount of company time and money employees can waste playing computer games, sending unimportant e-mail, or browsing the Internet. Junk e-mail, or *spam*, also causes waste. People receive hundreds of e-mail messages advertising products and services not wanted or requested. Not only does this waste time, but it also wastes paper and computer resources. Worse yet, spam messages often carry attached files with embedded viruses that can cause networks and computers to crash or allow hackers to gain unauthorized access to systems and data. Spam is considered a serious enough problem that Canada recently announced its own law called the Electronic Commerce Protection Act, which has a maximum penalty of up to $10 million for spammers.

A spam filter is software that attempts to block unwanted e-mail. One approach to filtering spam involves building lists of acceptable and unacceptable e-mail addresses. The lists can be created manually or automatically based on how the users keep or discard their e-mail. Another approach is automatic rejection of e-mail based on the content of the message or the appearance of keywords in the message. Rejected e-mail automatically goes to the spam or junk e-mail folder of your e-mail service. SPAMfighter, ChoiceMail, SpamEater Pro, and Spam Buster are among the most highly rated anti-spam software; they cost from $25 to $30.[4] Many e-mail programs have built-in spam filters.

A word of caution: some spam filters require e-mail addresses to be verified before e-mails from them are accepted. This can be disastrous for people in sales or customer service who frequently receive e-mails from people they do not know—the spam filter could block an e-mail from a customer or client with a valid reason for e-mailing. In one case, a spam filter blocked an e-mail about closing a real estate deal valued at around $175,000. The deal never closed and the real estate was sold to someone else because of the blocked e-mail.

Image-based spam is a new tactic spammers use to circumvent spam-filtering software that rejects e-mail based on the content of messages and the use of keywords. The message is presented in a graphic form that can be read by people but not computers. The images in this form of spam can be quite offensive.

When waste is identified, it typically points to one common cause: the improper management of information systems and resources.

Computer-Related Mistakes

Despite many people's distrust of them, computers rarely make mistakes. If users do not follow proper procedures, even the most sophisticated hardware cannot produce meaningful output. Mistakes can be caused by unclear expectations and a lack of feedback. A programmer might also develop a program that contains errors, or a data-entry clerk might enter the wrong data. Unless errors are caught early and prevented, the speed of computers can intensify mistakes. As information technology becomes faster, more complex, and more powerful, organizations and computer users face increased risks of experiencing the results of computer-related mistakes. Consider these examples from recent news reports.

- On May 6, 2010, the Dow Jones Industrial Average plunged over 1,000 points and the TSX dropped 452 points in less than half an hour for no apparent reason other than a massive overreaction by automatic computer trading programs.[5, 6]
- A software program used by the Mine Safety and Health Administration in the United States to identify patterns of safety violations failed to flag eight problems at the Upper Big Branch mine in West Virginia, where 29 workers died in an explosion. Officials claimed the error did not have an impact on the accident because improvements had already been made without the computer-generated warnings; nevertheless, the failure of the system is deeply disturbing.[7]
- A computer glitch caused all the ATM machines throughout United Arab Emirates to close down for an hour on a busy Saturday.[8]

PREVENTING COMPUTER-RELATED WASTE AND MISTAKES

To remain profitable in a competitive environment, organizations must use all resources wisely. To employ IS resources efficiently and effectively, employees and managers alike should strive to minimize waste and mistakes. This involves (1) establishing, (2) implementing, (3) monitoring, and (4) reviewing effective policies and procedures.

Establishing Policies and Procedures

The first step to prevent computer-related waste is to establish policies and procedures regarding efficient acquisition, use, and disposal of systems and devices. Computers permeate organizations today, and it is critical for organizations to ensure that systems are used to their full potential. As a result, most companies have implemented stringent policies on the acquisition of computer systems and equipment, including requiring a formal justification statement before computer equipment is purchased, definition of standard computing platforms (operating system, type of computer chip, minimum amount of RAM, etc.), and the use of preferred vendors for all acquisitions.

Prevention of computer-related mistakes begins by identifying the most common types of errors, of which there are surprisingly few. Types of computer-related mistakes include the following:

- Data-entry or data-capture errors
- Errors in computer programs
- Errors in handling files, including formatting a disk by mistake, copying an old file over a newer one, and deleting a file by mistake
- Mishandling of computer output
- Inadequate planning for and control of equipment malfunctions
- Inadequate planning for and control of environmental difficulties (such as electrical and humidity problems)
- Installing computing capacity inadequate for the level of activity
- Failure to provide access to the most current information by not adding new Web links and not deleting old links

To control and prevent potential problems caused by computer-related mistakes, companies have developed policies and procedures that cover the acquisition and use of computers. Training programs for individuals and workgroups as well as manuals and documents covering the use and maintenance of computer systems also help prevent problems. Other preventive measures include approval of certain systems and applications before they are implemented and used to ensure compatibility and cost-effectiveness, and a requirement that documentation and descriptions of certain applications be filed or submitted to a central office, including all cell formulas for spreadsheets and a description of all data elements and relationships in a database system. Such standardization can ease access and use for all personnel.

Many companies have established strong policies to prevent employees from wasting time using computers inappropriately at work. However, a Nielsen survey reported that 28 percent of office workers spend an average of 90 minutes per week at work viewing adult pornographic websites.[9]

After companies have planned and developed policies and procedures, they must consider how best to implement them. Nearly one hundred contract workers at Bruce Power, a Canadian nuclear power-generating company, were fired for reasons that had nothing to do with job performance, nuclear safety, or station security. They had violated the company's code of conduct with regard to inappropriate use of computer equipment by sending e-mail messages and accessing Internet sites that violated the code of conduct.[10]

Implementing Policies and Procedures

Implementing policies and procedures to minimize waste and mistakes varies according to the business conducted. Most companies develop such policies and procedures with advice from the firm's internal auditing group or its external auditing firm. The policies often focus on the implementation of source data automation, the use of data editing to ensure data accuracy and completeness, and the assignment of clear responsibility for data accuracy within each information system. Some useful policies to minimize waste and mistakes include the following:

- Changes to critical tables, HTML, and URLs should be tightly controlled, with all changes documented and authorized by responsible owners.
- A user manual should be available covering operating procedures and documenting the management and control of the application.
- Each system report should indicate its general content in its title and specify the time period covered.
- The system should have controls to prevent invalid and unreasonable data entry.
- Controls should exist to ensure that data input, HTML, and URLs are valid, applicable, and posted in the right time frame.
- Users should implement proper procedures to ensure correct input data.

Training is another key aspect of implementation. Many users are not properly trained in using applications, and their mistakes can be very costly.

Because more and more people use computers in their daily work, they should understand how to use them. Training is often the key to acceptance and implementation of policies and procedures. Because of the importance of maintaining accurate data and of people understanding their responsibilities, companies converting to ERP and e-commerce systems invest weeks of training for key users of the system's various modules.

Monitoring Policies and Procedures

To ensure that users throughout an organization are following established procedures, the next step is to monitor routine practices and take corrective action if necessary. By understanding what is happening in day-to-day activities, organizations can make adjustments or develop new procedures. Many organizations implement internal audits to measure actual results against established goals, such as percentage of end-user reports produced on time, percentage of data-input errors detected, number of input transactions entered per eight-hour shift, and so on.

The Société Générale scandal in France is a classic example of an individual employee circumventing internal policies and procedures. A low-level trader earning $2,700 per month on the arbitrage desk at the French bank created a series of fraudulent and unauthorized investment transactions that built a position of over $72 billion in European stock index futures. Eventually the house of cards collapsed, causing the bank to lose over $7 billion— even though a compliance officer at the bank had been alerted months in advance not once, but twice, that something unusual was going on. Since the scandal, the bank has taken several steps to improve its internal policies and procedures, tighten computer security, and adopt a more realistic approach to the potential for fraud.[11]

Reviewing Policies and Procedures

The final step is to review existing policies and procedures and determine whether they are adequate. During review, people should ask the following questions:

- Do current policies cover existing practices adequately? Were any problems or opportunities uncovered during monitoring?
- Does the organization plan any new activities in the future? If so, does it need new policies or procedures addressing who will handle them and what must be done?
- Are contingencies and disasters covered?

This review and planning allows companies to take a proactive approach to problem solving, which can enhance a company's performance, such as by increasing productivity and improving customer service. During such a review, companies are alerted to upcoming changes in information systems that could have a profound effect on many business activities.

Information systems professionals and users still need to be aware of the misuse of resources throughout an organization. Preventing errors and mistakes is one way to do so. Another is implementing in-house security measures and legal protections to detect and prevent a dangerous type of misuse: computer crime.

COMPUTER CRIME

Even good IS policies might not be able to predict or prevent computer crime. A computer's ability to process millions of pieces of data in less than one second makes it possible for a thief to steal data worth millions of dollars. Compared with the physical dangers of robbing a bank or retail store with a gun, a computer criminal with the right equipment and know-how can steal large amounts of money without leaving his or her home. The top five categories of computer crime reported to law enforcement organizations during 2009 were (1) undelivered merchandise or non-payment, (2) identity theft, (3) credit card fraud, and (4) auction fraud.[12] The following is a sample of recent computer crimes reported in 2010:

- Two Canadians were found guilty of defrauding U.S. citizens of more than $2.5 million. The pair tricked victims into believing that they had won large lottery prizes that could only be released only once the victim sent money to Canada to prepay taxes on the winnings.[13]

- Innovative Marketing caused Internet users in over 60 countries to waste more than $100 million by purchasing bogus antivirus and computer performance enhancement software. Victims were tricked into believing that their computers were infected with malware or had severe performance problems that could be fixed by purchasing and installing the bogus software.[14]
- Financial losses in excess of $2.4 million were incurred by victims of a "hack, pump, and dump" scheme. A group would hack into the victims' brokerage accounts and then use the accounts to make large purchases of thinly traded securities, causing the stock prices to become artificially inflated. The hackers would then sell the stocks at the high price before the victims were aware of what had happened.[15]

Although no one really knows how pervasive cybercrime is, a global study of 800 companies estimated that companies worldwide lost more than $1 trillion in 2008.[16] In Canada, publicly traded companies experience an estimated nine security breaches per year, resulting in average losses of more than $675,000 for each company and mass-marketing fraud, including spam, cost $59.3 million in 2009.[17,18] Unfortunately, these figures represent only a small fraction of total computer-related crimes, as many crimes go unreported because companies don't want the bad press or don't think that law enforcement could help. Such lack of publicity makes the job even tougher for law enforcement. Most companies that have been electronically attacked won't talk to the press. A big concern is loss of public trust and image—not to mention the fear of encouraging copycat hackers.

Today, computer criminals are a new breed—bolder and more creative than ever. With the increased use of the Internet, computer crime is now global. It's not just on Canadian shores that law enforcement has to battle cybercriminals. Regardless of its nonviolent image, computer crime is different only because a computer is used. It is still a crime. Part of what makes computer crime unique and difficult to combat is its dual nature—the computer can be both the tool used to commit a crime and the object of that crime.

THE COMPUTER AS A TOOL TO COMMIT CRIME

A computer can be used as a tool to gain access to valuable information and as the means to steal thousands or millions of dollars. It is, perhaps, a question of motivation—many people who commit computer-related crime claim they do it for the challenge, not for the money. Credit card fraud—whereby a criminal illegally gains access to another's line of credit with stolen credit card numbers—is a major concern for today's banks and financial institutions. In general, criminals need two capabilities to commit most computer crimes. First, the criminal needs to know how to gain access to the computer system. Sometimes, obtaining access requires knowledge of an identification number and a password. Second, the criminal must know how to manipulate the system to produce the desired result. Frequently, a critical computer password has been talked out of a person, a practice called **social engineering**. Or the attackers simply go through the garbage—**dumpster diving**—for important pieces of information that can help crack the computers or convince someone at the company to give them more access. In addition, over 2,000 websites offer the digital tools—for free—that will let people snoop, crash computers, hijack control of a machine, or retrieve a copy of every keystroke. While some of the tools were intended for legitimate use to provide remote technical support or monitor computer usage, hackers take advantage of them to gain unauthorized access to computers or data.

Chris Nickerson is a master at employing social engineering techniques with the nerve to attempt exploits criminals might avoid. Nickerson has a legitimate job serving as a security expert and helping organizations test their security defences. Businesses hire him to evaluate their vulnerability to social engineering crimes. Two of his jobs involved using social engineering techniques to gain access to an expensive jewellery store and car dealership. He was able to "acquire" expensive merchandise, including an exotic sports car.[19]

social engineering
Using social skills to get computer users to provide information that allows a hacker to access an information system or its data.

dumpster diving
Going through the trash of an organization to find secret or confidential information, including information needed to access an information system or its data.

Cyberterrorism

Cyberterrorism has been a concern for countries and companies around the globe. The Canadian government considered the potential threat of cyberterrorism serious enough that it established the Canadian Cyber Incident Response Centre (CCIRC). CCIRC is responsible for threat assessment, investigation, and coordinating the national response to any cyber security incident. The centre's focus is the protection of critical infrastructure, which provides telecommunications, energy, banking and finance, water systems, government operations, and emergency services. Successful cyber attacks against the facilities that provide these services could cause widespread and massive disruptions to the normal function of Canadian society.

A **cyberterrorist** is someone who intimidates or coerces a government or organization to advance political or social objectives by launching computer-based attacks against computers, networks, and the information stored on them.

International Multilateral Partnership Against Cyber Terrorism (IMPACT) is a global public and privately supported initiative against cyberterrorism. Its mission is to "bring together governments, academia, and cyber security experts to enhance the global community's capacity to prevent, defend against, and respond to cyber threats." It is headquartered in Malaysia's new planned township of science—a city named Cyberjaya.[20]

There are several sources of cyber attacks.[21] The most sophisticated threats come from intelligence and military services of foreign states. They attack to gain political, economic, commercial, or military advantage. Global terrorist groups may also launch cyber attacks. The third source is organized crime that uses cyber attacks to conduct identify theft, money laundering, and extortion.

cyberterrorist
Someone who intimidates or coerces a government or organization to advance political or social objectives by launching computer-based attacks against computers, networks, and the information stored on them.

Identity Theft

Identity theft is a crime in which an imposter obtains key pieces of personal identification information, such as Social Insurance Number or a driver's licence number, to impersonate someone else. The information is then used to obtain credit, merchandise, and/or services in the name of the victim or to provide the thief with false credentials. The perpetrators of these crimes employ such an extensive range of methods that investigating them is difficult.

In some cases, the identity thief uses personal information to open new credit accounts, establish cellular phone service, or open a new chequing account to obtain blank cheques. In other cases, the identity thief uses personal information to gain access to the person's existing accounts. Typically, the thief changes the mailing address on an account and runs up a huge bill before the person whose identity has been stolen realizes there is a problem. The Internet has made it easier for an identity thief to use the stolen information because transactions can be made without any personal interaction. In 2010, identity theft cost $9.4 million in Canada.[22]

identify theft
A crime in which an impostor obtains key pieces of personal identification information, such as Social Insurance Number or a driver's licence number, to impersonate someone else.

Internet Gambling

Many people enjoy Internet gambling as a recreational and leisure activity. Baccarat, bingo, blackjack, pachinko, poker, roulette, and sports betting are all readily available online. Internet gambling was estimated to generate $21 billion in 2010 and is growing at a rate of 20 percent per year.[23] Several provinces, including British Columbia and Ontario, plan to allow Internet gambling. The potential revenue from Internet gambling represents a major untapped source of income for governments.

THE COMPUTER AS A TOOL TO FIGHT CRIME

The computer is also used as a tool to fight computer crime. The computer and information systems are used to help in the recovery of stolen property, monitoring of sex offenders, and to better understand and diminish crime risks.

Recovery of Stolen Property

The Leads Online Web-based service system is used by law enforcement to recover stolen property in the United States. The system contains over 250 million records in its database. Data is entered into the system from pawnbrokers, secondhand dealers, and salvage yards. In some areas, state or local laws require that all such businesses register (with no charge for business owners) with LeadsOnline. The system allows law-enforcement officers to search the database by item serial number or by individual. The system even has a partnership with eBay that makes it possible to locate stolen merchandise that has been listed for sale or sold online.[24]

Monitoring Sex Offenders

The National Sex Offender Registry database is accessible to all police agencies across Canada. The registry assists police in investigating crimes of a sexual nature by providing information and the location of sex offenders.[25] Another use of technology is Cypertip. ca, Canada's tipline for reporting and protecting children from online sexual exploitation. The website promotes public education and prevention through online safety strategies and national awareness campaigns.[26]

Use of Geographic Information Systems

The ready availability of personal computers, coupled with the development of mapping and analysis software, has led law-enforcement agencies to use crime-related data, powerful analysis techniques, and Geographic Information Systems (GIS) to better understand and even diminish crime risks. The use of such software enables law-enforcement agencies to gain a quick overview of crime risk at a given address or in a given locale, as shown in Figure 2.1.

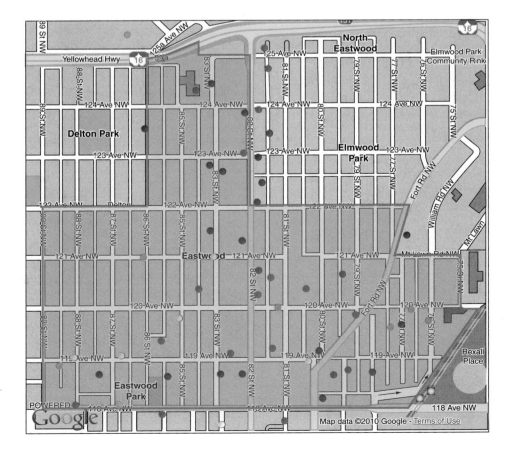

Figure 2.1

Mapping Crime Risk

Crime-fighting software data mines police calls by location and time of day to predict where the next crime may occur.

(Source: © CBC News.)

With GIS tools, law-enforcement agencies can analyze crime data relative to other factors, including the locations of common crime scenes (such as convenience stores and gas stations) and certain demographic data (such as age and income distribution).

THE COMPUTER AS THE OBJECT OF CRIME

A computer can also be the object of the crime, rather than the tool for committing it. See Table 2.1. Tens of millions of dollars' worth of computer time and resources are stolen every year. Each time system access is illegally obtained, data or computer equipment is stolen or destroyed, or software is illegally copied, the computer becomes the object of crime. These crimes fall into several categories: illegal access and use, data alteration and destruction, information and equipment theft, software and Internet piracy, computer-related scams, and international computer crime.

Table 2.1

Common Methods Used to Commit Computer Crimes

Methods	Examples
Add, delete, or change inputs to the computer system.	Delete records of absences from class in a student's school records.
Modify or develop computer programs that commit the crime.	Change a bank's program for calculating interest so it deposits rounded amounts in the criminal's account.
Alter or modify the data files used by the computer system.	Change a student's grade from C to A.
Operate the computer system in such a way as to commit computer crime.	Access a restricted government computer system.
Divert or misuse valid output from the computer system.	Steal discarded printouts of customer records from a company trash bin.
Steal computer resources, including hardware, software, and time on computer equipment.	Make illegal copies of a software program without paying for its use.
Offer worthless products for sale over the Internet.	Send e-mail requesting money for a worthless hair-growth product.
Blackmail executives to prevent release of harmful information.	Eavesdrop on an organization's wireless network to capture competitive data or scandalous information.
Blackmail company to prevent loss of computer-based information.	Plant a logic bomb and send a letter threatening to set it off unless paid a considerable sum.

hacker
A person who enjoys computer technology and spends time learning and using computer systems.

criminal hacker (cracker)
A computer-savvy person who attempts to gain unauthorized or illegal access to computer systems to steal passwords, corrupt files and programs, or even transfer money.

script bunny
A cracker with little technical savvy who downloads programs called scripts, which automate the job of breaking into computers.

insider
An employee, disgruntled or otherwise, working solo or in concert with outsiders to compromise corporate systems.

Illegal Access and Use

Crimes involving illegal system access and use of computer services are a concern to both government and business. Since the outset of information technology, computers have been plagued by criminal hackers. Originally, a **hacker** was a person who enjoyed computer technology and spent time learning and using computer systems. A **criminal hacker**, also called a **cracker**, is a computer-savvy person who attempts to gain unauthorized or illegal access to computer systems to steal passwords, corrupt files and programs, or even transfer money. In many cases, criminal hackers are people who are looking for excitement—the challenge of beating the system. Today, many people use the terms "hacker" and "cracker" interchangeably. **Script bunnies** admire crackers but have little technical savvy. They are crackers who download programs called *scripts* that automate the job of breaking into computers. **Insiders** are employees, disgruntled or otherwise, working solo or in concert with outsiders to compromise corporate systems. The biggest threat for many companies is not external hackers, but their own employees. Insiders have extra knowledge that makes them especially dangerous—they know logon IDs, passwords, and company procedures that help them evade detection.

Catching and convicting criminal hackers remains a difficult task. Although the method behind these crimes is often hard to determine, even if the method is known, tracking down the criminals can take a lot of time. It took five years to arrest and convict U. S. computer hacker Albert Gonzalez for leading a group of cybercriminals who hacked into the computer systems of major retailers and stole more than 90 million credit and debit card numbers. The loss to the various companies, banks, and insurers was estimated to be almost $200 million. Gonzalez was sentenced to 20 years in prison.[27]

Data and information are valuable corporate assets. The intentional use of illegal and destructive programs to alter or destroy data is as much a crime as destroying tangible goods. The most common of these programs are viruses and worms, which are software programs that, when loaded into a computer system, will destroy, interrupt, or cause errors in processing. Such programs are also called *malware*, and the growth rate for such programs is epidemic. It is estimated that hundreds of previously unknown viruses and worms emerge each day. Table 2.2 describes the most common types of malware.

Type of malware	Description
Logic bomb	A type of Trojan horse that executes when specific conditions occur. Triggers for logic bombs can include a change in a file by a particular series of keystrokes or at a specific time or date.
Rootkit	A set of programs that enable its user to gain administrator-level access to a computer or network. Once installed, the attacker can gain full control of the system and even obscure the presence of the rootkit from legitimate system administrators.
Trojan horse	A malicious program that disguises itself as a useful application or game and purposefully does something the user does not expect.
Variant	A modified version of a virus that is produced by the virus's author or another person by amending the original virus code.
Virus	Computer program file capable of attaching to disks or other files and replicating itself repeatedly, typically without the user's knowledge or permission.
Worm	Parasitic computer program that replicates but, unlike viruses, does not infect other computer program files. A worm can send the copies to other computers via a network.

Table 2.2

Common Types of Computer Malware

In some cases, a virus or a worm can completely halt the operation of a computer system or network for days until the problem is found and repaired. In other cases, a virus or a worm can destroy important data and programs. If backups are inadequate, the data and programs might never be fully functional again. The costs include the effort required to identify and neutralize the virus or worm and to restore computer files and data, as well as the value of business lost because of unscheduled computer downtime.

Criminal hackers used a clever Trojan horse program that, when installed on a victim's computer, altered the text displayed by HTML code to either erase evidence of a money transfer transaction entirely or alter the amount of the money transfer and bank balances. The gang used this Trojan horse to steal over €300,000 over three weeks from online customers of a German bank.[28]

Smartphones such as the iPhone and Google's Android phone that can run applications are also susceptible to malware.[29] Cybercriminals are distributing applications for smartphones that contain malware programmed to make calls to premium-rate phone numbers around the globe and run up large phone bills without the owner's knowledge.[30]

Spyware

spyware
Software that is installed on a personal computer to intercept or take partial control over the user's interaction with the computer without knowledge or permission of the user.

Spyware is software installed on a personal computer to intercept or take partial control over the user's interaction with the computer without the knowledge or permission of the user. Some forms of spyware secretly log keystrokes so that usersname and passwords may be captured. Other forms of spyware record information about the user's Internet surfing habits and sites that have been visited. Still other forms of spyware change personal computer settings so that the user experiences slow connection speeds or is redirected to Web pages other than those expected. Spyware is similar to a Trojan horse in that users unknowingly install it when they download freeware or shareware from the Internet.

The IE Antivirus spyware is a fake spyware remover that scares unwary computer users into buying it. It uses pop-up windows and fake system notifications to tell the user his computer is infected and that he needs to buy IE Antivirus. If the user inquires further, the computer is scanned without the program asking permission. The results of the scan are faked to show an alarming number of security risks. The user is then directed to a website that explains how to order the bogus antivirus software.

Government officials in India suspect China of infecting several computers with spyware in a section of the Indian Ministry of External Affairs that deals with sensitive Pakistani affairs. The spyware caused e-mails to be secretly sent to a third-party e-mail account. India claims the attacks are part of an attempt to map India's network infrastructure in preparation for future attacks designed to disable or disrupt it during a conflict.[31]

Information and Equipment Theft

password sniffer
A small program hidden in a network or a computer system that records identification numbers and passwords.

keystroke loggers
Software or hardware programmed to send a list of keystrokes typed by a user to a malicious person.

Data and information are assets or goods that can also be stolen. People who illegally access systems often do so to steal data and information. To obtain illegal access, criminal hackers require identification numbers and passwords. Some criminals try various identification numbers and passwords until they find ones that work. Using password sniffers is another approach. A **password sniffer** is a small program hidden in a network or a computer system that records identification numbers and passwords. In a few days, a password sniffer can record hundreds or thousands of identification numbers and passwords. **Keystroke loggers** are another means of stealing passwords or other user-entered data. They are software or hardware that is programmed to send a list of keystrokes typed by a user to a malicious person. Using a password sniffer or keystroke loggers, a criminal hacker can gain access to computers and networks to steal data and information, invade privacy, plant viruses, and disrupt computer operations.

In addition to theft of data and software, all types of computer systems and equipment have been stolen from offices. Portable computers such as laptops and portable storage devices (and the data and information stored in them) are especially easy for thieves to take.

In many cases, the data and information stored in these systems are more valuable than the equipment. Vulnerable data can be used in identity theft. In addition, the organization responsible receives a tremendous amount of negative publicity that can cause it to lose existing and potential customers. Often, the responsible organization offers to pay for credit monitoring services for those people affected in an attempt to restore customer goodwill and avoid lawsuits.

Safe Disposal of Personal Computers

Many companies donate personal computers they no longer need to schools, churches, or other organizations. Some sell them at a deep discount to their employees or put them up for sale on Internet auction sites such as eBay. However, care must be taken to ensure that all traces of any personal or company confidential data is completely removed. Simply deleting

INFORMATION SYSTEMS @ WORK

Data Theft an Ongoing Concern for Businesses

In 2008, the largest data theft occurred when 130 million credit card numbers were stolen from Heartland Payment System's servers. Heartland processes credit and debit card transactions for Visa, American Express, and other businesses. The data was stolen by hackers who infiltrated Heartland networks to gain access to the servers on which the data was stored.

As previously mentioned, computer hacker Albert Gonzalez was arrested for participating in the cybercrime ring that attacked Heartland and many others. The judge solicited valuable information about international cybercrime from Gonzalez prior to convicting him to 20 years in prison. Gonzalez informed the judge that international cybercrime rings have progressed from attacking individual businesses to attacking banks and organizations that handle large amounts of financial transaction data, such as Heartland.

Besides stealing the physical media on which data is stored and hacking into networks, data thieves also use collections of compromised computers called botnet armies to do their dirty work. For example, the Mariposa botnet, which was eventually dismantled in 2010, used 12.7 million infected PCs to steal credit card and bank account information. The botnet was shut down through a series of arrests in Spain. The Kneber botnet runs on infected computers spread across 126 countries and is designed to steal logon credentials for corporations, financial systems, and popular social networking and e-mail sites.

Often the data stolen in one attack is used to launch another attack or scam. For example, insurance company Aetna contacted 65,000 current and former employees letting them know that their e-mail addresses, and other private information may have been stolen from an external vendor's system. The company became aware of the theft when employees began receiving e-mails that referenced the stolen data.

Businesses aren't the only targets of data theft. The federal government has been victimized as well. In 2011, the Finance Department and Treasury Board departments had to temporarily shut down Internet access due to a significant attack the month before the federal budget was released. Last year the website of Defence Research and Development Canada, the scientific wing of the Canadian military, was disabled for several weeks due to a cyber attack. The Information Protection Centre, which acts as the main defence against cyber attacks, experiences roughly 20 million cyber security actions each month.

The Internet has become a major platform for criminal activity. Financial account information and personal information used for identity theft are often the goal of attacks, allowing hackers to rake in millions of dollars on the underground market. Hackers have many methods of attack, and no Internet-connected server can be considered 100 percent safe. It remains the responsibility of businesses to stay abreast of the latest security holes and patches, and to stay vigilant and watchful to react quickly when a data breach does occur. The best reaction to a data breach is immediate contact with those affected along with an offer to protect them from financial hardship.

Discussion Questions

1. What methods do hackers and thieves use to illegally access valuable information?
2. What is the best response for a business that has discovered private customer information stolen?

Critical Thinking Questions

1. What policies can and do financial institutions and governments put in place to protect consumers from data theft?
2. What practices can consumers use to help protect their own private information?

SOURCES: Weil, Nancy, "Gonzalez Sentenced to 20 Years for Heartland Break-in," Computerworld, *www.computerworld.com*, March 26, 2010; Bright, Peter, "Spanish Arrests Mark the End of Dangerous Botnet," *Ars Technica*, www.arstechnica. com, March 20, 2010; Vijayan, Jaikumar, "Over 75,000 Systems Compromised in Cyberattack," Computerworld, *www.computerworld.com*, February 18, 2010; Kirk, Jeremy, "Aetna Warns 65,000 about Web Site Data Breach," Computerworld, *www.computerworld.com*, May 28, 2009; Woods, Allan, "Cyber Attack Puts Ottawa's Security Strategy to the Test," *Toronto Star, www.thestar.com*, March 23, 2011.

files and emptying the Recycle Bin (or Trash) does not make it impossible for determined individuals to view the data. Be sure to use disk-wiping software utilities that overwrite all sectors of your disk drive, making all data unrecoverable. For example, Darik's Boot and Nuke (DBAN) is free and can be downloaded from the SourceForge website.

Acer, Apple, Asus, Dell, Fujitsu, HP, Lenovo, Sony, and Toshiba all offer some sort of recycling program. The program may exchange old computers for credits toward the purchase of a new computer. Other programs may provide a simple pick-up for no or a very small fee.

Patent and Copyright Violations

Works of the mind, such as art, books, films, formulas, inventions, music, and processes that are distinct and "owned" or created by a single person or group are called intellectual property. Copyright law protects authored works such as art, books, film, and music. Patent laws protect processes, machines, objects made by humans or machines, compositions of matter, and new uses of these items. Software is considered intellectual property and may be protected by copyright or patent law.

software piracy
The act of unauthorized copying or distribution of copyrighted software.

Software piracy is the act of unauthorized copying, downloading, sharing, selling, or installing of software. When you purchase software, you are purchasing a licence to use it; you do not own the actual software. The licence states how many times you can install the software. If you make more copies of the software than the licence permits, you are pirating.

The Canadian Alliance Against Software Theft (CAAST) and its sister organization Business Software Alliance (BSA) have become prominent software antipiracy organizations. Software companies, including Apple, Adobe, Hewlett-Packard, IBM, and Microsoft, contribute to the BSA. The BSA estimates that the 2009 global software piracy rate was 43 percent and amounted to $51 billion in lost sales.[32] Georgia, Zimbabwe, and Moldova have piracy rates exceeding 90 percent, while the United States has the lowest software piracy rate at just 20 percent.[33]

Penalties for software piracy can be severe. If the copyright owner brings a civil action against someone, the owner can seek to stop the person from using its software immediately and can also request monetary damages. The copyright owner can then choose between compensation for actual damages—which includes the amount it has lost because of the person's infringement, as well as any profits attributable to the infringement—and statutory damages, which can be as much as $20,000 for each program copied. In addition, the government can prosecute software pirates in criminal court for copyright infringement. If convicted, they could be fined up to $1 million or sentenced to jail for up to five years, or both.[34]

Another major issue with regard to copyright infringement is the downloading of music that is copyright protected. Estimates vary widely as to how much music piracy is costing the recording industry. The Canadian Recording Industry Association (CRIA) and other sources estimate that the global recording industry loses about $12.5 billion in revenue internationally to music piracy every year, including $23.5 million in Canada.[35, 36] However, independent research firm Jupiter Research believes that the losses are much lower.[37]

LimeWire, a music sharing service, was found guilty of copyright infringement in a case brought against it by the Recording Industry Association of America (RIAA). LimeWire boasts of 50 million unique monthly customers and downloads in excess of hundreds of thousands per day. Four percent of all Limewire users are Canadian. At a maximum of $150,000 per copyright violation, LimeWire faces fines in excess of $1 billion.[38, 39] According to CRIA's president, "The ruling kicks a leg out from under a major source of pirated music in Canada."[40]

In what represents the largest copyright infringement case in history, a class action lawsuit was filed on behalf of hundreds of authors against Google for copying and distributing their work without permission. Google has digitized millions of books to create a digital library and plans to provide Internet access to this vast storehouse of books. In setting up this storehouse, Google has asked that authors "opt out" of the program to allow access to their works rather than "opt in."[41]

Patent infringement is also a major problem for computer software and hardware manufacturers. It occurs when someone makes unauthorized use of another's patent. If a court determines that a patent infringement is intentional, it can award up to three times the amount of damages claimed by the patent holder. It is not unusual to see patent infringement awards in excess of $10 million. Recently, Microsoft was ordered to pay over $290 million in damages to i4i Inc., a small Canadian software company, for infringing on i4i's patent on technology used to open documents.

To obtain a patent or to determine if a patent exists in an area a company seeks to exploit requires a search by the Canadian Patent Office. Manufacturing firms, the financial community, consumer and public interest groups, and government leaders are demanding patent reform. One area that needs to be addressed is patent infringement. As Red Hat vice president and assistant general counsel Rob Tiller says, "The cost of software patent litigation since 1994 has vastly exceeded the profit generated by software patent licensing."[42]

HTC Corporation, maker of powerful mobile handsets, filed a complaint with the International Trade Commission (an independent U.S. federal agency that rules on cases involving imports that allegedly infringe intellectual property rights) against its competitor Apple. HTC claimed Apple violated five of its patents concerning cell phone directory hardware and software plus power management technology in portable devices. This came just a month after Apple filed patent infringement suits against HTC.[43]

Computer-Related Scams

People have lost hundreds of thousands of dollars on real estate, travel, stock, and other business scams. Today, many of these scams are being perpetrated with computers. Using the Internet, scam artists offer get-rich-quick schemes involving bogus real estate deals, tout "free" vacations with huge hidden costs, commit bank fraud, offer fake telephone lotteries, sell worthless penny stocks, and promote illegal tax-avoidance schemes. More than $14 million was lost in Canada in 2009 through e-mail, Internet, and text messaging schemes.[44]

Over the past few years, credit card customers of various banks have been targeted by scam artists trying to get personal information needed to use their credit cards. The scam works by sending customers an e-mail that includes a link that seems to direct users to their bank's website. At the site, they are greeted with a pop-up box asking them for their full debit card numbers, their personal identification numbers, and their credit card expiration dates. The problem is that the website is fake, operated by someone trying to gain access to customers' private information, a form of scam called *phishing*.

Travel situations seem to be a popular setting for phishers. A writer received an e-mail from a reader he had communicated with two years ago. "I don't mean to inconvenience you right now," the e-mail stated, "but I am stuck in London and need $940 to get home." Another ploy phishers use frequently is to claim that they lost their luggage at the airport and need some cash quickly.[45]

Vishing is similar to phishing. However, instead of using the victim's computer, it uses the victim's phone. The victim is typically sent a notice or message to call to verify account information. If the victim returns the message, the caller asks for personal information such as a credit card account number or name and address. The information gained can be used in identity theft to acquire and use credit cards in the victim's name. Vishing criminals can even spoof the caller ID that appears with the message to make it appear as if it came from a legitimate source.[46] The Spoof Card, sold online for less than $5 for 25 calls, causes phones to display a caller ID number specified by the caller rather than the actual number of the caller.[47]

International Computer Crime

Computer crime becomes more complex when it crosses borders. Money laundering is the practice of disguising illegally gained funds so that they seem legal. With the increase in electronic cash and funds transfer, some are concerned that terrorists, international drug dealers, and other criminals are using information systems to launder illegally obtained funds. An Australian arrested in Las Vegas was indicted for laundering more than $500 million in proceeds of U.S. gamblers and Internet gambling websites. He processed the gambling transactions in the United States to offshore accounts held by the gambling companies.[48]

PREVENTING COMPUTER-RELATED CRIME

Because of increased computer use today, greater emphasis is placed on the prevention and detection of computer crime. Although Canada has passed computer crime legislation, some believe that these laws are not effective because companies do not always actively detect and pursue computer crime, security is inadequate, and convicted criminals are not severely punished. However, all over Canada, private users, companies, employees, and public officials are making individual and group efforts to curb computer crime, and recent efforts have met with some success.

Crime Prevention by Government

The federal government and the provinces are taking a more proactive approach to identifying and preventing computer-related crime. There is better coordination between federal departments, such as the Royal Canadian Mounted Police (RCMP), provincial police forces, and international bodies in investigating computer crimes. The federal government has also established stronger privacy and copyright legislation and is strengthening the Canadian *Criminal Code* sections related to computer crime.[49] The Canadian Cyber Incident Response centre (CCIR) supports the Computer Emergency Response Team (CERT), which responds to network security breaches and monitors systems for emerging threats worldwide. Recent court cases and police reports involving computer crime show that lawmakers are ready to introduce new and tougher computer crime legislation.

Crime Prevention by Corporations

Companies are also taking crime-fighting efforts seriously. Many businesses have designed procedures and specialized hardware and software to protect their corporate data and systems. Specialized hardware and software, such as encryption devices, can be used to encode data and information to help prevent unauthorized use. As you will see in Chapter 7, encryption is the process of converting an original electronic message into a form that can be understood only by the intended recipients. A key is a variable value that is applied using an algorithm to a string or block of unencrypted text to produce encrypted text or to decrypt encrypted text. Encryption methods rely on the limitations of computing power for their effectiveness—if breaking a code requires too much computing power, even the most determined code crackers will not be successful. The length of the key used to encode and decode messages determines the strength of the encryption algorithm.

As employees move from one position to another at a company, they can build up access to several systems if inadequate security procedures fail to revoke access privileges. It is clearly not appropriate for people who have changed positions and responsibilities to still have access to systems they no longer use. To avoid this problem, many organizations create role-based system access lists so that only people filling a particular role (e.g., invoice approver) can access a specific system.

Fingerprint authentication devices provide security in the PC environment by using fingerprint recognition instead of passwords. Laptop computers from Lenovo, Toshiba, and others have built-in fingerprint readers used to log on and gain access to the computer system and its data. The 2 GB Fingerprint Biometric USB Flash Memory Stick Drive requires users to swipe their fingerprints and match them to one of up to 10 trusted users to access the data. The data on the flash drive can also be encrypted for further protection.[50]

Some USB flash drives have built-in fingerprint readers to protect the data on the device.

(Source: Enigma/Getstock.com.)

Crime-fighting procedures usually require additional controls on the information system. Before designing and implementing controls, organizations must consider the types of computer-related crime that might occur, the consequences of these crimes, and the cost and complexity of needed controls. In most cases, organizations conclude that the trade-off between crime and the additional cost and complexity weighs in favour of better system controls. Having knowledge of some of the methods used to commit crime is also helpful in preventing, detecting, and developing systems resistant to computer crime. Some companies actually hire former criminals to thwart other criminals.

The following list provides a set of useful guidelines to protect corporate computers from criminal hackers:

- Install strong user authentication and encryption capabilities on the corporate firewall.
- Install the latest security patches, which are often available at the vendor's Internet site.
- Disable guest accounts and null user accounts that let intruders access the network without a password.
- Do not provide overfriendly logon procedures for remote users (e.g., an organization that used the word "welcome" on their initial logon screen found they had difficulty prosecuting a criminal hacker).
- Restrict physical access to the server and configure it so that breaking into one server won't compromise the whole network.
- Dedicate one server to each application (e-mail, File Transfer Protocol, and domain name server).
- Turn audit trails on.
- Consider installing caller ID.
- Install a corporate firewall between your corporate network and the Internet.
- Install antivirus software on all computers and regularly download vendor updates.
- Conduct regular IS security audits.
- Verify and exercise frequent data backups for critical data.

Using Intrusion Detection Software

An **intrusion detection system (IDS)** monitors system and network resources and notifies network security personnel when it senses a possible intrusion. Examples of suspicious activities include repeated failed logon attempts, attempts to download a program to a

intrusion detection system (IDS)
Software that monitors system and network resources and notifies network security personnel when it senses a possible intrusion.

server, and access to a system at unusual hours. Such activities generate alarms that are captured on log files. When they detect an apparent attack, intrusion detection systems send an alarm, often by e-mail or pager, to network security personnel. Unfortunately, many IDSs frequently provide false alarms that result in wasted effort. If the attack is real, network security personnel must make a decision about what to do to resist the attack. Any delay in response increases the probability of damage. Use of an IDS provides another layer of protection in case an intruder gets past the outer security layers—passwords, security procedures, and corporate firewall.

Security Dashboard

security dashboard
Software that provides a comprehensive display on a single computer screen of all the vital data related to an organization's security defences, including threats, exposures, policy compliance, and incident alerts.

As you will see in Chapter 10, many organizations use **security dashboard** software to provide a comprehensive display on a single computer screen of all the vital data related to an organization's security defences, including threats, exposures, policy compliance, and incident alerts. The goal is to reduce the effort required for monitoring and to identify threats earlier. Data comes from a variety of sources, including firewalls, applications, servers, and other software and hardware devices.

Del Monte Foods, a leading manufacturer of food and pet products, employs over 5,400 people. The firm needed to provide an information infrastructure that would enable its employees to collaborate without risking the loss of proprietary company information. To that end, the company upgraded to software that provided protection against all forms of malware and could detect potential intrusions by unauthorized users. The firm also implemented a security dashboard that provides a snapshot of the data needed to identify and respond to security incidents immediately.[51]

Using Managed Security Service Providers (MSSPs)

Keeping up with computer criminals—and with new regulations—can be daunting for organizations. Criminal hackers are constantly poking and prodding, trying to breach the security defences of companies. Also, such legislation as the *Privacy Act* and the *Personal Information Protection and Electronic Documents Act* (PIPEDA), Bill 198 similar to *Sarbanes-Oxley*, and provincial laws require businesses to prove that they are securing their data. For most small and mid-sized organizations, the level of in-house network security expertise needed to protect their business operations can be quite costly to acquire and maintain. As a result, many are outsourcing their network security operations to managed security service providers (MSSPs) such as Counterpane, Guardent, IBM, Riptech, and Symantec. MSSPs monitor, manage, and maintain network security for both hardware and software. These companies provide a valuable service for IS departments drowning in reams of alerts and false alarms coming from virtual private networks (VPNs); antivirus, firewall, and intrusion detection systems; and other security monitoring systems. In addition, some provide vulnerability scanning and Web blocking and filtering capabilities.

IBM offers managed protection services that provide expert monitoring, management, and incident protection around the clock. The protection service is available for networks, servers, and desktops. When an Internet attack is detected, the service automatically blocks it without requiring human intervention. Taking the manual intervention step out of the process enables a faster response and minimizes damage from a criminal hacker. To encourage customers to adopt its service, IBM guarantees up to $50,000 in cash if the prevention service fails.[52]

Guarding Against Theft of Equipment and Data

Organizations need to take strong measures to guard against the theft of computer hardware and the data stored on it. Here are a few measures to be considered:

- Set clear guidelines on what kind of data (and how much of it) can be stored on vulnerable laptops. In many cases, private data or company confidential data may not be downloaded to laptops that leave the office.
- Require that data stored on laptops be encrypted and do spot checks to ensure that this policy is followed.

- Require that all laptops be secured using a lock and chain device so that they cannot be easily removed from an office area.
- Provide training to employees and contractors on the need for safe handling of laptops and their data. For example, laptops should never be left in a position where they can be viewed by the public, such as on the front seat of an automobile.
- Consider installing tracking software on laptops. The software sends messages via a wireless network to the specified e-mail address, pinpointing its location and including a picture of the thief (for those computers with an integrated Web cam).[53]

Crime Prevention for Individuals and Employees

This section outlines actions that individuals can take to prevent becoming a victim of computer crime, including identity theft, malware attacks, theft of equipment and data, and computer scams.

Identity Theft

Identity theft costs Canadian consumers, banks, and credit card firms an estimated $2 billion annually, according to the Canadian Council of Better Business Bureaus.[54] Consumers can protect themselves from identity theft by regularly checking their credit reports with major credit bureaus, following up with creditors if their bills do not arrive on time, not revealing any personal information in response to unsolicited e-mail or phone calls (especially Social Insurance Numbers and credit card account numbers), and shredding bills and other documents that contain sensitive information.

Some consumers contract with a service company that provides fraud monitoring services, helps you file required reports, and disputes unauthorized transactions in your accounts. Some services even offer identity theft guarantees of up to $1 million. Some of the more popular services include Trusted ID, Life Lock, Protect My ID, ID Watchdog, and Identity Guard.

The Canadian government passed a law in 2010 that created three new *Criminal Code* offences related to identity theft. The law gives courts the power to order offenders to pay restitution to victims of identity theft and also makes identity theft punishable by a prison term of up to five years for each offence.

Malware Attacks

The number of personal computers infected with malware (viruses, worms, spyware, etc.) has reached epidemic proportions. As a result of the increasing threat of malware, most computer users and organizations have installed **antivirus programs** on their computers. Such software runs in the background to protect your computer from dangers lurking on the Internet and other possible sources of infected files. The latest virus definitions are downloaded automatically when you connect to the Internet, ensuring that your PC's protection is current. To safeguard your PC and prevent it from spreading malware to your friends and co-workers, some antivirus software scans and cleans both incoming and outgoing e-mail messages. Some of the top rated anti-spyware software includes Symantec Norton Antivirus, Kaspersky Lab Anti-Virus, and Bit Defender Antivirus.[55]

antivirus program
Software that runs in the background to protect your computer from dangers lurking on the Internet and other possible sources of infected files.

Proper use of antivirus software requires the following steps:

1. *Install antivirus software and run it often.* Many of these programs automatically check for viruses each time you boot up your computer or insert a disk or CD, and some even monitor all e-mail, file transmissions, and copying operations.
2. *Update antivirus software often.* New viruses are created all the time, and antivirus software suppliers are constantly updating their software to detect and take action against these new viruses.
3. *Scan all removable media, including CDs, before copying or running programs from them.* Hiding on disks or CDs, viruses often move between systems. If you carry document or program files on removable media between computers at school or work and your home system, always scan them.

4. *Install software only from a sealed package or secure website of a known software company.* Even software publishers can unknowingly distribute viruses on their program disks or software downloads. Most scan their own systems, but viruses might still remain.

5. *Follow careful downloading practices.* If you download software from the Internet or a bulletin board, check your computer for viruses immediately after completing the transmission.

6. *If you detect a virus, take immediate action.* Early detection often allows you to remove a virus before it does any serious damage.

Many e-mail services and ISP providers offer free antivirus protection. For example, Rogers, Telus, and Bell offer free antivirus software.

Computer Scams

The following is a list of tips to help you avoid becoming a victim of a computer scam:

- Don't agree to anything in a high-pressure meeting or seminar. Insist on having time to think it over and to discuss your decision with someone you trust. If a company won't give you the time you need to check out an offer and think things over, you don't want to do business with them. A good deal now will be a good deal tomorrow; the only reason for rushing you is if the company has something to hide.

- Don't judge a company based on appearances. Flashy websites can be created and published in a matter of days. After a few weeks of taking money, a site can vanish without a trace in just a few minutes. You might find that the perfect money-making opportunity offered on a website was a money maker for the crook and a money loser for you.

- Avoid any plan that pays commissions simply for recruiting additional distributors. Your primary source of income should be your own product sales. If the earnings are not made primarily by sales of goods or services to consumers or sales by distributors under you, you might be dealing with an illegal pyramid.

- Beware of shills—people paid by a company to lie about how much they've earned and how easy the plan was to operate. Check with an independent source to make sure that the company and its offers are valid.

- Beware of a company's claim that it can set you up in a profitable home-based business but that you must first pay up front to attend a seminar and buy expensive materials. Frequently, seminars are high-pressure sales pitches, and the material is so general that it is worthless.

- If you are interested in starting a home-based business, get a complete description of the work involved before you send any money. You might find that what you are asked to do after you pay is far different from what was stated in the ad. You should never have to pay for a job description or for needed materials.

- Get in writing the refund, buy-back, and cancellation policies of any company you deal with. Do not depend on oral promises.

- Do your homework. Check with the Canadian Anti-fraud Centre (*www.antifraudcentre.ca*) before getting involved, especially when the claims about a product or potential earnings seem too good to be true.

If you need advice about an Internet or online solicitation, or if you want to report a possible scam, use the Online Reporting Form on the Anti-fraud Centre website, or call them at 1-888-495-8501.

PRIVACY ISSUES

Another important social issue in information systems involves privacy. Basically, the issue of privacy deals with this right to be left alone or to be withdrawn from public view. With information systems, privacy deals with the collection and use or misuse of data. Data is constantly being collected and stored on each of us. This data is often distributed over easily accessed networks and without our knowledge or consent. Concerns of privacy regarding this data must be addressed. Today many businesses have to handle many requests from law-enforcement agencies for information about its employees, customers, and suppliers. Indeed, some phone and Internet companies have full-time employees whose role it is to deal with information requests from local, provincial, and federal law-enforcement agencies.

With today's computers, the right to privacy is an especially challenging problem. More data and information are produced and used today than ever before. When someone is born, takes certain high school exams, starts a job, enrols in a college course, applies for a driver's licence, purchases a car, serves in the military, gets married, buys insurance, gets a library card, applies for a charge card or loan, buys a house, or merely purchases certain products, data is collected and stored somewhere in computer databases. A difficult question to answer is "Who owns this information and knowledge?" If a public or private organization spends time and resources to obtain data on you, does the organization own the data, and can it use the data in any way it desires? Government legislation answers these questions for federal agencies and private organizations.

Privacy and the Federal Government

The federal government has implemented a number of laws addressing personal privacy that are discussed in this section. The European Union has a data-protection directive that requires firms transporting data across national boundaries to have certain privacy procedures in place. This directive affects virtually any company doing business in Europe, and it is driving much of the attention being given to privacy in Canada and the United States.

Privacy at Work

The right to privacy at work is also an important issue. Employers are using technology and corporate policies to manage worker productivity and protect the use of IS resources. Employers are mostly concerned about inappropriate Web surfing, with 76 percent of employers monitoring the Web activity of their employees. Organizations also monitor employee's e-mail, with over half retaining and reviewing messages.[56] Statistics such as these have raised employee privacy concerns. In many cases, workers claim their right to privacy trumps their companies' rights to monitor employee use of IS resources.

E-Mail Privacy

E-mail also raises some interesting issues about work privacy. Federal law permits employers to monitor e-mail sent and received by employees. Furthermore, e-mail messages that have been erased from hard disks can be retrieved and used in lawsuits because the laws of discovery demand that companies produce all relevant business documents.

Instant Messaging Privacy

Using instant messaging (IM) to send and receive messages, files, and images introduces the same privacy issues associated with e-mail. As with e-mail, federal law permits employers to monitor instant messages sent and received by employees. Employers' major concern involves IMs sent by employees over their employer's IM network or using employer-provided phones. To protect your privacy and your employer's property, do not send personal or private IMs at work. Here are a few other tips:

- Choose a nonrevealing, nongender-specific, unprovocative IM screen name (Sweet Sixteen, 2hot4u, UCLAMBA all fail this test).
- Don't send messages you would be embarrassed to have your family members, colleagues, or friends read.
- Do not open files or click links in messages from people you do not know.
- Never send sensitive personal data such as credit card numbers, bank account numbers, or passwords via IM.

E-mail has changed how workers and managers communicate in the same building or around the world. E-mail, however, can be monitored and intercepted. As with other services such as cell phones, the convenience of e-mail must be balanced with the potential of privacy invasion.

(Source: © Huchen Lu/iStockphoto. com.)

Privacy and Personal Sensing Devices

Radio Frequency Identification (RFID) tags, essentially microchips with antenna, are embedded in many of the products we buy, such as medicine containers, clothing, library books, computer printers, car keys, and tires. RFID tags generate radio transmissions that, if appropriate measures are not taken, can lead to potential privacy concerns. Once these tags are associated with the individual who purchased the item, someone can potentially track individuals by the unique identifier associated with the RFID chip.

Privacy and the Internet

Some people assume that there is no privacy on the Internet and that you use it at your own risk. Others believe that companies with websites should have strict privacy procedures and be accountable for privacy invasion. Regardless of your view, the potential for privacy invasion on the Internet is huge. People wanting to invade your privacy could be anyone—criminal hackers, marketing companies, or corporate bosses. Your personal and professional information can be seized on the Internet without your knowledge or consent. E-mail is a prime target, as discussed previously. Sending an e-mail message is like having an open conversation in a large room—people can listen to your messages. When you visit a website on the Internet, information about you and your computer can be captured. When this information is combined with other information, companies can find out what you read, what products you buy, and what your interests are.

Most people who buy products on the Web say it's very important for a site to have a policy explaining how personal information is used, and the policy statement must make people feel comfortable and be extremely clear about what information is collected and what will and will not be done with it. However, many websites still do not prominently display their privacy policy or implement practices completely consistent with that policy. The real issue that Internet users need to be concerned with is what do content providers want to do with their personal information. If a site requests that you provide your name and address, you have every right to know why and what will be done with it. If you buy something and provide a shipping address, will it be sold to other retailers? Will your e-mail address be sold on a list of active Internet shoppers? And if so, you should realize that this e-mail list is no different from the lists compiled from the orders you place with catalogue retailers. You have the right to be taken off any mailing list.

A potential solution to some consumer privacy concerns is the screening technology called the **Platform for Privacy Preferences** (**P3P**) being proposed to shield users from sites that don't provide the level of privacy protection they desire. Instead of forcing users to find and read through the privacy policy for each site they visit, P3P software in a computer's browser will download the privacy policy from each site, scan it, and notify the user if the policy does not match his or her preferences. (Of course, unethical marketers can post a privacy policy that does not accurately reflect the manner in which the data is treated.) The World Wide Web Consortium, an international industry group whose members include Apple, Commerce One, Ericsson, and Microsoft, is supporting the development of P3P. Version 1.1 of the P3P was released in February 2006 and can be found at *www.w3.org/P3P/*.

> **Platform for Privacy Preferences (P3P)**
> A screening technology in Web browsers that shields users from websites that don't provide the level of privacy protection they desire.

The U.S. *Children's Online Privacy Protection Act* (COPPA) is directed at websites catering to children, requiring site owners to post comprehensive privacy policies and to obtain parental consent before they collect any personal information from children under 13 years of age. Website operators who violate the rule could be liable for civil penalties of up to $11,000 per violation. COPPA has made an impact in the design and operation of websites that cater to children. For example, Lions Gate Entertainment, the operator of the *www.thebratzfilm.com* website, had to modify its site after the Council of Better Business Bureaus determined the site failed to meet the COPPA requirements. The website requested personally identifiable information to register for the Bratz Newsletter and register for a chance to win a trip to the premiere of *The Bratz Movie* without first obtaining verifiable parental consent. Canada currently does not have specific laws comparable to COPPA that protect the privacy of children online.[57]

A social network service employs the Web and software to connect people for many purposes. There are thousands of such networks and some of the more popular social networking websites are Bebo, Facebook, Hi5, Imbee, MySpace, Namesdatabase, Tagged, and XuQa. Most of these websites allow you to easily create a user profile that provides personal details, photos, and even videos that can be viewed by other visitors to the website. Some of the websites have age restrictions or require that a parent register their preteen by providing a credit card to validate the parent's identity. Teens can provide information about where they live, go to school, their favourite music, and interests in hopes of meeting new friends. Unfortunately, they can also meet ill-intentioned strangers at these sites. Many documented encounters involve adults masquerading as teens attempting to meet young people for illicit purposes. Parents are advised to discuss potential dangers, check their children's profiles, and monitor their activities at such sites.

Internet Libel Concerns

Libel involves publishing an intentionally false written statement that is damaging to a person's or organization's reputation. Examples of Internet libel include an ex-husband posting lies about his wife on a blog, a disgruntled former employee posting lies about a company on a message board, and a jilted girlfriend posting false statements to her former boyfriend's Facebook account. Individuals can post information to the Internet using anonymous e-mail accounts or screen names. This makes it more difficult, but not impossible, to identify the libeller. Individuals, too, must be careful what they post on the Internet to avoid libel charges. In many cases, disgruntled former employees are being sued by their former employers for material posted on the Internet.

Filtering and Classifying Internet Content

To help parents control what their children see on the Internet, some companies provide *filtering software* to help screen Internet content. Many of these screening programs also prevent children from sending personal information over e-mail or through chat groups.

This stops children from broadcasting their name, address, phone number, or other personal information over the Internet. The two approaches used are filtering, which blocks certain websites, and rating, which places a rating on websites. According to the Internet Filter Review, five of the top-rated filtering software packages costing less than $50 are Net Nanny 6.5, CyberPatrol Parental Controls 7.7, PC Pandora 6.0, Safe Eyes 6.0, and OnLine Family Norton.[58]

Organizations also implement filtering software to prevent employees from visiting websites not related to work, particularly those involving gambling or those containing pornographic or other offensive material. Before implementing website blocking, the users must be informed about the company's policies and why they exist. It is best if the organization's Internet users, management, and IS organization work together to define the policy to be implemented. The policy should be clear about the repercussions to employees who attempt to circumvent the blocking measures.

The Internet Content Rating Association (ICRA) is a nonprofit organization whose members include Internet industry leaders such as America Online, British Telecom, IBM, and Microsoft. Its specific goals are to protect children from potentially harmful material, while safeguarding free speech on the Internet. Using the ICRA rating system, Web authors fill out an online questionnaire describing the content of their site—what is and isn't present. The broad topics covered include chat capabilities, the language used, nudity and sexual content, violence depicted, and other areas such as alcohol, drugs, gambling, and suicide. Based on the authors' responses, ICRA then generates a content label (a short piece of computer code) that the authors add to their site. Internet users (and parents) can set their browser to allow or disallow access to websites based on the objective rating information declared in the content label and their subjective preferences. Reliance on website authors to rate their own sites has its weaknesses, though. Website authors can lie when completing the ICRA questionnaire so that their site receives a content label that doesn't accurately reflect the site's content. In addition, many hate groups and sexually explicit sites don't have an ICRA rating, so they will not be blocked unless a browser is set to block all unrated sites. Unfortunately, this option would block out so many acceptable sites that it could make Web surfing useless. For these reasons, site labelling is currently at best a complement to other filtering techniques.

Fairness in Information Use

Selling information to other companies can be so lucrative that many companies will continue to store and sell the data they collect on customers, employees, and others. When is this information storage and use fair and reasonable to the people whose data is stored and sold? Do people have a right to know about data stored about them and to decide what data is stored and used? As shown in Table 2.3, these questions can be broken down into four issues that should be addressed: knowledge, control, notice, and consent.

In the past few decades, significant laws have been passed regarding a person's right to privacy. Others relate to business privacy rights and the fair use of data and information.

The *Privacy Act* and *Access to Information Act*

The major pieces of privacy legislation in Canada are the *Privacy Act* and the *Access to Information Act*. They impose obligations on federal government departments and agencies to respect privacy rights by limiting the collection, use, and disclosure of personal information. They also give individuals the right to access and correct personal information held by federal government organizations. Every Canadian province and territory has enacted similar privacy legislation.

Personal Information Protection and Electronic Documents Act (PIPEDA)

PIPEDA is concerned with how private-sector organizations can collect, use, and disclose personal information in their commercial activities. PIPEDA requires individuals' consent to have their personal information collected. The information must be collected for a reasonable purpose, used only for that purpose, and stored securely. The individual has the

Fairness Issues	Database Storage	Database Usage
The right to know	Knowledge	Notice
The ability to decide	Control	Consent
Knowledge	Should people know what data is stored about them?	In some cases, people are informed that information about them is stored in a corporate database. In others, they do not know that their personal information is stored in corporate databases.
Control	Should people be able to correct errors in corporate database systems?	This is possible with most organizations, although it can be difficult in some cases.
Notice	Should an organization that uses personal data for a purpose other than the original purpose notify individuals in advance?	Most companies don't do this.
Consent	If information on people is to be used for other purposes, should these people be asked to give their consent before data on them is used?	Many companies do not give people the ability to decide if information on them will be sold or used for other purposes.

Table 2.3

The Right to Know and the Ability to Decide Federal Privacy Laws and Regulations

right to inspect and review the accuracy of the information.[59] However, if there are existing laws that are similar to PIPEDA, these take precedence over PIPEDA. For example, the *Privacy Act* and several federal and provincial laws already deal with the protection of personal information in specific industries such as banking and consumer credit reporting.[60] One of the most famous PIPEDA cases is Canada's investigation against Facebook, described at the beginning of this chapter.

Electronic Commerce Protection Act (ECPA)

The *Electronic Commerce Protection Act* is Canada's law against spam and malware. It complements e-commerce legislation that has been enacted by the provinces and territories. The law forbids the installation on a computer of a program that could send an electronic message without the consent of the user. It also prohibits anyone in Canada from sending a commercial message to any electronic address unless the receiver has consented or has had a business transaction with the recipient in the previous 18 months. Penalties for breaking the law range from up to $1 million for individual violators to up to $10 million for organizations.[61]

Other Legislation

The *Investigative Powers for the 21st Century Act* (IP21C) was proposed in 2009 and had not been enacted at the time of writing this textbook. The law would require telecommunication and Internet service providers to assist police and federal bodies, such as the RCMP and the Canadian Security Intelligence Service (CSIS), in the investigation of crime using the Internet. The bill would require the service providers to maintain "intercept-capable" equipment on their networks and provide law-enforcement officials with timely access to the personal information about subscribers without the need for a warrant. Critics argue that the law removes many of the checks and balances that previously allowed the courts to ensure that law-enforcement agencies did not abuse their powers.

Corporate Privacy Policies

Even though privacy laws for private organizations are not very restrictive, most organizations are sensitive to privacy issues and fairness. They realize that invasions of privacy can hurt their business, turn away customers, and dramatically reduce revenues and profits.

Consider if a major international credit card company sold confidential financial information on millions of customers to other companies; the results could be disastrous. In a matter of days, the firm's business and revenues could be reduced dramatically. Therefore, most organizations maintain privacy policies, even though they are not required by law. Some companies even have a privacy bill of rights that specifies how the privacy of employees, clients, and customers will be protected. Corporate privacy policies should address a customer's knowledge, control, notice, and consent over the storage and use of information. They can also cover who has access to private data and when it can be used.

Multinational companies face an extremely difficult challenge in implementing data-collection and dissemination processes and policies because of the multitude of differing country or regional statutes. For example, Australia requires companies to destroy customer data (including backup files) or make it anonymous after it's no longer needed. Firms that transfer customer and personnel data out of Europe must comply with European privacy laws that allow customers and employees to access data about them and let them determine how that information can be used.

Websites for a few corporate privacy policies are shown in Table 2.4.

Table 2.4 **Corporate Privacy Policies**	**Company**	**URL**
	Research in Motion (RIM)	*www.rim.com/legal/privacy.shtml*
	Tim Hortons	*www.timhortons.com/ca/en/privacy.html*
	Bank of Montreal	*www.bmo.com/home/popups/global/privacy*
	Barrick Gold	*www.barrick.com/ContactUs/LegalPrivacy/default.aspx*
	Visa	*www.visa.ca/en/common/privacy.html*
	Imperial Oil	*www.imperialoil.ca/Canada-English/privacy.aspx*

A good database design practice is to assign a single unique identifier to each customer so each has a single record describing all relationships with the company across all its business units. That way, the organization can apply customer privacy preferences consistently throughout all databases. Failure to do so can expose the organization to legal risks—aside from upsetting customers who opted out of some collection practices.

Individual Efforts to Protect Privacy

Although numerous provincial and federal laws deal with privacy, the laws do not completely protect individual privacy. In addition, not all companies have privacy policies. As a result, many people are taking steps to increase their own privacy protection. Some of the steps you can take to protect personal privacy include the following:

- *Find out what is stored about you in existing databases.* Call the major credit bureaus to get a copy of your credit report. You are entitled to a free credit report every 12 months. You can also obtain a free report if you have been denied credit in the last 60 days. The major companies are Equifax Canada (1-800-465-7166, *www.equifax.ca*), TransUnion Canada (1-800-663-9980, *www.transunion.ca*). You can also submit an Access to Information request to a government agency that you suspect might have information stored on you.
- *Be careful when you share information about yourself.* Don't share information unless it is absolutely necessary. Every time you give information about yourself through an 800, 888, or 900 call, your privacy is at risk. Be vigilant in insisting that your doctor, bank, or financial institution not share information about you with others without your written consent.

- *Be proactive to protect your privacy.* You can get an unlisted phone number and ask the phone company to block caller ID systems from reading your phone number. If you change your address, don't fill out a change-of-address form with Canada Post; you can notify the people and companies that you want to have your new address. Destroy copies of your charge card bills and shred monthly statements before disposing of them in the garbage. Be careful about sending personal e-mail messages over a corporate e-mail system. You can also get help in avoiding junk mail and telemarketing calls by visiting the Canadian Marketing Association website at *www.the-cma.org*. Go to the Website and look under the Do Not Contact service section.
- *Take extra care when purchasing anything from a website.* Make sure that you safeguard your credit card numbers, passwords, and personal information. Do not do business with a site unless you know that it handles credit card information securely. Look for a seal of approval from organizations such as TRUSTe. When you open the Web page where you enter credit card information or other personal data, make sure that the Web address begins with *https* and check to see if a locked padlock icon appears in the Address bar or status bar. Do not provide personal information without reviewing the site's data privacy policy. Many credit card companies issue single-use credit card numbers on request. Charges appear on your usual bill, but the number is destroyed after a single use, eliminating the risk of stolen credit card numbers.

THE WORK ENVIRONMENT

The use of computer-based information systems has changed the makeup of the workforce. Jobs that require IS literacy have increased, and many less skilled positions have been eliminated. Corporate programs, such as reengineering and continuous improvement, bring with them the concern that as business processes are restructured and information systems are integrated within them, the people involved in these processes will be removed.

However, the growing field of computer technology and information systems has opened up numerous avenues to professionals and nonprofessionals of all backgrounds. Enhanced telecommunications has been the impetus for new types of business and has created global markets in industries once limited to domestic markets. Even the simplest tasks have been aided by computers, banking transactions,, smoothing order processing, and allowing people with disabilities to participate more actively in the workforce. As computers and other IS components drop in cost and become easier to use, more workers will benefit from the increased productivity and efficiency provided by computers. Yet, despite these increases in productivity and efficiency, information systems can raise other concerns.

Health Concerns

Organizations can increase employee effectiveness by paying attention to the health concerns in today's work environment. For some people, working with computers can cause occupational stress. Anxieties about job insecurity, loss of control, incompetence, and demotion are just a few of the fears workers might experience. In some cases, the stress can become so severe that workers might sabotage computer systems and equipment. Monitoring employee stress can alert companies to potential problems. Training and counselling can often help the employee and deter problems.

Heavy computer use can affect one's physical health as well. A job that requires sitting at a desk and using a computer for many hours a day qualifies as a sedentary job. Such work can double the risk of seated immobility thromboembolism (SIT), the formation of blood clots in the legs or lungs. People leading a sedentary lifestyle are also likely to experience an undesirable weight gain, which can lead to increased fatigue and greater risk of type 2 diabetes, heart problems, and other serious ailments.

ETHICAL AND SOCIETAL ISSUES

Is the Internet Eating Our Brains?

Since the rise of the Web, many have become concerned that humanity is becoming overly dependent on technology and the Internet. Others have countered that the benefits of the Internet far outweigh any dependency concerns.

Researchers at the University of Maryland asked 200 students to do without all digital media for one full day. The results of the study were startling. Many students in the study exhibited "signs of withdrawal, craving and anxiety" as their 24 hours of digital isolation ticked by. The psychological reactions were very similar to those of individuals with chemical addictions.

Students complained of feeling cut off from family and friends. Text messaging, e-mailing, and Facebook posts allow students to feel continuously connected to friends who provide support and comfort. Losing those connections left students feeling isolated and out of touch. Interacting with their social networks defined these students' daily lives and existence.

Although the American Psychiatric Association does not recognize Internet addiction as a formal disorder, it is clear that it is becoming an affliction of today's connected lifestyle. Canada has one of the highest rates of Internet usage in the world, and Canadians spend on average 42 hours a month surfing the Internet.[62] In South Korea, perhaps the most wired country in the world, the government is restricting access to popular online video games. This action was taken in response to numerous reports of out-of-control teens who refuse to log off their online games. South Korea has classified 2 million people as "Internet addicts." The government has started an educational program in grade schools to discourage students from obsessive Internet indulgence similar to programs used to discourage students from taking drugs.

Is our increasing use of the Internet an addiction or a natural evolution? Some see it as a positive progression for humankind, allowing us to pool our resources to accomplish more, while others think that it is eating our brains. In his book *The Shallows: What the Internet Is Doing to Our Brains*, Nicholas Carr makes the case that Internet use is damaging the way we

think. Carr believes that as we jump around the Web from topic to topic, we are rewiring our brains and reducing our ability to concentrate, remember, and reason.

The Internet represents a major societal change, and such major change always brings with it concern and criticism. Consider the words of English author Barnaby Rich 400 years ago regarding the mass production of books: "One of the great diseases of this age is the multitude of books that doth so overcharge the world that it is not able to digest the abundance of idle matter that is every day hatched and brought into the world."

Whether or not Internet addiction exists as a mental disorder, humanity would be wise to consider its dependency on the Internet and the implications of the loss of electronic technologies due to natural or economic disaster or military attack. How might a society survive the loss of essential network infrastructure or the electric grid?

Discussion Questions

1. In what manner are individuals becoming dependent on the Internet and digital technologies?
2. At what point do you think Internet use might be classified as an addiction? Do you know of anyone who you would classify as an Internet addict?

Critical Thinking Questions

1. Why do you think Internet addiction has become such a problem in South Korea? Do you think the same destiny awaits Canadians as we become increasingly digitally connected?
2. What action can be taken so that our dependency on the Internet poses less of a threat to our survival?

SOURCES: Slew, Walden, "U.S. Students Suffering from Internet Addiction: Study," Reuters, *www.reuters.com*, April 23, 2010; Yoon, Sangwon, "South Korea Cracks Down on Internet Addiction," NewsFactor, *www.newsfactor.com*, April 23, 2010; Johnston, Casey, "College Students Struggle to Go Without Media for 24 hours," *Ars Technica, www.arstechnica.com*, April 23, 2010; Snyder, Bill, "Nicholas Carr: The Internet Is Hurting Our Brains," *Computerworld, www.computerworld.com*, June 21, 2010.

Other work-related health hazards involve emissions from improperly maintained and used equipment. Some studies show that poorly maintained laser printers can release ozone into the air; others dispute the claim. Numerous studies on the impact of emissions from display screens have also resulted in conflicting theories. Although some medical authorities believe that long-term exposure can cause cancer, studies are not conclusive at this time. In any case, many organizations are developing conservative and cautious policies.

Most computer manufacturers publish technical information on radiation emissions from their computer monitors, and many companies pay close attention to this information. San Francisco was one of the first cities to propose a video display terminal (VDT) bill. The bill requires companies with 15 or more employees who spend at least four hours a day working with computer screens to give 15-minute breaks every two hours and adjustable chairs and workstations if employees request them.

In addition to the possible health risks from radio-frequency exposure, cell phone use has raised a safety issue—an increased risk of traffic accidents as vehicle operators become distracted while driving by talking on their cell phones (or operating their laptop computers, car navigation systems, or other computer devices). As a result, some provinces have made it illegal to operate a cell phone while driving.

From time to time, concern has been raised about heavy cell phone usage and an increased chance for brain cancer. A study by Interphone, an international collaboration, found there was no such risk except for perhaps a small percentage of the very heaviest cell phone users. Even here, the findings were inconclusive.[63]

Carpal tunnel syndrome (CTS) is an aggravation of the pathway for the nerves that travel through the wrist (carpal tunnel). CTS involves wrist pain, a feeling of tingling and numbness, and difficulty grasping and holding objects. In the late 1990s, many worker compensation claims were filed by people whose job required them to work at a keyboard many hours a day. However, a 2001 study by the Mayo Clinic found that heavy computer users (up to seven hours per day) had the same rate of carpal tunnel injury as the general population. It appears that CTS is caused by factors other than the repetitive motion of typing on a keyboard.

Avoiding Health and Environmental Problems

Many computer-related health problems are caused by a poorly designed work environment. The computer screen can be hard to read, with glare and poor contrast. Desks and chairs can also be uncomfortable. Keyboards and computer screens might be fixed in place or difficult to move. The hazardous activities associated with these unfavourable conditions are collectively referred to as *work stressors*. Although these problems might not be of major concern to casual users of computer systems, continued stressors such as repetitive motion, awkward posture, and eye strain can cause more serious and long-term injuries. If nothing else, these problems can severely limit productivity and performance.

The science of designing machines, products, and systems to maximize the safety, comfort, and efficiency of the people who use them, called **ergonomics**, has suggested some approaches to reducing these health problems. Ergonomic experts carefully study the slope of the keyboard, the positioning and design of display screens, and the placement and design of computer tables and chairs. Flexibility is a major component of ergonomics and an important feature of computer devices. People come in many sizes, have differing preferences, and require different positioning of equipment for best results. Some people, for example, want to place the keyboard in their laps; others prefer it on a solid table. Because of these individual differences, computer designers are attempting to develop systems that provide a great deal of flexibility. In fact, the revolutionary design of Apple's iMac computer came about through concerns for users' comfort. After using basically the same keyboard design for over a decade, Microsoft introduced a new split keyboard called the Natural Ergonomic Keyboard 4000. The keyboard provides improved ergonomic features such as improved angles that reduce motion and how

ergonomics
The science of designing machines, products, and systems to maximize the safety, comfort, and efficiency of the people who use them.

Research has shown that developing certain ergonomically correct habits can reduce the risk of adverse health effects when using a computer.

(Source: C Squared Studios/Photodisc/Getty Images.)

much you must stretch your fingers when you type. The design of the keyboard also provides more convenient wrist and arm postures, which make typing more convenient for users.

Computer users who work at their machines for more than an hour per day should consider using LCD screens, which are much easier on your eyes than CRT screens. If you stare at a CRT screen all day long, your eye muscles can become fatigued from the screen flicker and bright backlighting of the monitor. LCD screens provide a much better viewing experience for your eyes by virtually eliminating flicker while still being bright without harsh incandescence. Also, remember to blink! We tend to focus hard on the screen and blink much less than normal. The result is red, dry, itchy eyes. A few drops of artificial tears and changing your focus away from the screen periodically to rest the eyes has been found to help.

In addition to steps taken by hardware manufacturing companies, computer users must also take action to reduce repetitive stress injury (RSI) caused by overuse of the computer through repeated movements that affects muscles, tendons, or nerves in the arms, hands, or upper back. For example, when working at a workstation, the top of the monitor should be at or just below eye level. Your wrists and hands should be in line with your forearms, with your elbows close to your body and supported. Your lower back needs to be well supported. Your feet should be flat on the floor. Take an occasional break to get away from the keyboard and screen. Stand up and stretch while at your workplace. Do not ignore pain or discomfort. Many workers ignore early signs of RSI, and as a result, the problem becomes much worse and more difficult to treat.

It is never too soon to stop unhealthy computer work habits. Prolonged computer use under poor working conditions can lead to carpal tunnel syndrome, bursitis, headaches, and permanent eye damage. Strain and poor office conditions cannot be left unchecked. Unfortunately, at times we are all distracted by pressing issues such as the organization's need to raise productivity, improve quality, meet deadlines, and cut costs. We become complacent and fail to pay attention to the importance of healthy working conditions.[64]

ETHICAL ISSUES IN INFORMATION SYSTEMS

Ethical issues deal with what is generally considered right or wrong. Laws do not provide a complete guide to ethical behaviour. Just because an activity is defined as legal does not mean that it is ethical. For example, while is it legal to sell cigarettes in Canada, is it ethical for drugstores to sell cigarettes to smokers given medical evidence that smoking causes cancer? As a result, practitioners in many professions subscribe to a **code of ethics** that states the principles and core values that are essential to their work and, therefore, govern their behaviour, such as the Canadian Bar Association (CBA), Canadian Medical Association (CMA). The code can become a reference point for weighing what is legal and what is ethical. For example, doctors adhere to varying versions of the 2,000-year-old Hippocratic Oath, which medical schools offer as an affirmation to their graduating classes. Throughout this book there are "Ethical and Societal Issues" boxes in most chapters that discuss IS ethical issues.

code of ethics
A code that states the principles and core values that are essential to a set of people and that therefore govern their behaviour.

When faced with an ethical issue, it is important to identify the facts and the stakeholders (interested parties in the issue) and clearly define the conflict or dilemma. Once the issue has been defined, the next steps are to identify possible options and their potential consequences. There are several ethical principles or rules that could be followed in determining the appropriate outcome or action to an ethical issue. The Golden Rule—do unto others as you would have them do unto you—helps with assessing the fairness of the decision to the stakeholders. The utilitarian principle supports taking the action that achieves the higher or greater value such as freedom, privacy, and respect for the individual, while the risk aversion principle leads to taking the action that produces the least harm or least potential cost. Finally, Kant's categorical imperative would lead a person to undertake actions that would be right for everyone to do in every situation such as "It is best to tell the truth all the time."

Some IS professionals believe that their field offers many opportunities for unethical behaviour. They also believe that unethical behaviour can be reduced by top-level managers developing, discussing, and enforcing codes of ethics. Various IS-related organizations and associations promote ethically responsible use of information systems and have developed useful codes of ethics. Founded in 1947, the Association for Computing Machinery (ACM) is the oldest computing society and boasts more than 80,000 members in more than 100 countries. The ACM has a code of ethics and professional conduct that includes eight general moral imperatives that can be used to help guide the actions of IS professionals. These guidelines can also be used for those who employ or hire IS professionals to monitor and guide their work. These imperatives are outlined in the following list: As an ACM member I will ...

1. Contribute to society and human well-being.
2. Avoid harm to others.
3. Be honest and trustworthy.
4. Be fair and take action not to discriminate.
5. Honour property rights, including copyrights and patents.
6. Give proper credit for intellectual property.
7. Respect the privacy of others.
8. Honour confidentiality.

(Source: ACM Code of Ethics and Professional Conduct, *www.acm.org/about/code-of-ethics?searchterm=code+of+ethics* accessed June 15, 2010.)

The mishandling of the social issues discussed in this chapter—including waste and mistakes, crime, privacy, health, and ethics—can devastate an organization. The prevention of these problems and recovery from them are important aspects of managing information and information systems as critical corporate assets. More organizations are recognizing that people are the most important component of a computer-based information system and that long-term competitive advantage can be found in a well-trained, motivated, and knowledgeable workforce that adheres to a set of principles and core values that help guide their actions.

SUMMARY

Principle:

Policies and procedures must be established to avoid waste and mistakes associated with computer usage.

Computer waste is the inappropriate use of computer technology and resources in both the public and private sectors. Computer mistakes relate to errors, failures, and other problems that result in output that is incorrect and without value. At the corporate level, computer waste and mistakes impose unnecessarily high costs for an information system and reduce profits. Waste often results from poor integration of IS components, leading to duplication of efforts and overcapacity. Inefficient procedures also waste IS resources, as do thoughtless disposal of useful resources and misuse of computer time for games and personal use. Inappropriate processing instructions, inaccurate data entry, mishandling of IS output, and poor systems design all cause computer mistakes.

Preventing waste and mistakes involves establishing, implementing, monitoring, and reviewing effective policies and procedures. Companies should develop manuals and training programs to avoid waste and mistakes.

Principle:

Computer crime is a serious and rapidly growing area of concern requiring management attention.

Some crimes use computers as tools. For example, a criminal can use a computer to manipulate records, counterfeit money and documents, commit fraud via telecommunications links, and make unauthorized electronic transfers of money.

A cyberterrorist is someone who intimidates or coerces a government or organization to advance his or her political or social objectives by launching computer-based attacks against computers, networks, and the information stored on them.

Identity theft is a crime in which an impostor obtains key pieces of personal identification information to impersonate someone else. The information is then used to obtain credit, merchandise, and services in the name of the victim, or to provide the thief with false credentials.

Although Internet gambling is popular, its legality is questionable within Canada.

The computer is also used as a tool to fight crime. Law-enforcement agencies use GPS tracking devices and software to monitor the movement of registered sex offenders. Law-enforcement agencies use crime-related data and powerful analysis techniques, coupled with GIS systems, to better understand and even diminish crime risks.

A criminal hacker, also called a *cracker*, is a computer-savvy person who attempts to gain unauthorized or illegal access to computer systems to steal passwords, corrupt files and programs, and even transfer money. Script bunnies are crackers with little technical savvy. Insiders are employees, disgruntled or otherwise, working solo or in concert with outsiders to compromise corporate systems. The greatest fear of many organizations is the potential harm that can be done by insiders who know system logon IDs, passwords, and company procedures.

Computer crimes target computer systems and include illegal access to computer systems by criminal hackers, alteration and destruction of data and programs by viruses, and simple theft of computer resources.

Malware is a general term for software that is harmful or destructive. There are many forms of malware, including viruses, variants, worms, Trojan horse attacks, logic bombs, and rootkits. Spyware is software installed on a personal computer to intercept or take partial control over the user's interactions with the computer without knowledge or permission of the user. A password sniffer is a small program hidden in a network or computer system that records identification numbers and passwords.

Computer managers and law-enforcement agencies are emphasizing prevention and detection of computer crime. People can use antivirus software to detect the presence of all sorts of malware. Use of an intrusion detection system (IDS) provides another layer of protection in the event that an intruder gets past the outer security layers—passwords, security procedures, and corporate firewall. An IDS monitors system and network resources and notifies network security personnel when it senses a possible intrusion. Many small and mid-sized organizations are outsourcing their network security operations to managed security service providers (MSSPs), which monitor, manage, and maintain network security hardware and software. When discarding a computer, people should use disk-wiping utilities to avoid the loss of personal or confidential data even after deleting files and emptying the Recycle Bin (or Trash).

Software piracy might represent the most common computer crime. It is estimated that the software industry lost $51 billion in revenue in 2009 to software piracy. The global recording industry loses as much as $12.5 billion in revenue from music piracy each year. Patent infringement is also a major problem for computer software and hardware manufacturers.

Computer-related scams, including phishing and vishing, have cost people and companies thousands of dollars. Computer crime is an international issue.

Security measures, such as using passwords, identification numbers, and data encryption, help to guard against illegal computer access, especially when supported by effective control procedures. Virus-scanning software identifies and removes damaging computer programs. Organizations can use a security dashboard to provide a comprehensive display of vital data related to its security defences and threats.

Privacy issues are a concern with government agencies, e-mail use, corporations, and the Internet. The *Privacy Act*, *Access to Information Act* and PIPEDA established straightforward and easily understandable requirements for data collection, use, and distribution by federal agencies and private organizations. The *Investigative Powers for the 21st Century Act* requires Internet service providers and telephone companies to intercept Internet communication and turn over customer information without a warrant to law-enforcement authorities.

A business should develop a clear and thorough policy about privacy rights for customers, including database access. That policy should also address the rights of employees, including electronic monitoring systems and e-mail. Fairness in information use for privacy rights emphasizes knowledge, control, notice, and consent for people profiled in databases. People should know about the data that is stored about them and be able to correct errors in corporate database systems. If information on people is to be used for other purposes, they should be asked to give their consent beforehand. Each person has the right to know and the ability to decide.

Principle:

Jobs, equipment, and working conditions must be designed to avoid negative health effects from computers.

Jobs that involve heavy use of computers contribute to a sedentary lifestyle, which increases the risk of health problems. Some critics blame computer systems for emissions of ozone and electromagnetic radiation. Use of cell phones while driving has been linked to increased car accidents.

The study of designing and positioning computer equipment, called ergonomics, has suggested some approaches to reducing these health problems. Ergonomic design principles help to reduce harmful effects and increase the efficiency of an information system. RSI prevention includes keeping good posture, not ignoring pain or problems, performing stretching and strengthening exercises, and seeking proper treatment. Although they can cause negative health consequences, information systems can also be used to provide a wealth of information on health topics through the Internet and other sources.

Principle:

Practitioners in many professions subscribe to a code of ethics that states the principles and core values that are essential to their work.

A code of ethics states the principles and core values that are essential to the members of a profession or organization. Ethical computer users define acceptable practices more strictly than just refraining from committing crimes; they also consider the effects of their IS activities, including Internet usage, on other people and organizations. The Association for Computing Machinery developed guidelines and a code of ethics. Many IS professionals join computer-related associations and agree to abide by detailed ethical codes.

CHAPTER 2: SELF-ASSESSMENT TEST

Policies and procedures must be established to avoid waste and mistakes associated with computer usage.

1. Business managers and end users must work with IS professionals to implement and follow proper IS usage policies to ensure effective use of company resources. True or False?
2. Computer-related waste and mistakes are major causes of computer problems, contributing to unnecessarily high _____ and lost _____.
3. Preventing waste and mistakes involves establishing, implementing, _____, and reviewing effective policies and procedures.

Computer crime is a serious and rapidly growing area of concern requiring management attention.

4. A global study of 800 companies estimated that companies worldwide lost more than $1 trillion due to cybercrime in 2008. True or False?
5. Convincing someone to give out a critical password is an example of _____.
6. Someone who intimidates or coerces a government or organization to advance his or her political or social objectives by launching computer-based attacks against computers, networks, and the information stored on them is called a(n) _____.
7. Law-enforcement agencies have combined crime-related data, powerful analysis techniques, and _____ to better understand and even diminish crime risks.
8. A rootkit is a type of Trojan horse that executes when specific conditions occur. True or False?
9. What type of malware is capable of spreading itself from one computer to another?
   a. logic bomb
   b. Trojan horse
   c. virus
   d. worm
10. A(n) _____ is a modified version of a virus that is produced by the virus's author or another person amending the original virus code.
11. Deleting files and emptying the Recycle Bin (or Trash) ensures that others cannot view the personal data on your recycled computer. True or False?
12. _____ software provides a comprehensive display on a single computer screen of all the vital data related to an organization's security defences; this includes threats, exposures, policy compliance, and incident alerts.

Jobs, equipment, and working conditions must be designed to avoid negative health effects from computers.

13. A job that requires sitting at a desk and using a computer for many hours a day can double the risk of seated immobility _____, which is the formation of blood clots in the legs or lungs.

    Practitioners in many professions subscribe to a code of ethics that states the principles and core values that are essential to their work.

14. Just because an activity is defined as legal, it does not mean that it is ethical. True or False?

CHAPTER 2: SELF-ASSESSMENT TEST ANSWERS

(1) True (2) costs, profits (3) monitoring (4) True (5) social engineering (6) cyberterrorist (7) Geographic Information Systems (8) False (9) d (10) variant (11) False (12) Security dashboard (13) thromboembolism (14) True

REVIEW QUESTIONS

1. Discuss examples of computer waste.
2. What is a potential danger of using spam filters?
3. What factors make it difficult to determine the amount of computer-related crime?
4. What is social engineering?
5. Briefly discuss the seriousness with which the Canadian government views cyberterrorism.
6. How do you distinguish between a hacker and a criminal hacker?
7. Why are insiders one of the biggest threats for company computer systems?
8. What is a virus? What is a worm? How are they different?
9. What is vishing? What actions can you take to reduce the likelihood that you will be a victim of this crime?
10. What is filtering software? Why would organizations use such software?
11. What does intrusion detection software do? What are some of the issues with the use of this software?
12. What is the difference between a patent and a copyright? What copyright issues come into play when downloading software or music from a website?
13. Explain the difference between phishering and vishing.
14. What is ergonomics? How can it be applied to office workers?
15. What specific actions can you take to avoid spyware?
16. What is a code of ethics? Give an example.

DISCUSSION QUESTIONS

1. Discuss how policies and procedures can help prevent computer waste and mistakes.
2. Discuss at least three examples of the computer being used as a tool to fight crime.
3. Identify the risks associated with the disposal of obsolete computers. Discuss the steps that one must take to safely dispose of personal computers.
4. Identify five measures organizations can take to safeguard against the theft of computer hardware and the data stored on it.
5. Briefly discuss software piracy. What is it, how widespread is it, and who is harmed by it?
6. Identify and briefly discuss Canada's privacy laws.
7. Imagine that your friend regularly downloads copies of newly released, full-length motion pictures for free from the Internet and makes copies for others for a small fee. Do you think that this is ethical? Is it legal? Would you express any concerns to him?
8. Outline an approach, including specific techniques (e.g., dumpster diving, phishing, social engineering), that you could employ to gain personal data about the members of your class.
9. Your 12-year-old niece shows you a dozen or so photos of herself and a brief biography including address and cell phone number she plans to post on Facebook. What advice might you offer her about posting personal information and photos?
10. Imagine that you are a hacker and have developed a Trojan horse program. What tactics might you use to get unsuspecting victims to load the program onto their computer?
11. Briefly discuss the potential for cyberterrorism to cause a major disruption in our daily life. What are some likely targets of a cyberterrorist? What sort of action could a cyberterrorist take against these targets?
12. Do you believe that the RCMP should be able to collect Internet communication and personal information without a warrant? Why or why not?
13. Briefly discuss the differences between acting morally and acting legally. Give an example of acting legally and yet immorally.

PROBLEM-SOLVING EXERCISES

1. Access the websites for the Canadian Alliance Against Software Theft (CAAST), Motion Picture Association of America (MPAA), and Business Software Alliance (BSA) to get estimates of the amount of piracy worldwide for at least five years. Use a graphics package to develop a bar chart to show the amount of music, motion picture, and software piracy over a five-year time period.

2. Using spreadsheet software and appropriate forecasting routines, develop a forecast for the amount of piracy for next year. Document any assumptions you make in developing your forecast.

3. Do research on proposed changes to PIPEDA. Use presentation software to document these changes and present your position on the impact and legitimacy of these changes.

TEAM ACTIVITIES

1. The Digital Due Process Coalition includes the Internet's largest online service providers, such as Google, Microsoft, Facebook, AOL, and eBay. The coalition is pushing for updates in the U.S. and Canadian electronic privacy laws. Do research to find out more about this organization and the four principles it wants to see implemented in new or revised privacy legislation. Prepare to debate either side of this statement: the Digital Due Process Coalition is doing worthwhile work to improve the privacy of electronic data.

2. Have each member of your team access ten different websites and summarize their findings with regard to the existence of data privacy policy statements. Did the site have such a policy? Was it easy to find? Was it complete and easy to understand? Did you find any sites using the P3P standard or ICRA rating method?

WEB EXERCISES

1. Do research on the Web and find information about efforts being taken to speed up and improve the patent application process. What are the forces that are driving these changes? Write a brief report summarizing your findings.

2. Do research on the Web to find the latest information about Google's ongoing battle with China over the filtering of Internet search results. Write a brief report documenting your findings. Do you think that Google has acted in an ethical manner in regards to its response to China's request to filter search results?

3. Do research on the Canadian Cyber Incident Response Centre (CCIRC) and write a brief report summarizing its activities.

CAREER EXERCISES

1. You are a senior member of a marketing organization for a manufacturer of children's toys. A recommendation has been made to develop a website to promote and sell your firm's products as well as learn more about what parents and their children are looking for in new toys. Develop a list of considerations and laws that will affect the design of the website. Describe how these will limit the operation of your new site.

2. You have just begun a new position in customer relations for a retail organization that sells its products both online and in brick-and-mortar stores. Within your first week on the job, several customers have expressed concern about potential theft of customer data from the store's computer databases and identity theft. Who would you talk to within your organization to develop a satisfactory response to address your customers' concerns? What key points would you need to verify with the store's technical people?

CASE STUDIES

Case One

The "My SHC Community" Privacy Disaster

Sears Holdings Corporation (SHC) is the third largest retailer in the United States, owning both Sears Roebuck and Kmart. Like all retailers, Sears is heavily invested in marketing research. Discovering customers' interests and purchasing habits is essential to successful marketing and sales campaigns.

Gathering data on customer interests can be difficult. The Internet helps considerably by allowing businesses to analyze the actions of visitors on their sites. Though helpful, Web analytics provide only a small glimpse into the online activities of customers; businesses cannot see what users do elsewhere on the Web. Some businesses have tried, typically with disastrous effects, to track users around the Web. For example, online advertiser DoubleClick was charged with violations of privacy laws when it placed ads on many websites to track users' movements around the Web. More recently, Facebook has been scrutinized for its Open Graph technology that allows it and its partners to track users' movements around the Web.

Sears Holdings Corporation took its stab at tracking customers' online activities through a program it called My SHC Community. Customers of Sears and Kmart were encouraged to "become part of something new, something different." My SHC was framed as a "dynamic and highly interactive online community" where "your voice is heard and your opinion matters, and what you want and need counts!" Members were asked to install "research software" on their computers that would allow SHC to track their online browsing. To further entice customers to participate, SHC paid them $10 each.

After operating for several months, technology analysts discovered that the SHC "research" software collected a lot more information than users were aware of. It tracked not only URLs of Web pages visited, but also information typed into secure online forms. Such information included usernames and passwords, credit card numbers, online shopping cart contents, essentially everything the user typed and every page the user visited. When Harvard Business School assistant professor Ben Edelman learned of the situation, he accused SHC of distributing spyware. Shortly thereafter, the Federal Trade Commission (FTC) took up the case.

The FTC found that Sears Holdings did not sufficiently notify its customers about what information was being gathered by the software. The only notice of what the software actually did was buried on page 10 of the software licence that users may have glanced at before installing the software.

The FTC ordered Sears Holdings to discontinue distribution of the software, destroy all data gained from the experiment, and stop collecting data from copies of the software still running on customers' computers. Additionally, should Sears Holdings decide to attempt a similar experiment in the future, it must "clearly and prominently disclose the types of data the software will monitor, record, or transmit. This disclosure must be made prior to installation and separate from any user license agreement. Sears must also disclose whether any of the data will be used by a third party."

Sears Holdings has stated that while the software did collect sensitive user information, the company made "commercially viable efforts automatically to filter out confidential personally identifiable information such as user ID, password, credit card numbers, and account numbers, and made commercially viable efforts to purge our database of any such information if it was collected inadvertently."

Discussion Questions

1. What plan did Sears Holdings implement to gain more insight into customers' online shopping behaviour?
2. Why was the plan considered by a Harvard law professor and the FTC to be unethical and unlawful?

Critical Thinking Questions

1. If Sears Holdings had implemented its plan in accordance with FTC guidelines, do you think any customers would have been willing to sacrifice their privacy for $10?
2. What other methods might Sears Holdings and other companies consider implementing to gather information about customers' online habits and interests?

SOURCES: Anderson, Nate, "FTC Forces Sears, Kmart out of the Spyware Business," *Ars Technica*, www.arstechnica.com, September 13, 2009; McMillan, Robert, "Researcher Accuses Sears of Spreading Spyware," *PCWorld*, www.pcworld.com, January 2, 2008; My SHC Community Web page, *www.myshccommunity.com*, accessed June 26, 2010.

Case Two

U.S. Fights Fraud with Personal Certificates

One of the goals of the Obama administration has been to improve national information security to better protect the nation's infrastructure. Toward this goal, the president created a new post in his administration called the Cybersecurity Coordinator, appointing Howard Schmidt to the position.

One of Schmidt's first assignments was to develop a plan to effectively fight Internet fraud. Internet fraud is the most common type of Internet crime, covering a range of scams in which a buyer or seller assumes a false identity to trick someone out of money or merchandise. According to the FBI's Internet Crime Complaint Center, Internet fraud reports increased by 22.3 percent in 2009, with losses totalling close to $560 million. Among the most popular forms of fraud in 2009 were e-mail scams that used the FBI name to gain information (16.6 percent), undelivered merchandise or payment (11.9 percent), and advanced fee fraud (in which targets are asked to pay up front) (9.8 percent). The one fact that is consistent across all cases of fraud is the use of a false identity. If real identities were used, the fraudsters would be caught.

Cybersecurity coordinator Howard Schmidt has proposed a plan by which those involved in online transactions can be positively identified. Because credit cards and bank account numbers can be easily stolen and used by fraudsters, Schmidt's plan requires the possession of a smart identity card or digital certificate to buy and sell online.

The notion of national ID cards has been struck down by privacy advocates in the past, so Schmidt made his proposal a voluntary one. According to a draft plan, those who wish to authenticate their transactions would be able to acquire a secure identifier from a variety of service providers. Schwartz emphasizes that the system will balance efforts to maintain privacy while still collecting enough information about the card owner to ensure his identity.

Security vendors believe that the technology is already available for Schmidt's plan. For example, Google and Microsoft already have "single sign-on" systems where people can use their credentials to sign on to partner sites. In this scenario, Google or Microsoft maintains information about the user, while the partner sites are not provided access to that private information. A similar system could be used for online transaction authentication. What is needed is a national push for standards so that businesses and consumers can invest in a technology with some assurance that it will be long lasting.

Security experts have expressed scepticism that a voluntary system will be effective. Some argue that unless all Internet users are required to use the system, many transactions will remain vulnerable. The government must walk a fine line between privacy and ensuring secure transactions. Only time will tell what type of authentication system will be regarded as acceptable to government, consumers, and businesses.

Discussion Questions

1. Why does the U.S. government think it's necessary to intervene in online transactions?
2. Why might the use of digital certificates or smart identity cards to fight Internet fraud be controversial?

Critical Thinking Questions

1. How might a digital certificate or smart identity card system be implemented so that individuals' privacy is maintained and yet transactions are made more secure?
2. What ways might a smart card system backfire or present other security or privacy concerns?

SOURCES: 2009 IC3 Annual Report, IC3 website, *www.ic3.gov/media/annualreport/2009_IC3Report.pdf*, accessed July 15, 2010; Baldor, Lolita, "White House Unveils Cybersecurity Plans," NewsFactor Network, *www.newsfactor.com*, June 29, 2010; Stokes, Jon, "White House Wants to Help You 'Blog Anonymously'," *Ars Technica*, www.arstechnica.com, June 29, 2010; Markoff, John, "Taking the Mystery out of Web Anonymity," *New York Times, www.nytimes.com,* July 2, 2010.

Questions for Web Case

See the website for this book to read about the Altitude Online case for this chapter. Following are questions concerning this Web case.

Altitude Online: The Personal and Social Impact of Computers

Discussion Questions

1. Why do you think extending access to a corporate network beyond the business's walls dramatically elevates the risk to information security?
2. What tools and policies can be used to minimize that risk?

Critical Thinking Questions

1. Why does information security usually come at the cost of user convenience?
2. How do proper security measures help ensure information privacy?

NOTES

Sources for the opening vignette: Rebbapragada, Narasu, "What Is Your Facebook Data Worth?" *Computerworld, www.computerworld.com,* June 21, 2010; Bryant, Martin, "Ignore Facebook Open Graph at Your Peril—This Is Web 3.0," The Next Web, *http://thenextweb.com,* April 21, 2010; Helft, Miguel, "Zuckerberg on the Hot Seat," *New York Times, www.nytimes.com,* June 2, 2010; Levine, Barry, "Facebook Refuses Changes Urged by Privacy Groups," News Factor, *www.newsfactor.com,* June 18, 2010; Gaudin, Sharon, "More Than Half of Facebook Users May Quit Site, Poll Finds," *Computerworld, www.computerworld. com,* May 21, 2010; Kincaid, Jason, "WSJ: Facebook, MySpace and Others Share Identifying User Data With Advertisers," TechCrunch, *www.techcrunch.com,* May 20, 2010; Office of the Privacy Commissioner of Canada, "Facebook Agrees to Address Privacy Commissioner's Concerns," August 27, 2009. Retrieved from *www.priv.gc.ca/media/nr-c/2009/nr-c_090827_e.cfm,* on October 20, 2010.

1. Office of the Privacy Commissioner of Canada, "Facebook Agrees to Address Privacy Commissioner's Concerns," August 27, 2009, *www.priv. gc.ca/media/nr-c/2009/nr-c_090827_e.cfm,* accessed October 20, 2010.
2. O'Keefe, Ed, "Obama to Order Federal Agencies to Compile 'Do Not Pay' List'," *Washington Post,* June 18, 2010.

3. Bewley, Elizabeth, "Fraud Fight Uses 'Do Not Pay' List," *Cincinnati Enquirer,* June 19, 2010, page A12.
4. "Spam Filter Review for 2010," Top Ten Reviews, *http://spam-filter-review.toptenreviews.com,* accessed June 1, 2010.
5. Puzzanghera, Jim, "Regulators Still Working to Pinpoint Cause of Stock Market's Record Plunge," *Chicago Tribune,* May 11, 2010.
6. "Markets End Lower on Volatile Trading," *Globe and Mail, www. theglobeandmail.com/globe-investor/markets/markets-blog/markets-end-lower-in-volatile-trading/article1559459/,* accessed May 6, 2010.
7. Hananel, Sam, "Officials: Computer Error Affected Mine Scrutiny," *www. philly.com,* April 13, 2010.
8. Baxter, Elsa, "Computer Error Causes UAE Cash Machine Shutdown," *www. arabianbusiness.com/582494-computer-error-causes-uae-cash-machine-shutdown,* February 28, 2010.
9. Barlow, Daniel, "State to Block X-Rated Web Sites," *Time Argus,* timesargus.com/article/20100413/NEWS01/4130343/classifieds, April 13, 2010.
10. Hamilton, Tyler, "Dozens Fired at Bruce Power Over Web, E-Mail Use," *www.thestar.com/printarticle/693525,* September 10, 2009.

11 Doland, Angela, "Trial Opens for Accused French Rogue Trader," *Real Clear Markets*, www.realclearmarkets.com/news/ap/finance_business/2010/Jun/08/trial_opens_for_accused_french_rogue_trader.html, accessed June 8, 2010.

12 "Computer Crime Reports Increase 22% in 2009," *Crime News—Crime Prevention*, http://crimeinamerica.net/2010/03/16/computer-crime-reports-increase, March 16, 2010.

13 Department of Justice, "Two Canadians Guilty of Telemarketing Fraud," boston.fbi.gov/dojpressrel/pressrel09/bs081409a.htm, October 20, 2010.

14 "U.S. Indicts Ohio Man and Two Foreign Residents in Alleged Ukraine-Based 'Scareware' Fraud Scheme That Caused $100 Million in Losses to Internet Victims Worldwide," Department of Justice press release, http://chicago.fbi.gov/dojpressrel/pressrel10/cg052710.htm, May 27, 2010.

15 "Indian National Sentenced to 81 Months in Prison for Role in International Online Brokerage 'Hack, Pump, and Dump' Scheme," Department of Justice press release, www.cybercrime.gov/marimuthuSent.pdf, April 26, 2010.

16 "Unsecured Economies/Protecting Vital Information" McAfee, www.mcafee.com/us/about/press/corporate/2009/20090129_063500_j.html, accessed October 20, 2010.

17 Public Safety Canada, "Cyber Security," www.publicsafety.gc.ca/prg/em/cbr/csb-eng.aspx, accessed October 20, 2010.

18 Phone Busters, "Annual Statistical Report 2009," www.phonebusters.com/english/documents/AnnualStatisticalReport2009_003.pdf, accessed October 20, 2010.

19 Stasiukonis, Steve, "Security's Top 4 Social Engineers of All Time," dark reading blog, www.darkreading.com/blog/archives/2010/05/securitys_top_4.html, posted May 26, 2010.

20 IMPACT website, "Mission & Vision: About Us," www.impact-alliance.org/about_us.html, accessed June 10, 2010.

21 Public Safety Canada, "Canada's Cyber Security Strategy," www.publicsafety.gc.ca/prg/em/cbr/ccss-scc-eng.aspx#ftntb06, accessed October 20, 2010.

22 Canadian Anti-Fraud Centre, "Annual Statistical Report 2010," www.antifraudcentre-centreantifraude.ca/english/statistics_statistics.html, accessed March 23, 2011.

23 Zacharias, Jan, "Internet Gambling: Is It Worth It?", www.bcresponsiblegambling.ca/other/docs/internet_gambling_jan_zacharias.pdf, accessed October 20,2010.

24 Leads Online website, www.leadsonline.com/main/default.aspx, accessed June 19, 2010.

25 Royal Canadian Mounted Police, "National Sex Offender Registry," www.rcmp-grc.gc.ca/tops-opst/bs-sc/nsor-rnds/index-eng.htm, accessed October 20, 2010.

26 Cybertip.ca website, www.cybertip.ca/app/en/, accessed October 22, 2010.

27 Zetter, Kim, "TJX Hacker Gets 20 Years in Prison," *Wired*, March 25, 2010.

28 Zetter, Kim, "New Malware Rewrites Online Bank Statements to Cover Fraud," *Wired*, September 30, 2010.

29 "Kaspersky Predicts More iPhone, Android Attacks in 2010," *ABS CBN News*, www.abs-cbnnews.com, January 2, 2010.

30 Mills, Elinor, "Malware Found Lurking in Apps for Windows Mobile," *CNet News*, June 4, 2010.

31 Graham Cluley's blog, "Indian Government Computers Hit by Chinese Spyware Attack?" www.sophos.com/blogs/gc/g/2009/02/16, accessed June 20, 2010.

32 Duffy, Jim, "Software Piracy Rate Up 2% in 2009, Study Finds," *Network World*, May 11, 2010.

33 "Crime Rate: Software Piracy Rate (most recent) by Country," www.nationmaster.com/graph/cri_sof_pir_rat-crime-software-piracy-rate, accessed June 11, 2010.

34 Canadian Alliance Against Software Theft, "Canadian Copyright Law," www.caast.org/resources/canadiancopyrightlaw.php, accessed October 20, 2010.

35 "Piracy: Online and on the Street," www.riaa.com/physicalpiracy.php, accessed June 12, 2010.

36 Canadian Recording Industry Association, "Anti-Piracy," www.cria.ca/antipiracy.php#internet, October 20, 2010.

37 "Music Piracy Not That Bad, Industry Says," *CyberLaw Blog*, http://cyberlaw.org.uk/2009/01/18/music-piracy-not-that-bad-industry-says, January 18, 2009.

38 Kravets, David, "Recording Industry Says LimeWire on Hook for $1 Billion," *Wired*, June 8, 2010.

39 Kravets, David, "LimeWire Crushed in RIAA Infringement Lawsuit," *Wired*, May 12, 2010.

40 Canadian Recording Industry Association, "Canada's Recording Industry Welcomes US Federal Court Ruling against Limewire," CRIA, cria.ca/CIMA-CRIA Joint Release—Limewire 2010-05-13.pdf, May 13, 2010.

41 Craig, Brenda, "Google in Historic Lawsuit," Lawyers and Settlements website, www.lawyersandsettlements.com/articles/14118/copyright-infringement-news-5.html, May 12, 2010.

42 Paul, Ryan, "Red Hat Faces Another Patent Infringement Lawsuit over JBoss," *Ars Technica*, http://arstechnica/com/open-source/news, March 4, 2009.

43 "ITC to Probe Apple for HTC Patent Infringement," *Yahoo! News*, June 11, 2010.

44 Phonebusters, "Annual Statistical Report 2009," www.phonebusters.com/english/documents/AnnualStatisticalReport2009_003.pdf, accessed October 20, 2010.

45 Elliott, Christopher, "Travelers Vulnerable to 'Phishing' Scams," *CNN.com*, June 14, 2010.

46 Ledford, Jerri, "Vishing," http://idtheft.about.com/od/glossary/g/Vishing.htm, accessed June 18, 2010.

47 "SpoofCard," www.spoofcard.com, accessed June 18, 2010.

48 Hearns, Michael, "Australian in Las Vegas Suspected of Over 500 Million Laundered via Internet Gambling Web Sites," Money Laundering, http://laundering money.blogspot.com/2010/australian-in-las-vegas-suspected of.html, April 25, 2010.

49 "Government Re-introduces Legislation Targeting Identity Theft," www.justice.gc.ca/eng/news-nouv/nr-cp/2009/doc_32347.html, accessed October 21, 2010.

50 "2GB Fingerprint Biometric USB Flash Memory Stick Drive AFU-082," www.dinodirect.com/usb-flash-memory-stick-drive-finger-print-2gb-afu-082/AFFID-19.html, accessed June 15, 2010.

51 "Microsoft Case Studies: Del Monte Foods Premium-Quality Food Producer Drives Growth with Security-Enhanced Collaboration Solutions," www.microsoft.com/casestudies/Case_Study_Detail.aspx?casestudyid=4000007154, May 5, 2010.

52 "Managed Protection Services," www-935.ibm.com/services/us/index.wss/offering/iss/a1026962, accessed June 20, 2010.

53 Srikanth, A.D., "How to: Remotely Track Your Stolen Laptop?" Technology Bites, www.teknobites.com/2010/04/06/how-to-remotely-track-your-stolen-laptop, April 6, 2010.

54 "Tough Identity Theft Law Passed," www.cbc.ca/canada/story/2009/10/27/identity-theft027.html, accessed October 20, 2010.

55 "Top Standalone Antivirus Software for 2010," *PC World*, November 23, 2009.

56 "Survey: Many Companies Monitoring, Recording, Videotaping Employees," *Business Wire*, February 6, 2009.

57 "There Ought to be a Law: Protecting Children's Online Privacy in the 21st Century," www.gnb.ca/0073/PDF/Children'sOnlinePrivacy-e.pdf, November 19, 2009.

58 Rubenking, Neil J., "Keep Your Child Safe Online," *PC Magazine*, March 1, 2010.

59 Office of the Privacy Commissioner of Canada, "A Summary of the Personal Information Protection and Electronic Documents Act," www.ic.gc.ca/eic/site/oca-bc.nsf/eng/ca01460.html, accessed October 20, 2010.

60 Office of the Privacy Commissioner of Canada, "Privacy Legislation in Canada," www.priv.gc.ca/fs-fi/02_05_d_15_e.cfm, accessed October 20, 2010.

61 Soloman, Howard, "Four Tech-Related Bills Dead in Parliament," Network World Canada, January 4, 2010, www.itworldcanada.com/news/four-tech-related-bills-dead-in-parliament/139681, accessed October 21, 2010.

62 "Canada, Country Best Internet Addiction," http://wikifresh.co.cc/technology/canada-country-internet-addiction/, accessed May 24, 2011.

63 National Cancer Institute web page, "NCI Statement: International Study Shows No Increased Risk of Brain Tumours from Cell Phone Use," www.cancer.gov/newscenter/pressreleases/Interphone2010Results, May 17, 2020.

64 "Creating an Injury-Free Workplace—How to Avoid Corporate Complacency," http://businessinabullet.com/human-resources/cr..., June 27, 2010.

(Source: asharkyu/Shutterstock.com)

PART ·2·

Information Technology Concepts

CHAPTER · 3 ·

Hardware: Input, Processing, and Output Devices

(Source: asharkyu/Shutterstock.com)

PRINCIPLES

LEARNING OBJECTIVES

- Computer hardware must be carefully selected to meet the evolving needs of the organization and of its supporting information systems.

  - Describe the role of the central processing unit and main memory.

  - State the advantages of multiprocessing and parallel computing systems, and provide examples of the types of problems they address.

  - Describe the access methods, capacity, and portability of various secondary storage devices.

  - Identify and discuss the speed, functionality, and importance of various input and output devices.

  - Identify the characteristics of and discuss the usage of various classes of single-user and multi-user computer systems.

- The computer hardware industry is rapidly changing and highly competitive, creating an environment ripe for technological breakthroughs.

  - Describe Moore's Law and discuss its implications for future computer hardware developments.

  - Give an example of recent innovations in computer CPU chips, memory devices, and input/output devices.

- The computer hardware industry and users are implementing green computing designs and products.

  - Define the term "green computing" and identify the primary goals of this program.

  - Identify several benefits of green computing initiatives that have been broadly adopted.

Information Systems in the Global Economy
Turboinštitut d.d.

Exchanging Processing Power for Hydropower

Businesses are turning to various forms of renewable energy as they seek to reduce their carbon footprint and their impact on the climate. Among the most popular of renewable energy sources are wind and hydroelectric power. The process of turning wind and water into energy efficiently and affordably takes a considerable amount of science and engineering knowledge. Turboinštitut is a global company with a mission to promote water as an indispensable, sustainable, environmentally friendly source of energy, and to continuously improve hydraulic machine performance. Turboinštitut employs 135 scientists, engineers, and staff at its research facility located in Ljubljana, the capital of Slovenia.

Turboinštitut was established in 1948 by the Yugoslav government as a strategic centre for scientific and industrial research. Today it functions as an independent institute that has contributed its expertise in turbine research and development in the construction of hydro-fluid facilities (such as dams) in dozens of countries. The core of Turboinštitut's business is modelling, designing, and producing custom turbine hydraulics systems that meet the unique requirements of each installation and provide the maximum amount of energy from a water source. Turboinštitut's extensive research is carried out using computer simulations—more specifically, computational fluid dynamics (CFD)—to design highly successful hydro-energy installations.

Simulating the flow of water using CFD requires enormous amounts of computing capacity. As Turboinštitut has grown, its client base has expanded, and its turbine hydraulics systems have become more refined. More refined systems work smarter and can return more power from less water. However, they also require more processing power during their design. Turboinštitut's success, combined with its outdated computer hardware, has created a backlog of CFD tasks requiring computation. The company decided that it needed new hardware. Not just any hardware, but its own energy-efficient supercomputer that could deliver high performance with little power.

Whether the need is for calculating complex scientific models, for analyzing financial markets, or for supporting employees scattered around the globe, many businesses have needs similar to Turboinštitut's: to replace old, inefficient energy-consuming computing centres with new, powerful, compact, energy-efficient computing centres. Turboinštitut opted to collaborate with IBM to implement a supercomputing system it named Ljubljana Supercomputer Center (LSC) ADRIA. ADRIA uses blade servers (a type of server technology) that pack many processing circuit boards (blades) together in a single rack. Turboinštitut's ADRIA uses 256 clustered blade servers for a total of 2,048 processing cores—supercomputing power to match Turboinštitut's computational needs.

Processors work closely with various forms of storage to deliver high-performance services. ADRIA uses 4,096 GB (billions of bytes) of RAM and 10 TB (trillions of bytes) of an IBM storage system that has additional servers designed to rapidly deliver data as needed. The resulting system can perform calculations 50 times faster than Turboinštitut's previous system in half the amount of physical space. ADRIA enables Turboinštitut to make more than 10,000 complicated CFD analyses per year. ADRIA's highly efficient processors and advanced cooling system require much less power than the previous system. Aleš Petan, chief information officer, is pleased that the company's environmentally friendly mission is fulfilled not only by Turboinštitut's hydraulic research, designs, and products, but also by the company's information system infrastructure.

Today Turboinštitut carries out its complex water turbine design simulations on highly energy-efficient servers in a fraction of the time required with its previous system. This enables the company to save time and money and get products to clients more quickly, giving Turboinštitut a huge competitive advantage. Like Turboinštitut, businesses in many industries depend on the latest hardware to provide higher levels of efficiencies with less overhead—both financial and environmental. Although companies most often invest in servers to provide information and computational services and storage, all forms of hardware can yield savings. When selecting supercomputers, desktop computers, notebook computers, storage technologies, displays, scanners, and so on, businesses need technologies that provide the most power and speed and the highest level of efficiency and effectiveness.

As you read this chapter, consider the following:

- How does the type of hardware a company purchases—the size and amount of computers, the amount of storage, and the type of input and output devices—affect the way the company operates?
- Businesses are in constant flux, growing, diversifying, acquiring, and working to reduce costs. How do these conditions and requirements affect the purchase of the hardware on which information systems run?
- In the quest for the most efficient and effective systems, businesses must invest in state-of-the-art hardware to win a competitive advantage. How might a business decide when it is best to upgrade its hardware?

Why Learn About Hardware?

Organizations invest in computer hardware to improve worker productivity, increase revenue, reduce costs, provide better customer service, speed up time-to-market, and enable collaboration among employees. Organizations that don't make wise hardware investments are often stuck with outdated equipment that is unreliable and that cannot take advantage of the latest software advances. Such obsolete hardware can place an organization at a competitive disadvantage. Managers, no matter what their career field and educational background, are expected to help define the business needs that the hardware must support. In addition, managers must be able to ask good questions and evaluate options when considering hardware investments for their areas of the business. This is especially true in small organizations, which might not have information system specialists. Managers in marketing, sales, and human resources often help IS specialists assess opportunities to apply computer hardware and evaluate the options and features specified for the hardware. Managers in finance and accounting especially must keep an eye on the bottom line, guarding against overspending, yet be willing to invest in computer hardware when and where business conditions warrant it.

Today's use of technology is practical—it's intended to yield real business benefits, as demonstrated by Turboinštitut d.d. Using the latest information technology and providing additional processing capabilities can increase employee productivity, expand business opportunities, and allow for more flexibility. This chapter concentrates on the hardware component of a computer-based information system (CBIS). Recall that hardware refers to the physical components of a computer that perform the input, processing, storage, and output activities of the computer. When making hardware decisions, the overriding consideration of a business should be how hardware can support the objectives of the information system and the goals of the organization.

COMPUTER SYSTEMS: INTEGRATING THE POWER OF TECHNOLOGY

To assemble an effective and efficient system, you should select and organize components while understanding the trade-offs between overall system performance and cost, control, and complexity. For instance, when building a car, manufacturers try to match the intended use of the vehicle to its components. Race cars, for example, require special types of engines, transmissions, and tires. Selecting a transmission for a race car requires balancing how much engine power can be delivered to the wheels (efficiency and effectiveness) with how expensive the transmission is (cost), how reliable it is (control), and how many gears it has (complexity). Similarly, organizations assemble computer systems so that they are effective, efficient, and well suited to the tasks that need to be performed.

As auto manufacturers must match the intended use of a vehicle to its components, so too must business managers select the hardware components of an effective information system.

(Source: © Mark Jenkinson/CORBIS.)

People involved in selecting their organization's computer hardware must clearly understand current and future business requirements so they can make informed acquisition decisions. Consider the following examples of applying business knowledge to reach sound decisions on acquiring hardware.

- The Argus Machine Company, a custom parts and pipeline threading company in Edmonton, upgraded its aging, unreliable IT infrastructure to reduce its ongoing costs and improve customer services. The new IT system improved system performance, data management, and network security. Argus's new customer extranet enabled customers to track their orders and get current product information online.[1]
- The National Oceanic and Atmospheric Administration (NOAA) is a scientific agency whose mission is to understand and predict changes in the Earth's environment and conserve and manage coastal and marine resources. As part of meeting its mission, the NOAA produces daily weather forecasts and severe storm warnings. The NOAA recognized the need for more computing and backup capacity. As a result, it recently upgraded from a single computer to two more powerful computer systems to improve weather forecasts by processing more detailed information and increasing the resolution of weather conditions. The two new computers, dubbed Stratus and Cirrus, have four times the processing power of the previous system. In addition, the Stratus computer is backed up by the Cirrus, which is housed at a separate location. If the Stratus fails for any reason, the Cirrus can take over in just a few minutes.[2]

As these examples demonstrate, choosing the right computer hardware requires understanding its relationship to the information systems and the needs of the organization.

Hardware Components

Computer system hardware components include devices that perform input, processing, data storage, and output, as shown in Figure 3.1 on the next page. To understand how these hardware devices work together, consider an analogy from a paper-based office. Imagine a one-room office occupied by a single person named Dave. Dave (the processing device) can organize and manipulate data. Dave's mind (register storage) and his desk (primary storage) are places to temporarily store data. Filing cabinets fill the need for more permanent storage (secondary storage). In this analogy, the incoming and outgoing mail trays are sources of new data (input) or places to put the processed paperwork (output).

Figure 3.1

Hardware Components

These components include the input devices, output devices, communications devices, primary and secondary storage devices, and the central processing unit (CPU). The control unit, the arithmetic/logic unit (ALU), and the register storage areas constitute the CPU.

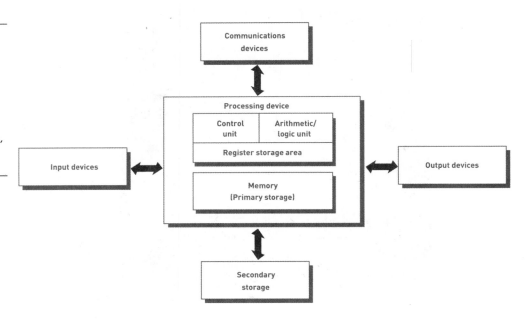

central processing unit (CPU)
The part of the computer that consists of three associated elements: the arithmetic/logic unit, the control unit, and the register areas.

arithmetic/logic unit (ALU)
The part of the CPU that performs mathematical calculations and makes logical comparisons.

control unit
The part of the CPU that sequentially accesses program instructions, decodes them, and coordinates the flow of data in and out of the ALU, the registers, the primary storage, and even secondary storage and various output devices.

register
A high-speed storage area in the CPU used to temporarily hold small units of program instructions and data immediately before, during, and after execution by the CPU.

primary storage (main memory; memory)
The part of the computer that holds program instructions and data.

Recall that any system must be able to process (organize and manipulate) data, and a computer system does so through an interplay between one or more central processing units and primary storage. Each **central processing unit** (**CPU**) consists of three associated elements: the arithmetic/logic unit, the control unit, and the register areas. The **arithmetic/ logic unit** (**ALU**) performs mathematical calculations and makes logical comparisons. The **control unit** sequentially accesses program instructions, decodes them, and coordinates the flow of data in and out of the ALU, the registers, the primary storage, and even secondary storage and various output devices. **Registers** are high-speed storage areas used to temporarily hold small units of program instructions and data immediately before, during, and after execution by the CPU. The *chip set* coordinates the communication between the CPU and other components of the computer. A given chip set is designed to work with a specific CPU. So for example, the X58 chip set is designed specifically to work with the Intel i7 processor. Because the chip set controls the communications to and from the CPU, it plays a crucial role in determining a system's performance.

Primary storage, also called **main memory** or **memory**, is closely associated with the CPU. Memory holds program instructions and data immediately before or after the registers. To understand the function of processing and the interplay between the CPU and memory, let's examine the way a typical computer executes a program instruction.

Hardware Components in Action

Executing any machine-level instruction involves two phases: instruction and execution. During the instruction phase, a computer performs the following steps:

- Step 1: Fetch instruction. The computer reads the next program instruction to be executed and any necessary data into the processor.
- Step 2: Decode instruction. The instruction is decoded and passed to the appropriate processor execution unit. Each execution unit plays a different role. The arithmetic/ logic unit performs all arithmetic operations; the floating-point unit deals with non-integer operations; the load/store unit manages the instructions that read or write to

memory; the branch processing unit predicts the outcome of a branch instruction in an attempt to reduce disruptions in the flow of instructions and data into the processor; the memory-management unit translates an application's addresses into physical memory addresses; and the vector-processing unit handles vector-based instructions that accelerate graphics operations.

The time it takes to perform the instruction phase (Steps 1 and 2) is called the **instruction time (I-time)**.

The second phase is execution. During the execution phase, a computer performs the following steps:

- Step 3: Execute instruction. The hardware element, now freshly fed with an instruction and data, carries out the instruction. This could involve making an arithmetic computation, logical comparison, bit shift, or vector operation.
- Step 4: Store results. The results are stored in registers or memory.

The time it takes to complete the execution phase (Steps 3 and 4) is called the **execution time (E-time)**.

After both phases have been completed for one instruction, they are performed again for the second instruction, and so on. Completing the instruction phase followed by the execution phase is called a **machine cycle**, as shown in Figure 3.2. Some processing units can speed processing by using **pipelining**, whereby the processing unit gets one instruction, decodes another, and executes a third at the same time. The Pentium 4 processor, for example, uses two execution unit pipelines. This means the processing unit can execute two instructions in a single machine cycle.

instruction time (I-time)
The time it takes to perform the fetch-instruction and decode-instruction steps of the instruction phase.

execution time (E-time)
The time it takes to execute an instruction and store the results.

machine cycle
The instruction phase followed by the execution phase.

pipelining
A form of CPU operation in which multiple execution phases are performed in a single machine cycle.

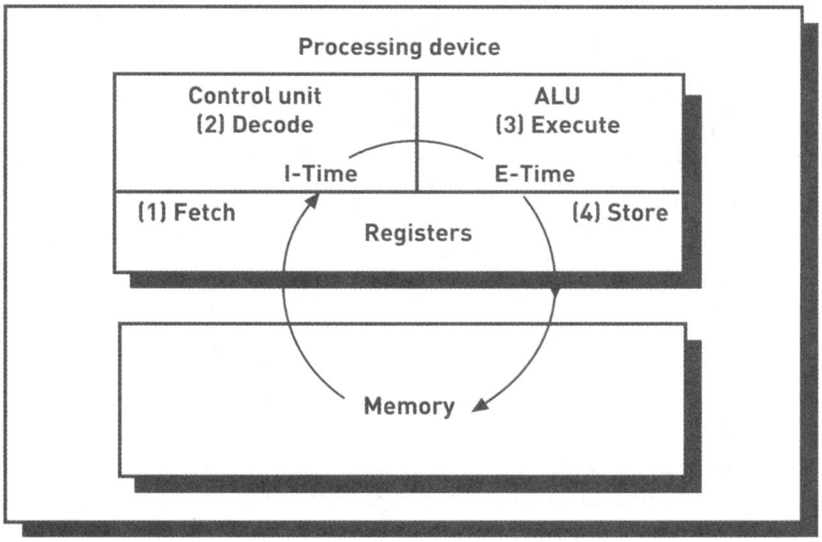

Figure 3.2

Execution of an Instruction

In the instruction phase, a program's instructions and any necessary data are read into the processor (1). Then the instruction is decoded so the central processor can understand what to do (2). In the execution phase, the ALU does what it is instructed to do, making either an arithmetic computation or a logical comparison (3). Then the results are stored in the registers or in memory (4). The instruction and execution phases together make up one machine cycle.

PROCESSING AND MEMORY DEVICES: POWER, SPEED, AND CAPACITY

The components responsible for processing—the CPU and memory—are housed together in the same box or cabinet, called the *system unit*. All other computer system devices, such as the monitor, secondary storage, and keyboard, are linked directly or indirectly into the system unit housing. In this section, we investigate the characteristics of these important devices.

Processing Characteristics and Functions

Because organizations want efficient processing and timely output, they use a variety of measures to gauge processing speed. These measures include the time it takes to complete a machine cycle and clock speed.

Machine Cycle Time

As you've seen, a computer executes an instruction during a machine cycle. The time in which a machine cycle occurs is measured in *nanoseconds* (one-billionth of one second) and *picoseconds* (one-trillionth of one second). Machine cycle time also can be measured by how many instructions are executed in one second. This measure, called **MIPS**, stands for millions of instructions per second. MIPS is another measure of speed for computer systems of all sizes.

Clock Speed

Each CPU produces a series of electronic pulses at a predetermined rate, called the **clock speed**, which affects machine cycle time. The control unit in the CPU manages the stages of the machine cycle by following predetermined internal instructions, known as **microcode**. You can think of microcode as predefined, elementary circuits and logical operations that the processor performs when it executes an instruction. The control unit executes the microcode in accordance with the electronic cycle, or pulses of the CPU "clock." Each microcode instruction takes at least the same amount of time as the interval between pulses. The shorter the interval between pulses, the faster each microcode instruction can be executed.

Because the number of microcode instructions needed to execute a single program instruction—such as performing a calculation or printing results—can vary, the clock speed is not directly related to the true processing speed of the computer.

Clock speed is often measured in **megahertz** (MHz, millions of cycles per second) or **gigahertz** (GHz, billions of cycles per second). Unfortunately, the faster the clock speed of the CPU, the more heat the processor generates. This heat must be dissipated to avoid corrupting the data and instructions the computer is trying to process. Also, chips that run at higher temperatures need bigger heat sinks, fans, and other components to eliminate the excess heat. This increases the size of the computer, which most users and manufactures like to keep small.

Chip and computer manufacturers are exploring various means to avoid heat problems in their new designs. Demand-based switching is a power management technology developed by Intel that varies the clock speed of the CPU so that it runs at the minimum speed necessary to allow optimum performance of the required operations. Manufacturers of portable electronic devices such as computers and cell phones are also seeking more effective sources of energy as portable devices grow increasingly power hungry. A number of companies are exploring the substitution of fuel cells for lithium ion batteries to provide additional, longer-lasting power. Fuel cells generate electricity by consuming fuel (often methanol), while traditional batteries store electricity and release it through a chemical reaction. A spent fuel cell is replenished in moments by simply refilling its reservoir or by replacing the spent fuel cartridge with a fresh one. Toshiba is experimenting with direct-methanol fuel cells (DMFCs), which could be used in digital audio players, wireless headsets for mobile phones, and personal computers.[3]

Cell Broadband Engine Architecture (or simply "Cell") is a microprocessor architecture that provides power-efficient, cost-effective, and high-performance processing for a wide range of applications. The Cell is an example of innovation across several organizations. A team from IBM Research joined forces with teams from IBM Systems Technology Group, Sony, and Toshiba to provide a breakthrough in performance for high-definition displays, recording equipment, and computer entertainment systems. The first commercial application of the Cell was in the Sony PlayStation 3 game console, where it performs at the rate of 2 trillion calculations per second. Toshiba plans to incorporate Cell in high-definition

---

MIPS
Millions of instructions per second, a measure of machine cycle time.

clock speed
A series of electronic pulses produced at a predetermined rate that affects machine cycle time.

microcode
Predefined, elementary circuits and logical operations that the processor performs when it executes an instruction.

megahertz (MHz)
Millions of cycles per second, a measure of clock speed.

gigahertz (GHz)
Billions of cycles per second, a measure of clock speed.

(HD) TV sets. IBM uses Cell processors to enhance the performance of the IBM System z9 mainframe computers.

Physical Characteristics of the CPU

Most CPUs are collections of digital circuits imprinted on silicon wafers, or chips, each no bigger than the tip of a pencil eraser. To turn a digital circuit on or off within the CPU, electrical current must flow through a medium (usually silicon) from point A to point B. The speed the current travels between points can be increased by either reducing the distance between the points or reducing the resistance of the medium to the electrical current.

Reducing the distance between points has resulted in ever smaller chips, with the circuits packed closer together. In the 1960s, shortly after patenting the integrated circuit, Gordon Moore, former chairman of the board of Intel (the largest maker of microprocessor chips), hypothesized that progress in chip manufacturing ought to make it possible to double the number of transistors (the microscopic on/off switches) on a chip roughly every two years. When actual results bore out his idea, the doubling of transistor densities on a single chip every two years became known as **Moore's Law**, and this "rule of thumb" has become a goal that chip manufacturers have met for over four decades. As shown in Figure 3.3, the number of transistors on a chip continues to climb.

Moore's Law
A hypothesis stating that transistor densities on a single chip will double every two years.

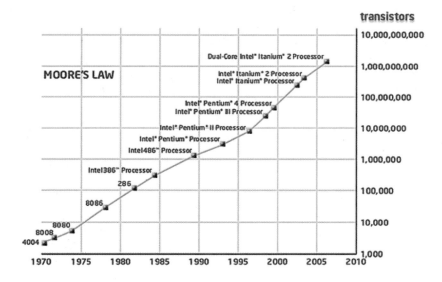

Figure 3.3

Moore's Law

Transistor densities on a single chip double about every two years.

(Source: Courtesy of Intel Corporation.)

In September 2009, Intel announced production of the world's first 32-nanometer microprocessor (a nanometer is one-billionth of a metre). At the same time, Intel stated that it is moving ahead with the development of a 22-nanometer chip that has more than 2.9 billion transistors packed into an area no bigger than your fingernail.[4]

Moore's Law enables chip makers to improve performance by putting more transistors on the same size chip while reducing the amount of power required to perform tasks. Intel's smallest and lowest power processor is called the Atom, which was designed for portable Internet-connected devices. See Figure 3.4 on the next page. Furthermore, because the chips are smaller, chip manufacturers can cut more chips from a single silicon wafer and thus reduce the cost per chip. As silicon-based components and computers perform better, they become cheaper to produce, and therefore more plentiful, more powerful, and more a part of our everyday lives.

Researchers are taking many approaches to continue to improve the performance of computers, such as using sophisticated tri-gate transistors, forming tiny computer circuits from carbon nanotubes only a nanometer in diameter, extreme miniaturization

Figure 3.4

The Intel Atom Chip

Intel released the low power-consuming Atom processor for use in the growing market of portable Internet-connected devices.

(Source: Courtesy of Intel Corporation.)

using radio waves to manipulate atoms into executing a simple computer program, and sending information between processors using light pulses instead of electrical signals.

Memory Characteristics and Functions

Main memory is located physically close to the CPU, but not on the CPU chip itself. It provides the CPU with a working storage area for program instructions and data. The chief feature of memory is that it rapidly provides the data and instructions to the CPU.

Storage Capacity

Like the CPU, memory devices contain thousands of circuits imprinted on a silicon chip. Each circuit is either conducting electrical current (on) or not conducting current (off). Data is stored in memory as a combination of on or off circuit states. Usually, 8 bits are used to represent a character, such as the letter *A*. Eight bits together form a **byte** (**B**). In most cases, storage capacity is measured in bytes, with 1 byte equivalent to one character of data. The contents of the Library of Congress, with over 126 million items and 530 miles of bookshelves, would require about 20 petabytes of digital storage. Table 3.1 lists units for measuring computer storage.

byte (B)
Eight bits that together represent a single character of data.

Table 3.1

Computer Storage Units

Name	Abbreviation	Number of Bytes
Byte	B	1
Kilobyte	KB	2^{10} or approximately 1,024 bytes
Megabyte	MB	2^{20} or 1,024 kilobytes (about 1 million)
Gigabyte	GB	2^{30} or 1,024 megabytes (about 1 billion)
Terabyte	TB	2^{40} or 1,024 gigabytes (about 1 trillion)
Petabyte	PB	2^{50} or 1,024 terabytes (about 1 quadrillion)
Exabyte	EB	2^{60} or 1,024 petabytes (about 1 quintillion)

Types of Memory

Computer memory can take several forms. Instructions or data can be temporarily stored in and read from **random access memory** (**RAM**). With the current design of RAM chips, they are volatile storage devices, meaning they lose their contents if the current is turned off or disrupted (as happens in a power surge, brownout, or electrical noise generated by lightning or nearby machines). RAM chips are mounted directly on the computer's main circuit board or in other chips mounted on peripheral cards that plug into the main circuit board. These RAM chips consist of millions of switches that are sensitive to changes in electric current.

RAM comes in many varieties. Static Random Access Memory (SRAM) is byte-addressable storage used for high-speed registers and caches. Dynamic Random Access Memory (DRAM) is byte-addressable storage used for the main memory in a computer. Double Data Rate Synchronous Dynamic Random Access Memory (DDR SDRAM) is an

random access memory (RAM)
A form of memory in which instructions or data can be temporarily stored.

improved form of DRAM that effectively doubles the rate at which data can be moved in and out of main memory. Other forms of RAM memory include DDR2, SDRAM, and DDR3 SDRAM.

Read-only memory (**ROM**), another type of memory, is nonvolatile, meaning that its contents are not lost if the power is turned off or interrupted. ROM provides permanent storage for data and instructions that do not change, such as programs and data from the computer manufacturer, including the instructions that tell the computer how to start up when power is turned on. ROM memory also comes in many varieties: programmable read-only memory (PROM), used to hold data and instructions that can never be changed; erasable programmable read-only memory (EPROM), which is programmable ROM that can be erased and reused; and electrically erasable programmable read-only memory (EEPROM), which is user-modifiable read-only memory that can be erased and reprogrammed repeatedly through the application of higher than normal electrical voltage.

Chip manufacturers are competing to develop a nonvolatile memory chip that requires minimal power, offers extremely fast write speed, and can store data accurately even after a large number of write-erase cycles. Such a chip could eliminate the need for RAM and simplify and speed up memory processing. Phase Change Memory (PCM), Ferroelectric random access memory (FeRAM), and magnetoresistive random access memory (MRAM) are three potential approaches to provide such a memory device.

Although microprocessor speed has doubled every 24 months over the past decades, memory performance has not kept pace. In effect, memory has become the principal bottleneck to system performance. **Cache memory** is a type of high-speed memory that a processor can access more rapidly than main memory to help to ease this bottleneck. See Figure 3.5. Frequently used data is stored in easily accessible cache memory instead of slower memory such as RAM. Because cache memory holds less data, the CPU can access the desired data and instructions more quickly than when selecting from data in main memory. Thus, the CPU can execute instructions faster, improving the overall performance of the computer system. Cache memory is available in three forms. The Level 1 (L1) cache is on the CPU chip. The Level 2 (L2) cache memory can be accessed by the CPU over a high-speed dedicated interface. The latest processors go a step further and place the L2 cache directly on the CPU chip itself and provide high-speed support for a tertiary Level 3 (L3) external cache.

read-only memory (ROM)
A nonvolatile form of memory.

cache memory
A type of high-speed memory that a processor can access more rapidly than main memory.

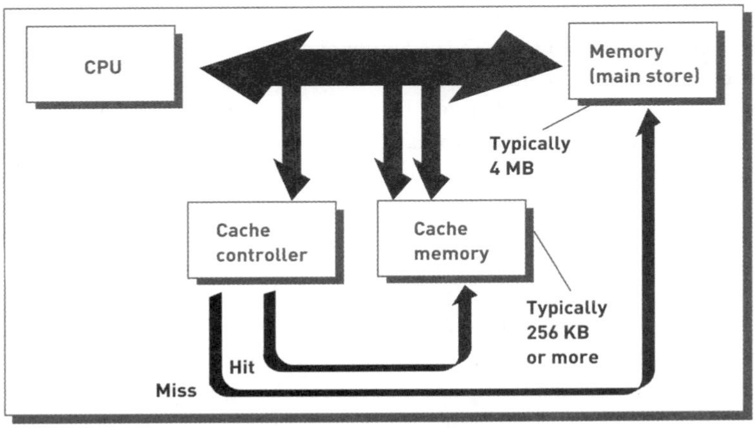

Figure 3.5

Cache Memory

Processors can access this type of high-speed memory faster than main memory. Located on or near the CPU chip, cache memory works with main memory. A cache controller determines how often the data is used, transfers frequently used data to cache memory, and then deletes the data when it goes out of use.

When the processor needs to execute an instruction, the instruction's operation code indicates whether the data will be in a register or in memory. If the operation code specifies a register as the source, it is taken from there. Otherwise, the processor looks for the data in the L1 cache, then the L2 cache, and then the L3 cache. If the data is not in any cache, the CPU requests the data from main memory. If the data is not even stored in main memory, the system has to retrieve the data from secondary storage. It can take from one to three clock cycles to fetch information from the L1 cache, while the CPU waits and does nothing. It takes 6 to 12 cycles to get data from an L2 cache on the processor chip. It can take dozens of cycles to fetch data from an L3 cache and hundreds of cycles to fetch data from secondary storage. Because this hierarchical arrangement of memory helps the CPU find data faster, it bridges a widening gap between processor speeds, which are increasing at roughly 50 percent per year, and DRAM access rates, which are climbing at only 5 percent per year.

Memory capacity contributes to the effectiveness of a CBIS. The specific applications of a CBIS determine the amount of memory required for a computer system. For example, complex processing problems, such as computer-assisted product design, require more memory than simpler tasks such as word processing. Also, because computer systems have different types of memory, they might need other programs to control how memory is accessed and used. In other cases, the computer system can be configured to maximize memory usage. Before purchasing additional memory, an organization should address all these considerations.

Multiprocessing

multiprocessing
The simultaneous execution of two or more instructions at the same time.

coprocessor
The part of the computer that speeds processing by executing specific types of instructions while the CPU works on another processing activity.

multicore microprocessor
A microprocessor that combines two or more independent processors into a single computer so they can share the workload and improve processing capacity.

Generally, **multiprocessing** involves the simultaneous execution of two or more instructions at the same time. One form of multiprocessing uses coprocessors. A **coprocessor** speeds processing by executing specific types of instructions while the CPU works on another processing activity. Coprocessors can be internal or external to the CPU and can have different clock speeds than the CPU. Each type of coprocessor performs a specific function. For example, a math coprocessor chip speeds mathematical calculations, while a graphics coprocessor chip decreases the time it takes to manipulate graphics.

A **multicore microprocessor** combines two or more independent processors into a single computer so that they can share the workload and boost processing capacity. In addition, a dual-core processor enables people to perform several tasks simultaneously, such as playing a game and burning a CD. Multicore processors that have a low clock speed and a shared cache (rather than separate dedicated caches for each processor core) can also reduce the heat generated by the computer without reducing its processing power. For example, the Intel Dual Core processor runs at 1.66 MHz compared to the single-core Pentium 4 processor, which runs at 3.2 GHz. AMD and Intel are battling for leadership in the multicore processor marketplace.

Both Intel and AMD have improved on dual processors by introducing quad-core and six-core chips. The Intel Core i7 is a family of several Intel processors based on Intel's Nehalem microcomputer architecture, which integrates four processors onto a single chip and lets them share a common L3 cache. The memory controller is also integrated onto the chip to provide a faster flow of data to and from main memory. The controller employs new technologies that enable faster communications between the CPU and other system components. The chips operate at 3.33 GHz and are built using the 45-nanometer manufacturing process. The next generation of Intel chips is code-named Gulftown and are being built to an even smaller scale using a new 32-nanometer manufacturing process. These chips support six processors. They will be even faster and more power efficient than Core i7 chips.[5]

AMD's quad-core Phenom II X64 Black Edition CPU operates at 3.4 GHz. Although the AMD clock speed is slightly faster than the Intel Core i7, comparing clock speed of two CPUs with different architectures means little. The entire computer system must be designed so that the CPU works well with main memory and the other components of the computer. The Intel Core i7 processor surpasses the AMD Phenom processor based on the results of various computing benchmarks.[6] AMD also recently introduced a six-core Phenom II processor chip.

IBM introduced its Power7 chip with eight processing cores. Because each core can process four tasks or threads, the chip provides a 32-core processor. By way of comparison, Intel's high-end Xeon processors, a strong IBM competitor, typically have four cores capable of supporting just two threads per core. With this powerful processor "electric utilities can move from processing less than one million meters per day, in a typical [power] grid, to more than 85 million reads per day in a smart grid."[7]

A **graphics processing unit (GPU)** is a specialized processor that offloads the tasks associated with 3D graphics rendering from the CPU. Such chips can generate breathtaking, interactive graphics on mobile devices, game consoles, and personal computers. The Apple iPhone 3GS uses an improved GPU that can support 3D rendering and high definition to provide a superb mobile gaming experience.[8] GPUs can also be used in certain applications that require massive vector operations to provide performance several orders of magnitude higher than a traditional CPU.[9]

When selecting a CPU, organizations must balance the benefits of processing speed with energy requirements and cost. CPUs with faster clock speeds and shorter machine cycle times require more energy to dissipate the heat generated by the CPU and are bulkier and more expensive than slower ones.

Parallel Computing

Parallel computing is the simultaneous execution of the same task on many processors to obtain results faster. Systems with thousands of such processors are known as **massively parallel processing systems**, a form of multiprocessing that speeds processing by linking hundreds or thousands of processors to operate at the same time, or in parallel, with each processor having its own bus, memory, disks, copy of the operating system, and applications. The processors might communicate with one another to coordinate when executing a computer program, or they might run independently of one another but under the direction of another processor that distributes the work to the other processors and collects their processing results. The dual-core processors mentioned earlier are a simple form of parallel computing.

The most frequent uses for parallel computing include modelling, simulation, and analyzing large amounts of data. Parallel computing is used in medicine to develop new imaging systems to complete ultrasound scans in less time with greater accuracy, for example, enabling doctors to provide better diagnosis to patients. Instead of building physical models of new products, engineers can create a virtual model of them and use parallel computing to test how the products work and then change design elements and materials as needed. Clothing designers can simulate the look and movement of new designs on virtual models, reducing the development time for a seasonal clothing collection to just over one month from the traditional six-month period.[10]

Grid computing is the use of a collection of computers, often owned by several individuals or organizations, to work in a coordinated manner to solve a common problem. Grid computing is a low-cost approach to parallel computing. The grid can include dozens, hundreds, or even thousands of computers that run collectively to solve extremely large processing problems. Key to the success of grid computing is a central server that acts as the grid leader and traffic monitor. This controlling server divides the computing task into subtasks and assigns the work to computers on the grid that have (at least temporarily) surplus processing power. The central server also monitors the processing, and if a member of the grid fails to complete a subtask, it restarts or reassigns the task. When all the subtasks are completed, the controlling server combines the results and advances to the next task until the whole job is completed.

IBM launched the World Community Grid project in 2004 to harness the unused computing power of personal and business computers into a large-scale public computing grid. Researchers at the University of Texas Medical Branch (UTMB) used the computer power of over one million devices attached to the grid to test drug candidates for new and drug-resistant flu strains, such as H1N1. Stan Watowich, the lead researcher at UTMB, claims that "we expect to identify new influenza drug candidates in less than a month. We can move from computer calculations into laboratory testing more quickly and with a sharper focus."[11]

graphics processing unit (GPU)
A specialized processor that offloads the tasks associated with 3D graphics rendering from the CPU.

parallel computing
The simultaneous execution of the same task on many processors to obtain results faster.

massively parallel processing systems
A form of multiprocessing that speeds processing by linking hundreds or thousands of processors to operate at the same time, or in parallel, with each processor having its own bus, memory, disks, copy of the operating system, and applications.

grid computing
The use of a collection of computers, often owned by several individuals or organizations, to work in a coordinated manner to solve a common problem.

SECONDARY STORAGE

Storing data safely and effectively is critical to an organization's success. Driven by many factors—such as needing to retain more data longer to meet government regulatory concerns, storing new forms of digital data such as audio and video, and keeping systems running under the onslaught of increasing volumes of e-mail—the amount of data that companies store digitally is increasing at a rate of more than 40 percent per year.[12] The social website MySpace.com has built one of the largest collections of business data in the world. MySpace captures between 7 and 10 billion events each day generated by its more than 130 million users worldwide.[13] One use of this enormous amount of data is to better target ads to MySpace users.[14]

For most organizations, the best overall data storage solution is likely a combination of different **secondary storage** options that can store large amounts of data, instructions, and information more permanently than allowed with main memory.

Compared with memory, secondary storage offers the advantages of nonvolatility, greater capacity, and greater economy. On a cost-per-megabyte basis, secondary storage is considerably less expensive than primary memory. See Table 3.2. The selection of secondary storage media and devices requires understanding their primary characteristics—access method, capacity, and portability.

secondary storage
Devices that store large amounts of data, instructions, and information more permanently than allowed with main memory.

Table 3.2

Cost Comparison for Various Forms of Storage

All forms of secondary storage cost considerably less per megabyte of capacity than SDRAM, although they have slower access times. A data cartridge costs about $0.18 per gigabyte, while SDRAM can cost around $22 per gigabyte—over 100 times more expensive.

(Source: Office Depot Web site, *www.officedepot.ca*, March 20, 2011.)

Description	Cost	Storage Capacity (GB)	Cost Per GB
50 4.7 GB DVD+R disks	$19.99	235	$0.085
500 GB portable hard drive	$89.99	500	$0.183
25 GB rewritable Blu-ray disk	$12.59	25	$0.504
8 GB flash drive	$39.99	8	$5.00
1 TB desktop external hard drive	$119.99	1,000	$0.120
2 GB DDR2 SDRAM memory upgrade	$43.95	2	$21.98

As with other computer system components, the access methods, storage capacities, and portability required of secondary storage media are determined by the information system's objectives. An objective of a credit card company's information system might be to rapidly retrieve stored customer data to approve customer purchases. In this case, a fast access method is critical. In other cases, such as equipping the Coca-Cola field sales force with pocket-sized personal computers, portability and storage capacity might be major considerations in selecting and using secondary storage media and devices.

In addition to cost, capacity, and portability, organizations must address security issues to allow only authorized people to access sensitive data and critical programs. Because the data and programs kept on secondary storage devices are so critical to most organizations, all of these issues merit careful consideration.

Access Methods

Data and information access can be either sequential or direct. **Sequential access** means that data must be accessed in the order in which it is stored. For example, inventory data might be stored sequentially by part number, such as 100, 101, 102, and so on. If you want to retrieve information on part number 125, you must read and discard all the data relating to parts 001 through 124.

Direct access means that data can be retrieved directly, without the need to pass by other data in sequence. With direct access, it is possible to go directly to and access the needed data—for example, part number 125—without having to read through parts 001

sequential access
A retrieval method in which data must be accessed in the order in which it is stored.

direct access
A retrieval method in which data can be retrieved without the need to read and discard other data.

through 124. For this reason, direct access is usually faster than sequential access. The devices used only to access secondary storage data sequentially are simply called **sequential access storage devices** (**SASDs**); those used for direct access are called **direct access storage devices** (**DASDs**).

Secondary Storage Devices

Secondary data storage is not directly accessible by the CPU. Instead, computers usually use input/output channels to access secondary storage and transfer the desired data using intermediate areas in primary storage. The most common forms of secondary storage devices include magnetic, optical, and solid state storage devices.

Magnetic Secondary Storage Devices

Magnetic storage uses tape or disk devices covered with a thin magnetic coating that enables data to be stored as magnetic particles.

Magnetic tape is a type of sequential secondary storage medium, now used primarily for storing backups of critical organizational data in the event of a disaster. Examples of tape storage devices include cassettes and cartridges measuring a few millimetres in diameter, requiring very little storage space

A **magnetic disk** is a direct-access storage device that represents bits using small magnetized areas and uses a read/write head to go directly to the desired piece of data. Because direct access allows fast data retrieval, this type of storage is ideal for companies that need to respond quickly to customer requests, such as airlines and credit card firms. For example, if a manager needs information on the credit history of a customer or the seat availability on a particular flight, the information can be obtained in seconds if the data is stored on a direct access storage device. Magnetic disk storage varies widely in capacity and portability. Hard disks, though more costly and less portable, are more popular because of their greater storage capacity and quicker access time. See Figure 3.6.

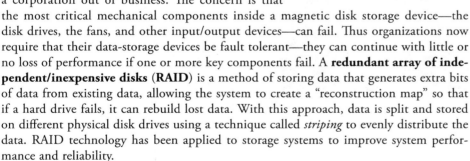

Putting an organization's data online involves a serious business risk—the loss of critical data can put a corporation out of business. The concern is that the most critical mechanical components inside a magnetic disk storage device—the disk drives, the fans, and other input/output devices—can fail. Thus organizations now require that their data-storage devices be fault tolerant—they can continue with little or no loss of performance if one or more key components fail. A **redundant array of independent/inexpensive disks** (**RAID**) is a method of storing data that generates extra bits of data from existing data, allowing the system to create a "reconstruction map" so that if a hard drive fails, it can rebuild lost data. With this approach, data is split and stored on different physical disk drives using a technique called *striping* to evenly distribute the data. RAID technology has been applied to storage systems to improve system performance and reliability.

RAID can be implemented in several ways. In the simplest form, RAID subsystems duplicate data on drives. This process, called **disk mirroring**, provides an exact copy that protects users fully in the event of data loss. However, to keep complete duplicates of current backups, organizations need to double the amount of their storage capacity. Other RAID methods are less expensive because they only partly duplicate the data, allowing storage managers to minimize the amount of extra disk space they must purchase to protect data. Optional second drives for personal computer users who need to mirror critical data are available for less than $100.

Point360 is a post-production company that edits, masters, reformats, and archives video files for its TV and film production clients. The firm implemented a RAID storage solution to provide a greater level of security and to manage the increasing amount of storage required by high-definition video and sophisticated visual effect rendering.[15]

sequential access storage device (SASD)
A device used to sequentially access secondary storage data.

direct access storage device (DASD)
A device used for direct access of secondary storage data.

magnetic tape
A type of sequential secondary storage medium, now used primarily for storing backups of critical organizational data in the event of a disaster.

magnetic disk
A direct-access storage device, with bits represented by magnetized areas.

Figure 3.6

Hard Disk

Hard disks provide direct access to stored data. The read/write head can move directly to the location of a desired piece of data, dramatically reducing access times compared to magnetic tape.

(Source: Courtesy of Seagate Technology.)

redundant array of independent/inexpensive disks (RAID)
A method of storing data that generates extra bits of data from existing data, allowing the system to create a "reconstruction map" so that if a hard drive fails, the system can rebuild lost data.

disk mirroring
A process of storing data that provides an exact copy that protects users fully in the event of data loss.

virtual tape
A storage device for less frequently needed data so that it appears to be stored entirely on tape cartridges, although some parts of it might actually be located on faster hard disks.

Virtual tape is a storage technology for less frequently needed data so that it appears to be stored entirely on tape cartridges, although some parts might actually be located on faster hard disks. The software associated with a virtual tape system is sometimes called a *virtual tape server*. Virtual tape can be used with a sophisticated storage-management system that moves data to slower but less costly forms of storage media as people use the data less often. Virtual tape technology can decrease data access time, lower the total cost of ownership, and reduce the amount of floor space consumed by tape operations. The IS organization at Boston Medical Center is responsible for maintaining over 400 TB of data associated with the operation of this 581-bed academic medical centre. The organization adopted a virtual tape management system to cope with a 50 percent annual data growth rate while keeping data storage costs under control and meeting strict regulatory requirements.[16]

Optical Secondary Storage Devices

optical storage device
A form of data storage that uses lasers to read and write data.

An **optical storage device** uses special lasers to read and write data. The lasers record data by physically burning pits in the disk. Data is directly accessed from the disk by an optical disk device, which operates much like a compact disk player. This optical disk device uses a low-power laser that measures the difference in reflected light caused by a pit (or lack thereof) on the disk.

compact disk read-only memory (CD-ROM)
A common form of optical disk on which data cannot be modified once it has been recorded.

A common optical storage device is the **compact disk read-only memory (CD-ROM)** with a storage capacity of 740 MB of data. After data is recorded on a CD-ROM, it cannot be modified—the disk is "read-only." A CD burner, the informal name for a CD recorder, is a device that can record data to a compact disk. *CD-recordable (CD-R)* and *CD-rewritable (CD-RW)* are the two most common types of drives that can write CDs, either once (in the case of CD-R) or repeatedly (in the case of CD-RW). CD-rewritable (CD-RW) technology allows PC users to back up data on CDs.

digital video disk (DVD)
A storage medium used to store software, video games, and movies.

A **digital video disk (DVD)** looks like a CD but can store about 135 minutes of digital video or several gigabytes of data. See Figure 3.7. Software, video games, and movies are often stored and distributed on DVDs. At a data transfer rate of 1.352 MB per second, the access speed of a DVD drive is faster than that of the typical CD-ROM drive.

DVDs have replaced recordable and rewritable CD discs (CD-R and CD-RW) as the preferred format for sharing movies and photos. Whereas a CD can hold about 740 MB of

Figure 3.7

Digital Video Disk and Player

DVDs look like CDs but have a greater storage capacity and can transfer data at a faster rate.

(Source: © Florea Marius Catalin/ iStockphoto.com.)

data, a single-sided DVD can hold 4.7 GB, with double-sided DVDs having a capacity of 9.4 GB. Several types of recorders and discs are currently in use. Recordings can be made on record-once discs (DVD-R and DVD+R) or on rewritable discs (DVD-RW, DVD+RW, and DVD-RAM). Not all types of rewritable DVDs are compatible with other types.

The Blu-ray high-definition video disk format based on blue laser technology stores at least three times as much data as a DVD now holds. The primary use for this new format is in home entertainment equipment to store high-definition video, though this format can also store computer data. A dual-layer Blu-ray disk can store 50 GB of data.

The Holographic Versatile Disk (HVD) is an advanced optical disk technology still in the development stage that would store more data than even the Blu-ray optical disk system. One approach to HVD records data through the depth of the storage media in three dimensions by splitting a laser beam in two—the signal beam carries the data, and the reference beam positions where the data is written and reads it. HVD devices are under development with the potential to transfer data at the rate of 1 to 20 GB per second and store up to 6 TB of data on a single optical disk.

Solid State Secondary Storage Devices

Solid state storage devices (SSDs) store data in memory chips rather than magnetic or optical media. These memory chips require less power and provide faster data access than magnetic data storage devices. In addition, SSDs have few moving parts, so they are less fragile than hard disk drives. All these factors make the SSD a preferred choice for portable computers. Two current disadvantages of SSD are their high cost per GB of data storage (roughly a 5:1 disadvantage compared to hard disks) and lower capacity compared to current hard drives. SSD is a rapidly developing technology, and future improvements will lower their cost and increase their capacity.

A Universal Serial Bus (USB) flash drive is one example of a commonly used SSD. See Figure 3.8. USB flash drives are external to the computer and are removable and rewritable. Most weigh less than an ounce and can provide storage of 1 GB to 64 GB. SanDisk manufactures flash drives that can store up to 64 GB based on technology it calls X4, which stores 4 bits of data in each of the millions of tiny storage elements on a chip called cells.[17]

Marketing Architects is a company of about 100 employees that provides radio, TV, and telephone marketing campaigns for its clients. The firm employs SSD technology to store data to provide faster data response time at lower storage costs compared to available alternatives.[18]

Figure 3.8

Flash Drive

Flash drives are solid state storage devices.

(Source: Lipsky/Shutterstock.com.)

Enterprise Storage Options

Businesses need to store large amounts of data created throughout the organization. Such large secondary storage is called *enterprise storage* and comes in three forms: attached storage, network-attached storage (NAS), and storage area networks (SANs).

Attached Storage

Attached storage methods include the tape, hard disks, and optical devices discussed previously, which are connected directly to a single computer. Attached storage methods, though simple and cost effective for single users and small groups, do not allow systems to share storage, and they make it difficult to back up data.

Because of the limitations of attached storage, firms are turning to network-attached storage (NAS) and storage area networks (SANs). These alternatives enable an organization to share data-storage resources among a much larger number of computers and users, resulting in improved storage efficiency and greater cost-effectiveness. In addition, they simplify data backup and reduce the risk of downtime. Nearly one-third of system downtime is a direct result of data-storage failures, so eliminating storage problems as a cause of downtime is a major advantage.

Network-Attached Storage

Network-attached storage (**NAS**) is hard disk storage that is set up with its own network address rather than being attached to a computer. Figure 3.9 (on the next page) shows a NAS storage device. NAS includes software to manage storage access and file management, relieving the users' computers of those tasks. The result is that both application software and files can be served faster because they are not competing for the same processor resources. Computer users can share and access the same information, even if they are using different types of computers. Common applications for NAS include consolidated storage, Internet and e-commerce applications, and digital media.

The Personal Genome Project (PGP) is aimed at helping people have their genome sequenced so that they can understand their risk profiles for disease, their physical and biological characteristics, and their personal ancestries. The project will use a NAS to store genetic data for up to 100,000 volunteers who participate in this research.[19]

Storage Area Network

A **storage area network** (**SAN**) is a special-purpose, high-speed network that provides direct connections among data-storage devices and computers across the enterprise.

network-attached storage (NAS) Hard disk storage that is set up with its own network address rather than being attached to a computer.

storage area network (SAN) A special-purpose, high-speed network that provides high-speed connections among data-storage devices and computers over a network.

Figure 3.9

NAS Storage Device

The Seagate BlackArmor NAS 440 has a capacity of 4,000 GB at a cost of $1,090, or $.27 per GB.

(Source: Courtesy of Seagate Technology.)

See Figure 3.10. A SAN also integrates different types of storage subsystems, such as multiple RAID storage devices and magnetic tape backup systems, into a single storage system. Use of a SAN offloads the network traffic associated with storage onto a separate network. The data can then be copied to a remote location, making it easier for companies to create backups and implement disaster recovery policies.

Using a SAN, an organization can centralize the people, policies, procedures, and practices for managing storage, and a data-storage manager can apply the data consistently across an enterprise. This centralization eliminates inconsistent treatment of data by different system administrators and users, providing efficient and cost-effective data-storage practices.

Deeley Harley-Davidson Canada, a motorcycle distributor, realized it was spending too much to manage its increasing volume of data. The company worked with Dell Canada to virtualize its storage area network. According to Kevin Peesker, a Dell Canada vice president, "Virtualization has pushed down data storage and management costs by as much as 80 percent over the past five years."[20]

A fundamental difference between NAS and SAN is that NAS uses file input/output, which defines data as complete containers of information, while SAN deals with block

Figure 3.10

Storage Area Network

A SAN provides high-speed connections among data-storage devices and computers over a network.

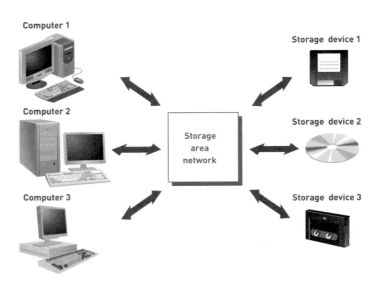

input/output, which is based on subsets of data smaller than a file. SAN manufacturers include EMC, Hitachi Data Systems Corporation, Xiotech, and IBM.

As organizations set up large-scale SANs, they use more computers and network connections than in a NAS environment, which become difficult to manage. In response, software tools designed to automate storage using previously defined policies are finding a place in the enterprise. Known as **policy-based storage management**, the software products from industry leaders such as Veritas Software Corporation, Legato Systems, Inc., EMC, and IBM automatically allocate storage space to users, balance the loads on servers and disks, and reroute networks when systems go down—all based on policies set up by system administrators.

policy-based storage management
Automation of storage using previously defined policies.

The trend in secondary storage is toward higher capacity, increased portability, and automated storage management. Organizations should select a type of storage based on their needs and resources. In general, storing large amounts of data and information and providing users with quick access makes an organization more efficient.

Storage as a Service

Storage as a service is a data storage model where a data storage service provider rents space to people and organizations. Users access their rented data storage via the Internet. Such a service enables the users to store and back up their data without requiring a major investment to create and maintain their own data storage infrastructure. Businesses can also choose pay-per-use services, where they rent space on massive storage devices housed either at a service provider (such as Hewlett-Packard or IBM) or on the customer's premises, paying only for the amount of storage they use. This approach is sensible for organizations with wildly fluctuating storage needs, such as those involved in the testing of new drugs or in developing software.

storage as a service
Storage as a service is a data storage model where a data storage service provider rents space to individuals and organizations.

Aviva, Amazon.com, EMC, Google, Microsoft, and ParaScale are a few of the storage as a service providers used by organizations. Amazon.com's Simple Storage Service (S3) provides storage as a service with a monthly cost of roughly $0.15 per GB stored and $0.10 per GB of data transferred into the Amazon.com storage.

Box.net, Carbonite, SugarSynch, Symantec, and Mozy are a few of the storage as a service providers used by individuals. This set of providers all charge less than $8 per month for up to 5 GB of storage.

INPUT AND OUTPUT DEVICES: THE GATEWAY TO COMPUTER SYSTEMS

Your first experience with computers is usually through input and output devices. These devices are the gateways to the computer system—you use them to provide data and instructions to the computer and receive results from it. Input and output devices are part of a computer's user interface, which includes other hardware devices and software that allow you to interact with a computer system.

As with other computer system components, an organization should keep its business goals in mind when selecting input and output devices. For example, many restaurant chains use handheld input devices or computerized terminals that let food servers enter orders efficiently and accurately. These systems have also cut costs by helping to track inventory and market to customers.

Characteristics and Functionality

In general, businesses want input devices that let them rapidly enter data into a computer system, and they want output devices that let them produce timely results. When selecting input and output devices, businesses also need to consider the form of the output they want, the nature of the data required to generate this output, and the speed and accuracy they need for both. Some organizations have very specific needs for output and input, requiring devices that perform specific functions. The more specialized the application, the more specialized the associated system input and output devices.

The speed and functions of input and output devices should be balanced with their cost, control, and complexity. More specialized devices might make it easier to enter data or output information, but they are generally more costly, less flexible, and more susceptible to malfunction.

The Nature of Data

Getting data into the computer—input—often requires transferring human-readable data, such as a sales order, into the computer system. "Human-readable" means data that people can read and understand. A sheet of paper containing inventory adjustments is an example of human-readable data. In contrast, machine-readable data can be read by computer devices (such as the universal bar code on many grocery and retail items) and is typically stored as bits or bytes. Inventory changes stored on a disk is an example of machine-readable data.

Some data can be read by people and machines, such as magnetic ink on bank cheques. Usually, people begin the input process by organizing human-readable data and transforming it into machine-readable data. Every keystroke on a keyboard, for example, turns a letter symbol of a human language into a digital code that the machine can manipulate.

Data Entry and Input

data entry
Converting human-readable data into a machine-readable form.

data input
Transferring machine-readable data into the system.

Getting data into the computer system is a two-stage process. First, the human-readable data is converted into a machine-readable form through **data entry**. The second stage involves transferring the machine-readable data into the system. This is **data input**.

Today, many companies are using online data entry and input—they communicate and transfer data to computer devices directly connected to the computer system. Online data entry and input places data into the computer system in a matter of seconds. Organizations in many industries require the instantaneous updating offered by this approach. For example, when ticket agents enter a request for concert tickets, they can use online data entry and input to record the request as soon as it is made. Ticket agents at other terminals can then access this data to make a seating check before they process another request.

Source Data Automation

source data automation
Capturing and editing data where it is initially created and in a form that can be directly input to a computer, thus ensuring accuracy and timeliness.

Regardless of how data gets into the computer, it should be captured and edited at its source. **Source data automation** involves capturing and editing data where it is originally created and in a form that can be directly input to a computer, thus ensuring accuracy and timeliness. For example, using source data automation, salespeople enter sales orders into the computer at the time and place they take the order. Any errors can be detected and corrected immediately. If an item is temporarily out of stock, the salesperson can discuss options with the customer. Prior to source data automation, orders were written on paper and entered into the computer later (usually by a clerk, not the person who took the order). Often the handwritten information wasn't legible or, worse yet, got lost. If problems occurred during data entry, the clerk had to contact the salesperson or the customer to "recapture" the data needed for order entry, leading to further delays and customer dissatisfaction.

Input Devices

Data entry and input devices come in many forms. They range from special-purpose devices that capture specific types of data to more general-purpose input devices. Some of the special-purpose data entry and input devices are discussed later in this chapter. First, we focus on devices used to enter and input general types of data, including text, audio, images, and video for personal computers.

Personal Computer Input Devices

A keyboard and a computer mouse are the most common devices used for entry and input of data such as characters, text, and basic commands. Some companies are developing keyboards that are more comfortable, more easily adjusted, and faster to use than standard keyboards. These ergonomic keyboards, such as the split keyboard by Microsoft and others, are designed to avoid wrist and hand injuries caused by hours of typing. Other keyboards include touch-pads that let you enter sketches on the touchpad while still using keys to enter text. Another innovation is wireless mice and keyboards, which keep a physical desktop free from clutter.

You use a computer mouse to point to and click symbols, icons, menus, and commands on the screen. The computer takes a number of actions in response, such as placing data into the computer system.

A keyboard and mouse are two of the most common devices for computer input. Wireless mice and keyboards are now readily available.

(Source: Dmitry Melnikov/ Shutterstock.com.)

Speech-Recognition Technology

Using **speech-recognition technology**, a computer equipped with a source of speech input, such as a microphone, can interpret human speech as an alternative means of providing data or instructions to the computer. The most basic systems require you to train the system to recognize your speech patterns or are limited to a small vocabulary of words. More advanced systems can recognize continuous speech without requiring you to break your speech into discrete words. Interactive voice response (IVR) systems allow a computer to recognize both voice and keypad inputs.

Companies that must constantly interact with customers are eager to reduce their customer support costs while improving the quality of their service. For example, Bell Canada uses "Emily," a custom-designed speech-recognition system to improve customer satisfaction by automatically routing callers to the correct department. Customers interact with the system using their natural voice and do not have to touch keys on their phone keypad.[21]

speech-recognition technology
Input devices that recognize human speech.

Digital Cameras

Digital cameras record and store images or video in digital form. When you take pictures, the images are electronically stored in the camera. You can download the images to a computer either directly or by using a flash memory card. After you store the images on the computer's hard disk, you can edit and print them, send them to another location, or paste them into another application. This saves time and money by eliminating the need to process film in order to share photos. For example, you can download a photo of your project team captured by a digital camera and then post it on a website or paste it into a project status report. Digital cameras have eclipsed film cameras used by professional pho-tographers for photo quality and features such as zoom, flash, exposure controls, special effects, and even video-capture capabilities. With the right software, you can add sound and handwriting to the photo.

digital camera
An input device used with a PC to record and store images and video in digital form.

Canon, Casio, Nikon, Olympus, Panasonic, Pentax, Sony, and other camera manufacturers offer full-featured, high-resolution digital camera models for under $250. Some manufacturers offer pocket-sized camcorders for under $150.

Terminals

Inexpensive and easy to use, terminals are simply input and display devices that have no processing capability of their own. They must transmit data input via keyboard, mouse, or some sort of scanning device to a computer to handle the data processing and storage. The computer system processes the data it receives and returns a response to the terminal. Terminals are frequently used in warehouses, on shipping docks, and on the factory floor. For such applications, terminals can greatly reduce the cost of owning and maintaining a computer system, and they provide a high degree of security because no data is stored on the terminal.

Scanning Devices

Scanning devices capture image and character data. A page scanner is like a copy machine. You either insert a page into the scanner or place it face down on the glass plate of the scanner, and then scan it. With a hand-held scanner, you manually move or roll the scanning device over the image you want to scan. Both page and hand-held scanners can convert monochrome or colour pictures, forms, text, and other images into machine-readable digits. Considering that North American enterprises generate an estimated 1 billion pieces of paper daily, many companies are looking to scanning devices to help them manage their documents and reduce the high cost of using and processing paper.

The Royal Canadian Mounted Police (RCMP) has implemented the Real Time Identification Project (RTID) to promote electronic fingerprint submissions for criminal record checks. The goal of the project is to complete 85 percent of civil requests submitted electronically within 72 hours compared to 120 days for paper-based fingerprint submissions.[22] Today's fingerprint scanning systems employ image enhancement software to remove scars, cuts, and breaks in the print that can make the print difficult to identify. The scanning systems operate very quickly and do not require the use of ink. The scanning system can be linked to a database that determines whether fingerprints match any in a criminal record database.[23]

Optical Data Readers

You can also use a special scanning device called an *optical data reader* to scan documents. The two categories of optical data readers are for optical mark recognition (OMR) and optical character recognition (OCR). You use OMR readers for grading tests and other purposes such as forms. With this technology, you use pencils to fill in bubbles or check boxes on OMR paper, which is also called a "mark sense form." OMR systems are used in standardized tests, including the SAT and GMAT tests, and to record votes in elections. In comparison, most OCR readers use reflected light to recognize and scan various machine-generated characters. With special software, OCR readers can also convert handwritten or typed documents into digital data. After being entered, this data can be shared, modified, and distributed over computer networks to hundreds or thousands of people.

The Montmagny-L'Islet Family Medicine Group operates three clinics in Quebec. The company implemented a paperless electronic medical records system to improve patient management and continuity of care among the doctors and nurses. All documents are scanned and medical notes and prescriptions are entered directly into the system. The system is also linked into the provincial medical imaging database to enable the clinic to receive patient X-rays electronically. The key benefits of the system are that staff are spending less time handling and looking for client information and the client information is more accurate and dependable, a change that has resulted in greater efficiency and fewer drug interactions, oversights, and delays in treatment decision making.[24]

Magnetic Ink Character Recognition (MICR) Devices

In the 1950s, the banking industry became swamped with paper cheques, loan applications, bank statements, and so on. The result was the development of magnetic ink character recognition (MICR), a system for reading banking data quickly. With MICR, data is placed on

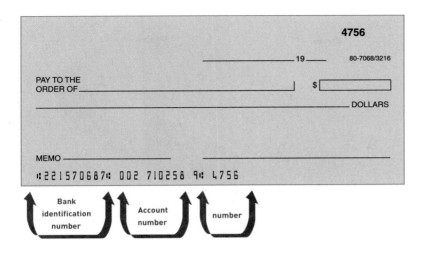

Figure 3.11

MICR Device

Magnetic ink character recognition technology codes data on the bottom of a cheque or other form using special magnetic ink, which is readable by people and computers. For an example, look at the bottom of a bank cheque.

(Source: Courtesy of NCR Corporation.)

the bottom of a cheque or other form using a special magnetic ink. Using a special character set, data printed with this ink is readable by people and computers. See Figure 3.11.

Magnetic Stripe Cards

A **magnetic stripe card** stores a limited amount of data by modifying the magnetism of tiny iron-based particles contained in a band on the card. The magnetic stripe is read by physically swiping the card at a terminal. For this reason, such cards are called a contact card. Magnetic stripe cards are commonly used in credit cards, transportation tickets, and driver's licences.

magnetic stripe card
A type of card that stores a limited amount of data by modifying the magnetism of tiny iron-based particles contained in a band on the card.

Chip-and-PIN Cards

Europe and Canada are taking steps to ban the use of magnetic stripe cards within the next few years in favour of the **chip-and-PIN card**, which uses "smart card" technology. This technology employs a computer chip that communicates with a card reader using radio frequencies. The cards do not need to be swiped at a terminal. Chip-and-PIN cards require different terminals from those used for magnetic stripe cards. However, the card holder is also required to enter a PIN at the point of sale. Such cards are more effective at preventing fraud than credit cards requiring a signature.[25] As a measure of the success of this technology, bank card fraud declined 23 percent during the first half of 2009 in the U.K.[26] Canadian banks and credit card issuers have mandated the use of chip-based credit cards by the end of 2010 to reduce the over $358 million in losses due to credit card fraud in 2009.[27, 28]

chip-and-PIN card
A type of card that employs a computer chip that communicates with a card reader using radio frequencies; it does not need to be swiped at a terminal.

Contactless Cards

A **contactless card** has an embedded chip that only needs to be held close to a terminal to transfer its data; no PIN number needs to be entered. American Express, MasterCard, and Visa issue some contactless cards. Visa Canada introduced its contactless debit card at the 2010 Winter Olympic Games in Vancouver.[29]

contactless card
A card with an embedded chip that only needs to be held close to a terminal to transfer its data; no PIN number needs to be entered.

Point-of-Sale Devices

Point-of-sale (**POS**) **devices** are terminals used to capture data for data entry. They are frequently used in retail operations to enter sales information into the computer system. The POS device then computes the total charges, including tax. In medical settings, POS devices are often used for remote monitoring in hospitals, clinics, laboratories, doctors' offices, and patients' homes. With network-enabled POS equipment, medical professionals can instantly get an update on the patient's condition, from anywhere at any time via a network or the Internet. POS devices use various types of input and output devices, such as keyboards, bar-code readers, scanning devices, printers, and screens. Much of the money that businesses spend on computer technology is for POS devices.

Many Canadian restaurants have introduced wireless, hand-held mobile POS devices. See Figure 3.12 on the next page. By sending orders to the kitchen and bar from the table and

point-of-sale (POS) device
A terminal used to enter data into the computer system.

Figure 3.12

Hand-held POS Terminal Device

Using a wireless, hand-held POS device, restaurant staff can take orders and payments on the floor.

(Source: Evgeny Tyzhinov/ Shutterstock.com.)

by receiving real-time updates of menu items that were sold out, servers can provide faster, better customer service. They can also securely process credit card payments and send the receipts to the printer directly from the tables, speeding up the payment process and turning over tables more efficiently.[30]

Automated Teller Machine (ATM) Devices

Another type of special-purpose input/output device, the automated teller machine (ATM) is a terminal that bank customers use to perform transactions with their bank accounts. Companies use various ATM devices, sometimes called *kiosks*, to support their business processes. Some can dispense tickets, such as for airlines, concerts, and soccer games. Some colleges use them to produce transcripts. Casino guests use buffet-entry kiosks to prepay their buffet meals with cash, credit, debit, or casino loyalty points. The kiosk then issues a receipt for guests to use to gain entry to the buffet.[31]

Pen Input Devices

By touching the screen with a pen input device, you can activate a command or cause the computer to perform a task, enter handwritten notes, and draw objects and figures. See Figure 3.13. Pen input requires special software and hardware. Handwriting recognition software can convert handwriting on the screen into text. The Tablet PC from Microsoft and its hardware partners can transform handwriting into typed text and store the "digital ink" just the way a person writes it. People can use a pen to write and send e-mail, add

Figure 3.13

Using a Pen Input Device

Using a pen input device directly on a 3D display, physicians can precisely trace organs at a very detailed level to prepare for a complex operation.

(Source: Courtesy of BioSkill.)

comments to Word documents, mark up PowerPoint presentations, and even hand-draw charts in a document. The data can then be moved, highlighted, searched, and converted into text. If perfected, this interface is likely to become widely used. Pen input is especially attractive if you are uncomfortable using a keyboard. The success of pen input depends on how accurately and at what cost handwriting can be read and translated into digital form.

Touch-Sensitive Screens

Advances in screen technology allow display screens to function as input as well as output devices. By touching certain parts of a touch-sensitive screen, you can start a program or trigger other types of action. Touch-sensitive screens can remove the need for a keyboard, which conserves space and increases portability. Touch-screens are frequently used at gas stations for customers to select grades of gas and request a receipt; on photocopy machines for selecting options; at fast-food restaurants for entering customer choices; at information centres for finding facts about local eating and drinking establishments; and at amusement parks to provide directions to patrons. They also are used in kiosks at airports and department stores. Touch-sensitive screens are also being considered for gathering votes in elections.

Technology consulting firm Roundarch is developing a prototype 17-inch screen panel to incorporate into the all-electric, high-performance Tesla Model S Sedan to provide the first-of-its-kind "infotainment" system, which includes high-definition radio, GPS navigation, a high-speed Internet connection to enable network browsing, and streaming audio.[32]

As touch-screens get smaller, the user's fingers begin to block the information on the display. Nanotouch technology is being explored as a means of overcoming this problem. Using this technology, users control the touch-screen from its backside so that fingers do not block the display. As the user's finger moves on the back of the display, a tiny graphical finger is projected onto the touch-screen. Such displays are useful for mobile audio players the size of a coin and cell phones the size of a matchbox.[33]

Bar-Code Scanners

A bar-code scanner employs a laser scanner to read a bar-coded label and pass the data to a computer. The bar-code reader may be stationary or hand-held to support a wide variety of uses. This form of input is used widely in store checkouts and warehouse inventory control. Bar codes are also used in hospitals, where a nurse scans a patient's wristband and then a bar code on the medication about to be administered; this practice helps prevent medication errors.[34]

Radio Frequency Identification

Radio Frequency Identification (RFID) is a technology that employs a microchip with an antenna to broadcast its unique identifier and location to receivers. The purpose of an RFID system is to transmit data by a mobile device, called a tag, which is read by an RFID reader and processed according to the needs of an IS program. One popular application of RFID is to place microchips on retail items and install in-store readers that track the inventory on the shelves to determine when shelves should be restocked. The RFID tag chip includes a special form of EPROM memory that holds data about the item to which the tag is attached. A radio frequency signal can update this memory as the status of the item changes. The data transmitted by the tag might provide identification, location information, or details about the product tagged, such as date manufactured, retail price, colour, or date of purchase.

Canada Revenue Agency (CRA) and Canada Post use a combination of RFID and bar-code technology to track mail shipments between CRA offices. RFID tags and bar codes are placed on each mail container to transmit real-time location data so that the CRA can track the movement of important documents between its offices.[35]

Radio Frequency Identification (RFID)
A technology that employs a microchip with an antenna to broadcast its unique identifier and location to receivers.

INFORMATION SYSTEMS @ WORK

Hand-held Computers Streamline National Inventory

When selecting the hardware for a particular information system, businesses often consider environmental factors. Before purchasing servers for a data centre, businesses calculate their available space. When purchasing PCs, businesses determine how mobile the computers should be by considering where employees will use the computers. Will the environment allow users to sit down and open a notebook; do they need to roam with a hand-held device? The goal is to achieve the best performance in the minimum amount of space at the lowest cost. Recently, the U.S. Census Bureau faced these decisions as it selected hardware for its data-collection agents.

The U.S. Census Bureau collects, stores, and processes more data than most businesses. In fact, many businesses learn about data collection and management by observing the U.S. Census Bureau's systems. Recently, the Census Bureau decided to remove the paperwork from its data-collection process. In 2006, the Census Bureau paid Harris Corporation $800 million to develop hand-held devices that census agents could use to collect data about U.S. citizens.

Originally, the bureau intended to use the devices for its two manual data-collection efforts: the Nonresponse Follow-up (NRFU), where agents visit the homes of citizens who do not reply to the bureau's Economic Census via mail (every five years); and for the Population and Housing Census. In the latter census, every 10 years agents complete a process called Address Canvassing (ADCan) to physically verify all 145 million home addresses in the United States. After delays, cost overruns, and pressure from the Government Accountability Office, the Census Bureau pared back its plans by deciding to continue with pen and paper for the NRFU but move forward with its paperless aspirations for ADCan. The resulting system uses 151,000 hand-held computers that Harris custom-designed for the Census Bureau to confirm address locations.

When selecting or designing hardware for an information system, developers must consider how the hardware fits into other systems and practices. As Harris created hand-held devices for census agents, it examined telecommunications, security, software, and database system requirements. It also studied how agents would use the device and in what types of settings. The resulting hand-held device uses the global positioning system (GPS) to pinpoint the location of an agent. With GPS technology, all an agent needs to do is select the address to verify on the device, visit the location of the address, and then record the GPS location.

As each agent verifies addresses, the data is stored in the hand-held device. Harris carefully analyzed storage capacity requirements to make sure the devices wouldn't become full. Periodically, the data is transferred to the Census Bureau's main database over a wireless cellular network. Because they transfer data in batches, census workers can use the hand-held device to collect data even where a cellular signal is not available, and then they can transfer a batch of data the next time they are in cellular range.

Harris adapted the hardware design to the needs of the Census Bureau. Because the bureau must maintain tight security over the data submitted to its database, Harris included a small fingerprint scanner so the device can be turned on only with the owner's fingerprint. Privacy is also an issue, so the devices store and send all data in an encrypted format. Out of the 151,000 devices, 100 were lost or stolen, but because of the security and privacy precautions, the devices could not be used to falsify or steal information. Harris also made sure the devices were easy to use and minimized stress on workers. To enter data into the device, census workers use a stylus on a touch-sensitive display. The displays on the devices were specially designed to be easy to read in outdoor lighting.

Based on testing results, the new devices are considered a huge success. When using paper and pen, the bureau achieved 95 percent accuracy in address canvassing. Using the new hand-held devices with GPS, the accuracy improved to 99.5 percent. Not only is the data more accurate, but census agents can complete their work more quickly.

The results to date prove that the Census Bureau can move toward a wireless census. The bureau hopes to expand the use of the hand-held computers in the next NRFU. Their goal is to eliminate paper altogether in 2020 by using Internet forms rather than mail-in forms.

Discussion Questions

1. What considerations did Harris Corporation take into account when designing devices for census agents?
2. Why did the original Census Bureau project fall short of its original goals? What do you think led to the difficulty?

Critical Thinking Questions

1. What industries, other than government, could benefit from the Census Bureau's experience with Harris Corporation?
2. What impediments could keep the U.S. Census Bureau from going completely paperless in 2020?

SOURCES: Lai, Eric, "Scaled-down e-Census Project 'a Great Success,' Bureau Says," *Computerworld*, July 30, 2009; Sybase, "Sybase and Harris Corporation Announce Success of the 2010 U.S. Census Address Canvassing Operation," Press release, www.sybase.com/detail?id=1065049, July 29, 2009.

Output Devices

Computer systems provide output to decision makers at all levels of an organization so they can solve a business problem or capitalize on a competitive opportunity. In addition, output from one computer system can provide input into another computer system. The desired form of this output might be visual, audio, or even digital. Whatever the output's content or form, output devices are designed to provide the right information to the right person in the right format at the right time.

Display Monitors

The display monitor is a device used to display the output from the computer. Because early monitors used a cathode-ray tube to display images, they were sometimes called *CRTs*. The cathode-ray tubes generate one or more electron beams. As the beams strike a phosphorescent compound (phosphor) coated on the inside of the screen, a dot on the screen called a pixel lights up. A **pixel** is a dot of colour on a photo image or a point of light on a display screen. It appears in one of two modes: on or off. The electron beam sweeps across the screen so that as the phosphor starts to fade, it is struck and lights up again.

A **plasma display** uses thousands of smart cells (pixels) consisting of electrodes and neon and xenon gases that are electrically turned into plasma (electrically charged atoms and negatively charged particles) to emit light. The plasma display lights up the pixels to form an image based on the information in the video signal. Each pixel is made up of three types of light—red, green, and blue. The plasma display varies the intensities of the lights to produce a full range of colours. Plasma displays can produce high resolution and accurate representation of colours to create a high-quality image.

LCD displays are flat displays that use liquid crystals—organic, oil-like material placed between two polarizers—to form characters and graphic images on a backlit screen. These displays are easier on your eyes than CRTs because they are flicker-free and brighter, and they do not emit the type of radiation that concerns some CRT users. In addition, LCD monitors take up less space and use less than half of the electricity required to operate a comparably sized CRT monitor. *Thin-film transistor (TFT) LCDs* are a type of liquid crystal display that assigns a transistor to control each pixel, resulting in higher resolution and quicker response to changes on the screen. TFT LCD monitors have displaced the older CRT technology and are available in sizes from 12 to 30 inches. Many companies now provide multimonitor solutions that enable users to see a wealth of related information at a single glance, as shown in Figure 3.14.

pixel
A dot of colour on a photo image or a point of light on a display screen.

plasma display
A type of display using thousands of smart cells (pixels) consisting of electrodes and neon and xenon gases which are electrically turned into plasma (electrically charged atoms and negatively charged particles) to emit light.

LCD display
Flat display that uses liquid crystals—organic, oil-like material placed between two polarizers—to form characters and graphic images on a backlit screen.

Figure 3.14

A Multimonitor Display

(Source: Justin Pumfrey/Getty Images.)

Organic light-emitting diode (OLED) uses a layer of organic material sandwiched between two conductors, which in turn are sandwiched between a glass top plate and a glass bottom plate. When electric current is applied to the two conductors, a bright, electro-luminescent light is produced directly from the organic material. OLEDs can provide sharper and brighter colours than LCDs and CRTs, and because they do not require a back-light, the displays can be half as thick as LCDs, and they are flexible. Another big advantage is that OLEDs do not break when dropped. OLED technology can also create 3D video

Organic light-emitting diode (OLED) display
Flat display that uses a layer of organic material sandwiched between two conductors that in turn are sandwiched between a glass top plate and a glass bottom plate so that when electric current is applied to the two conductors, a bright, electro-luminescent light is produced directly from the organic material.

displays by taking a traditional LCD monitor and then adding layers of transparent OLED films to create the perception of depth without the need for 3D glasses or laser optics. The iZ3D monitor is capable of displaying in both 2D and 3D mode. The manufacturer offered a 60-centimetre (22-inch) version of the monitor at a price of $300 to coincide with the debut of *Avatar*, a film directed by James Cameron.

Because most users leave their computers on for hours at a time, power usage is an important factor when deciding which type of monitor to purchase. Although the power usage varies from model to model, LCD monitors generally consume between 35 and 50 percent less power than plasma screens.[36] OLED monitors use even less power than LCD monitors.

Aspect ratio and screen size describe the size of the display screen. Aspect ratio is the ratio of the width of the display to its height. An aspect ratio of 4 to 3 is common. For widescreen LCD monitors used for viewing DVD movies in widescreen format, playing games, or displaying several screens side by side, an aspect ratio of 16 to 10 or 15 to 9 is preferred. The screen size is measured diagonally from the outside of the screen casing for CRT monitors and from the inside of the screen casing for LCD displays.

With today's wide selection of monitors, price and overall quality can vary tremendously. The quality of a screen image is measured by the number of horizontal and vertical pixels used to create it. Resolution is the total number of pixels contained in the display; the more pixels, the clearer and sharper the image. The size of the display monitor also affects the quality of the viewing. The same pixel resolution on a small screen is sharper than on a larger screen, where the same number of pixels is spread out over a larger area. Over the years, display monitor sizes have increased and display standards and resolutions have changed, as shown in Table 3.3.

Table 3.3

Common Display Monitor Standards and Associated Resolutions

Standard	Resolution (number of horizontal pixels x vertical pixels)
XGA (Extended Graphics Array)	1024 x 768
WXGA (Wide XGA)	1280 x 800
SXVGA (Super XGA)	1280 x 1024
WSXGA (Wide SGXA plus)	1680 x 1050
UXGA (Ultra XGA)	1600 x 1200
WUXGA (Wide Ultra XGA)	1920 x 1200
QXGA (Quad XGA)	2048 x 1536

Another way to measure image quality is the distance between one pixel on the screen and the next nearest pixel, which is known as *dot pitch*. The common range of dot pitch is from 0.25 mm to 0.31 mm. The smaller the dot pitch, the better the picture. A dot pitch of 0.28 mm or smaller is considered good. Greater pixel densities and smaller dot pitches yield sharper images of higher resolution.

The characteristics of screen colour depend on the quality of the monitor, the amount of RAM in the computer system, and the monitor's graphics adapter card. Digital Video Interface (DVI) is a video interface standard designed to maximize the visual quality of digital display devices such as flat-panel LCD computer displays.

Companies are competing on the innovation frontier to create thinner display devices for computers, cell phones, and other mobile devices. In its effort to gain an edge, LG Phillips has developed an extremely thin display that is only 0.15 mm thick, or roughly as thick as a human hair. The display is also so flexible that it can be bent or rolled up without being damaged. This flexible display opens possibilities for manufacturers to make cell phones and laptops with significantly larger displays but without increasing the size of the device itself, as the screen could be rolled up or folded and tucked away into a pocket.[37]

Printers and Plotters

One of the most useful and common forms of output is called *hard copy*, which is simply paper output from a printer. The two main types of printers are laser printers and inkjet printers, and they are available with different speeds, features, and capabilities. Some can be set up to accommodate paper forms, such as blank cheque forms and invoice forms. Newer printers allow businesses to create customized printed output for each customer from standard paper and data input using full colour. Ticket-receipt printers such as those used in restaurants, ATMs, and point-of-sale systems are in wide use.

The speed of the printer is typically measured by the number of pages printed per minute (ppm). Like a display screen, the quality, or resolution, of a printer's output depends on the number of dots printed per inch (dpi). A 600-dpi printer prints more clearly than a 300-dpi printer. A recurring cost of using a printer is the inkjet or laser cartridge that must be replaced periodically—every few thousand pages for laser printers and every 500 to 900 pages for inkjet printers.

Laser printers are generally faster than inkjet printers and can handle more volume than inkjet printers. Laser printers print 25 to 60 pages per minute (ppm) for black and white and 6 to 25 ppm for colour. Inkjet printers that can print 12 to 40 ppm for black and white and 5 to 20 ppm for colour are available for under $200.

For colour printing, inkjet printers print vivid hues and with an initial cost much less than colour laser printers. Inkjet printers can produce high-quality banners, graphics, greeting cards, letters, text, and photo prints. Hewlett-Packard introduced the CM8060 inkjet printers with a stationary print head that uses 60,000 nozzles to spray ink as the paper moves. The advantage of the new technology is the ability to print pages much faster (50 pages per minute for colour and 60 pages per minute for black and white).

A number of manufacturers offer multiple-function printers that can copy, print (in colour or black and white), fax, and scan. Such multifunctional devices are often used when people need to do a relatively low volume of copying, printing, faxing, and scanning. The typical price of multifunction printers ranges from $100 to $500, depending on features and capabilities. Because these devices take the place of more than one piece of equipment, they are less expensive to acquire and maintain than a standalone fax, plus a standalone printer, plus a standalone copier, and so on. Also, eliminating equipment that was once located on a countertop or desktop clears a workspace for other work-related activities. As a result, such devices are popular in homes and small office settings.

3D printers can be used to turn three-dimensional computer models into three-dimensional objects. One form of 3D printer uses an inkjet printing system to print an adhesive in the shape of a cross-section of the model. Next, a fine powder is sprayed onto the adhesive to form one layer of the object. This process is repeated thousands of times until the object is completed. 3D printing is commonly used in aerospace companies, auto manufacturers, and other design-intensive companies. It is especially valuable during the conceptual stage of engineering design when the exact dimensions and material strength of the prototype is not critical.

Plotters are a type of hard-copy output device used for general design work. Businesses typically use plotters to generate paper or acetate blueprints, schematics, and drawings of buildings or new products. Standard plot widths are 60 centimetres (24 inches) and 90 centimetres (36 inches), and the length can be whatever meets the need—from a few centimetres to many metres.

Digital Audio Players

A **digital audio player** is a device that can store, organize, and play digital music files. **MP3** (MPEG-1 Audio Layer-3) is a popular format for compressing a sound sequence into a very small file while preserving the original level of sound quality when it is played. By compressing the sound file, it requires less time to download the file and less storage space on a hard drive.

You can use many different music devices smaller than a deck of cards to download music from the Internet and other sources. These devices have no moving parts and can store hours of music. Apple expanded into the digital music market with an MP3 player (the iPod) and the iTunes Music Store, which allows you to find music online, preview it, and download it in a way that is safe, legal, and affordable. Other MP3 manufacturers include Dell, Sony, Samsung, Iomega, Creative, and Motorola, whose Rokr product is the first iTunes-compatible phone.

digital audio player
A device that can store, organize, and play digital music files.

MP3
A standard format for compressing a sound sequence into a small file.

The Apple's iPod Touch

(Source: © Simon Greig/Dreamstime. com.)

The Apple iPod Touch, with a 3.5-inch-wide screen, is a music player that also plays movies and TV shows, displays photos, and connects to the Internet. You can therefore use it to view YouTube videos, buy music online, check e-mail, and more. The display automatically adjusts the view when it is rotated from portrait to landscape. An ambient light sensor adjusts brightness to match the current lighting conditions.

E-Books

The digital media equivalent of a conventional printed book is called an e-book (short for electronic book). The Project Gutenberg Online Book Catalog lists over 30,000 free e-books and a total of over 100,000 e-books available. E-books can be downloaded from Project

Figure 3.15

E-book

(Source: Photosani/Shutterstock.com.)

Gutenberg (*www.gutenberg.org*) or many others onto personal computers or dedicated hardware devices known as e-book readers. The devices themselves cost around $250 to $350, and downloads of the bestselling books and new releases cost under $10. The Amazon.com Kindle, the Barnes and Noble Nook, the Samsung Papyrus, and the Sony Reader all use e-paper displays that look like printed pages, store contents without consuming power, and can be viewed using reflected light rather than the backlight required for LCD screens.[38] E-books weigh less than a third of a kilogram, are around one-half inch thick, and come with a display screen ranging from 5 to 8 inches. See Figure 3.15. E-books are more compact than most paperbacks so they can be easily held in one hand. On many e-readers, the size of the text can be magnified for readers with poor vision.

COMPUTER SYSTEM TYPES

In general, computers can be classified as either special purpose or general purpose. *Special-purpose computers* are used for limited applications, for example, by military and scientific research groups such as the RCMP and the National Research Council. Other applications include specialized processors found in appliances, cars, and other products. For example, automobile repair shops connect special-purpose computers to your car's engine to identify specific performance problems.

General-purpose computers are used for a variety of applications and to execute the business applications discussed in this text. General-purpose computer systems can be divided into two major groups: systems used by one user at a time and systems used by multiple concurrent users. Table 3.4 shows the general ranges of capabilities for various types of computer systems. General-purpose computer systems can range from small hand-held computers to massive supercomputers that fill an entire room. We will first cover single-user computer systems.

Table 3.4

Types of Computer Systems

Single-user computer systems can be divided into two groups— portable computers and nonportable computers.

Factor	Single-User Systems				
	Portable Computers				
	Handheld	**Laptop**	**Notebook**	**Notebook**	**Tablet**
Cost	$150–$400	$500–$1,500	$200–$800	$200–$800	$750–$2,500
Weight (kilograms)	< 0.14	< 3.5	< 2.5	< 1.5	< 2.5
Screen size (inches)	2.4–3.6	13.0–15.0	12.0–14.0	7.0–11.0	11.0–14.0
Typical use	Organize personal data	Improve worker productivity	Improve productivity of highly mobile worker	Access the Internet and e-mail	Capture data via pen input, improve worker productivity
	Nonportable Computers				
	Thin Client	**Desktop**	**Nettop**	**Workstation**	
Cost	$200–$800	$500–$2,500	<$300	$750–$5,000	
Weight (kilograms)	< 0.5	< 14	< 2.5	< 16	
Screen Size (inches)	10.0–15.0	13.0–27.0	Comes w/o monitor	13.0–27.0	
typical Use	Enter data and access the Internet	Improve worker productivity	Replace desktop with small, low-cost, low-energy computer	Perform engineering, CAD, and software development	
Factor	Multiple-User Computers				
	Server	**Mainframe**	**Supercomputer**		
Cost	$500–$50,000	> $100,000	> $250,000		
Weight (kilograms)	> 10	> 45	> 45		
Screen size (inches)	n/a	n/a	n/a		
Typical use	Perform network and Internet applications	Perform computing tasks for large organizations and provide massive data storage	Run scientific applications; perform intensive number crunching		

Portable Computers

Many computer manufacturers offer a variety of **portable computers**, those that are small enough to carry easily. Portable computers include hand-held computers, laptop computers, notebook computers, netbook computers, and tablet computers.

Handheld computers are single-user computers that provide ease of portability because of their small size—some are as small as a credit card. These systems often include a variety of software and communications capabilities. Most can communicate with desktop computers over wireless networks. Some even add a built-in GPS receiver with software that can integrate location data into the application. For example, if you click an entry in an electronic address book, the device displays a map and directions from your current location. Such a computer can also be mounted in your car and serve as a navigation system. One of the shortcomings of hand-held computers is that they require a lot of power relative to their size. Personal digital assistants and smartphones are two examples of handheld computers.

A **smartphone** combines the functionality of a mobile phone, camera, Web browser, e-mail tool, MP3 player, and other devices into a single hand-held device. See Figure 3.16.

portable computer
A computer small enough to carry easily.

hand-held computer
A single-user computer that provides ease of portability because of its small size.

smartphone
A phone that combines the functionality of a mobile phone, personal digital assistant, camera, Web browser, e-mail tool, and other devices into a single hand-held device.

Figure 3.16

BlackBerry Torch Smartphone

A smartphone combines the features of a mobile phone, personal digital assistant, camera, Web browser, e-mail tool, and other devices.

(Source: newsphoto/Getstock.com.)

Laptop Computers

A **laptop computer** is a personal computer designed for use by mobile users. It is small and light enough to sit comfortably on a user's lap. Laptop computers use a variety of flat panel technologies to produce a lightweight and thin display screen with good resolution. With regard to computing power, laptop computers can match most desktop computers and come with powerful CPUs as well as large-capacity primary memory and disk storage. This type of computer is highly popular among students and mobile workers who carry their laptops to meetings and classes. Many personal computer users now prefer a laptop computer over a desktop because of its portability, lower energy usage, and smaller space requirements. Since 2008 more portable computers have been sold in Canada than desktop computers.

laptop computer
A personal computer designed for use by mobile users; it is small and light enough to sit comfortably on a user's lap.

Notebook Computers

A **notebook computer** is an extremely lightweight computer that weighs less than 3 kilograms and can easily fit in a briefcase. It is smaller and lighter than a laptop computer.

The Apple MacBook Pro notebook computer is available with a 13-inch, 15-inch, or 17-inch screen, weighs less than 2.5 kilograms, and comes with a built-in battery that lasts up to 7 hours. When Eddie Bauer commissioned Dave Hahn, 15-time conqueror of Mount

notebook computer
Smaller than a laptop computer, an extremely lightweight computer that weighs less than 3 kilograms and can easily fit in a briefcase.

Everest, and a production crew to climb the world's highest peak as a way to promote its line of First Ascent professional climbing gear, the team packed MacBooks so they could blog and post photos and a few minutes of video edited on their computers.[39]

Netbook Computers

Netbook computers are the smallest (screen size of 7 to 10 inches), lightest (under 1.5 kilograms), and least expensive ($200 to $800) members of the laptop computer family. They are great for tasks that do not require a lot of computing power, such as sending and receiving e-mail or accessing the Internet. Many mobile workers have purchased them due to their portability and low cost.

However, netbook computers are not good for users who want to run demanding applications, have many applications open at one time, or need lots of data storage capacity. Netbooks come with a wireless network adapter but without an internal CD or DVD drive, and they have a limited amount of RAM memory and disk space. They often employ the Intel Atom CPU, which is specially designed to run on minimal power so that the computer can use small, lightweight batteries and avoid potential overheating problems without the need for fans and large heat sinks. Acer, Asus, Dell, Hewlett-Packard, MSI, and Toshiba manufacture the popular netbook computer.

netbook computer
The smallest, lightest, least expensive member of the laptop computer family.

Tablet Computers

Tablet computers are portable, lightweight computers with no keyboard that allow you to roam the office, home, or factory floor carrying the device like a clipboard. You can enter text with a writing stylus directly on the screen thanks to built-in handwriting recognition software. Other input methods include an optional keyboard or speech recognition. Tablet PCs that support input only via a writing stylus are called *slate computers*. The *convertible tablet PC* comes with a swivel screen and can be used as a traditional notebook or as a pen-based tablet PC.[40]

Tablet computers are especially popular with students and are frequently used in the health-care, retail, insurance, and manufacturing industries because of their versatility.

tablet computer
A portable, lightweight computer with no keyboard that allows you to roam the office, home, or factory floor carrying the device like a clipboard.

Apple iPad tablet computer.

(Source: ukscapes/Getstock.com.)

The Apple iPad is a tablet computer capable of running the same software that runs on the older Apple iPhone and iPod Touch devices, giving it a library of over 140,000 applications. It also runs software developed specifically for it. The device has a 9.7-inch screen and an on-screen keypad. It weighs 0.7 kilograms and supports Internet access over wireless networks.

Nonportable Single-User Computers

Nonportable single-user computers include thin client computers, desktop computers, nettop computers, and workstations.

thin client
A low-cost, centrally managed computer with essential but limited capabilities and no extra drives (such as CD or DVD drives) or expansion slots.

Thin Clients

A **thin client** is a low-cost, centrally managed computer with no extra drives (such as CD or DVD drives) or expansion slots. These computers have limited capabilities and perform only essential applications, so they remain "thin" with regard to the client applications they include. As stripped-down computers, they do not have the storage capacity or computing power of typical desktop computers, nor do they need it for the role they play. With no hard disk, they never pick up viruses or suffer a hard disk crash. Unlike personal computers, thin clients download data and software from a network when needed, making support, distribution, and updating of software applications much easier and less expensive. Thin-client manufacturers include Hewlett-Packard, Wyse, BOSaNOVA, and DTR Research.

Tokio Marine and Nichido Fire Insurance Company is one of the leading marine insurers in the world. The firm is deploying 30,000 thin-client systems and estimates that the total cost of ownership of the thin clients will be about 30 percent less than deploying full-fledged computers. In addition, because no data is stored on the thin-client systems, the firm will be able to implement a highly secure computing environment that carefully safeguards customer data.[41]

Desktop Computers

desktop computer
A relatively small, inexpensive, single-user computer that is highly versatile.

Desktop computers are single-user computer systems that are highly versatile. Named for their size, desktop computers can provide sufficient computing power, memory, and storage for most business computing tasks.

The Apple iMac is a family of Macintosh desktop computers first introduced in 1998, in which all the components (including the CPU, the disk drives, and so on) fit behind the display screen. The Intel iMac is available with Intel's new core i5 or i7 processors making such machines the first quad-core iMacs.

Nettop Computers

nettop computer
An inexpensive desktop computer designed to be smaller and lighter and consume much less power than a traditional desktop computer.

A **nettop computer** is an inexpensive (under $300) desktop computer designed to be smaller and lighter and to consume one-tenth the power of a traditional desktop computer. Figure 3.17 shows the Dell Studio Hybrid miniature desktop computer, which is about 20 percent the size of a regular desktop computer and uses 70 percent less power.[42] It is designed to perform basic processing tasks such as Internet surfing, document processing, and audio/video playback. Unlike netbook computers, nettop computers are not designed to be portable, they come without a monitor, but they may include an optical drive (CD/DVD). The CPU is typically an Intel Atom, AMD Geode, or another less powerful CPU. The CPU selection reduces the cost of the nettop computer and its power consumption

Figure 3.17

The Dell Studio Hybrid Miniature Desktop Computer

The Dell Studio Hybrid computer looks like an oversized hard drive. It is only about 20 percent the size of a regular desktop computer and uses 70 percent less power.

(Source: © 2011 Dell Inc. All Rights Reserved.)

but limits the processing power of the computer. Businesses are considering using nettop computers because they are inexpensive to buy and run, so they can improve an organization's profitability.

Workstations

Workstations are more powerful than personal computers but still small enough to fit on a desktop. They are used to support engineering and technical users who perform heavy mathematical computing, computer-aided design (CAD), and other applications requiring a high-end processor. Such users need very powerful CPUs, large amounts of main memory, and extremely high-resolution graphic displays. Workstations are typically much more expensive than the average desktop computer.

Blue Sky Studios used powerful workstations for rendering the animated feature *Ice Age: Dawn of the Dinosaurs*. The new workstations provided Blue Sky animators with more powerful design tools to create images for the film in a much shorter time period than previously possible.[43]

Multiple-User Computer Systems

Multiple-user computers are designed to support workgroups from a small department of two or three workers to large organizations with tens of thousands of employees and millions of customers. Multiple-user systems include servers, mainframe computers, and supercomputers.

Servers

A **server** is a computer used by many users to perform a specific task, such as running network or Internet applications. Servers typically have large memory and storage capacities, along with fast and efficient communications abilities. A Web server handles Internet traffic and communications. An enterprise server stores and provides access to programs that meet the needs of an entire organization. A file server stores and coordinates program and data files. Server systems consist of multi-user computers, including supercomputers, mainframes, and other servers. Often an organization will house a large number of servers in the same room where access to the machines can be controlled and authorized support personnel can more easily manage and maintain them from this single location. Such a facility is called a *server farm*.

The amazing 3D images of a futuristic world and the blue creatures from the movie *Avatar* were created by Weta Digital, Ltd., a visual effects company near Wellington, New Zealand. The 3D image rendering was performed on some 4,000 Hewlett-Packard blade servers in Weta's 10,000-square-foot server farm.[44]

Servers offer great **scalability**, the ability to increase the processing capability of a computer system so that it can handle more users, more data, or more transactions in a given period. Scalability is increased by adding more, or more powerful, processors. *Scaling up* adds more powerful processors, and *scaling out* adds many more equal (or even less powerful) processors to increase the total data-processing capacity.

Intel's Xeon chip line includes a design called the Nehalem-EX processor, which is targeted for more powerful servers. The processor has up to eight chips and supports a technology called hyperthreading, which enables each chip to conduct two sets of instructions, called threads. This means that the eight-chip processor could perform up to 16 tasks at once.[45]

Server manufacturers are also competing heavily to reduce the power required to operate their servers and making "performance per watt" a key part of their product differentiation strategy. Low power usage is a critical factor for organizations that run server farms of hundreds or even thousands of servers. Typical servers draw up to 220 watts, while new servers based on Intel's Atom microprocessor draw eight or less watts. The annual power savings from such low-energy usage servers can amount to tens of thousands of dollars.[46]

A virtual server is a method of logically dividing the resources of a single physical server to create multiple logical servers, each acting as its own dedicated machine. The

workstation
A more powerful personal computer used for mathematical computing, computer-aided design, and other high-end processing, but still small enough to fit on a desktop.

server
A computer used by many users to perform a specific task, such as running network or Internet applications.

scalability
The ability to increase the processing capability of a computer system so that it can handle more users, more data, or more transactions in a given period.

server administrator uses software to divide one physical server into many isolated virtual environments. For example, a single physical Web server might be divided into two virtual private servers. One of the virtual servers hosts the organization's live website, while the other hosts a copy of the website. The second private virtual server is used to test and verify updates to software before changes are made to the live website. The use of virtual servers is growing rapidly. In a typical data centre deployment of several hundred servers, companies using virtualization can build 12 virtual machines to every actual server with a resulting savings in capital and operating expenses (including energy costs) of millions of dollars per year. Gartner estimates that by 2012 nearly half of server workloads will run on virtual servers.[47]

blade server
A server that houses many individual computer motherboards that include one or more processors, computer memory, computer storage, and computer network connections.

The Dell Power Edge 1855 Chassis can hold up to 10 blade servers.

(Source: © 2011 Dell Inc. All Rights Reserved.)

A **blade server** houses many computer motherboards that include one or more processors, computer memory, computer storage, and computer network connections. These all share a common power supply and air-cooling source within a single chassis. By placing many blades into a single chassis, and then mounting multiple chassis in a single rack, the blade server is more powerful but less expensive than traditional systems based on mainframes or server farms of individual computers. In addition, the blade server approach requires much less physical space than traditional server farms.

Mainframe Computers

A **mainframe computer** is a large, powerful computer shared by dozens or even hundreds of concurrent users connected to the machine over a network. The mainframe computer must reside in a data centre with special heating, ventilating, and air-conditioning (HVAC) equipment to control temperature, humidity, and dust levels. In addition, most mainframes are kept in a secure data centre with limited access to the room. The construction and maintenance of a controlled-access room with HVAC can add hundreds of thousands of dollars to the cost of owning and operating a mainframe computer.

mainframe computer
A large, powerful computer often shared by hundreds of concurrent users connected to the machine via terminals.

The role of the mainframe is undergoing some remarkable changes as lower-cost, single-user computers become increasingly powerful. Many computer jobs that used to run on mainframe computers have migrated onto these smaller, less-expensive computers. This information-processing migration is called *computer downsizing*.

Mainframe computers have been the workhorses of corporate computing for more than 50 years. They can support hundreds of users simultaneously and can handle all of the core functions of a corporation.

(Source: Courtesy of IBM Corporation.)

The new role of the mainframe is as a large information-processing and data-storage utility for a corporation—running jobs too large for other computers, storing files and databases too large to be stored elsewhere, and storing backups of files and databases created elsewhere. For example, the mainframe can handle the millions of daily transactions associated with airline, automobile, and hotel and motel reservation systems. It can process the tens of thousands of daily queries necessary to provide data to decision support systems. Its massive storage and input/output capabilities enable it to play the role of a video computer, providing full-motion video to many concurrent users.

Telus Corporation is the second-largest telecommunications company in Canada and employs seven mainframe computers with a total processing power of 3,800 MIPs. Hundreds of Telus business applications run on these computers. In addition, Telus provides hosting services for its customers so they can meet their organization's data processing needs by using Telus mainframe computers.[48] "We have to run our business effectively, and first and foremost that means running IT efficiently," says Brad Palmer, director of Western Canada IT services at Telus.[49]

Supercomputers

Supercomputers are the most powerful computers with the fastest processing speed and highest performance. They are *special-purpose machines* designed for applications that require extensive and rapid computational capabilities. Originally, supercomputers were used primarily by government agencies to perform the high-speed number crunching needed in weather forecasting and military applications. With recent reductions in the cost of these machines, they are now used more broadly for commercial purposes.

supercomputers
The most powerful computer systems with the fastest processing speeds.

IBM is building the world's fastest computer for the U.S. Department of Energy for delivery in 2011. The Sequoia supercomputer will be able to perform calculations at the astonishing rate of 20 petaflops, or 20 quadrillion floating point operations per second. Table 3.5 describes the processing speeds of supercomputers. To put this into perspective, in one hour

Speed	Meaning
Gigaflops	1×10^9 flops
Teraflops	1×10^{12} flops
Petaflops	1×10^{15} flops

Table 3.5

Supercomputer Processing Speeds

the Sequoia will be able to perform a series of calculations that would take the entire population of the world over 320 years to complete using pocket calculators. Sequoia will be highly energy efficient for the job it does and will occupy 96 refrigerator-sized racks in a 3,400-square-foot room.[50] Table 3.6 lists the five most powerful supercomputers in use as of June 2010.[51]

Table 3.6

Five Most Powerful Operational Supercomputers (June 2010)[52]

Rank	System	Manufacturer	Location	Country	Speed (petaflops)
1	Jaguar	Cray	Department of Energy's Oak Ridge Laboratory	USA	1.759
2	Nebulae	Dawning	National Supercomputing Centre in Shenzhen	China	1.271
3	Roadrunner	IBM	Department of Energy's Los Alamos National Laboratory	USA	1.042
4	Kraken	Cray	National Institute for Computational Sciences/ University of Tennessee	USA	0.831
5	Jugene BlueGene/P	IBM	Forschungszentrum Juelich Research Center	Germany	0.826

IBM's Sequoia will be the fastest supercomputer in the world when it becomes operational in 2012 and can perform calculations at the rate of 20 petaflops—equivalent to an astounding 3 million computations by every human on the planet each second!

(Source: Courtesy of IBM Corporation.)

ETHICAL AND SOCIETAL ISSUES

Electronics Manufacturers Face the Global E-Waste Problem

The world is consuming and discarding increasing amounts of electronics products every year. The United States Environmental Protection Agency estimates that "over 2 billion computers, televisions, wireless devices, printers, gaming systems, and other devices have been sold since 1980." Have you considered where those devices end up when they become obsolete or worn out? It turns out that a large percentage of them are shipped to third-world countries where they are dismantled in salvaging operations that strip out valuable metals and burn the remaining parts. Ghana, Nigeria, Pakistan, India, and China have become the world's primary dumpsters for electronics salvaging.

The real problem with electronics waste, or e-waste, lies in the use of toxic heavy materials such as mercury, cadmium, beryllium, and lead, along with PVC plastic and hazardous chemicals like brominated flame retardants (BFR) that are included in electronics components. When dumped in landfills, these toxic components leach into the land over time and are released into the atmosphere. Burning computer components also releases these toxic components into the atmosphere, with deadly results to the people doing the burning in the short term, and a gradual eroding of the global environment in the long term.

The third-world countries that salvage electronics rarely take environmental precautions. Children are often used as labour, becoming sick after prolonged exposure to the toxic waste.

Organizations such as Greenpeace are going to great lengths to call attention to this global problem. They are encouraging electronics manufacturers to eliminate toxic materials from the products they sell. They also encourage manufacturers to provide incentives for their customers to properly recycle electronics devices when they are through with them. In its annual "Guide to Greener Electronics," Greenpeace ranks technology companies on their level of "green-ness" based on each company's manufacturing and recycling practices. For example, currently Nokia is ranked greenest due to its comprehensive voluntary take-back programs and recycling practices. Samsung is number two because it removed PVC from its LCD displays, BFR from some of its cell phones, and halogen from its chips and semiconductors. While Nokia and Samsung earned high points from Greenpeace, no company is currently ranked as being 100 percent green, and most are listed in the red with a lot of improvements still needed.

Some manufacturers are seeing green manufacturing practices as a method of gaining market share. The growing population of environmentally conscious consumers prefers to do business with green businesses. Apple has invested heavily in building its green reputation. It has worked to remove or dramatically reduce the amount of lead in its displays. It has eliminated or reduced dangerous chemicals, including arsenic and mercury, and compounds such as PVC and BFR. Apple operates recycling programs in 93 percent of the countries where Macs, iPhones, and iPods are sold. It even reduced packaging materials to a minimum to save trees and eliminate Styrofoam.

Apple is not unique in its efforts to reduce and safeguard e-waste but is considered the most progressive PC manufacturer by Greenpeace. Most other PC manufacturers are following suit. However, soon "going green" may not be a voluntary decision for electronics manufacturing. Legislation has been proposed in many Canadian provinces to address the e-waste issue. Legislation addresses how to manage current e-waste, develop recycling programs, and eliminate the use of toxic materials in electronics. Canada has fallen behind other countries in responding to the problem. The European Union has already passed two directives to deal with e-waste: the Restriction on the Use of Hazardous Substances (RoHS) and the Waste Electrical and Electronic Equipment (WEEE).

With increased attention turning toward the e-waste problem, optimism is increasing. One study estimates that if recycling initiatives continue to expand, the e-waste problem should reach a peak global volume of 73 million metric tons by 2015, and then begin to decline.

Discussion Questions

1. What concerns have been raised over e-waste?
2. What actions can electronics manufacturers take to address the e-waste problem?

Critical Thinking Questions

1. What laws, if any, do you think are necessary to address this problem? Why?
2. How might the global community cooperate to help speed up recovery?

SOURCES: Johnston, Casey, "Legislation Seeks to Deal with Growing Piles of E-Waste," *Ars Technica*, http://arstechnica.com, November 1, 2009; Lombardi, Candace, "Study: E-Waste Build-up Will Plateau by 2015," CNET news, *http://news.cnet.com*, May 6, 2009; Greenpeace E-Waste website, *www.greenpeace.org/international/campaigns/toxics/electronics*, accessed January 1, 2010; A Greener Apple Web page, *www.apple.com/hotnews/agreenerapple*, accessed January 1, 2010.

GREEN COMPUTING

Green computing is concerned with the efficient and environmentally responsible design, manufacture, operation, and disposal of IS related products, including all types of computers, printers, and printer materials, including cartridges and toner. Business organizations recognize that going green is in their best interests with regard to public relations, safety of employees, and the community at large. They also recognize that green computing presents an opportunity to substantially reduce total costs over the life cycle of their IS equipment. Green computing has three goals: reduce the use of hazardous material, enable companies to lower their power-related costs, and enable the safe disposal or recycling of some 700,000 tons of computers each year.

Computers contain many toxic substances, including beryllium, brominated flame retardants, cadmium, lead, mercury, polyvinyl chloride, and selenium. As a result, electronic manufacturing employees and suppliers at all steps along the supply chain and in the manufacturing process are at risk of unhealthy exposure. Computer users can also be exposed to these substances when using poorly designed or damaged devices. It is impossible to ensure safe recycling or disposal and so it's thought best to eliminate the use of toxic substances.[53] Indeed, recycling of used computers, monitors, and printers has raised concerns about toxicity and carcinogenicity of some of the substances. In many cases, recycling companies export large quantities of used electronics to companies in undeveloped countries. The disposal and reclamation operations must be extremely careful to avoid unsafe exposure in recycling operations and leaching of materials such as heavy metals from landfills and incinerator ashes. Unfortunately, many of these countries do not have strong environmental laws, and they sometimes fail to recognize the potential dangers of dealing with hazardous materials. In their defence, these countries point out that first-world countries were allowed to develop robust economies and rise up out of poverty without the restrictions of strict environmental policies.

One of the earliest initiatives toward green computing was the voluntary labelling program known as Energy Star. It was conceived of by the Environmental Protection Agency in 1992 to promote energy efficiency in hardware of all kinds. This resulted in the widespread adoption of sleep mode for electronic products. For example, the Windows Vista operating software has a broad set of centrally managed features that can help reduce power consumption by personal computers and monitors. "Sleep" is a low-power state that stores documents and programs running on the desktop in memory so that users can resume work quickly without going through a lengthy boot-up process.

The European Union Directive 2002/95/EC required that as of July 2006, all new electrical and electronic equipment cannot contain any of six banned substances in quantities exceeding certain maximum concentration values. The six banned substances are lead, mercury, cadmium, hexavalent chromium, polybrominated biphenyls, and polybrominated diphenylethers.[54] This directive applies to Canadian organizations selling equipment to members of the European Union and has encouraged Canadian manufacturers to meet the standards as well.

The Green Electronics Council manages the Electronic Product Environment Assessment Tool (EPEAT) to assist in the evaluation and purchase of green computing systems. The EPEAT assesses products against 51 life-cycle environmental criteria developed by representatives of the environmental community, manufacturers, private and public purchasers, resellers, recyclers, and other interested parties. These criteria are documented in IEEE Standard 1680 and have to do with the reduction of hazardous materials, the use of recycled materials, the design for recovery through recycling systems, product longevity, energy conservation, end of life management, the manufacturer's corporate environmental policy, and packaging.[55] The products evaluated against the EPEAT criteria are placed into one of three tiers based on their rating, as shown in Table 3.7. Table 3.8 shows the EPEAT ratings of three computer types.[56] (Both tables are on the next page.)

green computing
A program concerned with the efficient and environmentally responsible design, manufacture, operation, and disposal of IS related products.

Table 3.7

EPEAT Product Tiers

Tier	Number of Required Criteria That Must Be Met	Number of Optional Criteria That Must Be Met
Bronze	All 23	None
Silver	All 23	At least 50%
Gold	All 23	At least 75%

Table 3.8

EPEAT Ratings for Computers Registered in Canada

Computer Type	Bronze	Silver	Gold
Desktops	1	16	104
Notebooks	0	217	249
Workstations	0	0	13

Computer manufacturers such as Apple, Dell, and Hewlett-Packard have long competed on the basis of price and performance. As the difference among the manufacturers in these two arenas narrows, support for green computing is emerging as a new business strategy for these companies to distinguish themselves from the competition. Apple claims to have the "greenest lineup of notebooks" and is making progress at removing toxic chemicals. Dell's new mantra is to become "the greenest technology company on Earth." Hewlett-Packard highlights its long tradition of environmentalism and is improving its packaging to reduce use of materials. Hewlett-Packard is also urging computer users around the world to shut down their computers at the end of the day to save energy and reduce carbon emissions.

SUMMARY

Principle:

Computer hardware must be carefully selected to meet the evolving needs of the organization and its supporting information systems.

Computer hardware should be selected to meet specific user and business requirements. These requirements can evolve and change over time.

The central processing unit (CPU) and memory cooperate to execute data processing. The CPU has three main components: the arithmetic/logic unit (ALU), the control unit, and the register areas. Instructions are executed in a two-phase process called a machine cycle, which includes the instruction phase and the execution phase.

Computer system processing speed is affected by clock speed, which is measured in gigahertz (GHz). As the clock speed of the CPU increases, heat is generated that can corrupt the data and instructions the computer is trying to process. Bigger heat sinks, fans, and other components are required to eliminate the excess heat. This excess heat can also raise safety issues.

Primary storage, or memory, provides working storage for program instructions and data to be processed and provides them to the CPU. Storage capacity is measured in bytes. The chip set coordinates the communication between the CPU and other components of the computer.

A common form of memory is random access memory (RAM). RAM is volatile; loss of power to the computer erases its contents. RAM comes in many different varieties, including dynamic RAM (DRAM), synchronous DRAM (SDRAM), Double Data Rate SDRAM, and DDR2 SDRAM.

Read-only memory (ROM) is nonvolatile and contains permanent program instructions for execution by the CPU. Other nonvolatile memory types include programmable read-only memory (PROM), erasable programmable read-only memory (EPROM), electrically erasable PROM, and flash memory.

Cache memory is a type of high-speed memory that CPUs can access more rapidly than RAM.

A multicore microprocessor is one that combines two or more independent processors into a single computer so they can share the workload. Intel and AMD have introduced quad-core processors that are effective in working on problems involving large databases and multimedia.

Parallel computing is the simultaneous execution of the same task on many processors to obtain results more quickly. Massively parallel processing involves linking many processors to work together to solve complex problems.

Grid computing is the use of a collection of computers, often owned by many individuals or organizations, to work in a coordinated manner to solve a common problem.

Computer systems can store larger amounts of data and instructions in secondary storage, which is less volatile and has greater capacity than memory. The primary characteristics of secondary storage media and devices include access method, capacity, portability, and cost. Storage media can implement either sequential access or direct access. Common forms of secondary storage include magnetic storage devices such as tape, magnetic disk, virtual tape; optical storage devices such as optical disk, digital video disk (DVD), and holographic versatile disk (HVD), and solid state storage devices such as flash drives.

Redundant array of independent/inexpensive disks (RAID) is a method of storing data that generates extra bits of data from existing data, allowing the system to more easily recover data in the event of a hardware failure.

Network-attached storage (NAS) and storage area networks (SAN) are alternative forms of data storage that enable an organization to share data resources among a much larger number of computers and users for improved storage efficiency and greater cost-effectiveness.

The overall trend in secondary storage is toward direct-access methods, higher capacity, increased portability, and automated storage management. Interest in renting space on massive storage devices is increasing.

Input and output devices allow users to provide data and instructions to the computer for processing and allow subsequent storage and output. These devices are part of a user interface through which human beings interact with computer systems.

Data is placed in a computer system in a two-stage process: data entry converts human-readable data into machine-readable form; data input then transfers it to the computer. Common input devices include a keyboard, a mouse, speech recognition, digital cameras, terminals, scanning devices, optical data readers, magnetic ink character recognition devices, magnetic stripe cards, chip-and-PIN cards, contactless cards, point-of-sale devices, automated teller machines, pen input devices, touch-sensitive screens, bar-code scanners, and Radio Frequency Identification tags.

Display monitor quality is determined by aspect ratio, size, colour, and resolution. Liquid crystal display and organic light-emitting diode technology is enabling improvements in the resolution and size of computer monitors. Other output devices include printers, plotters, and digital audio players, and e-books.

Computer systems are generally divided into two categories: single user and multiple users. Single-user systems include hand-held, laptop, portable, thin client, desktop, and workstation computers.

Multi-user systems include servers, blade servers, mainframes, and supercomputers.

Principle:

The computer hardware industry is rapidly changing and is highly competitive, creating an environment ripe for technological breakthroughs.

CPU processing speed is limited by physical constraints such as the distance between circuitry points and circuitry materials. Moore's Law is a hypothesis stating that the number of transistors on a single chip doubles every two years. This hypothesis has been accurate since it was introduced in 1970.

Advances in tri-gate transistors, carbon nanotubes, and extreme miniaturization will result in faster CPUs.

Cell Broadband Engine Architecture is a microprocessor architecture developed by IBM, Sony, and Toshiba to provide more power-efficient, cost-effective, and higher-performance processing. This technology has numerous applications.

Manufacturers are competing to develop a nonvolatile memory chip that requires minimal power, offers extremely fast write speed, and can store data accurately even after it has been stored and written over many times. Such a chip could eliminate the need for RAM forms of memory. PCM, FeRAM, and MRAM are three potential solutions.

Principle:

The computer hardware industry and users are implementing green computing designs and products.

Green computing is concerned with the efficient and environmentally responsible design, manufacture, operation, and disposal of IT-related products.

Business organizations recognize that going green can reduce costs and is in their best interests with regard to public relations, safety of employees, and the community at large.

Three specific goals of green computing are to reduce the use of hazardous material, lower power-related costs, and enable the safe disposal and/or recycling of IT products.

Three key green computing initiatives are the Energy Star program to promote energy efficiency, the European Union Directive 2002/95/EC to reduce the use of hazardous materials, and use of the EPEAT tool to evaluate and purchase green computing systems.

CHAPTER 3: SELF-ASSESSMENT TEST

Computer hardware must be carefully selected to meet the evolving needs of the organization and its supporting information systems.

1. Obsolete computer hardware can place an organization at a competitive disadvantage. True or False?
2. The computer hardware that most organizations choose is virtually identical. True or False?
3. The overriding consideration for a business in making hardware decisions should be how the hardware supports the objectives of the information system and _____ of the organization.
4. Which represents a larger amount of data_____a terabyte or a gigabyte?
5. Which of the following components performs mathematical calculations and makes logical comparisons?
   a. the control unit
   b. the register
   c. the ALU
   d. the main memory
6. Executing an instruction by the CPU involves two phases: the instruction phase and the_____ phase.
7. _____ involves capturing and editing data when it is originally created and in a form that can be directly input to a computer, thus ensuring accuracy and timeliness.

The computer hardware industry is rapidly changing and highly competitive, creating an environment ripe for technological breakthroughs.

8. Many computer jobs that used to run on mainframe computers have migrated onto smaller, less expensive computers. This information-processing migration is called _____.
9. The transistor densities on a single chip double every two years. True or False?

The computer hardware industry and users are implementing green computing designs and products.

10. Green computing is about saving the environment; there are no real business benefits associated with this program. True or False?
11. The disposal and reclamation operations for IT equipment must be careful to avoid unsafe exposure to _____.

CHAPTER 3: SELF-ASSESSMENT TEST ANSWERS

(1) True (2) False (3) goals (4) terabyte (5) c (6) execution (7) Source data automation (8) computer downsizing (9) True (10) False (11) hazardous materials

REVIEW QUESTIONS

1. When determining the appropriate hardware components of a new information system, what role must the user of the system play?
2. What is the role of the chip set? How is it related to the CPU?

3. Identify and briefly discuss the fundamental characteristic that distinguishes RAM from ROM memory.
4. What is RFID technology? Identify three practical uses for this technology.

5. What issues can arise when the CPU runs at a very fast clock speed? What measures are manufacturers taking to deal with this problem?
6. What advantages do fuel cells offer over batteries for use in portable electronic devices? Do they have any disadvantages?
7. What is the difference between data entry and data input?
8. What is RAID storage technology?
9. Outline and briefly explain the two-phase process for executing machine-level instructions.
10. Why are the hardware components of a computer described as interdependent?
11. Identify the three components of the CPU and explain the role of each.

12. Distinguish between a netbook computer and a laptop computer. Distinguish between a nettop and desktop computer.
13. Identify three types of optical data storage devices. Compare them with regard to access method, capacity, portability, and cost per GB of storage.
14. Identify and briefly describe the various classes of desktop computers.
15. What is source data automation?
16. What is the overall trend in secondary storage devices?
17. Define the term "green computing" and state the primary goals of this program.
18. What is the EPEAT tool? How is it used?

DISCUSSION QUESTIONS

1. Briefly describe the concept of multiprocessing. How does parallel processing differ from multiprocessing?
2. Briefly discuss the advantages and disadvantages of installing thin clients for use in a university student computer lab versus nettop computers.
3. What is a quad-core processor? What advantages does it offer users? Are there any potential disadvantages?
4. Describe a practical business application that justifies the use of a multiple-monitor solution.
5. Briefly describe Moore's Law. What are the implications of this law? Are there any practical limitations to Moore's Law?
6. Identify and briefly discuss the advantages and disadvantages of solid state secondary storage devices compared to magnetic secondary storage devices.

7. Briefly discuss the advantages and disadvantages of attached storage, network-attached storage, and storage area networks in meeting enterprise data storage challenges.
8. If cost were not an issue, describe the characteristics of your ideal computer. What would you use it for? Would you choose a hand-held, portable, desktop, or workstation computer? Why?
9. How should organizations allocate grid computing resources so they address only the most important research projects?
10. Discuss potential issues that can arise if an organization is not careful in selecting a reputable service organization to recycle or dispose of its IS equipment.

PROBLEM-SOLVING EXERCISES

1. Use word-processing software to document what your needs are as a computer user and your justification for selecting either a desktop or portable computer. Find a website that allows you to order and customize a computer, and select those options that best meet your needs in a cost-effective manner. Assume that you have a budget of $750. Enter the computer specifications and associated costs from the website into an Excel spreadsheet that you cut and paste into the document defining your needs. E-mail the document to your instructor.

2. Develop a spreadsheet that compares the features, initial purchase price, and ongoing operating costs (paper, cartridges, and toner) for three colour laser printers. Now do the same for three inkjet printers. Write a brief memo on which printer you would choose and why. Cut and paste the spreadsheet into a document.
3. Use a database program to document at least six different computer CPUs, their manufacturers, and their associated chip sets.

TEAM ACTIVITIES

1. With one or two of your classmates, visit a retail store that employs Radio Frequency Identification chips to track inventory. Interview an employee involved in inventory control, and document the advantages and disadvantages they see in this technology.

2. With two or three of your classmates, visit a computer retail store and identify the most popular netbook or nettop computers. Interview members of the sales staff to find out why they think this particular computer is popular. Document the results of your interview.

WEB EXERCISES

1. Do research on the Web to identify the current state of development and production of advanced technology secondary storage devices. What are some of the most promising devices? What issues are associated with mass-producing these new devices? Write a brief report summarizing your findings.

2. Do research on the Web to learn more about the Electronic Product Environment Assessment Tool and the criteria it uses to evaluate products. Use the EPEAT tool to find out the rating for your current computer. Which company seems to have the greenest notebook computers? Write a brief report summarizing your findings.

CAREER EXERCISES

1. Imagine that you are going to buy a single hand-held device to improve your communication capabilities and organizational abilities. What tasks do you need it to perform? What features would you look for in this device? Visit a computer store or a consumer electronics store and identify the specific device and manufacturer that comes closest to meeting your needs at a cost under $325.

2. Your organization plans to acquire 250 new portable computers. The finance vice president has asked you to lead a project team assigned to define users' computer hardware needs and recommend the most cost-effective solution for meeting those needs. Who else (role, department) and how many people would you select to be a member of the team? How would you go about defining users' needs? Do you think that only one kind of portable computer will meet everyone's needs? Should you define multiple portable computers based on the needs of various classes of end user? What business justification can you define to substantiate this expenditure of roughly $250,000?

CASE STUDIES

Case One

Richard Ivey School of Business
The University of Western Ontario

Ivey

Ivey
Publishing

CAA Roadside App[1]

Professor Derrick Neufeld wrote this case solely to provide material for class discussion. The author does not intend to illustrate either effective or ineffective handling of a managerial situation.

---

1 This case has been written on the basis of published sources only. Consequently, the interpretation and perspectives presented in this case are not necessarily those of the Canadian Automobile Association or any of its employees.

The author may have disguised certain names and other identifying information to protect confidentiality.

Richard Ivey School of Business Foundation prohibits any form of reproduction, storage or transmission without its written permission. Reproduction of this material is not covered under authorization by any reproduction rights organization. To order copies or request permission to reproduce materials, contact Ivey Publishing, Richard Ivey School of Business Foundation, The University of Western Ontario, London, Ontario, Canada, N6A 3K7; phone (519) 661-3208; fax (519) 661-3882; e-mail cases@ivey.uwo.ca.

Copyright © 2010, Richard Ivey School of Business Foundation Version: 2010-11-04

Newsflash

"Couple stranded on logging road found safe and sound."

The 70-something couple was delivering phone books to neighbourhood residents in their remote Nova Scotia community but got their car stuck in a ditch on some back logging roads. A cell phone call to the RCMP might have solved their problem, except that the man and woman had become disoriented and were unable to explain where they were to the RCMP dispatcher.

This is exactly the kind of situation that the Canadian Automobile Association's (CAA) free Apple iPhone app, CAA Roadside, is designed to solve. Using this mobile application, a stranded motorist can quickly request roadside assistance at the tap of an icon. A message that includes the driver's CAA registration number, along with their iPhone location data, is automatically composed and forwarded to the CAA dispatch office. Once the dispatcher receives the message, assistance is sent to the coordinates. The app eliminates the need to call a number, wait on hold, recite a membership number, or explain a geographical location (although it does allow the driver to optionally speak with the CAA dispatcher, request 911 emergency assistance, or identify the closest CAA-approved auto repair locations).

"The number of Canadians that own iPhones is growing and this is just one of the ways that this technology is being adopted to improve our services," says Frank Fotia, CAA vice president of insurance, automotive, and corporate affairs. "Furthermore, this technology is not only handy to iPhone users, but it's also useful for our hearing-impaired members who can now request assistance electronically."

Location-aware technology finds its early origins in the Global Positioning System (GPS), a satellite-based navigational system created in 1973 by the U.S. Department of Defense. Since the U.S. government opened up this proprietary technology to commercial interests, a large GPS industry has emerged, and the technology has continued to evolve and expand. Today, mobile devices such as the Apple iPhone, BlackBerry Bold, and Motorola Droid provide robust location-aware hardware platforms by combining assisted GPS, digital compass, wifi, and cellular technologies. By using the software development kits (SDKs) and application programming interfaces (APIs) offered by these manufacturers, organizations can generate and deploy useful new apps to users very quickly and at low cost. There are many interesting location-aware applications, such as Google Maps, which can help you locate the nearest Starbucks, Tim Hortons, or nutritionist's office, and Proximate Global's face2face, which can help you find your nearby social networking friends.

Fortunately, the story of the stranded couple had a happy ending when a logging crew stumbled upon and rescued the elderly pair. Unfortunately, this was only after significant resources had already been expended by the RCMP, the Pictou County Ground Search Team, and the Department of Natural Resources, which had dispatched a helicopter search team.

Discussion Questions

1. What are the potential benefits to CAA of providing clients with the CAA Roadside app?
2. Was CAA wise to build this on the Apple iPhone platform as opposed to, say, the BlackBerry or Motorola platforms?
3. How might location-based technology that is built into mobile devices change the way you do things in the future?

SOURCES: J. Van Grove, "Mobile App Pinpoints Nearby Facebook and Twitter Friends," *Mashable/Tech*, July 10, 2010, *http://mashable.com/2010/07/10/ face2face/*, accessed July 21, 2010. "Couple Stranded on Logging Road Found Safe and Sound," *The New Glasgow News*, July 15, 2010, *http://www.ngnews.ca/ News/Local/2010-07-15/article-1570825/Couple-stranded-on-logging-road-found-safe-and-sound/1*, accessed July 20, 2010. "New CAA iPhone Application Enhances Assistance to Stranded Motorists," CAA News Release, July 6, 2010, *http://www. caa.ca/newsroom/newsroom-releases-details-e.cfm?newsItem=36&yearToShow=2010*, accessed July 20, 2010. Wikipedia, "Global Positioning System," *http:// en.wikipedia.org/wiki/Global_Positioning_System*, accessed July 20, 2010.

Case Two

Pepsi Bottler Goes Virtual

The G&J Pepsi-Cola Bottling Company employs over 1,600 people and uses a number of information systems, including Microsoft SharePoint, Microsoft Exchange, Microsoft SQL Server, and Oracle databases and file servers, all running on 78 servers from Dell and HP. That is, they were running on 78 servers until recently, when G&J's information systems manager, Christian Messer, performed what may seem like a miracle. He reduced the number of servers from 78 to 16 without any loss of system performance and with additional benefits.

Messer pulled off this feat by using virtualization technologies. You learned in this chapter that virtualization is a method of logically dividing the resources of a single physical server to create multiple logical servers, each acting as its own dedicated machine. Virtualization makes it possible to take advantage of unused resources on a single server. Prior to moving to virtualization, G&J was using only 10 percent of the computing resources available in its 78 servers.

Today, G&J uses 16 quad-core blade servers for a total of 64 processor cores. Messer uses VMware's hypervisor software to run two virtual machines on each core. G&J's server room looks bare these days with 16 physical servers rather than 78. Now running eight virtual servers each, the physical server is working much closer to its full potential. Messer figures that even with the dramatic reduction in servers, he is still only using 50 percent of the server's potential, which allows plenty of room for growth.

Along with virtual server technology, G&J has also invested in moving its storage hardware from tape drives to Dell's EqualLogic iSCSI storage-area network (SAN). The EqualLogic storage system uses virtual storage, which coordinates with the virtual servers' requirements. Messer believes that virtual storage is a must if you want to take full advantage of virtual servers. The combination has vastly reduced G&J's system recovery time. Recently, G&J's SQL server crashed. With its previous system, the recovery time would have taken eight to ten hours. With virtualization, the down time lasted only a half hour.

Virtualization provides many savings. It reduces space and energy requirements. It reduces hardware and maintenance costs. It also reduces system down time. Messer calculates that the new virtualized servers and storage saves the Pepsi bottler between $11,000 and $13,000 per year.

Discussion Questions

1. How did G&J reduce their servers from 78 to 16 without any loss in services?
2. What benefits do the combination of virtual servers and virtual storage provide?

Critical Thinking Questions

1. After hearing about the benefits of virtualization, what reasons might a company have for *not* immediately switching to virtual server technology?
2. How might a business use virtualization technologies to realize "green" advantages?

SOURCES: Brodkin, Jon, "Pepsi Bottler Swallows Skepticism, Gives Virtualization a Go," itBusiness.com, *www.itbusiness.ca*, December 15, 2008; G&J Pepsi Bottling Co. History, *www.gjpepsi.com/Columbus/history.asp*, accessed January 2, 2010.

Questions for Web Case

See the website for this book to read about the Altitude Online case for this chapter. Following are questions concerning this Web case.

Altitude Online: Choosing Hardware

Discussion Questions

1. How might Altitude Online determine what new hardware devices it requires to support the service that its employees use?
2. How will Altitude Online determine the computing power and storage requirements of the new system?

Critical Thinking Questions

1. What should Altitude Online do with its old computer hardware as it is replaced with new hardware?
2. Why do you think Altitude Online decided to phase in new desktop computers but replace mobile devices all at once?

NOTES

Sources for the opening vignette: IBM staff, "Turboinštitut Powers Green Energy Research with IBM BladeCenter," IBM Success Story, *www-01.ibm.com/software/success/cssdb.nsf/CS/ARBN-7T5LKQ?OpenDocument&Site=powersystems&cty=en_us*, June 26, 2009; Turboinštitut website, *www.turboinstitut.si*, accessed October 5, 2010; LSC ADRIA Web page, *www.turboinstitut.si/index.php?option=com_content&task=view&id=62*, accessed October 5, 2010.

1 Papp, David, "Manufacturer Boosts Productivity, Morale with IT overhaul," *PCworld*, July 9, 2010.
2 Thibodeau, Patrick, "U.S. Buys Weather Supercomputer with Twin Backup," *Computerworld*, September 8, 2009.
3 Toshiba Corporation, "Toshiba Launches Direct Methanol Fuel Cell in Japan as External Power for Mobile Electronic Devices," Press release, *www.toshiba.com/taec/news/press_releases/2009/dmfc_09_580.jsp*, October 22, 2009.
4 "Moore's Law Marches on at Intel," *PhysOrg.com*, *www.physorg.com/news172852816.html*, September 22, 2009.
5 Shah, Agam, "Intel's New Core i7 Chips Surface on Retail Sites," *Computerworld*, May 27, 2009.
6 Lai, Eric, "AMD's Latest Quad-Core Phenom CPU Ups Its Game," *Computerworld*, August 13, 2009.
7 Crothers, Brooke, "IBM Launches Power7 Chip, Systems," *Cnet*, February 7, 2010.
8 Keizer, Gregg, "iPhone 3G S Reveals 3x Speed Boost," *Computerworld*, June 19, 2009.
9 Shah, Agam, "Nvidia Launches Its Fastest Laptop Chip," *Computerworld*, March 3, 2009.
10 ACMA Computers, "Success Stories," Acma Computers website, *www.acma.com/acma/Casestudy.asp*, accessed January 16, 2010.
11 Shread, Paul, "Big Blue Takes on Swine Flu," *Grid Computing Planet*, May 12, 2009.
12 Forrester Consulting, "2009 Data Protection Budgets, Priorities, and Technology Adoption," Study commissioned by Hewlett-Packard Corporation, February 6, 2009.
13 Whitcomb, Aber, "MySpace Figures Out How to Do Massive Data Analysis on Commodity Systems," *InfoWorld*, May 26, 2009.
14 Perez, Juan Carlos, "MySpace to Open Source In-House Data Analysis," *IT World*, September 15, 2009.
15 "Media Distributors Introduces Industry's Most Affordable RAID Storage Solution for Professional Video Production Customers," Green Technology website, *http://green.tmcnet.com/news/2009/09/17/4375055.htm*, September 17, 2009.
16 Data Domain, "Boston Medical Center Presents on Reducing IT Costs and Simplifying Storage Management Using Data Domain," Press release, February 20, 2009.
17 Clark, Don, "SanDisk Says New Chips Will Lower Production Costs," *Wall Street Journal*, October 13, 2009.
18 "Mid-Sized Enterprises Among the First to Adopt Solid State Storage Solutions," Reuters, July 7, 2009.
19 "Genome Project Using Isilon's NAS," *GenomeWeb Daily News*, April 24, 2009.
20 Arellano, Nestor E., "Deeley Harley-Davidson Canada Wins This Virtualization," *itbusiness.ca*, May 5, 2010.
21 "Bell Canada Calls on Nuance Speech Solutions for Excellence in Customer Care," *www.crm2day.com/content/t6_librarynews_1.php?news_id=101059*, accessed September 26, 2010.
22 "How to Obtain a Certified Criminal Record Check", RCMP website, *www.rcmp-grc.gc.ca/cr-cj/fing-empr2-eng.htm*, accessed September 28, 2010.
23 "L-1 Identity Solutions Introduces New Live Scan Device for High Volume Civil Applications," L-1 Identify Solutions website, *http://ir.l1id.com*, July 14, 2009.
24 "The Montmagny Paperless Clinic," Canada Health Infoway, *www.infoway-inforoute.ca/lang-en/about-ehr/ehr-success-stories/montmagny-paperless-clinic*, accessed September 28, 2010.
25 Harzog, Beverly Blair, "U.S. Magnetic Stripe Credit Cards on Brink of Extinction?" *CreditCards.com*, August 4, 2009.
26 Zetter, Kim, "UK Bank Card Fraud Reduction Attributed to Use of Chip-and-PIN Card," *Threat Level*, October 8, 2009.
27 "Credit card Fraud," Canadian Bankers Association, *www.cba.ca/en/consumer-information/42-safeguarding-your-money/58-credit-card-fraud*, accessed September 28, 2010.
28 "Credit Card Fraud," RCMP, *www.rcmp-grc.gc.ca/scams-fraudes/cc-fraud-fraude-eng.htm*, accessed September 28, 2010.
29 "Visa to Unveil Its Contactless Debit Card at Games," *Contactless News*, October 9, 2009.
30 "Wireless Hand-held POS System Aid Restaurant Business," *Barcode.com*, *www.barcode.com/2009/08/wireless-hand-held-pos-system-aids-restaurant-business*, August 10, 2009.
31 Cooper, Caroline, "NEXTEP Announces Deployment of Casino Express Kiosks at Two Facilities," *Kiosk Marketplace*, September 22, 2009.
32 Buranosky, Paul, "Dave Meeker, Director of Emerging Technology at Roundarch, Interviewed on The Digital Scene Show," *impost*, accessed at *http://impost.roundarch.com/tag/touch-screen*, November 6, 2009.

33 Barber, Nick, "Nanotouch Technology Shrinks Touch-Screen Displays," *Computerworld*, April 7, 2009.

34 Fujitsu Computer Products of America, Inc., "Case Study: The University Hospital of Ulm Deploys the Mobile Electronic Patient File to Optimize Patient Care and Documentation," *www.hospitalnetwork.com/download.mvc/The-University-Hospital-Of-Ulm-Deploys-The-0001*, accessed October 5, 2010.

35 Lyngsoe Systems Ltd. video. "RFID: Tracking of Secure Shipment—Canada Post," *http://www.youtube.com/watch?v=3PorVZsRFeg*, accessed March 20, 2011.

36 Kondolojy, Amanda, "LCD Vs Plasma Monitors," eHow website, *www.ehow.com/about_4778386_lcd-vs-plasma-monitors.html*, accessed October 5, 2010.

37 Cheng, Jacqui, "Samsung and LG Phillips Announce Super-Thin OLEDs," *Ars Technica*, May 17, 2007.

38 Staff, "Solar Power—Yes, Life's Good," *The Daily Contributor*, October 12, 2009.

39 Ion, Florence, "Into Thin Air—Conquering Mt. Everest with a MacBook," *Mac|Life*, *www.maclife.com/print/5013*, October 2, 2009.

40 Stone, Brad, and Vance, Ashlee, "Just a Touch Away, the Elusive Tablet PC," *The New York Times*, October 5, 2009.

41 NEC Corporation, "NEC Deploys One of Japan's Largest Thin Client Systems for Tokio Marine," Press release, *www.nec.co.jp/press/en/0909/2901.html*, September 29, 2009.

42 "Dell Studio Hybrid Intel Dual-Core 2.1 GHz Miniature Desktop (26GB/160GB) $299.99," Tech Bargains, October 20, 2009.

43 Sun Microsystems, "Blue Sky Studios Deploys Sun Solution for Ice Age: Dawn of the Dinosaurs Film," Press release, *www.sun.com/aboutsun/pr/2009-07/sunflash.20090706.1.xml*, July 6, 2009.

44 Betts, Mitch, "Data Center Plays Supporting Role in Avatar," *Computerworld*, January 18, 2010.

45 Clark, Don, "Intel Plans to Expand Xeon Chip Line into Bigger Servers," *Wall Street Journal*, May 26, 2009.

46 Clark, Don, "Hints of a New Market for Cheap, Power-Sipping Servers," *Wall Street Journal*, May 25, 2009.

47 Messmer, Ellen, "Server Virtualization Now 18% of Server Workload," *InfoWorld*, October 20, 2009.

48 Fontecchio, Mark, "MIPS Growth a Concern for Mainframe Shops," *Data Center News*, September 23, 2009.

49 BMC, "BMC Software: Mainframe Users Gearing Up Now to Capitalize on Economic Recovery," Press release, *www.bmc.com/news/press-releases/2009/BMC-mainframe-users-capitalize-on-economic-recovery.html*, September 29, 2009.

50 "IBM Computer Will Have Power of 2 Million Laptops," *Reuters*, February 3, 2009.

51 Brodkin, Jon, "IBM, Cray Lead Top 500 Supercomputer Rankings," *Computerworld*, June 23, 2009.

52 "Top10 June 2010", *www.Top500.org*, accessed October 5, 2010.

53 Conger, Cristen, "Can My Computer Poison Me?" HowStuffWorks website, *http://computer.howstuffworks.com/computer-poison.htm/printable*, accessed October 5, 2010.

54 "Manufacturer's Corner X-Ray Fluorescence Analyzers," Empfasis website, *www.empf.org/empfasis/aug05/xray-flourescence-805.htm*, accessed October 5, 2010.

55 "Welcome to EPEAT," EPEAT website, *www.epeat.net*, accessed October 5, 2010.

56 Ibid.

CHAPTER · 4 ·

Software: Systems and Application Software

- **Systems software and application software are critical in helping individuals and organizations achieve their goals.**

  - Identify and briefly describe the functions of the two basic kinds of software.
  - Outline the role of the operating system and identify the features of several popular operating systems.

- **Organizations use off-the-shelf application software for common business needs and proprietary application software to meet unique business needs and provide a competitive advantage.**

  - Discuss how application software can support personal, workgroup, and enterprise business objectives.
  - Identify three basic approaches to developing application software and discuss the pros and cons of each.

- **Organizations should choose programming languages with functional characteristics that are appropriate for the task at hand and well suited to the skills and experience of the programming staff.**

  - Outline the overall evolution and importance of programming languages and differentiate among the generations of programming languages.

- **The software industry continues to undergo constant change; users need to be aware of recent trends and issues to be effective in their business and personal life.**

  - Identify several key software issues and trends that have an impact on organizations and individuals.

(Source: asharkyu/Shutterstock.com)

Information Systems in the Global Economy ⟩⟩
Rheinmetall AG

Social Network for a Global Business

Rheinmetall is a global manufacturer and supplier of automotive engine parts and defence equipment and technologies. Rheinmetall has its headquarters in Düsseldorf, Germany, and manufacturing facilities in dozens of locations across 16 countries. Its automotive division specializes in parts for every aspect of an engine, while its defence division is a leading supplier of defence and security equipment, including large mobile mortar combat systems and tanks.

By anyone's definition, Rheinmetall is a successful global enterprise. Seventy percent of its earnings come from international sales. Its 19,000 employees scattered around the globe are responsible for over $4 billion in sales each year.

As with most enterprises, teams perform most of the work at Rheinmetall. Teams often consist of experts located around the globe. They need to collaborate at every level: within one Rheinmetall location, among locations in the same country, and among locations in different countries and continents. Rheinmetall even encourages collaboration between its two divisions, which share one information system. To support its teams, the company depends on global network connections. Rheinmetall discovered that standard enterprise-wide information systems do not necessarily provide the best tools for global communication and collaboration.

Since 2002, Rheinmetall had been using an integrated enterprise system, an ERP system developed by SAP Corporation, with a desktop portal designed for enterprise-wide communication and collaboration. Although the system had been sufficient, it did not include the innovative collaborative features provided by the latest online software. By working with the SAP portal, Rheinmetall learned to appreciate the value of community, which whetted its appetite for more robust tools.

Rheinmetall went shopping for software that would provide community features to serve business needs. Common ways of communicating over the Internet such as Facebook, Twitter, and instant messaging are fine for everyday public use, but Rheinmetall decided that they were not appropriate for corporate use. The company needed a system it could manage so it could maintain control of the intellectual property and corporate knowledge that flowed through the online community. The company found what it was looking for at IBM.

IBM's Lotus collaboration software suite includes three components: IBM Lotus Connections, IBM Lotus Quickr, and IBM Lotus Sametime software. Like Facebook, Lotus Connections provides home pages and profiles for every Rheinmetall employee. It includes community features that allow employees to create professional networks with their collaborators. Lotus Connections has several forms of information and document-sharing software, including blogs, microblogs, wikis, and shared bookmarks.

Lotus Quickr is a content management and sharing system that lets users collaborate on shared documents. Teams can create a shared online workspace where they store documents and information. A team using Quickr can house team calendars, discussion forums, blogs, wikis, and other collaborative tools to help keep projects on track.

Lotus Sametime provides a set of integrated real-time communication services that support voice, data, and video communications. Team members can set up meetings on the Web or on the phone, sharing computer desktops and communicating through voice or video using the latest collaborative technologies. Sametime also makes it easy to find expert help within the organization at any time.

Rheinmetall worked with IBM to integrate the components of the three software packages into a single portal that can be accessed from desktop computers, notebooks, and smartphones. Using IBM software, Rheinmetall set up employee profiles and blogs, activity folders, online conferences, virtual team rooms, document libraries, and other mechanisms for supporting enterprise-wide collaboration and community.

The integrated suite of applications joins phone and Internet communications into a unified system that makes it easy for users to organize information and interactions. Being able to segregate communication into team rooms saves employees from being overwhelmed by information. Employees are making better use of resources and communication technology. For example, they no longer share documents through e-mail, but store them in virtual team rooms where team members can access and edit the documents.

The IBM Lotus collaboration software blends many types of business software—traditional software packages installed on user workstations and servers, custom-designed information systems that manage the flow of organizational information across an enterprise, and Internet-delivered software packages of all types, whether social networks or customer relationship management—into one coherent and powerful package. Rheinmetall employees around the world use this package to collaborate in online communities that makes them feel as though they are sharing an office suite. The software cuts across time zones, national borders, and corporate divisions to help employees collaborate efficiently and productively.

As you read this chapter, consider the following:

- What role does software play in an enterprise's ability to effectively communicate, produce goods and services, innovate, and operate?
- What considerations come into play when a company decides to purchase new software?

Why Learn About Software?

Software is indispensable for any computer system and the people using it. In this chapter, you will learn about systems software and application software. Without systems software, computers would not be able to accept data input from a keyboard, process data, or display results. Application software is one of the keys to helping you achieve your career goals. Sales representatives use software to enter sales orders and help their customers get what they want. Stock and bond traders use software to make split-second decisions involving millions of dollars. Scientists use software to analyze the threat of climate change. Regardless of your job, you most likely will use software to help you advance in your career and earn higher wages. You can also use software to help you prepare your personal income taxes, keep a budget, and keep in contact with friends and family online. Software can truly advance your career and enrich your life. We begin with an overview of software.

Software has a profound impact on individuals and organizations. It can make the difference between profits and losses, and between financial health and bankruptcy. As Figure 4.1 shows, companies recognize this impact, spending more on software than on computer hardware.

Figure 4.1

The Importance of Software in Business

Since the 1950s, businesses have greatly increased their expenditures on software compared with hardware.

AN OVERVIEW OF SOFTWARE

As you learned in Chapter 1, software consists of computer programs that control the workings of computer hardware. **Computer programs** are sequences of instructions for the computer. **Documentation** describes the program functions to help the user operate the computer system. Some documentation is given on screen or online, while other forms appear in external resources, such as printed manuals. People using commercially available software are usually asked to read and agree to End-User License Agreements (EULAs). After reading the EULA, you normally click an "I agree" button before you can use the program. Software can be one of two basic types: systems software and application software.

computer programs
Sequences of instructions for the computer.

documentation
Text that describes a program's functions to help the user operate the computer system.

Systems Software

Systems software is the set of programs that coordinates the activities and functions of the hardware and other programs throughout the computer system. Each type of systems software is designed for a specific CPU and class of hardware. The combination of a hardware configuration and systems software is known as a computer system platform.

Application software has the greatest potential to affect processes that add value to a business because it is designed for specific organizational activities and functions.

(Source: John McBride & Company Inc./The Image Bank/Getty Images.)

Application Software

Application software consists of programs that help users solve particular computing problems. In most cases, application software resides on the computer's hard disk before it is brought into the computer's memory and run. Application software can also be stored on CDs, DVDs, and even USB flash drives. An increasing amount of application software is available on the Web. Sometimes referred to as a *rich Internet application* (*RIA*), a Web-delivered software application combines hardware resources of the Web server and the PC to deliver valuable software services through a Web browser interface. Before a person, group, or enterprise decides on the best approach for acquiring application software, they should analyze their goals and needs carefully.

Supporting Individual, Group, and Organizational Goals

Every organization relies on the contributions of people, groups, and the entire enterprise to achieve its business objectives. Conversely, the organization also supports people, groups, and the enterprise by providing application software and information systems. One useful way of classifying the many potential uses of information systems is to identify the scope of the problems and opportunities that an organization addresses. This scope is

Microsoft Outlook is an application that workgroups can use to schedule meetings and coordinate activities.

(Source: Used with permission from Microsoft.)

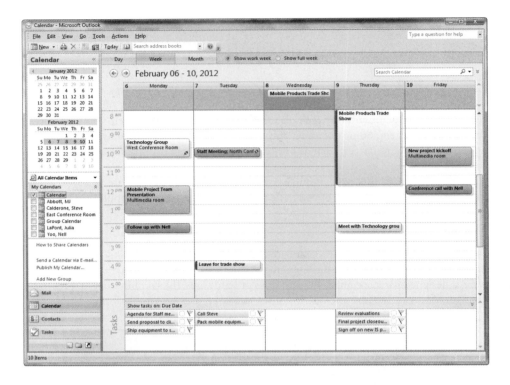

called the sphere of influence. For most companies, the spheres of influence are personal, workgroup, and enterprise. Table 4.1 shows how various kinds of software support these three spheres.

Table 4.1

Software Supporting Individuals, Workgroups, and Enterprises

Software	Personal	Workgroup	Enterprise
Systems software	Personal computer and workstation operating systems	Network operating systems	Server and mainframe operating systems
Application software	Word processing, spreadsheet, database, graphics	Electronic mail, group scheduling, shared work, and collaboration	General ledger, order entry, payroll, human resources

personal sphere of influence
The sphere of influence that serves the needs of an individual user.

personal productivity software
The software that enables users to improve their personal effectiveness, increasing the amount of work and quality of work they can do.

workgroup
Two or more people who work together to achieve a common goal.

workgroup sphere of influence
The sphere of influence that serves the needs of a workgroup.

Information systems that operate within the **personal sphere of influence** serve the needs of individual users. These information systems help users improve their personal effectiveness, increasing the amount and quality of work they can do. Such software is often called **personal productivity software**. For example, MindManager software from Mindjet provides tools to help people diagram complex ideas and projects using an intuitive graphic interface.[1]

When two or more people work together to achieve a common goal, they form a **workgroup**. A workgroup might be a large, formal, permanent organizational entity, such as a section or department, or a temporary group formed to complete a specific project. An information system in the **workgroup sphere of influence** helps a workgroup attain its common goals. Often, software designed for the personal sphere of influence can extend into the workgroup sphere. For example, people can use MindManager to share work for collaborative projects. People can also use online calendar software such as Google Calendar to store personal appointments and to schedule meetings with others.[2]

Information systems that operate within the **enterprise sphere of influence** support the firm in its interaction with its environment, which includes customers, suppliers, shareholders, competitors, special-interest groups, the financial community, and government agencies. This means the enterprise sphere of influence includes business partners, such as suppliers that provide raw materials; retail companies that store and sell a company's products; and shipping companies that transport raw materials to the plant and finished goods to retail outlets. For example, many enterprises use IBM Cognos software as a centralized Web-based system where employees, partners, and stakeholders can report and analyze corporate financial data.[3]

enterprise sphere of influence
The sphere of influence that serves the needs of the firm in its interaction with its environment.

SYSTEMS SOFTWARE

Controlling the operations of computer hardware is one of the most critical functions of systems software. Systems software also supports the application programs' problem-solving capabilities. Types of systems software include operating systems, utility programs, and middleware.

Operating Systems

An **operating system** (**OS**) is a set of programs that controls the computer hardware and acts as an interface with applications. See Figure 4.2. Operating systems can control one or more computers, or they can allow many users to interact with one computer. The various combinations of OSs, computers, and users include the following:

operating system (OS)
A set of computer programs that controls the computer hardware and acts as an interface with applications.

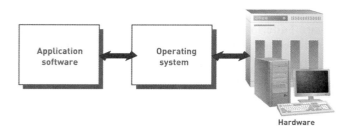

Hardware

Figure 4.2

The Role of Operating Systems

The role of the operating system is to act as an interface between application software and hardware.

- **Single computer with a single user.** This system is commonly used in a personal computer or a smartphone that supports one user at a time. Examples of OSs for this setup are Microsoft Windows, Mac OS X, and Google Android.
- **Single computer with many simultaneous users.** This system is typical of larger server or mainframe computers that can support hundreds or thousands of people, all using the computer at the same time. Examples of OSs that support this kind of system are UNIX, z/OS, and HP UX.
- **Many computers with many users.** This type of system is typical of a network of computers, such as a home network with several computers attached or a large computer network with hundreds of computers attached supporting many users, sometimes located around the world. Most PC operating systems double as network operating systems. Network server OSs include Red Hat Linux, Windows Server, and Mac OS X Server.
- **Special-purpose computers.** This type of system is typical of a number of computers with specialized functions, such as those that control sophisticated military aircraft, space shuttles, digital cameras, or home appliances. Examples of OSs for these purposes are Windows Embedded, Symbian, and some distributions of Linux.

The OS, which plays a central role in the functioning of the complete computer system, is usually stored on disk on general-purpose computers and in solid state memory on special-purpose computers such as cell phones and smartphones. After you start, or "boot up," a computer system, portions of the OS are transferred to memory as the system needs them. This process can take anywhere from a split second on a smartphone, to a few minutes on a desktop PC, to hours on a large mainframe or distributed computer systems. OS developers are continuously working to shorten the time required to boot devices from being shut down and wake devices from sleep mode. The move from hard disk drives (HDDs) to solid state drives (SSDs) in personal computers greatly reduces boot time. Windows 7 includes improvements to assist computers to sleep and resume more quickly.

You can also boot a computer from a CD, a DVD, or even a USB flash drive. A storage device that contains some or all of the OS is often called a *rescue disk* because you can use it to start the computer if you have problems with the primary hard disk.

The set of programs that make up the OS performs a variety of activities, including the following:

- Performing common computer hardware functions
- Providing a user interface and input/output management
- Providing a degree of hardware independence
- Managing system memory
- Managing processing tasks
- Sometimes providing networking capability
- Controlling access to system resources
- Managing files

kernel
The heart of the operating system and controls its most critical processes.

The **kernel**, as its name suggests, is the heart of the OS and controls its most critical processes. The kernel ties all of the OS components together and regulates other programs.

Common Hardware Functions

All applications must perform certain hardware-related tasks, such as the following:

- Get input from the keyboard or another input device
- Retrieve data from disks
- Store data on disks
- Display information on a monitor or printer

Each of these tasks requires a detailed set of instructions. The OS converts a basic request into the instructions that the hardware requires. In effect, the OS acts as an intermediary between the application and the hardware. The OS uses special software provided by device manufacturers, called device drivers, to communicate with and control a device. Device drivers are installed when a device is initially connected to the computer system.

User Interface and Input/Output Management

user interface
The element of the operating system that allows you to access and command the computer system.

command-based user interface
A user interface that requires you to give text commands to the computer to perform basic activities.

One of the most important functions of any OS is providing a **user interface**, which allows people to access and interact with the computer system. The first user interfaces for mainframe and personal computer systems were command based. A **command-based user interface** requires you to give text commands to the computer to perform basic activities. For example, the command ERASE 00TAXRTN would cause the computer to erase a file named 00TAXRTN. RENAME and COPY are other examples of commands used to rename files and copy files from one location to another. Today's systems engineers and administrators often use a command-based user interface to control the low-level functioning of computer systems. Most modern OSs (including popular graphical user interfaces such as Windows) provide a way to interact with the system through a command line. See Figure 4.3.

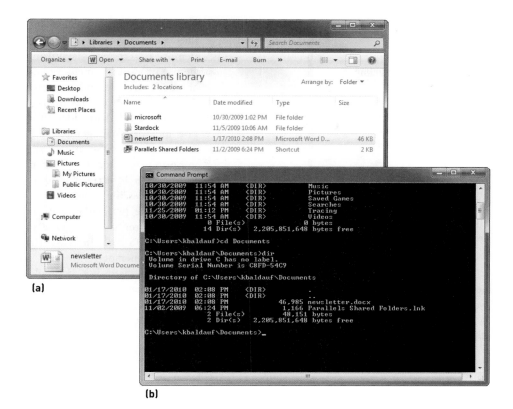

(a)

(b)

Figure 4.3

Command-Based and Graphical User Interfaces

Windows file system viewed with a GUI (a) and from the command prompt (b).

(Source: Used with permission from Microsoft.)

A **graphical user interface** (**GUI**) displays pictures (called *icons*) and menus that people use to send commands to the computer system. GUIs are more intuitive to use because they anticipate the user's needs and provide easy-to-recognize options. Today, the most widely used GUI is Microsoft Windows. As the name suggests, Windows is based on the use of a window, or a portion of the display screen dedicated to a specific application. The screen can display several windows at once.

Alan Kay and others at Xerox PARC (Palo Alto Research Center, located in California) were pioneers in investigating the use of icons and overlapping windows in an interface. GUIs were responsible for bringing computing to the mass market by making computers easier to use. While GUIs have traditionally been accessed using a keyboard and mouse, more recent technologies allow people to use touch-screens and spoken commands. Building on the success of the iPhone, due in no small part to its unique and advanced multitouch user interface, Windows 7 also provides strong support for interacting with its GUI through touch, which has spawned a new generation of PCs being sold with touch displays. Often these PCs are designed as an information appliance for use in the home. Sometimes such devices are referred to as nettops—desktop computers designed to conveniently and quickly access Internet information and services.

graphical user interface (GUI)
An interface that displays pictures (icons) and menus that people use to send commands to the computer system.

Hardware Independence

Software applications are designed to run on a particular operating system by using the operating system's **application program interface** (**API**), which provides software developers with tools they use to build application software without needing to understand the inner workings of the OS and hardware. See Figure 4.4 on the next page. Being able to develop software without concern for the specific underlying hardware is referred to as hardware independence. When new hardware technologies are introduced, the operating system is required to adjust to address those changes, not the application software that runs on the operating system.

application program interface (API)
An interface that allows applications to make use of the operating system.

Figure 4.4

Application Program Interface (API)

The API links application software to the operating system, providing hardware independence for software developers.

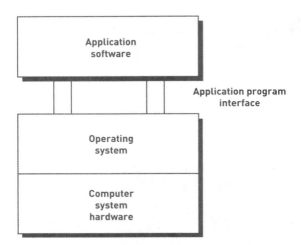

Memory Management

The OS also controls how memory is accessed, maximizing the use of available memory and storage to provide optimum efficiency. Most newer OSs manage memory better than older OSs. The memory-management feature of many OSs allows the computer to execute program instructions effectively and to speed processing. One way to increase the performance of an old computer is to upgrade to a newer OS and increase the amount of memory.

Most OSs support virtual memory, which allocates space on the hard disk to supplement the immediate, functional memory capacity of RAM. Virtual memory works by swapping programs or parts of programs between memory and one or more disk devices—a concept called paging. This reduces CPU idle time and increases the number of jobs that can run in a given time span.

Processing Tasks

The task-management features of today's OSs manage all processing activities. Task management allocates computer resources to make the best use of each system's assets. Task-management software lets one user run several programs or tasks at the same time (multitasking) and allows several users to use the same computer at the same time (time sharing).

An OS with multitasking capabilities allows a user to run more than one application at the same time. Most computer users take advantage of multitasking OSs without realizing how innovative they are. Without having to exit a program, you can work in one application, easily pop into another, and then jump back to the first program, picking up where you left off. Better still, while you're working in the *foreground* in one program, one or more other applications can be churning away, unseen, in the *background*. Background activities include tasks such as sorting a database, printing a document, or performing other lengthy operations that otherwise would monopolize your computer and leave you staring at the screen unable to perform other work. Multitasking can save users a considerable amount of time and effort.

Time sharing allows more than one person to use a computer system at the same time. For example, 15 customer service representatives might enter sales data into a computer system for a mail-order company at the same time. In another case, thousands of people might be simultaneously using an online computer service to get stock quotes and valuable business news.

The ability of the computer to handle an increasing number of concurrent users smoothly is called *scalability*. This feature is critical for systems expected to handle a large and possibly fluctuating number of users, such as a mainframe computer or a Web server. For example, Radisson Hotel Bangkok recently upgraded its systems to a collection of blade servers that adjusts to the hotel's current demands and that can easily be scaled to support more users in the future.[4] In this way, no resources are wasted, nor are the systems overtaxed.

Networking Capability

Most operating systems include networking capabilities so that computers can join together in a network to send and receive data and share computing resources. PCs running Mac, Windows, or Linux operating systems allow users to easily set up home or business networks for sharing Internet connections, printers, storage, and data. Windows 7 includes a Home-Group feature that makes it easy to share photos, music, files, and printers with others on a home network. Operating systems for larger server computers are designed specifically for computer networking environments.

Access to System Resources and Security

Because computers often handle sensitive data that can be accessed over networks, the OS needs to provide a high level of security against unauthorized access to the users' data and programs. Typically, the OS establishes a logon procedure that requires users to enter an identification code, such as a username, and a matching password. If the identification code is invalid or if the password does not match the identification code, the user cannot gain access to the computer. Some OSs require that users change their passwords frequently, such as every 20 to 40 days. Operating systems may also control what system resources a user may access. When a user successfully logs on to the system, the OS restricts access to only portions of the system for which the user has been authorized. The OS records who is using the system and for how long and reports any attempted breaches of security.

File Management

The OS manages files to ensure that files in secondary storage are available when needed and that they are protected from access by unauthorized users. Many computers support many users who store files on centrally located disks or tape drives. The OS keeps track of where each file is stored and who can access them. The OS must determine what to do if more than one user requests access to the same file at the same time. Even on stand-alone personal computers with only one user, file management is needed to track where files are located, what size they are, when they were created, and who created them.

Current Operating Systems

Today's operating systems incorporate sophisticated features and impressive graphic effects. Table 4.2 classifies a few current OSs by sphere of influence.

Personal	Workgroup	Enterprise
Microsoft Windows, Microsoft Windows Mobile	Microsoft Windows Server 2008	Microsoft Windows Server 2008
Mac OS X, Mac OS X iPhone	Mac OS X Server	
Linux	Linux	Linux
Google Android, Chrome OS		
Palm Web OS		
	UNIX	UNIX
	IBM i5/OS and z/OS	IBM i5/OS and z/OS
	HP-UX 11i	HP-UX 11i

Table 4.2

Operating Systems Serving Three Spheres of Influence

Microsoft PC Operating Systems

Since Microsoft developed PC-DOS and MS-DOS to support the IBM personal computer introduced in the 1980s, personal computer OSs have steadily evolved. *PC-DOS* and *MS-DOS* had command-driven interfaces that were difficult to learn and use. MS-DOS gave way to Windows, which opened the PC market to everyday users. Windows evolved through several versions, including Windows 1.01, 2.03, 3.0, 3.1, Windows 95, 98, Me,

Windows NT, Windows 2000, Windows XP, Windows Vista, and Windows 7. Each new version of OS has improved the ease of use, processing capability, reliability, and ability to support new computer hardware devices. Today, Microsoft has over 92 percent of the PC/ smartphone OS market. Apple holds 5.1 percent of the market, and Linux distributions and other OSs account for the rest.[5]

Windows XP (XP reportedly stands for the positive e*x*perience that you will have with your personal computer) was released in the fall of 2001. Previous consumer versions of Windows were notably unstable and crashed frequently, requiring frustrating and time-consuming reboots. With XP, Microsoft sought to bring reliability to the consumer.

In 2007, Microsoft released *Windows Vista* to the public, introducing it as the most secure version of Windows ever. Windows Vista includes design improvements that make it attractive and easy to use. The most advanced editions of Windows Vista include a 3D graphics interface called Aero. Windows Vista suffered some negative press when early adopters found that some software and hardware designed for Windows XP did not run on Vista. Many businesses decided not to upgrade from XP to Vista. Being content with XP, they held out to see what the next edition of Windows might bring.

The next version, *Windows 7*, was released in 2009 with improvements and new features. See Figure 4.5. Most analysts classified Windows 7 as "Vista done right."[6] Besides addressing some of the flaws in Windows Vista, Windows 7 introduced new windows manipulation functionality that allows users to more easily find, access, and work with information in files. It also features improved home networking capabilities and improved applications. Windows 7 has strong support for touch displays and netbooks, ushering in a new era of mobile computing devices. Windows 7 is available in three editions: Home Premium, Professional, and Ultimate. The Home Premium edition supports home computing and networking. The Professional edition adds an XP mode to run XP applications, business networking support, and auto backup. Windows 7 Ultimate adds extra security features and multilanguage support. Windows 7 is also available in a stripped-down edition, called Starter, for small mobile devices such as netbooks.

Windows 7 is available in configurations designed for 32-bit or 64-bit processors. Users running newer computers are advised to install the 64-bit version, if their computers can support it, to experience faster processor performance.[7] A Windows 7 Upgrade Advisor is

Figure 4.5

Microsoft Windows 7

(Source: Used with permission from Microsoft.)

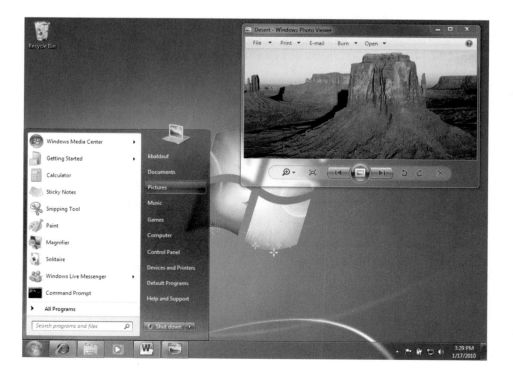

available from the Microsoft Windows website to analyze computers and recommend the most suitable version of Windows 7.

Bombardier Aerospace, one of Canada's largest global aerospace manufacturers, decided to upgrade from Windows 2000 to Windows 7 instead of Windows XP. The upgrade is expected to enhance security, reduce operating costs by $160,000 per year, and improve information access and productivity.[8]

Apple Computer Operating Systems

While IBM system platforms traditionally use Windows OSs and Intel microprocessors (often called *Wintel* for this reason), Apple computers have used non-Intel microprocessors designed by Apple, IBM, and Motorola along with the proprietary *Mac OS*. More recent Apple computers, however, use Intel chips. Although Wintel computers hold the largest share of the business PC market, Apple computers are also popular, especially in the fields of publishing, education, graphic arts, music, movies, and media. Software developed for the Macintosh often provides cutting-edge options for creative people. GarageBand, for example, is Macintosh software that allows you to create your own music the way a professional does, and it can make a PC sound like a small orchestra. Apple's Pro Tools is popular music production software for music professionals, and Final Cut is the software of choice for most professional video and motion picture producers.

The Apple OSs have also evolved over a number of years and often provide features not available from Microsoft. Recently, however, Windows and Mac platforms have evolved to share many of the same features as they compete for users. In July 2001, Mac OS X was released as an entirely new OS for the Mac based on the UNIX operating system. It included a new user interface, which provided a new visual appearance for users—including luminous and semitransparent elements, such as buttons, scroll bars, windows, and fluid animation to enhance the user's experience.

Since its first release, Apple has upgraded OS X several times. Lion (OS X v10.7) is the current version of OS X which competes with Windows 7. See Figure 4.6. Lion is said to be a refinement of the previous version of OS X. It includes an attractive 3D graphical user interface that Apple claims is more intuitive than Windows. Mission Control is a powerful feature that provides a comprehensive look at what's running on the Mac. It gives a bird's-eye view of things such as Dashboard and full-screen apps in one place. Macs are also considered very secure, with no widespread virus or spyware infections to date. Lion OS X is a 64-bit system, giving the OS and native Apple software a significant speed boost.

Because Mac OS X runs on Intel processors, Mac users can set up their computer to run both Windows Vista and Mac OS X and select which platform they want to work with when

Figure 4.6

Mac OS X Lion
(Source: Courtesy of Apple, Inc.)

Blended Platforms at LinkedIn

Although Microsoft Windows dominates the business desktop OS market, Macs are beginning to make inroads. The popular business-focused social network LinkedIn finds that its employees generally have a strong preference for one operating system over another. Rather than forcing employees to use one standard operating system and compatible software, LinkedIn allows its employees to choose either the Windows or Mac platform and sometimes even Linux.

Big Web companies such as LinkedIn hire a variety of specialists ranging from Web developers and software engineers to graphic artists, designers, accountants, and executives. Often professionals from different disciplines prefer one platform over another because of specific software tools designed for that platform.

Macs are especially popular with so-called techies: Web developers, software engineers, and programmers. They like the Mac platform because of its power and because it is based on the UNIX kernel. UNIX is popular with programmers who like to work from the command line. LinkedIn provides all of its software engineers with state-of-the-art Mac Pros (desktop PCs) and MacBooks (notebook PCs). LinkedIn uses this equipment as an enticement to attract top-of-the-line engineers. According to LinkedIn, "the Mac factor" has a big impact on developers' decisions to join the company. Some developers even set up their Macs to run both Mac OS X and Linux so that they can develop LinkedIn software to run in browsers on the Linux platform.

Artists and graphic designers are typically divided between Windows and Macs depending on what software they prefer to use. Aperture is popular photo editing software for the Mac. However, Photoshop and other popular graphics software from Adobe are available for both Windows and Mac. Generally speaking, Mac has a long history of appealing to digital media designers. It is especially popular with video and music producers.

For business applications, Microsoft Windows is typically king. It is rare to find a Mac in a business environment. LinkedIn product managers, accountants, human resources managers, executives, and other business staff have a choice of Microsoft Windows PCs or Macs. Surprisingly, 68 percent have chosen Macs. The general popularity of the Mac in Silicon Valley might be why LinkedIn has so many Mac users. Also, Microsoft Office and other business software are available for the Mac platform.

LinkedIn's IT department now provides services to all employees over the dual platform integrated network. Mac is completely compatible with Windows and has no problem sharing files and resources over a network. LinkedIn did not have to modify its network environment to accommodate both Macs and Windows PCs. As an increasing amount of computing takes place online rather than on the local PC, it is likely that the choice of PC platforms will become less important.

Discussion Questions

1. In what ways is LinkedIn unique in the options it provides its employees and in the choices it allows its employees to make?
2. If LinkedIn required all employees to use the same platform, how might that requirement detract from employee productivity?

Critical Thinking Questions

1. Do you think LinkedIn will serve as a trendsetter, with many businesses following suit?
2. What benefits does standardizing around one platform provide for businesses?

SOURCES: "LinkedIn. Not Just Your Ordinary Network," Apple Business Profiles, www.apple.com/business/profiles/linkedin, accessed March 20, 2011; LinkedIn website, www.linkedin.com, accessed March 20, 2011.

they boot their computer. Such an arrangement is called *dual booting*. While Macs can dual boot into Windows, the opposite is not true. Apple does not allow OS X to be run on any machine other than an Apple. However, Windows PCs can dual boot with Linux and other OSs.

Another option for using several operating systems is virtualization. Virtualization software, also referred to as virtual machine (VM) software, allows one operating system to run on top of another by creating a virtual machine on which the guest operating system can run. For example, VirtualBox software from Sun allows Linux to run in a window while the computer is running Windows or Mac OS. It can even allow Windows to run on a Mac, and practically any OS to run on any other.

Linux

Linux is an OS developed by Linus Torvalds in 1991 as a student in Finland. The OS is distributed under the GNU General Public Licence, and its source code is freely available to everyone. It is, therefore, called an open-source operating system. This doesn't mean, however, that Linux and its assorted distributions are necessarily free—companies and developers can charge money for a distribution as long as the source code remains available. Linux is actually only the kernel of an OS, the part that controls hardware, manages files, separates processes, and so forth. Several combinations of Linux are available, with various sets of capabilities and applications to form a complete OS. Each of these combinations is called a *distribution* of Linux. Many distributions are available as free downloads.

Linux is available on the Internet and from other sources. Popular versions include Red Hat Linux and Caldera OpenLinux. Several large computer vendors, including IBM, Hewlett-Packard, and Intel, support the Linux operating system. For example, IBM has hundreds of programmers working with Linux. Linux is a popular OS for servers, distributed systems, and even supercomputers. Most computer science and engineering graduates are familiar with Linux, so there is no shortage of programmers and engineers for Linux-based systems. The flexibility of the open architecture also makes it easy to customize Linux for different needs in different environments.

Linux is making inroads to the consumer PC market with their GUI distributions. Both Dell and Lenovo sell notebook computers running Ubuntu and SuSE Linux. Ubuntu is a user-friendly Linux distribution that is free to download and includes dozens of free software packages. See Figure 4.7. Some ultra-compact notebooks, netbooks, and other

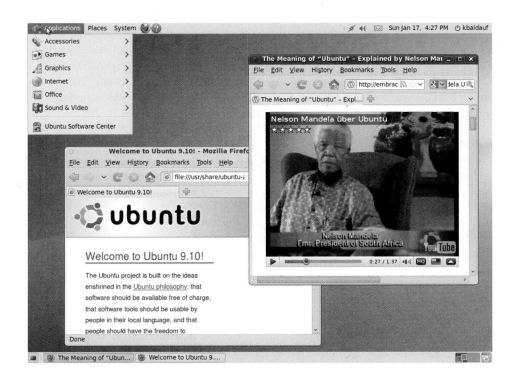

Figure 4.7

Ubuntu Linux Operating System

(Source: Courtesy of Canonical)

mobile devices use Linux to make the most of their limited system resources. Even some smartphones are developed around the Linux OS.[9]

Oxford Archaeology decided to switch from Microsoft Windows to Linux Ubuntu for its workforce. The 300 or so archaeologists and specialists employed by the company are dedicated to recording, protecting, and preserving archaeological artifacts for the betterment of humanity. The company's information systems manager decided that, over the long term, the open-source alternative would save the company money and give it more flexibility than a closed and proprietary system such as Microsoft Windows. The company describes Ubuntu as an excellent platform for the GIS, mapping, and geospacial systems on which Oxford Archaeology depends.[10]

Google Chrome OS

Over the years, Google has extended its reach from providing the most popular search engine to application software (Google Docs), mobile operating system (Android), Web browser (Chrome), and more recently, PC operating system—*Chrome OS*. Chrome OS is a Linux-based operating system designed for netbooks and nettops, which are notebooks and desktop PCs primarily designed to access Web-based information and services such as e-mail, Web browsing, social networks, and Google online applications.[11] A typical configuration for Chrome OS includes desktop links to Google Docs, Gmail, Google Maps, Facebook, and other online services.

Chrome OS was announced in 2009 when netbooks were becoming popular. The OS is designed to run on inexpensive low-power computers. Google advertises that Chrome boots in seconds and is virtually impervious to viruses. An open-source version of Chrome OS, named Chromium OS, was made available at the end of 2009. Because it is open-source software, developers can customize the source code to run on different platforms, incorporating unique features.

However, the future success of Chrome OS is questionable.[12] It has tough competition to contend with. Microsoft has developed a netbook version of Windows 7, and Apple's OS X has mobile versions as well. Google's Android OS designed for smartphones is also being customized to run on netbooks. However, even if Chrome OS does not survive long, it has driven Microsoft and Apple to move more toward Web-delivered applications, which will help both its browser business and Google Docs.

Workgroup Operating Systems

To keep pace with user demands, the technology of the future must support a world in which network usage, data storage requirements, and data processing speeds increase at a dramatic rate. This rapid increase in communications and data processing capabilities pushes the boundaries of computer science and physics. Powerful and sophisticated OSs are needed to run the servers that meet these business needs for workgroups.

Windows Server

Microsoft designed *Windows Server* to perform a host of tasks that are vital for websites and corporate Web applications. For example, Microsoft Windows Server can be used to coordinate large data centres. The OS also works with other Microsoft products. It can be used to prevent unauthorized disclosure of information by blocking text and e-mails from being copied, printed, or forwarded to other people. Microsoft *Windows Server 2008* delivers benefits such as a powerful Web server management system, virtualization tools that allow various operating systems to run on a single server, advanced security features, and robust administrative support.

UNIX

UNIX is a powerful OS originally developed by AT&T for minicomputers—the predecessors of servers that are larger than PCs and smaller than mainframes. UNIX can be used on many computer system types and platforms, including workstations, servers, and mainframe computers. UNIX also makes it much easier to move programs and data among computers or to connect mainframes and workstations to share resources. There are many variants of UNIX—including HP/UX from Hewlett-Packard, AIX from IBM, UNIX SystemV from UNIX Systems Lab, Solaris from Sun Microsystems, and SCO from Santa Cruz Operations. Mac OS X boasts that it uses a UNIX kernel for maximum stability and security.

The online marketplace eBay uses Sun Microsystems servers, software, storage, and services to run its operations. Sun's Solaris operating system manages eBay's systems, including database servers, Web servers, tape libraries, and identity management systems. The online auction company found that when it switched to Sun and Solaris, system performance increased by 20 percent.[13] The 2010 Vancouver Olympics also used Solaris to manage daily operations and share real-time results with billions across the world.[14]

Red Hat Linux

Red Hat Software offers a Linux network OS that taps into the talents of tens of thousands of volunteer programmers who generate a steady stream of improvements for the Linux OS. The *Red Hat Linux* network OS is very efficient at serving Web pages and can manage a cluster of up to eight servers. Linux environments typically have fewer virus and security problems than other OSs. Distributions such as SuSE and Red Hat have proven Linux to be a very stable and efficient OS.

Mac OS X Server

The *Mac OS X Server* is the first modern server OS from Apple Computer and is based on the UNIX OS. The most recent version is OS X Server 10.7 Lion. It includes support for 64-bit processing, along with several server functions and features that allow the easy management of network and Internet services such as e-mail, website hosting, calendar management and sharing, wikis, and podcasting.

Enterprise Operating Systems

Mainframe computers, often referred to as "Big Iron," provide the computing and storage capacity to meet massive data processing requirements and offer many users high performance and excellent system availability, strong security, and scalability. In addition, a wide range of application software has been developed to run in the mainframe environment, making it possible to purchase software to address almost any business problem. As a result, mainframe computers remain a popular computing platform for mission-critical business applications for many companies. Examples of mainframe OSs include z/OS from IBM, HP-UX from Hewlett-Packard, and Linux.

z/OS

The z/OS is IBM's first 64-bit enterprise OS. It supports IBM's z900 and z800 lines of mainframes that can come with up to sixteen 64-bit processors. (The z stands for zero downtime.) The OS provides several new capabilities to make it easier and less expensive for users to run large mainframe computers. The OS has improved workload management and advanced e-commerce security. The IBM zSeries mainframe, like previous generations of IBM mainframes, lets users subdivide a single computer into many smaller servers, each of which can run a different application. In recognition of the widespread popularity of a competing OS, z/OS allows partitions to run a version of the Linux OS. This means that a company can upgrade to a mainframe that runs the Linux OS.

Germany's largest health insurance company, AOK, recently replaced its core systems with two IBM mainframe servers running z/OS. The company chose z/OS based on its reputation for high reliability and performance. AOK also uses IBM Tivoli software to assist in automating tasks in the mainframe infrastructure and storage management system. AOK is legally responsible for storing records for 30 years for its more than 25 million policy holders.[15] That level of responsibility requires the highest levels of system reliability.

HP-UX and Linux

The *HP-UX* is a robust UNIX-based OS from Hewlett-Packard designed to handle a variety of business tasks, including online transaction processing and Web applications. It supports

Internet, database, and business applications on server and mainframe enterprise systems. It can work with Java programs and Linux applications. The OS comes in four versions: foundation, enterprise, mission critical, and technical. HP-UX supports Hewlett-Packard's computers and those designed to run Intel's Itanium processors.

Red Hat Linux, described in the previous section, can also be used as an enterprise-level operating system. ResMed, a leading provider of equipment for the management of respiratory disorders, recently migrated its servers to Red Hat Linux. The company was relying on outdated Sun Solaris servers, and ResMed decided it was time to replace them. Moving to 80 servers running Red Hat enterprise Linux, and taking advantage of server virtualization provided by Red Hat's unique KVM hypervisor technology, increased server performance and stability and saved the company $200,000 over the price quoted for a similar UNIX-based system.[16]

Operating Systems for Small Computers, Embedded Computers, and Special-Purpose Devices

New OSs and other software are changing the way we interact with smartphones, cell phones, digital cameras, TVs, and other digital electronic devices. These OSs are also called *embedded operating systems*, or just *embedded systems* because they are typically embedded within a device. Embedded systems are typically designed to perform specialized tasks. For example, an automotive embedded system might be responsible for controlling fuel injection. A digital camera's embedded system supports taking and viewing photos and may include a limited set of editing tools. An embedded system controlling an MRI machine controls a powerful magnetic field to acquire 3D images of the body. A GPS device uses an embedded system to help people find their way around town. See Figure 4.8. Some of the more popular OSs for devices are described in the following section.

Figure 4.8

GPS Devices Use Embedded Operating Systems

A GPS device uses an embedded system to acquire information from satellites, display your current location on a map, and direct you to your destination.

(Source: © Roberta Casaliggi/iStockphoto.com.)

Cell Phone Embedded Systems and Operating Systems

Cell phones have traditionally used embedded systems to provide communication and limited personal information management services to users. *Symbian*, the world's most popular cell phone embedded OS, has traditionally provided voice and text communication, an address book, and a few other basic applications. When RIM introduced the BlackBerry smartphone in 2002, the mobile phone's capabilities were vastly expanded. Since then, cell phone embedded systems have transformed into full-fledged personal computer OSs such as the iPhone OS, Google Android, and Microsoft Windows Mobile. Even traditional embedded systems such as Palm OS (now WebOS) and Symbian have evolved into PC operating systems, with APIs and software development kits that allow developers to design hundreds of applications providing a myriad of mobile services.

Windows Embedded

Windows Embedded is a family of Microsoft OSs included with or embedded into small computer devices. Windows Embedded includes several versions that provide computing power for TV set-top boxes, automated industrial machines, media players, medical devices, digital cameras, PDAs, GPS receivers, ATMs, gaming devices, and business devices such as cash registers. Microsoft Auto provides a computing platform for automotive software such as Ford Sync. The Ford Sync system uses an in-dashboard display and wireless networking technologies to link automotive systems with cell phones and portable media players. See Figure 4.9.

Figure 4.9

Microsoft Auto and Ford Sync

The Ford Sync system, developed on the Microsoft Auto operating system, allows drivers to wirelessly connect cell phones and media devices to automotive systems.

(Source: Bloomberg/Getty Images.)

Proprietary Linux-Based Systems

Because embedded systems are usually designed for a specific purpose in a specific device, they are usually proprietary, or custom-created and owned by the manufacturer. Sony's Wii, for example, uses a custom-designed OS based on the Linux kernel. Linux is a popular choice for embedded systems because it is free and highly configurable. In October 2009, Nokia released the N900 smartphone—the first Linux-based smartphone.[17] Linux has been used in many embedded systems, including e-book readers, ATM machines, cell phones, networking devices, and media players. At least nine distributions of Linux are designed for embedded systems. Linux is a major competitor to Symbian in the cell phone market and to Microsoft Embedded in most other markets.

Utility Programs

Utility programs help to perform maintenance or correct problems with a computer system. For example, some utility programs merge and sort sets of data, keep track of computer jobs being run, compress files of data before they are stored or transmitted over a network (thus saving space and time), and perform other important tasks. Some utility programs can help computer systems run better and longer without problems.

Another type of utility program allows people and organizations to take advantage of unused computer power over a network. Often called *grid computing*, the approach can be very efficient and less expensive than purchasing additional hardware or computer equipment. CERN, home of the Large Hadron Collider (LHC), the world largest scientific instrument, is also home to one of the world's largest scientific grid computing and storage systems. The LHC Computing Grid (LCG) project provides scientists around the world with access to shared computer power and storage systems over the Internet.[18]

Utility programs can also help to secure and safeguard data. For example, the publishing and motion picture industries use digital rights management (DRM) technologies to prevent copyright-protected books and movies from being unlawfully copied. The files storing the intellectual property are encoded so that software running on e-book readers and media players recognizes and plays only legally obtained copies. DRM has been criticized for infringing on the freedom and rights of customers. Record companies have already moved away from DRM technologies in an effort to win the appreciation of their customers.

utility program
Program that helps to perform maintenance or correct problems with a computer system.

Although many PC utility programs come installed on computers (see Figure 4.10), you can also purchase utility programs separately. The following sections examine some common types of utilities.

Figure 4.10

Security and System Utilities on Windows 7

Windows 7 includes powerful security and system utilities, but still requires users to download and install additional virus protection.

(Source: Used with permission from Microsoft.)

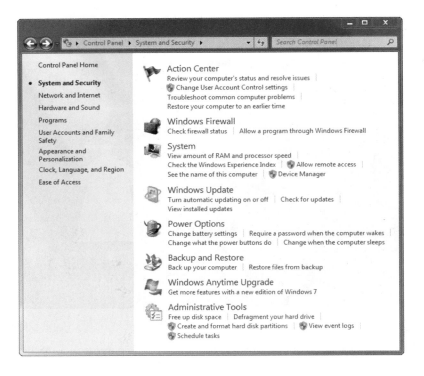

Hardware Utilities

Some hardware utilities are available from companies such as Symantec, which produces Norton Utilities. Hardware utilities can check the status of all parts of the PC, including hard disks, memory, modems, speakers, and printers. Disk utilities check the hard disk's boot sector, file allocation tables, and directories, and analyze them to ensure that the hard disk is not damaged. Disk utilities can also optimize the placement of files on a crowded disk.

Security Utilities

Computer viruses and spyware from the Internet and other sources can be a nuisance—and sometimes can completely disable a computer. Antivirus and anti-spyware software can be installed to constantly monitor and protect the computer. If a virus or spyware is found, often it can be removed. This software runs continuously in the background to keep new viruses and spyware from entering the system. To keep current and make sure that the software checks for the latest threats, it can be easily updated over the Internet. It is also a good idea to protect computer systems with firewall software. Firewall software filters incoming and outgoing packets, making sure that neither hackers nor their tools are attacking the system. Some software assists in keeping private data from being accessed from a computer system and works to protect you from scams and fraud. Symantec, McAfee, and Microsoft are the most popular providers of security software.

File-Compression Utilities

File-compression programs can reduce the amount of disk space required to store a file or reduce the time it takes to transfer a file over the Internet. Both Windows and Mac operating systems let you compress or decompress files and folders. A zip file has a .zip extension, and its contents can be easily unzipped to their original size. *MP3 (Motion Pictures Experts Group-Layer 3)* is a popular file-compression format used to store, transfer, and play music and audio files, such as podcasts—audio programs that can be downloaded from the Internet. MP3 can compress files 10 times smaller than the original file while maintaining almost CD-quality sound. Software, such as iTunes and Windows Media Player, are used to store, organize, and play MP3 music files. Video, photographs, and other digital media also use compression to reduce file size.

Spam Filtering Utilities

Receiving unwanted e-mail (spam) can be a frustrating waste of time. E-mail software and services include spam-filtering utilities to assist users with these annoyances. E-mail filters identify spam by learning what the user considers spam and routing it to a junk mail folder. However, this method is insufficient for protecting enterprise-level e-mail systems where spam containing viruses is a serious threat. Businesses often use additional spam-filtering software from companies including Cisco, Barracuda Networks, and Google at the enterprise level to intercept dangerous spam as it enters the corporate e-mail system.

Network and Internet Utilities

A broad range of network- and systems-management utility software is available to monitor hardware and network performance and trigger an alert when a server is crashing or a network problem occurs. Advanced website monitoring utilities, available from companies such as Atwatch, HP, and Uptrends, provide a detailed analysis of Web server functionality and traffic. The software alerts administrators before problems build to dangerous levels. Because businesses depend on their internal networks and Web presence, downtime can seriously affect a business's bottom line.

Server and Mainframe Utilities

Some utilities enhance the performance of servers and mainframe computers. IBM has created systems-management software that allows a support person to monitor the growing number of desktop computers in a business attached to a server or mainframe computer. With this software, the support people can sit at their personal computers and check or diagnose problems, such as a hard disk failure on a network computer. The support people can even repair individual systems anywhere on the organization's network, often without having to leave their desks. The direct benefit is to the system manager, but the business also gains from having a smoothly functioning information system. Utility programs can meet the needs of a single user, workgroup, or enterprise, as listed in Table 4.3. These programs perform many useful tasks, from finding information to improving system performance.

Table 4.3

Examples of Utility Programs

Personal	Workgroup	Enterprise
Software to compress data so that it takes less hard disk space	Software that maintains an archive of changes made to a shared document	Software to archive contents of a database by copying data from disk to tape
Software that assists in determining which files to delete to free up disk space	Software that monitors group activity to determine levels of participation	Software that monitors network traffic and server loads
Antivirus and anti-spyware software for PCs	Software that reports unsuccessful user logon attempts	Software that reports the status of a particular computer job

Similar to the virtual machine software discussed earlier, *server virtualization software* allows a server to run more than one operating system at the same time. For example, you could run four different virtual servers simultaneously on one physical server. Virtual server technology also allows firms to use server resources more efficiently, which saves expense.

While server virtualization has become popular with businesses, some are also experimenting with desktop virtualization.[19] In desktop virtualization, an employee's personal computer desktop environment is stored and run on a server while being manipulated by the user on a PC just as though it resides in the PC. Desktop virtualization allows companies to control the exact configuration of all PCs, providing increased security and convenient maintenance.

Other Utilities

Utility programs are available for almost every conceivable task or function. For example, you can use utilities such as PCmover from Laplink and Apple's Migration Assistant to migrate software and data from an old computer to a new one. You can use Microsoft Windows Rights Management Services with Microsoft Office programs to manage and protect important corporate documents. Widgit Software has developed an important software utility that helps people with visual disabilities use the Internet. The software converts icons and symbols into plain text that can be easily seen. Key logging software allows a manager to see every keystroke a worker makes on a computer system. Monitoring software can catalogue the Internet sites that employees visit and the time that employees are working at their computer. Parental control software allows parents to control what their children can access on the computer and Web. Keyboard shortcut utilities allow users to map common tasks to defined keyboard combinations. For example, Ctrl+Shift+W might open Wikipedia in a browser on the desktop. The authors and editors of this textbook used an FTP (file transfer protocol) utility to transfer files back and forth between their PCs and the publisher's server.

In addition, you can use search utilities to find important files and documents on your PC, on a network, or on the Internet. The following list provides some popular categories of utilities found at *download.cnet.com*.

Antivirus software	File management	Parental control
Automation software	Firewall software	Password managers
Backup software	FTP software	Photo sharing and publishing
Bookmark managers	Internet security software suites	Printer software
CD and DVD burners	iTunes utilities	Privacy software
Clipboard software	Keyboard shortcut utilities	Remote access software
Corporate security software	Maintenance and optimization	Screen saver, theme, and wallpaper
Data transfer and syncing	Media management	Software launchers
Desktop customization	Monitoring software	Spyware removers
Diagnostic	Music management software	Video capture
Download managers	Music ripper and converter software	Video converting
Encryption software	Online storage and backup	Virtual desktop managers
File compression	P2P and file-sharing software	Wireless networking software

Middleware

middleware
Software that allows various systems to communicate and exchange data.

Middleware is software that allows various systems to communicate and exchange data. Middleware is often developed to address situations where a company acquires different types of information systems through mergers, acquisitions, or expansion and wants the systems to share data and interact. Middleware can also serve as an interface between the Internet and private corporate systems. For example, middleware can be used to transfer a request for information from a corporate customer on the corporate website to a traditional database on a mainframe computer and return the results to the customer on the Internet.

Nestlé Nespresso, a subsidiary of the Nestlé group involved in coffee products, uses middleware productively. It used middleware called Fusion from Oracle to pull data from Nestlé corporate databases around the world to build a data warehouse. It used the warehouse to provide detailed client segmentation data to marketing and sales people, which allowed the company to target customers that were more likely to make purchases.[20]

The use of middleware to connect disparate systems has evolved into an approach for developing software and systems called SOA. A **service-oriented architecture (SOA)** uses modular application services to allow users to interact with systems and systems to interact with each other. Systems developed with SOA are flexible and ideal for businesses that need a system to expand and evolve over time. SOA modules can be reused for a variety of purposes, which reduces development time. Because SOA modules are designed using programming standards so they can interact with other modules, rigid custom-designed middleware software is not needed to connect systems. Sears Canada used SOA to minimize the systems development time required to integrate its legacy systems with more than 3,000 suppliers. Moving to SOA allowed systems engineers to increase code reuse by 5 to 15 percent for major savings in time and money.[21]

service-oriented architecture (SOA)
A modular method of developing software and systems that allows users to interact with systems and systems to interact with each other.

APPLICATION SOFTWARE

As discussed earlier in this chapter, the primary function of application software is to apply the power of the computer to give people, workgroups, and the entire enterprise the ability to solve problems and perform specific tasks. When you need the computer to do something, you use one or more application programs. The application programs interact with systems software, and the systems software then directs the computer hardware to perform the necessary tasks. Applications help you perform common tasks, such as create and format documents, perform calculations, or manage information. Some applications are more specialized. A pharmaceutical company, for example, has developed application software to detect the early signs of Parkinson's disease. The new software can help doctors predict the disease by detecting slight trembling in speech patterns not detectable by the human ear. Application software is used throughout the medical profession to save and prolong lives. For example, the North York General Hospital in Ontario uses content management software to improve communication across the organization and extend the existing intranet.[22]

The functions performed by application software are diverse and range from personal productivity to business analysis. For example, application software can help sales managers track sales of a new item in a test market. Software from IntelliVid monitors video feeds from store security cameras and notifies security when a shopper is behaving suspiciously. Most of the computerized business jobs and activities discussed in this book involve application software. We begin by investigating the types and functions of application software.

Overview of Application Software

Proprietary software and off-the-shelf software are important types of application software. **Proprietary software** is one-of-a-kind software designed for a specific application and owned by the company, organization, or person that uses it. Proprietary software can give a company a competitive advantage by providing services or solving problems in a unique manner, better than methods used by a competitor. **Off-the-shelf software** is mass-produced by software vendors to address needs that are common across businesses, organizations, or individuals. For example, Amazon.ca uses the same off-the-shelf payroll software as many businesses but uses custom-designed proprietary software on its website that allows visitors to more easily find items to purchase. The relative advantages and disadvantages of proprietary software and off-the-shelf software are summarized in Table 4.4 on the next page.

proprietary software
One-of-a-kind software designed for a specific application and owned by the company, organization, or person that uses it.

off-the-shelf software
Software mass-produced by software vendors to address needs that are common across businesses, organizations, or individuals.

Proprietary Software		Off-the-Shelf Software	
Advantages	**Disadvantages**	**Advantages**	**Disadvantages**
You can get exactly what you need in the way of features, reports, and so on.	It can take a long time and significant resources to develop required features.	The initial cost is lower because the software firm can spread the development costs over many customers.	An organization might have to pay for features that are not required and never used.
Being involved in the development offers control over the results.	In-house system development staff may become hard pressed to provide the required level of ongoing support and maintenance because of pressure to move on to other new projects.	The software is likely to meet the basic business needs—you can analyze existing features and the performance of the package before purchasing.	The software might lack important features, thus requiring future modification or customization. This can be very expensive because users must adopt future releases of the software as well.
You can modify features that you might need to counteract an initiative by competitors or to meet new supplier or customer demands. A merger with or acquisition of another firm also requires software changes to meet new business needs.	The features and performance of software that has yet to be developed presents more potential risk.	The package is likely to be of high quality because many customer firms have tested the software and helped identify its bugs.	The software might not match current work processes and data standards.

Table 4.4

A Comparison of Proprietary and Off-the-Shelf Software

application service provider (ASP)
A company that provides software, support, and the computer hardware on which to run the software from the user's facilities over a network.

Software as a Service (SaaS)
A service that allows businesses to subscribe to Web-delivered business application software by paying a monthly service charge or a per-use fee.

Many companies use off-the-shelf software to support business processes. Forrester Research reported that 80 percent of enterprises use Microsoft Office.[23] Key questions for selecting off-the-shelf software include the following: (1) Will the software run on the OS and hardware you have selected? (2) Does the software meet the essential business requirements that have been defined? (3) Is the software manufacturer financially solvent and reliable? and (4) Does the total cost of purchasing, installing, and maintaining the software compare favourably to the expected business benefits? Some off-the-shelf programs can be modified, in effect blending the off-the-shelf and customized approaches.

Another approach to obtaining a customized software package is to use an application service provider. An **application service provider** (**ASP**) is a company that can provide the software, support, and computer hardware on which to run the software from the user's facilities over a network. Some vendors refer to the service as *on-demand software*. An ASP can also simplify a complex corporate software package so that it is easier for the users to set up and manage. ASPs provide contract customization of off-the-shelf software, and they speed deployment of new applications while helping IS managers avoid implementation headaches, reducing the need for many skilled IS staff members and decreasing project start-up expenses. Such an approach allows companies to devote more time and resources to more important tasks. For example, Rapid Advance, a leading cash advance service for small to medium-sized businesses (SMBs), uses Business Objects and Crystal Reports, applications served by SAP Corporation, to manage its business intelligence (BI). The system provides real-time access to sales information, business partner information, and critical corporate reports.[24]

Using an ASP makes the most sense for relatively small, fast-growing companies with limited IS resources. It is also a good strategy for companies that want to deploy a single, functionally focused application quickly, such as setting up an e-commerce website or supporting expense reporting. Contracting with an ASP might make less sense, however, for larger companies that have major systems and their technical infrastructures already in place.

The high overhead of an ASP designing, running, managing, and supporting many customized applications for many businesses has led to another form of software distribution known as **Software as a Service** (**SaaS**), which allows businesses to subscribe to

Web-delivered business application software by paying a monthly service charge or a per-use fee. Like ASP, SaaS providers maintain software on their own servers and provide access to it over the Internet. SaaS usually uses a Web browser–based user interface. For example, SaaS provider SuccessFactors offers a SaaS solution for evaluating employee performance.[25] The Web-based software analyzes an employee's level of success in meeting goals using information from business intelligence and ERP systems. Many business activities are supported by SaaS. Vendors include Oracle, SAP, Net Suite, Salesforce, and Google. SaaS can reduce expenses by sharing its running applications among many businesses. For example, Sears and Walmart might use CRM software provided by a common SaaS provider. Providing one high-quality SaaS application to thousands of businesses is much more cost-effective than custom-designing software for each business.

SaaS and new Web development technologies have led to a new paradigm in computing called cloud computing. Cloud computing refers to the use of computing resources, including software and data storage, on the Internet (the cloud) rather than on local computers. The emergence of powerful Web programming languages and techniques, such as AJAX, lets developers create Web-based software that rivals traditional installed software. Rather than installing, storing, and running software on your own computer, with cloud computing, you use the Web browser to access software stored and delivered from a Web server. Typically the data generated by the software is also stored on the Web server. For example, Tableau software allows users to import database or spreadsheet data to create powerful visualizations that provide useful information.[26] Cloud computing provides the benefit of being able to easily collaborate with others by sharing documents on the Internet. Table 4.5 provides examples of cloud computing.

Application	Description
37signals	Project management and personal information management
Amazon Web Services	Storage and server platforms for cloud computing applications
Buzzword	High-quality word processing software from Adobe
Google Docs and Google Apps	Productivity applications, including word processing, spreadsheets, and presentation software
Icloud and eyeOS	Web-based operating systems
Microsoft Azure	An online Windows platform that supports custom-designed cloud computing applications
Nozbe	To-do list and organizer
Photoshop.com	Photo editing
Salesforce.com	CRM solutions for all sizes of business
Slide Rocket	High-quality presentation software
Zoho	A wide selection of productivity and business applications, including all of the above plus customer resource management (CRM), Web conferencing, database, invoicing, reporting, and human resources software

Table 4.5

Cloud Computing Applications and Platforms

Starbucks used cloud computing services from Salesforce.com when it designed its online community at *www.mystarbucksidea.com*. The site allows Starbucks to converse with its customers to find out how they feel about Starbucks and its products. The customer interactions are stored in a CRM system at Saleforce.com and accessed by Starbucks managers and executives using Salesforce.com's online reporting tools. The cloud computing solution has recorded 77,000 customer suggestions and hundreds of thousands of comments and votes, resulting in 25 new Starbucks products and services.[27]

ASP, SaaS, and cloud computing involve some risks. For example, sensitive information could be compromised in a number of ways, including unauthorized access by employees or computer hackers; the host might not be able to keep its computers and network up and running as consistently as necessary; or a disaster could disable the host's data centre, temporarily putting an organization out of business. These are legitimate concerns that all of these technologies continue to address. Read the Ethical and Societal Issues box for more information on this topic.

Personal Application Software

Hundreds of computer applications can help people at school, home, and work. New computer software under development and existing GPS technology, for example, will allow people to see 3D views of where they are, along with directions and 3D maps to where they would like to go. The features of some popular types of personal application software are summarized in Table 4.6. In addition to these general-purpose programs, thousands of

Table 4.6
Examples of Personal Application Software

Type of Software	Explanation	Example
Word processing	Create, edit, and print text documents	Microsoft Word Corel WordPerfect Google Docs Apple Pages Sun Writer
Spreadsheet	Provide a wide range of built-in functions for statistical, financial, logical, database, graphics, and date and time calculations	Microsoft Excel IBM Lotus 1-2-3 Google Spreadsheet Apple Numbers Sun Calc
Database	Store, manipulate, and retrieve data	Microsoft Access IBM Lotus Approach Borland dBASE Sun Base
Graphics	Develop graphs, illustrations, and drawings	Adobe Illustrator Adobe FreeHand
Project management	Plan, schedule, allocate, and control people and resources (money, time, and technology) needed to complete a project according to schedule	Microsoft Project Symantec On Target Scitor Project Scheduler Symantec Time Line
Financial management	Provide income and expense tracking and reporting to monitor and plan budgets (some programs have investment portfolio management features)	Intuit Quicken
Desktop publishing (DTP)	Use with personal computers and high-resolution printers to create high-quality printed output, including text and graphics; various styles of pages can be laid out; art and text files from other programs can also be integrated into published pages	Quark XPress Microsoft Publisher Adobe PageMaker Corel Ventura Publisher Apple Pages

other personal computer applications perform specialized tasks: to help you do your taxes, get in shape, lose weight, get medical advice, write wills and other legal documents, repair your computer, fix your car, write music, and edit your pictures and videos. This type of software, often called *user software* or *personal productivity software*, includes the general-purpose tools and programs that support individual needs.

Word Processing

Word processing applications are installed on most PCs today. These applications come with a vast array of features, including those for checking spelling, creating tables, inserting formulas, creating graphics, and much more. See Figure 4.11. Much of the work required to create this book used the popular word processing software Microsoft Word.

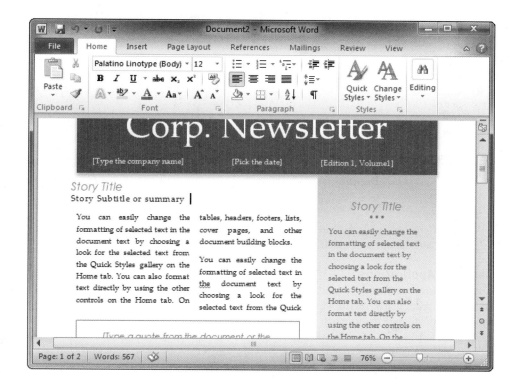

Figure 4.11

Word Processing Program

Word processing applications such as Microsoft Word can be used to write letters, professional documents, work reports, and term papers.

(Source: Used with permission from Microsoft.)

A team of people can use a word processing program to collaborate on a project. The authors and editors who developed this book, for example, used the Track Changes and Reviewing features of Microsoft Word to track and make changes to chapter files. With these features, you can add comments or make revisions to a document that a co-worker can review and either accept or reject.

Spreadsheet Analysis

Spreadsheets are powerful tools for manipulating and analyzing numbers and alphanumeric data. Individuals and organizations use spreadsheets. Features of spreadsheets include formulas, statistical analysis, built-in business functions, graphics, limited database capabilities, and much more. See Figure 4.12 on the next page. The business functions include calculation of depreciation, present value, internal rate of return, and the monthly payment on a loan, to name a few. Optimization is another powerful feature of many spreadsheet programs. *Optimization* allows the spreadsheet to maximize or minimize a quantity subject to certain constraints. For example, a small furniture manufacturer that produces chairs and tables might want to maximize its profits. The constraints could be a limited supply of lumber, a limited number of workers who can assemble the chairs and tables, or a limited amount of various hardware fasteners that might be required. Using an optimization feature, such as

Figure 4.12

Spreadsheet Program

Spreadsheet programs such as Microsoft Excel should be considered when calculations are required.

(Source: Used with permission from Microsoft.)

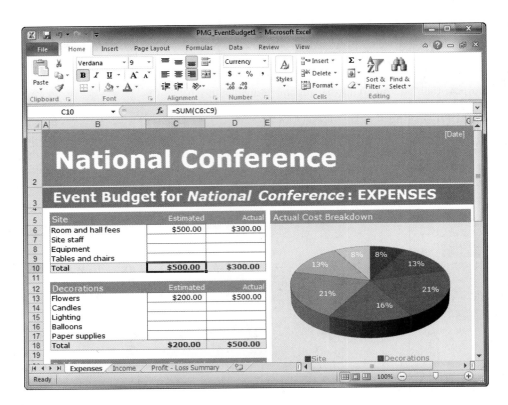

Solver in Microsoft Excel, the spreadsheet can determine what number of chairs and tables to produce with labour and material constraints to maximize profits.

Database Applications

Database applications are ideal for storing, organizing, and retrieving data. These applications are particularly useful when you need to manipulate a large amount of data and produce reports and documents. Database manipulations include merging, editing, and sorting data. The uses of a database application are varied. You can keep track of a CD collection, the items in your apartment, tax records, and expenses. A student club can use a database to store names, addresses, phone numbers, and dues paid. In business, a database application can help process sales orders, control inventory, order new supplies, send letters to customers, and pay employees. Database management systems can be used to track orders, products, and customers; analyze weather data to make forecasts for the next several days; and summarize medical research results. A database can also be a front end to another application. For example, you can use a database application to enter and store income tax information, then export the stored results to other applications, such as a spreadsheet or tax-preparation application.

Presentation Graphics Program

It is often said that a picture is worth a thousand words. With today's graphics programs, it is easy to develop attractive graphs, illustrations, and drawings that assist in communicating important information. See Figure 4.13. Presentation graphics programs can be used to develop advertising brochures, announcements, and full-colour presentations, and to organize and edit photographic images. If you need to make a presentation at school or work, you can use a special type of graphics program called a presentation application to develop slides and then display them while you are speaking. Because of their popularity, many colleges and departments require students to become proficient at using presentation graphics programs.

Many graphics programs, including Microsoft Office PowerPoint, consist of a series of slides. Each slide can be displayed on a computer screen, printed as a handout, or

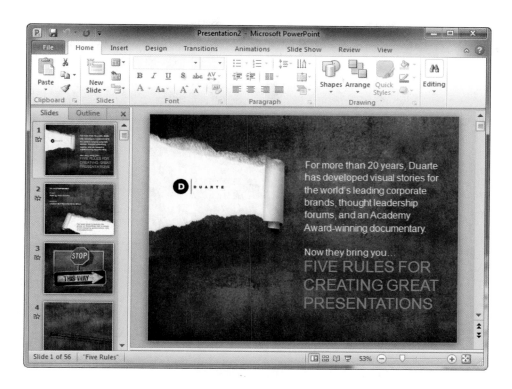

Figure 4.13

Presentation Graphics Program

Presentation graphics programs such as Microsoft PowerPoint can help you make a presentation at school or work.

(Source: Used with permission from Microsoft.)

(more commonly) projected onto a large viewing screen for audiences. Powerful built-in features allow you to develop attractive slides and complete presentations. You can select a template for a type of presentation, such as recommending a strategy for managers, communicating news to a sales force, giving a training presentation, or facilitating a brainstorming session. The presentation graphics program lets you create a presentation step by step, including applying colour and attractive formatting. You can also design a custom presentation using the many types of charts, drawings, and formatting available. Most presentation graphics programs come with many pieces of *clip art*, such as drawings and photos of people meeting, medical equipment, telecommunications equipment, entertainment, and much more.

Personal Information Managers

Personal information management (PIM) software helps people, groups, and organizations store useful information, such as a list of tasks to complete or a set of names and addresses. PIM software usually provides an appointment calendar, an address book or contacts list, and a place to take notes. In addition, information in a PIM can be linked. For example, you can link an appointment with a sales manager in the calendar to information on the sales manager in the address book. When you click the appointment in the calendar, a window opens displaying information on the sales manager from the address book. Microsoft Outlook is an example of very popular PIM software. Increasingly, PIM software is moving online where it can be accessed from any Internet connected device. See Figure 4.14 on the next page.

Some PIMs allow you to schedule and coordinate group meetings. If a computer or hand-held device is connected to a network, you can upload the PIM data and coordinate it with the calendar and schedule of others using the same PIM software on the network. You can also use some PIMs to coordinate e-mails to invite others to meetings. As users receive their invitations, they click a link or button to be automatically added to the guest list. Goodmans LLP, a Canadian law firm, implemented a custom-designed Microsoft Outlook–based application in combination with its telephone system to automatically track time spent on client phone calls. The company expects to recover as many as 10,000 unbilled hours annually.[28]

Figure 4.14

Personal Information Management Software

iGoogle and other Web portals support PIM by allowing users to access calendars, to-do lists, e-mail, social networks, contacts, and other information all from one page.

(Source: Google.)

software suite

A collection of single programs packaged together in a bundle.

Table 4.7

Major Components of Leading Software Suites

Software Suites and Integrated Software Packages

A **software suite** is a collection of single programs packaged together in a bundle. Software suites can include a word processor, spreadsheet program, database management system, graphics program, communications tools, organizers, and more. Some suites support the development of Web pages, note taking, and speech recognition so that applications in the suite can accept voice commands and record dictation. Software suites offer many advantages. The software programs have been designed to work similarly, so after you learn the basics for one application, the other applications are easy to learn and use. Buying software in a bundled suite is cost-effective; the programs usually sell for a fraction of what they would cost individually.

Microsoft Office, Corel WordPerfect Office, Lotus SmartSuite, and Sun Microsystems OpenOffice are examples of popular general-purpose software suites for personal computer users. Microsoft Office has the largest market share. OpenOffice is an open-source software suite derived from Sun Microsystems's StarOffice. Each of these software suites includes a spreadsheet program, word processor, database program, and graphics presentation software. All can exchange documents, data, and diagrams. See Table 4.7. In other words, you can create a spreadsheet and then cut and paste that spreadsheet into a document created using the word processing application.

Personal Productivity Function	Microsoft Office	Lotus Symphony	Corel WordPerfect Office	Oracle StarOffice	Apple iWork	Google
Word Processing	Word	Documents	WordPerfect	Writer	Pages	Docs
Spreadsheet	Excel	Spreadsheets	Quattro Pro	Calc	Numbers	Spreadsheet
Presentation Graphics	PowerPoint	Presentations	Presentations	Impress	Keynote	Presentation
Database	Access		Paradox	Base		

Forrester Research reports that 80 percent of enterprise customers use some version of Microsoft Office. The latest version is Office 2010, available in seven editions: Starter, Home and Student, Home and Business, Standard, Professional, Professional Academic, and Professional Plus. Each edition includes a subset of 10 applications. Office 2010 introduced a new feature for the product: Office Web Apps, which are online versions of Word, Excel, PowerPoint, and OneNote. Office Web Apps are expected to compete with online applications from Google, Zoho, and others.

In addition to suites, some companies produce *integrated application packages* that contain several programs. For example, Microsoft Works is one program that contains basic word processing, spreadsheet, database, address book, calendar, and other applications. Although not as powerful as stand-alone software included in software suites, integrated software packages offer a range of capabilities for less money.

Some companies offer Web-based productivity software suites that require no installation—only a Web browser. Zoho, Google, and Thinkfree offer free online word processing, spreadsheet, presentation, and other software that require no installation on the PC. Adobe has developed Acrobat.com, which features an impressive online suite: Buzzword for word processing, Tables for spreadsheet and database applications, and Presentations for presentation graphics. See Figure 4.15. Documents created with the software can be stored on the Web server. Currently these online applications are not as powerful and robust as installed software such as Microsoft Office. However, as the technology becomes more powerful and network connection speeds increase, users will probably need to install less software on their PCs and turn instead to using software online. After observing this trend, Microsoft responded with an online version of some of its popular Office applications. The online versions of Word, Excel, PowerPoint, and OneNote are tightly integrated with their desktop counterparts for easy sharing of documents among computers and collaborators.[29]

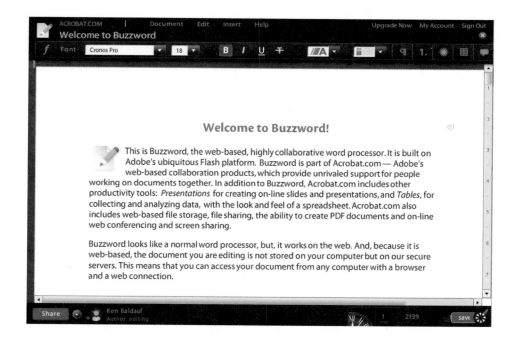

Figure 4.15

Web Suites

Adobe Acrobat.com provides a suite of online applications, including Buzzword, with cutting-edge interface designs.

(Source: Adobe product screenshot reprinted with permission from Adobe Systems Incorporated.)

Other Personal Application Software

In addition to the software already discussed, people can use many other interesting and powerful application software tools. In some cases, the features and capabilities of these applications can more than justify the cost of an entire computer system. TurboTax, for example, is a popular tax-preparation program. You can find software for creating Web pages and sites, composing music, and editing photos and videos editing. Many people use educational and reference software, and entertainment, games, and leisure software. Engineers, architects, and designers often use computer-aided design (CAD) software to design and develop buildings, electrical systems, plumbing systems, and more. Autosketch, CorelCAD, and AutoCad are examples of CAD software. Other programs perform a wide array of statistical tests. Colleges and universities often have a number of courses in statistics that use this type of application software. Two popular applications in the social sciences are SPSS and SAS.

Mobile Application Software

Recall that operating systems designed for smartphones include OS X iPhone, Android, and WebOS. The APIs and software development kits designed for these mobile operating systems have given software developers the opportunity to develop applications specifically for mobile use on a small display. Besides the valuable mobile applications that come with the OS, tens of thousands of applications have been developed by third parties for the iPhone. iPhone users download and install these so-called apps using Apple's App Store. Many iPhone apps are free, others range in price from 99 cents to hundreds of dollars. For example, the BarMax iPhone App helps law students prepare for the California bar exam for $999.99.[30] Thousands of mobile apps are also available in the Android Market for users of Android handsets. The Palm WebOS has released its software development kit and might soon have many applications available beyond the dozens that are currently available. Table 4.8 lists typical mobile application categories.

Table 4.8

Categories of Mobile Applications for Smartphones

Category	Description
Books and reference	Access e-books, subscribe to journals, or look up information in Webster's or Wikipedia
Business and finance	Track expenses, trade stocks, and access corporate information systems
Entertainment	Access all forms of entertainment, including movies, television programs, music videos, and local night life
Games	Play a variety of games, from 2D games such as Pacman and Tetris to 3D games such as Need for Speed, Rock Band, and The Sims
Health and fitness	Track workout and fitness progress, calculate calories, and even monitor your speed and progress from your wirelessly connected Nike shoes
Lifestyle	Find good restaurants, select wine for a meal, record workout progress, and more
Music	Find, listen to, and create music
News and weather	Access major news and weather providers, including CBC, *Globe and Mail, National Post,* and the Weather Channel.
Photography	Organize, edit, view, and share photos taken on your camera phone
Productivity and utilities	Create grocery lists, practise PowerPoint presentations, work on spreadsheets, synchronize with PC files, and more
Social networking	Connect with others via major social networks, including Facebook, Twitter, and MySpace
Sports	Keep up with your favourite team or track your own golf scores
Travel and navigation	Use the GPS in your smartphone to get turn-by-turn directions, find interesting places to visit, access travel itineraries, and more

Apple's App store was a bigger success than anyone anticipated. In less than a year, more than a billion applications were downloaded from the App store. Now more than three times that many have been downloaded and more than 100,000 applications are available.[31] The rapid growth in popularity of Apple's App store caused other businesses and organizations to adopt similar models. Popular smartphones platforms all have some form of software development kit and app store. Sun Microsystems has created a store for Java applications. Even the U.S. federal government is jumping on the bandwagon. In 2009 it launched an app store for federal agencies to use in finding cloud computing applications.[32]

Workgroup Application Software

Workgroup application software is designed to support teamwork, whether team members are in the same location or dispersed around the world. This support can be accomplished with software known as *groupware* that helps groups of people work together effectively. Microsoft Exchange Server, for example, has groupware and e-mail features. Also called *collaborative software*, the approach allows a team of managers to work on the same production problem, letting them share their ideas and work via connected computer systems. The "Three Cs" rule for successful implementation of groupware is summarized in Table 4.9.

workgroup application software
Software that supports teamwork, whether team members are in the same location or dispersed around the world.

Quality	Description
Convenient	If it's too hard to use, it's not used; it should be as easy to use as the telephone.
Content	It must provide a constant stream of rich, relevant, and personalized content.
Coverage	If it isn't conveniently accessible, it might never be used.

Table 4.9

Ernst & Young's "Three Cs" Rule for Groupware

Examples of workgroup software include group scheduling software, electronic mail, and other software that enables people to share ideas. Lotus Notes from IBM, for example, lets companies use one software package and one user interface to integrate many business processes. Lotus Notes can allow a global team to work together from a common set of documents, have electronic discussions using threads of discussion, and schedule team meetings. As the program matured, Lotus added services to it and renamed it Domino (Lotus Notes is now the name of the e-mail package.) Now an entire third-party market has emerged to build collaborative software based on Domino.

Web-based software is ideal for group use. Because documents are stored on an Internet server, anyone with an Internet connection can access them easily. Google provides options in its online applications that allow users to share documents, spreadsheets, presentations, calendars, and notes with other specified users or everyone on the Web. This makes it convenient for several people to contribute to a document without concern for software compatibility or storage. Google also provides a tool for creating Web-based forms and surveys. When invited parties fill out the form, the data is stored in a Google spreadsheet. See Figure 4.16.

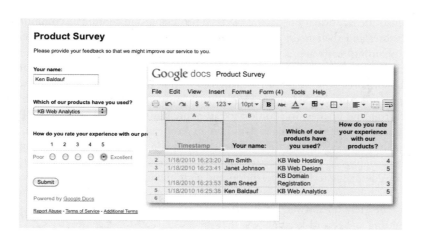

Figure 4.16

Google Forms

Google forms are used to collect information online and store it in a spreadsheet.

(Source: Google.)

An increasing number of software applications are moving online to support group document and information sharing. Google applications let users share notes, calendars, documents, spreadsheets, and presentations. At the Ta-Da Lists website (*www.tadalists.com*), users can share to-do lists with others in a group. Microsoft offers Office Live Workspace for sharing documents, spreadsheets, and other Office files online. If you have digital information you wish to share, you can probably find an online service where you can share it and control who can access it.

Enterprise Application Software

Software that benefits an entire organization—enterprise application software—can also be developed specifically for the business or purchased off the shelf. Some software vendors, such as SAP, specialize in developing software for enterprises. One of the first enterprise applications was a payroll program for Lyons Bakeries in England, developed in 1954 on the Leo 1 computer. Many organizations are moving to integrated enterprise software that supports supply chain management (movement of raw materials from suppliers through shipment of finished goods to customers). Following are some applications that can be addressed with enterprise software.

Accounts payable	Invoicing
Accounts receivable	Manufacturing control
Airline industry operations	Order entry
Automatic teller systems	Payroll
Cash-flow analysis	Receiving
Cheque processing	Restaurant management
Credit and charge card administration	Retail operations
Distribution control	Sales ordering
Fixed asset accounting	Savings and time deposits
General ledger	Shipping
Human resource management	Stock and bond management
Inventory control	Tax planning and preparation

Organizations can no longer respond to market changes using nonintegrated information systems based on overnight processing of the previous day's business transactions, conflicting data models, and obsolete technology. Walmart and many other companies have sophisticated information systems to speed processing and coordinate communications between stores and their main offices. Many corporations are turning to ERP (enterprise resource planning) software, a set of integrated programs that manage a company's vital business operations for an entire multi-site, global organization. Thus an ERP system must be able to support many legal entities, languages, and currencies. Although the scope can vary from vendor to vendor, most ERP systems provide integrated software to support manufacturing and finance. In addition to these core business processes, some ERP systems might support business functions such as human resources, sales, and distribution. The primary benefits of implementing ERP software include eliminating inefficient systems, easing adoption of improved work processes, improving access to data for operational decision making, standardizing technology vendors and equipment, and enabling supply chain management. By contrast, small businesses usually do not need complex enterprise application software. They rely on software such as Intuit QuickBooks and Sage's Simply Accounting for accounting and record-keeping.

Application Software for Information, Decision Support, and Specialized Purposes

Specialized application software for information, decision support, and other purposes is available in every industry. For example, many schools and colleges use Blackboard or other learning management software to organize class materials and grades.[33] Genetic researchers, as another example, are using software to visualize and analyze the human genome. Music executives use decision support software to help pick the next hit song. Sophisticated decision support software is also being used to increase the cure rate for cancer by analyzing about 100 scans of a cancerous tumour to create a 3D view of the tumour. Software can then consider thousands of angles and doses of radiation to determine the best program of radiation therapy. The software analysis takes only minutes but the results can save years or decades of life for the patient. As you will see in future chapters, information, decision support, and specialized systems are used in businesses of all sizes and types to increase profits or reduce costs. But how are all these systems actually developed and built? The answer is through the use of programming languages, discussed next.

PROGRAMMING LANGUAGES

Both system and application software are written in coding schemes called *programming languages*. The primary function of a programming language is to provide instructions to the computer system so that it can perform a processing activity. IS professionals work with **programming languages**, which are sets of keywords, symbols, and rules for constructing statements that people can use to communicate instructions to a computer. Programming involves translating what a user wants to accomplish into instructions that the computer can understand and execute. Programming involves translating what a user wants to accomplish into a code that the computer can understand and execute. *Program code* is the set of instructions that signal the CPU to perform circuit-switching operations. In the simplest coding schemes, a line of code typically contains a single instruction such as "Retrieve the data in memory address X." As discussed in Chapter 3, the instruction is then decoded during the instruction phase of the machine cycle. Like writing a report or a paper in English, writing a computer program in a programming language requires the programmer to follow a set of rules. Each programming language uses symbols, keywords, and commands that have special meanings and usage. Each language also has its own set of rules, called the **syntax** of the language. The language syntax dictates how the symbols, keywords, and commands should be combined into statements capable of conveying meaningful instructions to the CPU. Rules such as "statements must terminate with a semicolon" and "variable names must begin with a letter" are examples of a language's syntax. A variable is a quantity that can take on different values. Program variable names such as SALES, PAYRATE, and TOTAL follow the syntax because they start with a letter, whereas variables such as %INTEREST, $TOTAL, and #POUNDS do not.

programming languages
Sets of keywords, commands, symbols, and a system of rules for constructing statements by which humans can communicate instructions to a computer.

syntax
A set of rules associated with a programming language.

The Evolution of Programming Languages

The desire for faster, more efficient, more powerful information processing has pushed the development of new programming languages. The evolution of programming languages is typically discussed in terms of generations of languages. See Table 4.10 on the next page.

Visual, Object-Oriented, and Artificial Intelligence Languages

Today, programmers often use visual and object-oriented languages. In the future, they will likely be using artificial intelligence languages to a greater extent. In general, these languages are easier for nonprogrammers to use, compared with older generation languages.

Generation	Language	Approximate Development Date	Sample Statement or Action
First	Machine language	1940s	00010101
Second	Assembly language	1950s	MVC
Third	High-level language	1960s	READ SALES
Fourth	Query and database languages	1970s	PRINT EMPLOYEE NUMBER IF GROSS PAY>1000
Beyond Fourth	Natural and intelligent languages	1980s	IF gross pay is greater than 40, THEN pay the employee overtime pay

Table 4.10

The Evolution of Programming Languages

Visual programming uses a graphical or "visual" interface combined with text-based commands. Prior to visual programming, programmers were required to describe the windows, buttons, text boxes, and menus that they were creating for an application by using only text-based programming language commands. With visual programming, the software engineer drags and drops graphical objects such as buttons and menus onto the application form. Then, using a programming language, the programmer defines the capabilities of those objects in a separate code window. Visual Basic was one of the first visual programming interfaces. Today, software engineers use Visual Basic .NET, Visual C++, Visual C# (# is pronounced "sharp" as in music), Visual J#, and other visual programming tools.

Many people refer to visual programming interfaces such as Visual C# as "visual programming languages." This is fine for casual references, but a lesser-known category of programming language is more truly visual. With a true visual programming language, programmers create software by manipulating programming elements only graphically, without the use of any text-based programming language commands. Examples include Alice, Mindscript, and Microsoft Visual Programming Language, which is used for programming robotics. Visual programming languages are ideal for teaching novices the basics about programming without requiring them to memorize programming language syntax.

Some programming languages separate data elements from the procedures or actions that will be performed on them, but another type of programming language ties them together into units called *objects*. An object consists of data and the actions that can be performed on the data. For example, an object could be data about an employee and all the operations (such as payroll calculations) that might be performed on the data. Programming languages that are based on objects are called *object-oriented programming languages*. C++ and Java are the most popular general-purpose object-oriented programming languages. Languages used for Web development such as Javascript and PHP are also object-oriented. In fact, most popular languages in use today take the object-oriented approach—and for good reason.

Using object-oriented programming languages is like constructing a building using prefabricated modules or parts. The object containing the data, instructions, and procedures is a programming building block. The same objects (modules or parts) can be used repeatedly. One of the primary advantages of an object is that it contains reusable code. In other words, the instruction code within that object can be reused in different programs for a variety of applications, just as the same basic prefabricated door can be used in two different houses. An object can relate to data on a product, an input routine, or an order processing routine. An object can even direct a computer to execute other programs or to retrieve and manipulate data. So a sorting routine developed for a payroll application could be used in both a billing program and an inventory control program. By reusing program code, programmers can write programs for specific application problems more quickly. See Figure 4.17. By combining existing program objects with new ones, programmers can easily and efficiently develop new object-oriented programs to accomplish organizational goals.

Programming languages used to create artificial intelligence or expert systems applications are often called *fifth-generation languages* (*5GLs*). FLEXPERT, for example, is an expert system used to perform plant layout and to help companies determine the best placement for equipment and manufacturing facilities. Fifth-generation languages are sometimes called

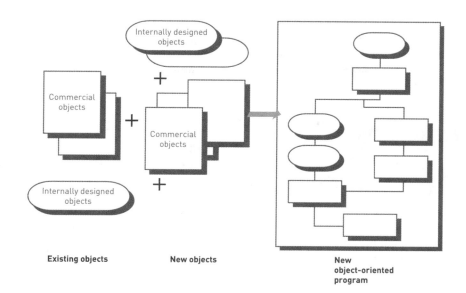

Existing objects   New objects   New object-oriented program

Figure 4.17

Reusable Code in Object-Oriented Programming

By combining existing program objects with new ones, programmers can easily and efficiently develop new object-oriented programs to accomplish organizational goals. Note that these objects can be either commercially available or designed internally.

natural languages because they use even more English-like syntax than 4GLs. They allow programmers to communicate with the computer by using normal sentences. For example, computers programmed in fifth-generation languages can understand queries such as "How many athletic shoes did our company sell last month?"

With third-generation and higher-level programming languages, each statement in the language translates into several instructions in machine language. A special software program called a **compiler** converts the programmer's source code into the machine-language instructions, which consists of binary digits, as shown in Figure 4.18. A compiler creates a two-stage process for program execution. First, the compiler translates the program into a machine language; second, the CPU executes that program. Another approach is to use an

compiler
A special software program that converts the programmer's source code into the machine-language instructions, which consists of binary digits.

Figure 4.18

How a Compiler Works

A compiler translates a complete program into a complete set of binary instructions (Stage 1). After this is done, the CPU can execute the converted program in its entirety (Stage 2).

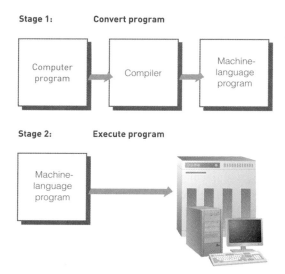

Stage 1: Convert program

Computer program → Compiler → Machine-language program

Stage 2: Execute program

Machine-language program →

Program execution

interpreter, which is a language translator that carries out the operations called for by the source code. An interpreter does not produce a complete machine-language program. After the statement executes, the machine-language statement is discarded, the process continues for the next statement, and so on.

The majority of software used today is created using an integrated development environment. An *integrated development environment*, or *IDE*, combines all the tools required

Figure 4.19

Emulator for Android Smartphones

To develop for the Android, you use an SDK with a mobile device emulator so you can prototype, develop, and test Android applications without transferring them to a physical device.

(Source: Google.)

for software engineering into one package. For example, the popular IDE Microsoft Visual Studio includes an editor that supports several visual programming interfaces and languages, a compiler and interpreter, programming automation tools, a debugger (a tool for finding errors in the code), and other tools that provide convenience to the developer.

Software Development Kits (SDKs) often serve the purpose of an IDE for a particular platform. For example, software developers for Google's Android smartphone platform use Java (an object-oriented programming language) along with the Eclipse SDK. They use special code libraries provided by Google for Android functionality, and they test out their applications in an Android Emulator. See Figure 4.19.

IDEs and SDKs have made software development easier than ever. Many novice coders and some who might have never considered developing software are publishing applications for popular platforms such as Facebook and the iPhone.

SOFTWARE ISSUES AND TRENDS

Because software is such an important part of today's computer systems, issues such as software bugs, licensing, upgrades, and global software support have received increased attention. We highlight several major software issues and trends in this section: software bugs, copyrights, software licensing, freeware and open-source software, software upgrades, and global software support.

Software Bugs

A software bug is a defect in a computer program that keeps it from performing as it is designed to perform. Some software bugs are obvious and cause the program to terminate unexpectedly. Other bugs are subtler and allow errors to creep into your work. Computer and software vendors say that as long as people design and program hardware and software, bugs are inevitable. The following list summarizes tips for reducing the impact of software bugs.

- Register all software so that you receive bug alerts, fixes, and patches.
- Check the manual or read-me files for solutions to known problems.
- Access the support area of the manufacturer's website for patches.
- Install the latest software updates.
- Before reporting a bug, make sure that you can re-create the circumstances under which it occurs.
- After you can re-create the bug, call the manufacturer's tech support line.
- Consider waiting before buying the latest release of software to give the vendor a chance to discover and remove bugs. Many schools and businesses don't purchase software until the first major revision with patches is released.

Copyrights and Licences

Most software products are protected by law using copyright or licensing provisions. Those provisions can vary, however. In some cases, you are given unlimited use of software on one or two computers. This is typical with many applications developed for personal computers. In other cases, you pay for your usage—if you use the software more, you pay more. This

ETHICAL AND SOCIETAL ISSUES

Software-Driven Cars

Today's vehicles—cars, SUVs, and trucks—use sophisticated software as an interface between the driver and the mechanics of the engine. Just as an operating system is used as an interface to computer hardware, automotive system software is used as an interface to automotive hardware. When a driver presses the accelerator or brake, or turns the steering wheel, it may feel as though he or she is interacting directly with the mechanics of the vehicle, but in reality, those actions are used as input for the software actually controlling the mechanics.

Electronic systems and software account for roughly 40 percent of the cost of manufacturing today's vehicles. Those electronic systems—the circuit boards and software that run on them—are manufactured by suppliers that specialize in automotive subsystems. Dozens of such subsystems are delivered to automotive manufacturers, including Ford and Toyota, where they are integrated into the complex systems that make up today's engines. If you have engine trouble, it is likely to be a failure on the part of one of the electronic subsystems.

Great care is taken in the design of the software that controls critical systems—systems on which life may depend, such as braking, acceleration, and steering. However, as manufacturers move to new, fuel-efficient technologies such as those used in hybrid cars, these systems are becoming more complex and increasingly difficult to troubleshoot. For example, Toyota's hybrid vehicle, the Prius, has three electronic braking systems that work together to safely stop the car while generating electricity. The first software system controls the standard brake pads, increasing pressure on the brake pads as the driver increases pressure on the brake pedal. The second software system is the Antilock Braking System (ABS) that senses the traction level between the tire and road, and compensates for icy and slippery conditions. The third software system is the regenerative brake system, a component of Toyota's hybrid Synergy Drive, which collects energy from the turning wheels to recharge the battery that runs the car's secondary electric motors.

The three braking systems on the Toyota Prius continuously collect data from different sources and combine that information to effectively slow or stop the car. In the case of the 2010 Prius, those systems had a minor software bug that caused the brakes to hesitate momentarily when the driver applied a small amount of pressure. While the bug was not life threatening—the brakes worked with increased pressure—it did cause some Prius drivers a moment of panic. Toyota had to recall over 100,000 vehicles to install a software patch.

Software flaws in automobiles may not be any more dangerous than hardware flaws. After all, an imperfection in a Prius brake pad might have had even more disastrous results. However, depending on software does cause consumers additional concerns. From their experience with PCs, many people expect software to crash. However, with automotive software and other critical software, a software crash can become a life-threatening event. Concerns stem not only from software bugs but from the possibility of hacking and viruses. Suppose a hacker or terrorist group infiltrated a manufacturer's workforce and implanted a virus in a software system that caused braking systems to simultaneously shut down at a specified time and date.

Automobiles are just one example of the many ways that people depend on properly functioning software. Businesses and governments recognize the importance of software stability and are funding extensive research to provide guaranteed safe and reliable software solutions.

Discussion Questions

1. Why do you think the Toyota recall created a large stir in the media, causing strong consumer reaction?
2. What actions did Toyota take to restore consumer confidence in its products following the troubles with its software? Do you think its actions were effective? Why or why not?

Critical Thinking Questions

1. What other critical systems do people, organizations, countries, and the world depend on to use properly functioning software?
2. Can software ever be truly trustworthy? Why or why not?

SOURCES: Mitchell, Robert, "Toyota's Lesson: Software Can Be Unsafe at Any Speed," *Computerworld*, www.computerworld.com, February 5, 2010; Tabuchi, Hiroko, "Toyota Is to Recall 2010 Prius Model Cars for Brakes," *New York Times*, www.nytimes.com, February 7, 2010; "Toyota Announces Voluntary Recall on 2010 Model-Year Prius to Update ABS Software," Toyota website, www.toyota.com/recall/abs.html, accessed February 13, 2010.

approach is becoming popular with software placed on networks or larger computers. Most of these protections prevent you from copying software and giving it to others. Some software now requires that you *register* or *activate* it before it can be fully used. This is another way software companies prevent illegal distribution of their products.

When people purchase software, they don't actually own the software but rather are licensed to use the software on a computer. This is called a single-user licence. A **single-user licence** permits you to install the software on one computer, or sometimes two computers, used by one person. A single-user licence does not allow you to copy and share the software with others. Table 4.11 describes different types of software licences. Licences that accommodate several users are usually provided at a discounted price.

single-user licence
A software licence that permits only one person to use the software, typically on only one computer.

Table 4.11

Software Licences

Licence	Description
Single-user licence	Permits you to install the software on one computer, or sometimes two computers, used by one person.
Multi-user licence	Specifies the number of users allowed to use the software and can be installed on each user's computer. For example, a 20-user licence can be installed on 20 computers for 20 users.
Concurrent-user licence	Designed for network-distributed software, this licence allows any number of users to use the software, but only a specific number of users to use it at the same time.
Site licence	Permits the software to be used anywhere on a particular site, such as a college campus, by everyone on the site.

Freeware and Open-Source Software

Some software developers are less interested in profiting from their intellectual property and have developed alternative copyrights and licensing agreements. *Freeware* is software that is made available to the public for free. Software developers might give away their product for several reasons. Some want to build customer interest and name recognition. Others simply don't need the money and want to make a valuable donation to society. Still others, such as those associated with the Free Software Foundation (*www.fsf.org*), believe that all software should be free. Some freeware is placed in the public domain where anyone can use the software free of charge. Creative works that reach the end of their term of copyright revert to the public domain. Table 4.12 shows some examples of freeware.

Table 4.12

Examples of Freeware

Software	Description
Thunderbird	E-mail and newsgroup software
Pidgin	Instant messaging software
Adobe Reader	Software for viewing Adobe PDF documents
AVG Anti-Virus	Antivirus security software
WinPatrol	Anti-spyware software
IrfanView	Photo-editing software

Freeware differs slightly from free software. Freeware simply implies that the software is distributed for free. The term "free software" was coined by Richard Stallman and the Free Software Foundation and implies that the software is not only freeware, but it is also open source. **Open-source software** is distributed, typically for free, with the source code also available so that it can be studied, changed, and improved by its users. Open-source software evolves from the combined contribution of its users. Table 4.13 provides examples of popular open-source software applications.

open-source software
Software that is distributed, typically for free, with the source code also available so that it can be studied, changed, and improved by its users.

Software	Category
Linux	Operating system
Open Office	Application software
MySQL	Database software
Mozilla Firefox	Internet browser
Gimp	Photo editing
OpenProj	Project management
Grisbi	Personal accounting
Thunderbird	E-mail

Table 4.13

Examples of Open-Source Software

Open-source software is not completely devoid of restrictions. Much of the popular free software in use today is protected by the GNU General Public License (GPL). The GPL grants you the right to do the following:

- Run the program for any purpose
- Study how the program works and adapt it to your needs
- Redistribute copies so you can help others
- Improve the program and release improvements to the public

Software under the GPL is typically protected by a "copyleft" (a play on the word copyright), which requires that any copies of the work retain the same licence. A copylefted work cannot be owned by any one person, and no one is allowed to profit from its distribution. The Free Software Directory (*http://directory.fsf.org*) lists over 5,000 software titles in 22 categories licensed under the GPL.

Why would an organization run its business using software that's free? Can something that's given away over the Internet be stable, reliable, or sufficiently supported to place at the core of a company's day-to-day operations? The answer is surprising—many believe that open-source software is often *more* reliable and secure than commercial software. How can this be? First, by making a program's source code readily available, users can fix any problems they discover. A fix is often available within hours of the problem's discovery. Second, with the source code for a program accessible to thousands of people, the chances of a bug being discovered and fixed before it does any damage are much greater than with traditional software packages. Whole Foods Market recently switched to a Linux-based platform and reports increased productivity and reduced costs due to more efficient system administration.[34]

However, using open-source software does have some disadvantages. Although open-source systems can be obtained for next to nothing, the up-front costs are only a small piece of the total cost of ownership that accrues over the years that the system is in place. Some claim that open-source systems contain many hidden costs, particularly for user support or solving problems with the software. Licensed software comes with guarantees and support services that open-source software does not. Still, many businesses appreciate the additional freedom that open-source software provides. The question of software support is the biggest stumbling block to the acceptance of open-source software at the corporate level. Getting support for traditional software packages is easy—you call a company's toll-free support number or access its website. But how do you get help if an open-source package doesn't work as expected? Because the open-source community lives on the Internet, you look there for help. Through use of Internet discussion areas, you can communicate with others who use the same software, and you might even reach someone who helped develop it. Users of popular open-source packages can get correct answers to their technical questions within a few hours of asking for help on the appropriate Internet forum. Another approach is to contact one of the many companies emerging to support and service such software—for example, Red Hat for Linux, C2Net for Apache, and Sendmail, Inc., for Sendmail. These companies offer high-quality, for-pay technical assistance.

Software Upgrades

Software companies revise their programs and sell new versions periodically. Such upgrades typically cost less than a new installation of a product. Software upgrades vary widely in the benefits that they provide, and what some people call a benefit others might call a drawback. Some upgrades, such as the move from Microsoft Office 2003 to Office 2007, provide a new and improved user interface that makes the product easier to use. Others, such as Windows 7 and Mac OS Lion, improve the stability of the product and offer improvements in performance. Most software upgrades offer new features and capabilities as well. Deciding whether to upgrade to a new version of software can be a challenge for corporations and people with a large investment in software. Should the newest version be purchased when it is released? Some users do not always get the most current software upgrades or versions, unless it includes significant improvements or capabilities. Instead, they might upgrade to newer software only when it offers vital new features. When software companies stop supporting older software versions or releases, some customers feel forced to upgrade to the newer software.

Global Software Support

Large global companies have little trouble persuading vendors to sell them software licences for even the most far-flung outposts of their company. But can those same vendors provide adequate support for their software customers in all locations? Supporting local operations is one of the biggest challenges IS teams face when putting together standardized, company-wide systems. Slower technology growth markets, such as Eastern Europe and Latin America, might not have any official vendor presence. Instead, large vendors such as Sybase, IBM, and Hewlett-Packard typically contract with local providers to support their software.

One approach that has been gaining acceptance in North America is to outsource global support to one or more third-party distributors. The user company can still negotiate its licence with the software vendor directly, but it then hands the global support contract to a third-party supplier. The supplier acts as a middleman between software vendor and user, often providing distribution, support, and invoicing.

In today's computer systems, software is an increasingly critical component. Whatever approach people and organizations take to acquire software, everyone must be aware of the current trends in the industry. Informed users are wise consumers.

SUMMARY

Principle:

Systems software and application software are critical in helping individuals and organizations achieve their goals.

Software consists of programs that control the workings of the computer hardware. The two main categories of software are systems software and application software. Systems software is a collection of programs that interacts between hardware and application software and includes operating systems, utility programs, and middleware. Application software can be proprietary or off the shelf and enables people to solve problems and perform specific tasks.

An operating system (OS) is a set of computer programs that controls the computer hardware to support users' computing needs. An OS converts an instruction from an application into a set of instructions needed by the hardware. This intermediary role allows hardware independence. An OS also manages memory, which involves controlling storage access and use by converting logical requests into physical locations and by placing data in the best storage space, including virtual memory.

An OS manages tasks to allocate computer resources through multitasking and time sharing. With multitasking, users can run more than one application at a time. Time sharing allows more than one person to use a computer system at the same time.

The ability of a computer to handle an increasing number of concurrent users smoothly is called *scalability*, a feature critical for systems expected to handle a large number of users.

An OS also provides a user interface, which allows users to access and command the computer. A command-based user interface requires text commands to send instructions; a graphical user interface (GUI), such as Windows, uses icons and menus.

Software applications use the OS by requesting services through a defined application program interface (API). Programmers can use APIs to create application software without having to understand the inner workings of the OS. APIs also provide a degree of hardware independence so that the underlying hardware can change without necessarily requiring a rewrite of the software applications.

Over the years, many popular OSs have been developed. OSs for personal computers include many versions of Microsoft Windows, culminating in the most recent version, Windows 7. While Microsoft Windows has held a monopoly in the PC OS market for well over a decade, the Mac OS X has recently increased its market share, and Linux has grown in popularity for inexpensive mobile computers such as netbooks. There are several options for OSs in the enterprise as well, depending on the type server. UNIX is a powerful OS that can be used on many computer system types and platforms, from workstations to mainframe systems. UNIX makes it easy to move programs and data among computers or to connect mainframes and workstations to share resources. Linux is the kernel of an OS whose source code is freely available to everyone. Several variations of Linux are available, with sets of capabilities and applications to form a complete OS—for example, Red Hat Linux. z/OS and MPE iX are OSs for mainframe computers. Some OSs, such as Mac OS X iPhone, Windows Mobile, Windows Embedded, Symbian, Android, WebOS, and variations of Linux, have been developed to support mobile communications and consumer appliances. When an OS is stored in solid state memory, embedded in a device, it is referred to as an embedded operating system, or an embedded system for short.

Utility programs can perform many useful tasks and often come installed on computers along with the OS. This software is used to merge and sort sets of data, keep track of computer jobs being run, compress files of data, protect against harmful computer viruses, monitor hardware and network performance, and perform dozens of other important tasks. Virtualization software simulates a computer's hardware architecture in software so that computer systems can run operating systems and software designed for other architectures, or run several operating systems simultaneously on one system. Middleware is software that allows different systems to communicate and transfer data back and forth. A service-oriented architecture (SOA) uses modular application services to allow users to interact with systems and systems to interact with each other.

Principle:

Organizations use off-the-shelf application software for common business needs and proprietary application software to meet unique business needs, providing a competitive advantage.

Application software applies the power of the computer to solve problems and perform specific tasks. One useful way of classifying the many potential uses of information systems is to identify the scope of problems and opportunities addressed by a particular organization or its sphere of influence. For most companies, the spheres of influence are personal, workgroup, and enterprise.

User software, or personal productivity software, includes general-purpose programs that enable users to improve their personal effectiveness, increasing the quality and amount of work that can be done. Software that helps groups work together is often called workgroup application software. It includes group scheduling software, electronic mail, and other software that enables people to share ideas. Enterprise software that benefits the entire organization, called enterprise resource planning software, is a set of integrated programs that help manage a company's vital business operations for an entire multi-site, global organization.

Three approaches to acquiring application software are to build proprietary application software, buy existing programs off the shelf, or use a combination of customized and off-the-shelf application software. Building proprietary software (in-house or on contract) has the following advantages: the organization gets software that more closely matches its needs; by being involved with the development, the organization has further control over the results; and the organization has more flexibility in making changes. The disadvantages include the following: it is likely to take longer and cost more to develop, the in-house staff will be hard pressed to provide ongoing support and maintenance, and there is a greater risk that the software features will not work as expected or that other performance problems will occur.

Purchasing off-the-shelf software has many advantages. The initial cost is lower, there is a lower risk that the software will fail to work as expected, and the software is likely to be of higher quality than proprietary software. Some disadvantages are that the organization might pay for features it does not need, the software might lack important features requiring expensive customization, and the system might require process reengineering.

Some organizations have taken a third approach—customizing software packages. This approach usually involves a mixture of the preceding advantages and disadvantages and must be carefully managed.

An application service provider (ASP) is a company that provides the software, support, and computer hardware on which to run the software from the user's facilities over a network. ASPs customize off-the-shelf software on contract and speed deployment of new applications while helping IS managers avoid implementation headaches. ASPs reduce the need for many skilled IS staff members and also lower a project's start-up expenses. Software as a Service (SaaS) allows businesses to subscribe to Web-delivered business application software by paying a monthly service charge or a per-use fee.

SaaS and recent Web development technologies have led to a new paradigm in computing called cloud computing. Cloud computing refers to the use of computing resources, including software and data storage, on the Internet (the cloud), not on local computers. Rather than installing, storing, and running software on your own computer, with cloud computing, you access software stored on and delivered from a Web server.

Although hundreds of computer applications can help people at school, home, and work, the most popular applications are word processing, spreadsheet analysis, database, graphics, and personal information management. A software suite, such as SmartSuite, WordPerfect, StarOffice, or Microsoft Office, offers a collection of these powerful programs sold as a bundle.

With the increased popularity of mobile computing, many new mobile applications, commonly referred to as apps, have been developed. Nearly as many applications are designed for smartphones such as the iPhone as for PCs. Popular categories of mobile apps include games, music and entertainment, social networking, news and weather, travel and navigation, business, and sports.

Many thousands of applications are designed for businesses and work groups. Business software generally falls under the heading of information systems that support common business activities such as accounts receivable, accounts payable, inventory control, and other management activities. Enterprise resource planning software combines business operations into one large, centrally administered, enterprise-wide system.

Principle:

Organizations should choose programming languages with functional characteristics that are appropriate for the task at hand and are well suited to the skills and experience of the programming staff.

All software programs are written in coding schemes called *programming languages*, which provide instructions to a computer to perform some processing activity. The several classes of programming languages include machine, assembly, high-level, query and database, object-oriented, and visual programming languages.

Programming languages have changed since their initial development in the early 1950s. In the first generation, computers were programmed in machine language, and in the second, assembly languages were used. The third generation consists of many high-level programming languages that use English-like statements and commands. They must be converted to machine language by special software called a compiler and include BASIC, COBOL, FORTRAN, and others. Fourth-generation languages include database and query languages such as SQL.

Fifth-generation programming languages combine rules-based code generation, component management, visual programming techniques, reuse management, and other advances. Object-oriented programming languages—such as Smalltalk, C++, and Java—use groups of related data, instructions, and procedures called *objects*, which serve as reusable modules in various programs. These languages can reduce program development and testing time. Java can be used to develop applications on the Internet. Visual programming environments, integrated development environments (IDEs), and software development kits (SDKs) simplified and streamlined the coding process and have made it easier for more people to develop software.

Principle:

The software industry continues to undergo change; users need to be aware of recent trends and issues to be effective in their business and personal lives.

Software bugs, software licensing and copyrighting, open-source software, shareware and freeware, software upgrades, and global software support are all important software issues and trends.

A software bug is a defect in a computer program that keeps it from performing in the manner intended. Software bugs are common, even in key pieces of business software.

Freeware is software that is made available to the public for free. Open-source software is freeware that also has its source code available so that others may modify it. Open-source software development and maintenance is a collaborative process, with developers around the world using the Internet to download the software, communicate about it, and submit new versions of the software.

Software upgrades are an important source of increased revenue for software manufacturers and can provide useful new functionality and improved quality for software users.

Global software support is an important consideration for large, global companies putting together standardized, company-wide systems. A common solution is outsourcing global support to one or more third-party software distributors.

CHAPTER 4: SELF-ASSESSMENT TEST

Systems software and application software are critical in helping individuals and organizations achieve their goals.

1. Which of the following is an example of a command-driven operating system?
   a. XP
   b. Snow Lion
   c. MS DOS
   d. Windows 7
2. Application software, such as Microsoft Excel, manipulates the computer hardware directly. True or False?
3. _____ is an open-source OS that is used in all computer platforms: PC, server, embedded, smartphones, and others.
4. Spam filtering is a function of the operating system. True or False?
5. What do some companies use to run multiple operating systems on a single computer?
   a. multitasking
   b. middleware
   c. service-oriented architecture
   d. virtualization

Organizations use off-the-shelf application software for common business needs and proprietary application software to meet unique business needs providing a competitive advantage.

6. Controlling the operations of computer hardware is one of the most critical functions of application software. True or False?
7. What type of software enables users to improve their effectiveness, increasing the amount of work they can do and its quality?
   a. personal productivity software
   b. operating system software
   c. utility software
   d. graphics software
8. Optimization can be found in which type of application software?
   a. spreadsheets
   b. word processing programs
   c. personal information management programs
   d. presentation graphics programs
9. _____ software is one-of-a-kind software designed for a specific application and owned by the company, organization, or person that uses it.

10. What allows businesses to subscribe to Web-delivered business application software by paying a monthly service charge or a per-use fee?
    a. Software as a Service (SaaS)
    b. an application service provider (ASP)
    c. proprietary software
    d. off-the-shelf software

Organizations should choose programming languages with functional characteristics that are appropriate for the task at hand and well suited to the skills and experience of the programming staff.

11. What type of licence is used for most software purchased to run on a personal computer?
    a. site
    b. concurrent-user
    c. multi-user
    d. single-user
12. One of the primary advantages of _____ programming is that it employs reusable code modules that save developers from having to start coding from scratch.
13. Each programming language has its own set of rules, called the _____ of the language.
14. A compiler converts a programmer's source code into the machine-language instructions consisting of binary digits. True or False?

The software industry continues to undergo constant change; users need to be aware of recent trends and issues to be effective in their business and personal life.

15. What type of software allows users to tweak the software to their own needs?
    a. freeware
    b. off-the-shelf software
    c. open-source software
    d. software in the public domain
16. What type of licence is an enterprise likely to purchase for software that it intends for all of its employees to use while on site?

CHAPTER 4: SELF-ASSESSMENT TEST ANSWERS

(1) c (2) False (3) Linux (4) False (5) d (6) False (7) a (8) a (9) Proprietary (10) a (11) d (12) object-oriented (13) syntax (14) True (15) c (16) site licence

REVIEW QUESTIONS

1. What is the difference between systems software and application software? Give four examples of personal productivity software.
2. What steps can a user take to correct software bugs?
3. Identify and briefly discuss two types of user interfaces provided by an operating system. What are the benefits and drawbacks of each?
4. What is a software suite? Give several examples.
5. Name four operating systems that support the personal sphere of influence.
6. What is a service-oriented architecture (SOA)?
7. What is multitasking?
8. Define the term "utility software" and give two examples.
9. Identify the two primary sources for acquiring application software.
10. What is cloud computing? What are the pros and cons of cloud computing?
11. What is open-source software? What are the benefits and drawbacks for a business that uses open-source software?
12. What does the acronym API stand for? What is the role of an API?
13. Briefly discuss the advantages and disadvantages of frequent software upgrades.
14. Describe the term "enterprise resource planning (ERP) system." What functions does such a system perform?
15. What is the difference between freeware and open-source software?

DISCUSSION QUESTIONS

1. Assume that you must take a computer-programming course next semester. What language do you think would be best for you to study? Why? Do you think that a professional programmer needs to know more than one programming language? Why or why not?
2. You are going to buy a personal computer. What operating system features are important to you? What operating system would you select, and why?
3. Identify the fundamental types of application software. Discuss the advantages and disadvantages of each type.
4. You are using a new release of an application software package. You think that you have discovered a bug. Outline the approach that you would take to confirm that it is indeed a bug. What actions would you take if it truly were a bug?
5. How can application software improve the effectiveness of a large enterprise? What are some of the benefits associated with implementation of an enterprise resource planning system? What are some of the issues that could keep the use of enterprise resource planning software from being successful?
6. Define the term "Software as a Service (SaaS)." What are some of the advantages and disadvantages of employing a SaaS? What precautions might you take to minimize the risk of using one?
7. Describe three personal productivity software packages you are likely to use the most. What personal productivity software packages would you select for your use?
8. Contrast and compare three popular OSs for personal computers.
9. If you were the IT manager for a large manufacturing company, what issues might you have with the use of open-source software? What advantages might there be for use of such software?
10. Identify four types of software licences frequently used. Which approach does the best job of ensuring a steady, predictable stream of revenue from customers? Which approach is most fair for the small company that makes infrequent use of the software?
11. How have software development kits (SDKs) influenced software development?
12. How can virtualization save a company a lot of money?

PROBLEM-SOLVING EXERCISES

1. Develop a six-slide presentation on cloud computing that provides several examples of commercial cloud computing services, outlines the benefits and drawbacks, and concludes with your thoughts on the future of cloud computing.
2. Use a spreadsheet package to prepare a simple monthly budget and forecast your cash flow—both income and expenses for the next six months (make up numbers rather than using actual ones). Now use a graph to plot

the total monthly income and monthly expenses for six months. Cut and paste both the spreadsheet and the graph into a word processing document that summarizes your (fictitious) financial situation.

3. Use a database program to enter five software products you are likely to use at work. List the name, vendor or manufacturer, cost, and features in the columns of a database table. Use a word processor to write a report on the software. Copy the database table into the word processing program.

TEAM ACTIVITIES

1. Form a group of three or four classmates. Find articles from business periodicals, search the Internet, or interview people on the topic of software bugs. How frequently do they occur, and how serious are they? What can software users do to encourage defect-free software? Compile your results for an in-class presentation or a written report.

2. Form a group of three or four classmates. Identify and contact an employee of any local business or organization. Interview the individual and describe the application software the company uses and discuss the importance of the software to the organization. Write a brief report summarizing your findings.

3. Team members should learn how to use a PC operating system with which they are unfamiliar. Explore how to launch applications, minimize and maximize windows, close applications, view files on the system, and change system settings such as the wallpaper. Team members should collaborate on a report, using the track changes features of Word or collaborative features of Google Docs to summarize your findings and opinions on at least three PC OSs.

WEB EXERCISES

1. Use the Web to research four productivity software suites from various vendors (see *http://en.wikipedia.org/wiki/Office_Suite*). Create a table in a word processing document to show what applications are provided by the competing suites. Write a few paragraphs on which suite you think best matches your needs and why.

2. Use the Internet to search for three popular freeware utilities that you would find useful. Write a report that describes the features of these three utility programs.

3. Visit *http://downloads.cnet.com* and explore the many applications that can be found there. List five applications that you discover and would like to try. Explain each application's usefulness.

4. Do research on the Web about application software that is used in an industry that is of interest to you. Write a brief report describing how the application software can be used to increase profits or reduce costs.

CAREER EXERCISES

1. What personal computer OS would help you the most in your next professional job? Why? What features are the most important to you?

2. Think of your ideal job. Describe five application software packages that could help you advance in your career. If the software package doesn't exist, describe the kinds of software packages that could help you in your career.

CASE STUDIES

Case One
BlueStar Profits from SOA and Open Source

BlueStar Energy Services, founded in Illinois in 2002, buys and sells electricity in Illinois, Maryland, Pennsylvania, and Washington D.C. Its customers include businesses and residential customers looking to get the best deal on electricity custom-suited to their needs. BlueStar is a certified Green-e Energy Renewable Energy Certificate (REC) marketer, providing its customers with power from renewable energy sources and traditional sources with an option to earn carbon credits or buy carbon offsets. Carbon credits and offsets are tools that allow companies to balance overall carbon emissions between companies with high and low energy requirements.

Brokering electricity in today's volatile and fluctuating energy marketplace is a complex process. BlueStar works with the companies that generate power, companies that control power transmission across the United States, and local distribution companies to access power from various sources and deliver it to its customers. In order to profit from this business, BlueStar must streamline and automate the flow of information with its partners in the industry to make the process as efficient as possible. CTO Tom Keen explains that the trick is to buy smart and deliver in an optimal way, which requires careful management of the flow of information. The challenge is that each of its partners uses different software that stores data in different formats.

Keen worked closely with BlueStar executives to establish the company's goals and enterprise architecture. This architecture defined the technology needs of the business. Keen initially set out to find off-the-shelf software that might accommodate its needs but soon discovered that, while many software packages are designed for utility companies, none met the unique requirements of BlueStar. BlueStar needed software that could accept input in various formats from its business partners' systems and process it to provide BlueStar with usable information. Keen eventually decided to build the software in-house exactly to BlueStar specifications.

Rather than designing one large software application from scratch, Keen decided to use open-source software to create a service-oriented architecture that addressed each of the corporate processes individually. Using open-source software provided the stability that Keen desired. He explains that with open-source software, bugs are well documented and can be easily avoided. Commercial software companies don't allow access to the source code, so bugs remain unknown to the users.

Keen and his team of programmers partitioned the business needs into narrowly defined domains. Once identified, software was developed to independently serve those needs while communicating with each other by passing data back and forth. This flexible SOA business infrastructure automates many of the tasks involved in negotiating with suppliers, partners, and customers. The modular design of SOA allows developers to tweak the software to accommodate new needs as the market changes.

Because BlueStar's information systems were created to the specific requirements of the enterprise architecture, the information systems and how the business is managed are interdependent. Keen built the systems that now contribute to the success of the company. He also established the software engineering principles and practices that are the cornerstones of IS operations. They include practices such as the software engineering life cycle, domain-driven design, model-driven development, continuous integration, and several other approaches to software development. Today, 50 programmers trained in these practices work for BlueStar at a development centre in Lima, Peru. By using offshore resources for their continuous software improvement processes, BlueStar has enjoyed considerable savings. In fact, between offshore resources and use of open-source software and SOA, the company estimates that it has saved $24 million over the past five years—an incredible amount in difficult economic times.

Tom Keen and his work have earned awards and recognition over the past few years. In 2008, BlueStar earned a top 10 business award from *InfoWorld* for its successful SOA implementation. Tom Keen was named one of the top 25 CTOs by *InfoWorld* in 2009.

Discussion Questions

1. Why did BlueStar decide to develop proprietary software rather than purchase off-the-shelf software?
2. What advantages did open-source software and SOA provide to the development process?

Critical Thinking Questions

1. Tom Keen believes that the open-source community is better at managing software bugs than commercial software vendors. Do you agree with his reasoning? Why or why not?
2. What types of software development projects are best suited for a service-oriented architecture (SOA)?

SOURCES: Dineley, Doug, "BlueStar Energy Uses Stepwise SOA to Reinvent Its IT," *InfoWorld*, www.infoworld.com/t/soa-service-oriented-architecture/bluestar-energy-uses-stepwise-soa-reinvent-its-it-431, May 29, 2009; Gruman, Galen, "The Best CTOs of 2009," *InfoWorld*, www.infoworld.com/t/it-management/best-ctos-2009-133, June 1, 2009; Dineley, Doug, "BlueStar Sparks Energy Services with SOA," *CIO*, www.cio.com/article/464359/Bluestar_Sparks_Energy_Services_with_SOA, November 19, 2008; BlueStar website, www.bluestarenergy.com/company.html, accessed January 24, 2010.

Case Two
Office Depot Gets SaaSy

Like most businesses, Office Depot has been searching for ways to boost its market share and increase revenue in times when money is tight. Glenn Trommer, director of e-commerce and implementation services at Office Depot, and his team work closely with the sales department looking for ways that technology can assist with sales.

One area identified as needing improvement was in Office Depot's ordering system for its business customers. Some of the transaction requests from business customers were not compatible with Office Depot's ordering software. In other words, customers could not specify their needs using the existing system.

Office Depot's competitors, however, did not suffer from the same problem, and so were able to fill orders and satisfy customers that Office Depot could not.

Office Depot needed software that could better integrate the order-placing systems used by its customers with its own order processing system. Trommer and his team had three options: they could design proprietary software themselves, they could purchase software off the shelf and customize it to their needs, or they could hire the services of a company that specializes in integration software. Because of its financial restraints, Trommer decided that investing in software as a service (SaaS) for its integration needs would allow the business to get the best return on its investment in the shortest amount of time. Trommer, his team, and Office Depot sales managers ultimately chose Hubspan, which provides a cloud-based integration platform called Integration-as-a-service.

Hubspan's system was placed between Office Depot's and its business customers to interpret customer needs into a format that Office Depot could process. Trommer and his team worked with Hubspan to educate the service provider on Office Depot's selling approach, sales cycle, and data formats. In a short time, the new system was in place without any inconvenience to customers.

Since its adoption, Integration-as-a-service has provided Office Depot with a "significant" increase in incremental revenue—revenue generated by big corporate customers who had previously been driven to Office Depot competitors. The increase in revenue has led to an increase in market share for Office Depot. Trommer says, "In these tough economic times [it's] really helped us gain market share with very little investment."

Trommer appreciates that Hubspan's Integration-as-a-service is secure, reliable, and scalable. He is considering expanding its use to transactions with Office Depot's own vendors. The short implementation time, low technical requirements, flexibility, and low cost made SaaS a perfect solution for Office Depot's problem.

Discussion Questions

1. Why did Office Depot decide to use SaaS rather than developing its own software or purchasing off-the-shelf solutions?

2. What benefits do SaaS solutions provide to businesses like Office Depot?

Critical Thinking Questions

1. In general, which types of problems are best suited for SaaS solutions?

2. What risks, if any, is Office Depot taking by trusting its data and operations to Hubspan?

SOURCES: Violino, Bob, "Integration as a Service at Office Depot," *CIO Insight, www.cioinsight.com/c/a/Services/Integration-as-a-Service-at-Home-Depot-474099/1,* September 24, 2009; Hubspan website, *www.hubspan.com,* accessed January 24, 2010.

Questions for Web Case

See the website for this book to read about the Altitude Online case for this chapter. Following are questions concerning this Web case.

Altitude Online: Choosing Software

Discussion Questions

1. Why do you think Altitude Online uses two PC platforms—Windows and Mac—rather than standardizing on one? What are the benefits and drawbacks of their decision?

2. Why do you think a business is required to keep copies of all of its software licences?

Critical Thinking Questions

1. How much freedom should a company like Altitude Online allow for its employees to choose their own personal application software? Why might a company prefer to standardize around specific software packages?

2. What benefits might be provided to an advertising media company like Altitude Online by upgrading to the latest media development and production software? How might upgrading provide the company with a competitive advantage?

NOTES

Sources for the opening vignette: "Rheinmetall AG Improves Its Project Processes with an Integrated Collaboration Software Suite," IBM Success Story, *www-01.ibm.com/software/success/cssdb.nsf/CS/LMCM-7RJRNY?OpenDocument&Site=lotus&cty=en_us,* April 30, 2009 ; Lotus Quickr website, *www-01.ibm.com/software/lotus/products/quickr/teams.html,* accessed January 23, 2010; Lotus Connections website, *www-01.ibm.com/software/lotus/products/connections,* accessed January 23, 2010; Lotus Sametime website, *www-01.ibm.com/software/lotus/sametime,* accessed January 23, 2010; Rheinmetall website, *www.rheinmetall.de,* accessed January 23, 2010.

1   Boulton, Clint, "Mindjet MindManager 8 for Mac Integrates with Apple Apps," *eweek, www.eweek.com,* January 27, 2010.
2   Dunn, Scott, "Master Your Schedule with Google Calendar," *PC World,* August 2008, p. 110.

3   "Leading Energy Management Firm Streamlines Global Reporting, Increases Synergies, Thanks to Powerful IBM Cognos Solution," IBM Case Study, *www-01.ibm.com/software/success/cssdb.nsf/cs/SANS-82GM69?OpenDocument&Site=cognos&cty=en_us,* accessed February 10, 2010.
4   "Radisson Hotel Says 'Yes, I Can' with HP," HP Success Stories, *http://h20195.www2.hp.com/V2/GetPDF.aspx/4AA2-4452EEW.pdf,* accessed January 17, 2010.
5   "Top Operating System Share Trend," Market Share Research website, *http://marketshare.hitslink.com/os-market-share.aspx?qprid=9;* Elmer-DeWitt, Philip, "Survey: Mac OS Hit Record 7.3% Share in December; iPhone up 33%," *Fortune, http://apple20.blogs.fortune.cnn.com/2008/01/01/survey-mac-os-hit-record-73-share-in-december-iphone-up-33,* January 1, 2008.

6   Pogue, David, "Windows 7 Keeps the Good, Tries to Fix Flaws," *New York Times*, October 21, 2009.

7   DeCarlo, Matthew, "Should You Install Windows 7 32-bit or 64-bit?" *TechSpot, www.techspot.com*, July 29, 2009.

8   "Bombardier Aerospace" Microsoft Case Study, *www.microsoft.com/ canada/casestudies/Case_Study_Detail.aspx?casestudyid=4000006572*, accessed October 8, 2010.

9   Whitney, Lance, "Linux-Based OS Drives News Nokia N900," *Cnet, http:// news.cnet.com*, August 27, 2009.

10 "Ubuntu Is the Open Source Platform of Choice for Oxford Archaeology," Ubuntu Case Studies, *www.ubuntu.com/products/casestudies/oxford- archaeology*, accessed September 22, 2009.

11 Tweney, Dylan, "Google Chrome OS: Ditch Your Hard Drives, the Future Is the Web," *Wired, www.wired.com*, November 19, 2009.

12 Spring, Tom, "Google's Chrome OS: Game-Changing Failure?" *PC World*, September 2009, p. 12.

13 "eBay Inc.," Sun Customer Snapshot website, *www.sun.com/customers/ index.xml?c=ebay.xml&submit=Find*, accessed January 17, 2010.

14 "Sun Solutions Helps Vancouver 2010 Organizing Committee Build Com- plex Infrastructure for the 2010 Winter Games," Oracle website, *www. oracle.com/us/corporate/customers/060505.pdf*, accessed October 6, 2010.

15 "IBM eServer zSeries Systems and GDPS Help AOK Bavaria Create a Healthy Environment for Growth," IBM Success Stories, May 1, 2009, *www-01.ibm.com/software/success/cssdb.nsf/CS/JFTD-6VESNY?OpenDocum ent&Site=eserverzseries&cty=en_us*.

16 "Resmed Breathes Easy with Impressive Cost Savings with Red Hat and Jboss Solutions," Red Hat Success Stories, *http://customers.redhat.com*, accessed February 13, 2010.

17 Kinnander, Ola, "Nokia to Roll Out Phone Based on Linux Software," *Wall Street Journal*, August 28, 2009, Technology Section, p. B4.

18 "ProCurve Networking Partners with CERN to Unlock the Secrets of the Universe," HP Success Story, *http://h20195.www2.hp.com/v2/ GetDocument.aspx?docname=4AA2-2318EEW&doctype=success%20 story&doclang=EN_GB&searchquery=All%20sizes|All%20Industries|grid%20 computing&cc=us&lc=en*, accessed January 17, 2010.

19 George, Randy, "Desktop Virtualization," *InformationWeek*, August 17, 2009, p. 18.

20 "Nestlé Nespresso S.A. Provides Its Decision-Makers with High-Value- Added Actionable Data," Oracle Customer Snapshot, *www.oracle.com/ customers/snapshots/nestle-nespresso-snapshot.pdf*, accessed February 13, 2010.

21 IBM staff, "Sears Canada increases code reuse by 5%-15% with SOA solution," IBM Case Study, *www-01.ibm.com/software/success/cssdb.nsf/ CS/CPOR-7RM272?OpenDocument&Site=wssoftware&cty=en_us*, accessed April 20, 2009.

22 Revize Staff, "Case Study – North York General Hospital – Toronto Canada," *http://revize.com/case_studies.html*, accessed October 6, 2010.

23 Montalbano, Elizabeth, "Forrester: Microsoft Office in No Danger From Competitors," *PC World, www.pcworld.com/businesscenter/article/166123/ forrester_microsoft_office_in_no_danger_from_competitors.html?tk=nl_ dnx_h_crawl*, June 4, 2009.

24 "Customer: RapidAdvance," SAP Case Study, *www.ondemand.com/ customers/rapidadvance.asp*, accessed January 17, 2010.

25 Weier, Mary Hayes, "SuccessFactors Shows SaaS's Next Challenge," *InformationWeek*, September 14, 2009, p. 15.

26 Lai, Eric, "Forget Mashups: Tableau Software Wants Data Junkies to Do the 'Viz'," *Computerworld, www.computerworld.com*, February 11, 2010.

27 "Powered by Salesforce CRM's Idea Community, My Starbucks Idea Brews Customer Feedback at Starbucks," Salesforce Success Story, *www.sales- force.com/customers/distribution-retail/starbucks.jsp*, accessed January 17, 2010.

28 "Goodmans LLP: Law Firm Could Regain 10,000 Billable Hours Annually with Unified Communications," *www.microsoft.com/canada/casestudies/ Case_Study_Detail.aspx?casestudyid=4000008156*, accessed October 8, 2010.

29 Burrows, Peter, "Microsoft Defends Its Empire," *Businessweek*, July 6, 2009, p. 28.

30 Siegler, M.G., "BarMax: The $1,000 iPhone App That Might Actually Be Worth It," *TechCrunch, http://techcrunch.com/2010/01/17/ most-expensive-iphone-app-barmax*, January 17, 2010.

31 Blair, Nancy, "Apple: Three Billion Downloads from iPhone App Store," *USA Today, http://content.usatoday.com/communities/technologylive/ post/2010/01/apple-three-billion-downloads-from-iphone-app-store/1*, January 5, 2010.

32 Sutter, John D., "U.S. Government Sets Up Online 'App Store'," CNN, *www.cnn.com*, accessed September 16, 2009.

33 Schaffhauser, Dian, "Florida Virtual to Extend Use of LMS to Students," *The Journal, www.thejournal.com*, January 22, 2010.

34 "Whole Foods Market: 2009 Red Hat Innovator of the Year," Red Hat Linux Success Stories, *http://customers.redhat.com/category/industry/ consumer*, accessed January 17, 2010.

CHAPTER · 5 ·

Database Systems, Data Centres, and Business Intelligence

PRINCIPLES	LEARNING OBJECTIVES
▪ **Data management and modelling are key aspects of organizing data and information.**	▪ Define general data management concepts and terms, highlighting the advantages of the database approach to data management. ▪ Describe logical and physical database design considerations, the function of data centres, and the relational database model.
▪ **A well-designed and well-managed database is an extremely valuable tool in supporting decision making.**	▪ Identify the common functions performed by all database management systems, and identify popular database management systems.
▪ **The number and types of database applications will continue to evolve and yield real business benefits.**	▪ Identify and briefly discuss business intelligence, data mining, and other database applications.

(Source: asharkyu/Shutterstock.com)

Information Systems in the Global Economy
Aquent

Leveraging Database Technology to Empower Marketing Professionals

Aquent is a global leader in marketing staffing. The company works with *Fortune 500* marketing organizations to fill positions with highly qualified professionals drawn from a pool of thousands of marketing experts worldwide. Aquent works to place brand managers, copywriters, data analysts, Web designers, search-engine optimizers, and other specialists in full-time positions as well as short-term contract positions. According to Aquent, the industry is changing from one in which marketing experts join a company and work their way up the corporate ladder, to one in which marketing projects are hired out to specialists who move from company to company applying unique high-level skills to challenging projects. Aquent believes that it plays a key role in enabling this new era of marketing. It provides challenging projects for marketing professionals to hone their skills and advance in their field, while elevating the quality and effectiveness of marketing efforts within organizations.

Aquent has unique database and information system needs. Its clients are both large corporations and individuals. Although its primary business is staffing, it also provides ancillary services such as project management, translation and localization, and health-care consulting. Its information systems must produce a wide range of reports to meet a variety of business needs. These needs include staffing levels and requirements, human resource usage, gross profit, pay rates, and many others. Because the company works with many organizations, it must manage diverse payroll schemes and schedules. Aquent also manages systems that allow it to provide insurance and retirement benefits to many of the marketing professional talent that it represents. The databases that support these wide-ranging and diverse systems are about as complicated as a business's databases can be.

To get a handle on all its data, Aquent uses a database management system that collects operational data from around the world and stores it in a central data mart managed by the SAP Corporation. Each night the system refreshes the data stored in the data mart with updates from data centres in Sydney, London, and Boston. A backup of the data is stored in Aquent's data centre in Boston.

Aquent executives, managers, and personnel access the data through a Web-based system provided by SAP. SAP takes responsibility for storing and managing Aquent's database and providing a robust database management system (DBMS) accessed through a Web browser. This approach to database management, where a company outsources its DBMS to a service provider, is referred to as Database as a Service or DaaS.

Aquent uses a business intelligence (BI) system to create ad-hoc and annual reports. Aquent regional managers run individual reports for Asia Pacific, Europe, and North America. They also run reports that cover all regions using common criteria to examine. Executives can get a high-level view of trends in corporate data and use BI tools to drill down into the data to discover specific areas of the business that require attention.

Aquent uses SAP data-mining technology to examine data in the data mart and discover patterns and anomalies that cue decision makers to examine problems and opportunities. Predictive analysis tools help to provide managers with insight into the future based on an analysis of the past. Using these tools, Aquent can determine future demand for marketing professionals and ensure it can meet that demand. It may also determine a future lack of demand so that Aquent can advise some professionals to consider jobs in other related areas.

Using a central data mart and joining operations around the world, Aquent can more easily view itself as a multinational company. The distances among its global divisions are greatly reduced by its ability to combine corporate data and evaluate it both by region and in its totality.

As you read this chapter, consider the following:

- What role do databases play in the overall effectiveness of information systems?
- What techniques do businesses use to maximize the value of the information provided from databases?

Why Learn About Database Systems, Data Centres, and Business Intelligence?

A huge amount of data is entered into computer systems every day. Where does all this data go, and how is it used? How can it help you on the job? In this chapter, you will learn about database systems and business intelligence tools that can help you make the most effective use of information. If you become a marketing manager, you can access a vast store of data on existing and potential customers from surveys, their Web habits, and their past purchases. This information can help you sell products and services. If you become a corporate lawyer, you will have access to past cases and legal opinions from sophisticated legal databases. This information can help you win cases and protect your organization legally. If you become a human resource (HR) manager, you will be able to use databases and business intelligence tools to analyze the impact of raises, employee insurance benefits, and retirement contributions on long-term costs to your company. Regardless of your field of study in school, using database systems and business intelligence tools will likely be a critical part of your job. In this chapter, you will see how you can use data mining to extract valuable information to help you succeed. This chapter starts by introducing basic concepts of database management systems.

A database is an organized collection of data. Like other components of an information system, a database should help an organization achieve its goals. A database can contribute to organizational success by providing managers and decision makers with timely, accurate, and relevant information based on data. For example, Comic Relief, in London, England, raises money to assist the needy by hosting entertainment events featuring comedians. The organization uses a database to determine which clips in its televised fundraiser generate the highest emotional response from the public to determine whether the clip should be repeated.[1]

Databases also help companies generate information to reduce costs, increase profits, track past business activities, and open new market opportunities. In some cases, organizations collaborate in creating and using international databases. Six organizations, including the Organization of Petroleum Exporting Countries (OPEC), International Energy Agency (IEA), and the United Nations, use a database to monitor the global oil supply.

A database provides an essential foundation for an organization's information and decision support system. Without a well-designed, accurate database, executives, managers, and others do not have access to the information they need to make good decisions. For example, during the 2010 oil spill disaster in the Gulf of Mexico, a database was used to pinpoint spill-related damage along the coast. Software was designed to collect reports from residents and volunteers up and down the coast through phone calls, text messages, and e-mail. The incident and its location were recorded in a database. The Louisiana Bucket Brigade's website provided a map displaying detailed information about oil spill–related damage. Volunteers used the information to focus their attention on areas that needed the most help.[2]

A database is also the foundation of most systems development projects. If the database is not designed properly, the systems development effort can be like a house of cards, collapsing under the weight of inaccurate and inadequate data. Because data is so critical to an organization's success, many firms develop databases to help them access data more efficiently and use it more effectively. This typically requires a well-designed database management system and a knowledgeable database administrator.

A **database management system** (**DBMS**) consists of a group of programs that manipulate the database and provide an interface between the database and its users and other application programs. Usually purchased from a database company, a DBMS provides a single point of management and control over data resources, which can be critical to maintaining the integrity and security of the data. A database, a DBMS, and the application programs that use the data make up a database environment. A **database administrator** (**DBA**) is a skilled and trained IS professional who directs all activities related to an organization's database, including providing security from intruders. People hack into databases for various reasons. Consider the Latvian computer expert who hacked into a government database to make public the salary information of government officials. He intended to show the people that during the country's severe economic problems, government officials continued receiving high salaries.[3] In 2010, the names, birth dates, and Social Security numbers of 3.3 million students were stolen from a database owned by a student loan company.[4] Such data breaches have become commonplace for organizations because many databases are now accessible from the Internet. Data quality and accuracy also continue to be important issues for DBAs. For example, in Uckfield, England, government records for Pauline Grant and her farm became jumbled due to a land registry error. The mix-up resulted in a pig named Blossom on Grant's farm receiving mail encouraging her to vote in the upcoming election.[5]

Databases and database management systems are becoming even more important to businesses as they deal with increasing amounts of digital information. A report from marketing research firm IDC called "The Digital Universe Decade—Are You Ready?" estimates the size of the digital universe to be 1.2 zettabytes, or 1.2 trillion gigabytes.[6] If a tennis ball were one byte of information, a zettabyte-sized ball would be around the size of a million Earths. Furthermore, between 2009 and 2020, the amount of information humanity creates will grow by a factor of 44, storage capacity will grow by a factor of 30, and the estimated investment in database infrastructure and administration will grow by only a factor of 1.4. IDC recommends that organizations move now to create policies, tools, and standards to accommodate the approaching tidal wave of digital data and information.

> **database management system (DBMS)**
> A group of programs that manipulate the database and provide an interface between the database and the user of the database and other application programs.

> **database administrator (DBA)**
> A skilled IS professional who directs all activities related to an organization's database.

DATA MANAGEMENT

Without data and the ability to process it, an organization could not successfully complete most business activities. It could not pay employees, send out bills, order new inventory, or produce information to assist managers in decision making. As you recall, data consists of raw facts, such as employee numbers and sales figures. For data to be transformed into useful information, it must first be organized in a meaningful way.

The Hierarchy of Data

Data is generally organized in a hierarchy that begins with the smallest piece of data used by computers (a bit) and progresses through the hierarchy to a database. A bit (a binary digit) represents a circuit that is either on or off. Bits can be organized into units called *bytes*. A byte is typically eight bits. Each byte represents a **character**, which is the basic building block of most information. A character can be an uppercase letter (A, B, C... Z), lowercase letter (a, b, c... z), numeric digit (0, 1, 2... 9), or special symbol (., !, +, −, /, ...).

Characters are put together to form a field. A **field** is typically a name, number, or combination of characters that describes an aspect of a business object (such as an employee, a location, or a truck) or activity (such as a sale). In addition to being entered into a database, fields can be computed from other fields. *Computed fields* include the total, average, maximum, and minimum value. A collection of data fields all related to one object, activity, or

> **character**
> A basic building block of most information, consisting of uppercase letters, lowercase letters, numeric digits, or special symbols.

> **field**
> Typically a name, number, or combination of characters that describes an aspect of a business object or activity.

record
A collection of data fields all related to one object, activity, or individual.

file
A collection of related records.

hierarchy of data
Bits, characters, fields, records, files, and databases.

individual is called a **record**. By combining descriptions of the characteristics of an object, activity, or individual, a record can provide a complete description of it. For instance, an employee record is a collection of fields about one employee. One field includes the employee's name, another field contains the address, and still others the phone number, pay rate, earnings made to date, and so forth. A collection of related records is a **file**—for example, an employee file is a collection of all company employee records. Likewise, an inventory file is a collection of all inventory records for a particular company or organization. Some database software refers to files as tables.

At the highest level of this hierarchy is a *database*, a collection of integrated and related files. Together, bits, characters, fields, records, files, and databases form the **hierarchy of data**. See Figure 5.1. Characters are combined to make a field, fields are combined to make a record, records are combined to make a file, and files are combined to make a database. A database houses not only all these levels of data but also the relationships among them.

Figure 5.1

The Hierarchy of Data

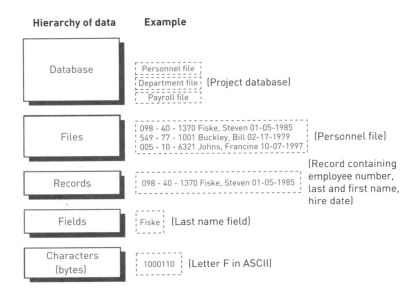

Data Entities, Attributes, and Keys

entity
A general class of people, places, or things for which data is collected, stored, and maintained.

attribute
A characteristic of an entity.

data item
The specific value of an attribute.

Entities, attributes, and keys are important database concepts. An **entity** is a general class of people, places, or things (objects) for which data is collected, stored, and maintained. Examples of entities are employees, inventory, and customers. Most organizations organize and store data as entities.

An **attribute** is a characteristic of an entity. For example, employee number, last name, first name, hire date, and department number are attributes for an employee. See Figure 5.2. The inventory number, description, number of units on hand, and location of the inventory item in the warehouse are attributes for items in inventory. Customer number, name, address, phone number, credit rating, and contact person are attributes for customers. Attributes are usually selected to reflect the relevant characteristics of entities such as employees or customers. The specific value of an attribute, called a **data item**, can be found in the fields of the record describing an entity.

Most organizations use attributes and data items. Many governments use attributes and data items to help in criminal investigations. The United States Federal Bureau of Investigation is building a huge database of people's physical characteristics or biometrics.[7] At a cost of $1 billion, the database management system named Next Generation Identification will catalogue digital images of faces, fingerprints, and palm prints of U.S.

Employee #	Last name	First name	Hire date	Dept. number	
005-10-6321	Johns	Francine	10-07-1997	257	ENTITIES (records)
549-77-1001	Buckley	Bill	02-17-1979	632	
098-40-1370	Fiske	Steven	01-05-1985	598	

KEY FIELD

ATTRIBUTES (fields)

Figure 5.2

Keys and Attributes

The key field is the employee number. The attributes include last name, first name, hire date, and department number.

citizens and visitors. Each person in the database is an entity, each biometric category is an attribute, and each image is a data item. The information will be used as a forensics tool and to increase homeland security.

As discussed earlier, a collection of fields about a specific object is a record. A **key** is a field or set of fields in a record that identifies the record. A **primary key** is a field or set of fields that uniquely identifies the record. No other record can have the same primary key. For an employee record, such as the one shown in Figure 5.2, the employee number is an example of a primary key. The primary key is used to distinguish records so that they can be accessed, organized, and manipulated. Primary keys ensure that each record in a file is unique. For example, eBay Canada assigns an "Item number" as its primary key for items to make sure that bids are associated with the correct item. See Figure 5.3.

key
A field or set of fields in a record that is used to identify the record.

primary key
A field or set of fields that uniquely identifies the record.

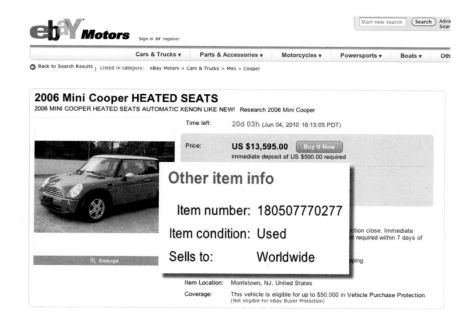

Figure 5.3

Primary Key

eBay assigns an Item number as a primary key to keep track of each item in its database.

(Source: These materials have been reproduced with the permission of eBay Inc. © 2011 EBAY INC. ALL RIGHTS RESERVED.)

Locating a particular record that meets a specific set of criteria might be easier and faster using a combination of secondary keys. For example, a customer might call a mail-order company to place an order for clothes. The order clerk can easily access the customer's mailing and billing information by entering the primary key—usually a customer number—but if the customer does not know the correct primary key, a secondary key such as last name can be used. In this case, the order clerk enters the last name, such as Adams. If several customers have a last name of Adams, the clerk can check other fields, such as address, first name, and so on, to find the correct customer record. After locating the correct customer record, the order can be completed and the clothing items shipped to the customer.

The Database Approach

At one time, information systems referenced specific files containing relevant data. For example, a payroll system would use a payroll file. Each distinct operational system used data files dedicated to that system. This approach to data management is called the **traditional approach to data management**.

Today, most organizations use the **database approach to data management**, where a variety of information systems share a pool of related data. A database offers the ability to share data and information resources. Federal databases, for example, often include the results of DNA tests as an attribute for convicted criminals. The information can be shared with law-enforcement officials throughout Canada.

To use the database approach to data management, additional software—a database management system (DBMS)—is required. As previously discussed, a DBMS consists of a group of programs that can be used as an interface between a database and the user of the database. Typically, this software acts as a buffer between the application programs and the database itself. Figure 5.4 illustrates the database approach.

---

traditional approach to data management
An approach to data management whereby each distinct operational system used data files dedicated to that system.

database approach to data management
An approach to data management whereby a pool of related data is shared by a variety of information systems.

Figure 5.4

The Database Approach to Data Management

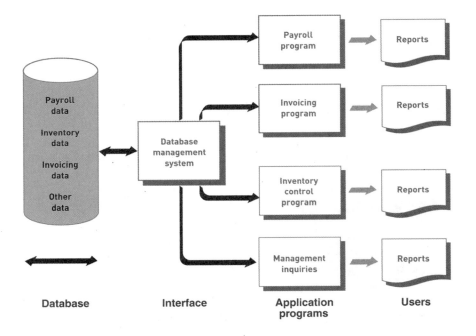

Table 5.1 lists some of the primary advantages of the database approach, and Table 5.2 lists some disadvantages.

As you can see from the Tables 5.1 and 5.2, the advantages of the database approach far outweigh the disadvantages. For that reason, nearly all businesses use databases of various types and sizes to collect important data that fuels information systems and decision making. Many modern databases serve entire enterprises, encompassing much of the data of the organization. Often, distinct yet related databases are linked to provide enterprise-wide databases. For example, Canada Health Infoway, a not-for-profit foundation made up of federal, provincial, and territorial health departments, uses centralized electronic health record databases to provide information to doctors, pharmacists, and other health-care professionals.

Table 5.1

Advantages of the Database Approach

Advantages	Explanation
Improved strategic use of corporate data	Accurate, complete, up-to-date data can be made available to decision makers where, when, and in the form they need it. The database approach can also give greater visibility to the organization's data resource.
Reduced data redundancy	Data is organized by the DBMS and stored in only one location. This results in a more efficient use of system storage space.
Improved data integrity	With the traditional approach, some changes to data were not reflected in all copies of the data. The database approach prevents this problem because no separate files are maintained.
Easier modification and updating	The DBMS coordinates data modifications and updates. Programmers and users do not have to know where the data is physically stored. Data is stored and modified once. Modification and updating is also easier because the data is commonly stored in only one location.
Data and program independence	The DBMS organizes the data independently of the application program, so the application program is not affected by the location or type of data. Introduction of new data types not relevant to a particular application does not require rewriting that application to maintain compatibility with the data file.
Better access to data and information	Most DBMSs have software that makes it easy to access and retrieve data from a database. In most cases, users give simple commands to get important information. Relationships between records can be more easily investigated and exploited, and applications can be more easily combined.
Standardization of data access	A standardized, uniform approach to database access means that all application programs use the same overall procedures to retrieve data and information.
A framework for program development	Standardized database access procedures can mean more standardization of program development. Because programs go through the DBMS to gain access to data in the database, standardized database access can provide a consistent framework for program development. In addition, each application program need address only the DBMS, not the actual data files, reducing application development time.
Better protection of the data	Accessing and using centrally located data is easier to monitor and control. Security codes and passwords can ensure that only authorized people have access to particular data and information in the database, thus ensuring privacy.
Shared data and information resources	The cost of hardware, software, and personnel can be spread over many applications and users. This is a primary feature of a DBMS.

Table 5.2

Disadvantages of the Database Approach

Disadvantages	Explanation
More complexity	DBMSs can be difficult to set up and operate. Many decisions must be made correctly for the DBMS to work effectively. In addition, users have to learn new procedures to take full advantage of a DBMS.
More difficult to recover from a failure	With the traditional approach to file management, a failure of a file affects only a single program. With a DBMS, a failure can shut down the entire database.
More expensive	DBMSs can be more expensive to purchase and operate than traditional file management. The expense includes the cost of the database and specialized personnel, such as a database administrator, who is needed to design and operate the database. Additional hardware might also be required.

DATA MODELLING AND DATABASE CHARACTERISTICS

Because today's businesses have so many elements, they must keep data organized so that it can be used effectively. A database should be designed to store all data relevant to the business and provide quick access and easy modification. Moreover, it must reflect the business processes of the organization. When building a database, an organization must carefully consider these questions:

- *Content.* What data should be collected and at what cost?
- *Access.* What data should be provided to which users and when?
- *Logical structure.* How should data be arranged so that it makes sense to a given user?
- *Physical organization.* Where should data be physically located?

The Canadian federal government carefully considers what information it should make accessible and what information should remain private. News agencies, research labs, and analysts can use the Statistics Canada website (*www.statcan.gc.ca*) to connect databases directly to government records, Canadian statistics, and other information.

Data Centre

data centre
A climate-controlled building or set of buildings that house database servers and the systems that deliver mission-critical information and services.

Databases, and the systems that manipulate them, can be physically stored on computers as small as a PC or as large as mainframes and data centres. A **data centre** is a climate-controlled building or set of buildings that house database servers and the systems that deliver mission-critical information and services. Data centres of large organizations are often distributed among several locations, but a recent trend has many organizations consolidating their data centres into a few large facilities. For example, the Canadian federal government is working to save millions of dollars by consolidating hundreds of data centres into fewer than 10 facilities.[8] Microsoft constructed a $550-million, 400,000-square-foot data centre on 44 acres in San Antonio. Google invested $600 million for a mega data centre in Lenoir, North Carolina, and $750 million for another in Goose Creek, South Carolina. Clearly, storing and managing data is a serious business.

Traditional data centres consist of warehouses filled with row upon row of server racks and powerful cooling systems to compensate for the heat generated by the processors. Microsoft,[9] Google,[10] and others have adopted a new modular data centre approach, which uses large shipping containers like the ones that transport consumer goods around the world. The huge containers, such as the HP POD, are packed with racks of servers prewired and cooled to easily connect and set up. Microsoft constructed a 700,000-square-foot data centre in Northlake, Illinois. It is considered to be one of the largest in the world, taking up 16 football fields of space. The mega facility is filled with 220 shipping containers packed with servers. Microsoft says that a new shipping container can be wheeled into place and connected to the Internet within hours.[11] See Figure 5.5.

Modular data centres are becoming popular around the world due to their convenience and efficiencies. Taiwan's Technology Research Institute is working to create standards for modular data centres in shipping containers that they say will reduce the costs of these units by half while increasing ease of use and reducing energy demands.[12]

While a company's data sits in large supercooled data centres, the people accessing that data are typically in offices spread across the country or around the world. In fact, the expectation of data centre specialists such as Hewlett-Packard CEO Mark Hurd is that in the near future, the only personnel on duty at data centres will be security guards. Data centres are approaching the point of automation where they can run and manage themselves while being monitored remotely. This is referred to as a "lights out" environment. HP has moved to automated data centres, reducing its IT staffing needs by 3,000.[13]

As data centres continue to increase the quantity of data that they store and process, their energy demands are becoming an increasingly significant portion of the total energy

Figure 5.5

Modular Data Centre

Modular data centres use large shipping containers such as the IBM Portable Modular Data Center, which transports consumer goods around the world.

(Source: Courtesy of IBM Corporation.)

demands of humanity. Businesses and technology vendors are working to develop green data centres that run more efficiently and require less energy for processing and cooling.

Data Modelling

When organizing a database, key considerations include determining what data to collect, who will have access to it, and how they might want to use it. After determining these details, an organization can create the database. Building a database requires two different types of designs: a logical design and a physical design. The *logical design* of a database is an abstract model of how the data should be structured and arranged to meet an organization's information needs. The logical design involves identifying relationships among the data items and grouping them in an orderly fashion. Because databases provide both input and output for information systems throughout a business, users from all functional areas should assist in creating the logical design to ensure that their needs are identified and addressed. The *physical design* starts from the logical database design and fine-tunes it for performance and cost considerations (such as improved response time, reduced storage space, and lower operating cost). The person who fine-tunes the physical design must have an in-depth knowledge of the DBMS. For example, the logical database design might need to be altered so that certain data entities are combined, summary totals are carried in the data records rather than calculated from elemental data, and some data attributes are repeated in more than one data entity. These are examples of **planned data redundancy**, which is done to improve the system performance so that user reports or queries can be created more quickly.

One of the tools database designers use to show the logical relationships among data is a data model. A **data model** is a diagram of entities and their relationships. Data modelling usually involves understanding a specific business problem and analyzing the data and information needed to deliver a solution. When done at the level of the entire organization, this is called enterprise data modelling. **Enterprise data modelling** is an approach that starts by investigating the general data and information needs of the organization at the strategic level and then examines more specific data and information needs for the various functional areas and departments within the organization. Various models have been developed to help managers and database designers analyze data and information needs. An entity-relationship diagram is an example of such a data model.

planned data redundancy
A way of organizing data in which the logical database design is altered so that certain data entities are combined, summary totals are carried in the data records rather than calculated from elemental data, and some data attributes are repeated in more than one data entity to improve database performance.

data model
A diagram of data entities and their relationships.

enterprise data modelling
Data modelling done at the level of the entire enterprise.

ETHICAL AND SOCIETAL ISSUES

Mega Data Centres and Their Environmental Impact

To keep up with the unprecedented amount of information being generated, businesses need to invest in larger and larger data centres. Many businesses find it more economical to outsource their data centre needs. Dozens of mega data centres are being constructed around the world for a variety of uses.

Mega data centres typically cost hundreds of millions of dollars and consume acres of property. One of the world's largest was constructed for $301 million by Next Generation Data, outside of Newport in South Wales. The 750,000-square-foot (70,000-square-metre) facility has enough space to house 19,000 server racks that each holds a dozen servers. The facility hopes to serve hundreds of businesses, many located in nearby London. Its first two tenants, BT and Logica, signed contracts worth a combined $29 million.

Next Generation Data can provide its customers with certain guarantees of service and data protection. To guard against terrorist attacks, the data centre has "triple-skinned walls, bomb-proof glass, prison-grade perimeter fencing, infrared detection, biometric recognition, and ex-special forces security guards." The data centre's network is equally protected, and all systems have failback systems to guard against hardware or electrical failure.

The biggest environmental impact of mega data centres is their energy consumption for the processing, storage, and cooling required. The Next Generation Data data centre outside Newport has its own energy substation that provides 90 megavolt-amperes of electrical power. That's roughly equivalent to the requirements of a city of 400,000 people. Multiply this by the dozens of other mega data centres going online, including huge facilities such as Microsoft's new 700,000-square-foot centre near Chicago, and the energy requirements increase around the world. Adding the energy needs of mega data centres to the increasing energy demands of developing countries with huge populations such as China and India results in unprecedented worldwide energy consumption.

When coal-burning power plants fulfill these energy demands, they add carbon to the atmosphere, which many scientists argue accelerates climate change. A number of efforts are underway to counteract the growing demand for data centres. Hardware manufacturers are producing servers that are more efficient, requiring half the energy as their predecessors to do twice the work. As new data centres go into operation, they are implementing new energy-efficient technologies. Gradually, as old wasteful systems break down, managers will migrate data to new green systems.

The Newport data centre uses fresh air cooling and Energy Star–rated equipment to help reduce its impact on the environment. The Environmental Protection Agency has recently released Energy Star standards for servers and is developing standards for enterprise storage as well. Such standards give hardware and software manufacturers targets to shoot for to keep systems running efficiently with less energy.

In light of environmental pressures and public sentiment, many companies are making pledges to reduce the energy requirements of information systems. Disney recently pledged to reduce its electricity consumption by 20 percent by 2013. By measuring Power Usage Effectiveness (PUE), companies can compare IS equipment power requirements to environmental power requirements. A PUE of 2—the industry average—indicates that processing and cooling are requiring equal amounts of energy. Disney and others hope to invest in technologies that have significantly lower energy requirements. Google discovered that adjusting thermostats in its data centres up from a frigid 15 to 27 degrees Celsius helped to lower its PUE to 1.5.

Without a doubt, data centres will continue consuming increasing amounts of real estate. Through a combination of techniques and technologies that include consolidation, more efficient servers, more effective cooling techniques, and alternative energy sources, expanding data centres can reduce their impact on the environment.

Discussion Questions

1. Why is the increase in data centre construction a concern for the environment?
2. What efforts can help to minimize the impact of data centres on the environment?

Critical Thinking Questions

1. Companies are finding it necessary to weigh the value of storing information against the value of affecting the environment. Write a few paragraphs outlining the importance of both and describing how companies might financially benefit from protecting both.
2. If you were a systems administrator for a data centre, what steps would you take to create and manage a data centre to store the maximum amount of valuable data with the minimum impact on the environment?

SOURCES: Niccolai, James, "750,000-sq.-ft. Data Center Opens in Wales," *Computerworld*, March 15, 2010, *www.computerworld.com*; Lawson, Stephen, "EPA Drafting Energy Star Standards for Enterprise Storage," *Computerworld*, May 10, 2010, *www.computerworld.com*; Brodkin, Jon, "Disney, Verizon Go Green in the Data Center," *Computerworld*, October 6, 2009, *www.computerworld.com*; Niccolai, James, "Google: Crank up the Heat in Your Data Center," *Computerworld*, April 29, 2010, *www.computerworld.com*.

Entity-relationship (ER) diagrams use basic graphical symbols to show the organization of and relationships between data. In most cases, boxes in ER diagrams indicate data items or entities contained in data tables, and diamonds show relationships between data items and entities. In other words, ER diagrams show data items in tables (entities) and the ways they are related.

ER diagrams help ensure that the relationships among the data entities in a database are correctly structured so that any application programs developed are consistent with business operations and user needs. In addition, ER diagrams can serve as reference documents after a database is in use. If changes are made to the database, ER diagrams help design them. Figure 5.6 shows an ER diagram for an order database. In this database design, one salesperson serves many customers. This is an example of a one-to-many relationship, as indicated by the one-to-many symbol (the "crow's-foot") shown in Figure 5.6. The ER diagram also shows that each customer can place one-to-many orders; each order includes one-to-many line items; and many line items can specify the same product (a many-to-one relationship). This database can also have one-to-one relationships. For example, one order generates one invoice.

entity-relationship (ER) diagrams
Data models that use basic graphical symbols to show the organization of and relationships between data.

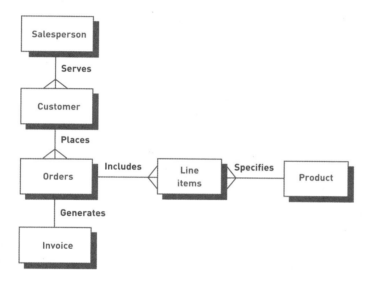

Figure 5.6

An Entity-Relationship (ER) Diagram for a Customer Order Database

Development of ER diagrams helps ensure that the logical structure of application programs is consistent with the data relationships in the database.

The Relational Database Model

Although there are a number of different database models, including flat files, hierarchical models, and network models, the relational model has become the most popular, and use of this model will continue to increase. The **relational model** describes data using a standard tabular format; all data elements are placed in two-dimensional tables, called *relations*, which are the logical equivalent of files. The tables in relational databases organize data in rows and columns, simplifying data access and manipulation. It is normally easier for managers to understand the relational model than other database models. See Figure 5.7 on the next page.

Databases based on the relational model include IBM DB2, Oracle, Sybase, Microsoft SQL Server, Microsoft Access, and MySQL. Oracle is currently the market leader in general-purpose databases, with about half of the multibillion-dollar database market. Oracle's most recent edition of its relational database, 11g, is highly sophisticated and uses database grids that allow a single database to run across a cluster of computers.[14]

In the relational model, each row of a table represents a data entity—a record—and each column of the table represents an attribute—a field. Each attribute can accept only certain values. The allowable values for these attributes are called the **domain**. The domain for a particular attribute indicates what values can be placed in each column of the relational table. For instance, the domain for an attribute such as gender would be limited to male or female. A domain for pay rate would not include negative numbers. In this way, defining a domain can increase data accuracy.

relational model
A database model that describes data in which all data elements are placed in two-dimensional tables, called *relations*, which are the logical equivalent of files.

domain
The allowable values for data attributes.

Figure 5.7

A Relational Database Model

In the relational model, all data elements are placed in two-dimensional tables, or relations. As long as they share at least one common element, these relations can be linked to output useful information.

Data Table 1: Project Table

Project	Description	Dept. number
155	Payroll	257
498	Widgets	632
226	Sales manual	598

Data Table 2: Department Table

Dept.	Dept. name	Employee No.
257	Accounting	005-10-6321
632	Manufacturing	549-77-1001
598	Marketing	098-40-1370

Data Table 3: Manager Table

Employee No.	Last name	First name	Hire date	Dept. number
005-10-6321	Johns	Francine	10-07-1997	257
549-77-1001	Buckley	Bill	02-17-1979	632
098-40-1370	Fiske	Steven	01-05-1985	598

Manipulating Data

After entering data into a relational database, users can make inquiries and analyze the data. Basic data manipulations include selecting, projecting, and joining. **Selecting** involves eliminating rows according to certain criteria. Suppose a project table contains the project number, description, and department number for all projects a company is performing. The president of the company might want to find the department number for Project 226, a sales manual project. Using selection, the president can eliminate all rows but the one for Project 226 and see that the department number for the department completing the sales manual project is 598.

Projecting involves eliminating columns in a table. For example, a department table might contain the department number, department name, and employee number of the manager in charge of the project. A sales manager might want to create a new table with only the department number and the employee number of the manager in charge of the sales manual project. The sales manager can use projection to eliminate the department name column and create a new table containing only the department number and employee number.

Joining involves combining two or more tables. For example, you can combine the project table and the department table to create a new table with the project number, project description, department number, department name, and employee number for the manager in charge of the project.

As long as the tables share at least one common data attribute, the tables in a relational database can be **linked** to provide useful information and reports. Being able to link tables to each other through common data attributes is one of the keys to the flexibility and power of relational databases. Suppose the president of a company wants to find out the name of the manager of the sales manual project and the length of time the manager has been with the company. Assume that the company has the manager, department, and project tables shown in Figure 5.7. A simplified ER diagram showing the relationship between these tables is

selecting
Manipulating data to eliminate rows according to certain criteria.

projecting
Manipulating data to eliminate columns in a table.

joining
Manipulating data to combine two or more tables.

linking
Data manipulation that combines two or more tables using common data attributes to form a new table with only the unique data attributes.

shown in Figure 5.8. Note the crow's-foot by the project table. This indicates that a department can have many projects. The president would make the inquiry to the database, perhaps via a personal computer. The DBMS would start with the project description and search the project table to find out the project's department number. It would then use the department number to search the department table for the manager's employee number. The department number is also in the department table and is the common element that links the project table to the department table. The DBMS uses the manager's employee number to search the manager table for the manager's hire date. The manager's employee number is the common element between the department table and the manager table. The final result is that the manager's name and hire date are presented to the president as a response to the inquiry. See Figure 5.9.

One of the primary advantages of a relational database is that it allows tables to be linked, as shown in Figure 5.9. This linkage reduces data redundancy and allows data to be organized more logically. The ability to link to the manager's employee number stored once in the manager table eliminates the need to store it many times in the project table.

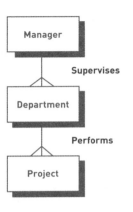

Figure 5.8

A Simplified ER Diagram Showing the Relationship Between the Manager, Department, and Project Tables

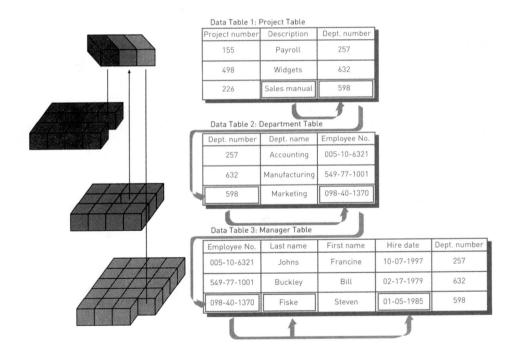

Figure 5.9

Linking Data Tables to Answer an Inquiry

In finding the name and hire date of the manager working on the sales manual project, the president needs three tables: project, department, and manager. The project description (Sales manual) leads to the department number (598) in the project table, which leads to the manager's employee number (098-40-1370) in the department table, which leads to the manager's name (Fiske) and hire date (01-05-1985) in the manager table.

The relational database model is by far the most widely used. It is easier to control, more flexible, and more intuitive than other approaches because it organizes data in tables. As shown in Figure 5.10 (on the next page), a relational database management system, such as Access, provides tips and tools for building and using database tables. In this figure, the database displays information about data types and indicates that additional help is available. The ability to link relational tables also allows users to relate data in new ways without having to redefine complex relationships. Because of the advantages of the relational model, many companies use it for large corporate databases, such as those for marketing and accounting. The relational model can also be used with personal computers and mainframe systems. A travel reservation company, for example, can develop a fare-pricing system by using relational database technology that can handle millions of daily queries from online travel companies such as Expedia.ca, Travelocity.ca, and Orbitz.ca.

Figure 5.10

Building and Modifying a Relational Database

Relational databases provide many tools, tips, and shortcuts to simplify the process of creating and modifying a database.

(Source: Used with permission from Microsoft.)

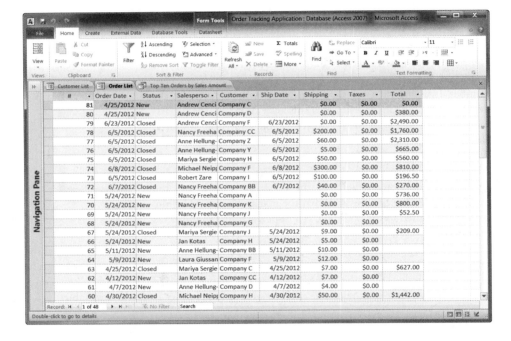

Data Cleanup

As discussed in Chapter 1, valuable data is accurate, complete, economical, flexible, reliable, relevant, simple, timely, verifiable, accessible, and secure. The database must also be properly designed. The purpose of **data cleanup** is to develop data with these characteristics. Consider a database for a fitness centre designed to track member dues. The table contains the attribute name, phone number, gender, dues paid, and date paid. See Table 5.3. As the records in Table 5.3 show, Anita Brown and Sim Thomas have paid their dues in September. Sim has paid his dues in two installments. Note that no primary key uniquely identifies each record. As you will see next, this problem must be corrected.

data cleanup
The process of looking for and fixing inconsistencies to ensure that data is accurate and complete.

Table 5.3

Fitness Centre Dues

Name	Phone	Gender	Dues Paid	Date Paid
Brown, A.	468-3342	Female	$30	September 15
Thomas, S.	468-8788	Male	$15	September 15
Thomas, S.	468-5238	Male	$15	September 25

Because Sim Thomas has paid dues twice in September, the data in the database is now redundant. The name, phone number, and gender for Thomas are repeated in two records. Notice that the data in the database is also inconsistent: Thomas has changed his phone number, but only one of the records reflects this change. Further reducing this database's reliability is the lack of a primary key to uniquely identify Sim Thomas's record. The first Thomas could be Sim Thomas, but the second might be Steve Thomas. These problems and irregularities in data are called *anomalies*. Data anomalies often result in incorrect information, causing database users to be misinformed about actual conditions. Anomalies must be corrected.

To solve these problems in the fitness centre's database, we can add a primary key, such as member number, and put the data into two tables: a Fitness Centre Members table with gender, phone number, and related information, and a Dues Paid table with dues paid and date paid. (See Tables 5.4 and 5.5.) Both tables include the member number attribute so that they can be linked.

Member No.	Name	Phone	Gender
SN123	Brown, A.	468-3342	Female
SN656	Thomas, S.	468-5238	Male

Table 5.4

Fitness Centre Members

Member No.	Dues Paid	Date Paid
SN123	$30	September 15
SN656	$15	September 15
SN656	$15	September 25

Table 5.5

Dues Paid

The relations in Table 5.4 and Table 5.5 reduce the redundancy and eliminate the potential problem of having two different phone numbers for the same member. Also note that the member number gives each record in the Fitness Centre Members table a primary key. Because the Dues Paid table lists two payment entries ($15 each) with the same member number (SN656), one person clearly made the payments, not two different people. Formalized approaches, such as *database normalization*, are often used to clean up problems with data.

DATABASE MANAGEMENT SYSTEMS

Creating and implementing the right database system ensures that the database will support both business activities and goals. But how do we actually create, implement, use, and update a database? The answer is found in the database management system. As discussed earlier, a DBMS is a group of programs used as an interface between a database and application programs or a database and the user. The capabilities and types of database systems, however, vary considerably. For example, Twitter, Google, Brightkite, and other Internet companies that provide GPS location applications are discussing the creation of a "Unified Database of Places." Rather than each company building proprietary databases of business and attraction locations, they would like to pool resources to build one huge database of places that includes details on every location on earth; such data would fuel applications like Google Street View.[15] Indeed, DBMSs are used to manage all kinds of data for all kinds of purposes.

Overview of Database Types

Database management systems can range from small, inexpensive software packages to sophisticated systems costing hundreds of thousands of dollars. The following sections discuss a few popular alternatives. See Figure 5.11 on the next page for one example.

Flat File

A flat file is a simple database program whose records have no relationship to one another. Flat file databases are often used to store and manipulate a single table or file; they do not use any of the database models discussed previously, such as the relational model. Many spreadsheet and word processing programs have flat file capabilities. These software packages can sort tables and make simple calculations and comparisons. Microsoft OneNote is designed to let people put ideas, thoughts, and notes into a flat file. In OneNote, each note can be placed anywhere on a page or in a box on a page, called a *container*. Pages are organized into sections and subsections that appear as coloured tabs. After you enter a note, you can retrieve, copy, and paste it into other applications, such as word processing and

Figure 5.11

Microsoft OneNote

Microsoft OneNote lets you gather any type of information and then retrieve, copy, and paste the information into other applications, such as word processing and spreadsheet programs.

(Source: Used with permission from Microsoft.)

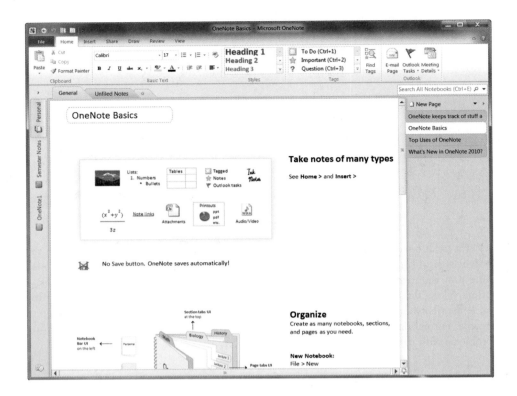

spreadsheet programs. The University of Toronto's Faculty of Medicine uses OneNote to enable medical students to capture information in varied ways and easily organize, search, and share notes and research.[16]

Similar to OneNote, EverNote is a free online database service that can store notes and other pieces of information. Considering the amount of information today's high-capacity hard disks can store, the popularity of databases that can handle unstructured data will continue to grow.

Single User

A database installed on a personal computer is typically meant for a single user. Microsoft Office Access and FileMaker Pro are designed to support single-user implementations. Microsoft InfoPath is another example of a database program that supports a single user. This software is part of the Microsoft Office suite, and it helps people collect and organize information from a variety of sources. InfoPath has built-in forms that can be used to enter expense information, timesheet data, and a variety of other information.

Multiple Users

Small, midsize, and large businesses need multi-user DBMSs to share information throughout the organization over a network. These more powerful, expensive systems allow dozens or hundreds of people to access the same database system at the same time. Popular vendors for multi-user database systems include Oracle, Microsoft, Sybase, and IBM. Many single-user databases, such as Microsoft Access, can be implemented for multi-user support over a network, though they often are limited in the number of users they can support.

All DBMSs share some common functions, such as providing a user view, physically storing and retrieving data in a database, allowing for database modification, manipulating data, and generating reports. These DBMSs can handle the most complex data processing tasks, and because they are accessed over a network, one database can serve many locations around the world. For example, the Canadian National Railway (CN), one of North America's largest railway companies, uses an enterprise-wide database to link its 22,500 employees and improve operations.[17]

Providing a User View

Because the DBMS is responsible for access to a database, one of the first steps in installing and using a large database involves "telling" the DBMS the logical and physical structure of the data and the relationships among the data for each user. This description is called a **schema** (as in schematic diagram). Large database systems, such as Oracle, typically use schemas to define the tables and other database features associated with a person or user. A schema can be part of the database or a separate schema file. The DBMS can reference a schema to find where to access the requested data in relation to another piece of data.

schema
A description of the entire database.

Creating and Modifying the Database

Schemas are entered into the DBMS (usually by database personnel) via a data definition language. A **data definition language** (**DDL**) is a collection of instructions and commands used to define and describe data and relationships in a specific database. A DDL allows the database's creator to describe the data and relationships that are to be contained in the schema. In general, a DDL describes logical access paths and logical records in the database. Figure 5.12 shows a simplified example of a DDL used to develop a general schema. The use of the letter *X* in Figure 5.12 reveals where specific information concerning the database should be entered. File description, area description, record description, and set description are terms the DDL defines and uses in this example. Other terms and commands can be used, depending on the DBMS employed.

data definition language (DDL)
A collection of instructions and commands used to define and describe data and relationships in a specific database.

```
SCHEMA DESCRIPTION
SCHEMA NAME IS XXXX
AUTHOR        XXXX
DATE          XXXX
FILE DESCRIPTION
    FILE NAME IS XXXX
      ASSIGN XXXX
    FILE NAME IS XXXX
      ASSIGN XXXX
AREA DESCRIPTION
    AREA NAME IS XXXX
RECORD DESCRIPTION
    RECORD NAME IS XXXX
    RECORD ID IS XXXX
    LOCATION MODE IS XXXX
    WITHIN XXXX AREA FROM XXXX THRU XXXX
SET DESCRIPTION
    SET NAME IS XXXX
    ORDER IS XXXX
    MODE IS XXXX
    MEMBER IS XXXX
    .
    .
    .
```

Figure 5.12

Using a Data Definition Language to Define a Schema

Another important step in creating a database is to establish a **data dictionary**, a detailed description of all data used in the database. The data dictionary contains the following information:

data dictionary
A detailed description of all the data used in the database.

- Name of the data item
- Aliases or other names that may be used to describe the item
- Range of values that can be used
- Type of data (such as alphanumeric or numeric)
- Amount of storage needed for the item
- Notation of the person responsible for updating it and the various users who can access it
- List of reports that use the data item

A data dictionary can also include a description of data flows, the way records are organized, and the data processing requirements. Figure 5.13 shows a typical data dictionary entry.

Figure 5.13

A Typical Data Dictionary Entry

NORTHWESTERN MANUFACTURING

PREPARED BY:	D. BORDWELL
DATE:	04 AUGUST 2011
APPROVED BY:	J. EDWARDS
DATE:	13 OCTOBER 2011
VERSION:	3.1
PAGE:	1 OF 1
DATA ELEMENT NAME:	PARTNO
DESCRIPTION:	INVENTORY PART NUMBER
OTHER NAMES:	PTNO
VALUE RANGE:	100 TO 5000
DATA TYPE:	NUMERIC
POSITIONS:	4 POSITIONS OR COLUMNS

For example, the information in a data dictionary for the part number of an inventory item can include the following information:

- Name of the person who made the data dictionary entry (D. Bordwell)
- Date the entry was made (August 4, 2011)
- Name of the person who approved the entry (J. Edwards)
- Approval date (October 13, 2011)
- Version number (3.1)
- Number of pages used for the entry (1)
- Part name (PARTNO)
- Other part names that might be used (PTNO)
- Range of values (part numbers can range from 100 to 5,000)
- Type of data (numeric)
- Storage required (four positions are required for the part number)

A data dictionary is valuable in maintaining an efficient database that stores reliable information with no redundancy, and it makes it easy to modify the database when necessary. Data dictionaries also help computer and system programmers who require a detailed description of data elements stored in a database to create the code to access the data.

Storing and Retrieving Data

One function of a DBMS is to be an interface between an application program and the database. When an application program needs data, it requests the data through the DBMS. Suppose that to calculate the total price of a new car, a pricing program needs price data on the engine option—six cylinders instead of the standard four cylinders. The application program requests this data from the DBMS. In doing so, the application program follows a logical access path. Next, the DBMS, working with various system programs, accesses a storage device, such as disk drives, where the data is stored. When the DBMS goes to this storage device to retrieve the data, it follows a path to the physical location (physical access path) where the price of this option is stored. In the pricing example, the DBMS might go to a disk drive to retrieve the price data for six-cylinder engines. This relationship is shown in Figure 5.14.

This same process is used if a user wants to get information from the database. First, the user requests the data from the DBMS. For example, a user might give a command, such as LIST ALL OPTIONS FOR WHICH PRICE IS GREATER THAN 200 DOLLARS. This

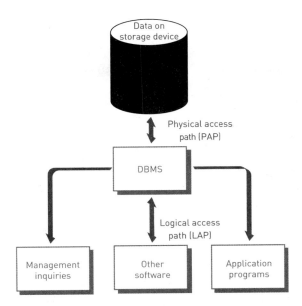

Figure 5.14

Logical and Physical Access Paths

is the logical access path (LAP). Then the DBMS might go to the options price section of a disk to get the information for the user. This is the physical access path (PAP).

Two or more people or programs attempting to access the same record at the same time can cause a problem. For example, an inventory control program might attempt to reduce the inventory level for a product by 10 units because 10 units were just shipped to a customer. At the same time, a purchasing program might attempt to increase the inventory level for the same product by 200 units because inventory was just received. Without proper database control, one of the inventory updates might be incorrect, resulting in an inaccurate inventory level for the product. **Concurrency control** can be used to avoid this potential problem. One approach is to lock out all other application programs from access to a record if the record is being updated or used by another program.

concurrency control
A method of dealing with a situation in which two or more users or applications need to access the same record at the same time.

Manipulating Data and Generating Reports

After a DBMS has been installed, employees, managers, and consumers can use it to review reports and obtain important information. For example, the Canada Consumer Product Safety Act requires companies to report serious incidents related to their products to Health Canada. Using a DBMS, a company can manage this requirement.

Some databases use *Query by Example (QBE)*, which is a visual approach to developing database queries or requests. Like Windows and other GUI operating systems, you can perform queries and other database tasks by opening windows and clicking the data or features you want. See Figure 5.15 on the next page.

In other cases, database commands can be used in a programming language. For example, C++ commands can be used in simple programs that will access or manipulate certain pieces of data in the database. Here's another example of a DBMS query: SELECT * FROM EMPLOYEE WHERE JOB_CLASSIFICATION = "C2". The asterisk (*) tells the program to include all columns from the EMPLOYEE table. In general, the commands that are used to manipulate the database are part of the **data manipulation language** (DML). This specific language, provided with the DBMS, allows managers and other database users to access and modify the data, to make queries, and to generate reports. Again, the application programs go through schemas and the DBMS before getting to the data stored on a device such as a disk.

data manipulation language (DML)
A specific language, provided with a DBMS, which allows users to access and modify the data, to make queries, and to generate reports.

In the 1970s, D. D. Chamberlain and others at the IBM Research Laboratory in San Jose, California, developed a standardized data manipulation language called *Structured Query Language (SQL)*, pronounced like the word *sequel* or spelled out as *SQL*. The EMPLOYEE

Figure 5.15

Query by Example

Some databases use Query by Example (QBE) to generate reports and information.

(Source: Used with permission from Microsoft.)

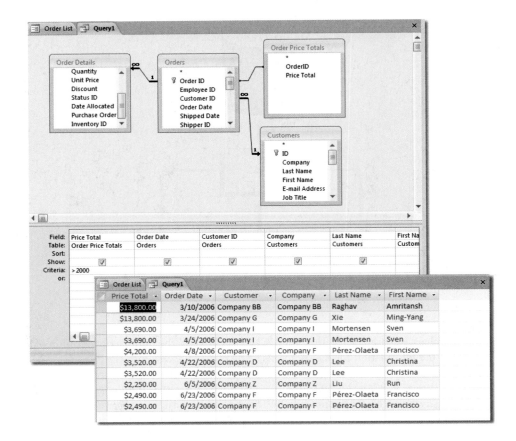

query shown earlier is written in SQL. In 1986, the American National Standards Institute (ANSI) adopted SQL as the standard query language for relational databases. Since ANSI's acceptance of SQL, interest in making SQL an integral part of relational databases on both mainframe and personal computers has increased. SQL has many built-in functions, such as average (AVG), the largest value (MAX), the smallest value (MIN), and others. Table 5.6 contains examples of SQL commands.

SQL lets programmers learn one powerful query language and use it on systems ranging from PCs to the largest mainframe computers. See Figure 5.16. Programmers and database users also find SQL valuable because SQL statements can be embedded into many

Table 5.6

Examples of SQL Commands

SQL Command	Description
SELECT ClientName, Debt FROM Client WHERE Debt > 1000	This query displays all clients (ClientName) and the amount they owe the company (Debt) from a database table called Client for clients who owe the company more than $1,000 (WHERE Debt > 1000).
SELECT ClientName, ClientNum, OrderNum FROM Client, Order WHERE Client.ClientNum=Order.ClientNum	This command is an example of a join command that combines data from two tables: the client table and the order table (FROM Client, Order). The command creates a new table with the client name, client number, and order number (SELECT ClientName, ClientNum, OrderNum). Both tables include the client number, which allows them to be joined. This is indicated in the WHERE clause, which states that the client number in the client table is the same as (equal to) the client number in the order table (WHERE Client.ClientNum= Order.ClientNum).
GRANT INSERT ON Client to Guthrie	This command is an example of a security command. It allows Bob Guthrie to insert new values or rows into the Client table.

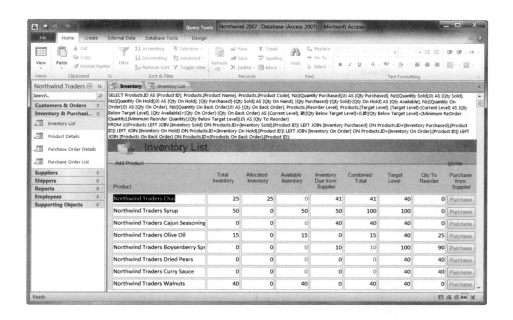

Figure 5.16

Structured Query Language

Structured Query Language (SQL) has become an integral part of most relational databases, as shown by this screen from Microsoft Access 2010.

(Source: Used with permission from Microsoft.)

programming languages, such as the widely used C++, Java, and COBOL. Because SQL uses standardized and simplified procedures for retrieving, storing, and manipulating data, the popular database query language can be easy to understand and use.

After a database has been set up and loaded with data, it can produce desired reports, documents, and other outputs. See Figure 5.17. These outputs usually appear in screen displays or hard-copy printouts. The output-control features of a database program allow you to select the records and fields you want to appear in reports. You can also make calculations specifically for the report by manipulating database fields. Formatting controls and organization options (such as report headings) help you to customize reports and create flexible, convenient, and powerful information-handling tools.

Monthly Sales Report

Monthly Sales Report

Sunday, July 29, 2007   5:36:07 PM

June, 2006

Product	Sales
Northwind Traders Boysenberry Spread	$2,250.00
Northwind Traders Dried Apples	$1,590.00
Northwind Traders Fruit Cocktail	$1,560.00
Northwind Traders Chocolate	$1,020.00
Northwind Traders Dried Pears	$900.00
Northwind Traders Cajun Seasoning	$660.00
Northwind Traders Coffee	$230.00
Northwind Traders Clam Chowder	$96.50
June Sales Total	$8,306.50

Page 1 of 1

Figure 5.17

Database Output

A database application offers sophisticated formatting and organization options to produce the right information in the right format.

(Source: Used with permission from Microsoft.)

A DBMS can produce a wide variety of documents, reports, and other output that can help organizations achieve their goals. The most common reports select and organize data to present summary information about some aspect of company operations. For example, accounting reports often summarize financial data such as current and past-due accounts. Many companies base their routine operating decisions on regular status reports that show the progress of specific orders toward completion and delivery.

Database Administration

Database systems require a skilled database administrator (DBA), who is expected to have a clear understanding of the fundamental business of the organization, be proficient in the use of selected database management systems, and stay abreast of emerging technologies and new design approaches. The role of the DBA is to plan, design, create, operate, secure, monitor, and maintain databases. Typically, a DBA has a degree in computer science or management information systems and some on-the-job training with a particular database product or more extensive experience with a range of database products. See Figure 5.18.

Figure 5.18

Database Administrator

The role of the database administrator (DBA) is to plan, design, create, operate, secure, monitor, and maintain databases.

(Source: Pinchuk Alexey/Shutterstock. com.)

The DBA works with users to decide the content of the database—to determine exactly what entities are of interest and what attributes are to be recorded about those entities. Thus, personnel outside of IS must have some idea of what the DBA does and why this function is important. The DBA can play a crucial role in the development of effective information systems to benefit the organization, employees, and managers.

The DBA also works with programmers as they build applications to ensure that their programs comply with database management system standards and conventions. After the database is built and operating, the DBA monitors operations logs for security violations. Database performance is also monitored to ensure that the system's response time meets users' needs and that it operates efficiently. If there is a problem, the DBA attempts to correct it before it becomes serious.

A database failure can cause huge financial losses for a business. A failure due to mechanical problems, controller failures, viruses or attacks, or human failure can cause productivity in an organization to grind to a halt. Databases accessible from the Internet are at a higher level of risk from hackers and viruses than databases stored on private servers. For example, an SQL injection attack uses a Web form to issue SQL commands to a database over the Internet. The SQL command might prompt the database to reveal private data, or it might corrupt the data in the database. SQL injection attacks were used to steal 130 million credit and debit card numbers from databases owned by Heartland Payment Systems, TJX Companies, and other businesses in 2009.[18] In 2010, the Open Web Application Security Project (OWASP) listed injection attacks as the top security threat for Web applications. A large responsibility of a DBA is to protect the database from attack or other forms of failure. DBAs use security software, preventive measures, and redundant systems to keep data safe and accessible.

Some organizations have also created a position called the **data administrator**, a nontechnical, but important position responsible for defining and implementing consistent

data administrator
A nontechnical position responsible for defining and implementing consistent principles for a variety of data issues.

principles for a variety of data issues, including setting data standards and data definitions that apply across all the databases in an organization. For example, the data administrator would ensure that a term such as "customer" is defined and treated consistently in all corporate databases. This person also works with business managers to identify who should have read or update access to certain databases and to selected attributes within those databases. This information is then communicated to the database administrator for implementation. The data administrator can be a high-level position reporting to top-level managers.

Popular Database Management Systems

Some popular DBMSs for single users are Microsoft Access and FileMaker Pro. The complete DBMS market encompasses software used by professional programmers and that runs on midrange servers, mainframes, and supercomputers. The entire market generates billions of dollars per year in revenue for companies such as IBM, Oracle, and Microsoft.

Like other software products, a number of open-source database systems are available, including PostgreSQL and MySQL. Open-source software was described in Chapter 4. In addition, many traditional database programs are now available on open-source operating systems. The popular DB2 relational database from IBM, for example, is available on the Linux operating system. The Sybase IQ database and other databases are also available on the Linux operating system.

A new form of database system is emerging that some refer to as *Database as a Service* (*DaaS*); others call it Database 2.0. DaaS is similar to Software as a Service (SaaS). Recall that a SaaS system is one in which the software is stored on a service provider's servers and is accessed by the client company over a network. In DaaS, the database is stored on a service provider's servers and accessed by the client over a network, typically the Internet. In DaaS, database administration is provided by the service provider. SaaS and DaaS are both part of the larger cloud computing trend. Recall from Chapter 3 that cloud computing uses a giant cluster of computers that run high-performance applications. In cloud computing, all information systems and data are maintained and managed by service providers and delivered over the Internet. Businesses and individuals are freed from having to install, service, maintain, upgrade, and safeguard their systems.

More than a dozen companies are moving in the DaaS direction. They include Google, Microsoft, Oracle, Amazon, Intuit, MyOwnDB, and Trackvia. Oracle's DaaS combines cloud computing with grid computing and virtualization to provide cost-effective, reliable, and scalable database solutions.[19] Oracle provides both private clouds—accessible only to users on a private network—and public clouds—accessible to the public over the Internet. Canada Yellow Pages developed an API using cloud computing and Amazon's Web Services to provide Web developers with access to its 1.5 million listings. Where.com, for example, uses the API to provide a local search and recommendation service to discover places and events in specific geographic areas.[20] Procter and Gamble consolidated hundreds of projects into a single cloud database, a move that saved operational costs and reduced meeting time and data entry time for employees.[21]

Special-Purpose Database Systems

In addition to the popular database management systems just discussed, some specialized database packages are used for specific purposes or in specific industries. For example, RexBook from Urbanspoon is an iPad App designed for restaurants that uses a special-purpose online database to store and manage dining reservations.[22] Another unique special-purpose DBMS for biologists called Morphbank (*www.morphbank.net*) allows researchers from around the world to continually update and expand a library of over 96,000 biological images to share with the scientific community and the public. Apple's iTunes software uses a special-purpose database system that includes fields for song name, rating, file size, time, artist, album, and genre. When iTunes users go to the iTunes store and search for an artist, they are actually querying the central iTunes database. See Figure 5.19 on the next page.

Figure 5.19

iTunes Database

Apple's iTunes software uses a database to catalogue and access music.

(Source: Courtesy of Apple, Inc.)

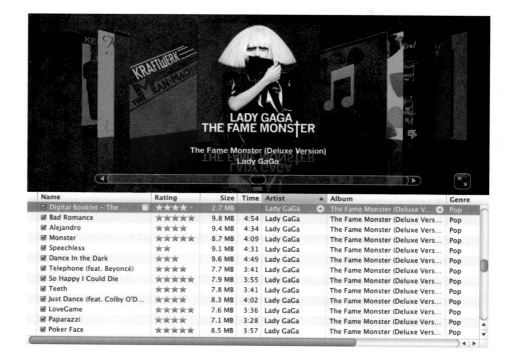

Selecting a Database Management System

The database administrator often selects the best database management system for an organization. The process begins by analyzing database needs and characteristics. The information needs of the organization affect the type of data that is collected and the type of database management system that is used. Important characteristics of databases include the following:

- *Database size*: The number of records or files in the database
- *Database cost*: The purchase or lease costs of the database
- *Concurrent users*: The number of people who need to use the database at the same time
- *Performance*: How fast the database can update records
- *Integration*: The ability to work seamlessly with other applications and databases
- *Vendor*: The reputation and financial stability of the database vendor

Using Databases with Other Software

Database management systems are often used with other software and with the Internet. A DBMS can act as a front-end application or a back-end application. A *front-end application* is one that people interact with directly. Marketing researchers often use a database as a front end to a statistical analysis program. The researchers enter the results of market questionnaires or surveys into a database. The data is then transferred to a statistical analysis program to determine the potential for a new product or the effectiveness of an advertising campaign. A *back-end application* interacts with other programs or applications; it only indirectly interacts with people or users. When people request information from a website, the website can interact with a database (the back end) that supplies the desired information. For example, you can connect to a university website to find out whether the university's library has a book you want to read. The website then interacts with a database that contains a catalogue of library books and articles to determine whether the book you want is available. See Figure 5.20.

In some situations, front-end systems cannot connect directly to a back-end database due to compatibility issues. Middleware solutions, such as Oracle's Fusion software, are available to connect systems seamlessly, interpreting data from a variety of sources and translating it to a format compatible with the database.

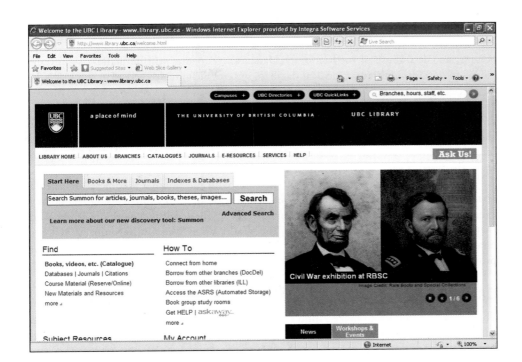

Figure 5.20

Library Website

Many university libraries provide Web access to their databases.

(Source: The University of British Columbia Library website (2011). Used with permission.)

DATABASE APPLICATIONS

Today's database applications manipulate the content of a database to produce useful information. Common manipulations are searching, filtering, synthesizing, and assimilating the data, using a number of database applications. These applications allow users to link the company databases to the Internet, set up data warehouses and marts, use databases for strategic business intelligence, place data at different locations, use online processing and open connectivity standards for increased productivity, develop databases with the object-oriented approach, and search for and use unstructured data, such as graphics, audio, and video.

Linking the Company Database to the Internet

The ability to link databases to the Internet is one reason the Internet is so popular. A large percentage of corporate databases are accessed over the Internet through a standard Web browser. Being able to access bank account data, student transcripts, credit card bills, product catalogues, and a host of other data online is convenient for individual users and increases effectiveness and efficiency for businesses and organizations. Amazon.ca, eHarmony.ca, eBay.ca, and many others have made billions of dollars by combining databases, the Internet, and smart business models.

Google, Microsoft, and others have developed Personal Health Record (PHR) systems designed to provide physicians and patients a single storage location for all medical records, accessed through a Web browser.[23] Google Health and Microsoft HealthVault provide "patient-centred" health records that empower patients to more easily participate in their own health care. In the United States, President Obama is pushing to establish electronic health (e-health) records for all Americans prior to 2015 by making $17 billion available to e-health projects and programs. In Canada, Canada Health Infoway was established to promote and standardize health information technology systems across Canada. The creation of electronic drug-information records is expected to result in $436 million in savings and efficiencies through improved drug-cost management, fewer adverse drug interactions, and less abuse of medication.[24] Database companies will be making significant efforts to develop health and medical database systems that are accessible on the Internet.

Access to private medical information over the public Web has some privacy advocates concerned. However, the convenience that the system offers by dramatically reducing the amount of paper forms to fill out and store, along with the reduction of clerical errors through streamlined data management procedures, has most in the field supporting the move to a centralized system. Encryption and authentication technologies will be used to make the systems as secure as possible.

Developing a seamless integration of databases with the Internet is sometimes called a *semantic Web*. A semantic Web provides metadata with all Web content using technology called the Resource Description Framework (RDF).[25] The result is a more organized Web that acts like one large database system. The World Wide Web Consortium (W3C) has established standards, including an RDF, for a semantic Web in hopes of bringing content providers onboard.

Data Warehouses, Data Marts, and Data Mining

The raw data necessary to make sound business decisions is stored in a variety of locations and formats. This data is initially captured, stored, and managed by transaction processing systems that are designed to support the day-to-day operations of the organization. For decades, organizations have collected operational, sales, and financial data with their online transaction processing (OLTP) systems. The data can be used to support decision making through data warehouses, data marts, and data mining.

Data Warehouses

data warehouse
A large database that collects business information from many sources in the enterprise, covering all aspects of the company's processes, products, and customers, in support of management decision making.

A **data warehouse** is a database that holds business information from many sources in the enterprise, covering all aspects of the company's processes, products, and customers. The data warehouse provides business users with a multidimensional view of the data they need to analyze business conditions. Data warehouses allow managers to *drill down* to get more detail or *roll up* to take detailed data and generate aggregate or summary reports. A data warehouse is designed specifically to support management decision making, not to meet the needs of transaction processing systems. A data warehouse stores historical data that has been extracted from operational systems and external data sources. See Figure 5.21. This operational and external data is "cleaned up" to remove inconsistencies and integrated to create a new information database that is more suitable for business analysis.

Data warehouses typically start out as very large databases, containing millions and even hundreds of millions of data records. As this data is collected from the various production systems, a historical database is built that business analysts can use to track changes in an organization over time and analyze current conditions. To keep it fresh and accurate, the data warehouse receives regular updates. Old data that is no longer needed is purged from the data warehouse. Updating the data warehouse must be fast, efficient, and automated, or the ultimate value of the data warehouse is sacrificed. It is common for a data warehouse to contain from 3 to 10 years of current and historical data. Data-cleaning tools can merge data from many sources into one database, automate data collection and verification, delete unwanted data, and maintain data in a database management system.

Data warehouses can also acquire data from unique sources. Oracle's Warehouse Management software, for example, can accept information from Radio Frequency Identification (RFID) technology, which is being used to tag products as they are shipped or moved from one location to another. Honda Italia, the world leader in powered two-wheel vehicle manufacturing, uses RFID to feed its data warehouse with information about production. Each vehicle component is tagged with an RFID chip so it can be tracked through the entire production process. The RFID-based system provides highly detailed information to

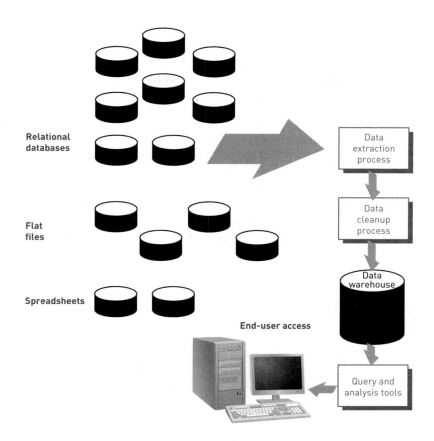

Figure 5.21

Elements of a Data Warehouse

production managers who can tweak production to quickly identify problems and improve supply with little or no wasted effort or resources.[26]

The primary advantage of data warehousing is the ability to relate data in innovative ways. However, a data warehouse for a large organization can be extremely difficult to establish, with the typical cost exceeding $2 million. Table 5.7 compares online transaction processing (OLTP) and data warehousing.

Table 5.7

Comparison of OLTP and Data Warehousing

Characteristic	OLTP Database	Data Warehousing
Purpose	Support transaction processing	Support decision making
Source of data	Business transactions	Multiple files and databases—data internal and external to the firm
Data access allowed to users	Read and write	Read only
Primary data access mode	Simple database update and query	Simple and complex database queries with increasing use of data mining to recognize patterns in the data
Primary database model employed	Relational	Relational
Level of detail	Detailed transactions	Often summarized data
Availability of historical data	Very limited—typically a few weeks or months	Several years
Update process	Online and ongoing process as transactions are captured	Periodic process, once per week or once per month
Ease of process	Routine and easy	Complex, must combine data from many sources; data must go through a data cleanup process
Data integrity issues	Each transaction must be closely edited	Major effort to "clean" and integrate data from many sources

data mart
A subset of a data warehouse, used by small and medium-sized businesses and departments within large companies to support decision making.

Data Marts

A **data mart** is a subset of a data warehouse. Data marts bring the data warehouse concept—online analysis of sales, inventory, and other vital business data that has been gathered from transaction processing systems—to small and medium-sized businesses and to departments within larger companies. Rather than store all enterprise data in one monolithic database, data marts contain a subset of the data for a single aspect of a company's business—for example, finance, inventory, or personnel. In fact, a specific area in the data mart might contain more detailed data than the data warehouse.

Data marts are most useful for smaller groups who want to access detailed data. A warehouse contains summary data that can be used by an entire company. Because data marts typically contain tens of gigabytes of data, as opposed to the hundreds of gigabytes in data warehouses, they can be deployed on less powerful hardware with smaller secondary storage devices, delivering significant savings to an organization. Although any database software can be used to set up a data mart, some vendors deliver specialized software designed and priced specifically for data marts. Companies such as Sybase, Software AG, and Microsoft have products and services that make it easier and cheaper to deploy these scaled-down data warehouses. The selling point: data marts put targeted business information into the hands of more decision makers.

data mining
An information-analysis tool that involves the automated discovery of patterns and relationships in a data warehouse.

Data Mining

Data mining is an information-analysis tool that involves the automated discovery of patterns and relationships in a data warehouse. Like gold mining, data mining sifts through mountains of data to find a few nuggets of valuable information. For example, Reader's Digest Canada uses data mining to gain a better understanding its major market segments, identify profitable subsets of these markets, and analyze new markets.[27]

Data mining's objective is to extract patterns, trends, and rules from data warehouses to evaluate (i.e., predict or score) proposed business strategies, which will improve competitiveness, increase profits, and transform business processes. It is used extensively in marketing to improve customer retention; cross-selling opportunities; campaign management; market, channel, and pricing analysis; and customer segmentation analysis (especially one-to-one marketing). In short, data-mining tools help users find answers to questions they haven't thought to ask.

E-commerce presents another major opportunity for effective use of data mining. Attracting customers to websites is tough; keeping them there and ensuring they return is even tougher. For example, when retail websites launch deep-discount sales, they cannot easily determine how many first-time customers are likely to come back and buy again. Nor do they have a way of understanding which customers acquired during the sale are more likely to jump on future sales. As a result, companies are gathering data on user traffic through their websites and storing the data in databases. This data is then analyzed using data-mining techniques to personalize the website and develop sales promotions targeted at specific customers. Facebook has angered users on several occasions for sharing members' data with commercial partners who then use the information in data mining that fuels targeted marketing campaigns. Some members feel that the practice is a violation of their privacy.[28]

predictive analysis
A form of data mining that combines historical data with assumptions about future conditions to predict outcomes of events, such as future product sales or the probability that a customer will default on a loan.

Predictive analysis is a form of data mining that combines historical data with assumptions about future conditions to predict outcomes of events, such as future product sales or the probability that a customer will default on a loan. Retailers use predictive analysis to upgrade occasional customers into frequent purchasers by predicting what products they will buy if offered an appropriate incentive. Genalytics, Magnify, NCR Teradata, SAS Institute, Sightward, SPSS, and Quadstone have developed predictive analysis tools. Predictive analysis software can be used to analyze a company's customer list and a year's worth of sales data to find new market segments that could be profitable.

The Canadian Bankers Association has received international recognition for using intelligence analytical techniques to assist police departments in fighting ATM card fraud crimes by identifying crime hotspots, crime mapping, day of week matrices, and predictive analysis on next-target locations.[29]

Traditional DBMS vendors are well aware of the great potential of data mining. Thus, companies such as Oracle, Sybase, Tandem, and Red Brick Systems are all incorporating data-mining functionality into their products. Table 5.8 summarizes a few of the most frequent applications for data mining.

Application	Description
Branding and positioning of products and services	Enable the strategist to visualize the different positions of competitors in a given market using performance (or other) data on dozens of key features of the product and then to condense all that data into a perceptual map of only two or three dimensions.
Customer churn	Predict current customers who are likely to switch to a competitor.
Direct marketing	Identify prospects most likely to respond to a direct marketing campaign (such as a direct mailing).
Fraud detection	Highlight transactions most likely to be deceptive or illegal.
Market basket analysis	Identify products and services that are most commonly purchased at the same time (e.g., nail polish and lipstick).
Market segmentation	Group customers based on who they are or on what they prefer.
Trend analysis	Analyze how key variables (e.g., sales, spending, promotions) vary over time.

Table 5.8

Common Data-Mining Applications

Business Intelligence

The use of databases for business-intelligence purposes is closely linked to the concept of data mining. **Business intelligence** (**BI**) involves gathering enough of the right information in a timely manner and usable form and analyzing it so that it can have a positive effect on business strategy, tactics, or operations. Petro-Canada, for example, uses a BI system to analyze its financial and operating data. BI turns data into useful information that is then distributed throughout an enterprise. It provides insight into the causes of problems and, when implemented, can improve business operations. The Royal Bank of Canada, Canada's largest bank, uses SAS software to provide business intelligence to its divisions in the areas of customer management, performance management, campaign management, channel management, marketing analytics, decision support, and service pricing.[30]

Competitive intelligence is one aspect of business intelligence and is limited to information about competitors and the ways that knowledge affects strategy, tactics, and operations. Competitive intelligence is a critical part of a company's ability to see and respond quickly and appropriately to the changing marketplace. Competitive intelligence is not espionage—the use of illegal means to gather information. In fact, almost all the information a competitive-intelligence professional needs can be collected by examining published information sources, conducting interviews, and using other legal, ethical methods. Using a variety of analytical tools, a skilled competitive-intelligence professional can by deduction fill the gaps in information already gathered.

The term **counterintelligence** describes the steps an organization takes to protect information sought by "hostile" intelligence gatherers. One of the most effective counterintelligence measures is to define "trade secret" information relevant to the company and control its dissemination.

Data loss prevention (**DLP**) refers to systems designed to lock down data within an organization. DLP software from RSA, Symantec, Code Green, Safend, Trend Micro, Sophos, and others are designed to identify, monitor, and protect data wherever it may exist on a system. That includes data stored on disk, passing over a network, in databases, in files, in e-mail, and elsewhere. DLP is a powerful tool for counterintelligence and is a necessity in complying with government regulations that require companies to safeguard private customer data.[31]

business intelligence (BI)
The process of gathering enough of the right information in a timely manner and usable form and analyzing it to have a positive impact on business strategy, tactics, or operations.

competitive intelligence
One aspect of business intelligence limited to information about competitors and the ways that knowledge affects strategy, tactics, and operations.

counterintelligence
The steps an organization takes to protect information sought by "hostile" intelligence gatherers.

data loss prevention (DLP)
Systems designed to lock down—to identify, monitor, and protect—data within an organization.

The Database That Drives the Austrian Turnpike

ASFINAG Maut Service GmbH is the company responsible for planning, financing, building, maintaining, and operating the Austrian turnpike and highway system—all 2,100 kilometres of it. As with most European countries, Austria has relied on manually collected tolls to finance its highway system. Recently, the country turned to state-of-the-art database-driven systems to transport its highways into the 21st century.

Bernd Datler, head of system development for ASFINAG Maut Service GmbH, calls it "the world's first fully automated, free-flowing tolling system for commercial vehicles." ASFINAG hired Austrian IS service provider Raiffeisen Informatik GmbH to implement a system that would tag and track over 700,000 commercial vehicles across Austrian roads, automatically billing each vehicle according to complicated specifications.

The database that supports this massive system would have to contend with a variety of data formats and high frequency of data input. It would feed numerous systems to serve a variety of needs.

The fully automated, free-flowing tolling system begins with driver registration. Drivers can register online, by phone, or at local sales centres. The registration process collects information about the driver, the vehicle, and the company that employs the driver. This information is fed into the database and is accessed by a customer relationship management (CRM) system as needed. Upon registration, drivers are provided with a radio transceiver box that is mounted to the dashboard of the commercial vehicle.

The 800 tollgates along Austrian highways were fitted with special microwave receivers that connect with the boxes on drivers' dashboards without the drivers needing to stop. As drivers pass a tollgate, data is continuously collected and entered into the database as transactions. Rather than billing a flat rate, the automated system allows for custom rates to be applied. Fees are calculated based on several criteria, including the size of the vehicle, whether it is full or empty, the time of day, and the vehicle's emission class. These last two criteria can be used to motivate drivers to travel at off-peak times and to use vehicles with low emissions.

The database also collects photographic data. Cameras mounted at tollgates photograph every vehicle to catch unregistered vehicles. The photos are used to see vehicle tags and registration to track down the vehicle's owner. The photo system is also used to collect tolls from noncommercial vehicles that use a registration sticker on the windshield.

Drivers can access their toll information online using a Web-based portal that delivers real-time reporting. Data is automatically transferred into a data warehouse, where ASFINAG managers have access to powerful business intelligence (BI) tools that allow them to generate reports on highway usage from several perspectives. The system manages 2.5 million transactions per week, without the need for any human intervention. Invoices are automatically generated in the customer's native language and are delivered electronically. The system was designed to be interoperable as well, reading not only Austrian-registered vehicles, but also vehicles registered in Switzerland, Germany, and Italy.

All in all, the project took over 100 Raiffeisen Informatik IS professionals 18 months to complete. The team met its deadline and hit its goals measured by quality, functionality, and costs.

Discussion Questions

1. What unique challenges did the ASFINAG project present for database installation, administration, and security?
2. How does the "world's first fully automated, free-flowing tolling system for commercial vehicles" benefit drivers and the highway system?

Critical Thinking Questions

1. What business functions are supported by the database at ASFINAG?
2. What database applications discussed in the chapter are used in conjunction with the ASFINAG database?

SOURCES: "Raiffeisen Informatik—SAP Software Powers Outsourced Toll-Collection System," SAP Customer Success Story, *www.sap.com/solutions/sapbusinessobjects/customers*, accessed May 15, 2010; ASFINAG website, *www.asfinag.at/en*, accessed May 15, 2010.

Distributed Databases

Distributed processing involves placing processing units at different locations and linking them via telecommunications equipment. A **distributed database**—a database in which the data can be spread across several smaller databases connected through telecommunications devices—works on much the same principle. A user in the Montreal branch of a clothing manufacturer, for example, might make a request for data that is physically located at corporate headquarters in Milan, Italy. The user does not have to know where the data is physically stored. See Figure 5.22.

distributed database
A database in which the data can be spread across several smaller databases connected via telecommunications devices.

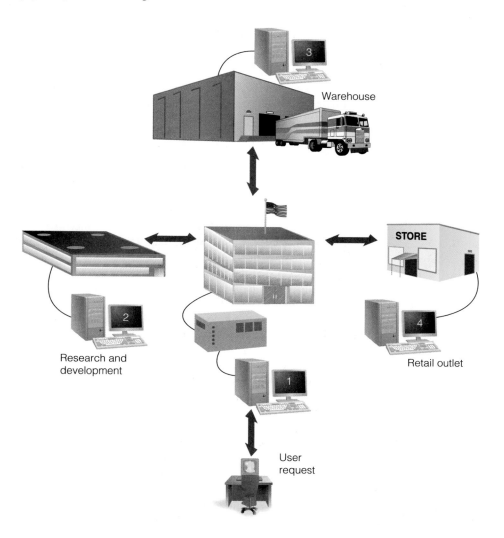

_____

| **Figure 5.22** |

The Use of a Distributed Database

For a clothing manufacturer, computers might be located at corporate headquarters, in the research and development centre, in the warehouse, and in a company-owned retail store. Telecommunications systems link the computers so that users at all locations can access the same distributed database, no matter where the data is actually stored.

_____

Distributed databases give corporations and other organizations more flexibility in how databases are organized and used. Local offices can create, manage, and use their own databases, and people at other offices can access and share the data in the local databases. Giving local sites more direct access to frequently used data can improve organizational effectiveness and efficiency significantly. The Edmonton Police Service, for example, has hundreds of officers searching for information located on servers in offices around the city.

Despite its advantages, distributed processing creates additional challenges in integrating different databases (information integration) and maintaining data security, accuracy, timeliness, and conformance to standards. Distributed databases allow more users direct access at different sites; however, controlling who accesses and changes data is sometimes difficult. Also, because distributed databases rely on telecommunications lines to transport data, access to data can be slower.

replicated database
A database that holds a duplicate set of frequently used data.

To reduce telecommunications costs, some organizations build a replicated database. A **replicated database** holds a duplicate set of frequently used data. The company sends a copy of important data to each distributed processing location when needed or at predetermined times. Each site sends the changed data back to update the main database on an update cycle that meets the needs of the organization. This process, often called *data synchronization*, is used to make sure that replicated databases are accurate, up to date, and consistent with each other. A railroad, for example, can use a replicated database to increase punctuality, safety, and reliability. The primary database can hold data on fares, routings, and other essential information. The data can be continually replicated and downloaded on a read-only basis from the master database to hundreds of remote servers across the country. The remote locations can send back to the main database the latest figures on ticket sales and reservations.

Online Analytical Processing (OLAP)

online analytical processing (OLAP)
Software that allows users to explore data from a number of perspectives.

For nearly two decades, multidimensional databases and their analytical information display systems have provided flashy sales presentations and trade show demonstrations. All you have to do is ask where a certain product is selling well, for example, and a colourful table showing sales performance by region, product type, and time frame appears on the screen. Called **online analytical processing (OLAP)**, these programs are now being used to store and deliver data warehouse information efficiently. The leading OLAP software vendors include Microsoft, Cognos, SAP, Business Objects, MicroStrategy, Applix, Infor, and Oracle. Blue Mountain, Ontario's largest mountain resort, uses OLAP to allow its analysts, managers, and executives to quickly view and understand large sets of complex data. The resort includes 13 business lines, including restaurants, ski ticketing, call centres, and lodging. Decision makers use the OLAP system to view their data across many dimensions and drill down to access specifics.[32]

The value of data ultimately lies in the decisions it enables. Powerful information-analysis tools in areas such as OLAP and data mining, when incorporated into a data warehousing architecture, bring market conditions into sharper focus and help organizations deliver greater competitive value. OLAP provides top-down, query-driven data analysis; data mining provides bottom-up, discovery-driven analysis. OLAP requires repetitive testing of user-originated theories; data mining requires no assumptions and instead identifies facts and conclusions based on patterns discovered. OLAP, or multidimensional analysis, requires a great deal of human ingenuity and interaction with the database to find information in the database. A user of a data-mining tool does not need to figure out what questions to ask; instead, the approach is "Here's the data, tell me what interesting patterns emerge." For example, a data-mining tool in a credit card company's customer database can construct a profile of fraudulent activity from historical information. Then this profile can be applied to all incoming transaction data to identify and stop fraudulent behaviour, which might otherwise go undetected. Table 5.9 compares OLAP and data mining.

Table 5.9

Comparison of OLAP and Data Mining

Characteristic	OLAP	Data Mining
Purpose	Supports data analysis and decision making	Supports data analysis and decision making
Type of analysis supported	Top-down, query-driven data analysis	Bottom-up, discovery-driven data analysis
Skills required of user	Must be very knowledgeable of the data and its business context	Must trust in data-mining tools to uncover valid and worthwhile hypotheses

Object-Relational Database Management Systems

object-oriented database
A database that stores both data and its processing instructions.

An **object-oriented database** uses the same overall approach of objected-oriented programming that was discussed in Chapter 4. With this approach, both the data and the processing instructions are stored in the database. For example, an object-oriented database could store monthly expenses and the instructions needed to compute a monthly budget from those expenses. A traditional DBMS might store only the monthly expenses. The popular Internet phone service Skype has been pleased with its object-oriented database from PostgreSQL. The object-oriented nature of the database allowed Skype to develop the database as the company grew and evolved.[33] Object-oriented databases are useful when a database contains complex data that needs to be processed quickly and efficiently.

In an object-oriented database, a *method* is a procedure or action. A sales tax method, for example, could be the procedure to compute the appropriate sales tax for an order or sale—for example, multiplying the total amount of an order by 7 percent, if that is the local sales tax. A *message* is a request to execute or run a method. For example, a sales clerk could issue a message to the object-oriented database to compute sales tax for a new order. Many object-oriented databases have their own query language, called *object query language* (*OQL*), which is similar to SQL, discussed previously.

An object-oriented database uses an **object-oriented database management system** (**OODBMS**) to provide a user interface and connections to other programs. Computer vendors who sell or lease OODBMSs include Versant and Objectivity. Many organizations are selecting object-oriented databases for their processing power. Versant's OODBMS, for example, is being used by companies in the telecommunications, defense, online gaming, and health-care industries, and by government agencies. The *Object Data Standard* is a design standard created by the *Object Database Management Group* (*www.odmg.org*) for developing object-oriented database systems.

An **object-relational database management system** (**ORDBMS**) provides a complete set of relational database capabilities plus the ability for third parties to add new data types and operations to the database. These new data types can be audio, images, unstructured text, spatial, or time series data that require new indexing, optimization, and retrieval features. Each of the vendors offering ORDBMS facilities provides a set of application programming interfaces to allow users to attach external data definitions and methods associated with those definitions to the database system. They are essentially offering a standard socket into which users can plug special instructions. DataBlades, Cartridges, and Extenders are the names applied by Oracle and IBM to describe the plug-ins to their respective products. Other plug-ins serve as interfaces to Web servers.

object-oriented database management system (OODBMS) A group of programs that manipulate an object-oriented database and provide a user interface and connections to other application programs.

object-relational database management system (ORDBMS) A DBMS capable of manipulating audio, video, and graphical data.

Visual, Audio, and Other Database Systems

In addition to raw data, organizations are finding a need to store large amounts of visual and audio signals in an organized fashion. Credit card companies, for example, enter pictures of charge slips into an image database using a scanner. The images can be stored in the database and later sorted by customer name, printed, and sent to customers along with their monthly statements. Image databases are also used by physicians to store X-rays and transmit them to clinics away from the main hospital. Financial services, insurance companies, and government branches are using image databases to store vital records and replace paper documents. Drug companies often need to analyze many visual images from laboratories. Visual databases can be stored in some object-relational databases or special-purpose database systems. Many relational databases can also store images.

Combining and analyzing data from different databases is an increasingly important challenge. Global businesses, for example, sometimes need to analyze sales and accounting data stored around the world in different database systems. Companies such as IBM have developed *virtual database systems* to allow different databases to work together as a unified database system. The process of joining separate databases into one is sometimes referred to as a *federated database system*. World-renowned insurer Lloyd's of London joined its database with that of International Underwriting Association (IUA), creating a virtual database that ensured improved customer service at a lower cost.[34]

In addition to visual, audio, and virtual databases, other special-purpose database systems meet particular business needs. *Spatial data technology* involves using a database to store and access data according to the locations it describes and to permit spatial queries and analysis. MapInfo software from Pitney Bowes allows businesses such as Home

Spatial data technology is used by
law-enforcement agencies to provide
protection where it is most needed.

(Source: © David R. Frazier
Photolibrary, Inc./Alamy.)

Depot, Rexall, and TD Canada Trust to choose the optimal location for new stores based on geospatial demographics. It also can be used to assist law-enforcement agencies and emergency response teams to prepare for emergencies and provide community protection in an efficient manner.[35] The software provides information about local competition, populations, and traffic patterns to predict how a business will fare in a particular location. Builders and insurance companies use spatial data to make decisions related to natural hazards. Spatial data can even be used to improve financial risk management with information stored by investment type, currency type, interest rates, and time. Spatial data technology is a powerful tool that geographic information systems (GIS) use to plot information on a map.

SUMMARY

Principle:

Data management and modelling are key aspects of organizing data and information.

Data is one of the most valuable resources that a firm possesses. It is organized into a hierarchy that builds from the smallest element to the largest. The smallest element is the bit, a binary digit. A byte (a character such as a letter or numeric digit) is made up of eight bits. A group of characters, such as a name or number, is called a field (an object). A collection of related fields is a record; a collection of related records is called a file. The database, at the top of the hierarchy, is an integrated collection of records and files.

An entity is a generalized class of objects for which data is collected, stored, and maintained. An attribute is a characteristic of an entity. Specific values of attributes—called data items—can be found in the fields of the record describing an entity. A data key is a field within a record that is used to identify the record. A primary key uniquely identifies a record, while a secondary key is a field in a record that does not uniquely identify the record.

Traditional file-oriented applications are often characterized by program-data dependence, meaning that they have data organized in a manner that cannot be read by other programs. To address problems of traditional file-based data management, the database approach was developed. Benefits of this approach include reduced data redundancy, improved data consistency and integrity, easier modification and updating, data and program independence, standardization of data access, and more efficient program development.

When building a database, an organization must consider content, access, logical structure, and physical organization of the database. Many enterprises build a data centre to house the servers that physically store databases and the systems that deliver mission-critical information and services. One of the tools that database designers use to show the logical structure and relationships among data is a data model. A data model is a map or diagram of entities and their relationships. Enterprise data modelling involves analyzing the data and information needs of an entire organization. Entity-relationship (ER) diagrams can be used to show the relationships among entities in the organization.

The relational model places data in two-dimensional tables. Tables can be linked by common data elements, which are used to access data when the database is queried. Each row represents a record, and each column represents an attribute (or field). Allowable values for these attributes are called the domain. Basic data manipulations include selecting, projecting, and joining. The relational model is easier to control, more flexible, and more intuitive than the other models because it organizes data in tables.

Principle:

A well-designed and well-managed database is an extremely valuable tool in supporting decision making.

A DBMS is a group of programs used as an interface between a database and its users and other application programs. When an application program requests data from the database, it follows a logical access path. The actual retrieval of the data follows a physical access path. Records can be considered in the same way: a logical record is what the record contains; a physical record is where the record is stored on storage devices. Schemas are used to describe the entire database, its record types, and their relationships to the DBMS.

A DBMS provides four basic functions: providing user views, creating and modifying the database, storing and retrieving data, and manipulating data and generating reports. Schemas are entered into the computer via a data definition language, which describes the data and relationships in a specific database. Another tool used in database management is the data dictionary, which contains detailed descriptions of all data in the database.

After a DBMS has been installed, the database can be accessed, modified, and queried via a data manipulation language. A more specialized data manipulation language is the query language, the most common being Structured Query Language (SQL). SQL is used in several popular database packages today and can be installed on PCs and mainframes.

Popular single-user DBMSs include Corel Paradox and Microsoft Access. IBM, Oracle, and Microsoft are the leading DBMS vendors. Database as a Service (DaaS), or Database 2.0, is a new form of database service in which clients lease use of a database on a service provider's site.

A database administrator (DBA) plans, designs, creates, operates, secures, monitors, and maintains databases. Attacks on databases such as SQL injection attacks are an all-too-common threat that DBAs must guard against. Selecting a DBMS begins by analyzing the information needs of the organization. Important characteristics of databases include the size of the database, the number of concurrent users, its performance, the ability of the DBMS to be integrated with other systems, the features of the DBMS, the vendor considerations, and the cost of the database management system.

Principle:

The number and types of database applications will continue to evolve and yield real business benefits.

Traditional online transaction processing (OLTP) systems put data into databases very quickly, reliably, and efficiently, but they do not support the types of data analysis that today's businesses and organizations require. To address this need, organizations are building data warehouses, which are relational database management systems specifically designed to support management decision making. Data marts are subdivisions of data warehouses, which are commonly devoted to specific purposes or functional business areas.

Data mining, which is the automated discovery of patterns and relationships in a data warehouse, is a practical approach to generating hypotheses about the data that can be used to predict future behaviour.

Predictive analysis is a form of data mining that combines historical data with assumptions about future conditions to forecast outcomes of events such as future product sales or the probability that a customer will default on a loan.

Business intelligence is the process of getting enough of the right information in a timely manner and usable form and analyzing it so that it can have a positive effect on business strategy, tactics, or operations. Competitive intelligence is one aspect of business intelligence limited to information about competitors and the ways that information affects strategy, tactics, and operations. Competitive intelligence is not espionage—the use of illegal means to gather information. Counterintelligence describes the steps an organization takes to protect information sought by "hostile" intelligence gatherers. Data loss prevention (DLP) refers to systems designed to lock down data within an organization.

With the increased use of telecommunications and networks, distributed databases, which allow many users and different sites access to data that may be stored in different physical locations, are gaining in popularity. To reduce telecommunications costs, some organizations build replicated databases, which hold a duplicate set of frequently used data.

Multidimensional databases and online analytical processing (OLAP) programs are being used to store data and allow users to explore the data from a number of different perspectives.

An object-oriented database uses the same overall approach of object-oriented programming, first discussed in Chapter 4. With this approach, both the data and the processing instructions are stored in the database. An object-relational database management system (ORDBMS) provides a complete set of relational database capabilities, plus the ability for third parties to add new data types and operations to the database. These new data types can be audio, video, and graphical data that require new indexing, optimization, and retrieval features.

In addition to raw data, organizations are finding a need to store large amounts of visual and audio signals in an organized fashion. A number of special-purpose database systems are also being used.

CHAPTER 5: SELF-ASSESSMENT TEST

Data management and modelling are key aspects of organizing data and information.

1. What group of programs manipulates the database and provides an interface between the database, the user of the database, and other application programs?
   a. a GUI
   b. an operating system
   c. a DBMS
   d. a productivity software

2. A(n) _____ is a skilled and trained IS professional who directs all activities related to an organization's database.

3. A field is made up of multiple records. True or False?

4. What field or set of fields uniquely identifies a database record?
   a. an attribute
   b. a data item
   c. a key
   d. a primary key

5. The _____ approach provides a pool of related data shared by many information systems.

6. Many businesses store their database and related systems in climate-controlled facilities called _____.

7. What database model places data in two-dimensional tables?
   a. the relational model
   b. the network model
   c. the normalized model
   d. the hierarchical model

A well-designed and well-managed database is an extremely valuable tool in supporting decision making.

8. Which of the following involves combining two or more database tables?
   a. projecting
   b. joining
   c. selecting
   d. data cleanup

9. Because the DBMS is responsible for providing access to a database, one of the first steps in installing and using a database involves telling the DBMS the logical and physical structure of the data as well as what relationships exist among the data in the database. This description of an entire database is called a(n) _____.

10. The commands used to access and report information from the database are part of which of the following languages?
    a. data definition language
    b. data manipulation language
    c. data normalization language
    d. schema

11. Access is a popular DBMS for which of the following?
    a. personal computers
    b. graphics workstations
    c. mainframe computers
    d. supercomputers

12. A trend in database management, known as Database as a Service, places the responsibility of storing and managing a database on a service provider. True or False?

The number and types of database applications will continue to evolve and yield real business benefits.

13. A(n) _____ holds business information from many sources in the enterprise, covering all aspects of the company's processes, products, and customers.

14. What information-analysis tool involves the automated discovery of patterns and relationships in a data warehouse?

    a. a data mart

    b. data mining

    c. predictive analysis

    d. business intelligence

15. _____ allows users to predict the future based on database information from the past and present.

16. The process of gathering information in a timely manner and in a usable form so that it positively affects business strategy, tactics, and operations is called _____.

CHAPTER 5: SELF-ASSESSMENT TEST ANSWERS

(1) c (2) database administrator (3) False (4) d (5) database (6) data centres (7) a (8) b (9) schema (10) b (11) a (12) True (13) data warehouse (14) b (15) Predictive analysis (16) business intelligence

REVIEW QUESTIONS

1. What is an attribute? How is it related to an entity?
2. Define the term "database." How is it different from a database management system?
3. What is the hierarchy of data in a database?
4. What is a relation, and what is its importance to relational databases?
5. What is the purpose of a primary key? How is it useful in controlling data redundancy?
6. What is the purpose of data cleanup?
7. What are the advantages of the database approach over the traditional approach to database management?
8. What is data modelling? What is its purpose? Briefly describe three commonly used data models.
9. What is a data centre, and why are they becoming increasingly important?
10. What is a database schema, and what is its purpose?
11. How can a data dictionary be useful to database administrators and DBMS software engineers?
12. Identify important characteristics in selecting a database management system.
13. What is the difference between a data definition language (DDL) and a data manipulation language (DML)?
14. What is the difference between projecting and joining?
15. What is a distributed database system?
16. What is a data warehouse, and how is it different from a traditional database used to support OLTP?
17. What is meant by the "front end" and the "back end" of a DBMS?
18. What is the relationship between the Internet and databases?
19. What is data mining? What is OLAP? How are they different?
20. What is an ORDBMS? What kind of data can it handle?
21. What is business intelligence? How is it used?
22. What is predictive analysis, and how does it assist businesses in gaining competitive advantage?
23. In what circumstances might a database administrator consider using an object-oriented database?

DISCUSSION QUESTIONS

1. You have been selected to represent the student body on a project to develop a new student database for your school. What is the first step in developing the database? What actions might you take to fulfill this responsibility to ensure that the project meets the needs of students and is successful?
2. Your company wants to increase revenues from its existing customers. How can data mining be used to accomplish this objective?
3. You are going to design a database for your school's outdoors club to track its activities. Identify the database characteristics most important to you in choosing a DBMS. Which of the database management systems described in this chapter would you choose? Why? Is it important for you to know what sort of computer the database will run on? Why or why not?
4. Make a list of the databases in which data about you exists. How is the data in each database captured? Who updates each database and how often? Is it possible for you to request a printout of the contents of your data record from each database? What data privacy concerns do you have?

5. If you were the database administrator for the iTunes store, how might you use predictive analysis to determine which artists and movies will sell most next year?

6. You are the vice president of information technology for a large, multinational consumer packaged goods company (such as Procter & Gamble or Unilever). You must make a presentation to persuade the board of directors to invest $5 million to establish a competitive-intelligence organization—including people, data-gathering services, and software tools. What key points do you need to make in favour of this investment? What arguments can you anticipate that the board might make?

7. Identity theft, where people steal personal information, continues to be a problem for consumers and businesses. Assume that you are the database administrator for a corporation with a large database that is accessible from the Web. What steps would you implement to prevent people from stealing personal information from the corporate database?

8. What roles do databases play in your most favourite online activities and websites?

PROBLEM-SOLVING EXERCISES

1. Develop a simple data model for the music you have on your digital music player or in your CD collection, where each row is a song. For each row, what attributes should you capture? What will be the primary key for the records in your database? Describe how you might use the database to expand your music exposure and enjoyment.

2. A video movie rental store is using a relational database to store information on movie rentals to answer customer questions. Each entry in the database contains the following items: Movie Number (the primary key), Movie Title, Year Made, Movie Type, Rating, Number of Copies on Hand, and Quantity Owned. Movie Types are comedy, family, drama, horror, science fiction, and western. Movie ratings are G (General), PG (Parental Guidance), 14A, 18A, and R (Restricted). Use a single-user database management system to build a data-entry screen to enter this data. Build a small database with at least 10 entries.

3. To improve service to their customers, the salespeople at the video rental store have proposed a list of changes being considered for the database in the previous exercise.

From this list, choose two database modifications and modify the data-entry screen to capture and store this new information.
Proposed changes:
a. To help store clerks locate the newest releases, add the date that the movie was first available.
b. Add the director's name.
c. Add the names of three primary actors in the movie.
d. Add a rating of one, two, three, or four stars.
e. Add the number of Academy Award nominations.

4. Your school maintains information about students in several interconnected database files. The student_contact file contains student contact information. The student_grades file contains student grade records, and the student_financial file contains financial records, including tuition and student loans. Draw a diagram of the fields these three files might contain, identify which field is a primary key in each file, and show which fields serve to relate one file to another. Use Figure 5.6 as a guide.

TEAM ACTIVITIES

1. In a group of three or four classmates, communicate with the person at your school who supervises information systems. Find out how many databases are used by your school and for what purpose. Also find out what policies and procedures are in place to protect the data stored from identity thieves and other threats.

2. As a team of three or four classmates, interview business managers from three different businesses that use databases. What data entities and data attributes are contained in each database? What database company did each company select to provide their database, and why? How do they access the database to perform analysis? Have they received training in any query or reporting tools? What do they like about their databases, and what could be improved? Do any of them use data-mining or OLAP techniques? Weighing the information obtained, select one of these databases as being most strategic for the firm and briefly present your selection and the rationale for the selection to the class.

3. Imagine that you and your classmates are a research team developing an improved process for evaluating loan applicants for automobile purchases. The goal of the research

is to predict which applicants will become delinquent or forfeit their loan. Those who score well on the application will be accepted, and those who score exceptionally well will be considered for lower-rate loans. Prepare a brief report for your instructor addressing these questions:

a. What data do you need for each loan applicant?

b. What data might you need that is not typically requested on a loan application form?

c. Where might you get this data?

d. Take a first cut at designing a database for this application. Using the material in this chapter on designing a database, draw the logical structure of the relational tables for this proposed database. In your design, include the data attributes you believe are necessary for this database, and show the primary keys in your tables. Keep the size of the fields and tables as small as possible to minimize required disk drive storage space. Fill in the database tables with the sample data for demonstration purposes (10 records). After your design is complete, implement it using a relational DBMS.

WEB EXERCISES

1. Use a Web search engine to find information on specific products for one of the following topics: business intelligence, object-oriented databases, or Database as a Service. Write a brief report describing what you found, including a description of the database products and the companies that developed them.

2. More information is being produced than can currently be stored in data centres, and yet, existing data centres are consuming huge amounts of energy, putting a strain on the environment and on budgets. Go online to research "Green Data Centre" to learn what can be done to store more data using fewer resources. Students with the most creative and useful suggestions may be awarded extra credit.

CAREER EXERCISES

1. What type of data is stored by businesses in a professional field that interests you? How many databases might be used to store that data? How would the data be organized within each database? How can techniques like data loss prevention (DLP) be used to protect critical databases?

2. How could you use business intelligence (BI) to do a better job at work? Give some specific examples of how BI can give you a competitive advantage.

CASE STUDIES

Case One

Richard Ivey School of Business
The University of Western Ontario

Ivey

Ivey
Publishing

Canada Health Infoway[1]

Professor Derrick Neufeld wrote this case solely to provide material for class discussion. The author does not intend to illustrate either effective or ineffective handling of a managerial situation.

---

1 This case has been written on the basis of published sources only. Consequently, the interpretation and perspectives presented in this case are not necessarily those of the Canadian Health Infoway or any of its employees.

The author may have disguised certain names and other identifying information to protect confidentiality.

Richard Ivey School of Business Foundation prohibits any form of reproduction, storage, or transmission without its written permission. Reproduction of this material is not covered under authorization by any reproduction rights organization. To order copies or request permission to reproduce materials, contact Ivey Publishing, Richard Ivey School of Business Foundation, The University of Western Ontario, London, Ontario, Canada, N6A 3K7; phone (519) 661-3208; fax (519) 661-3882; e-mail cases@ivey.uwo.ca.

Copyright © 2010, Richard Ivey School of Business Foundation Version: 2011-01-04

Emergency 9-1-1

Luc Boucher was unconscious when he was wheeled into the hospital emergency room. In order to assess, diagnose, and treat him properly, the doctors and nurses needed to know his health history, quickly. Boucher could not speak for himself, but his electronic health record (EHR), a secure, digital file containing his medical history, indicated that he was a Type 1 diabetic whose insulin dosage had recently been increased by his physician. Boucher's EHR also included up-to-date information from his dietician and endocrinologist. The emergency room staff used this vital data to craft a care plan for Boucher and avoided what could easily have become a life-threatening situation.

Canada's universal health-care system is made up of a great number of providers (e.g., physicians, surgeons, ophthalmologists, dentists, nurses, therapists, technicians), working at tens of thousands of facilities (e.g., hospitals, clinics, laboratories, ambulatory services) from coast to coast to coast. Providing Canadians with an integrated and high-quality health-care experience in this diverse, highly dispersed, professionally specialized context is extraordinarily challenging and costly. Annual health-care spending in Canada now exceeds $180 billion or more than $5,300 per person, on average.

Karen Madill, a former nurse, suffers from serious health problems herself. "My health is very, very complicated.... I developed lupus and then fibromyalgia, then osteoporosis and auto-immune hepatitis. I'm on about 30 different medications for various things. And now I've got asthma." Treating chronic health conditions like Madill's is very challenging for doctors and patients; prescription drugs are essential, but they can be lethal if drug interactions occur. Madill was happy to join a pilot project called EMRxtra that allowed pharmacists to directly access physicians' electronic medical records. According to Dr. David Crookston, a family physician who participated in the project, "Pharmacists tell us that, most of the time, access to the medical chart clears up any misunderstanding or questions they might have about why a doctor is sending them a particular prescription." Systems like EMRxtra allow physicians and pharmacists to easily collaborate and provide the best advice and care for the patient.

Canada Health Infoway is a national, nonprofit organization whose purpose is to deeply integrate health-care services through the use of information technology. Broadly speaking, integration means combining parts in such a way as to form a unified whole. Technically speaking, integrating an information system leads to improved information quality (e.g., accuracy, timeliness, relevancy, and accessibility). Practically speaking, deeply integrating the health-care system equates to things like increased patient participation in health care, decreased wait times, efficient chronic disease management, access to better care in remote communities, and reduced adverse drug interactions.

Daniel Girard, an avid outdoorsman from Northern Ontario, underwent a bone marrow transplant at Toronto's Princess Margaret Hospital (PMH). Because Girard's long-term medical follow-up required biweekly visits to a highly specialized medical team at PMH, he had to consider moving to Toronto. However, thanks to the University Health Network's (UHN) Telehealth videoconferencing system, Girard was able to return home and resume his active lifestyle, while receiving care from the PMH medical team remotely. Janice Wright, a registered nurse and nurse practitioner, explained, "The complexity after transplant is managing the patient's symptoms. Often that means one or two follow-up appointments a week. For Daniel, that is a 1,600-kilometre round trip. During the telemedicine appointment, I can use the digital

stethoscope to listen to his chest and the magnification camera to make an oral assessment. Furthermore, it has enabled us to bring our expertise to the local communities." According to Dr. Ed Brown, chief executive officer of the Ontario Telemedicine Network, "The next great step for us is to be right in the patient's home, and that's really where telemedicine is going." Says Girard: "Telemedicine has been a godsend to me."

The kind of deeply integrated health-care system that Luc Boucher, Karen Madill, and Daniel Girard experienced requires a well-planned, sophisticated information system. Such a large-scale, multi-stakeholder system is expensive, complicated, and imperfect—and yet it is essential to the health of Canadians, and perhaps to our national identity.

Discussion Questions

1. Consider the last time you used Canada's health-care system. Was the experience positive or negative? What role did information quality play?
2. What do you think of the purpose of Infoway? Do you believe that "deep integration" is required in the Canadian health-care system?
3. What kinds of challenges do you believe Canada Health Infoway will face in completing its vision? How long will it take to achieve complete integration?

SOURCES: Canada Health Infoway website, *www.infoway-inforoute.ca/lang-en*, accessed July 23, 2010. Dalton, S., and McGonigle, S., "Videoconferencing Technology Helps Patients Manage Follow-up Care," *Hospital News*, February 2009, *www.hospitalnews.com/modules/magazines/mag.asp?ID=3&IID=116&AID=1502*, accessed July 21, 2010. "Health-care Spending in Canada to Exceed $180 Billion This Year," Canadian Institute for Health Information, November 19, 2009, *www.cihi.ca/cihiweb/dispPage.jsp?cw_page=media_20091119_e*, accessed July 23, 2010. Wang, R., and Strong, D., "Beyond Accuracy: What Data Quality Means to Data Consumers," *Journal of Management Information Systems*, 1996, 12(4), pp. 5–34.

Case Two

Using Databases to Map Human Migration

National Geographic was established in 1888 to advance human understanding of the world's cultural, historical, and natural resources. National Geographic is a nonprofit organization that has contributed greatly to scientific research. One of the most recent examples of its contribution to science is the Genographic Project.

According to the National Geographic website, the Genographic Project is a "landmark study of the human journey." Scientists believe that we all descended from a common group of ancestors who lived in Africa some 60,000 years ago. Over the millennia, that group reproduced and migrated to populate the entire globe. The Genographic Project intends to map that migration to allow individuals to trace their ancestry back through time and location using advanced DNA research.

Dozens of researchers distributed around the world have been engaged in genetic research of indigenous cultures. DNA is being collected from select individuals and stored in a database where sequences can be automatically studied. Comparing commonalities between DNA strands allows researchers to draw conclusions about where an individual originated and where his or her ancestors may have migrated to and from.

Stage 2 of the study brings in the general public. Volunteers from around the world can sign up online to become part of the study and trace their own heritages and family migrations. For $99, anyone can purchase a Genographic Project kit, which includes abundant information and a swab for gathering DNA from the inside of the mouth. The DNA sample is sent to the Genographic Project by mail. Participants can trace the progress of the research on their DNA online. Once analyzed, the participant is provided with historical information about their ancestors and migration paths dating back to that African community 60,000 years ago.

The same data-mining and business intelligence tools used by businesses to find correlations between business data is applied to the DNA information stored by the Genographic Project. Advanced trend mapping and analysis tools provide a deeper understanding of mutation rates and DNA-merging behaviour. The participation of over 300,000 volunteers has created one of the world's largest repositories of genetic information, providing new insight into our migratory history and fuelling collaboration on new projects.

Without the automation provided by database tools, this research would not be possible. Dr. Spencer Wells, National Geographic Explorer-in-Residence and scientific director of the project, stated that "with hundreds of thousands of samples, researchers could easily become lost in our collected data. But, by working with IBM, we can distil this information into something useful—research breakthroughs and new findings."

Discussion Questions

1. What role do database and DBMS play in assisting with the Genographic Project?
2. What type of data is stored in the genographic database, and how might it be organized into the data hierarchy discussed in this chapter?

Critical Thinking Questions

1. How is the manipulation of genographic data similar to the manipulation of business data? What DBMS tools and techniques are shared by both?

2. How does National Geographic's investment in this DBMS assist other researchers? How might this data be shared using the database concepts taught in this chapter?

SOURCES: "National Geographic, as Part of Its Genographic Project, Tracks Human Migration Across the Millennia via DNA Analysis," IBM Case Studies, July 28, 2009, *www-01.ibm.com/software/success/cssdb.nsf/CS/LMCM-7U7U29?OpenDocument&Site =wssoftware&cty=en_us*; Genographic Project website, *https://genographic. nationalgeographic.com*, accessed May 15, 2010.

Questions for Web Case

See the website for this book to read about the Altitude Online case for this chapter. Following are questions concerning this Web case.

Altitude Online: Using Databases and Business Intelligence

Discussion Questions

1. What work is involved in merging several databases into one central database, as Altitude Online is doing?
2. Why do you think Altitude Online found it necessary to hire a database administrator? How will the ERP affect the responsibilities of IS personnel across the organization?

Critical Thinking Questions

1. In a major move such as this, what opportunities can Altitude Online take advantage of as it totally revamps its database system that it perhaps wouldn't consider before?
2. Why do you think Altitude Online is beginning work on its database prior to selecting an ERP vendor?

NOTES

Sources for the opening vignette: "Aquent: Staffing Firm Uses SAP BusinessObjects Software Tools to Deliver Talent," SAP Customer References, 2009, *www.sap.com/usa/solutions/sapbusinessobjects/customers*; "Aquent Enterprise Resource Technology Group," *www.ertgroup.com/index.php/aquent*, accessed May 15, 2010; "Aquent—About Us," *http://aquent.us/learn_more/ about_us*, accessed May 15, 2010.

1   "Just-in-Time Intelligence Helps Comic Relief Boost Donations 25% While Reducing Failure Risk," Oracle Customer Snapshot, August 2009, *www.oracle.com/customers/snapshots/comic-relief-obiee-snapshot.pdf*.
2   Wheaton, Sarah, "New Technology Generates Database on Spill Damage," *New York Times*, May 4, 2010, *www.nytimes.com/2010/05/05/ us/05brigade.html*.
3   Kirk, Jeremy, "Latvian Police Decline to Hold Database Hacker," *Computerworld*, May 14, 2010, *www.computerworld.com/s/article/9176781/ Latvian_police_decline_to_hold_database_hacker?source=rss_news*.
4   Kirk, Jeremy, "Company Says 3.3M Student Loan Records Stolen," *Computerworld*, March 20, 2010, *www.computerworld.com/s/article/9174312/ Company_says_3.3M_student_loan_records_stolen?source=rss_news*.

5   "Pig Received Voter Registration Reminder," UPI, May 12, 2010, *www. upi.com*.
6   "The Digital Universe Decade—Are You Ready?," IDC, May 2010, *www. emc.com/collateral/demos/microsites/idc-digital-universe/iview.htm*.
7   "Beyond Fingerprints: The FBI's Next Generation Database," *Home Security Newswire*, January 27, 2009, *http://homelandsecuritynewswire.com/ beyond-fingerprints-fbis-next-generation-database*.
8   Bruce, Peter, "Technology Roadmap for the Government of Canada," ICA Presentation, October 2009, *www.ica-it.org*, accessed August 5, 2011.
9   Miller, Rich, "Microsoft Goes All-in on Container Data Centers," *Data Center Knowledge*, December 2, 2008, *www.datacenterknowledge.com/ archives/2008/12/02/microsoft-goes-all-in-on-container-data-centers*.
10   Miller, Rich, "Google Unveils Its Container Data Center," *Data Center Knowledge*, April 1, 2009, *www.datacenterknowledge.com/ archives/2009/04/01/google-unveils-its-container-data-center*.
11   Miller, Rich, "Microsoft to Open Two Massive Data Centers," *Data Center Knowledge*, June 29, 2009, *www.datacenterknowledge.com*.
12   Nystedt, Dan, "Project Aims to Halve Cost of a Data Center," *InfoWorld*, June 2, 2010, *www.infoworld.com*.

13   Thibodeau, Patrick, "HP Job Cuts Point to Shifting IT Skills," *Computerworld*, June 1, 2010, *www.computerworld.com*.

14   Oracle Database website, *www.oracle.com/us/products/database*, accessed May 14, 2010.

15   Siegler, M.G., "The Unified Database of Places Is Coming Soon. Or Maybe Never," *TechCrunch*, May 8, 2010, *http://techcrunch. com/2010/05/08/place-database/?utm_source=feedburner&utm_ medium=feed&utm_campaign=Feed:+Techcrunch+(TechCrunch)&utm_ content=Google+Reader*.

16   "University of Toronto, Microsoft OneNote 2003 Is Helping Today's Medical Students to Become Tomorrow's Doctors," Microsoft Case Studies, February 18, 2005., *www.microsoft.com/casestudies/Case_Study_Detail. aspx?casestudyid=4000006922*.

17   "Canadian National Railway Company: Enabling a Service-Led Railway with SAP ERP," SAP Case Study, 2006,*/www.sap.com/canada/solutions/ pdf/Canadian_National_Railway.pdf*.

18   Vijayan, Jaikumar, "U.S. Says SQL Injection Caused Major Breaches," *Computerworld News Digest*, August 27/24, 2009, p. 4.

19   Oracle Cloud Computing website, *www.oracle.com/us/technologies/cloud*, accessed May 11, 2010.

20   Williams, Alex, "Canada Yellow Pages Launches API: A Picture of a Modern Service," Readwriteweb.com, September 24, 2010, *www.read-writeweb.com/cloud/2010/09/canada-yellow-pages-launches-a.php*.

21   McCann, Liz, "Case Study: Online Database Applications at Proctor & Gamble," Intuit website, January 28, 2010, *http://quickbase.intuit.com/ blog/2010/01/28/case-study-online-database-applications-at-procter-gamble*.

22   Schonfeld, Erick, "Urbanspoon Wants to Challenge OpenTable with Its RezBook IPad App," *TechCrunch*, May 19, 2010, *www.techcrunch.com*.

23   Ackerman, Kate, "Personal Health Records May Not Be So Personal," *iHealthBeat*, May 14, 2010, *www.ihealthbeat.org/features/2010/personal-health-records-may-not-be-so-personal.aspx*.

24   "Drug Information Systems to Generate $436 Million in Benefits in 2010," *www.infoway-inforoute.ca/about-infoway/news/news-releases/ 640-drug-information-systems-to-generate-436-million-in-benefits-in-2010-*, accessed October 9, 2010.

25   Resource Description Framework (RDF) website, accessed May 11, 2010, *www.w3.org/RDF*.

26   "Honda Italia Industriale Teams with IBM to Jump-start a Significant Business Transformation Project by Adopting RFID Technology for Its Production Processes," IBM Case Study, April 26, 2010, *www-01.ibm. com/software/success/cssdb.nsf/cs/GMMY-84SLG2?OpenDocument&Site=gic ss67snsr&cty=en_us*.

27   "Direct Marketing at Reader's Digest," Data-Mining-software.com, accessed October 9, 2010, *www.data-mining-software.com/data_mining_ examples.htm#RD*.

28   "Facebook Loses Friends over Privacy Settings," *The Economic Times*, May 15, 2010, *http://economictimes.indiatimes.com/infotech/internet/ Facebook-loses-friends-over-privacy-settings/articleshow/5934675.cms*.

29   "CBA Intelligence Unit Wins IALEIA Award," Criminal Intelligence Service Canada, *www.cisc.gc.ca/annual_reports/annual_report_2009/ environmental_crime_2009_e.html*, accessed October 10, 2010.

30   "RBC Vaults Ahead with SAS® Business Intelligence," SAS, *www.sas.com/ success/RBC.html*, accessed October 9, 2010.

31   George, Randy, "An Ounce of Loss Prevention," *Information Week*, July 6, 2009, p. 39.

32   "Case Study: Blue Mountain," IBM Case Studies, May 10, 2010, *www-01. ibm.com/software/success/cssdb.nsf/CS/LWIS-7LPTPY?OpenDocument&Site =cognos&cty=en_us*.

33   "PostgreSQL at Skype," Skype Developer Zone website, *https://developer. skype.com/SkypeGarage/DbProjects/SkypePostgresqlWhitepaper*, accessed May 11, 2010.

34   "Mainframe Integration Works for Giants of the Insurance Industry," Attunity Customer Case Study, *www.attunity.com/Data/Uploads/Case%20 Studies/Lloyds%20CS.pdf*, accessed May 11, 2010.

35   "Case Study—Cumberland County," Pitney Bowes Case Studies, *www. pbinsight.com/resources/case-studies/details/cumberland-county*, accessed May 11, 2010.

CHAPTER
· 6 ·

Telecommunications and Networks

PRINCIPLES	LEARNING OBJECTIVES
■ **A telecommunications system consists of several fundamental components.**	■ Identify and describe the fundamental components of a telecommunications system.
	■ Discuss two broad categories of telecommunications media and their associated characteristics.
	■ Briefly describe several options for short-range, medium-range, and long-range communications.
■ **Networks are an essential component of an organization's information technology infrastructure.**	■ Identify the benefits of using a network.
	■ Describe three distributed processing alternatives and discuss their basic features.
	■ Identify several telecommunications hardware devices and discuss their functions.
■ **Network applications are essential to organizational success.**	■ List and describe several network applications that organizations benefit from today.

(Source: asharkyu/Shutterstock.com)

Information Systems in the Global Economy
Procter & Gamble

Telepresence: The Next Best Thing to Being There

Procter & Gamble (P&G) has invested heavily in a technology that allows its employees to attend a morning meeting in Kobe, Japan, have lunch with business partners in Barcelona, Spain, attend an afternoon round table discussion in Istanbul, Turkey, and get home in time to see their children's soccer game in Toronto. No, P&G didn't purchase a fleet of X-15s (the fastest aircraft in the world), nor did it invent teleportation. What P&G did was to install telepresence equipment in more than 75 of its global locations.

When it comes to global enterprises, few are bigger than P&G. P&G is an $80-billion company, with 135,000 employees spread across 80 countries, delivering well-known consumer brands such as Pampers, Puffs, Crest, Gillette, and two dozen others to more than 3 billion people in 180 countries.

P&G was founded on principles of collaboration. Its executives and managers are strong believers in the value of solutions developed through a collaborative effort. It's from these beliefs that its recent "Connect and Develop" strategy was born. Connect and Develop involves using new technologies to increase communication among all employees and especially those with expert knowledge.

It was in this spirit that P&G decided to invest in Cisco Telepresence technologies. Telepresence uses existing corporate high-speed networks to create video links between local or global endpoints. High-definition video cameras and microphones are installed in conference rooms to capture the participants sitting around a semicircular conference table. Large displays are mounted on a wall across from the people to display life-size images of remote participants. Stereo speakers match the participant's voice with the location of the participant's video image. This creates the illusion of several people seated around an oval table, when in reality, half of them are in some other location perhaps halfway around the world.

P&G calls its 75 telepresence conference rooms "Video Collaboration Studios." They range in capacity from a few people to dozens. While P&G won't divulge how much the total installation cost, a typical telepresence room can cost more than $250,000. P&G says that it is well worth the investment. It estimates that it saves $4 for every $1 invested due to savings in travel and productivity.

P&G employees use the Video Collaboration Studios as much as 80 percent of a 50-hour workweek. Participants can use Live Meeting software from Microsoft to enable any presenter to project his or her computer screen for others to see a spreadsheet, slide presentation, document, or photo. The system also makes it easier for P&G specialists and experts to share their knowledge with others across the company. P&G executives have even sealed partnership deals without needing to fly in their prospective partners.

The Cisco Telepresence system is easy to operate. Meetings are scheduled using calendaring software such as Microsoft Outlook. At the time of the meeting, video connections are established with a simple one-button click. P&G also arranged for Cisco to monitor its networks to make sure all runs smoothly. Cisco help is available via telepresence, also with a one-button click at any time.

Telepresence assists P&G in meeting its goals in becoming a green company. The reduction in travel helps reduce its carbon footprint, and sharing information electronically has reduced its need for paper. Telepresence has also assisted P&G in meeting its financial goals by increasing productivity, reducing the time employees spend in transit, and increasing communication and collaborative opportunities. Telepresence also helps P&G stay in close communication with its business partners and build new partnerships.

Like many companies, P&G leverages telecommunications technologies to stream-line the flow of information between its employees, which improves productivity and increases market share and profits. Besides telepresence, P&G also uses instant messaging, wikis, phone chat, and other online communications to maximize the flow of information across the enterprise. Whether it's virtual travel via telepresence or a short text message, an appropriate telecommunications infrastructure is one of the big keys to success.

As you read this chapter, consider the following:

- What services do new telecommunications and network technologies offer to assist individuals and organizations in being more effective?
- What role do telecommunications play in connecting organizations and growing the global economy?

Why Learn About Telecommunications and Networks?

Effective communication is essential to the success of every major human undertaking, whether it's building great cities, waging war, or running a modern organization. Today we use electronic messaging and networking to enable people everywhere to communicate and interact effectively without requiring face-to-face meetings. Regardless of your chosen major or career field, you will need the communications capabilities provided by telecommunications and networks, especially if your work involves the supply chain. Among all business functions, supply chain management probably uses telecommunications and networks the most because it requires cooperation and communications among workers in inbound logistics, warehouse and storage, production, finished product storage, outbound logistics, and most important, with customers, suppliers, and shippers. All members of the supply chain must work together effectively to increase the value perceived by the customer, so partners must communicate well. Other employees in human resources, finance, research and development, marketing, and sales positions must also use communications technology to communicate with people inside and outside the organization. To be a successful member of any organization, you must be able to take advantage of the capabilities that these technologies offer you. This chapter begins by discussing the importance of effective communications.

In today's high-speed global business world, organizations need always-on, always-connected computing for travelling employees and for network connections to their key business partners and customers. As we saw in the opening vignette, forward-thinking companies such as Procter & Gamble hope to increase revenue, reduce time to market, and enable collaboration with their suppliers, customers, and business partners by using telecommunications systems. Here are just a few additional examples of organizations using telecommunications and networks to move ahead.

- In the face of a slowdown in the economy, many organizations are substituting video teleconferencing meetings for business travel in order to cut costs. British Telecom estimates that it saved $330 million per year on avoided travel costs and time saved. Microsoft estimates that it saves $90 million per year. Procter & Gamble and Deloitte have installed dozens of videoconferencing systems around the world and are saving millions each month in reduced travel expenses.[1]
- eBay, Google, Microsoft, and Yahoo—all Web competitors—are promoting themselves by providing free Wi-Fi access to people at several airports, on various airlines, and at hotels. For example, people who connect to the Internet through a hot spot at an airport are shown a Web page that allows them to donate to a charity and have the donation matched by Google.[2]
- It is estimated that 54 percent of physicians own a smartphone and are increasingly using them as a valuable tool to provide patient services. Physicians can download applications to their phones that enable them to check drug references, perform common medical calculations, consult normal lab value charts, use decision support tools, and view electronic medical records.[3]

- Thousands of companies use Webcasts to inform and educate potential customers about their products and services.
- The UNAIDS organization is using telecommunications to provide millions of people living in developing countries with access to health-care information and services. Mobile phones are being used as low-cost tools for HIV data collection, epidemic tracking, and training of health workers.[4]

AN OVERVIEW OF TELECOMMUNICATIONS

"Telecommunications" refers to the electronic transmission of signals for communications, by means such as telephone, radio, and television. Telecommunications is creating profound changes in business because it lessens the barriers of time and distance. Advances in telecommunications technology allow us to communicate rapidly with business partners, clients, and co-workers almost anywhere in the world. Telecommunications also reduces the amount of time needed to transmit information that can drive and conclude business actions. Telecommunications is changing not only the way organizations operate, but the nature of commerce itself. As networks connect to one another and transmit information more freely, a competitive marketplace demands excellent quality and service from all organizations.

Figure 6.1 shows a general model of telecommunications. The model starts with a sending unit (1) such as a person, a computer system, a terminal, or another device that originates the message. The sending unit transmits a signal (2) to a telecommunications device (3). The telecommunications device—a hardware component that facilitates electronic communication—performs many tasks, which can include converting the signal into a different form or from one type to another. The telecommunications device then sends the signal through a medium (4). A **telecommunications medium** is any material substance that carries an electronic signal to support communications between a sending and receiving device. Another telecommunications device (5) connected to the receiving device (6) receives the signal. The process can be reversed, and the receiving unit (6) can send a message to the original sending unit (1). An important characteristic of telecommunications is the speed at which information is transmitted, which is measured in bits per second (bps). Common speeds are in the range of thousands of bits per second (Kbps) to millions of bits per second (Mbps) and even billions of bits per second (Gbps).

telecommunications medium
Any material substance that carries an electronic signal to support communications between a sending and receiving device.

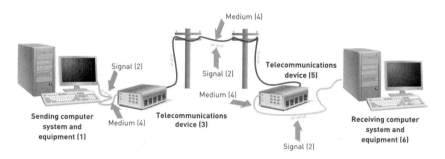

Figure 6.1

Elements of a Telecommunications System

Telecommunications devices relay signals between computer systems and transmission media.

A **networking protocol** is a set of rules, algorithms, messages, and other mechanisms that enable software and hardware in networked devices to communicate effectively. The goal is to ensure fast, efficient, error-free communications and to enable hardware, software, and equipment manufacturers and service providers to build products that interoperate effectively. The Institute of Electrical and Electronics Engineers (IEEE) is a leading standards-setting organization whose IEEE 802 network standards are the basis for many telecommunications devices and services. The International Telecommunication Union (ITU) is a specialized agency of the United Nations with headquarters in Geneva, Switzerland. The international standards produced by the ITU are known as Recommendations and carry a high degree of formal international recognition.

networking protocol
A set of rules, algorithms, messages, and other mechanisms that enable software and hardware in networked devices to communicate effectively.

Communications between two people can occur synchronously or asynchronously. With synchronous communications, the receiver gets the message as soon as it is sent. Voice and phone communications are examples of synchronous communications. With asynchronous communications, the receiver gets the message after some delay—a few seconds, to minutes or hours or even days after the message is sent. Sending a letter through the post office or e-mail over the Internet are examples of asynchronous communications. Both types of communications are important in business.

At Athabasca University in Alberta, all courses are offered via distance learning using telecommunications hardware and software that enables instructors to connect to students anywhere in Canada and around the world. Students can elect to attend a synchronous class where they and the instructor all attend the online course at the same time. Students can see and hear the instructor in real time and interact by asking questions. Other students can attend asynchronous classes, in which they participate at any time that is convenient to them. They see a video of the instructor, and if they have questions, they can correspond with the instructor via e-mail.

Telecommunications technology enables businesspeople to communicate with co-workers and clients from remote locations.

(Source: Betsie Van der Meer/Stone/ Getty Images.)

simplex channel
A communications channel that can transmit data in only one direction and is seldom used for business telecommunications.

half-duplex channel
A communications channel that can transmit data in either direction, but not simultaneously.

full-duplex channel
A communications channel that permits data transmission in both directions at the same time; a full-duplex channel is like two simplex channels.

channel bandwidth
The rate at which data is exchanged, usually measured in bits per second (bps).

broadband communications
A relative term but generally means a telecommunications system that can exchange data very quickly.

Basic Telecommunications Channel Characteristics

The transmission medium carries messages from the source of the message to its receivers. A transmission medium can be divided into one or more telecommunications channels, each capable of carrying a message. Telecommunications channels can be classified as simplex, half-duplex, or full-duplex.

A **simplex channel** can transmit data in only one direction and is seldom used for business telecommunications. Doorbells and the radio operate using a simplex channel. A **half-duplex channel** can transmit data in either direction, but not simultaneously. For example, A can begin transmitting to B over a half-duplex line, but B must wait until A is finished to transmit back to A. Personal computers are usually connected to a remote computer over a half-duplex channel. A **full-duplex channel** permits data transmission in both directions at the same time, so a full-duplex channel is like two simplex channels. Private leased lines or two standard phone lines are required for full-duplex transmission.

Channel Bandwidth

In addition to the direction of data flow supported by a telecommunications channel, you must consider the speed at which data can be transmitted. Telecommunications **channel bandwidth** refers to the rate at which data is exchanged, usually measured in bits per second (bps)—the broader the bandwidth, the more information can be exchanged at one time. **Broadband communications** is a relative term, but it generally means a telecommunications system that can transmit data very quickly. For example, for wireless networks, broadband lets you send and receive data at a rate greater than 1.5 Mbps.

Telecommunications professionals consider the capacity of the channel when they recommend transmission media for a business. In general, today's organizations need more bandwidth than they did even a few years ago for increased transmission speed to carry out their daily functions.

Circuit Switching and Packet Switching

Circuit switching and packet switching are two different means for routing data from the communications sender to the receiver.

In a **circuit switching network**, a dedicated circuit is first established to create a path that connects the communicating devices. This path is committed and then used for the duration of the communication. Because it is dedicated, the circuit cannot be used to support communications from other users or sending devices until the circuit is released and a new connection is set up. The traditional telephone network is a circuit switching network.

In a **packet switching network**, no fixed path is created between the communicating devices, and the data is broken into packets for sending over the network. Each packet is transmitted individually and is capable of taking various paths from sender to receiver. Because the communication paths are not dedicated, packets from many users and communicating devices can travel over the same communication path. Once all the packets forming a message arrive at the destination, they are compiled into the original message. The Internet is an example of a packet switching network that employs the packet switching protocol called TCP/IP.

The advantage of a circuit switching network is that it provides for the nonstop transfer of data without the overhead of assembling and disassembling data into packets and determining which routes packets should follow. Circuit switching networks are best when data must arrive in exactly the same order in which it is sent. This is the case with most real-time data such as live audio and video.

Packet switching networks are more efficient at using the channel bandwidth because packets from several conversations can share the same communications links. However, there can be delays in the delivery of messages due to network congestion and the loss of packets or the delivery of packets out of order. Thus packet switching networks are used to communicate data that can withstand some delays in transmission, such as e-mail messages and the sending of large data files. Another key consideration is the type of telecommunications media to use.

circuit switching network
A network that sets up a circuit between the sender and receiver before any communications can occur; this circuit is maintained for the duration of the communication and cannot be used to support any other communications until the circuit is released and a new connection is set up.

packet switching network
A network in which no fixed path is created between the communicating devices, and the data is broken into packets with each packet transmitted individually and is capable of taking various paths from sender to recipient.

Telecommunications Media

Each telecommunications media type can be evaluated according to characteristics such as cost, capacity, and speed. In designing a telecommunications system, the transmission media selected depends on the amount of information to be exchanged, the speed at which data must be exchanged, the level of concern for data privacy, whether the users are stationary or mobile, and many other business requirements. The transmission media are selected to support the communications goals of the organization systems at the lowest cost, but to still allow for possible modifications should business requirements change. Transmission media can be divided into two broad categories: *guided transmission media*, in which telecommunications signals are guided along a solid medium, and *wireless*, in which the telecommunications signal is broadcast over airwaves as a form of electromagnetic radiation.

Guided Transmission Media Types

Guided transmission media are available in many types. Table 6.1, on the next page, summarizes the guided media types by physical media type. These guided transmission media types are discussed in the sections following the table.

Table 6.1

Guided Transmission Media
Types

Media Type	Description	Advantages	Disadvantages
Twisted-pair wire	Twisted pairs of copper wire, shielded or unshielded	Used for telephone service; widely available	Transmission speed and distance limitations
Coaxial cable	Inner conductor wire surrounded by insulation	Cleaner and faster data transmission than twisted-pair wire	More expensive than twisted-pair wire
Fibre-optic cable	Many extremely thin strands of glass bound together in a sheathing; uses light beams to transmit signals	Diameter of cable is much smaller than coaxial; less distortion of signal; capable of high transmission rates	Expensive to purchase and install
Broadband over power lines	Data is transmitted over standard high-voltage power lines	Can provide Internet service to rural areas where cable and phone service may be nonexistent	Can be expensive and may interfere with ham radios and police and fire communications

Twisted-Pair Wire

Twisted-pair wire contains two or more twisted pairs of wire, usually copper, as shown in Figure 6.2. Proper twisting of the wire keeps the signal from "bleeding" into the next pair and creating electrical interference. Because the twisted-pair wires are insulated, they can be placed close together and packaged in one group. Hundreds of wire pairs can be grouped into one large wire cable.

Twisted-pair wires are classified by category (Category 2, 3, 5, 5E, and 6—there was no Category 1, and Category 4 is no longer used). The lower categories are used primarily in homes. Higher categories are used in networks and can carry data at higher speeds. For example, 10-Gigabit Ethernet is a standard for transmitting data in full-duplex mode at the speed of 10 billion bits per second for limited distances over Category 5 or 6 twisted-pair wire. The 10-Gigabit Ethernet cable can be used for the high-speed links that connect groups of computers or to move data stored in large databases on large computers to stand-alone storage devices.

Coaxial Cable

Figure 6.2 (middle) also shows a typical coaxial cable, similar to that used in cable television installations. When used for data transmission, coaxial cable falls in the middle of the guided transmission media in terms of cost and performance. The cable itself is more expensive than twisted-pair wire but less than fibre-optic cable (discussed next). However, the cost of installation and other necessary communications equipment makes it difficult to compare the total costs of each medium. Coaxial cable offers cleaner and crisper data transmission (less noise) than twisted-pair wire. It also offers a higher data transmission rate.

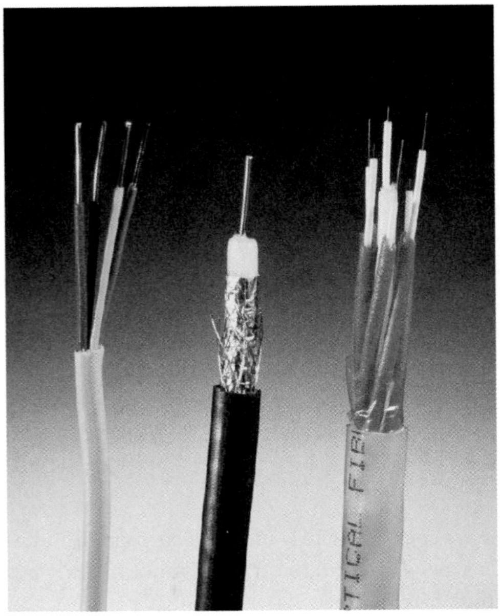

Figure 6.2

Types of Guided Transmission Media

Twisted-pair wire (left), coaxial cable (middle), fibre-optic cable (right)

(Source: © Phil Degginger/Stone/ Getty Images.)

Many cable companies, such as Rogers and Shaw, aggressively court customers for telephone service, enticing them away from phone companies by offering highly discounted rates for bundled high-speed Internet and phone services along with TV and making new movies available on demand the same day as the DVD is released.

Fibre-Optic Cable

Fibre-optic cable, consisting of many extremely thin strands of glass or plastic bound together in a sheathing (also known as a jacket), transmits signals with light beams. See Figure 6.2. These high-intensity light beams are generated by lasers and are conducted along the transparent fibres. These fibres have a thin coating, called *cladding*, which works like a mirror, preventing the light from leaking out of the fibre. The much smaller diameter of fibre-optic cable makes it ideal when there is no room for bulky copper wires—for example, in crowded conduits, which can be pipes or spaces carrying both electrical and communications wires. Fibre-optic cable and associated telecommunications devices are more expensive to purchase and install than their twisted-pair wire counterparts, although the cost is decreasing.

Ryerson University's Rogers Communications Centre building in Ontario was the first media building in Canada to be wired to handle 10-Gigabit Ethernet desktop applications. The building also acts as a fibre-optic hub with 144 fibre-optic cables to connect buildings across the campus. These networks link the Rogers Communications Centre both locally at unparalleled network speed and globally through the Internet.[5]

FiOS is a bundled set of communications services, including Internet, telephone, and TV, that operates over a total fibre-optic communications network. With this service, fibre-optic cable is run from the carrier's local exchange all the way to the customer's premises. (Cable networks often use fibre optic in their network backbone that connects their local exchanges, but do not run fibre optic to the customer's premises.) FiOS is offered in select areas from Telus in Canada and Verizon in the United States. At the top speed for FiOS of 50 Mbps, it would take just 16 minutes to download a 2-hour movie (500 MB). This same task would take 53 minutes over a 15-Mbps cable network.[6] A shortcoming of this service is that if there is a power outage at the premises, there is no FiOS service. A battery backup unit is advisable to avoid this potential problem.

Broadband over Power Lines

Many utilities, cities, and organizations are experimenting with *broadband over power lines* (*BPL*) to provide Internet access to homes and businesses over standard high-voltage power lines. This form of BPL is called *access BPL*. A system called *in-premise BPL* can be used to create a local area network using the building's wiring. A potential problem with BPL is that transmitting data over unshielded power lines can interfere with both amateur (ham) radio broadcasts and police and fire radios. However, BPL can provide Internet service in rural areas where broadband access has lagged because electricity is more prevalent in homes than cable or even telephone lines.

Wireless Communications Options

Wireless communications coupled with the Internet is revolutionizing how and where we gather and share information, collaborate in teams, listen to music or watch videos, and stay in touch with our families, friends, and co-workers while on the road. With wireless capability, a coffee shop can become our living room and the bleachers at a ball park can become our office. The many advantages and freedom provided by wireless communications are causing many organizations to consider moving to an all-wireless environment.

Wireless transmission involves the broadcast of communications in one of three frequency ranges: radio, microwave, or infrared frequencies, as shown in Table 6.2 on the next page. In some cases, the use of wireless communications is regulated and the signal must be broadcast within a specific frequency range to avoid interference with other wireless transmissions. For example, radio and TV stations must gain approval to use a certain frequency to broadcast their signals. Where wireless communications are not regulated, there is a high potential for interference between signals.

With the spread of wireless network technology to support devices such as smartphones, mobile computers, and cell phones, the telecommunications industry needed new protocols to define how these hardware devices and their associated software would operate on the networks provided by telecommunications carriers. More than 70 active groups are setting standards at the regional, national, and global levels, resulting in a dizzying array of communications standards and options. Some of the more widely used wireless communications options are discussed next.

Table 6.2

Frequency Ranges Used for
Wireless Communications

Technology	Description	Advantages	Disadvantages
Radio frequency range	Operates in the 3KHz–300 MHz range	Supports mobile users; costs are dropping	Signal highly susceptible to interception
Microwave—terrestrial and satellite frequency range	High-frequency radio signal (300 MHz–300 GHz) sent through atmosphere and space (often involves communications satellites)	Avoids cost and effort to lay cable or wires; capable of high-speed transmission	Must have unobstructed line of sight between sender and receiver; signal highly susceptible to interception
Infrared frequency range	Signals in the 300 GHz–400 THz frequency range sent through air as light waves	Lets you move, remove, and install devices without expensive wiring	Must have unobstructed line of sight between sender and receiver; transmission effective only for short distances

Short-Range Wireless Options

Many wireless solutions provide communications over very short distances, including Near Field Communications, Bluetooth, ultra wideband, infrared transmission, and ZigBee.

Near Field Communication (NFC)

Near Field Communication (**NFC**) is a very short-range wireless connectivity technology designed for consumer electronics, cell phones, and credit cards. Once two NFC-enabled devices are in close proximity (touching or a few centimetres apart), they exchange the necessary communications parameters and passwords to enable Bluetooth, Wi-Fi, or other wireless communications between the devices. Because only two devices participate in the communications, NFC establishes a peer-to-peer network.

Photos stored on an NFC-enabled cell phone can be sent from the phone to an NFC-enabled big-screen TV simply by touching the "hot spot" of the TV with the digital camera. This causes a peer-to-peer network to be established and communications to flow. Speed-pass is a contactless payment system based on NFC that enables Esso customers to pay for purchases easily and safely by waving their keytag across an area of a gasoline pump, car wash kiosk, or convenience store terminal.[7] Visa is introducing a card payment system that uses a cell phone with an embedded NFC chip to communicate its credit card number to a payment terminal.[8]

Bluetooth

Bluetooth is a wireless communications specification that describes how cell phones, computers, printers, and other electronic devices can be interconnected over distances of 3 metres to 10 metres at a rate of about 2 Mbps. Bluetooth allows users of multifunctional devices to synchronize with information in a desktop computer, send or receive faxes, print, and, in general, coordinate all mobile and fixed computer devices. The Bluetooth technology is named after the 10th-century Danish King Harald Blatand, or Harold Bluetooth in English. He had been instrumental in uniting warring factions in parts of what is now Norway, Sweden, and Denmark—just as the technology named after him is designed to allow collaboration among differing devices such as computers, phones, and other electronic devices.

A communications application has been developed by researchers at the University of Glasgow to support "ad hoc networking." It enables up to eight mobile phone users to send direct mobile-to-mobile messages, not through their cell phone networks but via Bluetooth with an expanded distance capability of a few hundred yards. The application is of interest for fans in a sports stadium who want to quickly and easily exchange messages about the game. Normally in such an environment, it can be difficult to even find a mobile phone signal. Even if a signal is found, it can take a long time to set up the call and deliver a

Near Field Communication (NFC)
A very short-range wireless connectivity technology designed for cell phones and credit cards.

Bluetooth
A wireless communications specification that describes how cell phones, computers, faxes, personal digital assistants, printers, and other electronic devices can be interconnected over distances of 3 to 10 metres at a rate of about 2 Mbps.

message to another user. According to Dr. Matthew Chalmers, leader of the effort, "Chat and banter need to be immediate. If a disputed goal is scored or a yellow card awarded, you want to hear what others have to say about it straight away, from their vantage point in the stadium. Direct mobile-to-mobile communication can make this happen."[9]

Ultra Wideband

Ultra wideband (UWB) communications is fundamentally different from all other communication techniques because UWB signals are extremely short electromagnetic pulses lasting just 50 to 1,000 picoseconds. (One picosecond is one-trillionth or one-millionth of one-millionth of a second.) The pulses are transmitted across a broad range of radio frequencies of several gigahertz. UWB provides several advantages over other communications means such as high throughput rate, the ability to transmit virtually undetected and impervious to interception or jamming, and no interference with current communications services.

Potential UWB applications include wirelessly connecting printers and other devices to desktop computers or enabling completely wireless home multimedia networks. UWB products are considered too expensive at this time to have broad market appeal, but prices are coming down.[10]

ultra wideband (UWB)
A form of short-range communications that employs extremely short electromagnetic pulses lasting just 50 to 1,000 picoseconds that are transmitted across a broad range of radio frequencies of several gigahertz.

Infrared Transmission

Infrared transmission sends signals at a frequency of 300 GHz and above—higher than those of microwaves but lower than those of visible light. Infrared transmission is frequently used in wireless networks, intrusion detectors, home entertainment remote control, and fire sensors. Infrared transmission requires line-of-sight transmission and short distances—such as a few yards. Infrared transmission allows hand-held computers to transmit data and information to larger computers within the same room and to connect a display screen, printer, and mouse to a computer.

infrared transmission
A form of communications that sends signals at a frequency of 300 GHz and above—higher than those of microwaves but lower than those of visible light.

ZigBee

ZigBee is a form of wireless communications frequently used in security systems and heating and cooling control systems. ZigBee is a relatively low-cost technology and requires little power, which allows longer life with smaller batteries.

The Province of Ontario wants to be a leader in energy conservation. By the end of 2010, most homes and small businesses had Smart Meters that use ZigBee technology. The Smart Meters enable the electrical utilities to charge users higher rates during peak energy demand periods and lower rates during lower demand periods. With smart metering, users have better options for managing and reducing their energy costs.[11]

ZigBee
A form of wireless communications frequently used in security systems and heating and cooling control systems.

Medium-Range Wireless Options

Wi-Fi is a wireless telecommunications technology brand owned by the Wi-Fi Alliance, which consists of about 300 technology companies, including AT&T, Dell, Microsoft, Nokia, and Qualcomm. The alliance exists to improve the interoperability of wireless local area network products based on the IEEE 802.11 series of telecommunications standards.

With a Wi-Fi wireless network, the user's computer, smartphone, or cell phone has a wireless adapter that translates data into a radio signal and transmits it using an antenna. A wireless access point, which consists of a transmitter with an antenna, receives the signal and decodes it. The access point then sends the information to the Internet over a wired connection, as shown in Figure 6.3 on the next page. When receiving data, the wireless access point takes the information from the Internet, translates it into a radio signal, and sends it to the device's wireless adapter. These devices typically come with built-in wireless transmitters and software to enable them to alert the user to the existence of a Wi-Fi network. The area covered by one or more interconnected wireless access points is called a "hot spot." Current Wi-Fi access points have a maximum range of about 100 metres outdoors and 30 metres within a dry-walled building. Wi-Fi has proven so popular that hot spots are established in places such as airports, coffee shops, college campuses, libraries, and restaurants.

Wi-Fi
A medium-range wireless telecommunications technology brand owned by the Wi-Fi Alliance.

Figure 6.3

Wi-Fi Network

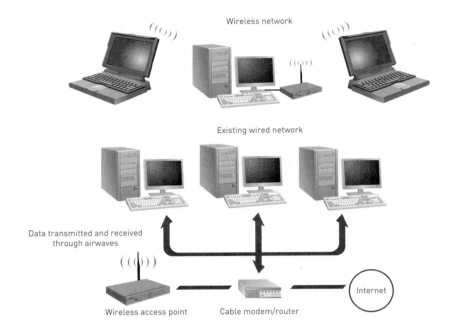

More than 100 city governments in the United States have implemented municipal Wi-Fi networks for use by meter readers and other municipal workers and to partially subsidize Internet access to their citizens and visitors. Supporters of the networks believe that the presence of such networks stimulates economic development by attracting new businesses. Critics doubt the long-term viability of municipal Wi-Fi networks because the technology cannot easily handle rapidly increasing numbers of users. Also, because municipal Wi-Fi networks use an unlicensed bandwidth available to any user and they operate at up to 30 times the power of existing home and business Wi-Fi networks, critics claim interference is inevitable with these networks. Competing Internet service providers (cable, telephone, and satellite, for example) complain that municipal Wi-Fi networks are subsidized to such an extent that they have an unfair competitive cost advantage. There has been limited development of municipal Wi-Fi networks in Canada due to our geography and more interest in Internet and mobile access.[12]

The availability of free Wi-Fi within a hotel's premises has become very popular with the business traveller. The Aloft and Element hotels, part of the Starwood chain, cater to the extended-stay traveller. Both hotels have recently added free Wi-Fi service in their rooms and lobbies. At the other end of the accommodations spectrum, The Four Seasons Hotels and Resorts also offer free Wi-Fi. Many other hotels offer or are considering adding free Wi-Fi.[13]

Wide Area Wireless Network Types

Many solutions provide wide area network options, including satellite and terrestrial microwave transmission, wireless mesh, 3G, 4G, and WiMAX.

Microwave Transmission

Microwave is a high-frequency (300 MHz–300 GHz) signal sent through the air, as shown in Figure 6.4. Terrestrial (Earth-bound) microwaves are transmitted by line-of-sight devices, so that the line of sight between the transmitter and receiver must be unobstructed. Typically, microwave stations are placed in a series—one station receives a signal, amplifies it, and retransmits it to the next microwave transmission tower. Such stations can be located roughly 50 kilometres apart before the curvature of the Earth makes it impossible for the towers to "see" one another. Microwave signals can carry thousands of channels at the same time.

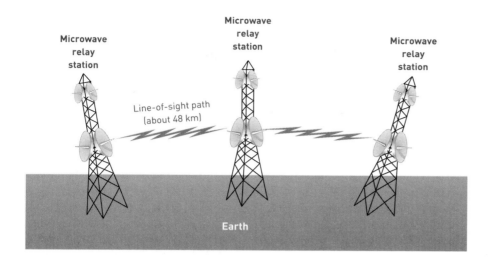

Figure 6.4

Microwave Communications

Because they are line-of-sight transmission devices, microwave dishes are frequently placed in relatively high locations, such as mountains, towers, or tall buildings.

A communications satellite also operates in the microwave frequency range. See Figure 6.5. The satellite receives the signal from the Earth station, amplifies the relatively weak signal, and then rebroadcasts it at a different frequency. The advantage of satellite communications is that satellites can receive and broadcast over large geographic regions. Such problems as the curvature of the Earth, mountains, and other structures that block the line-of-sight microwave transmission make satellites an attractive alternative. Geostationary, low-Earth orbit, and small mobile satellite stations are the most common forms of satellite communications.

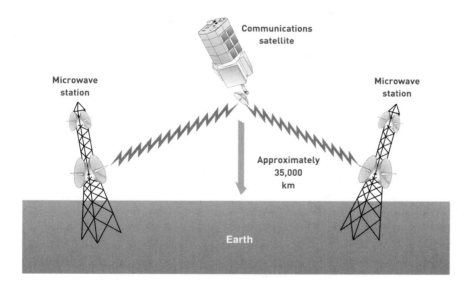

Figure 6.5

Satellite Transmission

Communications satellites are relay stations that receive signals from one Earth station and rebroadcast them to another.

A *geostationary satellite* orbits the Earth directly over the equator, approximately 35,800 kilometres above the Earth, so that it appears stationary. Environment Canada relies on the Geostationary Operational Environmental Satellite program for weather imagery and quantitative data to support weather forecasting, severe storm tracking, and meteorological research.

A *low-Earth orbit (LEO) satellite* system employs many satellites, each in an orbit at an altitude of less than 1,600 kilometres. The satellites are spaced so that, from any point on the Earth at any time, at least one satellite is on a line of sight. Iridium Communications Inc. provides a global communications network that spans the entire Earth using 66 satellites in a near polar orbit at an altitude of 780 kilometres. Calls are routed among the satellites to create a reliable connection between call participants that cannot be disrupted by natural disasters such as earthquakes, tsunamis, or hurricanes that knock out ground-based wireless towers and wire or cable-based networks.[14] Iridium phones were the primary source of communication in New Orleans after Hurricane Katrina in 2005 and after the major earthquake in China in 2008.[15]

A *very small aperture terminal* (*VSAT*) is a satellite ground station with a dish antenna smaller than three metres in diameter. The U.S. Army is buying thousands of VSATs under a five-year $5-billion contract. Paul Brown, technical adviser for the Defence Communications and Army Transmission Systems, explains, "In a war zone, a soldier who needs to order parts would typically have to get into his vehicle and drive from one outlying camp to another. Providing them with a VSAT solution allows them to stay within the wire of their base and communicate directly to order those parts. VSATs save lives; that's a critical piece."[16]

Wireless Mesh

wireless mesh
A form of communication that uses many Wi-Fi access points to link a series of interconnected local area networks to form a wide area network capable of serving a large campus or entire city.

Wireless mesh uses many Wi-Fi access points to link a series of interconnected local area networks to form a wide area network capable of serving a large campus or entire city. Communications are routed among network nodes by allowing for continuous connections and reconfiguration around blocked paths by "hopping" from node to node until a connection can be established. Mesh networks are very robust: if one node fails, all the other nodes can still communicate with each other, directly or through one or more intermediate nodes.

Asia Pacific Breweries Singapore implemented a mesh control network to provide a higher level of automation and control to its production and quality processes. As a result, the brewer improved its speed to market for new beers while still preserving its high quality and consistent taste standards.[17]

3G Wireless Communications

3G wireless communications supports wireless voice and broadband speed data communications in a mobile environment. It is called 3G for "third generation" of solutions for wireless voice and data communications. Additional capabilities include mobile video, mobile e-commerce, location-based services, mobile gaming, and the downloading and playing of songs.

The ITU established a single standard for cellular networks in 1999. The goal was to standardize future digital wireless communications and allow global roaming with a single handset. Called IMT-2000, now referred to as 3G, this standard provides for faster transmission speeds in the range of 2 to 4 Mbps. Originally, 3G was supposed to be a single, unified, worldwide standard, but the 3G standards effort split into several different standards.

Global System for Mobile Communications (GSM)
A globally accepted standard for digital cellular communications.

One standard is the Universal Mobile Telephone System (UMTS), which is the preferred choice of European countries that use **Global System for Mobile** (**GSM**) communications, a digital cellular communications standard used by over 3 billion people in more than 200 countries.[18]

Another 3G-based standard is Code-Division Multiple Access (CDMA), which is used in Australia, Canada, China, India, Israel, Mexico, South Korea, the United States, and Venezuela.

The wide variety of 3G cellular communications protocols can support many business applications. The challenge is to enable these protocols to intercommunicate and support fast, reliable, global wireless communications. Existence of these standards enables network operators to select from a large number of competitive hardware suppliers.

The four primary 3G communications carriers in Canada are Rogers, Telus, Sasktel, and Bell Canada. These carriers compete vigorously for new customers and market share. However, the 3G networks of these carriers do not always live up to their marketing hype, which typically boasts the best coverage and broadband transmission speeds (defined by industry analysts as 1.5 Mbps for downloads and 250 Kbps for uploads). Coverage can be disappointing, with users in many locations unable to link to their carrier's 3G network. In addition, the transmission speed may be less than advertised due to the number of users on a cell tower at a given time, the device used, the local geography, whether the user is stationary

Building Out the Broadband Infrastructure in Canada

In 2010, the government of Canada announced it was providing $225 million over three years for the development and implementation of a strategy to extend broadband coverage to nearly 250,000 households in underserviced rural areas in Canada.

Areas of the country that do not have broadband access are generally rural areas with low population densities or areas of poverty where people can't afford to pay for high-speed Internet service. Telecommunications companies do not have the incentive to invest in providing high-speed Internet to these areas because the money to be made is significantly less than the investment required to build the infrastructure. Historically in such cases, the government has intervened to make sure that all of its citizens are served. The government has subsidized many such efforts, such as building railroad lines and highway systems. Access to high-speed Internet is considered as valuable as these other national infrastructures in providing citizens with the ability to participate in society.

The federal government has determined which households do not currently have access to high-speed Internet and is in the process of determining which proposals are best for these unserved areas. Naturally, the telecom companies are concerned that the government may intrude on business opportunities. So each proposal is checked against telecom records to confirm that the area is not already served by an existing telecommunications company. Many telecom companies have not applied for stimulus funding because the financial aid comes with a requirement that the network is open to everyone and cannot favour some services over others. These stipulations are referred to as *network neutrality*, and when it comes to network services, commercial telecom companies are rarely neutral—their interests lie with their investors.

Besides fibre-optic solutions, wide area wireless technologies are also being explored to bring high-speed Internet to rural areas. Emerging 4G wireless technologies such as WiMAX and Long Term Evolution (LTE) hold much promise as ideal solutions for low-population areas because one tower can provide high-speed Internet to hundreds of homes over a range of kilometres, sparing the expense of running expensive fibre.

By building out the national broadband infrastructure using the latest telecommunications technologies, the Canadian government intends to provide all Canadians with equal access to the benefits of digital information and communication. It is also hoped that improving communication networks across the country will encourage economic development, spur innovation, and improve the quality of life across the country.

Discussion Questions

1. Why has the Canadian government made broadband Internet a national priority?
2. What challenges will the Canadian government face in implementing a national broadband infrastructure?

Critical Thinking Questions

1. Do you think that it is necessary for the government to intervene in providing broadband Internet to Canadians? Why or why not?
2. Do you think that improved national broadband access will encourage economic development and improve the quality of life across Canada?

or mobile, and the amount of interference from nearby buildings or mountains.[19] China Mobil operates the world's largest 3G network, which covered some 70 percent of China's cities at the end of 2009. Its 3G network is based on a unique Time-Division Synchronous Code Division Multiple Access (TD-SCDMA) technology. A rapid growth was expected in the number of users of the 3G network—from 3 million by the end of 2009 to at least 50 million by the end of 2010.[20]

4G Wireless Communications

Fourth-generation broadband mobile wireless is expected to deliver more advanced versions of enhanced multimedia, smooth streaming video, universal access, portability across all types of devices, and eventually, worldwide roaming capability. 4G will also provide increased data transmission rates in the 20 to 40 Mbps range.

AT&T announced that it would have a fully ready 4G cellular network based on Long Term Evolution (LTE) in 2011. This put AT&T about one year behind Verizon, which planned to start its own 4G LTE network in 2010. LTE has the potential to download data at up to 100 Mbps.[21] T-Mobile is also planning a 4G network based on LTE. Table 6.3 shows the evolution of 3G and 4G networks.

Meanwhile, telecommunications operator Teliasonera implemented a 4G network in Norway in 2009. In a public demonstration, the network downloaded a 7 megabyte MP3 file in just one second.[22] Canada will not have full 4G cellular networks until at least 2012.

Table 6.3

Evolution of 3G and 4G Networks

Communication Transport Technology	Transmission Speed
3G Networks That Descended from GSM	
GPRS (General Packet Radio Service)	114 Kbps
EDGE (Enhanced Data GSM Environment	384 Kbps
W-CDMA (Wideband CDMA also known as Universal Mobil Telecommunications or UMTS)	1.92 Mbps
HSDPA (High-Speed Downlink Packet Access)	14 Mbps
LTE (Evolved UMTS Terrestrial Radio Access)	100 Mbps
3G Networks That Descended from IMT-2000	
CDMA2000 1xRTT (One-time radio transmission technology)	144 Kbps
CDMA 1xEV-DO (Evolution-Data Optimized)	2.4 Mbps
CDMA2000 1xEV-DO (Evolution-Data and Voice Optimized)	3.1 Mbps
W-CDMA (Wideband CDMA, also known as Universal Mobil Telecommunications or UMTS)	288 Mbps
4G Networks	
LTE (Evolved UMTS Terrestrial Radio Access)	100 Mbps
W-CDMA (Wideband CDMA, also known as Universal Mobil Telecommunications or UMTS)	288 Mbps

Worldwide Interoperability for Microwave Access (WiMAX)

Worldwide Interoperability for Microwave Access (WiMAX)
The common name for a set of IEEE 802.16 wireless metropolitan area network standards that support various types of communications access.

Worldwide Interoperability for Microwave Access (WiMAX) is the common name for a set of IEEE 802.16 wireless metropolitan area network standards that support various types of communications access. In many respects, WiMAX operates like Wi-Fi, only over greater distances and at faster transmission speeds. A WiMAX tower connects directly to the Internet via a high-bandwidth, wired connection. A WiMAX tower can also communicate with another WiMAX tower using a line-of-sight, microwave link. The distance between the WiMAX tower and an antenna can be as great as 50 kilometres. WiMAX can support data communications at a rate of 70 Mbps. Fewer WiMAX base stations are required to cover the same geographical area than when Wi-Fi technology is used. Mobile WiMAX refers to systems built based on the 802.16e standard and provides both fixed and mobile access over the same network infrastructure. Fixed WiMAX is based on the 802.16-2004 standard designed to deliver communications to homes and offices, but it cannot support mobile users. WiMAX is considered a 4G service.

Rogers Communications and Bell Canada established a joint venture, Inukshuk, to construct a Canada-wide broadband network based on the WiMAX standard. The network is expected to cover around 45 cities and 100 rural areas and remote communities across Canada.[23] Both Rogers and Bell are currently marketing their services as a portable way to access the Internet for rural and urban customers. Consumer adoption of the Inukshuk network services has been slow due to the slower speeds and high monthly costs compared to wireless and wired Internet access.

Clearwire Corporation is a wireless Internet service provider founded by cellular phone pioneer Craig McCaw. In 2008, Sprint and Clearwire in the United States pooled their WiMAX assets and obtained over $3.2 billion in capital from Intel, Comcast, and Google to create a new, independent company (Clearwire Communications) whose goal is to build a national mobile broadband network across the United States. Clearwire operates the 4G mobile WiMAX network, and Sprint and Comcast sell airtime on the network. This enables the companies to compete with the wireless data offerings of AT&T and Verizon.[24]

To date, Clearwire has launched its 4G WiMAX network (Clear) in about two dozen markets. Clear residential modems provide up to 6 Mbps download speeds, while mobile Internet customers can expect to receive up to 4 Mbps download speeds. In late 2009, Sprint, Comcast, Time Warner Cable, Intel, and other investors anted up another $1.5 billion to finance further expansion of the 4G service.[25]

To supply the necessary phones, computer chips, and other equipment, Sprint is working with Intel, Motorola, Nokia, and Samsung to provide WiMAX-capable PC cards, gaming devices, laptops, cameras, and even phones. Sprint also plans to implement a business model much different from the typical cellular model. Sprint's strategy is to allow any WiMAX-compliant device to run on its network. Users will be able to buy such devices at a variety of retail stores and will not be required to sign a contract with Sprint to use the network.

WiMAX is a key component of Intel's broadband wireless strategy to deliver innovative mobile platforms for "anytime, anywhere." Centrino is a marketing initiative from Intel. Intel touts that its Centrino laptops deliver improved performance, have a longer battery life, and can access a variety of wireless networks, including WiMAX. To qualify for the Centrino label, a laptop computer provider must use a combined chip set, mobile CPU, and wireless interface from Intel. So although Apple uses Intel laptop components in its MacBooks, it cannot advertise them as Centrinos because they do not use the Intel wireless chipset. Dell, Fujitsu, Lenovo, Panasonic, Samsung, and Toshiba are among the manufacturers that produce laptop computers with the Centrino label.[26]

Intel is also producing a computer chipset called Kilmer Peak that will support three versions of WiMAX operating at 2.3 GHz, 2.5 GHz, and 3.5 GHz. The Kilmer Peak chipset is designed for installation in the Calpella Arrandale notebook.[27] Higher-end notebook computers will have WiMAX technology that uses a chip called Rosedale. WiMAX cards that plug into a slot in the computer will also be available.

Most telecommunications experts agree that WiMAX is an attractive option for developing countries with little or no wireless telephone infrastructure. However, it is not clear whether WiMAX will be as successful in developed countries such as the United States and Canada, where regular broadband is plentiful and cheap, and where 3G wireless networks already cover most major metropolitan areas. In addition, AT&T, Verizon Wireless, Rogers Communications, and Bell Canada have chosen a different direction and plan to upgrade their wireless networks with the LTE communications technology.

NETWORKS AND DISTRIBUTED PROCESSING

computer network
The communications media, devices, and software needed to connect two or more computer systems or devices.

A **computer network** consists of communications media, devices, and software needed to connect two or more computer systems or devices. The computers and devices on the networks are also called *network nodes*. After they are connected, the nodes can share hardware and software and data, information, and processing jobs. Increasingly, businesses are linking computers in networks to streamline work processes and enable employees to collaborate on projects. If a company uses networks effectively, it can grow into an agile, powerful, and creative organization, giving it a long-term competitive advantage. Organizations can use networks to share hardware, programs, and databases. Networks can transmit and receive information to improve organizational effectiveness and efficiency. They enable geographically separated workgroups to share documents and opinions, which fosters teamwork, innovative ideas, and new business strategies.

Network Types

Depending on the physical distance between nodes on a network and the communications and services it provides, networks can be classified as personal area, local area, metropolitan area, or wide area.

Personal Area Networks

personal area network (PAN)
A network that supports the interconnection of information technology within a range of 10 metres or so.

A **personal area network** (**PAN**) is a wireless network that connects information technology devices close to one person. With a PAN, you can connect a laptop, digital camera, and portable printer without cables. You can download digital image data from the camera to the laptop and then print it on a high-quality printer—all wirelessly.

PANiQ electronics enables users to transform their clothing into a wearable PAN that controls their iPhone, iPod, cell phones, walkie-talkies, and other electronic devices. Users can play, pause, or adjust the volume of their devices while freeing up their hands and keeping their devices stored safely in their pockets. The user connects a ribbon cable in the garment to the PANiQ controller to activate the smart fabric buttons sewn into the clothing. Then they connect the PANiQ controller to the electronic device. Clothing from several major clothing manufacturers can be purchased with PANiQ capability.[28]

Local Area Networks

local area network (LAN)
A network that connects computer systems and devices within a small area, such as an office, home, or several floors in a building.

A network that connects computer systems and devices within a small area such as an office, home, or several floors in a building is a **local area network** (**LAN**). Typically, LANs are wired into office buildings and factories, as shown in Figure 6.6. Although LANs often use unshielded twisted-pair wire, other media—including fibre-optic cable—is also popular. Increasingly, LANs are using some form of wireless communications. You can build LANs to connect personal computers, laptop computers, or powerful mainframe computers.

Docklands Light Railway is one of the first light rail systems in Britain and carries over 67 million passengers per year. Serco Docklands, the operator of the railway, is upgrading its existing LAN to support the railway's rollout of new services and applications, including a novel public address system that services 32 railway stations and is controlled by personal computer workstations at a single control centre. The system will also provide passengers with audio-visual updates to keep track of the comings and goings of the various rail cars.[29]

A basic type of LAN is a simple peer-to-peer network that a small business might use to share files and hardware devices such as printers. In a peer-to-peer network, you set up each computer as an independent computer, but you let other computers access specific files on its hard drive or share its printer. These types of networks have no server. Instead, each computer is connected to the next machine. Examples of peer-to-peer networks are Windows for Workgroups, Windows NT, Windows 2000, AppleShare, and Windows 7 homegroup. Performance of the computers on a peer-to-peer network is usually slower because one computer is actually sharing the resources of another computer.

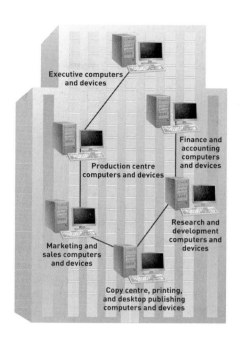

Figure 6.6

Typical LAN

All network users within an office building can connect to each other's devices for rapid communication. For instance, a user in research and development could send a document from her computer to be printed at a printer located in the desktop publishing centre.

Care must be exercised in placing sensitive data and documents on peer-to-peer servers. A junior member of the U.S.A. House Ethics Committee took home an electronic copy of a 22-page report detailing ethics probes involving some 30 members of Congress. He loaded it onto his home computer, which ran peer-to-peer networking software. Not surprisingly, the document was siphoned away to the file-sharing network where it was accessible to thousands of other computers.[30]

With more people working at home, connecting home computing devices and equipment into a unified network is on the rise. Small businesses are also connecting their systems and equipment. A home or small business can connect network resources, computers, printers, scanners, and other devices. A person working on one computer, for example, can use data and programs stored on another computer. In addition, several computers on the network can share a single printer. To make home and small business networking a reality, many companies are offering networking standards, devices, and procedures.

Metropolitan Area Networks

A **metropolitan area network** (**MAN**) is a telecommunications network that connects users and their computers in a geographical area that spans a campus or city. A MAN might redefine the many networks within a city into a single larger network or connect several LANs into a single campus LAN.

Grupo AMSA S.A. is a privately owned textile manufacturing company located in Lima, Peru. It operates three production plants that are roughly 10 kilometres apart from one another. The company implemented a MAN to support wireless communications among the three plants. The network provides high-speed data, voice, and Internet traffic among the locations, enabling effective planning, tracking, and controlling of operations at all three facilities.[31]

Wide Area Networks

A **wide area network** (**WAN**) is a telecommunications network that connects large geographic regions. A WAN might be privately owned or rented and includes public (shared users) networks. When you make a long-distance phone call or access the Internet, you are using a WAN. WANs usually consist of computer equipment owned by the user, together with data communications equipment and telecommunications links provided by various carriers and service providers. See Figure 6.7 on the next page.

WANs often provide communications across national borders, which involves national and international laws regulating the electronic flow of data across international boundaries or

metropolitan area network (MAN)
A telecommunications network that connects users and their computers in a geographical area that spans a campus or city.

wide area network (WAN)
A telecommunications network that connects large geographic regions.

Figure 6.7

Wide Area Network

WANs are the basic long-distance networks used around the world. The actual connections between sites, or nodes (shown by dashed lines), might be any combination of guided and wireless media. When you make a long-distance telephone call or access the Internet, you are using a WAN.

North America

transborder data flow. Many countries, including those in the European Union, have strict laws placing limits on the transmission of personal data about customers and employees across national borders.

The Canadian Department of National Defence developed its own internal communications network called the Defence Wide Area Network (DWAN). DWAN is used to access applications and share confidential information within the Department of National Defence across Canada.[32] China Datang Corporation is a state-owned corporation with 88 subsidiaries, including several large power generation plants. Its operations span 21 provinces of China and required the implementation of a WAN covering virtually the entire country. The network ensures high-quality voice, video, and data communications among the sites connected to the network.[33]

Basic Processing Alternatives

When an organization needs to use two or more computer systems, it can implement one of three basic processing alternatives: centralized, decentralized, or distributed. With **centralized processing**, all processing occurs in a single location or facility. This approach offers the highest degree of control because a single centrally managed computer performs all data processing. The Ticketmaster.ca reservation service is an example of a centralized system. One central computer with a database stores information about all events and records the purchases of seats. Ticket clerks at various ticket-selling locations can enter order data and print the results, or customers can place orders directly over the Internet.

With **decentralized processing**, processing devices are placed at various remote locations. Each processing device is isolated and does not communicate with any other processing device. Decentralized systems are suitable for companies that have independent operating units, such as 7-Eleven, where each of its 460 Canadian stores is managed to meet local retail conditions. Each store has a computer that runs several business applications, such as cash register operations, gasoline pump monitoring, and merchandising.

With **distributed processing**, processing devices are placed at remote locations but are connected to each other via a network. One benefit of distributed processing is that managers can allocate data to the locations that can process it most efficiently. Most grocery companies set up each store with its own computer to support store operations such as customer

centralized processing
An approach to processing wherein all processing occurs in a single location or facility.

decentralized processing
An approach to processing wherein processing devices are placed at various remote locations.

distributed processing
An approach to processing wherein processing devices are placed at remote locations but are connected to each other via a network.

checkout and inventory management. These computers are connected to a network so that sales data gathered by each store's computer can be sent to a huge data repository on a main-frame computer for efficient analysis by marketing analysts and product supply chain managers.

Ongoing terrorist attacks around the world and the heightened sensitivity to natural disasters (such as the 2010 earthquakes in Chile and Haiti and the series of three blizzards in the mid-Atlantic and northeast sections of the United States in early 2010) have motivated many companies to distribute their workers, operations, and systems much more widely, a reversal of the previous trend toward centralization. The goal is to minimize the consequences of a catastrophic event at one location while ensuring uninterrupted systems availability.

File Server Systems

Users can share data through file server computing, which allows authorized users to download entire files from certain computers designated as file servers. After downloading data to a local computer, a user can analyze, manipulate, format, and display data from the file, as shown in Figure 6.8.

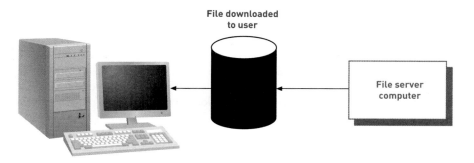

File downloaded to user

File server computer

Figure 6.8

File Server Connection

The file server sends the user the entire file that contains the data requested. The user can then analyze, manipulate, format, and display the downloaded data with a program that runs on the user's personal computer.

Client/Server Systems

In **client/server architecture**, computer servers are dedicated to special functions, such as database management, printing, communications, and program execution. Each server is accessible by all computers on the network. Servers can be computers of all sizes; they store both application programs and data files and are equipped with operating system software to manage the activities of the network. The server distributes programs and data to the other computers (clients) on the network as they request them. An application server holds the programs and data files for a particular application, such as an inventory database. The client or the server can do the processing.

A client is any computer (often a user's personal computer) that sends messages requesting services from the servers on the network. A client can converse with many servers concurrently. For example, a user at a personal computer initiates a request to extract data that resides in a database somewhere on the network. A data request server intercepts the request and determines on which database server the data resides. The server then formats the user's request into a message that the database server will understand. When it receives the message, the database server extracts and formats the requested data and sends the results to the client. The database server sends only the data that satisfies a specific query—not the entire file. See Figure 6.9. As with the file server

client/server architecture
An approach to computing wherein computer servers are dedicated to special functions, such as database management, printing, communications, and program execution.

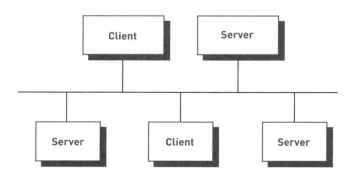

Client   **Server**

Server   **Client**   **Server**

Figure 6.9

Client/Server Connection

Computer servers are dedicated to special functions. Each server is accessible by all computers on the network.

approach, when the downloaded data is on the user's machine, it can then be analyzed, manipulated, formatted, and displayed by a program that runs on the user's personal computer.

Table 6.4 lists the advantages and disadvantages of client/server architecture.

Table 6.4	**Advantages**	**Disadvantages**
Advantages and Disadvantages of Client/Server Architecture	Moving applications from mainframe computers and terminal-to-host architecture to client/server architecture can yield significant savings in hardware and software support costs.	Moving to client/server architecture is a major two- to five-year conversion process.
	Minimizes traffic on the network because only the data needed to satisfy a user query is moved from the database to the client device.	Controlling the client/server environment to prevent unauthorized use, invasion of privacy, and viruses is difficult.
	Security mechanisms can be implemented directly on the database server through the use of stored procedures.	Using client/server architecture leads to a multivendor environment with problems that are difficult to identify and isolate to the appropriate vendor.

LaserPro is a client/server application used by lenders in more than 2,800 of the approximately 7,500 banks in the United States to generate the paperwork needed to offer consumer, real estate, and commercial loans. Based on loan officer responses to system prompts, this document assembly system creates the loan documents by selecting and customizing text from more than 13,000 standard paragraphs. The system includes a legal and compliance knowledge base of state and federal loan regulations to ensure that the documents it generates conform to all laws.[34] The system increases loan officer productivity and ensures that all documents meet the rapidly evolving set of regulations for loans.

Telecommunications Hardware

Networks require various telecommunications hardware devices to operate, including personal digital assistants and smartphones, modems, multiplexers, front-end processors, private branch exchanges, switches, bridges, routers, and gateways.

Apple iPhone

The iPhone is a combination mobile phone, widescreen iPod, and Internet access device.

(Source: Iain Masterton/Getstock.com.)

Smartphones

As discussed in Chapter 3, a smartphone combines the functionality of a mobile phone, personal digital assistant, camera, Web browser, e-mail tool, MP3 player, and other devices into a single hand-held device. For example, the Apple iPhone is a combination mobile phone, widescreen iPod, and Internet access device capable of supporting e-mail and Web browsing. An iPhone user can connect to the Internet via Wi-Fi.

Smartphones have their own software operating systems and are capable of running applications that have been created for their particular operating system. As a result, the capabilities of smartphones will continue to evolve as new applications become available. The Apple iPhone (iPhone OS), BlackBerry (RIM OS), and Palm (Palm OS) smartphones come with their own proprietary operating systems. The Android, Microsoft Windows Mobile, and Symbian operating systems are used on various manufacturers' smartphones.

Smartphone applications are developed by the manufacturers of the hand-held device, by the operators of the communications network on which they operate, and by third-party software developers. More than 125,000 Apple iPhone applications can be downloaded from the Apple Apps for iPhone online store. BlackBerry, Palm, and Android-based phones sell their apps through their own online stores—BlackBerry App World, Palm Pre Applications, and Android Market.

Droid Smartphone

The Droid smartphone is manufactured by Motorola and uses the Android operating system from Google.

(Source: George Frey/Stringer/Getty News Images.)

The Nexus One is a smartphone that uses Google's Android mobile operating system. The device is manufactured according to Google's specifications by Taiwan's HTC Corporation. The phone is similar in size and shape to the iPhone but boasts a higher resolution, enhanced 3D graphics, and speech-to-text features that enable the user to dictate Facebook and Twitter updates. The Nexus One can be bought directly from Google over the Web and comes "unlocked," meaning it is not restricted to use on a single network provider. Google offers it for use with Rogers Wireless, Telus, Bell, Videotron, and Wind Mobile.

Each of the smartphones listed in Table 6.5 comes with phone capabilities, a digital camera, video recorder, GPS tracking capability, digital player, Internet browser, and e-mail tool.

Feature	Samsung Galaxy	BlackBerry Torch 9800	Apple iPhone 4 GS
Approximate cost without a contract (Fall 2010)	$500	$600	$650
Screen size (inches)	3.2	3.2	3.5
Dimensions (cm)	11.5 X 5.6 X 1.2	11.1 X 6.2 X 1.5	11.5 X 5.9 X 0.9
Memory	8 GB	4 GB	16 GB

Table 6.5

Popular Smartphones

Modems

At each stage of the communications process, transmission media of differing types and capacities may be used. If you use an analog telephone line to transfer data, it can accommodate only an analog signal. Because a computer generates a digital signal represented by bits, you need a special device to convert the digital signal to an analog signal, and vice versa; see Figure 6.10.

Figure 6.10

How a Modem Works

Digital signals are modulated into analog signals, which can be carried over existing phone lines. The analog signals are then demodulated back into digital signals by the receiving modem.

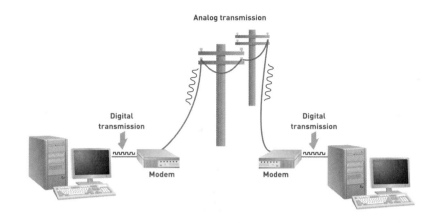

modem
A telecommunications hardware device that converts (modulates and demodulates) communications signals so they can be transmitted over the communication media.

A cable modem can deliver network and Internet access up to 500 times faster than a standard modem and phone line.

(Source: © Norman Chan/iStockphoto.com.)

Translating data from digital to analog is called *modulation*, and translating data from analog to digital is called *demodulation*. Thus, these devices are modulation/demodulation devices, or **modems**. Penril/Bay Networks, Hayes, Microcom, Motorola, and U.S. Robotics are modem manufacturers.

Modems can dial telephone numbers, originate message sending, and answer incoming calls and messages. Modems can also perform tests and checks on how well they are operating. Some modems can vary their transmission rates based on detected error rates and other conditions. Cellular modems in laptop personal computers allow people on the go to connect to wireless networks and communicate with other users and computers.

With a cellular modem, you can connect to other computers while in your car, on a boat, or in any area that has cellular transmission service. You can use PC memory card expansion slots for standardized credit card–sized PC modem cards, which work like standard modems. PC modems are becoming increasingly popular with notebook and portable computer users.

Cable company network subscribers use a cable modem, which has a low initial cost and can transmit at speeds up to 10 Mbps. The cable modem is always on, so you can be connected to the Internet around the clock. Digital subscriber line (DSL) refers to a family of services that provides high-speed digital data communications service over the wires of the local telephone company. Subscribers use a DSL modem to connect their computers to this service.

Multiplexers

multiplexer
A device that combines data from multiple data sources into a single output signal that carries many channels, thus reducing the number of communications links needed, therefore lowering telecommunications costs.

A **multiplexer** is a device that combines data from multiple data sources into a single output signal that carries many channels, thus reducing the number of communications links needed and, therefore, lowering telecommunications costs. See Figure 6.11. Multiplexing is commonly used on long-distance phone lines, combining many individual phone calls onto a single long-distance line without affecting the speed or quality of an individual call. At the receiving end, a demultiplexer chooses the correct destination from the many possible destinations and routes each individual call to its correct destination.

Front-End Processors

front-end processors
Special-purpose computers that manage communications to and from a large computer serving hundreds or even thousands of users.

Front-end processors are special-purpose computers that manage communications to and from a large computer serving hundreds or even thousands of users. They poll user devices to see if they have messages to send; facilitate efficient, error-free communications; perform message and transaction switching; and provide multiplexing and transaction security. Front-end processors also provide end-to-end transaction management and reporting—important functions needed to support mission critical transaction environments such as banking,

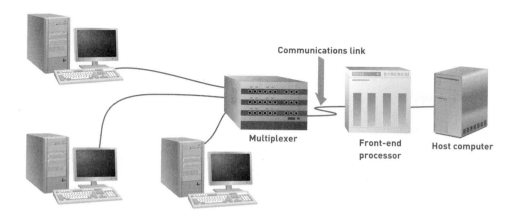

Figure 6.11

Use of a Multiplexer to Consolidate Data Communications onto a Single Communications Link

Communications link

Multiplexer

Front-end processor

Host computer

Telecommunications networks require state-of-the-art computer software technology to continuously monitor the flow of voice, data, and image transmission over billions of circuit kilometres worldwide.

(Source: Roger Tully/Stone/Getty Images.)

point-of-sale, and health-care applications. By performing this work, the front-end processor relieves the primary computer system of much of the overhead processing associated with telecommunications.

Private Branch Exchange (PBX)

A **private branch exchange** (**PBX**) is a telephone switching exchange that serves a single organization. It enables users to share a certain number of outside lines (trunk lines) to make telephone calls to people outside the organization. This sharing reduces the number of trunk lines required, which reduces the organization's telephone expense. With a PBX, you typically need to dial only three or four digits to reach anyone else within the organization. The PBX can also provide many other functions, such as voice mail, voice paging, three-way calling, call transfer, and call waiting. Centrex is a form of PBX with all switching occurring at the local telephone office instead of on the organization's premises. An IP-PBX can convert voice communications into packets of data for routing over the Internet.

Switches, Bridges, Routers, and Gateways

Telecommunications hardware devices switch messages from one network to another at high speeds. A **switch** uses the physical device address in each incoming message on the network to determine to which output port it should forward the message to reach another device on the same network. A **bridge** connects two LANs using the same telecommunications protocol. A **router** forwards data packets across two or more distinct networks toward their destinations

private branch exchange (PBX)
A telephone switching exchange that serves a single organization.

switch
A telecommunications device that uses the physical device address in each incoming message on the network to determine to which output port it should forward the message to reach another device on the same network.

bridge
A telecommunications device that connects two LANs using the same telecommunications protocol.

router
A telecommunications device that forwards data packets across two or more distinct networks toward their destinations, through a process known as routing.

gateway
A telecommunications device that serves as an entrance to another network.

network operating system (NOS)
Systems software that controls the computer systems and devices on a network and allows them to communicate with each other.

network-management software
Software that enables a manager on a networked desktop to monitor the use of individual computers and shared hardware (such as printers); scan for viruses; and ensure compliance with software licences.

encryption
The process of converting an original message into a form that can be understood only by the intended receiver.

encryption key
A variable value that is applied (using an algorithm) to a set of unencrypted text to produce encrypted text or to decrypt encrypted text.

through a process known as routing. Often, an Internet service provider (ISP) installs a router in a subscriber's home that connects the ISP's network to the network within the home. A **gateway** is a network device that serves as an entrance to another network.

Telecommunications Software

A **network operating system** (**NOS**) is systems software that controls the computer systems and devices on a network and allows them to communicate with each other. The NOS performs the similar functions for the network as operating system software does for a computer, such as memory and task management and coordination of hardware. When network equipment (such as printers, plotters, and disk drives) is required, the NOS makes sure that these resources are used correctly. Novell NetWare, Windows 2000, Windows 2003, and Windows 2008 are common network operating systems.

Because companies use networks to communicate with customers, business partners, and employees, network outages or slow performance can mean a loss of business. Network management includes a wide range of technologies and processes that monitor the network and help identify and address problems before they can create a serious impact.

Software tools and utilities are available for managing networks. With **network-management software**, a manager on a networked personal computer can monitor the use of individual computers and shared hardware (such as printers); scan for viruses; and ensure compliance with software licences. Network-management software also simplifies the process of updating files and programs on computers on the network—a manager can make changes through a communications server instead of having to visit each individual computer. In addition, network-management software protects software from being copied, modified, or downloaded illegally. It can also locate telecommunications errors and potential network problems. Some of the many benefits of network-management software include fewer hours spent on routine tasks (such as installing new software), faster response to problems, and greater overall network control.

Today, most IS organizations use network-management software to ensure that their network remains up and running and that every network component and application is performing acceptably. The software enables IS staff to identify and resolve fault and performance issues before they affect customers and service. The latest network-management technology even incorporates automatic fixes—the network-management system identifies a problem, notifies the IS manager, and automatically corrects the problem before anyone outside the IS department notices it.

Data Synch Systems provides remote network monitoring for over 50 customers. The organization minimized customer interruptions and saved over $80,000 in site visit expenses by using network-management software.[35]

Securing Data Transmission

The interception of confidential information by unauthorized individuals can compromise private information about employees or customers, reveal marketing or new product development plans, or cause organizational embarrassment. Organizations with widespread operations need a way to maintain the security of communications with employees and business partners, wherever their facilities are located.

Guided media networks have an inherently secure feature; only devices physically attached to the network can access the data. Wireless networks, on the other hand, are surprisingly often configured by default to allow access to any device that attempts to "listen to" broadcast communications. Action must be taken to override the defaults.

Encryption of data is one approach taken to protect the security of communications over both wired and wireless networks. **Encryption** is the process of converting an original message into a form that can be understood only by the intended receiver. An **encryption key** is a variable value that is applied (using an algorithm) to a set of unencrypted text to produce encrypted text or to decrypt encrypted text. See Figure 6.12. The key is chosen from one of a large number of possible encryption keys. The longer the key, the greater the number of possible encryption keys. An encryption protocol based on a 56-bit key, for

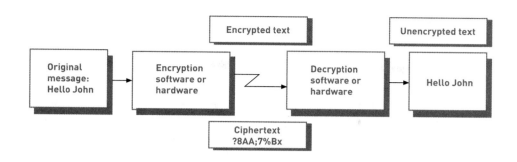

Figure 6.12

Encryption Process

example, has 2^{56} different possible keys, while one based on a 128-bit key has 2^{128} different possible keys. Of course, it is essential that the key be kept secret from possible interceptors. A hacker who obtains the key by whatever means can recover the original message from the encrypted data.

Encryption methods rely on the limitations of computing power for their security—if breaking a code requires too much computing power, even the most determined hacker cannot be successful.

Bertelsmann AG is a major international media company with interests in TV, books, magazines, music, media services, and media clubs in more than 60 countries. The company implemented PGP Encryption to protect the confidentiality of the e-mails of its 97,000 employees. Of particular concern was sensitive data about employees, customers, mergers, and acquisitions.[36]

Securing Wireless Networks

WEP and WPA are the two main approaches to securing wireless networks such as Wi-Fi and WiMAX. Wired equivalent privacy (WEP) used to use encryption based on a 64-bit key, which has been upgraded to a 128-bit key. WEP represents an early attempt at securing wireless communications and is not difficult for hackers to crack. Most wireless networks now use the Wi-Fi Protected Access (WPA) security protocol that offers significantly improved protection over WEP.

The following steps, while not foolproof, help safeguard a wireless network:

- Connect to the router and change the default logon (admin) and password (password) for the router. These defaults are widely known by hackers.
- Create a service set identifier (SSID). This is a 32-character unique identifier attached to the header portion of packets sent over a wireless network that differentiates one network from another. All access points and devices attempting to connect to the network must use the same SSID.
- Configure the security to WPA. Surprisingly, many routers are shipped with encryption turned off.
- Disable SSID broadcasting. By default, wireless routers broadcast a message communicating the SSID so wireless devices within range (such as a laptop) can identify and connect to the wireless network. If a device doesn't know the wireless network's SSID, it cannot connect. Disabling the broadcasting of the SSID will discourage all but the most determined and knowledgeable hackers.
- Configure each wireless computer on the network to access the network by setting the security to WPA and entering the same password entered on the router.

War driving involves hackers driving around with a laptop and antenna trying to detect insecure wireless access points. Once connected to such a network, the hacker can gather enough traffic to analyze and crack the encryption.

The Kasumi encryption code is a 128-bit code that was planned to be used to encrypt communications on nearly 1.2 billion phone sets that operate on 3G wireless networks. However, three researchers have shown that it is possible to break this code in a matter of hours, causing reconsideration of the broad rollout of this code.[37]

Virtual Private Network (VPN)

virtual private network (VPN)
A private network that uses
a public network (usually the
Internet) to connect many remote
locations.

The use of a virtual private network is another means used to secure the transmission of communications. A **virtual private network** (**VPN**) is a private network that uses a public network (usually the Internet) to connect many remote locations. A VPN provides network connectivity over a potentially long physical distance and thus can be considered a form of wide area network. VPNs support secure, encrypted connections between a company's private network and remote users through a third-party service provider. Telecommuters, salespeople, and frequent travellers find the use of a VPN to be a safe, reliable, low-cost way to connect to their corporate intranets. Often users are provided with a security token that displays a constantly changing password to log on to the VPN. This solution avoids the problem of users forgetting their password while providing added security through use of a password constantly changing every 30 to 60 seconds.

The Canadian Forces Health Information System provides a fully integrated computerized health information system for the Department of Defence. Since safeguarding members' privacy and confidentiality of health information was important, a VPN was implemented on the existing DWAN, discussed earlier in this chapter.[38]

TELECOMMUNICATIONS SERVICES AND NETWORK APPLICATIONS

Telecommunications and networks are a vital part of today's information systems. In fact, it is hard to imagine how organizations could function without them. For example, when a business needs to develop an accurate monthly production forecast, a manager simply downloads sales forecast data gathered directly from customer databases. Telecommunications provides the network link, allowing the manager to access the data quickly and generate the production report, which supports the company's objective of better financial planning. This section looks at some of the more significant telecommunications services and network applications.

Cellular Phone Services

The cell phone has become ubiquitous and is an essential part of life in the 21st century. Although many of the people who live in developing countries do not have ready access to clean drinking water, electricity, or the Internet, according to the International Telecommunications Union (ITC) more than half of these individuals were expected to have mobile phones by 2012.[39]

Cellular phones operate using radio waves to provide two-way communications. With cellular transmission, a local area such as a city is divided into cells. As a person with a cellular device such as a mobile phone moves from one cell to another, the cellular system passes the phone connection from one cell to another; see Figure 6.13. The signals from the cells

Figure 6.13

Typical Cellular Transmission Scenario

Using a cellular car phone, the caller dials the number (1). The signal is sent from the car's antenna to the low-powered cellular antenna located in that cell (2). The signal is sent to the regional cellular phone switching office, also called the *mobile telephone subscriber office* (MTSO) (3). The signal is switched to the local telephone company switching station located nearest the call destination (4). Now integrated into the regular phone system, the call is switched to the number originally dialled (5), all without the need for operator assistance.

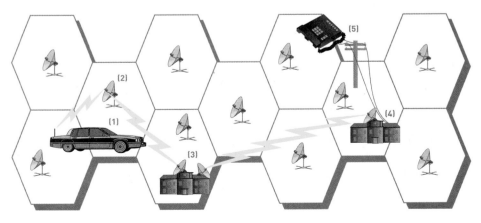

are transmitted to a receiver and integrated into the regular phone system. Cellular phone users can thus connect to anyone who has access to either a cell phone or regular phone service, whether it's a child at home, your friend on the road, or a business associate in another country. Because cellular transmission uses radio waves, people with special receivers can listen to cellular phone conversations, so they are not secure.

More and more workers rely on their mobile phones as their primary business phones. However, they frequently encounter problems with poor coverage and can find it difficult to place calls or conduct an extended conversation. A picocell is a miniature cellular base station designed to serve a very small area such as part of a floor inside a building. Many communications companies now offer picocell solutions to boost cell phone signals or enable the cell phone to operate over other wireless networks, thus guaranteeing a strong, reliable cell signal. Cell phones may also be linked to a cordless phone via a Bluetooth connection so that if someone calls you on your cell, you can answer the call on the cordless phone. This improves the range of cell phone coverage and eliminates dropped calls, especially for those times you cannot find your cell phone in time.[40]

Picocells are being installed to provide service on aircraft to enable passengers to use their cell phones. Picocells also enable aircraft crew to update approach charts and access management networks while parked at the gate. By controlling when picocells are available, pilots can block mobile calls during take-off, landing, and turbulence.[41]

Digital Subscriber Line (DSL) Service

A **digital subscriber line** (**DSL**) is a telecommunications service that delivers high-speed Internet access to homes and small businesses over the existing phone lines of the local telephone network. See Figure 6.14. Most home and small business users are connected to an *asymmetric DSL (ADSL)* line designed to provide a connection speed from the Internet to the user (download speed) that is three to four times faster than the connection from the user back to the Internet (upload speed). ADSL does not require an additional phone line and yet provides "always-on" Internet access. A drawback of ADSL is that the farther the subscriber is from the local telephone office, the poorer the signal quality and the slower the transmission speed. ADSL provides a dedicated connection from each user to the phone company's local office, so the performance does not decrease as new users are added. Cable modem users generally share a network loop that runs through a neighbourhood so that adding users means lowering the transmission speeds. *Symmetric DSL (SDSL)* is used mainly by small businesses; it does not allow you to use the phone at the same time, but the speed of receiving and sending data is the same.

digital subscriber line (DSL)
A telecommunications service that delivers high-speed Internet access to homes and small businesses over the existing phone lines of the local telephone network.

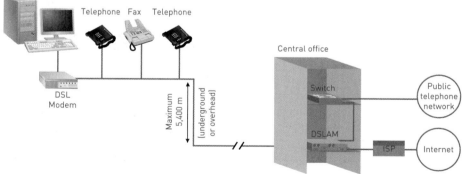

Figure 6.14

Digital Subscriber Line (DSL)

At the local telephone company's central office, a DSL Access Multiplexer (DSLAM) takes connections from many customers and multiplexes them onto a single, high-capacity connection to the Internet. Subscriber phone calls can be routed through a switch at the local telephone central office to the public telephone network.

Linking Personal Computers to Mainframes and Networks

One of the most basic ways that telecommunications connect users to information systems is by connecting personal computers to mainframe computers so that data can be downloaded or uploaded. For example, a user can download a data file or document file from a database to a personal computer. Some telecommunications software programs instruct the computer to connect to another computer on the network, download or send information, and then disconnect from the telecommunications line. These programs are called *unattended systems* because they perform the functions automatically, without user intervention.

Voice Mail

voice mail
Technology that enables users to send, receive, and store verbal messages to and from other people around the world.

With **voice mail**, users can send, receive, and store verbal messages to and from other people around the world. Some voice mail systems assign a code to a group of people. Suppose the code 100 stands for all the sales representatives in a company. If anyone calls the voice mail system, enters the number 100, and leaves a message, all the sales representatives receive the same message. Call management systems can be linked to corporate e-mail and instant messaging systems. Calls to employees can be generated from instant messages or converted into e-mail messages to ensure quicker access and response.

Voice Mail-to-Text Services

voice mail-to-text service
A service that captures voice mail messages, converts them to text, and sends them to an e-mail account.

Voice mail is more difficult to manage than e-mail because you must deal with messages one by one without knowing who has called you and without being able to prioritize the messages. In recognition of these shortcomings of voice mail, several services (e.g., Jott, SpinVox, GotVoice, and SimulScribe) are now available to convert speech to text so that you can manage voice mails more effectively. If you subscribe to a **voice mail-to-text service**, your voice mail no longer reaches your phone service provider's voice mail service. Instead, it is rerouted to the voice-to-text service, translated into text, and then sent to your regular e-mail account or a special account for converted e-mail messages. You can also temporarily disable the voice-to-text service and receive voice messages.

Reverse 911 Service

reverse 911 service
A communications system that delivers emergency notifications to users in a selected geographical area.

Reverse 911 service is a communications system at delivers recorded emergency notifications to users in a selected geographical area. The technology employs databases of phone numbers and contact information. Some systems can send over 250,000 voice or text messages per hour via phone, pager, cell phone, and e-mail. A reverse 911 system was implemented in 2011 to allow Montreal residents to receive emergency health or safety information from the city.[42]

Home and Small Business Networks

Small businesses and many families own more than one computer and want to set up a simple network to share printers or an Internet connection; access shared files such as photos, MP3 audio files, spreadsheets, and documents on different machines; play games that support several concurrent players; and send the output of network-connected devices, such as a security camera or DVD player, to a computer.

One simple solution is to establish a wireless network that covers your home or small business. To do so, you can buy an 802.11n access point, connect it to your cable modem or DSL modem, and then use it to communicate with all your devices. For less than $100, you can purchase a combined router, firewall, Ethernet hub, and wireless hub in one small device. Computers in your network connect to this box with a wireless card, which is connected by cable or DSL modem to the Internet. This enables each computer in the network to access the Internet. The firewall filters the information coming from the Internet into your network. You can configure it to reject information from offensive websites or potential hackers. The router can also encrypt all wireless communications to keep your network secure.

In addition, you can configure your computers to share printers and files. Windows 7 and Windows Vista include a Network and Sharing Centre that helps with network configuration. Some of the basic configuration steps include assigning each computer to a workgroup and giving it a name, identifying the files you want to share (placing an optional password on some files), and identifying the printers you want to share.

Electronic Document Distribution

electronic document distribution
A process that enables the sending and receiving of documents in a digital form without being printed (although printing is possible).

Electronic document distribution lets you send and receive documents in a digital form without printing them (although printing is possible). It is much faster to distribute electronic documents via networks than to mail printed forms. Viewing documents on screen instead of printing them also saves paper and document storage space. Accessing and retrieving electronic documents is also much faster.

Call Centres

A call centre is a location where an organization handles customer and other telephone calls, usually with some amount of computer automation. Call centres are used by customer service organizations, telemarketing companies, computer product help desks, charitable and political campaign organizations, and any organization that uses the telephone to sell or support its products and services. An automatic call distributor (ACD) is a telephone facility that manages incoming calls, handling them based on the number called and an associated database of instructions. Call centres frequently employ an ACD to validate callers, place outgoing calls, forward calls to the right party, allow callers to record messages, gather usage statistics, balance the workload of support personnel, and provide other services.

The National Do Not Call Registry was set up in 2008 by the Canadian Radio-television and Telecommunications Commission (CRTC). Telemarketers who call numbers on the list face penalties of up to $15,000 per call. More than 8.5 million consumers have signed on to the list by logging on to the site *www.dncl.gc.ca*. Even though you have registered, you will still receive calls from political organizations, charities, and telephone surveyors. You can also receive calls from companies with which you have an existing business relationship, such as your bank or credit card companies.[43] Although the registry has greatly reduced the number of unwanted calls to consumers, it has created several compliance-related issues for direct marketing companies.

Offshore call centres provide technical support services for many technology vendors and their customers.

(Source: © STR/AFP/Getty Images.)

Telecommuting and Virtual Workers and Workgroups

Employees are performing more and more work away from the traditional office setting. Many enterprises have adopted policies for **telecommuting** so that employees can work away from the office using computing devices and networks. This means workers can be more effective and companies can save money on office and parking space and office equipment. According to a recent study by Forrester Research, 17 percent of North American enterprises and 14 percent of European enterprises report having employees who spend at least 20 percent of their time away from their normal work desk or work from home.[44]

Telecommuting is popular among workers for several reasons. Parents find that eliminating the daily commute helps balance family and work responsibilities. Qualified workers who otherwise might be unable to participate in the normal workforce (e.g., those who are physically challenged or who live in rural areas too far from the city office to commute regularly) can use telecommuting to become productive workers. When gas prices soar, telecommuting can help workers reduce significant expenses. Extensive use of telecommuting can lead to decreased need for office space, potentially saving a large company millions of dollars. Corporations

telecommuting
The use of computing devices and networks so that employees can work effectively away from the office.

are also being encouraged by public policy to try telecommuting as a means of reducing their carbon footprint and traffic congestion. Large companies also view telecommuting as a means to distribute their workforce and reduce the impact of a disaster at a central facility.

Some types of jobs are well-suited to telecommuting, including jobs held by salespeople, secretaries, real estate agents, computer programmers, and legal assistants, to name a few. Telecommuting also requires a certain personality type to be effective. Telecommuters need to be strongly self-motivated, organized, and focused on their tasks with minimal supervision and have a low need for social interaction. Jobs unsuitable for telecommuting include those that require frequent face-to-face interaction, need much supervision, and have many short-term deadlines. Employees who choose to work at home must be able to work independently, manage their time well, and balance work and home life.

Studies found that in 2009 40 percent of public- and private-sector firms in Canada offered employees the opportunity to telework compared with only 25 percent in 2007 and that approximately 10 percent of the country's workforce worked at least one day a week away from the office.[45] There is also a growing trend within Canada of cross-broader telecommuting—Canadian-based telecommuters who work for or provide services to companies or customers in the United States and internationally.

Electronic Meetings

videoconferencing
A set of interactive telecommunications technologies that enable people at various locations to communicate using simultaneous two-way video and audio transmissions.

Videoconferencing is a set of interactive telecommunications technologies that enable people at various locations to communicate using simultaneous two-way video and audio transmissions. Videoconferencing can reduce travel expenses and time, and it can increase managerial effectiveness through faster response to problems, access to more people, and less duplication of effort by geographically dispersed sites. Almost all videoconferencing systems combine video and phone call capabilities with data or document conferencing, as shown in Figure 6.15. You can see the other person's face, view the same documents, and swap notes and drawings. With some systems, callers can change live documents in real time. Many businesses find that the document- and application-sharing feature of the videoconference enhances group productivity and efficiency. It also fosters teamwork and can save corporate travel time and expense.

Figure 6.15

Videoconferencing

Videoconferencing allows participants to conduct long-distance meetings "face to face" while eliminating the need for costly travel.

(Source: © Comstock/Getty Images.)

Group videoconferencing is used daily in a variety of businesses as an easy way to connect work teams. Members of a team meet in a specially prepared videoconference room equipped with sound-sensitive cameras that automatically focus on the person speaking, large TV-like monitors for viewing the participants at the remote location, and high-quality speakers and microphones. Videoconferencing costs have declined steadily, while video quality and synchronization of audio to video—once weak points for the technology—have improved.

Ryder Levett Bucknall is a global property and construction consulting organization with more than 2,000 employees spread around the world. The organization recently implemented videoconferencing systems in its seven U.K. offices. Mark Evans, IT manager for the firm, says, "We were faced with a dilemma: colleagues and project teams in different offices needed to communicate and collaborate. But rising travel costs and the associated carbon emissions meant travelling to and from meetings wasn't financially or environmentally responsible. [Videoconferencing] helps us work smarter all the way around. Not only have we reduced expenses and our carbon footprint, but we've also increased productivity and client satisfaction, which makes everyone happy."[46]

Electronic Data Interchange

Electronic data interchange (EDI) is a way to communicate data from one company to another and from one application to another in a standard format, permitting the recipient to perform a standard business transaction, such as processing purchase orders. Connecting corporate computers among organizations is the idea behind EDI, which uses network systems and follows standards and procedures that can process output from one system directly as input to other systems—without human intervention. EDI can link the computers of customers, manufacturers, and suppliers, as shown in Figure 6.16. This technology eliminates the need for paper documents and substantially cuts down on costly errors. Customer orders and inquiries are transmitted from the customer's computer to the manufacturer's computer. The manufacturer's computer determines when new supplies are needed and can place orders by connecting with the supplier's computer.

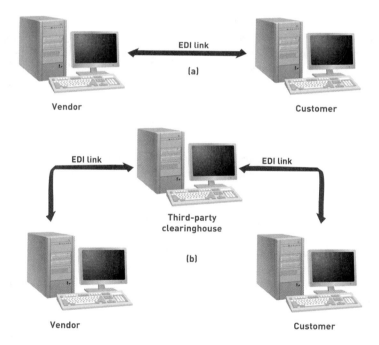

Vendor — EDI link (a) — **Customer**

EDI link — **Third-party clearinghouse** — EDI link (b)

Vendor — **Customer**

Figure 6.16

Two Approaches to Electronic Data Interchange

Many organizations now insist that their suppliers use EDI systems. Often, the vendor and customer (a) have a direct EDI connection or (b) the link is provided by a third-party clearinghouse that converts data and performs other services for the participants.

General Motors uses EDI to drive global innovation across its supply chain consisting of more than 19,000 suppliers. Ralph Szygenda, CIO of General Motors, states, "We exchange millions of production-critical EDI messages each month between our suppliers and our facilities. EDI gives us a reliable, cost-effective messaging solution that will further improve our processes and drive real-time integration with our suppliers."[47]

Electronic Funds Transfer

Electronic funds transfer (EFT) is a system of transferring money from one bank account directly to another without any paper money changing hands. It is used for both credit transfers, such as payroll payments, and for debit transfers, such as mortgage payments.

The benefits of EFT include reduced administrative costs, increased efficiency, simplified bookkeeping, and greater security. One of the most widely used EFT programs is direct deposit, which deposits employee payroll cheques directly into the designated bank accounts. The two primary components of EFT, wire transfer and automated clearing house (ACH), are summarized in Table 6.6.

Table 6.6

Comparison of ACH Payments and Wire Transfers

	ACH Payments	Wire Transfers
When does payment clear?	Overnight	Immediately
Can payment be cancelled?	Yes	No
Is there a guarantee of sufficient funds?	No	Yes
What is the approximate cost per transaction?	$0.25	$10–$40

Unified Communications

Unified communications provides a simple and consistent user experience across all types of communications, such as instant messaging, fixed and mobile phone, e-mail, voice mail, and Web conferencing. The concept of *presence* (knowing where one's desired communication participants are and if they are available at this instant) is a key component of unified communications. The goal is to reduce the time required to make decisions and communicate results, thus greatly improving productivity.

All the ways that unified communications can be implemented rely on fast, reliable communications networks. Typically, users have a device capable of supporting the various forms of communications (e.g., laptop with microphone and video camera or a smartphone) that is loaded with software that supports unified communications. The users' devices also connect to a server that keeps track of the presence of each user.

Global Positioning System Applications

The Global Positioning System (GPS) is a global navigation satellite system that uses two dozen satellites roughly 17,000 kilometres above the Earth. These satellites are used as reference points to calculate positions on Earth to an accuracy of a few metres or even less. GPS receivers have become as small as a cell phone and relatively inexpensive, making the technology readily accessible. The technology was originally developed for national defence and military applications. The technology has migrated to consumer devices and is used in navigational and location tracking devices. GPS receivers are commonly found in autos, boats, planes, laptop computers, and cell phones.[48]

To determine its position, a GPS receiver receives the signals from four GPS satellites and determines its exact distance from each satellite. (While the position of the receiver could be determined with just three measurements, a fourth distance measurement helps to adjust for any impreciseness in the other three measurements.)[49] This is done by very accurately measuring the time it takes for a signal to travel at the speed of light from the satellite to the receiver (distance = time $\times$ 300,000 kilometres/second). It then uses these distances to triangulate the precise location of the receiver in terms of latitude, longitude, and altitude.

GPS tracking technology has become the standard by which fleet managers monitor the movement of their cars, trucks, and vehicles. GPS tracking quickly exposes inefficient routing practices, wasted time on the job, and speeding. Even small fleet operators can achieve significant benefits from the use of GPS tracking.

Computer-based navigation systems are also based on GPS technology. These systems come in all shapes and sizes and with varying capabilities—from PC-based systems installed in automobiles for guiding you across the country to hand-held units you carry while

Henny Penny Moves to Unified Communications

Henny Penny is a global manufacturer and supplier of high-end restaurant food preparation and storage equipment, such as fryers, rotisseries, freezers, and warmers. Henny Penny has offices around the world, including sites in Canada, Paris, Beirut, Moscow, and China. Its products are popular in 100 countries due to the high quality of the products and its customer service.

Henny Penny works with manufacturers in China to produce its equipment, selling it through global distributors. As with all global enterprises, providing efficient and economical communication among employees, manufacturers, and distributors has been a challenge for Henny Penny. It has also been a priority for the company because its reputation depends on its ability to react quickly to customer needs. Recently, a surge in business made Henny Penny's call centre operators unusually busy, leaving customers on hold longer than normal. This, combined with high travel expenses, helped Henny Penny decide that it was time to improve its telecommunications system.

Upon investigating its options, Henny Penny's communications manager, Brad Fletcher, was impressed by the opportunities available through unified communications. He and the company's executives became convinced that combining computer-based communications, voice communications, and video communications into one system would help the company better manage its global communications.

Henny Penny ripped out its old Avaya PBX telephone system and replaced it with a computer-based unified communications system. Now Henny Penny employees and its partners communicate using Internet Protocol (IP) phones that support text, voice, and video communications. The IP phones are linked to employee computers to support group videoconferences with desktop space for sharing presentations and files.

The new unified communications system was costly to install but has saved Henny Penny considerable expense in several areas, paying for itself in its first year. The new system is used to hold two-day meetings with distributors to update them on the latest products and enhancements. It is also used for week-long distributor training sessions and for weekly meetings of the global sales force. The new system saves Henny Penny $131,250 annually by replacing travel to China with video meetings that allow people in Ohio to visually inspect the manufacturing process. In one year, the company avoided 15 ten-day trips to China by replacing them with video communications.

The unified system has transformed Henny Penny's call centre into an organized system that gets answers to customers quickly. One central operator greets the phoning customers, records their name and question, and quickly transfers them to an expert that is best suited to assist them—all managed through a sophisticated computer-based system. The new system reduces hold times by 50 percent, with 96 percent of the calls addressed in under 30 seconds, giving the company by far the highest customer satisfaction rating in the industry.

The new system has also helped improve the quality of life for Henny Penny employees. They can get more done with less effort. When a teleconference is scheduled with manufacturers in China for 5:00 a.m., those involved can participate from home. Brad Fletcher says that the company is becoming "borderless," where work no longer has to take place only at the office, but can take place from any location with an Internet connection. In the next stage of development, Henny Penny plans to add the ability to access its unified communications system from smartphones.

Discussion Questions

1. Why did Henny Penny decide that it was time to improve its communications system?
2. In what ways did a unified communications system help Henny Penny?

Critical Thinking Questions

1. Considering the benefits of unified communications that this article highlights, what are some of the drawbacks of replacing face-to-face meeting with video?
2. In your opinion, what business activities should require a physical, face-to-face meeting?

SOURCES: Greene, Tim, "Cisco Unified Communications Saves Money for Henny Penny," *ITWorld, www.itworld.com/networking/78494/cisco-unified-communications-saves-money-henny-penny*, September 24, 2009; "Manufacturer Improves Responsiveness and Saves Money," Cisco Customer Case Study, *www.cisco.com/en/US/prod/collateral/voicesw/ps6788/vcallcon/ps556/case_study_c36-558384.pdf*, accessed February 16, 2010; Henny Penny website, *www.hennypenny.com*, accessed February 16, 2010; Cisco Unified Communications website, *www.cisco.com/en/US/products/sw/voicesw/index.html#~all-prod*, accessed February 16, 2010.

A Global Positioning System (GPS) can guide you along a route whether you are mobile or on foot.

(Source: © Doug Berry/iStockphoto. com.)

hiking. All systems need a GPS antenna to receive satellite signals to pinpoint your location. On most of these systems, your location is superimposed on a map stored on CDs or a DVD. Portable systems can be moved from one car to another or carried in your backpack. Some systems come with dynamic rerouting capability, where the path recommended depends on weather and road conditions, which are continually transmitted to your car via a receiver connected to a satellite radio system.

Most of the major Canadian wireless carriers offer cell phones that include an additional GPS antenna and internal GPS chip that can pinpoint a given location within a hundred metres or so. (The accuracy really depends on the accuracy of the timing mechanism of the cell phone. A tiny timing error can result in an error of 300 metres.) Some employers use GPS-enabled phones to track their employees' locations. The Whereifone locator phone provides GPS coordinates and can dial emergency phone numbers. Parents and caregivers can track the phone's location by phone or online and can receive notification if it leaves a designated safe area.

Google employs the Latitude software to enable people with mobile phones and other wireless devices to share their location with friends and family. The software relies on cell phone towers or global positioning systems to determine their location and plot it on a Google map for others to see.[50] Google has also announced that it will offer detailed turn-by-turn directions to users of the Motorola Droid cell phone.[51]

SUMMARY

Principle:

A telecommunications system consists of several fundamental components.

In a telecommunications system, the sending unit transmits a signal to a telecommunications device, which performs a number of functions such as converting the signal into a different form or from one type to another. The telecommunications device then sends the signal through a medium that carries the electronic signal. The signal is received by another telecommunications device that is connected to the receiving computer.

A networking protocol defines the set of rules that governs the exchange of information over a telecommunications channel to ensure fast, efficient, error-free communications and to enable hardware, software, and equipment manufacturers and service providers to build products that interoperate effectively. There is a myriad of telecommunications protocols, including international, national, and regional standards.

Communications among people can occur synchronously or asynchronously.

A transmission medium can be divided into one or more communications channels, each capable of carrying a message. Telecommunications channels can be classified as simplex, half-duplex, or full-duplex.

Channel bandwidth refers to the rate at which data is exchanged, usually expressed in bits per second.

A circuit switching network uses a dedicated path for the duration of the communications. A packet switching network does not employ a dedicated path for communications and breaks data into packets for transmission over the network.

The telecommunications media that physically connect data communications devices can be divided into two broad categories: guided transmission media and wireless media. Guided transmission media include twisted-pair wire, coaxial cable, fibre-optic cable, and broadband over power lines. Wireless transmission involves the broadcast of communications in one of three frequency ranges: radio, microwave, or infrared.

Wireless communications solutions for very short distances include near field communications, Bluetooth, ultra wideband, infrared transmission, and ZigBee. Wi-Fi is a popular wireless communications solution for medium-range distances. Wireless communications methods for long distances include satellite and terrestrial microwave transmission, wireless mesh, 3G and 4G cellular communications service, and WiMAX.

Principle:

Networks are an essential component of an organization's information technology infrastructure.

The geographic area covered by a network determines whether it is called a personal area network (PAN), local area network (LAN), metropolitan area network (MAN), or wide area network (WAN).

The electronic flow of data across international and global boundaries is often called transborder data flow.

When an organization needs to use two or more computer systems, it can follow one of three basic data processing strategies: centralized (all processing at a single location, high degree of control), decentralized (many processors that do not communicate with one another), or distributed (many processors that communicate with each other). Distributed processing minimizes the consequences of a catastrophic event at one location while ensuring uninterrupted systems availability.

A client/server system is a network that connects a user's computer (a client) to one or more host computers (servers). A client is often a PC that requests services from the server, shares processing tasks with the server, and displays the results.

Popular telecommunications devices are personal digital assistants (PDAs), smartphones, modems, multiplexers, front-end processors, PBX systems, switches, bridges, routers, and gateways.

Telecommunications software performs important functions, such as error checking and message formatting. A network operating system controls the computer systems and devices on a network, allowing them to communicate with one another. Network-management software enables a manager to monitor the use of individual computers and shared hardware, scan for viruses, and ensure compliance with software licences.

The interception of confidential information by unauthorized parties is a major concern for organizations. Encryption of data and the use of virtual private networks are two common solutions to this problem. Special measures must be taken to secure wireless networks.

Principle:

Network applications are essential to organizational success.

Telecommunications and networks are creating profound changes in business because they remove the barriers of time and distance.

The effective use of networks can turn a company into an agile, powerful, and creative organization, giving it a long-term competitive advantage. Networks let users share hardware, programs, and databases across the organization. They can transmit and receive information to improve organizational effectiveness and efficiency. They enable geographically separated workgroups to share documents and opinions, which fosters teamwork, innovative ideas, and new business strategies.

The wide range of telecommunications and network applications includes cellular phone services, digital subscriber line (DSL), linking personal computer to mainframes, voice mail, voice-to-text services, reverse 911 service, home and small business networks, electronic document distribution, call centres, telecommuting, videoconferencing, electronic data interchange, electronic funds transfer, unified communications, and global positioning system applications.

CHAPTER 6: SELF-ASSESSMENT TEST

A telecommunications system consists of several fundamental components.

1. Videoconferencing is an example of asynchronous communications. True or False?
2. Any material that carries an electronic signal to support communications is called a(n) _____.
3. Which of the following defines a set of rules, algorithms, messages, and other mechanisms that enable software and hardware in networked devices to communicate effectively?
   a. the network channel
   b. the network bandwidth
   c. the network protocol
   d. circuit switching
4. Which of the following are two broad categories of transmission media?
   a. guided and wireless
   b. shielded and unshielded
   c. twisted and untwisted
   d. infrared and microwave
5. In a(n) _____ network, no fixed path is created between the communicating devices, and the data is broken into packets for sending over the network.
6. Bluetooth is a wireless communications specification that describes how cell phones, computers, faxes, smartphones, printers, and other electronic devices can be interconnected over distances of less than 9 metres at a rate of 2 Mbps. True or False?

Networks are an essential component of an organization's information technology infrastructure.

7. A(n) _____ is a network that connects computer systems and devices within a small area, such as an office, home, or several floors in a building.

8. 7-Eleven is an example of an organization that uses decentralized processing to help its stores meet local retail conditions. True or False?
9. What device combines data from several data sources into a single output channel that carries several channels?
   a. modem
   b. multiplexer
   c. front-end processor
   d. PBX

Network applications are essential to organizational success.

10. _____ is a telecommunications service that delivers high-speed Internet access to homes and small businesses over the existing phone lines of the local telephone network.
11. _____ is a communications system that delivers recorded emergency notifications to users in a selected geographic area.
12. Telecommuting enables organizations to save money because less office space, parking space, and office equipment are required. True or False?
13. _____ is a system of transferring money from one bank account directly to another without any paper money changing hands.

CHAPTER 6: SELF-ASSESSMENT TEST ANSWERS

(1) False (2) media (3) c (4) a (5) packet switching (6) True (7) LAN (8) True (9) b (10) Digital subscriber line (11) Reverse 911 (12) True (13) Electronic funds transfer

REVIEW QUESTIONS

1. What is meant by broadband communications?
2. Describe the elements and steps involved in the telecommunications process.
3. What is a telecommunications protocol?
4. What are the names of the three primary frequency ranges used in wireless communications?
5. What is a shared workspace? Provide an example of how a project team might use a shared workspace.
6. What is VPN? How do organizations use this technology?
7. What is the difference between near field communication and ultra wideband?
8. Is telecommuting aimed solely at enabling employees to work from home? Explain your answer.

9. What is the difference between Wi-Fi and WiMAX communications?
10. What roles do the bridge, router, gateway, and switch play in a network?
11. Distinguish between a PAN, LAN, MAN, and WAN.
12. What are some of the advantages of videoconferencing? Describe a recent meeting you attended that could have used videoconferencing.
13. What is EFT? What is the difference between ACH payments and wire transfers?
14. Identify two approaches to securing the transmission of confidential data.
15. What is meant by the term "presence"?

DISCUSSION QUESTIONS

1. What are the risks of transmitting data over an unsecured Wi-Fi network? What steps are necessary to secure a Wi-Fi Protected Access network?
2. Why is an organization that employs centralized processing likely to have a different management decision-making philosophy than an organization that employs distributed processing?
3. Briefly discuss the evolution of wireless 3G and 4G communications.
4. Identify the fundamental differences between a file server system and a client/server system.
5. Briefly discuss the pros and cons of e-mail versus voice mail. Under what circumstances would you use each?
6. Develop a set of at least five criteria to use to determine if a given job is a good candidate for telecommuting.
7. Briefly explain how the GPS global navigation satellite system determines the position of a transmitter.

PROBLEM-SOLVING EXERCISES

1. You have been hired as a telecommunications consultant to help an organization select and purchase 500 smartphones for its sales force to use. Develop a list of key business requirements so that salespeople can use a smartphone effectively. Identify three different possible candidate smartphones. Which one would you recommend and why? Summarize your selection process and support your recommendation in a one-page memo.
2. As the CIO of a hospital, you are convinced that installing a wireless network and providing portable computers to nurses and doctors is a necessary step to reduce costs and improve patient care. Use PowerPoint or similar software to make a convincing presentation to management for adopting such a program. Your presentation must identify benefits and potential issues that must be overcome to make such a program a success.

TEAM ACTIVITIES

1. With two or three of your classmates, develop a proposal to install videoconferencing equipment in one of your school's classrooms so that students can view lectures or conduct conferences with others at remote videoconferencing facilities. What sort of equipment is required, who provides this equipment, and what does it cost to install and operate?
2. Form a team to identify the public locations (such as an airport, public library, or café) in your area where wireless LAN connections are available. Visit at least two locations and write a brief paragraph discussing your experience at each location trying to connect to the Internet.

WEB EXERCISES

1. Do research on the Web to identify the latest 4G communications developments. In your opinion, which carrier's 4G network is the most widely deployed? Write a short report on what you found.
2. Go online to find current information about the extent of telecommuting. Has the rate of telecommuting been increasing or decreasing in the past two years? What trends are predicted for the future? Would telecommuting be an attractive option to you? Why or why not? Briefly summarize your findings in a written report.

CAREER EXERCISES

1. Consider a future job position with which you are familiar through work experience, coursework, or a study of industry performance. How might you use some of the telecommunications and network applications described in this chapter in this job?
2. Do research to assess potential career opportunities in the telecommunications or networking industry. Consider resources such as the Human Resources and

Skills Development (HRDC), *Network World*, and *Computerworld*. Are there particular positions within these industries that offer good opportunities? What sort of background and education is required for candidates for these positions? You might be asked to summarize your findings for your class in a written or oral report.

CASE STUDIES

Case One
MAFIABOY[1]

 Richard Ivey School of Business
The University of Western Ontario — **IVEY** | Ivey Publishing

Professor Derrick Neufeld wrote this case solely to provide material for class discussion. The author does not intend to illustrate either effective or ineffective handling of a managerial situation. The author may have disguised certain names and other identifying information to protect confidentiality.

Richard Ivey School of Business Foundation prohibits any form of reproduction, storage or transmission without its written permission. Reproduction of this material is not covered under authorization by any reproduction rights organization. To order copies or request permission to reproduce materials, contact Ivey Publishing, Richard Ivey School of Business Foundation, The University of Western Ontario, London, Ontario, Canada, N6A 3K7; phone (519) 661-3208; fax (519) 661-3882; e-mail cases@ivey.uwo.ca.

Copyright © 2010, Richard Ivey School of Business Foundation Version: 2011-01-04

DISTRIBUTED DENIAL OF SERVICE ATTACK

Jack Hutchins, president of Aget Clothing, shook his head as he stared at the 1,000-plus page server log from the night before. According to Tim Shelley, Aget's part-time technology support person, the distributed denial of service (DDoS) attack had been 100 percent effective in shutting down Aget's Web services. Fortunately the attack occurred at 1:15 a.m. and lasted only 12 minutes, so that customer impact was minimal ... this time. But Hutchins worried about next time. He had asked Shelley to provide more information about the attack and what they could do about it and in response had received a stack of books, magazine articles, and white papers dealing with information technology (IT) security.

Hutchins's concerns were well founded, as attested by many recent news headlines: "Computer virus uses Canada Post scam," "Saskatchewan teen charged with hacking New York City-based website," "Gambler hit by online glitch unhappy with BC Lottery Corporation response." IT security failures strike fear into the hearts of technology-savvy business executives who cannot help but wonder, "Will we be next?" A 2009 study by the University of Toronto and Telus Corporation revealed that threats originate both from inside the organization (e.g., unauthorized access to information by employees) and outside (e.g., software viruses), with an average annual loss exceeding $834,000 per firm. DDoS attacks are a particularly debilitating threat, and Canada has earned a notorious reputation in this area thanks to one Canadian teenager.

Canada had developed some notoriety as a source of DDoS attacks. In the year 2000, 15-year-old Michael Calce sat at his computer in Montreal, contemplating which Web server to attack next. Three years earlier his best friend had died in a car accident, spawning a sense of powerlessness in the young boy. As he processed his new reality, Calce submerged himself in the dark side of the Web, eventually seeking out methods to attack online systems. Says Calce, "With these tools in hand, I began to feel like I was in control of the Internet, rather than the other way around. The sense of power and possibility was intoxicating." From the apparent safety of his alter ego, "Mafiaboy," Calce launched DDoS attacks on the very largest Web companies: Amazon, CNN, Dell, eBay, Yahoo!, and others. His activities rendered the servers unresponsive to legitimate customers for hours at a time and drew the attention of the financial markets and senior political leaders in Canada, the United States, and abroad. Some estimates pegged total damages from Mafiaboy's exploits at $1.7 billion. The fact that the devastating attacks were accomplished using such inexpensive and ubiquitous technologies as a PC and Internet connection was concerning enough, but that a mere teenager accomplished them was downright terrifying. The authorities eventually tracked down Calce, but only because he bragged about his exploits in some online chat rooms. He was sentenced to a year of probation, allowed only restricted use of the Internet, and given a small fine.

While a DDoS attack may sound technically sophisticated, in fact most are based on a simple and unimaginative idea: the prank telephone call. Imagine a naughty child who picks

---

[1]This case has been written on the basis of published sources only. Consequently, the interpretation and perspectives presented in this case are not necessarily those of Michael Calce.

up the telephone, calls a number at random, makes a joke, and then hangs up. To the victim, this single call might be a minor nuisance. If the child calls the same victim several times in a row, the victim might become annoyed at the inane disturbances. However, if the prankster gets 100 friends to call the same victim continuously, legitimate calls would no longer have a chance to get through. The victim's telephone system would have become compromised. Likewise, in a typical brute-force DDoS attack, the hacker may connect with thousands of software "bots" running on remote Internet-connected PCs (typically compromised using trojan viruses) and instruct them to contact a particular Web server at a given time. The server tries to respond to this incoming flood of requests, but it quickly becomes overloaded with the sheer volume of connection requests. Legitimate users have no chance to get through. The hacker can evade capture via "spoofing," that is, by modifying the return address on malicious data packets. In hacker parlance, the server has been "pwned" (see http://en.wikipedia.org/wiki/Pwn).

Just as technology evolves rapidly, cyber criminal behaviours such as DDoS attacks have become increasingly prevalent and sophisticated, and responding to them remains a challenge and depends on a few key factors. For example, if the content of the incoming DDoS packets is in some way characterizable, it may be possible to filter out (ignore) them and accept only legitimate packets. If the target of the attack is on a particular back-end resource or application, as opposed to the front-end network server, then load-balancing or authentication techniques may be configured to minimize the impact. If the DDoS packets are originating from a constrained geographical locale, a distributed server architecture may be designed to provide localized protection (e.g., duplicate servers in North America and Europe to handle the traffic from those regions).

As Hutchins pondered the attack, he felt decidedly unsettled about the state of his firm's IT security. True, since enabling the online sales channel five months ago, revenue had grown by $1.2 million or 4 percent. And yet, a major security breach that resulted in the shutdown of systems or theft of customer data could do irreparable damage to the firm. Perhaps the company should retreat from online sales and return to emphasizing traditional retail approaches.

Discussion Questions

1. Did Calce's punishment fit the crime?
2. How much computer expertise do you believe is required to launch a DDoS attack today?
3. Hackers clearly pose a threat to online business such as Amazon and eBay since, if their servers are inaccessible, the companies' business activity can be interrupted. Why should traditional (non IT-focused) businesses pay attention to hacker threats?
4. Should Hutchins retreat from doing business online?

SOURCES: "Mafiaboy Hacker Makes Amends," *Vancouver Sun*, June 28, 2010, *www.vancouversun.com/story_print.html?id=3210336&sponsor=*, accessed August 8, 2010. Calce. M., and Silverman, C., "Mafiaboy: A Portrait of the Hacker as a Young Man," Penguin Canada, 2010. "Saskatchewan Teen Charged with Hacking New York City-based Website," *Saskatoon StarPhoenix*, August 20, 2010, *www.thestarphoenix.com*, accessed August 23, 2010. "Gambler Hit by Online Glitch Unhappy with BCLC Response," CTV News, July 28, 2010, *www.ctvbc.ctv.ca/servlet/an/local/CTVNews/20100728*, accessed August 23, 2010. Taylor, L.C., "Computer Virus Uses Canada Post Scam," TheStar.com, April 23, 2010, *www.thestar.com/news/sciencetech/technology/article/799689*, accessed August 23, 2010. LeFort, A., and Hejazi, W., "2009 Rotman-TELUS Joint Study on Canadian IT Security Practices," *http://promo.telus.com/2009/Manage_Risk/index.html*, accessed August 23, 2010. Mirkovic, J., and Reiher, P., "A Taxonomy of DDoS Attack and DDoS Defence Mechanisms," *ACM SIGCOMM Computer Communication Review*, 34(2), 2004.

Case Two

Adidas Turns to Cellular Network for Inventory Data

The Adidas Group is a global leader in the sporting goods industry, offering a large portfolio of products in virtually every country in the world. Adidas Group brands include Adidas, Reebok, and TaylorMade—Adidas Golf. The Adidas Group headquarters is in Herzogenaurach, Germany, with 170 subsidiaries located around the world.

Adidas America is the U.S. division of the Adidas Group, employing around 2,000 people at its offices and distribution centres across the country. Recently, Adidas America discovered an inexpensive way to use telecommunications technologies to help its sales force become more productive.

Adidas sales representatives spend a lot of time travelling, paying visits to customers that range from small private sporting shops to large franchises. One major inconvenience for the sales force and the customers it calls on lies in checking current inventory levels for order placement. For years, a salesperson was required to phone Adidas customer service representatives (CSRs) to find out which products were in stock and which were sold out. Because Adidas inventory fluctuates frequently, this important information is needed to keep customers from being frustrated by back-ordered products. Having to phone for the information was frustrating for sales representatives as well as customers who would have to wait while the salesperson talked on the phone. It also over-burdened the CSRs, whose main job wasn't inventory reporting but assisting customers.

Adidas America information systems group thought it had a solution. It set up a VPN to enable customer representatives to securely connect to the corporate data from their laptops and access the inventory data directly. However, what looks good on paper doesn't always work well when implemented. Customer service employees were not comfortable visiting customers with their laptop computers, because they had to make the customer wait while they booted up and looked up information. Instead, they would typically take the customer's order, then check inventory later, getting back to the customer if there were product shortages. This certainly wasn't the intended workflow, and the solution ended up being as bad as the original problem.

Adidas sales force automation manager Tim Oligmueller was struck by an idea while attending a telecommunications trade show. He realized that the BlackBerry smartphones the sales force used could do much more than deliver e-mail and make phone calls. He saw demonstrations of BlackBerry phones that ran sophisticated business information systems. Oligmueller realized that the solution was in the salespeople's pockets all along. All that was required was for Adidas to invest in BlackBerry's Mobile Data System and Enterprise Server, and for the information system group to develop its own sales force and CRM applications.

Within two weeks and with an investment of less than $10,000, Oligmueller and his team had deployed a mobile information system that now allows salespeople to quickly and effortlessly access inventory data without inconveniencing customers or CSRs. Now salespeople can provide customers with the information they need to make quicker purchasing decisions on the spot. Salespeople and CSRs spend less time on the phone with each other, freeing both sides to be more productive. Customers are impressed with the improved service and technological innovativeness of the company. Salespeople can e-mail catalogues and order information to the customer as they converse. The new system has increased customer's confidence in doing business with Adidas.

Adidas is looking to many other wireless applications that can assist the sales force and others in the organization. As with all of the examples provided in this chapter, telecommunications technologies provide Adidas with rapid access to information when and where it is needed, empowering the company to maximize its productivity and potential and gain a competitive advantage.

Discussion Questions

1. Describe the problem that plagued Adidas's sales force that was addressed through a telecommunications solution.
2. Why do you think the hand-held solution was better than the laptop computer solution?

Critical Thinking Questions

1. What other types of information, besides inventory, might salespeople like to have access to over their BlackBerry phones?
2. What security concerns might arise over mobile access to private corporate information?

SOURCES: "Adidas America Equips Sales Team with Powerful Wireless Sales Tool," BlackBerry Case Study, *www.blackberry.com/products/pdfs/Adidas_LOB_CS_Final.pdf*, accessed February 20, 2010; About Adidas Web page, *www.adidas.com/us/shared/aboutadidas.asp*, accessed February 20, 2010; Schultz, Beth, "Realizing Rapid ROI Through Mobility," Computerworld White Paper, *www.slide-share.net/PingElizabeth/rapid-roirealizing-rapid-roi-through-mobility*, accessed February 20, 2010.

Questions for Web Case

See the website for this book to read about the Altitude Online case for this chapter. Following are questions concerning this Web case.

Altitude Online: Telecommunications and Networks

Discussion Questions

1. What telecommunications equipment is needed to fulfill Altitude Online's vision?
2. Why is it necessary to lease a line from a telecommunications company?

Critical Thinking Questions

1. What types of services will be provided over Altitude Online's network?
2. What considerations should Jon and his team take into account as they select telecommunications equipment?

NOTES

Sources for the opening vignette: "Procter & Gamble Revolutionizes Collaboration with Cisco Telepresence," Cisco website, *www.cisco.com/en/US/solutions/ns669/vid_pg.html*, accessed February 14, 2010; Hamblen, Matt, "PepsiCo to Deploy Telepresence from Cisco and BT Globally," *Computerworld*, *www.computerworld.com*, February 2, 2010; Hamblen, Matt, "Firms Use Collaboration Tools to Tap the Ultimate IP—Worker Ideas," *Computerworld*, *www.computerworld.com*, September 2, 2009; "Video Collaboration Studios," Computerworld Honors Program, 2008, *www.cwhonors.org/viewCaseStudy2008.asp?NominationID=697*.

1   Winston, Andrew, "Will Videoconferencing Kill Business Class Travel?" *Harvard Business Publishing*, August 3, 2009.
2   Svensson, Peter, "Google, Yahoo, eBay, and Microsoft Use Free Wi-Fi Hot Spots as Marketing Lure," *Associated Press*, November 10, 2009.
3   Dolan, Pamela Lewis, "Knowledge on Call: Finding New Uses for Smartphones," *American Medical News*, January 5, 2009.
4   "Telecom: Tools Connecting the World and Communicating About HIV," UNAIDS Web page, *www.unaids.org/en/KnowledgeCentre/Resources/FeatureStories/archive/2009/20091005_telecom.asp*, accessed October 5, 2009.
5   Ryerson University, "Rogers Communication Centre—Mission," *www.rcc.ryerson.ca/about/mission/index.htm*, accessed October 10, 2010.
6   Verizon FiOS Internet Web page, *www22.verizon.com/Residential/FiOSInternet/FiOSvsCable/FiOSvsCable.htm*.
7   Speedpass website, "How It Works: Overview," *www.essoextra.com/programs/SpeedpassHome.page*, accessed October 10, 2010.

8   Hansell, Saul, "Visa Introduces a Credit Card on a Phone," *New York Times*, April 10, 2009.
9   "New Bluetooth Application Will Let Sports Fans Share Experiences in Real Time," *Science Daily*, July 9, 2009.
10   Fleishman, Greg, "UWB Groups Shutters, Sends Tech to Bluetooth, USB Groups," *ars technica*, March 16, 2007.
11   "Smart Meters: A New Way to Think about Electricity," Ontario Ministry of Energy website, *www.mei.gov.on.ca/en/energy/conservation/smartmeters/*, accessed October 10, 2010.
12   Crow, Barbara, Longford, Graham, et al., "Engaging Citizens in Community Wi-Fi: Insights from Three Canadian Case Studies" presentation at CICT Conference 2006, *www.cwirp.org/files/CICT_WiFi_case_studies.pdf*, accessed October 10, 2010.
13   "Hotel Chatter Annual Wi-Fi Report 2009," *www.hotelchatter.com/special/Best_WiFi_Hotels_2009*, accessed January 6, 2010.
14   Iridium Everywhere Web page, *www.iridium.com/about/globalnetwork.php*, accessed November 18, 2009.
15   Wells, Jane, "Iridium Satellite Is Back and Ready for Liftoff," *CNBC.com*, February 26, 2009.
16   Rosenberg, Barry, "VSAT Proves Crucial to Battlefield Communications," *Defense Systems*, June 5, 2009.
17   "IPS Implements Mesh Control Network for SE Asia Beverage Industry," *Automation*, February 11, 2009.
18   "Data Explained," *Vodaworld Online*, December 26, 2009, *www.vodaworld.co.za/showarticle.asp?id=2200*.

19 Hamblen, Matt, "3G Networks Don't Deliver Speeds Users Expect, Gartner Says," *Computerworld*, January 27, 2009.

20 Nystedt, Dan, "China Mobile's 3G Coverage to Rapidly Expand," *Computerworld*, November 18, 2009.

21 "AT&T Promises Formal 4G Service in 2011," *electronista*, February 17, 2009.

22 "Success Stories—Teliasonera in Norway Pioneers the 4G Wireless Broadband Services in the World," Huawei website, *www.huawei.com/publications/view.do?id=6035&cid=11341&pid=2043*, accessed March 12, 2010.

23 Industry Canada, "Frequency Allocation for Maravedis Projects an Accumulated 21 Million and *WiMAX*," *www.ic.gc.ca/eic/site/ict-tic.nsf/eng/it07902.html, accessed October 11, 2010.*

24 Goldstein, Phil, "Intel: Clearwire Has Sufficient Capital," FierceWireless website, *www.fiercewireless.com*, February 12, 2009.

25 Associated Press, "Sprint, Others Give Clearwire $1.5 B in Financing," *www.moneycentral.msn.com*, accessed November 10, 2009.

26 "Intel to Launch Centrino WiMAX 6250 Codenamed Kilmer Peak in Q1 2010," *Going Wimax.com*, November 10, 2009, *www.goingwimax.com/intel-to-launch-centrino-wimax-6250-codenamed kilmer-peak-in-q1-2010*.

27 Lemon, Summer, "Intel in WiMAX Push with Kilmer Peak Release," *Computerworld UK*, November 9, 2009.

28 Akhtar, Iyaz, "PANiQ's Clothing Line Lets You Control Your Toys," *Gadgetell*, January 22, 2009.

29 "Docklands Light Railway on Track for Growth with New Cisco LAN and VoIP-Based Public Address System," *New Blaze*, February 10, 2009.

30 Thorpe, Simon, "Peer-to-Peer Network Exposes Document Detailing US Congress Ethics Probes," November 2, 2009, *http://blogs.oracle.com/irm/2009/11peer-to-peer_network_exposes_d.html*, accessed March 12, 2010.

31 "Netkrom Customer Success Stories Metropolitan Backbone Network," *www.netkrom.com/success_stories_lima.html*, accessed December 29, 2009.

32 "The CFHIS Security Solution," National Defense website, *www.mdn.ca/health-sante/proj/cfhis-sisfc/secur-eng.asp*, accessed October 10, 2010.

33 "NE20 Serves Datang Power WAN," *www.huawei.com/products/datacomm/catalog.do?id=361*, accessed December 29, 2009.

34 "LaserPro," Harland Financial Solutions website, *www.harlandfinancialsolutions.com/search.php?searchStr=laserpro*, accessed March 12, 2010.

35 Packet Trap Networks home page, *www.packettrap.com*, accessed October 11, 2010.

36 "Bertelsmann AG: Strategic Information Security in a Distributed Enterprise Environment," PGP website, *www.pgp.com/insight/customers/customer_profile_bertelsmann.html*, accessed March 12, 2010.

37 Vijayan, Jaikumar, "Researchers Use PC to Crack Encryption for Next-Gen GSM Networks," *The Industry Standard*, January 14, 2010.

38 National Defence website, accessed October 11, 2010.

39 "Telecom: Tools Connecting the World and Communicating About HIV," UNAIDS Web page, *www.unaids.org/en/KnowledgeCentre/Resources/FeatureStories/archive/2009/20091005_telecom.asp*. accessed October 5, 2009.

40 Target website, "Panasonic Link-to-Cell Cordless Phone," *www.target.com/Panasonic-Link-to-Cell-Cordless-Phone -KX-TH1212B/dp/B00138*, accessed January 20, 2010.

41 "Pilots 'Can Control Mobile Use' Via Picocells," *Picocell Industry News*, December 19, 2009.

42 "Reverse 911 Service Coming to Montreal," CBC News, February 2, 2011.

43 CRTC website, "National Do Not Call List," *www.crtc.gc.ca/eng/dncl/brochure_consumer.htm*, accessed October 10, 2010.

44 Arellano, Nester, "Cross-Border Telecommuting on the Rise in Canada," IT Business.ca, April 1, 2009, *www.itbusiness.ca/it/client/en/home/News.asp?id=52634*, accessed October 11, 2010.

45 Beizer, Doug, "DSIA Will Use Telework to Retain Displaced Employees," *Federal Computer Week*, September 4, 2009.

46 "Ryder Levett Bucknall Deploys LifeSize HD Video Conferencing Systems Across UK Offices," LifeSize Web page, October 1, 2009, *www.lifesize.com/Company/News_and_Events/Press_ Releases/2009/Rider_Levet_Bucknall*, accessed November 20, 2009.

47 "Covisint Customer Success Stories—General Motors," *www.covisint.com/customers/successStories/gm.shtml*, accessed December 11, 2009.

48 "Understanding GPS Technology," *beagle software*, *www.beaglesoft.com/gpstechnology.htm*, accessed November 20, 2009.

49 Ibid.

50 Liedtke, Michael, "Google's Latest—Tracking People by Cell Phone," *KATU.com News Portland Oregon*, February 6, 2009, www.katu.com/internal?st=print&if=39243012&path=/news, accessed November 20, 2009.

51 Gustafson, Krystina, "Cell Phones Get Better at Tracking People," *www.cnbc.com/id/33622833*, accessed November 5, 2009.

CHAPTER
· 7 ·

The Internet, Web, Intranets, and Extranets

PRINCIPLES	LEARNING OBJECTIVES
▪ **The Internet provides a critical infrastructure for delivering and accessing information and services.**	▪ Briefly describe how the Internet works, including methods for connecting to it and the role of Internet service providers.
▪ **Originally developed as a document-management system, the World Wide Web has grown to become a primary source of news and information, an indispensable conduit for commerce, and a popular hub for social interaction, entertainment, and communication.**	▪ Describe the World Wide Web and how it works. ▪ Explain the use of markup languages, Web browsers, and Web servers. ▪ Identify and briefly describe the process of creating software applications for the Web.
▪ **The Internet and Web provide numerous resources for finding information, communicating and collaborating, socializing, conducting business and shopping, and being entertained.**	▪ List and describe several sources of information on the Web. ▪ Describe methods of finding information on the Web. ▪ List and describe several forms of online communication, along with the benefits and drawbacks of each, in terms of convenience and effectiveness. ▪ Explain Web 2.0 and provide examples of Web 2.0 sites. ▪ List and describe sources of online media and entertainment. ▪ Explain how Web resources are used to support shopping and travel. ▪ Briefly name and describe two useful Internet utilities.
▪ **Popular Internet and Web technologies have been applied to business networks in the form of intranets and extranets.**	▪ Explain how intranets and extranets use Internet and Web technologies, and describe how the two differ.

(Source: asharkyu/Shutterstock.com.)

Information Systems in the Global Economy
Avon

Avon Expands to Facebook and the Cloud

Since 1886, Avon has been well known for its women's cosmetics. Today, Avon is the world's largest direct seller, with 6.2 million independent sales representatives in more than 100 countries and annual revenue of more than $10 billion. Over the years, the Avon catalogue has expanded to include several brands, including Avon Color, Avon Skincare, Avon Bath & Body, Avon Hair Care, Avon Wellness, Avon Fragrance, M-The Men's Catalogue, and mark., a new brand designed for young women.

Like all successful large corporations, Avon has leveraged Internet and Web technologies to the benefit of its customers, sales representatives, and shareholders. Recently, Avon corporate leaders became aware of the growing use of social media (such as Facebook, Twitter, and MySpace) and its potential as a marketing, communication, and customer relationship management (CRM) tool. The company has also become sold on the benefits of cloud computing. Cloud computing refers to the use of Internet servers—now known as the cloud—to deliver applications and information to users anywhere, anytime. Avon hired the cloud computing experts at Appirio and the SaaS CRM specialists at Salesforce to combine Internet technologies and create a cutting-edge system that allows sales representatives to reach more customers. Appirio calls the system a cloud of clouds.

Avon decided to test the social media waters with its youngest and hippest brand, mark. According to Avon.com, mark. is the "number two trend brand in the world" and "celebrates remarkable young women who are making their mark in the world." The young women who sell and buy mark. products are connected to online social networks. Avon found that this group no longer responds to e-mail marketing campaigns. Most communicate primarily using social networks rather than e-mail. It made good business sense to appeal to them through their social networks, where each has a complex social graph involving hundreds of friends, each connected to other users, groups, and businesses.

To serve this young and vibrant market, Avon worked with Appirio to develop a Facebook application for its mark. sales representatives. The application, named mark. book, allows Avon sales representatives to send product announcements to a select group of Facebook friends that are likely to find a particular product enticing. The mark.book application uses descriptive tags for Facebook friends that allow the representatives to easily categorize them by their interests, age, region, and other revealing characteristics. For example, using mark.book, a representative can send a wall post to friends who are graduating from college or university informing them of cosmetics that are useful for job interviews. The wall post includes a link to an Avon page that provides more information about the product. The Avon Web page can track who has visited from Facebook and provide the representative with follow-up information.

Avon's Facebook application is connected to Avon's cloud-based CRM system from Salesforce through middleware designed by Appirio. Salesforce allows mark. representatives to manage sales campaigns and offers made through the Facebook application using a convenient dashboard application. The Salesforce dashboard can also analyze key words and tags used to push promotions to Facebook friends and provide insight into what tags yield the best results. A higher-level dashboard lets senior managers track all sales through the Facebook application to reward representatives with high sales and track areas of growth and opportunity.

Avon's cloud of clouds application combines the Facebook cloud with the Salesforce cloud to provide a convenient Web interface to powerful sales, marketing, and CRM systems. Sales have doubled for the 1,000-plus mark. representatives who are using the new system. The social media approach is believed to be twice as effective for mark. customers as e-mail campaigns. Avon has effectively used mark.book as a vehicle to drive the company to the next generation of direct selling. Where once "Avon ladies" rang doorbells singing "Avon calling," today "mark.girls" post offers to their Facebook friends who are likely to find the offers appealing.

Avon and others, with the help of companies like Appirio, are discovering rich new opportunities for businesses on the Internet and Web. Internet and Web technologies are evolving at a rapid pace, and businesses need to stay on their toes to profit from rapid technological advances.

As you read this chapter, consider the following:

- What unique features of the Internet and Web make them popular choices for many business communication applications?
- In what ways do people use the Internet and Web to improve their quality of life? How do businesses use these technologies to improve the bottom line?

Why Learn About the Internet?

To say that the Internet has had a big impact on organizations of all types and sizes would be an understatement. Since the early 1990s, when the Internet was first used for commercial purposes, it has affected all aspects of business. Businesses use the Internet to sell and advertise their products and services, reaching out to new and existing customers. If you are undecided about a career, you can use the Internet to investigate career opportunities and salaries using sites such as *www.monster.ca* and *workopolis.ca*. Most companies have Internet sites that list job opportunities, descriptions, qualifications, salaries, and benefits. If you have a job, you probably use the Internet daily to communicate with co-workers and your boss. People working in every field and at every level use the Internet in their work. Purchasing agents use the Internet to save millions of dollars in supplies every year. Travel and events-management agents use the Internet to find the best deals on travel and accommodations. Automotive engineers use the Internet to work with other engineers around the world developing designs and specifications for new automobiles and trucks. Property managers use the Internet to find the best prices and opportunities for commercial and residential real estate. Whatever your career, you will probably use the Internet daily. This chapter starts by exploring how the Internet works and then investigates the many exciting opportunities for using the Internet to help you achieve your goals.

The Internet is the world's largest computer network. Recall from Chapter 1 that the Internet is actually a collection of interconnected networks, all freely exchanging information using a common set of protocols. The Internet began as an experiment linking together research institutes and universities. Over time, more organizations were connected to the Internet, followed by homes and businesses, until today, when it is difficult to find a computer that is not connected to the Internet. More than 750 million computers, or hosts,[1] make up today's Internet, supporting nearly 2 billion users. Those numbers are expected to continue growing.[2] Figure 7.1 shows the staggering growth of the Internet, as measured by the number of Internet host sites, or domain names. Domain names are discussed later in the chapter.

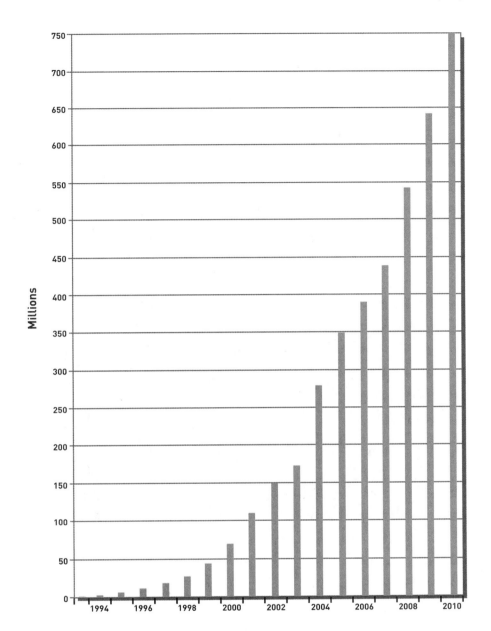

Figure 7.1

Internet Growth: Number of Internet Domain Names

(Source: Data from "The Internet Domain Survey," *www.isc.org*.)

USE AND FUNCTIONING OF THE INTERNET

The Internet is truly international in scope, with users on every continent—including Antarctica. More than 26 million people in Canada (77.7 percent of the population) use the Internet. Although Canada has high Internet penetration among its population, it does not constitute the majority of people online. Of all the people using the Internet, citizens of Asian countries make up 42.0 percent, Europeans 24.2 percent, and North Americans only 13.5 percent.[3] China has by far the most Internet users at 420 million, which is more people than the total U.S. population, but is only 31.6 percent of China's total population. The Internet is expanding around the globe, though at differing rates for each country. For example, most Internet use in South Korea is through high-speed broadband connections, and over 81 percent of the population is online. By contrast, north of the border in North Korea, the government prohibits Internet use and other civil liberties. Not coincidentally, South Korea has a vibrant thriving economy, while North Korea is globally isolated and economically unstable. Being connected to the Internet provides global economic opportunity to individuals, businesses, and countries.

The freedom of expression provided by the Internet has been a source of controversy in many countries. The government of China, for example, blocks Internet content that it decides is subversive or threatening to "national unity."[4] Ireland, France, Australia, and several other countries have blocked Internet access to individuals caught illegally downloading copyrighted material.[5] Other countries have blocked content that is considered blasphemous to their national religions.[6] Even Canada blocks some Web content.[7] However, the Internet includes so many connections that completely controlling its flow of information is next to impossible.

China has over 420 million Internet users online, which is only 32 percent of its population.[8]

(Source: Reuters/Landov.)

ARPANET
A project started by the U.S. Department of Defense (DoD) in 1969 as both an experiment in reliable networking and a means to link the DoD and military research contractors, including many universities doing military-funded research.

Internet Protocol (IP)
A communication standard that enables computers to route communications traffic from one network to another as needed.

The ancestor of the Internet was the **ARPANET**, a project started by the U.S. Department of Defense (DoD) in 1969. The ARPANET was both an experiment in reliable networking and a means to link the DoD and military research contractors, including many universities doing military-funded research. (*ARPA* stands for the Advanced Research Projects Agency, the branch of the DoD in charge of awarding grant money. The agency is now known as DARPA—the added *D* is for *Defense*.) The ARPANET was highly successful, and every university in the country wanted to use it. This swift growth made the ARPANET difficult to manage, particularly its large and rapidly growing number of university sites. The ARPANET was eventually broken into two networks: MILNET, which included all military sites, and a new, smaller ARPANET, which included all the nonmilitary sites. The two networks remained connected, however, through use of the **Internet Protocol** (**IP**), which enables computers to route communications traffic from one network to another as needed. All the networks connected to the Internet use IP so they can communicate. Table 7.1 outlines a brief history of the Internet.

Today, people, universities, and companies are attempting to make the Internet faster and easier to use. To speed Internet access, a group of corporations and universities called the University Corporation for Advanced Internet Development (UCAID) is working on a faster, alternative Internet. Called Internet2 (I2), Next Generation Internet (NGI), or Abilene, depending on the universities or corporations involved, the new Internet offers the potential of faster Internet speeds—up to 2 Gbps per second or more.[9] The *National LambdaRail* (*NLR*) is a cross-country, high-speed (10 Gbps) fibre-optic network dedicated

Year	No. of Internet Hosts	Internet Milestone
1970	13	AT&T installs the first cross-country link to connect networks across the United States
1973	35	ARPANET goes international as it expands overseas to University College in London, England, and the Royal Radar Establishment in Norway
1984	1,024	ARPANET divided into two subnetworks: MILNET, for military needs, and ARPANET, for research
1990	313,000	The ARPANET project officially concluded, and "the Internet" turned over to the public, managed by the Internet Society (ISOC)
1991	617,000	The Commercial Internet Exchange (CIX) Association established, allowing businesses to connect to the Internet
1993	1,500,000	The first Web browser, Mosaic, released to Internet users
1994	3,864,000	Birth of online banking and Web-based transactions
1996	12,881,000	Internet2 established
2003	171,638,297	National LambdaRail established
2004	285,139,107	The emergence of Web 2.0 and the Web as a computing platform
2007	489,774,269	The release of the iPhone, putting the Internet in the pockets of millions of users
2009	681,064,561	The rise of location-based Internet apps that provide location-aware services using GPS

Table 7.1

A Brief History of the Internet

to research in high-speed networking applications.[10] The NLR provides a "unique national networking infrastructure" to advance networking research and next-generation network-based applications in science, engineering, and medicine. This new high-speed fibre-optic network will support the ever-increasing need of scientists to gather, transfer, and analyze massive amounts of scientific data.

How the Internet Works

In the early days of the Internet, the major telecommunications (telecom) companies around the world agreed to connect their networks so that users on all the networks could share information over the Internet. These large telecom companies are called *network service providers* (*NSPs*). Examples are Bell Canada, Sprint, British Telecom, and AT&T. The cables, routers, switching stations, communication towers, and satellites that make up these networks are the hardware over which Internet traffic flows. The combined hardware of these and other NSPs—the fibre-optic cables that span the globe over land and under the sea—makes up the Internet **backbone**.

The Internet transmits data from one computer, called a *host*, to another. See Figure 7.2 on the next page. If the receiving computer is on a network to which the first computer is directly connected, it can send the message directly. If the receiving and sending computers are not directly connected to the same network, the sending computer relays the message to another computer that can forward it. The message is typically sent through one or more routers to reach its destination. It is not unusual for a message to pass through a dozen or more routers on its way from one part of the Internet to another.

The Internet routes data packets over the network backbone from router to router to reach their destinations.

backbone
One of the Internet's high-speed, long-distance communications links.

Figure 7.2

Routing Messages over
the Internet

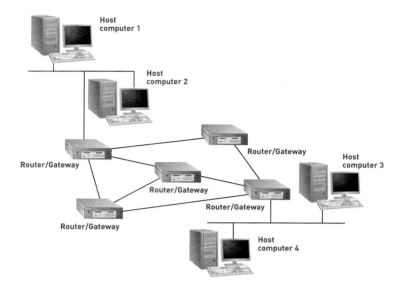

**Transmission Control
Protocol (TCP)**
The widely used transport-layer
protocol that most Internet
applications use with IP.

IP address
A 64-bit or 128-bit number that
identifies a computer on the
Internet.

Uniform Resource Locator (URL)
A Web address that specifies the
exact location of a Web page
using letters and words that map
to an IP address and a location
on the host.

The various telecommunications networks that are linked to form the Internet work much the same way—they pass data around in chunks called *packets*, each of which carries the addresses of its sender and its receiver along with other technical information. The set of conventions used to pass packets from one host to another is the IP. Many other protocols are used in connection with IP. The best known is the **Transmission Control Protocol** (**TCP**). Many people use "TCP/IP" as an abbreviation for the combination of TCP and IP used by most Internet applications. After a network following these standards links to the Internet's backbone, it becomes part of the worldwide Internet community.

Each computer on the Internet has an assigned address, called its IP address, that identifies it on the Internet. An **IP address** is a 64-bit number that identifies a computer on the Internet. The 64-bit number is typically divided into four bytes and translated to decimal; for example, 69.32.133.79. The Internet will soon be upgraded to IPv6, which uses 128-bit addresses to provide for many more devices.[11] Because people prefer to work with words rather than numbers, a system called the Domain Name System (DNS) was created. Domain names such as *www.cengage.com* are mapped to IP addresses such as 69.32.133.79 using the DNS. If you type either www.cengage.com or 69.32.133.79 into your Web browser, you will access the same website.

A **Uniform Resource Locator** (**URL**) is a Web address that specifies the exact location of a Web page using letters and words that map to an IP address and a location on the host. The URL gives those who provide information over the Internet a standard way to designate where Internet resources such as servers and documents are located. Consider the URL for Course Technology, http://www.cengage.com/coursetechnology.

The "http" specifies the access method and tells your software to access a file using the Hypertext Transport Protocol. This is the primary method for interacting with the Internet. In many cases, you don't need to include http:// in a URL because it is the default protocol. The "www" part of the address sometimes, but not always, signifies that the address is associated with the World Wide Web service. The URL *www.cengage.com* is the domain name that identifies the Internet host site. The part of the address following the domain name—/coursetechnology—specifies an exact location on the host site.

Domain names must adhere to strict rules. They always have at least two parts, with each part separated by a dot (period). For some Internet addresses, the far right part of the domain name is the country code, such as au for Australia, ca for Canada, dk for Denmark, fr for France, de (Deutschland) for Germany, and jp for Japan. Many Internet addresses have a code denoting affiliation categories, such as com for business sites and edu for education sites. Table 7.2 contains a few popular categories. The far left part of the domain name identifies the host network or host provider, which might be the name of a university or business. Countries outside of Canada may use top-level domain affiliations different from the ones described in the table.

Affiliation ID	Affiliation
com	Business sites
gc.ca	Federal government sites
net	Networking sites
org	Nonprofit organization sites
mobi	Mobile-compatible sites for smartphones

Table 7.2

Canadian Top-Level Domain Affiliations

The Internet Corporation for Assigned Names and Numbers (ICANN) is responsible for managing IP addresses and Internet domain names. One of its primary concerns is to make sure that each domain name represents only one individual or entity—the one that legally registers it. For example, if your teacher wanted to use *www.course.com* for a course website, he or she would discover that domain name has already been registered by Course Technology and is not available. ICANN uses companies called *accredited domain name registrars* to handle the business of registering domain names. For example, you can visit *www.godaddy.com*, an accredited registrar, to find out if a particular name has already been registered; if not, you can register the name for around $13 per year. Once you do so, ICANN will not allow anyone else to use that domain name as long as you pay the yearly fee.

Accessing the Internet

Although you can connect to the Internet in numerous ways, Internet access is not distributed evenly throughout the world or even throughout a city. Which access method you choose is determined by the size and capability of your organization or system, your budget, and the services available to you. See Figure 7.3.

Figure 7.3

Several Ways to Access the Internet

Users can access the Internet several ways, including using a LAN server, telephone lines, a high-speed service, or a wireless network.

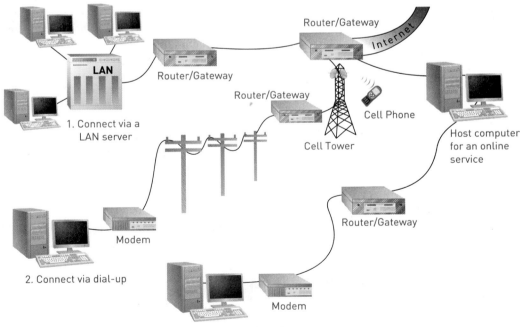

1. Connect via a LAN server

2. Connect via dial-up

Connect via high-speed service

Connecting via LAN Server

This approach is used by businesses and organizations that manage a local area network (LAN). By connecting a server on the LAN to the Internet using a router, all users on the LAN are provided access to the Internet. Business LAN servers are typically connected to the Internet at very fast data rates, sometimes in the hundreds of Mbps. In addition, you can share the higher cost of this service among several dozen LAN users to allow a reasonable cost per user.

Connecting via Internet Service Providers

Internet service provider (ISP)
An organization that provides Internet access to people.

Companies and residences unable to connect directly to the Internet through a LAN server must access the Internet through an Internet service provider. An **Internet service provider** (**ISP**) is an organization that provides Internet access to people. Thousands of organizations serve as ISPs, ranging from universities that make the Internet available to students and faculty, to small Internet businesses, to major telecommunications giants such as Rogers, Bell Canada, and Telus. To connect to the Internet through an ISP, you must have an account with the service provider (for which you usually pay) along with software (such as a browser) and devices (such as a computer or smartphone) that support a connection via TCP/IP.

Perhaps the least expensive but slowest connection provided by ISPs is a dial-up connection. A *dial-up Internet connection* uses a modem and standard phone line to "dial up" and connect to the ISP server. Dial-up is considered the slowest of connections because it is restricted by the 56 Kbps limitation of traditional phone line service. A dial-up connection also ties up the phone line so that it is unavailable for voice calls. Although dial-up was originally the only way to connect to the Internet from home, it is rapidly becoming replaced by high-speed services.

Several "high-speed" Internet services are available for home and business. They include cable modem connections from cable television companies, DSL connections from phone companies, and satellite connections from satellite companies. These technologies were discussed in Chapter 6. High-speed services provide data transfer rates between 1 and 15 Mbps. Some businesses and universities use the very fast T1 or T3 lines to connect to the Internet. T1 and T3 support high data rates, but have additional value compared to DSL and cable connections because they can send many signals simultaneously.

In addition to connecting to the Internet through wired systems such as phone lines and television cables, wireless Internet over cellular and Wi-Fi networks have become common. Thousands of public Wi-Fi services are available in coffee shops, airports, hotels, and elsewhere, where Internet access is provided free, for an hourly rate, or for a monthly subscription fee. In 2010, McDonald's became the biggest provider of free wireless in the United States when it began offering free Wi-Fi at 11,000 of its 13,000 restaurants.[12] Many businesses have followed suit, using free Wi-Fi access as a tool to attract customers. Wi-Fi is even making its way into aircraft, allowing business travellers to be productive during air travel by accessing e-mail and corporate networks.

Cell phone carriers also provide Internet access for handsets, notebooks, and tablets. New 4G mobile phone services rival wired high-speed connections enjoyed at home and work. Rogers, Bell, Telus, and other popular carriers are working to bring 4G service to subscribers, beginning in large metropolitan areas. Rogers' HSPA+ network provides up to 21 Mbps.[13] Bell and Telus are rolling out Long-Term Evolution (LTE) networks that promise to be even faster. By purchasing data plans, users can connect to these networks with smartphones and computers. Table 7.3 compares data transfer speeds and popular Internet services based on 2011 quotes from Rogers, Bell, and Skyway West.

Table 7.3

Internet Service Options Compared

Service	Download Speed Per Monthly Cost: Standard Plan	Download Speed Per Monthly Cost: Premium Plan
Cable	3 Mbps/$35.99	50 Mpbs/$99.99
DSL	2 Mbps/$24.95	25 Mbps/$55.95
Satellite	1 Mbps/$69.99	5 Mbps/$399.99
Cellular	1 Mbps/$30.00	21 Mbps/$65.00
Dial-up	56 Kbps/$19.95	N/A

When Apple introduced the iPhone, one of its slogans was the "Internet in your pocket." The iPhone proves the popularity of and the potential for Internet services over a handset. Many other smartphones followed hot on the heels of the iPhone, offering similar services on all the cellular networks. More recently, the iPhone 4 brought video calling into vogue, while the iPad and other tablets provide anywhere, anytime access to all types of Internet services on a larger display.

Most ISP services are assumed to provide any Internet service in unlimited capacity. Unlimited Internet access is becoming less common, however, as ISPs work to reign in bandwidth hogs who ISPs claim are slowing down service for normal users. Rogers implemented a 175 GB per month cap for its heaviest Internet users, charging $0.50 for each GB that a subscriber goes over the cap.[14]

Connecting Wirelessly

The iPad connects to the Internet over cellular or Wi-Fi networks.

(Source: Stefan Sollfors/Alamy.)

Cloud Computing

Cloud computing refers to a computing environment where software and storage are provided as an Internet service and accessed with a Web browser. As Internet connection speeds increase and wireless Internet access broadens, more computing activities are being delivered over the Internet rather than from software installed on PCs. Google and Yahoo! store the e-mail of many users, along with calendars, contacts, and to-do lists. Facebook provides social interaction and can store personal photos, as can Flickr and a dozen other photo sites. Pandora delivers music, and YouTube delivers movies. Google Docs, Microsoft Web Apps, Zoho, 37signals, Flypaper, Adobe Buzzword, and others provide Web-delivered productivity and information management software. Soon, it seems, most computing will take place on Internet servers through the Web browser. Communications, contacts, photos, documents, music, and media will be available to you from any Internet-connected device. This is the world of cloud computing.

The term "cloud computing" comes from the use of a cloud in network diagrams to represent the Internet in an abstract sense. See Figure 7.4. Cloud computing service providers manage their services much like a utility company manages its resources. The processing and storage requirements of all its clients can be spread over numerous servers. As business grows, more servers are added. If one server fails, others pick up the slack. Cloud computing is extremely scalable and often takes advantage of virtualization technologies.

cloud computing
A computing environment where software and storage are provided as an Internet service and are accessed with a Web browser.

Figure 7.4

Cloud Computing

Cloud computing uses applications and resources delivered via the Web.

(Source: Helder Almeida/Shutterstock.com.)

Danger in the Cloud

The general public has embraced cloud computing more readily than many businesses. Millions of people trust cloud computing technologies from Google to store their e-mail, appointment calendars, and address books. They trust Facebook to store their photos and personal information. Businesses have been more hesitant to trust Internet firms with their valuable corporate information—and with good cause.

Cloud computing services do fail, leaving users unable to access programs or data. It is not uncommon for Google, Twitter, Microsoft, Facebook, and other online companies to experience server outages. In other cases, cloud computing services have lost customer data. Perhaps the most notable was the catastrophe with T-Mobile's Sidekick smartphone service. In October 2009, T-Mobile informed its thousands of Sidekick users that it had lost their data and might not be able to recover it. It advised the users not to turn off their cell phones, as the data stored on them would be irrecoverable. The Sidekick uses a cloud computing data service from a Microsoft subsidiary ironically named Danger, Inc., to back up user data from smartphones. The data stored includes user contacts, calendars, notes, photos, text messages, and other data typically stored on mobile phones. The cloud storage system for this data failed and had no backup system in place. As angry Sidekick users posted comments online, the failure gained the attention of businesses and consumers.

In the end, much of the data was recovered, and those who lost data were compensated with a $100 credit. Still, the incident is considered a black eye for T-Mobile and cloud computing. Similar incidents such as Gmail outages cause businesses to be leery about trusting cloud computing with important data.

The City of Los Angeles has decided to trust Google and its online applications rather than using traditional software such as Microsoft Office. The decision was not made lightly. The $75-million contract came with several stipulations. Google has agreed to pay a considerable penalty if a security breach occurs. Google is legally responsible for any release of data in violation of a nondisclosure agreement. The city's data must also be encrypted, stored on a dedicated server, and kept in the United States with limited access.

Such assurances are essential if cloud computing is going to live up to its potential for businesses. Microsoft wants to see new laws designed to offer protection for data stored in the cloud and to enact stiffer penalties for hackers who attempt to illegally access it. Microsoft hopes that government support for cloud computing will spread globally so that data can be safe wherever it is stored within the global business infrastructure. "We need a free trade agreement for data," says Brad Smith, senior vice president and general counsel at Microsoft.

Without government assistance, open standards, and international cooperation, some fear that cloud computing will be controlled by two or three big companies, leaving smaller companies unable to compete. Users may be locked into one service provider's proprietary system. Open standards, on the other hand, would allow customers to easily transfer their cloud computing services from one company to another. Smith calls for cloud computing vendors to band together to establish open standards for data storage that provide transparency for security and privacy. "Simply put, it should not be enough for service providers simply to say that their services are private and secure," Smith said. "There needs to be some transparency about why this is the case."

Jonathan Rochelle, a group product manager at Google, suggests that cloud computing isn't any more dangerous than storing data on your own PC or server. "While it feels more comfortable, the same way the money under your mattress feels more comfortable, it may not be the best way to manage your information," suggests Rochelle. The point is that the public is willing to trust banks and companies with their financial well-being, so why not trust the companies that provide cloud computing services with your information?

Discussion Questions

1. Would you be comfortable storing all of your data, including personal data, media, and professional data, in the cloud rather than on your own PC? Why or why not?
2. What assurances and practices do you feel are necessary from cloud computing firms to earn the trust of businesses and the public?

Critical Thinking Questions

1. What role can government(s) play in helping cloud computing realize its potential?
2. Why do you think Microsoft, a company that has been historically opposed to open standards, is now lobbying for them?

SOURCES: Weinschenk, Carl, "T-Mobile Resumes Sidekick Sales Despite Costly Risk," NewsFactor, www.newsfactor.com/story.xhtml?story_id=70139&full_skip=1, November 17, 2009; Resende, Patricia, "L.A. Cloud Contract Goes to Google Over Microsoft," News-Factor, www.newsfactor.com/story.xhtml?story_id=69765, October 28, 2009; Thibodeau, Patrick, "Microsoft Seeks Legal Protections for Data Stored in Cloud," CIO, www.cio.com/article/520724/Microsoft_Seeks_Legal_Protections_for_Data_Stored_in_Cloud?source=rss_all, January 21, 2010; Gross, Grant, "Microsoft Calls for Cloud Computing Transparency," ITWorld, www.itworld.com/government/93452/microsoft-calls-cloud-computing-transparency?utm_source=feedburner&utm_medium=feed&utm_campaign=Feed%3A+Itw orldToday+%28ITworld+Today%29, January 20, 2010; Dunn, John E., "Internet Heading for 'Perfect Storm'," CIO, www.cio.com/article/519770/Internet_Heading_for_Perfect_Storm_?source=rss_all, January 20, 2010.

Cloud computing offers tremendous advantages to businesses.[15] By outsourcing business information systems to the cloud, a business saves on system design, installation, and maintenance. Employees can also access corporate systems from any Internet-connected computer using a standard Web browser. For example, RezBook by Urbanspoon is a cloud computing application (often called an "app" for short) designed for the iPad to manage reservations for restaurants. Hosts and wait staff in a restaurant use their iPads to access the system stored on an Internet server to check for open tables, track each table's progress through a meal, and store and access customer reservations.[16]

In addition to cloud applications such as Rezbook, cloud computing is also used to provide online storage. Some companies, including Microsoft and Google, provide free online storage (with capacity limitations) for access from any Internet-connected computer. Dropbox, SugarSync, and others include file backup and synchronization services to their cloud storage offerings.

In business, cloud computing is often referred to as Software as a Service (SaaS), and the vendors that provide the software are application service providers (ASPs). Salesforce.com is an example of SaaS as applied to customer relationship management (CRM). Servicing more than 50,000 businesses, Salesforce provides hundreds of CRM applications for a wide variety of business types. Employees of those businesses can use a Web browser to access customer data, stored on Salesforce servers, from their desktops, notebooks, and cell phones. Businesses that use Salesforce.com don't have to worry about supporting complicated CRM software on their servers, installing updates and security patches, and troubleshooting problems. The SaaS provider manages it all.

Cloud computing can have several methods of deployment. Those that have been discussed thus far are considered public cloud services. *Public cloud* refers to service providers that offer their cloud-based services to the general public, whether that is an individual using Google calendar or a corporation using Salesforce.com. There is also a *private cloud* deployment, where cloud technology is used within the confines of a private network. Corus Automotive Engineering Group found that private cloud technology from Univa UD was ideal for managing its massive parallel processing technical applications. The cloud technology improved application performance by 32 percent with 57 percent fewer server resources, and it required 80 percent less time in administration.[17] Some businesses like private cloud computing because it provides more control over infrastructure and security than public cloud computing.[18]

Businesses may elect to combine public cloud and private cloud services to create a *hybrid cloud*. Amazon, for example, provides a virtual private cloud (VPC) service that allows companies to create a private cloud on its public cloud infrastructure connecting through a virtual private network (VPN). A VPN provides a secure and private connection over the Internet. In another version of cloud computing, known as a *community cloud*, several businesses share cloud computing resources.

As cloud computing grows, the power and storage capacity of users' computers can diminish. The popularity of netbooks, which are small notebook computers designed primarily for accessing Web applications, and nettops, their desktop equivalents, indicate this direction toward cloud computing. High-speed wireless access, a Web browser, and a decent keyboard and display are all you really need for computing in the cloud.

THE WORLD WIDE WEB

The World Wide Web was developed by Tim Berners-Lee at CERN, the European Organization for Nuclear Research in Geneva, Switzerland. He originally conceived of it as an internal document-management system. From this modest beginning, the Web has grown to become a primary source of news and information, an indispensable conduit for commerce, and a popular hub for social interaction, entertainment, and communication.

How the Web Works

Although the terms "Internet" and "Web" are often used interchangeably, technically, the two are different technologies. The Internet is the infrastructure on which the Web exists. The Internet is made up of computers, network hardware such as routers and fibre-optic cables, software, and the TCP/IP protocols. The **Web**, on the other hand, consists of server and client software, the hypertext transfer protocol (http), standards, and markup languages that combine to deliver information and services over the Internet.

The Web was designed to make information easy to find and organize. It connects billions of documents, which are now called Web pages, stored on millions of servers around the world. These are connected to each other using **hyperlinks**, specially denoted text or graphics on a Web page, that, when clicked, open a new Web page containing related content. Using hyperlinks, users can jump between Web pages stored on various Web servers—creating the illusion of interacting with one big computer. Because of the vast amount of information available on the Web and the wide variety of media, the Web has become the most popular means of information access in the world today.

In short, the Web is a hyperlink-based system that uses the client/server model. It organizes Internet resources throughout the world into a series of linked files, called pages, accessed and viewed using Web client software called a **Web browser**. Internet Explorer, Firefox, Chrome, Safari, and Opera are five popular Web browsers. See Figure 7.5. A collection of pages on one particular topic, accessed under one Web domain, is called a website. The Web was originally designed to support formatted text and pictures on a page. It has evolved to support many more types of information and communication, including user interactivity, animation, and video. Web *plug-ins* help provide additional features to standard websites. Adobe Flash and Real Player are examples of Web plug-ins.

Web
Server and client software, the hypertext transfer protocol (http), standards, and markup languages that combine to deliver information and services over the Internet.

hyperlink
Highlighted text or graphics in a Web document, that, when clicked, opens a new Web page containing related content.

Web browser
Web client software such as Internet Explorer, Firefox, Chrome, Safari, and Opera used to view Web pages.

Figure 7.5

Mozilla Firefox

Web browsers such as Firefox let you access Internet resources such as this customizable Web portal from Google.

(Source: Google.)

Hypertext Markup Language (**HTML**) is the standard page description language for Web pages. HTML is defined by the World Wide Web Consortium (referred to as "W3C") and has developed through numerous revisions. It is currently in its fifth revision—HTML5. HTML tells the browser about font characteristics, paragraph formatting, page layout, image placement, and hyperlinks and how to display the content of a Web page. HTML uses tags, which are codes that tell the browser how to format the text or graphics: as a heading, list, or body text, for example. Website creators "mark up" a page by placing **HTML tags** before and after one or more words. For example, to have the browser display a sentence as a heading, you place the <h1> tag at the start of the sentence and an </h1> tag at the end of the sentence. When you view this page in your browser, the sentence is displayed as a heading. HTML also provides tags to import objects stored in files, such as photos, pictures, audio, and movies, into a Web page. In short, a Web page is made up of three components: text, tags, and references to files. The text is your Web page content, the tags are codes that mark the way words will be displayed, and the references to files insert photos and media into the Web page at specific locations. All HTML tags are enclosed in a set of angle brackets (< and >), such as <h2>. The closing tag has a forward slash in it, such as </b> for closing bold. Consider the following text and tags:

```
<html>

<head>

<title>Table of Contents</title>

<link href="style.css" rel="stylesheet" type="text/css" />

</head>

<body style="background-color:#333333">

<div id="container">

<p><img src="header.png" width="602" height="78" /></p>

<h1 align=center>Principles of Information Systems</h1>

<ol>

<li>An Overview</li>

<li>Information Technology Concepts</li>

<li>Business Information Systems</li>

<li>Systems Development</li>

<li>Information Systems in Business and Society</li>

</ol>

</div>

</body>

</html>
```

The <html> tag identifies this as an HTML document. HTML documents are divided into two parts: the <head> and the <body>. The <body> contains everything that is viewable in the Web browser window, and the <head> contains related information such as a <title> to place on the browser's title bar. The background colour of the page is specified in

Hypertext Markup Language (HTML)
The standard page description language for Web pages.

HTML tags
Codes that tell the Web browser how to format text—as a heading, as a list, or as body text—and whether images, sound, and other elements should be inserted.

Figure 7.6

HTML Code Interpreted by a Browser

The example HTML code as interpreted by the Firefox Web browser on a Mac.

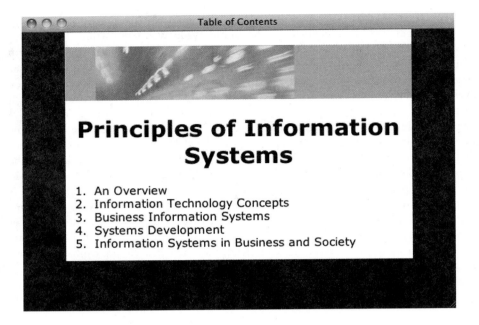

the <body> tag using a hexadecimal code. The heading "Principles of Information Systems" is identified as the largest level 1 heading with the <h1> tag, typically a 16- to 18-point font, centred on the page. The <ol> tag indicates an ordered list, and the <li> tags indicate list items. The resulting Web page is shown in Figure 7.6.

HTML5 provides many advantages over its predecessors. For the first time, HTML supports delivery of rich media without the need for *plug-ins* (applications that help Web browsers perform tasks such as playing videos). When combined with other common Web development tools, HTML5 can use local storage, deliver native audio and video, provide geolocation services, and provide a number of other useful applications.[19]

HTML works hand in hand with another markup language called CSS. **CSS**, which stands for **Cascading Style Sheet**, has become a popular tool for designing groups of Web pages. CSS uses special HTML tags to globally define font characteristics for a variety of page elements as well as how those elements are laid out on the Web page. Rather than having to specify a font for each occurrence of an element throughout a document, formatting can be specified once and applied to all occurrences. CSS styles are often defined in a separate file and then can be applied to many pages on a website. In the previous example code, you may have noticed the <link> tag that refers to an external style sheet file, style.css.

The following CSS code defines an area of a Web page to hold text that will be called "menu" in the HTML for the Web page. It then defines what the <h1> tag should look like when used in the menu area. Once this code is placed in a .css file, a website designer can link any Web page to that file and then can use this formatting repeatedly by simply referring to the "menu" style.

Cascading Style Sheet (CSS)
A markup language for defining the visual design of a Web page or group of pages.

```
#menu {

       float: left;

       width: 110px;

       padding: 12px 0px 0px 12px;

       margin: 20px 12px 0px 20px;

       border: 1px solid #FFFFFF;

}
```

```
#menu  h1{

    font-size: 90%;

    font-weight: bold;

    color: #FFFFFF;

}
```

Extensible Markup Language (**XML**) is a markup language designed to transport and store data on the Web. Rather than using predefined tags like HTML, XML allows the coder to create custom tags that define data. For example, the following XML code identifies the components of a book.

Extensible Markup Language (XML)
The markup language designed to transport and store data on the Web.

```
<book>

<chapter>Hardware</chapter>

<topic>Input Devices</topic>

<topic>Processing and Storage Devices</topic>

<topic>Output Devices</topic>

</book>
```

XML is extremely useful for organizing Web content and making data easy to find. Many websites use CSS to define the design and layout of Web pages, XML to define the content, and HTML to join the content (XML) with the design (CSS). See Figure 7.7 on the next page. This modular approach to Web design allows you to change the visual design without affecting the content and to change the content without affecting the visual design.

Web Programming Languages

Many of the services offered on the Web are delivered through the use of programs and scripts. A Web program may be something as simple as a menu that expands when you click it or as complicated as a full-blown spreadsheet application. Web applications may run on the Web server, delivering the results of the processing to the user, or they may run directly on the client—the user's PC. These two categories are commonly referred to as client-side and server-side software. JavaScript is a popular programming language for client-side applications. Using JavaScript, you can create interactive Web pages that respond to user actions. JavaScript can be used to validate data entry in a Web form, to display photos in a slideshow style, to embed simple computer games in a Web page, and to provide a currency conversion calculator.

Asynchronous JavaScript and XML (AJAX) is a popular programming platform that evolved from JavaScript for developing rich Internet applications (RIAs) such as Google Docs. AJAX combines HTML, CSS, XML, JavaScript, and other Web technologies to create interactive Web applications that rival desktop applications. Programs built with AJAX run smoothly on the client PC, occasionally exchanging messages with the server. Many of today's most popular online applications, including Gmail, Google Docs, Flickr, and Facebook were developed with AJAX.

Java is an object-oriented programming language from Sun Microsystems based on the C++ programming language, which allows small programs, called *applets*, to be embedded within an HTML document. When the user clicks the appropriate part of an HTML page to retrieve an applet from a Web server, the applet is downloaded onto the client workstation, where it begins executing. Unlike other programs, Java software can run on any type of computer. Java can be used to develop client-side or server-side applications. Programmers use Java to make Web pages come alive, adding splashy graphics, animation, and real-time updates.

Java
An object-oriented programming language from Sun Microsystems based on the C++ programming language, which allows applets to be embedded within an HTML document.

Figure 7.7

XML, CSS, and HTML

Today's websites are created using XML to define content, CSS to define the visual style, and HTML to put it all together.

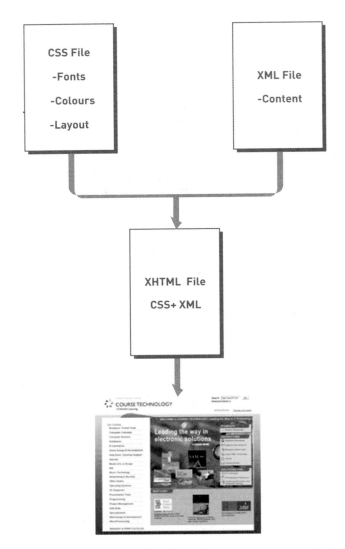

Hypertext Preprocessor, or *PHP*, is an open-source programming language that is popular for server-side application development. Unlike some other Web programming languages, PHP is easy to use because its code, or instructions, can be embedded directly into HTML code. PHP can be used with a variety of database management systems, such as MySQL, DB2, Oracle, Informix, and many others. PHP's flexibility, power, and ease of use make it popular with many Web developers. Perl is another popular server-side programming language.

Adobe Flash and *Microsoft Silverlight* provide development environments for creating rich Web animation and interactive media. Both Flash and Silverlight require the user to install a browser plug-in to run. Flash became so common that popular browsers included it as a standard feature. The introduction of HTML5 in 2010 provided Web developers the ability to create interactive Web content and media natively in HTML without the need for Flash or Silverlight. A number of technology companies, led by Apple, are moving away from Flash to HTML5.[20] See Figure 7.8.

Web Services

Web services consist of standards and tools that streamline and simplify communication among websites, promising to revolutionize the way we develop and use the Web for business and personal purposes. Internet companies, including Amazon, eBay, and Google, are now using Web services. Amazon, for example, has developed Amazon Web Services (AWS) to make the contents of its huge online catalogue available to other websites or software applications.

HTML5 Showcase
The demos below show how Apple's Safari web browser supports the
capabilities of web standards such as HTML5, CSS3, and JavaScript.

◄ Back to overview

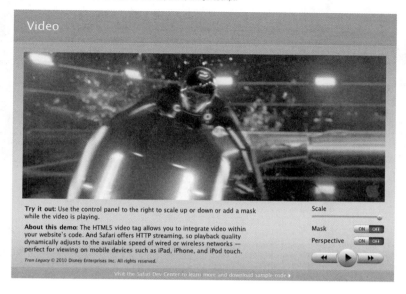

Figure 7.8

HTML5 Video

HTML5 supports interactive media,
including video and audio.

(Source: Courtesy of Apple, Inc.)

The key to Web services is XML. Just as HTML was developed as a standard for formatting Web content into Web pages, XML is used within a Web page to describe and transfer data between Web service applications. XML is easy to read and has wide industry support. In addition to XML, three other components are used in Web service applications:

1. SOAP (Simple Object Access Protocol) is a specification that defines the XML format for messages. SOAP allows businesses, their suppliers, and their customers to communicate with each other. It provides a set of rules that makes it easier to move information and data over the Internet.
2. WSDL (Web Services Description Language) provides a way for a Web service application to describe its interfaces in enough detail to allow a user to build a client application to talk to it. In other words, it allows one software component to connect to and work with another software component on the Internet.
3. UDDI (Universal Discovery Description and Integration) is used to register Web service applications with an Internet directory so that potential users can easily find them and carry out transactions over the Web.

Developing Web Content and Applications

The art of Web design involves working within the technical limitations of the Web to make appealing designs that effectively communicate information to users. Popular tools for creating Web pages and managing websites are Adobe Dreamweaver, Microsoft Expression Web, and Nvu. See Figure 7.9 on the next page. Today's Web development applications allow developers to create websites using software that resembles a word processor. The software includes features that allow the developer to work directly with the HTML code or to use auto-generated code. Web development software also helps the designer keep track of all files in a website and the hyperlinks that connect them.

Web application frameworks have arisen to simplify Web development by providing the foundational code—or framework—for a professional, interactive website, allowing developers to customize the code to specific needs. They include popular development software such as Drupal and Joomla! and range in complexity from WordPress, which allows nonprogrammers to create websites, to Ruby on Rails, which requires significant experience with programming. Web application frameworks that support full enterprise-level needs are

Web application framework
Web development software that
provides the foundational code—
or framework—for a professional,
interactive website, allowing
developers to customize the code
to specific needs.

Figure 7.9

Creating Web Pages

Microsoft Expression Web makes Web design nearly as easy as using a word processor.

(Source: Used with permission from Microsoft.)

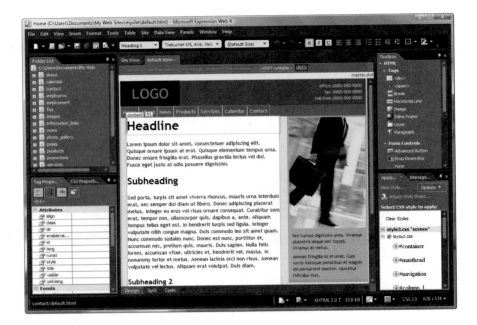

referred to as online content management systems or frameworks. Most frameworks use a database to store and deliver Web content. The Michael Bublé website was developed using the Drupal framework.[21]

Websites are typically developed on personal computers and then uploaded to a Web server. Although a business may manage its own Web server, the job is often outsourced to a Web hosting company. Web hosts maintain Web servers, storage systems, and backup systems, and they provide Web development software and frameworks, Web analytics tools, and e-commerce software when required. A Web host can charge $15 or more per month, depending on the services delivered. Some Web hosting sites also include domain name registration and website design services.

Many products make it easy to develop Web content and interconnect Web services, discussed in the next section. Microsoft, for example, provides a development and Web services platform called .NET, which allows developers to use various programming languages to create and run programs, including those for the Web. The .NET platform also includes a rich library of programming code to help build XML Web applications. Other popular Web development platforms are Sun JavaServer Pages, Microsoft ASP, and Adobe Cold Fusion.

INTERNET AND WEB APPLICATIONS

The types of Internet and Web applications available are vast and ever expanding. The most common and popular uses for the Internet and Web can be categorized as follows:

- Publishing information
- Assisting users in finding information
- Supporting communication and collaboration
- Building online community
- Providing software applications
- Providing a platform for expressing ideas and opinions
- Delivering media of all types
- Providing a platform for commerce
- Supporting travel and navigation

Online Information Sources

The Web has become the most popular medium for distributing and accessing information. Consumers increasingly rely on online resources to inform major life events such as weddings, buying a home, changing jobs, and having a baby. The Web has become the most popular source for daily news, surpassing newspapers and television. Academic researchers use the Web to share their findings with others in their field; most academic publications have moved from paper to the Web. Businesses rely on the Web for storing and delivering corporate information internally to employees and externally to business partners, customers, and the press. The Web has become the first place people look when faced with a challenge or question.

News and Opinion

The Web is a powerful tool for keeping informed about local, provincial, national, and global news. It allows the public to actively research issues and become more knowledgeable about current events. Traditional news media deliver the news through television, radio, and newspapers. These media provide the news that they consider to be of interest to the general public. Items of special or unique interest may be replaced with more general stories. By contrast, the Web has an abundance of special-interest coverage. It also has the capacity to provide deeper analysis of the subject matter. For example, during military conflicts overseas, online news services provide news articles in text, audio, and video. Clicking links allows you to find out more about geographic regions by viewing maps, for example; you could also link to historical coverage of international relations and learn about the battle equipment being deployed.

Most newspaper, radio, and television news services have expanded to provide online news coverage. This trend has put the various forms of media in direct competition with each other as their online format expands to include text, photos, audio, and video. Text and photos are supported by the HTML standard. Video (sometimes called a Webcast) and audio are provided in the browser through plug-in technology and in podcasts. See Figure 7.10. Bringing the news to the Web is eliminating the lines of distinction between traditional newspaper, radio, and television news sources.

Most city newspapers have turned to the Web to save themselves from financial hardship and even bankruptcy as increasing numbers of subscribers are giving up newspaper

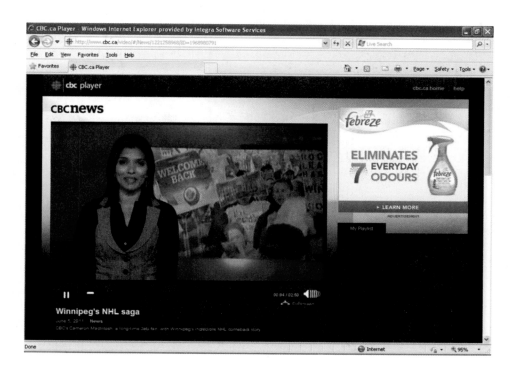

Figure 7.10

News Webcast

Online news is available in text, audio, and video formats, providing the ability to do in-depth research into stories.

(Source: © CBC News.)

subscriptions for online news sources.[22] The leading international news agencies have a strong online presence as well. Reuters, the Associated Press, and the BBC provide online sources of global news and information for media companies and the general population.

While traditional news sources migrate to the Web, new sources are emerging from online companies. News websites from Google, Yahoo!, Digg, and Newsvine provide popular or interesting news stories from a variety of news sources.

In a trend some refer to as social journalism or citizen journalism, ordinary citizens are more involved in reporting the news than ever before. The online community is taking journalism into its hands and reporting the news from each person's perspective, using an abundance of online tools. YouTube has launched a channel dedicated to citizen journalism called CitizenTube. The channel features breaking news videos captured by everyday citizens and uploaded to YouTube.[23] For example, during one week, users on CitizenTube uploaded videos of a plane crash near Destin, Florida, celebrations in the streets of Uruguay over its World Cup match, and floods in Mexico. With 24 hours of videos being uploaded to YouTube every minute, a wealth of insightful news-related videos are available.

Although social journalism provides important news not available elsewhere, its sources may not be as reliable as mainstream media sources. It is sometimes difficult to discern news from opinion. In 2010, many organizations joined a coalition to ask the FCC (the equivalent to the CRTC in Canada) to open a probe on "hate speech" and "misinformation" in the media. They were concerned about broadcasts and websites that spread misinformation and hate speech under the guise of legitimate news.[24] News from nonprofessional journalists, reporting without the strict guidelines of formal news agencies, may be biased, misrepresented, mistaken, or perhaps even deliberately misleading. Many citizen journalists would be quick to point out that mainstream media may also be biased in its reporting of the news.

Education and Training

As a tool for sharing information and a primary repository of information on all subjects, the Web is ideally suited for education and training. Advances in interactive Web technologies further support important educational relationships between teacher and student and among students. See Figure 7.11. The Web can play a major role in education from pre-kindergarten through adult continuing education. In today's highly competitive and rapidly changing professional environments, more professionals are turning to the Web to learn skills that will enhance their professional value.

Figure 7.11

Skillsoft Online Professional Training and Certification

The Internet supports education from pre-kindergarten to lifelong learning.

(Source: Courtesy of SkillSoft Corporation.)

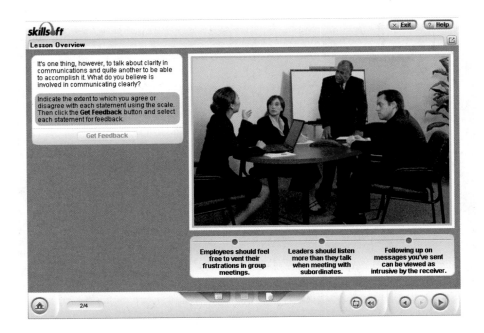

Even before children enter school, they are engaged with educational content on the Web at sites such as JumpStart.com. Primary schools use the Web to inform parents of school schedules and activities. Teachers give elementary school students research exercises in the classroom and at home that use Web resources. By high school, students have integrated the Web into daily study habits. Teachers manage class Web pages that contain information and links for students to use in homework exercises.

Most university and college-level courses rely on the Web to enhance learning. Educational support products, such as Blackboard, provide an integrated Web environment that includes virtual chat for class members; a discussion group for posting questions and comments; access to the class syllabus and agenda, student grades, and class announcements; and links to class-related material. Some course websites even deliver filmed lectures using Webcasting technology. Such environments can complement the traditional classroom experience or be the sole method of course delivery.

Conducting classes over the Web with no physical class meetings is called *distance education*. Many colleges and universities offer distance education classes, which provide a convenient method for nontraditional students to attend college or university. Nontraditional students include older students who have job or family obligations that might otherwise prohibit them from attending college. Distance education offers them a way of working through class material on a flexible schedule. Some schools offer entire degree programs through distance education.

In a program it calls Open Courseware, the Massachusetts Institute of Technology (MIT) offers all of its courses free online. See Figure 7.12. Students who take courses via Open Courseware do not earn credit toward a degree or have access to teachers, but they can benefit from the knowledge gained. Since MIT's move online, many other schools have followed suit. Organizations such as the Open Courseware Consortium and the Center for Open Sustainable Learning have been established to support open education around the world.

Figure 7.12

MIT's Open Courseware

(Source: Courtesy of OpenCourseWare Consortium/MIT.)

Beyond traditional education, many corporations offer professional job skills training over the Web. Job seekers often use these services to acquire specialized business or technical training. Some of the training leads to certification. Certification verifies a person's skill and understanding in a particular area. It has become very important, especially for some technical skill sets, to assure an employer that a job applicant truly has the skills claimed. Many corporations and organizations also provide on-the-job training for current employees to expand their skills.

Museums, libraries, private businesses, government agencies, and many other types of organizations and individuals offer educational materials online for free or a fee. Consider eHow, the website that claims to teach you "how to do just about everything!" Certiport offers training and testing for technology certification, such as for Microsoft and Adobe products.

Business Information

Throughout this book you see numerous examples of how businesses depend on the Internet and Web to provide access to information and services within and outside the enterprise. Many businesses use the Web browser as an interface to corporate information systems. This is certainly the case with cloud computing systems.

Businesses often use Internet and Web-based systems for knowledge management within the enterprise. Information systems within the organization may be accessed through Web portals and dashboards that provide a single source for all business-related news and information. Such portals may extend beyond the walls of the office to notebooks and smartphones through Internet connections.

Providing news and information about a business and its products through the company's website and online social media can assist in increasing a company's exposure to the general public and improving its reputation. Providing answers to common product questions and customer support online can help keep customers coming back for more. For example, natural food company Kashi uses its website to promote healthy living, with a blog about leading a natural lifestyle, recipes, tools for dieters, and personal stories from Kashi employees. The website helps build a community around the Kashi brand and promotes awareness of Kashi's philosophy and products.[25]

Personal and Professional Advice and Support

Websites now support every subject and activity of importance. As people confront life's challenges, they can find Web resources that can educate and prepare them to succeed. Examples include *www.theknot.ca*, which provides information and advice about getting married; *www.whattoexpect.com* provides information and support for expectant parents; and the Canadian Mortgage and Housing Corporation website at *www.cmhc-schl.gc.ca* provides all the information a prospective home buyer needs.

Medical and health websites such as Public Health Canada (*www.publichealth.gc.ca*) assist in diagnosing health problems and advising on treatments. Online forums and support groups provide information and access to resources for every disease. For example, the Canadian Cancer Society provides free support resources for cancer victims at *www.cancer.ca*. Many physicians and hospitals provide abundant educational information online to assist their patients.

The Web is an excellent source of job-related information. People looking for their first jobs or seeking information about new job opportunities can find a wealth of information on the Web. Search engines, such as Google or Bing (discussed next), can be a good starting point for searching for specific companies or industries. You can use a directory on Yahoo!'s home page, for example, to explore industries and careers. Most medium-sized and large companies have websites that list open positions, salaries, benefits, and people to contact for further information. The IBM website, *www.ibm.com/ca*, has a link to "Jobs." When you click this link, you can find information on jobs with IBM around the world. Some sites can help you develop a résumé and assist you during your job search. They can also help you develop an effective cover letter for a résumé, prepare for a job interview, negotiate an employment contract, and more. In addition, several Internet sites specialize in helping you find job information and even apply for jobs online, including *www.monster.ca, www.workopolis.com,* and *www.careerbuilder.ca*.

Search Engines and Web Research

The fundamental purpose of the Web is to make it easier to find information from diverse Internet sources. However, the Web has become so large that many complain of information overload, or the inability to find the information they need due to the overabundance of information. To relieve the strain of information overload, Web developers have provided Web search engines to help organize and index Web content.

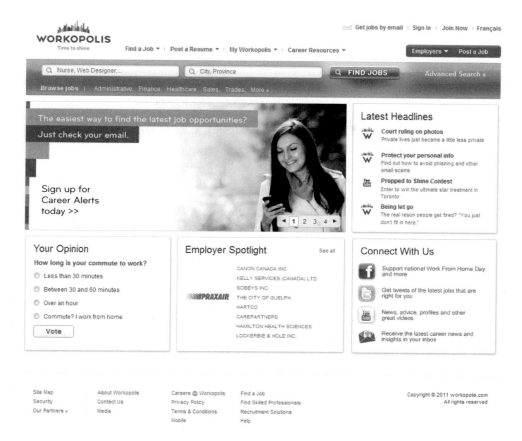

Several Internet sites specialize in helping people get job information and even apply for jobs online.

(Source: Courtesy of Workopolis.)

A **search engine** is a valuable tool that enables you to find information on the Web by specifying words or phrases known as keywords, which are related to a topic of interest. You can also use operators such as OR and NOT for more precise search results. Table 7.4 provides examples of the use of operators in Google searches as listed on Google's help page (*www.google.ca/help/cheatsheet.html*).

search engine
A valuable tool that enables you to find information on the Web by specifying words that are key to a topic of interest, known as keywords.

Table 7.4

Using Operators in Google Web Searches

Keywords and Operator Entered	Search Engine Interpretation
vacation Hawaii	The words "vacation" and "Hawaii"
Maui OR Hawaii	Either the word "Maui" or the word "Hawaii"
"To each his own"	The exact phrase "To each his own"
virus-computer	The word virus, but not the word computer
Star Wars Episode +I	The movie title "Star Wars Episode," including the Roman numeral I
~auto loan	Loan information for both the word "auto" and its synonyms, such as "truck" and "car"
define:computer	Definitions of the word "computer" from around the Web
red * blue	The words "red" and "blue" separated by one or more words

Search engines have become the biggest application on the Web. Search giant Google has become one of the world's most profitable companies, with more than $16.5 billion in annual revenue. Google is so successful that it has launched its own trading floor to invest more than $20 billion of cash and short-term investments it has generated. Web search has become such a profitable business because it's an application that everyone on the Web uses. Search engine companies make money through advertisements. Because everyone on the Web uses a search engine, advertisers are keen to pay to have their ads posted on search pages.

The search engine market is dominated by Google, which owns around 85 percent of the global market. Yahoo! is second, with around 6 percent; Microsoft Bing is third, with about 3 percent; and China's Baidu has 2.6 percent. Baidu gained considerable market share when Google discontinued operations in China in protest over China's censoring practices. The rest of the market is divided among other companies such as Ask.com, AOL, and Mahalo. Google has taken advantage of its market dominance to expand into other Web-based services, most notably e-mail, scheduling, maps, Web-based applications, and cell phone software.

To help users get the information they want from the Web, most search engines use an automated approach that scours the Web with automated programs called spiders. These spiders follow all Web links in an attempt to catalogue every Web page by topic; each Web page is analyzed and ranked using unique algorithms, and the resulting information is stored in a database. Google maintains more than 4 billion indexed Web pages on 30 clusters of up to 2,000 computers each, totalling over 30 petabytes of data.

A keyword search at Yahoo!, Bing, or Google isn't a search of the Web but rather a search of a database that stores information about Web pages. The database is continuously checked and refreshed so that it is an accurate reflection of the current status of the Web.

Some search companies have experimented with human-powered and human-assisted search. Human-powered search provides search results created by human researchers. Because the system is human powered, the search results are typically more accurate, definitive, and complete. With human-powered search, you do not need to examine a long list of search results to find what you are looking for. Each search leads to one page of information on your topic with links to more sources of information. The downside of human-powered search is that it takes a lot of effort. Although an automated search engine can find information on any word in the dictionary (and more), human-powered search provides information only on the most popular key terms. For example, human-powered search engine Mahalo has built search results pages for 25,000 topics.

The website *www.liveperson.com* takes human-power one step further and allows visitors to chat and seek advice from human experts. The Web service contracts thousands of experts in a wide variety of fields to answer questions from users for a small fee.

The Bing search engine has attempted to innovate with its design. Bing refers to itself as a decision engine, providing more than just a long list of links in its search results. Bing also includes media—music, videos, and games—in its search results.[26] See Figure 7.13.

A meta search engine allows you to run keyword searches on several search engines at once. For example, a search run from *www.dogpile.com* returns results from Google, Yahoo!, MSN, Ask, and other search engines.

Figure 7.13

Microsoft Bing Decision Engine

Microsoft calls its search engine a decision engine to distinguish it from other search software.

(Source: Used with permission from Microsoft.)

Today's heated competition in the search engine market is pressing the big players to expand their services. Table 7.5 lists some of the newer search engine services available and those currently being developed.

Table 7.5

Search Engine Services

Service	What it does
Alerts	Receive news and results of your searches via e-mail
Answers	Ask a question, set a price, get an answer
Catalogues	Search and browse mail-order catalogues
Desktop Search for Enterprise	Search your company's network
Images	Search for images on the Web
Local	Find local businesses and services
Maps	View maps and get directions
Mobile	Search the Web from your cell phone
News	Search thousands of news stories
Personalized Search Page	Customize your search page with current news and weather
Print	Search the full text of books
Ride Finder	Find a taxi, limousine, or shuttle using real-time position of vehicles
Scholar; University Search	Search through journal articles, abstracts, and other scholarly literature; search a specific school's website
Search by Location	Filter results by geographic location
Search History	Maintain a history of past searches and the websites that produced results
Search Toolbar	Access search from the toolbar of your browser or from your operating system taskbar
Shopping	Find the best deal on consumer products
Video	Search recent TV programs online

Savvy business owners know that the results gained from search engines are tools that draw visitors to certain websites. Many businesses invest in search engine optimization (SEO)—a process for driving traffic to a website by using techniques that improve the site's ranking in search results. Normally, when a user gets a list of results from a Web search, the links listed highest on the first page of search results have a far greater chance of being clicked. SEO professionals therefore try to get the websites of their businesses to be listed with as many appropriate keywords as possible. They study the algorithms that search engines use, and then they alter the contents of their Web pages to improve the page's chance of being ranked number one. SEO professionals use *Web analytics software* to study detailed statistics about visitors to their sites.

In addition to search engines, you can use other Internet sites to research information. Wikipedia, an online encyclopaedia with over 3.3 million English-language entries created and edited by millions of users, is another example of a website that can be used to research information. See Figure 7.14 on the next page. In Hawaiian, *wiki* means quick, so a "Wikipedia" provides quick access to information. The website is both open source and open editing, which means that people can add or edit entries in the encyclopaedia at any time. Besides being self-regulating, Wikipedia articles are vetted by around 1,700 administrators. However, even with so many administrators, it is possible that some entries are inaccurate and biased.

Figure 7.14

Wikipedia

Wikipedia captures the knowledge of tens of thousands of experts.

(Source: Courtesy of the Wikimedia Foundation.)

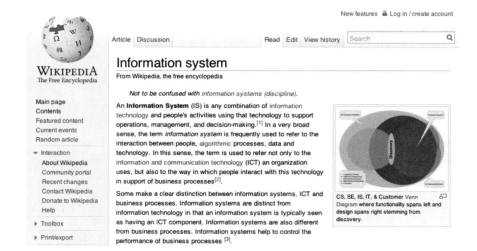

While Wikipedia is the best-known, general-purpose wiki, many other wikis are designed for special purposes. Wikimedia, the nonprofit organization behind Wikipedia, has wikis for books, news, media, and open learning. Zoho, Wikispaces, Wetpaint, and others provide tools to create wikis for any use. You can search thousands of wikis at the search engine *www.wiki.com*. A wiki can be used in an enterprise to enable the sharing of information between employees, training for new employees, or customer support for products.[27]

The wiki approach to content development is referred to as *crowd sourcing*, which uses the combined effort of many individuals to accomplish some task. Another example of crowd sourcing is the OpenStreetMap.org project. OpenStreetMap uses a wiki and the power of the crowd to develop a detailed map of the world.[28]

Online research is greatly assisted by traditional resources that have migrated from libraries to websites. The most reliable sources of information can be found at your library's website. The books, reference materials, journals, and other periodicals that are housed in your college, university, or local library have undergone quality-control evaluation to earn the right to sit on the shelves. Books and periodicals considered fundamental to any given field are typically stocked in the library. Library resources are professionally analyzed and categorized in a logical manner that is easy to navigate. Best of all, the most knowledgeable of researchers—librarians—are available to assist you with your project. Most libraries have online catalogues that allow you to search for books and journal articles from the comfort of your home.

Besides online catalogues, libraries typically provide links to public and sometimes private research databases on the Web. Online research databases allow visitors to search for information in thousands of journal, magazine, and newspaper articles. Information database services are valuable because they offer the best in quality and convenience. They conveniently provide full-text articles from reputable sources over the Web. College, university, and public libraries typically subscribe to many databases to support research. One of the most popular private databases is LexisNexis Academic Universe. LexisNexis provides access to full-text documents from over 5,900 news, business, legal, medical, and reference publications. You can access the information through a standard keyword search engine. See Figure 7.15. The sources from which LexisNexis draws include these:

- National and regional newspapers, wire services, broadcast transcripts, international news sources, and non–English-language sources
- Canadian federal and provincial case law, codes, regulations, legal news, law reviews, and international legal information
- Business news journals, company financial information, reports, and industry and market news

Figure 7.15

LexisNexis

A search at LexisNexis on "Internet in Canada" yields hundreds of full-text articles.

(Source: © Copyright 2011 LexisNexis, a division of Reed Elsevier Inc. All Rights Reserved. LexisNexis and the Knowledge Burst logo are registered trademarks of Reed Elsevier Properties Inc. and are used with the permission of LexisNexis.)

Web Portals

A **Web portal** is a Web page that combines useful information and links and acts as an entry point to the Web—they typically include a search engine, a subject directory, daily headlines, and other items of interest. Many people choose a Web portal as their browser's home page (the first page you open when you begin browsing the Web), so the two terms are used interchangeably. Portals provide a convenient starting point for Web exploration in a general or a specific context. They allow users to have convenient access to their most frequently used Web resources.

Many Web pages have been designed to serve as Web portals. iGoogle, Yahoo!, AOL, and MSN are examples of horizontal portals; "horizontal" refers to the fact that these portals cover a wide range of topics. My Yahoo! and iGoogle allow users to custom-design their page, selecting from hundreds of widgets—small applications that deliver information and services. Yahoo! also integrates with Facebook so that Facebook users can access their friends and news streams from the My Yahoo! portal.[29] See Figure 7.16.

Vertical portals are pages that provide information and links for special-interest groups. For example, the portal at *www.iVillage.com* focuses on items of interest to women, and *www.ca.AskMen.com* is a vertical portal for men.

Many businesses set up corporate portals for their employees. Corporate portals (sometimes called dashboards) provide access to work-related resources such as corporate news and information, along with access to business tools, databases, and communication tools to support collaboration. Some businesses use a corporate portal to provide employees with work-related online content and to limit access to other Web content.

Web portal
A Web page that combines useful information and links and acts as an entry point to the Web—they typically include a search engine, a subject directory, daily headlines, and other items of interest. Many people choose a Web portal as their browser's home page (the first page you open when you begin browsing the Web).

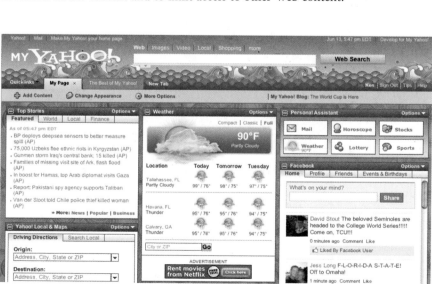

Figure 7.16

MyYahoo! Personalized Portal

Personalized portals contain custom designs and widgets.

(Source: Reproduced with permission of Yahoo! Inc. © 2011 Yahoo! Inc. YAHOO! and the YAHOO! logo are registered trademarks of Yahoo! Inc.)

Communication and Collaboration

The Internet and Web provide many applications for communication and collaboration. Whether they are text-based applications such as e-mail or telepresence systems that use high-definition video and audio that allow individuals from anywhere in the world to meet around a table, Internet communications supports many levels of communication.

Various forms of Internet communication and collaboration can be measured by their convenience and effectiveness. E-mail, for example, is very convenient since it is asynchronous— messages are left for others to view at their discretion; however, e-mail is not very effective for communications that require a quick back-and-forth dialogue. E-mail also lacks a way to communicate voice inflections, facial expressions, and body language. Telepresence and video communication is less convenient since it is synchronous—meaning the individuals involved must meet together at the same time—and it involves a lot of equipment. However, it is a very effective form of communication because it includes voice inflection, facial expressions, and body language, along with the ability to share documents and converse in a natural style.

The many forms of Internet communication include instant messaging, chat, virtual chat, blogging, microblogging, status updates, Internet phone, video chat and conferencing, virtual chat, and Web conferencing. When selecting a communication method, first consider the importance of the exchange and what needs to be shared. The most effective and meaningful communications are typically the least convenient. Although the value of an in-person, face-to-face meeting should not be underestimated, many communications benefit from the convenience provided by the Internet.

E-mail

E-mail is a useful form of Internet communication that supports text communication, HTML content, and sharing documents as e-mail attachments. E-mail is accessed through Web-based systems or through dedicated e-mail applications such as Microsoft Outlook and Mozilla Thunderbird. E-mail can also be distributed through enterprise systems to desktop computers, notebook computers, and smartphones.

Many people use online e-mail services such as Hotmail, MSN, and Gmail. See Figure 7.17. Online e-mail services store messages on the server, not the user's computer, so users need to be connected to the Internet to view, send, and manage e-mail. Other people prefer to use software such as Outlook, Apple Mail, or Thunderbird, which retrieve e-mail from the server and deliver it to the user's PC. Post Office Protocol (POP) is used to transfer messages from e-mail servers to your PC. POP allows you to save your e-mail on your own PC, making it easier to manage and organize messages and to keep the messages private and secure. Another protocol called Internet Message Access Protocol (IMAP) allows you to view e-mail using Outlook or other e-mail software, but without downloading and storing the messages locally. Some users prefer this method because it allows them to view messages from any Internet-connected PC.

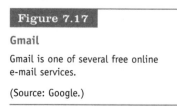

Figure 7.17

Gmail

Gmail is one of several free online e-mail services.

(Source: Google.)

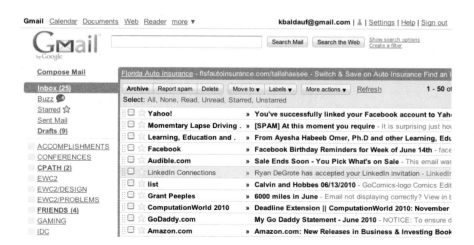

Business users who access e-mail from smartphones such as the BlackBerry take advantage of a technology called push e-mail. Push e-mail uses corporate server software that transfers, or pushes, e-mail to the handset as soon as it arrives at the corporate e-mail server. To the BlackBerry user, it appears as though e-mail is delivered directly to the handset. Push e-mail allows the user to view e-mail from any mobile or desktop device connected to the corporate server. This arrangement allows users flexibility in where, when, and how they access and manage e-mail.

Some companies use bulk e-mail to send legitimate and important information to sales representatives, customers, and suppliers around the world. With its popularity and ease of use, however, some people think this leads to too much e-mail. Many messages are copies sent to long lists of corporate users. Users are taking steps to cope with and reduce the mountain of e-mail. Some companies have banned the use of copying others on e-mails unless it is critical. Some e-mail services scan for possible junk or bulk mail, called *spam*, and the service deletes it or places it in a separate folder. More than half of all e-mail can be considered spam. While

BlackBerry users have instant access to e-mail sent to their business accounts.

(Source: Marvin Woodyatt/Photoshot/ Landov.)

spam-filtering software can prevent or discard unwanted messages, other software products can help users sort and answer large amounts of legitimate e-mail. For example, software from ClearContext, Seriosity, and Xobni rank and sort messages based on sender, content, and date, allowing individuals to focus on the most urgent and important messages first.

Instant Messaging

Instant messaging is online, real-time communication between two or more people who are connected to the Internet. See Figure 7.18 on the next page. With instant messaging, participants build buddy lists, or contact lists, that let them see which contacts are currently logged on to the Internet and available to chat. You can send messages to one of your online buddies, which opens a small dialogue box on your buddy's computer and allows the two of you to chat via the keyboard. Although chat typically involves exchanging text messages with one other person, more advanced forms of chat are emerging. Today's instant messaging software supports not only text messages, but also sharing images, sounds, files, and voice communications. Popular instant messaging services include America Online Instant Messenger (AIM), MSN Messenger, Google Talk, and Yahoo!.

instant messaging
A method that allows two or more people to communicate online in real time using the Internet.

Figure 7.18

Instant Messaging

Instant messaging lets you converse with another Internet user by exchanging messages instantaneously.

(Source: Spencer Grant/PhotoEdit.)

Micro blogging, Status Updates, and News Feeds

Twitter is a Web application that allows members to report on what they are doing throughout the day. Referred to as a micro blogging service, Twitter allows users to send short text updates (up to 140 characters) from a cell phone or Web account to their Twitter followers. While Twitter has been hugely successful for personal use, businesses are finding value in the service as well. Business people use Twitter to stay in close touch with associates by sharing their location and activities throughout the day. Businesses also find Twitter to be a rich source of consumer sentiment that can be tapped to improve marketing, customer relations, and product development. Many businesses have a presence on Twitter, dedicating personnel to communicate with customers by posting announcements and reaching out to individual users. Seneca College, one of Canada's largest colleges, uses Twitter to build relationships with its students.

The popularity of Twitter has caused social networks such as Facebook, LinkedIn, and MySpace to include Twitter-like news feeds. Facebook users share their thoughts and activities with their friends by posting messages to Facebook's News Feed.

Conferencing

Some Internet technologies support real-time online conferencing. Teleconferences have been a popular form of remote conferencing for many years. Participants dial into a common phone number to share a multiparty phone conversation. The Internet has made it possible for those involved in teleconferences to share computer desktops. Using services such as WebEx or GoToMeeting, conference participants log on to common software that allows them to broadcast their computer display to the group. This is quite useful for presenting with PowerPoint, demonstrating software, training, or collaborating on documents. Participants verbally communicate by phone or PC microphone. Some conferencing software uses Web cams to broadcast video of the presenter and group participants. Telepresence, as discussed in Chapter 6's opening case, takes videoconferencing to the ultimate level. Baxter Healthcare Corporation finds that using telepresence systems enables "faster decision making and problem solving … streamlining the way projects move through the system."[30]

You don't need to be a big business to enjoy the benefits of video conversations. Free software is available to make video chat easy to use for anyone with a computer, a Web cam, and a high-speed Internet connection. Online applications such as Google Chat and Microsoft Messenger support video connections between Web users. For spontaneous, random video chat with strangers, you can use *www.Chatroulette.com* and Internet Conga Line.[31] Software such as Apple iChat and Skype provide computer-to-computer video chat so users can speak to each other face to face. In addition to offering text, audio, and video chat on computers, Skype offers its video phone service over Internet-connected TVs. Recent Internet-connected sets from Panasonic and Samsung ship with the Skype software preloaded. You attach a Web cam to your TV to video-chat from your sofa.

Some people, businesses, and organizations hold meetings in virtual space. Virtual worlds such as Second Life allow users to take on a virtual presence through the use of avatars—3D characters that navigate a virtual landscape. IBM saved $320,000 by holding its annual world conference in Second Life rather than a physical conference centre.[32] Many businesses are developing presences in Second Life in hopes of reaching more customers. A study at Florida State University found that "users who interact with a brand in a virtual world environment are far more likely to purchase brand products than users who interact with a brand through traditional advertising mediums."[33]

Web 2.0

Over the past several years, the Web has evolved from a one-directional resource where users only obtain information to a two-directional resource where users obtain and contribute information. Consider websites such as YouTube, Wikipedia, and Facebook as examples. The Web has also grown in power to support full-blown software applications such as Google Docs and is becoming a computing platform itself. These two major trends in how the Web is used and perceived have created dramatic changes in how people, businesses, and organizations use the Web, creating a paradigm shift to **Web 2.0**.

Web 2.0
The Web as a computing platform that supports software applications and the sharing of information among users.

The Social Web

The original Web—Web 1.0—provided a platform for technology-savvy developers and the businesses and organizations that hired them to publish information for the general public to view. The introduction of user-generated content supported by Wikipedia, blogging, and podcasting made it clear that those using the Web were also interested in contributing to its content. This led to the development of websites with the sole purpose of supporting user-generated content and user feedback.

Websites such as YouTube and Flickr allow users to share video and photos with other people, groups, and the world. Microblogging sites such as Twitter allow people to post thoughts and ideas throughout the day for friends to read. See Figure 7.19. Social bookmarking sites such as *www.digg.com* and *www.delicious.com* allow users to pool their votes to determine what online news stories and Web pages are most interesting at any given time of the day. Similarly, Epinions and many retail websites allow consumers to voice their opinions about products. All these popular websites serve as examples of how the Web has transformed to become the town square where people share information, ideas, and opinions; meet with friends; and make new acquaintances.

Figure 7.19

Twitter

Twitter provides a forum for public sentiment.

(Source: Courtesy of Twitter.)

Social networking websites provide Web-based tools for users to share information about themselves with people on the Web and to find, meet, and converse with other members. Facebook, MySpace, and LinkedIn are the most popular social networking sites. LinkedIn is unique in that it is designed for professional use to assist its members with creating and maintaining valuable professional connections. Ning provides tools for Web users to create their own social networks dedicated to a topic or interest.[34]

Social network sites provide members with a personal Web page and allow them to post photos and information about themselves. Social networking sites allow members to send messages to each other and post comments on each other's pages. Members accumulate friends through invitation. Special interest groups can be created and joined as well.

Facebook provides an application development platform so that technically proficient members can create applications to run within Facebook. This has led to hundreds of widgets that Facebook users can add to their pages. For example, Facebook has applications to connect to people with similar music tastes, display a daily horoscope, share videos, find "Mr. or Ms. Right," express a mood, play games of all sorts, and do much more. Some Facebook applications have been extremely lucrative for their publishers. For example, the game Farmville has 70 million active monthly players. Participants purchase "farm cash" to develop online farms, which translates to millions of dollars for Zynga, the creator of the game. Analysts estimate that $1 billion was spent on social gaming in 2010.[35]

Social networks have become very popular for finding old friends, staying in touch with current friends, and making new friends. Besides their personal value, social networks provide a wealth of consumer information and opportunity to businesses as well. Businesses can use social networks to "address their tribes." In his book *Tribes*, Seth Godin makes the point that business and personal relationships are tribal, and social networks are an ideal tool for communicating with your tribe.[36] Businesses can observe social network users to determine their tastes and interests. Such data can be mined to discover consumer trends to guide product design and offerings.[37] Advertisers can target certain groups based on consumer information gleaned from social networking.[38]

Some businesses are including social networking features in their workplaces. The use of social media in business is called Enterprise 2.0. Enterprise 2.0 applications such as Salesforce's Chatter bring Facebook-like interaction to the workplace. Employees post profiles, making it easy to find colleagues with knowledge that is useful to the work environment. News feeds provide a constant patter of interaction and discussion about work-related topics. While many see Enterprise 2.0 applications as revitalizing forces in the workplace, others worry that they are distracting.[39] Schools are following the Web 2.0 model as well. Schoology is a learning management system (LMS) with a social network design.[40] Students and teachers interact through a news feed for a learning experience that extends well beyond the classroom walls.

Rich Internet Applications

The introduction of powerful Web-delivered applications such as Google Docs, Adobe Photoshop Express, Xcerion Web-based OS, and Microsoft Office Web Apps have elevated the Web from an online library to a platform for computing. Many of the computer activities traditionally provided through software installed on a PC can now be carried out using rich Internet applications (RIAs) in a Web browser without installing any software. A **rich Internet application** is software that has the functionality and complexity of traditional application software but runs in a Web browser and does not require local installation. See Figure 7.20. RIAs are the result of continuously improving programming languages and platforms designed for the Web.

Most RIAs take advantage of being online by emphasizing their collaborative benefits. Microsoft and Google both support online document sharing and collaborative editing. *37signals.com* provides online project management, contact management, calendar, and group chat applications. Microsoft SharePoint provides businesses with

rich Internet application (RIA)
Software that has the functionality and complexity of traditional application software but does not require local installation and runs in a Web browser.

Figure 7.20

Rich Internet Application

SlideRocket is a rich Internet application for creating vibrant online presentations.

(Source: Courtesy of SlideRocket.)

collaborative workspaces and social computing tools to allow people at different locations to work on projects together.

Blogging and Podcasting

A **Web log**, typically called a **blog**, is a website that people can create and use to write about their observations, experiences, and opinions on a wide range of topics. The community of blogs and bloggers is often called the *blogosphere*. A *blogger* is a person who creates a blog, while *blogging* refers to the process of placing entries on a blog site. A blog is like a journal. When people post information to a blog, it is placed at the top of the blog page. Blogs can include links to external information and an area for comments submitted by visitors. Video content can also be placed on the Internet using the same approach as a blog. This is often called a *video log* or *vlog*.

Internet users may subscribe to blogs using a technology called Really Simple Syndication (RSS). RSS is a collection of Web technologies that allow users to subscribe to Web content that is frequently updated, such as news sites and blogs. With RSS, you can receive a blog update and the latest headlines without actually visiting the blog or news website. Software used to subscribe to RSS feeds is called *aggregator software*. Google Reader is a popular aggregator for subscribing to blogs.

To set up a blog, you can go to the website of a blog service provider, such as *www.blogger.com* or *www.wordpress.com*, create a username and password, select a theme, choose a URL, follow any other instructions, and start making your first entry. People who want to find a blog on a certain topic can use blog search engines, such as Technorati, Feedster, and Blogdigger. You can also use Google to locate a blog.

A corporate blog can be useful for communicating with customers, partners, and employees. However, companies and their employees need to be cautious about the legal risks of blogging. Blogging can expose a corporation and its employees to charges of defamation, copyright and trademark infringement, invasion of privacy, and revealing corporate secrets.

A *podcast* is an audio broadcast over the Internet. The name podcast originated from Apple's *iPod* combined with the word *broadcast*. A podcast is like an audio blog. Using PCs, recording software, and microphones, you can record podcast programs and place them on the Internet. Apple's iTunes provides free access to tens of thousands of podcasts, sorted by topic and searchable by key word. See Figure 7.21 on the next page. After you find a podcast, you can download it to your PC (Windows or Mac), to an MP3 player such as the iPod, or any smartphone. You can also subscribe to podcasts using RSS software included in iTunes and other digital audio software.

While you are driving, walking, or making a meal, you can listen to podcasts of radio programs, whether from the Canadian Broadcast Corporation (CBC) or a local radio station. Canadapodcasts.ca lists a variety of podcasts from the CBC, TSN, and other contributors. Colleges and universities often use blogs and podcasts to deliver course material to students.

Web log (blog)
A website that people can create and use to write about their observations, experiences, and opinions on a wide range of topics.

Figure 7.21

iTunes Podcasts

iTunes provides free access to tens of thousands of podcasts.

(Source: Courtesy of Apple, Inc.)

Online Media and Entertainment

Like news and information, all forms of media and entertainment have followed their audiences online. Improvements in bandwidth have made it possible to access even high-definition movies online. Music, movies, television program episodes, user-generated videos, e-books, and audio books are all available online to download and purchase or stream.

content streaming
A method for transferring large media files over the Internet so that the data stream of voice and pictures plays more or less continuously as the file is being downloaded.

Content streaming is a method of transferring large media files over the Internet so that the data stream of voice and pictures plays more or less continuously as the file is being downloaded. For example, rather than wait for an entire 5 MB video clip to download before they can play it, users can begin viewing a streamed video as it is being received. Content streaming works best when the transmission of a file can keep up with the playback of the file.

Music

The Internet and the Web have made music more accessible than ever, with artists distributing their songs through online radio, subscription services, and download services. The Web has had a dramatic impact on the music industry, causing unprecedented changes in marketing and distribution. Digital distribution has allowed artists to distribute music directly to fans without the need for record companies. It has also opened the door to music piracy and illegal distribution of music that is legally protected by copyright.

Internet radio is similar to local AM and FM radio except that it is digitally delivered to your computer over the Internet, providing many more choices of stations. For example, *www.live365.com* provides access to thousands of radio stations in more than 200 musical genre categories. Some stations charge a subscription fee, but most do not.

Other Web-delivered streaming music services depart from the traditional radio format and create a more personalized service. Online services such as Pandora and Last.fm build radio stations around the listener's tastes by learning what the listener likes and doesn't like. These services base song selections on artists that the listener specifies as favourites and related artists that the service believes play a similar style of music. In this way, the listener can hear tracks from the requested artist along with other music in the same vein.

Compressed music formats such as MP3 have made music swapping over the Internet a convenient and popular activity. File-sharing software such as BitTorrent provides a means by which some music fans copy and distribute music, often without consideration of copyright law. The result is a popular music distribution system that is largely illegal and difficult to control, and which cuts deeply into the recording industry's profits. In addition, it is not always safe to swap files with strangers. Downloaded music files may actually be viruses renamed to look like MP3 files. Music industry giants have pulled together to win back customers by offering legal and safe electronic music distribution at a reasonable price that provides services and perks not offered by file-sharing networks.

Several legal music download services are available. Apple's iTunes was one of the first online music services to find success. Since its release, the iTunes Music Store has become the largest music retailer in the world. Microsoft, Amazon, Walmart, and other retailers also sell music online. The going rate for music downloads is 89 to 99 cents per song. Downloaded music may include digital rights management (DRM) technology that prevents or limits the user's ability to make copies or to play the music on several players.

Music services that use a subscription model of distribution include Napster, Rhapsody, Yahoo! Music, and AOL Music. For an annual fee, these music services offer access to a catalogue of millions of songs from the Big Five labels—Universal Music, Sony Music, Warner Music, BMG, and EMI—and from independent artists. After months of legal struggles unsuccessfully fighting recording company lawsuits, popular file-sharing service LimeWire has also moved to a subscription model of music distribution.[41]

Podcasts are yet another way to access music on the Web. Many independent artists provide samples of their music through podcasts. Podcast Alley features around 8,000 music-related podcasts from unsigned artists.

Movies, Video, and Television

With increasing amounts of Internet bandwidth going to more homes, streaming video and television are becoming commonplace. Once content with small, low-quality YouTube videos, the public now craves professionally produced video. Some are connecting their computers to high-definition television sets to access television and even motion-picture quality programming. The Web and TV are rapidly merging into a single integrated system available from home entertainment systems, PCs, and cell phones.

Television is expanding to the Web in leaps and bounds. Websites such as Hulu and Internet-based television platforms like Joost in the United States provide television programming from hundreds of providers, including most mainstream television networks. Joost attracts an estimated 67 million viewers per month.[42] Hulu provides a premium service called Hulu Plus that provides an extended menu of programming to iPhones, iPads, TVs, and more for $10 per month. Hulu CEO Jason Kilar says the service complements rather than replaces cable TV. But most analysts agree that it's only a matter of time until cable is challenged by Internet-based television programming.[43] Many TV networks, including GlobalTV and CTV in Canada, offer online full-length streamed episodes of popular programs, including season premieres that are released before airing on television. Clicker.com serves as a television guide to most online programming. Apple iTunes offers television programs from ABC, AMC, CBS, CNN, E!, FOX, PBS, MTV, and many other networks—some for free, but most for around $3 an episode. Once purchased, the program can be downloaded and viewed on a computer, iPod, iPhone, or iPad. By no means does Apple have a corner on this market. Television and movie programming is available for every platform, including PC, smartphone, and tablet.

Motion pictures are also making their way to Internet distribution. Subscription services such as Netflix Canada allow members to rent DVDs by mail and to stream movies over the Web to their computers or TVs. Apple iTunes is also in the motion picture business. Users of the service can rent or purchase movies from the iTunes store and download them to a computer.

Television programs and motion pictures are typically distributed online in a controlled manner. Streaming video does not provide access to the entire video file, which makes it difficult to produce copies. Purchased downloaded video is typically protected with DRM technology. The TV and movie industries are doing all they can to prevent pirating. Still, illegally copied and shared movie and video files take up a large percentage of Internet bandwidth. Some Internet service providers have deliberately interfered with movie uploads and downloads over BitTorrent networks in an effort to free up bandwidth for legitimate Internet business.

No discussion of Internet video would be complete without mentioning YouTube. YouTube supports the online sharing of user-created videos. Every day, people upload hundreds of thousands of videos to YouTube and view hundreds of millions of these videos. YouTube videos are relatively short and cover a wide range of categories from the nonsensical to college lectures. Other video streaming sites include Google Video, Yahoo! Video, Metacafe, and AOL Video.

E-Books and Audio Books

An e-book is a book stored digitally, rather than on paper, and read on a display using e-book reader software. E-books have been available for quite a while, nearly as long as computers. However, it wasn't until the introduction of Amazon's e-book reading device, the Kindle, in 2007 that they gained more widespread acceptance. Several features of the Kindle appeal to the general public. First, the Kindle features ePaper, a display that does not include backlighting like traditional displays. Some feel that ePaper is less harsh on your eyes than using a backlit display. Second, the Kindle is light and compact, similar in size and weight to a paperback book, but thinner than most books. Finally, Amazon created a vast library of e-books that could be purchased and downloaded to the Kindle. By 2009, dozens of electronics manufacturers were offering e-book readers.

Apple's iPad changed the e-book industry by providing a product that is similar to but larger than the Kindle. The iPad also includes a colour backlit display. As an e-book reader, the iPad functions much like the Kindle; however, the iPad provides thousands of applications in addition to e-books. Apple offers users much the same selection of books as Kindle users. Amazon has even developed a Kindle application that runs on the iPad so users can access their Kindle libraries on the iPad. The iPad has launched a computing revolution, with dozens of manufacturers designing their own slate computers to act as e-book readers, media players, Internet devices, and more.

Besides using the Kindle, iPad, and other slate devices, you can access e-books on the Web, download them as PDF files to view on your computer, or read them on your smartphone. There are dozens of e-book formats. Some are proprietary, such as Kindle's .azw format, which can be viewed only on a Kindle. Other formats are open, such as Open eBook's .opf format and the .epub format, both of which can be read on many different devices and software packages, including Apple's iPad.

Google has partnered with libraries to digitize over 10 million books in its Google Books Library Project. A Google search includes searching for information in its Google Books Library. Google Books includes digital copies of in-copyright books, out-of-copyright books, and books from publishers with whom Google has partnered. Search results from Google Books may include snippets of information about the book and where to buy it or, in the case of out-of-copyright books, the entire contents. Google has made an effort to open its own e-book store, but so far it has been blocked by U.S. courts because of worries that Google would obtain monopoly power over the industry.

There have been major efforts to bring library resources to the Internet.[44] Unesco and the United States Library of Congress have joined forces to develop the World Digital Library (WDL). The WDL is an online resource containing more than 1,200 cultural entries from around the world. Available in Arabic, Chinese, English, French, Portuguese, Russian, and Spanish, the WDL is intended to promote international and intercultural understanding and to help bridge the digital divide.

Audio books have become more popular due to the success of the iPod and the iPhone and services such as *www.audible.com*. Audio books either are read by a narrator without much inflection or varying voices, or can be performed by actors who add dramatic interpretations of the book to the reading. Audio books may be abridged (consolidated and edited for audio format) or unabridged (read word for word from the book). Audio book services may allow you to purchase books individually or sign up for a membership and receive a new book each month. Audio books can be transferred from PC to a portable device such as an iPod or Kindle.

Online Games

Video games have become a huge industry. The industry is expected to grow from $52.5 billion in 2009 to $86.8 billion in global sales by 2014.[45] Many video games are available online. They include single-user, multi-user, and massively multi-user games. The Web offers a multitude of games for all ages. Whether you're looking for Nickelodeon's Sponge Bob games, solitaire, or massively multiplayer online role-playing games (MMORPG), a wide variety of offerings suit every taste. Of course, the Web provides a medium for downloading single-player games to your desktop, notebook, hand-held device, or cell phone device, but the power of the Web is most apparent with multiplayer games. Table 7.6 lists the various genres of online multiplayer games.

Type	Description
Action	Fast-paced games requiring accuracy and quick reflexes
Board	Games involving play on a virtual game board
Card	Games involving the use of a virtual deck of cards
Flight Simulation	Games that involve taking on the role of a pilot in a historic biplane, modern aircraft, or a futuristic starship
Multi-User Dimension or Multi-User Dungeon (MUD)	Text-based games that make up for their lack of graphics with diverse and immersive game play
Role-Playing Games (RPG)	Games in which you take on the persona of a game character
Sims (Simulations)	Games in which you create your own character that lives in a simulated environment
Sports	Games involving sports like baseball, football, basketball, or golf
Strategy	Games that feature planning, tactics, and diplomacy
Trivia/Puzzle	Games that require a good memory or problem-solving skills

Table 7.6

Multiplayer Online Games

Although most multiplayer games are free, some of the best charge fees. You may need to purchase software or pay monthly, yearly, or per-play subscription fees. The popular MMORPG World of Warcraft costs $20 or more for the software and $14.99 per 30 days of game time.

Game consoles such as the Wii, Xbox, and PlayStation provide multiplayer options for online gaming over the Internet. Subscribers can play with or against other subscribers in 3D virtual environments. They can even talk to each other using a microphone headset. Microsoft's Xbox LIVE provides features that allow users to keep track of their buddies online and match up with other players who are of the same skill level.

Although currently illegal in most of Canada, online gambling is a billion-dollar global industry. Online casinos, poker rooms, sports and racing bookies, and bingo halls are found in abundance online. Poker is particularly popular because it pits player against player and allows the more skillful to win. Online gaming companies PartyGaming and Empire Online are so large that they sell shares on the London Stock Exchange. Some worry that the convenience of online gambling increases the possibility of addiction and is a risk to the public good.

Shopping Online

Shopping on the Web can be convenient, easy, and cost effective. You can buy almost anything via the Web—books, clothing, cars, and sports equipment are just a few of the categories. You can even buy medical advice on the Web. Amazon.ca sells short stories by popular authors for 49 cents per story. My Virtual Model works with clothing retailers to provide visitors with a virtual model on which to try clothes that they may want to purchase. Dell.com and many other computer retailers provide tools that allow shoppers to specify every aspect and component of a computer system to purchase. GroceryGateway.com would be happy to deliver groceries to your doorstep. Products and services abound online.

Many online shopping options are available to Web users. E-tail stores—online versions of retail stores—provide access to many products that may be unavailable in local stores. Sears, Costco, Walmart, and many others carry only a percentage of their inventory in their retail stores; the other inventory is available online. To add to their other conveniences, many websites offer free shipping and pickup for returned items that don't fit or otherwise meet a customer's needs.

Starbucks blends online shopping with coffee house visits in its iPhone applications. Customers can use the applications to design new coffee beverages and order and pay for them at the Starbucks counter with a swipe of the iPhone over a bar-code reader.[46]

Like your local shopping mall, cybermalls provide access to a collection of stores that aim to meet your every need. Cybermalls are typically aligned with popular Web portals such as Yahoo!, AOL, and MSN. Websites such as *www.mySimon.com*, *www.DealTime.com*, *www.PriceSCAN.com*, *www.PriceGrabber.com*, and *www.NexTag.com* provide product price quotations from numerous e-tailers to help you to find the best deal. An application for Android smartphones called Compare Everywhere allows users to compare the price of an item offered by many retailers. Even if the best price is offered at your local warehouse store, shopping online provides the assurance that you are getting the best deal.

Shopping online not only makes it easy to find the best price, it also provides the means to make an informed decision about what you're buying. Many websites offer reviews of products purchased online. You can read about the experiences of other consumers before spending money on a new camera, backpack, or car.

Online clearinghouses, Web auctions, and marketplaces provide a platform for businesses and individuals to sell their products and belongings. Online clearinghouses such as *www.uBid.com* provide a method for manufacturers to liquidate stock and for consumers to find a good deal. Outdated or overstocked items are put on the virtual auction block and users bid on the items. The highest bidder(s) when the auction closes gets the merchandise—often for less than 50 percent of the advertised retail price. Credit card numbers are collected at the time that bids are placed. A good rule to keep in mind is not to place a bid on an item unless you are prepared to buy it at that price.

The most popular online auction or marketplace is *www.eBay.com*. See Figure 7.22. eBay provides a public platform for global trading where anyone can buy, sell, or trade practically anything. eBay offers a wide variety of features and services that enable members to buy and sell on the site quickly and conveniently. Buyers have the option to purchase

Figure 7.22

eBay.com provides an online marketplace where anyone can buy, sell, or trade practically anything.

(Source: These materials have been reproduced with the permission of eBay Inc. © 2011 EBAY INC. ALL RIGHTS RESERVED.)

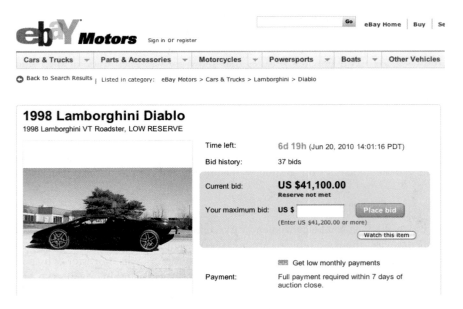

items at a fixed price or in auction-style format, where the highest bid wins the product. Information about auction items on eBay includes how much time is left in the auction, the current highest bid, as well as details about the item and seller. On any given day, millions of items are listed on eBay across thousands of categories.

Auction houses such as eBay accept limited liability for problems that buyers or sellers may experience in their transactions. Transactions that make use of eBay's PayPal service are protected. Others may be risky. Participants should be aware that auction fraud is the most prevalent type of fraud on the Internet.

Craigslist is a network of online communities that provides free online classified advertisements. It is a popular online marketplace for purchasing items from local individuals. Many shoppers turn to Craigslist rather than going to the classifieds in the local paper.

Businesses benefit from shopping online as well. *Global supply management (GSM)* online services provide methods for businesses to find the best deals on the global market for raw materials and supplies needed to manufacture their products. *Electronic exchanges* provide an industry-specific Web resource created to deliver a convenient centralized platform for B2B e-commerce among manufacturers, suppliers, and customers. You can read more about this topic in Chapter 8.

Travel, Geolocation, and Navigation

The Web has had a profound effect on the travel industry and the way people plan and prepare for trips. From getting assistance with short trips across town to planning long holidays abroad, travellers are turning to the Web to save time and money and overcome much of the risk involved in visiting unknown places.

Travel websites such as *www.travelocity.ca*, *www.expedia.ca*, and *www.priceline.com* help travellers find the best deals on flights, hotels, car rentals, vacation packages, and cruises. Priceline offers a slightly different approach from Travelocity and Expedia. It allows shoppers to name a price they're willing to pay for a ticket and then works to find an airline that can meet that price. After flights have been reserved, travellers can use these websites to book hotels and rental cars, often at discounted prices.

Travel agencies, resorts, airlines, cruise lines, and all businesses associated with travel have a strong online presence. Map websites like Bing Maps and Google Maps are invaluable for finding your way to and around destinations; you can even view your destination from street view. Websites like *www.tripit.com* allow you to organize all of your travel plans, including flights, car rentals, hotel reservations, restaurants, and landmarks in one easy-to-access Web page. Today, most travel begins on the Web.

Mapping and geolocation tools are among the most popular and successful Web applications. MapQuest, Google Maps, and Bing Maps are examples. See Figure 7.23. By offering free street maps for cities around the world, these tools help travellers find their way. Provide

Figure 7.23

Bing Maps

Mapping software such as Bing Maps provide streetside views of Times Square.

(Source: Used with permission from Microsoft.)

your departure location and destination, and these online applications produce a map that displays the fastest route. Now with GPS technologies, these tools can detect your current location and provide directions from where you are.

Google Maps also provides extensive location-specific business information, satellite imagery, up-to-the-minute traffic reports, and Street View. Street View is the result of Google employees driving the streets of the world's cities in vehicles with high-tech camera gear, taking 360-degree images. These images are integrated into Google Maps to allow users to get a "street view" of an area that can be manipulated as if they were actually walking down the street looking around. Bing Maps takes it a step further with high-resolution aerial photos and street-level 3D photographs.

Map applications like Google Maps provide tool kits that allow them to be combined with other Web applications. For example, Google Maps can be used in conjunction with Twitter to display the location where various tweets were posted. Likewise, Google Maps combined with Flickr can overlay photos of specific geographic locations. Combined Web applications are commonly referred to as a *mashup*.

Mapping software packages from Google and Microsoft overlay road maps onto high-resolution satellite images of Earth to produce a zoomable view of the planet. You can view the planet from 1.5 kilometres out in space, zoom in to view a country or province, and then zoom in further to view cities, roads, and buildings.

Geographic information systems (GIS) provide geographic information layered over a map. For example, Google Earth provides options for viewing traffic, weather, local photos and videos, underwater features such as shipwrecks and marine life, local attractions, businesses, and places of interest. Software such as Google Latitude and Loopt allow you to find your friends on a map—with their permission—and will automatically notify you if a friend is near.

Geo-tagging is technology that allows for tagging information with an associated location. For example, Flickr and other photo software and services allow photos to be tagged with the location they were taken. Once tagged, it becomes easy to search for photos taken in Alberta for example. Geo-tagging also makes it easy to overlay photos on a map, as Google Maps and Bing Maps have done. Twitter, Facebook, and other social networks have made it possible for users to geo-tag photos, comments, tweets, and posts.

Geolocation information does pose a risk to privacy and security. Many people prefer for their location to remain unknown, at least to strangers, and often to acquaintances and even friends. Recently, criminals have made use of location information to determine when people are away from their residences so that they can burglarize without fear of interruption.

Figure 7.24

Layar Augmented Reality

Layar overlays local business information over images captured on a smartphone's camera.

(Source: Courtesy of Layar.)

Augmented reality applications take geolocation one step further. Using your phone's camera, GPS information, compass information, local business information, and sometimes a form of artificial intelligence called pattern recognition, applications such as Google Goggles and Layar can overlay local information over the image you view from your camera.[47] With this technology, as you pan around an intersection viewing the image through your camera, you will see information about nearby businesses and points of interest. See Figure 7.24. Location-based advertisements may inform you that a nearby business will honour a coupon delivered to your phone as a text message.

Internet Utilities

Just as the Web is an application that runs on the Internet to provide a framework for delivering information and services, other applications have

INFORMATION SYSTEMS @ WORK

Selling Real Estate with Google Maps

The REA Group, headquartered in Australia, started its business in 1995 with $24,000 AUD (Australian dollars) and the belief that the Web would grow to become a dominant tool for the real estate industry. The company worked with Australian realtors to develop effective online real estate advertising. Before long, its website, *www.realestate.com.au*, became the most popular real estate portal in Australia. Today the REA Group has 18 Web portals and operations in 12 countries, including Belgium, France, Germany, Hong Kong, Italy, Luxembourg, New Zealand, and the United Kingdom, with an annual revenue of over AUD $156 million.

As online map software such as Google Maps arrived on the scene, the REA Group immediately saw its potential for the real estate market. CEO Simon Baker believes that shoppers want to see as much information about a property as possible before contacting an agent. The REA Group purchased simple mapping software to add to its real estate Web portals. Unfortunately, the software was slow to load, and key features such as zooming in and out worked inconsistently in different Web browsers. Even worse, the software failed to plot some coordinates accurately.

Fortunately, mapping technology improved over time, and the REA Group became impressed with the features provided by Google Maps. In particular, the company appreciated that Google Maps could be customized to meet the needs of the real estate industry and could easily be embedded into Web pages. The REA Group dropped its previous mapping technology and moved to Google Maps.

The API Premier version of Google Maps allows businesses to associate information with map coordinates. Google Maps embedded in *www.realestate.com.au* allows shoppers to see home locations on a map using a map view, a satellite view, hybrid view, terrain view, or street view. Shoppers can click the house icons on the map to view details and price. Google Maps also provides detailed property boundary lines. Those shopping for real estate can combine Google Maps and interior photos of the home to get a fairly thorough inspection before taking time for a physical visit. The REA Group believes that the embedded map is the most important feature of the online shopping experience.

Additionally, shoppers can perform structured and geographic searches for property. They can also use the embedded Google search bar to look for nearby schools, restaurants, attractions, and businesses. The REA Group plans to extend the capabilities of Google Maps with an assortment of overlays that provide information on a particular geographic region.

After the REA Group added Google Maps to its Australian site, it witnessed a steady boost in traffic and sales leads. Rather than competing with real estate agents, the software provides the agents with well-informed customers ready to buy, allowing the agents to make more sales with less effort. More recently, the company has rolled out the technology to its U.K. and Luxembourg sites and is currently continuing to extend the software to its remaining sites.

In 2009, the REA Group provided over 1.5 billion maps through its real estate portals, making it one of the largest map providers in the world. CEO Simon Baker says that "with the mapping technology from Google, we're able to enhance the user experience, increase site stickiness, and improve the quality and accuracy of the data being displayed."

Discussion Questions

1. How has Google Maps improved the online shopping experience for visitors to *www.realestate.com.au*?
2. How does Google Maps help real estate agents in their work?

Critical Thinking Questions

1. What might the REA Group have done to avoid the problems it experienced with its first mapping software?
2. How might a company like the REA Group make money?

SOURCES: "Global Real Estate Portal Network Adds Google Maps to Enhance Customers' House Hunting Experience," Google Maps Case Study, *www.google.com/enterprise/maps/reagroup.html*, accessed January 23, 2010; The REA Group website, *www.rea-group.com*, accessed January 24, 2010; *realestate.com.au*, accessed January 24, 2010.

been designed to run on the Internet for other purposes. Many of these applications serve as utilities for accessing and maintaining resources on the Internet. A few such utilities that predate the Web and http, and still remain useful, are Telnet, SSH, and FTP.

Telnet is a network protocol that enables users to log on to networks remotely over the Internet. Telnet software uses a command-line interface that allows the user to work on a remote server directly. Because Telnet is not secured with encryption, most users are switching to *secure shell* (*SSH*), which provides Telnet functionality through a more secure connection.

File Transfer Protocol (**FTP**) is a protocol that supports file transfers between a host and a remote computer. See Figure 7.25. Using FTP, users can copy files from one computer to another. For example, the authors and editors of this book used an FTP site provided by the publisher, Cengage Learning, to share and transfer important files during the publication process. Chapter files and artwork, for example, were uploaded to a Cengage Learning FTP site and downloaded by authors and editors to review. Like Telnet, FTP connections are not encrypted and are therefore not secure. Many users are switching to secure FTP (SFTP) for more secure file transfers.

File Transfer Protocol (FTP)
A protocol that provides a file transfer process between a host and a remote computer and allows users to copy files from one computer to another.

Figure 7.25

FTP Applications

FTP applications allow you to transfer files between computers by clicking and dragging them from one window to another.

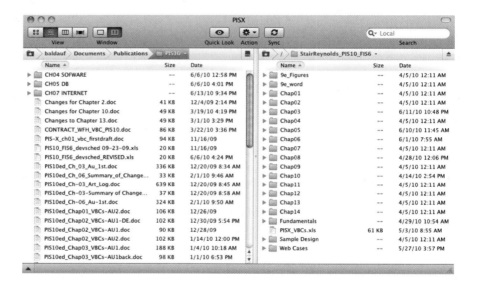

INTRANETS AND EXTRANETS

Recall from Chapter 1 that an intranet is an internal corporate network built using Internet and World Wide Web standards and technologies. Employees of an organization use it to gain access to corporate information. After getting their feet wet with public websites that promote company products and services, corporations are seizing the Web as a swift way to streamline—even transform—their organizations. These private networks use the infrastructure and standards of the Internet and the World Wide Web. Using an intranet offers one considerable advantage: many people are already familiar with Internet technology, so they need little training to make effective use of their corporate intranet.

An intranet is an inexpensive yet powerful alternative to other forms of internal communication, including conventional computer networks. One of an intranet's most obvious virtues is its ability to reduce the need for paper. Because Web browsers run on any type of computer, the same electronic information can be viewed by any employee. That means that all sorts of documents (such as internal phone books, procedure manuals, training manuals, and requisition forms) can be inexpensively converted to electronic form on the Web, easily distributed, and constantly updated. An intranet provides employees with an easy and intuitive approach to accessing information that was previously difficult to obtain. For example, it is an ideal way to provide information to a mobile sales force that needs access to rapidly changing information.

A growing number of companies offer limited access to their private corporate network for selected customers and suppliers. Such networks are referred to as extranets; they connect people who are external to the company. An **extranet** is a network that links selected resources of the intranet of a company with its customers, suppliers, or other business partners. Like intranets, an extranet is built around Web technologies.

Security and performance concerns are different for an extranet than for a website or network-based intranet. User authentication and privacy are critical on an extranet so that information is protected. Obviously, the network must perform well to provide quick response to customers and suppliers. Table 7.7 summarizes the differences between users of the Internet, intranets, and extranets.

extranet
A network based on Web technologies that links selected resources of a company's intranet with its customers, suppliers, or other business partners.

Type	Users	Need User ID and Password?
Internet	Anyone	No
Intranet	Employees and managers	Yes
Extranet	Business partners	Yes

Table 7.7

Summary of Internet, Intranet, and Extranet Users

Secure intranet and extranet access applications usually require the use of a *virtual private network* (VPN), a secure connection between two points on the Internet. VPNs transfer information by encapsulating traffic in IP packets and sending the packets over the Internet, a practice called **tunnelling**. Most VPNs are built and run by ISPs. Companies that use a VPN from an ISP have essentially outsourced their networks to save money on wide area network equipment and personnel.

tunnelling
The process by which VPNs transfer information by encapsulating traffic in IP packets over the Internet.

SUMMARY

Principle:

The Internet provides a critical infrastructure for delivering and accessing information and services.

The Internet is truly international in scope, with users on every continent. The Internet started with ARPANET, a project sponsored by the U.S. Department of Defense (DoD). Today, the Internet is the world's largest computer network. Actually, it is a collection of interconnected networks, all freely exchanging information. The Internet transmits data from one computer (called a host) to another. The set of conventions used to pass packets from one host to another is known as the Internet Protocol (IP). Many other protocols are used with IP. The best known is the Transmission Control Protocol (TCP). TCP is so widely used that many people refer to the Internet protocol as TCP/IP, the combination of TCP and IP used by most Internet applications. Each computer on the Internet has an assigned IP address for easy identification. A Uniform Resource Locator (URL) is a Web address that specifies the exact location of a Web page (using letters and words that map to an IP address) and the location on the host.

Cloud computing refers to a computing environment where software and storage are provided as an Internet service and accessed with a Web browser, rather than installed and stored on PCs. As Internet connection speeds improve and wireless Internet access becomes pervasive, computing activities are increasing. Cloud computing offers tremendous advantages. By outsourcing business information systems to the cloud, a business saves on system design, installation, and maintenance. Employees can also access corporate systems from any Internet-connected computer using a standard Web browser.

People can connect to the Internet backbone in several ways: via a LAN whose server is an Internet host, or via a dial-up connection, high-speed service, or wireless service. An Internet service provider (ISP) is any organization that provides access to the Internet. To use this type of connection, you must have an account with the service provider and software that allows a direct link via TCP/IP.

Principle:

Originally developed as a document-management system, the World Wide Web has grown to become a primary source of news and information, an indispensable conduit for commerce, and a popular hub for social interaction, entertainment, and communication.

The Web is a collection of tens of millions of servers providing information via hyperlink technology to billions of users worldwide. Thanks to the high-speed Internet circuits connecting them and to hyperlink technology, users can jump between Web pages and servers effortlessly—creating the illusion of using one big computer. Because of its ability to handle multimedia objects and hypertext links between distributed objects, the Web is emerging as the most popular means of information access on the Internet today.

As a hyperlink-based system that uses the client/server model, the Web organizes Internet resources throughout the world into a series of linked files, called pages, accessed and viewed using Web client software, called a Web browser. Internet Explorer, Firefox, Chrome, Safari, and Opera are popular Web browsers. A collection of pages on one particular topic, accessed under one Web domain, is called a website.

Hypertext Markup Language (HTML) is the standard page description language for Web pages. The HTML tags tell the browser how to format the text: as a heading, as a list, or as body text, for example. HTML also indicates where images, sound, and other elements should be inserted. Some other Web standards have become nearly equal to HTML in importance, including Extensible Markup Language (XML), Cascading Style Sheets (CSS), and Wireless Markup Language (WML).

Web 2.0 refers to the Web as a computing platform that supports software applications and the sharing of information among users. Over the past few years, the Web has been changing from a one-directional resource where users find information, to a two-directional resource where users find and share information. The Web has also grown in power to support complete software applications and is becoming a computing platform itself. A Rich Internet Application (RIA) is software that has the functionality and complexity of traditional application software, but runs in a Web browser and does not require local installation. Java, PHP, AJAX, MySQL, .NET, and Web application frameworks are all used to create interactive Web pages.

Principle:

The Internet and Web provide numerous resources for finding information, communicating and collaborating, socializing, conducting business and shopping, and being entertained.

The types of Internet and Web applications available are vast and ever expanding. The most common and popular uses for the Internet and Web can be categorized as publishing information, assisting users in finding information, supporting communication and collaboration, building online community, providing software applications, providing a platform for expressing ideas and opinions, delivering media of all types, providing a platform for commerce, and supporting travel and navigation.

The Web has become the most popular medium for distributing and accessing information. It is a powerful tool for keeping informed about local, provincial, national, and global news. As a tool for sharing information and a primary repository of information on all subjects, the Web is ideally suited for education and training. Museums, libraries, private businesses, government agencies, and many other types of organizations and individuals offer educational materials online for free or a fee. Many businesses use the Web browser as an interface to corporate information systems. Websites have sprung up to support every subject and activity of importance.

A search engine is a valuable tool that enables you to find information on the Web by specifying words that are key to a topic of interest—known as keywords. Some search companies have experimented with human-powered and human-assisted search. In addition to search engines, you can use other Internet sites to research information. Wikipedia, an online encyclopaedia with over 3.3 million English-language entries created and edited by millions of users, is another example of a website that can be used to research information. Although Wikipedia is the best-known, general-purpose wiki, other wikis are designed for special purposes. Online research is also greatly assisted by traditional resources that have migrated from libraries to websites such as online databases.

A Web portal is a Web page that combines useful information and links into one page and that often acts as an entry point to the Web—the first page you open when you begin browsing the Web. A Web portal typically includes a search engine, a subject directory, daily headlines, and other items of interest. They can be general or specific in nature.

The Internet and Web provide many applications for communication and collaboration. E-mail is an incredibly useful form of Internet communication that not only supports text communication, but also supports HTML content and file sharing as e-mail attachments. Instant messaging is online, real-time communication between two or more people who are connected to the Internet. Referred to as a microblogging service, Twitter allows users to send short text updates (up to 140 characters long) from a cell phone or the Web to their Twitter followers. A number of Internet technologies support real-time online conferencing. The Internet has made it possible for those involved in teleconferences to share computer desktops. Using services such as WebEx or GoToMeeting, conference participants log on to common software that allows them to broadcast their computer displays to the group. Telepresence systems use high-resolution video and audio with high-definition displays to make it appear that conference participants are actually sitting around a table.

Over the past several years, the Web has evolved from a one-directional resource where users only obtain information to a two-directional resource where users obtain and contribute information. Websites such as YouTube and Flickr allow users to share video and photos with other people, groups, and the world. Microblogging sites like Twitter allow people to post thoughts and ideas throughout the day for friends to read. Social bookmarking sites such as www.digg.com and www.delicious.com allow users to pool their votes to determine what online news stories and Web pages are most interesting at any given time of the day. Similarly, Epinions and many retail websites allow consumers to voice their opinions about products. Social networking websites provide Web-based tools for users to share information about themselves with people on the Web and to find, meet, and converse with other members.

Many of the computer activities traditionally provided through software installed on a PC can now be carried out using RIAs in a Web browser without installing any software. RIAs are the result of continuously improving programming languages and platforms designed for the Web.

A Web log, typically called a blog, is a website that people can create and use to write about their observations, experiences, and opinions on a wide range of topics. Internet users may subscribe to blogs using a technology called Really Simple Syndication (RSS). RSS is a collection of Web technologies that allow users to subscribe to Web content that is frequently updated. With RSS, you can receive a blog update without actually visiting the blog website. A *podcast* is an audio broadcast over the Internet.

Like news and information, all forms of media and entertainment have followed their audiences online. The Internet and the Web have made music more accessible than ever, with artists distributing their songs through online radio, subscription services, and download services. With increasing amounts of Internet bandwidth available, streaming video and television are becoming commonplace. E-books have been available for quite a while, nearly as long as computers. However, it wasn't until the birth of Amazon's e-book reading device, the Kindle, in 2007 that they gained more widespread acceptance. Online games include the many different types of single-user, multi-user, and massively multi-user games played on the Internet and the Web.

Many online shopping options are available to Web users. E-tail stores—online versions of retail stores—provide access to many products that may be unavailable in local stores. Like your local shopping mall, cybermalls provide access to a collection of stores that aim to meet your every need. Online clearinghouses, Web auctions, and marketplaces provide a platform for businesses and individuals to sell their products and belongings.

The Web has had a profound effect on the travel industry and the way people plan and prepare for trips. From getting assistance with short trips across town to planning long holidays abroad, travellers are turning to the Web to save time and money and overcome much of the risk involved in visiting unknown places. Mapping and geolocation tools are among the most popular and successful Web applications. MapQuest, Google Maps, and Bing Maps are examples. Geo-tagging is technology that allows for tagging information with an associated location. Augmented reality applications take geolocation one step further. Using your phone's camera, GPS information, compass information, local business information, and sometimes a form of artificial intelligence called pattern recognition, applications like Google Goggles and Layar can overlay local information on the image you view from your camera.

Just as the Web is an application that runs on the Internet to provide a framework for delivering information and services, other applications have been designed to run on the Internet for other purposes. Telnet is a network protocol that enables users to log on to networks remotely over the Internet. Because Telnet is not secured with encryption, most users are switching to secure shell (SSH), which provides Telnet functionality through a more secure connection. File Transfer Protocol (FTP) is a protocol that supports file transfers between a host and a remote computer. Like Telnet, FTP connections are not encrypted and are therefore not secure. Many users are switching to secure FTP (SFTP) for more secure file transfers.

Principle:

Popular Internet and Web technologies have been applied to business networks in the form of intranets and extranets.

An intranet is an internal corporate network built using Internet and World Wide Web standards and products. Because Web browsers run on any type of computer, the same electronic information can be viewed by any employee. That means that all sorts of documents can be converted to electronic form on the Web and constantly be updated.

An extranet is a network that links selected resources of the intranet of a company with its customers, suppliers, or other business partners. It is also built around Web technologies. Security and performance concerns are different for an extranet than for a website or network-based intranet. User authentication and privacy are critical on an extranet. Obviously, the network must perform well to provide quick response to customers and suppliers.

CHAPTER 7: SELF-ASSESSMENT TEST

The Internet provides a critical infrastructure for delivering and accessing information and services.

1. The _____ was the ancestor of the Internet and was developed by the U.S. Department of Defense.

2. Canada has more Internet users than China. True or False?

3. On the Internet, what enables traffic to flow from one network to another?
   a. Internet Protocol
   b. ARPANET
   c. Uniform Resource Locator
   d. LAN server

4. Each computer on the Internet has an address called the Transmission Control Protocol. True or False?

5. In what computing environment are software and storage provided as an Internet service and accessed with a Web browser?
   a. cloud computing
   b. Internet Society (ISOC)
   c. The Web
   d. America Online (AOL)

6. A(n) _____ is an organization that provides people with access to the Internet.

Originally developed as a document-management system, the World Wide Web has grown to become a primary source of news and information, an indispensable conduit for commerce, and a popular hub for social interaction, entertainment, and communication.

7. CSS is a markup language designed to transport and store data on the Web. True or False?

8. Which technology was developed to assist in easily specifying the visual appearance of Web pages in a website?
   a. HTML
   b. XHTML
   c. XML
   d. CSS

9. Many of today's most popular online applications, including Gmail, Google Docs, Flickr, and Facebook, were developed with _____.

10. What is the standard page description language for Web pages?
    a. Home Page Language
    b. Hypermedia Language
    c. Java
    d. Hypertext Markup Language

11. Web development software that provides the foundational code—or framework—that developers use to customize the code to specific needs for a professional, interactive website is called a(n) _____.

The Internet and Web provide numerous resources for finding information, communicating and collaborating, socializing, conducting business, shopping, and being entertained.

12. Websites such as www.digg.com and www.delicious.com are examples of _____ websites.
    a. media sharing
    b. social network
    c. social bookmarking
    d. content streaming

13. A(n) _____ is a valuable tool that enables you to find information on the Web by specifying words or phrases (known as keywords) related to a topic of interest.

14. Which of the following is an example of a microblogging service?
    a. Facebook
    b. WordPress
    c. Twitter
    d. YouTube

15. _____ uses high-resolution video and audio with high-definition displays that allow individuals from anywhere in the world to meet and make it appear that conference participants are actually sitting around a table.

Popular Internet and Web technologies have been applied to business networks in the form of intranets and extranets.

16. A(n) _____ is a network based on Web technology that links customers, suppliers, and others to the company.

17. An intranet is an internal corporate network built using Internet and World Wide Web standards and products. True or False?

CHAPTER 7: SELF-ASSESSMENT TEST ANSWERS

(1) ARPANET (2) False (3) a (4) False (5) a (6) Internet service provider (ISP) (7) False (8) d (9) AJAX (10) d (11) Web Application Framework (12) c (13) search engine (14) c (15) Telepresence (16) extranet (17) True

REVIEW QUESTIONS

1. What is the Internet? Who uses it and why?
2. What is ARPANET?
3. What is TCP/IP? How does it work?
4. Explain the naming conventions used to identify Internet host computers.
5. What is a Web browser? Provide four examples.
6. What is cloud computing?
7. Briefly describe three ways to connect to the Internet. What are the advantages and disadvantages of each approach?
8. What is an Internet service provider? What services does it provide?
9. How do Web application frameworks assist Web developers?
10. What are the advantages and disadvantages of e-mail?
11. What is a podcast?
12. How do human-powered search engines work?
13. For what are Telnet and FTP used, respectively?
14. What is content streaming?
15. What is instant messaging?
16. What is the Web? Is it another network like the Internet or a service that runs on the Internet?
17. What is a URL, and how is it used?
18. What is augmented reality, and how is it useful?
19. What is an intranet? Provide three examples of the use of an intranet.
20. What is an extranet? How is it different from an intranet?
21. Describe at least three important Internet issues.

DISCUSSION QUESTIONS

1. Social networks are widely used. Describe how this technology could be used in a business setting. Are there any drawbacks or limitations to using social networks in a business setting?
2. Your company is about to develop a new website. Describe how you could use Web services for your site.
3. Why is it important to have an organization that manages IP addresses and domain names?
4. What are the benefits and risks involved in using cloud computing?
5. Which Internet service option provides the best value in Mbps per dollar?
6. Describe how a company could use a blog and podcasting.
7. Briefly describe how the Internet phone service operates. Discuss the potential impact that this service could have on traditional telephone services and carriers.
8. Why is XML an important technology?
9. How do HTML, CSS, and XML work together to create a Web page?
10. What value does SEO provide to businesses?
11. Identify three companies with which you are familiar that are using the Web to conduct business. Describe their use of the Web.
12. What are the defining characteristics of a Web 2.0 site?
13. Name four forms of Internet communication and describe the benefits and drawbacks of each.
14. What social concerns surround geolocation technologies?
15. One of the key issues associated with the development of a website is getting people to visit it. If you were developing a website, how would you inform others about it and make it interesting enough that they would return and tell others about it?
16. Downloading music, radio, and video programs from the Internet is easier and more regulated than in the past, but some companies are still worried that people will illegally obtain copies of this programming without paying the artists and producers royalties. If you were an artist or producer, what would you do?
17. How could you use the Internet if you were a travelling salesperson?
18. Briefly summarize the differences in how the Internet, a company intranet, and an extranet are accessed and used.

PROBLEM-SOLVING EXERCISES

1. Do research on the Web to find several social networking sites. After researching these sites, use a word processor to write a report comparing and contrasting the services. Also discuss the advantages and potential problems of sharing personal information online. What information collected by social networking sites do you think should be kept private from the general public?

2. Develop a brief proposal for creating a business website. How could you use Web services to make creating and maintaining the website easier and less expensive? Develop a simple spreadsheet to analyze the income you need to cover your website and other business expenses.

3. Think of a business that you might like to establish. Use a word processor to define the business in terms of what product(s) or service(s) it provides, where it is located, and its name. Go to *www.godaddy.com* and find an appropriate domain name for your business that is not yet taken. Shop around online for the best deal on website hosting. Write a paragraph about your experience finding a name, why you chose the name that you did, and how much it will cost you to register the name and host a site.

4. You have been hired to research the use of a blog for a company. Develop a brief report on the advantages and disadvantages of using a blog to advertise corporate products and services. Using a graphics program, prepare a slide show to help you make a presentation about your findings.

5. Investigate the ways Twitter is used by its members. Write a short review that classifies the many different types of posts (tweets). If you use (or were to use) Twitter, what types of posts do you (or would you) make?

TEAM ACTIVITIES

1. With your teammates, identify a company that is making effective use of Web 2.0 technologies on its website. Write a review of the site and why you believe it is effective.

2. Use Flickr.com to have a photo contest. Each group member should post four favourite photos taken by that member. Share account information among your group members, and then use photo comment boxes to vote on your favourite photos. The photo with the most favourable comments wins.

3. Your group will use Web 2.0 sites to organize a social gathering. First choose a group name based on the type of social event you are planning. This could be an actual event that group members will attend, such as "Pizza Extravaganza." Use your Facebook account, or a temporary account set up for the purpose of this exercise, to create a group page and use it to communicate with group members. Use the group page to establish who will be the group leader. Each member should use Google Calendar to post his or her activities for the week the event is to take place. Share your calendars with everyone in the group. The group leader should examine everyone's online calendar to determine a date and time when everyone is available for the event. Create the event and invite the other group members using Google Calendar and Gmail. The leader should create a document using Google Docs that lists details of the event—the title, the purpose, activities on the agenda, food that will be available, the responsibilities of those attending, etc. Share the document with group members. Group members should share their ideas by editing the document. The group leader should judiciously decide which edits to keep and which to reject. Present your instructor with information to join your Facebook group and to view your calendars and Google doc. Write a summary of your experiences with this exercise.

4. Each team member should use a different search engine to find information about podcasting. Meet as a team and decide which search engine was the best for this task. Write a brief report to your instructor summarizing your findings.

WEB EXERCISES

1. This chapter covers a number of powerful Internet tools, including Internet phones, search engines, browsers, e-mail, microblogs, AJAX, and intranets. Pick one of these topics and find more information about that topic on the Internet. You might be asked to develop a report or send an e-mail message to your instructor about what you found.

2. The Internet can be a powerful source of information about various industries and organizations. Locate several industry or organization websites. Which website is the best designed? Which one provides the most amount of information?

3. Research some of the potential disadvantages of using the Internet, such as privacy, fraud, or unauthorized websites. Write a brief report on what you found.

4. Set up an account on *www.twitter.com* and invite a few friends to join. Use Twitter to send messages to your friends on their cell phones, keeping everyone posted on what you are doing throughout the day. Write a review of the service for your instructor.

CAREER EXERCISES

1. Use the Internet to explore starting salaries, benefits, and job descriptions for a career in developing or managing a website. Monster.ca is a good place to start.

2. Consider how the Internet and Web can be useful to businesses in fields that interest you. Select two such businesses and research how they use the Web. Write up the results of your research, including the benefits of the Web to these businesses and recommendations for how they might extend their use of the Web to increase profits.

CASE STUDIES

Case One

Open Text Corporation[1]

Richard Ivey School of Business
The University of Western Ontario

IVEY | Ivey Publishing

Professor Derrick Neufeld wrote this case solely to provide material for class discussion. The author does not intend to illustrate either effective or ineffective handling of a managerial situation. The author may have disguised certain names and other identifying information to protect confidentiality.

Richard Ivey School of Business Foundation prohibits any form of reproduction, storage or transmission without its written permission. Reproduction of this material is not covered under authorization by any reproduction rights organization. To order copies or request permission to reproduce materials, contact Ivey Publishing, Richard Ivey School of Business Foundation, The University of Western Ontario, London, Ontario, Canada, N6A 3K7; phone (519) 661-3208; fax (519) 661-3882; e-mail cases@ivey.uwo.ca.

Copyright © 2010, Richard Ivey School of Business Foundation Version: 2011-01-04

Knowledge Management Tools

A good decision is based on knowledge and not on numbers.
— Plato
Waterloo, Ontario-based Open Text Corporation may not be a household name, but it is extremely well known among *Fortune 500* companies. With 39 percent year-over-year earnings growth,

Open Text ranks among the 100 fastest-growing companies in the world and is the largest Canadian commercial software firm. For the last 15 years, the company has been developing computer software to support enterprise content management (ECM), defined by the Association for Information and Image Management as "the strategies, methods and tools used to capture, manage, store, preserve and deliver content and documents related to organizational processes." Many of the largest companies in the world rely on software from Open Text to help them effectively capture and manage their knowledge stores.

Hyatt, the premier global hotel company, found it increasingly difficult to deliver a consistently strong customer service experience across its 424 hotel and resort properties, which spanned 45 countries with differing time zones, currencies, languages, and cultures. Over time, different business units had attempted to set up local portals to resolve the problem, but content and branding were inconsistent, and key capabilities such as search and personalization were lacking. To solve the problem, Hyatt corporate adopted several Open Text software modules to create HyattConnect, a globally centralized, online meeting platform whose purpose was to "promote community, facilitate day-to-day work, and enable the sharing of information" among Hyatt employees. According to Robb Webb, Hyatt's chief human resources officer, "Using Open Text, associates working in our corporate office and at Hyatt properties can quickly update and locate fundamental information and benefit from the knowledge of other individuals, regardless of location. That translates into more time dedicated to our guests."

Siemens AG, a $100-billion, high-growth technology conglomerate with 450,000 employees, needed a single knowledge management and Web-publishing application to support virtual collaboration across dispersed geographic and organizational boundaries and to replace 26 discrete document management systems that had emerged over time. Building on two Open Text software modules, a company-wide system called Siemens

[1]This case has been written on the basis of published sources only. Consequently, the interpretation and perspectives presented in this case are not necessarily those of Open Text Corporation or any of its employees.

ShareNet was developed. The new system was used to manage documents and coordinate projects over time and space. It also seamlessly interfaced with the company's SAP R/3 enterprise system. Chief information officer Jan Dressel described the result of using Open Text's Livelink package to integrate Nexus, an internal project designed to automate highly mundane tasks, with Siemens' SAP system: "Because Livelink provides a powerful electronic workflow, coupled with e-mail routing with a view into a database, this software can quickly eliminate reams of paper and labour from such tasks. ... As one example, we lowered the cost of obtaining an airline ticket by more than 60 percent by 'self serve' through the Nexus portal rather than going to an outside travel agent."

EnCana, a $10-billion natural gas and oilsands company headquartered in Calgary, Alberta, was wasting time. Engineers needing a specific document would spend a great deal of time and energy searching for that document. As one EnCana data analyst put it, "Sometimes it took a day to find [the required document]. ... [It was often] faster to reproduce it or reorder it from the service company than trying to locate it within the organization." To solve the problem, EnCana used Open Text to create an integrated document repository that was linked to EnCana's map-based geographic information system (GIS). Geophysicists, geological engineers, and other geo-technical users could now locate and instantly retrieve all documents associated with an asset (e.g., a region, field, well, pipeline) by simply clicking on a well-understood, map-based interface. As a result, the geo-specialists could stay focused and productive.

Many other organizations such as Lockheed Martin, Electronic Arts, Mercedes, Sprint, Unilever, Owens Corning, and Barclays Bank have offered similar stories of turning to Open Text software to help manage their unstructured information. Tom Jenkins, Open Text's chief strategy officer, believes that advances in Internet and cloud computing technologies are enabling extraordinary access and control over massive, disparate knowledge sources from around the world. As the content on the Internet continues to deepen and evolve, users will increasingly demand the ability to "mash up" the content in new and useful ways. Jenkins argued, "If Canada misses out on any part of [the information revolution], we really put the next generation at risk."

Discussion Questions

1. What is "unstructured information," and why is difficult to manage?
2. What business benefits did these organizations gain by improving their knowledge-management processes?
3. Do you agree or disagree with Jenkins, that missing out on any part of the information revolution will put the next generation of Canadians at risk? Explain.

SOURCES: Carter, C., "Internet's Evolution Raises Stakes for Canada's Culture and Competitiveness," *Toronto Star,* October 5, 2010, *www.thestar.com/news/ sciencetech/technology/article/870764--internet-s-evolution-raises-stakes-for- canada-s-culture-and-competitiveness,* accessed October 31, 2010. Multiple pages, Open Text Corporation website, 2010, *www.opentext.com,* accessed October 31, 2010. Multiple pages, Association for Information and Image Management website, 2010, *www.aiim.org/What-is-ECM-Enterprise-Content-Management,* accessed October 31, 2010. "100 fastest growing companies," *Fortune,* 2010, *http:// money.cnn.com/magazines/fortune/fortunefastestgrowing/2010/full_list/,* accessed October 31, 2010.

Case Two
Barriers to Enterprise 2.0

Web 2.0 and social media such as Facebook, Wikipedia, and You-Tube have transformed life for many people, providing new ways to connect with friends and share information and media. While social Web 2.0 sites have become popular with the general public, managers have had a difficult time deciding how these technologies can benefit their businesses.

The use of Web 2.0 technologies and social media in the enterprise has been dubbed Enterprise 2.0. In most instances, Enterprise 2.0 is an extension of a corporate intranet; it is sealed off for access to employees only. VPN technology may be used to allow employee access from any Internet-connected device using a corporate login.

Some companies have been extremely successful with the implementation of Enterprise 2.0. Cisco, one of the world's largest technology companies, has implemented Enterprise 2.0 for its 65,000 employees. Cisco is the global leader in the design, manufacturing, and sales of networking and communications technologies and services. Cisco created a Facebook-like application for its employees to assist in finding subject-matter experts within the organization. Like Facebook users, Cisco employees create profiles within the system that include their professional areas of expertise. When other employees need assistance with a problem, a quick search of the system will lead them to an expert within the organization.

Cisco also provides a video wiki used for training on various products and technologies and a Wikipedia-like application for sharing knowledge across the Enterprise. A number of mashup applications have been developed to draw information from the main Enterprise 2.0 applications to address specific needs. For example, one mashup can be used to quickly contact technical support staff.

Initially, Cisco experienced some cultural pushback in the planning stage of its Enterprise 2.0 applications. A highly sceptical group of engineers thought that the company was wasting resources on needless technologies. Ultimately, the technologies have created real improvements for Cisco's business models.

Cisco is in a vast minority of companies that have successfully implemented Enterprise 2.0; however, it is likely that many companies will be following Cisco's lead. Traditional business culture often acts as a barrier to the adoption of Web 2.0 technologies. There is often a prevailing notion that posting to social networks is wasting time rather than being productive and doesn't constitute "real work." In reality, people are most productive when interacting with networks of colleagues.

Another barrier to Enterprise 2.0 is a concern that social networks act as gateways to chaos, generating an unmanageable amount of mostly worthless data. The response to this argument is to provide tools that allow users to filter out the junk to get an optimal signal-to-noise ratio. Those who have been successful with Enterprise 2.0 find that getting users to generate as much noise and activity as possible creates the most valuable information to mine.

Yet another barrier to implementing Enterprise 2.0 is fear that the social network will be used as a "digital soapbox for disgruntled employees." This issue, as with the others, can be handled with proper management of the system and employees. If employees have grounds for complaining, management can more easily address those issues through the open forum of a social network.

In general, Enterprise 2.0 has been slow to take off due to an inability to easily show a return on investment. Social networks within an enterprise provide a soft return that is sometimes difficult to quantify. Successful Enterprise 2.0 implementations typically have two things in common: they are built to support key business processes, and they are not expected to show a ROI.

Discussion Questions

1. What Web 2.0 applications can provide benefits to employees in a business environment?
2. What barriers exist in some businesses that hamper the adoption of Enterprise 2.0?

Critical Thinking Questions

1. How might an information system administrator make a case for the implementation of Enterprise 2.0 when no ROI can be easily demonstrated?
2. In a large global enterprise, how might Enterprise 2.0 applications be organized so as to provide local benefits as well as global benefits?

SOURCES: Bennett, Elizabeth, "Web 2.0 in the Enterprise 2.0," *CIO Insight*, July 13, 2009; Gardner, W. David, "Enterprise 2.0: How Cloud Computing Is Challenging CIOs," *Information Week*, June 15, 2010, *www.informationweek.com*.

Questions for Web Case

See the website for this book to read about the Altitude Online case for this chapter. Following are questions concerning this Web case.

Altitude Online: The Internet, Web, Intranets, and Extranets

Discussion Questions

1. What impact will the new ERP system have on Altitude Online's public-facing website? How will it affect its intranet?
2. What types of applications will be available from the employee dashboard?

Critical Thinking Questions

1. Altitude Online employees have various needs, depending on their position within the enterprise. How might the dashboard and intranet provide custom support for individual employee needs?
2. What Web 2.0 applications should Altitude Online consider for its dashboard? Remember that the applications must be available only on the secure intranet.

NOTES

Sources for the opening vignette: "Appirio Customer Success: Avon," Appirio website, accessed June 18, 2010, *www.appirio.com/customers/cust_avon.php*; Salesforce force.com product website, accessed June 18, 2010; Avon's mark website, accessed June 18, 2010, *http://shop.avon.com/shop/product_list.aspx?cat_type=B&bnd=1&level1_id=300&level2_id=469&dept_id=469&omnCode=Mark*; Hamm, Steve, "How Cloud Computing Will Change Business," *Bloomberg Business Week*, June 15, 2009, *www.businessweek.com/magazine/content/09_24/b4135042942270.htm*.

1 The ISC Domain Survey, *http://www.isc.org/solutions/survey*, accessed June 8, 2010.
2 Internet Usage Statistics, *www.internetworldstats.com/stats.htm*, accessed June 8, 2010.
3 Internet Usage World Stats website, *www.internetworldstats.com*, accessed October 11, 2010.
4 McDonald, Scott, "China Vows to Keep Blocking Online Content," NewsFactor, June 8, 2010, *www.newsfactor.com*.
5 Anderson, Nate, "Internet Disconnections Come to Ireland, Starting Today," *Ars Technica*, May 24, 2010, *www.arstechnica.com*.
6 Greene, Patrick Allen, "Pakistan Blocks Facebook over 'Draw Mohammed Day,'" CNN, May 19, 2010, *www.cnn.com*.
7 Hanchard, Doug, "Why China, U.S., Canada, U.K., Australia, New Zealand All Block Internet Content," *www.zdnet.com/blog/government/why-china-us-canada-uk-australia-new-zealand-all-block-internet-content/6996*, accessed June 8, 2011.

8 "Internet World Stats: Usage and Population Statistics," *www.internetworldstats.com/stats3.htm#asia*, accessed March 11, 2011.
9 Internet2 website, *www.internet2.edu*, accessed June 8, 2010.
10 National LambdaRail website, *www.nlr.net*, accessed June 8, 2010.
11 Miller, Rich, "Facebook Begins Deploying IPv6," Data Center Knowledge, June 10, 2010, *www.datacenterknowledge.com*.
12 Levine, Barry, "You Want Wi-Fi with That? McDonalds to Make Wi-Fi Free," NewsFactor, December 16, 2009, *www.newsfactor.com*.
13 Rogers website, *www.rogers.com/web/content/wireless_network?customer_type=Business*, accessed October 11, 2010.
14 Rogers website, "Compare Internet Packages," *www.rogers.com*, accessed October 10, 2010.
15 Gaskin, James, "Clouds Now Strong Enough to Support Your Business," *Computerworld*, October 6, 2009, *www.computerworld.com*.
16 Schonfeld, Erick, "Urbanspoon Wants to Challenge OpenTable With Its Rezbook iPad App," TechCrunch, May 19, 2010, *www.techcrunch.com*.
17 "Private Cloud RIO Study: Corus AEG," *Infoworld*, June 2010, *www.infoworld.com/d/cloud-computing/wp/private-cloud-roi-study-corus-aeg-720*.
18 Linthicum, David, "Why Private Clouds Are Surging: It's the Control, Stupid!," *Infoworld*, June 3, 2010, *www.infoworld.com*.
19 Claburn, Thomas, "Google Launches Web Site Promoting HTML5," Information Week, June 22, 2010, *www.informationweek.com*.
20 Vernon, Amy, "Mozilla likes HTML5 over Flash," Network World, June 25, 2010, *www.networkworld.com*.

21 Michael Bublé website, *www.michaelbuble.com/en-ca,* accessed March 11, 2011.

22 Lefkow, Chris, "News Corp. Makes Digital Journalism Moves," AFP, June 14, 2010, *www.google.com/hostednews/afp/article/ALeqM5icelpR1yDjP9I YJcvx1kz_hybyzw.*

23 Hogg, Chris, "YouTube Announces 'News Feed' Showcasing Top Citizen Journalism," Digital Journal, June 15, 2010, *www.digitaljournal.com.*

24 Lassar, Matthew, "FCC Asked to Monitor 'Hate Speech,' 'Misinformation' Online," *Ars Technica,* June 1, 2010, *www.arstechnica.com.*

25 Kashi website, *www.kashi.ca,* accessed October 11, 2010.

26 Pegaroro, Rob, "Bing Adds Music, Videos, Games," *Washington Post,* June 23, 2010, *http://voices.washingtonpost.com.*

27 Porter, Alan, "Getting over the Barriers to Wiki Adoption," *Ars Technica,* February 13, 2010, *www.arstechnica.com.*

28 Anderson, Nate, "OpenStreetMap: Crowd-sourcing the World, a Street at a Time," *Ars Technica,* June 1, 2010, *www.arstechnica.com.*

29 Noyes, Katherine, "Facebook Quickens Yahoo's Pulse," E-Commerce Times, June 7, 2010, *www.ecommercetimes.com.*

30 "ROI with Cisco Telepresence," Cisco Telepresence Case Study, March 2009, *www.cisco.com/en/US/prod/collateral/ps7060/ps8329/ ps8330/9599/TelePresence_Research_Brief_Final_03_20_09.pdf.*

31 Butcher, Mike, "Internet Conga Line—A New Take on ChatRoulette Which Feels Safer," TechCrunch, June 23, 2010, *www.techcrunch.com.*

32 "IBM Saves $320,000 with Second Life Meeting," Virtual Worlds News, February 27, 2009, *www.virtualworlds news.com.*

33 "Study: Brands Sell in Virtual Worlds," Virtual Worlds News, July 1, 2010, *www.virtualworldsnews.com.*

34 Saint, Nick, "Ning Makes It Easier for Its Network Creators to Make Money," SFGate, June 16, 2010, *www.sfgate.com.*

35 Graham, Jefferson, "Zynga Plants 'Farmville' App," PhysOrg, July 5, 2010, *www.physorg.com.*

36 Pombriant, Denis, "Talking to Your Tribe," *Ecommerce Times,* March 13, 2010, *www.ecommercetimes.com.*

37 Naone, Erica, "Getting a Grip on Online Buzz," Technology Review, February 9, 2010, *www.technologyreview.com.*

38 Wauters, Robin, "Measuring the Value of Social Media Advertising," TechCrunch, April 20, 2010, *www.techcrunch.com.*

39 Nakano, Chelsi, "Enterprise 2.0 Roll-up: Social Computing Is Destroying the Enterprise, Yet Solutions Arrive in Waves," CRM Newswire, June 24, 2010, *www.crmnewswire.com.*

40 Wauters, Robin, "Schoology Raises $1.25 Million for Learning Management Software," TechCrunch, June 7, 2010, *www.techcrunch.com.*

41 Vijayan, Jaikumar, "Embattled LimeWire to Launch Subscription Music Service," *Computerworld,* June 21, 2010, *www.computerworld.com.*

42 Wauters, Robin, "Joost Video Network Stuns with Big Reach: 67 Million Viewers Per Month," TechCrunch, April 14, 2010, *www.techcrunch.com.*

43 Hollister, Sean, "Hulu CEO: We're 'Complementary' to Cable," Engadget, July 1, 2010, *www.engadget.com.*

44 Fowler, Geoffrey, "Libraries Have a Novel Idea," *Wall Street Journal,* June 29, 2010, *online.wsj.com.*

45 PricewaterhouseCoopers, "Consumer Behaviour Drives Change; Entertainment and Media Players Seek New Roles in Digital Value Chain," June 15, 2010

46 Hamblen, Matt, "Starbucks Expands Pay-by-iPhone Pilot to 1,000 Stores," *Computerworld,* March 31, 2010, *www.computerworld.com.*

47 Stevenson, Reed, "There's Something in the Air: Augmented Reality," Reuters, December 4, 2009, *www.reuters.com.*

PART
· 3 ·

Business Information Systems

(Source: Lukiyanova Natalia/frenta/Shutterstock.com.)

CHAPTER
· 8 ·
Electronic and Mobile Commerce

PRINCIPLES	LEARNING OBJECTIVES
■ **Electronic and mobile commerce are evolving, providing new ways of conducting business that present both potential benefits and problems.**	■ Describe the current status of various forms of e-commerce, including B2B, B2C, C2C, and e-Government. ■ Outline a multistage purchasing model that describes how e-commerce works. ■ Define m-commerce and identify some of its unique challenges.
■ **E-commerce and m-commerce can be used in many innovative ways to improve the operations of an organization.**	■ Identify several e-commerce and m-commerce applications. ■ Identify several advantages associated with the use of e-commerce and m-commerce.
■ **Although e-commerce and m-commerce offer many advantages, users must be aware of and protect themselves from many threats associated with this technology.**	■ Identify the major issues that represent significant threats to the continued growth of e-commerce and m-commerce.
■ **Organizations must define and execute a strategy to be successful in e-commerce and m-commerce.**	■ Outline the key components of a successful e-commerce and m-commerce strategy.
■ **E-commerce and m-commerce require the careful planning and integration of a number of technology infrastructure components.**	■ Identify the key components of technology infrastructure that must be in place for e-commerce and m-commerce to work. ■ Discuss the key features of the electronic payment systems needed to support e-commerce and m-commerce.

(Source: Lukiyanova Natalia/frenta/Shutterstock.com.)

Information Systems in the Global Economy
Tommy Hilfiger

Hilfiger Leaves E-Commerce to the Experts

Tommy Hilfiger is one of the world's leading brands of premium lifestyle clothing. Hilfiger clothing reflects styling that is popular around the world. Hilfiger clothing is distributed in over 65 countries through high-class fashion shops, department stores, and over 900 of its own retail stores.

In 2009, Hilfiger decided it was time to focus on improving its online sales. Its Web store had been respectable but had not implemented any of the latest e-commerce tools for driving sales.

Executives at Hilfiger recognize that the company's core competencies lie in fashion, marketing, and merchandising. Hilfiger has no interest in becoming an IT company, building an IT department, or investing in servers and computing equipment. It didn't take long for the company to decide that its e-commerce systems should be outsourced. Whatever system Hilfiger used would have to be powerful and yet easy for businespeople to interact with.

Hilfiger director of e-commerce Tom Davis reviewed several popular e-commerce hosting services. E-commerce hosts provide everything needed for an e-commerce site, including hardware, software, databases, networking, and support, for an annual fee. Of all the companies Davis evaluated, ATG struck him as being the best fit for Hilfiger's needs. ATG's Commerce OnDemand platform is a fully hosted e-commerce system that includes the latest and most advanced e-commerce tools and techniques. The ATG Business Control Center is an easy-to-use interface that allows companies to enter products into an online catalogue. It also uses set price points, arranges products within the site, builds promotions, and sets shipping fees.

Tom Davis worked with engineers at ATG to implement the new Hilfiger site within 120 days. During the first months of operation, Hilfiger merchandising staff experimented with the site, introducing more products each week and working to improve conversion rates (the percentage of visitors that purchase products). In order to boost cross-sales, the staff manually entered one-to-one product relationships, so that when a customer views an item or checks out, another related item is recommended.

The process of hand-coding the related item recommendations required a significant time investment. After three months, Davis discovered that the recommendations had no significant impact on sales and so he gave up the effort. ATG came to the rescue with an e-commerce tool called ATG Recommendations. ATG Recommendations works dynamically to recommend products that a customer is likely to find appealing, using a sophisticated predictive algorithm that combines data from the merchandise catalogue, the site structure, historical and current shopper behaviour, and aggregate shopper behaviour.

Implementing the new ATG Recommendations system took less than four weeks and required minimal changes to the site. Hilfiger found that the software was well worth the investment. After only one month, the Recommendations system increased online sales by 16 percent. You can view the Recommendations system at the bottom of every product page as a series of merchandise photos that "people who viewed this also viewed."

Hilfiger learned that its approach to manually adding recommendations failed because it was primarily recommending products that it was keen to sell. ATG Recommendations was successful because it recommends items that it calculates a customer would want, without regard to Hilfiger's priorities. The only business rule that governs the Recommendations system is that recommendations are not made that might reduce an order's value.

Over time, Hilfiger expanded its use of ATG Recommendations, tying it to e-mail campaigns, a Top Sellers page, a Gift Guide feature, integrating it into higher level pages, and a Last Chance Recommendations at checkout. Through ATG Recommendations, Hilfiger can expose customers to a wider breadth of products on each page as well as products that the customer is likely to find appealing.

Hilfiger's new e-commerce site has been incredibly successful. In its first holiday season, the new site doubled the company's online revenue. Davis says that "the likelihood of checkout is three times higher for those shoppers who interacted with Recommendations than those who did not."

Outsourcing the e-commerce business to an experienced e-commerce company has freed Hilfiger employees to concentrate on what they do best: planning promotions and strategies to optimize their products' exposure and further increase sales.

As you read this chapter, consider the following:

- What advantages does e-commerce offer sellers and vendors over traditional shopping venues?
- What are the limitations of e-commerce? What doesn't sell well online, and why are some shoppers uncomfortable shopping online?

Why Learn About Electronic and Mobile Commerce?

Electronic and mobile commerce have transformed many areas of our lives and careers. One fundamental change has been the manner in which companies interact with their suppliers, customers, government agencies, and other business partners. As a result, most organizations today have or are considering setting up business on the Internet. To be successful, all members of the organization need to plan and participate in that effort. As a sales or marketing manager, you will be expected to help define your firm's e-commerce business model. Customer service employees can expect to participate in the development and operation of their firm's website. As a human resource or public relations manager, you will likely be asked to provide website content for use by potential employees and shareholders. Analysts in finance need to know how to measure the business impact of their firm's Web operations and how to compare that to competitors' efforts. Clearly, as an employee in today's organization, you must understand what the potential role of e-commerce is, how to capitalize on its many opportunities, and how to avoid its pitfalls such as consumers' lack of trust and privacy concerns. The emergence of m-commerce adds an exciting new dimension to these opportunities and challenges. This chapter begins by providing a brief overview of the dynamic world of e-commerce.

AN INTRODUCTION TO ELECTRONIC COMMERCE

electronic commerce
Conducting business activities (e.g., distribution, buying, selling, marketing, and servicing of products or services) electronically over computer networks.

Electronic commerce is the conducting of business activities (e.g., distribution, selling, marketing, and servicing of products or services) electronically over computer networks. This includes any business transaction executed electronically between companies (business-to-business), companies and consumers (business-to-consumer), consumers and other consumers (consumer-to-consumer), public sector and business (government-to-business), and the public sector to citizens (government-to-citizen).

Business activities that are strong candidates for conversion to e-commerce are ones that are paper-based, time-consuming, and inconvenient activities for customers. Over the last five years, Internet sales in Canada have increased at a double-digit pace. Although private and public sector Internet sales exceed $62.7 billion, they still represent less than 2 percent of total revenue for private-sector firms.[1]

Business-to-Business (B2B) E-Commerce

Business-to-business (B2B) e-commerce is a subset of e-commerce where all the partici-pants are organizations. B2B e-commerce is a useful tool for connecting business partners in a virtual supply chain to reduce costs. Although the business-to-consumer market grabs more of the news headlines, the B2B market is considerably larger and is growing more rapidly.

An organization will use both *buy-side e-commerce* to purchase goods and services from its suppliers and *sell-side e-commerce* to sell products to its customers. Buy-side e-commerce activities may include identifying and comparing competitive suppliers and products, nego-tiating and establishing prices and terms, ordering and tracking shipments, and steering organizational buyers to preferred suppliers and products.

Sell-side e-commerce activities may include enabling the purchase of products online, providing information for customers to evaluate the organization's goods and services, encouraging sales and generating leads from potential customers, providing a portal of information of interest to the customer, and enabling interactions among a community of consumers.

In Canada, business-to-business sales accounted for 62 percent of online sales.[2] In a study, firms were more like to purchase than sell goods and services online, and the main benefits for firms to use the Internet were lower costs and better coordination with suppliers and customers.[3]

business-to-business (B2B) e-commerce
A subset of e-commerce where all the participants are organizations.

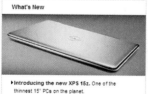

Dell sells its products through the Dell.ca website.

(Source: © 2011 Dell Inc. All Rights Reserved.)

Business-to-Consumer (B2C) E-Commerce

Early **business-to-consumer (B2C) e-commerce** pioneers competed with the traditional "brick-and-mortar" retailers in an industry selling their products directly to consumers. For example, in 1995, upstart Amazon.com challenged well-established booksellers. Amazon did not become profitable until 2003; the firm has grown from selling only books on a U.S.-based website to selling a wide variety of products through international websites in Canada, China, France, Germany, Japan, and the United Kingdom. Although B2C e-commerce repre-sents less than 3 percent of total Canadian retail sales, B2C e-commerce sales are expected to grow at a compound rate of 10.6 percent each year from $13.8 billion in 2007 to $22.8 billion in 2012.[4] One reason for the steady growth is that shoppers find many goods and services are

business-to-consumer (B2C) e-commerce
A form of e-commerce in which customers deal directly with an organization and avoid intermediaries.

cheaper when purchased via the Web, including stocks, books, newspapers, airline tickets, and hotel rooms. They can also compare information about automobiles, cruises, loans, insurance, and home prices, for example, to find better values. Canadians have adopted B2C e-commerce at a slower rate than in the United States. According to the Canadian Retail Council, "Canadians tend to do product research, window shopping and price comparisons online, then make those purchases in stores."[5]

More than just a tool for placing orders, the Internet is an extremely useful way to compare prices, features, value, and other customers' opinions. Internet shoppers can, for example, access sites such as eBay Shopping.com, Google Product Search, Shopzilla, PriceGrabber, Yahoo! Shopping, or Excite to browse the Internet and obtain lists of items, prices, and merchants. Many B2C merchants have added what is called "social commerce" to their websites by creating a section where shoppers can go to see only those products that have been reviewed and listed by other shoppers.

By using B2C e-commerce to sell directly to consumers, producers or providers of consumer products can eliminate the middlemen, or intermediaries, between them and the consumer. In many cases, this squeezes costs and inefficiencies out of the supply chain and can lead to higher profits for businesses and lower prices for consumers. The elimination of intermediate organizations between the producer and the consumer is called *disintermediation*.

Dell Canada is an example of a manufacturer that has successfully embraced this model to achieve a strong competitive advantage. People can specify a unique computer online, and Dell assembles the components and ships the computer directly to the consumer within five days.

Following a successful pilot project involving over 5,000 consumers, Procter and Gamble (P&G), the consumer goods marketer with annual sales of more than $80 billion, launched a business-to-consumer website. This initiative, called the estore, represents a major change for the company as its products are normally sold indirectly to consumers through major retailers. Although most sales will continue to be through retailers, P&G will use the estore to gain a better understanding of its consumers as well as build stronger consumer relationships. However, the website has generated some ill will between P&G and the major retailers as it reduces their in-store sales of P&G products. The site is owned and operated by PFSWeb and currently sells P&G products to only U.S. consumers.[6] Johnson & Johnson and Nestle have established limited e-commerce campaigns in Canada. Some of the largest B2C retailers are Amazon, Dell, and Sears.[7]

Consumer-to-Consumer (C2C) E-Commerce

consumer-to-consumer (C2C) e-commerce
A subset of e-commerce that involves consumers selling directly to other consumers.

Consumer-to-consumer (C2C) e-commerce is a subset of e-commerce that involves electronic transactions between consumers using a third party to facilitate the process. eBay is an example of a C2C e-commerce site; customers buy and sell items to each other through the site. Founded in 1995, eBay has become one of the most popular websites in the world, although the number of items listed for sale and their value declined sharply from January 2009 to November 2009 as the number of visitors fell 37 percent due to a number of factors, including the poor economic environment.[8]

Other C2C sites include Craigslist, Kijiji, eBid, ePier, Ubid, and Tradus. The growth of C2C is responsible for reducing the use of the classified pages of a newspaper to advertise and sell personal items, and so it has had a negative impact on that industry. On the other hand, C2C has created an opportunity for many people to make a living out of selling items on auction websites.

Table 8.1 summarizes the key factors that differentiate among B2B, B2C, and C2C e-commerce.

e-Government

e-Government
The use of information and communications technology to simplify the sharing of information, speed formerly paper-based processes, and improve the relationship between citizens and government.

e-Government is the use of information and communications technology to simplify the sharing of information, speed formerly paper-based processes, and improve the relationship between citizens and government. Government-to-citizen (G2C), government-to-business (G2B), and government-to-government (G2G) are all forms of e-Government, each with different applications.

Factors	B2B	B2C	C2C
Value of sale	Thousands or millions of dollars	Tens or hundreds of dollars	Tens of dollars
Length of sales process	Days to months	Days to weeks	Hours to days
Number of decision makers involved	Several people to a dozen or more	One or two	One or two
Uniformity of offer	Typically a uniform product offering	More customized product offering	Single product offering, one of a kind
Complexity of buying process	Extremely complex, much room for negotiation on price, payment and delivery options, quantity, quality, options and features	Relatively simple, limited discussion over price and payment and delivery options	Relatively simple, limited discussion over payment and delivery options; negotiation over price
Motivation for sale	Driven by a business decision or need	Driven by an individual consumer's need or emotion	Driven by an individual consumer's need or emotion

Table 8.1

Differences Between B2B, B2C, and C2C

Citizens can use G2C applications to submit their federal tax returns online, apply for student loans, and access government service programs. At the Action Plan website (*www.actionplan.gc.ca*), Canadians can view where federal stimulus money is being allocated.[9] The federal government also developed a central website, Service Canada (*www.servicecanada.gc.ca*), to assist individuals in applying for Employment Insurance, the Canada Pension Plan, and other federal assistance programs.[10]

G2B applications support the purchase of materials and services from private industry by government procurement offices, enable firms to bid on government contracts, and help businesses receive information about current government regulations related to their operations. *Canadabusiness.ca* enables businesses to access information about how to sell products and services to local, provincial, and federal government agencies.

G2G applications are designed to improve communications among the various levels of government. The next section describes a basic model that supports products for purchase via e-commerce methods.

Multistage Model for E-Commerce

A successful e-commerce system must address the many stages that consumers experience in the sales life cycle. At the heart of any e-commerce system is the user's ability to search for and identify items for sale; select those items and negotiate prices, terms of payment, and delivery date; send an order to the vendor to purchase the items; pay for the product or service; obtain product delivery; and receive after-sales support. Figure 8.1 (on the next page) shows how e-commerce can support each of these stages. Product delivery can involve tangible goods delivered in a traditional form (e.g., clothing delivered via a package service) or goods and services delivered electronically (e.g., software downloaded over the Internet).

Search and Identification

An employee ordering parts for a storeroom at a manufacturing plant would follow the steps shown in Figure 8.1. The company would store a wide range of office supplies, spare parts, and maintenance supplies in the storeroom. The employee prepares a list of needed items—for example, fasteners, piping, and plastic tubing. Typically, for each item carried in the storeroom, a corporate buyer has already identified a preferred supplier based on the vendor's price competitiveness, level of service, quality of products, and speed of delivery. The employee then logs on to the Internet and goes to the website of the preferred supplier.

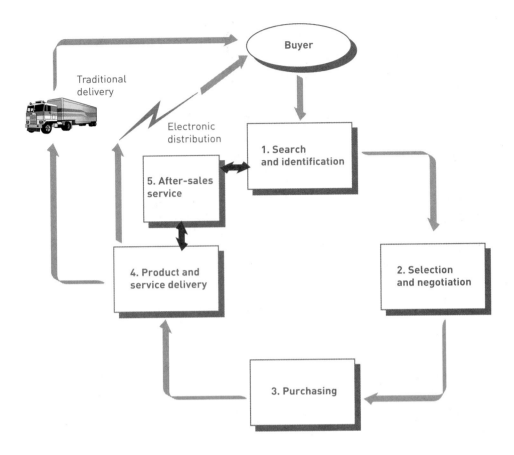

Figure 8.1

Multistage Model for
E-Commerce (B2B and B2C)

From the supplier's home page, the employee can access a product catalogue and browse until finding the items that meet the company's specifications. The employee fills out a request-for-quotation form by entering the item codes and quantities needed. When the employee completes the quotation form, the supplier's Web application calculates the total charge of the order with the most current prices and shows the additional cost for various forms of delivery—overnight, within two working days, or the next week. The employee might elect to visit other suppliers' Web home pages and repeat this process to search for additional items or obtain competing prices for the same items.

Selection and Negotiation

After the price quotations have been received from each supplier, the employee examines them and indicates, by clicking the request-for-quotation form, which items to order from a given supplier. The employee also specifies the desired delivery date. This data is used as input into the supplier's order processing TPS. In addition to price, an item's quality and the supplier's service and speed of delivery can be important in the selection and negotiation process.

B2B e-commerce systems need to support negotiation between a buyer and the selected seller over the final price, delivery date, delivery costs, and any extra charges. However, this is not a fundamental requirement of most B2C systems, which offer their products for sale on a "take-it-or-leave-it basis."

Purchasing Products and Services Electronically

The employee completes the purchase order specifying the final agreed-to terms and prices by sending a completed electronic form to the supplier. Complications can arise in paying for the products. Typically, a corporate buyer who makes several purchases from the supplier each year has established credit with the supplier in advance, and all purchases are billed to a corporate account. But when individual consumers make their first, and perhaps only, purchase from the supplier, additional safeguards and measures are required. Part of the purchase transaction can involve the customer providing a credit card number. Another approach to paying for goods and services purchased over the Internet is using electronic money, which can be exchanged for hard cash, as discussed later in the chapter.

The 3M Company is a $25-billion firm that produces thousands of imaginative products in a variety of markets, including health care, highway safety, office products, and abrasives and adhesives. 3M Canada has established a purchasing portal for its customers at *http://solutions.3mcanada.com/wps/portal/3M/en_CA/Partners/Suppliers*. Authorized customers can log on to this portal and search by keyword to find 3M products for which their firm may have already negotiated favourable terms.

Product and Service Delivery

Electronic distribution can be used to download software, music, pictures, video, and written material through the Internet faster and for less expense than shipping the items via a package delivery service. Most products, however, cannot be delivered over the Internet, so they are delivered in a variety of other ways: overnight carrier, regular mail service, truck, or rail. In some cases, the customer might elect to drive to the supplier and pick up the product.

Many manufacturers and retailers have outsourced the physical logistics of delivering merchandise to cybershoppers—those who take care of the storing, packing, shipping, and tracking of products. To provide this service, UPS, Federal Express, Canada Post, and other delivery firms have developed software tools and interfaces that directly link customer ordering, manufacturing, and inventory systems with their own system of highly automated warehouses, call centres, and worldwide shipping networks. The goal is to make the transfer of all information and inventory—from the manufacturer to the delivery firm to the consumer—fast and simple.

For example, when a customer orders a printer at the Hewlett-Packard (HP) website, that order actually goes to FedEx, which stocks all the products that HP sells online at a dedicated e-distribution facility. FedEx ships the order, which triggers an e-mail notification to the customer that the printer is on its way and an inventory notice to HP that the FedEx warehouse now has one less printer in stock. See Figure 8.2. For product returns, HP enters return information into its own system, which is linked to FedEx. This signals a FedEx courier to pick up the unwanted item at the customer's house or business. Customers don't need to fill out shipping labels or package the item. Instead, the FedEx courier uses information transmitted over the Internet to a computer in his truck to print a label from a portable printer attached to his belt. FedEx has control of the return, and HP can monitor its progress from start to finish.

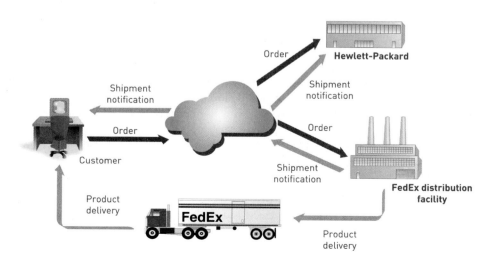

Figure 8.2

Product and Information Flow for HP Printers Ordered over the Web

After-Sales Service

In addition to capturing the information to complete the order, comprehensive customer information is captured from the order and stored in the supplier's customer database. This information can include customer name, address, telephone numbers, contact person, credit history, and some order details. For example, if the customer later contacts the supplier to complain that not all items were received, that some arrived damaged, or even that the product provides unclear instructions, all customer service representatives can retrieve the order information from the database via a computing/communications device. Companies are adding the capability to answer many after-sales questions to their websites, such as how to maintain a piece of equipment, how to effectively use the product, and how to receive repairs under warranty.

E-Commerce Challenges

A company must overcome many challenges to convert its business processes from the traditional form to e-commerce processes, especially for B2C e-commerce. As a result, not all e-commerce ventures are successful. This section summarizes four key challenges: (1) defining an effective e-commerce model and strategy, (2) dealing with consumer privacy concerns, (3) overcoming consumers' lack of trust, and (4) overcoming global issues.

Figure 8.3

Three Basic Components of a Successful E-Commerce Model

Content
Industry news
Economic news
Stock prices

Commerce
Consumers and businesses buying and selling

Community
Message boards
Chat rooms

Defining an Effective E-Commerce Model and Strategy

The first major challenge is for the company to define an effective e-commerce model and strategy. Although companies can select from a number of approaches, the most successful e-commerce models have three basic components: community, content, and commerce, as shown in Figure 8.3. Message boards and chat rooms can build a loyal *community* of people who are interested in and enthusiastic about the company and its products and services. Providing useful, accurate, and timely *content*—such as industry and economic news and stock quotes—is a sound approach to encourage people to return to your website time and time again. *Commerce* involves consumers and businesses paying to purchase physical goods, information, or services that are posted or advertised online.

Dealing with Consumer Privacy Concerns

While about half of Canadian Internet users have purchased an item online, one-half (48 percent) of all Canadians, whether or not they went online, reported being very concerned about online credit card use.[11] In addition to having an effective e-commerce model and strategy, companies must carefully address consumer privacy concerns and overcome consumers' lack of trust.

Following are a few examples of security beaches in which personal data was compromised.

- Heartland Payment Systems found evidence of malicious software that compromised 100 million credit card transactions that crossed its network each month. It is estimated that hackers stole over 130 million credit and debit card numbers. Heartland was sued and eventually agreed to pay some $60 million to cover losses by Visa credit and debit cardholders.[12]

- PlayNow.com, B.C. Lottery Corp's regulated casino—the first of its kind in Canada — was shut down just hours after it was launched in 2010. Personal, private information of some players was exposed to other players.[13]
- According to a Telus/University of Toronto study, the average annual cost of security breaches in government organizations more than tripled to $1 million in 2009, up from $321,000 in 2008. Governments are custodians of confidential information, and breaches tend to be related to **identity theft**.[14] According to the Privacy Commissioner of Canada, "Identity theft is the unauthorized collection and use of your personal information, usually for criminal purposes."[15] Thieves may use consumers' credit card numbers to charge items to their accounts, use identification information to apply for a new credit card or a loan in their names, or use their name and Social Insurance Number to receive government benefits.

Companies must be prepared to make a substantial investment to safeguard their customers' privacy or run the risk of losing customers and generating potential class action law suits (see Heartland Payment Systems mentioned earlier) should the data be compromised. Most websites invest in the latest security technology and employ highly trained security experts to protect their customers' data.

identify theft
Someone using your personally identifying information without your permission to commit fraud or other crimes.

Overcoming Consumers' Lack of Trust

Lack of trust in online sellers is one of the most frequently cited reasons for consumers being not willing to purchase online. Can they be sure that the company or person with which they are dealing is legitimate and will send the item(s) they purchase from them? What if there is a problem with the product or service when it is received—for example, if it does not match the description on the website, is the wrong size or wrong colour, is damaged during the delivery process, or does not work as advertised?

Online marketers must create specific trust-building strategies for their websites by analyzing their customers, products, and services. A perception of trustworthiness can be created by implementing one or more of the following strategies:

- Demonstrate a strong desire to build an ongoing relationship with customers by giving first-time price incentives, offering loyalty programs, or eliciting and sharing customer feedback.
- Demonstrate that the company has been in business for a long time.
- Make it clear that considerable investment has been made in the website.
- Provide brand endorsements from well-known experts or well-respected individuals.
- Demonstrate participation in appropriate regulatory programs or industry associations.
- Display website accreditation by the Better Business Bureau, VeriSign, or TRUSTe programs.

Here are some tips to help online shoppers avoid problems:

- Buy only from a well-known website you can trust—one that advertises on national media, is recommended by a friend, or receives strong ratings in the media.
- Look for a seal of approval from organizations such as the Better Business Bureau, VeriSign, or TRUSTe. See Figure 8.4.
- Review the website's privacy policy to be sure that you are comfortable with its conditions before you provide personal information.
- Determine what the website policy is for return of products purchased.
- Be wary if you must enter any personal information other than what's required to complete the purchase (name, credit card number, address, and telephone number).

Figure 8.4

Better Business Bureau and TRUSTe Seals of Approval

(Source: Left: Courtesy of The Council of Better Business Bureaus. Right: Courtesy of TrustE.)

- Do not, under any conditions, ever provide information such as your Social Insurance Number, bank account numbers, or your mother's maiden name.
- When you open the Web page where you enter credit card information or other personal data, make sure that the Web address begins with "https," and check to see if a locked padlock icon appears in the Address bar or status bar, as shown in Figure 8.5.
- Consider using virtual credit cards, which expire after one use when doing business.
- Before downloading music, change your browser's advanced settings to disable access to all computer areas that contain personal information.

Figure 8.5

Website Security

Website that uses "https" in the address and a secure site lock icon.

Overcoming Global Issues

E-commerce and m-commerce offer enormous opportunities by allowing manufacturers to buy supplies at a low cost worldwide. They also offer enterprises the chance to sell to a global market right from the start. Moreover, they offer great promise for developing countries, helping them to enter the prosperous global marketplace, which helps to reduce the gap between rich and poor countries. People and companies can get products and services from around the world, instead of around the corner or across town. These opportunities, however, come with numerous obstacles and issues, first identified in Chapter 1 as challenges associated with all global systems.

- *Cultural challenges*: Great care must be taken to ensure that a website is appealing, easy to use, and inoffensive to people around the world.
- *Language challenges*: Language differences can make it difficult to understand the information and directions posted on a website.
- *Time and distance challenges*: Significant time differences make it difficult for some people to be able to speak to customer service representatives or to get technical support.
- *Infrastructure challenges*: The website must support access by customers using a wide variety of hardware and software devices.
- *Currency challenges*: The website must be able to state prices and accept payment in a variety of currencies.
- *Local, provincial, and national law challenges*: The website must operate in conformance to a wide variety of laws that cover a variety of issues, including the protection of trademarks and patents, the sale of copyrighted material, the collection and safeguarding of personal or financial data, the payment of sales taxes and fees, and much more.

AN INTRODUCTION TO MOBILE COMMERCE

As discussed briefly in Chapter 1, mobile commerce (m-commerce) relies on the use of mobile, wireless devices, such as cell phones and smartphones, to place orders and conduct business. Handset manufacturers such as Ericsson, Motorola, Nokia, and Qualcomm are working with communications carriers such as Bell, Telus, and Rogers to develop such wireless devices, related technology, and services. The Internet Corporation for Assigned Names and Numbers (ICANN) created a .mobi domain to help attract mobile users to the Web. mTLD Top Level Domain Ltd of Dublin, Ireland, administers this domain and helps to ensure that the .mobi destinations work quickly, efficiently, and effectively with user handsets.

Mobile Commerce in Perspective

The market for m-commerce in North America is maturing much later than in Western Europe and Japan for several reasons. In North America, responsibility for network infrastructure is fragmented among many providers, consumer payments are usually made by credit card, and many Americans are unfamiliar with mobile data services. In most Western European countries, communicating via wireless devices is common, and consumers are much more willing to use m-commerce. Japanese consumers are generally enthusiastic about new technology and are much more likely to use mobile technologies for making purchases.

Nearly 450 million users worldwide accessed the Internet via mobile devices in 2009. It is estimated that the number of mobile devices accessing the Internet will exceed 1 billion by 2013.[16] The number of mobile websites is expected to grow rapidly because of advances in wireless broadband technologies, the development of new and useful applications, and the availability of less costly but more powerful handsets. Indeed, the website Mobil Mammoth highlights a new mobile website every day.[17] Experts point out that the relative clumsiness of mobile browsers and security concerns must be overcome to ensure rapid m-commerce growth.

M-Commerce Websites

A number of retailers have established special websites for users of mobile devices. Two popular mobile sites are Best Buy and Sunglass Hut.[18] Mdog.com is a portal for your mobile device's Web browser. You direct your browser to mdog.com and many of your favourite websites (e.g., eBay, Craigslist, Wikipedia, Citysearch, and MySpace) and blogs are displayed in a format convenient for your mobile device. Another interesting service can be accessed from Twitter by sending a shopping-related question to @imshopping. Your question is routed to an appropriate expert who can provide unbiased opinions and links to products within about 15 minutes. (Experts are rated over time based on their answers.) The expert's response is a URL link to a page at IMshopping.com that will provide a longer answer than the 140-character limit imposed by Twitter.[19]

Advantages of Electronic and Mobile Commerce

Conversion to an e-commerce or m-commerce system enables organizations to reduce the cost of doing business, speed the flow of goods and information, increase the accuracy of order processing and order fulfillment, and improve the level of customer service.

Reduce Costs

By eliminating or reducing time-consuming and labour-intensive steps throughout the order and delivery process, more sales can be completed in the same period and with increased accuracy. With increased speed and accuracy of customer order information, companies can reduce the need for inventory—from raw materials to safety stocks and finished goods—at all the intermediate manufacturing, storage, and transportation points.

Speed the Flow of Goods and Information

When organizations are connected via e-commerce, the flow of information is accelerated because electronic connections and communications are already established. As a result, information can flow from buyer to seller easily, directly, and rapidly.

Increase Accuracy
By enabling buyers to enter their own product specifications and order information directly, human data-entry error on the part of the supplier is eliminated.

Improve Customer Service
Increased and more detailed information about delivery dates and current status can increase customer loyalty. In addition, the ability to consistently meet customers' desired delivery dates with high-quality goods and services eliminates any incentive for customers to seek other sources of supply.

ELECTRONIC AND MOBILE COMMERCE APPLICATIONS

E-commerce and m-commerce are being used in innovative and exciting ways. This section examines a few of the many B2B, B2C, C2C, and m-commerce applications in retail and wholesale, manufacturing, marketing, advertising, price comparison, couponing, investment and finance, banking, and e-boutiques.

Retail and Wholesale

electronic retailing (e-tailing)
The direct sale of products or services by businesses to consumers through electronic storefronts, typically designed around an electronic catalogue and shopping cart model.

E-commerce is being used extensively in retailing and wholesaling. **Electronic retailing**, sometimes called *e-tailing*, is the direct sale of products or services by businesses to consumers through electronic storefronts, which are typically designed around the familiar electronic catalogue and shopping cart model. Companies such as Office Depot and Walmart have used the same model to sell wholesale goods to employees of corporations. Tens of thousands of electronic retail websites sell everything from soup to nuts. See Table 8.2.

Table 8.2

Top-Rated B2C Websites (Spring 2009)

(Source: Burns, Enid, "Study: Consumer Satisfaction in E-Commerce Slips," ClickZ, May 11, 2009, *www.clickz.com/3633686*, accessed March 14, 2010.)

Website	ACSI Index	Products Sold
Amazon.com	84	Books, music, DVDs, and more
Avon.com	81	Beauty, health, and fitness products
TigerDirect.com	79	Computers and computer-related products
VictoriaSecret.com	78	Lingerie and women's clothing

cybermall
A single website that offers many products and services at one Internet location.

Cybermalls are another means to support retail shopping. A **cybermall** is a single website that offers many products and services at one Internet location—similar to a regular shopping mall. An Internet cybermall pulls many buyers and sellers into one virtual place, easily reachable through a Web browser. For example, the Dogwood Mall allows Internet shoppers to search for products and services from British Columbia. Etailers Mall allows shoppers to shop at dozens of bath, body, candle, cosmetics, and jewellery e-tailers on the Internet.

A key sector of wholesale e-commerce is spending on manufacturing, repair, and operations (MRO) goods and services—from simple office supplies to mission-critical equipment, such as the motors, pumps, compressors, and instruments that keep manufacturing facilities running smoothly. MRO purchases often approach 40 percent of a manufacturing company's total revenues, but the purchasing system can be haphazard, without automated controls. In addition to these external purchase costs, companies face significant internal costs resulting from outdated and cumbersome MRO management processes. For example, studies show that a high percentage of manufacturing downtime is often caused by not having the right part at the right time in the right place. The result is lost productivity and capacity. E-commerce software for plant operations provides powerful comparative searching capabilities to enable managers to identify functionally equivalent items, helping them spot opportunities to combine purchases for cost savings. Comparing various suppliers, coupled with consolidating more spending with fewer suppliers, leads to decreased costs. In addition, automated workflows are typically based on industry best practices, which can streamline processes.

Manufacturing

One approach taken by many manufacturers to raise profitability and improve customer service is to move their supply chain operations onto the Internet. Here they can form an **electronic exchange** to join with competitors and suppliers alike to buy and sell goods, trade market information, and run back-office operations, such as inventory control, as shown in Figure 8.6. This approach has greatly speeded up the movement of raw materials and finished products among all members of the business community and has reduced the amount of inventory that must be maintained. It has also led to a much more competitive marketplace and lower prices. Private exchanges are owned and operated by a single company. The owner uses the exchange to trade exclusively with established business partners. Public exchanges are owned and operated by industry groups. They provide services and a common technology platform to their members and are open, usually for a fee, to any company that wants to use them.

electronic exchange
An electronic forum where manufacturers, suppliers, and competitors buy and sell goods, trade market information, and run back-office operations.

Figure 8.6

Model of an Electronic Exchange

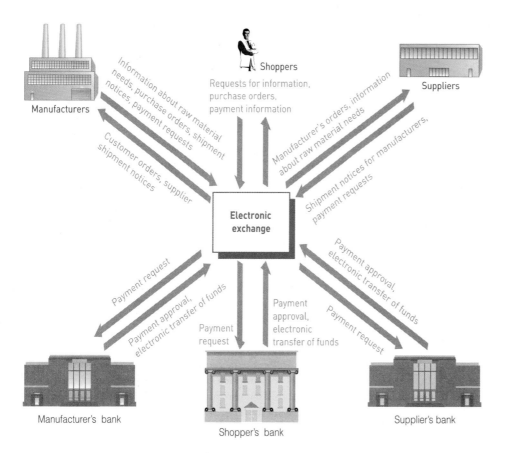

Avendra is a private exchange that provides access to a $3-billion supply chain of goods and services from over 900 suppliers to about 4,500 customers in the hospitality industry. The exchange was formed by ClubCorp, Fairmont Hotels, Hyatt,

Intercontinental Hotels Group, and Marriott International in 2001.[20] Not only do customers benefit from cost savings generated by Avendra's volume purchasing, they can draw on Avendra's extensive hospitality expertise to select those products that best meet their needs and budgets.

Several strategic and competitive issues are associated with the use of exchanges. Many companies distrust their corporate rivals and fear they might lose trade secrets through participation in such exchanges. Suppliers worry that online marketplaces will drive down the prices of goods and favour buyers. Suppliers also can spend a great deal of money in the setup to participate in multiple exchanges. For example, more than a dozen new exchanges have appeared in the oil industry, and the printing industry is up to more than 20 online marketplaces. Until a clear winner emerges in particular industries, suppliers are more or less forced to sign on to several or all of them. Yet another issue is potential government scrutiny of exchange participants—when competitors get together to share information, it raises questions of collusion or antitrust behaviour.

Many companies that already use the Internet for their private exchanges have no desire to share their expertise with competitors. At Walmart, the world's number-one retail chain, executives turned down several invitations to join exchanges in the retail and consumer goods industries. Walmart is pleased with its in-house exchange, Retail Link, which connects the company to 7,000 worldwide suppliers that sell everything from toothpaste to furniture.

Marketing

The nature of the Web enables firms to gather more information about customer behaviour and preferences as customers and potential customers gather information and make their purchase decisions. Analysis of this data is complicated because of the Web's interactivity and because each visitor voluntarily provides or refuses to provide personal data such as name, address, e-mail address, telephone number, and demographic data. Internet advertisers use the data to identify specific portions of their markets and target them with tailored advertising messages. This practice, called **market segmentation**, divides the pool of potential customers into subgroups usually defined by demographic characteristics, such as age, gender, marital status, income level, and geographic location.

In the past, market segmentation has been difficult for B2B marketers because firmographic data (addresses, financials, number of employees, industry classification code) was difficult to obtain. Now however, Nielsen, a marketing and media information company, has developed its Business-Facts database that provides this information for over 13 million businesses. Using this data, analysts can estimate potential sales for each business and rank it against all other prospects and customers.

Advertising

Mobile ad networks distribute mobile ads to publishers such as mobile websites, application developers, and mobile operators. Mobile ad impressions are generally bought at a cost per thousand (CPM), cost per click (CPC), or cost per action (CPA, in which the advertiser pays only if the customer clicks through and then buys the product or service). The main measures of success are the number of users reached, click through rate (CTR), and the number of actions users take, such as the number of downloads prompted by the ad.[21] The advertiser is keenly interested in this data to measure the effectiveness of its advertising spending and may pay extra to purchase the data from the mobile ad network or a third party. Generally, there are three types of mobile ad networks—blind, premium blind, and premium networks—though no clear lines separate them. The characteristics of these mobile advertising networks are summarized in Table 8.3.

AdMob is a mobile advertising provider that serves up ads for display on mobile devices and in applications like those that run on the Android and iPhone. With AdMob, smartphone application developers can distribute their apps for free and recover their costs over time by payments from advertisers.[22]

Table 8.3

Characteristics of Three Types of Mobile Advertising Networks

Characteristic	Blind Networks	Premium Blind Networks	Premium Networks
Degree to which advertisers can specify where ads are run	Can specify country and content channel (e.g., news, sports, or entertainment) on which the add will run but not specific website	Most advertising is blind, but for an additional charge, the advertiser can buy a specific spot on a website of their choice	Big brand advertisers can secure elite locations on top-tier destinations
Predominant pricing model and typical rate	CPC ($0.01 per click)	CPM ($20 per thousand impressions)	CPM ($40 per thousand impressions)
Examples	Admoda/Adultmoda AdMob BuzzCity InMobi	Jumptap Madhouse Millennial Media Quattro Wireless	Advertising.com/AOL Hands Microsoft Mobile Advertising Nokia Interactive Advertising Pudding Media YOC Group

Because m-commerce devices usually have a single user, they are ideal for accessing personal information and receiving targeted messages for a particular consumer. Through m-commerce, companies can reach individual consumers to establish one-to-one marketing relationships and communicate whenever it is convenient—in short, anytime and anywhere. According to one recent study, 51 percent of the consumers in 11 countries during the 2009 holiday season used their mobile phones to perform in-store activities including shopping, seeking peer feedback on products, obtaining product information, and capturing coupons.[23]

Consumers are increasingly using mobile phones to purchase goods and perform other transactions online.

(Source: © ICP/Alamy.)

Price Comparison

A growing number of companies provide a mobile phone service that enables shoppers to compare prices and products on the Web. Google Product Search works for iPhone and Android handsets. The shopper enters the name of the product into the Google search field and clicks "See Shopping Results" to display a list of suppliers and prices. You can also request consumer reviews and technical specification for a specific choice.[24] Frucall allows users to enter the bar code of a product and then it finds and displays the best online prices for any product with that bar code. You can also read reviews or purchase the item immediately by clicking a button.[25]

Couponing

Shoppers can sign up with individual retailers to request that their coupons are sent directly to their cell phone. Shoppers can also subscribe to mobile coupon aggregators such as Clip mobile or Dealcetera.com to receive promotions from many retailers. Mobile coupons are more likely to be redeemed (15 to 20 percent) than paper coupons (less than 1 percent).[26]

Target was the first national retailer in the United States to offer a scannable mobile coupon program. After opting into this program (via *m.target.com*), shoppers receive a text message with a link to a mobile Web page that contains various offers, all accessible under a single bar code. They redeem the coupons by scanning the bar code displayed on their Web-enabled phones at the checkout. Target customers can also use their mobile phones to access their Target Mobile GiftCards, check product availability at various Target store locations, administer their Target gift registries and lists, browse Target weekly ads, and receive text and e-mail notifications of deals.[27]

Valpak Canada has launched a free mobile coupon application for smartphone users that delivers over 17,000 offers. The application allows users to search for coupons by categories such as auto, beauty, dining, and health. It uses the phone's GPS to identify stores near you with offers, sorts the stores by distance from your current location, and provides directions to any selected store.[28]

As with any new technology, m-commerce will succeed only if it provides users with real benefits. Companies involved in m-commerce must think through their strategies carefully and ensure that they provide services that truly meet customers' needs.

Investment and Finance

The Internet has revolutionized the world of investment and finance. Perhaps the changes have been so significant because this industry had so many built-in inefficiencies and so much opportunity for improvement.

The brokerage business adapted to the Internet faster than any other arm of finance. The allure of online trading that enables investors to do quick, thorough research and then buy shares in any company in a few seconds and at a fraction of the cost of a full-commission firm has brought many investors to the Web.

Banking

Online banking customers can check balances of their savings, chequing, and loan accounts; transfer money among accounts; and pay their bills. These customers enjoy the convenience of not writing cheques by hand, tracking their current balances, and reducing expenditures on envelopes and stamps. In addition, paying bills online is good for the environment by reducing the amount of paper used, thus saving trees and reducing greenhouse gases.

All the major banks and many of the smaller banks in Canada enable their customers to pay bills online; many support bill payment via cell phone or other wireless device. Banks are eager to gain more customers who pay bills online because such customers tend to stay with the bank longer, have higher cash balances, and use more of the bank's products and services. To encourage the use of this service, many banks have eliminated all fees associated with online bill payment.

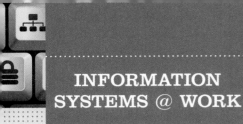

Virtual Models Sell Clothes at Sears.com

Sears was one of first businesses to develop a mail-order catalogue business. For decades, the Sears catalogue has been a popular method of ordering products for those unable or unwilling to travel to a department store. There isn't much difference between ordering from a catalogue and ordering from many e-commerce sites. Customers peruse a catalogue filled with photos and descriptions of products, then phone in or enter their order and await delivery. More recently, however, digital technologies have been developed that provide e-commerce sites with powerful tools to drive sales—especially for products that have traditionally been difficult to sell online.

While books, music, and airline tickets are relatively easy to sell online, physical merchandise—especially clothing—is much more challenging. Shoppers like to try on clothing and see how outfit components look together. Trying on clothes and experimenting with clothing combinations has been impossible to do online, and so most shoppers prefer to shop in stores for their clothes.

3D technologies have been able to provide online shoppers with the next best thing to being there. IBM and a company named My Virtual Model partnered to provide powerful e-commerce tools for online clothing stores such as Sears.

My Virtual Model provided a custom-designed 3D virtual model for shoppers to use to see how clothes look when tried on. Each customer used online tools to create a custom virtual model that closely resembled their own physical characteristics. Body size and shape, skin colour, hair colour and style, and facial features could be customized to look like the customer. You could even upload a photo of your face to create an exact virtual twin. Once created, the virtual model could be used to try on clothing from the online catalogue. Mix and match shirts, pants, shoes, skirts, hats, all kinds of apparel to find a combination that suited your tastes and appearance. The model could be rotated to view the clothes from all angles.

Sears combined My Virtual Model with IBM's WebSphere Commerce software to provide a visual catalogue of apparel that could be dragged onto a virtual model. The system provided additional social networking features that allowed shoppers to share images of themselves in various outfits with friends online to solicit their feedback and suggestions. Sears and other retailers found that shoppers are more likely to feel confident about a purchase when friends offer encouragement. Retailers that used My Virtual Model with social networking functionality saw a 30 to 40 percent increase in sales conversion rates. Due to technical issues, however, Sears discontinued using My Virtual Model's software.

Some analysts believe that the use of social networking and 3D technologies will propel the next generation of e-commerce and assist retailers in invigorating sales. One study found that 81 percent of consumers who use social networks seek shopping advice from friends and followers. Seventy-four percent of social network users say that their social network influences their buying decisions. It is only logical for businesses to pursue social networks for e-commerce.

The impact of social networks on sales is sometimes referred to as the "Twitter effect." Bad publicity for a product on Twitter can have a devastating effect on sales. Increasing numbers of shoppers rely on social networks for advice while shopping online and in stores. It is not unusual to find shoppers in store aisles consulting their social network via an iPhone or other smartphone prior to tossing an item into their shopping cart.

Companies such as CrossView specialize in what they call cross-channel enablement: developing strategies for improving the shopping experience across all shopping environments and covering brand reputation across all online influences. Businesses are realizing that consumers are drawing information that shapes their shopping decisions from numerous sources, including social networks, television and newspaper ads, and in-store promotions. Businesses are responding to this by taking a holistic approach to advertising and marketing. Companies such as Sears are combining the latest technologies with social networking tools and traditional marketing techniques to create new and powerful ways to influence and win over consumers.

Discussion Questions

1. What recent technologies are being harnessed to invigorate e-commerce sales?
2. Why is it important for retailers to turn to social networking as a tool for building positive brand recognition?

Critical Thinking Questions

1. How might a company respond to negative publicity on social networks like Twitter?
2. What other types of products might benefit from the integration of virtual 3D technologies with e-commerce sites?

SOURCES: Walsh, Lawrence, "Solution Providers Transform Retail, E-Commerce," Channel Insider, September 1, 2009, www.channelinsider.com/c/a/IBM/Solution-Providers-Transform-Retail-eCommerce-122473; "Sears Transforms the Online Shopping Experience with Help From IBM and My Virtual Model," IBM Press Release, September 17, 2008; My Virtual Model website, http://corpo.mvm.com, accessed April 1, 2010.

Consumers who have enrolled in mobile banking and downloaded the mobile application to their cell phones can check their credit card balances before making major purchases and can avoid credit rejections. They can also transfer funds from savings to chequing accounts to avoid an overdraft.

CIBC offers mobile banking via an application download. The application is custom-designed for the unique features and capabilities of the iPhone, Blackberry, and Android smartphones. The user can check balances, transfer funds, pay bills, and find the nearest ATM or bank branch. The application uses advanced encryption technology to protect against unauthorized access.[29]

E-Boutiques

An increasing number of websites offer personalized shopping consultations for shoppers interested in upscale, contemporary clothing—dresses, sportswear, denim, handbags, jewellery, shoes, and gifts. Key to the success of websites such as luxualboutique and Rubysky is a philosophy of high customer service and strong, personal client relationships. Online boutique shoppers complete a personal shopping profile by answering questions about body measurements, profession, interests, preferred designers, and areas of shopping where they would welcome assistance. Shoppers are then given suggestions on what styles and designers might work best and where they can be found—online or in brick-and-mortar shops.

Gilt is a private (invited members only), limited-time sales website where shoppers compete against each other for exclusive designer apparel and accessories. Items on the website typically sell out within 36 hours. The exclusive membership helps Gilt know who its customers are and to more clearly see what they like and don't like. The website has 1.6 million members. Those who use an iPad can see all the key information on one screen and then quickly tap through the sales process and drag items from the screen to their cart.[30] Although the website can be accessed by several mobile devices, an iPad with its larger screen size, along with its ability to zoom and flip through images with the swipe of a finger, makes Gilt look more like a magazine.[31]

THREATS TO ELECTRONIC AND MOBILE COMMERCE

Businesses must deal with a host of issues to ensure that e-commerce and m-commerce transactions are safe and consumers are protected. The following sections summarize a number of threats to e-commerce and m-commerce, along with practical ideas on how to minimize the impact of these threats.

Security

Many organizations that accept credit cards to pay for items purchased via e-commerce have adopted the Payment Card Industry (PCI) security standard. This standard spells out measures and security procedures to safeguard the card issuer, the cardholder, and the merchant. Some of the measures include installing and maintaining a firewall configuration to control access to computers and data; never using software or hardware vendor-supplier defaults for system passwords; and requiring merchants to protect stored data, encrypt transmission of cardholder information across public networks, use and regularly update antivirus software, and restrict access to sensitive data on a need-to-know basis.

Various measures are being implemented to increase the security associated with the use of credit cards at the time of purchase. Address Verification System is a check built into the payment authorization request that compares the address on file with the card issuer to the billing address provided by the cardholder. The Card Verification Number technique is a check of the additional digits printed on the back of the card. Visa has Advanced Authorization, a Visa-patented process that provides an instantaneous rating of that transaction's potential for fraud to the financial institution that issued the card. The card issuer can then send an immediate response to the merchant whether to accept or decline the transaction. The technology is now being applied to every Visa credit card purchase today. Visa estimates that this technique will reduce fraudulent credit card charges by 40 percent.

To reduce fraud two-factor authorization is recommended. This approach adds another identity check along with the password system such as "verified by Visa." A number of multifactor authentication schemes can be used, such as biometrics, one-time passwords, or hardware tokens that plug into a USB port on the computer and generate a password that matches the ones used by a bank's security system. Currently, the use of biometric technology to secure online transactions is rare for both cost and privacy reasons. It can be expensive to outfit every merchant with a biometric scanner, and it is difficult to convince consumers to supply something as personal and distinguishing as a fingerprint. In spite of this, a growing number of financial service firms are considering biometric systems.

Theft of Intellectual Property

Intellectual property includes works of the mind such as books, films, music, processes, and software, which are unique and are owned or created by a single entity. The owner of the intellectual property is entitled to certain rights in relation to the subject matter of the intellectual property. Thus, copyright law protects authored works such as books, film, images, music, and software from unauthorized copying. Patents can also protect software as well as business processes, formulae, compounds, and inventions. Information that has significant value for a firm and for which strong measures are taken to protect it is a trade secret. This too is protected under various laws. Although concerns about intellectual property and digital rights management (discussed next) apply to creative works distributed traditionally through brick-and-mortar retailers and libraries, these issues are more urgent for e-commerce because computers and the Internet make it easy to access, copy, and distribute digital content.

Digital rights management (DRM) refers to the use of any of several technologies to enforce policies for controlling access to digital media such as movies, music, and software. Many digital content publishers state that DRM technologies are needed to prevent revenue loss due to illegal duplication of their copyrighted works. While the costs of movie piracy can only be estimated imprecisely, the Motion Picture Association of America (MPAA) placed the direct cost to its member companies at $6 billion, with total costs (including loss of jobs and tax revenue) to the global industry at about $18 billion for 2005.[32] On the other hand, many digital content users argue that DRM and associated technologies lead to a loss of user rights. For example, users can purchase a music track online for under a dollar through Apple's iTunes music store. They can then burn that song to a CD and transfer it to an iPod. However, the purchased music files are encoded in the AAC format supported by iPods and protected by FairPlay, a DRM technology developed by Apple. To the consternation of music lovers, many music devices are not compatible with the AAC format and cannot play iTunes' protected files.

Fraud

The first wave of Internet crime consisted mostly of online versions of offline hoaxes, the usual get-rich-quick schemes. For example, many people received pleas from desperate Nigerians trying to enlist their help in transferring funds out of their country. More recently, however, fraud artists have begun to exploit the Internet to execute more sophisticated ploys, using fake websites and spam. In 2010, Canadians lost over $15 million due to Internet, e-mail, and text fraud.[33]

Phishing entails sending bogus messages purportedly from a legitimate institution to pry personal information from customers by convincing them to go to a "spoofed" website. The spoofed website appears to be a legitimate site but actually collects personal information from unsuspecting victims. Phishing scams are frequently disguised as requests for donations from a charitable organization. Sadly, criminals take advantage of the generosity of others following every natural disaster by sending out tens of thousands of bogus

intellectual property
Includes works of the mind such as books, films, music, processes, and software, which are unique and are owned or created by a single entity.

digital rights management (DRM)
Refers to the use of any of several technologies to enforce policies for controlling access to digital media such as movies, music, and software.

phishing
A practice that entails sending bogus messages purportedly from a legitimate institution to pry personal information from customers by convincing them to go to a "spoofed" website.

requests for donations from charitable organizations. Unfortunately, many generous but naive people provide personal information or bank account data. When Haiti was hit by a powerful earthquake, cybercriminals used this as an opportunity to launch phishing attacks requesting donations for the victims.[34] Another phishing scam with the subject line "download and upgrade Adobe PDF Reader–Writer for Windows" included a fake Adobe logo and requested users to click a link to a website that would download malicious code to their machines.[35]

click fraud
A problem arising in a pay-per-click online advertising environment where additional clicks are generated beyond those that come from actual, legitimate users.

Click fraud can arise in a pay-per-click online advertising environment when additional clicks are generated beyond those that come from actual, legitimate users. In pay-per-click advertising, the advertiser pays when a user clicks its ad to visit its website. The additional clicks may be generated by an illegitimate user, automated script, or some other means. These bogus clicks generate revenue for the advertising network such as Google or Yahoo!. Several marketers filed a suit against Facebook for click fraud. Facebook put in place a number of measures to ensure that it charges advertisers only for legitimate clicks; however, it appears those measures were not foolproof. Facebook claims that its contracts with advertisers state that they agree to accept the risk of fraudulent clicks. The issue is still in litigation as of this writing.[36]

Online auction fraud represents a major source of complaints both in Canada and abroad. The majority of the problems come from so-called person-to-person auctions, which account for roughly half the auction sites. On these sites, it is up to the buyer and seller to resolve details of payment and delivery; the auction sites offer no guarantees. Sticking with auction sites such as eBay (*www.ebay.ca*) that ensure the delivery and quality of all the items up for bidding can help buyers avoid trouble. However, even then, you can become a victim of auction fraud if the item you buy is stolen or counterfeit. An individual sold over $1 million worth of counterfeit software on eBay between 2001 and 2007. He was arrested, tried, found guilty, sentenced to 41 months in jail, and ordered to pay restitution.[37]

Invasion of Consumer Privacy

Online consumers are more at risk today than ever before. One of the primary factors causing higher risk is *online profiling*—the practice of Web advertisers recording online behaviour for the purpose of producing targeted advertising. **Clickstream data** is the data gathered based on the websites you visit and the items you click. From the marketers' perspective, the use of online profiling allows businesses to market to customers electronically one to one. The benefit to customers is personalized, more effective service; the benefit to providers is the increased business that comes from building relationships and encouraging customers to return for subsequent purchases. However, what may be considered one person's customer relationship building can be viewed by others as a manipulative and potentially harmful marketing technique.

clickstream data
The data gathered based on the websites you visit and the items you click.

Lack of Internet Access

The *digital divide* is a term that describes the difference between people who do and do not use modern technology such as computers, the Internet, telephone, and television to improve their standard of living. For example, it is estimated that of the roughly 1 billion Internet users worldwide, only 20 million (2 percent) are in the less-developed nations. The lack of universal Internet access makes it impossible to conduct e-commerce with many of the world's people. The digital divide exists not only between more and less developed countries but within countries between economic classes, the educated and uneducated, and those who live in cities and those who live in rural areas. Obviously, the lack of Internet access creates a barrier to further e-commerce expansion.

Legal Jurisdiction

Companies engaging in e-commerce must be careful that their sales do not violate the rules of various provincial or other legal jurisdictions. Examples of illegal sales are sales to those who cannot obtain cigarettes or wine because of their age.

Taxation

Canadian businesses and consumers must be aware of taxation issues when conducting e-commerce. Internet-based merchants need to apply sales tax only when buyers live in a province where the company has physical facilities, or "nexus."[38] E-commerce businesses try to avoid the complexity of dealing with the nonstandard taxation rules by setting up their Internet sales operations as legally separate companies with no physical presence outside of where their computers and warehouses are located. The provinces find it very difficult to collect sales taxes on Internet purchases. Total e-commerce B2C sales were estimated to be about $16 billion in 2009.[39] An average sales tax rate of 6 percent yields an estimate of almost $1 billion in lost sales tax revenue.

STRATEGIES FOR SUCCESSFUL E-COMMERCE AND M-COMMERCE

With all the constraints to e-commerce just covered, a company must develop an effective website—one that is easy to use and accomplishes the goals of the company, yet is safe, secure, and affordable to set up and maintain. The next sections examine several issues for a successful e-commerce site.

Defining the Website Functions

When building a website, you should first decide which tasks the site must accomplish. Most people agree that an effective website is one that creates an attractive presence and that meets the needs of its visitors, including the following:

- Obtaining general information about the organization
- Obtaining financial information for making an investment decision in the organization
- Learning the organization's position on social issues
- Learning about the products or services that the organization sells
- Buying the products or services that the company offers
- Checking the status of an order
- Getting advice or help on effective use of the products
- Registering a complaint about the organization's products
- Registering a complaint concerning the organization's position on social issues
- Providing a product testimonial or an idea for product improvement or new product
- Obtaining information about warranties or service and repair policies for products
- Obtaining contact information for a person or department in the organization

After a company determines which objectives its site should accomplish, it can proceed to the details of developing the site.

As the number of e-commerce shoppers increases and they become more comfortable—and more selective—making online purchases, a company might need to redefine the basic business model of its site to capture new business opportunities. For example, consider the major travel sites such as Expedia, Travelocity, CheapTickets, Orbitz, and Priceline. These sites used to specialize in one area of travel—inexpensive airline tickets. Now they offer a full range of travel products, including airline tickets, auto rentals, hotel rooms, tours, and last-minute trip packages. Expedia provides in-depth hotel details to help comparison shoppers and even offers 360-degree visual tours and expanded photo displays. It also entices flexible travellers to search for rates, compare airfares, and configure hotel and air prices at the same time. Expedia has developed numerous hotel partnerships to reduce costs and help secure great values for consumers. Meanwhile, Orbitz has launched a special full-service program for corporate business travellers.

Establishing a Website

Companies large and small can establish websites. Some companies elect to develop their sites in house, but this requires learning HTML, Java, and Web design software. Many firms, especially those with few or no experienced Web developers, have decided that to outsource the building of their websites gets the websites up and running faster and cheaper than doing it themselves.

Website hosting companies such as Canada Web Hosting and Cirrus Tech Ltd. make it possible to set up a Web page and conduct e-commerce within a matter of days and with little up-front cost.

These companies can also provide free hosting for your store; but to allow visitors to pay for merchandise with credit cards, you need a merchant account with a bank. If your company doesn't already have one, it must establish one.

Web development firm services range from providing organizations with pre-built templates and website builder tools to enable customers to build their own websites to full-service Web design and development with custom-designed websites.

storefront broker
A company that acts as an intermediary between your website and online merchants who have the products and retail expertise.

Another model for setting up a website is the use of a **storefront broker**, a business that serves as an intermediary between your website and online merchants who have the actual products and retail expertise. The storefront broker deals with the details of the transactions, including who gets paid for what, and is responsible for bringing together merchants and reseller sites. The storefront broker is similar to a distributor in standard retail operations, but in this case no product moves—only electronic data flows back and forth. Products are ordered by a customer at your site, orders are processed through a user interface provided by the storefront broker, and the product is shipped by the merchant.

Inst.biz is a software firm that, among other things, helps clients to set up an electronic storefront. Clients include Cross Canada Stitching, a distributor of high-quality cross stitching supplies, and Mortgage Architects, a national mortgage broker.[40]

Building Traffic to Your Website

The Internet includes hundreds of thousands of e-commerce websites. With all those potential competitors, a company must take strong measures to ensure that the customers it wants to attract can find its website. The first step is to obtain and register a domain name, which should say something about your business. For instance, stuff4u might seem to be a good catchall, but it doesn't describe the nature of the business—it could be anything. If you want to sell soccer uniforms and equipment, then you'd try to get a domain name such as *www. soccerstuff4u.com*, *www.soccerequipment.com*, or *www.stuff4soccercoaches.com*. The more specific the Web address, the better.

The next step to attracting customers is to make your site search-engine friendly by improving its rankings. Following are several ideas on how to do this.

meta tag
An HTML code, not visible on the displayed Web page, that contains keywords representing your site's content, which search engines use to build indexes pointing to your website.

- Include a meta tag in your store's home page. A **meta tag** is an HTML code, not visible on the displayed Web page, that contains a description of your site's content. Some search engines use the meta tag description on search-engine result pages, which can improve click-through rates. However, the usefulness of meta tags in improving a website's ranking on search-engine results has decreased dramatically due to the increased sophistication of search engines.
- Use website traffic data analysis software to turn the data captured in the Web log file into useful information. This data can tell you the URLs from which your site is being accessed, the search engines and keywords that find your site, and other useful information. Using this data can help you identify search engines to which you need to market your website, allowing you to submit your Web pages to them for inclusion in the search engine's index.
- Provide quality, keyword-rich content. Be careful not to use too many keywords, as search engines often ban sites that do this. Judiciously place keywords throughout your site, ensuring that the Web content is sensible and easy to read by humans as well as search engines.

- Add new content to the website on a regular basis. Again, this makes the site attractive to humans as well as search engines.
- Acquire links to your site from other reputable websites that are popular and related to your website. Avoid the use of low-quality links as they can actually hurt your website's rating.

The use of the Internet is growing rapidly in markets throughout Europe, Asia, and Latin America. Obviously, companies that want to succeed on the Web cannot ignore this global shift. Companies must be aware that consumers outside the United States will access sites with a variety of devices and so they should modify their site design accordingly. In Europe, for example, closed-system iDTVs (integrated digital televisions) are becoming popular for accessing online content, with some 80 million European households now using them. Because such devices have better resolution and more screen space than the PC monitors that North American consumers use to access the Internet, iDTV users expect more ambitious graphics. Successful global firms operate with a portfolio of sites designed for each market, with shared sourcing and infrastructure to support the network of stores, and with local marketing and business development teams to take advantage of local opportunities. Service providers continue to emerge to solve the cross-border logistics, payments, and customer service needs of these global retailers.

Maintaining and Improving Your Website

Website operators must constantly monitor the traffic to their sites and the response times experienced by visitors. AMR Research, an independent research analysis firm, reports that Internet shoppers expect service to be better than or equal to their in-store experience.

Nothing will drive potential customers away faster than experiencing unreasonable delays while trying to view or order your products or services. To keep pace with technology and increasing traffic, it might be necessary to modify the software, databases, or hardware on which the website runs to ensure acceptable response times.

Avnet is a global distributor of literally millions of electronic components, and each part has dozens of technical components. The company established a B2B e-commerce website so that established customers could purchase a large volume of a specific part. The site was recently redesigned to accept orders from organizations representing new customers who want to purchase small volumes for test purposes before finalizing their product designs. Under the original setup, it took these customers an excessive amount of time to order small quantities because they were required to register at the site and undergo credit checks. The website now streamlines the ordering process for such new customers. New customers don't have to register before ordering, the search engine was redesigned to be easier to use, credit checks were loosened, shipping rates were simplified so that customers could see their total charge before placing orders, and an online chat function was added to provide immediate assistance.[41]

Website operators must also continually be alert to new trends and developments in the area of e-commerce and be prepared to take advantage of new opportunities. For example, recent studies show that customers more frequently visit websites they can customize. **Personalization** is the process of tailoring Web pages to specifically target individual consumers. The goal is to meet the customer's needs more effectively, make interactions faster and easier, and, consequently, increase customer satisfaction and the likelihood of repeat visits. Building a better understanding of customer preferences also can aid in cross-selling related products and more expensive products. The most basic form of personalization involves using the consumer's name in an e-mail campaign or in a greeting on the Web page. Amazon uses a more advanced form of personalization, in which the website greets each repeat customer by name and recommends a list of new products based on the customer's previous purchases.

Businesses use two types of personalization techniques to capture data and build customer profiles. *Implicit personalization* techniques capture data from actual customer Web sessions—primarily based on which pages were viewed and which weren't. *Explicit*

personalization
The process of tailoring Web pages to specifically target individual consumers.

North Face Website Mixes Business, Philanthropy, and Humanity

The North Face is a company dedicated to developing performance apparel, equipment, and footwear for the world's most accomplished extreme outdoor athletes as well as for everyday enthusiasts. The North Face was established in 1966 as an outdoor sports shop. Over the years, the North Face brand has grown to include all types of garments, equipment, and footwear for climbers, mountaineers, extreme skiers, snowboarders, endurance runners, and explorers. Today the North Face operates 36 retail stores and distributes to hundreds of additional retail locations worldwide.

Recently, the North Face decided to take its products directly to customers online with a new B2C e-commerce site. The North Face wanted the site to reflect the brand's "Never Stop Exploring" spirit. The company's reputation for high technical quality, philanthropy, and athletic inspiration needed to be expressed in the design and content of the site. The site needed to use state-of-the-art technologies to provide flawless service to visitors, using a design that was inspiring. Anything less would be detrimental to the North Face image.

The North Face worked with three technology companies to accomplish its B2C e-commerce goals. IBM and Zobrist Consulting Group partnered to provide the infrastructure for the site. Fluid, an online retail specialist, was responsible for developing the site organization and visual design.

The foundation of the e-commerce functionality for the site was provided by IBM Websphere Commerce Enterprise software. Websphere manages an inventory database, provides the online TPS, and interacts with the company's primary business systems to create an integrated system. Zobrist also installed IBM Lotus Web Content Management software that provides an easy-to-use interface for North Face employees to update website content. Zobrist also integrated IBM OmniFind Discovery Edition into the system to customize each visitor's experience. OmniFind uses artificial intelligence to analyze user intent to display products that the customer is likely to find interesting.

When Zobrist was finished developing the underlying architecture for the system, North Face turned to Fluid to custom-design the look and feel of the site. Fluid analyzed detailed "user flows" for all types of visitors. For example, it studied how a "surgical" shopper, one that is product-driven and knows exactly what product to purchase, would navigate the site to access a product quickly and efficiently. It also studied how an "enthusiast" who lives the outdoors lifestyle might want to browse and interact with the site.

After completing its research, Fluid's resulting design for NorthFace.com was progressive and unique. It provides a "visceral, first-person experience" that immerses the visitor in outdoor colours, images, descriptions, and videos. It integrates the North Face products into this environment, with a strong emphasis on North Face–sponsored expeditions and athletes. It also spotlights the company's environmental initiatives. The design includes tools that make the products easy to examine and purchase. The overall result is a site that provides a technically advanced appearance and functionality, highlights North Face's philanthropic aspects along with the company's zest for the human spirit and the great outdoors, and is distinct from any competitor's site.

In the final stages of development, Zobrist returned to the site to apply search engine optimization (SEO) techniques. One of the techniques transforms cryptic URLs to common, descriptive URLs for interior site pages. This may sound easy to implement, but it is actually quite the opposite. Websites that provide customized pages based on customer usage typically automate the creation of page URLs so the Web server can determine what customized content to display. This results in a complex URL that looks like this:

http://www.northface.com/b/ref=sa_menu_bo0?ie=UTF8&node=283155&pf_rd_p

When search engines discover links such as this, they skip over them. Zobrist applied techniques to the NorthFace.com's merchandise database, and the applications that access it, so that the resulting URLs look like this:

http://www.thenorthface.com/catalog/sc-gear/women-s-jackets-vests.html

This URL will be recognized by search engines and easily referenced when someone searches for "North Face women's jackets."

The combined effort of IBM, Zobrist, and Fluid provided North Face with a state-of-the-art e-commerce site that truly reflects the company's high technical quality as well as its spirit. The site includes community features such as a blog and social networking features that foster the community that has developed around the North Face brand. All of this adds up to an environment that promotes North Face, makes visitors want to invest in the brand, and supports convenient e-commerce transactions.

Discussion Questions

1. What unique challenges did the North Face project pose for online retail specialist Fluid?
2. What SEO technique did Zobrist apply to improve North Face's chances of being recognized by search engines?

Critical Thinking Questions

1. Why do you think North Face used two companies for the development of its e-commerce site? What benefits did this approach provide? What challenges?
2. What risk does a company such as North Face acquire when using state-of-the-art technologies in hopes to impress visitors? What advice would you give to developers looking to implement the latest Web technologies?

SOURCES: "The North Face, Exploring Peak Performance," Fluid Case Study, *www.fluid.com/company/studies*, accessed April 10, 2010; "A Leading Producer of High-Performance Outdoor Gear Chooses IBM to Deploy a High-Performance Computing Platform Tailor made for Its Business," IBM Case Study, *www-01.ibm.com/software/success/cssdb.nsf/CS/CPOR-7PY6YP?OpenDocument&Site=corp&cty=en_us*, accessed May 5, 2010; Johnson, Nathania, "Zobrist Offers Search Friendly URL Service for IBM Websphere Commerce Customers," Internet Marketing, July 16, 2009, *http://blog.searchenginewatch.com/090716-233321*.

personalization techniques capture user-provided information, such as information from warranties, surveys, user registrations, and contest-entry forms completed online. Data can also be gathered through access to other data sources such as marketing affiliates (firms that share marketing data). Marketing firms aggregate this information to build databases containing a huge amount of consumer behavioural data. During each customer interaction, powerful algorithms analyze both types of data in real time to predict the consumer's needs and interests. This analysis makes it possible to deliver new, targeted information before the customer leaves the site. Because personalization depends on gathering and using personal user information, privacy issues are a major concern.

These tips and suggestions are only a few ideas that can help a company set up and maintain an effective e-commerce site. With technology and competition changing constantly, managers should read articles in print and on the Web to keep up to date on ever-evolving issues.

Now that we've examined how to establish e-commerce effectively, let's look at some of the technical issues related to e-commerce systems and the technology that makes it possible.

TECHNOLOGY INFRASTRUCTURE REQUIRED TO SUPPORT E-COMMERCE AND M-COMMERCE

Successful implementation of e-business requires significant changes to existing business processes and substantial investment in IS technology. These technology components must be chosen carefully and integrated to support a large volume of transactions with customers, suppliers, and other business partners worldwide. Online consumers complain that poor website performance (e.g., slow response time, inadequate customer support, and lost orders) drives them to abandon some e-commerce sites in favour of those with better, more reliable performance. This section provides a brief overview of the key technology infrastructure components. See Figure 8.7.

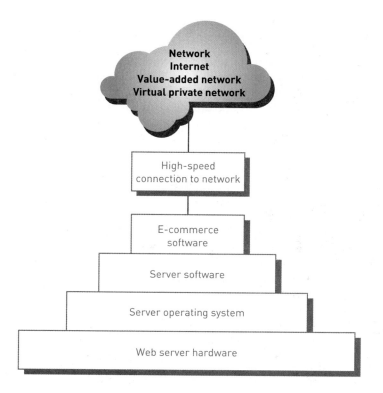

Figure 8.7

Key Technology Infrastructure Components

Hardware

A Web server hardware platform complete with the appropriate software is a key ingredient to e-commerce infrastructure. The amount of storage capacity and computing power required of the Web server depends primarily on two things: the software that must run on the server and the volume of e-commerce transactions that must be processed. The most successful e-commerce solutions are designed to be highly scalable so that they can be upgraded to meet unexpected user traffic.

A key decision facing a new e-commerce company is whether to host its own website or to let someone else do it. Many companies decide that using a third-party Web service provider is the best way to meet initial e-commerce needs. The third-party company rents space on its computer system and provides a high-speed connection to the Internet, which minimizes the initial out-of-pocket costs for e-commerce start-up. The third party can also provide personnel trained to operate, troubleshoot, and manage the Web server.

Web Server Software

In addition to the Web server operating system, each e-commerce website must have Web server software to perform fundamental services, including security and identification, retrieval and sending of Web pages, website tracking, website development, and Web page development. The two most widely used Web server software packages are Apache HTTP Server (51 percent market share) and Microsoft Internet Information Services (35 percent market share).[42]

E-Commerce Software

After you have located or built a host server, including the hardware, operating system, and Web server software, you can begin to investigate and install e-commerce software to support five core tasks: catalogue management to create and update the product catalogue, product configuration to help customers select the necessary components and options, shopping cart facilities to track the items selected for purchase, e-commerce transaction processing, and Web traffic data analysis to provide details to adjust the operations of the website.

Mobile Commerce Hardware and Software

For m-commerce to work effectively, the interface between the wireless, hand-held device and its user must improve to the point that it is nearly as easy to purchase an item on a wireless device as it is to purchase it on a PC. In addition, network speed must improve so that users do not become frustrated. Security is also a major concern, particularly in two areas: the security of the transmission itself and the trust that the transaction is being made with the intended party. Encryption can provide secure transmission. Digital certificates, discussed later in this chapter, can ensure that transactions are made between the intended parties.

The hand-held devices used for m-commerce have several limitations that complicate their use. Their screens are small, perhaps no more than several square centimetres, and might be able to display only a few lines of text. Their input capabilities are limited to a few buttons, so entering data can be tedious and error-prone. They also have less processing power and less bandwidth than desktop computers, which are usually hardwired to a high-speed LAN. They also operate on limited-life batteries. For these reasons, it is currently impossible to directly access many websites with a hand-held device. Web developers must rewrite Web applications so that users with hand-held devices can access them.

To address the limitations of wireless devices, the industry has undertaken a standardization effort for their Internet communications. The Wireless Application Protocol (WAP) is a standard set of specifications for Internet applications that run on hand-held, wireless devices. It effectively serves as a Web browser for such devices.

Electronic Payment Systems

Electronic payment systems are a key component of the e-commerce infrastructure. Current e-commerce technology relies on user identification and encryption to safeguard business transactions. Actual payments are made in a variety of ways, including electronic cash and smart, credit, charge, and debit cards. Websites that accept several payment types convert more visitors to purchasing customers than merchants who offer only a single payment method.

Authentication technologies are used by many organizations to confirm the identity of a user requesting access to information or assets. A **digital certificate** is an attachment to an e-mail message or data embedded in a website that verifies the identity of a sender or website. A **certificate authority (CA)** is a trusted third-party organization or company that issues digital certificates. The CA is responsible for guaranteeing that the people or organizations granted these unique certificates are, in fact, who they claim to be. Digital certificates are used by the SSL protocol, explained below, to verify the purchaser and supplier identities and improve the level of security of online electronic transactions.

> **digital certificate**
> An attachment to an e-mail message or data embedded in a website that verifies the identity of a sender or website.

> **certificate authority (CA)**
> A trusted third-party organization or company that issues digital certificates.

Secure Sockets Layer

All online shoppers fear the theft of credit card numbers and banking information. To help prevent this type of identity theft, the **Secure Sockets Layer (SSL)** communications protocol is used to secure sensitive data. The SSL communications protocol includes a handshake stage, which authenticates the server (and the client, if needed), determines the encryption and hashing algorithms to be used, and exchanges encryption keys. Following the handshake stage, data might be transferred. The data is always encrypted, ensuring that your transactions are not subject to interception or "sniffing" by a third party. Although SSL handles the encryption part of a secure e-commerce transaction, a digital certificate is necessary to provide server identification.

> **Secure Sockets Layer (SSL)**
> A communications protocol used to secure sensitive data during e-commerce.

Electronic Cash

Electronic cash is an amount of money that is computerized, stored, and used as cash for e-commerce transactions. Typically, consumers must open an account with an electronic cash service provider by providing identification information. When the consumers want to withdraw electronic cash to make a purchase, they access the service provider via the Internet and present proof of identity—a digital certificate issued by a certification authority or a username and password. After verifying a consumer's identity, the system debits the consumer's account and credits the seller's account with the amount of the purchase. PayPal, BillMeLater, MoneyZap, and TeleCheck are four popular forms of electronic cash.

> **electronic cash**
> An amount of money that is computerized, stored, and used as cash for e-commerce transactions.

The PayPal service of eBay enables any person or business with an e-mail address to securely, easily, and quickly send and receive payments online. To send money, you enter the recipient's e-mail address and the amount you want to send. You can pay with a credit card, debit card, or funds from a chequing account. The recipient gets an e-mail that says, "You've got cash!" Recipients can then collect their money by clicking a link in the e-mail that takes them to *www.paypal.ca*. To receive the money, the user also must have a credit card or chequing account to accept fund transfers. To request money for an auction, invoice a customer, or send a personal bill, you enter the recipient's e-mail address and the amount you are requesting. The recipient gets an e-mail and instructions on how to pay you using PayPal. PayPal has 78 million active accounts in 190 markets and makes payments in 19 currencies around the world.[43]

Credit, Charge, Debit, and Smart Cards

Many online shoppers use credit and charge cards for most of their Internet purchases. A credit card, such as Visa or MasterCard, has a preset spending limit based on the user's credit history, and each month the user can pay all or part of the amount owed. Interest is charged on the unpaid amount. Online verification by Visa and MasterCard is being implemented to reduce fraud. The user is required to enter a password and card verification number on the back of the card when using the card for online purchases. A charge card, such as American Express, carries no preset spending limit, and the entire amount charged to the card is due at the end of the billing period. Charge cards do not involve lines of credit and do not accumulate interest charges. American Express became the first company to offer disposable credit card numbers in 2000. Debit cards look like credit cards, and they operate like cash or a personal cheque but offer a higher level of security since they require a personal identification number (PIN) to use them.

The **smart card** is a credit card–sized device with an embedded microchip to provide electronic memory and processing capability. Smart cards can be used for a variety of purposes, including storing a user's financial facts, health insurance data, credit card numbers, and network identification codes and passwords. They can also store monetary values for spending.

Smart cards are better protected from misuse than conventional credit, charge, and debit cards because the smart-card information is encrypted. Transit passes, ATM bank cards, and "chip and PIN" credit cards are examples of smart cards. Conventional credit, charge, and debit cards clearly show your account number on the face of the card. The card number, along with a forged signature, is all that a thief needs to purchase items and charge them against your card. The "chip and PIN" credit cards provide a higher level of security since the card and the PIN are required. With many smart cards there is no external number that a thief can use and no physical signature a thief can forge. Table 8.4 compares various types of payment systems.

The Dragon Hotel is a four-star, 527-room facility located in a scenic and tourist-friendly portion of Hangzhou, China. The hotel invested $150 million to provide its clientele with a unique, personalized experience in its effort to become the first five-star hotel in the province of Zhejiang. It installed a smart card system "to automatically register visitors upon their arrival, direct them to their rooms, customize temperature settings to established preferences, and even record their attendance at conference events."[44]

smart card
A credit card–sized device with an embedded microchip to provide electronic memory and processing capability.

Table 8.4

Comparison of Payment Systems

Payment System	Description	Advantages	Disadvantages
Credit card	Carries preset spending limit based on the user's credit history	Each month the user can pay all or part of the amount owed	Unpaid balance accumulates interest charges—often at a high rate of interest
Charge card	Looks like a credit card but carries no preset spending limit	Does not involve lines of credit and does not accumulate interest charges	The entire amount charged to the card is due at the end of the billing period
Debit card	Looks like a credit card or automated teller machine (ATM) card	Operates like cash or a personal cheque	Money is immediately deducted from user's account balance
Smart card	Is a credit card device with embedded microchip capable of storing facts about card holder	Better protected from misuse than conventional credit, charge, and debit cards because the smart-card information is encrypted	Not widely used in the United States

Electronic Bill Presentment and Payment

With the process of electronic bill presentment and payment, a vendor posts an image of your invoice on the Internet and alerts you by e-mail that your bill has arrived, thus eliminating the paper bill. The customer then pays the bill using a credit card or through processing an electronic fund transfer. Some services, such as epost by Canada Post and CheckFree, consolidate subscribers' bills, such as monthly utility bills from various sources, so that they can be paid all at once.

P-Card

A **p-card (procurement card or purchasing card)** is a credit card used to streamline the traditional purchase order and invoice payment processes. The p-card is typically issued to selected employees who must follow company rules and guidelines that may include a single purchase limit, a monthly spending limit, or merchant category code restrictions. Due to an increased risk of unauthorized purchases, each p-card holder's spending activity is reviewed periodically by someone independent of the cardholder to ensure adherence to the guidelines. Environment Canada is a federal government department with approximately 4,700 employees located across Canada. The department began a p-card program to handle small-dollar purchases and limited use of the p-card to specific employees who could make individual purchases up to a maximum amount. Users must file expense reports and have the report signed by their supervisor. The program has reduced the effort and costs associated with procurement.[45]

p-card (procurement card or purchasing card)
A credit card used to streamline the traditional purchase order and invoice payment processes.

Payments Using Cell Phones

A number of companies are exploring more convenient ways to enable payments by cell phones by converting cell phones into virtual chequebooks or credit cards so that users can simply use the touch pad to send payments. Two options are available: payments linked to your bank account and payments added to your phone bill. The goals are to make the payment process as simple and secure as possible and for it to work on many different phones and through many different cell phone service providers—not simple tasks. Fortunately, the intelligence built into the iPhone, BlackBerry, and other smartphones can make this all possible.[46]

Obopay is developing a service that enables people to transmit money from one another via text messaging. The MasterCard MoneySend service (currently in use in India) builds upon the Obopay technology. With MoneySend, funds transferred to a Maestro or MasterCard card can be available within one or two banking days. Users get an immediate confirmation that the funds have been successfully transferred. The recipient can access the transferred funds by making a purchase anywhere Maestro or MasterCard cards are accepted or by withdrawing cash at a participating ATM that accepts MasterCard cards and offers cash.[47]

Boku is attempting to start up a cell phone payment system based on the use of cell phone numbers rather than credit card numbers. The advantage is that while most people know their cell phone numbers, few remember their credit card numbers. The system sends a text message to the buyers asking them to authorize the purchase. If authorized, a charge for the purchase then appears on the buyer's mobile phone bill.

SUMMARY

Principle:

Electronic and mobile commerce are evolving, providing new ways of conducting business that present both potential benefits and problems.

Electronic commerce is the conducting of business activities (e.g., distribution, buying, selling, marketing, and servicing of products or services) electronically over computer networks. Business-to-business (B2B) e-commerce allows manufacturers to buy at a low cost worldwide, and it offers enterprises the chance to sell to a global market. B2B e-commerce is currently the largest type of e-commerce. Business-to-consumer (B2C) e-commerce enables organizations to sell directly to consumers, eliminating intermediaries. In many cases, this squeezes costs and inefficiencies out of the supply chain and can lead to higher profits and lower prices for consumers. Consumer-to-consumer (C2C) e-commerce involves consumers selling directly to other consumers. Online auctions are the chief method by which C2C e-commerce is currently conducted. e-Government involves the use of information and communications technology to simplify the sharing of information, improve formerly paper-based processes, and improve the relationship between citizens and government.

A successful e-commerce system must address the many stages consumers experience in the sales life cycle. At the heart of any e-commerce system is the ability of the user to search for and identify items for sale; select those items; negotiate prices, terms of payment, and delivery date; send an order to the vendor to purchase the items; pay for the product or service; obtain product delivery; and receive after-sales support.

From the perspective of the provider of goods or services, an effective e-commerce system must be able to support the activities associated with supply chain management and customer relationship management.

A firm must overcome three key challenges to convert its business processes from the traditional form to e-commerce processes: (1) it must define an effective e-commerce model and strategy; (2) it must deal effectively with consumer privacy concerns; and (3) it must successfully overcome consumers' lack of trust.

Mobile commerce is the use of wireless devices such as cell phones and smartphones to facilitate the sale of goods or services—anytime, anywhere. The market for m-commerce in North America is expected to mature much later than in Western Europe and Japan. Numerous retailers have established special websites for users of mobile devices.

Principle:

E-commerce and m-commerce can be used in many innovative ways to improve the operations of an organization.

Electronic retailing (e-tailing) is the direct sale from a business to consumers through electronic storefronts designed around an electronic catalogue and shopping cart model.

A cybermall is a single website that offers many products and services at one Internet location.

Manufacturers are joining electronic exchanges, where they can work with competitors and suppliers to use computers and websites to buy and sell goods, trade market information, and run back-office operations such as inventory control. They are also using e-commerce to improve the efficiency of the selling process by moving customer queries about product availability and prices online.

The Web allows firms to gather much more information about customer behaviour and preferences than they could using other marketing approaches. This new technology has greatly enhanced the practice of market segmentation and enabled companies to establish closer relationships with their customers.

The Internet has revolutionized the world of investment and finance, especially online stock trading and online banking. The Internet has also created many options for electronic auctions, where geographically dispersed buyers and sellers can come together.

Online real estate services and e-boutiques are readily available.

The numerous m-commerce applications include mobile banking, mobile price comparison, mobile advertising, and mobile coupons.

Principle:

Although e-commerce and m-commerce offer many advantages, users must be aware of and protect themselves from many threats associated with this technology.

Businesses and people use e-commerce and m-commerce to reduce transaction costs, speed the flow of goods and information, improve the level of customer service, and enable the close coordination of actions among manufacturers, suppliers, and customers.

E-commerce and m-commerce also enable consumers and companies to gain access to worldwide markets. They offer great promise for developing countries, enabling them to enter the prosperous global marketplace, and hence helping to reduce the gap between rich and poor countries.

Because e-commerce and m-commerce are global systems, they face cultural, language, time and distance, infrastructure, currency, product and service, and provincial, regional, and national law challenges.

Revolutionary change always raises new issues, and e-commerce is no exception. Among the issues that must be addressed are security, theft of intellectual property, fraud, invasion of consumer privacy, lack of Internet access, return on investment, legal jurisdiction, and taxation.

Principle:

Organizations must define and execute a strategy to be successful in e-commerce and m-commerce.

Most people agree that an effective website is one that creates an attractive presence and meets the needs of its visitors. E-commerce start-ups must decide whether they will build and operate the website themselves or outsource this function. Website hosting services and storefront brokers provide alternatives to building your own website.

To build traffic to your website, you should register a domain name that is relevant to your business, make your site search-engine friendly by including a meta tag in your home page, use website traffic data analysis software to attract additional customers, and modify your website so that it supports global commerce. Website operators must constantly monitor the traffic and response times associated with their sites and adjust software, databases, and hardware to ensure that visitors have a good experience when they visit.

Principle:

E-commerce and m-commerce require the careful planning and integration of a number of technology infrastructure components.

A number of infrastructure components must be chosen and integrated to support a large volume of transactions with customers, suppliers, and other business partners worldwide. These components include hardware, Web server software, and e-commerce software.

M-commerce presents additional infrastructure challenges, including improving the ease of use of wireless devices, addressing the security of wireless transactions, and improving network speed. The Wireless Application Protocol (WAP) is a standard set of specifications to enable development of m-commerce software for wireless devices. WAP uses the Wireless Markup Language, which is designed for effectively displaying information on small devices. The development of WAP and its derivatives addresses many m-commerce issues.

Electronic payment systems are a key component of the e-commerce infrastructure. A digital certificate is an attachment to an e-mail message or data embedded in a Web page that verifies the identity of a sender or a website. To help prevent the theft of credit card numbers and banking information, the Secure Sockets Layer (SSL) communications protocol is used to secure all sensitive data. Several electronic cash alternatives require the purchaser to open an account with an electronic cash service provider and to present proof of identity whenever payments are to be made. Payments can also be made by credit, charge, debit, smart cards, and p-cards.

CHAPTER 8: SELF-ASSESSMENT TEST

Electronic and mobile commerce are evolving, providing new ways of conducting business that present both potential benefits and problems.

1. An organization will use _____ e-commerce to purchase goods and services from its suppliers and _____ e-commerce to sell products to its customers.
2. Which form of e-commerce is the largest?
3. What is the elimination of intermediate organizations between the producer and the consumer called?
4. The sole objective of e-Government is to improve communications between citizens and the federal government. True or False?
5. The market for m-commerce in North America is more advanced compared to Western Europe and Japan. True or False?

E-commerce and m-commerce can be used in many innovative ways to improve the operations of an organization.

6. Which of the following is a single website that offers many products and services at one Internet location?
   a. e-tailer
   b. Web service
   c. cybermall
   d. Premium networks
7. The practice of _____ divides the pool of potential customers into subgroups, which are usually defined by demographic characteristics.

8. An advancement in online bill payment that allows the biller to post an image of your statement on the Internet via e-mail so you can direct your bank to pay it is called _____.

Although e-commerce and m-commerce offer many advantages, users must be aware of and protect themselves from many threats associated with this technology.

9. According to the text, which of the following is a frequent advantage of converting to an e-commerce supply chain?
   a. a decrease in transportation costs
   b. an increase in available product inventory
   c. acquisition of expensive information systems technology
   d. an improved level of customer service
10. The use of any of several technologies to enforce policies for controlling access to digital media is called _____.

Organizations must define and execute a strategy to be successful in e-commerce and m-commerce.

11. After your website is established and successful, you do not need to redefine your site's basic business model. True or False?
12. Website operators can take several actions to improve how they are ranked by search engines. True or False?

E-commerce and m-commerce require the careful planning and the integration of a number of technology infrastructure components.

13. Poor website performance can drive consumers to abandon a website in favour of those with better, more reliable performance. True or False?

14. _____ contain variable information and are built to respond to a specific website visitor's request for information.

CHAPTER 8: SELF-ASSESSMENT TEST ANSWERS

(1) buy-side; sell-side (2) B2B (3) disintermediation (4) false (5) false (6) c (7) market segmentation (8) electronic bill presentment (9) d (10) digital rights management (11) false (12) true (13) true (14) Dynamic Web pages

REVIEW QUESTIONS

1. What is buy-side e-commerce? What is sell-side e-commerce?
2. State two reasons for the steady growth of online purchases as a percent of total retail sales.
3. What is a key benefit for producers of using B2C e-commerce to sell directly to the consumer, thus eliminating middlemen?
4. Identify the five stages consumers experience in the sales life cycle that must be supported by a successful e-commerce system.
5. Identify three key challenges that an organization must overcome to convert its business processes from the traditional form to e-commerce processes.
6. What is identity theft? Provide several tips for online shoppers to avoid identity theft.
7. Outline at least three specific trust-building strategies for an organization to gain the trust of consumers.
8. What is mobile commerce?
9. What is electronic retailing? What is an electronic exchange?
10. What is market segmentation? What has happened recently that makes it easier for B2B marketers to perform market segmentation?
11. What is the Wireless Application Protocol? Is it universally accepted? Why or why not?
12. Why is it necessary to continue to maintain and improve an existing website?
13. What role do digital certificates and certificate authorities play in e-commerce?
14. Briefly explain the differences among smart, credit, charge, debit cards, and p-cards.
15. Because e-commerce and m-commerce systems are global systems, what are some of the global challenges that they face?
16. Identify the key elements of the technology infrastructure required to successfully implement e-commerce within an organization.

DISCUSSION QUESTIONS

1. Describe the process of electronic bill presentment. Outline some potential problems in using this form of billing customers.
2. Why are many manufacturers and retailers outsourcing the physical logistics of delivering merchandise to shoppers? What advantages does such a strategy offer? What are the potential issues or disadvantages?
3. What does it mean to define the functions of a website? What are some of the possible functions?
4. What do you think are the biggest barriers to wide-scale adoption of m-commerce by consumers?
5. Walmart, the world's largest retail chain, has turned down several invitations to join exchanges in the retail and consumer goods industries. Is this good or bad for the overall Canadian economy? Why?
6. Identify and briefly describe three m-commerce applications you have used.
7. Discuss the use of e-commerce to improve spending on manufacturing, repair, and operations (MRO) of goods and services.
8. Summarize the key differences between B2B, B2C, and C2C e-commerce.
9. Outline the key steps in developing a corporate global e-commerce strategy.
10. Identify three kinds of business organizations that would have difficulty in becoming a successful e-commerce organization.

PROBLEM-SOLVING EXERCISES

1. Develop a set of criteria you would use to evaluate various business-to-consumer websites based on factors such as ease of use, protection of consumer data, and security of payment process. Develop a simple spreadsheet containing these criteria. Evaluate five popular websites using the criteria you developed. What changes would you recommend to the Web developer of the site that scored lowest?

2. Use the charting capability of your spreadsheet software to plot the growth of B2C e-commerce and retail sales for the period 2000 to the present. Using current growth rates, predict the year that B2C e-commerce will exceed 10 percent of retail sales. Document any assumptions you make.

3. Your washing machine just gave out and must be replaced within the week! Use your Web-enabled smartphone (or borrow a friend's) to perform a price and product comparison to identify the manufacturer and model that best meets your needs and the retailer with the lowest delivered cost. Obtain peer input to validate your choice. Write a brief summary of your experience and identify the websites you found most useful.

TEAM ACTIVITIES

1. Imagine that your team has been hired as consultants to provide recommendations to boost the traffic to a website that sells environmentally friendly ("green") household cleaning products. Identify as many ideas as possible for how you can increase traffic to this website. Next, rank your ideas from best to worst.

2. As a team, develop a set of criteria that you would use to evaluate the effectiveness of a mobile advertising campaign to boost the sales of one of your firm's products. Identify the measures you would use and the data that must be gathered.

WEB EXERCISES

1. Do research on the Web to find out more about the American Consumer Satisfaction Index methodology developed by the University of Michigan. Write a brief report about this methodology and explain how it was applied to rate B2C websites. Using this information, develop a list of at least six recommendations for someone developing a B2C website.

2. Do research on the Web to find a dozen websites that offer mobile coupons. Separate the sites into two groups: those that provide coupons for a single retailer and those that aggregate coupons for many retailers. Produce a table that summarizes your results and shows the approximate number of coupons available at each site.

CAREER EXERCISES

1. Do research and write a brief report on the impact of mobile advertising on sales and marketing.

2. For your chosen career field, describe how you might use or be involved with e-commerce. If you have not chosen a career yet, answer this question for someone in marketing, finance, or human resources.

CASE STUDIES

Case One

Mazda Provides Dealers with Customized E-Commerce Sites

Since 1968 when the first Mazda vehicles arrived in Canada, Mazda has built nearly 170 dealerships across the country. Besides building its on-ground business in Canada, Mazda has also been building its online business. Customers can go online to check out the latest models viewed as 3D images that can be rotated in numerous photos and even in videos. Shoppers can choose to view models in various colours and with various features. You can build your dream car with all the options you like to see how it will look and get a quote on price. You can even use the site to compare Mazda cars to other cars from other manufacturers.

Mazda dealerships' websites also provide e-commerce features that allow customers to shop for and purchase auto parts and accessories online. The Mazda parts site has been centrally administered and shared by all dealerships. While sharing this site allows Mazda to maintain control of its brand and business, it fails to provide dealerships with the freedom they need to run special regional sales and promotions.

Mazda worked with IBM to design a solution that would please both the dealerships and Mazda headquarters. IBM WebSphere Commerce includes a feature called extended sites that ideally addresses Mazda's dilemma. Using WebSphere, Mazda was able to design and set up its catalogue of accessories and parts. WebSphere includes a transaction processing system that connected to Mazda's 15-year-old mainframe-based ordering and inventory system.

Once the parts and accessories site was created, WebSphere allowed each dealer to customize a version of the site. So, while all dealers shared the same parts and accessories catalogue and all sales were routed to a common ordering and inventory system, dealers had the freedom to adjust their own prices in accordance with local economies and special promotions. The customization tools that WebSphere provided to dealers were so simple that most dealers could set up a local site within 15 minutes.

Mazda's new approach to e-commerce provides its dealerships with better support while dramatically improving its dealerships' ability to sell parts and accessories. The new site especially appeals to younger shoppers who are more likely to purchase parts and accessories and to shop online rather than visit a dealership. Because the catalogue of parts is shared across dealerships, Mazda can maintain a consistent brand message. Finally, the improved service to customers and support for local promotions provided by the new e-commerce sites have increased the number of customers that visit the dealerships.

Discussion Questions

1. Why were dealers unhappy with Mazda's one-size-fits-all e-commerce site for auto parts and accessories?
2. Why do you think it was unrealistic for each dealership to run its own unique and independent parts e-commerce site?

Critical Thinking Questions

1. What other businesses would benefit from the model of one central shared catalogue with customization options?
2. Why do you think Mazda decided to outsource its e-commerce site to IBM?

SOURCES: "Mazda Helps Its Dealers Create Their Own Online Parts and Accessories Stores Using the Latest Release of IBM WebSphere Commerce Software," IBM Case Study, February 6, 2009, www-01.ibm.com/software/success/cssdb.nsf/CS/CPOR-7P239T?OpenDocument&Site=corp&cty=en_us; Mazda website, www.mazda.ca, accessed June 10, 2011; WebSphere Commerce website, www-01.ibm.com/software/genservers/commerceproductline, accessed April 1, 2010.

Case Two

Wrangler Sells Direct Online

The Wrangler Jeans story begins in 1904, when C. C. Hudson bought several sewing machines from his previous employer, leased space over a grocery store, and started the Hudson Overall Company. Fifteen years later, the name of the business was changed to Blue Bell Overall Company. Over decades of growth and acquisitions, Blue Bell became Wrangler and expanded to produce and sell western-style clothing for men, women, and children around the world. Today, one in every five pairs of jeans sold globally is made by Wrangler.

In 2009, Wrangler decided to open its first B2C e-commerce site. Wrangler had several goals for the new site. It needed to provide visitors with a view into the spirit behind the Wrangler brand. Wrangler wanted to use the site to feature and promote various products as the market dictated. They also wanted the site to use the latest technologies to show that Wrangler is tech savvy and to empower Wrangler's marketing department with new ways to present its products.

One Wrangler slogan is "Enduring American freedom; it's in the spirit of people who work hard, have fun, and recognize courageous individuality." Wrangler's website design expresses this concept with large, bold photos of down-home scenes featuring country music and rodeo stars alongside hard-working individuals and people just hanging out.

Wrangler's new site uses background image fade-ins with rotating product image overlays that allow Wrangler to feature different products as needed. Behind the scenes, the site is delivered in a Flash version and a pure HTML version, both fully integrated to support all browser requirements. Although this approach requires additional development time, it allows the site to "garner better natural search rankings."

Wrangler included additional database functionality to provide different views of products. For example, a visitor can click Jeans to go directly to the Jeans page, or browse through product collections listed under themes that include Rodeo & Riding, Workwear & Safety, Music & Dancing, and Hanging Out. Each theme opens with a large splash screen that Wrangler marketing uses to promote its brand in the selected environment. For example, clicking Music & Dancing opens a large photo of country music legend George Strait, with a paragraph on Wrangler's importance to those involved in country music and dancing.

The site uses the latest technologies to provide interesting page and page element presentations and site navigation. The latest technologies are also used on the back end to make sure that pages are loaded and refreshed extremely quickly. It features a single-page checkout system that makes the checkout process quick and efficient. It also features a powerful search utility that provides an alternative to the traditional drill-down approach to navigation.

Wrangler's new site took four months to develop and was completed on-time and on-budget. Wrangler has benefited from additional sales provided by its new B2C e-commerce site. Equally valuable is the insight the company gains about customer interests and the platform it provides for Wrangler marketing to experiment with product and brand promotions.

Discussion Questions

1. How does Wrangler's new B2C e-commerce site assist Wrangler's brand recognition and marketing efforts?
2. What goals did Wrangler set for its e-commerce site? Visit *www.wrangler.com*. Do you think its new site meets those goals?

Critical Thinking Questions

1. Wrangler targets a very specific type of person with its marketing and website. How would you describe that group? What risks and benefits do companies assume when they target specific types of individuals? Do you think it pays off for Wrangler? Why?
2. The Wrangler site incorporates a lot of dynamic visual elements. How do these elements affect a shopper? What types of products are best suited for this type of marketing approach?

SOURCES: Todé, Chantel, "Wrangler Launches First e-Commerce Portal," DMNews, September 10, 2009, *www.dmnews.com/wrangler-launches-first-e-commerce-portal/article/148482*; "Wrangler," Zobrist Success Story, *www.zobristinc.com/our_clients/success_stories/Wrangler*, accessed April 10, 2010; Wrangler website, *www.wrangler.com*, accessed April 10, 2010.

Questions for Web Case

See the website for this book to read about the Altitude Online case for this chapter. The following are questions concerning this Web case.

Altitude Online: E-Commerce Considerations

Discussion Questions

1. How does Altitude Online's website contribute to the company's commerce?
2. How will the new ERP system affect Altitude Online's Web presence?

Critical Thinking Questions

1. How can companies like Altitude Online, which sell services rather than physical products, use e-commerce to attract customers and streamline operations?
2. Fluid Inc. is similar to Altitude Online in the services it offers. What features of the Fluid website, *www.fluid.com*, do you think are effective for e-commerce? How might you design the site differently?

NOTES

Sources for the opening vignette: "ShopTommy.com Dresses for Online Success—OnDemand," ATG Case Studies, *www.atg.com/resource-library/case-studies/CS-Tommy-Hilfiger.pdf*, accessed March 31, 2010; Tommy Hilfiger website, *www.tommy.com*, accessed March 31, 2010; ATG website, I, accessed March 31, 2010.

1 *The Daily*, "Electronic Commerce and Technology," *www.statcan.gc.ca/daily-quotidien/080424/dq080424a-eng.htm*, accessed October 22, 2010.
2 Ibid.
3 Ibid.
4 "Canada B2C E-Commerce: A Work in Progress," emarketer, *www.emarketer.com/Report.aspx?code=emarketer_2000547*, accessed October 23, 2010.
5 Lasalle, Luann, "Canadian Retailers Still Adopting e-Commerce, Social Media to Woo Consumers," *The Kitchener – Waterloo Record*, July 13, 2010, *www.news.therecord.com/article/744979*, accessed October 23, 2010.
6 O'Reilly, Joseph, "P&G Explores B2C," *Inbound Logistics*, February 10, 2010, *www.inboundlogistics.com/articles/trends/trends0210.shtml*, accessed March 6, 2010.
7 *Internet Retailer: Top 500 Guide*, 2009 edition, *www.internetretailer.com/top500/list.asp*, accessed March 8, 2010.
8 "The Biggest Online Winners and Losers for 2009: eBay Traffic Collapse," *24/7 Wall St*, December 16, 2009, *http://247wallst.com/2009/12/16/the-biggest-online-winners-and-losers-for-2009-ebay-traffic-collapse*, accessed March 7, 2010.

9 Canada's Economic Action Plan, *www.actionplan.gc.ca*, accessed October 23, 2010.
10 Service Canada, *www.servicecanada.gc.ca*, accessed October 23, 2010.
11 Statistics Canada, "E-commerce: Shopping on the Internet," *www.statcan.gc.ca/daily-quotidien/100927/dq100927a-eng.htm*, accessed October 23, 2010.
12 "A Chronology of Data Breaches," The Privacy Rights Clearing House, *www.privacyrights.org/ar/ChronDataBreaches.htm#CP*, accessed March 22, 2010.
13 Thomas, Knowlton, "B.C. Lottery Corporation Officially Admits to Security Breaches on North America's First Online Casino," *www.techvibes.com/blog/bc-lottery-corporation-officially-admits-to-security-breaches-on-north-americas-first-online-casino*, accessed October 23, 2010.
14 "Kavur, Jennifer, "Cost of IT Security Breaches Jump 97 Per Cent," itWorldCanada, *www.itworldcanada.com/news/cost-of-it-security-breaches-jumps-97-per-cent/138878*, accessed June 11, 2011.
15 The Office of the Privacy Commissioner of Canada, *www.priv.gc.ca/fs-fi/02_05_d_10_e.cfm*, accessed June 11, 2011.
16 Shah, Agam, "IDC: 1 Billion Mobile Devices Will Go Online by 2013," *Computerworld*, December 9, 2009.
17 Mobile Mammoth website, *www.mobilemammoth.com*, accessed March 24, 2010.
18 "Leslie Linevsky on e-Marketing—2010 Top 10 Mobile Shopping Sites," *www.catalogs.com/blog*, accessed March 24, 2010.
19 Hansberry, Ed, "Shopping Service Opens up on Twitter," *InformationWeek*, April 30, 2009.

20 Avendra, LLC Profile, Hoovers, *www.hoovers.com/company/Avendra_Llc/ryxskci-1.html*, accessed March 26, 2010.

21 "mobiThinking Guide to Mobile Advertising Networks (2010)," *mobilethinking.com/mobile-ad-network-guide*, accessed March 29, 2010.

22 Weintraub, Seth, "Google to Acquire AdMob for $750 Million in Stock," *Computerworld*, November 9, 2009.

23 "Motorola 2009 Retail Holiday Season Shopper Study," January 11, 2010, *http://mediacenter.motorola.com/imagelibrary/detail.aspx?MediaDetailsID=861*, accessed March 29, 2010.

24 Purdy, Kevin, "Google Product Search Goes Mobile," April 24, 2009, *http://lifehacker.com/5225858/google-product-search-goes-mobile*, accessed March 27, 2010.

25 Frucall website, *www.frucall.com*, accessed March 27, 2010.

26 Wortham, Jenna, "Coupons You Don't Clip, Sent to Your Cellphone," *New York Times*, August 29, 2009.

27 "Target Launches First Ever Scannable Mobile Coupon Program," *Super-Market Industry News*, March 11, 2010.

28 "Valpak Mobile Coupons 2010," March 19, 2010, *webfloss.com/Valpak-mobile-coupons-2010*, accessed March 28, 2010.

29 "Mobile Applications," CIBC website, *www.cibc.com/ca/how-to-bank/mobile.html*, accessed June 11, 2011.

30 Muir, Courtney, "Gilt Groupe iPad App Compromises 2 Percent of Sales in First 3 Days," *Mobile Commerce Daily*, April 12, 2010.

31 Miller, Claire Cain, "On the iPad, Gilt Is for All Kinds of Shoppers," *New York Times*, April 2, 2010.

32 Hiltzik, Michael, "Casual Purchase of Counterfeit DVD Shines Light on Piracy," *Los Angeles Times*, January 4, 2010.

33 Phone Busters, "Annual Statistical Report 2010," *www.phonebusters.com/english/ documents/Annual 2010 CAFC.pdf*, accessed June 11, 2011.

34 Silva, Veronica C., "Cybercriminals Exploit Haiti Tragedy with Malware," *PC World*, February 21, 2010.

35 Messmer, Ellen, "Phishing Scam Targets Users of Adobe PDF Reader," *Network World*, January 28, 2010.

36 Davis, Wendy, "Facebook Asks Court to Dismiss Click Fraud Cases," Media Post News, February 1, 2010, *www.mediapost.com/publications/?fa=Articles.showArticle&art_aid=121682*, accessed April 2, 2010.

37 Gross, Grant, "Virginia Man to Serve Prison Term for Selling Counterfeit Software," *Computerworld*, October 23, 2009.

38 About.com, "Small Business: Canada—Charging Provincial Sales Taxes on Online Sales," http://sbinfocanada.about.com/od/pst/a/PSTecommerce.htm, accessed June 11, 2011.

39 "Canada B2C E-Commerce: A Work in Progress," emarketer, *www.emarketer.com/Report.aspx?code=emarketer_2000547*, accessed June 11, 2011.

40 "Customers—Portfolio," Inst.biz website, *www.insta.biz*, accessed October 23, 2010.

41 Phillips, Steve, "Global CIO: Avnet Tears Up the B2B E-Commerce Play-book," *InformationWeek,* June 15, 2009.

42 McDonough, Michele, "Microsoft Internet Information Services Basics," Bright Hub website, August 22, 2009, *www.brighthub.com/computing/hardware/articles/16160.aspx*, accessed March 26, 2010.

43 "About Us," PayPal website, *https://www.paypal-media.com/aboutus.cfm*, accessed March 21, 2010.

44 "The Dragon Hotel Uses Smart Card Technology to Deliver a World-Class, Personalized Experience," IBM website, *www-01.ibm.com/software/success/cssdb.nsf/CS/LMCM-7XBP7B?OpenDocument&Site=corp&cty=en_us*, accessed March 22, 2010.

45 "Local Purchase Order Case Study," Environment Canada, *www.ec.gc.ca/ae-ve/default.asp?lang=En&n=B86CCD28&offset=2&toc=show*, accessed October 24, 2010.

46 Miller, Claire Cain, and Richtel, Matt, "Investors Bet on Payments via Cellphone," *New York Times*, June 22, 2009.

47 MasterCard MoneySend, *www.mastercard.com/in/personal/en/moneysend/index.html*, accessed June 11, 2011.

CHAPTER
· 9 ·

Enterprise Systems

- **An organization must have information systems that support routine, day-to-day activities and that help a company add value to its products and services.**

- Identify the basic activities and business objectives common to all transaction processing systems.

- Describe the transaction processing systems associated with the order processing, purchasing, and accounting business functions.

- Identify key control and management issues associated with transaction processing systems.

- **A company that implements an enterprise resource planning system is creating a highly integrated set of systems, which can lead to many business benefits.**

- Discuss the advantages and disadvantages associated with the implementation of an enterprise resource planning system.

- Identify the challenges that multinational corporations face in planning, building, and operating their transaction processing systems.

(Source: Lukiyanova Natalia/frenta/Shutterstock.com.)

Information Systems in the Global Economy
FedEx

Fed Ex Fuses Multiple Enterprise Systems

Nearly everyone has heard of FedEx. The well-known shipping company has an extensive reach into more than 220 countries and territories, employs more than 280,000 "team members," and earns annual revenue of more than $35.5 billion.

While FedEx has widespread name recognition, not everyone is aware of its many divisions. FedEx is actually a collection of eight companies: FedEx Express, FedEx Ground, FedEx Freight, FedEx Office, FedEx Custom Critical, FedEx Trade Networks, FedEx SupplyChain, and FedEx Services. Each company has unique information it manages to serve its customers. Effectively collecting and managing that information at the enterprise level requires the use of sophisticated information systems.

Tim Robertson, IT manager at FedEx, was overwhelmed by the complexity of managing a diverse set of information systems. He knew that FedEx needed to standardize and simplify its many company-run systems. Robertson wanted a single system for managing shipping across all FedEx companies, a single system for managing customer information across FedEx companies, and a single invoice system—he wanted to eliminate the walls that separated the information systems of each of the FedEx companies. FedEx needed an enterprise resource planning system (ERP) to gain control of its massive tangle of information systems. Recall that an ERP is a set of integrated programs that manage a company's vital business operations.

FedEx systems administrators worked years in developing a central enterprise database for collecting all the information from its many companies; this proved to be a time-consuming task. Robertson and his team wanted to standardize the systems across the FedEx companies. The team worked with an ERP vendor to standardize FedEx systems and unify them through the use of an open application server platform. An application server would provide a middle-tier layer that would integrate all the information systems and processes across FedEx systems.

Robertson's team developed a group of applications called FedEx Unified Strategic Information Optimization Network, or FUSION. FUSION includes components for shipping, customer resources management (CRM), and revenue. Each of these components uses a middleware system and application server that provides FedEx companies, partners, and customers with a single Web-based application for shipment tracking and account reporting.

The new system has powerful tools that allow FedEx developers to spend less time coding and managing infrastructure, and more time solving business problems. Recently, FUSION has expanded to include an integrated transaction processing system called Tuxedo. Tuxedo manages millions of transactions a day for FedEx through Web-based systems that are accessed directly by customers or by FedEx representatives. Tuxedo includes order processing systems, accounting systems, and purchasing systems that integrate fully with the business systems provided by the FUSION ERP.

Today, FUSION and Tuxedo provide all the core business applications across the FedEx enterprise. FedEx is pleased with the performance and reliability of the ERP. Because it is based on open standards, the system allows for flexibility and scaling over time. FedEx system engineers no longer have to force data from different systems into a common data warehouse. Nor do they have to service dozens of different systems across the eight FedEx companies. FedEx managers and executives are empowered by the ability to get an up-to-the-second view of enterprise-wide operations and conditions on which to base critical business decisions.

As you read this chapter, consider the following:

- How does the efficiency and effectiveness of a business's transaction processing systems affect the overall well-being of the business?
- What types of information systems are critical to a business's success, and how are they related one to another?

Why Learn About Enterprise Systems?

Organizations today are moving from a collection of nonintegrated transaction processing systems (TPS) to highly integrated enterprise-wide systems to manage business processes and corporate information. As mentioned in Chapter 1, enterprise systems support a wide range of business activities, including supply chain management, customer relationship management, human resources, and accounting. Although these systems were initially thought to be cost-effective only for very large companies, even small and midsized companies are now implementing them to reduce costs and improve service.

In our service-oriented economy, outstanding customer service has become a goal of virtually all companies. To provide good customer service, employees who work directly with customers—whether in sales, customer service, or marketing—require high-quality transaction processing systems and accurate information. Such workers might use an enterprise system to check the inventory status of ordered items, view the production planning schedule to tell the customer when the item will be in stock, or enter data to schedule a delivery to the customer.

No matter what your role, it is very likely that you will provide input to or use the output from your organization's enterprise systems. Your effective use of these systems will be essential to raise the productivity of your firm, improve customer service, and enable better decision making. Thus, it is important that you understand how these systems work and what their capabilities and limitations are.

enterprise system
A system central to the organization that ensures information can be shared across all business functions and all levels of management to support the running and managing of a business.

An **enterprise system** is central to an organization and ensures that information can be shared across all business functions and all levels of management to support the running and managing of a business. Enterprise systems employ a database of key operational and planning data that can be shared throughout the company. This eliminates the problems of lack of information and inconsistent information caused by multiple transaction processing systems that support only one business function or one department in an organization. Examples of enterprise systems include enterprise resource planning systems (ERP) that support supply chain processes, such as order processing, inventory management, and purchasing and customer relationship management systems (CRM) that support sales, marketing, and customer service–related processes.

As demonstrated in the opening vignette, businesses rely on enterprise systems to perform many of their daily activities in areas such as product supply, distribution, sales, marketing, human resources, manufacturing, accounting, and taxation so that work is performed quickly, without waste or mistakes. Without such systems, recording and processing business transactions would consume huge amounts of an organization's resources. This collection of processed transactions also forms a storehouse of data invaluable to decision making. The ultimate goal is to satisfy customers and provide a competitive advantage by reducing costs and improving service.

This chapter begins by presenting an overview of transaction processing systems.

AN OVERVIEW OF TRANSACTION PROCESSING SYSTEMS

Every organization has many *transaction processing systems* (*TPSs*) that capture and process the detailed data necessary to update records about the fundamental business operations of the organization. These systems include order entry, inventory control, payroll, accounts payable, accounts receivable, and the general ledger, to name just a few. The input to these systems includes basic business transactions, such as customer orders, purchase orders, receipts, time cards, invoices, and customer payments. The processing activities include data collection, data editing, data correction, data manipulation, data storage, and document production. The result of processing business transactions is that the organization's records are updated to reflect the status of the operation at the time of the last processed transaction.

A TPS also provides valuable input to management information systems, decision support systems, and knowledge management systems, first discussed in Chapter 1. A transaction processing system serves as the foundation for these other systems. See Figure 9.1.

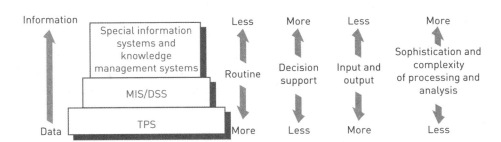

Figure 9.1

TPS, MIS/DSS, and Special Information Systems in Perspective

Transaction processing systems support routine operations associated with customer ordering and billing, employee payroll, purchasing, and accounts payable. TPSs don't provide much support for decision making.

TPSs use a large amount of input and output data to update the official records of the company about orders, sales, customers, and so on. St-Hubert, a family restaurant chain in Quebec and Ontario, integrated its point-of-sale transaction processing system and ERP systems. The integration saved time, improved processing times, and increased the accuracy of daily sales transactions.[1] Because TPSs often perform activities related to customer contacts—such as order processing and invoicing—these information systems play a critical role in providing value to the customer. For example, by capturing and tracking the movement of each package, shippers such as FedEx Canada and United Parcel Service (UPS) Canada can provide timely and accurate data on the exact location of a package. Shippers and receivers can access an online database and, by providing the airbill number of a package, find the package's current location. If the package has been delivered, they can see who signed for it (a service that is especially useful in large companies where packages can become "lost" in internal distribution systems and mailrooms). Such a system provides the basis for added value through improved customer service.

Traditional Transaction Processing Methods and Objectives

With **batch processing systems**, business transactions are accumulated over a period of time and prepared for processing as a single unit or batch. See Figure 9.2a on the next page. Transactions are accumulated for the length of time needed to meet the needs of the users of that system. For example, it might be important to process invoices and customer payments for the accounts receivable system daily. On the other hand, the payroll system might receive time cards and process them biweekly to create paycheques, update employee earnings records, and distribute labour costs. The essential characteristic of a batch processing system is that there is some delay between an event and the eventual processing of the related transaction to update the organization's records.

Wagjag, an online company, uses batch processing in a unique way. The company finds deals in local Canadian cities for events, restaurants, and activities and then promotes the deals to its members for a limited time period. Interested members sign up and pay for deals that they are interested in. The purchases are held as a batch. If enough members pay to get the deal, the payments are processed as a batch and a printable

batch processing system
A form of data processing where business transactions are accumulated over a period of time and prepared for processing as a single unit or batch.

Figure 9.2

Batch versus Online Transaction Processing

(a) Batch processing inputs and processes data in groups. (b) In online processing, transactions are completed as they occur.

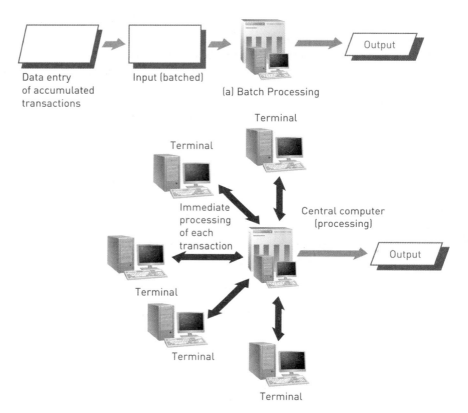

Data entry of accumulated transactions → Input (batched) → (a) Batch Processing → Output

Terminal

Terminal

Immediate processing of each transaction

Central computer (processing)

Output

Terminal

Terminal

Terminal

(b) Online Transaction Processing

online transaction processing (OLTP)
A form of data processing where each transaction is processed immediately, without the delay of accumulating transactions into a batch.

electronic coupon is sent to each member. If there are not enough members interested, the deal expires and the members get their money back.[2]

With **online transaction processing (OLTP)**, each transaction is processed immediately, without the delay of accumulating transactions into a batch, as shown in Figure 9.2b. Consequently, at any time, the data in an online system reflects the current status. This type of processing is essential for businesses that require access to current data such as airlines, ticket agencies, and stock investment firms. Many companies find that OLTP helps them provide faster, more efficient service—one way to add value to their activities in the eyes of the customer. More and more companies are using the Internet to capture and process transaction data such as customer orders and shipping information from e-commerce applications.

Trimac Corporation, located in Calgary, Alberta, is a bulk hauling carrier with 140 branch offices and some 3,000 tractors and 6,000 trailers driving 355 million kilometres per year. The firm uses an OLTP system to perform all tasks associated with order entry, dispatching, trip planning, and driver payment.[3]

(Source: Courtesy of TruckPix.)

TPS applications do not always run using online processing. For many applications, batch processing is more appropriate and cost-effective. Payroll transactions and billing are typically done via batch processing. Specific goals of the organization define the method of transaction processing best suited for the various applications of the company.

Figure 9.3 shows the traditional flow of key pieces of information from one TPS to another for a typical manufacturing organization.

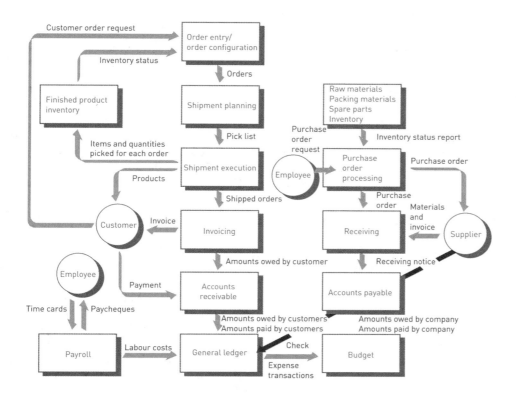

Figure 9.3

Integration of a Firm's TPS

Because of the importance of transaction processing, organizations expect their TPSs to accomplish a number of specific objectives, including the following:

- Capture, process, and update databases of business data required to support routine business activities.
- Ensure that the data is processed accurately and completely.
- Avoid processing fraudulent transactions.
- Produce timely user responses and reports.
- Reduce clerical and other labour requirements.
- Help improve customer service.
- Achieve competitive advantage.

A TPS typically includes the following types of systems:

- *Order processing systems.* Running these systems efficiently and reliably is so critical that the order processing systems are sometimes referred to as the lifeblood of the organization. The processing flow begins with the receipt of a customer order. The finished product inventory is checked to see if sufficient inventory is on hand to fill the order. If sufficient inventory is available, the customer shipment is planned to meet the customer's desired receipt date. A product pick list is printed at the warehouse from which the order is to be filled on the day the order is planned to be shipped. At the warehouse, workers gather the items needed to fill the order and enter the item identifier and quantity for each item to update the finished product inventory. When the order is complete and sent on its way, a customer invoice is created.

- *Accounting systems.* The accounting systems must track the flow of data related to all the cash flows that affect the organization. As mentioned earlier, the order processing system generates an invoice for customer orders that have been shipped. This information is also sent to the accounts receivable system to update the customer's account. When the customer pays the invoice, the payment information is used to update the customer's account. The necessary accounting transactions are sent to the general ledger system to keep track of amounts owed and amounts paid. Similarly, as the purchasing systems generate purchase orders and those items are received, information is sent to the accounts payable system to manage the amounts owed by the company. Data about amounts owed and paid by customers to the company and from the company to vendors and others are sent to the general ledger system that records and reports all financial transactions for the company.
- *Purchasing systems.* The traditional transaction processing systems that support the purchasing business function include inventory control, purchase order processing, receiving, and accounts payable. Employees place purchase order requests in response to shortages identified in inventory control reports. Purchase order information flows to the receiving system and accounts payable systems. A record of receipt is created upon receipt of the items ordered. When the invoice arrives from the supplier, it is matched to the original order and the receiving report, and a cheque is generated if all data is complete and consistent.

In the past, organizations knitted together a hodgepodge of systems to accomplish the transaction processing activities shown in Figure 9.3. Some of the systems might have been applications developed using in-house resources, some may have been developed by outside contractors, and others may have been off-the-shelf software packages. Much customization and modification of the different software was necessary for all the applications to work together efficiently. In some cases, it was necessary to print data from one system and manually reenter it into other systems. Of course, this increased the amount of effort required and increased the likelihood of processing delays and errors.

The approach taken today by many organizations is to implement an integrated set of transaction processing systems from a single or limited number of software vendors that handles most or all of the transaction processing activities shown in Figure 9.3. The data flows automatically from one application to another with no delay or need to reenter data.

Table 9.1 summarizes some of the ways that companies can use transaction processing systems to achieve competitive advantage.

Table 9.1

Examples of Transaction Processing Systems for Competitive Advantage

Competitive Advantage	Example
Customer loyalty increased	Customer interaction system to monitor and track each customer interaction with the company
Superior service provided to customers	Tracking systems that customers can access to determine shipping status
Better relationship with suppliers	Internet marketplace to allow the company to purchase products from suppliers at discounted prices
Superior information gathering	Order configuration system to ensure that products ordered will meet customer's objectives
Costs dramatically reduced	Warehouse management system employing RFID technology to reduce labour hours and improve inventory accuracy
Inventory levels reduced	Collaborative planning, forecasting, and replenishment to ensure the right amount of inventory is in stores

Depending on the specific nature and goals of the organization, any of these objectives might be more important than others. By meeting these objectives, TPSs can support corporate goals such as reducing costs; increasing productivity, quality, and customer satisfaction; and running more efficient and effective operations. For example, overnight delivery companies such as FedEx expect their TPSs to increase customer service. These systems can locate a client's package at any time, from initial pickup to final delivery. This improved customer information allows companies to produce timely information and be more responsive to customer needs and queries.

Transaction Processing Systems for Small and Medium-Size Enterprises (SMEs)

Many software packages provide integrated transaction processing systems for small and medium-size enterprises (SMEs), where small is an enterprise with fewer than 50 employees and medium is one with fewer than 250 employees.[4] These systems are typically easy to install and operate and usually have a low total cost of ownership, with an initial cost of a few hundred to a few thousand dollars. Such systems are highly attractive to firms that have outgrown their current software but cannot afford a complex, high-end integrated system. Table 9.2 presents some of the software that is available.

Vendor	Software	Type of TPS Offered	Target Customers
AccuFund	AccuFund	Financial reporting and accounting	Nonprofit, municipal, and government organizations
OpenPro	OpenPro	Complete ERP solution, including financials, supply chain management, e-commerce, customer relationship management, and retail POS system	Manufacturers, distributors, and retailers
Intuit	QuickBooks	Financial reporting and accounting	Manufacturers, professional services, contractors, nonprofits, and retailers
Sage	Timberline	Financial reporting, accounting, and operations	Contractors, real estate developers, and residential builders
Sage	Simply Accounting	Financial reporting and accounting	Manufacturers, professional services, contractors, nonprofits, and retailers

Table 9.2

Sample of Integrated TPS Software for SMEs

Megavolt Design, a small website development and graphic design company located in Quebec, uses Simply Accounting, one of the most popular small business programs in Canada. Simply Accounting was chosen due to its ease of use and flexible billing features. The software provides the owner with tools to manage the company and employees effectively.[5]

TRANSACTION PROCESSING ACTIVITIES

Along with having common characteristics, all TPSs perform a common set of basic data processing activities. TPSs capture and process data that describes fundamental business transactions. This data is used to update databases and to produce a variety of reports for people both within and outside the enterprise. The business data goes through a **transaction processing cycle** that includes data collection, data editing, data correction, data manipulation, data storage, and document production. See Figure 9.4 on the next page.

transaction processing cycle
The process of data collection, data editing, data correction, data manipulation, data storage, and document production.

Figure 9.4

Data Processing Activities Common to Transaction Processing Systems

data collection
Capturing and gathering all data necessary to complete the processing of transactions.

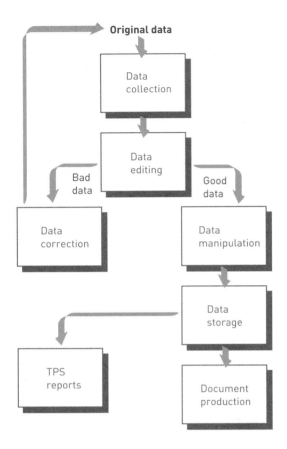

Data Collection

Capturing and gathering all data necessary to complete the processing of transactions is called **data collection**. In some cases, it can be done manually, such as by collecting handwritten sales orders or changes to inventory. In other cases, data collection is automated via special input devices such as scanners, point-of-sale devices, and terminals.

Data collection begins with a transaction (e.g., taking a customer order) and results in data that serves as input to the TPS. Data should be captured at its source and recorded accurately in a timely fashion, with minimal manual effort, and in an electronic or digital form that can be directly entered into the computer. This approach is called source data automation. An example of source data automation is an automated device at a retail store that speeds the checkout process—either UPC codes read by a scanner or RFID signals picked up when the items approach the checkout stand. Using both UPC bar codes and RFID tags is quicker and more accurate than having a clerk enter codes manually at the cash register. The product ID for each item is determined automatically, and its price retrieved from the item database. The point-of-sale TPS uses the price data to determine the customer's bill. The store's inventory and purchase databases record the number of units of an item purchased, along with the price and the date and time of the purchase. The inventory database generates a management report notifying the store manager to reorder items that have fallen below the reorder quantity. The detailed purchases database can be used by the store or sold to marketing research firms or manufacturers for detailed sales analysis. See Figure 9.5.

Figure 9.5

Point-of-Sale Transaction Processing System

The purchase of items at the checkout stand updates a store's inventory database and its database of purchases.

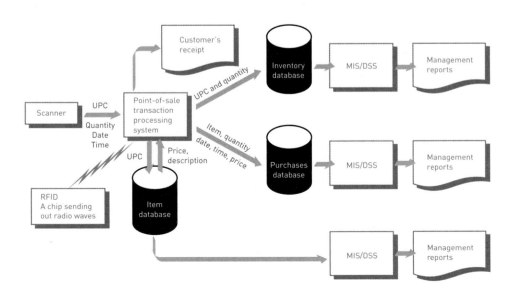

Many grocery stores combine point-of-sale scanners and coupon printers. The systems are programmed so that each time a specific product—for example, a box of cereal—crosses a checkout scanner, an appropriate coupon—perhaps a milk coupon—is printed. Companies can pay to be promoted through the system, which is then reprogrammed to print those companies' coupons if the customer buys a competitive brand. These TPSs help grocery stores increase profits by improving their repeat sales and bringing in revenue from other businesses.

Data Editing

An important step in processing transaction data is to check data for validity and completeness to detect any problems, a task called **data editing**. For example, quantity and cost data must be numeric and names must be alphabetic; otherwise, the data is not valid. Often, the codes associated with an individual transaction are edited against a database containing valid codes. If any code entered (or scanned) is not present in the database, the transaction is rejected.

data editing
The process of checking data for validity and completeness.

Data Correction

It is not enough simply to reject invalid data. The system should also provide error messages that alert those responsible for editing the data. Error messages must specify the problem so proper corrections can be made. **Data correction** involves reentering data that was not typed or scanned properly. For example, a scanned UPC code must match a code in a master table of valid UPCs. If the code is misread or does not exist in the table, the checkout clerk is given an instruction to rescan the item or type the information manually.

data correction
The process of reentering data that was not typed or scanned properly.

Data Manipulation

Another major activity of a TPS is **data manipulation**, the process of performing calculations and other data transformations related to business transactions. Data manipulation can include classifying data, sorting data into categories, performing calculations, summarizing results, and storing data in the organization's database for further processing. In a payroll TPS, for example, data manipulation includes multiplying an employee's hours worked by the hourly pay rate. Overtime pay, federal and provincial tax withholdings, and deductions are also calculated.

data manipulation
The process of performing calculations and other data transformations related to business transactions.

Data Storage

Data storage involves updating one or more databases with new transactions. After being updated, this data can be further processed and manipulated by other systems so that it is available for management reporting and decision making. Thus, although transaction databases can be considered a by-product of transaction processing, they have an effect on nearly all other information systems and decision-making processes in an organization.

data storage
The process of updating one or more databases with new transactions.

Document Production and Reports

Document production involves generating output records, documents, and reports. These can be hard-copy paper reports or displays on computer screens (sometimes referred to as soft copy). Printed paycheques, for example, are hard-copy documents produced by a payroll TPS, whereas an outstanding balance report for invoices might be a soft-copy report displayed by an accounts receivable TPS. Often, results from one TPS flow downstream to become input to other systems, as shown earlier in Figure 9.5, which might use the results of updating the inventory database to create the stock exception report (a type of management report) of items whose inventory level is below the reorder quantity.

In addition to major documents such as cheques and invoices, most TPSs provide other useful management information and decision support, such as printed or on-screen reports that help managers and employees perform various activities. A report showing current inventory is one example; another might be a document listing items ordered from a

document production
The process of generating output records and reports.

supplier to help a receiving clerk check the order for completeness when it arrives. A TPS can also produce reports required by provincial and federal agencies, such as statements of tax withholding and quarterly income statements.

ENTERPRISE RESOURCE PLANNING AND CUSTOMER RELATIONSHIP MANAGEMENT

As defined in Chapter 1, enterprise resource planning (ERP) is a set of integrated software programs that manage a company's vital business operations for an entire organization, even a complex, multi-site, global organization. Recall that a business process is a set of coordinated and related activities that takes one or more types of input and creates an output of value to the customer of that process. The customer might be a traditional external business customer who buys goods or services from the firm. An example of such a process is capturing a sales order, which takes customer input and generates an order. The customer of a business process might also be an internal customer, such as a worker in another department of the firm. For example, the shipment process generates the internal documents workers need in the warehouse and shipping departments to pick, pack, and ship orders. At the core of the ERP system is a database that is shared by all users so that all business functions have access to current and consistent data for operational decision making and planning, as shown in Figure 9.6.

Figure 9.6

Enterprise Resource Planning System

An ERP integrates business processes and the ERP database.

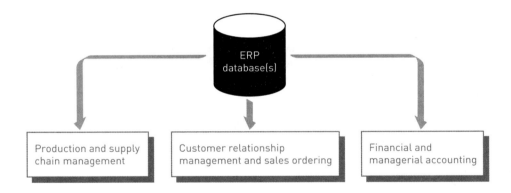

An Overview of Enterprise Resource Planning

ERP systems evolved from materials requirement planning (MRP) systems developed in the 1970s. These systems tied together the production planning, inventory control, and purchasing business functions for manufacturing organizations. During the late 1980s and early 1990s, many organizations recognized that their legacy TPSs lacked the integration needed to coordinate activities and share valuable information across all the business functions of the firm. As a result, costs were higher and customer service poorer than desired. Large Canadian organizations were the first to take on the challenge of implementing ERP. As they did, they uncovered many advantages as well as some disadvantages summarized in the following sections.

Advantages of ERP

Increased global competition, new needs of executives for control over the total cost and product flow through their enterprises, and ever-more-numerous customer interactions drive the demand for enterprise-wide access to real-time information. ERP offers integrated software from a single vendor to help meet those needs. The primary benefits of implementing ERP include improved access to data for operational decision making,

Kabbani Integrates and Secures Information with ERP

Kabbani Construction Group (KCG) was founded in 1980 as a small roofing subcontractor in Jeddah, Saudi Arabia. Since then it has grown to be a leading specialized engineering contracting company in the Persian Gulf and Middle East regions with three office locations in Saudi Arabia and others in Cairo, Egypt; Doha, Qatar; Dubai, UAE; Beirut-Lebanon; and Manama, Bahrain. Today KCG owns 22 companies with 156 branches spread over nine countries employing over 8,000 employees.

KCG has 10 divisions, each specializing in a unique area of construction. They include waterproofing and thermal insulation, concrete repair and industrial flooring, constructions and maintenance, pool and marine division, security and networking, and specialized oil and gas engineering.

As with many rapidly growing companies, KCG experienced growing pains in its IT infrastructure as they acquired numerous systems and then merged them with its information system infrastructure. Each business unit managed its own financial systems and maintained its own data. When managers needed to make enterprise-wide decisions, they had to request data from each division and manually integrate it into a data warehouse.

The isolated systems also made it difficult for KCG to properly enforce security policies and access rules. Too many employees had access to confidential corporate data. Mahmoud Kassim Al-Awar, chief applications officer for Kabbani Construction Group, proposed that KCG integrate the information systems from all divisions into one enterprise resource planning (ERP) system. The proposal was met with some scepticism. Division managers were leery of having to retrain staff on a new system. However, when upper management gave the proposal a thumbs-up, work commenced on the ERP.

KCG worked with consultants from the Right Group to deploy Microsoft Dynamics AX 4.0 across the enterprise. The Right Group was selected because of its familiarity with the needs of construction companies. They assisted KCG in customizing the system to meet the business requirements.

A centralized database was designed to capture all data from the 10 divisions of KCG. Local systems were adjusted to store transaction and financial data directly in the central database rather than in local databases. Microsoft Dynamics also provided valuable reporting tools to cover all core business functions, including accounts receivable, trial balance, and cash flow reports. Critical to a construction company, the new system provides powerful project management features and reports. For example, project managers appreciate being able to run a report that shows the internal resources required to finish a project on time.

Using Microsoft Dynamics, systems administrators can enforce security policies across the organization, making sure that employees have access only to information they need to complete their jobs. Sensitive data is restricted to only those who have the clearance to view it. Records are kept to show who accessed what data and when, providing auditors with clues in cases of security breaches.

The Right Group provided training sessions to assist in smoothing the transition to the new system. Originally, only 110 employees used the new system. As others saw how easy the system is to use and how valuable the results are, they started using the system. Mahmoud Kassim Al-Awar lists the benefits as being much faster report generation, a reduced workload, improved security, and more efficiently managed projects.

Discussion Questions

1. What made Kabbani Construction Group an ideal candidate for an ERP system?
2. What concerns did Kabbani Construction Group have about implementing an ERP system?

Critical Thinking Questions

1. What advantages did the ERP system provide for Kabbani Construction Group, and which were particularly well suited to a construction company?
2. How can an ERP system improve information security with an organization?

SOURCES: "Kabbani Construction Group," Microsoft Dynamics customer stories in construction, March 31, 2010, *www.microsoft.com/dynamics/en/us/customer-stories-construction-detail.aspx?casestudyid=4000006807*; Kabbani Construction Group website, *www.kcg.cc*, accessed May 2, 2010.

elimination of inefficient or outdated systems, improvement of work processes, and technology standardization. ERP vendors have also developed specialized systems that provide effective systems for specific industries and market segments.

Improved Access to Data for Operational Decision Making

ERP systems operate via an integrated database, using one set of data to support all business functions. The systems can support decisions on optimal sourcing or cost accounting, for instance, for the entire enterprise or business units from the start, rather than gathering data from many business functions and then trying to coordinate that information manually or reconciling data with another application. The result is an organization that looks seamless, not only to the outside world but also to the decision makers who are deploying resources within the organization. The data is integrated to facilitate operational decision making and allows companies to provide greater customer service and support, strengthen customer and supplier relationships, and generate new business opportunities.

Elimination of Costly, Inflexible Legacy Systems

Adoption of an ERP system enables an organization to eliminate dozens or even hundreds of separate systems and replace them with a single, integrated set of applications for the entire enterprise. In many cases, these systems are decades old, the original developers are long gone, and the systems are poorly documented. As a result, the systems are extremely difficult to fix when they break, and adapting them to meet new business needs takes too long. They become an anchor around the organization that keeps it from moving ahead and remaining competitive. An ERP system helps match the capabilities of an organization's information systems to its business needs—even as these needs evolve.

The Royal Canadian Mint (RCM) is a Crown corporation that produces and markets coins to Canadians and customers around the world. Their existing legacy applications were difficult to use and expensive to support and upgrade. RCM replaced their legacy systems with Microsoft's Dynamics AX ERP system to streamline operations, customer relationship, and supply chain processes. The new system also supported RCM's new customer-centric focus and lean manufacturing.[6]

Improvement of Work Processes

Competition requires companies to structure their business processes to be as effective and customer oriented as possible. ERP vendors do considerable research to define the best business processes. They gather requirements of leading companies within the same industry and combine them with research findings from research institutions and consultants. The individual application modules included in the ERP system are then designed to support these **best practices**, the most efficient and effective ways to complete a business process. Thus, implementation of an ERP system ensures good work processes based on best practices. For example, for managing customer payments, the ERP system's finance module can be configured to reflect the most efficient practices of leading companies in an industry. This increased efficiency ensures that everyday business operations follow the optimal chain of activities, with all users supplied the information and tools they need to complete each step.

best practices
The most efficient and effective ways to complete a business process.

Upgrade of Technology Infrastructure

When implementing an ERP system, an organization has an opportunity to upgrade the information technology (such as hardware, operating systems, and databases) that it uses. While centralizing and formalizing these decisions, the organization can eliminate the hodgepodge of many hardware platforms, operating systems, and databases it is currently using—most likely from a variety of vendors. Standardizing on fewer technologies and vendors reduces ongoing maintenance and support costs as well as training for those who must support the infrastructure.

Allen Candy, a leading Canadian confectioner, used ERP technology to bring about ongoing improvements in business processes and productivity. Upgrading the company's ERP system enabled the company to eliminate the need for manual entry of manufacturing orders, use electronic data interchange (EDI) with its suppliers and distributors, and improve materials requirements planning.[7]

Disadvantages of ERP Systems

Unfortunately, implementing ERP systems can be difficult and error-prone. Some of the major disadvantages of ERP systems are the expense and time required for implementation, the difficulty in implementing the many business process changes that accompany the ERP system, the problems with integrating the ERP system with other systems, the risks associated with making a major commitment to a single vendor, and the risk of implementation failure.

Expense and Time in Implementation

Getting the full benefits of ERP takes time and money. Although ERP offers many strategic advantages by streamlining a company's TPSs, large firms typically spend two to five years and millions of dollars to successfully implement an ERP system. Indeed, one ERP implementation consultant states "that a typical ERP implementation introduces so many complex, difficult technical and business issues that just making it to the finish line with one's shirt on is considered a win."[8]

Some firms run out of time and budget before an ERP system can be completed. Waste Management, Inc. sued its ERP vendor to recover more than $100 million in project-related expenses plus unrealized savings and benefits from a failed ERP software implementation. The sales agreement was signed in October 2005 with a commitment that the system would be up and running in December 2006. However, the system was never finished.

Difficulty Implementing Change

In some cases, a company has to radically change how it operates to conform to the ERP's work processes—its best practices. These changes can be so drastic to long-time employees that they retire or quit rather than adapt to the change. This exodus can leave a firm short of experienced workers. Sometimes, the best practices simply are not appropriate for the firm because they cause great work disruptions.

Difficulty Integrating with Other Systems

Most companies have other systems that must be integrated with the ERP system, such as financial analysis programs, e-commerce operations, and other applications. These companies can experience difficulties linking their organization's ERP system with their B2B or B2C systems that communicate with suppliers, customers, distributors, and other business partners. An AMR Research study discovered that for major companies, delays in their ERP deployments due to a lack of integration between their ERP and B2B systems can cost over $1 million per month in lost sales revenue. The study also found that over a third of the data in ERP systems comes from customers, suppliers, and others outside the firm—further emphasizing the need to integrate external trading partner transactions and data with ERP systems.[9]

Difficulty in Loading Data into New ERP System

A major amount of work is required to load existing data from various sources into a new ERP database. The new ERP system may have the capability to store hundreds or even thousands of data items (such as customer name, bill-to address, and product description). The required data items depend on the scope of ERP implementation. If certain processes or transactions are not included within the scope of implementation, there will be less data to load. This process includes the following three key steps.

1. Data mapping is the examination of each data item required for the new ERP system and determining where that data item will come from. While most of the data for the new system will come from the files of existing legacy systems, some data items may need to be pulled from manual systems or even created for the new system.
2. Data cleanup is required because the legacy systems are likely to contain data that is inaccurate, incomplete, or inconsistent. For example, the same customer may be listed many times in existing customer files with varying bill-to addresses, or products may appear in the inventory files that have not been produced for years.
3. Data loading can be performed either by using data conversion software that reads the old data and converts it into a format for loading it into the database or by end users entering data via the input screens of the new system.

Risks in Using One Vendor

The high cost to switch to another vendor's ERP system makes it extremely unlikely that a firm will do so. After a company has adopted an ERP system, the vendor has less incentive to listen and respond to customer concerns. The high cost to switch also increases risk—in the event the ERP vendor allows its product to become outdated or goes out of business. Selecting an ERP system involves choosing not only the best software product but also the right long-term business partner. It was unsettling for many companies that had implemented PeopleSoft, JD Edwards, or Siebel Systems enterprise software when these firms were acquired by Oracle.

Risk of Implementation Failure

Implementing an ERP system, particularly for a large organization, is extremely challenging and requires tremendous amounts of resources, the best IS and businesspeople, and plenty of management support. Unfortunately, as illustrated in the examples above, ERP installations occasionally fail, and problems with an ERP implementation can require expensive solutions.

The following list provides tips for avoiding many common causes for failed ERP implementations:

- Assign a full-time executive to manage the project.
- Appoint an experienced, independent resource to provide project oversight and to verify and validate system performance.
- Allow sufficient time for transition from the old way of doing things to the new system and new processes.
- Plan to spend considerable time and money training people; many project managers recommend that $10,000 to $20,000 per employee be budgeted for training of personnel.
- Define metrics to assess project progress and to identify project-related risks.
- Keep the scope of the project well defined and contained to essential business processes.
- Be wary of modifying the ERP software to conform to your firm's business practices.

Leading ERP Systems

ERP systems are commonly used in manufacturing companies, colleges and universities, professional service organizations, retailers, and health-care organizations. The business needs for each of these types of organizations vary greatly. Thus, no one ERP software solution from a single vendor is "best" for all organizations. SAP is the largest and most recognized ERP systems provider among Fortune 1000 and Global 5000 organizations with more than 35,000 customers in over 120 countries. The scope of its ERP software encompasses accounting, distribution, financial, manufacturing, human resources, and payroll functions. Oracle has accumulated an impressive customer list and set of ERP systems through its acquisition of PeopleSoft (including JD Edwards) and Siebel Systems. Its challenge is to integrate all those products through Project Fusion. Infor is the third-largest ERP software manufacturer and has several different ERP systems that appeal to midsized organizations. The Microsoft Dynamics ERP system is very popular among small and medium-size businesses.

Interestingly, although Microsoft and SAP market competing enterprise software, they also partnered with one another in the development of Duet, a set of technologies that enables SAP users to access and interact with their back-end ERP system via a familiar Microsoft Outlook interface. The goal is to boost worker productivity without additional training. Easy access to key back-end data helps SAP and Microsoft users make faster and more informed business decisions.

ERP for Small and Medium-Size Enterprises (SMEs)

Organizations that are successful in implementing ERP are not limited to large Canadian businesses. SMEs (both for-profit and not-for-profit) can achieve real business benefits from their ERP efforts. Many SMEs elect to implement open-source ERP systems from vendors such as Apache, Compiere, and OpenBravo. With open-source software, anyone can see and modify the source code to customize it to meet their needs. Such systems are much less costly to acquire and are relatively easy to modify to meet business needs. Frequent reasons for customization are that customization is needed for your other business systems to work

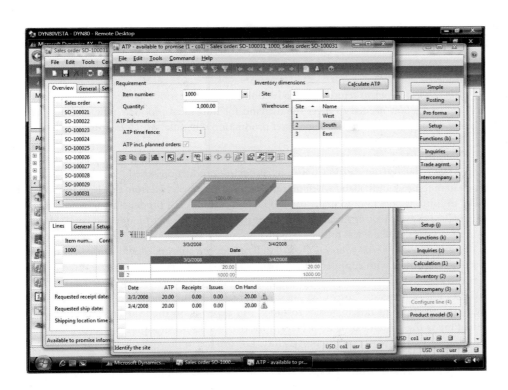

Microsoft Dynamics is an ERP system that is very popular among small and medium-size businesses.

(Source: Used with permission from Microsoft.)

with the ERP package, you need additional data fields and/or different field sizes than comes with the standard system, and customization is needed to meet regulatory requirements. A wide range of software service organizations can perform the system development and maintenance.

The following section outlines the use of an ERP system within a manufacturing organization to support what is known as supply chain management.

Supply Chain Management (SCM)

Supply chain management (SCM) includes the planning, execution, and control of all activities involved in raw material sourcing and procurement, conversion of raw materials to finished products, and the warehousing and delivery of the finished product to customers. The goal of SCM is to reduce costs and improve customer service, while at the same time reducing the overall investment in inventory in the supply chain.

Another way to think about SCM is that it is the management of materials, information, and finances as they move in a process from supplier to manufacturer to wholesaler to retailer to consumer. The material flow includes the inbound movement of raw materials from supplier to manufacturer as well as the outbound movement of finished products from manufacturer to wholesaler, retailer, and customer. The information flow involves the capture and transmission of orders and invoices among suppliers, manufacturer, wholesalers, retailers, and customers. The financial flow consists of payment transactions among suppliers, manufacturers, wholesalers, retailers, customers, and their financial institutions.

The ERP system for a manufacturing organization typically encompasses SCM activities and manages the flow of materials, information, and finances. Manufacturing ERP systems follow a systematic process for developing a production plan that draws on the information available in the ERP system database.

The process starts with *sales forecasting* to develop an estimate of future customer demand. This initial forecast is at a fairly high level with estimates made by product group rather than by each individual product item. The sales forecast extends for months into the future; it might be developed using an ERP software module or produced by other means using specialized software and techniques. Many organizations are moving to a collaborative process with major customers to plan future inventory levels and production rather than relying on an internally generated sales forecast.

supply chain management (SCM)
A system that includes planning, executing, and controlling all activities involved in raw material sourcing and procurement, converting raw materials to finished products, and warehousing and delivering the finished product to customers.

The *sales and operations plan* (*S&OP*) takes demand and current inventory levels into account and determines the specific product items that need to be produced and when to meet the forecast future demand. Production capacity and any seasonal variability in demand must also be considered.

Demand management refines the production plan by determining the amount of weekly or daily production needed to meet the demand for individual products. The output of the demand management process is the master production schedule, which is a production plan for all finished goods.

Detailed scheduling uses the production plan defined by the demand management process to develop a detailed production schedule specifying production scheduling details, such as which item to produce first and when production should be switched from one item to another. A key decision is how long to make the production run for each product. Longer production runs reduce the number of machine setups required, thus reducing production costs. Shorter production runs generate less finished product inventory and reduce inventory holding costs.

Materials requirement planning (*MRP*) determines the amount of and timing for placing raw material orders with suppliers. The types and amounts of raw materials required to support the planned production schedule are determined by the existing raw material inventory and the "bill of materials," or BOM—a sort of "recipe" of ingredients needed to make each item. The quantity of raw materials to order also depends on the lead time and lot sizing. Lead time is the amount of time it takes from the placement of a purchase order until the raw materials arrive at the production facility. Lot size has to do with discrete quantities that the supplier will ship and the amount that is economical for the producer to receive or store. For example, a supplier might ship a certain raw material in units of 36,000-kilogram rail cars. The producer might need 43,000 kilometres of the raw material. A decision must be made to order one or two rail cars of the raw material.

Purchasing uses the information from MRP to place purchase orders for raw materials with qualified suppliers. Typically, purchase orders are released so that raw materials arrive just in time to be used in production and to minimize warehouse and storage costs. Often, producers will allow suppliers to tap into data via an extranet that enables them to determine what raw materials the producer needs, minimizing the effort and lead time to place and fill purchase orders.

Production uses the high-level production schedule to plan the details of running and staffing the production operation. This more detailed schedule takes into account employee, equipment, and raw material availability along with detailed customer demand data.

The right supply chain ERP system allowed Ridley, a manufacturer and distributor of animal feed and nutrition products in the United States and Canada, to better manage its purchasing and manufacturing processes of more than 47,000 product variations. The company mixes feed based on specific customer requirements and needed a system that provided it with the flexibility to buy raw materials in bulk and track costs and revenue by customer. The system will save the company more than $1.1 million a year in staffing and maintenance costs.[10]

Sales ordering is the set of activities that must be performed to capture a customer sales order. A few of the essential steps are recording the items to be purchased, setting the sales price, recording the order quantity, determining the total cost of the order including delivery costs, and confirming the customer's available credit. Should the item(s) the customer wants to order be out of stock, the sales order process should communicate this fact and suggest other items that could substitute for the customer's initial choice. Setting sales prices can be quite complicated; sales prices include quantity discounts, promotions, and incentives. After the total cost of the order is determined, a company must check the customer's available credit to see if this order is within the credit limit. Figure 9.7 shows a sales order entry window in SAP business software.

ERP systems do not work directly with production machines, so they need a way to capture information about what was produced. This data must be passed to the ERP accounting modules to keep an accurate count of finished product inventory. Many companies have personal computers on the production floor that count the number of cases of each product item by scanning a UPC code on the packing material. Other approaches for capturing production quantities include the use of RFID chips and manually entering the data via a PDA.

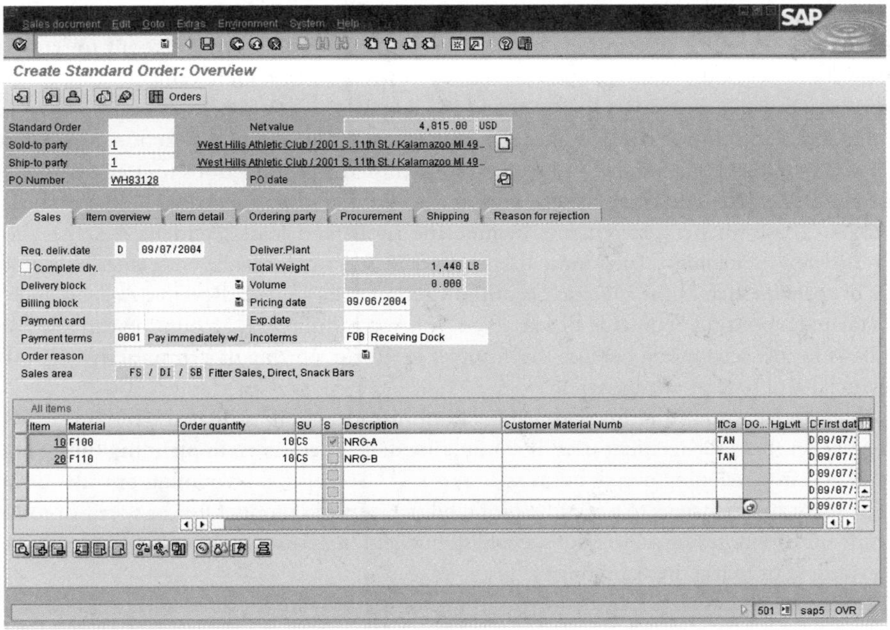

Figure 9.7

Sales Order Entry Window
(Source: Courtesy of SAP.)

Separately, production-quality data can be added based on the results of quality tests run on a sample of the product for each batch of product produced. Typically, this data includes the batch identification number, which identifies the production run and the results of various product quality tests.

Retailers as well as manufacturers use demand forecasting to match production to consumer demand and to allocate products to stores. For example, Just White Shirts offers top-quality, 100 percent cotton dress shirts and socks directly to its customers at competitive prices. The company's ERP system seamlessly ties together the online ordering and accounting activities. Call centre staff can instantly access customer information, process an order, and have it shipped directly or to a retail outlet for customer pick-up. Customer service has greatly improved, and the company has been able to reduce call centre and warehouse distribution staff.[11] According to Wayne Usie of JDA Software, "To compete effectively in today's dynamic retail landscape and positively impact sales and margins, businesses must provide their consumers with the desired merchandise. This requires flawless planning and execution by bringing together the best people, processes, and technologies."[12]

Financial and Managerial Accounting and ERP

The general ledger is the main accounting record of a business. It is often divided into categories, including assets, liabilities, revenue, expenses, and equity. These categories, in turn, are subdivided into subledgers to capture details such as cash, accounts payable, and accounts receivable. The business processes required to capture and report these accounting details are essential to the operation of any organization and are frequently included within the scope of an organization's ERP system. In the ERP system, input to the general ledger occurs simultaneously with the input of a business transaction to a specific module. Here are several examples of how this occurs:

- An order clerk records a sale and the ERP system automatically creates an accounts receivable entry indicating that a customer owes money for goods received.
- A buyer enters a purchase order and the ERP system automatically creates an accounts payable entry in the general ledger registering that the company has an obligation to pay for goods that will be received at some time in the future.
- A dock worker enters a receipt of purchased materials from a supplier, and the ERP system automatically creates a general ledger entry to increase the value of inventory on hand.
- A production worker withdraws raw materials from inventory to support production, and the ERP system generates a record to reduce the value of inventory on hand.

Thus, the ERP system captures transactions entered by workers in all functional areas of the business. The ERP system then creates the associated general ledger record to track the financial impact of the transaction. This set of records is an extremely valuable resource that companies can use to support financial and managerial accounting.

Financial accounting consists of capturing and recording all the transactions that affect a company's financial state and then using these documented transactions to prepare financial statements to external decision makers, such as stockholders, suppliers, banks, and government agencies. These financial statements include the profit and loss statement, balance sheet, and cash flow statement. They must be prepared in strict accordance with rules and guidelines of agencies such as the Ontario Securities Commission, Canada Revenue Agency, and the Canadian Accounting Standards Board. Data gathered for financial accounting can also form the basis for tax accounting because this involves external reporting of a firm's activities to the provincial and federal tax agencies.

Managerial accounting involves using "both historical and estimated data in providing information that management uses in conducting daily operations, in planning future operations, and in developing overall business strategies."[13] Managerial accounting provides data to enable the firm's managers to assess the profitability of a given product line or specific product, identify underperforming sales regions, establish budgets, make profit forecasts, and measure the effectiveness of marketing campaigns.

All transactions that affect the financial state of the firm are captured and recorded in the database of the ERP system. This data is used in the financial accounting module of the ERP system to prepare the statements required by various users. The data can also be used in the managerial accounting module of the ERP system along with various assumptions and forecasts to perform various analyses such as generating a forecasted profit and loss statement to assess the firm's future profitability.

Using an ERP with financial and managerial accounting systems can contribute significantly to a company's success. Osprey Media Group Inc. operates 32 small community newspapers in Ontario. Prior to implementing a centralized ERP, each community newspaper used separate accounting packages. Extracting, processing, and then consolidating accounting data was time-consuming and staff-intensive. The different accounting records made it difficult to extract comparable management information. This onerous consolidation process made it difficult to create detailed reports that would enable financial benchmarking and help determine the newspapers' most effective practices. Osprey implemented a standardized financial management reporting system, which has improved productivity, provided higher-quality information, and facilitated collaboration among the accounting groups. Osprey can now benchmark and compare newspaper operations so that senior management can make more informed decisions.[14]

Business Intelligence and ERP

As discussed in Chapter 5, business intelligence (BI) involves gathering enough of the right information in a timely manner and usable form and analyzing it to shine a spotlight on the organization's performance. BI has become recognized as an essential component of an organization's ERP system. BI tools are used to access all the operational data captured in the ERP database and analyze performance on a daily basis, highlight areas for improvement, and monitor the results of business strategies. The most widely used BI software comes from SAP, IBM, Oracle, and Microsoft, with JasperSoft and Pentaho offering open-source solutions.

In the retail industry, BI can enable retailers to gain customer knowledge and improve sales visibility across the enterprise so the firm can react to and better predict customer demand and maximize sales. Bell Mobility, a division of Bell Canada, experienced challenges in determining customer profitability. Due to disparate business applications and databases, customer service representatives (CSR) could not advise customers of new promotions or sell customers additional products prior to implementing Infor's CRM system. The system enabled CSRs to present tailored promotions to customers, resulting in a 50 percent customer response rate to offers and increased revenue.[15]

Customer Relationship Management

As discussed in Chapter 1, a **customer relationship management (CRM) system** helps a company manage all aspects of customer encounters, including marketing and advertising, sales, customer service after the sale, and programs to keep loyal customers. See Figure 9.8. The goal of CRM is to understand and anticipate the needs of current and potential customers to increase customer retention and loyalty, while optimizing the way that products and services are sold. CRM is used primarily by people in the sales, marketing, and service organizations to capture and view data about customers and to improve communications. Businesses implementing CRM systems report benefits such as improved customer satisfaction, increased customer retention, reduced operating costs, and the ability to meet customer demand.

customer relationship management (CRM) system
A system that helps a company manage all aspects of customer encounters, including marketing and advertising, sales, customer service after the sale, and programs to retain loyal customers.

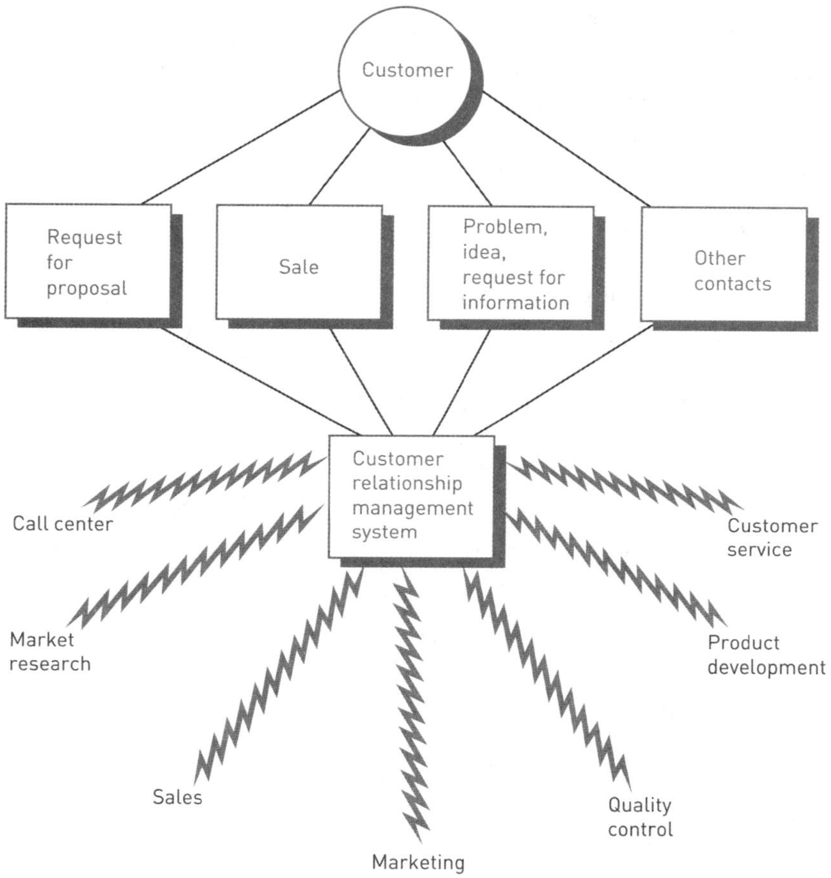

Figure 9.8

Customer Relationship Management System

CRM software automates and integrates the functions of sales, marketing, and service in an organization. The objective is to capture data about every contact a company has with a customer through every channel and store it in the CRM system so the company can truly understand customer actions. CRM software helps an organization build a database about its customers that describes relationships in sufficient detail so that management, salespeople, customer service providers—and even customers—can access information to match customer needs with product plans and offerings, remind them of service requirements, and know what other products they have purchased.

Control Panel Systems' (CPS) mishmash of nonintegrated applications to track customer data, deliver quotes, and create sales orders threatened the growth of the company. Customer information collected by the sales force had to be manually reentered into the company's financial system to process the sales. As a result, the company adopted an integrated ERP/CRM system that provided seamless processes between the sale force and head office staff. Recording all customer information in one database resulted in improved customer relationships and operational efficiency.[16]

The key features of a CRM system are the following:

- *Contact management:* The ability to track data on individual customers and sales leads and access that data from any part of the organization.
- *Sales management:* The ability to organize data about customers and sales leads and then to prioritize the potential sales opportunities and identify appropriate next steps.
- *Customer support:* The ability to support customer service representatives so that they can quickly, thoroughly, and appropriately address customer requests and resolve customers' issues while at the same time collecting and storing data about those interactions.
- *Marketing automation:* The ability to capture and analyze all customer interactions, generate appropriate responses, and gather data to create and build effective and efficient marketing campaigns.
- *Analysis:* The ability to analyze customer data to identify ways to increase revenue and decrease costs, identify the source of the firm's "best customers," and determine how to retain them and find more of them.
- *Social networking:* The ability to create and join sites like Facebook, where salespeople can make contacts with potential customers.
- *Access by smartphones*: The ability to access Web-based customer relationship management software by devices such as the BlackBerry or Apple iPhone.
- *Import contact data*: The ability for users to import contact data from various data service providers such as Jigsaw, which offers company-level contact data that can be downloaded for free directly into the CRM application.

Figure 9.9 shows the SAP Contact Manager.

Figure 9.9

SAP Contact Manager

(Source: Courtesy of SAP.)

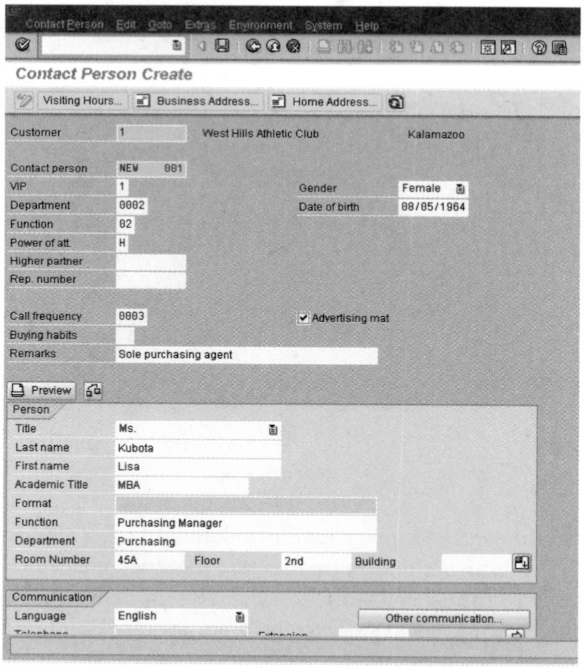

The focus of CRM involves much more than installing new software. Moving from a culture of simply selling products to placing the customer first is essential to a successful CRM deployment. Before any software is loaded onto a computer, a company must retrain employees. Who handles customer issues and when must be clearly defined, and computer systems need to be integrated so that all pertinent information is available immediately, whether a customer calls a sales representative or customer service representative. In addition to using stationary computers, most CRM systems can now be accessed via wireless devices.

ISM, Inc. is a CRM strategic adviser that has rigorously tested the available CRM packages each year since 1990. For example, in 2009 each CRM package was rated according to 217 selection criteria, including 102 business functions and 51 technical features. Packages are divided into those suitable for use by large organizations and those for SMEs. The detailed ratings for the top 15 packages in each group are available at a cost of $995.[17] Table 9.3 lists vendors whose CRM software solution was ranked in the top 15 for three consecutive years (2007–2009).

Top-Rated CRM Solutions for Large Organizations	Top-Rated CRM Solutions for SMEs
Amdocs CRM (Amdocs)	Ardexus MODE (Ardexus)
Firstwave CRM (Firstwave)	Microsoft Dynamics CRM (Microsoft)
Infor CRM (Infor Global Solutions)	NetSuite CRM (NetSuite)
ExSellence (Optima Technologies)	Relavis CRM (Relavis)
PeopleSoft CRM (Oracle)	Sage CRM (Sage)
Salesforce CRM (Salesforce.com)	Salesforce CRM (Salesforce.com)
	Salespage CRM (Salespage Technologies)
	StayInFront CRM (StayInFront)

Table 9.3

Top-Rated Enterprise CRM Solutions 2007–2009

Hosted Software Model for Enterprise Software

Many business application software vendors are pushing the use of the hosted software model for SMEs. The goal is to help customers acquire, use, and benefit from the new technology while avoiding much of the associated complexity and high start-up costs. Applicor, Intacct, NetSuite, SAP, and Workday are among the software vendors who offer hosted versions of their ERP or CRM software at a cost of $50 to $200 per month per user.

This pay-as-you-go approach is appealing to SMEs because they can experiment with powerful software capabilities without making a major financial investment. Organizations can then dispose of the software without large investments if the software fails to provide value or otherwise misses expectations. Also, using the hosted software model means the small business firm does not need to employ a full-time IT person to maintain key business applications. The small business firm can expect additional savings from reduced hardware costs and costs associated with maintaining an appropriate computer environment (such as air conditioning, power, and an uninterruptible power supply).

Table 9.4 lists the advantages and disadvantages of hosted software.

Advantages	Disadvantages
Decreased total cost of ownership	Potential availability and reliability issues
Faster system start-up	Potential data security issues
Lower implementation risk	Potential problems integrating the hosted products of different vendors
Management of systems outsourced to experts	Savings anticipated from outsourcing may be offset by increased effort to manage vendor

Table 9.4

Advantages and Disadvantages of Hosted Software Model

INTERNATIONAL ISSUES ASSOCIATED WITH ENTERPRISE SYSTEMS

Enterprise systems must support businesses that interoperate with customers, suppliers, business partners, shareholders, and government agencies in many countries. Different languages and cultures, disparities in IS infrastructure, varying laws and customs rules, and many currencies are among the challenges that must be met by an enterprise system of a multinational company. The following sections highlight these issues.

Different Languages and Cultures

Teams composed of people from several countries speaking different languages and familiar with different cultures might not agree on a single work process. In some cultures, people do not routinely work in teams in a networked environment. Despite these complications, many multinational companies can establish close connections with their business partners and roll out standard IS applications for all to use. However, those standard applications often don't account for all the differences among business partners and employees operating in other parts of the world. They sometimes require extensive and costly customization. For example, even though English has become a standard business language among executives and senior managers, many people within organizations do not speak English. As a result, software might need to be designed with local language interfaces to ensure the successful implementation of a new system. Customization might also be needed for date fields; the Canadian date format is month/day/year, the European format is day/month/year, and Japan uses year/month/day. Sometimes, users might also have to implement manual processes to override established formatting to enable systems to function correctly.

Disparities in Information System Infrastructure

Many countries' telecommunications services are controlled by a central government or operated as a monopoly, with no incentives to provide fast and inexpensive customer service. For example, much of Latin America lags behind the rest of the world in Internet usage, and online marketplaces are rare. This gap makes it difficult for multinational companies to meet online with their Latin American business partners. The lack of a robust or a common information infrastructure can also create problems. Even something as mundane as the power plug on a piece of equipment built in one country might not fit into the power socket of another country.

Varying Laws and Customs Rules

Numerous laws can affect the collection and dissemination of data. For example, labour laws in some countries prohibit the recording of worker performance data. Also, some countries have passed laws limiting the transborder flow of data linked to individuals. Specifically, European Community Directive 95/96/EC of 1998 requires that any company doing business within the borders of the 25 European Union member nations protect the privacy of customers and employees. It bars the export of data to countries that do not have data-protection standards comparable to the European Union's.

Trade custom rules between nations are international laws that set practices for two or more nations' commercial transactions. They cover imports and exports and the systems and procedures dealing with quotas, visas, entry documents, commercial invoices, foreign trade zones, payment of duty and taxes, and many other related issues. For example, the North American Free Trade Agreement (NAFTA) of 1994 created trade custom rules to address the flow of goods throughout the North American continent. Most of these custom rules and their changes over time create significant complications for people who must keep enterprise systems consistent with the rules.

Multiple Currencies

The enterprise system of multinational companies must conduct transactions in many currencies. To do so, a set of exchange rates is defined, and the information systems apply these rates to translate from one currency to another. The systems must be current with foreign currency exchange rates; handle reporting and other transactions, such as cash receipts; issue vendor payments and customer statements; record retail store payments; and generate financial reports in the currency of choice.

ETHICAL AND SOCIETAL ISSUES

Google Pulls Out of China

Companies that serve customers around the world often need to make adjustments so that the products and services they provide adhere to local laws. Conforming to the local laws of the countries in which you do business is not typically a major issue, unless those laws contradict the company's ethical values. Such was the case when Google decided to pull out of China.

The story begins in December 2009 when Google and dozens of other companies and government organizations were the targets of a cyber attack based in China. The purpose of the attacks was to gain access to the accounts of Chinese dissidents and journalists. For Google, the attack served as the final straw in building tensions between Google and the Chinese government. For years, the Chinese government required Google to filter search results served to Chinese citizens—a requirement that Google regards as unethical. China also occasionally required Google's China office to provide account information of Chinese bloggers that had criticized the government. In some cases, the information provided by Google reportedly resulted in arrests and even torture.

After it was clear to Google that the December attack could not have occurred without government sponsorship, Google laid down an ultimatum: Google would continue operations in China only if it was allowed to provide unfiltered search results. Google used the hacking incident as a lever to raise the ethical concerns it has with China laws. China responded to the hacking allegation by downplaying the incident and reiterating that all businesses in China are bound to uphold China's laws.

After months of closed-door negotiations, with China holding firm to its stance, Google closed the doors on its search engine in China, following through on its promise. But, rather than eliminating its filters on *www.google.cn* and risking the arrest of its China-based employees, Google redirected requests for *google.cn* to its Hong Kong search engine, *www.google. com.hk*, where it maintains unfiltered Chinese-language search results. Shortly after the switch, China was quick to apply its own censoring filters to the Internet DNS servers that feed its country.

Google's decision to close google.cn was shocking because of the large monetary sacrifice it required. China has the world's largest population and has one of the most rapidly growing economies. Google gave up a large competitive advantage in exchange for a clean conscience. Google's move is causing many companies that do business in China to re-evaluate their own motivations and convictions.

So far, while many have applauded Google's decision, only a few have followed suit. Popular Web hosting company GoDaddy stopped registering domain names for the .cn domain. That decision came after the Chinese government demanded personal information about people who had purchased domain names from GoDaddy. Microsoft has stated that it intends to continue expanding its business in China. Even Google continues other operations in China and looks forward to robust sales of Google Android phones in China in coming years.

China isn't the only country where Google censors content based on government-imposed policies. Using the site *www. google.com/governmentrequests*, Google lists governments that require the company to censor content. Brazil, Germany, India, the United Kingdom, South Korea, and the United States rank high on the list. Granted, censorship is sometimes justified, such as in cases where it protects populations from physical harm. However, many feel that it is not justified when it is used to silence dissident opinions, such as in China. Increasingly, technology companies such as Google and Internet service providers are assuming responsibility for policing Internet content. Google's stance against China's censorship has shown that the company is clearly uncomfortable with its role as a censor and causes some to wonder if it may not follow up with changes in policy elsewhere. Google's chief legal officer wrote that the China issue "goes to the heart of a much bigger global debate about freedom of speech."

Google's experience in China provides an extreme example of the considerations faced by technology companies providing services abroad. Similar considerations are faced by all kinds of international companies at varying levels of complexity. While most companies comply with local laws and customs in the countries in which they operate without complaint, Google chose to use its financial power and influence to make a statement about its company's ethical position on political censorship.

Discussion Questions

1. What constraints imposed by China combined to cause Google to close its Chinese search engine?
2. What pressures might cause businesses to set aside ethical considerations to do business in China?

Critical Thinking Questions

1. Some have argued that Google's exit from China might have actually harmed the growth of democracy around the world. How might Google have positively influenced democracy if it had stayed in China?
2. What constraints might China place on a business like Walmart, or India on a restaurant like McDonald's? How do those constraints differ from those placed on Google in China?

SOURCES: Perez, Juan Carlos, "Google Stops Censoring in China," *Computerworld*, March 22, 2010, *www.computerworld.com*; Gross, Grant, "GoDaddy to Stop Registering .cn Domain Names," *Computerworld*, March 24, 2010, *www.computerworld. com*; Naone, Erica, "Google and Censorship," *Technology Review*, March 26, 2010, *www.technologyreview.com*; Wills, Ken, "China State Media Accuses Google of Political Agenda," Reuters, March 21, 2010, *www.reuters.com*.

SUMMARY

Principle:

An organization must have information systems that support routine, day-to-day activities and that help a company add value to its products and services.

Transaction processing systems (TPSs) are at the heart of most information systems in businesses today. A TPS is an organized collection of people, procedures, software, databases, and devices used to capture fundamental data about events that affect the organization (transactions) and that use that data to update the official records of the organization.

The methods of transaction processing systems include batch and online. Batch processing involves the collection of transactions into batches, which are entered into the system at regular intervals as a group. Online transaction processing (OLTP) allows transactions to be entered as they occur.

Order processing systems capture and process customer order data from receipt of order through creation of a customer invoice.

Accounting systems track the flow of data related to all the cash flows that affect the organization.

Purchasing systems support the inventory control, purchase order processing, receiving, and accounts payable business functions.

Organizations today, including SMEs, typically implement an integrated set of TPSs from a single or limited number of software vendors to meet their transaction processing needs.

Organizations expect TPSs to accomplish a number of specific objectives, including processing data generated by and about transactions, maintaining a high degree of accuracy and information integrity, compiling accurate and timely reports and documents, increasing labour efficiency, helping provide increased and enhanced service, and building and maintaining customer loyalty. In some situations, an effective TPS can help an organization gain a competitive advantage.

All TPSs perform the following basic activities: data collection, which involves the capture of source data to complete a set of transactions; data editing, which checks for data validity and completeness; data correction, which involves providing feedback of a potential problem and enabling users to change the data; data manipulation, which is the performance of calculations, sorting, categorizing, summarizing, and storing data for further processing; data storage, which involves placing transaction data into one or more databases; and document production, which involves outputting records and reports.

Principle:

A company that implements an enterprise resource planning system is creating a highly integrated set of systems, which can lead to many business benefits.

Enterprise resource planning (ERP) is software that supports the efficient operation of business processes by integrating activities throughout a business, including sales, marketing, manufacturing, logistics, accounting, and staffing.

Implementing an ERP system can provide many advantages, including providing access to data for operational decision making; elimination of costly, inflexible legacy systems;

providing improved work processes; and creating the opportunity to upgrade technology infrastructure.

Some of the disadvantages associated with an ERP system are that they are time consuming, difficult, and expensive to implement, and they can be difficult to integrate with other systems.

Many SMEs are implementing ERP systems to achieve organizational benefits. In many cases, they are choosing open-source systems because of the lower total cost of ownership and their ability to be easily modified.

No one ERP software system is "best" for all organizations. SAP, Oracle, Infor, and Microsoft are among the leading ERP suppliers.

Although the scope of ERP implementation can vary, most firms use ERP systems to support financial and managerial accounting and business intelligence. Most manufacturing organizations use ERP to support the supply chain management activities of planning, executing, and controlling all tasks involved in raw material sourcing and procurement, conversion of raw materials to finished products, and the warehousing and delivery of finished product to customers.

The production and supply chain management process starts with sales forecasting to develop an estimate of future customer demand. This initial forecast is at a fairly high level, with estimates made by product group rather than by individual product item. The sales and operations plan takes demand and current inventory levels into account and determines the specific product items that need to be produced and when to meet the forecast future demand. Demand management refines the production plan by determining the amount of weekly or daily production needed to meet the demand for individual products. Detailed scheduling uses the production plan defined by the demand management process to develop a detailed production schedule specifying details, such as which item to produce first and when production should be switched from one item to another. Materials requirement planning determines the amount and timing for placing raw material orders with suppliers. Purchasing uses the information from materials requirement planning to place purchase orders for raw materials and transmit them to qualified suppliers. Production uses the detailed schedule to plan the logistics of running and staffing the production operation. The individual application modules included in the ERP system are designed to support best practices, the most efficient and effective ways to complete a business process.

Organizations are implementing CRM systems to manage all aspects of customer encounters including marketing and advertising, sales, customer service after the sale, and programs to keep and retain loyal customers.

Business application software vendors are experimenting with the hosted software model to see if the approach meets customer needs and is likely to generate significant revenue. This approach is especially appealing to SMEs due to the low initial cost, which makes it possible to experiment with powerful software capabilities.

Numerous complications arise that multinational corporations must address in planning, building, and operating their enterprise systems. These challenges include dealing with different languages and cultures, disparities in IS infrastructure, varying laws and customs, and many currencies.

CHAPTER 9: SELF-ASSESSMENT TEST

An organization must have information systems that support routine, day-to-day activities and that help a company add value to its products and services.

1. A key characteristic of an enterprise system is that it uses a database of key operational and planning data that can be _____.

2. The result of processing business transactions is that the organization's records are updated to reflect the status of the operation at the time of the _____.

3. Which of the following is not one of the basic components of a TPS?
   a. databases
   b. networks
   c. procedures
   d. analytical models

4. A form of TPS where business transactions are immediately processed is called _____.

5. Capturing data at its source and recording it accurately in an electronic form that can be directly entered into the computer are the principles behind _____.

6. Which of the following is a set of transaction processing systems sometimes referred to as the lifeblood of the organization?
   a. purchasing systems
   b. accounting systems
   c. order processing systems
   d. human resource systems

7. Business data goes through a(n) _____ that includes data collection, data editing, data correction, data manipulation, data storage, and documentation production.

8. Inventory control, purchase order processing, receiving, and accounts payable systems make up a set of systems that support the _____ business function.

9. The _____ transaction processing system manages the cash flow of the company by keeping track of the money owed to the company.

A company that implements an enterprise resource planning system is creating a highly integrated set of systems, which can lead to many business benefits.

10. Many multinational companies roll out standard IS applications for all to use. However, standard applications often don't account for all the differences among business partners and employees operating in other parts of the world. Which of the following is a frequent modification that is needed for standard software?
    a. Software might need to be designed with local language interfaces to ensure the successful implementation of a new IS.
    b. Customization might be needed to handle date fields correctly.
    c. Users might also have to implement manual processes and overrides to enable systems to function correctly.
    d. all of the above

11. Which of the following is not a primary benefit of implementing an ERP system?
    a. elimination of inefficient systems
    b. easing adoption of improved work processes
    c. improving access to data for operational decision making
    d. ease of implementation

12. The individual application modules included in an ERP system are designed to support _____, the most efficient and effective ways to complete a business process.

13. Most companies can implement an ERP system without major difficulty. True or False?

14. Only large, multinational companies can justify the implementation of ERP systems. True or False?

CHAPTER 9: SELF-ASSESSMENT TEST ANSWERS

(1) shared by all (2) last processed transaction (3) d (4) online transaction processing (5) source data automation (6) c (7) transaction processing cycle (8) purchasing (9) accounts receivable (10) d (11) d (12) best practices (13) False (14) False

REVIEW QUESTIONS

1. Enterprise information systems employ a single database of key data that can be shared by all. What problem associated with the use of multiple TPSs does this eliminate?

2. What basic transaction processing activities are performed by all transaction processing systems?

3. Provide an example where the use of a batch processing system to handle transactions is appropriate. Provide an example of where the use of online transaction processing is appropriate.

4. Why would an SME choose to customize and implement an open-source ERP system rather than buy a proprietary ERP system?

5. Identify four complications that multinational corporations must address in planning, building, and operating their ERP systems.
6. How does materials requirement planning support the purchasing process? What are some of the issues and complications that arise in materials requirement planning?
7. What is the role of a CRM system? What sort of benefits can such a system produce for a business?
8. What are the business processes included with the scope of supply chain management?

9. Why is the general ledger application key to the generation of accounting information and reports?
10. What is the difference between managerial and financial accounting?
11. What is the role of the general ledger system in keeping track of the financial transactions of the organization? How is it used?
12. List and briefly describe the set of activities that must be performed by the sales ordering module of an ERP system to capture a customer sales order.

DISCUSSION QUESTIONS

1. Assume that you are the owner of a landscaping firm serving hundreds of customers in your area. Identify the kinds of customer information you would like your firm's CRM system to capture. How might this information be used to provide better service or increase revenue? Identify where or how you might capture this data.
2. What are the primary benefits that can be achieved through supply chain management?
3. In what ways is the implementation of a hosted ERP system simpler and less risky for an SME than for a large, multinational corporation?
4. Briefly discuss how business intelligence tools can integrate with an ERP system.
5. What are some of the challenges and potential problems of implementing a CRM system and CRM mindset in a firm's employees? How might you overcome these?
6. You are a member of the organization's finance organization. The firm is considering the implementation of an

ERP system. Make a convincing argument for finance and accounting to be included within the scope of the ERP implementation.
7. Your friend has been appointed the project manager of your firm's ERP implementation system. What advice would you offer to help ensure the success of the project?
8. What sort of benefits should the suppliers and customers of a firm that has successfully implemented an ERP system expect to see? What sort of issues might arise for suppliers and customers during an ERP implementation?
9. Many organizations are moving to a collaborative process with their major customers to get their input on planning future inventory levels and production rather than relying on an internally generated demand forecast. Explain how such a process might work. What issues and concerns might a customer have in entering into an agreement to do this?

PROBLEM-SOLVING EXERCISES

1. Imagine that you are the new IS manager for a large multinational company. Surprisingly, the firm still operates with a hodgepodge of transaction processing systems—some are software packages from various vendors and some systems are developed in-house. Use a graphics package (such as PowerPoint) to prepare a slide presentation you will make to senior company managers to convince them that it is time to implement a comprehensive ERP system. What sort of resistance and objections do you expect to encounter? How would you overcome these? Include appropriate slides to cover this as well.

2. Use a spreadsheet program to develop a sales forecasting system for a new car dealership that can estimate monthly sales for each make and model based on historical sales data and various parameters. Suggestion: Assume that this month's sales will be the same as the sales for this month last year except for adjustments due to the cost of gas and each make of car's litres per kilometre. You can further refine the model to take into account change in interest rates for new cars or other parameters you wish to include. Document the assumptions you make in building your model.

TEAM ACTIVITIES

1. Your team members should interview several business managers at a firm that has implemented a CRM system. Interview them to define the scope and schedule for the overall project. Make a list of what they see as the primary benefits of the implementation. What were the biggest hurdles they had to overcome? Did the firm need to retrain its employees to place greater emphasis on putting the customer first?

2. As a team, develop a list of seven key criteria that an SME manufacturing firm should consider in selecting an ERP system. Discuss each criterion and assign a weight representing the relative importance of that criterion. Develop a simple spreadsheet to use in scoring various ERP alternatives.

WEB EXERCISES

1. Do research on the Web and find a website that offers a demo of an ERP or CRM system. View the demo, perhaps more than once. Write a review of the software based on the demo. What are its strengths and weaknesses? What additional questions about the software do you have? E-mail your questions to the vendor and document their response to your questions.

2. Using the Web, identify several software services firms that offer consulting services to help organizations to implement ERP or CRM systems. Gain an understanding of what sort of services they offer and become familiar with several of their success stories. If you had to choose one of the software services firms to assist your SME organization, which one would you choose, and why?

CAREER EXERCISES

1. Imagine that you are a prescription drug salesperson for a large pharmaceutical firm and that you make frequent sales calls on physicians and other primary care providers. The purpose of these sales calls is to acquaint them with your firm's products and get them to prescribe your products to their patients. Describe the basic functionality you would want in your organization's CRM system for it to support you in preparing and making presentations to these people.

2. ERP software vendors need business systems analysts that understand both information systems and business processes. Make a list of six or more specific qualifications needed to be a strong business systems analyst supporting an ERP implementation within a medium-sized global organization.

CASE STUDIES

Case One

Skullcraft Goes Big Time with ERP

Skullcraft began as a dream of Rick Alden, a ski and skateboard fanatic, who saw a business opportunity in selling stylized headphones designed for extreme sports enthusiasts. In 2003, he began designing high-end headphones with a radical stylized design that would appeal to skaters and skiers. He was the first to provide the ability to switch between music listening and cell phone conversations over headphones. Combined, these ideas put Skullcraft headphones on the map.

Rick began marketing his headphones to specialty ski and skate shops. The unique approach caught on, and the Skullcraft brand began quickly spreading among the target demographic. With a 200 to 300 percent annual growth rate, Rick next approached large department and discount stores with Skullcraft products. He and his associates were shocked when Circuit City, Target, and Best Buy all expressed an interest in carrying Skullcraft products at the same time. It was at that point Rick and his team realized that Skullcraft was going to be big.

Although Skullcraft's products were widely distributed, the company remained small. With only 26 employees in an office in Park City, Utah, Skullcraft found itself in an unusual position. It was a small business that needed to handle large amounts of transactions. In 2007, the company was rivalling Sony in the U.S. headphone market, with sales of up to $37 million. Ironically, Skullcraft's finance department was managing its books with Excel spreadsheets and QuickBooks. IT manager Beth Siron knew it was time for the company to think big about information systems. Even though Skullcraft was technically a small business, Beth believed it was time to invest in an ERP system.

After evaluating many systems, it was clear to Beth that the ideal ERP for Skullcraft was SAP's Business ByDesign. Business ByDesign is a fully hosted system, so Skullcraft wouldn't need to invest in its own information system infrastructure or staff. The last thing Skullcraft managers wanted to be bothered with was managing a technology infrastructure. Business ByDesign is Web-based, so Skullcraft staff can access it anywhere, anytime. It enables big business best practices for managing financials, customer relationships, human resources, projects, procurement, and the supply chain in a format accessible to small businesses.

Beth Siron supervised the implementation of SAP's Business ByDesign, leaving other Skullcraft staff to continue with business as usual. This decision was important since the adoption took place just prior to the company's busiest quarter. She interviewed SAP users and mapped out the business processes. She handled the scoping and basic testing, supported data migration, and trained the users. The system implementation was a huge success. Skullcraft especially appreciates the ability to track products through the supply chain and forecast demand.

With an industrial-strength ERP system in place, Skullcraft is ready to chase its dreams. The company intends to begin pursuing international markets and expanding its presence in retail stores. Although the business has boomed, Skullcraft staff stay true to their original passions—skateboarding around the office and hitting the slopes when the powder falls.

Discussion Questions

1. What inspired Skullcraft to pursue an ERP even though the company has only 26 employees?
2. What features caused Skullcraft to choose SAP's Business ByDesign?

Critical Thinking Questions

1. How do you think Skullcraft was able to maintain a small staff while increasing production 200 to 300 percent annually?
2. Do you think Skullcraft is unusual in its size and needs? What other businesses can you think of that fit the Skullcraft model?

SOURCES: Dunn, Angela, "Headphones for Extreme Sports," SAP SPECTRUM magazine, December 6, 2009, *http://en.sap.info/headphones-for-extreme-sports/10547*; Skullcandy website, *www.skullcandy.com*, accessed May 2, 2009; SAP Business ByDesign website, *www.sap.com/sme/solutions/businessmanagement/businessbyde-sign/index.epx*, accessed May 2, 2009.

Case Two
Dubai Bank Improves Customer Satisfaction with CRM

Dubai Bank is one of the top Islamic banks based in Dubai, United Arab Emirates, with 25 branches across the UAE and total assets of AED 14.4 billion. Banking is a highly competitive business in Dubai, a city of glass-and-steel skyscrapers and state-of-the-art massive engineering projects, rooted in oil money, and growing in leaps and bounds. Banks work hard to win over customers with lavish lobbies, financial incentives, and impeccable customer service.

As Dubai Bank grew, adding services and customers, it became apparent that the bank needed a way to easily gather customer information. Dubai Bank customers often had data spread across three separate databases—one for account information, another for credit card information, and yet another for investments and loans. If customers held several bank accounts, separate database records were created and even more information was duplicated.

The complexity of customer information systems caused Dubai Bank agents frustration in finding information and setting up new accounts. Even worse was the aggravation it caused valuable customers. If a customer phoned customer service with a question, the agent might have to access up to eight systems to collect customer information, leaving the customer waiting on the line. If the customer followed up the next day with a visit to the bank, the teller would have no knowledge of the previous discussion with customer service, further aggravating the customer.

When customers set up a new account, agents were required to fill out multiple applications. Credit checks needed to be performed manually. With this level of customer service, Dubai Bank was having a difficult time keeping customers.

Faizal Eledath, chief information officer at Dubai Bank, recognized the need for an enterprise-wide customer relationship management (CRM) system. He sought a system that would integrate all customer records into one cohesive system, providing agents and managers detailed information about each customer through a single interface.

Dubai Bank is recognized as an Islamic institution that strictly adheres to the Shari'a principles—that is, the sacred law of Islam. These principles include conducting business with the highest level of transparency, integrity, fairness, respect, and care. Dubai Bank's information systems would need to support its Islamic principles.

Dubai Bank hired information systems consultant Veripark to assist in building the ideal CRM for the bank. Dubai made its choice based on positive past experiences it shared with Veripark and the Microsoft products it represents. Veripark selected Microsoft's Dynamics CRM package that integrates all critical operational banking systems, including credit cards, data warehouse, wealth management, and risk systems into the CRM.

The new CRM provides bank representatives with a 360-degree view of the customer, where information can be entered and accessed through a single interface. Veripark customized the package to comply with Islamic banking regulations. Business process automation is programmed into the system to further assist the bank in its strict adherence to Shari'a principles.

The new CRM system records information from all customer interaction with the bank. If a customer makes a withdrawal from an ATM, it is recorded in the CRM. When a customer phones customer service, notes are recorded in the system as well. Whenever a customer has a need, a bank representative can easily review the customer's history and quickly recommend a course of action.

Since the installation of its new CRM system, both customers and bank agents are much happier. Customer service agents can now provide speedy service because information is provided in one interface rather than eight. New accounts are created in a quarter of the time previously required. Compliance with Islamic banking requirements are assured and automated, without involving additional effort on the part of bank officials or agents. Most importantly, Dubai Bank knows and understands its customers more deeply, and it can use that information to provide services and implement programs that increase customer satisfaction.

Discussion Questions

1. What conditions brought Dubai Bank to the realization that it could benefit from a CRM system?
2. How did the CRM system make life easier for Dubai Bank agents and customers?

Critical Thinking Questions

1. Dubai Bank had regulations imposed on it by the Islamic faith that affected its information systems. What types of regulations are imposed on Canadian banks that have a similar impact?
2. How can the information collected by a CRM system be used to gain insight and boost a business's profits? Provide some examples.

SOURCES: "Dubai Bank," Microsoft Case Studies, March 26, 2010, www.microsoft.com/casestudies/Case_Study_Detail.aspx?casestudyid=4000006766; Dubai Bank website, www.dubaibank.ae, accessed May 2, 2010.

Questions for Web Case

See the website for this book to read about the Altitude Online case for this chapter. Following are questions concerning this Web case.

Altitude Online: Enterprise System Considerations

Discussion Questions

1. Judging from the ERP features, how important is an ERP to the functioning of a business? Explain.
2. What consideration do you think led Altitude Online to decide to host the ERP on its own servers rather than using SaaS? What are the benefits and drawbacks of both approaches?

Critical Thinking Questions

1. What challenges lie ahead for Altitude Online as it rolls out its new ERP system?
2. How might the ERP affect Altitude Online's future growth and success?

NOTES

Sources for the opening vignette: Baum, David, "Server It Up!" Oracle Magazine, Jan/Feb, 2009, www.oracle.com/technology/oramag/oracle/09-jan/o19appserver.html; Babcock, Charles, "Tuxedo Emerges as Part of Oracle Fusion Middleware," InformationWeek, January 23, 2009, www.informationweek.com/news/software/integration/showArticle.jhtml?articleID=212902078&queryText=FedEx%20FUSION; FedEx Facts, FedEx website, www.informationweek.com/news/software/integration/showArticle.jhtml?articleID=212902078&queryText=FedEx%20FUSION, accessed May, 2, 2010.

1 St-Hubert Case Study, InfoSynergique, www.synergique.qc.ca/en/default_005.html, accessed October 13, 2010.
2 WagJag website, www.wagjag.com, accessed June 11, 2011.
3 "Trimac Corporation," Sybase website, www.sybase.com/detail?id=1033799, accessed June 11, 2011.
4 Ward, Susan, "SME," http://sbinfocanada.about.com/od/businessinfo/g/SME.htm, accessed April 8, 2010.
5 "Megavolt Design Energizes Its Operations with Simply Accounting by Sage Enterprise," Sage website, accessed October 13, 2010.
6 "Customer Case Study: The Royal Canadian Mint for Their Money After Improving Its IT Processes with Microsoft Dynamics AX," Microsoft Case Studies, www.microsoft.com/canada/casestudies/Case_Study_Detail.aspx?casestudyid=4000006445, accessed June 11, 2011.
7 "Customer Case Study: Candy Maker Sharpens Competitive Edge, Drives Productivity and Insight with ERP Upgrade," Microsoft Case Studies, www.microsoft.com/canada/casestudies/Case_Study_Detail.aspx?casestudyid=4000006948, accessed October 15, 2010.
8 All, Ann, "Who's to Blame for Failed ERP Project that Prompted SAP Lawsuit?" April 1, 2008, www.itbusinessedge.com/cm/blogs/all/whos-to-blame-for-failed-erp-project-that-prompted-sap-lawsuit/?cs=11588, accessed June 10, 2011.

9 "ERP Project Delays Due to B2B Rollouts Cost Manufacturers More than $1 Million Per Month," September 21, 2009, http://news.gxs.com/index.php/2009/09/erp-project-delays-due-to-b2b-rollouts-cost-manufactureres-than-$1-million-per-month, accessed April 20, 2010.
10 "Customer Case Study: Ridley, the Right Supply-Chain Decision Saves Animal Feed and Nutrition Provider $1 Million," Microsoft Case Studies, www.microsoft.com/canada/casestudies/Case_Study_Detail.aspx?casestudyid=4000004023, accessed October 15, 2010.
11 "Success Stories: Just White Shirts," www.sageaccpac.com/Company/News_Room/Success_Stories/details?CID=1D530149-3B17-0001-491E-17B06BC01401, accessed October 15, 2010.
12 "Chico's FAS, Inc. Completes Rapid Implementation of JDA's Allocation and Workforce Management Solutions," Internet Retailer, April 7, 2010.
13 Glossary of terms at www.crfonline.org/oc/glossary/m.html, accessed April 24, 2010.
14 "Success Stories: Osprey Media Group, Inc.," www.sageaccpac.com/Company/News_Room/Success_Stories/details?CID=1D530153-A6CB-0001-52E4-134FB2B01B40, accessed October 15, 2010.
15 "Bell Rings up Big Revenues with Infor CRM," www.infor.com/content/casestudies/119289/, accessed June 11, 2011.
16 "Success Stories: Sage Software gets CPS Back on Track," www.sageaccpac.com/Company/News_Room/Success_Stories/details?CID=88390625-1875-9688-8438-140625, accessed October 15, 2010.
17 "Top 15 Reviews," www.ismguide.com/index.php?option=com_content&view=article&id=17&Itemid=101, accessed April 23, 2010.

CHAPTER · 10 ·

Information and Decision Support Systems

(Source: Lukiyanova Natalia/frenta/Shutterstock.com.)

PRINCIPLES	LEARNING OBJECTIVES
▪ **Good decision-making and problem-solving skills are key to developing effective information and decision support systems.**	▪ Define the stages of decision making. ▪ Discuss the importance of implementation and monitoring in problem solving.
▪ **The management information system (MIS) must provide the right information to the right person in the right format at the right time.**	▪ Explain the uses of MISs and describe their inputs and outputs. ▪ Discuss information systems in the functional areas of business organizations.
▪ **Decision support systems (DSSs) are used when the problems are unstructured.**	▪ List and discuss important characteristics of DSSs that give them the potential to be effective management support tools. ▪ Identify and describe the basic components of a DSS.
▪ **Specialized support systems, such as group support systems (GSSs) and executive support systems (ESSs), use the overall approach of a DSS in situations such as group and executive decision making.**	▪ State the goals of a GSS and identify the characteristics that distinguish it from a DSS. ▪ Identify the fundamental uses of an ESS and list the characteristics of such a system. ▪ List and discuss other special-purpose systems.

Information Systems in the Global Economy
Tru-Test

MIS Reports Guide Decision Makers at Tru-Test

Tru-Test, the world's leading manufacturer of livestock scales, milk-metering equipment, and electric fencing, specializes in livestock and pasture management. Based on extensive research and development, Tru-Test has created technologies that allow their products to stand head and horns above the competition. Tru-Test livestock scales have a patented algorithm that makes it possible to weigh livestock while they're moving. Ranchers can weigh 500 sheep per hour or 150 cattle per hour—far more than with traditional scales. Tru-Test milk meters use an advanced technology and design for precise and accurate milk sampling and testing during the milking process. The company's electric fencing uses a patented Cyclic Wave technology that supports a safer and more economic use of electricity from AC, DC, or solar sources. Like business information systems, Tru-Test products allow ranchers to work more efficiently and maximize the return on their livestock investment.

Tru-Test is headquartered in Auckland, New Zealand, with offices and operations in Canada, Australia, the United States, and Mexico. Tru-Test has more than 400 staff worldwide and customers spread across 70 countries. During its lifetime, Tru-Test has expanded and diversified into four business units that house eight brands. The business units are Livestock Management, Pasture Management and Animal Containment, Shearing Equipment, and Contract Manufacturing. As with all successful businesses, Tru-Test has experienced growth pains trying to keep up with its ever-expanding amount of information. Recently Tru-Test took steps to gain control of its information and to leverage it to support wise strategic business planning.

Through a period of sustained growth and several acquisitions, Tru-Test found itself supporting nine separate information systems. It was clear that the first step toward information management was to merge those nine systems into one central system. Tru-Test chose an ERP system from JD Edwards to manage finances, procurement, customer service, warehousing, and manufacturing. The ERP system is housed on servers at Tru-Test headquarters, and limited access is made available to Tru-Test subsidiaries around the world through virtual desktop software from Citrix.

The impact of the new ERP system was immediately felt across Tru-Test. CFO Ian Hadwin states that "the standardization of business processes across the group on a single centralized architecture is easier to manage." The new system performs basic financial tasks much more quickly and efficiently than the previous system. This allows employees to be more productive while operating costs decrease. But the largest benefit is in the power that the new system provides to corporate decision makers.

The management information systems that make up the ERP provide Tru-Test decision makers with a variety of reports that contain detailed information about the state of the company. Scheduled reports on sales and inventory provide production and warehouse managers with the information they need to make sure sales are fulfilled in a timely manner. Tru-Test can now accurately forecast demand for its products and implement a just-in-time production model, reducing its inventory to precisely match demand. Eliminating surplus stock means an increase in profits for the company.

Tru-Test extended its demand planning to all areas of its business using Demantra, specialized software from Oracle. Demantra is a group support system designed to support demand planning across an enterprise. Using enterprise data from the ERP and models designed to represent various business activities, Demantra assists managers in sales, operations, manufacturing, marketing, and other business areas with planning for the future.

Tru-Test's database of customers and customer interactions supports a powerful CRM system. Reports from the CRM system provide sales information that allows decision makers in marketing to launch more effective marketing campaigns. The finance department has designed reports that allow for reliable revenue forecasting.

Reports providing Tru-Test top management with important corporate facts, called key indicators, support high-level decisions that steer the company toward meeting its goals. Gaining control of its information, collecting it into a centralized database, and mining it for valuable information depend on Tru-Test's ability to meet and exceed its goals to maximize profits with a minimum investment.

As you read this chapter, consider the following:

- How is an MIS used in the various functional areas of a business?
- How do an MIS and DSS affect a company's business practices and its ability to compete in a market?

Why Learn About Information and Decision Support Systems?

You have seen throughout this book how information systems can make you more efficient and effective through the use of database systems, the Internet, e-commerce, transaction processing systems, and many other technologies. The true potential of information systems, however, is in helping you and your co-workers make more informed decisions. This chapter shows you how to slash costs, increase profits, and uncover new opportunities for your company using management information and decision support systems. Transportation coordinators can use management information reports to find the least expensive way to ship products to market and to solve bottlenecks. A loan committee at a bank or credit union can use a group support system to help determine who should receive loans. Store managers can use decision support systems to help them decide what and how much inventory to order to meet customer needs and increase profits. An entrepreneur who owns and operates a temporary storage company can use vacancy reports to help determine what price to charge for new storage units. Everyone can be a better problem solver and decision maker. This chapter shows you how information systems can help. It begins with an overview of decision making and problem solving.

As shown in the opening vignette, information and decision support are the lifeblood of today's organizations. Thanks to information and decision support systems, managers and employees can obtain useful information in real time. As discussed in Chapter 9, TPS and ERP systems capture a wealth of data. When this data is filtered and manipulated, it can provide powerful support for managers and employees. The ultimate goal of management information and decision support systems is to help managers and executives at all levels make better decisions and solve important problems. The result can be increased revenues, reduced costs, and the realization of corporate goals. Many companies, for example, are using Internet video sharing and social networking sites such as YouTube, MySpace, and Facebook to reduce advertising costs.[1] No matter what type of information and decision support system you use, its primary goal should be to help you and others become better decision makers and problem solvers.

DECISION MAKING AND PROBLEM SOLVING

Every organization needs effective decision makers. YouTube, the popular video-sharing Internet site, made a decision to distribute programming from Time Warner, CNN, and the Cartoon Network to help the company generate ad revenues.[2] The company is also exploring new ad formats to help generate additional revenues and profits.

In most cases, strategic planning and the overall goals of the organization set the course for decision making, helping employees and business units achieve their objectives and goals. Often, information systems also assist with problem solving, helping people make better decisions and save lives. For example, several pharmacies in Canada maintain drug information systems that watch for possible serious drug interactions based on customer prescriptions.

Decision Making as a Component of Problem Solving

In business, one of the highest compliments you can receive is to be recognized by your colleagues and peers as a "real problem solver." Problem solving is a critical activity for any business organization. After identifying a problem, the process of solving the problem begins with decision making. A well-known model developed by Herbert Simon divides the **decision-making phase** of the problem-solving process into three stages: intelligence, design, and choice. This model was later incorporated by George Huber into an expanded model of the entire problem-solving process. See Figure 10.1.

The first stage in the problem-solving process is the **intelligence stage**. During this stage, you identify and define potential problems or opportunities. You also investigate resource and environmental constraints. For example, if you were a British Columbian farmer, during the intelligence stage you would explore the possibilities of shipping fruit from your farm in B.C. to stores in Nova Scotia. The perishability of the fruit and the maximum price that consumers in Nova Scotia are willing to pay for the fruit are problem constraints. As another example, researchers are gathering information during the intelligence stage about a new encryption approach to protect sensitive data that was introduced in a Ph.D. dissertation.[3] The new approach would allow calculations on encrypted data instead of removing the encryption to make the calculations, which could make the data vulnerable to theft or privacy concerns. According to one researcher, "It's like one of those boxes with the gloves that are used to handle toxic chemicals. All the manipulation happens inside the box." If successful, this new approach could have a dramatic impact on data security techniques.

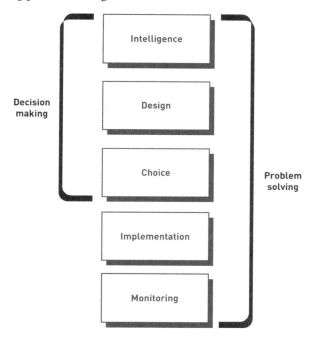

In the **design stage**, you develop alternative solutions to the problem and evaluate their feasibility. In the fruit example, you would consider the alternative methods of shipment, including the transportation times and costs associated with each. During this stage, you might determine that shipment by rail to Nova Scotia and then by truck to the customers is not feasible because the fruit would spoil. In another example, many hedge funds and investment firms are developing high-frequency trading systems during the design stage that increase speed and potential profitability.[4] High-frequency trading, also called flash trading, allows individuals and companies to make money by placing trades on very fast computers and high-speed telecommunications lines whenever prices fluctuate slightly during the trading day.[5] These profits would not be available using normal computers and trading approaches. Some regulatory agencies, such as the Ontario Securities Commission (OSC), are considering limiting or banning some types of high-frequency trading.

decision-making phase
The first part of problem solving, including three stages: intelligence, design, and choice.

Figure 10.1

How Decision Making Relates to Problem Solving

The three stages of decision making—intelligence, design, and choice—are augmented by implementation and monitoring to result in problem solving.

intelligence stage
The first stage of decision making, in which you identify and define potential problems or opportunities.

design stage
The second stage of decision making, in which you develop alternative solutions to the problem and evaluate their feasibility.

choice stage
The third stage of decision making, which requires selecting a course of action.

problem solving
A process that goes beyond decision making to include the implementation stage.

implementation stage
A stage of problem solving in which a solution is put into effect.

monitoring stage
The final stage of the problem-solving process, in which decision makers evaluate the implementation.

programmed decision
A decision made using a rule, procedure, or quantitative method.

The last stage of the decision-making phase, the **choice stage**, requires selecting a course of action. In the fruit example, you might select the method of shipping fruit by air from your farm to Nova Scotia as the solution. The choice stage would then conclude with selection of an air carrier. As you will see later, various factors influence choice; the act of choosing is not as simple as it might first appear.

Problem solving includes and goes beyond decision making. It also includes the **implementation stage**, when the solution is put into effect. For example, if your decision is to ship fruit to Nova Scotia as air freight using a specific carrier, implementation involves informing your field staff of the new activity, getting the fruit to the airport, and actually shipping the product to Nova Scotia.

The final stage of the problem-solving process is the **monitoring stage**. In this stage, decision makers evaluate the implementation to determine whether the anticipated results were achieved and to modify the process in light of new information. Monitoring can involve feedback and adjustment. For example, after the first shipment of fruit from British Columbia to Nova Scotia, you might learn that the flight of your chosen air freight firm routinely stops in Toronto, Ontario, where the plane sits on the runway for a number of hours while loading additional cargo. If this unforeseen fluctuation in temperature and humidity adversely affects the fruit, you might have to readjust your solution to include a new carrier that does not make such a stop, or perhaps you would consider a change in fruit packaging. In another case, a popular GPS company monitored the performance of one of its marine navigation systems and determined that the GPS device incorrectly computed water depths.[6] As a result of the monitoring stage, the company issued a worldwide recall of all affected devices.

Programmed versus Nonprogrammed Decisions

In the choice stage, various factors influence the decision maker's selection of a solution. One factor is whether the decision can be programmed. **Programmed decisions** are made using a rule, procedure, or quantitative method. For example, to say that inventory should be ordered when inventory levels drop to 100 units is a programmed decision because it adheres to a rule. Programmed decisions are easy to computerize using traditional information systems. For example, you can easily program a computer to order more inventory when levels for a certain item reach 100 units or less. Cisco Systems, a large computer equipment and server manufacturing company, controls its inventory and production levels using programmed decisions embedded into its computer systems.[7] The programmed decision-making process has improved forecasting accuracy and reduced the possibility of

Ordering more products when inventory levels drop to specified levels is an example of a programmed decision.

(Source: Bloomberg via Getty Images.)

manufacturing the wrong types of inventory, a change that has saved money. Management information systems can also reach programmed decisions by providing reports on problems that are routine and in which the relationships are well defined (in other words, they are structured problems).

Nonprogrammed decisions deal with unusual or exceptional situations. In many cases, these decisions are difficult to quantify. Determining the appropriate training program for a new employee, deciding whether to develop a new type of product line, and weighing the benefits and drawbacks of installing an upgraded pollution control system are examples. Each of these decisions contains unique characteristics, and standard rules or procedures might not apply to them. Today, decision support systems help solve many nonprogrammed decisions, in which the problem is not routine and rules and relationships are not well defined (unstructured or ill-structured problems). These problems can include deciding the best location for a manufacturing plant or whether to rebuild a hospital that was severely damaged by a flood.

nonprogrammed decision
A decision that deals with unusual or exceptional situations.

Optimization, Satisficing, and Heuristic Approaches

In general, computerized decision support systems can either optimize or satisfice. An **optimization model** finds the best solution, usually the one that will best help the organization meet its goals.[8] For example, an optimization model can find the best route to ship products to markets, given certain conditions and assumptions. Descartes, a leading provider of software-as-a-service logistic solutions located in Waterloo, Ontario, sells a route and sequencing optimization system that can reduce fuel costs by up to 15 percent for fleet operators.[9] In another case, Xerox has developed an optimization system to increase printer productivity and reduce costs, called Lean Document Production (LDP) solutions.[10] The optimization routine was able to reduce labour costs by 20 to 40 percent in some cases. Marriott International used optimization to help determine the optimal price of a group or block of rooms. The optimization routine helped Marriott increase revenues and profits as a result.[11]

Optimization models use problem constraints. A limit on the number of available work hours in a manufacturing facility is an example of a problem constraint. Shermag, a furniture manufacturing company with headquarters in Sherbrooke, Quebec, used an optimization program to reduce raw materials costs, including wood, in its manufacturing operations.[12] The optimization program, which used the C++ programming language and CPLEX optimization software, helped the company reduce total costs by more than 20 percent. Some spreadsheet programs, such as Excel, have optimizing features, as shown in Figure 10.2 on the next page. Optimization software also allows decision makers to explore various alternatives.[13]

optimization model
A process to find the best solution, usually the one that will best help the organization meet its goals.

A **satisficing model** is one that finds a good—but not necessarily the best—solution to a problem. Satisficing is used when modelling the problem properly to get an optimal decision would be too difficult, complex, or costly. Satisficing normally does not look at all possible solutions but only at those likely to give good results. Consider a decision to select a location for a new manufacturing plant. To find the optimal (best) location, you must consider all cities in Canada or the world. A satisficing approach is to consider only five or ten cities that might satisfy the company's requirements. Limiting the options might not result in the best decision, but it will likely result in a good decision, without spending the time and effort to investigate all cities. Satisficing is a good alternative modelling method because it is sometimes too expensive to analyze every alternative to find the best solution.

satisficing model
A model that will find a good— but not necessarily the best— solution to a problem.

Heuristics, also known as "rules of thumb," are commonly accepted guidelines or procedures that usually find a good solution. A heuristic that baseball team managers use is to place batters most likely to get on base at the top of the lineup, followed by the power hitters who can drive them in to score. An example of a heuristic used in business is to order four months' supply of inventory for a particular item when the inventory level drops to 20 units or less; although this heuristic might not minimize total inventory costs, it can serve as a good rule of thumb to avoid stockouts without maintaining excess inventory. Symantec, a provider of antivirus software, has developed an antivirus product that is based on heuristics.[14] The software can detect viruses that are difficult to detect using traditional antivirus software techniques.

heuristics
Commonly accepted guidelines or procedures that usually find a good solution.

Figure 10.2

Optimization Software

Some spreadsheet programs, such as Microsoft Excel, have optimizing routines. This figure shows Solver, which can find an optimal solution given certain constraints.

(Source: Used with permission from Microsoft.)

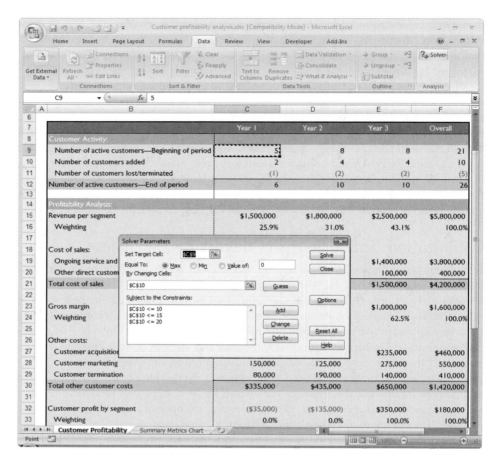

The Benefits of Information and Decision Support Systems

The information and decision support systems covered in this chapter and the next help individuals, groups, and organizations make better decisions, solve problems, and achieve their goals. These systems include management information systems, decision support systems, group support systems, executive support systems, knowledge management systems, and a variety of special-purpose systems. As shown in Figure 10.3, the benefits are a measure of increased performance of these systems versus the cost to deliver them. The plus sign (+) by the arrow from *performance* to *benefits* indicates that increased performance has a positive impact on benefits. The minus sign (−) from *cost* to *benefits* indicates that increased cost has a negative impact on benefits.

Figure 10.3

The Benefits of Information and Decision Support Systems

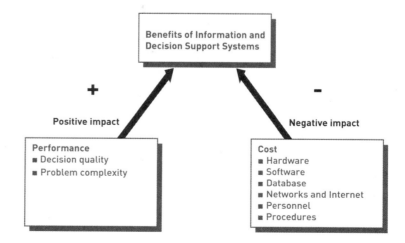

The performance of these systems is typically a function of decision quality and problem complexity. Decision quality can result in increased effectiveness, increased efficiency, higher productivity, and many other measures first introduced in Chapter 1.[15] Problem complexity depends on how hard the problem is to solve and implement. The cost of delivering these systems are the expenditures of the information technology components covered in Part II of this book, including hardware, software, databases, networks and the Internet, people, and procedures. But how do these systems actually deliver benefits to the individuals, groups, and organizations that use them? It depends on the system. We begin our discussion with traditional management information systems.

AN OVERVIEW OF MANAGEMENT INFORMATION SYSTEMS

A management information system (MIS) is an integrated collection of people, procedures, databases, and devices that provides managers and decision makers with information to help achieve organizational goals. MISs can often give companies and other organizations a competitive advantage by providing the right information to the right people in the right format and at the right time.

Management Information Systems in Perspective

The primary purpose of an MIS is to help an organization achieve its goals by providing managers with insight into the regular operations of the organization so that they can control, organize, and plan more effectively. One important role of the MIS is to provide the right information to the right person in the right format at the right time. In short, an MIS provides managers with information, typically in reports, that supports effective decision making and provides feedback on daily operations. Figure 10.4 (on the next page) shows the role of MISs within the flow of an organization's information. Note that business transactions can enter the organization through traditional methods, or via the Internet, or via an extranet connecting customers and suppliers to the firm's ERP or transaction processing systems. The use of MISs spans all levels of management. That is, they provide support to and are used by employees throughout the organization.

Inputs to a Management Information System

As shown in Figure 10.4, data that enters an MIS originates from both internal and external sources, including a company's supply chain. The most significant internal data sources for an MIS are the organization's various TPS and ERP systems and related databases. External sources of data can include customers, suppliers, competitors, and stockholders, whose data is not already captured by the TPS, as well as other sources, such as the Internet. As discussed in Chapter 5, companies also use data warehouses and data marts to store valuable business information. Business intelligence, also discussed in Chapter 5, can be used to turn a database into useful information throughout the organization. According to one study, almost 70 percent of consumer goods companies surveyed said they are going to make business intelligence available to more employees in the future.[16]

Outputs of a Management Information System

The output of most MISs is a collection of reports that are distributed to managers. Many MIS reports come from an organization's databases. These reports can be tailored for each user and can be delivered in a timely fashion. Today, many hospitals and health-care facilities use their health-related databases to streamline MIS reports, reduce recordkeeping costs, and save lives by avoiding medical errors in diagnoses, treatments, and adverse drug

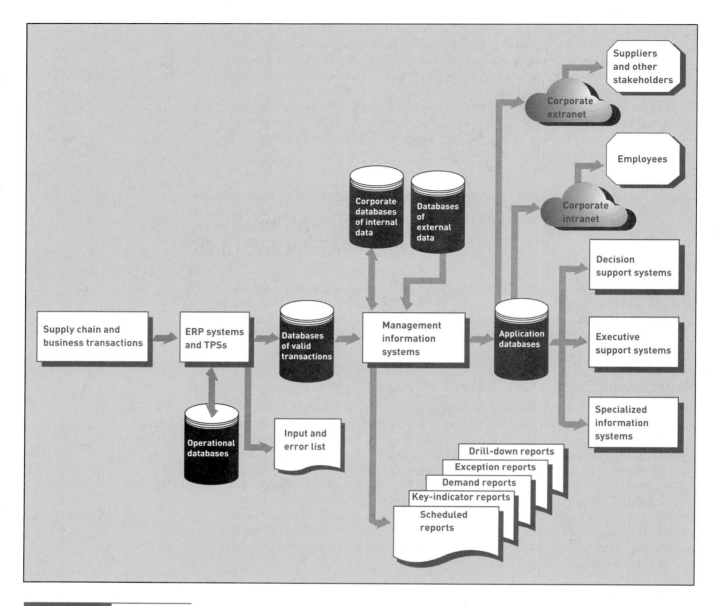

Figure 10.4

Sources of Managerial Information

The MIS is just one of many sources of managerial information. Decision support systems, executive support systems, and expert systems also assist in decision making.

interactions.[17] The Canadian Food Inspection Agency (CFIA) is responsible for managing public health risks associated with the food supply and transmission of animal disease to humans. CFIA used IBM Cognos BI software to design a more centralized system that offers users streamlined and easy-to-understand reports accessible via the Web.[18] Clorox Canada uses customer-based and brand-based dashboards to provide reporting and analysis of key operational metrics, focusing on sales, inventory, and budgeting.[19] Microsoft makes a reporting system called Business Scorecard Manager to give decision makers timely information about sales and customer information.[20] The software, which competes with Business Objects and Cognos, can integrate with other Microsoft software products, including Microsoft Office Excel. Hewlett-Packard's OpenView Dashboard is another MIS package that can quickly and efficiently render pictures, graphs, and tables that show how a business is functioning.

Management reports can come from various company databases, data warehouses, and other sources. These reports include scheduled reports, key-indicator reports, demand reports, exception reports, and drill-down reports. See Figure 10.5 on page 404.

Southwest Airlines Applies MIS to Customer Service

Perhaps one of the most frustrating parts of long-distance travel is dealing with unexpected flight delays, which can be caused by weather, aircraft mechanical problems, overbooked flights, or other unexpected circumstances. Delays strand travellers for hours or sometimes even for days.

Some airlines make attempts to notify passengers about flight delays as soon as they become evident in hopes of saving the passenger needless waiting. Southwest Airlines has been doing this for years. Southwest prides itself on clever, unique approaches to customer service that it calls "The Southwest Way." The airline makes special efforts to satisfy customers who have been inconvenienced. Fred Taylor is Southwest's senior manager of Proactive Customer Service Communications. The *New York Times* has nicknamed Fred Southwest's "Chief Apology Officer." It's Fred's job to make sure customers who experience difficulties are presented with options that leave them feeling satisfied. When Fred found out that Southwest was given a low score for its flight notification service in a *Wall Street Journal* poll, he took action.

Although information systems are typically credited for providing business managers and decision makers with information they can use, they also supply information that customers can use. Information generated by MISs and DSSs can act as a service to a company's customers, such as with Google Search, or as a value added, such as UPS package tracking. Another example is Amazon, which uses information about purchases customers have made on the Amazon website to recommend other products that might interest them. Fred Taylor of Southwest Airlines wanted to empower his customers with up-to-the-minute reports on flight information. Not only would his system notify travellers of flight delays but also of gate changes, opportunities to upgrade, cancellations and rescheduling, and other information that can assist travellers with their preparations.

Fred decided that the best way to inform passengers of preflight information was by phone. Southwest does not have access to all passengers' e-mail addresses or cell phone numbers, so it cannot depend on e-mail or text messaging. It does, however, have access to all customers' phone numbers. Fred and his team reviewed a dozen services that offer automated phone messaging systems. It settled on Varolii Corporation, which specializes in helping companies stay in touch with employees and customers through personalized automated phone messages.

Fred and his team had to develop an MIS that pulled information from its reservation database provided by Sabre reservations systems and from Southwest's own database that manages flight information. The output of the MIS needed to be a report containing passenger names and phone numbers of those who had reservations on flights that were changed, along with details about the disruption. This information had to be delivered in a format that Varolii's system could take as input. The reports also had to be generated quickly so that passengers received the notification as it was delivered to Southwest personnel. In the early testing of the system, Fred received a call from a flustered gate attendant who had a line of passengers asking about a gate change notification. The passengers had received notification before the attendant! After that, a slight delay was programmed into the system to make sure that the information was disseminated to the right people at the right time.

As Fred and his crew rolled out the new system, they included a failsafe to make sure no misinformation was mistakenly sent to passengers. Each notification requires a human review prior to sending the information to Varolii for phoning. Once a notification gets approved, customers' phones ring within seconds. Upon answering, the customer hears a chime, indicating an automated message, and a personable voice that proclaims, "This is Southwest Airlines calling." The message continues with details on flight information, advice on how to proceed, and ends with the offer to connect the customer to a service representative.

Southwest is now collecting travellers' cell phone numbers and e-mail addresses so it can extend its service to other forms of communication. Its Chief Apology Officer continues to explore new ways to apply information systems to making customers happy.

Discussion Questions

1. What were the unique aspects and requirements of Southwest's customer notification MIS?
2. How does this information assist Southwest in gaining a competitive advantage?

Critical Thinking Questions

1. In what other ways could airline information systems assist with increasing customer satisfaction?
2. Many banks use Varolii's phone service for notifying customers who are late making loan payments. What are the benefits and drawbacks of using automated communications systems compared to human communication?

SOURCES: Carr, David, "Southwest Upgrades Customer Service," CIO Insight, August 31, 2009, *www.cioinsight.com/index2.php?option=content&task=view&i d=882809&pop=1&hide_ads=1&page=0&hide_js=1*; Southwest Airlines website, www.southwest.com, accessed March 24, 2010; Varolii website *www.varolii.com*, accessed March 24, 2010.

(a) Scheduled Report

Daily Sales Detail Report

Prepared: 08/10/08

Order #	Customer ID	Salesperson ID	Planned Ship Date	Quantity	Item #	Amount
P12453	C89321	CAR	08/12/08	144	P1234	$3,214
P12453	C89321	CAR	08/12/08	288	P3214	$5,660
P12454	C03214	GWA	08/13/08	12	P4902	$1,224
P12455	C52313	SAK	08/12/08	24	P4012	$2,448
P12456	C34123	JMW	08/13/08	144	P3214	$720
....	....	....	....	....	....	....

(b) Key-Indicator Report

Daily Sales Key-Indicator Report

	This Month	Last Month	Last Year
Total Orders Month to Date	$1,808	$1,694	$1,914
Forecasted Sales for the Month	$2,406	$2,224	$2,608

(c) Demand Report

Daily Sales by Salesperson Summary Report

Prepared: 08/10/08

Salesperson ID	Amount
CAR	$42,345
GWA	$38,950
SAK	$22,100
JWN	$12,350
....	....

(d) Exception Report

Daily Sales Exception Report—Orders Over $10,000

Prepared: 08/10/08

Order #	Customer ID	Salesperson ID	Planned Ship Date	Quantity	Item #	Amount
P12345	C89321	GWA	08/12/08	576	P1234	$12,856
P22153	C00453	CAR	08/12/08	288	P2314	$28,800
P23023	C32832	JMN	08/11/08	144	P2323	$14,400
....	....	....	....	....	....	....

(e) First-Level Drill-Down Report

Earnings by Quarter (Millions)

		Actual	Forecast	Variance
2nd Qtr.	2008	$12.6	$11.8	6.8%
1st Qtr.	2008	$10.8	$10.7	0.9%
4th Qtr.	2008	$14.3	$14.5	-1.4%
3rd Qtr.	2008	$12.8	$13.3	-3.8%

(f) Second-Level Drill-Down Report

Sales and Expenses (Millions)

Qtr: 2nd Qtr. 2008	Actual	Forecast	Variance
Gross Sales	$110.9	$108.3	2.4%
Expenses	$ 98.3	$ 96.5	1.9%
Profit	$ 12.6	$ 11.8	6.8%

(g) Third-Level Drill-Down Report

Sales by Division (Millions)

Qtr: 2nd Qtr. 2008	Actual	Forecast	Variance
Beauty Care	$ 34.5	$ 33.9	1.8%
Health Care	$ 30.0	$ 28.0	7.1%
Soap	$ 22.8	$ 23.0	-0.9%
Snacks	$ 12.1	$ 12.5	-3.2%
Electronics	$ 11.5	$ 10.9	5.5%
Total	$110.9	$108.3	2.4%

(h) Fourth-Level Drill-Down Report

Sales by Product Category (Millions)

Qtr: 2nd Qtr. 2008 Division: Health Care	Actual	Forecast	Variance
Toothpaste	$12.4	$10.5	18.1%
Mouthwash	$ 8.6	$ 8.8	-2.3%
Over-the-Counter Drugs	$ 5.8	$ 5.3	9.4%
Skin Care Products	$ 3.2	$ 3.4	-5.9%
Total	$30.0	$28.0	7.1%

Figure 10.5

Reports Generated by an MIS

The types of reports are (a) scheduled, (b) key indicator, (c) demand, (d) exception, and (e–h) drill down.

(Source: From REYNOLDS. *Information Systems for Managers*, 3E. © 1995 South-Western, a part of Cengage Learning, Inc. Reproduced by permission. www.cengage.com/permissions.)

scheduled report
A report produced periodically, such as daily, weekly, or monthly.

key-indicator report
A summary of the previous day's critical activities, typically available at the beginning of each workday.

demand report
A report developed to give certain information at someone's request rather than on a schedule.

Scheduled Reports

Scheduled reports are produced periodically, such as daily, weekly, or monthly. For example, a production manager could use a weekly summary report that lists total payroll costs to monitor and control labour and job costs. Monthly bills are also examples of scheduled reports. Toronto Hydro, for example, provides customers with comparative monthly energy usage on its bills to encourage better energy conservation. Other scheduled reports can help managers control customer credit, performance of sales representatives, inventory levels, and more.

A **key-indicator report** summarizes the previous day's critical activities and is typically available at the beginning of each workday. These reports can summarize inventory levels, production activity, sales volume, and the like. Key-indicator reports are used by managers and executives to take quick, corrective action on significant aspects of the business. Some believe that the Canadian economy will slowly recover in the next several years as a result of important key-indicator reports, including production rates and retail sales figures.[21]

Demand Reports

Demand reports are developed to provide certain information upon request. In other words, these reports are produced on demand rather than on a schedule. Like other reports discussed in this section, they often come from an organization's database system. For example, an executive might want to know the production status of a particular item—a demand report can be generated to provide the requested information by querying the company's database. Suppliers and customers can also use demand reports. FedEx, for example, provides demand reports on its website to allow customers to track packages from their source to their final destination. Other examples of demand reports are reports requested by executives to show the hours worked by a particular employee and total sales to date for a product. Today, many demand reports are generated from the Internet or using cloud computing.[22] Jive Software, for example, allows employees to search large databases and get important demand reports using key words and natural-language questions. The software can also generate useful graphics, including pie charts and bar graphs.

Exception Reports

Exception reports are reports that are automatically produced when a situation is unusual or requires management action. For example, a manager might set a parameter that generates a report of all inventory items with fewer than the equivalent of five days of sales on hand. This unusual situation requires prompt action to avoid running out of stock on the item. The exception report generated by this parameter would contain only items with fewer than five days of sales in inventory.

As with key-indicator reports, exception reports are most often used to monitor aspects important to an organization's success. In general, when an exception report is produced, a manager or executive takes action. Parameters, or *trigger points*, should be set carefully for an exception report. Trigger points that are set too low might result in too many exception reports; trigger points that are too high could mean that problems requiring action are overlooked. For example, if a manager at a large company wants a report that contains all projects over budget by $100 or more, the system might retrieve almost every company project. The $100 trigger point is probably too low. A trigger point of $10,000 might be more appropriate.

exception report
A report automatically produced when a situation is unusual or requires management action.

Drill-Down Reports

Drill-down reports provide increasingly detailed data about a situation. Using these reports, analysts can see data at a high level first (such as sales for the entire company), then at a more detailed level (such as the sales for one department of the company), and then a very detailed level (such as sales for one sales representative). Most accounting software packages provide drill-down report features so managers can drill down from summarized information into more levels of detail to individual transactions if they want. Companies and organizations of all sizes and types use drill-down reports.

drill-down report
A report providing increasingly detailed data about a situation.

Characteristics of a Management Information System

Scheduled, key-indicator, demand, exception, and drill-down reports have all helped managers and executives make better, more timely decisions. In general, MISs perform the following functions:

- Provide reports with fixed and standard formats.
- Produce hard-copy and soft-copy reports.
- Use internal data stored in the computer system.
- Allow users to develop custom reports.
- Require user requests for reports developed by systems personnel.

FUNCTIONAL ASPECTS OF THE MIS

Most organizations are structured along functional areas. This functional structure is usually apparent from an organization chart, which typically shows a hierarchy in roles or positions. Some traditional functional areas include finance, manufacturing, marketing, human resources, and other specialized information systems. The MIS can also be divided along those functional lines to produce reports tailored to individual functions. See Figure 10.6 on the next page.

Financial Management Information Systems

A **financial MIS** provides financial information for executives and for a broader set of people who need to make better decisions on a daily basis. Reuters, for example, has developed an automated reporting system that scans articles about companies for stock traders to determine if the news is favourable or unfavourable. The reports can result in buy orders if the

financial MIS
An information system that provides financial information for executives and for a broader set of people who need to make better decisions on a daily basis.

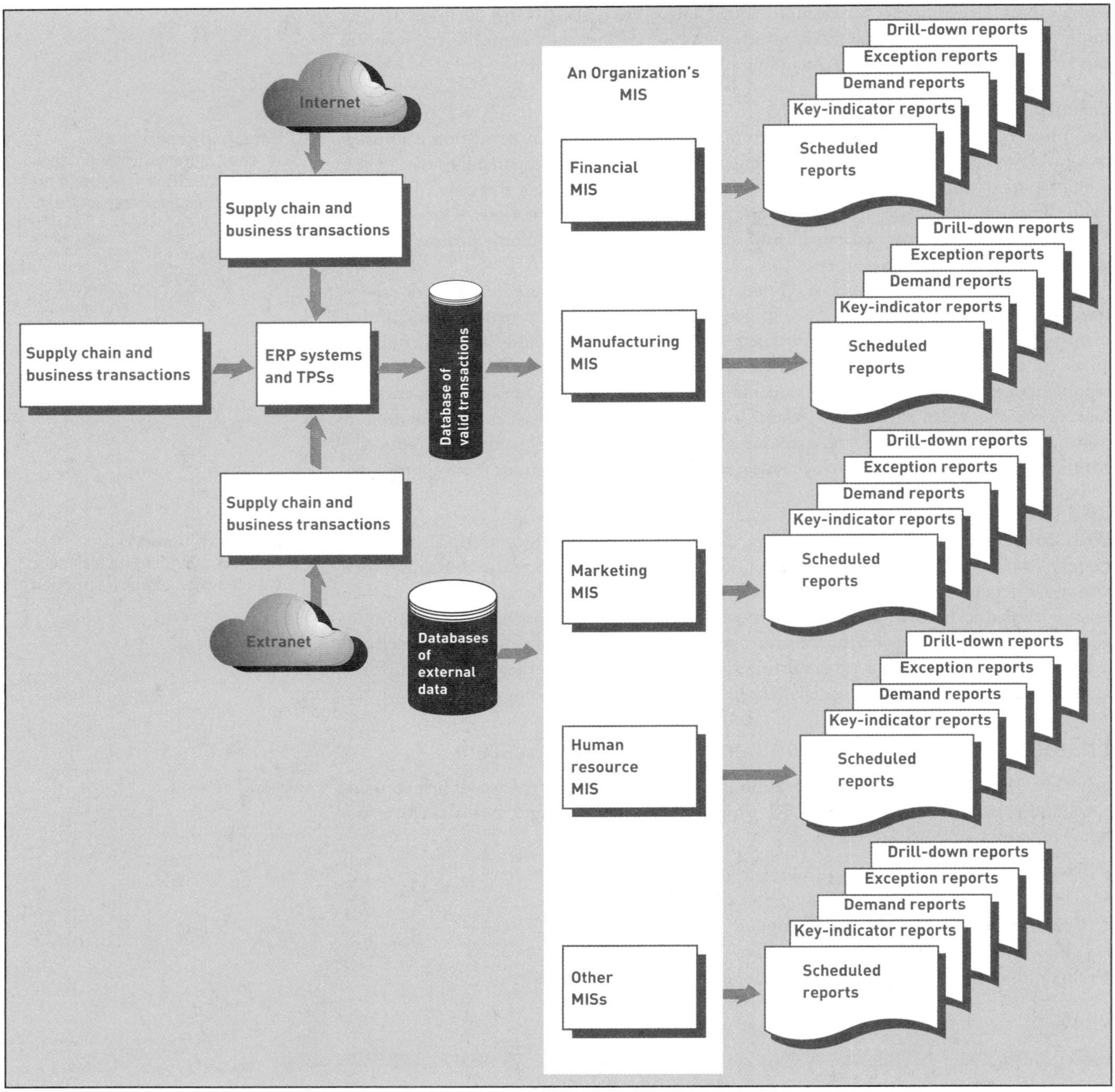

Figure 10.6

An Organization's MIS

The MIS is an integrated collection of functional information systems, each supporting particular functional areas.

news is positive or sell orders if the news is negative. Eventually, the system will be tied into machine trading that doesn't require trade orders generated by people.[23] Websites can also provide financial information. For example, websites such as Canadamortgage.com provide information on current mortgage rates from Canadian lenders. People in Europe, Japan, and other countries are also starting to use their smartphones and mobile devices to transfer money directly to other people to make loans or repay them.[24] Financial MISs are often used to streamline reports of transactions. Most financial MISs perform the following functions:

- Integrate financial and operational information from many sources, including the Internet, into a single system.
- Provide easy access to data for both financial and nonfinancial users, often through the use of a corporate intranet to access corporate Web pages of financial data and information.

- Make financial data immediately available to shorten analysis turnaround time.
- Enable analysis of financial data along several dimensions—time, geography, product, plant, and customer.
- Analyze historical and current financial activity.
- Monitor and control the use of funds over time.

Figure 10.7 shows typical inputs, function-specific subsystems, and outputs of a financial MIS, including profit and loss, auditing, and uses and management of funds. Some of the financial MIS subsystems and outputs are outlined below.

Figure 10.7

Overview of a Financial MIS

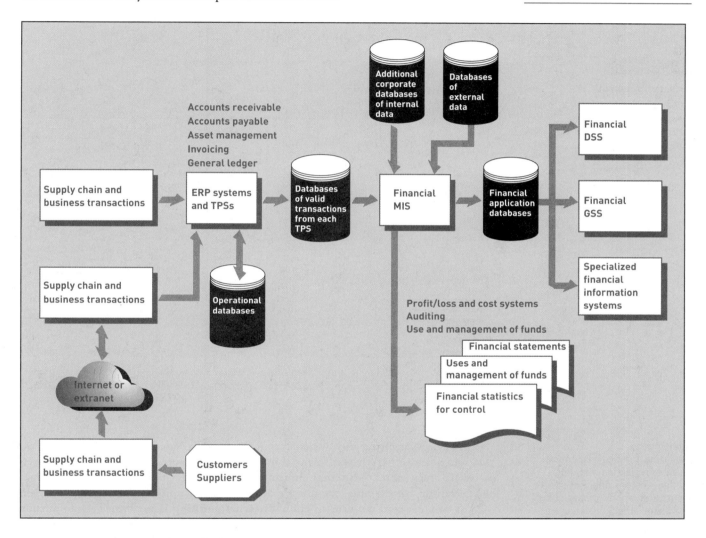

Financial institutions use information systems to analyze historical and current investment data for clients.

(Source: StockLite/Shutterstock.com.)

profit centre
A department within an organization that focuses on generating profits.

revenue centre
A division within a company that generates sales or revenues.

cost centre
A division within a company that does not directly generate revenue.

Profit/loss and cost systems. Many departments within an organization are **profit centres**, which means that they focus on generating profits. An investment division of a large insurance or credit card company is an example of a profit centre. See Figure 10.8. Other departments can be **revenue centres**, which are divisions within the company that focus primarily on generating sales or revenues, such as a marketing or sales department. Still other departments can be **cost centres**, which are divisions within a company that do not directly generate revenue, such as manufacturing or research and development. In most cases, information systems are used to compute revenues, costs, and profits.

Figure 10.8

Income Statement

An income statement shows a corporation's business results, including all revenues, earnings, expenses, costs, and taxes.

Projected Five-Year Income Statement

Upland International
Recreational Products Division
Projected Five-Year Income Statement

Prepared: 4/29/2013

| | | | | Tax Rate | 33% |
| | | | | Cost of Goods | 75% |

	Year 1	Year 2	Year 3	Year 4	Year 5
Revenues	$3,200,000	$3,541,382	$3,919,184	$4,337,290	$4,800,000
Cost of Sales	$2,400,000	$2,656,037	$2,939,388	$3,252,967	$3,600,000
Gross Profit	**$800,000**	**$885,346**	**$979,796**	**$1,084,322**	**$1,200,000**
Accounting	$12,600	$14,112	$15,805	$17,702	$19,826
Advertising & Promotion	$37,800	$42,336	$47,416	$53,106	$59,479
Insurance	$3,600	$4,032	$4,516	$5,058	$5,665
Maintenance	$8,640	$9,677	$10,838	$12,139	$13,595
Utilities	$13,680	$15,322	$17,160	$19,219	$21,526
Miscellaneous	$4,300	$4,816	$5,394	$6,041	$6,766
Total General Expenses	**$80,620**	**$90,294**	**$101,130**	**$113,265**	**$126,857**
Earnings before Interest, Depr. & Tax	$719,380	$795,051	$878,666	$971,057	$1,073,143
Depreciation Expense	$141,550	$120,459	$102,511	$87,237	$74,238
Operating Profit	**$577,830**	**$674,592**	**$776,156**	**$883,821**	**$998,905**
Interest Expense	$65,733	$53,102	$39,490	$24,822	$9,016
Earnings Before Taxes	**$512,097**	**$621,490**	**$736,665**	**$858,998**	**$989,889**
Estimated Tax	$168,992	$205,092	$243,099	$283,469	$326,663
Net Income	**$343,105**	**$416,398**	**$493,566**	**$575,529**	**$663,226**

auditing
Analyzing the financial condition of an organization and determining whether financial statements and reports produced by the financial MIS are accurate.

internal auditing
Auditing performed by individuals within the organization.

external auditing
Auditing performed by an outside company.

- *Auditing.* **Auditing** involves analyzing the financial condition of an organization and determining whether financial statements and reports produced by the financial MIS are accurate.[25] **Internal auditing** is performed by individuals within the organization. For example, the finance department of a corporation might use a team of employees to perform an audit. **External auditing** is performed by an outside company, usually an accounting or consulting firm such as PricewaterhouseCoopers or Deloitte & Touche. Computer systems are used in all aspects of internal and external auditing. Even with internal and external audits, some companies can mislead investors and others with fraudulent accounting statements. One of Canada's largest accounting fraud cases was Livent Inc.'s $500-million accounting fraud. The company improperly recorded expenses in an effort to increase its profitability.[26]
- *Uses and management of funds.* Internal uses of funds include purchasing additional inventory, updating plants and equipment, hiring new employees, acquiring other companies, buying new computer systems, increasing marketing and advertising, purchasing raw materials or land, investing in new products, and increasing research and development. External uses of funds are typically investment related. Companies often use financial MISs to invest excess funds in such external revenue

generators as bank accounts, stocks, bonds, bills, notes, futures, options, and foreign currency. A number of powerful personal finance applications also help people manage and use their money.[27] Several Canadian banks provide budgeting tools on their websites to help people budget their expenditures. Yahoo Finance (*http://ca.finance.yahoo.com*), Google Finance (*www.google.ca/finance*), and Globe Investor (*www.globeinvestor.com*) are just a couple of Internet sites that can be used to monitor personal investments.

Manufacturing Management Information Systems

Without question, advances in information systems have revolutionized manufacturing. As a result, many manufacturing operations have been dramatically improved over the last decade. The use of computerized systems is emphasized at all levels of manufacturing—from the shop floor to the executive suite. Dell Computer has used both optimization and heuristic software to help it manufacture a larger variety of products.[28] Dell was able to double its product variety, while saving about $1 million annually in manufacturing costs. Figure 10.9 gives an overview of some of the manufacturing MIS inputs, subsystems, and outputs.

Figure 10.9

Overview of a Manufacturing MIS

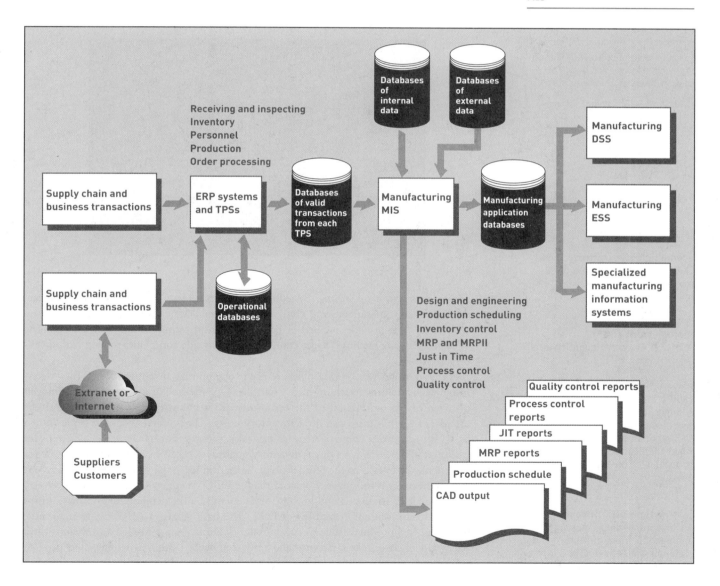

The manufacturing MIS subsystems and outputs are used to monitor and control the flow of materials, products, and services through the organization. As raw materials are converted to finished goods, the manufacturing MIS monitors the process at almost every stage. New technology could make this process easier. Using specialized computer chips and tiny radio transmitters, companies can monitor materials and products through the entire manufacturing process. Procter & Gamble and Walmart have funded research into this manufacturing MIS. According to a survey of manufacturing companies, increased efficiency, lower costs, and new products and services are important manufacturing MIS features that can increase profitability and success.[29]

The success of an organization can depend on the manufacturing function. Some common information subsystems and outputs used in manufacturing are provided in the following list:

- *Design and engineering.* Manufacturing companies often use computer-aided design (CAD) with new or existing products.[30] For example, Boeing (*www.boeing.ca*) uses a CAD system to develop a complete digital blueprint of an aircraft before it begins the manufacturing process. As mock-ups are built and tested, the digital blueprint is constantly revised to reflect the most current design. Using such technology helps Boeing reduce manufacturing costs and the time to design a new aircraft.

Computer-aided design (CAD) is used in the development and design of complex products or structures.

(Source: © Dennis Hallinan/Alamy Images.)

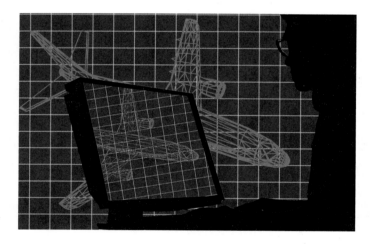

economic order quantity (EOQ)
The quantity that should be reordered to minimize total inventory costs.

reorder point (ROP)
A critical inventory quantity level.

material requirements planning (MRP)
A set of inventory-control techniques that help coordinate thousands of inventory items when the demand of one item is dependent on the demand for another.

just-in-time (JIT) inventory
An inventory management approach in which inventory and materials are delivered just before they are used in manufacturing a product.

- *Master production scheduling.* Scheduling production and controlling inventory are critical for any manufacturing company. The overall objective of master production scheduling is to provide detailed plans for both short-term and long-range scheduling of manufacturing facilities. Some companies hire outside companies to help with inventory control.
- *Inventory control.* Most techniques are used to minimize inventory costs. They determine when and how much inventory to order. One method of determining the amount of inventory to order is called the **economic order quantity** (**EOQ**). This quantity is calculated to minimize the total inventory costs. The "When to order?" question is based on inventory usage over time. Typically, the question is answered by a **reorder point** (**ROP**), which is a critical inventory quantity level. When the inventory level for a particular item falls to the reorder point, or critical level, the system generates a report so that an order is immediately placed for the EOQ of the product. Another inventory technique used when demand for one item depends on the demand for another is called **material requirements planning** (**MRP**). The basic goals of MRP are to determine when finished products, such as automobiles or airplanes, are needed and then to work backward to determine deadlines and resources needed, such as engines and tires, to complete the final product on schedule. **Just-in-time** (**JIT**) **inventory** and manufacturing is an approach that maintains inventory at the lowest levels without sacrificing

the availability of finished products. With this approach, inventory and materials are delivered just before they are used in a product. Many drug manufacturing companies use JIT to produce flu vaccinations just before they are needed for the flu season to make sure the vaccinations are freshest and the most effective.[31] JIT, however, can result in some organizations running out of inventory when demand exceeds expectations or there are problems with the manufacturing process.

- *Process control.* Managers can use a number of technologies to control and streamline the manufacturing process. For example, computers can directly control manufacturing equipment, using systems called **computer-assisted manufacturing** (**CAM**).[32] CAM systems can control drilling machines, assembly lines, and more. **Computer-integrated manufacturing** (**CIM**) uses computers to link the components of the production process into an effective system. CIM's goal is to tie together all aspects of production, including order processing, product design, manufacturing, inspection and quality control, and shipping. A **flexible manufacturing system** (**FMS**) is an approach that allows manufacturing facilities to rapidly and efficiently change from making one product to another. In the middle of a production run, for example, the production process can be changed to make a different product or to switch manufacturing materials. By using an FMS, the time and cost to change manufacturing jobs can be substantially reduced and companies can react quickly to market needs and competition. For example, Chrysler used an FMS to quickly change from manufacturing diesel minivans with right-hand drive to gasoline minivans with left-hand drive.[33]

computer-assisted manufacturing (CAM)
A system that directly controls manufacturing equipment.

computer-integrated manufacturing (CIM)
Using computers to link the components of the production process into an effective system.

flexible manufacturing system (FMS)
An approach that allows manufacturing facilities to rapidly and efficiently change from making one product to making another.

Computer-assisted manufacturing systems control complex processes on the assembly line and provide users with instant access to information.

(Source: © Phototake/Alamy Images.)

- *Quality control and testing.* With increased pressure from consumers and a general concern for productivity and high quality, today's manufacturing organizations are placing more emphasis on **quality control**, a process that ensures that the finished product meets the customers' needs. Information systems are used to monitor quality and take corrective steps to eliminate possible quality problems.

quality control
A process that ensures that the finished product meets the customers' needs.

Marketing Management Information Systems

A **marketing MIS** supports managerial activities in product development, distribution, pricing decisions, promotional effectiveness, and sales forecasting.[34] Marketing functions are increasingly being performed on the Internet. Some companies make gifts to people who write reviews on blogs or the Internet, which can result in favourable, biased reviews.[35] Companies such as Salesforce (*www.salesforce.com*) offer a range of applications over the Internet, including customer relationship management (CRM), and many other programs that help a company's marketing efforts.[36] Salesforce generates about $1 billion in revenues annually. Newer marketing

marketing MIS
An information system that supports managerial activities in product development, distribution, pricing decisions, promotional effectiveness, and sales forecasting.

companies, such as Tagga Media. (*www.tagga.com*), are placing ads on cell phones and mobile devices with Internet access. Cara Foods, which owns restaurant chains such as Swiss Chalet, Harvey's, Milestones, redesigned its mobile marketing strategy to give each Cara brand a unique feel. The change resulted in a 175 percent higher click-through rate on mobile websites, and customers who visited one Cara restaurant tended to try other Cara restaurants as well.[37] One marketing research firm estimates that some companies spend millions of dollars annually on social networking Internet sites to promote their products and services online.[38]

Some marketing departments are actively using the Internet to advertise their products and services and keep customers happy using services such as Facebook (*www.facebook.com*). YouTube (*www.youtube.com*), the video-sharing Internet site, sells video ads on its site to companies, including Ford and BMW. After about 10 seconds, the video ad disappears unless the user clicks it. Corporate marketing departments also use social networking sites, such as Second Life (*www.secondlife.com*), to advertise their products and perform marketing research. Porter Airlines (*www.flyporter.com*), Canada's third-largest airline, uses blogs and Twitter to listen to customers and improve customer service. Porter staff at head office scan Twitter looking for references to the airline. In one instance, a customer who was dissatisfied with waiting in line tweeted her dissatisfaction from her smartphone. By the time the customer had reached the ticket counter, local Porter staff were ready for her and directly addressed her complaint.[39] According to an Internet consultant, "Twitter is a digital handshake. It's one of the fastest ways you can reach out to people." Figure 10.10 shows the inputs, subsystems, and outputs of a typical marketing MIS.

Subsystems for the marketing MIS include marketing research, product development, promotion and advertising, and product pricing. These subsystems and their outputs help marketing managers and executives increase sales, reduce marketing expenses, and develop plans for future products and services to meet the changing needs of customers.

Figure 10.10

Overview of a Marketing MIS

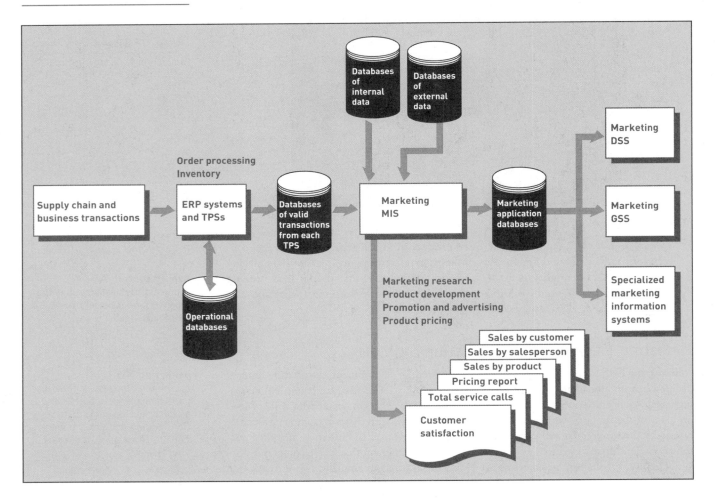

- *Marketing research*. The purpose of marketing research is to conduct a formal study of the market and customer preferences. Computer systems are used to help conduct and analyze the results of surveys, questionnaires, pilot studies, and interviews. BMW, the German luxury car maker, performs marketing research using search engines to determine customer preferences and to target ads to people who might want to buy one of its cars.[40] Hyundai Motors asked a group of men and women to look at certain parts of a new Hyundai car while wearing head caps with wires attached to their skulls to try to determine customer preferences.[41] According to one company executive, "We want to know what consumers think about a car before we start manufacturing thousands of them." In addition to knowing what you buy, marketing research can determine where you buy.

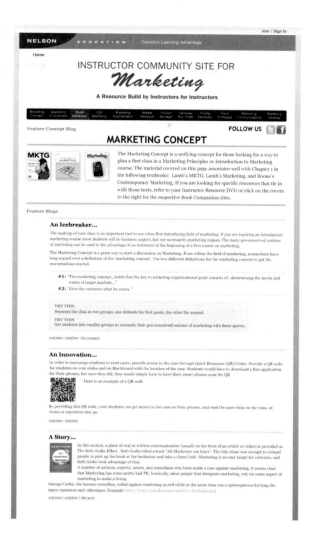

Corporate marketing departments use social networking sites, such as Second Life (*www.secondlife.com*), to advertise their products and perform marketing research.

(Source: Courtesy of Nelson Education Ltd.)

This can help in developing new products and services and tailoring ads and promotions. With the use of GPS, marketing firms can promote products to phones and other mobile devices by knowing your location. Internet sites such as Loopt (*www.loopt.com*), BrightKite (*www.brightkite.com*), and Latitude by Google (*www.google.com/latitude/intro.html*) allow you to locate people, stores, restaurants, and other businesses and landmarks that are close to you.[42] Using GPS and location analysis from cell phone towers, advertisers will be able to promote products and services in stores and shops that are close to people with cell phones.[43] In other words, you could receive

Marketing research data yields valuable information for the development and marketing of new products.

(Source: © Michael Newman/ PhotoEdit.)

ads on your cell phone for a burger restaurant as you walk or drive close to it. Other marketing research companies, such as Betawave (*www.betawave.com*), are performing marketing research on customer engagement and attentiveness in responding to ads.[44] If successful, this marketing research might result in advertisers charging more for higher levels of customer engagement and attentiveness, instead of charging for the number of viewers of a particular advertisement.

- *Product development.* Product development involves the conversion of raw materials into finished goods and services and focuses primarily on the various attributes of the product and its supply chain. Sysco Canada, a food distribution company, uses software and databases to prepare and ship over 20 million tons of meat, produce, and other food items to restaurants and other outlets every year.[45] The huge company supplies one out of three cafeterias, sports stadiums, restaurants, and other food outlets. Many factors, including plant capacity, labour skills, engineering issues, and materials are important in product development decisions. In many cases, a computer program analyzes these various factors and selects the appropriate mix of labour, materials, plant and equipment, and engineering designs. Make-or-buy decisions can also be made with the assistance of computer programs.

- *Promotion and advertising.* One of the most important functions of any marketing effort is promotion and advertising. Product success is a direct function of the types of advertising and sales promotion done. Increasingly, organizations are using the Internet to advertise and sell products and services. Johnson & Johnson used Internet cartoons instead of extensive TV advertising to promote a popular baby lotion. The goal is to target ads to a specific group of people who are likely to purchase the advertised goods and services. Today, about $2.0 billion is spent annually on local TV ads, about $2.0 billion on newspapers ads, and about $1.9 billion on Internet ads.[46] Companies are also trying to measure the effectiveness of different advertising approaches, such as TV and Internet advertising. Several companies, including ScanScout (*www.scanscout.com*), are trying to match video content on the Internet with specific ads that cater to those watching the videos.[47] Cell phones are also becoming very popular advertising outlets.[48] Burger King, Lions Gate Entertainment, and other companies are now promoting their products on games and other applications for Apple's iPhone and other devices.[49] In some cases, the advertising is hidden within free gaming applications. When you download and start playing the game, the advertising pops up on the phone. Other companies, like Honda Motors and Marriott International, are placing ads on mobile search engines available on phones and other mobile devices.[50] Increased use of the Internet to place advertisements, however, has made some computers and mobile devices vulnerable to virus attacks.[51]

Cell phones are becoming increasingly popular advertising outlets.

(Source: PRNewsFoto/State Farm Insurance Companies.)

- *Product pricing.* Product pricing is another important and complex marketing function. Retail price, wholesale price, and price discounts must be set. Most companies try to develop pricing policies that will maximize total sales revenues. Computers are often used to analyze the relationship between prices and total revenues. Traditionally, executives used costs to determine prices. They simply added a profit margin to total costs to guarantee a decent profit. Today, however, more executives look at the marketplace to determine product pricing.

- *Sales analysis.* Computerized sales analysis is important to identify products, sales personnel, and customers that contribute to profits and those that do not. This analysis can be done for sales and ads that help generate sales. According to Ford's marketing chief, "It's almost like we're getting price guarantees on how well our ad is doing, and that's close to the Holy Grail for me." IBM used the OnTarget sales analysis tool to identify new sales opportunities with existing customers.[52] The sales analysis tool helps IBM assign sales personnel to sales opportunities to improve both sales and profitability. Several reports can be generated to help marketing managers make good sales decisions; see Figure 10.11. The sales-by-product report lists all major products and their sales for a specified period of time. This report shows which products are doing well and which need improvement or should be discarded altogether. The sales-by-salesperson report lists total sales for each salesperson for each week or month. This report can also be subdivided by product to show which products are being sold by each salesperson. The sales-by-customer report is a tool that can be used to identify high- and low-volume customers.

(a) Sales by Product

Product	August	September	October	November	December	Total
Product 1	34	32	32	21	33	152
Product 2	156	162	177	163	122	780
Product 3	202	145	122	98	66	633
Product 4	345	365	352	341	288	1,691

(b) Sales by Salesperson

Salesperson	August	September	October	November	December	Total
Jones	24	42	42	11	43	162
Kline	166	155	156	122	133	732
Lane	166	155	104	99	106	630
Miller	245	225	305	291	301	1,367

(c) Sales by Customer

Customer	August	September	October	November	December	Total
Ang	234	334	432	411	301	1,712
Braswell	56	62	77	61	21	277
Celec	1,202	1,445	1,322	998	667	5,634
Jung	45	65	55	34	88	287

Figure 10.11

Reports Generated to Help Marketing Managers Make Good Decisions

(a) This sales-by-product report lists all major products and their sales for the period from August to December. (b) This sales-by-salesperson report lists total sales for each salesperson for the same time period. (c) This sales-by-customer report lists sales for each customer for the period. Like all MIS reports, totals are provided automatically by the system to show managers at a glance the information they need to make good decisions.

Human Resource Management Information Systems

A **human resource MIS (HRMIS)**, also called the *personnel MIS*, is concerned with activities related to previous, current, and potential employees of the organization. The HRMIS is being used more and more to oversee and manage part-time, virtual work teams, and job sharing in additional to traditional job titles and duties.[53] Because the personnel function relates to all other functional areas in the business, the HRMIS plays a valuable role in ensuring organizational success. Some of the activities performed by this important MIS include workforce analysis and planning, hiring, training, job and task assignment, and many other personnel-related issues. An effective HRMIS allows a company to keep personnel costs at a minimum, while serving the required business processes needed to achieve corporate goals. Although human resource information systems focus on cost reduction, many of today's HR systems concentrate on hiring and managing existing employees to get the total potential of the human talent in the organization. Figure 10.12 (on the next page) shows some of the inputs, subsystems, and outputs of the human resource MIS.

Human resource subsystems and outputs range from the determination of human resource needs and hiring through retirement and outplacement. Most medium and large organizations have computer systems to assist with human resource planning, hiring,

human resource MIS (HRMIS)
An information system that is concerned with activities related to previous, current, and potential employees of an organization, also called a personnel MIS.

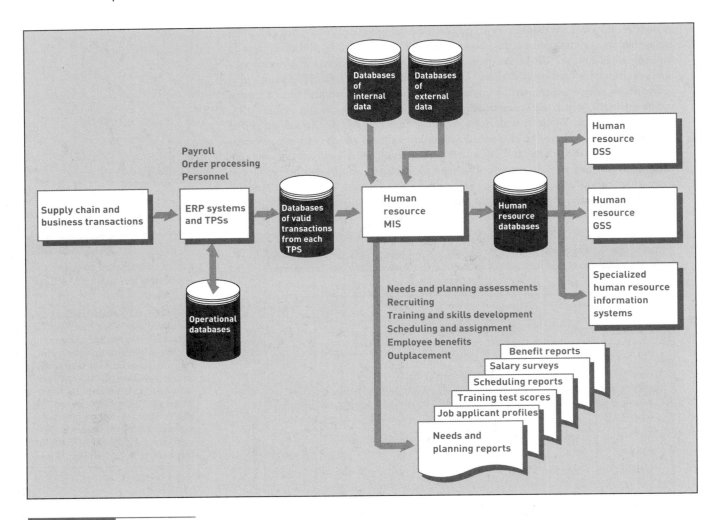

Figure 10.12

Overview of a Human Resource MIS

training and skills inventorying, and wage and salary administration. Outputs of the HR MIS include reports, such as human resource planning reports, job application review profiles, skills inventory reports, and salary surveys. Most human resource departments start with planning, discussed next.

Human resource MIS subsystems help to determine personnel needs and match employees to jobs.

(Source: Image Source/Getty Images.)

- *Human resource planning.* One of the first aspects of any human resource MIS is determining personnel and human needs. The overall purpose of this MIS subsystem is to put the right number and type of employees in the right jobs when they are needed, including internal employees who work exclusively for the organization and outside workers who are hired when they are needed. Some experts believe that workers should be managed like a supply chain, using supply chain management (SCM) and just-in-time techniques.

- *Personnel selection and recruiting.* If the human resource plan reveals that additional personnel are required, the next logical step is recruiting and selecting personnel. Companies seeking new employees often use computers to schedule recruiting efforts and to test potential employees' skills. Many companies now use the Internet to screen for job applicants. Applicants use a template to load their résumés onto the Internet site. HR managers can then access these résumés and identify applicants they are interested in interviewing.

- *Training and skills inventory.* Some jobs, such as programming, equipment repair, and tax preparation, require very specific training for new employees. Other jobs may require general training about the organizational culture, orientation, dress standards, and expectations of the organization. When training is complete, employees often take computer-scored tests to evaluate their mastery of skills and new material.

- *Scheduling and job placement.* Employee schedules are developed for each employee, showing job assignments over the next week or month. Job placements are often determined based on skills inventory reports showing which employee might be best suited to a particular job. Sophisticated scheduling programs are often used in the airline industry, the military, and many other areas to get the right people assigned to the right jobs at the right time.

- *Wage and salary administration.* Another human resource MIS subsystem involves determining wages, salaries, and benefits, including medical benefits and pension plans. Wage data, such as industry averages for positions, can be taken from the corporate database and manipulated by the human resource MIS to provide wage information and reports to higher levels of management.

- *Outplacement.* Employees leave a company for a variety of reasons. Outplacement services are offered by many companies to help employees make the transition. *Outplacement* can include job counselling and training, job and executive search, retirement and financial planning, and a variety of severance packages and options. Many employees use the Internet to plan their future retirement or to find new jobs, using job sites such as *www.monster.ca.*

Other Management Information Systems

In addition to finance, manufacturing, marketing, and human resource MISs, some companies have other functional management information systems. For example, most successful companies have well-developed accounting functions and a supporting accounting MIS. Also, many companies use geographic information systems for presenting data in a useful form.

Accounting MISs

In some cases, accounting works closely with financial management. An **accounting MIS** performs a number of important activities, providing aggregate information on accounts payable, accounts receivable, payroll, and many other applications. The organization's enterprise resource planning and transaction processing system captures accounting data, which is also used by most other functional information systems.

accounting MIS
An information system that provides aggregate information on accounts payable, accounts receivable, payroll, and many other applications.

Some smaller companies hire outside accounting firms to assist them with their accounting functions. These outside companies produce reports for the firm using raw accounting data. In addition, many excellent integrated accounting programs are available for personal computers in small companies. Depending on the needs of the small organization and its staff's computer experience, using these computerized accounting systems can be a very cost-effective approach to managing information.

geographic information system (GIS)
A computer system capable of assembling, storing, manipulating, and displaying geographic information, that is, data identified according to its location.

Geographic Information Systems

Increasingly, managers want to see data presented in graphical form. A **geographic information system** (**GIS**) is a computer system capable of assembling, storing, manipulating, and displaying geographically referenced information; that is, data identified according to its location. Google, for example, has developed a GIS that combines geothermal information with its mapping applications to help identify carbon emissions.[54] Another Google GIS has been developed to map flu trends around the world by tracking flu inquiries on its website. Rona, one of Canada's largest hardware and home renovation retailers, uses a GIS system to profile customer sales and optimize its marketing and distribution strategies. The system also provides suppliers and distributors with better customer information.[55] It is possible to use GIS to analyze customer preferences and shopping patterns in various locations using GPS and location analysis from cell phone towers.[56] In addition, a number of applications follow the location of people and places using GPS, including Loopt (*www.loopt.com*), Where (*www.where.com*), and Google Latitude.[57] Some people are concerned about privacy concerns with these GPS applications.[58]

Google Latitude tracks the physical location of people who give their permission to be tracked.

(Source: Google.)

We saw earlier in this chapter that management information systems (MISs) provide useful summary reports to help solve structured and semistructured business problems. Decision support systems (DSSs) offer the potential to assist in solving both semistructured and unstructured problems. These systems are discussed next.

AN OVERVIEW OF DECISION SUPPORT SYSTEMS

A decision support system (DSS) is an organized collection of people, procedures, software, databases, and devices used to help make decisions that solve problems. The focus of a DSS is on decision-making effectiveness when faced with unstructured or semistructured business problems. Decision support systems offer the potential to generate higher profits, lower costs, and better products and services. Decision support systems, although skewed somewhat toward the top levels of management, can be used at all levels. The Royal Bank of Canada avoided $15 million in credit fraud losses by using a DSS.[59] Indigo Books and Music uses a DSS to identify its high-value customers and predict when and what type of products its customers will purchase based on past purchases.[60] DSSs are also used in government, law enforcement, and nonprofit organizations. See Figure 10.13.

Characteristics of a Decision Support System

Decision support systems have many characteristics that allow them to be effective management support tools. Of course, not all DSSs work the same. The following list shows some important characteristics of a DSS.

- Provide rapid access to information.
- Handle large amounts of data from different sources.
- Provide report and presentation flexibility.
- Offer both textual and graphical orientation.
- Support drill-down analysis.
- Perform complex, sophisticated analyses and comparisons using advanced software packages.
- Support optimization, satisficing, and heuristic approaches. See Figure 10.14.
- Perform simulation analysis—the ability of the DSS to duplicate the features of a real system, where probability or uncertainty is involved.

Figure 10.13

Decision support systems are used by health-care professionals in many settings.

(Source: Konstantin Sutyagin/ iStockphoto.com.)

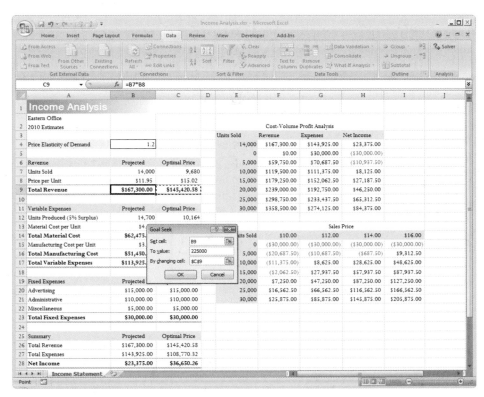

Figure 10.14

With a spreadsheet program, a manager can enter a goal and the spreadsheet will determine the input needed to achieve the goal.

Amenities Inc. Gets a Grip on Pachinko Information

Just as Las Vegas has its casinos and slot machines, Japan has pachinko parlours and pachinko machines. Pachinko is a game played on vertical boards where small metal balls are flung to the top and cascade down through numerous metal pins. If a ball happens to land in one of the cups, points are scored and more balls are released. Winning scores collect prizes.

Amenities Inc. owns 16 pachinko parlours in Japan, as well as cinemas, karaoke booths, bowling alleys, and restaurants. In 2005, Amenities became the first in the pachinko industry to adopt an ERP system to manage its data and provide useful information for business decision making. In 2008, Amenities installed a business intelligence platform to further benefit from the information it gathered about its businesses and customers. More recently, Amenities began a quest to organize and display information in a manner that better supports strategic decision making.

Until recently, Amenities used a decision-making process referred to as the plan-do-check-act (PDCA) approach. This is a model based on the scientific method that begins with a hypothesis (plan), tested by an experiment (do), followed by an examination of results (check), and adjustments applied based on observations (act), which cycles back to the planning stage. Amenities realized that the PDCA approach was not ideal for the strategic decisions it needed to make in the pachinko industry. It thought that a more appropriate model was the observe, orient, decide, and act (OODA) approach. OODA is used by the military in combat operations and in business to gain advantages in tough competitive markets.

The OODA model is designed to defeat an adversary and survive. It depends on on-going observation and analysis of a situation. It requires an information system that can supply up-to-the minute information about the business, its competitors, and the environment in which it operates. Over the years, Amenities had built such an information system. Now it needed to focus on getting relevant data to its decision makers.

Amenities purchased three software packages intended to deliver the right information to the right people at the right time in the right format. SAP BusinessObjects Web Intelligence software is designed to allow decision makers to access business reports through a Web browser interface. SAP Business Objects Live Office software is designed to obtain and analyze data directly in Microsoft Excel and Word. Xcelsius software is designed to provide a dashboard that graphically displays key indicators. This was combined with Crystal Reports software that provides additional visual reporting tools.

Armed with this arsenal of MIS tools, Amenities CIO Kazuo Yoshida set out to deliver useful information to its decision makers. For corporate executives, a dashboard was designed that included three key indicator charts and meters: profits and losses, sales amounts, and customer amounts. The charts were integrated with the company's groupware, so that every time executives check e-mail or collaborate online, they get a quick glimpse of the company's current health. If the graphs indicate anything unusual, an executive can click the graph to drill down into more detailed information.

Lower-ranked business managers within Amenities have a similar dashboard showing key indicators that include bar graphs for sales, profits, and expenses with goals and current status listed side by side. The layout allows managers to easily see their current degree of success in achieving key indicators and corporate goals. Managers also have access to interactive forms that allow them to submit daily reports to headquarters.

Amenities' new information delivery system allows its decision makers to have up-to-the-minute corporate information. If a competitor launches a one-day promotion, managers can react before midday. Executives can quickly react to significant sales declines by launching ad-hoc promotional events. Unexpected sales increases allow executives to recognize new opportunities and quickly take advantage of them. With its ERP system, business intelligence system, and reporting tools in place, Amenities will continue to refine the manner in which it delivers valuable information to individuals who are able to act upon it and improve its position in the market.

Discussion Questions

1. What information system components did Amenities use to get the right information to the right people at the right time in the right format?
2. Why did Amenities decide to combine its dashboard charts and meters with its groupware?

Critical Thinking Questions

1. What advantages did Amenities think it could gain by adopting an OODA approach to decision making?
2. How might real-time and continuous access to key indicator data influence a business' decision making?

SOURCES: "Amenities—Sap Software Optimizes Decision Making and Information Quality," SAP Success Stories, www.sap.com/solutions/sapbusinessobjects/sme/reporting-dashboarding/customers/index.epx, accessed March 23, 2010.

Capabilities of a Decision Support System

Developers of decision support systems strive to make them more flexible than management information systems and to give them the potential to assist decision makers in a variety of situations. DSSs can assist with all or most problem-solving phases, decision frequencies, and varying degrees of problem structure. DSS approaches can also help at all levels of the decision-making process. A single DSS might provide only a few of these capabilities, depending on its uses and scope.

Support for Problem-Solving Phases

The objective of most decision support systems is to assist decision makers with the phases of problem solving. As previously discussed, these phases include intelligence, design, choice, implementation, and monitoring. A specific DSS might support only one or a few phases. By supporting all types of decision-making approaches, a DSS gives the decision maker a great deal of flexibility in getting computer support for decision-making activities.

Support for Various Decision Frequencies

Decisions can range on a continuum from one-of-a-kind to repetitive decisions. One-of-a-kind decisions are typically handled by an ad hoc DSS. An **ad hoc DSS** is concerned with situations or decisions that come up only a few times during the life of the organization; in small businesses, they might happen only once. For example, a company might need to decide whether to build a new manufacturing facility in another area of the country. Repetitive decisions are addressed by an institutional DSS. An **institutional DSS** handles situations or decisions that occur more than once, usually several times per year or more. An institutional DSS is used repeatedly and refined over the years. Examples of institutional DSSs include systems that support portfolio and investment decisions and production scheduling. These decisions might require decision support numerous times during the year. Between these two extremes are decisions that managers make several times, but not routinely.

Support for Various Problem Structures

As discussed previously, decisions can range from highly structured and programmed to unstructured and nonprogrammed. **Highly structured problems** are straightforward, requiring known facts and relationships. **Semistructured** or **unstructured problems**, on the other hand, are more complex. The relationships among the pieces of data are not always clear, the data might be in a variety of formats, and the data might be difficult to manipulate or obtain. In addition, the decision maker might not know the information requirements of the decision in advance.

Support for Various Decision-Making Levels

Decision support systems can provide help for managers at various levels within the organization. Operational managers can get assistance with daily and routine decision making. Tactical decision makers can use analysis tools to ensure proper planning and control. At the strategic level, DSSs can help managers by providing analysis for long-term decisions requiring both internal and external information. See Figure 10.15.

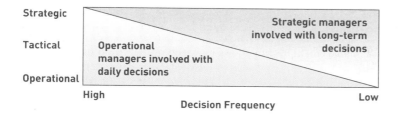

A Comparison of DSS and MIS

A DSS differs from an MIS in numerous ways, including the type of problems solved, the support given to users, the decision emphasis and approach, and the type, speed, output, and development of the system used. Table 10.1 (on the next page) lists brief descriptions of these differences.

ad hoc DSS
A DSS concerned with situations or decisions that come up only a few times during the life of the organization.

institutional DSS
A DSS that handles situations or decisions that occur more than once, usually several times per year or more. An institutional DSS is used repeatedly and refined over the years.

highly structured problems
Problems that are straightforward and require known facts and relationships.

semistructured or unstructured problems
More complex problems in which the relationships among the pieces of data are not always clear, the data might be in a variety of formats, and the data is often difficult to manipulate or obtain.

Figure 10.15

Decision-Making Level

Strategic managers are involved with long-term decisions, which are often made infrequently. Operational managers are involved with decisions that are made more frequently

Factor	DSS	MIS
Problem Type	Can handle unstructured problems that cannot be easily programmed.	Normally used only with structured problems.
Users	Supports individuals, small groups, and the entire organization. In the short run, users typically have more control over a DSS.	Supports primarily the organization. In the short run, users have less control over an MIS.
Support	Supports all aspects and phases of decision making; it does not replace the decision maker—people still make the decisions.	In some cases, makes automatic decisions and replace the decision maker.
Emphasis	Emphasizes actual decisions and decision-making styles.	Usually emphasizes information only.
Approach	Serves as a direct support system that provides interactive reports on computer screens.	Typically serves as an indirect support system that uses regularly produced reports.
System	Uses computer equipment that is usually online (directly connected to the computer system) and related to real time (providing immediate results). Computer terminals and display screens are examples—these devices can provide immediate information and answers to questions.	Uses printed reports that might be delivered to managers once per week, so it cannot provide immediate results.
Speed	Is flexible and can be implemented by users, so it usually takes less time to develop and is better able to respond to user requests.	Provides response time usually longer than a DSS.
Output	Produces reports that are usually screen oriented, with the ability to generate reports on a printer.	Is oriented toward printed reports and documents.
Development	Has users who are usually more directly involved in its development. User involvement usually means better systems that provide superior support. For all systems, user involvement is the most important factor for the development of a successful system.	Is frequently several years old and often was developed for people who may no longer be performing the work supported by the MIS.

Table 10.1

Comparison of DSSs and MISs

COMPONENTS OF A DECISION SUPPORT SYSTEM

dialogue manager
A user interface that allows decision makers to easily access and manipulate the DSS and to use common business terms and phrases.

At the core of a DSS are a database and a model base. In addition, a typical DSS contains a user interface, also called **dialogue manager**, which allows decision makers to easily access and manipulate the DSS and to use common business terms and phrases. Finally, access to the Internet, networks, and other computer-based systems permits the DSS to tie into other powerful systems, including the TPS or function-specific subsystems. Figure 10.16 shows a conceptual model of a DSS. Specific DSSs might not have all the components shown in Figure 10.16.

The Database

The database management system allows managers and decision makers to perform *qualitative analysis* on the company's vast stores of data in databases, data warehouses, and data marts, discussed in Chapter 5. A *data-driven DSS* primarily performs qualitative analysis based on the company's databases.[61] Data-driven DSSs tap into vast stores of information contained in the corporate database, retrieving information on inventory, sales, personnel, production, finance, accounting, and other areas. TD Securities used a pilot program from IBM called "stream computing" that allows the trading company to analyze 5 million pieces of data per second before the data is placed into corporate databases.[62] The data-driven DSS helps TD Securities sort through an immense amount of data and place profitable security trades automatically. According to a company executive,

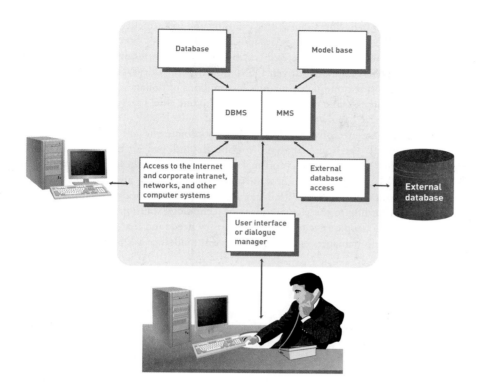

Figure 10.16

Conceptual Model of a DSS

DSS components include a model base; database; external database access; access to the Internet and corporate intranet, networks, and other computer systems; and a user interface or dialogue manager.

"In this business, quicker decisions are better decisions. If you fall behind, you're dealing with stale data and that puts you at a disadvantage." Exeros, which was acquired by IBM, provides technology and software to help companies sift through a mountain of data and return valuable information and decision support.[63] Data mining and business intelligence, introduced in Chapter 5, are often used in a data-driven DSS. Data-driven DSSs can also be used in emergency medical situations to make split-second, life-or-death treatment decisions. Data-driven medical DSSs allow doctors to access the complete medical records of a patient.[64]

A database management system can also connect to external databases to give managers and decision makers even more information and decision support. External databases can include the Internet, libraries, and government databases. Access to a combination of internal and external databases can give key decision makers a better understanding of the company and its environment. Travelocity.ca, for example, uses software to mash up, or tie together, information from airlines, hotels, car rental companies, and activities to build a travel itinerary. Other companies, including ING Direct and the Weather Network, use similar software packages to integrate data from different sources into data-driven DSSs.

The Model Base

The **model base** allows managers and decision makers to perform *quantitative analysis* on both internal and external data. A *model-driven DSS* primarily performs mathematical or quantitative analysis. Health Canada designed a DSS to assist in determining the effects of health-care trends.[65] Model-driven DSSs have been developed for submarine warfare, search and rescue missions, health-care information, and crop analysis. The model base gives decision makers access to a variety of models so that they can explore different scenarios and see their effects. Ultimately, it assists them in the decision-making process. Procter & Gamble, maker of Pringles potato chips, Pampers diapers, and hundreds of other consumer products, used a model-driven DSS to streamline how raw materials and products flow from suppliers to customers. The model-driven DSS has saved the company hundreds of millions of dollars in supply chain-related costs. Model-driven DSSs are excellent at

model base
Part of a DSS that provides decision makers access to a variety of models and assists them in decision making.

predicting customer behaviours. Some stock trading and investment firms use sophisticated model-driven DSSs to make trading decisions and huge profits. Some experts believe that a slight time advantage in computerized trading programs can result in millions of dollars of trading profits. Not all model-driven DSSs, however, provide superior results. In 2009, for example, many stock trading companies lost millions of dollars with models that didn't accurately predict stock market trends.[66] According to one chief investment officer of a large hedge fund, "We have been wrong more than usual."

model management software (MMS)
Software that coordinates the use of models in a DSS.

Model management software (**MMS**) can coordinate the use of models in a DSS, including financial, statistical analysis, graphical, and project-management models. Depending on the needs of the decision maker, one or more of these models can be used. See Table 10.2. What is important is how the mathematical models are used, not the number of models that an organization has available. In fact, too many model-based tools can be a disadvantage. According to the vice president of technology solutions at Allstate Insurance Company, "Usually people have more tools than they need, and that can be distracting."[67] MMS can often help managers effectively use several models in a DSS.

Model Type	Description	Software
Financial	Provides cash flow, internal rate of return, and other investment analysis	Spreadsheet, such as Microsoft Excel
Statistical	Provides summary statistics, trend projections, hypothesis testing, and more	Statistical programs, such as SPSS or SAS
Graphical	Assists decision makers in designing, developing, and using graphic displays of data and information	Graphics programs, such as Microsoft PowerPoint
Project Management	Handles and coordinates large projects; also used to identify critical activities and tasks that could delay or jeopardize an entire project if they are not completed in a timely and cost-effective fashion	Project management software, such as Microsoft Project

Table 10.2

Model Management Software

DSSs often use financial, statistical, graphical, and project-management models.

The User Interface or Dialogue Manager

The user interface or dialogue manager allows users to interact with the DSS to obtain information. It assists with all aspects of communications between the user and the hardware and software that constitute the DSS. In a practical sense, to most DSS users, the user interface is the DSS. Upper-level decision makers are often less interested in where the information came from or how it was gathered than that the information is both understandable and accessible.

GROUP SUPPORT SYSTEMS

The DSS approach has resulted in better decision making for all levels of individual users. However, many DSS approaches and techniques are not suitable for a group decision-making environment. A **group support system** (**GSS**), also called a *group decision support system* and a *computerized collaborative work system*, consists of most of the elements in a DSS, plus software to provide effective support in group decision-making settings. See Figure 10.17.

group support system (GSS)
Software application that consists of most elements in a DSS, plus software to provide effective support in group decision making; also called *group support system* or *computerized collaborative work system*.

Group support systems are used in most industries, governments, and the military. Kraft, for example, used iPhones and other mobile devices to help managers and workers stay connected and work together on important projects.[68] Collaboration using GSS can also save money. TransUnion, a large credit reporting company, reduced computer-related costs by about $2.5 million annually by investing $50,000 in a corporate social networking Internet site to improve collaboration.[69] According to the chief technology officer, "The savings mostly come out of teams that would have historically said 'Buy me more hardware' or 'I need a new software tool' who figured out how to solve their problems

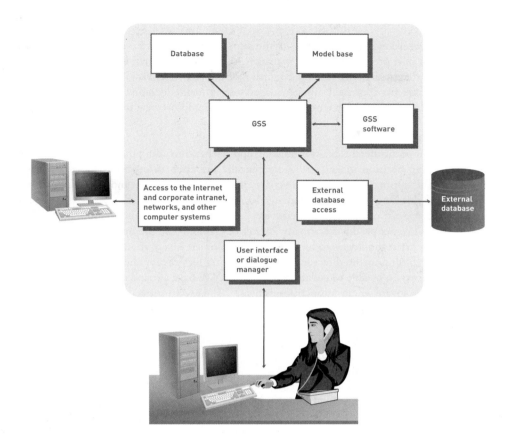

Figure 10.17

Configuration of a GSS

A GSS contains most of the elements found in a DSS, plus software to facilitate group member communications.

without asking for those things." Social networking Internet sites, such as Facebook and MySpace, can be used to support group decision making.[70] Many organizations have used Facebook or have developed their own social networking sites to help their employees collaborate on important projects. With Ning (*www.ning.com*), for example, companies and individuals can create their own social networking sites. Many companies are using Ning and similar social networking sites to stay in contact with their customers.[71] Some executives, however, believe that social networking Internet sites are a waste of time and corporate resources.

Characteristics of a GSS That Enhance Decision Making

It is often said that two heads are better than one. When it comes to decision making, a GSS's unique characteristics have the potential to result in better decisions. Developers of these systems try to build on the advantages of individual support systems while adding new approaches unique to group decision making. For example, some GSSs can allow the exchange of information and expertise among people without direct face-to-face interaction, although some face-to-face meeting time is usually beneficial. The following sections describe some characteristics that can improve and enhance decision making.

Special Design

The GSS approach acknowledges that special procedures, devices, and approaches are needed in group decision-making settings. These procedures must foster creative thinking, effective communications, and good group decision-making techniques.

Ease of Use

Like an individual DSS, a GSS must be easy to learn and use. Systems that are complex and hard to operate will seldom be used. Many groups have less tolerance than do individual decision makers for poorly developed systems.

Flexibility

Two or more decision makers working on the same problem might have different decision-making styles and preferences. Each manager makes decisions in a unique way, in part because of different experiences and cognitive styles. An effective GSS not only has to support the different approaches that managers use to make decisions, but also must find a means to integrate their different perspectives into a common view of the task at hand.

Decision-Making Support

A GSS can support different decision-making approaches, including the **delphi approach**, in which group decision makers are geographically dispersed throughout the country or the world. This approach encourages diversity among group members and fosters creativity and original thinking in decision making. In another approach, called **brainstorming**, members offer ideas "off the top of their heads," fostering creativity and free thinking. The $80-billion consumer products company Procter & Gamble used the Internet, videoconferencing, and other technologies to brainstorm and think creatively about new products and services.[72] According to the director of global business services for the company, "It is an absolute necessity to be able to collaborate every day. We have a mandate to brainstorm, to listen, and to innovate where competition is fierce." The **group consensus approach** forces members in the group to reach a unanimous decision. The Workplace Hazardous Materials Information System (WHMIS) was developed using a group consensus approach. With the **nominal group technique**, each decision maker can participate; this technique encourages feedback from individual group members, and the final decision is made by voting, similar to a system for electing public officials.

Anonymous Input

Many GSSs allow anonymous input, where the person giving the input is not known to other group members. For example, some organizations use a GSS to help rank the performance of managers. Anonymous input allows the group decision makers to concentrate on the merits of the input without considering who gave it. In other words, input given by a top-level manager is given the same consideration as input from employees or other members of the group. Some studies have shown that groups using anonymous input can make better decisions and have superior results compared with groups that do not use anonymous input.

Reduction of Negative Group Behaviour

One key characteristic of any GSS is the ability to suppress or eliminate group behaviour that is counterproductive or harmful to effective decision making. In some group settings, dominant individuals can take over the discussion, which can prevent other members of the group from participating. In other cases, one or two group members can sidetrack or subvert the group into areas that are nonproductive and do not help solve the problem at hand. Other times, members of a group might assume they have made the right decision without examining alternatives—a phenomenon called *groupthink*. If group sessions are poorly planned and executed, the result can be a tremendous waste of time. Today, many GSS designers are developing software and hardware systems to reduce these types of problems. Procedures for effectively planning and managing group meetings can be incorporated into the GSS approach. A trained meeting facilitator is often employed to help lead the group decision-making process and to avoid groupthink. See Figure 10.18.

Parallel and Unified Communication

With traditional group meetings, people must take turns addressing various issues. One person normally talks at a time. With a GSS, every group member can address issues or make comments at the same time by entering them into a PC or workstation. These comments and issues are displayed on every group member's PC or workstation immediately. *Parallel communication* can speed meeting times and result in better decisions. Organizations are using unified communications to support group decision making. *Unified communications* ties together and integrates various communications systems, including traditional

delphi approach
A decision-making approach in which group decision makers are geographically dispersed; this approach encourages diversity among group members and fosters creativity and original thinking in decision making.

brainstorming
A decision-making approach that consists of members offering ideas "off the top of their heads."

group consensus approach
A decision-making approach that forces members in the group to reach a unanimous decision.

nominal group technique
A decision-making approach that encourages feedback from individual group members, and the final decision is made by voting, similar to the way public officials are elected.

Figure 10.18

Using the GSS Approach

A trained meeting facilitator can help lead the group decision-making process and avoid groupthink.

(Source: © Mlenny Photography/ iStockphoto.com.)

phones, cell phones, e-mail, text messages, and the Internet. With unified communications, members of a group decision-making team use a wide range of communications methods to help them collaborate and make better decisions.

Automated Recordkeeping

Most GSSs can keep detailed records of a meeting automatically. Each comment that is entered into a group member's PC or workstation can be anonymously recorded. In some cases, literally hundreds of comments can be stored for future review and analysis. In addition, most GSS packages have automatic voting and ranking features. After group members vote, the GSS records each vote and makes the appropriate rankings.

GSS Software

GSS software, often called *groupware* or *workgroup software*, helps with joint work group scheduling, communication, and management. Software from Autodesk, for example, has GSS capabilities that allow group members to work together on the design of manufacturing facilities, buildings, and other structures. Designers, for example, can use Autodesk's Buzzsaw Professional Online Collaboration Service, which works with AutoCAD, a design and engineering software product from Autodesk.

One popular package, IBM's Lotus Notes, can capture, store, manipulate, and distribute memos and communications that are developed during group projects. It can also incorporate knowledge management, discussed in Chapter 5, into the Lotus Notes Package. Some companies standardize on messaging and collaboration software, such as Lotus Notes. Lotus Connections (*www-01.ibm.com/software/lotus/products/connections/features.html*) is a feature of Lotus Notes that allows people to post documents and information on the Internet. The feature is similar to popular social networking sites such as Facebook, LinkedIn, and MySpace, but is designed for business use. Microsoft has invested billions of dollars in GSS software to incorporate collaborative features into its Office suite and related products. Office Communicator (*www.microsoft. com/unifiedcommunications*), for example, is a Microsoft product developed to allow better and faster collaboration. Other GSS software packages include Collabnet, OpenMind, and Team-Ware. All these tools can aid in group decision making. *Shared electronic calendars* can be used to coordinate meetings and schedules for decision-making teams. Using electronic calendars, team leaders can block out time for all members of the decision-making team.

A number of additional collaborative tools are available on the Internet. Sharepoint (*www.microsoft.com*), WebOffice (*www.weboffice.com*), and BaseCamp (*www.basecamphq. com*) are just a few examples. Fuze Meeting (*www.fuzemeeting.com*) provides video collaboration tools on the Internet.[73] The service can automatically bring participants into a live chat, allow workers to share information on their computer screens, and broadcast video content in high definition. Twitter (*www.twitter.com*) and Jaiku (*www.jaiku.com*) are Internet sites that some organizations use to help people and groups stay connected and coordinate work schedules. Yammer (*www.yammer.com*) is an Internet site that helps companies provide short answers to frequently asked questions. Managers and employees must first log into their private company network on Yammer to get their questions answered. Sermo (*www.sermo.com*) is a social networking site used by doctors to collaborate with other doctors, share their medical experiences, and even help make diagnoses. Teamspace (*www.teamspace.com*) is yet another collaborative software package that assists teams to successfully complete projects. Many of these Internet packages embrace the use of Web 2.0 technologies. Some executives, however, worry about security and corporate compliance issues with any new technology.

In addition to stand-alone products, GSS software is increasingly being incorporated into existing software packages. Today, some transaction processing and enterprise resource planning packages include collaboration software. Some ERP producers (see Chapter 9), for example, have developed groupware to facilitate collaboration and to allow users to integrate applications from other vendors into the ERP system of programs. In addition to groupware, GSSs use a number of tools discussed previously, including the following:

- E-mail, instant messaging (IM), and text messaging (TM)
- Videoconferencing
- Group scheduling
- Project management
- Document sharing

GSS Alternatives

Group support systems can take on a number of network configurations, depending on the needs of the group, the decision to be supported, and the geographic location of group members. GSS alternatives include a combination of decision rooms, local area networks, teleconferencing, and wide area networks.

decision room
A room that supports decision making, with the decision makers in the same building, combining face-to-face verbal interaction with technology to make the meeting more effective and efficient.

- The **decision room** is a room that supports decision making, with the decision makers in the same building, combining face-to-face verbal interaction with technology to make the meeting more effective and efficient. It is ideal for situations in which decision makers are located in the same building or geographic area and the decision makers are occasional users of the GSS approach. Hewlett-Packard, for example, has developed the Halo system (*www.hp.com/halo/introducing.html*), which uses identical rooms containing a number of high-resolution screens and other devices to facilitate group decision making.[74] In some cases, the decision room might have a few computers and a projector for presentations. In other cases, the decision room can be fully equipped with a network of computers and sophisticated GSS software. A typical decision room is shown in Figure 10.19.

Figure 10.19

The GSS Decision Room

For group members who are in the same location, the decision room is an optimal GSS alternative. This approach can use both face-to-face and computer-mediated communication. By using networked computers and computer devices, such as project screens and printers, the meeting leader can pose questions to the group, instantly collect their feedback, and, with the help of the governing software loaded on the control station, process this feedback into meaningful information to aid in the decision-making process.

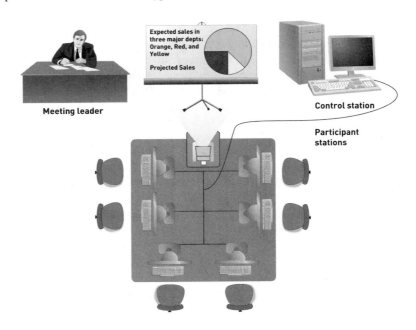

- The *local area decision network* can be used when group members are located in the same building or geographic area and under conditions in which group decision making is frequent. In these cases, the technology and equipment for the GSS approach is placed directly into the offices of the group members.
- *Teleconferencing* is used when the decision frequency is low and the location of group members is distant. These distant and occasional group meetings can tie together many GSS decision-making rooms across the country or around the world.
- The *wide area decision network* is used when the decision frequency is high and the location of group members is distant. In this case, the decision makers require frequent or constant use of the GSS approach. This GSS alternative allows people to work in **virtual workgroups**, where teams of people located around the world can work on common problems.

virtual workgroups
Teams of people located around the world working on common problems.

EXECUTIVE SUPPORT SYSTEMS

Because top-level executives often require specialized support when making strategic decisions, many companies have developed systems to assist executive decision making. This type of system, called an **executive support system** (**ESS**), is a specialized DSS that includes all the hardware, software, data, procedures, and people used to assist senior-level executives within the organization. In some cases, an ESS, also called an *executive information system* (*EIS*), supports decision making of members of the board of directors, who are responsible to stockholders. These top-level decision-making strata are shown in Figure 10.20. Canada Post developed an ESS to transform the company from an information-rich environment to a knowledge-rich environment. The comprehensive and integrated ESS supported Canada Post's strategic priorities. According to Cal Hart, VP Business Transformation, the ESS was what "we need[ed] to make business transformation a success and realize our goals."[75] Nova Chemicals uses an ESS to monitor plant performance. The real-time access to information has led to higher productivity and asset utilization, and quicker identification of business opportunities, resulting in higher profits.[76]

executive support system (ESS)
Specialized DSS that includes all hardware, software, data, procedures, and people used to assist senior-level executives within the organization.

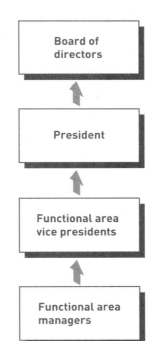

Figure 10.20

The Layers of Executive Decision Making

An ESS can also be used by individuals at middle levels in the organizational structure. Once targeted at the top-level executive decision makers, ESSs are now marketed to and used by employees at other levels in the organization.

Executive Support Systems in Perspective

An ESS is a special type of DSS, and, like a DSS, is designed to support higher-level decision making in the organization. The two systems are, however, different in important ways. DSSs provide a variety of modelling and analysis tools to enable users to thoroughly analyze problems—that is, they allow users to *answer* questions. ESSs present structured information about aspects of the organization that executives consider important. The characteristics of an ESS are summarized in the following list:

- Are tailored to individual executives
- Are easy to use
- Have drill-down abilities
- Support the need for external data
- Can help with situations that have a high degree of uncertainty
- Have a future orientation
- Are linked with value-added business processes

Capabilities of Executive Support Systems

The responsibility given to top-level executives and decision makers brings unique problems and pressures to their jobs. This section discusses some of the characteristics of executive decision making that are supported through the ESS approach. ESSs take full advantage of data mining, the Internet, blogs, podcasts, executive dashboards, social networking sites, and many other technological innovations. As you will note, most of these decisions are related to an organization's overall profitability and direction. An effective ESS should have the capability to support executive decisions with components such as strategic planning and organizing, crisis management, and more.

Support for Defining an Overall Vision

One of the key roles of senior executives is to provide a broad vision for the entire organization. This vision includes the organization's major product lines and services, the types of businesses it supports today and in the future, and its overriding goals.

Support for Strategic Planning

strategic planning
Determining long-term objectives by analyzing the strengths and weaknesses of the organization, predicting future trends, and projecting the development of new product lines.

ESSs also support strategic planning. **Strategic planning** involves determining long-term objectives by analyzing the strengths and weaknesses of the organization, predicting future trends, and projecting the development of new product lines. It also involves planning the acquisition of new equipment, analyzing merger possibilities, and making difficult decisions concerning downsizing and the sale of assets if required by unfavourable economic conditions.

Support for Strategic Organizing and Staffing

Top-level executives are concerned with organizational structure. For example, decisions concerning the creation of new departments or downsizing the labour force are made by top-level managers. Overall direction for staffing decisions and effective communication with labour unions are also major decision areas for top-level executives. ESSs can help executives analyze the impact of staffing decisions, potential pay raises, changes in employee benefits, and new work rules.

Support for Strategic Control

Another type of executive decision relates to strategic control, which involves monitoring and managing the overall operation of the organization. Goal seeking can be done for each major area to determine what performance these areas need to achieve to reach corporate expectations. Effective ESS approaches can help top-level managers make the most of their existing resources and control all aspects of the organization.

Support for Crisis Management

Even with careful strategic planning, a crisis can occur. Major incidents, including natural disasters, fires, and terrorist activities, can totally shut down major parts of the organization. Handling these emergencies is another responsibility for top-level executives. In many cases, strategic emergency plans can be put into place with the help of an ESS. These contingency plans help organizations recover quickly if an emergency or crisis occurs.

Decision making is a vital part of managing businesses strategically. IS systems such as information and decision support, group support, and executive support systems help employees by tapping existing databases and providing them with current, accurate information. The increasing integration of all business information systems—from TPSs to MISs to DSSs—can help organizations monitor their competitive environment and make better-informed decisions. Organizations can also use specialized business information systems, discussed in the next chapter, to achieve their goals.

SUMMARY

Principle:

Good decision-making and problem-solving skills are key to developing effective information and decision support systems.

Every organization needs effective decision making and problem solving to reach its objectives and goals. Problem solving begins with decision making. A well-known model developed by Herbert Simon divides the decision-making phase of the problem-solving process into three stages: intelligence, design, and choice. During the intelligence stage, potential problems or opportunities are identified and defined. Information is gathered that relates to the cause and scope of the problem. Constraints on the possible solution and the problem environment are investigated. In the design stage, alternative solutions to the problem are developed and explored. In addition, the feasibility and implications of these alternatives are evaluated. Finally, the choice stage involves selecting the best course of action. In this stage, the decision makers evaluate the implementation of the solution to determine whether the anticipated results were achieved and to modify the process in light of new information learned during the implementation stage.

Decision making is a component of problem solving. In addition to the intelligence, design, and choice steps of decision making, problem solving also includes implementation and monitoring. Implementation places the solution into effect. After a decision has been implemented, it is monitored and modified if necessary.

Decisions can be programmed or nonprogrammed. Programmed decisions are made using a rule, procedure, or quantitative method. Ordering more inventory when the level drops to 100 units or fewer is an example of a programmed decision. A nonprogrammed decision deals with unusual or exceptional situations. Determining the best training program for a new employee is an example of a nonprogrammed decision.

Decisions can use optimization, satisficing, or heuristic approaches. Optimization finds the best solution. Optimization problems often have an objective such as maximizing profits given production and material constraints. When a problem is too complex for optimization, satisficing is often used. Satisficing finds a good, but not necessarily the best, decision. Finally, a heuristic is a "rule of thumb" or commonly used guideline or procedure used to find a good decision.

Principle:

The management information system (MIS) must provide the right information to the right person in the right format at the right time.

A management information system is an integrated collection of people, procedures, databases, and devices that provides managers and decision makers with information to help achieve organizational goals. An MIS can help an organization achieve its goals by providing managers with insight into the regular operations of the organization so that they can control, organize, and plan more effectively and efficiently. The primary difference between the reports generated by the TPS and those generated by the MIS is that MIS reports support managerial decision making at the higher levels of management.

Data that enters the MIS originates from both internal and external sources. The most significant internal sources of data for the MIS are the organization's various TPSs and ERP systems. Data warehouses and data marts also provide important input data for the MIS. External sources of data for the MIS include extranets, customers, suppliers, competitors, and stockholders.

The output of most MISs is a collection of reports that are distributed to managers. These reports include scheduled reports, key-indicator reports, demand reports, exception reports, and drill-down reports. Scheduled reports are produced periodically, such as daily, weekly, or monthly. A key-indicator report is a special type of scheduled report. Demand reports are developed to provide certain information at a manager's request. Exception reports are automatically produced when a situation is unusual or requires management action. Drill-down reports provide increasingly detailed data about situations.

Management information systems have a number of common characteristics, including producing scheduled, demand, exception, and drill-down reports; producing reports with fixed and standard formats; producing hard-copy and soft-copy reports; using internal data stored in organizational computerized databases; and having reports developed and implemented by IS personnel or end users. More and more MIS reports are being delivered over the Internet and through mobile devices, such as cell phones.

Most MISs are organized along the functional lines of an organization. Typical functional management information systems include financial, manufacturing, marketing, human resources, and other specialized systems. Each system is composed of inputs, processing subsystems, and outputs. The primary sources of input to functional MISs include the corporate strategic plan, data from the ERP system and TPS, information from supply chain and business transactions, and external sources, including the Internet and extranets. The primary outputs of these functional MISs are summary reports that assist in managerial decision making.

A financial management information system provides financial information to all financial managers within an organization, including the chief financial officer (CFO). Subsystems are profit/loss and cost systems, auditing, and use and management of funds.

A manufacturing MIS accepts inputs from the strategic plan, the ERP system and TPS, and external sources, such as supply chain and business transactions. The systems involved support the business processes associated with the receiving and inspecting of raw material and supplies; inventory tracking of raw materials, work in process, and finished goods; labour and personnel management; management of assembly lines, equipment, and machinery; inspection and maintenance; and order processing. The subsystems involved are design and engineering, master production scheduling and inventory control, process control, and quality control and testing.

A marketing MIS supports managerial activities in the areas of product development, distribution, pricing decisions, promotional effectiveness, and sales forecasting. Subsystems include marketing research, product development, promotion and advertising, and product pricing.

A human resource MIS is concerned with activities related to employees of the organization. Subsystems include human resource planning, personnel selection and recruiting, training and skills inventories, scheduling and job placement, wage and salary administration, and outplacement.

An accounting MIS performs a number of important activities, providing aggregate information on accounts payable, accounts receivable, payroll, and many other applications. The organization's ERP system or TPS captures accounting data, which is also used by most other functional information systems. Geographic information systems provide regional data in graphical form.

Principle:

Decision support systems (DSSs) are used when the problems are unstructured.

A decision support system (DSS) is an organized collection of people, procedures, software, databases, and devices working to support managerial decision making. DSS characteristics include the ability to handle large amounts of data; obtain and process data from a variety of sources; provide report and presentation flexibility; support drill-down analysis; perform complex statistical analysis; offer textual and graphical orientations; support optimization, satisficing, and heuristic approaches; and perform what-if, simulation, and goal-seeking analysis.

DSSs provide support assistance through all phases of the problem-solving process. Different decision frequencies also require DSS support. An ad hoc DSS addresses unique, infrequent decision situations; an institutional DSS handles routine decisions. Highly structured problems, semistructured problems, and unstructured problems can be supported by a DSS. A DSS can also support different managerial levels, including strategic, tactical, and operational managers. A common database is often the link that ties together a company's TPS, MIS, and DSS.

The components of a DSS are the database, model base, user interface or dialogue manager, and a link to external databases, the Internet, the corporate intranet, extranets, networks, and other systems. The database can use data warehouses and data marts. A data-driven DSS primarily performs qualitative analysis based on the company's databases. Data-driven DSSs tap into vast stores of information contained in the corporate database, retrieving information on inventory, sales, personnel, production, finance, accounting, and other areas. Data mining is often used in a data-driven DSS. The model base contains the models used by the decision maker, such as financial, statistical, graphical, and project-management models. A model-driven DSS primarily performs mathematical or quantitative analysis. Model management software (MMS) is often used to coordinate the use of models in a DSS. The user interface provides a dialogue management facility to assist in communications between the system and the user. Access to other computer-based systems permits the DSS to tie into other powerful systems, including the TPS or function-specific subsystems.

Principle:

Specialized support systems, such as group support systems (GSSs) and executive support systems (ESSs), use the overall approach of a DSS in situations such as group and executive decision making.

A group support system (GSS), also called a *computerized collaborative work system*, consists of most of the elements in a DSS, plus software to provide effective support in group decision-making settings. GSSs are typically easy to learn and use and can offer specific or general decision-making support. GSS software, also called *groupware*, is specially designed to help generate lists of decision alternatives and perform data analysis. These packages let people work on joint documents and files over a network. Newer Web 2.0 technologies are being used to a greater extent in delivering group decision-making support. Text messages and the Internet are also commonly used in a GSS.

The frequency of GSS use and the location of the decision makers will influence the GSS alternative chosen. The decision room alternative supports users in a single location who meet infrequently. Local area decision networks can be used when group members are located in the same geographic area and users meet regularly. Teleconferencing is used when decision frequency is low and the location of group members is distant. A wide area network is used when the decision frequency is high and the location of group members is distant.

Executive support systems (ESSs) are specialized decision support systems designed to meet the needs of senior management. They serve to indicate issues of importance to the organization, indicate new directions the company might take, and help executives monitor the company's progress. ESSs are typically easy to use, offer a wide range of computer resources, and handle a variety of internal and external data. In addition, the ESS performs sophisticated data analysis, offers a high degree of specialization, and provides flexibility and comprehensive communications capabilities. An ESS also supports individual decision-making styles. Some of the major decision-making areas that can be supported through an ESS are providing an overall vision, strategic planning and organizing, strategic control, and crisis management.

CHAPTER 10: SELF-ASSESSMENT TEST

Good decision-making and problem-solving skills are key to developing effective information and decision support systems.

1. Developing decision alternatives is done during what decision-making stage?
   a. the initiation stage
   b. the intelligence stage
   c. the design stage
   d. the choice stage
2. Problem solving is one of the stages of decision making. True or False?
3. A "rule of thumb" or commonly accepted guideline is called a(n) _____.
4. Deciding to order inventory when inventory levels drop to 500 units is an example of what type of decision?
   a. synchronous decision
   b. asynchronous decision
   c. nonprogrammed decision
   d. programmed decision
5. A(n) _____ model will find the best solution to help an organization meet its goals.
6. A satisficing model is one that will find a good problem solution, but not necessarily the best problem solution. True or False?

The management information system (MIS) must provide the right information to the right person in the right format at the right time.

7. What summarizes the previous day's critical activities and is typically available at the beginning of each workday?
   a. a key-indicator report
   b. a demand report
   c. an exception report
   d. a database report
8. MRP and JIT are subsystems of which of the following?
   a. the marketing MIS
   b. the financial MIS
   c. the manufacturing MIS
   d. the auditing MIS
9. Another name for the _____ MIS is the personnel MIS because it is concerned with activities related to employees and potential employees of the organization.

Decision support systems (DSSs) are used when the problems are unstructured.

10. The focus of a decision support system is on decision-making effectiveness when faced with unstructured or semistructured business problems. True or False?
11. The _____ component in a decision support system allows a decision maker to perform quantitative analysis.
12. What component of a decision support system allows decision makers to easily access and manipulate the DSS as well as use common business terms and phrases?
   a. the knowledge base
   b. the model base
   c. the user interface
   d. the expert system

Specialized support systems, such as group support systems (GSSs) and executive support systems (ESSs), use the overall approach of a DSS in situations such as group and executive decision making.

13. What decision-making technique allows voting group members to arrive at a final group decision?
   a. groupthink
   b. anonymous input
   c. nominal group technique
   d. delphi
14. A type of software that helps with joint work group scheduling, communication, and management is called _____.
15. The local area decision network is the ideal GSS alternative for situations in which decision makers are located in the same building or geographic area and the decision makers are occasional users of the GSS approach. True or False?
16. A(n) _____ supports the actions of members of the board of directors, who are responsible to stockholders.

CHAPTER 10: SELF-ASSESSMENT TEST ANSWERS

(1) c (2) False (3) heuristic (4) d (5) optimization (6) True (7) a (8) c (9) human resource (10) True (11) model base (12) c (13) c (14) groupware or workgroup software (15) False (16) executive information system (EIS)

REVIEW QUESTIONS

1. What is a satisficing model? Describe a situation when it should be used.
2. What is the difference between intelligence and design in decision making?
3. What is the difference between a programmed decision and a nonprogrammed decision? Give several examples of each.
4. What are the basic kinds of reports produced by an MIS?
5. How can a social networking site be used in a DSS?
6. What are the functions performed by a financial MIS?
7. Describe the functions of a manufacturing MIS.
8. List and describe some other types of MISs.
9. What are the stages of problem solving?
10. What is the difference between decision making and problem solving?
11. How can location analysis be used in a marketing research MIS?

12. Describe the difference between a structured and an unstructured problem and give an example of each.
13. Define *decision support system*. What are its characteristics?
14. Describe the difference between a data-driven and a model-driven DSS.
15. What is the difference between what-if analysis and goal-seeking analysis?
16. What are the components of a decision support system?
17. State the objective of a group support system (GSS) and identify three characteristics that distinguish it from a DSS.
18. How can social networking sites be used in a GSS?
19. How does an executive support system differ from a decision support system?
20. Identify three fundamental uses for an executive support system.

DISCUSSION QUESTIONS

1. Select an important problem you had to solve during the last two years. Describe how you used the decision-making and problem-solving steps discussed in this chapter to solve the problem.
2. Describe how a GSS can be used at your college or university.
3. Discuss how a social networking site can be used in an information and decision support system.
4. Describe a financial MIS for a *Report on Business 1000* manufacturer of food products. What are the primary inputs and outputs? What are the subsystems?
5. How can a strong financial MIS provide strategic benefits to a firm?
6. Why is auditing so important in a financial MIS? Give an example of an audit that failed to disclose the true nature of the financial position of a firm. What was the result?
7. Describe two industries where a marketing MIS is critical to sales and success.
8. You have been hired to develop a management information system and a decision support system for a manufacturing company. Describe what information you would include in printed reports and what information you would provide using a screen-based decision support system.

9. Pick a company and research its human resource management information system. Describe how the system works. What improvements could be made to the company's human resource MIS?
10. You have been hired to develop a DSS for a car company such as Ford or GM. Describe how you would use both data-driven and model-driven DSSs.
11. Describe how you would use Twitter in one of the MISs or DSSs discussed in this chapter.
12. What functions do decision support systems support in business organizations? How does a DSS differ from a TPS and an MIS?
13. How is decision making in a group environment different from individual decision making, and why are information systems that assist in the group environment different? What are the advantages and disadvantages of making decisions as a group?
14. You have been hired to develop group support software for your university. Describe the features you would include in your new GSS software.
15. Imagine that you are the vice president of manufacturing for a *Report on Business 1000* manufacturing company. Describe the features and capabilities of your ideal ESS.

PROBLEM-SOLVING EXERCISES

1. Use the Internet to research social networking sites to support managerial decision making. Use a word processor to describe what you discovered. Develop a set of slides using a graphics program to deliver a presentation on the use of social networking sites in developing an information and decision support system.

2. Review the summarized consolidated statement of income for the manufacturing company whose data is shown here. Use graphics software to prepare a set of bar charts that shows the data for this year compared with the data for last year.
   a. This year, operating revenues increased by 3.5 percent, while operating expenses increased 2.5 percent.
   b. Other income and expenses decreased to $13,000.
   c. Interest and other charges increased to $265,000.

Operating Results (in millions)

Operating Revenues	$2,924,177
Operating Expenses (including taxes)	2,483,687
Operating Income	440,490
Other Income and Expenses	13,497
Income Before Interest and Other Charges	453,987
Interest and Other Charges	262,845
Net Income	191,142
Average Common Shares Outstanding	147,426
Earnings per Share	1.30

If you were a financial analyst tracking this company, what detailed data might you need to perform a more complete analysis? Write a brief memo summarizing your data needs.

3. As the head buyer for a major supermarket chain, you are constantly being asked by manufacturers and distributors to stock their new products. Over 50 new items are introduced each week. Many times, these products are launched with national advertising campaigns and special promotional allowances to retailers. To add new products, the amount of shelf space allocated to existing products must be reduced or items must be eliminated altogether. Develop a marketing MIS that you can use to estimate the change in profits from adding or deleting an item from inventory. Your analysis should include input such as estimated weekly sales in units, shelf space allocated to stock an item (measured in units), total cost per unit, and sales price per unit. Your analysis should calculate total annual profit by item and then sort the rows in descending order based on total annual profit.

TEAM ACTIVITIES

1. Using only e-mail, text messaging, or Twitter, have your team collaborate on a decision of your choice. Each team member should write a brief report on his or her experiences. In addition to the individual reports, your team should collaborate on a group report that describes the different perceptions of each team member and make recommendations about the use of e-mail, text messaging, or Twitter in group decision making.

2. Have your team make a group decision about how to solve the most frustrating aspect of college or university life. Appoint one or two members of the team to disrupt the meeting with negative group behaviour. After the meeting, have your team describe how to prevent this negative group behaviour. What GSS software features would you suggest to prevent the negative group behaviour your team observed?

3. Have your team design a marketing MIS for a medium-sized retail store. Describe the features and characteristics of your marketing MIS. How could you achieve a competitive advantage over a similar retail store with your marketing MIS?

WEB EXERCISES

1. Use a search engine such as Yahoo! or Google to explore two or more companies that produce and sell groupware or collaborative software. Would you find the features of the groupware or collaborative software useful in completing team projects in your classes? You might be asked to develop a report or send an e-mail message to your instructor about what you found.

2. Use the Internet to explore the use of GPS and location analysis on cell phones and other mobile devices to market and sell products and services. Summarize your findings in a report.

3. Software, such as Microsoft Excel, is often used to find an optimal solution to maximize profits or minimize costs. Search the Internet using Yahoo!, Google, or another search engine to find other software packages that offer optimization features. Write a report describing one or two of the optimization software packages. What are some of the features of the package?

CAREER EXERCISES

1. What decisions are critical for success in a career that interests you? What specific types of reports could help you make better decisions on the job? Give three specific examples.

2. Describe how you could use a GSS to help you in a career of your choice. What features in the GSS would be the most helpful to you in advancing your career? Which features would not be helpful?

CASE STUDIES

Case One

3D Digital City Model Assists Vancouver City Officials and Departments

Information provided as output from information management systems and decision support systems is typically provided in text and numbers on paper or an electronic display. A smaller percentage of MIS and DSS output may take the form of photographs or even video, such as passport photos or security camera recordings. Businesses and organizations are discovering that 3D output provides rich information for some applications.

The city of Vancouver, British Columbia, has recently joined a digital cities initiative sponsored by Autodesk, creator of 3D Design and Visualization software. The goal of the initiative is to create a realistic digital 3D rendering of all the buildings and structures in various cities. Vancouver is the third city to join the initiative. The first city, Salzburg, Austria, intends to use its 3D digital model to guide new development while remaining true to the historic architecture of the city. The second city, Incheon, South Korea, is using its 3D digital model to guide construction of a new portion of the city that will "fully integrate [a] digital lifestyle with an integrated sensor network, high-speed Internet communications, TV and cable services, as well as computer-scheduled transportation." City planners and designers will use the virtual city to simulate real-world scenarios and assist them in decision making and information sharing.

Vancouver plans to use its 3D digital model to guide improvements to its physical 3D infrastructure. An interactive 3D digital model can more effectively communicate city plans with city departments and citizens. Dan Campbell, graphics planner for the city, believes that a 3D interactive model will eliminate confusion and difference in interpretation when it comes to discussing plans for the city. A 3D model requires much less explanation than a 2D map.

The software tools provided by Autodesk are a combination of GIS, computer aided design (CAD), building information modelling (BIM), and gaming software. They allow the intricate details of city structures to be rendered in 3D. City planners can click buildings to access schematics and detailed information. The game engines allow users to view city streets from any perspective. You can easily switch from street view to aerial view to soar around town like a virtual hawk. The software even renders building shadows as they exist in reality. This function is very useful for cities like London, which has a "right to light" law that restricts the construction of buildings that will cast others into shadow all day.

3D models created from databases of physical specifications provide decision makers with information that can be more intuitively interpreted. As computing processing power increases and software tools become easier to manipulate, it is likely that an increasing amount of MIS and DSS output will take on 3D proportions.

Discussion Questions

1. How are 3D digital city models assisting city officials in Salzburg, Incheon, and Vancouver?
2. What insight can 3D digital models provide that 2D maps and building specifications can't?

Critical Thinking Questions

1. Besides city planning, what other types of businesses and applications might 3D modelling assist with?
2. What input is required for an MIS that outputs a 3D model? What types of information might the 3D model reveal?

SOURCES: Arellano, Nestor, "Vancouver Embarks on Digital City Project," itWorld-Canada.com, April 14, 2009, *www.itworldcanada.com/ViewArticle.aspx?url=vancouver-embarks-on-digital-city-project*; Autodesk Digital Cities Web page, *http://usa.autodesk.com/adsk/servlet/index?siteID=123112&id=11053875*, accessed March 24, 2010.

Case Two
Accurate Reports Place Umbrella over Arts

Arts Umbrella began with a few art enthusiasts who have a love for children and wanted to provide inexpensive art lessons to a few dozen students in a small rented space in Vancouver, British Columbia. Today, Arts Umbrella is a world-class art centre with 150 staff and faculty, 300 volunteers, and tens of thousands of students between the ages of 2 and 19. The Arts Umbrella central facility offers over 650 classes per week, ranging from beginner classes to professional level, including courses in architecture, cartooning, computer and classical animation, dance, film making, media arts, painting and drawing, printmaking, photography, sculpture, theatre, and video game design. Many of its students can afford its modest tuition, but others take advantage of grant funding that covers their tuition.

Arts Umbrella is a nonprofit organization that depends on the kindness and generosity of its supporters to operate. It has an army of volunteers who find people interested in donating to the cause.

Arts Umbrella maintains its data and financial records in an information system designed for nonprofit organizations called Raiser's Edge from Blackbaud, Inc. In the past, Arts Umbrella staff would spend days each month providing projections and creating reports that detailed the centre's fundraising efforts. The data would be exported from Raiser's Edge into an Excel spreadsheet and manipulated in the spreadsheet. If staff members discovered an error in the data, they would have to correct the data in Raiser's Edge and re-export it into the spreadsheet. The entire process left Arts Umbrella administrators and its board of directors less than confident in the results and projections.

Arts Umbrella consulted with SAP and discovered that its Crystal Reports software could integrate with the Raiser's Edge database to create real-time reports. After installation, customization, and training, Arts Umbrella staff started to produce reports anytime with a click of the mouse—reports that previously required days to create. Now, since the data in the report is a direct reflection of the data in the database, corrections to the database are reflected immediately in the reports.

The adoption of Crystal Reports into its information system has transformed the ability of Arts Umbrella to solicit contributions. Arts Umbrella has identified four characteristics that serve as strong indicators of whether a prospect is likely to pledge. This allows the centre to predict with a high degree of certainty who will pledge and who will not. Arts Umbrella uses this information to coach its canvassers on how to transform prospects into pledgers. For example, a canvasser may learn that one particular prospect is currently at a 10 percent chance of contributing. The system can inform the organization of what to do to increase that percentage to 70 percent.

The Arts Umbrella board of directors now has more confidence in the centre and its prospects. Contributions have increased significantly since the implementation of Crystal Reports, allowing Arts Umbrella to service more students.

Discussion Questions

1. How did the use of Crystal Reports streamline the process of creating reports for Arts Umbrella staff?
2. Why did the use of Crystal Reports increase confidence within the organization?

Critical Thinking Questions

1. How do the goals of nonprofit organizations differ from profit-driven organizations? How might that difference influence the use of MISs and DSSs?
2. Besides tracking donations, what other information do you think is valuable to an organization like Arts Umbrella? What types of reports might provide decision makers with insight into that information?

SOURCES: "ARTS UMBRELLA—Art Center Cuts Reporting Time with Crystal Reports® Software," SAP Success Stories, www.sap.com/solutions/sapbusinessobjects/sme/reporting-dashboarding/customers/index.epx, accessed March 23, 2010; Blackbaud Internet Solutions website, www.blackbaud.com, accessed March 23, 2010; Arts Umbrella website, www.artsumbrella.com, accessed March 23, 2010.

Questions for Web Case

See the website for this book to read about the Altitude Online case for this chapter. The following are questions concerning this Web case.

Altitude Online: Information and Decision Support System Considerations

Discussion Questions

1. What functional areas of Altitude Online are supported by MISs?
2. How do MISs and DSSs provide a value add to Altitude Online's products?

Critical Thinking Questions

1. How do you think MISs and DSSs assist Altitude Online's top executives in guiding the direction of the company?
2. How can the quality of information systems affect Altitude Online's ability to compete in the online marketing industry?

NOTES

Sources for the opening vignette: "Tru-Test Consolidates Applications, Integrates Business Units, and Increases Margins," Oracle Case Studies, *www.oracle.com/customers/solutions/bi.html*, accessed March 23, 2010; Tru-Test website, *www.tru-test.com*, accessed March 23, 2010; Citrix website, *www.citrix.com*, accessed March 23, 2010; Demantra Web page, *www.oracle.com/demantra*, accessed March 23, 2010.

1 Steel, Emily, "Marketers Take Search Ads Beyond Search Engines," *Wall Street Journal*, January 20, 2009, p. B4.
2 Vascellaro, Jessica, "YouTube Pumps More Ads into Lineup," *Wall Street Journal*, August 20, 2009, p. B1.
3 Greenberg, Andy, "The Blindfolded Calculator," *Forbes*, July 13, 2009, p. 40.
4 Patterson, Scott, and Rogow, Geoffrey, "What's Behind High-Frequency Trading," *Wall Street Journal*, August 1, 2009, p. B1.
5 Smith, Randall, "The Flash Trading Thorn in NYSE's Side," *Wall Street Journal*, August 31, 2009, p. C1.
6 Ricknas, Mikael, "GPS Algorithm Error Prompts Garmin Recall," *PC World*, August 2009, p. 30.
7 Brandel, William, "Free Up Cash," *Computerworld*, August 17, 2009, p. 28.
8 Gnanlet, A., et al., "Sequential and Simultaneous Decision Making for Optimizing Health Care," *Decision Sciences*, May 2009, p. 295.
9 "Battling the Fuel Cost Frenzy with Route Optimization and Wireless Tracking Services," Descartes Systems Group, *www.descartes.com/resources/whitepapers/ds_wp_battling_fuel_cost.pdf*, accessed June 11, 2011.
10 Rai, S., et al., "LDP—O.R. Enhanced Productivity Improvements for the Printing Industry," *Interfaces*, January 2009, p. 69.
11 Hormby, S., et al., "Marriott International Increases Revenue by Implementing a Group Pricing Optimizer," *Interfaces*, January-February, 2010, p. 47.
12 D'Amours, S., et al., "Optimization Helps Shermag Gain Competitive Advantage," *Interfaces*, July-August, 2009, p. 329.
13 *www.cmis.csiro.au*, accessed July 7, 2009.
14 "Norton Internet Security 2010," *New Zealand Herald*, October 5, 2009.
15 Weier, Mary Hayes, "Collaboration Is Key to Increased Efficiency," *Information Week*, September 14, 2009, p. 90.
16 Claburn, Thomas, "BI and the Web Are Front and Center," *Information Week*, September 14, 2009, p. 85.
17 Ioffe, Julia, "Tech Rx For Health Care," *Fortune*, March 16, 2009, p. 36.
18 "Canadian Food Inspection Agency Gains Valuable Insight into Data and Centralized Business Intelligence Solution, Thanks to IBM Cognos Products and Services," *www-01.ibm.com/software/success/cssdb.nsf/CS/SANS-86QHD3?OpenDocument&Site=cognos&cty=en_us*, accessed June 11, 2011.
19 "Clorox Canada: An IBM Cognos Solution for Sales, Inventory and Budgeting," *www-01.ibm.com/software/success/cssdb.nsf/CS/SANS-7YRM72?OpenDocument&Site=cognos&cty=en_us*, accessed October 15, 2010.
20 *www.microsoft.com/dynamics/product/business_scorecard_manager.mspx*, July 07, 2009.
21 "Leading Indicators, August 2010," Statistics Canada, *www.statcan.gc.ca/daily-quotidien/100922/dq100922b-eng.htm*, September 22, 2010.
22 Jackson-Higgins, Kelly, "Jive Wikis Meet SAP Analytics," *Information Week*, July 6, 2009, p. 15.
23 Cui, Carolyn, "Computer-Trading Models Meet Match," *Wall Street Journal*, April 20, 2009, p. C3.
24 Feldman, Amy, "Buddy, Can You E-Mail Me 100 Bucks?" *BusinessWeek*, November 23, 2009, p. 68.
25 Kelly, C., "Turning an F Into Fun," *Computerworld*, May 26, 2008, p. 32.

26 "Livent Co-Founder Found Guilty of Fraud, Forgery," CTV Toronto, *http://toronto.ctv.ca/servlet/an/local/CTVNews/20090325/Livent_trial_090325/20090325?hub=Toronto*, March 25, 2009.
27 Banjo, Shelly, "The Best Online Tools for Personal Finance," *Wall Street Journal*, June 8, 2009, p. R1.
28 *www.dell.com*, accessed October 12, 2009.
29 Weier, Mary Hayes, "Collaboration Is Key to Increased Efficiency," *Information Week*, September 14, 2009, p. 90.
30 "CimatronE to Power Live Cutting," *Drug Week*, October 9, 2009, p. 1550.
31 Linblad, C., and Maurer, H., "A Drumbeat of Deals," *BusinessWeek*, October 12, 2009, p. 4.
32 "Education in Paper Magazine," *Weekly Times*, July 8, 2009, p. 16.
33 Van Alphen, Tony, "Chrysler Adds Right-Hand Drive Minivan," *Toronto Star*, September 9, 2009, p. B03.
34 Sandler, Kathy, "Web Ad Sales in Britain Overtake TV," *Wall Street Journal*, September 30, 2009, p. B7.
35 Schatz, Amy, "U.S. Seeks To Restrict Gifts Made to Bloggers," *Wall Street Journal*, October 6, 2009, p. A1.
36 Hempel, Jessi, "Salesforce Hits Its Stride," *Fortune*, March 2, 2009, p. 29.
37 Arelanno, Nestor, "Canadian Firms Win Big with Mobile Marketing," *www.itbusiness.ca/it/client/en/home/News.asp?id=57173*, April 13, 2010.
38 "Can You Believe What You Read on the Web," *Parade*, June, 21, 2009, p. 8.
39 Levy, Carmi, "Airline Uses Twitter, Other Social Tools to Revolutionize Customer Service," *Toronto Star*, October 10, 2010, *www.thestar.com/business/companies/porter/article/871979--airlines-use-twitter-other-social-tools-to-revolutionize-customer-service*, accessed October 16, 2010.
40 Hof, Robert, "Google's New Ad Weapon," *BusinessWeek*, June 22, 2009, p. 52.
41 Dornan, David and Jules, "Battle for the Brain," *Forbes*, November 16, 2009, p. 76.
42 "Loopt Now Available in the Android Market," *Drug Week*, January 2, 2009, p. 1852.
43 Baker, Stephen, "The Next Net," *BusinessWeek*, March 9, 2009, p. 42.
44 Helm, Burt, "Online Ads: Beyond Counting Clicks," *BusinessWeek*, March 9, 2009, p. 56.
45 Yang, Jia L., "Veggie Tales," *Fortune*, June 8, 2009, p. 25.
46 Bailey, Katie, "Ad Spend on the Rebound: Group M," *www.mediaincanada.com/articles/mic/20100628/adspendgroupm.html*, accessed October 16, 2010.
47 Vascellaro, Jessica, "Radio Tunes Out Google," *Wall Street Journal*, May 12, 2009, p. A1.
48 Lowry, Tom, "Pandora: Unleashing Mobile Phone Ads," *BusinessWeek*, June 1, 2009, p. 52.
49 Kane, Y., "iPhone Gets Bigger as Ad Medium," *Wall Street Journal*, May 12, 2009, p. B6.
50 Vascellaro, Jessica, and Steel, Emily, "Something New Gains with Something Borrowed," *Wall Street Journal*, June 5, 2009, p. B6.
51 Steel, Emily, "Web Ad Sales Open Door to Viruses," *Wall Street Journal*, June 15, 2009, p. B7.
52 Lawrence, Rick, et al., "Operations Research Improves Sales Force Productivity at IBM," *Interfaces*, January-February 2010, p. 33.
53 Moy, Patsy, "Sharing Just the Job for Women," *The Standard*, October 12, 2009.
54 Hardy, Quentin, "High Network Individual," *Forbes*, March 16, 2009, p. 20.
55 "Rona Case Study," Esri Canada, *www.esricanada.com/en_resources/files/EC1_0057_1002_1A_Rona.pdf*, accessed June 11, 2011.
56 Baker, Stephen, "The Next Net," *BusinessWeek*, March 9, 2009, p. 42.

57 Mossberg, Walter, "Tracking Friends the Google Way," *Wall Street Journal*, February 4, 2009, p. D2.

58 Wingfield, Nick, "Sharing Where You Are When You Care to Share," *Wall Street Journal*, May 21, 2009, p. D1.

59 "SAS Helps Royal Bank of Canada Avoid $15 Million in Credit Fraud Losses," *www.sas.com/offices/NA/canada/en/success/SAS-RBC.html*, accessed June 11, 2011.

60 "SAS Helps Indigo Get Personal with Reading Enthusiasts," *www.sas.com/offices/NA/canada/en/success/Indigo.html*, accessed June 11, 2011.

61 Zweig, Jason, "Data Mining Isn't a Good Bet for Stock-Market Predictions," *Wall Street Journal*, August 8, 2009, p. B1.

62 Hamm, Steve, "Big Blue Goes into Analysis," *BusinessWeek*, April 27, 2009, p. 16.

63 McDougall, Paul, "IBM Takes Aim at Data Deluge," *Information Week*, May 11, 2009, p. 24.

64 Ilie, V., et al., "Paper Versus Electronic Medical Records," *Decision Sciences*, May 2009, p. 213.

65 "About Health Canada: Applied Research and Analysis Directorate," Health Canada website, *www.hc-sc.gc.ca/ahc-asc/branch-dirgen/spb-dgps/arad-draa/index-eng.php*, accessed June 11, 2011.

66 Cui, Carolyn, "Computer-Trading Models Meet Match," *Wall Street Journal*, April 20, 2009, p. C3.

67 Mitchell, Robert, "BI On A Budget," *Computerworld*, September 14, 2009, p. 23.

68 Weier, Mary Hayes, "Business Gone Mobile," *Information Week*, March 30, 2009, p. 23.

69 Murphy, Chris, "TransUnion Finds Cost Savings, Seeks More," *Information Week*, March 23, 2009, p. 24.

70 Hempel, Jessi, "How Facebook Is Taking Over Our Lives," *Fortune*, March 2, 2009, p. 49.

71 Stern, Jack, "Build a Social Network for Your Business," *PC World*, December 2009, p. 31.

72 Hamblen, Matt, "Finding the Stars with Bright Ideas," *Computerworld*, September 14, 2009, p. 10.

73 Stern, Zack, "Collaboration Online with Fuze Meeting Service," *PC World*, March 2009, p. 34.

74 Scheck, J., and White, B., "Telepresence Is Taking Hold," *Wall Street Journal*, May 6, 2009, p. B6.

75 "SAP Customer Success Story, Canada Post: An Innovative Leader in the Global Postal Community Achieves Business Transformation with mySAP Business Suite," *www.sap.com/canada/solutions/pdf/Canada_Post_BSuite.pdf*, accessed June 11, 2011.

76 "SAP Customer Success Story, NOVA Chemicals, Sap x MII Helps Chemical Company to Integrate Processes Across the Board," *www.sap.com/canada/solutions/pdf/CS_Nova_Chemicals.pdf*, accessed June 12, 2011.

CHAPTER
· 11 ·

Knowledge Management and Specialized Information Systems

PRINCIPLES	LEARNING OBJECTIVES
■ **Knowledge management allows organizations to share knowledge and experience among managers and employees.**	■ Discuss the differences between data, information, and knowledge. ■ Describe the role of the chief knowledge officer (CKO). ■ List some of the tools and techniques used in knowledge management.
■ **Artificial intelligence systems form a broad and diverse set of systems that can replicate human decision making for certain types of well-defined problems.**	■ Define the term "artificial intelligence" and state the objective of developing artificial intelligence systems. ■ List the characteristics of intelligent behaviour and compare the performance of natural and artificial intelligence systems for each of these characteristics. ■ Identify the major components of the artificial intelligence field and provide one example of each type of system.
■ **Expert systems can enable a novice to perform at the level of an expert but must be developed and maintained very carefully.**	■ List the characteristics and basic components of expert systems. ■ Identify at least three factors to consider in evaluating the development of an expert system. ■ Outline and briefly explain the steps for developing an expert system. ■ Identify the benefits associated with the use of expert systems.
■ **Multimedia and virtual reality systems can reshape the interface between people and information technology by offering new ways to communicate information, visualize processes, and express ideas creatively.**	■ Discuss the use of multimedia in a business setting. ■ Define the term "virtual reality" and provide three examples of virtual reality applications.
■ **Specialized systems can help organizations and individuals achieve their goals.**	■ Discuss examples of specialized systems for organizational and individual use.

(Source: Lukiyanova Natalia/frenta/Shutterstock.com.)

Information Systems in the Global Economy
Capgemini

Managing Corporate Knowledge on a Global Scale

Capgemini is a global business and IT consulting company headquartered in Paris, France. It employees 90,000 business and IT specialists distributed across more than 30 countries in North America, Europe, and the Asia Pacific region.

Capgemini has four divisions to address client needs. Its consulting services analyze corporate clients' business infrastructure and practices to help companies more easily reach their goals. The technology services division of Capgemini integrates information systems to transform clients' technology infrastructure to better meet corporate needs. The consulting and technology divisions work closely together to assist Capgemini clients. Capgemini also has an outsourcing services division that allows clients to outsource noncore business functions such as finance, accounting, procurement, and IT. Finally, Capgemini's local professional services division provides on-site IT support to large corporations.

Global enterprises such as Capgemini depend on virtual connections rather than face-to-face communication to share information and knowledge. Because it isn't practical for Capgemini's 90,000 employees to meet as a physical community and share information, the company must provide its employees with online tools to create a robust virtual community. In general, companies use online tools to distribute and share corporate knowledge and wisdom. Employees can access that knowledge to find ready answers to questions, respond to problems, and move the company forward in a unified manner.

Capturing and distributing the knowledge of professionals within an organization is referred to as knowledge management (KM). A KM system supports a company's progress and keeps valuable knowledge within the organization even as knowledgeable employees leave. KM systems need to easily collect information acquired by knowledge workers, catalogue and store that information, and, most importantly, provide employees throughout the organization with easy access to the information when they need it. Capgemini CTO Andy Mulholland saw opportunity in Web 2.0 technologies as a basis for the company's global KM system.

Web 2.0 technologies allow community members to contribute their knowledge to a pool using tools such as community posts, blogs, and wikis. Associating descriptive tags with each entry makes it easy to organize community input into categories that can help others search and find useful information later. Community members can also rank information according to its value, which means others are likely to find the best solutions to problems.

Capgemini supplemented Web 2.0 social media tools with Google Apps to allow community members to easily collaborate on projects. Google Apps can also be used as a repository for shared documents, including documents that assist employees with common corporate procedures—an important component of a KM system.

Andy Mulholland and his team designed a corporate Web portal based on a service-oriented architecture. The portal combines all of the Web 2.0 social media and Google Apps into an integrated KM system that Capgemini's 90,000 employees can use. They can search for solutions in each corporate division or throughout the enterprise. The launch of the new KM portal at Capgemini has produced measurable cost savings by helping employees acquire knowledge faster and by increasing collaboration.

The Web 2.0-based KM system at Capgemini is one of many common types of special-purpose systems developed to meet a corporate need. Specialized systems are designed to streamline operations, automate tasks, and take advantage of the latest technologies to serve unique needs and assist businesses in achieving their goals.

As you read this chapter, consider the following:

- What steps can a business take to retain corporate knowledge within the business?
- How can computer intelligence be harnessed to serve corporate needs in various industries?
- How can people and businesses make the best use of specialized systems?

Why Learn About Specialized Information Systems?

Knowledge management and specialized information systems are used in almost every industry. If you are a manager, you might use a knowledge management system to support decisive action to help you correct a problem. If you are a production manager at an automotive company, you might oversee robots that attach windshields to cars or paint body panels. As a young stock trader, you might use a special system called a *neural network* to uncover patterns and make millions of dollars trading stocks and stock options. As a marketing manager for a PC manufacturer, you might use virtual reality on a website to show customers your latest laptop and desktop computers. If you are in the military, you might use computer simulation as a training tool to prepare you for combat. In a petroleum company, you might use an expert system to determine where to drill for oil and gas. You will see many additional examples of using these specialized information systems throughout this chapter. Learning about these systems will help you discover new ways to use information systems in your day-to-day work.

Like other aspects of an information system, the overall aims of knowledge management and the specialized systems discussed in this chapter is to help people and organizations achieve their goals. In this chapter, we explore knowledge management, artificial intelligence, and many other specialized information systems, including expert systems, robotics, vision systems, natural language processing, learning systems, neural networks, genetic algorithms, intelligent agents, multimedia, and virtual reality.

KNOWLEDGE MANAGEMENT SYSTEMS

Chapter 1 defines and discusses data, information, and knowledge. Recall that *data* consists of raw facts, such as an employee number, number of hours worked in a week, inventory part numbers, or sales orders. A list of the quantity available for all items in inventory is an example of data. When these facts are organized or arranged in a meaningful manner, they become information. You might recall from Chapter 1 that *information* is a collection of facts organized so that they have additional value beyond the value of the facts themselves. An exception report of inventory items that might be out of stock in a week because of high demand is an example of information. *Knowledge* is the awareness and understanding of a set of information and the ways that information can be made useful to support a specific task or reach a decision. Knowing the procedures for ordering more inventory to avoid running out is an example of knowledge. In a sense, information tells you what has to be done (low inventory levels for some items), while knowledge tells you how to do it (make two important phone calls to the right people to get the needed inventory shipped overnight). See Figure 11.1.

A *knowledge management system (KMS)* is an organized collection of people, procedures, software, databases, and devices used to create, store, share, and use the organization's

Figure 11.1

The Differences Between Data, Information, and Knowledge

Data	There are 20 PCs in stock at the retail store.
Information	The store will run out of inventory in a week unless more is ordered today.
Knowledge	Call 800-555-2222 to order more inventory.

knowledge and experience.[1] KMSs cover a wide array of systems, such as software that contains some KMS components and dedicated systems designed specifically to capture, store, and use knowledge.

Overview of Knowledge Management Systems

Like the other systems discussed throughout the book, including information and decision support systems, knowledge management systems attempt to help organizations achieve their goals. For businesses, this usually means increasing profits or reducing costs. One study of a large information systems consulting firm found an $18.60 return on every dollar invested in its knowledge management system, representing over 1,000 percent return on investment (ROI).[2] This outstanding ROI was a result of time and cost savings from superior knowledge retrieval and usage. Acquired Intelligence, a British Columbia company, developed a KMS for the University of Victoria to assess graduate school applicants. The system decreased the amount of time taken to process applications by automating the review by faculty members of acceptable applicants. For nonprofit organizations, KM can mean providing better customer service or providing special needs to people and groups.

A KMS can involve different types of knowledge.[3] *Explicit knowledge* is objective and can be measured and documented in reports, papers, and rules. For example, knowing the best road to take to minimize drive time from home to the office when a major highway is closed is explicit knowledge. It can be documented in a report or a rule, as in "If the TransCanada highway is closed, take Highway 6." *Tacit knowledge*, on the other hand, is hard to measure and document and typically is not objective or formalized. Knowing the best way to negotiate with a foreign government about nuclear disarmament or a volatile hostage situation often requires a lifetime of experience and a high level of skill. These are examples of tacit knowledge. It is difficult to write a detailed report or a set of rules that would always work in every hostage situation. Many organizations actively attempt to convert tacit knowledge to explicit knowledge to make the knowledge easier to measure, document, and share with others.[4]

Data and Knowledge Management Workers and Communities of Practice

The personnel involved in a KMS include data workers and knowledge workers. Secretaries, administrative assistants, bookkeepers, and similar data-entry personnel are often called *data workers*. As mentioned in Chapter 1, *knowledge workers* are people who create, use, and disseminate knowledge.[5] They are usually professionals in science, engineering, or business, and they usually work in offices and belong to professional organizations. Other examples of knowledge workers are writers, researchers, educators, and corporate designers. See Figure 11.2.

Figure 11.2

Knowledge Workers

Knowledge workers are people who create, use, and disseminate knowledge, including professionals in science, engineering, business, and other areas.

(Source: © Silvia Jansen/iStockphoto. com.)

chief knowledge officer (CKO)
A top-level executive who helps the organization use a KMS to create, store, and use knowledge to achieve organizational goals.

The **chief knowledge officer (CKO)** is a top-level executive who helps the organization work with a KMS to create, store, and use knowledge to achieve organizational goals. The CKO is responsible for the organization's KMS and typically works with other executives and vice presidents, including the chief executive officer (CEO), chief financial officer (CFO), and others.

Some organizations and professions use *communities of practice (COP)* to create, store, and share knowledge. A COP is a group of people dedicated to a common discipline or practice, such as open-source software, auditing, medicine, or engineering. A group of oceanographers investigating climate change or a team of medical researchers looking for new ways to treat lung cancer are examples of COPs. COPs excel at obtaining, storing, sharing, and using knowledge. A study of knowledge workers in a large insurance company showed that a COP shares information better, solves problems more collaboratively, and is more committed to sharing best practices.[6]

Obtaining, Storing, Sharing, and Using Knowledge

Obtaining, storing, sharing, and using knowledge is the key to any KMS. MWH Global (*www.mwhglobal.com*), with offices in Canada, uses a KMS to create, disseminate, and use knowledge specializing in environmental engineering, construction, and management activities worldwide. The company has about 7,000 employees and 170 offices around the world. Using a KMS often leads to additional knowledge creation, storage, sharing, and usage. Drug companies and medical researchers invest billions of dollars in creating knowledge on cures for diseases. An example is Ubika Corporation. Ubika provides data and model management to knowledge-driven advanced analytics for the financial services industry such as financial and valuation research, investment research, data analytics and knowledge processes such as "equity research publishing."[7] Knowledge management systems can also diminish the reliance on paper reports, which reduces costs and helps protect the environment.[8] According to one expert, "Going green has become a topic of increased attention lately, but it's nothing new to knowledge management." Although knowledge workers can act alone, they often work in teams to create or obtain knowledge. See Figure 11.3.

Figure 11.3

Knowledge Management System

Obtaining, storing, sharing, and using knowledge is the key to any KMS.

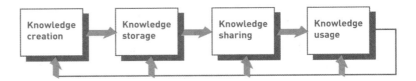

After knowledge is created, it is often stored in a *knowledge repository* that includes documents, reports, files, and databases.[9] The knowledge repository can be located both inside the organization and outside. Some types of software can store and share knowledge contained in documents and reports. Adobe Acrobat PDF files, for example, allow you to store corporate reports, tax returns, and other documents and send them to others over the Internet.[10] The publisher and the authors of this book used PDF files to store, share, and edit each chapter. Traditional databases, data warehouses, and data marts, discussed in Chapter 5, often store the organization's knowledge. Specialized knowledge bases in expert systems, discussed later in this chapter, can also be used.

Because knowledge workers often work in groups or teams, they can use collaborative work software and group support systems (discussed in Chapter 10) to share knowledge, such as groupware, meeting software, and collaboration tools. Intranets and password-protected Internet sites also provide ways to share knowledge. Many businesses, however, use patents, copyrights, trade secrets, Internet firewalls, and other measures to keep prying eyes from seeing important knowledge that is expensive and hard to create.

Using a knowledge management system begins with locating the organization's knowledge. This is often done using a *knowledge map* or directory that points the knowledge worker to the needed knowledge. Drug companies have sophisticated knowledge maps that include database and file systems to allow scientists and drug researchers to locate previous medical studies. Medical researchers, university professors, and even textbook authors use Lexis-Nexis to locate important knowledge. Corporations often use the Internet or corporate Web portals to help their knowledge workers find knowledge stored in documents and reports.

Technology to Support Knowledge Management

KMSs use a number of tools discussed throughout the book. In Chapter 1, for example, we explored the importance of *organizational learning* and *organizational change*. An effective KMS is based on learning new knowledge and changing procedures and approaches as a result. A manufacturing company, for example, might learn new ways to program robots on the factory floor to improve accuracy and reduce defective parts. The new knowledge will likely cause the manufacturing company to change how it programs and uses its robots. In Chapter 5, we investigated the use of *data mining* and *business intelligence*. These powerful tools can be important in capturing and using knowledge. Enterprise resource planning tools, such as SAP, include knowledge management features. In Chapter 10, we showed how *groupware* can improve group decision-making and collaboration. Groupware can also be used to help capture, store, and use knowledge. Of course, hardware, software, databases, telecommunications, and the Internet, discussed in Part II, are important technologies used to support most knowledge management systems.

Hundreds of organizations provide specific KM products and services.[11] In addition, researchers at colleges and universities have developed tools and technologies to support knowledge management. Canadian companies spend millions of dollars on knowledge management technology every year. Companies such as IBM have many knowledge management tools in a variety of products, including Lotus Notes, discussed in Chapter 10. Microsoft offers a number of knowledge management tools, including Digital Dashboard, which is based on the Microsoft Office suite. Digital Dashboard integrates information from a variety of sources, including personal, group, enterprise, and external information and documents. Other tools from Microsoft include Web Store Technology, which uses wireless technology to deliver knowledge to any location at any time; Access Workflow Designer, which helps database developers create effective systems to process transactions and keep work flowing through the organization; and related products. Some additional knowledge management organizations and resources are summarized in Table 11.1. In addition to these tools, several artificial intelligence and special-purpose technologies and tools, discussed next, can be used in a KMS.

Company	Description	Website
CortexPro	Knowledge management collaboration tools	www.cortexpro.com[12]
Delphi Group	A knowledge management consulting company	www.delphigroup.com[13]
Knowledge Management Resource Center	Knowledge management sites, products and services, magazines, and case studies	www.kmresource.com[14]
Knowledge Management Solutions, Inc.	Tools to create, capture, classify, share, and manage knowledge	www.kmsi.us[15]
Knowledge Management Web Directory	A directory of knowledge management websites	www.knowledge-manage.com[16]
KnowledgeBase	Content creation and management	www.knowledgebase.net[17]
Law Clip Knowledge Manager	A service that collects and organizes text, Web links, and more from law-related websites	www.lawclip.com[18]
Knowledge Management Consortium International	Offers knowledge management training and support	www.kmci.org/index.html[19]

Table 11.1

Additional Knowledge Management Organizations and Resources

An Overview of Artificial Intelligence

At a Dartmouth College conference in 1956, John McCarthy proposed the use of the term *artificial intelligence* (*AI*) to describe computers with the ability to mimic or duplicate the functions of the human brain. For example, advances in AI have led to systems that can recognize complex patterns.

Many AI pioneers attended this first conference; a few predicted that computers would be as "smart" as people by the 1960s. The prediction has not yet been realized, but the benefits of artificial intelligence in business and research can be seen today, and research continues.

Science fiction novels and popular movies have featured scenarios of computer systems and intelligent machines taking over the world. Computer systems such as Hal in the classic movie *2001: A Space Odyssey* and those in the movie *A.I.* and many other movies are futuristic glimpses of what might be. These accounts are fictional, but they show many computer systems that use the notion of AI. These systems help to make medical diagnoses, explore for natural resources, determine what is wrong with mechanical devices, and assist in designing and developing other computer systems.

Science fiction movies give us a glimpse of the future, but many practical applications of artificial intelligence exist today, among them medical diagnostics and development of computer systems.

(Source: TWENTIETH CENTURY-FOX FILM CORPORATION/THE KOBAL COLLECTION.)

Artificial Intelligence in Perspective

artificial intelligence systems
People, procedures, hardware, software, data, and knowledge needed to develop computer systems and machines that demonstrate the characteristics of intelligence.

Artificial intelligence systems include the people, procedures, hardware, software, data, and knowledge needed to develop computer systems and machines that demonstrate characteristics of intelligence. Artificial intelligence can be used by most industries and applications. Researchers, scientists, and experts on how human beings think are often involved in developing these systems.

The Nature of Intelligence

intelligent behaviour
The ability to learn from experiences and apply knowledge acquired from those experiences; to handle complex situations; to solve problems when important information is missing; to determine what is important and to react quickly and correctly to a new situation; to understand visual images, process and manipulate symbols, be creative and imaginative; and to use heuristics.

From the early AI pioneering stage, the research emphasis has been on developing machines with the ability to "learn" from experiences and apply knowledge acquired from those experiences; to handle complex situations; to solve problems when important information is missing; to determine what is important and to react quickly and correctly to a new situation; to understand visual images, process and manipulate symbols, be creative and imaginative; and to use heuristics, which together is considered **intelligent behaviour**.[20] In a book called *The Singularity Is Near* and in articles by and about him, Ray Kurzweil predicts computers will have humanlike intelligence in 20 years.[21] The author also foresees that by 2045 human and machine intelligence might merge. Machine intelligence, however, is hard to achieve.

The *Turing Test* attempts to determine whether the responses from a computer with intelligent behaviour are indistinguishable from responses from a human being. No computer has passed the Turing Test, developed by Alan Turing, a British mathematician. The Loebner Prize offers money and a gold medal for anyone developing a computer that can pass the Turing Test (see *www.loebner.net*). Some of the specific characteristics of intelligent behaviour include the ability to do the following:

- *Learn from experience and apply the knowledge acquired from experience.* Learning from past situations and events is a key component of intelligent behaviour and is a natural ability of humans, who learn by trial and error. This ability, however, must be carefully programmed into a computer system. Today, researchers are developing systems that can "learn" from experience.[22] For instance, computerized AI chess software can learn to improve while playing human competitors. In one match, Garry Kasparov competed against a personal computer with AI software developed in Israel, called Deep Junior. This match was a 3–3 tie, but Kasparov picked up something the machine would have no interest in—$700,000. The 20 questions (20q) website, *www.20q.net*, is another example of a system that learns.[23] The website is an artificial intelligence game that learns as people play.

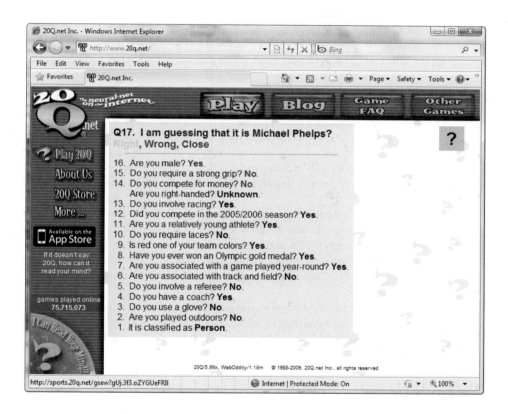

20Q is an online game where users play the popular game Twenty Questions against an artificial intelligence foe.

(Source: © 1988–2011. 20Q is a registered trademark of 20Q.net Inc. All related titles, logos and characters are trademarks of 20Q.net Inc. All rights reserved. © 2011. I can read your mind ... is a registered trademark of 20Q.net Inc.)

- *Handle complex situations.* People are often involved in complex situations. In a business setting, top-level managers and executives must handle a complex market, challenging competitors, intricate government regulations, and a demanding workforce. Even human experts make mistakes in dealing with these situations. Very careful planning and elaborate computer programming are necessary to develop systems that can handle complex situations.
- *Solve problems when important information is missing.* An integral part of decision making is dealing with uncertainty. Often, decisions must be made with little information or inaccurate information because obtaining complete information is too costly or impossible. Today, AI systems can make important calculations, comparisons, and decisions even when information is missing.

perceptive system
A system that approximates the way a person sees, hears, and feels objects.

- *Determine what is important.* Knowing what is truly important is the mark of a good decision maker. Developing programs and approaches to allow computer systems and machines to identify important information is not a simple task.

- *React quickly and correctly to a new situation.* A small child, for example, can look over an edge and know not to venture too close. The child reacts quickly and correctly to a new situation. Computers, on the other hand, do not have this ability without complex programming.

- *Understand visual images.* Interpreting visual images can be extremely difficult, even for sophisticated computers. Moving through a room of chairs, tables, and other objects can be trivial for people but extremely complex for machines, robots, and computers. Such machines require an extension of understanding visual images, called a **perceptive system**. Having a perceptive system allows a machine to approximate the way a person sees, hears, and feels objects. Military robots, for example, use cameras and perceptive systems to conduct reconnaissance missions to detect enemy weapons and soldiers.[24] Detecting and destroying them can save lives.

- *Process and manipulate symbols.* People see, manipulate, and process symbols every day. Visual images provide a constant stream of information to our brains. By contrast, computers have difficulty handling symbolic processing and reasoning. Although computers excel at numerical calculations, they aren't as good at dealing with symbols and three-dimensional objects. Recent developments in machine-vision hardware and software, however, allow some computers to process and manipulate some symbols.

- *Be creative and imaginative.* Throughout history, some people have turned difficult situations into advantages by being creative and imaginative. For instance, when defective mints with holes in the middle arrived at a candy factory, an enterprising entrepreneur decided to market these new mints as LifeSavers instead of returning them to the manufacturer. Ice cream cones were invented at the St. Louis World's Fair when an imaginative store owner decided to wrap ice cream with a waffle from his grill for portability. Developing new products and services from an existing (perhaps negative) situation is a human characteristic. While software has been developed to enable a computer to write short stories, few computers can be imaginative or creative in this way.

- *Use heuristics.* For some decisions, people use heuristics (rules of thumb arising from experience) or even guesses. In searching for a job, you might rank the companies you are considering according to profits per employee. Today, some computer systems, given the right programs, obtain good solutions that use approximations instead of trying to search for an optimal solution, which would be technically difficult or too time consuming.

- This list of traits only partially defines intelligence. Unlike the terminology used in virtually every other field of IS research, in which the objectives can be clearly defined, the term *intelligence* is a formidable stumbling block. Another challenge is linking a human brain to a computer.[25]

The Brain Computer Interface

Developing a link between the human brain and the computer is another exciting area that touches all aspects of artificial intelligence. Called *Brain Computer Interface (BCI)*, the idea is to directly connect the human brain to a computer and have human thought control computer activities.[26] Two exciting studies conducted at the Massachusetts General Hospital in Boston will attempt to use a chip called BrainGate to connect a human brain to a computer. If successful, the BCI experiment will allow people to control computers and artificial arms and legs through thought alone. The objective is to give people without the ability to speak or move (called Locked-in Syndrome) the ability to communicate and move artificial limbs using advanced BCI technologies. Honda Motors has developed a BCI system that allows a person to complete certain operations, like bending a leg, with 90 percent accuracy.[27] The new system uses a special helmet that can measure and transmit brain activity to a computer.

The Major Branches of Artificial Intelligence

AI is a broad field that includes several specialty areas, such as expert systems, robotics, vision systems, natural language processing, learning systems, and neural networks (see Figure 11.4). Many of these areas are related; advances in one can occur simultaneously with or result in advances in others.

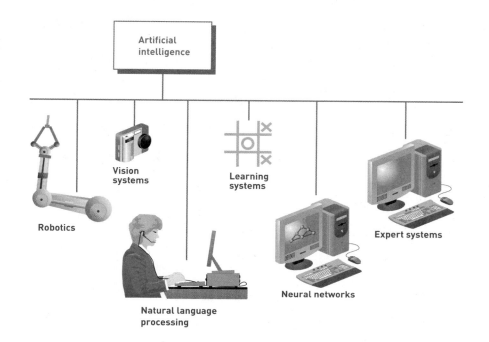

Figure 11.4

A Conceptual Model of Artificial Intelligence

Expert Systems

An expert system consists of hardware and software that stores knowledge and makes inferences, similar to those of a human expert.[28] Because of their many business applications, expert systems are discussed in more detail in the next several sections of the chapter.

Robotics

Robotics involves developing mechanical or computer devices that can paint cars, make precision welds, and perform other tasks that require a high degree of precision or are tedious or hazardous for human beings. The word "robot" comes from a play by Karel Capek in the 1920s, when he used the word "robota" to describe factory machines that do drudgery work but then revolt.[29] The use of robots has expanded and is likely to increase in the future. For many businesses, robots are used to do the three Ds—dull, dirty, and dangerous jobs. Manufacturers use robots to locate, assemble, and paint products.[30] Some robots, such as the ER series by Intelitek (*www.intelitek.com*), can be used for training or entertainment. Contemporary robotics combines both high-precision machine capabilities and sophisticated controlling software. The controlling software in robots is what is most important for AI.

When Canadians think about robotics, the first thing they might think of is the Canadarm, the well-known space tool from MacDonald, Detteiler and Associates (MDA). The field of robotics has many applications, and research into these unique devices continues. The following are a few examples:

- For Inspiration and Recognition in Science and Technology (FIRST) is a high school robotics competition in which teams have six weeks to design and build a robot. A team from Ontario brought home the silver medal and an Excellence in Engineering Award in the 2010 International Robotics Competition.[31]

robotics
Mechanical or computer devices that perform tasks requiring a high degree of precision or that are tedious or hazardous for humans.

WebEx Uses AI-Powered Analytics to Focus Sales Force

WebEx is an online conferencing service that allows participants to view a common computer screen broadcasted over an Internet connection while they converse over the phone. With WebEx, a salesperson or academic researcher could present a PowerPoint presentation from his or her office to interested people scattered around the world. Software developers use WebEx to demonstrate products to clients. Corporations use WebEx to hold online meetings and train new employees. Other people use WebEx for so-called webinars (seminars on the Web) that launch new ideas or products and for help desk operations and customer support.

WebEx is not the only company with an online conferencing product. It fights for market share like most commercial enterprises. WebEx has a large sales force that searches for potential clients, or leads, and then works to turn leads into customers. In sales, it is often difficult to predict which leads will pan out and which will dry up. Because of this, sales representatives sometimes waste time working with leads who have no intention of becoming paying customers. Sales forces use various lead management systems to help ensure that leads will eventually close a deal. The rate at which leads decide to close a deal and become a customer is referred to as the lead-to-close rate. A successful sales force works hard to improve its lead-to-close rate.

To determine which leads will turn into sales you must predict the future. You can make accurate predictions if you understand history, current facts, and trends. What types of behaviour and conditions have led to sales in the past? Do those behaviours and conditions exist in a current scenario? Are past trends the same as current trends?

To accurately predict the future of a sale, it helps to study and understand customer behaviour, past and present. This practice is sometimes referred to as behavioural analytics. Some businesses specialize in behavioural analytics. They collect information about customers, study it thoroughly, and then provide a detailed report on the characteristics of likely customers. More recently, new behavioural analytics software can analyze leads and customers and then advise a sales representative on which leads to pursue.

WebEx selected a SaaS solution from Quantivo Corporation to assist its sales force in improving its lead-to-close rate. The system collects data from WebEx's CRM system along with financial records, website analytics, and WebEx's lead management system. It provides this information to sophisticated AI algorithms. Using data-mining techniques, the Quantivo software "learns" from past sales successes and failures to determine which lead characteristics make for likely sales. Using that information, the system creates lead profiles that the sales force uses to identify current prospects that are ready to buy. Customers and potential customers are also evaluated over time to determine critical touch points, which are opportunities when they may be open to further investment.

Quantivo is easy to use so that sales representatives unfamiliar with the details of behavioural analytics can understand the customer qualities to identify. WebEx also uses the software to identify market segments on which to concentrate the efforts of its entire sales force so they can win more market share with less investment. Sales managers can also evaluate sales patterns relative to individual sales representatives, competitors, sales regions, and other filters.

The amount of information that Quantivo processes in a few seconds or minutes would take a human analyst days or weeks to calculate. Because Quantivo is programmed with machine intelligence to identify profile attributes that lead to sales, it carries out this otherwise human activity continuously and tirelessly, providing new valuable lead data every day. All the sales representative needs to do is enter data collected about each new lead, and Quantivo takes it from there.

Discussion Questions

1. How does Quantivo assist a sales force in being more productive and a company in gaining market share?
2. What role does AI play in Quantivo's operations?

Critical Thinking Questions

1. What specific customer data do you think would assist Quantivo in determining if a lead is likely to become a customer?
2. How might the information provided by Quantivo assist a sales rep in seeking out new and unknown leads?

SOURCES: Schwartz, Joe, "Cisco WebEx Improves Sales Lead-to-Close Rates with Quantivo," *Information Management*, May 2009, *www.information-management.com*; "What Can Behavioural Analytics Do For Me?", Quantivo website, *www.quantivo.com/resources/me_sales.php*, accessed February 2, 2010; "What Is WebEx," WebEx website, *www.webex.com*, accessed February 2, 2010.

- Braintech (*Braintech.com*), a British Columbia company, specializes in intelligent machine vision and robot vision software. The company's software is used around the world in assembly lines at Ford, Toyota, and GM.[32]
- MDA has contracted with the Canadian Space Agency (CSA) to provide advanced technology for CSA's Exploration Surface Mobility program. MDA will lead a team that will design, build, and test a Mars Exploration and Science Rover (MESR) Prototype.[33]
- Robots are used in a variety of ways in medicine. MDA has used its experience in space robotics to develop advanced medical robots. Using real-time magnetic resonance images and a pair of mechanical hands, surgeons can perform operations ranging from repairs of blood vessels to removal of a brain tumour at tolerances down to mere millimetres. A surgeon controls the NeuroArm using levers at a computer workstation in a room next to the operating theatre.
- The Hybrid Assistive Limb (HAL) lab is developing a robotic suit to help paraplegics and stroke victims move so they can perform basic functions. The suit helps with lifting heavy objects, walking long distances, or performing other basic movements that can't be done otherwise. HAL was also the name of an artificial-intelligence computer in the classic movie *2001: A Space Odyssey.* The letters in HAL are each one letter up from the letters in IBM.
- In the military, robots are moving beyond movie plots to become remotely operated vehicles that are deployed to conduct dangerous tasks, such as bomb disposal. Allen-Vanguard Corporation, located in Ottawa, offers counterterrorist equipment systems for defeating and mitigating terrorist devices. Its remotely operated bomb disposal robots have been sold to military and police customers in Canada, the United States, Europe, and Asia.

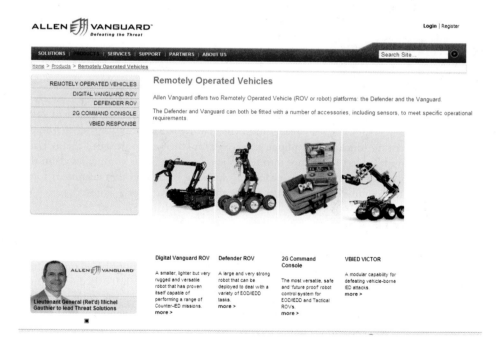

Allen Vanguard's remotely controlled Vanguard and Defender robots are used by military and police forces worldwide.

(Source: Courtesy of Allen Vanguard.)

Although most of today's robots are limited in their capabilities, future robots will find wider applications in banks, restaurants, homes, doctors' offices, and hazardous working environments such as nuclear stations. The Repliee Q1 and Q2 robots from Japan are ultra-humanlike robots or androids that can blink, gesture, speak, and even appear to breathe (*www.ed.ams.eng.osaka-u.ac.jp/development/Android_RreplieeQ2_e.html*). See Figure 11.5 on the next page. Microrobotics, also called *micro-electro-mechanical systems (MEMS)*, are also being developed (*www.memsnet.org/mems/what-is.html*). MEMS can be used in a person's bloodstream to monitor the body and in air bags, cell phones, refrigerators, and more.

Figure 11.5

The Repliee Q2 Robot from Japan

(Source: AP Photo/Katsumi Kasahara.)

vision systems
The hardware and software that permit computers to capture, store, and manipulate visual images.such as English.

natural language processing
Processing that allows the computer to understand and react to statements and commands made in a "natural" language, such as English.

Dragon Systems' NaturallySpeaking 10 uses continuous voice recognition, or natural speech, allowing the user to speak to the computer at a normal pace without pausing between words. The spoken words are transcribed immediately onto the computer screen.

(Source: Courtesy of Nuance.)

learning systems
A combination of software and hardware that allows the computer to change how it functions or how it reacts to situations based on feedback it receives.

Vision Systems

Another area of AI involves vision systems. **Vision systems** include hardware and software that permit computers to capture, store, and manipulate visual images.[34] Vision systems are effective at identifying people based on facial features. Nvidia's GeForce 3D is software that can display images on a computer screen that are three-dimensional when viewed with special glasses.[35]

Natural Language Processing and Voice Recognition

As discussed in Chapter 4, **natural language processing** allows a computer to understand and react to statements and commands made in a "natural" language, such as English.[36] Google, for example, has a service called Google Voice Local Search that allows you to dial a toll-free number and search for local businesses using voice commands and statements. Many companies provide natural language processing help over the phone. When you call the help phone number, you are typically given a menu of options and asked to speak your responses. Many people, however, are frustrated talking to a machine instead of a human.

In some cases, voice recognition is used with natural language processing. *Voice recognition* involves converting sound waves into words. After converting sounds into words, natural language processing systems react to the words or commands by performing a variety of tasks. Bell Canada and Rogers have implemented voice-recognition and natural language processing technology to replace the existing touchpad telephone menu system when customers call them. Using voice recognition to convert recordings into text is also possible. Some companies claim that voice-recognition and natural language processing software is so good that customers forget they are talking to a computer and start discussing the weather or sports scores.

Learning Systems

Another part of AI deals with **learning systems**, a combination of software and hardware that allows a computer to change how it functions or how it reacts to situations based on feedback it receives. For example, some computerized games have learning abilities. If the computer does not win a game, it remembers not to make the same moves under the same conditions again.[37] IBM, for example, has developed a computer called Watson, named after one of its founders, that challenged humans in the popular TV program *Jeopardy*.[38] The objective was to demonstrate how a sophisticated computer system can challenge humans and provide fast, accurate answers to difficult questions. *Reinforcement Learning* is a learning system involving sequential decisions with learning taking place between each decision.[39] Reinforcement learning often involves sophisticated computer programming and optimization techniques, first discussed in Chapter 10. The computer makes a decision, analyzes the results, and then makes a better decision based on the analysis. The process, often called *dynamic programming*, is repeated until it is impossible to make improvements in the decision.

Learning systems software requires feedback on the results of actions or decisions. At a minimum, the feedback needs to indicate whether the results are desirable (winning a game) or undesirable (losing a game). The feedback is then used to alter what the system will do in the future.

Neural Networks

An increasingly important aspect of AI involves neural networks, also called neural nets. A **neural network** is a computer system that can act like or simulate the functioning of a human brain. The systems can use massively parallel processors in an architecture that is based on the human brain's own mesh-like structure. In addition, neural network software simulates a neural network using standard computers. Neural networks can process many pieces of data at the same time and learn to recognize patterns.[40] For example, in the Joint Strike Fighter program, the aerospace and defence sector in Canada designed a neural network to help identify aircraft repair and maintenance problems.[41] Some oil and gas exploration companies use a program called the Rate of Penetration based on neural networks to monitor and control drilling operations. The neural network program helps engineers slow down or speed up drilling operations to help increase drilling accuracy and reduce costs.

More businesses are firing up neural nets to help them navigate ever-thicker forests of data and make sense of a myriad of customer traits and buying habits. Computer Associates has developed Neugents (*www.neugents.com*), neural intelligence agents that "learn" patterns and behaviours and predict what will happen next. For example, Neugents can track the habits of insurance customers and predict which ones will not renew an automobile policy. They can then suggest to an insurance agent what changes to make in the policy to persuade the consumer to renew it.

AI Trilogy, available from the Ward Systems Group (*www.wardsystems.com*), is a neural network software program that can run on a standard PC. The software can make predictions with NeuroShell Predictor and classify information with NeuroShell Classifier. See Figure 11.6. The software package also contains GeneHunter, which uses a special type of algorithm called a genetic algorithm to get the best result from the neural network system.

neural network
A computer system that can simulate the functioning of a human brain.

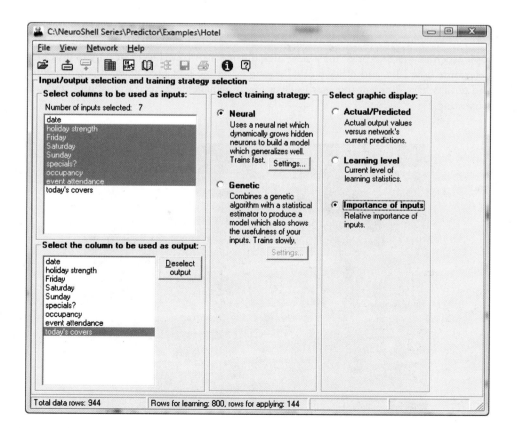

Figure 11.6

Neural Network Software

NeuroShell Predictor uses recognized forecasting methods to look for future trends in data.

(Source: Courtesy of Ward Systems Group, Inc.)

(Genetic algorithms are discussed in a moment.) Some pattern-recognition software uses neural networks to analyze hundreds of millions of bank, brokerage, and insurance accounts involving a trillion dollars to uncover money laundering and other suspicious money transfers.

Other Artificial Intelligence Applications

A few other artificial intelligence applications exist in addition to those just discussed. A **genetic algorithm**, also called a genetic program, is an approach to solving large, complex problems in which many repeated operations or models change and evolve until the best one emerges.[42] The approach is based on the theory of evolution that requires (1) variation and (2) natural selection. The first step is to change or vary competing solutions to the problem. This can be done by changing the parts of a program or by combining different program segments into a new program, mimicking the evolution of species, in which the genetic makeup of a plant or animal mutates or changes over time. The second step is to select only the best models or algorithms, which continue to evolve. Programs or program segments that are not as good as others are discarded—a process similar to what happens in natural selection in which only the best species survive and continue to evolve. This process of variation and selection continues until the genetic algorithm yields the best possible solution to the original problem. A genetic algorithm can be used to help schedule airline crews to meet flight requirements, while minimizing total costs.[43] Natural Selection, a San Diego company, originally developed a genetic algorithm that attempted to analyze past inventions and suggest future ones.[44] Although the original genetic algorithm was not an immediate success, the approach has been used by General Electric and others to cut costs and streamline delivery routes of products.

An **intelligent agent** (also called an *intelligent robot* or *bot*) consists of programs and a knowledge base used to perform a specific task for a person, a process, or another program. Like a sports agent who searches for the best endorsement deals for a top athlete, an intelligent agent often searches to find the best price, schedule, or solution to a problem. The programs used by an intelligent agent can search large amounts of data as the knowledge base refines the search or accommodates user preferences. Often used to search the vast resources of the Internet, intelligent agents can help people find information on any topic, such as the best price for a new digital camera. An intelligent agent can also help determine how land and other natural resources can be best used when different people and groups have different interests, such as forest management, recreational uses, and tree harvesting.[45]

genetic algorithm
An approach to solving large, complex problems in which many related operations or models change and evolve until the best one emerges.

intelligent agent
Programs and a knowledge base used to perform a specific task for a person, a process, or another program; also called *intelligent robot* or *bot*.

NASA's Jet Propulsion Laboratory has an agent that monitors inventory, planning, and scheduling equipment ordering to keep costs down, as well as food storage facilities. These agents usually monitor complex computer networks that can keep track of the configuration of each computer connected to the network.

(Source: NASA.)

AN OVERVIEW OF EXPERT SYSTEMS

As mentioned earlier, an expert system behaves similarly to a human expert in a particular field. Like human experts, computerized expert systems use heuristics, or rules of thumb, to arrive at conclusions or make suggestions. One company uses the Lantek expert system to cut and fabricate metal into finished products for the automotive, construction, and mining industries. The expert system helped reduce raw material waste and increase profits. The U.S. Army uses the Knowledge and Information Fusion Exchange (KnIFE) expert system to help soldiers in the field make better military decisions based on successful decisions made in previous military engagements.

Expert systems are used in metal fabrication plants to aid in decision making.

(Source: © H. Mark Weidman Photography/Alamy.)

When to Use Expert Systems

Sophisticated expert systems can be difficult, expensive, and time consuming to develop. This is especially true for large expert systems implemented on mainframes. The following is a list of factors that normally make expert systems worth the expenditure of time and money. People and organizations should develop an expert system if it can do any of the following:

- Provide a high potential payoff or significantly reduce downside risk
- Capture and preserve irreplaceable human expertise
- Solve a problem that is not easily solved using traditional programming techniques
- Develop a system more consistent than human experts
- Provide expertise needed at a number of locations at the same time or in a hostile environment that is dangerous to human health
- Provide expertise that is expensive or rare
- Develop a solution faster than human experts can
- Provide expertise needed for training and development to share the wisdom and experience of human experts with many people

Components of Expert Systems

An expert system consists of a collection of integrated and related components, including a knowledge base, an inference engine, an explanation facility, a knowledge base acquisition facility, and a user interface. A diagram of a typical expert system is shown in Figure 11.7. In this figure, the user interacts with the interface, which interacts with the inference engine. The inference engine interacts with the other expert system components. These components must work together to provide expertise. This figure shows the inference engine coordinating the flow of knowledge to other components of the expert system. Note that different knowledge flows can exist, depending on what the expert system is doing and on the specific expert system involved.

Figure 11.7

Components of an Expert System

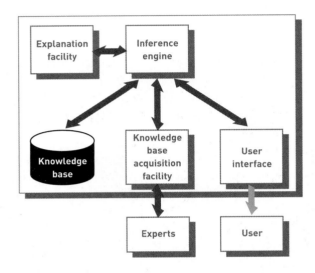

The Knowledge Base

knowledge base
The collection of data, rules, procedures, and relationships that must be followed to achieve value or the proper outcome.

The **knowledge base** stores all relevant information, data, rules, cases, and relationships that the expert system uses. As shown in Figure 11.8, a knowledge base is a natural extension of a database (presented in Chapter 5) and an information and decision support system (presented in Chapter 10). A knowledge base must be developed for each unique application. For example, a medical expert system contains facts about diseases and symptoms. The following are some tools and techniques that can be used to create a knowledge base.[46]

Figure 11.8

The Relationships Between Data, Information, and Knowledge

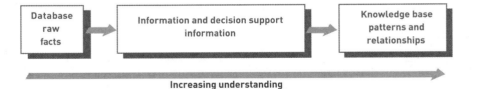

rule
A conditional statement that links conditions to actions or outcomes.

IF-THEN statements
Rules that suggest certain conclusions.

- *Using rules.* A **rule** is a conditional statement that links conditions to actions or outcomes. In many instances, these rules are stored as **IF-THEN statements**, which are rules that suggest certain conclusions. For example: "If a certain set of network conditions exists, then a certain network problem diagnosis is appropriate." In an expert system for a weather forecasting operation, for example, the rules could state that if certain temperature patterns exist with a given barometric pressure and certain previous weather patterns over the last 24 hours, then a specific forecast will be made, including temperatures, cloud coverage, and wind-chill factor. IBM has used a rule-based expert system to help detect execution errors in its large mainframe computers.[47] Figure 11.9 shows how to use expert system rules in determining whether a person should receive a mortgage loan from a bank. These rules can be placed in

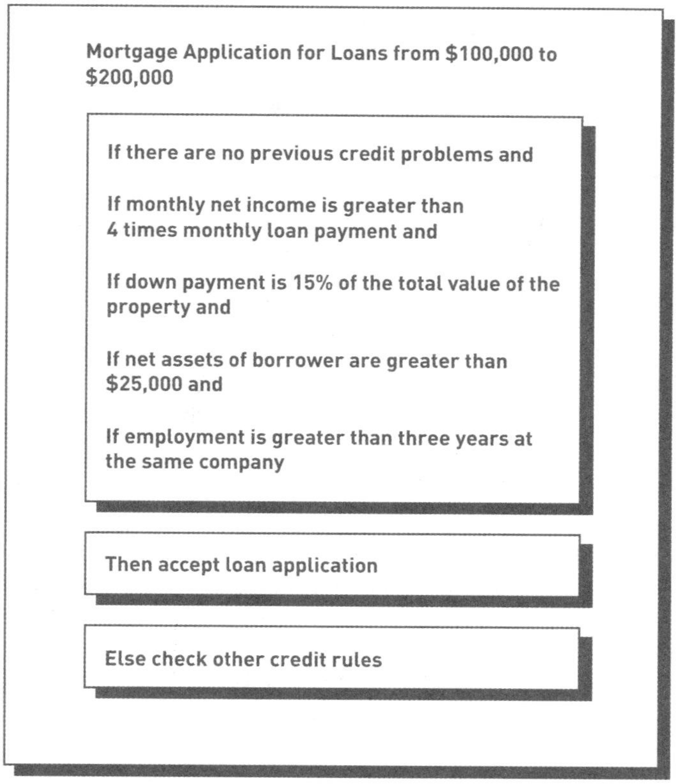

Figure 11.9

Rules for a Credit Application

Mortgage Application for Loans from $100,000 to $200,000

If there are no previous credit problems and

If monthly net income is greater than 4 times monthly loan payment and

If down payment is 15% of the total value of the property and

If net assets of borrower are greater than $25,000 and

If employment is greater than three years at the same company

Then accept loan application

Else check other credit rules

almost any standard program language (discussed in Chapter 4) using "IF-THEN" statements or into special expert systems shells and products, discussed later in the chapter. In general, as the number of rules that an expert system knows increases, the precision of the expert system also increases.

- *Using cases.* An expert system can use cases in developing a solution to a current problem or situation. This process involves (1) finding cases stored in the knowledge base that are similar to the problem or situation at hand, and (2) modifying the solutions to the cases to fit or accommodate the current problem or situation. For example, a company might use an expert system to determine the best location for a new service facility in Manitoba. The expert system might identify two previous cases involving the location of a service facility where labour and transportation costs were also important—one in Quebec and the other in Alberta. The expert system can modify the solution to these two cases to determine the best location for a new facility in Manitoba. In another situation, a case-based expert system was used to help determine how jobs were assigned in a chip fabrication factory.[48]

The Inference Engine

The overall purpose of an **inference engine** is to seek information and relationships from the knowledge base and to provide answers, predictions, and suggestions similar to the way a human expert would. In other words, the inference engine is the component that delivers the expert advice. Consider the expert system that forecasts future sales for a product. One approach is to start with a fact such as "The demand for the product last month was 20,000 units." The expert system searches for rules that contain a reference to product demand. For example, "IF product demand is over 15,000 units, THEN check the demand for competing products." As a result of this process, the expert system might use information on the demand for competitive products. Next, after searching additional rules, the expert

inference engine
Part of the expert system that seeks information and relationships from the knowledge base and provides answers, predictions, and suggestions similar to the way a human expert would.

system might use information on personal income or national inflation rates. This process continues until the expert system can reach a conclusion using the data supplied by the user and the rules that apply in the knowledge base.

The Explanation Facility

explanation facility
Component of an expert system that allows a user or decision maker to understand how the expert system arrived at certain conclusions or results.

An important part of an expert system is the **explanation facility**, which allows a user or decision maker to understand how the expert system arrived at certain conclusions or results. A medical expert system, for example, might reach the conclusion that a patient has a defective heart valve given certain symptoms and the results of tests on the patient. The explanation facility allows a doctor to find out the logic or rationale of the diagnosis made by the expert system. The expert system, using the explanation facility, can indicate all the facts and rules that were used in reaching the conclusion, which the doctors can look at to determine whether the expert system is processing the data and information correctly and logically.

The Knowledge Acquisition Facility

A difficult task in developing an expert system is the process of creating and updating the knowledge base. In the past, when more traditional programming languages were used, developing a knowledge base was tedious and time consuming. Each fact, relationship, and rule had to be programmed into the knowledge base. In most cases, an experienced programmer had to create and update the knowledge base.

knowledge acquisition facility
Part of the expert system that provides a convenient and efficient means of capturing and storing all the components of the knowledge base.

Today, specialized software allows users and decision makers to create and modify their own knowledge bases through the knowledge acquisition facility, as shown in Figure 11.10. The purpose of the **knowledge acquisition facility** is to provide a convenient and efficient means of capturing and storing all components of the knowledge base.[49] Knowledge acquisition software can present users and decision makers with easy-to-use menus. After entering the appropriate attributes, the knowledge acquisition facility correctly stores information and relationships in the knowledge base, making the knowledge base easier and less expensive to set up and maintain.

Figure 11.10

Knowledge Acquisition Facility

The knowledge acquisition facility acts as an interface between experts and the knowledge base.

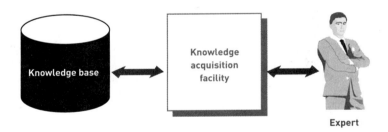

The User Interface

The main purpose of the user interface is to make an expert system easier for users and decision makers to develop and use. At one time, skilled computer personnel created and operated most expert systems; today, the user interface permits decision makers to develop and use their own expert systems. A typical user interface between a user and the expert system for the credit application shown in Figure 11.9 follows.

EXPERT SYSTEM: Are there any previous credit problems?

USER: No.

EXPERT SYSTEM: Is the applicant's net income greater than four times the monthly loan payment?

USER: Yes.

EXPERT SYSTEM: Is the down payment greater than 15 percent of the property value?

USER: Yes.

EXPERT SYSTEM: Are the net assets of the borrower greater than $25,000?

USER: Yes.

EXPERT SYSTEM: Has the borrower worked more than three years at the same company?

USER: Yes.

EXPERT SYSTEM: **Accept the loan application.**

Participants in Developing and Using Expert Systems

Typically, several people are involved in developing and using an expert system. See Figure 11.11.

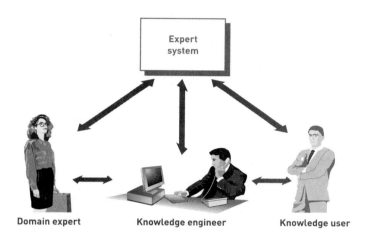

Figure 11.11

Participants in Expert Systems Development and Use

Domain expert   Knowledge engineer   Knowledge user

There are a number of participants in the development and use of an expert system. The **domain expert** is the person or group with the expertise or knowledge the expert system is trying to capture (domain). In most cases, the domain expert is a group of human experts. Research has shown that good domain experts can increase the overall quality of an expert system.[50] A **knowledge engineer** is a person who has training or experience in the design, development, implementation, and maintenance of an expert system, including training or experience with expert system shells. Knowledge engineers can help transfer the knowledge from the expert system to the knowledge user.[51] The **knowledge user** is the person or group who uses and benefits from the expert system. Knowledge users do not need any previous training in computers or expert systems.

domain expert
The person or group with the expertise or knowledge the expert system is trying to capture (domain).

knowledge engineer
A person who has training or experience in the design, development, implementation, and maintenance of an expert system.

knowledge user
The person or group who uses and benefits from the expert system.

Expert Systems Development Tools and Techniques

Theoretically, expert systems can be developed from any programming language. Since the introduction of computer systems, programming languages have become easier to use, more powerful, and better able to handle specialized requirements. In the early days of expert systems development, traditional high-level languages, including Pascal, FORTRAN, and COBOL, were used, as shown in Figure 11.12 on page 461. LISP was one of the first special languages developed and used for artificial intelligence applications. PROLOG was also developed for AI applications. Since the 1990s, however, other expert system products (such as shells) have become available that remove the burden of programming, allowing nonprogrammers to develop and benefit from the use of expert systems.

Expert System Shells and Products

An *expert system shell* is a collection of software packages and tools used to design, develop, implement, and maintain expert systems. Expert system shells are available for both personal computers and mainframe systems. Some shells are inexpensive, costing less than

ETHICAL AND SOCIETAL ISSUES

Austin Energy First to Implement a Smart Grid

The power generators that provide homes and businesses in the United States with electricity are responsible for 40 percent of the country's energy consumption. Transportation is second, consuming around 29 percent of the country's energy. Creating efficiencies in energy consumption in these two sectors could greatly decrease our dependency on non-renewable resources. The solution would also reduce carbon emissions, resulting in economic, environmental, and social benefits.

One solution that has become popular for saving electricity involves special-purpose systems referred to as Intelligent Utility Networks (IUNs), or smart grid technologies. In 2009, the U.S. Department of Energy distributed $3.4 billion in financial stimulus funding to launch 100 smart grid projects across the country. By that time, Austin Energy in Austin, Texas, had already rolled out its smart grid and was designing what it calls Smart Grid 2.0. The lessons Austin Energy learned and its pioneering spirit have served as guidelines for other companies now embarking on smart grid projects.

In 2003, Austin Energy worked with IBM and Ascendant Technology (an IT consulting company) to launch its IUN initiative, which it calls Smart Grid 1.0. So how can a utility network be intelligent or smart? As you are learning in this chapter, computers can be programmed to carry out tasks the way a domain expert does, even making judgment calls based on past experience. However, to act intelligently, the computers that control a utility network need access to consumption and production information. That means the first steps in transforming a traditional electric grid into a smart grid are replacing traditional electricity meters with digital meters and deploying sensors across the network to collect production and flow information.

Digital meters, also called smart meters, collect detailed information about electric consumption and wirelessly report it to the electric company using standard Internet protocols. It took Austin Energy five years to install 410,000 smart meters for its customers. Additionally, Austin Energy installed 86,000 smart thermostats that also contribute information to the smart grid. They installed 2,500 sensors on the grid, along with 3,000 computers, additional servers, and network gear to collect and process the information. By October 2008, Austin Energy was processing hundreds of terabytes of data flowing in from meters and sensors, which provided detailed consumption data every 15 minutes.

With access to detailed utility network data, Austin Energy can now determine where energy is most required on its network at any time of the day. Using a distributed system, rather than one central power distribution point, Austin Energy automates the supply of electricity to various points on its grid as needed. The intelligent network can foresee power outages and make adjustments to prevent them.

Austin Energy is also experimenting with many forms of alternative energy sources. Its smart grid makes it possible for energy consumers to produce energy (through solar, wind, or other generation methods) and provide it back to the network for credit. Tracking energy consumption and production and efficiently routing electricity to where it is most urgently needed becomes too laborious for human operators. Instead, Austin Energy programmed its knowledge into its computer systems, which are better equipped to manage the huge amounts of continuously streaming data.

Having access to detailed energy information empowers both consumers and policy makers so they can make wiser decisions. Consumers using a smart grid can go online to view and evaluate their energy consumption patterns, perhaps finding that minor changes in lifestyle could create major savings in energy consumption. Policy makers can determine whether the country's energy supply is being consumed wisely, and in times of crisis can make decisions that maintain essential systems.

Austin Energy is sold on the idea that information empowers. The second phase of its initiative, Smart Grid 2.0, extends its reach into the homes and businesses of its consumers. Using smart appliances and smart thermostats, Austin Energy can assist consumers in learning how to best consume energy within their domain. Austin Energy is even looking at ways to use electric car batteries as a household backup power supply; an electric car charging in the garage could reverse its current to provide five hours of electricity to the home during power failures.

By analyzing energy consumption in a highly detailed fashion, smart grids can assist the country in squeezing the most usefulness out of every watt produced. Austin Energy found that it saved 660 megawatts of electricity in its first month using America's first smart grid.

Discussion Questions

1. How can smart grids provide economic, environmental, and social benefits?
2. What are the key components in a smart grid system?

Critical Thinking Questions

1. Why do you think the U.S. government decided to invest billions of dollars to jump-start smart grids across the country?
2. What privacy concerns, if any, might arise from Austin Energy's Smart Grid 2.0 project?

SOURCES: Fehrenbacher, Katie, "Smart Grid Stimulus Funding Revealed!" Earth-2Tech, October 27, 2009, *http://earth2tech.com*; Carvallo, Andres, "LIGHTSON: Austin Energy Delivers First Smart Grid in the US," Electric Energy Online, *www.electricenergyonline.com*, accessed February 2, 2010; Carvallo, Andres, "Austin Energy Plans Its Smart Grid 2.0," CIO Master, April 18, 2009, *www.ciomaster.com*; LaMonica, Martin, "Will Anyone Pay for the 'Smart' Power Grid," Cnet News, May 16, 2007, *news.cnet.com*; "Austin Energy Smart Grid Program," Austin Energy website, *www.austinenergy.com/About%20Us/Company%20Profile/smartGrid*, accessed February 2, 2010.

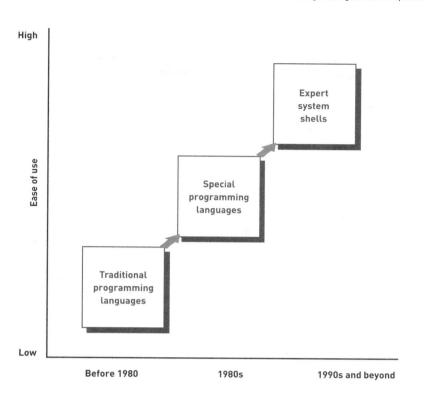

Figure 11.12

Expert Systems Development

Software for expert systems development has evolved greatly since 1980, from traditional programming languages to expert system shells.

$500. In addition, off-the-shelf expert system shells are complete and ready to run. The user enters the appropriate data or parameters, and the expert system provides output to the problem or situation. Table 11.2 lists a few expert system products.

Name of Product	Application and Capabilities
Exsys Corvid	An expert system tool that simulates a conversation with a human expert from Exsys (*www.exsys.com*)[52]
EZ-Xpert	A rule-based expert system that results in complete applications in the C++ or Visual Basic programming languages by EZ-Xpert (*www.ez-xpert.com*)[53]
G2	Assists in oil and gas operations
HazMat Loader	Analyzes hazardous materials in truck shipments (*http://hazmat.dot.gov*)
Imprint Business Systems	Has an expert system that helps printing and packaging companies manage their businesses (*www.imprint-mis.co.uk*)
Lantek Expert System	Helps metal fabricators reduce waste and increase profits (*www.lantek.es*)

Table 11.2

Popular Expert System Products

MULTIMEDIA AND VIRTUAL REALITY

The use of multimedia and virtual reality has helped many companies achieve a competitive advantage and increase profits. The approach and technology used in multimedia is often the foundation of virtual reality systems, discussed later in this section. Although these specialized information systems are not used by all organizations, they can play a key role for many. We begin with a discussion of multimedia.

Overview of Multimedia

multimedia
Text, graphics, video, animation, audio, and other media that can be used to help an organization efficiently and effectively achieve its goals.

Multimedia is text, graphics, video, animation, audio, and other media that can be used to help an organization efficiently and effectively achieve its goals. Multimedia can be used to create stunning brochures, presentations, reports, and documents. Although not all organizations use the full capabilities of multimedia, most use text and graphics capabilities.

Text and Graphics

All large organizations and most small and medium-sized ones use text and graphics to develop reports, financial statements, advertising pieces, and other documents used internally and externally. Internally, organizations use text and graphics to communicate policies, guidelines, and much more to managers and employees. Externally, organizations use text and graphics to communicate to suppliers, customers, federal and provincial organizations, and a variety of other stakeholders. Text can have different sizes, fonts, and colours. Graphics can include photographs, illustrations, drawings, a variety of charts, and other still images. Graphic images can be stored in a variety of formats, including JPEG (Joint Photographic Experts Group format) and GIF (Graphics Interchange Format).

While standard word-processing programs are an inexpensive and simple way to develop documents and reports that require text and graphics, most organizations use specialized software. Adobe Illustrator, for example, can be used to create attractive and informative charts, illustrations, and brochures. The software can also be used to develop digital art, reference manuals, and profit and loss statements. Adobe Photoshop is a sophisticated and popular software package that can be used to edit photographs and other visual images. Once created, these documents and reports can be saved in an Adobe PDF (Portable Document Format) file and sent over the Internet or saved on a CD or similar storage device.

Microsoft Silverlight can be used to add high-definition video and animation to Internet sites and other programming.[54] CTV used Silverlight when it broadcast the 2010 Olympics. PowerPoint, also by Microsoft, can be used to develop a presentation that is displayed on a large viewing screen with sound and animation. There are many other graphics programs, such as Paint and PhotoDraw by Microsoft and CorelDraw. Many graphics programs can create 3D images. James Cameron's movie *Avatar* used sophisticated computers and 3D imaging to create one of the most profitable movies in history.[55] Once used primarily in movies, 3D technology can be used by companies to design products such as motorcycles, jet engines, bridges, and more.[56] Autodesk, for example, makes exciting 3D software that companies can use to design large skyscrapers and other buildings.[57] The software can also be used by Hollywood animators to develop exciting movies. The technology used to produce 3D movies is now available with TVs. Due to technical challenges, it may take a few years for Canadian TV carriers to offer full 3D programming. Graphics software and systems can be used to help scientists understand our universe, doctors perform delicate surgeries, military specialists guide unmanned drones used to locate and destroy enemy targets, geologists locate oil and gas, and many more applications. See Figure 11.13.

Audio

Audio includes music, human voices, recorded sounds, and a variety of computer-generated sounds. Audio can be stored in a variety of file formats, including MP3 (Motion Picture Experts Group Audio Layer 3), WAV (wave format), MIDI (Musical Instrument Digital Interface), and other formats. When audio files are played while they are being downloaded from the Internet, it's called *streaming audio.*

Input to audio software includes audio recording devices like microphones, imported music or sound from CDs or audio files, MIDI instruments that can create music and sounds directly, and other audio sources. Once stored, audio files can be edited and augmented

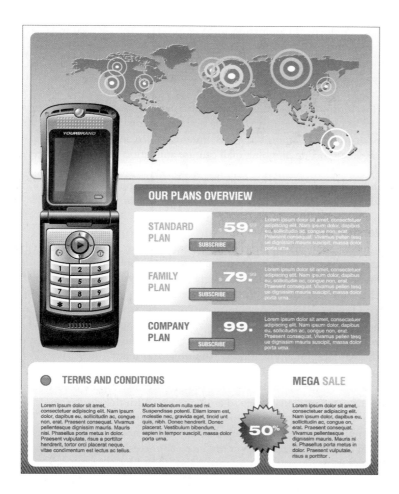

Figure 11.13

Digital Graphics

Businesses create graphics such as charts, illustrations, and brochures using software such as Adobe Photoshop or Adobe Illustrator.

(Source: Viktor Gmyria/Shutterstock.com.)

using audio software, such as Apple's QuickTime, Microsoft's Sound Recorder, and Adobe's Audition. Audio files are used by scientists to monitor ocean life, submarines for navigation and enemy ship detection, radio stations to broadcast news and music, and law enforcement to catch criminals. Once edited, audio files can also be used to enhance presentations, create music, broadcast satellite radio signals, develop audio books, record podcasts for iPods and other audio players, provide realism to movies, and enhance video and animation.

Apple Soundtrack Pro provides editing tools for editing and producing audio files in a variety of formats.

(Source: Courtesy of Apple, Inc.)

Video and Animation

The moving images of video and animation are typically created by rapidly displaying one still image after another. Video and animation can be stored in AVI (Audio Video Interleave) files used with many Microsoft applications, MPEG (Motion Picture Experts Group format) files, and MOV (QuickTime format) files used with many Apple applications. When video files are played while they are being downloaded from the Internet, it's called *streaming video.* On the Internet, Java applets (small downloadable programs) and animated GIF files can be used to animate or create "moving" images.

A number of video and animation software products can be used to create and/or edit video and animation files. Many video and animation programs can create realistic 3D moving images. Adobe's Premiere and After Effects and Apple's Final Cut Pro can be used to edit video images taken from cameras and other sources. Final Cut Pro, for example, has been used to edit and produce full-length motion pictures shown in movie theatres. Adobe Flash and LiveMotion can be used to add motion and animation to Web pages.

There are many business uses of video and animation. Companies that develop computer-based or Internet training materials often use video and audio software. An information kiosk at an airport or shopping mall can use animation to help customers check into a flight or get information. Of course, movie studios use audio and video techniques to make standard and animated movies. Pixar, for example, used sophisticated animation software to create dazzling 3D movies. The exact process can be seen at Pixar's website.[58]

File Conversion and Compression

Most multimedia applications are created, edited, and distributed in a digital file format, such as the ones discussed above. Older inputs to these applications, however, can be in an analog format from old home movies, magnetic tape, vinyl records, or similar sources. In addition, there are older digital formats that are no longer popular or used. In these cases, the analog and older digital formats must be converted into a newer digital format before they can be edited and processed by today's multimedia software. This can be done with a conversion program or specialized hardware. Some of the multimedia software discussed above, such as Adobe Premium, Adobe Audition, and many others, have this analog-to-digital conversion capability. Standalone software and specialized hardware can also be used.[59] Grass Valley, for example, is a hardware device that can be used to convert analog video to digital video or digital video to analog video. With this device, you can convert old VHS tapes to digital video files or digital video files to an analog format.

Because multimedia files can be large, it's sometimes necessary to compress files in order to make them easier to download from the Internet or send as e-mail attachments. Many of the multimedia software programs discussed above can be used to compress files. In addition, there are standalone file conversion programs, such as WinZip, that can be used to compress many file formats.

Designing a Multimedia Application

Designing multimedia applications requires careful thought and a systematic approach. The overall approach to modifying any existing application or developing a new one is discussed in the next chapters on systems development. There are, however, some additional considerations in developing a multimedia application. Multimedia applications can be printed on beautiful brochures, placed into attractive corporate reports, uploaded to the Internet, or displayed on large screens for viewing. Because these applications are typically more expensive than preparing documents and files in a word-processing program, it is important to spend time designing the best possible multimedia application. Designing a multimedia application requires that the end use of the document or file be carefully considered. For example, some text styles and fonts are designed for Internet display. Because different computers and Web browsers display information differently, it is a good idea to select styles, fonts, and presentations based on computers and browsers that are likely to display the multimedia application. Because large files can take much longer to load into a Web page, smaller files are usually preferred for Web-based multimedia applications.

Overview of Virtual Reality

The term "virtual reality" was initially coined by Jaron Lanier, founder of VPL Research, in 1989. Originally, the term referred to *immersive virtual reality*, in which the user becomes fully immersed in an artificial, 3D world that is completely generated by a computer. Immersive virtual reality can represent any 3D setting, real or abstract, such as a building, an archaeological excavation site, the human anatomy, a sculpture, or a crime scene reconstruction.

Through immersion, the user can gain a deeper understanding of the virtual world's behaviour and functionality. The Canadian government, for example, invested $1.5 million to develop a virtual reality rehabilitation system for injured Canadian Forces personnel.[60]

A **virtual reality system** enables one or more users to move and react in a computer-simulated environment. Virtual reality simulations require special interface devices that transmit the sights, sounds, and sensations of the simulated world to the user. These devices can also record and send the speech and movements of the participants to the simulation program, enabling users to sense and manipulate virtual objects much as they would real objects. This natural style of interaction gives the participants the feeling that they are immersed in the simulated world. For example, an auto manufacturer can use virtual reality to help it simulate and design factories.

virtual reality system
A system that enables one or more users to move and react in a computer-simulated environment.

Interface Devices

To see in a virtual world, often the user wears a head-mounted display (HMD) with screens directed at each eye. The HMD also contains a position tracker to monitor the location of the user's head and the direction in which the user is looking. Using this information, a computer generates images of the virtual world—a slightly different view for each eye—to match the direction that the user is looking, and displays these images on the HMD. Many companies sell or rent virtual-reality interface devices, including Virtual Realities (*www.vrealities.com*), Amusitronix (*www.amusitronix.com*), and I-O Display Systems (*www.i-glassesstore.com*).

The Electronic Visualization Laboratory at the University of Illinois at Chicago introduced a room constructed of large screens on three walls and the floor on which the graphics are projected. The CAVE, as this room is called, provides the illusion of immersion by projecting stereo images on the walls and floor of a room-sized cube (*http://cave.ncsa.uiuc.edu*). Several persons wearing lightweight stereo glasses can enter and walk freely inside the CAVE. A head-tracking system continuously adjusts the stereo projection to the current position of the leading viewer.

Users hear sounds in the virtual world through earphones. The information reported by the position tracker is also used to update audio signals. When a sound source in virtual space is not directly in front of or behind the user, the computer transmits sounds to arrive at one ear a little earlier or later than at the other and to be a little louder or softer and slightly different in pitch.

The *haptic* interface, which relays the sense of touch and other physical sensations in the virtual world, is the least developed and perhaps the most challenging to create.[61] A Japanese virtual reality company has developed a haptic interface device that can be placed on a person's fingertips to give an accurate feel for game players, surgeons, and others.[62] Currently, with the use of a glove and position tracker, the computer locates the user's hand and measures finger movements. The user can reach into the virtual world and handle objects; however, it is difficult to generate the sensations of a person tapping a hard surface, picking up an object, or running a finger across a textured surface. Touch sensations also have to be synchronized with the sights and sounds users experience. Today, some virtual reality developers are even trying to incorporate taste and smell into virtual reality applications.[63] According to a virtual reality researcher at the University of Warwick Digital Lab in the United Kingdom, "The crucial thing for virtual reality is that it will hit all five senses in a highly realistic manner. . . . We need to have smell, we need to have taste."

Forms of Virtual Reality

Aside from immersive virtual reality, virtual reality can also refer to applications that are not fully immersive, such as mouse-controlled navigation through a 3D environment on a graphics monitor, stereo viewing from the monitor via stereo glasses, stereo projection systems, and others. *Augmented reality*, a newer form of virtual reality, has the potential to superimpose digital data over real photos or images.[64] GPS maps, for example, can be combined with real pictures of stores and streets to help you locate your position or find your way to a new destination. Using augmented reality, you can point a smartphone camera at a historic landmark such as a castle, museum, or other building and have information about the landmark appear on your screen, including a brief description of the landmark, admission price, and hours of operation. Although still in its early phases of implementation, augmented reality has the potential to become an important feature of tomorrow's smartphones and similar mobile devices.

Some virtual reality applications allow views of real environments with superimposed virtual objects. Telepresence systems (such as telemedicine and telerobotics) immerse a viewer in a real world that is captured by video cameras at a distant location and allow for the remote manipulation of real objects via robot arms and manipulators. Many believe that virtual reality will reshape the interface between people and information technology by offering new ways to communicate information, visualize processes, and express ideas creatively.

Using virtual reality technology, health professionals can perform remote medical procedures or examinations, even virtual surgery.

(Source: AP Photo/Jens Meyer.)

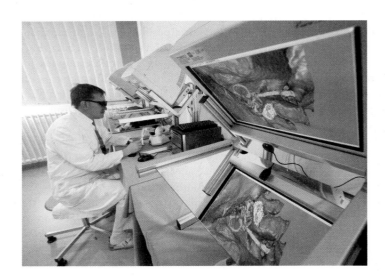

Virtual Reality Applications

You can find thousands of applications of virtual reality, with more being developed as the cost of hardware and software declines and as people's imaginations are opened to the potential of virtual reality. The following are a few virtual reality applications in medicine, education and training, business, and entertainment.

Medicine

Barbara Rothbaum, the director of the Trauma and Recovery Program at the U.S. Emory University School of Medicine and cofounder of Virtually Better, uses an immersive virtual reality system to help in the treatment of anxiety disorders.[65] One VR program, called SnowWorld, helps treat burn patients.[66] Using VR, the patients can navigate through icy terrain and frigid waterfalls. VR helps because it gets a patient's mind off the pain. In Canada, one study looked at the effectiveness of using the Wii gaming system in rehabilitating stroke patients.[67]

Education and Training

Virtual environments are used in education to bring exciting new resources into the classroom. According to the founder of Mantis Development Corporation, a software company that specialized in digital media and virtual reality, "In order to learn, you need to engage the mind, and immersive education is engaging."[68] In development for more than 10 years, *3D Rewind Rome* is a virtual reality show developed at a virtual reality lab at University of California Los Angeles (UCLA).[69] The show is historically accurate with over 7,000 reconstructed buildings.

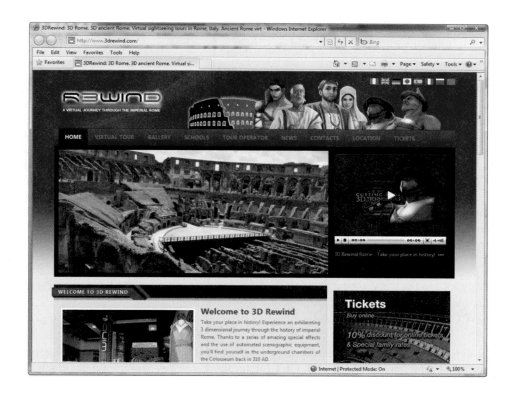

3D Rewind Rome is based on more than 10 years of research by archaeologists and historians coordinated by the University of California, Los Angeles.

(Source: Courtesy of 3DRewind.)

Virtual technology has also been applied by the military. To help with aircraft maintenance, a virtual reality system has been developed to simulate an aircraft and give a user a sense of touch, while computer graphics provide a sense of sight and sound. The user sees, touches, and manipulates the various parts of the virtual aircraft during training. Also, the Department of National Defence uses a virtual-reality training lab to simulate various war scenarios.[70]

Business and Commerce

Virtual reality has been used in all areas of business. Boeing used virtual reality to help it design and manufacture airplane parts and new planes, including the 787 Dreamliner. Boeing used 3D PLM from Dassault Systems.[71] One health-care institution in the United States used Second Life to create a virtual hospital when it started construction of a real multimillion-dollar hospital. The purpose of the Second Life virtual hospital was to show clients and staff the layout and capabilities of the new hospital. Second Life has also been

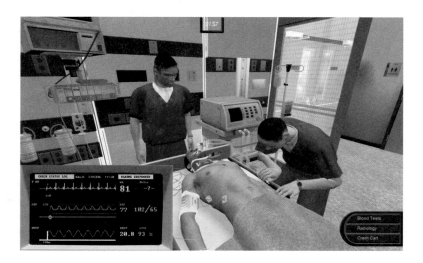

Although it looks like a video game, Pulse!! is a serious training tool for nurses and physicians developed by Breakaway.

(Source: Pulse!! is a research project of Texas A&M University-Corpus Christi in collaboration with the Office of Navel Research and Breakaway Ltd. Courtesy of BreakAway Ltd.)

used in business and recruiting. Second Life (*www.secondlife.com*) also allows people to play games, interact with avatars, and build structures, such as homes. A number of companies are using VR in advertising.[72]

Entertainment

Computer-generated image technology, or CGI, has been around since the 1970s. Many movies use this technology to bring realism to the silver screen, including *Avatar, Finding Nemo, Spider-Man II*, and *Star Wars Episode II—Attack of the Clones*. A team of artists rendered the roiling seas and crashing waves of *Perfect Storm* almost entirely on computers using weather reports, scientific formulas, and their imagination. Other films that have used CGI technology include *Dinosaur* with its realistic talking reptiles, *Titan A.E.*'s beautiful 3D spacescapes, and the casts of computer-generated crowds and battles in *Gladiator* and *The Patriot*. CGI can also be used for sports simulation to enhance the viewers' knowledge and enjoyment of a game. SimCity (*http://simcity.ea.com/*), a virtual reality game, allows people to experiment with decisions related to urban planning.

SPECIALIZED SYSTEMS

In addition to artificial intelligence, expert systems, and virtual reality, other interesting specialized systems have appeared. MIT's Fab Labs project (*http://fab.cba.mit.edu*), for example, has a goal to let anyone manufacture almost anything using specialized equipment and computers.[73] It is hoped that Fab Labs will be able to produce a wide range of products, such as computers and roof panels. Stanford University researchers are experimenting with batteries made out of special paper that can be folded, crumpled, or even soaked in a liquid, and still work.[74]

Many special-purpose systems help overcome disabilities or improve health, often called *assistive technology*. The *Eagle Eyes* tool allows people with physical disabilities to control a computer by moving their head or eyes.[75] Using electrodes placed on a person's head, a camera connected to a computer detects head or eye movements and controls the operation of the computer. The chip maker Intel has developed the Intel Reader, which can help blind people read books using a "text-to-speech" processor.[76] The i-Limb from Touch Bionics (*www.touchbionics.com*) is an artificial hand that uses special-purpose systems and software to allow people who can't move their hands or arms to grip objects.[77] The i-Limb, which has movable fingers and a rotating thumb, won second place in the 2009 Technology Innovation Awards competition. A California company is testing a digital, digestible chip that patients can swallow.[78] Once swallowed, the chip travels through the digestive system and sends important information back to doctors, including whether a patient is taking his or her medications. Today, more hospitals and health-care facilities are using the Internet to connect doctors to patients in distant locations.[79] In one case, a physician used Internet video to check on the treatment of a stroke patient located 25 kilometres away to make sure the drugs being used weren't increasing the chance of bleeding in the brain. After reviewing CT scans and the behaviour of the patient, the doctor made specific drug recommendations. The patient's wife believes the special-purpose Internet video connection saved her husband's life.

Segway is an electric scooter that uses sophisticated software, sensors, and gyro motors to transport people through warehouses, offices, downtown sidewalks, and other spaces (*www.segway.com*). Originally designed to transport people around a factory or around town, more recent versions are being tested by the military for gathering intelligence and transporting wounded soldiers to safety. General Motors has developed a two-person prototype electric car with two wheels that uses Segway technology.[80] Segway has also been used to play polo instead of using horses.[81] Called Segway Polo, the sport has attracted many players, including one of the founders of Apple Computer. According to the head of Germany's Funky-Move Turtle's Polo team, "They couldn't drive very well, and they crashed into each other a lot, but their ball handling was amazing."

Some forensics experts are now experimenting with computer software that can draw images of crime suspects based only on the DNA collected at the crime scene.[82] Some lawmakers, however, are concerned about privacy invasion with this use of DNA to target or identify possible crime suspects. In the United States, the FBI is developing a special-purpose computer system that will allow it to compare a photo of a fugitive with photos from drivers' licences from around the country.[83] If successful, the new system could help the agency locate, capture, and prosecute criminals trying to escape the justice system.

A number of special-purpose systems are now available in vehicles. Ford Motor Company and Microsoft have developed a voice-activated system called *Sync* that can play music, make phones calls, and more. The Advanced Warning System by Mobileye warns drivers to keep a safe distance from other vehicles and drivers. Automotive software allows cars and trucks to connect to the Internet. The software can do such things as track a driver's speed and location and allow gas stations to remotely charge for fuel and related services. More cars in the future will use special-purpose systems.[84] According to GM's global director of electrical controls, "The embedded systems are about to hit 50% of the value of the car." Improvements are also being made in bridges and roadways. Several bridges in Manitoba have smart sensors that measure and report on any potential structural problems.[85]

Microsoft's Surface is a touch-screen computer that uses a glass-top display. It looks like a coffee table or dining room table with a built-in computer. Some manufacturing is being done with inkjet printers that "print" 3D parts. For example, a printer can spray layers of polymers onto circuit boards to form transistors and other electronic components. Some new computers can even be worn on your body. Smith Drug, for example, used a wearable computer by Vocollect, Inc. (*www.vocollect.com*) to help its employees monitor inventory levels. The waist-worn computer, which includes a headset with a microphone and speaker, dramatically increases productivity and helps eliminate errors.

Microsoft Surface recognizes the phone on its surface and offers additional features, colours, and plan options for it.

(Source: Used with permission from Microsoft.)

Companies use special-purpose tracking devices, chips, and bar codes for a variety of purposes. As mentioned previously, *Radio Frequency Identification (RFID)* tags that contain small chips with information about products or packages can be quickly scanned to perform inventory control or trace a package as it moves from a supplier to a company to its customers. Coca-Cola will test a drink-dispensing machine that will have the ability to dispense over 100 different types of soft drinks, juices, and teas.[86] The drink dispenser uses 30 flavour cartridges, each with a unique RFID tag. After a customer selects a drink, an RFID reader collects data on what customers are ordering to determine which drinks are the most popular. When attached to clothing and worn close to a mirror, some RFID tags will display sizes, styles, colour, suggested accessories, and images of models wearing the clothing on the mirror or a display screen. Airline companies are now starting to use RFID tags and sophisticated software to improve baggage handling and processing.[87] It is hoped that the new tags will reduce lost luggage, which is expensive for the airlines and very frustrating for passengers. According to an airline expert, "Our industry has been slow to adopt new technology, especially when it comes to passengers and baggage processing, but we're getting there." Another technology is being used to create "smart containers" for ships, railroads, and trucks. NaviTag (*http://navitag.com/*) and other companies are developing communications systems that allow containers to broadcast the contents, location, and condition of shipments to shipping and cargo managers. A railroad company can use standard radio messages to generate shipment and tracking data for customers and managers.

One special application of computer technology is derived from a branch of mathematics called **game theory**, which involves the use of information systems to develop competitive strategies for people, organizations, or even countries. Two competing businesses in the same market can use game theory to determine the best strategy to achieve their goals. Game theory was used to develop a better security system for an airport.[88] The game theory application used ARMOR (Assistant for Randomized Monitoring over Routes) software to help determine the best monitoring and patrolling strategies to enhance airport security. The military can also use game theory to determine the best military strategy to win a conflict against another country, and individual investors can use game theory to determine the best strategies when competing against other investors. Groundbreaking work on game theory was pioneered by John Nash, the mathematician whose life was profiled in the book and film *A Beautiful Mind*.

Informatics, another specialized system, combines traditional disciplines, such as science and medicine, with computer systems and technology. *Bioinformatics*, for example, combines biology and computer science. Also called *computational biology*, bioinformatics has been used to help map the human genome and conduct research on biological organisms. Using sophisticated databases and artificial intelligence, bioinformatics helps unlock the secrets of the human genome, which could eventually prevent diseases and save lives. Some universities have courses on bioinformatics and offer bioinformatics certification. Medical informatics combines traditional medical research with computer science. Journals such as *Healthcare Informatics* report current research on applying computer systems and technology to reduce medical errors and improve health care. Informatics can also be used in finance to develop sophisticated and profitable modelling programs that can analyze market risks and potential.[89]

game theory
The use of information systems to develop competitive strategies for people, organizations, or even countries.

informatics
A specialized system that combines traditional disciplines, such as science and medicine, with computer systems and technology.

SUMMARY

Principle:

Knowledge management allows organizations to share knowledge and experience among managers and employees.

Knowledge is an awareness and understanding of a set of information and the ways that information can be made useful to support a specific task or reach a decision. A knowledge management system (KMS) is an organized collection of people, procedures, software, databases, and devices used to create, store, share, and use the organization's knowledge and experience. Explicit knowledge is objective and can be measured and documented in reports, papers, and rules. Tacit knowledge is hard to measure and document and is typically not objective or formalized.

Knowledge workers are people who create, use, and disseminate knowledge. They are usually professionals in science, engineering, business, and other areas. The chief knowledge officer (CKO) is a top-level executive who helps the organization use a KMS to create, store, and use knowledge to achieve organizational goals. Some organizations and professions use communities of practice (COP) to create, store, and share knowledge. A COP is a group of people or a community dedicated to a common discipline or practice, such as open-source software, auditing, medicine, engineering, and other areas.

Obtaining, storing, sharing, and using knowledge is the key to any KMS. The use of a KMS often leads to additional knowledge creation, storage, sharing, and usage. Many tools and techniques can be used to create, store, and use knowledge. These tools and techniques are available from IBM, Microsoft, and other companies and organizations.

Principle:

Artificial intelligence systems form a broad and diverse set of systems that can replicate human decision making for certain types of well-defined problems.

The term "artificial intelligence" is used to describe computers with the ability to mimic or duplicate the functions of the human brain. The objective of building AI systems is not to replace human decision making but to replicate it for certain types of well-defined problems.

Intelligent behaviour encompasses several characteristics, including the abilities to learn from experience and apply this knowledge to new experiences; handle complex situations and solve problems for which pieces of information might be missing; determine relevant information in a given situation; think in a logical and rational manner and give a quick and correct response; and understand visual images and process symbols. Computers are better than people at transferring information, making a series of calculations rapidly and accurately, and making complex calculations, but human beings are better than computers at all other attributes of intelligence.

Artificial intelligence is a broad field that includes several key components, such as expert systems, robotics, vision systems, natural language processing, learning systems, and neural networks. An expert system consists of the hardware and software used to produce systems that behave as a human expert would in a specialized field or area (e.g., credit analysis). Robotics uses mechanical or computer devices to perform tasks that require a high degree of precision or are tedious or hazardous for humans (e.g., stacking cartons on a pallet). Vision systems include hardware and software that permit computers to capture, store, and manipulate images and pictures (e.g., face-recognition software). Natural language processing allows the computer to understand and react to statements and commands made in a "natural" language, such as English. Learning systems use a combination of software and hardware to allow a computer to change how it functions or reacts to situations based on feedback it receives (e.g., a computerized chess game). A neural network is a computer system that can simulate the functioning of a human brain (e.g., disease diagnostics system). A genetic algorithm is an approach to solving large, complex problems in which a number of related operations or models change and evolve until the best one emerges. The approach is based on the theory of evolution, which requires variation and natural selection. Intelligent agents consist of programs and a knowledge base used to perform a specific task for a person, a process, or another program.

Principle:

Expert systems can enable a novice to perform at the level of an expert but must be developed and maintained very carefully.

An expert system consists of a collection of integrated and related components, including a knowledge base, an inference engine, an explanation facility, a knowledge acquisition facility, and a user interface. The knowledge base is an extension of a database, discussed in Chapter 5, and an information and decision support system, discussed in Chapter 10. It contains all the relevant data, rules, and relationships used in the expert system. The rules are often composed of IF-THEN statements, which are used for drawing conclusions.

The inference engine processes the rules, data, and relationships stored in the knowledge base to provide answers, predictions, and suggestions the way a human expert would.

The explanation facility of an expert system allows the user to understand what rules were used in arriving at a decision. The knowledge acquisition facility helps the user add or update knowledge in the knowledge base. The user interface makes it easier to develop and use the expert system.

The people involved in the development of an expert system include the domain expert, the knowledge engineer, and the knowledge users. The domain expert is the person or group who has the expertise or knowledge being captured for the system. The knowledge engineer is the developer whose job is to extract the expertise from the domain expert. The knowledge user is the person who benefits from the use of the developed system.

Expert systems can be implemented in several ways. Previously, traditional high-level languages, including Pascal, FORTRAN, and COBOL, were used. LISP and PROLOG are two languages specifically developed for creating expert systems from scratch. A faster and less expensive way to acquire an expert system is to purchase an expert system shell or existing package. The shell program is a collection of software packages and tools used to design, develop, implement, and maintain expert systems.

The benefits of using an expert system go beyond the typical reasons for using a computerized processing solution. Expert systems display "intelligent" behaviour, manipulate symbolic information and draw conclusions, provide portable knowledge, and can deal with uncertainty. Expert systems can be used to solve problems in many fields or disciplines and can assist in all stages of the problem-solving process. Past successes have shown that expert systems are good at strategic goal setting, planning, design, decision making, quality control and monitoring, and diagnosis.

Applications of expert systems and artificial intelligence include credit granting and loan analysis, catching cheats and terrorists, budgeting, games, information management and retrieval, AI and expert systems embedded in products, plant layout, hospitals and medical facilities, help desks and assistance, employee performance evaluation, virus detection, repair and maintenance, shipping, and warehouse optimization.

Principle:

Multimedia and virtual reality systems can reshape the interface between people and information technology by offering new ways to communicate information, visualize processes, and express ideas creatively.

Multimedia is text, graphics, video, animation, audio, and other media that can be used to help an organization efficiently and effectively achieve its goals. Multimedia can be used to create stunning brochures, presentations, reports, and documents. Although not all organizations use the full capabilities of multimedia, most use text and graphics capabilities. Other applications of multimedia are audio, video, and animation. File compression and conversion are often needed in multimedia applications to import or export analog files and to reduce file size when storing multimedia files and sending them to others. Designing a multimedia application requires careful thought to get the best results and achieve corporate goals.

A virtual reality system enables one or more users to move and react in a computer-simulated environment. Virtual reality simulations require special interface devices that transmit the sights, sounds, and sensations of the simulated world to the user. These devices can also record and send the speech and movements of the participants to the simulation program. Thus, users can sense and manipulate virtual objects much as they would real objects. This natural style of interaction gives the participants the feeling that they are immersed in the simulated world.

Virtual reality can also refer to applications that are not fully immersive, such as mouse-controlled navigation through a three-dimensional environment on a graphics monitor, stereo viewing from the monitor via stereo glasses, stereo projection systems, and others. Some virtual reality applications allow views of real environments with superimposed virtual objects. Augmented reality, a newer form of virtual reality, has the potential to superimpose digital data over real photos or images. Virtual reality applications are found in medicine, education and training, real estate and tourism, and entertainment.

Principle:

Specialized systems can help organizations and individuals achieve their goals.

A number of specialized systems have recently appeared to assist organizations and individuals in new and exciting ways. Segway, for example, is an electric scooter that uses sophisticated software, sensors, and gyro motors to transport people through warehouses, offices, downtown sidewalks, and other spaces. It was originally designed to transport people around a factory or around town, but more recent versions are being tested by the military for gathering intelligence and transporting wounded soldiers to safety. Radio Frequency Identification (RFID) tags are used in a variety of settings. Game theory involves the use of information systems to develop competitive strategies for people, organizations, and even countries. Informatics combines traditional disciplines, such as science and medicine, with computer science. Bioinformatics and medical informatics are examples. A number of special-purpose telecommunications systems can be placed in products for varied uses.

CHAPTER 11: SELF-ASSESSMENT TEST

Knowledge management allows organizations to share knowledge and experience among managers and employees.

1. _____ knowledge is objective and can be measured and documented in reports, papers, and rules.
2. What type of person creates, uses, and disseminates knowledge?
   a. a knowledge worker
   b. an information worker
   c. a domain expert
   d. a knowledge engineer

3. A community of practice (COP) is a group of people or a community dedicated to a common discipline or practice, such as open-source software, auditing, medicine, and engineering. True or False?

Artificial intelligence systems form a broad and diverse set of systems that can replicate human decision making for certain types of well-defined problems.

4. The Turing Test attempts to determine whether the responses from a computer with intelligent behaviour are indistinguishable from the responses of a human. True or False?

5. _____ are rules of thumb arising from experience or even guesses.

6. What is not an important attribute for artificial intelligence?
   a. the ability to use sensors
   b. the ability to learn from experience
   c. the ability to be creative
   d. the ability to make complex calculations

7. _____ involves mechanical or computer devices that can paint cars, make precision welds, and perform other tasks that require a high degree of precision or are tedious or hazardous for human beings.

8. What branch of artificial intelligence involves a computer understanding and reacting to spoken statements in English or another language?
   a. expert systems
   b. neural networks
   c. natural language processing
   d. vision systems

9. A(n) _____ is a combination of software and hardware that allows the computer to change how it functions or reacts to situations based on feedback it receives.

Expert systems can enable a novice to perform at the level of an expert but must be developed and maintained very carefully.

10. What is a disadvantage of an expert system?
    a. its inability to solve complex problems
    b. its inability to deal with uncertainty
    c. limitations to relatively narrow problems
    d. its inability to draw conclusions from complex relationships

11. A(n) _____ is a collection of software packages and tools used to develop expert systems that can be implemented on most popular PC platforms to reduce development time and costs.

12. A heuristic consists of a collection of software and tools used to develop an expert system that will reduce development time and costs. True or False?

13. What stores all relevant information, data, rules, cases, and relationships used by the expert system?
    a. the knowledge base
    b. the data interface
    c. the database
    d. the acquisition facility

14. A disadvantage of an expert system is the inability to provide expertise needed at a number of locations at the same time or in a hostile environment that is dangerous to human health. True or False?

15. What allows a user or decision maker to understand how the expert system arrived at a certain conclusion or result?
    a. the domain expert
    b. the inference engine
    c. the knowledge base
    d. the explanation facility

16. An important part of an expert system is the _____, which seeks information and relationships from the knowledge base to provide answers similar the way a human expert would.

17. In an expert system, the domain expert is the individual or group who has the expertise or knowledge one is trying to capture in the expert system. True or False?

Multimedia and virtual reality systems can reshape the interface between people and information technology by offering new ways to communicate information, visualize processes, and express ideas creatively.

18. _____ can be used to create stunning brochures, presentations, reports, and documents.

19. What type of virtual reality is used to make human beings feel as though they are in a three-dimensional setting, such as a building, an archaeological excavation site, the human anatomy, a sculpture, or a crime scene reconstruction?
    a. cloud
    b. relative
    c. immersive
    d. visual

Specialized systems can help organizations and individuals achieve their goals.

20. _____ involves the use of information systems to develop competitive strategies for people, organizations, or even countries.

CHAPTER 11: SELF-ASSESSMENT TEST ANSWERS

(1) explicit (2) a (3) True (4) True (5) Heuristics (6) d (7) Robotics (8) c (9) learning system (10) c (11) expert system shell (12) False (13) a (14) False (15) d (16) inference engine (17) True (18) multimedia (19) c (20) game theory

REVIEW QUESTIONS

1. What is a knowledge management system?
2. What is a community of practice?
3. What is a chief knowledge officer? What are his or her duties?
4. What is a vision system? Discuss two applications of such a system.
5. What is natural language processing? What are the three levels of voice recognition?
6. Describe three examples of the use of robotics. How can a microrobot be used?
7. What is a learning system? Give a practical example of such a system.
8. What is a neural network? Describe two applications of neural networks.
9. Under what conditions is the development of an expert system likely to be worth the effort?
10. Identify the basic components of an expert system and describe the role of each.
11. Describe several business uses of multimedia.
12. What is virtual reality? Give three examples of its use.
13. Expert systems can be built based on rules or cases. What is the difference between the two?
14. Describe the roles of the domain expert, the knowledge engineer, and the knowledge user in expert systems.
15. What is informatics? Give three examples.
16. Describe game theory and its use.
17. Identify three special interface devices developed for use with virtual reality systems.
18. Identify and briefly describe three specific virtual reality applications.
19. What is informatics? How is it used?
20. Give three examples of other specialized systems.

DISCUSSION QUESTIONS

1. What are the requirements for a computer to exhibit human-level intelligence? How long will it be before we have the technology to design such computers? Do you think we should push to accelerate such a development? Why or why not?
2. You work for an insurance company as an entry-level manager. The company contains both explicit and tacit knowledge. Describe the types of explicit and tacit knowledge that might exist in your insurance company. How you would capture each type of knowledge?
3. Describe the duties of a chief knowledge officer.
4. What are some of the tasks at which robots excel? Which human tasks are difficult for robots to master? What fields of AI are required to develop a truly perceptive robot?
5. Describe how natural language processing could be used in a university setting.
6. Discuss how learning systems can be used in a military war simulation to train future officers and field commanders.
7. You have been hired to develop an expert system for a university career placement centre. Develop five rules a student could use in selecting a career.
8. What is the relationship between a database and a knowledge base?
9. Imagine that you are developing the rules for an expert system to select the strongest candidates for a medical school. What rules or heuristics would you include?
10. Describe how game theory can be used in a business setting.
11. Describe how a university might use multimedia.
12. What application of virtual reality has the most potential to generate increased profits in the future?
13. Describe a situation RFID could be used in a business setting.

PROBLEM-SOLVING EXERCISES

1. You are a senior vice president of a company that manufactures kitchen appliances. You are considering using robots to replace up to ten of your skilled workers on the factory floor. Using a spreadsheet, analyze the costs of acquiring several robots to paint and assemble some of your products versus the cost savings in labour. How many years would it take to pay for the robots from the savings in fewer employees? Assume that the skilled workers make $20 per hour, including benefits.

2. Assume that you have just won a lottery worth $100,000. You have decided to invest half the amount in the stock market. Develop a simple expert system to pick ten stocks to consider. Using your word-processing program, create seven or more rules that could be used in such an expert system. Create five cases and use the rules you developed to determine the best stocks to pick.

3. Use a graphics program, such as PowerPoint, to develop a brochure for a small restaurant. Contrast your brochure to one that could have been developed using a specialized multimedia application for developing brochures. Write a report using a word-processing application on the advantages of a multimedia application compared to a graphics program.

TEAM ACTIVITIES

1. Do research with your team to identify KMSs in three different businesses or nonprofit organizations. Describe the types of tacit and explicit knowledge that would be needed by each organization or business.
2. Have your team develop a game between two contestants, where the winning contestant receives fake money. At random, pick two team members to play the game against each other. Have your other team members write a report on the winning strategy and how the game could be improved.
3. Have your team members explore the use of a special-purpose system in an industry of your choice. Describe the advantages and disadvantages of this special-purpose system.

WEB EXERCISES

1. Use the Internet to find information about the use of multimedia in a business setting. Describe what you found.
2. This chapter discussed several examples of expert systems. Search the Internet for two examples of the use of expert systems. Which one has the greatest potential to increase profits for a medium-sized firm? Explain your choice.
3. Use the Internet to get information about the application of game theory in business or the military. Write a report about what you found.

CAREER EXERCISES

1. Describe how a COP can be used to help advance your career.
2. Describe the roles and salaries of two people involved in multimedia applications, such as movie production, sound production, or another multimedia application.

CASE STUDIES

Case One
MITRE Taps the Brain Trust of Top U.S. Experts

MITRE Corporation is responsible for managing the Research and Development (R&D) Centers for several American government agencies. MITRE also researches new technologies that may assist in solving its clients' problems.

More than 7,000 scientists, engineers, and support specialists work in labs managed by MITRE, and most have master's or doctoral degrees. Staff members are engaged in hundreds of different projects across the company. Each staff member possesses valuable technical, operational, and domain knowledge that MITRE wants to tap to its full value and potential. When knowledge management (KM) systems came on the scene in the mid-1990s, MITRE immediately saw the benefit for its researchers and has been tinkering with KM ever since.

With so many research specialists engaged across its labs, the value of tapping each other's knowledge and collaborating on projects is immense. However, it's a challenge to interact efficiently with low overhead while researchers are simultaneously working on hundreds of separate projects. For knowledge management, MITRE takes a gradual learn-while-you-go approach.

MITRE's first step in providing knowledge management was to simply track its research staff. A people locator was developed as part of the larger MITRE Information Infrastructure (MII). The people locator works like an electronic phone book, identifying which employees worked on which assignments over time. The system drew information from the existing project management systems and human resource systems. Using the people locator, staff could find colleagues with useful knowledge based on previous work or the sponsoring organization.

As MITRE researchers used the people finder, developers refined the system based on user feedback. Over time, they introduced additional capabilities. For example, they added an Expertise Finder to help find researchers with expertise in special areas. MITRE also included a library of best practices for systems engineering and project management in the system. MITRE experimented with technology exchange meetings and an annual Innovation Exchange, which allowed researchers to share their successes with colleagues. When they found new technologies and ideas useful, developers added them to the KM system. More recently, MITRE has experimented with Web 2.0 technologies similar to Facebook and Wikipedia for its KM system.

MITRE's approach to KM has been evolutionary. New ideas are piloted and those proven valuable and viable are kept in the system. The success of MITRE's KM system is in its unique approach to KM as a journey with continuous improvements.

Discussion Questions

1. Why is KM extremely valuable in areas of research and development?
2. How do the different components of MITRE's KM system assist in spreading knowledge throughout its labs and in storing knowledge for use in the future?

Critical Thinking Questions

1. What unique challenges do research and development labs provide for KM implementation?
2. What is the benefit of MITRE's evolutionary approach to KM?

SOURCES: Swanborg, Rick, "Mitre's Knowledge Management Journey," *CIO*, February 27, 2009, *www.cio.com*; "About MITRE," MITRE website, *www.mitre.org/about*, accessed January 31, 2010.

Case Two
JEA Uses AI to Optimize Water Delivery

JEA supplies much of the Jacksonville, Florida, area with electricity, water, and sewer services. The JEA water system uses 150 artesian wells to tap the Florida Aquifer, distributing water to 44 water treatment plants and then down 5,600 kilometres of underground water pipes to businesses and residences.

Making sure that its wells are producing enough water to meet customer demand is a tricky and sometimes wasteful process. Reservoirs accommodate anticipated demand, often overcompensating to make sure they have enough water to accommodate an unusually high demand. When too much water is kept on hand, the quality of the water decreases (due to salt intrusion), and the health of the well decreases (due to inactivity).

Recently, JEA decided to put artificial intelligence to work assisting its wells in pumping just enough water to meet

customer demand. It purchased AI-based software from Gensym and created a neural network to predict hourly consumption of water over a given time frame. The neural network is trained using previous water-usage data. The consumption forecasts created by the neural net are fed into an expert system. The expert system allocates the total anticipated demand to the 44 water treatment plants and artesian well pumps.

The schedule for hourly water production is fed into automated systems in the production and treatment plant to control production and delivery of the water. The Gensym software allows JEA engineers to define inputs (including reservoir sensors and meter-reading) and outputs (such as controls on equipment) to optimize the production and flow of water through the JEA system.

It took JEA six months to develop and implement the optimized expert system and automation. The system has resulted in better use of reservoir capacity by filling reservoirs only to levels required with each hour of operation. The needs-based production has minimized costs while maximizing water quality. Salt intrusion has been reduced and the health of the wells is increasing. As JEA rolls out its new system to all of its wells and treatment plants, it will enjoy considerable benefits and savings, including lower energy costs and reduced equipment failures from smarter pumping.

Discussion Questions

1. What problem did JEA face that required the use of an expert system and automation?
2. What benefits were provided by JEA's new automated system?

Critical Thinking Questions

1. What are the components of JEA's new system, and what tasks does each component accomplish?
2. What other industries might benefit from a Gensym optimization and automation system like JEA's? Why?

SOURCES: Gensym Staff, "Success Story: JEA," Gensym website, *www.gensym.com*, accessed January 31, 2010; "About JEA," JEA website, *www.jea.com/about*, accessed January 31, 2010.

Questions for Web Case

See the website for this book to read about the Altitude Online case for this chapter. Following are questions concerning this Web case.

Altitude Online: Knowledge Management and Other Considerations

Discussion Questions

1. Why do you think it is a good idea for Altitude Online to maintain records of all advertising projects?
2. How can social networks and blogs serve as knowledge management systems?

Critical Thinking Questions

1. What challenges lie in filling a wiki with information provided by employees?
2. What other tools could Altitude Online use to capture employee knowledge, build community, and reward productive employees?

NOTES

Sources for the opening vignette: Gruman, Galen, "Capgemini Adopts Social Networking Tools for Knowledge Management," *Computerworld*, June 1, 2009, *www.computerworld.com*; "Capgemini—Who We Are," Capgemini website, *www.us.capgemini.com/about*, accessed January 31, 2010; Fitzgerald, Michael, "Why Social Computing Aids Knowledge Management," *CIO*, June 13, 2008, *www.cio.com*.

1   "Knowledge Management in Practice," *Information Today*, June 2009, p. 48.

2   Aaron, Bruce, "Determining the Business Impact of Knowledge Management," *Performance Improvement*, April 2009, p. 35.

3   Nguyen, Le, et al., "Acquiring Tacit and Explicit Marketing Knowledge from Foreign Partners in IJVs," *Journal of Business Research*, November 2007, p. 1152.

4   Gerard, J., et al., "Empirically Testing Explicit and Tacit Knowledge Assumptions," *The Business Review*, Summer 2009, p. 1.

5   Holtshouse, Dan, "The Future of Knowledge Workers," *KM World*, September 2009, p. 2.

6   Hemmasi, M., and Csanda C., "The Effectiveness of Communities of Practice," *Journal of Managerial Issues*, Summer 2009, p. 262.

7   *www.ubikacorp.com*, accessed October 17, 2010.

8   Lamont, Judith, "Knowledge Management: Naturally Green," *KM World*, February 2009, p. 5.

9   Subramenian, A., and Soh, P., "Contributing Knowledge to Knowledge Repositories," *Information Resources Management Journal*, January 2009, p. 45.

10   "Adobe Creative Suite 3," *www.adobe.com/products/creativesuite*, accessed July 20, 2009.

11   McKellar, Hugh, "100 Companies That Matter in Knowledge Management," *KM World*, March 2009, p. 18.

12   *www.cortexpro.com*, accessed July 19, 2009.

13   *www.delphigroup.com*, accessed July 19, 2009.

14   *www.kmresource.com*, accessed July 19, 2009.

15   *www.kmsi.us*, accessed July 19, 2009.

16   *www.knowledge-manage.com*, accessed July 19, 2009.

17   *www.knowledgebase.net*, accessed October 26, 2009.

18   *www.lawclip.com*, accessed July 19, 2009.

19   *www.kmci.org/index.html*, accessed July 19, 2009.

20   Gomes, Lee, "When Smart Is Dumb," *Forbes*, April 13, 2009, p. 42.

21   O'Keefe, Brian, "The Smartest, the Nuttiest Futurist on Earth," *Fortune*, May 14, 2007, p. 60.

22   Markoff, John, "IBM Computer Program to Take on Jeopardy," *New York Times*, April 27, 2009, p. 11.

23   *www.20q.net*, accessed July 20, 2009.

24   Harris, Mark, "Stand Aside, Soldier, We Robots Are in Command," *Sunday Times*, May 31, 2009, p. 4.

25   Fahey, Jonathan, "Reconnecting the Brain," *Forbes*, December 28, 2009, p. 48.

26   "Mind-Machine Meld: Brain-Computer Interfaces for ALS, Paralysis," *Alzheimer Research Forum*, June 22, 2009, *www.alzforum.org/new/detail.asp?id=2173*, accessed July 21, 2009.

27   Rowley, Ian, "Drive, He Thought," *BusinessWeek*, April 20, 2009, p. 10.

28   Zebda, A., and McEacham, M., "Accounting Expert Systems," *The Business Review*, December 2008, p. 11.

29   Abate, Tom, "Future Moving From I, Robot to My Robot," *Rocky Mountain News*, February 26, 2007, p. 8.

30   *www.irobot.com*, accessed July 20, 2009.

31   *www.firstroboticscanada.org/site/node/974*, accessed October 17, 2010.

32   *www.braintech.com*, accessed October 17, 2010.

33   *sm.mdacorporation.com/news/pr22092010.html*, accessed October 17, 2010.

34   Thryft, A., "Vision Systems Enables Zero Defects," *Test & Measurement*, October 2009, p. 48.

35   Wildstrom, Stephen, "Coming at You: 3D On Your PC," *BusinessWeek*, January 19, 2009, p. 65.

36   Koit, M., et al., "Towards Computer-Human Interaction in Natural Language," *International Journal of Computer Applications in Technology*, Vol. 34, 2009, p. 291.

37   Young, Peyton, "Learning by Trial and Error," *Games and Economic Behavior*, March 2009, p. 626.

38   "IBM Developing Computing System to Challenge Humans on America's Favourite Quiz Show, Jeopardy," IBM Press Room, *www-03.ibm.com/press/us/en/pressrelease/27324.wss*, accessed July 22, 2009.

39   Gosavi, Abhijit, "Reinforcement Learning," *Informs*, Spring 2009, p. 178.

40   Dengiz, B., et al., "Optimization of Manufacturing Systems Using a Neural Network," *The Journal of the Operational Research Society*, September 2009, p. 1191.

41   Industry Canada, "Canadian Aerospace and Defence Industry—Maintenance Repair and Overhaul Technologies," *www.ic.gc.ca/eic/site/ad-ad.nsf/eng/ad03851.html*, accessed October 17, 2010.

42   He, J., et al., "A Hybrid Parallel Genetic Algorithm for Yard Crane Scheduling," *Transportation Research*, January 2009, p. 136.

43   Souai, N., et al., "Genetic Algorithm Based Approach for the Integrated Airline Crew-Pairing and Rostering Problem," *European Journal of Operations Research*, December 16, 2009, p. 674.

44   Reena, J., "Dusting Off a Big Idea in Hard Times," *BusinessWeek*, June 22, 2009, p. 44.

45   Bone, C., and Dragicevic, S., "GIS and Intelligent Agents," *Transactions in GIS*, June 2009, p. 253.

46   Ahmed, M., et al., "Handling Imprecision and Uncertainty in Software Development," *Information and Software Technology*, March 2009, p. 640.

47   Sinz, C., et al., "Detection of Dynamic Execution Errors in IBM System Automation Rule-Based Expert System," *Information and Software Technology*, November 1, 2002, p. 857.

48   Chiu, C., et al., "A Case-Based Expert Support System for Due-Date Assignment in Wafer Fabrication," *Journal of Intelligent Manufacturing*, June-August, 2003, p. 14.

49   Wagner, W., "Knowledge Acquisition for Marketing Expert Systems," *Marketing Intelligence & Planning*, Vol. 23, 2005, p. 403.

50   Guimareas, T., et al., "Empirically Testing Some Important Factors for Expert System Quality," *The Quality Management Journal*, Vol. 13, 2006, p. 7.

51   Feng, W., et al., "Understanding Expert Systems Applications from a Knowledge Transfer Perspective," *Knowledge Management Research & Practices*, June 2009, p. 131.

52   EXSYS, *www.exsys.com*, accessed July 21, 2009.

53   EZ-Xpert Expert System, *www.ez-xpert.com*, accessed July 21, 2009.

54   Wingfield, Nick, "Silverlight Is Still Racing Flash," *Wall Street Journal*, September 15, 2009, p. B4.

55   Betts, Mitch, "Data Center Plays Supporting Role in Avatar," *Computerworld*, January 18, 2010, p. 4.

56   Copeland, Michael, "3-D Gets Down to Business," *Fortune*, March 30, 2009, p. 32.

57   Foust, Dean, "Top Performing Companies," *BusinessWeek*, April 6, 2009, p. 40.

58   "How We Do It," *www.pixar.com/howwedoit/index.html#*, accessed July 18, 2009.

59   West, Jackson, "Digitize All of Your Old Analog Media, Easily," *PC World*, August 2009, p. 104.

60   "Minister of National Defence Announces New Virtual Reality System at the Glenrose Rehabiliation Hospital," Canada News Centre, *news.gc.ca*, April 18, 2010.

61 *http://osl-www.colorado.edu/Research/haptic/hapticInterface.shtml*, accessed July 20, 2009.

62 "AIST Brings Feel of Reality into Virtual Reality," June 11, 2007, p. 1.

63 Madrigal, Alexis, "Researchers Want to Add Touch, Taste, Smell to Virtual Reality," *Wired Science*, March 4, 2009, p. 1.

64 Wildstrom, Stephen, "Augmented Reality," *BusinessWeek*, November 20, 2009, p. 75.

65 *www.emory.edu/EMORY_MAGAZINE/winter96/rothbaum.html*, accessed July 20, 2009.

66 *www.temple.edu/ispr/examples/ex03_07_23.html*, accessed July 20, 2009.

67 Saposnik, G., Mamdani, M., Bayley, M., Thorpe, K., Hall, J., Cohen, L., Teasell, R., and on behalf of the Steering Committee and EVREST Study Group* for the Stroke Outcome Research Canada (SORCan) Working Group (2010), "Effectiveness of Virtual Reality Exercises in Stroke Rehabilitation (EVREST): Rationale, Design, and Protocol of a Pilot Randomized Clinical Trial Assessing the Wii Gaming System," *International Journal of Stroke*, 5: 47–51. doi: 10.1111/j.1747-4949.2009.00404.x.

68 Walsh, Aaron, "Dossier," *Computerworld*, August 17, 2009, p. 12.

69 Vorais, Richard, "Ancient Rome 2.0," *Forbes*, March 16, 2009, p. 68.

70 "403 Squadron Virtual Battle Space Training Simulator," www.forces.gc.ca/site/Commun/ml-fe/article-eng.asp?id=2544, accessed October 17, 2010.

71 *www.3ds.com/home*, accessed July 20, 2009.

72 Vranica, Suzanne, "Madison Avenue Flirts with 3D," *Wall Street Journal*, May 26, 2009, p. B10.

73 Corcoran, Elizabeth, "Fab Labs," *Forbes*, August 24, 2009, p. 32.

74 Gaudin, Sharon, "Nanotech Creates Batteries Out of Paper," *Computerworld*, December 21, 2009, p. 6.

75 "Eagle Eyes Project," *www.bc.edu/schools/csom/eagleeyes*, accessed June 22, 2009.

76 Mossberg, Walter, "Intel Makes Leap in Device to Aid Impaired Readers," *Wall Street Journal*, November 19, 2009, p. D1.

77 "Innovation Awards," *Wall Street Journal*, September 14, 2009, p. R3.

78 Clark, Don, "Take Two Digital Pills and Call Me in the Morning," *Wall Street Journal*, August 4, 2009, p. A6.

79 Worthen, Ben, "Doctor, Can You See Me Now?" *Wall Street Journal*, October 20, 2009, p. D1.

80 Choi, K., "GM Daewood Auto," *Wall Street Journal*, April 8, 2009, p. B3.

81 Greenburg, Z., "Segway Owners Are Challenging the Notion that Polo Should Be Played on Horseback," *Forbes*, October 19, 2009, p. 242.

82 Naik, Gautam, "To Sketch a Thief," *Wall Street Journal*, March 27, 2009, p. A9.

83 "FBI Scanning Driver Photos for Fugitives," *Tampa Tribune*, p. 15.

84 Franklin, Curtis, "Pimp My Dash," *Information Week*, November 16, 2009, p. 22.

85 Morre, Sean, "Building Better Bridges," InnovationCanada.ca, *www.innovationcanada.ca/en/articles/building-better-bridges*, accessed October 17, 2010.

86 Weier, Mary Hayes, "RFID-Based Dispensers," *Information Week*, June 8, 2009, p. 30.

87 Michaels, Daniel, "Airline Industry Gets Smarter with Bags," *Wall Street Journal*, September 30, 2009, p. B5.

88 Pita, J. et al., "Using Game Theory for Los Angeles Airport Security," *AI Magazine*, spring 2009, p. 43.

89 Flood, M., "Embracing Change: Financial Informatics and Risk Analysis," *Quantitative Finance*, April 2009, p. 243.

INTEGRATIVE CASE

Richard Ivey School of Business
The University of Western Ontario

Ivey
Publishing

RBC Investments—Portfolio Planning Initiative

Professor Derrick Neufeld prepared this case solely to provide material for class discussion. The author does not intend to illustrate either effective or ineffective handling of a managerial situation. The author may have disguised certain names and other identifying information to protect confidentiality.

Richard Ivey School of Business Foundation prohibits any form of reproduction, storage or transmission without its written permission. Reproduction of this material is not covered under authorization by any reproduction rights organization. To order copies or request permission to reproduce materials, contact Ivey Publishing, Richard Ivey School of Business Foundation, The University of Western Ontario, London, Ontario, Canada, N6A 3K7; phone (519) 661-3208; fax (519) 661-3882; e-mail cases@ivey.uwo.ca.

Copyright © 2005, Richard Ivey School of Business Foundation Version: (A) 2010-10-20

Blake Hellam reflected on his first intense week as head of Strategic Resource Planning and Management at Royal Bank of Canada Investments (RBCI). A 17-year veteran in the bank, Hellam had moved over to the investment side of the business to accept this new job just five days earlier. As his first assignment,

Hellam had been asked by his new boss, Chief Strategy Officer Chris Crosby, to develop a "dashboard" mechanism for strategically assessing and managing RBCI's NIE spend—that is, all non-interest expenses, excluding brokerage fees, associated with providing value-adding services to RBCI's clients.

After a full week of analysis, two things were apparent to Hellam. First, the four major business units within RBCI were operating independently, neither collaborating on projects nor sharing information. Second, most of the NIE spend was related to information technology (IT) projects, both in process and planned or requested. Considering that RBCI was spending nearly $700,000[1] per day on service delivery, Crosby and the rest of the senior management team were extremely eager to see what Hellam would propose.

Royal Bank of Canada Financial Group

Royal Bank of Canada (RBC) was Canada's largest bank. With $450 billion in assets, RBC served more than 11 million clients through 1,300 retail branches and 5,000 automated teller machines (ATMs), as well as remote telephone and Web banking services. Royal Bank was originally founded in 1864, in Halifax, Nova Scotia, as the Merchants Bank. The brand name "RBC Financial Group" was introduced in 2001 to reflect the diverse range of businesses that were part of the bank. The group was organized into five business units: Investments, Banking, Insurance, Capital Markets and Global Services (see Exhibit 1).[2]

---

[1] All amounts in Canadian dollars unless otherwise specified. Numbers that are not publicly available have been disguised.
[2] *For a more detailed history of the bank, visit www.rbc.com/history/index.html.*

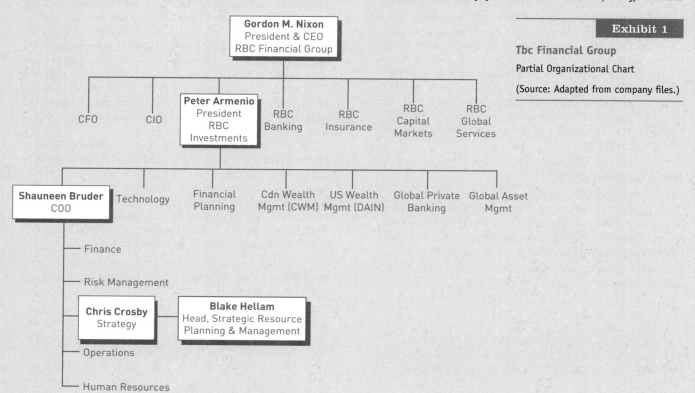

Exhibit 1

Tbc Financial Group

Partial Organizational Chart

(Source: Adapted from company files.)

President and CEO Gordon M. Nixon described the bank's goals and strategic objectives:

> Our three key goals are to be recognized as the undisputed lead provider of integrated financial services in Canada, a best-in-class provider of personal and business financial services in the U.S. and a premier provider of selected global financial services. . . . To reach our goals, we have set four key priorities—strong fundamentals, superior client experience, North American expansion, and cross-enterprise leverage.[3]

The bank appeared to be making excellent progress in terms of meeting most of its strategic priorities. The client experience, defined as "everything the client sees, hears, feels, touches and does when interacting with us,"[4] was being improved by building deeper client relationships through creative application of information technology, such as:

- New digital imaging systems that improved cheque processing and cheque tracing speeds;
- The RBC *eLearning Reference Tool* that was used to train sales agents about RBC insurance products;
- *ClientLink*, a contact and portfolio management application that helped investment advisors better service clients' needs;
- *FX Direct*, a 24-7 online trading system that supported corporate and institutional clients.

North American expansion was also well underway. The bank had recently made 12 U.S. acquisitions totaling approximately US$5.5 billion, including Centura Banks (U.S. banking), Liberty Life Insurance (U.S. life insurance) and Dain Rauscher (U.S. brokerage). The bank was also leveraging cross-enterprise benefits by sharing best practices across business units, and integrating services where possible (e.g., the *RBC Snowbird Package* was developed by bundling existing services to provide an integrated mix of Canadian and U.S. financial services to Canadians who vacation and live in the Southern United States during the winter months).

However, the bank had also failed to meet several of its fundamental performance priorities. For example, share price valuation, earnings growth and revenue growth were lower than targeted.[5] The desire to improve bottom-line financial performance was a key factor driving Hellam's activities in his new role in RBC Investments.

RBC Investments

RBC's Investments division was organized into four business units: Canadian Wealth Management (investment brokerage unit), U.S. Wealth Management (through Dain Rauscher, Inc.), Global Private Banking (international banking unit) and Global Asset Management (mutual fund management business unit).

Three overarching business strategies were driving activities in each of these units:

- To develop broader and deeper relationships with clients by using segmentation strategies to develop specific solutions for specific client groups;
- To transform our distribution models to ensure that our financial consultants and advisors have more time to focus on their clients; and
- To focus on improving operational infrastructure and processes to efficiently support growth

The resulting product and service offerings were implicitly dependent on information technologies:

> RBC Investments provides wealth management services including full-service and self-directed brokerage, financial planning, investment counselling, personal trust, private banking and investment management products and services to clients in Canada, the U.S. and internationally. Products and services are delivered through the RBC Royal Bank branch network across Canada, RBC Investments offices, RBC Dain Rauscher branches in the U.S., private banking offices and other locations worldwide. Services are also delivered via the Internet and telephone.[6]

RBCI net income and return on investment (ROE) had been trending favorably over the past five quarters. RBCI contributed approximately 18 per cent to RBC Financial Group's bottom line.

Blake Hellam

Blake Hellam joined RBC in 1987. His career had been focused primarily in retail banking, including 10 years in field sales and branch management, and the last seven years in head office roles. Strategic planning and integration were common themes running through Hellam's prior experiences in the Bank. For example, in his most recent role as senior manager, Business Markets Strategic Initiatives, Hellam directed a variety of strategic planning activities including client value proposition alignment, business case development, testing, integration and implementation across a variety of small and medium enterprise (SME) business groups nationally. He had also held other senior roles in strategic planning and strategic integration. It was this background that prepared Hellam for his new role, head of Strategic Resource Planning and Management.

Hellam's key job responsibility was to develop behavioral as well as practical mechanisms for tracking, prioritizing and optimizing project funding and resource allocation decisions across the four RBCI business units, in support of a six-quarter rolling forecast approach to business performance planning. A high level summary of key operational systems maintained within one of RBC Investment's four major business units, the Canadian Wealth Management Group, is illustrated in Exhibit 2.

The Portfolio Management Challenge

RBCI had, over the last several years, operated more as a "holding company" than as a truly interwoven "strategic business unit" of the RBC Financial Group. Hellam wryly explained:

---

[3] www.rbc.com/investorrelations/ar_03/html/letters/letter2.html.

[4] www.rbc.com/investorrelations/ar_03/html/priorities/superior.html.

[5] www.rbc.com/investorrelations/ar_03/html/priorities/fundamentals. html.

[6] www.rbc.com/investorrelations/ar_03/html/overview/investments. html.

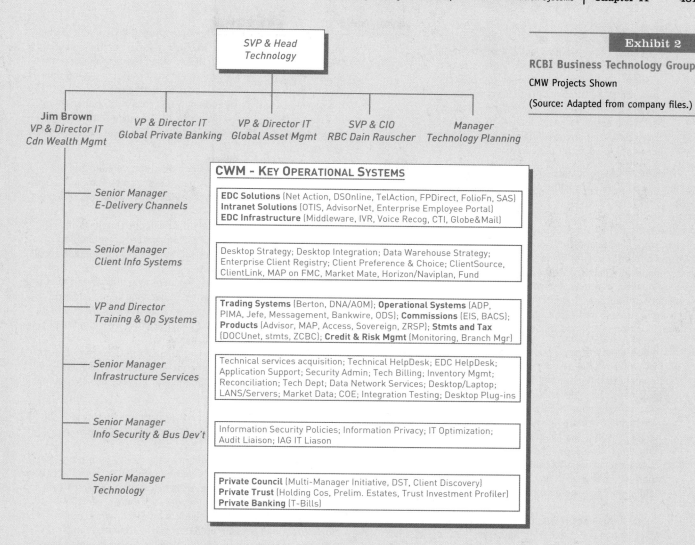

Exhibit 2

RCBI Business Technology Group
CMW Projects Shown
(Source: Adapted from company files.)

SVP & Head
Technology

Jim Brown
VP & Director IT
Cdn Wealth Mgmt

VP & Director IT
Global Private Banking

VP & Director IT
Global Asset Mgmt

SVP & CIO
RBC Dain Rauscher

Manager
Technology Planning

Senior Manager
E-Delivery Channels

Senior Manager
Client Info Systems

VP and Director
Training & Op Systems

Senior Manager
Infrastructure Services

Senior Manager
Info Security & Bus Dev't

Senior Manager
Technology

CWM – KEY OPERATIONAL SYSTEMS

EDC Solutions (Net Action, DSOnline, TelAction, FPDirect, FolioFn, SAS)
Intranet Solutions (OTIS, AdvisorNet, Enterprise Employee Portal)
EDC Infrastructure (Middleware, IVR, Voice Recog, CTI, Globe&Mail)

Desktop Strategy; Desktop Integration; Data Warehouse Strategy;
Enterprise Client Registry; Client Preference & Choice; ClientSource,
ClientLink, MAP on FMC, Market Mate, Horizon/Naviplan, Fund

Trading Systems (Berton, DNA/AOM); **Operational Systems** (ADP,
PIMA, Jefe, Messagement, Bankwire, ODS); **Commissions** (EIS, BACS);
Products (Advisor, MAP, Access, Sovereign, ZRSP); **Stmts and Tax**
(DOCUnet, stmts, ZCBC); **Credit & Risk Mgmt** (Monitoring, Branch Mgr)

Technical services acquisition; Technical HelpDesk; EDC HelpDesk;
Application Support; Security Admin; Tech Billing; Inventory Mgmt;
Reconciliation; Tech Dept; Data Network Services; Desktop/Laptop;
LANS/Servers; Market Data; COE; Integration Testing; Desktop Plug-ins

Information Security Policies; Information Privacy; IT Optimization;
Audit Liaison; IAG IT Liason

Private Council (Multi-Manager Initiative, DST, Client Discovery)
Private Trust (Holding Cos, Prelim. Estates, Trust Investment Profiler)
Private Banking (T-Bills)

"The general expectation of business unit heads was to 'deliver your business plan at the end of the year, you manage the how.'" Although this strategy gave individual unit managers a great deal of autonomy and incentive to perform well, Hellam knew that it also resulted in a suboptimal allocation and use of overall resources. For instance, it was not uncommon for two or more businesses to request independent funding to design and develop highly similar IT-based client services. Collaboration across business units was rare.

Due to increasing market pressures and opportunities, Peter Armenio, president of RBC Investments, wished to adopt a portfolio approach to manage resources more strategically. The overriding objective was to better utilize, align and integrate resources across marketing, operations, information technology and other areas, and in the process to gain bottom-line efficiencies while improving service delivery effectiveness.

Unlike RBC Banking, which had historically sought organic growth (e.g., by developing and introducing new products and services to attract and grow clients), RBC Investments had engaged in an aggressive growth through acquisition strategy. In the previous decade, the four RBCI business units had acquired dozens of new firms. Each of these acquisitions had numerous information systems in operation as well as new IS projects planned for future rollout. In the process of

acquisition, some of these systems were dropped in favor of existing RBCI systems, but many were considered unique to the individual business and were retained, at least for the short run. As a result, today there were more than 300 different information systems in operation within RBCI, running on a variety of different hardware platforms and operating systems.

For example, the Canadian Wealth Management (CWM) group within RBCI was operating approximately 100 different applications on a variety of hardware platforms (including Tandem and IBM mainframes, Hewlett-Packard mid-range equipment and numerous brands of desktop-level machines) and operating systems platforms (from hardware-specific systems, to Unix, to Windows). According to Jim Brown, vice-president (VP) and director of IT for the CWM group, this technological diversity resulted both through a combination of business acquisitions, as well as decisions along the way to adopt packaged software solutions to provide particular functionalities. Brown explained that the pressure to develop new applications was unrelenting:

> We have an annual planning cycle, which starts in May, and so you always get a build-up. By May we receive up to 150 new project requests . . . to put this into perspective the CWM IT department has around 300 people in

total; there is no way we can do them all, much less fund them. We do a quick assessment of the project request in terms of cost, size and priority, and there's always over 100 projects left. We cycle through this process several more times, and by September or October we identify 30 to 40 active projects, and 50 to 75 pending projects. So at any given time we are actively developing 30 to 40 projects.

Within the last two years, cross-business information technology collaboration had started to occur more frequently within RBCI. The IT directors began getting together for funding status updates weekly, and made formal reports monthly. Also, because each project went through a predefined gating process to track timing and costs on an ongoing basis, there were multiple opportunities for IT personnel and business sponsors to communicate and reflect on a project's status throughout its development. However, Brown observed that cross-business collaboration between IT personnel occurred much more easily when individuals shared a common framework:

> When there's a common understanding of the underlying business structure there are not a lot of problems. But when you take it up a level, and try to integrate two fundamentally different businesses, it's like another world in many ways. The infrastructure people—the telecommunications and hardware people for instance—are specialists in their own right. They know their work, but don't necessarily understand the business. It takes a lot more effort to work together. I suppose you get that in any large organization, as people become more specialized.

The four RBCI businesses (CWM, Global Private Banking, Global Asset Management and Dain Rauscher) had four distinct cultures, and because of the high number of recent acquisitions, many additional subcultures as well. For example, a Dain broker in St. Paul, Minnesota, a trust officer in the Channel Islands, and a mutual fund analyst in Toronto could easily have competing interests (high net worth clients) and local systems that would prevent them from "talking the same language." Distinctive leadership styles within the businesses could also lead to integration issues, as there was little obvious incentive to collaborate on a day-to-day basis. Compensation, resources, turf protection and unit-level strategic direction were always thorny issues.

Total NIE (non-interest expense) spending exceeded $3 billion. Approximately $250 million of this total was spent on new initiatives, in three main categories:

- Infrastructure ($100 million "lights on" spending and maintenance, plus approximately $75 million in discretionary infrastructure spending);
- In-flight discretionary business-specific initiatives from previous years ($15 million) and
- New discretionary business-specific initiatives ($60 million).

According to Hellam, the $75 million spent in categories two and three included a "mixed bag of initiatives, applications, build-outs and enhancements."

Hellam also suspected there were substantial inefficiencies within the $75 million in discretionary infrastructure spending. "We're cowpathing," he said, referring to the problem described by Don Tapscott[7] that occurs when organizations use information technology to automate existing inefficient processes (i.e., the paved cowpaths may look new and improved, but nothing has really changed since the paths still meander and are inherently inefficient). The discretionary projects were classified into four groups:

- *Active-Projects* were those systems that were already developed and in service (e.g., *Guest Access Redesign* was an active project that related to RBCI's Action Direct self-serve online brokerage).
- *Active-Enhancements* referred to approved projects in process, whose purpose was to upgrade active projects (e.g., *NetAction:Enhancement Release* was an upgrade to the NetAction system).
- *Planned-Projects* were discretionary new initiatives that the business unit was interested in pursuing (e.g., *Telaction* was a voice recognition system that would allow clients to interact with their Action Direct account over the telephone, using natural language commands).
- *Planned-Enhancements* were proposed initiatives to update active projects (e.g., *NetAction FY2005 Enhancements* was a project that included a bundle of upgrades to the online brokerage system).

Basic information about each project was historically captured and stored in an MS Access database (see partial report in Exhibit 3).

The Access database was fairly easy to use by a program office administrator, and provided a useful inventory of active and proposed projects. However, because information in the database was not dynamically updated, at any given time certain project data were accurately reflected, while other project data had become outdated and inaccurate. Thus, the database was not very useful as a prediction or planning tool. For example, there was no way to easily analyze or prioritize a newly proposed project in relation to all of the other existing projects within or across the four main business units. According to Hellam:

> To date, there has been a small measure of business level planning/prioritization, and nearly zero at the overall platform level ... The chief operating officer (COO) [Shauneen Bruder] is looking for an informational framework or dashboard that "isn't bureaucratic." This is investment-speak for "keep me nimble"!

Bruder and Crosby had hoped to take a dashboard view to the "top of the house"—that is, to both the RBCI Operating Committee and to RBC Financial Group's "group council" (comprising RBC's chief executive officer [CEO], chief financial officer [CFO], chief information officer [CIO], and the five vice-chairs). They hoped it would become a mechanism for sharing and developing a resource-based management perspective at RBCI, and ideally across the entire financial group. In a nut-

---

7 Don Tapscott, *The Digital Economy: Promise and Peril in the Age of Networked Intelligence*, McGraw-Hill, New York, 1996, p. 82.

Potential Carryover & New/Re-introduced Discretionary Initiatives ($,000)

Exhibit 3

**Partial Project Report from
MS Access Database**

(Source: Adapted from company files.)

Ref#	Project Name	BU Priority	Stage	3YR Benefits	YTD Actual	Current FY Forecast			Next FY Forecast		C-fwd
						Capital IT NIE Leased BU NIE Total			Capital IT NIE BU NIE Total		
Canadian Wealth Management Group – Action Direct											
Active – Projects											
812	Common Account Opening ...		D&T								
1707.1	Enterprise NIVR Migration ...		CTD								
1655	Guest Access Redesign		D&T								
1153	NetAction 3.0		D&T								Yes
812.82	Project Mercury - Print&Submit ...		IMP								
1707	Technology Contact Centre ...		IMP								
Active – Enhancements											
1484	ADA Release		IMP								
1343	ClientSource - AD Release ...		D&T								
1573	NetAction::Enhancement Rel ...		D&T								
1829	NetAction::eServices Enhance ...		D&T								
Planned – Projects											
1975	Bankwire	5	CON								
1959	Mercury Phase II ...	1	CON								
1935	Natural Language Intranet ...	2	CON								
812.9	Project Mercury::Mercury ...		CHA								
1934	Real Time Financial Info ...	2	CON								Yes
1885	Telaction - IVR Voice Authent ...	2	CON								
1884	Telaction - Natural Language ...	2	CON								
645.6	Trading Systems::IR Order ...		CON								
Planned – Enhancements											
1879	E-service Enhancements ...	1	CON								
1878	NetAction Enhancements ...	1	CON								
1936	Other AD enhancements ...	2	CON								
	Action Direct Total										

Canadian Wealth Management Group – CWMG Infrastructure
Active – Projects

> **Canadian Wealth Management Group**
> 9-page report includes:
>
> - 43 Active Projects
> - 27 Active Enhancements
> - 96 Planned Projects
> - 25 Planned Enhancements
>
> (CWM is one of four business groups within RBC Investments)

shell, Hellam needed to develop a plan and a set of tools to move RBC Investments away from the current suboptimal discretionary spending approach, toward a more integrated and holistic resource allocation strategy. As illustrated in Exhibit 4, the idea was to make the same investment (in this example, $60 million) to produce a higher net benefit ($90 million versus $76 million).

To add to this project management problem, there were very few standards in place to guide RBCI managers who had a new project idea. Project champions and designers would do their

best to assemble what they considered to be "appropriate" data in order to sell a new project idea, but as these various proposals were aggregated from different business units—each of which had its own unique culture, leadership styles, norms and vocabularies—decision-makers at higher levels had a very difficult time assessing the relative benefits of one project versus another. As a result, proposals were frequently far too detailed (providing a comprehensive business case when the core idea was questionable), or alternatively not nearly detailed enough (failing to provide an adequate sense of the core idea).

'Discretionary' spending

Exhibit 4

**Discrete versus Integrated
"Discretionary" Spending**

(Source: Adapted from company files.)

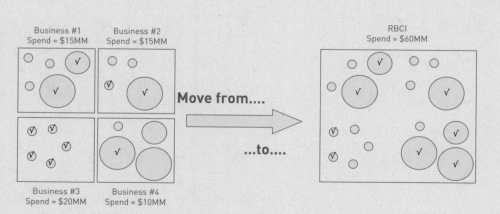

Total discretionary spend = $60MM

Net expected benefit = $76MM

Total discretionary spend = $60MM

Net expected benefit = $90MM

> More effective use of resource through a portfolio approach to selecting initiatives based on limited resources

Next Steps

Hellam had covered a lot of ground in a week, and felt he had a decent handle on the overall scope of the challenge. Yet he knew he had only just begun. Any new strategies and techniques could not be developed in a vacuum, but had to take into account current realities. As new tools and templates were developed, they would have to be integrated with today's Rube Goldberg[8] strategies and operations.

Hellam's immediate challenge was to develop a dashboard mechanism to allow RBCI to strategically organize, track and manage projects, in order to minimize NIE spend while maximizing benefits. Just as a jet pilot relies on a small number of cockpit instruments to provide critical information about altitude, airspeed, attitude and related flight information, so too the senior leaders at RBCI needed a dashboard with a small number of reliable and valid strategic indicators to fly the ship. What instruments should be included on the dashboard to help senior decision-makers assess and prioritize a proposed project? Could the dashboard also be used as a means of communicating between senior decision-makers and project champions (e.g., as a means to provide early input on a project idea, so that champions did not put too much effort into a doomed project, or too little effort into a brilliant idea)? How should Hellam go about constructing the instruments with his available raw materials?

More broadly speaking, what principles should guide the selection or rejection of particular projects? Modern portfolio theory examines how investors go about optimizing their expected returns and considers such concepts as diversification (reducing volatility by investing in many unrelated instruments), hedging (investing in assets to offset risk), the efficient frontier (the optimal portfolio for a given level of risk) and so on. Could these concepts inform the development of an IT portfolio approach at RBCI?

In addition to the challenge of constructing a valid and useful dashboard, Hellam felt that he would need to invest some serious effort to promote the notion of strategic alignment. What steps would be necessary to educate and gain senior leadership support? What about managers and project champions in the bank? Was it even rational to think about collapsing systems that were undoubtedly deeply integrated with core business processes within each business unit? Or should he expect leaders, managers and project champions to embrace strategic alignment as a boon for their departments and the bank as a whole?

As he allowed himself to relax for just a moment, Hellam's attention shifted to the family vacation that would start the following week. Thank goodness he had negotiated to keep his holiday plans intact before accepting this new appointment! Perhaps he would find the answers he needed on the golf course . . .

Student Assignment Questions

1. How should existing and new projects be categorized and prioritized at RBC Investments?
2. Describe the instruments you would include on the project dashboard. What role will each instrument play in helping Crosby and his superiors to select or reject projects for funding?
3. Refer to the "Discretionary Spending" exhibit. How are RBCI business unit leaders likely to respond to the idea of "erasing the lines"?
4. Describe the key action steps you must take to successfully implement your new IT portfolio approach.

---

[8] See www.rubegoldberg.com, accessed January 29, 2010.

(Source: Chepko Danil Vitalevich/Shutterstock.com.)

PART
• 4 •

Systems
Development

CHAPTER · 12 ·

Systems Development: Investigation and Analysis

PRINCIPLES	LEARNING OBJECTIVES

- **Effective systems development requires a team effort from stakeholders, users, managers, systems development specialists, and various support personnel, and it starts with careful planning.**

  - Identify the key participants in the systems development process and discuss their roles.
  - Define the term "information systems planning" and list several reasons for initiating a systems project.

- **Systems development often uses tools to select, implement, and monitor projects, including prototyping, rapid application development, CASE tools, and object-oriented development.**

  - Discuss the key features, advantages, and disadvantages of the traditional, prototyping, rapid application development, and end-user systems development life cycles.
  - Identify several factors that influence the success or failure of a systems development project.
  - Discuss the use of CASE tools and the object-oriented approach to systems development.

- **Systems development starts with investigation and analysis of existing systems.**

  - State the purpose of systems investigation.
  - Discuss the importance of performance and cost objectives.
  - State the purpose of systems analysis and discuss some of the tools and techniques used in this phase of systems development.

(Source: Chepko Danil Vitalevich/Shutterstock.com.)

Information Systems in the Global Economy
LEGO

LEGO Builds Information Systems from Modular Blocks

LEGO blocks are one of the best-known toys in the world. Founded in 1932 in Denmark by the Kirk Kristiansen family, which still owns the company, the LEGO Group has grown to 8,000 employees, providing fun building toys to children in more than 130 countries. The word LEGO is derived from an abbreviation of the two Danish words "leg godt," which translates to "play well." Children can "play well" with LEGO blocks because of the modular framework which allows children to explore their creativity and to solve problems.

Recently LEGO has enjoyed a resurgence of popularity. The company has experienced growing net profits over the past decade, with 2009 annual net profits increasing by 63 percent to Danish Krone (DKK) 2,204 million. LEGO is building and riding its tidal wave of success by diversifying and growing its product line. Its popular LEGO and DUPLO blocks take advantage of the latest media fads by offering kits for popular titles such as *Star Wars*, *Toy Story*, *SpongeBob*, and *Space Police*. Its Bionicle line is popular with tweens, and its Mindstorms computer-driven robots appeal to technically and scientifically minded children and young adults. Adults enjoy LEGO's more complicated kits such as its Architecture line. Recently, LEGO expanded into software games that duplicate their physical block packages in virtual reality software. The company has also launched LEGO Universe—a massively multiplayer online game (MMOG). The LEGO Group has even opened Discovery Centers featuring educational LEGO activities and theme parks featuring more than 50 LEGO-themed rides, shows, and attractions in Denmark, the U.K., the U.S., and Germany. By continuously reshaping itself, LEGO has reenergized its brand, leading to unprecedented growth for the company.

The rapid growth of the LEGO Group has provided substantial challenges for its information systems. Until recently, its mainframe-based enterprise system could not provide the flexibility to keep up with the rapid changes of the toy market. LEGO systems engineers were tasked with upgrading LEGO systems to handle the company's growth and its diverse business model. LEGO required a system that could support the needs of a large enterprise while being flexible and nimble enough to accommodate rapid change. Esben Viskum, senior director of the LEGO Service Centre, defines rapid change as the ability to "respond to the market quickly, using short product development processes without losing control of cost and quality, and being able to manage both people and operations effectively and efficiently."

After considering the problem, LEGO systems analysts decided that the best system for the task would need to be as modular and standardized as the LEGO blocks themselves. A modular standardized model would make it possible for the company to quickly expand into new markets.

LEGO system analysts spent months evaluating LEGO's current systems and data to determine the exact needs for the new system. Next, the team performed numerous feasibility studies to confirm that they could build the new system within their economic, technical, operational, and time constraints.

Because the new system would be large and comprehensive, the LEGO team would require the assistance of information system market leaders. LEGO selected SAP as the software foundation of its enterprise-wide systems. This foundation included SAP ERP Human Capital Management software and SAP Product Lifecycle Management software. Esben Viskum defines these as "business-critical" solutions.

LEGO selected IBM for the system infrastructure, including servers and storage. Esben Viskum says that IBM provided the "best way to deliver robust operations, and provide a repeatable template for each new LEGO venture."

The resulting system clearly supports LEGO's corporate goals. According to Viskum, LEGO wants to become "a much larger business, with the products, sales, and infrastructure to become truly robust." Its new enterprise systems will allow it to do just that. LEGO plans to expand with new sales offices, manufacturing plants, and retail shops. The SAP/IBM system provides a cookie-cutter approach to stamping out new business extensions with information systems that support local operations integrated into the system.

LEGO's investment of €45 million in its new systems is estimated to produce business benefits of €150 million—a threefold payback. The savings result from improved information delivery, which provides managers with better control and allows executives to respond more quickly and effectively to opportunities and problems.

As you read this chapter, consider the following:

- What situations can arise within a business to trigger new systems development initiatives?
- What are the best methods for a business to use in approaching new systems development projects?

Why Learn About Systems Development?

Throughout this book, you have seen many examples of the use of information systems in a variety of careers. But where do you start to acquire these systems or have them developed? How can you work with IS personnel, such as systems analysts and computer programmers, to get what you need to succeed on the job or in your own business? This chapter, the first of two chapters on systems development, provides the answers to these questions. You will see how you can initiate the systems development process and analyze your needs with the help of IS personnel. You will also see how you can use the systems development approach to start your own business. Systems investigation and systems analysis are the first two steps of the systems development process. This chapter provides specific examples of how new or modified systems are initiated and analyzed in a number of industries. In this chapter, you will learn how your project can be planned, aligned with corporate goals, rapidly developed, and much more. We start with an overview of the systems development process.

When an organization needs to accomplish a new task or change a work process, how does it do so? It develops a new system or modifies an existing one. Systems development is the activity of creating new systems or modifying existing systems. It refers to all aspects of the process—from identifying problems to solve or opportunities to exploit to implementing and refining the chosen solution.

AN OVERVIEW OF SYSTEMS DEVELOPMENT

In today's businesses, managers and employees in all functional areas work together and use business information systems. As a result, they are helping with development and, in many cases, leading the way. Users might request that a systems development team determine whether they should purchase a few PCs or create an attractive website using the tools discussed in Chapter 7. In another case, an entrepreneur might use systems development to build an Internet site to compete with large corporations. A number of individuals, for example, have developed applications for Apple's iPhone that are sold on Apple's applications store (App Store).[1] According to Steve Jobs, one of the founders of Apple Computer, "The App Store is like nothing the industry has ever seen before in both scale and quality. With 1.5 billion apps downloaded, it is going to be very hard for others to catch up."

This chapter and the next provide you with a deeper appreciation of the systems development process. The System Design Life Cycle (SDLC) methodology will be used to explain the five phases used in developing information systems: investigation, analysis, design, implementation and maintenance and review. Corporations and nonprofit organizations use systems development to achieve their goals. This chapter will also help you avoid systems development failures or projects that go over budget. As mentioned in an earlier chapter, over $1 billion was wasted when the province of Ontario's electronic health record project failed to operate as intended.[2]

Participants in Systems Development

Effective systems development requires a team effort. The team usually consists of stakeholders, users, managers, systems development specialists, and various support personnel. This team, called the *development team*, is responsible for determining the objectives of the information system and delivering a system that meets these objectives. Selecting the best IS team for a systems development project is critical to project success.[3] A *project* is a planned collection of activities that achieves a goal, such as constructing a new manufacturing plant or developing a new decision support system. Nevsun Resources, a Canadian mining operation, used a software package called Unifier to oversee its large African mining operations.[4] The company used the project management software to obtain real-time reviews of its mining projects in remote areas, such as Africa.

All projects have a defined starting point and ending point, normally expressed as dates such as August 4 and December 11. Most IS budgets have a significant amount of funds allocated for new systems development efforts. In one survey of insurance companies, survey respondents indicated that about 35 percent of IS spending is for new systems development projects.[5] A *project manager* is responsible for coordinating all people and resources needed to complete a project on time. The project manager can make the difference between project success and failure. In systems development, the project manager can be an IS person inside the organization or an external consultant. Project managers need technical, business, and people skills. In addition to completing the project on time and within the specified budget, the project manager is usually responsible for controlling project quality, training personnel, facilitating communications, managing risks, and acquiring any necessary equipment, including office supplies and sophisticated computer systems. Research studies have shown that project management success factors include good leadership from executives and project managers, a high level of trust in the project and its potential benefits, and the commitment of the project team and organization to successfully complete the project and implement its results. Research has also shown that project escalation, where the goals and costs of a project dramatically increase, can be a major obstacle to successful project implementation.[6]

In the context of systems development, **stakeholders** are people who, either themselves or through the organization they represent, ultimately benefit from the systems development project. **Users** are people who will interact with the system regularly. They can be employees, managers, or suppliers. For large-scale systems development projects, where the investment in and value of a system can be high, it is common for senior-level managers, including the functional vice presidents (of finance, marketing, and so on), to be part of the development team.

stakeholders
People who, either themselves or through the organization they represent, ultimately benefit from the systems development project.

users
People who will interact with the system regularly.

Because stakeholders ultimately benefit from the systems development project, they often work with others in developing a computer application.

(Source: © Jacob Wackerhausen/ iStockphoto.com.)

systems analyst
A professional who specializes in analyzing and designing business systems.

programmer
A specialist responsible for modifying or developing programs to satisfy user requirements.

Depending on the nature of the systems project, the development team might include systems analysts and programmers, among others. A **systems analyst** is a professional who specializes in analyzing and designing business systems. Systems analysts play various roles while interacting with the stakeholders and users, management, vendors and suppliers, external companies, programmers, and other IS support personnel. See Figure 12.1. Like an architect developing blueprints for a new building, a systems analyst develops detailed plans for the new or modified system. The **programmer** is responsible for modifying or developing programs to satisfy user requirements. Like a contractor constructing a new building or renovating an existing one based on an architect's drawings, the programmer takes the plans from the systems analyst and builds or modifies the necessary software.

Figure 12.1

Role of the Systems Analyst

The systems analyst plays an important role in the development team and is often the only person who sees the system in its totality. The one-way arrows in this figure do not mean that there is no direct communication between other team members. These arrows just indicate the pivotal role of the systems analyst—a person who is often called on to be a facilitator, moderator, negotiator, and interpreter for development activities.

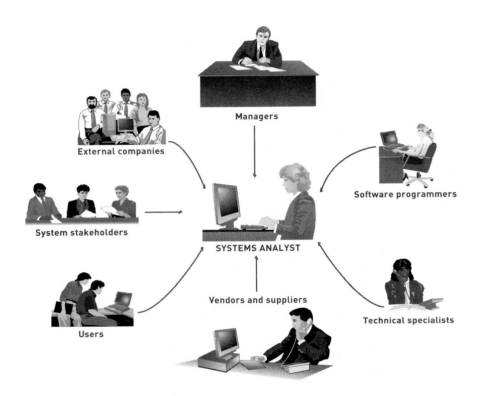

The other support personnel on the development team are mostly technical specialists, including database and telecommunications experts, hardware engineers, and supplier representatives. It is becoming more common for companies to open IS departments with a team of systems analysts and other IS personnel in foreign countries.[7] Equifax, for example, has systems analysts and a systems development staff in Santiago, Chile, to develop financial programs to help the credit-rating company. Yahoo! is another company that has established systems development staffs in foreign countries. For small businesses, the development team might consist only of a systems analyst and the business owner as the primary stakeholder. For larger organizations, formal IS staff can include hundreds of people involved in a variety of activities, including systems development.

Individual Systems Developers and Users

For decades, systems development was oriented toward corporations and corporate teams or groups. The major participants were discussed above. While this continues to be an important part of systems development, we are seeing individual systems developers and users to a greater extent.

An *individual systems developer* is a person who performs all the systems development roles, including systems analyst, programmer, technical specialist, and other roles described in the above section. Although individual systems developers can create applications for a group or entire organization, many specialize in developing applications for individuals. A large number of these applications are available for smartphones and other hand-held computing devices. Individual developers from around the world, for example, are using the steps of systems development to create unique applications for the iPhone.[8] In addition, Apple has special tools for iPhone application developers, including GPS capabilities, turn-by-turn directions, instant messaging, cut-and-paste features, and audio streaming to make it easier for people to craft unique applications.[9] Apple is also allowing systems developers to charge users in a variety of ways, including fixed prices and subscription fees through Apple's App Store. Ted Sullivan, for example, has developed a free download called Game Changer that he hopes to make available on Apple's App Store.[10] The application will collect baseball statistics from kids' baseball games and send them to the iPhones of parents, relatives, and others. Sullivan hopes to make millions of dollars from advertisers and monthly subscription fees for the service. Before an individual developer can have his or her application placed or sold on Apple's application store, however, Apple must approve or select the application.[11] Apple has tens of thousands of applications that can be downloaded and used.

Other companies also have application stores. BlackBerry has an application store, called App World, and Google has Android Market store.[12] Google also has a systems development tool called Wave that lets individual developers collaborate and communicate with others in creating documents.[13] Other people can add text, multimedia, and a variety of applications to a document. According to a Wave cofounder, "We're banking on Wave having a very large impact, but a lot of it depends on our ability to explain this to users. That's part of the reason why we're putting this out early to developers." Some applications, such as Google's Secure Data Connector, allow data to be downloaded from secure corporate databases, including customer and supplier information.[14]

Individual users acquire applications for both personal and professional use.[15] Cisco, the large networking company, has developed an iPhone application to help individual security personnel respond to IS and computer-related threats.[16] The application, called Security Intelligence Operations To Go, can instantly notify security professionals of security attacks as they occur and can help them recover if they occur. Another personal application turns an iPhone into a flute that can be played by blowing into the microphone and pushing keys on a virtual keyboard.[17] The program costs 99 cents but has generated about $1 million for the developer, an assistant professor of music. Another application is a sophisticated patient monitoring system for doctors and other health-care professionals.[18] Individual applications can be used to compare prices of products, analyze loans, locate organic food, find reliable repair services, and locate an apartment.[19] You can also turn a smartphone or PDA into a powerful scientific or financial calculator.[20] Other applications can synchronize with popular calendar and contact applications on laptop or desktop computers.[21] Applications can cost as little as $1 or as much as $100, including games, a compass and maps to show your direction and location, word processing and spreadsheet programs, airline flight information, and much more. Although most people purchase individual applications from authorized websites, unauthorized application stores that are not supported by the smartphone or cellular company can be used to purchase or acquire useful applications.[22]

It is also possible for one person to be both an individual developer and user. The term **end-user systems development** describes any systems development project in which business managers and users assume the primary effort. User-developed systems range from the very small (such as a software routine to merge form letters) to those of significant organizational value (such as customer contact databases for the Web).[23] Like any systems developer, individual developers and end users should follow the approach and techniques of the systems development process described in this and the next chapter. Even if you develop *your own* applications, you will likely want to have an IS department develop applications for you that are too complex or time consuming to develop on your own. In this case, you will be involved in initiating systems development, discussed next.

end-user systems development
Any systems development project in which the primary effort is undertaken by a combination of business managers and users.

Many end users today are demonstrating their systems development capability by designing and implementing their own PC-based systems.

(Source: India Today Group/Getty Images.)

Initiating Systems Development

Systems development initiatives arise from all levels of an organization and are both planned and unplanned.[24] Systems development projects are initiated for many reasons, as shown in Figure 12.2.

The increased use of the *cloud computing* approach, discussed in Chapter 7 and other chapters, has many IS professionals looking into using the Internet to run applications such as word processing, spreadsheet analysis, and others, instead of putting these applications on desktop or laptop computers.[25] The Victoria Order of Nurses (VON), Canada's largest

Figure 12.2

Typical Reasons to Initiate a Systems Development Project

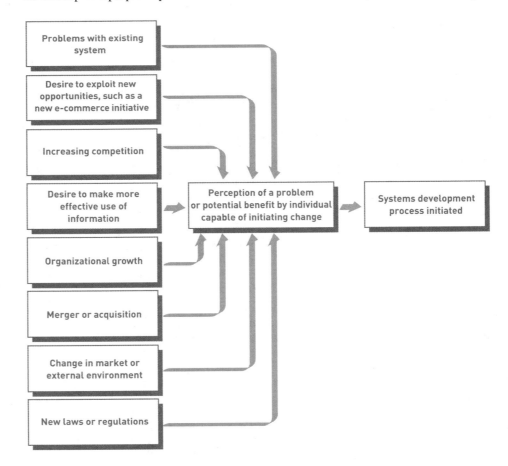

U.S. Federal Government IS Project to Save Billions

Information systems development initiatives are prompted by a wide variety of motivations. A recent systems development initiative was launched by the U.S. federal government in an effort to save taxpayers billions of dollars in government operating expenses and to reduce the impact of government data centres on the natural environment.

Basically, the U.S. government wants to get out of the data centre business. The federal government currently runs 1,100 data centres across the country. It intends to reduce this number to just 12 over the next few years. To do so, the government will outsource its data centre needs to SaaS providers that operate in the cloud. It will then consolidate its remaining operations, which store sensitive and confidential data, using new technologies, such as virtualization, that can accomplish more with fewer servers. By reducing its data centres by 90 percent, the federal government reduces both its spending and its greenhouse gas emissions.

One of the first steps in the federal government's move to the cloud was to set up an app store for federal agencies. The app store at *www.apps.gov* provides links to business apps, productivity apps, social media apps, and IT services provided by Software as a Service (SaaS), Infrastructure as a Service (IaaS), and Platform as a Service (PaaS) vendors. These vendors are vetted by the government as complying with government security and privacy regulations. Federal agencies can discover and adopt cloud services from this one website, assisting in their own systems development projects.

The General Services Administration (GSA), which is responsible for the site, has also published a website at *www.info. apps.gov* that assists agencies in understanding the benefits of cloud computing and finding applications that can be useful. The hope is that agencies will see the savings and benefits in cloud services and start offloading data and applications from government data centres onto cloud services.

Meanwhile, as efforts are made to sell federal agencies on the cloud, an intense review of government data centres is underway. Once a detailed accounting is completed for the

1,100 data centres, federal CIO Vivek Kundra and his team will begin implementing consolidation plans. These plans are guided by four high-level goals: promote green IT, reduce cost, increase IT security, and shift IT investments to more efficient computing platforms and technologies (namely cloud computing). Kundra hopes to take this opportunity to apply best practices from the private sector.

The U.S. federal government's data centre project is being called the largest data consolidation project ever. It illustrates the trend of data moving from small, privately owned data centres to huge data centres owned by service providers. Microsoft, Google, Amazon, and other cloud vendors are working hard to bring their systems up to compliance with government regulations so that they can provide services to government agencies. The government's consolidation efforts will benefit many commercial service vendors, as well as the government agencies and U.S. taxpayers.

Discussion Questions

1. Why does the U.S. federal government want to get out of the data centre business?
2. What benefits does cloud computing and data centre consolidation provide to the government and taxpayers?

Critical Thinking Questions

1. What businesses and industries will benefit from the federal government's plans?
2. Who, if anyone, will be negatively affected by the federal government's plans?

SOURCES: Claburn, Thomas, "Government Embraces Cloud Computing, Launches App Store," InformationWeek, September 15, 2010, *www.informationweek.com/ news/government/cloud-saas/showArticle.jhtml?articleID=220000493&queryText= apps.gov*; Hoover, J. Nicholas, "Feds Advance Cloud Adoption Plans," Information-Week, May 21, 2010, *www.informationweek.com/news/government/cloud-saas/ showArticle.jhtml?articleID=224900701&pgno=1&queryText=&isPrev=*; Miller, Rich, "Feds Commence Huge Data Center Consolidation," Data Center Knowledge, March 1, 2010, *www.datacenterknowledge.com/archives/2010/03/01/ feds-commence-huge-data-center-consolidation*.

national nonprofit organization for home and community care, initiated a cloud computing systems development project to improve patient care and make the organization more cost-efficient.[26] Cloud computing applications, however, have additional systems development challenges, such as making sure that the data and programs on the Internet are safe and secure from hackers and corporate spies. Amazon offers Elastic Compute Cloud for organizations and individuals that pay only for the computing resources they use.[27]

Mergers and acquisitions can trigger many systems development projects.[28] Even with similar information systems, the procedures, culture, training, and management of the information systems are often different, requiring a realignment of the IS departments. Of course, systems development can be initiated because existing systems and procedures failed or caused problems.

Systems development can also be initiated when a vendor no longer supports an older system or older software. When this support is no longer available, companies are often forced to upgrade to new software and systems, which can be expensive and require additional training. This lack of support is a dilemma for many companies trying to keep older systems operational.

Governments can foster new systems development projects in the public and private sectors. The Canadian federal government, for example, granted $500 million to Canada Health Infoway to encourage greater use of electronic records.[29] In the wake of recent financial scandals, the government also instituted corporate financial reporting rules under Bill 198, similar to the *Sarbanes-Oxley Act* in the United States. These regulations have caused many companies to initiate systems development efforts. To comply with this law, companies can spend hundreds of thousands or millions of dollars in new systems development efforts. Many IS projects are also funded by federal government stimulus programs initiated in 2009.

Information Systems Planning and Aligning Corporate and IS Goals

Information systems planning and aligning corporate and IS goals are important aspects of any systems development project. Achieving a competitive advantage is often the overall objective of systems development.

Information Systems Planning

information systems planning
Translating strategic and organizational goals into systems development initiatives.

The term **information systems planning** refers to translating strategic and organizational goals into systems development initiatives. See Figure 12.3.[30] Proper IS planning ensures that specific systems development objectives support organizational goals. Long-range planning can also be important and can result in getting the most from a systems development effort. It can also align IS goals with corporate goals and culture, which is discussed next.

Figure 12.3

Information Systems Planning

Information systems planning transforms organizational goals outlined in the strategic plan into specific systems development activities.

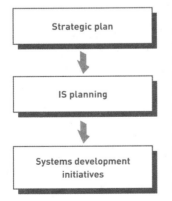

Strategic plan

IS planning

Systems development initiatives

Aligning Corporate and IS Goals

Aligning organizational goals and IS goals is critical for any successful systems development effort.[31] Because information systems support other business activities, IS staff and people in other departments need to understand each other's responsibilities and tasks. Most corporations have as primary goals increasing their profits and their return on investment (ROI), first introduced in Chapter 1. ROI is a key metric for technology initiatives, and the business case needs to include both initial development costs and subsequent maintenance costs. Another difficult aspect of aligning corporate and IS goals is the changing nature of business goals and priorities.[32]

Specific systems development initiatives can spring from the IS plan, but the IS plan must also provide a broad framework for future success. The IS plan should guide development of the IS infrastructure over time. Another benefit of IS planning is that it ensures better use of IS resources—including funds, personnel, and time for scheduling specific projects. The steps of IS planning are shown in Figure 12.4.

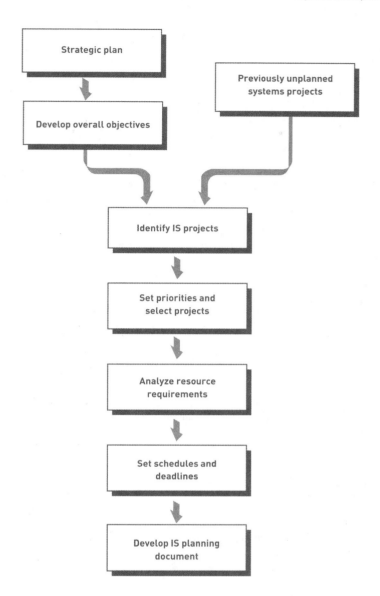

Figure 12.4

The Steps of IS Planning

Some projects are identified through overall IS objectives, whereas additional projects, called *unplanned projects*, are identified from other sources. All identified projects are then evaluated based on their organizational priority.

Developing a Competitive Advantage

In today's business environment, many companies seek systems development projects that will provide them with a competitive advantage. Thinking competitively usually requires creative and critical analysis. By looking at problems in new or different ways and by introducing innovative methods to solve them, many organizations have gained a significant competitive advantage.

Creative analysis involves investigating new approaches to existing problems. By looking at problems in new or different ways and by introducing innovative methods to solve them, many firms have gained a competitive advantage. Typically, these new solutions are inspired by people and events not directly related to the problem. Sir Isaac Newton, for example, watched something as simple as an apple fall from a tree as he developed the laws of gravity. Albert Einstein modified Newton's laws of gravity to create special and general relativity watching trains and thinking about the constant speed of light from different vantage points. Today, physicists are once again using creative analysis to dream about nine or more dimensions that could modify Einstein's theories with an approach called "string theory." It is hoped that string theory will explain everything from the gravity of large planets and stars to the movement of the smallest particles known to today's scientists. Researchers are starting to investigate brain patterns to better understand creative analysis

creative analysis
The investigation of new approaches to existing problems.

Hess Information Systems Take the Long View

Hess Corporation is a global energy company engaged in the exploration for and production of crude oil and natural gas. Hess has offices in 18 countries across six continents, with key headquarters in Houston, London, Kuala Lumpur (Malaysia), and Woodbridge (New Jersey).

Like most smart, mature companies, Hess aligns its information systems with long-term organizational goals and strategies. The focus on long term, however, was further emphasized with the arrival of a new CIO, Jeff Steinhorn. Steinhorn discovered that the Hess information systems group had historically taken a short-term approach to project planning. The company had its IS personnel focused on supporting near-term initiatives and the separate needs of each business division. No one was analyzing how these smaller short-term projects were assisting the company as a group at the highest level to meet its long-term objectives.

While this short-sighted approach served Hess adequately during the years that the company was focused solely on the oil business, it became more important as the company diversified for IS to assist in high-level long-term goals. In the past decade, Hess has expanded into natural gas and electricity. It was clear to Steinhorn that the company's IS initiatives needed to support and connect the organization's more diverse interests over the long haul.

Bobby Cameron at Forrester Research says that Steinhorn's predicament is not unique. The majority of new CIOs find themselves addressing the same problem. This is the result of the recent trend of organizations moving to use IS in ways important to the organization as a whole. Although businesses have traditionally called upon IS to support various initiatives, enterprise IS is a current force that drives business processes and spurs innovation. With this in mind, more and more IS initiatives are aligned with high-level, long-term organizational goals.

Steinhorn began by centralizing the data source that fed all information systems. Since IS projects had been conducted in each business division, the divisions weren't sharing important information such as customer records and market information. A central data store would eliminate data redundancy and improve data accuracy.

Next, Steinhorn set out to develop a five-year IS strategic plan. Once established, Steinhorn had to work to gain senior management approval. Senior management was resistant to change, and Steinhorn had not yet proved himself within the organization. Steinhorn brought some of the Hess's best-regarded IS managers onto the planning team and, with their assistance, gained senior management support.

Steinhorn also had trouble gaining the support of division executives who were accustomed to viewing IS as a support facility rather than a contributor to organizational goals and objectives. Steinhorn finally won them over by selling them on the ROI of long-term planning. Steinhorn persuaded them by showing that the costs of his plan were one-tenth as much as the benefits would return.

Steinhorn's five-year plan was divided into three components:

Business or "B" projects that assist in improving business processes, reducing costs, and increasing revenue.

Enabler or "E" projects that provided decision makers with information that enabled them to make better decisions, including business intelligence and analytical systems.

Process or "P" projects that assisted the IS group in organizing and standardizing its own work processes.

Within nine months of Steinhorn's five-year plan, 17 projects had been kicked off and seven were completed. This included a major upgrade of the company's SAP retail energy system.

Under its "P" project category, Steinhorn's group developed standardized systems for application development, project management, and IS governance. Steinhorn also implemented a performance tracking and scorecard system with which project success could be gauged. These advances in IS project management dramatically improved the quality and efficiency of the IS team's work.

With each successful project, Steinhorn's efforts are gaining increased support across Hess. The three divisions of Hess—oil, gas, and electricity—have become more interested in working together. Approaching IS from a long-term, enterprise level "has really elevated the decision-making to help decide where it's best to invest IT dollars to get the greatest returns," says William Hanna, vice president of electric operations at Hess and a program sponsor for the IT strategic planning initiative.

Discussion Questions

1. What challenges did Steinhorn face when he took the job as CIO of Hess?
2. Why are many businesses switching to a long-term, enterprise-wide emphasis for IS projects?

Critical Thinking Questions

1. How did Steinhorn organize IS projects under his five-year plan? What other categories of projects might you have included?
2. Why did Steinhorn face resistance from top-level managers and executives? What smart moves did he make to win them over?

SOURCES: "Amerada Hess Uses SAP Oil & Gas to Reduce Cost of Joint-Venture Activity," SAP Customer Implementation Success, accessed May 23, 2010, *www.sap.com/industries/oil-gas/pdf/50026246.pdf;* Hess website, accessed May 23, 2010, *www.hess.com;* Hoffman, Thomas, "Hess Builds a Project Pipeline with Long-Term Vision," *Computerworld,* April 7, 2008, *www.computerworld.com/s/article/314711/Building_an_IT_Project_Pipeline?taxonomyId=74&pageNumber=1.*

and innovation and how it can be applied to help people solve today's problems.[33] A lack of creative analysis and innovation can lead to a loss in competitiveness and long-term profitability.[34]

Critical analysis requires unbiased and careful questioning of whether system elements are related in the most effective ways.[35] It involves considering the establishment of new or different relationships among system elements and perhaps introducing new elements into the system. Critical analysis in systems development involves the following actions:

- *Questioning statements and assumptions.* Questioning users about their needs and clarifying their initial responses can result in better systems and more accurate predictions. Too often, stakeholders and users specify certain system requirements because they assume that their needs can be met only that way.
- *Identifying and resolving objectives and orientations that conflict.* Each department in an organization can have different objectives and orientations. The buying department might want to minimize the cost of spare parts by always buying from the lowest-cost supplier, but engineering might want to buy more expensive, higher-quality spare parts to reduce the frequency of replacement. These differences must be identified and resolved before a new purchasing system is developed or an existing one modified.

critical analysis
The unbiased and careful questioning of whether system elements are related in the most effective ways.

Establishing Objectives for Systems Development

The overall objective of systems development is to achieve business goals, not technical goals, by delivering the right information to the right person at the right time. The impact a particular system has on an organization's ability to meet its goals determines the true value of that system to the organization. Although all systems should support business goals, some systems are more pivotal in continued operations and goal attainment than others. These systems are called **mission-critical systems**. An order processing system, for example, is usually considered mission-critical. Without it, few organizations could continue daily activities, and they clearly would not meet set goals.

The goals defined for an organization also define the objectives that are set for a system. A manufacturing plant, for example, might determine that minimizing the total cost of owning and operating its equipment is critical to meet production and profit goals. **Critical success factors (CSFs)** are factors that are essential to the success of certain functional areas of an organization.[36] The CSF for manufacturing—minimizing equipment maintenance and operating costs—would be converted into specific objectives for a proposed system. One specific objective might be to alert maintenance planners when a piece of equipment is due for routine preventative maintenance (e.g., cleaning and lubrication). Another objective might be to alert the maintenance planners when the necessary cleaning materials, lubrication oils, or spare parts inventory levels are below specified limits. These objectives could be accomplished either through automatic stock replenishment via electronic data interchange or through the use of exception reports.

Regardless of the particular systems development effort, the development process should define a system with specific performance and cost objectives. The success or failure of the systems development effort will be measured against these objectives.

mission-critical systems
Systems that play a pivotal role in an organization's continued operations and goal attainment.

critical success factors (CSFs)
Factors that are essential to the success of a functional area of an organization.

Performance Objectives

The extent to which a system performs as desired can be measured through its performance objectives. System performance is usually determined by factors such as the following:

- *The quality or usefulness of the output.* Is the system generating the right information to the right people in a timely fashion? A glitch in a software program for a large computer company, for example, delayed it from paying commissions to some of its salespeople.[37] According to a former salesperson, "You'd be foolish to think people aren't frustrated."

- *The accuracy of the output.* Is the output accurate, and does it reflect the true situation? As a result of people and organizations losing most or all of their money to financial Ponzi schemes in 2009, accuracy is becoming more important, and top corporate officers are being held responsible for the accuracy of all corporate reports.[38]
- *The speed at which output is generated.* Is the system generating output in time to meet organizational goals and operational objectives? Objectives such as customer response time, the time to determine product availability, and throughput time are examples. Kanetix (*Kanetix.ca*) has developed a website that allows customers to get fast quotes on auto insurance and related insurance products from a variety of companies all through one website. They hope the increased speed of outputting quotes and offering multiple insurance company quotes will translate into more customers. Some hedge funds and trading firms use speed to make highly profitable trades that require powerful computer systems and sophisticated mathematical analysis.[39] The results of the high-speed trading are numerous buy or sell recommendations that are output from fast, powerful computers.[40]
- *The flexibility of the system.* Is the information system flexible and adaptable enough to produce a variety of reports and documents, depending on current conditions and the needs of the organization?[41]
- *The ease of use of the application.* Developing applications that can be easily used by managers and employees is an important goal for any systems development process.
- *The scalability of the resulting system.* As mentioned in Chapter 4, *scalability* allows an information system to handle business growth and increased business volume. The number of trades processed at the Toronto Stock Exchange, for example, has grown from 7.6 billion a month in 2006 to more than 9.7 billion a month in 2010.[42,43] This incredible growth requires a highly scalable information system.
- *The risk of the system.* One important objective of many systems development projects is to reduce risk. According to a survey of IS professionals, controlling access to critical data, data and file encryption, and securing any off-site IS facilities are effective ways to reduce risk and protect an organization's critical data resources.[44]

In some cases, the achievement of performance objectives can be easily measured (e.g., by tracking the time it takes to determine product availability). In other cases, it is sometimes more difficult to ascertain in the short term. For example, it might be difficult to determine how many customers are lost because of slow responses to customer inquiries regarding product availability. Even though it can be difficult to measure how IS spending helps an organization achieve its goals, many companies are increasing their IS spending. According to one survey, about 55 percent of responding insurance companies increased IS spending in 2009 and 2010.[45]

Cost Objectives

Organizations can spend more than is necessary during a systems development project. The benefits of achieving performance goals should be balanced with all costs associated with the system, including the following:

- *Development costs.* All costs required to get the system up and running should be included. Some computer vendors give cash rewards to companies using their systems to reduce costs and act as an incentive.
- *Costs related to the uniqueness of the system application.* A system's uniqueness has a profound effect on its cost. An expensive but reusable system might be preferable to a less costly system with limited use.
- *Fixed investments in hardware and related equipment.* Developers should consider costs of such items as computers, network-related equipment, and environmentally controlled data centres in which to operate the equipment.
- *Ongoing operating costs of the system.* Operating costs include costs for personnel, software, supplies, and resources such as the electricity required to operate the system. The U.S. and Canadian federal governments, for example, are investigating ways to cut operating costs by consolidating data centres, eliminating unnecessary IS projects, and exploring the use of cloud computing.[46,47] For many IS operations, ongoing operating costs are much higher than development or acquisition costs.

SYSTEMS DEVELOPMENT LIFE CYCLES

The systems development process is also called a *systems development life cycle* (SDLC) because the activities associated with it are ongoing. As each system is built, the project has timelines and deadlines, until at last the system is installed and accepted. The life of the system continues as it is maintained and reviewed. If the system needs significant improvement beyond the scope of maintenance, if it needs to be replaced because of a new generation of technology, or if the IS needs of the organization change significantly, a new project will be initiated and the cycle will start over.

A key fact of systems development is that the later in the SDLC an error is detected, the more expensive it is to correct. See Figure 12.5. One reason for the mounting costs is that if an error is found in a later phase of the SDLC, the previous phases must be reworked to some extent. Another reason is that the errors found late in the SDLC affect more people. For example, an error found after a system is installed might require retraining users when a "work-around" to the problem has been found. Thus, experienced systems developers prefer an approach that will catch errors early in the project life cycle.

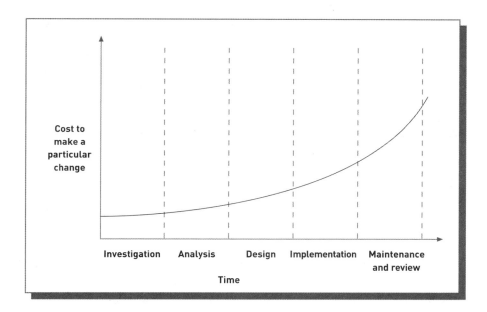

Figure 12.5

Relationship Between Timing of Errors and Costs

The later that system changes are made in the SDLC, the more expensive these changes become.

Common systems development life cycle approaches are traditional, prototyping, rapid application development (RAD), and individual development. Prototyping and the use of fourth-generation languages (used in RAD) are often incorporated into the traditional SDLC. In addition, companies can outsource the systems development process. With some companies, these approaches are formalized and documented so that systems developers have a well-defined process to follow; other companies use less formalized approaches. Keep Figure 12.5 in mind as you are introduced to alternative SDLCs in the next section.

The Traditional Systems Development Life Cycle

Traditional systems development efforts can range from a small project, such as purchasing an inexpensive computer program, to a major undertaking, such as installing a large computer system at a corporation or university. The steps of traditional systems development might vary from one company to the next, but most approaches have five common phases: investigation, analysis, design, implementation, and maintenance and review. See Figure 12.6 on the next page.

Figure 12.6

The Traditional Systems Development Life Cycle

Sometimes, information learned in a particular phase requires cycling back to a previous phase.

systems investigation
The systems development phase during which problems and opportunities are identified and considered in light of the goals of the business.

systems analysis
The systems development phase involving the study of existing systems and work processes to identify strengths, weaknesses, and opportunities for improvement.

systems design
The systems development phase that defines how the information system will do what it must do to obtain the solution.

systems implementation
The systems development phase involving the creation or acquisition of various system components detailed in the systems design, assembling them, and placing the new or modified system into operation.

systems maintenance and review
The systems development phase that ensures the system operates and modifies the system so that it continues to meet changing business needs.

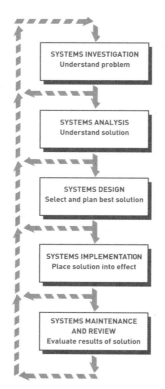

In the **systems investigation** phase, potential problems and opportunities are identified and considered in light of the goals of the business. Systems investigation attempts to answer the questions "What is the problem, and is it worth solving?" The primary result of this phase is a defined development project for which business problems or opportunity statements have been created, to which some organizational resources have been committed, and for which systems analysis is recommended. **Systems analysis** attempts to answer the question "What must the information system do to solve the problem?" This phase involves studying existing systems and work processes to identify strengths, weaknesses, and opportunities for improvement. The major outcome of systems analysis is a list of requirements and priorities. **Systems design** seeks to answer the question "How will the information system do what it must do to obtain the solution?" The primary result of this phase is a technical design that either describes the new system or describes how existing systems will be modified. The system design details system outputs, inputs, and user interfaces; specifies hardware, software, database, telecommunications, personnel, and procedure components; and shows how these components are related. **Systems implementation** involves creating or acquiring the various system components detailed in the systems design, assembling them, and placing the new or modified system into operation. An important task during this phase is to train the users. Systems implementation results in an installed, operational information system that meets the business needs for which it was developed. It can also involve phasing out or removing old systems which can be difficult for existing users.

The purpose of **systems maintenance and review** is to ensure that the system operates and to modify the system so that it continues to meet changing business needs. As shown in Figure 12.6, a system under development moves from one phase of the traditional SDLC to the next.

The traditional SDLC allows for a large degree of management control. However, a major problem is that the user does not use the solution until the system is nearly complete. Table 12.1 lists advantages and disadvantages of the traditional SDLC.

Prototyping

Prototyping takes an iterative approach to the systems development process.[48] During each iteration, requirements and alternative solutions to the problem are identified and analyzed, new solutions are designed, and a portion of the system is implemented. Users are then

Table 12.1

Advantages and Disadvantages of Traditional SDLC

prototyping
An iterative approach to the systems development process in which at each iteration requirements and alternative solutions to a problem are identified and analyzed, new solutions are designed, and a portion of the system is implemented.

Advantages	Disadvantages
Formal review at the end of each phase allows maximum management control.	Users get a system that meets the needs as understood by the developers; this might not be what the users really needed.
This approach creates considerable system documentation.	Documentation is expensive and time consuming to create. It is also difficult to keep current.
Formal documentation ensures that system requirements can be traced back to stated business needs.	Often, user needs go unstated or are misunderstood.
It produces many intermediate products that can be reviewed to see whether they meet the users' needs and conform to standards.	Users cannot easily review intermediate products and evaluate whether a particular product (e.g., a data flow diagram) meets their business requirements.

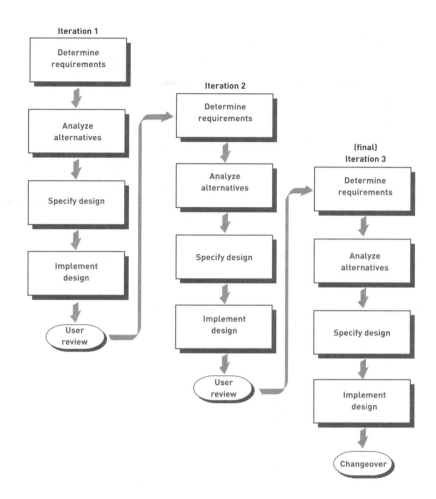

Figure 12.7

Prototyping

Prototyping is an iterative approach to systems development.

encouraged to try the prototype and provide feedback. See Figure 12.7. Prototyping begins with creating a preliminary model of a major subsystem or a scaled-down version of the entire system. For example, a prototype might show sample report formats and input screens. After they are developed and refined, the prototypical reports and input screens are used as models for the actual system, which can be developed using an end-user programming language such as Visual Basic. The first preliminary model is refined to form the second- and third-generation models, and so on, until the complete system is developed. See Figure 12.8.

Prototypes can be classified as operational or nonoperational. An *operational prototype* is a prototype that works—accesses real data files, edits input data, makes necessary computations and comparisons, and produces real output. A *nonoperational prototype* is a mock-up or model that that includes output and input specifications and formats. The advantages and disadvantages of prototyping are summarized in Table 12.2.

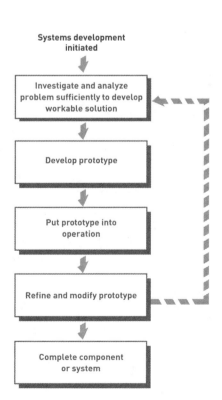

Figure 12.8

Refining During Prototyping

Each generation of prototype is a refinement of the previous generation based on user feedback.

Table 12.2

Advantages and Disadvantages
of Prototyping

Advantages	Disadvantages
Users can try the system and provide constructive feedback during development.	Each iteration builds on the previous one. The final solution might be only incrementally better than the initial solution.
An operational prototype can be produced in weeks.	Formal end-of-phase reviews might not occur. Thus, it is very difficult to contain the scope of the prototype, and the project never seems to end.
As solutions emerge, users become more positive about the process and the results.	System documentation is often absent or incomplete because the primary focus is on development of the prototype.
Prototyping enables early detection of errors and omissions.	System backup and recovery, performance, and security issues can be overlooked in the haste to develop a prototype.

Rapid Application Development, Agile Development, and Other Systems Development Approaches

rapid application development (RAD)
A systems development approach that employs tools, techniques, and methodologies designed to speed application development.

Rapid application development (**RAD**) employs tools, techniques, and methodologies designed to speed application development. These tools can also be used to make systems development projects more flexible and agile to be able to rapidly change with changing conditions and environments.[49] Vendors such as Computer Associates International, IBM, and Oracle market products targeting the RAD market. Rational Software, a division of IBM, has a RAD tool called Rational Rapid Developer to make developing large Java programs and applications easier and faster. Rational allows both systems developers and users to collaborate on systems development projects using Team Concert, which is like a social networking site for IBM developers and users.[50] RAD tools Advantage Gen, formerly known as COOL:Gen from Computer Associates International, and Optimalj from Compuware (*www.compuware.com*) can be used to rapidly generate computer code from business models and specifications.

RAD should not be used on every software development project. In general, it is best suited for DSSs and MISs and less suited for TPSs. During a RAD project, the level of participation of stakeholders and users is much higher than in other approaches. Table 12.3 lists advantages and disadvantages of RAD.

Table 12.3

Advantages and Disadvantages
of RAD

Advantages	Disadvantages
For appropriate projects, this approach puts an application into production sooner than any other approach.	This intense SDLC can burn out systems developers and other project participants.
Documentation is produced as a by-product of completing project tasks.	This approach requires systems analysts and users to be skilled in RAD systems development tools and RAD techniques.
RAD forces teamwork and lots of interaction between users and stakeholders.	RAD requires a larger percentage of stakeholders' and users' time than other approaches.

Other approaches to rapid development, such as *agile development* or *extreme programming (XP)*, allow the systems to change as they are being developed.[51] Agile development requires cooperation and frequent face-to-face meetings with all participants, including systems developers and users, as they modify, refine, and test how the system meets users' needs and what its capabilities are.[52] Organizations are using agile development to a greater extent today to improve the results of systems development, including global systems development projects requiring IS resources distributed in different locations.[53] Agile development can be a good approach when the requirements of a new or modified system aren't completely known in advance.[54] According to one IS professional, "Agile is perfect when you're not sure what you're getting into." Agile development is also called Dynamic Systems Development Method, Crystal, Agile Modelling, and several others. [55]

Extreme programming (XP) uses pairs of programmers who work together to design, test, and code parts of the systems they develop.[56] Research has shown that a pair of programmers usually outperforms the average individual programmer and on a level with the organization's best programmers.[57] The iterative nature of XP helps companies develop robust systems with fewer errors. Sabre Airline Solutions, a $2-billion computer company serving the airline travel industry, used XP to eliminate programming errors and shorten program development times.

In addition to the systems development approaches discussed previously, a number of other agile and innovative systems development approaches have been created by computer vendors and authors of systems development books. These approaches all attempt to deliver better systems in a shorter amount of time. A few agile development tools are listed below.

Adaptive Software Development (ASD). Adaptive Software Development grew out of rapid application development techniques and stresses an iterative process that involves analysis, design, and implementation at each cycle or iteration. The approach was primarily developed by James Highsmith.

Lean Software Development. Lean Software Development came from a book with the same title by Mary and Tom Poppendieck. The approach comes from lean manufacturing practices used by Toyota and stresses continuous learning, just-in-time decision making, empowering systems development teams, and the elimination of waste.[58]

Rational Unified Process (RUP). Rational Unified Process is an iterative systems development approach developed by IBM and includes a number of tools and techniques that are typically tailored to fit the needs of a specific company or organization. RUP uses an iterative approach to software development that stresses quality as the software is changed and updated over time.[59] Many companies have used RUP to their advantage.[60]

Feature-Driven Development (FDD). Originally used to complete a systems development project at a large bank, Feature-Driven Development is an iterative systems development approach that stresses the features of the new or modified system and involves developing an overall model, creating a list of features, planning by features, designing by features, and building by features.[61]

Crystal Methodologies. Crystal Methodologies is a family of systems development approaches developed by Alistair Cockburn that concentrates on effective team work and the reduction of paperwork and bureaucracy to make development projects faster and more efficient.

Outsourcing and On-Demand Computing

Many companies hire an outside consulting firm or computer company that specializes in systems development to take over some or all of its development and operations activities.[62] The drug company Pfizer, for example, used outsourcing to allow about 4,000 of its employees to outsource some of their jobs to other individuals or companies around the globe.[63] ENMAX, Alberta's largest electrical energy company, used outsourcing to help it innovate and find creative methods of providing natural gas and flexible billing services. According to ENMAX's commercial and institutional operations manager, its relationship with the outsourcing company "provides superior customer service, which gives us a competitive advantage."[64] Table 12.4 (on the next page) describes the circumstances in which outsourcing is a good idea.

Small and medium-sized firms are using outsourcing to a greater extent today to cut costs and acquire needed technical expertise that would be difficult to afford with in-house personnel.[65] According to one outsourcing expert, "The downturn is making it harder for companies to tie outsourcing to broader goals than basic cost cutting." The market for outsourcing services for small and medium-sized firms is expected to increase by 15 percent

Reason	Example
When a company believes it can cut costs	Toronto Pearson International Airport outsourced its IT infrastructure, including ticket kiosks and flight information networks. The incentive was to change from bundled landing fees to charging airlines usage-based fees.
When a firm has limited opportunity to distinguish itself competitively through a particular IS operation or application	Desjardins Group, the largest financial cooperative in Canada, outsourced its centralized IT infrastructure operations and hosting services to optimize financial returns.
When outsourcing does not strip the company of technical know-how required for future IS innovation	Firms must ensure that their IS staffs remain technically up to date and have the expertise to develop future applications.
When the firm's existing IS capabilities are limited, ineffective, or technically inferior	A company might use outsourcing to help it make the transition from a centralized mainframe environment to a distributed client/server environment.
When a firm is downsizing	A firm may use outsourcing as part of a program to reduce the number of employees and expenses.

Table 12.4

When to Use Outsourcing for Systems Development

Figure 12.9

Outsourcing

With consultants located in offices around the world, including Russia, China, and Israel, IBM offers outsourcing services and generates over $50 billion in revenues each year.

(Source: Toma Babovic/laif/Redux.)

annually through 2012 and beyond. Reducing costs, obtaining state-of-the-art technology, eliminating staffing and personnel problems, and increasing technological flexibility are reasons that companies have used the outsourcing and on-demand computing approaches.

A number of companies and nonprofit organizations offer outsourcing and on-demand computing services—from general systems development to specialized services. IBM's Global Services, for example, is one of the largest full-service outsourcing and consulting services.[66] IBM has consultants located in offices around the world and generates over $50 billion in revenues each year. Electronic Data Systems (EDS) is another large company that specializes in consulting and outsourcing.[67] EDS has approximately 140,000 employees in almost 60 countries and has more than 9,000 clients worldwide. EDS, which was acquired by Hewlett-Packard, generates over $20 billion annually.[68] Accenture is another company that specializes in consulting and outsourcing.[69] The company has more than 75,000 employees in 47 countries, with annual revenues that exceed $20 billion. Wipro Technologies, headquartered in India, is another worldwide outsourcing company with more than $4 billion in annual revenues.[70] Amazon, the large online retailer of books and other products, will

offer on-demand computing to individuals and other companies of all sizes, allowing them to use Amazon's computer expertise and database capacity. Individuals and companies pay only for the computer services they use. See Figure 12.9.

Outsourcing has some disadvantages, however. ENMAX cancelled its 10-year outsourcing contract with a large consulting company based on cost overruns, chronic inefficiencies, and a decline in service levels.[71] Internal expertise can be lost and loyalty can suffer under an outsourcing arrangement. When a company outsources, key IS personnel with expertise in technical and business functions are no longer needed. When these IS employees leave, their experience with the organization and expertise in information systems is lost. For some companies, it can be difficult to achieve a competitive advantage when competitors are using the same computer or consulting company. When the outsourcing or on-demand computing is done offshore or in a foreign country, some people raise security concerns. How will important data and trade secrets be guarded? In other cases, the outsourcing company can be involved in illegal activities or fail to deliver the products and services it promised.[72] The manager of one outsourcing company was accused of fraud for falsely reporting higher revenues, profits, and cash on hand. The manager compared the fraud to "riding a tiger, not knowing how to get off without being eaten."

FACTORS AFFECTING SYSTEMS DEVELOPMENT SUCCESS

Successful systems development means delivering a system that meets user and organizational needs—on time and within budget. Achieving a successful systems development project, however, can be difficult. Rogers Communications, for example, had problems with its billing system. Three hundred thousand customers were affected by a programming error in calculating multi-product discounts. The company overcharged customers a total of $30 million.[73] Getting users and stakeholders involved in systems development is critical for most systems development projects. Some researchers believe that how a systems development project is managed and run is one of the best indicators of systems development success.[74] Having the support of top-level managers is also important. In addition to user involvement and top management support, other factors can contribute to successful systems development efforts—at a reasonable cost. These factors are discussed next.

Degree of Change

A major factor that affects the quality of systems development is the degree of change associated with the project. The scope can vary from enhancing an existing system to major reengineering. The project team needs to recognize where they are on this spectrum of change.

Continuous Improvement Versus Reengineering

As discussed in Chapter 1, continuous improvement projects do not require a lot of changes or retraining of people; thus, they have a high degree of success.[75] Typically, because continuous improvements involve minor improvements, these projects also have relatively modest benefits. On the other hand, reengineering involves fundamental changes in how the organization conducts business and completes tasks. The factors associated with successful reengineering are similar to those of any development effort, including top management support, clearly defined corporate goals and systems development objectives, and careful management of change. Major reengineering projects tend to have a high degree of risk but also a high potential for major business benefits. See Figure 12.10 on the next page.

Managing Change

The ability to manage change is critical to the success of systems development. New systems inevitably involve change. Unfortunately, not everyone adapts easily, and the increasing complexity of systems can multiply the problems. Some systems developers believe that system complexity is a major cause of systems development failures.[76] It is essential to recognize existing or potential problems (particularly the concerns of users) and deal with them before they become a serious threat to the success of the new or modified system. Here are several of the most common problems that often need to be addressed as a result of new or modified systems:

- Fear that the employee will lose his job, power, or influence within the organization
- Belief that the proposed system will create more work than it eliminates
- Reluctance to work with "computer people"

Figure 12.10

The degree of change can greatly affect the probability of a project's success.

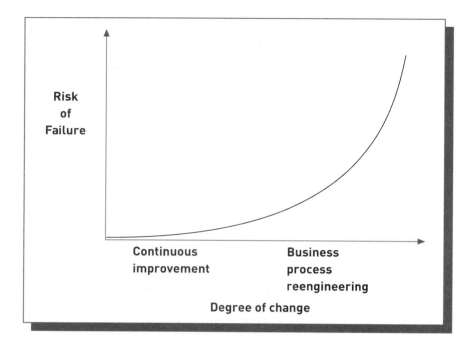

• Anxiety that the proposed system will negatively alter the structure of the organization
• Belief that other problems are more pressing than those solved by the proposed system or that the system is being developed by people unfamiliar with "the way things need to get done"
• Unwillingness to learn new procedures or approaches

The Importance of Planning

The bigger the project, the more likely that poor planning will lead to significant problems. Many companies find that large systems projects fall behind schedule, go over budget, and do not meet expectations. Although proper planning cannot guarantee that these types of problems will be avoided, it can minimize the likelihood of their occurrence. Good systems development is not automatic. Certain factors contribute to the failure of systems development projects. These factors and the countermeasures to eliminate or alleviate the problem are summarized in Table 12.5.

Organizational experience with the systems development process is also an important factor for systems development success.[77] The *Capability Maturity Model (CMM)* is one way to measure this experience.[78] It is based on research done at Carnegie Mellon University and

Table 12.5

Project Planning Issues That Frequently Contribute to Project Failure

Factor	Countermeasure
Solving the wrong problem	Establish a clear connection between the project and organizational goals.
Poor problem definition and analysis	Follow a standard systems development approach.
Poor communication	Set up communications procedures and protocols.
Project is too ambitious	Narrow the project focus to address only the most important business opportunities.
Lack of top management support	Identify the senior manager who has the most to gain from the success of the project and recruit this person to champion the project.
Lack of management and user involvement	Identify and recruit key stakeholders to be active participants in the project.

work done by the Software Engineering Institute (SEI). CMM is a measure of the maturity of the software development process in an organization. CMM grades an organization's systems development maturity using five levels: initial, repeatable, defined, managed, and optimized.

Use of Project Management Tools

Project management involves planning, scheduling, directing, and controlling human, financial, and technological resources for a defined task whose result is achievement of specific goals and objectives. Corporations and nonprofit organizations use these important tools and techniques.

A **project schedule** is a detailed description of what is to be done. Each project activity, the use of personnel and other resources, and expected completion dates are described. A **project milestone** is a critical date for the completion of a major part of the project, such as program design, coding, testing, and release (for a programming project). The **project deadline** is the date the entire project is to be completed and operational—when the organization can expect to begin to reap the benefits of the project.

In systems development, each activity has an earliest start time, earliest finish time, and slack time, which is the amount of time an activity can be delayed without delaying the entire project. The **critical path** consists of all activities that, if delayed, would delay the entire project. These activities have zero slack time. Any problems with critical-path activities will cause problems for the entire project. To ensure that critical-path activities are completed in a timely fashion, formalized project management approaches have been developed. Tools such as Microsoft Project are available to help compute these critical project attributes.

Although the steps of systems development seem straightforward, larger projects can become complex, requiring hundreds or thousands of separate activities. For these systems development efforts, formal project management methods and tools are essential. A formalized approach called **Program Evaluation and Review Technique** (**PERT**) creates three time estimates for an activity: shortest possible time, most likely time, and longest possible time. A formula is then applied to determine a single PERT time estimate. A **Gantt chart** is a graphical tool used for planning, monitoring, and coordinating projects; it is essentially a grid that lists activities and deadlines. Each time a task is completed, a marker such as a darkened line is placed in the proper grid cell to indicate the completion of a task. See Figure 12.11 on the next page.

Both PERT and Gantt techniques can be automated using project management software. Project management software helps managers determine the best way to reduce project completion time at the least cost. Several project management software packages are identified in Table 12.6 on the next page.

Use of Computer-Aided Software Engineering (CASE) Tools

Computer-aided software engineering (**CASE**) tools automate many of the tasks required in a systems development effort and encourage adherence to the SDLC, thus instilling a high degree of rigour and standardization to the entire systems development process. Oracle Designer by Oracle (*www.oracle.com*) and Visible Analyst by Visible Systems Corporation (*www.visible.com*) are examples of CASE tools. Oracle Designer is a CASE tool that can help systems analysts automate and simplify the development process for database systems. Other CASE tools include Embarcadero Describe (*www.embarcadero.com*), Popkin Software (*www.popkin.com*), Rational Software (part of IBM), and Visio (a charting and graphics program) from Microsoft.

CASE tools that focus on activities associated with the early stages of systems development are often called *upper-CASE* tools. These packages provide automated tools to assist with systems investigation, analysis, and design activities. Other CASE packages, called *lower-CASE* tools, focus on the later implementation stage of systems development and can automatically generate structured program code.

project schedule
A detailed description of what is to be done.

project milestone
A critical date for the completion of a major part of the project.

project deadline
The date the entire project is to be completed and operational.

critical path
Activities that, if delayed, would delay the entire project.

Program Evaluation and Review Technique (PERT)
A formalized approach for developing a project schedule.

Gantt chart
A graphical tool used for planning, monitoring, and coordinating projects.

computer-aided software engineering (CASE)
Tools that automate many of the tasks required in a systems development effort and encourage adherence to the SDLC.

Figure 12.11

Sample Gantt Chart

A Gantt chart shows progress through systems development activities by putting a bar through appropriate cells.

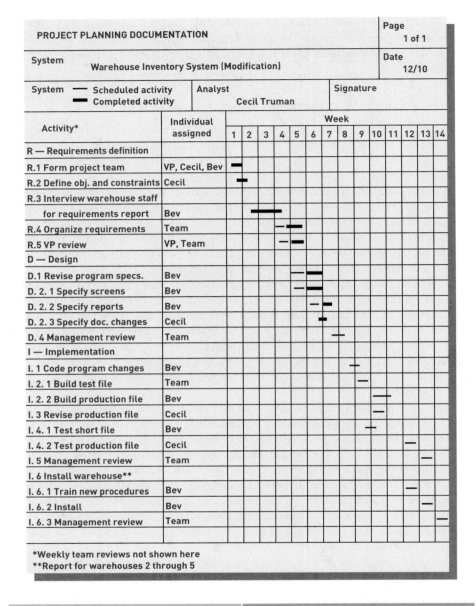

PROJECT PLANNING DOCUMENTATION															Page 1 of 1		

System: **Warehouse Inventory System (Modification)** — Date: 12/10

System — Scheduled activity / Completed activity — Analyst: Cecil Truman — Signature

Activity*	Individual assigned	Week													
		1	2	3	4	5	6	7	8	9	10	11	12	13	14
R — Requirements definition															
R.1 Form project team	VP, Cecil, Bev	▬													
R.2 Define obj. and constraints	Cecil		▬												
R.3 Interview warehouse staff															
for requirements report	Bev			▬											
R.4 Organize requirements	Team					▬									
R.5 VP review	VP, Team					▬									
D — Design															
D.1 Revise program specs.	Bev						▬								
D. 2. 1 Specify screens	Bev						▬								
D. 2. 2 Specify reports	Bev							▬							
D. 2. 3 Specify doc. changes	Cecil							▬							
D. 4 Management review	Team								▬						
I — Implementation															
I. 1 Code program changes	Bev									▬					
I. 2. 1 Build test file	Team										▬				
I. 2. 2 Build production file	Bev											▬			
I. 3 Revise production file	Cecil											▬			
I. 4. 1 Test short file	Bev										▬				
I. 4. 2 Test production file	Cecil												▬		
I. 5 Management review	Team												▬		
I. 6 Install warehouse**															
I. 6. 1 Train new procedures	Bev												▬		
I. 6. 2 Install	Bev													▬	
I. 6. 3 Management review	Team														▬

*Weekly team reviews not shown here
**Report for warehouses 2 through 5

Table 12.6

Selected Project Management Software

Software	Vendor
OpenPlan	Welcom (*www.welcom.com*)
Microsoft Project	Microsoft (*www.microsoft.com*)
Unifier	Skire (*www.skire.com*)

Object-Oriented Systems Development

The success of a systems development effort can depend on the specific programming tools and approaches used. As mentioned in Chapter 4, object-oriented (OO) programming languages allow the interaction of programming objects (recall that an object consists of both data and the actions that can be performed on the data). So, an object could be data about an employee and all the operations (such as payroll, benefits, and tax calculations) that might be performed for that employee. Developing programs and applications using OO programming languages involves constructing modules and parts that can be reused in other programming projects.

Chapter 4 discussed a number of programming languages that use the object-oriented approach, including Visual Basic, C++, and Java. These languages allow systems developers to take the OO approach, making program development faster and more efficient and resulting in lower costs. Modules can be developed internally or obtained from an external source. After a company has the programming modules, programmers and systems analysts can modify them and integrate them with other modules to form new programs.

Object-oriented systems development (**OOSD**) combines the logic of the systems development life cycle with the power of object-oriented modelling and programming.[79] OOSD follows a defined systems development life cycle, much like the SDLC. The life cycle phases are usually completed with many iterations. Object-oriented systems development typically involves the following tasks:

- *Identifying potential problems and opportunities within the organization that would be appropriate for the OO approach.* This process is similar to traditional systems investigation. Ideally, these problems or opportunities should lend themselves to the development of programs that can be built by modifying existing programming modules.
- *Defining what kind of system users require.* This analysis means defining all the objects that are part of the user's work environment (object-oriented analysis). The OO team must study the business and build a model of the objects that are part of the business (such as a customer, an order, or a payment). Many of the CASE tools discussed in the previous section can be used, starting with this step of OOSD.
- *Designing the system.* This process defines all the objects in the system and the ways they interact (object-oriented design). Design involves developing logical and physical models of the new system by adding details to the object model started in analysis.
- *Programming or modifying modules.* This implementation step takes the object model begun during analysis and completed during design and turns it into a set of interacting objects in a system. Object-oriented programming languages are designed to allow the programmer to create classes of objects in the computer system that correspond to the objects in the actual business process. Objects such as customer, order, and payment are redefined as computer system objects—a customer screen, an order entry menu, or a dollar sign icon. Programmers then write new modules or modify existing ones to produce the desired programs.
- *Evaluation by users.* The initial implementation is evaluated by users and improved. Additional scenarios and objects are added, and the cycle repeats. Finally, a complete, tested, and approved system is available for use.
- *Periodic review and modification.* The completed and operational system is reviewed at regular intervals and modified as necessary.

object-oriented systems development (OOSD)
An approach to systems development that combines the logic of the systems development life cycle with the power of object-oriented modelling and programming.

SYSTEMS INVESTIGATION

As discussed earlier in the chapter, systems investigation is the first phase in the traditional SDLC of a new or modified business information system. The purpose is to identify potential problems and opportunities and consider them in light of the goals of the company. Some stock trading companies that automatically place buy and sell orders based on news items are investigating their automated trading systems.[80] The automated stock trading programs caused the stock of a large airline company to fall after an erroneous news item surfaced on an online news report. In general, systems investigation attempts to uncover answers to the following questions:

- What primary problems might a new or enhanced system solve?
- What opportunities might a new or enhanced system provide?
- What new hardware, software, databases, telecommunications, personnel, or procedures will improve an existing system or are required in a new system?
- What are the potential costs, both variable and fixed?
- What are the associated risks?

Initiating Systems Investigation

Because systems development requests can require considerable time and effort to implement, many organizations have adopted a formal procedure for initiating systems development, beginning with systems investigation. The **systems request form** is a document filled out by someone who wants the IS department to initiate systems investigation. This form typically includes the following information:

systems request form
A document filled out by someone who wants the IS department to initiate systems investigation.

- Problems in or opportunities for the system
- Objectives of systems investigation
- Overview of the proposed system
- Expected costs and benefits of the proposed system

The information in the systems request form helps to rationalize and prioritize the activities of the IS department. Based on the overall IS plan, the organization's needs and goals, and the estimated value and priority of the proposed projects, managers make decisions regarding the initiation of each systems investigation for such projects.

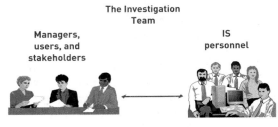

The Investigation Team

Managers, users, and stakeholders

IS personnel

- Undertakes feasibility analysis
- Establishes systems development goals
- Selects systems development methodology
- Prepares systems investigation report

Figure 12.12

The Systems Investigation Team

The team consists of upper- and middle-level managers, a project manager, IS personnel, users, and stakeholders.

Participants in Systems Investigation

After a decision has been made to initiate systems investigation, the first step is to determine what members of the development team should participate in the investigation phase of the project. Members of the development team change from phase to phase. See Figure 12.12. The systems investigation team can be diverse, with members located around the world. Cooperation and collaboration are keys to successful investigation teams in these cases. The members of the development team who participate in investigation are then responsible for gathering and analyzing data, preparing a report justifying systems development, and presenting the results to top-level managers.

feasibility analysis
Assessment of the technical, economic, legal, operational, and schedule feasibility of a project.

technical feasibility
Assessment of whether the hardware, software, and other system components can be acquired or developed to solve the problem.

economic feasibility
The determination of whether the project makes financial sense and whether predicted benefits offset the cost and time needed to obtain them.

Feasibility Analysis

A key step of the systems investigation phase is **feasibility analysis**, which assesses technical, economic, legal, operational, and schedule feasibility. See Figure 12.13. **Technical feasibility** is concerned with whether the hardware, software, and other system components can be acquired or developed to solve the problem.

Economic feasibility determines whether the project makes financial sense and whether predicted benefits offset the cost and time needed to obtain them. Economic feasibility can involve cash flow analysis such as that done in internal rate of return (IRR) or total cost of ownership (TCO) calculations, first discussed in Chapter 1. Spreadsheet programs, such as IBM Lotus and Microsoft Excel, have built-in functions to compute internal rate of return and other cash flow measures.

Legal feasibility determines whether laws or regulations can prevent or limit a systems development project. Legal feasibility involves an analysis of existing and future laws to determine the likelihood of legal action against the systems development project and the possible consequences.

Operational feasibility is a measure of whether the project can be put into action or operation. It can include logistical and motivational

Figure 12.13

Technical, Economic, Legal, Operational, and Schedule Feasibility

T echnical

E conomic

L egal

O perational

S chedule

legal feasibility
The determination of whether laws or regulations may prevent or limit a systems development project.

operational feasibility
The measure of whether the project can be put into action or operation.

(acceptance of change) considerations. Motivational considerations are important because new systems affect people and data flows and can have unintended consequences. As a result, power and politics might come into play, and some people might resist the new system.

Schedule feasibility determines whether the project can be completed in a reasonable amount of time—a process that involves balancing the time and resource requirements of the project with other projects.

schedule feasibility
The determination of whether the project can be completed in a reasonable amount of time.

Object-Oriented Systems Investigation

The object-oriented approach can be used during all phases of systems development, from investigation to maintenance and review. Consider a kayak rental business in Vancouver. B.C., where the owner wants to computerize its operations, including renting kayaks to customers and adding new kayaks into the rental program. See Figure 12.14. As you can see, the kayak rental clerk rents kayaks to customers and adds new kayaks to the current inventory available for rent. The stick figure is an example of an *actor*, and the ovals each represent an event, called a *use case*. In our example, the actor (the kayak rental clerk) interacts with two use cases (rent kayaks to customers and add new kayaks to inventory). The use case diagram is part of the Unified Modelling Language (UML) that is used in object-oriented systems development.

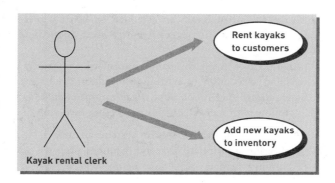

Figure 12.14

Use Case Diagram for a Kayak Rental Application

The Systems Investigation Report

The primary outcome of systems investigation is a **systems investigation report**, also called a *feasibility study*. This report summarizes the results of systems investigation and the process of feasibility analysis and recommends a course of action: continue on into systems analysis, modify the project in some manner, or drop it. A typical table of contents for the systems investigation report is shown in Figure 12.15.

The systems investigation report is reviewed by senior management, often organized as an advisory committee, or **steering committee**, consisting of senior management and users from the IS department and other functional areas. These people help IS personnel with their decisions about the use of information systems in the business and give authorization to pursue further systems development activities. After review, the steering committee might agree with the recommendation of the systems development team, or it might

systems investigation report
A summary of the results of the systems investigation and the process of feasibility analysis and recommendation of a course of action.

Figure 12.15

A Typical Table of Contents for a Systems Investigation Report

steering committee
An advisory group consisting of senior management and users from the IS department and other functional areas.

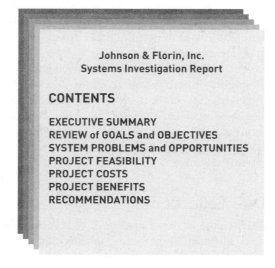

Johnson & Florin, Inc.
Systems Investigation Report

CONTENTS

EXECUTIVE SUMMARY
REVIEW of GOALS and OBJECTIVES
SYSTEM PROBLEMS and OPPORTUNITIES
PROJECT FEASIBILITY
PROJECT COSTS
PROJECT BENEFITS
RECOMMENDATIONS

suggest a change in project focus to concentrate more directly on meeting a specific company objective. Another alternative is that everyone might decide that the project is not feasible, and they would cancel the project.

SYSTEMS ANALYSIS

After a project has been approved for further study, the next step is to answer the question "What must the information system do to solve the problem?" The overall emphasis of analysis is gathering data on the existing system, determining the requirements for the new system, considering alternatives within these constraints, and investigating the feasibility of the solutions. The primary outcome of systems analysis is a prioritized list of systems requirements.

General Considerations

Systems analysis starts by clarifying the overall goals of the organization and determining how the existing or proposed information system helps meet them. A manufacturing company, for example, might want to reduce the number of equipment breakdowns. This goal can be translated into one or more informational needs. One need might be to create and maintain an accurate list of each piece of equipment and a schedule for preventative maintenance. Another need might be a list of equipment failures and their causes.

Analysis of a small company's information system is usually straightforward. On the other hand, evaluating an existing information system for a large company can be a long, tedious process. As a result, large organizations evaluating a major information system normally follow a formalized analysis procedure, involving these steps:

1. Assembling the participants for systems analysis
2. Collecting appropriate data and requirements
3. Analyzing the data and requirements
4. Preparing a report on the existing system, new system requirements, and project priorities

Participants in Systems Analysis

The first step in formal analysis is to assemble a team to study the existing system. This group includes members of the original investigation team—from users and stakeholders to IS personnel and management. Most organizations usually allow key members of the development team to not only analyze the condition of the existing system, but also to perform other aspects of systems development, such as design and implementation.

After the participants in systems analysis are assembled, this group develops a list of specific objectives and activities. A schedule for meeting the objectives and completing the specific activities is also devised, along with deadlines for each stage. They also draw up a statement of the resources required at each stage, such as clerical personnel, supplies, and so forth. Major milestones are normally established to help the team monitor progress and determine whether problems or delays occur in performing systems analysis.

Data Collection

The purpose of data collection is to seek additional information about the problems or needs identified in the systems investigation report. During this process, the strengths and weaknesses of the existing system are emphasized.

Identifying Sources of Data
Data collection begins by identifying and locating the various sources of data, including both internal and external sources. See Figure 12.16.

Internal Sources	External Sources
Users, stakeholders, and managers	Customers
Organization charts	Suppliers
Forms and documents	Stockholders
Procedure manuals and policies	Government agencies
Financial reports	Competitors
IS manuals	Outside groups
Other measures of business process	Journals, etc.
	Consultants

Figure 12.16

Internal and External Sources of Data for Systems Analysis

Collecting Data

After data sources have been identified, data collection begins. Figure 12.17 shows the steps involved. Data collection might require a number of tools and techniques, such as interviews, direct observation, and questionnaires.

Interviews can either be structured or unstructured. In a **structured interview**, the questions are written in advance. In an **unstructured interview**, the questions are not written in advance; the interviewer relies on experience in asking the best questions to uncover the inherent problems of the existing system and the needs of the employee or department. An advantage of the unstructured interview is that it allows the interviewer to ask follow-up or clarifying questions immediately.

With **direct observation**, one or more members of the analysis team directly observe the existing system in action. One of the best ways to understand how the existing system functions is to work with the users to discover how data flows in certain business tasks. Determining the data flow entails direct observation of users' work procedures, their reports, current screens (if automated already), and so on. From this observation, members of the analysis team determine which forms and procedures are adequate and which need improvement. Direct observation requires a certain amount of skill. The observer must be able to see what is really happening and not be influenced by attitudes or feelings. This approach can reveal important problems and opportunities that would be difficult to obtain using other data collection methods. An example would be observing the work procedures, reports, and computer screens associated with an accounts payable system being considered for replacement.

When many data sources are spread over a wide geographic area, **questionnaires** might be the best method. Like interviews, questionnaires can be either structured or unstructured. In most cases, a pilot study is conducted to fine-tune the questionnaire. A follow-up questionnaire can also capture the opinions of those who do not respond to the original questionnaire.

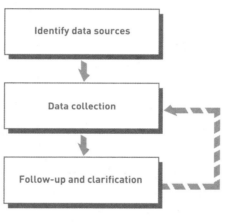

Figure 12.17

The Steps in Data Collection

structured interview
An interview where the questions are written in advance.

unstructured interview
An interview where the questions are not written in advance.

direct observation
Directly observing the existing system in action by one or more members of the analysis team.

questionnaires
A method of gathering data when the data sources are spread over a wide geographic area.

Direct observation is a method of data collection. One or more members of the analysis team directly observes the existing system in action.

(Source: © Kriss Russell/iStockphoto. com.)

Other data collection techniques can also be employed. In some cases, telephone calls work well. Activities can also be simulated to see how the existing system reacts. Thus, fake sales orders, stockouts, customer complaints, and data-flow bottlenecks can be created to see how the existing system responds to these situations. **Statistical sampling**, which involves taking a random sample of data, is another technique. For example, suppose that you want to collect data that describes 10,000 sales orders received over the last few years. Because it is too time consuming to analyze each of the sales orders, you can collect a random sample of 100 to 200 sales orders from the entire batch. You can assume that the characteristics of this sample apply to all 10,000 orders.

statistical sampling
Selecting a random sample of data and applying the characteristics of the sample to the whole group.

Data Analysis

The data collected in its raw form is usually not adequate to determine the effectiveness of the existing system or the requirements for the new system. The next step is to manipulate the collected data so that the development team members who are participating in systems analysis can use the data. This manipulation is called **data analysis**. Data and activity modelling and using data-flow diagrams and entity-relationship diagrams show the relationships among various objects, associations, and activities. Other common tools and techniques for data analysis include application flowcharts, grid charts, CASE tools, and the object-oriented approach.

data analysis
The manipulation of collected data so that the development team members who are participating in systems analysis can use the data.

Data Modelling

Data modelling, first introduced in Chapter 5, is a commonly accepted approach to modelling organizational objects and associations that employ both text and graphics. How data modelling is employed, however, is governed by the specific systems development methodology.

Data modelling is most often accomplished through the use of entity-relationship (ER) diagrams. Recall from Chapter 5 that an entity is a generalized representation of an object type—such as a class of people (employee), types of events (sales), categories of things (desks), or different locations (city). Recall also that entities possess certain attributes. Objects can be related to other objects in many ways. An entity-relationship diagram, such as the one shown in Figure 12.18a, describes a number of objects and the ways they are associated. An ER diagram (or any other modelling tool) cannot by itself fully describe a business problem or solution because it lacks descriptions of the related activities. It is, however, a good place to start because it describes object types and attributes about which data might need to be collected for processing.

Activity Modelling

To fully describe a business problem or solution, the related objects, associations, and activities must be described. Activities in this sense are events or items that are necessary to fulfil the business relationship or that can be associated with the business relationship in a meaningful way.

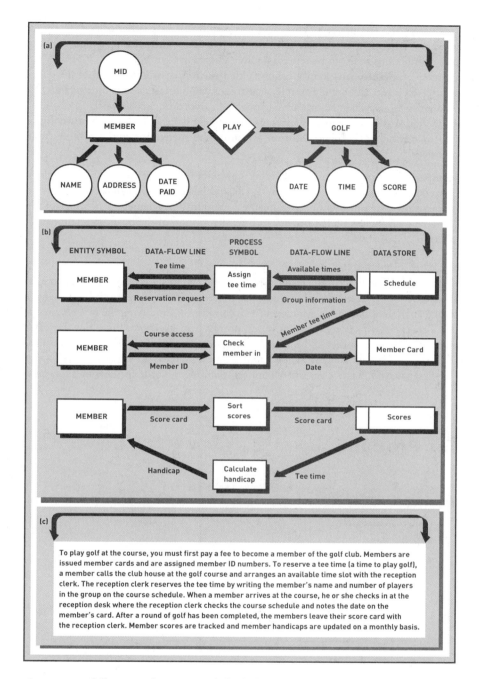

Figure 12.18

Data and Activity Modelling

(a) An entity-relationship diagram. (b) A data-flow diagram. (c) A semantic description of the business process.

(Source: From SANDERS. *Data Modeling*, 1E © 1995 South-Western, a part of Cengage Learning, Inc. Reproduced by permission. www. cengage.com/permissions.)

Activity modelling is often accomplished through the use of data-flow diagrams. A **data-flow diagram (DFD)** models objects, associations, and activities by describing how data can flow between and around various objects. DFDs work on the premise that every activity involves some communication, transference, or flow that can be described as a data element. DFDs describe the activities that fulfil a business relationship or accomplish a business task, not how these activities are to be performed. That is, DFDs show the logical sequence of associations and activities, not the physical processes. A system modelled with a DFD could operate manually or could be computer based; if computer based, the system could operate with a variety of technologies.

DFDs are easy to develop and easily understood by nontechnical people. Data-flow diagrams use four primary symbols, as illustrated in Figure 12.18b.

- *Data flow.* The **data-flow line** includes arrows that show the direction of data element movement.

data-flow diagram (DFD)
A model of objects, associations, and activities that describes how data can flow between and around various objects.

data-flow line
Arrows that show the direction of data element movement.

process symbol
Representation of a function that is performed.

entity symbol
Representation of either a source or destination of a data element.

data store
Representation of a storage location for data.

- *Process symbol.* The **process symbol** reveals a function that is performed. Computing gross pay, entering a sales order, delivering merchandise, and printing a report are examples of functions that can be represented with a process symbol.
- *Entity symbol.* The **entity symbol** shows either the source or destination of the data element. An entity can be, for example, a customer who initiates a sales order, an employee who receives a paycheque, or a manager who receives a financial report.
- *Data store.* A **data store** reveals a storage location for data. A data store is any computerized or manual data storage location, including magnetic tape, disks, a filing cabinet, or a desk.

Comparing entity-relationship diagrams with data-flow diagrams provides insight into the concept of top-down design. Figures 12.18a and b show an entity-relationship diagram and a data-flow diagram for the same business relationship—namely, a member of a golf club playing golf. Figure 12.18c provides a brief description of the business relationship for clarification.

application flowcharts
Diagrams that show relationships among applications or systems.

Application Flowcharts

Application flowcharts show the relationships among applications or systems. Assume that a small business has collected data about its order processing, inventory control, invoicing, and marketing analysis applications. Management is thinking of modifying the inventory control application. The raw facts collected, however, do not help in determining how the applications are related to each other and to the databases required for each. These relationships are established through data analysis with an application flowchart; see Figure 12.19. Using this tool for data analysis makes clear the relationships among the order processing functions.

Figure 12.19

A Telephone Order Process Application Flowchart

The flowchart shows the relationships among various processes.

(Source: Courtesy of SmartDraw Software, LLC.)

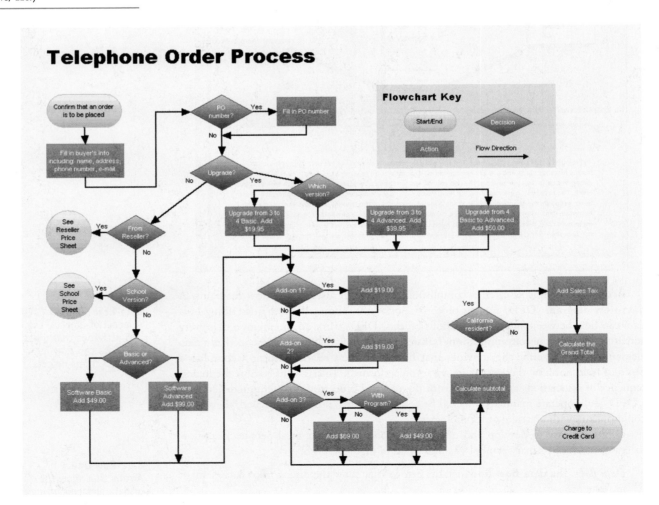

In the simplified application flowchart in Figure 12.19, you can see that the telephone order clerk provides important data to the system about items such as versions, quantities, and prices. The system calculates sales tax and order totals. Any changes made to this order processing system could affect the company's other systems, such as inventory control and marketing.

Grid Charts

A **grid chart** is a table that shows relationships among various aspects of a systems development effort. For example, a grid chart can reveal the databases used by the various applications. See Figure 12.20.

grid chart
A table that shows relationships among the various aspects of a systems development effort.

Databases → Applications	Customer database	Inventory database	Supplier database	Accounts receivable database
Order processing application	X	X		
Inventory control application		X	X	
Marketing analysis application	X	X		
Invoicing application	X			X

Figure 12.20

A Grid Chart

The chart shows the relationships among applications and databases.

The simplified grid chart in Figure 12.20 shows that the customer database is used by the order processing, marketing analysis, and invoicing applications. The inventory database is used by the order processing, inventory control, and marketing analysis applications. The supplier database is used by the inventory control application, and the accounts receivable database is used by the invoicing application. This grid chart shows which applications use common databases and reveals that, for example, any changes to the inventory control application must investigate the inventory and supplier databases.

CASE Tools

As discussed earlier, many systems development projects use CASE tools to complete analysis tasks. Most computer-aided software engineering tools have generalized graphics programs that can generate a variety of diagrams and figures. Entity-relationship diagrams, data-flow diagrams, application flowcharts, and other diagrams can be developed using CASE graphics programs to help describe the existing system. During the analysis phase, a **CASE repository**—a database of system descriptions, parameters, and objectives—will be developed.

CASE repository
A database of system descriptions, parameters, and objectives.

Requirements Analysis

The overall purpose of **requirements analysis** is to determine user, stakeholder, and organizational needs. For an accounts payable application, the stakeholders could include suppliers and members of the purchasing department. Questions that should be asked during requirements analysis include the following:

requirements analysis
The determination of user, stakeholder, and organizational needs.

- Are these stakeholders satisfied with the current accounts payable application?
- What improvements could be made to satisfy suppliers and help the purchasing department?

One of the most difficult procedures in systems analysis is confirming user or systems requirements. In some cases, communications problems can interfere with determining these requirements. For example, an accounts payable manager might want a better procedure for tracking the amount owed by customers. Specifically, the manager wants a weekly report that shows all customers who owe more than $1,000 and are more than 90 days past due on their accounts. A financial manager might need a report that summarizes the total amount owed by customers to consider whether to loosen or tighten credit limits. A sales manager might want to review the amount owed by a key customer relative to sales to that same customer. The purpose of requirements analysis is to capture these requests in detail. Numerous tools and techniques can be used to capture systems requirements.

Asking Directly

asking directly
An approach to gather data that asks users, stakeholders, and other managers about what they want and expect from the new or modified system.

One the most basic techniques used in requirements analysis is asking directly. **Asking directly** is an approach that asks users, stakeholders, and other managers about what they want and expect from the new or modified system. This approach works best for stable systems in which stakeholders and users clearly understand the system's functions. The role of the systems analyst during the analysis phase is to critically and creatively evaluate needs and define them clearly so that the systems can best meet them.

Critical Success Factors

Another approach uses critical success factors (CSFs). As discussed earlier, managers and decision makers are asked to list only the factors that are critical to the success of their areas of the organization.[81] A CSF for a production manager might be adequate raw materials from suppliers; a CSF for a sales representative could be a list of customers currently buying a certain type of product. Starting from these CSFs, the system inputs, outputs, performance, and other specific requirements can be determined.

The IS Plan

As we have seen, the IS plan translates strategic and organizational goals into systems development initiatives. The IS planning process often generates strategic planning documents that can be used to define system requirements. Working from these documents ensures that requirements analysis will address the goals set by top-level managers and decision makers. See Figure 12.21. There are unique benefits to applying the IS plan to define systems requirements. Because the IS plan takes a long-range approach to using information technology within the organization, the requirements for a system analyzed on the basis of the IS plan are more likely to be compatible with future systems development initiatives.

Figure 12.21

Converting Organizational Goals into Systems Requirements

Screen and Report Layout

screen layout
A technique that allows a designer to quickly and efficiently design the features, layout, and format of a display screen.

Developing formats for printed reports and screens to capture data and display information are some of the common tasks associated with developing systems. Screens and reports relating to systems output are specified first to verify that the desired solution is being delivered. Manual or computerized screen and report layout facilities are used to capture both output and input requirements.

Using a **screen layout**, a designer can quickly and efficiently design the features, layout, and format of a display screen. In general, users who interact with the screen frequently can be presented with more data and less descriptive information; infrequent users should have more descriptive information presented to explain the data that they are viewing. See Figure 12.22.

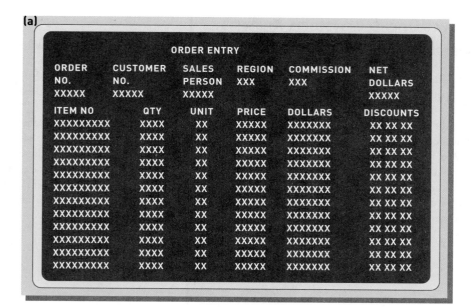

Figure 12.22

Screen Layouts

(a) A screen layout chart for frequent users who require little descriptive information.

(b) A screen layout chart for infrequent users who require more descriptive information.

Report layout allows designers to diagram and format printed reports. Reports can contain data, graphs, or both. Graphic presentations allow managers and executives to quickly view trends and take appropriate action, if necessary.

Screen layout diagrams can document the screens users desire for the new or modified application. Report layout charts reveal the format and content of various reports that the application will prepare. Other diagrams and charts can be developed to reveal the relationship between the application and outputs from the application.

report layout
A technique that allows designers to diagram and format printed reports.

Requirements Analysis Tools

A number of tools can be used to document requirements analysis, including CASE tools. As requirements are developed and agreed on, entity-relationship diagrams, data-flow diagrams, screen and report layout forms, and other types of documentation are stored in the CASE repository. These requirements might also be used later as a reference during the rest of systems development or for a different systems development project.

Object-Oriented Systems Analysis

The object-oriented approach can also be used during systems analysis. Like traditional analysis, problems or potential opportunities are identified during object-oriented analysis. Identifying key participants and collecting data is still performed. But instead of analyzing the existing system using data-flow diagrams and flowcharts, the team uses an object-oriented approach.

The section "Object-Oriented Systems Investigation" introduced a kayak rental example. A more detailed analysis of that business reveals that there are two classes of kayaks: single kayaks for one person and tandem kayaks that can accommodate two people. With the OO approach, a class is used to describe different types of objects, such as single and tandem kayaks. The classes of kayaks can be shown in a generalization/specialization hierarchy diagram; see Figure 12.23. KayakItem is an object that will store the kayak identification number (ID) and the date the kayak was purchased (datePurchased).

Figure 12.23

Generalization/Specialization Hierarchy Diagram for Single and Tandem Kayak Classes

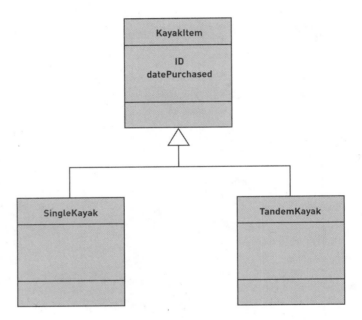

Of course, there could be subclasses of customers, life vests, paddles, and other items in the system. For example, price discounts for kayak rentals could be given to seniors (people over 65 years) and students. Thus, the customer class could be divided into regular, senior, and student customer subclasses.

The Systems Analysis Report

Systems analysis concludes with a formal systems analysis report. It should cover the following elements:

- The strengths and weaknesses of the existing system from a stakeholder's perspective
- The user/stakeholder requirements for the new system (also called the *functional requirements*)
- The organizational requirements for the new system
- A description of what the new information system should do to solve the problem

Suppose analysis reveals that a marketing manager thinks a weakness of the existing system is its inability to provide accurate reports on product availability. These requirements and a preliminary list of the corporate objectives for the new system will be in the systems analysis report. Particular attention is placed on areas of the existing system that could be improved to meet user requirements. The table of contents for a typical report is shown in Figure 12.24.

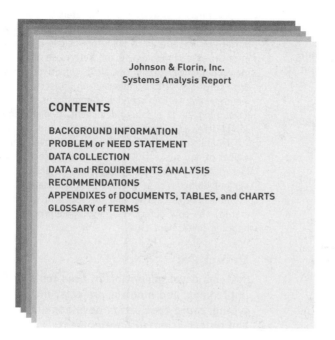

Johnson & Florin, Inc.
Systems Analysis Report

CONTENTS

BACKGROUND INFORMATION
PROBLEM or NEED STATEMENT
DATA COLLECTION
DATA and REQUIREMENTS ANALYSIS
RECOMMENDATIONS
APPENDIXES of DOCUMENTS, TABLES, and CHARTS
GLOSSARY of TERMS

Figure 12.24

A Typical Table of Contents for a Report on an Existing System

The systems analysis report gives managers a good understanding of the problems and strengths of the existing system. If the existing system is operating better than expected or the necessary changes are too expensive relative to the benefits of a new or modified system, the systems development process can be stopped at this stage. If the report shows that changes to another part of the system might be the best solution, the development process might start over, beginning again with systems investigation. Or, if the systems analysis report shows that it will be beneficial to develop one or more new systems or to make changes to existing ones, then systems design, which is discussed in Chapter 13, begins.

SUMMARY

Principle:

Effective systems development requires a team effort from stakeholders, users, managers, systems development specialists, and various support personnel, and it starts with careful planning.

The systems development team consists of stakeholders, users, managers, systems development specialists, and various support personnel. The development team determines the objectives of the information system and delivers to the organization a system that meets its objectives.

Stakeholders are people who, either themselves or through the area of the organization they represent, ultimately benefit from the systems development project. Users are people who will interact with the system regularly. They can be employees, managers, customers, or suppliers. Managers on development teams are typically representative of stakeholders or can be stakeholders themselves. In addition, managers are most capable of initiating and maintaining change. For large-scale systems development projects, where the investment in and value of a system can be quite high, it is common to have senior-level managers be part of the development team.

A systems analyst is a professional who specializes in analyzing and designing business systems. The programmer is responsible for modifying or developing programs to satisfy user requirements. Other support personnel on the development team include technical specialists, either employees from the IS department or outside consultants. Depending on the magnitude of the systems development project and the number of IS development specialists on the team, the team might also include one or more IS managers. At some point in your career, you will likely be a participant in systems development. You could be involved in a systems development team—as a user, as a manager of a business area or project team, as a member of the IS department, or maybe even as a CIO.

Individuals are involved as systems developers and users. An individual systems developer is a person who performs all the systems development roles, including analyst, programmer, technical specialist, etc. An individual user acquires applications for both personal and professional use through a number of sources, including Apple's App Store, popular with iPhone users. The term *end-user systems development* describes any systems development project in which the primary effort is undertaken by a combination of business managers and users. Today, more individuals are becoming entrepreneurs and developing applications for cell phones and other devices.

Systems development projects are initiated for many reasons, including the need to solve problems with an existing system, to exploit opportunities to gain competitive advantage, to increase competition, to make use of effective information, to spur organizational growth, to handle a merger or corporate acquisition, and to address a change in the market or external environment. External pressures, such as potential lawsuits or terrorist attacks, can also prompt an organization to initiate systems development.

Information systems planning refers to the translation of strategic and organizational goals into systems development initiatives. Benefits of IS planning include a long-range view of information technology use and better use of IS resources. Planning requires developing overall IS objectives; identifying IS projects; setting priorities and selecting projects; analyzing resource requirements; setting schedules, milestones, and deadlines; and developing the IS planning document. IS planning can result in a competitive advantage through creative and critical analysis.

Establishing objectives for systems development is a key aspect of any successful development project. Critical success factors (CSFs) can identify important objectives. Systems development objectives can include performance goals (quality and usefulness of the output and the speed at which output is generated) and cost objectives (development costs, fixed costs, and ongoing investment costs).

Principle:

Systems development often uses tools to select, implement, and monitor projects, including prototyping, rapid application development, CASE tools, and object-oriented development.

The five phases of the traditional SDLC are investigation, analysis, design, implementation, and maintenance and review. Systems investigation identifies potential problems and opportunities and considers them in light of organizational goals. Systems analysis seeks a general understanding of the solution required to solve the problem; the team studies the existing system in detail and identifies weaknesses. Systems design creates new or modifies existing system requirements. Systems implementation encompasses programming, testing, training, conversion, and operation of the system. Systems maintenance and review entails monitoring the system and performing enhancements or repairs.

Advantages of the traditional SDLC include the following: It provides for maximum management control, creates considerable system documentation, ensures that system requirements can be traced back to stated business needs, and produces many intermediate products for review. Its disadvantages include the following: Users may get a system that meets the needs as understood by the developers, the documentation is expensive and difficult to maintain, users' needs go unstated or might not be met, and users cannot easily review the many intermediate products produced.

Prototyping is an iterative approach that involves defining the problem, building the initial version, having users work with and evaluate the initial version, providing feedback, and incorporating suggestions into the second version. Prototypes can be fully operational or nonoperational, depending on how critical the system under development is and how much time and money the organization has to spend on prototyping.

Rapid application development (RAD) uses tools and techniques designed to speed application development. Its use reduces paper-based documentation, automates program source code generation, and facilitates user participation in development activities. RAD can use newer programming techniques, such as agile development or extreme programming.

Many companies hire an outside consulting firm that specializes in systems development to take over some or all of its systems development activities. This approach is called *outsourcing*. Reasons for outsourcing include companies' belief that they can cut costs, achieve a competitive advantage without having the necessary IS personnel in-house, obtain state-of-the-art technology, increase their technological flexibility, and proceed with development despite downsizing. Many companies offer outsourcing services, including computer vendors and specialized consulting companies.

A number of factors affect systems development success. The degree of change introduced by the project, continuous improvement and reengineering, organizational experience with systems development, the use of project management tools, and the use of CASE tools and the objected-oriented approach are all factors that affect the success of a project. The greater the amount of change a system will endure, the greater the degree of risk and often the greater the amount of reward. Continuous improvement projects do not require significant business process or IS changes, while reengineering involves fundamental changes in how the organization conducts business and completes tasks. Successful systems development projects often involve such factors as support from top management, strong user involvement, use of a proven methodology, clear project goals and objectives, concentration on key problems and straightforward designs, staying on schedule and within budget, good user training, and solid review and maintenance programs.

The use of automated project management tools enables detailed development, tracking, and control of the project schedule. Effective use of a quality assurance process enables the project manager to deliver a high-quality system and to make intelligent trade-offs among cost, schedule, and quality. CASE tools automate many of the systems development tasks, thus reducing an analyst's time and effort while ensuring good documentation. Object-oriented systems development can also be an important success factor. With the object-oriented systems development (OOSD) approach, a project can be broken down into a group of objects that interact. Instead of requiring thousands or millions of lines of detailed computer instructions or code, the systems development project might require a few dozen or maybe a hundred objects.

Principle:

Systems development starts with investigation and analysis of existing systems.

In most organizations, a systems request form initiates the investigation process. Participants in systems investigation can include stakeholders, users, managers, employees, analysts, and

programmers. The systems investigation is designed to assess the feasibility of implementing solutions for business problems, including technical, economic, legal, operational, and schedule feasibility. Internal rate of return (IRR) analysis is often used to help determine a project's economic feasibility. An investigation team follows up on the request and performs a feasibility analysis that addresses technical, economic, legal, operational, and schedule feasibility.

If the project under investigation is feasible, major goals are set for the system's development, including performance, cost, managerial goals, and procedural goals. Many companies choose a popular methodology so that new IS employees, outside specialists, and vendors will be familiar with the systems development tasks set forth in the approach. A systems development methodology must be selected. Object-oriented systems investigation is being used to a greater extent today. The use case diagram is part of the Unified Modelling Language that is used to document object-oriented systems development. As a final step in the investigation process, a systems investigation report should be prepared to document relevant findings.

Systems analysis is the examination of existing systems, which begins after a team receives approval for further study from management. Additional study of a selected system allows those involved to further understand the system's weaknesses and potential areas for improvement. An analysis team assembles to collect and analyze data on the existing system.

Data collection methods include observation, interviews, questionnaires, and statistical sampling. Data analysis manipulates the collected data to provide information. The analysis includes grid charts, application flowcharts, and CASE tools. The overall purpose of requirements analysis is to determine user and organizational needs.

Data analysis and modelling is used to model organizational objects and associations using text and graphical diagrams. Analysts do this through the use of entity-relationship (ER) diagrams. Activity modelling often uses data-flow diagrams (DFDs), which model objects, associations, and activities by describing how data can flow between and around various objects. DFDs use symbols for data flows, processing, entities, and data stores. Application flowcharts, grid charts, and CASE tools are also used during systems analysis.

Requirements analysis determines the needs of users, stakeholders, and the organization in general. Asking directly, using critical success factors, and determining requirements from the IS plan can be used. Often, screen and report layout charts are used to document requirements during systems analysis.

Like traditional analysis, teams often identify problems or potential opportunities during object-oriented analysis. Object-oriented systems analysis can involve using diagramming techniques, such as a generalization/specialization hierarchy diagram.

CHAPTER 12: SELF-ASSESSMENT TEST

Effective systems development requires a team effort from stakeholders, users, managers, systems development specialists, and various support personnel, and it starts with careful planning.

1. _____ is the activity of creating or modifying existing business systems. It refers to all aspects of the process—from identifying problems to be solved or opportunities to be exploited to the implementation and refinement of the chosen solution.

2. Who ultimately benefits from a systems development project?
   a. computer programmers
   b. systems analysts
   c. stakeholders
   d. senior-level managers

3. _____ involves questioning statements and assumptions.

4. Like a contractor constructing a new building or renovating an existing one, the chief information officer (CIO) takes the plans from the systems analyst and builds or modifies the necessary software. True or False?

5. The term _____ refers to the translation of strategic and organizational goals into systems development initiatives.

6. What involves investigating new approaches to existing problems?
   a. critical success factors
   b. systems analysis factors
   c. creative analysis
   d. critical analysis

Systems development often uses tools to select, implement, and monitor projects including prototyping, rapid application development, CASE tools, and object-oriented development.

7. What kind of development uses tools, techniques, and methodologies designed to speed application development?
   a. rapid application development
   b. joint optimization
   c. prototyping
   d. extended application development

8. Agile development allows systems to change as they are being developed. True or False?

9. _____ takes an iterative approach to the systems development process. During each iteration, the team identifies and analyzes requirements and alternative solutions to the problem, designs new solutions, and implements a portion of the system.

10. Rapid application development (RAD) employs tools, techniques, and methodologies designed to speed application development. True or False?

11. What consists of all activities that, if delayed, would delay the entire project?
    a. deadline activities
    b. slack activities
    c. RAD tasks
    d. the critical path

Systems development starts with investigation and analysis of existing systems.

12. The systems request form is a document that is filled out during systems analysis. True or False?

13. Feasibility analysis is typically done during which systems development stage?
    a. investigation
    b. analysis
    c. design
    d. implementation

14. Data modelling is most often accomplished through the use of _____, whereas activity modelling is often accomplished through the use of _____.

15. The overall purpose of requirements analysis is to determine user, stakeholder, and organizational needs. True or False?

CHAPTER 12: SELF-ASSESSMENT TEST ANSWERS

(1) Systems development (2) c (3) Critical analysis (4) False (5) information systems planning (6) c (7) a (8) True (9) Prototyping (10) True (11) d (12) False (13) a (14) entity-relationship (ER) diagrams, data-flow diagrams (15) True

REVIEW QUESTIONS

1. What is an IS stakeholder?
2. What is the goal of IS planning? What steps are involved in IS planning?
3. What are the typical reasons to initiate systems development?
4. What is the difference between creative analysis and critical analysis?
5. What is the difference between a programmer and a systems analyst?
6. What is the difference between a Gantt chart and PERT?
7. What is the difference between systems investigation and systems analysis? Why is it important to identify and remove errors early in the systems development life cycle?
8. What is end-user systems development?
9. List factors that have a strong influence on project success.
10. What is the purpose of systems analysis?
11. What are the steps of object-oriented systems development?
12. Define the different types of feasibility that systems development must consider.
13. What are the objectives of agile development?
14. What is the result or outcome of systems analysis? What happens next?

DISCUSSION QUESTIONS

1. Why is it important for business managers to have a basic understanding of the systems development process?
2. Briefly describe the role of a system user in the systems investigation and systems analysis stages of a project.
3. How could you use critical analysis to help you develop a better information system for your college or university?
4. You have decided to become an IS entrepreneur and develop applications for the iPhone and other mobile devices. Describe what applications you would develop and how you would do it.
5. Your company wants to develop or acquire a new sales program to help sales representatives identify new customers. Describe what factors you would consider in deciding whether to develop the application in-house or outsource the application to an outside company.
6. You have been hired by your university to find an outsourcing company to perform the payroll function. What are your recommendations? Describe the advantages and disadvantages of the outsourcing approach for this application.
7. You have been hired as a project manager to develop a new website in the next six months for a store that sells music and books online. Describe how project management tools, such as a Gantt chart and PERT, might be used.
8. For what types of systems development projects might prototyping be especially useful? What are the characteristics of a system developed with a prototyping technique?
9. Assume that you work for an insurance company. Describe three applications that are critical to your business. What tools would you use to develop applications?
10. How important are communications skills to IS personnel? Consider this statement: "IS personnel need a combination of skills—one-third technical skills, one-third business skills, and one-third communications skills." Do you think this is true? How would this affect the training of IS personnel?
11. You have been hired to perform systems investigation for a French restaurant owner in a large metropolitan area. She is thinking of opening a new restaurant with a state-of-the-art computer system that would allow customers to place orders on the Internet or at kiosks at restaurant tables. Describe how you would determine the technical, economic, legal, operational, and schedule feasibility for the restaurant and its proposed computer system.
12. Discuss three reasons why aligning overall business goals with IS goals is important.
13. You are the chief information officer for a medium-sized retail store and would like to develop an extranet to allow your loyal customers to see and buy your products on the Internet. Describe how you would determine the requirements for the new system.

PROBLEM-SOLVING EXERCISES

1. For a business of your choice, use a graphics program to develop one or more Use Case diagrams and one or more Generalized/Specialized Hierarchy diagrams for your new business, using the object-oriented approach.
2. You have been hired to develop a payroll program for a medium-sized company. At a minimum, the application should have an hours-worked table that contains how many hours each employee worked and an employee table that contains information about each employee, including hourly pay rate. Design and develop these tables that could be used in a database for the payroll program.

TEAM ACTIVITIES

1. Your team should interview people involved in systems development in a local business or at your college or university. Describe the process used. Identify the users, analysts, and stakeholders for a systems development project that has been completed or is currently under development.
2. Your team has been hired to determine the requirements and layout of the Web pages for a company that sells fishing equipment over the Internet. Using the approaches discussed in this chapter, develop a rough sketch of at least five Web pages that you would recommend. Make sure to show the important features and the hyperlinks for each page.
3. Your team has been hired to use systems development to produce a billing program for a small heating and air conditioning company. Develop a flowchart that shows the major features and components of your billing program.

WEB EXERCISES

1. Cloud computing, where applications such as word processing and spreadsheet analysis are delivered over the Internet, is becoming more popular. You have been hired to analyze the potential of a cloud computing application that performs payroll and invoicing over the Internet from a large Internet company. Describe the systems development steps and procedures you would use to analyze the feasibility of this approach.
2. Using the Internet, explore the use of agile systems development approaches for two companies. Write a report that describes the advantages and disadvantages of the agile systems development approach for these companies.

CAREER EXERCISES

1. Pick a career that you are considering. What type of information system would help you on the job? Perform technical, economic, legal, operational, and schedule feasibility for an information system you would like developed.
2. Using the Internet, research career opportunities in which you would develop applications for the iPhone and similar smartphones. Write a report on what you found. Compare the career opportunities in developing applications for these types of devices to a career as a traditional computer programmer.

CASE STUDIES

Case One

BMW Streamlines IS with App Virtualization

The number of enterprise software applications that a business supports can dramatically affect its operating expenses. The installation and maintenance of software on enterprise PCs can easily consume all of the efforts of an IS departments, keeping IS professionals from otherwise contributing to the organization.

One recent study found that the most successful companies have on average only 20 applications per 1,000 users. Supporting more applications creates an overly complex technology environment with a strong likelihood of redundant or unnecessary applications. Maintaining 20 applications per 1,000 users suggest a strong alignment between applications and business objectives.

Many businesses are launching systems development projects to reduce or gain control of enterprise application bloat. BMW provides a great example of one such effort.

BMW found itself supporting 1,000 apps across 80,000 PCs at its 24 production sites and 250 offices in 13 countries. While many of BMW's apps were remotely packaged, tested, and installed by a firm in India, many others required a physical service call to the PC for installation. BMW estimates the cost at $54 per visit. The company could provide users with administrative accounts to perform their own installations, but only at a huge risk to system security and stability.

BMW systems engineers found a solution in Microsoft Application Virtualization (App-V). A virtual application is launched from a PC the same way as installed applications. The difference is that virtual applications are served up from an application server over the corporate LAN rather than a local installation. Virtual apps use Web service technologies to combine network resources and local resources for storing and running applications.

Using application virtualization, BMW systems group needed to install only Microsoft App-V on its 80,000 PCs. Once installed, App-V allows users to run one of dozens of applications from BMW servers without having to install each individual application on each PC. BMW is rolling out virtualized apps gradually. In November 2009, the company went live with 20 virtual applications to 500 employees. By May 2010, 60 applications were virtualized and all new PCs were receiving the virtualization treatment. Thousands more installations were completed in 2010.

App-V has been useful in a number of ways. Using App-V, the company ran a virtual version of Office 2010 alongside local installations of Office 2007. This allowed employees to gradually migrate to the new version of Office. The company is in the middle of upgrading its PCs from Windows XP to Windows 7. Virtualization allows it to run incompatible Windows XP applications on Windows 7 and 64-bit versions of software on 32-bit PCs. Virtualization provides the added benefit of allowing employees to access their virtual applications from home PCs.

But the biggest advantage for the company is in the money saved from using application virtualization. Systems engineers no longer have to install software on individual PCs. Software is installed and maintained on application servers, then distributed to the PCs over the network. Virtualization provides systems engineers with more control over software installations, increasing information security, and offers better system stability. By December 2009, the automaker had virtualized more than 400 applications, saving the company $200,000 in installation costs.

Discussion Questions

1. How does the amount of software applications supported by an organization reflect on that organization's efficiency?
2. What is application virtualization, and how can it reduce information system costs?

Critical Thinking Questions

1. What lessons can be learned from BMW's experience when it comes to systems development initiatives that require software purchases?
2. Some companies are reducing expenses by allowing employees to use their own computers for work. What complexities does this add to a company's technology environment? What benefits does it provide to users?

SOURCES: O'Neill, Shane, "BMW Takes a Sharp Turn Toward App Virtualization," CIO, May 20, 2010, www.cio.com; Betts, Mitch, "The Best Companies Have Fewer Applications, Study Says," Computerworld, May 24, 2010; Microsoft Application Virtualization website, accessed May 25, 2010, www.microsoft.com/systemcenter/appv/default.mspx.

Case Two

Hotwire.com Gains Control of Hotel Partner Information

Hotwire.com advertises four-star hotels at two-star prices throughout North America and Europe. By building businesses partnerships with more than 7,000 hotels across North America, Hotwire assists its hotel partners in filling otherwise empty rooms and helps its customers by finding them rates discounted by as much as 60 percent.

Hotwire maintains a wealth of information about each of its 7,000 hotel partners. Besides basics such as location, amenities, customer reviews, and prices, it also maintains information about the number of available rooms. Much of the information Hotwire tracks changes frequently. Maintaining accurate and up-to-date information is a key to success in this highly competitive business.

Until recently, Hotwire maintained its hotel information on shared Excel spreadsheets. Hotwire employees kept the information up to date by accessing the shared spreadsheets over the corporate network. Various applications drew information from the spreadsheets to provide Hotwire the information it needed to provide its customers with deals. Unfortunately, the system was prone to errors and extremely difficult to maintain.

Hotwire systems analysts considered the problem and possible solutions. The data that the system manipulated was well defined, as were the processes that were applied to the data. The problem lay in the manner in which the data was stored and accessed.

It was clear to Hotwire analysts that a centralized database-driven system would allow Hotwire to gain better control over its data. Hotwire analysts considered costs and benefits of designing its own database and DBMS compared to outsourcing the service to a provider. Upon evaluation of the requirements for the system, they discovered that the data Hotwire was managing could be easily managed by a Customer Relationship Management (CRM) system, even though its partner hotels were not exactly customers.

Hotwire systems analysts evaluated a variety of CRM systems and found the one from Salesforce to be most effective and feasible with regard to cost and technology. The Salesforce CRM allows Hotwire employees to access hotel data through a user-friendly Web-based interface from any Internet-connected computer. Hotwire data is securely stored and maintained on Salesforce servers, relieving Hotwire of that costly responsibility. Hotwire system engineers customize the CRM to deliver the information and reports needed by Hotwire managers and systems.

The new system has improved data reliability and accuracy, allowing better management of the information, happier customers, and improved relationships with Hotwire partners.

Discussion Questions

1. How do you think system engineers determined that it was a good time to invest in this information systems development project?
2. What benefits did Salesforce provide Hotwire.com over its previous system?

Critical Thinking Questions

1. What considerations are required in deciding whether to host your own system or outsource to a vendor like Salesforce?

2. How can Hotwire gauge the success of this information systems development project?

SOURCES: "Hotwire Uses Salesforce CRM to Keep Tabs on More Than 7,000 Hotel Partners Across North America," Salesforce success stories, *www.salesforce.com*, accessed May 25, 2010; Salesforce CRM website, *www.salesforce.com/crm/products.jsp*, accessed May 25, 2010; About Hotwire, *www.hotwire.com/about-hotwire/pressroom/factSheet.jsp*, accessed May 25, 2010.

Questions for Web Case

See the website for this book to read about the Altitude Online case for this chapter. Following are questions concerning this Web case.

Altitude Online: Systems Investigation and Analysis Considerations

Discussion Questions

1. What important activities did Jon's team engage in during the Systems Investigation stage of the Systems Development Life Cycle?
2. Why are all forms of feasibility considerations especially important for an ERP development project?

Critical Thinking Questions

1. Why is the quality of the systems analysis report crucial to the successful continuation of the project?
2. Why do you think Jon felt the need to travel to communicate with Altitude Online colleagues rather than using e-mail or phone conferencing? What benefit does face-to-face communication provide in this scenario?

NOTES

Sources for the opening vignette: "LEGO Creates Model Business Success with SAP and IBM," IBM Success Stories, May 19, 2010, *www-01.ibm.com/software/success/cssdb.nsf/CS/STRD-85KGS6?OpenDocument&Site=bladecenter&cty=en_us*; "LEGO—About Us," accessed May 23, 2010, *www.lego.com/eng/info*.

1   Kane, Y., "Seeking Fame in Apple's Sea of Apps," *Wall Street Journal*, July 15, 2009, p. B1.
2   "Ehealth Scandal a $1B Waste: Auditor," CBC News, October 7, 2009, */www.cbc.ca/canada/toronto/story/2009/10/07/ehealth-auditor.html*, accessed October 17, 2010.
3   Anderson, Howard, "Project Triage: Skimpy Must Die," *Information Week*, March 16, 2009, p. 14.
4   Soat, John, "IT Leaders Are Wrestling with How to Bring Informal Collaboration into Rigorous Processes," *Information Week*, July 20, 2009, p. 17.
5   Hoover, N., "Insurers Spend on IT to Cut Costs Elsewhere," *Information Week*, September 14, 2009, p. 88.
6   Harvey, Paul, and Victorovich, Lisa, "The Influence of Forward-Looking Antecedents, Uncertainty, and Anticipatory Emotions on Project Escalation," *Decision Sciences*, November 2009, p. 759.
7   Jana, Reena, "South America's New IT Hub," *BusinessWeek*, August 24, 2009, p. 73.

8   Kane, Yukare Iwatani, "Apple Woos Developers with New iPhone," *Wall Street Journal*, March 18, 2009, p. B6.
9   Kane, "Apple Woos Developers with New iPhone Tools."
10 Woolsey, Matt, "New Ball Game," *Forbes*, March 2, 2009, p. 50.
11 O'Brien, Jeffrey, "The Wizards of Apps," *Fortune*, May 25, 2009, p. 29.
12 Reena, J., and Burrows, P., "An All-Out Online Assault on the iPhone," *BusinessWeek*, April 6, 2009, p. 74.
13 Albro, Edward, "Google's Wave," *PC World*, August 2009, p. 14.
14 Weier, Mary H., "Google Tries to Make App Engine Practical," *Information Week*, April 13, 2009, p. 13.
15 MacMillan, D., et al., "The App Economy," *BusinessWeek*, November 2, 2009, p. 45.
16 Perez, Marin, "The iPhone as IT Security Tool," *Information Week*, November 30, 2009, p. 18.
17 Boudreau, John, "iPhone Has Musical Hit," *Tampa Tribune*, March 30, 2009, p. 8.
18 Wildstrom, Stephen, "The Unstoppable iPhone," *BusinessWeek*, June 29, 2009, p. 63.
19 Mossberg, W., and Bhehret K., "A Shopping Trip to the App Store for Your iPhone," *Wall Street Journal*, July 23, 2009, p. D1.
20 Pressman, Aaron, "Figuring Your Finances," *BusinessWeek*, December 15, 2008, p. 78.

21 Wildstrom, Stephan, "A Stroll Through iPhone App Store," *BusinessWeek*, July 28, 2009, p. 74.

22 Kane, Y., "Breaking Apple's Grip on the iPhone," *Wall Street Journal*, March 6, 2009, p. B1.

23 Aedo, I., et al., "End User Oriented Strategies," *Information Processing & Management*, January 2010, p. 11.

24 Hookway, J., "How Team of Geeks Cracked Spy Trade," *Wall Street Journal*, September 4, 2009, p. A1.

25 Wildstrom, Stephen, "What to Entrust to the Cloud," *BusinessWeek*, April 6, 2009, p. 89.

26 "The Growing Need for 'cloud' computing'," *European Hospital*, March 2, 2010, www.european-hospital.com/en/article/6966-The_growing_need_for_'cloud'_computing.html, accessed October 17, 2010.

27 Conry-Murray, Andrew, "What's in the Public Cloud," *Information Week*, September 7, 2009, p. 37.

28 Mehta, M., et al., "Strategic Alignment in Mergers and Acquisitions," *The Journal of the Association of Information Systems*, March 2007, p. 143.

29 "Canada's Economic Action Plan: Budget 2009," www.budget.gc.ca/2009/plan/bpc1-eng.html, accessed October 18, 2010.

30 Cordoba, J., "Critical Reflection in Planning Information Systems," *Information Systems Journal*, March 2009, p. 123.

31 Preston, D., and Karahanna, E., "Antecedents of IS Strategic Alignment," *Information Systems Research*, June 2009, p. 159.

32 Evans, Bob, "Stop Aligning IT with the Business," *Information Week*, January 19, 2009, p. 68.

33 Hotz, Robert, "A Wandering Mind Heads Straight Toward Insight," *Wall Street Journal*, June 19, 2009, p. A11.

34 Mandel, Michael, "Innovation Interrupted," *BusinessWeek*, June 15, 2009, p. 35.

35 Moreno, V., et al., "Strategic Alignment and Its Antecedents: A Critical Analysis," *Journal of Global Information Technology Management*, No. 12, 2009, p. 33.

36 Chow, W., et al., "Determinants of the Critical Success Factors of Disaster Recovery Planning for Information Systems," *Information Management & Computer Security*, Vol. 17, 2009, p. 248.

37 Scheck, J., "H-P Is on Quest to Fix Software Glitch," *Wall Street Journal*, August 5, 2009, p. B2.

38 Henriques, Diana, "Madoff Victims Sue SEC for Negligence," *Boston Globe*, October 15, 2009, p. 9.

39 Duhigg, Charles, "Traders Profit with Computers High Speed," *New York Times*, July 24, 2009.

40 Patterson, Scott, "Faster, Faster," *Wall Street Journal*, March 29, 2010, p. C1.

41 Agerfalk, P., et al., "Flexible and Distributed Information Systems Development," *Information Systems Research*, September 2009, p. 317.

42 "TMX Group—Consolidated Trading Statistics September 2010," TMX Group, www.tmx.com/en/pdf/MonthlyTradingSummary.pdf, accessed October 18, 2010.

43 "TSX Trading Volume Jumps in January, Listings Fall," Reuters, February 7, 2007, www.reuters.com/article/idUSN0743026120070207, accessed October 18, 2010.

44 Fratto, Mike, "What's Your Appetite for Risk?" *Information Week*, June 22, 2009, p. 25.

45 Hoover, N., "Insurers Spend on IT to Cut Costs Elsewhere," *Information Week*, September 14, 2009, p. 88.

46 Gohring, Nancy, "Federal CIO Calls for Monitoring Gov't IT," *Computerworld*, March 22, 2010, p. 8.

47 Daneck, Jirka, "Cloud Computing and the Canadian Environment," October 6, 2009, www.scribd.com/full/20818613?access_key=key-gn8m346gk59rv7di3qv, accessed October 18, 2010.

48 Web, Warren, "Prototyping Kit Shortens Embedded-Systems-Development Schedule," *EDN*, April 9, 2009, p. 8.

49 Goodhue, D., et al., "Addressing Business Agility Challenges with Enterprise Systems," *MIS Quarterly Executive*, June 2009, p. 73.

50 Babcock, Charles, "IBM Adds Social Networking to Rational Team Development," *Information Week*, June 2, 2009, p. 24.

51 Vidgen, R., et al., "Coevolving Systems and the Organization of Agile Software Development," *Information Systems Research*, September 2009, p. 355.

52 Tubbs, Jerry, "Team Building Goes Viral," *Information Week*, February 22, 2010, p. 47.

53 Sarker, Saonee, and Sarker, Suprateek, "Exploring Agility in Distributed Information Systems Development Teams," *Information Systems Research*, September 2009, p. 440.

54 Erickson, J., "Agile Development," *Information Week*, April 27, 2009, p. 31.

55 Conboy, Kieran, "Agility from First Principles," *Information Systems Research*, September, 2009, p. 329.

56 Tolfo, C., et al., "The Influence of Organizational Culture on the Adoption of Extreme Programming," *The Journal of Systems and Software*, November 2008, p. 1955.

57 Balijepally, V., et al., "Are Two Heads Better Than One for Software Development?" *MIS Quarterly*, March 2009, p. 91.

58 West, Dave, "Agile Processes Go Lean," *Information Week*, April 27, 2009, p. 32.

59 "The Rational Unified Process," www-306.ibm.com/software/awdtools/rup/support..., accessed June 2, 2008.

60 "Rational Case Studies," www-01.ibm.com/software/success/cssdb.nsf/softwareL2VW?OpenView&Start=1&Count=30&RestrictToCategory=rational_RationalUnifiedProcess, accessed June 2, 2008.

61 Kettunen, Petri, "Adopting Key Lesson from Agile Manufacturing to Software Product Development," *Technovation*, June 2009, p. 408.

62 Weier, M., "How GM's CIO Looks at IT Restructuring," *Information Week*, June 8, 2009, p. 20.

63 McGregor, Jena, "The Chore Goes Offshore," *BusinessWeek*, March 23, 2009, p. 50.

64 "ENMAX Learns to Operate in a Deregulated World," www.electricityforum.com/news/aug08/Learningtooperatedinaderegulatedmarket.html, accessed October 18, 2010.

65 McGee, M., "Pay for Performance," *Information Week*, March 23, 2009, p. 32.

66 IBM website, www.ibm.com, accessed June 2, 2008.

67 EDS website, www.eds.com, accessed June 2, 2008.

68 Scheck, J., and Worthen, B., "Hewlett-Packard Takes Aim at IBM," *Wall Street Journal*, May 4, 2008, p. B1.

69 Accenture website, www.accenture.com, accessed June 2, 2008.

70 Sheth, N., "Wipro Sets Outsourcing Sights on Emerging Markets," *Wall Street Journal*, May 13, 2009, p. B4B.

71 "Cancellation of Expensive, Inefficient Outsourcing Contract in Alberta Sparks Renewed Demand for Review in BC," www.cope378.ca/cancellation-expensive-inefficient-outsourcing-contract-alberta-sparks-renewed-demands-review-bc, July 24, 2008.

72 "Indian IT Upheaval," *Information Week*, January 19, 2009, p. 22.

73 "Rogers Identifies and Corrects Billing Inaccuracy Affecting up to Five Percent of Customers," www.digitaljournal.com/pr/59329, June 18, 2010.

74 Tiwana, A., "Governance-Knowledge Fit in Systems Development Projects," *Information Systems Research*, June 2009, p. 180.

75 Pereira, Rudy, "Embrace a Culture of Continuous Improvement," *Credit Union Magazine*, October 2009, p. 62.

76 Betts, Mitch, "The No. 1 Cause of IT Failure: Complexity," *Computerworld*, December 21, 2009, p. 4.

77 Capability Maturity Model for Software home page, www.sei.cmu.edu, accessed June 2, 2008.

78 Shang, S., et al., "Understanding the Effectiveness of the Capability Maturity Model," *Total Quality Management & Business Excellence*, Vol. 20, 2009, p. 219.

79 "An Object-Oriented Graphical Modelling for Power System Analysis," *International Journal of Modelling & Simulation*, Vol. 29, 2009, p. 71.

80 Ovide, S., and Vascellaro, J., "UAL Story Blame Is Placed on Computer," *Wall Street Journal*, September 10, 2008, p. B3.

81 Sebora, T., et al., "Critical Success Factors for E-Commerce Entrepreneurship," *Small Business Economics*, March, 2009, p. 303.

CHAPTER
· 13 ·

Systems Development: Design, Implementation, Maintenance, and Review

PRINCIPLES	LEARNING OBJECTIVES

■ **Designing new systems or modifying existing ones should always help an organization achieve its goals.**

- State the purpose of systems design and discuss the differences between logical and physical systems design.

- Describe the process of design modelling and the diagrams used during object-oriented design.

- Discuss the issues involved in environmental design.

- Define the term "RFP" and discuss how this document is used to drive the acquisition of hardware and software.

- Describe the techniques used to make systems selection evaluations.

■ **The primary emphasis of systems implementation is to make sure that the right information is delivered to the right person in the right format at the right time.**

- State the purpose of systems implementation and discuss the activities associated with this phase of systems development.

- List the advantages and disadvantages of purchasing versus developing software.

- Discuss the software development process and list some of the tools used in this process, including object-oriented program development tools.

■ **Maintenance and review add to the useful life of a system but can consume large amounts of resources. These activities can benefit from the same rigorous methods and project management techniques applied to systems development.**

- State the importance of systems and software maintenance and discuss the activities involved.

- Describe the systems review process.

(Source: Chepko Danil Vitalevich/Shutterstock.com.)

NEL

Information Systems in the Global Economy ⟫
Ryder

Ryder Implements Customer Resource Management System

Perhaps you've seen Ryder trucks on the highway and you consider the company just another U.S. trucking company. In reality, those unassuming trucks are a small part of Ryder's large global presence in several far-reaching industries.

Ryder System, Inc. is a *Fortune 500* company that operates in North America, Latin America, Europe, and Asia. It has three divisions: Fleet Management Solutions (FMS), which provides corporations with fleets of trucks and maintenance on them; Dedicated Contract Carriage (DCC), which provides shipping services (the trucks you see on the highways); and Supply Chain Solutions (SCS), which manages the transportation of raw materials to finished products.

Ryder was ranked among InternetWeek's top 100 U.S. companies for "effectiveness in using the Internet to achieve tangible business benefits." However, an organization as large as Ryder takes time to fully migrate into the Internet age. Until recently, Ryder's SCS division was using relatively archaic methods for maintaining information about customers. Its Customer Resource Management (CRM) system was outdated and inefficient. Ryder used a Microsoft Access database and Excel spreadsheets to track sales leads and contracts. One week a month was dedicated to e-mailing spreadsheets to Ryder offices around the world informing them of customer status. Ryder decided it needed a centralized CRM system where all its employees could access customer information in real time. Such a system would help the company in retaining customers, closing deals, and responding to new sales opportunities.

In the systems analysis phase of development, Ryder decided that the new CRM system should be Web-based, so that employees could have easy access through a Web browser. Ryder executives wanted employees in all business areas to have access to the system, including sales, engineering, pricing, legal, and human resources. Each of these areas would benefit from having detailed information about current and prospective customers.

Once the system design was established and approved, the development team moved to implement the system. It didn't take long for the team to decide to outsource the development. Many professional information systems companies have invested millions in building and refining CRM systems over decades. Ryder would take advantage of that expertise rather than developing its own system from scratch.

Ryder conferred with two information system research and advisory firms, Gartner and Forrester, to gain insight into its options. Ryder learned that it could install a CRM system on its own servers, for which it would then be responsible for maintenance, or it could store and run a CRM system on a provider's servers and let the provider bear the burden of maintenance. Based on what it learned from Gartner and Forrester, Ryder evaluated several CRM systems, including those from SalesLogix, Siebel, and Salesforce. Ultimately, Ryder decided on the Salesforce CRM as the system that best met its requirements, could be implemented in the least amount of time, provided flexibility, and would require the least amount of investment in both the short term and long term.

It took just 30 days to install the initial Salesforce CRM. However, the speed with which the system was implemented is in no way indicative of a careless operation. Ryder spent considerable time laying out a roadmap for long-term success. They focused on producing high-quality data that led to the reengineering of business processes. Ryder decided on a phased rollout, getting fundamentals right for high-priority needs and expanding to other business operations over time.

The first task was to combine all of Ryder's customer data and pipeline information from numerous databases into one central Salesforce data warehouse. The development team cleaned the database, eliminating duplicate data and creating relationships between entities. They designed numerous reports to meet many needs. They introduced the system as a pilot to a small sales team. After a month and a few tweaks, the system was expanded to the entire U.S. sales force. Expansion of the system into 11 countries followed shortly thereafter.

With a centralized source for all customer data, Ryder employees have increased productivity. They no longer waste time trying to find information scattered across numerous locations. With access to real-time data, executives are spending less time on administrative tasks and more time on mission-critical business processes.

Salesforce CRM also automates the workflow to provide information related to the sales process to other business units when opportunities appear. For example, engineers are notified of customers' needs that affect their operations, and the pricing department is involved when new contracts are negotiated. Pulling together teams for customer contracts has helped Ryder to accelerate close rates. Salesforce CRM has provided Ryder's sales force with more than $200 million in new proposals over the course of a year and a significant improvement in retention of multimillion-dollar contracts.

Ryder continues to evaluate its Salesforce CRM system, expanding and refining its usefulness across its global organization. Because Salesforce manages the cloud-based system, Ryder is not burdened with maintaining hardware or software and is assured that its valuable data is continuously backed up and safe from disaster.

As you read this chapter, consider the following:

- After a company develops specifications for a new information system, what steps should it take to implement the system successfully?
- What important factors should be considered when implementing, maintaining, and reviewing an information system?

Why Learn About Systems Development?

Information systems are designed and implemented for employees and managers every day. A manager at a hotel chain can use an information system to look up client preferences. An accountant at a manufacturing company can use an information system to analyze the costs of a new plant. A sales representative for a music store can use an information system to determine which CDs to order and which to discount because they are not selling. A computer engineer can use an information system to help determine why a computer system is running slowly. Information systems have been designed and implemented for almost every career and industry. An individual can use systems development and implementation to create applications for smartphones for profit or enjoyment. This chapter shows how you can be involved in designing and implementing an information system that will directly benefit you on the job. It also shows how to avoid errors and how to recover from disasters. This chapter starts with describing how systems are designed.

The way an information system is designed, implemented, and maintained profoundly affects the daily functioning of an organization. Like investigation and analysis covered in Chapter 12, the design, implementation, maintenance, and review covered in this chapter strive to achieve organizational goals, such as reducing costs, increasing profits, or improving customer service. We begin this chapter with a discussion of systems design.

SYSTEMS DESIGN

systems design
The stage of systems development that answers the question "How will the information system solve a problem?"

The purpose of **systems design** is to answer the question "How will the information system solve a problem?" The primary result of the systems design phase is a technical design that details system outputs, inputs, and user interfaces; specifies hardware, software, databases, telecommunications, personnel, and procedures; and shows how these components are related. The new or modified system should take advantage of the latest developments in technology. Many companies, for example, are using cloud computing, where applications are run on the Internet instead of being developed and run within the company or organization.[1] One advantage of using cloud computing is easier management of information systems because everything is in one place on the Internet. General Electric, for example, is developing a "private" cloud that can be accessed and used only by General Electric's employees and managers.[2] According to General Electric's CTO, "You get efficiencies when you start to manage that as a single entity. You can flex that capacity across applications, back it up, monitor it, and manage it as one entity." However, relying on cloud computing has potential disadvantages.[3] One important risk is security. Someone might be able to hack into the Internet and access sensitive and critical data.[4] Another risk is availability. If the Internet site that is providing the cloud computing application is unavailable or having technical problems, critical applications may not be available. Some users have also complained about slow access and execution times for applications that use cloud computing.[5]

Systems design is typically accomplished using the tools and techniques discussed in Chapter 12. Depending on the specific application, these methods can be used to support and document all aspects of systems design. Two key aspects of systems design are logical and physical design.

Logical and Physical Design

As discussed in Chapter 5, design has two dimensions: logical and physical. The **logical design** refers to what the system will do; it describes the functional requirements of a system. Today, for example, many stock exchanges, large hedge funds, and institutional stock investors include speed as a critical logical design element for new computer trading systems.[6] The objective is to increase profits by being faster in placing electronic trades than traditional computerized trading systems. Without logical design, the technical details of the system (such as which hardware devices should be acquired) often obscure the best solution. Logical design involves planning the purpose of each system element, independent of hardware and software considerations. The logical design specifications that are determined and documented include output, input, process, file and database, telecommunications, procedures, controls and security, and personnel and job requirements.

Security is always an important logical design issue for corporations and governments. In one survey, CIOs estimated that their organizations lost more than $4 billion annually in intellectual property theft as a result of inadequate security measures.[7] One Internet security firm estimated that losses due to security breaches were approximately $1 trillion in 2008.

The **physical design** refers to how a computer system accomplishes tasks, including what each component does and how the components work together. Physical design specifies the characteristics of the system components necessary to put the logical design into action. In this phase, the characteristics of the hardware, software, database, telecommunications, personnel, and procedure and control specifications must be detailed. These physical design components were discussed in Part 2 on technology.

Object-Oriented Design

Logical and physical design can be accomplished using either the traditional approach or the object-oriented (OO) approach to systems development. Both approaches use a variety of design models to document the new system's features and the development team's understandings and agreements. Many organizations today are turning to OO development because of its increased flexibility. This section outlines a few OO design considerations and diagrams.

Using the OO approach, you can design key objects and classes of objects in the new or updated system.[8] This process includes considering the problem domain, the operating environment, and the user interface. The problem domain involves the classes of objects related to solving a problem or realizing an opportunity. In our example of the Vancouver, B.C., kayak rental shop, first introduced in Chapter 12, KayakItem in Figure 12.23 is an

logical design
A description of the functional requirements of a system.

physical design
The specification of the characteristics of the system components necessary to put the logical design into action.

example of a problem domain object that will store information on kayaks in the rental program. The operating environment for the rental shop's system includes objects that interact with printers, system software, and other software and hardware devices. The user interface for the system includes objects that users interact with, such as buttons and scroll bars in a Windows program.

During the design phase, you also need to consider the sequence of events that must happen for the system to function correctly. For example, you might want to design the sequence of events for adding a new kayak to the rental program. The event sequence is often called a *scenario*, and it can be diagrammed in a sequence diagram. See Figure 13.1.

Figure 13.1

A Sequence Diagram to Add a
New KayakItem Scenario

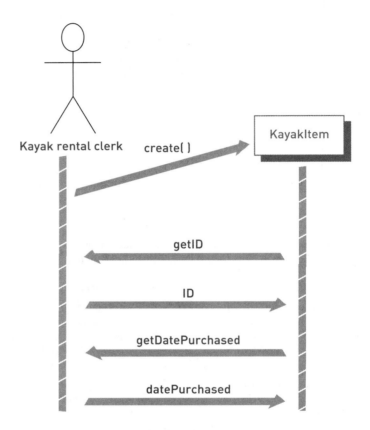

You read a sequence diagram starting at the top and moving down.

1. The Create arrow at the top is a message from the kayak rental clerk to the KayakItem object to create information on a new kayak to be placed into the rental program.
2. The KayakItem object knows that it needs the ID for the kayak and sends a message to the clerk requesting the information. See the getID arrow.
3. The clerk then types the ID into the computer. This is shown with the ID arrow. The data is stored in the KayakItem object.
4. Next, KayakItem requests the purchase date. This is shown in the getDatePurchased arrow.
5. Finally, the clerk types the purchase date into the computer. The data is also transferred to KayakItem object. This is shown in the datePurchased arrow at the bottom of Figure 13.1.

This scenario is only one example of a sequence of events. Other scenarios might include entering information about life jackets, paddles, suntan lotion, and other accessories. The same types of use case and generalization/specialization hierarchy diagrams discussed in Chapter 12 can be created for each event, and additional sequence diagrams will also be needed.

Interface Design and Controls

Designing a good interface for users leads to greater satisfaction with the system and better security. A *sign-on procedure* requiring identification numbers, passwords, and other safeguards is available with most systems to improve security and unauthorized use. With a *menu-driven system* (see Figure 13.2), users simply pick what they want to do from a list of alternatives. Most people can easily operate these types of systems. In addition, many designers incorporate a *help facility* into the system or applications program. When users want to know more about a program or feature or what type of response is expected, they can activate the help facility. Computer programmers can develop *lookup tables* to simplify and shorten data entry. For example, if you are entering a sales order for a company, you can type its abbreviation, such as ABCO. The program searches the customer table, normally stored on a disk, and looks up all the information pertaining to the company abbreviated ABCO that you need to complete the sales order.

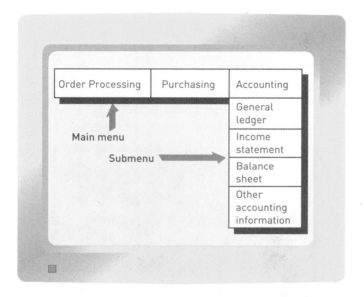

Figure 13.2

Menu-Driven System

A menu-driven system allows you to choose what you want from a list of alternatives.

Design of System Security and Controls

After specifying security features during the logical design phase discussed above, designers must develop specific system security and controls for all aspects of the IS, including hardware, software, database systems, telecommunications, and Internet operations. These key considerations involve error prevention, detection, and correction; disaster planning and recovery; and systems controls.

Preventing, Detecting, and Correcting Errors

The most cost-effective time to deal with potential errors is early in the design phase. Every possibility should be considered, even minor problems. One company, for example, had installed backup electrical generators in case of a power failure. When a fuel truck crashed near its facility and spilled its flammable cargo, the city shut down all power to the area and didn't let the company use its electrical generators, fearing it could cause an explosion or severe fire. This relatively minor incident of a car crash completely shut down the company's IS centre until the spill could be cleaned up. In addition to minor problems, other important security and control measures, including disaster planning and recovery and adequate backup procedures, must be considered.

Disaster Planning and Recovery

Disaster planning is the process of anticipating and providing for disasters. The purpose of disaster planning is to ensure *business continuity*, where the organization's critical applications, data, and information systems are continuously available.[9] Some computer companies have developed systems that claim to have continuous availability.[10] Disasters can range from a minor problem to a major catastrophe. A disaster can be an act of nature (a flood, fire, or earthquake) or a human act (terrorism, human error, labour unrest, or erasure of an important file). Disaster planning often focuses primarily on two issues: maintaining the integrity of corporate information and keeping the information system running until normal operations can be resumed.

Disaster recovery is the implementation of the disaster plan. According to a Harris Interactive survey, over 70 percent of IS managers considered disaster planning recovery as important or critical. Unfortunately, with the recent economic slump, many organizations are cutting their disaster recovery budgets.[11] See Figure 13.3.

disaster recovery
The implementation of the disaster plan.

Figure 13.3

Disaster Recovery Efforts

(Source: CP PHOTO/St. John's Telegram/Joe Gibbons.)

The primary tools used in disaster planning and recovery are hardware, software, and database, telecommunications, and personnel backups. Most of these systems were discussed in Part 2 on information technology concepts. For some companies, personnel backup can be critical. Without IS employees, the IS department can't function. Hot and cold sites can be used to back up hardware. A duplicate, operational hardware system that is ready for use (or immediate access to one through a specialized vendor) is an example of a **hot site**. If the primary computer has problems, the hot site can be used immediately as a backup. However, the hot site cannot be affected by the same disaster. Increasingly, organizations are using virtualization to create a hot site that keeps key applications and databases available on a virtual computer that can take over if a disaster renders the main information system inoperable.[12] Another approach is to use a **cold site**, also called a *shell*, which is a computer environment that includes rooms, electrical service, telecommunications links, data storage devices, and similar equipment. If a primary computer has a problem, backup computer hardware is brought into the cold site, and the complete system is made operational. Files and databases can be protected by making a copy of all files and databases changed during

hot site
A duplicate, operational hardware system or immediate access to one through a specialized vendor.

cold site
A computer environment that includes rooms, electrical service, telecommunications links, data storage devices, and the like; also called a *shell*.

the last few days or the last week, a technique called **incremental backup**. This approach to backup uses an **image log**, which is a separate file that contains only changes to applications. Whenever an application is run, an image log is created that contains all changes made to all files. If a problem occurs with a database, an old database with the last full backup of the data, along with the image log, can be used to re-create the current database. Organizations can also hire outside companies to help them perform disaster planning and recovery. Fusepoint, for example, offers data backup as one of its products (*www.fusepoint.com*). For individuals and some applications, backup copies of important files can be placed on the Internet. *Failover* is another approach to database backup.[13] When a database fails or is no longer functioning, failover automatically switches applications and other programs that use the database to a redundant or replicated database so there is no interruption of service. SteelEye's LifeKeeper (*www.steeleye.com*) and Continuous Protection by NeverFail (*www.neverfailgroup.com*) are examples of failover software. Failover is especially important for applications that must be operational at all times.

incremental backup
A backup copy of all files changed during the last few days or the last week.

image log
A separate file that contains only changes to applications.

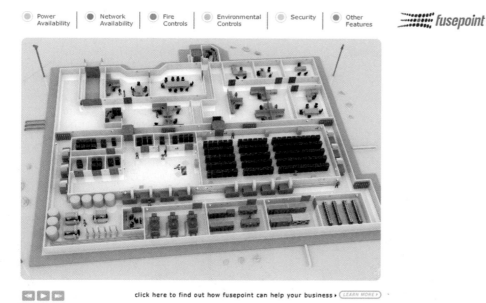

Companies that suffer a disaster can employ a disaster recovery service, which can secure critical data backup information. These service companies can also provide a facility from which to operate and communications equipment to stay in touch with customers.

(Source: Courtesy of Savvis.)

Systems Controls

Most IS departments establish tight **systems controls**, which are rules and procedures, to maintain data security. Security lapses, fraud, and the invasion of privacy can present difficult challenges. In one case, a futures and options trader for a British bank lost about $1 billion. A simple systems control might have prevented a problem that caused the 200-year-old bank to collapse. With the increased use of virtualization and cloud computing, systems controls become even more important.[14] It can be more challenging to provide data security with virtualization, and cloud computing has risks of improper access to sensitive information and denial of service on the Internet. Many companies are also developing systems controls to preserve important information in case a company faces legal action and is required by law to produce corporate e-mails, documents, and other important data, often called *electronic discovery* or *e-discovery*.[15] Many types of systems controls can be developed, documented, implemented, and reviewed. These controls touch all aspects of the organization. See Table 13.1 on the next page.

After controls are developed, they should be documented in standards manuals that indicate how the controls are to be implemented. They should then be implemented and frequently reviewed. It is common practice to measure the extent to which control techniques are used and to take action if the controls have not been implemented.

systems controls
Rules and procedures to maintain data security.

Controls	Description
Table 13.1 Using Systems Controls to Enhance Security	
Input controls	Maintain input integrity and security. Their purpose is to reduce errors while protecting the computer system against improper or fraudulent input. Input controls range from using standardized input forms to eliminating data-entry errors and using tight password and identification controls.
Processing controls	Deal with all aspects of processing and storage. The use of passwords and identification numbers, backup copies of data, and storage rooms that have tight security systems are examples of processing and storage controls.
Output controls	Ensure that output is handled correctly. In many cases, output generated from the computer system is recorded in a file that indicates the reports and documents that were generated, the time they were generated, and their final destinations.
Database controls	Deal with ensuring an efficient and effective database system. These controls include the use of identification numbers and passwords, without which a user is denied access to certain data and information. Many of these controls are provided by database management systems.
Telecommunications controls	Provide accurate and reliable data and information transfer among systems. Telecommunications controls include firewalls and encryption to ensure correct communication while eliminating the potential for fraud and crime.
Personnel controls	Make sure that only authorized personnel have access to certain systems to help prevent computer-related mistakes and crime. Personnel controls can involve the use of identification numbers and passwords that allow only certain people access to particular data and information. ID badges and other security devices (such as smart cards) can prevent unauthorized people from entering strategic areas in the information systems facility.

Many companies use biometric devices to prevent unauthorized access to sensitive areas in the information systems facility.

(Sources: © Mario Arruda/iStockphoto.com (left) and Michal Mrozek/Shutterstock.com (right).)

 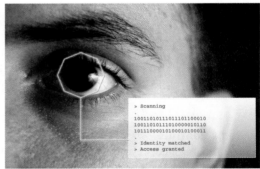

Environmental Design Considerations

environmental design
Also called *green design*, it involves systems development efforts that slash power consumption, require less physical space, and result in systems that can be disposed of in a way that does not negatively affect the environment.

Developing new systems and modifying existing ones in an environmentally sensitive way is becoming important for many IS departments. **Environmental design**, also called *green design*, involves systems development efforts that slash power consumption, require less physical space, and result in systems that can be disposed of in a way that doesn't negatively affect the environment.[16] One survey revealed that over 40 percent of CEOs said that their information system would play a very important role in reducing the organization's environmental impact. According to one IS analyst, "The green issue is not going to go away. There's too much at stake."[17]

Today, companies are using innovative ways to design efficient systems and operations, including using virtual servers to save energy and space, pushing cold air under data centres to cool equipment, using software to efficiently control cooling fans, building facilities with more insulation, and even collecting rainwater from roofs to cool equipment.[18] Nissan, for example, used virtual server technology to reduce its number of servers from about 160 to about 30, saving energy and money.[19] Reducing the number of servers has slashed electricity costs by more than 30 percent for the automotive company.[20] The GreenStar Network project could make Canada the largest Internet service provider with almost no carbon footprint. The project will use cloud computing and a virtual infrastructure of linked data centres across Canada. The data centres will run on renewable green energy.[21] Outsourcing companies are also involved with environmental design. According to the chief information officer of Wipro, a large consulting and outsourcing company, "Our main priority is to deliver infrastructure services to drive energy savings. This includes building management systems, LEED (Leadership in Energy and Environmental Design) certifications, consolidation of data centres, and virtualization."[22] The Canadian LEED rating system was adapted from the U.S. Green Building Council and includes a number of standards for the construction and operation of buildings.

Many companies are developing products and services to help save energy. PC companies, such as Hewlett-Packard and others, are designing computers that use less power and are made from recycled materials.[23] Some PCs consume energy even when they are turned off. Cell phone manufacturers are also starting to manufacture phones that consume less electricity.[24] EMC has developed new disk drives that use substantially less energy. Voltaic Generator (*www.voltaicsystems.com/bag*) has developed a solar PC case that charges batteries from sunlight and other light sources.[25] The solar-powered bag can power computers, cell phones, and other electronic devices. Environmental design also involves developing software and systems that help organizations reduce power consumption for other aspects of their operations. Carbonetworks and Optimum Energy, for example, have developed software products that reduce energy costs by helping companies determine when and how to use electricity. UPS developed its own software to reduce the distances its trucks and other vehicles drive by routing them more efficiently. The new software helped UPS cut million of kilometres per year, slash fuel costs, and reduce carbon emissions.

Hewlett-Packard, Dell Computer, and others have developed procedures and machines to dispose of old computers and computer equipment in environmentally friendly ways.[26] VenJuvo (*www.venjuvo.com*) and other companies recycle old electronics equipment, offering cash in some cases, depending on the age and type of equipment.[27] Old computers and computer equipment are fed into machines that shred them into small pieces and sort them into materials that can be reused. The process is often called *green death*. The Canadian federal government also rates products with the *Energy Star* designation to help people select products that save energy. Today, utility companies are providing their corporate and individual customers with "smart meters" and specialized software that can help them reduce their power consumption and electric bills.[28]

Generating Systems Design Alternatives

Generating systems design alternatives often involves getting the involvement of single vendor or several vendors.[29] If the new system is complex, the original development team might want to involve other personnel in generating alternative designs. In addition, if new hardware and software are to be acquired from an outside vendor, a formal request for proposal (RFP) can be made.

Request for Proposals

The **request for proposal** (**RFP**) is a document that specifies in detail required resources such as hardware and software. The RFP is an important document for many organizations involved with large, complex systems development efforts. Smaller, less-complex systems often do not require an RFP. A company that is purchasing an inexpensive piece of software that will run on existing hardware, for example, might not need to go through a formal RFP process.

request for proposal (RFP)
A document that specifies in detail required resources such as hardware and software.

Companies such as Hewlett-Packard and Dell Computer dispose of old computers and computer equipment in environmentally friendly ways.

(Source: © 2011 Dell Inc. All Rights Reserved.)

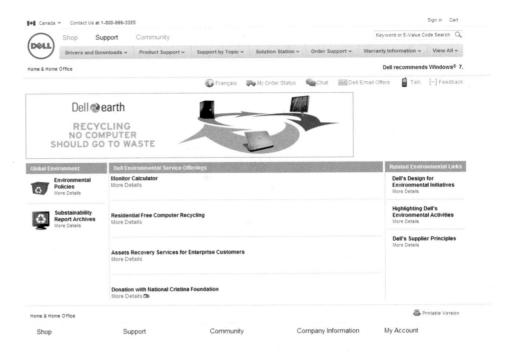

In some cases, separate RFPs are developed for different needs. For example, a company might develop separate RFPs for hardware, software, and database systems. The RFP communicates these needs to vendors, and it provides a way to evaluate whether the chosen vendor has delivered what was expected. In some cases, the RFP is part of the vendor contract. The table of contents for a typical RFP is shown in Figure 13.4.

Figure 13.4

A Typical Table of Contents for a Request for Proposal

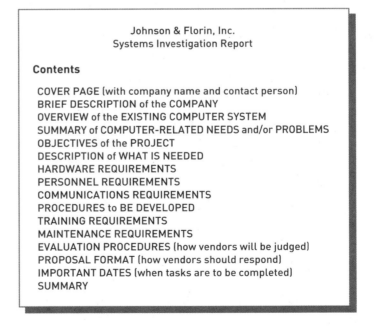

Johnson & Florin, Inc.
Systems Investigation Report

Contents

COVER PAGE (with company name and contact person)
BRIEF DESCRIPTION of the COMPANY
OVERVIEW of the EXISTING COMPUTER SYSTEM
SUMMARY of COMPUTER-RELATED NEEDS and/or PROBLEMS
OBJECTIVES of the PROJECT
DESCRIPTION of WHAT IS NEEDED
HARDWARE REQUIREMENTS
PERSONNEL REQUIREMENTS
COMMUNICATIONS REQUIREMENTS
PROCEDURES to BE DEVELOPED
TRAINING REQUIREMENTS
MAINTENANCE REQUIREMENTS
EVALUATION PROCEDURES (how vendors will be judged)
PROPOSAL FORMAT (how vendors should respond)
IMPORTANT DATES (when tasks are to be completed)
SUMMARY

Financial Options

When acquiring computer systems, several choices are available, including purchase, lease, or rent. Cost objectives and constraints set for the system play a significant role in the choice, as do the advantages and disadvantages of each. In addition, traditional financial tools, including net present value and internal rate of return, can be used. Table 13.2 summarizes the advantages and disadvantages of these financial options.

Renting (Short-Term Option)	
Advantages	**Disadvantages**
No risk of obsolescence	No ownership of equipment
No long-term financial investment	High monthly costs
No initial investment of funds	Restrictive rental agreements
Maintenance usually included	
Leasing (Intermediate to Long-Term Option)	
Advantages	**Disadvantages**
No risk of obsolescence	High cost of cancelling lease
No long-term financial investment	Longer time commitment than renting
No initial investment of funds	No ownership of equipment
Less expensive than renting	
Purchasing (Long-Term Option)	
Advantages	**Disadvantages**
Total control over equipment	High initial investment
Can sell equipment at any time	Additional cost of maintenance
Can depreciate equipment	Possibility of obsolescence
Low cost if owned for a number of years	Other expenses, including taxes and insurance

Table 13.2

Advantages and Disadvantages of Acquisition Options

Determining which option is best for a particular company in a given situation can be difficult. Financial considerations, tax laws, the organization's policies, its sales and transaction growth, marketplace dynamics, and the organization's financial resources are all important factors. In some cases, lease or rental fees can amount to more than the original purchase price after a few years.

Evaluating and Selecting a Systems Design

Evaluating and selecting the best design involves achieving a balance of system objectives that will best support organizational goals. Normally, evaluation and selection involves both a preliminary and a final evaluation before a design is selected.

A **preliminary evaluation** begins after all proposals have been submitted. The purpose of this evaluation is to dismiss unwanted proposals. Several vendors can usually be eliminated by investigating their proposals and comparing them with the original criteria. The **final evaluation** begins with a detailed investigation of the proposals offered by the remaining vendors. The vendors should be asked to make a final presentation and to fully demonstrate the system. The demonstration should be as close to actual operating conditions as possible. Figure 13.5 (on the next page) illustrates the evaluation process.

preliminary evaluation
An initial assessment whose purpose is to dismiss the unwanted proposals; begins after all proposals have been submitted.

final evaluation
A detailed investigation of the proposals offered by the vendors remaining after the preliminary evaluation.

Evaluation Techniques

The exact procedure used to make the final evaluation and selection varies from one organization to the next. Some were first introduced in Chapter 1, including return on investment (ROI), earnings growth, market share, customer satisfaction, and total cost of ownership (TCO). In addition, four other approaches are commonly used: group consensus, cost/benefit analysis, benchmark tests, and point evaluation.

Group Consensus

In **group consensus**, a decision-making group is appointed and given the responsibility of making the final evaluation and selection. Usually, this group includes the members of the development team who participated in either systems analysis or systems design. This approach might be used to evaluate which of several screen layouts or report formats is best.

group consensus
Decision making by a group that is appointed and given the responsibility of making the final evaluation and selection.

Figure 13.5

The Stages in Preliminary and Final Evaluations

The number of possible alternatives decreases as the firm gets closer to making a final decision.

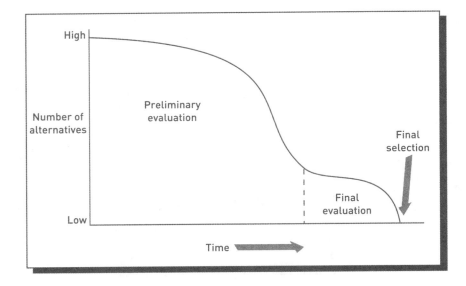

cost/benefit analysis
An approach that lists the costs and benefits of each proposed system. After they are expressed in monetary terms, all the costs are compared with all the benefits.

Cost/Benefit Analysis

Cost/benefit analysis is an approach that lists the costs and benefits of each proposed system. After they are expressed in monetary terms, all the costs are compared with all the benefits. Table 13.3 lists some of the typical costs and benefits associated with the evaluation and selection procedure. This approach is used to evaluate options whose costs can be quantified, such as which hardware or software vendor to select.

Table 13.3

Cost/Benefit Analysis Table

Costs	Benefits
Development costs	Reduced costs
Personnel	Fewer personnel
Computer resources	Reduced manufacturing costs Reduced inventory costs More efficient use of equipment Faster response time Reduced downtime or crash time Less spoilage
Fixed Costs	**Increased Revenues**
Computer equipment	New products and services
Software	New customers
One-time licence fees for software and maintenance	More business from existing customers Higher price as a result of better products and services
Operating Costs	**Intangible Benefits**
Equipment lease and/or rental fees	Better public image for the organization
Computer personnel (including salaries, benefits, etc.)	Higher employee morale Better service for new and existing customers
Electric and other utilities	The ability to recruit better employees
Computer paper, tape, and disks	Position as a leader in the industry
Other computer supplies	System easier for programmers and users
Maintenance costs	Insurance

Benchmark Tests

A **benchmark test** is an examination that compares computer systems operating under the same conditions.[30] Most computer companies publish their own benchmark tests, but some forbid disclosure of benchmark tests without prior written approval. Thus, one of the best approaches is for an organization to develop its own tests and then use them to compare the equipment it is considering. This approach might be used to compare the end-user system response time on two similar systems. Several independent companies and journals also rate computer systems.

Point Evaluation

One of the disadvantages of cost/benefit analysis is the difficulty of determining the monetary values for all the benefits. An approach that does not use monetary values is a **point evaluation system**. Each evaluation factor is assigned a weight, in percentage points, based on importance. Then each proposed information system is evaluated in terms of this factor and given a score, such as one ranging from 0 to 100, where 0 means that the alternative does not address the feature at all and 100 means that the alternative addresses that feature perfectly. The scores are totalled, and the system with the greatest total score is selected. When using point evaluation, an organization can list and evaluate hundreds of factors. Figure 13.6 shows a simplified version of this process. This approach is used when there are many options to be evaluated, such as which software best matches the needs of a particular business.

	Factor's importance	System A		System B	
		Evaluation	Weighted evaluation	Evaluation	Weighted evaluation
Hardware	35%	95 35%	33.25	75 35%	26.25
Software	40%	70 40%	28.00	95 40%	38.00
Vendor support	25%	85 25%	21.25	90 25%	22.50
Totals	100%		82.5		86.75

Freezing Design Specifications

Near the end of the design stage, some organizations prohibit further changes in the design of the system. Freezing systems design specifications means that the user agrees in writing that the design is acceptable. See Figure 13.7. Other organizations, however, allow or even encourage design changes. These organizations often use agile or rapid systems development approaches, introduced in Chapter 12.

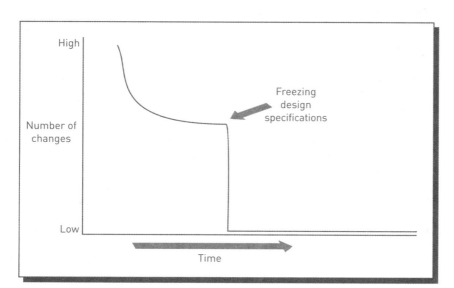

benchmark test
An examination that compares computer systems operating under the same conditions.

point evaluation system
An evaluation process in which each evaluation factor is assigned a weight, in percentage points, based on importance. Then each proposed system is evaluated in terms of each factor and given a score ranging from 0 to 100. The scores are totalled, and the system with the greatest total score is selected.

Figure 13.6

An Illustration of the Point Evaluation System

In this example, software has been given the most weight (40 percent), compared with hardware (35 percent) and vendor support (25 percent). When system A is evaluated, the total of the three factors amounts to 82.5 percent. System B's rating, on the other hand, totals 86.75 percent, which is closer to 100 percent. Therefore, the firm chooses system B.

Figure 13.7

Freezing Design Specifications

The Contract

One of the most important steps in systems design is to develop a good contract if new computer facilities are being acquired. A good contract should have provisions for monitoring systems development progress, ownership and property rights of the new or modified system, contingency provisions in case something doesn't work as expected, and dispute resolution if something goes wrong.[31] Finding the best terms where everyone makes a profit can be difficult. Most computer vendors provide standard contracts; however, such contracts are designed to protect the vendor, not necessarily the organization buying the computer equipment. Some organizations include penalty clauses in the contract, in case the vendor does not meet its obligation by the specified date. Typically, the request for proposal becomes part of the contract. This saves a considerable amount of time in developing the contract, because the RFP specifies in detail what is expected from the vendors.

Figure 13.8

A Typical Table of Contents for a Systems Design Report

design report
The primary result of systems design, reflecting the decisions made and preparing the way for systems implementation.

The Design Report

System specifications are the final results of systems design. They include a technical description that details system outputs, inputs, and user interfaces as well as all hardware, software, databases, telecommunications, personnel, and procedure components and the way these components are related. The specifications are contained in a **design report**, which is the primary result of systems design. The design report reflects the decisions made for systems design and prepares the way for systems implementation. The contents of the design report are summarized in Figure 13.8.

SYSTEMS IMPLEMENTATION

systems implementation
A stage of systems development that includes hardware acquisition, software acquisition or development, user preparation, hiring and training of personnel, site and data preparation, installation, testing, start-up, and user acceptance.

After the information system has been designed, a number of tasks must be completed before the system is installed and ready to operate. This process, called **systems implementation**, includes hardware acquisition, programming and software acquisition or development, user preparation, hiring and training of personnel, site and data preparation, installation, testing, start-up, and user acceptance. The typical sequence of systems implementation activities is shown in Figure 13.9.

Virtualization, first introduced in Chapter 3, has had a profound impact on many aspects of systems implementation.[32] Virtualization can result in a consistent systems development environment, higher programmer productivity, and meeting critical deadlines.[33] As discussed earlier, virtualization can be environmentally friendly, reducing power consumption and requiring less space for equipment. Virtualization, however, introduces important implementation considerations, including security and backup procedures. Virtualization is being used to acquire hardware, software, databases, and other capabilities. IBM has developed the VMControl tool to help companies implement virtual servers from various vendors.[34] We start our discussion of systems implementation with hardware acquisition.

Acquiring Hardware from an IS Vendor

To obtain the components for an information system, organizations can purchase, lease, or rent computer hardware and other resources from an IS vendor. An *IS vendor* is a company that offers hardware, software, telecommunications systems, databases, IS personnel, or other computer-related resources. Types of IS vendors include general computer manufacturers (such as IBM and Hewlett-Packard), small computer manufacturers (such as Dell and Sony), peripheral equipment manufacturers (such as Epson and SanDisk), computer dealers and distributors (such as Future Shop and Best Buy), and chip makers (such as Intel and AMD). Some of the most successful vendors are IBM (hardware and other services), Oracle (databases), Apple (personal computers), Microsoft (software), Accenture (IS consulting), and many others.[35] In addition, many new hardware vendors provide specialized equipment and services.[36] Venture capital firms have invested hundreds of millions of dollars in new hardware vendors. Hardware vendors can provide very small or very large systems. Many companies have several hardware vendors, but managing them can be difficult.[37] Different vendors must compete against each other to get an outsourcing contract with the organization. Then the selected vendors must work together to develop an effective information system at a good price. Open communications among the outsourcing vendors is critical. Each vendor's work and pricing should be transparent and available to all the other outsourcing vendors. Over time, it is best to have a set of trusted, reliable outsourcing vendors that can be used in future systems development projects.

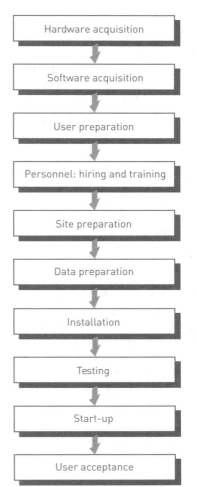

Figure 13.9

Typical Steps in Systems Implementation

Computer dealers, such as Best Buy, manufacture build-to-order computer systems and sell computers and supplies from other vendors.

(Source: Daniel Acker/Bloomberg via Getty Images.)

In addition to buying, leasing, or renting computer hardware, companies can pay only for the computing services that they use. Called "pay-as-you-go," "on-demand," or "utility" computing, this approach requires an organization to pay only for the computer power it uses, as it would pay for a utility such as electricity. Hewlett-Packard offers its clients a "capacity-on-demand" approach, in which organizations pay according to the computer resources actually used, including processors, storage devices, and network facilities.

Companies can also purchase used computer equipment. This option is especially attractive to firms that are experiencing an economic slowdown. Companies often use traditional Internet auctions to locate used or refurbished equipment. Popular Internet auction sites sometimes sell more than $1 billion of computer-related equipment annually, and companies can purchase equipment for about 20 or 30 cents on the dollar. However, buyers need to beware: prices are not always low, and equipment selection can be limited on Internet auction sites. Also, used equipment rarely comes with warranties or support.

Acquiring Software: Make or Buy?

make-or-buy decision
The decision regarding whether to obtain the necessary software from internal or external sources.

As with hardware, application software can be acquired in several ways. As previously mentioned, it can be purchased from external developers or developed in-house. This decision is often called the **make-or-buy decision**. A comparison of the two approaches is shown in Table 13.4. Today, most software is purchased. Individuals and organizations can purchase software from a number of online application stores or retail stores located around the country. General Electric had an important make-or-buy decision for an Internet application that would provide critical data for its employees and managers.[38] The company tries to buy the necessary software when possible. According to the company's chief technology officer, "We're trying to avoid building GE code, because we don't have the energy to figure out how to do this right all by ourselves." As mentioned in Chapter 4, companies can also purchase open-source software from Red Hat and many other open-source software companies, including programs that use the Internet and cloud computing approaches.[39] Research has shown that many programmers and systems developers freely join groups to develop and refine open-source software.[40]

Table 13.4

Comparison of Off-the-Shelf and Developed Software

Factor	Developed (Make)	Off-the-Shelf (Buy)
Cost	High cost	Low cost
Needs	Custom software more likely to satisfy your needs	Might not get what you need
Quality	Quality can vary depending on the programming team	Can assess the quality before buying
Speed	Can take years to develop	Can acquire it now
Competitive advantage	Can develop a competitive advantage with good software	Other organizations can have the same software and same advantage

Externally Acquired Software and Software as a Service (SaaS)

A company planning to purchase or lease software from an outside company has many options. Commercial off-the-shelf development is often used. The *commercial off-the-shelf (COTS)* development process involves the use of commonly available products from software vendors. It combines software from various vendors into a finished system. In many cases, it is necessary to write some original software from scratch and combine it with purchased or leased software. For example, a company can purchase or lease software from several software vendors and combine it into a single software program.

Organizations are also acquiring more virtualization software from software vendors, including operating systems and application software. Windows Server, for example, provides virtualization tools that allow multiple operating systems to run on a single server. Quebecor used VMware on its servers to reduce the number of servers by 90 percent and power needs by 60 percent.[41] Virtualization software such as VMware is also being used by businesses to safeguard private data.

Medical Centre Moves Patient Records to Cloud

Beth Israel Deaconess Medical Center (BID) is a large teaching hospital associated with Harvard Medical School that serves Boston and surrounding communities. BID is one of the top four recipients of biomedical research funding from the National Institutes for Health, winning nearly $200 million annually.

Moving to an electronic health record system (EHRS) has been a priority for BID for years. In 2008, long before the U.S. federal government offered stimulus funds for EHRS, BID rolled out its own EHRS. BID was motivated to move to an EHRS by requirements imposed by insurance companies. So-called pay-for-performance insurance plans require highly detailed and real-time documentation that is possible only through EHRS.

BID knew its 300 physicians would approve an EHRS, but earning the approval of the 900 other physicians associated with BID, but not owned by BID, was a bigger challenge. Many of those 900 physicians own small practices with limited resources. Along with their staff, they work 10-hour days, processing 40 patients a day, and have little time to invest in learning new technology. BID decided to invest in an EHRS for its own physicians, gambling that its associated physicians would eventually witness the value of an EHRS and buy in.

BID evaluated many EHRSs, weighing their benefits against their drawbacks. The systems analysts designing the EHRS were at a disadvantage because they didn't know exactly how many physicians and medical records the system would need to accommodate. They needed a system that could be scaled to match the amount of data. For this reason, they decided on a SaaS cloud computing system.

The solution came from a company named eClinicalWorks, which licenses its software to BID and provides the hosted service. The hosted service runs on virtual servers that make it easy to add more storage and processing resources as they are needed, without any interruption to service. For example, BID recently updated its security to a stronger form of encryption. The upgrade placed too much strain on the servers, so BID spent $20,000 to add more virtual resources to the service provider's hosted servers. The same scenario without virtualization would have cost BID $325,000 for additional hardware. This is a convincing argument in support of both virtualization and SaaS cloud computing services.

The medical industry in the United States has unique information security requirements placed on it by local and federal governments designed to provide patient privacy. Because of this, the move to EHRSs has been slow. The system designed by eClinicalWorks uses a thin client device that connects to PCs to encrypt medical data as it leaves the PC and decrypt data as it arrives. Other than that, the system requires no complicated software or setup, and it runs in a standard Web browser. The system also has an offline mode, so that records can be accessed even when clients are not connected to the network. Each time computers connect to eClinicalWorks, the records are synchronized with records on the server.

Because eClinicalWorks is easy to set up and use, BID associates are more likely to join the system. There are many other incentives as well. Besides the obvious convenience of access to medical records anywhere anytime, the EHRS also provides record-keeping automation. Medical practices often hire several employees just to process the paperwork required by Medicaid and private insurers. The EHRS automates those processes, dramatically reducing the need for staff. BID has made the EHRS a requirement for associates who want to take advantage of the medical centre's administrative, clinical, and technical support.

BID associates have been quick to see the benefits of the eClinicalWorks EHRS and are migrating to the new system. No longer do BID patients have to fill out forms in triplicate every time they visit a new physician or specialist. No longer do BID physicians have to dig through file cabinets for patient records—they have access to them anywhere, anytime on their tablet computers. No longer does staff have to work full time filling out insurance claims. The eClinicalWorks EHRS provides all these services, and because it is hosted in the cloud, maintenance is not a concern for BID information systems staff.

Discussion Questions

1. What motivated BID to invest in an EHRS?
2. Why did BID decide on the eClinicalWorks SaaS as its EHRS system?

Critical Thinking Questions

1. What special considerations does the medical industry face when implementing information systems?
2. What benefits are provided to medical centres, physicians, and patients by an EHRS?

SOURCES: Fogarty, Kevin, "Cloud Servers Help Hospital with Digital Record," Computerworld, www.computerworld.com/s/article/9160918/Cloud_servers_help_hospital_with_digital_records?taxonomyId=154&pageNumber=1, February 23, 2010; Beth Israel Deaconess Medical Center website, www.bidmc.org, accessed March 5, 2010; eClinicalWorks website, www.eclinicalworks.com/products.php, accessed March 5, 2010.

As mentioned in Chapter 4, *Software as a Service* (*SaaS*) allows businesses to subscribe to Web-delivered application software by paying a monthly service charge or a per-use fee.[42] Instead of acquiring software externally from a traditional software vendor, SaaS allows individuals and organizations to access needed software applications over the Internet. Companies such as Google are using the cloud computing approach to deliver word processing, spreadsheet programs, and other software over the Internet.

In-House Developed Software

Another option is to make or develop software internally. UPS, for example, used IS personnel including systems analysts and the people who will be using the application to develop in-house software.[43] Getting users involved with in-house software development can be critical to a successful systems development project. The vice president of IS at UPS commented about user input, "They know they'll have to go back to their teams and consume it." Programmer productivity is also important for in-house developed software.[44] According to one software expert, "A programmer coding at full throttle is keeping zillions of things in their head at once."

Some advantages inherent with in-house–developed software include meeting user and organizational requirements and having more features and increased flexibility in customization and changes. Software programs developed within a company also have greater potential for providing a competitive advantage because competitors cannot easily duplicate them in the short term. Companies can also reuse software they developed for another application.[45] IBM, for example, modified software that catches card counters and cheats at gambling casinos so that the same software could be used to identify illegal immigrants. IBM expects to generate about $1 billion in revenues from immigration agencies around the world by modifying its software in this way. If software is to be developed internally, a number of tools and techniques can be used. A few of the tools and techniques used to develop in-house software are briefly discussed below.

- **CASE and object-oriented approaches.** As mentioned in Chapter 12, CASE tools and the object-oriented approach are often used during software development.
- **Cross-platform development.** One software development technique, called **cross-platform development**, allows programmers to develop programs that can run on computer systems that have different hardware and operating systems, or platforms. Web service tools, such as .NET by Microsoft, introduced in Chapter 7, are examples. With cross-platform development, the same program can run on both a personal computer and a mainframe or on two different types of PCs.
- **Integrated development environment.** The combination of the tools needed for programming with a programming language in one integrated package is called an **integrated development environment** (IDE). An IDE allows programmers to use simple screens, customized pull-down menus, and graphical user interfaces. Visual Studio from Microsoft is an example of an IDE. Oracle Designer, which is used with Oracle's database system, is another example of an IDE. Eclipse Workbench (*www.eclipse-workbench.com*) supports IDEs that can be used with the Java, C, and C++ programming languages. Eclipse Workbench includes a debugger and a compiler, along with other tools.
- **Documentation.** With internally developed software, documentation is always important. **Technical documentation** is written details used by computer operators to execute the program and by analysts and programmers to solve problems or modify the program. In technical documentation, the purpose of every major piece of computer code is written out and explained. Key variables are also described. **User documentation** is developed for the people who use the program. This type of documentation shows how the program can and should be used, in easy-to-understand language. Incorporating a description of the benefits of the new application into user documentation can help stakeholders understand the reasons for the program and can speed user acceptance.

cross-platform development
A software development technique that allows programmers to develop programs that can run on computer systems having different hardware and operating systems, or platforms.

integrated development environments (IDEs)
A development approach that combines the tools needed for programming with a programming language into one integrated package.

technical documentation
Written details used by computer operators to execute the program and by analysts and programmers to solve problems or modify the program.

user documentation
Written descriptions developed for people who use a program, shows how the program can and should be used, in easy-to-understand language.

Acquiring Database and Telecommunications Systems

Because databases are a blend of hardware and software, many of the approaches discussed earlier for acquiring hardware and software also apply to database systems, including open-source databases. *Virtual databases* and *database as a service* (*DaaS*) are popular ways to acquire database capabilities.[46] The University of British Columbia, the City of Edmonton, and Wendy's restaurants, for example, use the DaaS approach to manage many of their database operations from the Internet.[47] Walmart gives its customers more information on how its databases are acquired and used.[48] According to Walmart's chief privacy officer, "We want to provide customers with more control over their own data, which is a big topic today for relationships with customers and their privacy."

With the increased use of e-commerce, the Internet, intranets, and extranets, telecommunications is one of the fastest-growing applications for today's organizations. Like database systems, telecommunications systems require a blend of hardware and software. For personal computer systems, the primary piece of hardware is a modem. For client/server and mainframe systems, the hardware can include multiplexers, concentrators, communications processors, and a variety of network equipment. Communications software will also have to be acquired from a software company or developed in-house. Again, the earlier discussion on acquiring hardware and software also applies to the acquisition of telecommunications hardware and software. As discussed in Chapter 12 and previous chapters, individuals and organizations are using the Internet and cloud computing more than ever to implement many new systems development efforts.[49] Systems analysts and programmers are also starting to use the Internet to develop applications.[50] CBC Hockey's iPhone app was one of the top downloaded applications from Apple's application store.[51]

User Preparation

User preparation is the process of readying managers, decision makers, employees, other users, and stakeholders for the new systems. This activity is an important but often ignored area of systems implementation. When a new operating system or application software package is implemented, user training is essential. In some cases, companies decide not to install the latest software because the amount of time and money needed to train employees is too much. Because user training is so important, some companies provide training for their clients, including in-house, software, video, Internet, and other training approaches.

user preparation
The process of readying managers, decision makers, employees, other users, and stakeholders for new systems.

Providing users with proper training can help ensure that the information system is used correctly, efficiently, and effectively.

(Source: Konstantin Chagin/ Shutterstock.com)

IS Personnel: Hiring and Training

Depending on the size of the new system, an organization might have to hire, and in some cases train, new IS personnel. An IS manager, systems analysts, computer programmers, data-entry operators, and similar personnel might be needed for the new or modified system.

The eventual success of any system depends on how it is used not only by the end users, but also by the IS personnel within the organization. Training programs should be conducted for the IS personnel who will be using the computer system. These programs are similar to those for the users, although they can be more detailed in the technical aspects of the systems. Effective training will help IS personnel use the new system to perform their jobs and support other users in the organization. IBM and many other companies are using online and simulated training programs to cut training costs and improve effectiveness.[52]

Site Preparation

site preparation
Preparation of the location of a new system.

The location of the new system needs to be prepared, a process called **site preparation**. For a small system, site preparation can be as simple as rearranging the furniture in an office to make room for a computer. With a larger system, this process is not so easy because it can require special wiring and air conditioning. A special floor, for example, might have to be built, under which the cables connecting the various computer components are placed, and a new security system might be needed to protect the equipment. Today, developing IS sites that are energy efficient is important for most systems development implementations. Security is also important for site preparation.[53] One company, for example, installed special security kiosks that let visitors log on and request a meeting with a company employee. The employee can see the visitor on his or her computer screen and accept or reject the visitor. If the visitor is accepted, the kiosk prints a visitor pass.

Data Preparation

data preparation, or data conversion
Making sure all files and databases are ready to be used with new computer software and systems.

Data preparation, or **data conversion**, involves making sure that all files and databases are ready to be used with new computer software and systems. If an organization is installing a new payroll program, the old employee-payroll data might have to be converted into a format that can be used by the new computer software or system. After the data has been prepared or converted, the computerized database system or other software will then be used to maintain and update the computer files.

Installation

installation
The process of physically placing the computer equipment on the site and making it operational.

Installation is the process of physically placing the computer equipment on the site and making it operational. Although normally the manufacturer is responsible for installing computer equipment, someone from the organization (usually the IS manager) should oversee the process, making sure that all equipment specified in the contract is installed at the proper location. After the system is installed, the manufacturer performs several tests to ensure that the equipment is operating as it should.

Testing

unit testing
Testing of individual programs.

system testing
Testing the entire system of programs.

volume testing
Testing the application with a large amount of data.

integration testing
Testing all related systems together.

acceptance testing
Conducting any tests required by the user.

Good testing procedures are essential to make sure that the new or modified information system operates as intended.[54] Inadequate testing can result in mistakes and problems. Problems with a project to consolidate data centre servers, for example, resulted in more than 160,000 Internet sites being shut down. The company that was trying to consolidate its database servers was hosting the Internet sites. Some Internet sites were down for more than six days. Better testing may have prevented these types of problems.

Several forms of testing should be used, including testing each program (**unit testing**), testing the entire system of programs (**system testing**), testing the application with a large amount of data (**volume testing**), and testing all related systems together (**integration testing**), as well as conducting any tests required by the user (**acceptance testing**). Figure 13.10

lists the types of testing. In addition to these forms of testing, there are different types of testing, including alpha and beta testing, discussed next.

Alpha testing involves testing an incomplete or early version of the system; **beta testing** involves testing a complete and stable system by end users. Alpha-unit testing, for example, is testing an individual program before it is completely finished. Beta-unit testing, on the other hand, is performed after alpha testing, when the individual program is complete and ready for use by end users. After seven months of beta testing, HMV launched its own online music store. The president of HMV Canada believes that due to the "extensive testing and consumer feedback we've received to date, we are confident that hmvdigital.ca is a digital offering that will impress consumers."[55] Vodafone used an innovative way to beta-test its systems development efforts to deliver mobile applications.[56] It created a website called *www.betavine.com* that anyone, from customers to software professionals, can use to test mobile applications for Vodafone's networks and other wireless networks.

Unit testing is accomplished by developing test data that will force the computer to execute every statement in the program. In addition, each program is tested with abnormal data to determine how it will handle problems.

System testing requires the testing of all the programs together. It is not uncommon for the output from one program to become the input for another. So system testing ensures that program output can be used as input for another program within the system. Volume testing ensures that the entire system can handle a large amount of data under normal operating conditions. Integration testing ensures that the new programs can interact with other major applications. It also ensures that data flows efficiently and without error to other applications. For example, a new inventory control application might require data input from an older order processing application. Integration testing would be done to ensure smooth data flow between the new and existing applications.

Finally, acceptance testing makes sure that the new or modified system is operating as intended. Run times, the amount of memory required, disk access methods, and more can be tested during this phase. Acceptance testing ensures that all performance objectives defined for the system are satisfied. Involving users in acceptance testing can help them understand and effectively interact with the new system. Acceptance testing is the final check of the system before start-up. In addition to the forms of testing described above, some companies are using *security testing* for critical software.[57] Security testing makes sure that sensitive data remains protected from hackers and corporate spies.

Start-Up

Start-up, also called *cutover*, begins with the final tested information system. When start-up is finished, the system is fully operational. Start-up can be critical to the success of the organization. If not done properly, the results can be disastrous. In one case, a small manufacturing company that decided to stop an accounting service used to send out bills on the same day they were going to start their own program to send out bills to customers. The manufacturing company wanted to save money by using their own billing program developed by an employee. The new program didn't work, the accounting service wouldn't help because they were upset about being terminated, and the manufacturing company wasn't able to send out any bills to customers for more than three months. The manufacturing company almost went bankrupt.

Various start-up approaches are available; see Figure 13.11 on the next page. **Direct conversion** (also called *plunge* or *direct cutover*) involves stopping the old system and starting the new system on a given date. Direct conversion is usually the least desirable approach because of the potential for problems and errors when the old system is shut off and the new system is turned on at the same instant.

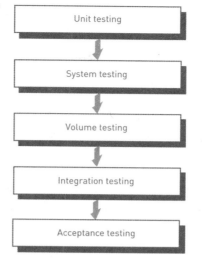

Figure 13.10

Types of Testing

alpha testing
Testing an incomplete or early version of the system.

beta testing
Testing a complete and stable system.

start-up
The process of making the final tested information system fully operational.

direct conversion (also called *plunge* or *direct cutover*)
Stopping the old system and starting the new system on a given date.

Figure 13.11

Start-Up Approaches

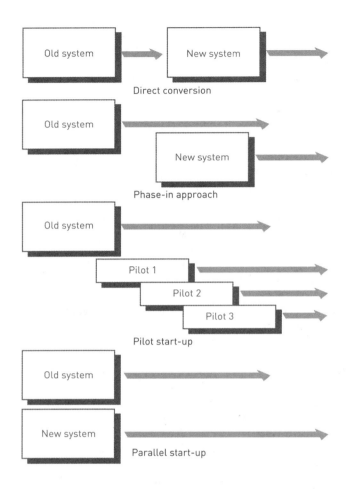

Direct conversion

Phase-in approach

Pilot start-up

Parallel start-up

phase-in approach
Slowly replacing components of the old system with those of the new one; this process is repeated for each application until the new system is running every application and performing as expected; also called a *piecemeal approach*.

pilot start-up
Running the new system for one group of users rather than all users.

parallel start-up
Running both the old and new systems for a period of time and comparing the output of the new system closely with the output of the old system; any differences are reconciled. When users are comfortable that the new system is working correctly, the old system is eliminated.

user acceptance document
A formal agreement signed by the user that states that a phase of the installation or the complete system is approved.

The **phase-in approach** is a popular technique preferred by many organizations. In this approach, sometimes called a *piecemeal approach*, components of the new system are slowly phased in while components of the old one are slowly phased out. When everyone is confident that the new system is performing as expected, the old system is completely phased out. This gradual replacement is repeated for each application until the new system is running every application. In some cases, the phase-in approach can take months or years.

Pilot start-up involves running the new system for one group of users rather than all users. For example, a manufacturing company with many retail outlets throughout the country could use the pilot start-up approach and install a new inventory control system at one of the retail outlets. When this pilot retail outlet runs without problems, the new inventory control system can be implemented at other retail outlets. Telus used a pilot approach to test a new billing information system.

Parallel start-up involves running both the old and new systems for a period of time. The output of the new system is compared closely with the output of the old system, and any differences are reconciled. When users are comfortable that the new system is working correctly, the old system is eliminated.

User Acceptance

Most computer manufacturers use a formal **user acceptance document**—a formal agreement the user signs stating that a phase of the installation or the complete system is approved. This is a legal document that usually removes or reduces the IS vendor's liability for problems that occur after the user acceptance document has been signed. Because this document is so important, many companies get legal assistance before they sign the acceptance document. Stakeholders can also be involved in acceptance testing to make sure that the benefits to them are indeed realized.

SYSTEMS OPERATION AND MAINTENANCE

Systems operation involves all aspects of using the new or modified system in all kinds of operating conditions. Getting the most out of a new or modified system during its operation is the most important aspect of systems operations for many organizations. Throughout this book, we have seen many examples of information systems operating in a variety of settings and industries. Thus we will not cover the operation of an information system in detail in this section. To provide adequate support, many companies use a formal help desk. A *help desk* consists of computer systems, manuals, people with technical expertise, and other resources needed to solve problems and give accurate answers to questions. If you are having trouble with your PC and call a toll-free number for assistance, you might reach a help desk in India, China, or another country.

Systems maintenance involves checking, changing, and enhancing the system to make it more useful in achieving user and organizational goals. Organizations can perform systems maintenance in-house, or they can hire outside companies to perform maintenance for them.[58] Many companies that use database systems from Oracle or SAP, for example, often hire these companies to maintain their database systems. Systems maintenance is important for individuals, groups, and organizations. Individuals, for example, can use the Internet, computer vendors, and independent maintenance companies, such as nerds4hire (*nerds4hire.com*), Geek Squad (*www.geeksquad.com*), SCI Canada (*scicanada.com*), and others. Organizations often have personnel dedicated to maintenance.

Software maintenance for purchased software can be 20 percent or more of the purchase price of the software annually.[59] While some CIOs complain about the high cost of software maintenance, others believe it is worth the cost. According to one CIO, "We've never viewed maintenance as a black hole you put your money into. Maintenance is part of the game." The maintenance process can be especially difficult for older software. A *legacy system* is an old system that might have been patched or modified repeatedly over time. An old payroll program in COBOL developed decades ago and frequently changed is an example of a legacy system. Legacy systems can be very expensive to maintain, and it can be difficult to add new features to some legacy systems. With about 11 million lines of older computer code, a large railroad company wasn't able to add the new features customers wanted.[60] At some point, it becomes less expensive to switch to new programs and applications than to repair and maintain the legacy system. Maintenance costs for older legacy systems can be 50 percent of total operating costs in some cases.

Software maintenance is a major concern for most organizations. In some cases, organizations encounter major problems that require recycling the entire systems development process. In other situations, minor modifications are sufficient to remedy problems. Hardware maintenance is also important. Companies such as IBM have developed *autonomic computing* (*www.ibm.com/autonomic*), in which computers are programmed to manage and maintain themselves.[61] The goal is for computers to be self-configuring, self-protecting, self-healing, and self-optimizing. Being self-configuring allows a computer to handle new hardware, software, or other changes to its operating environment. Being self-protecting means a computer can identify potential attacks, prevent them when possible, and recover from attacks if they occur. Being self-healing means a computer can fix problems when they occur, and being self-optimizing allows a computer to run faster and get more done in less time.

Getting rid of old equipment is an important part of maintenance. The options include selling it on Web auction sites such as eBay, recycling the equipment at a computer-recycling centre, and donating it to a charitable organization, such as a school, library, or religious organization. When discarding old computer systems, it is always a good idea to permanently remove sensitive files and programs. Companies such as McAfee and Blancco (*www.blancco.com*) have software to help people remove data and

systems operation
Use of a new or modified system.

systems maintenance
A stage of systems development that involves checking, changing, and enhancing the system to make it more useful in achieving user and organizational goals.

Tasty Baking Moves Data Centre

People who live in the northeast region of the United States should be familiar with TastyKakes. Dozens of TastyKake products such as Butterscotch Krimpets, Peanut Butter Kandy Kakes, and Cream Filled Buttercream Iced Chocolate Cupcakes are available in grocery stores and convenience marts across Pennsylvania, Ohio, New Jersey, Virginia, and Maryland.

TastyKakes are baked in Philadelphia, Pennsylvania, at the Tasty Baking company headquarters. In 1922, Tasty Baking moved into a large building and warehouse in northern Philadelphia, where it housed both its industrial bakery and its business offices. When computer-based information systems were introduced in the 1940s, Tasty Baking cleared out a floor of its building and set up its first data centre. Over time, that floor became crowded with IBM computers, data storage units, and a growing information systems staff to run it all. The information systems, running on the computers ranging from workstations to mainframes, controlled both the manufacturing processes, as well as business operations.

Tasty Baking's information systems remained in that same space for decades, until 2009, when the company built two beautiful new buildings, one for business offices and another for baking. The buildings are located across town on Philadelphia's south side in the Philadelphia Navy Yard. Given two years' notice prior to the move, Tasty Baking's information systems staff had plenty of time to prepare for the move.

Brendan H. O'Malley, Tasty Baking vice president and CIO, decided that the move provided an excellent opportunity for the company to upgrade its information systems infrastructure. O'Malley decided to use a phase-in approach for the system upgrade and move. They would purchase new servers and storage units and set them up in the old building. When moving day arrived, all they would have to do is transfer the hardware to the new location, plug it in, and resume operations. In 2007, O'Malley sent out a request for proposals for new servers, storage units, and supportive infrastructure.

The combination of modern server technology and server virtualization allowed Tasty Baking to reduce its number of servers from 45 to 15. The new servers were installed in the old server room, where the decades of cables lay tangled like spaghetti under the floor panels. Cabling was always difficult to track, a source of frustration for systems engineers. The company's recently upgraded ERP system was copied to the new servers, and in a few days, the new system was up and running in the old location.

Tasty Baking's information system staff practised the procedures that would be necessary the day of the move, shutting down systems and bringing them back online in an orderly fashion. O'Malley took the opportunity to set up a new disaster recovery system using a set of backup servers. The backup system was set up side by side with the primary system. After the backup system was working, it was transported to a facility 130 kilometres from headquarters. There, any emergency that shut down the main system was unlikely to affect the backup system. Installing the backup system provided an excellent practice run for relocating the data centre.

In the weeks prior to moving day, O'Malley's team installed all the cables in the new facility using a sophisticated cable management system. Moving day for the data centre was on a Friday. Servers were shut down at 2:00 p.m. and then loaded onto a moving van. Upon arrival at the new location, they were moved into location and connected together using well-marked cables that were already in place. By 3:00 a.m. Saturday, all servers, storage, and networking gear were up and running as though their environment never changed.

Using a WAN and LAN, the servers were connected to the old Tasty Baking office building and the new adjoining industrial baking complex. Tasty Baking's employees came to work on Sunday to test the system so that they could be assured of normal operations when work resumed Monday. No one could tell any difference in how the system functioned.

With a new top-of-the-line data centre in place, the rest of the move proceeded smoothly over the next months, with no interruption in normal day-to-day operations. Tasty Baking's information systems staff is enjoying their new environment, with spacious offices with windows—quite an improvement over its old cramped basement environment. Systems are much easier to expand and maintain with the well-organized cable management system. The 13-hour move has received positive recognition by several analysts who agree that it could not have been planned and executed more perfectly.

Discussion Questions

1. What did Tasty Baking do to prepare for moving its data centre?
2. Why was it a good idea to install the disaster recovery system prior to the move?

Critical Thinking Questions

1. Why did Tasty Baking decide to move its data centre first? Why not last?
2. How did having a two-year warning assist Tasty Baking information systems staff with preparing for the move? If they had only two months, how would preparation have differed?

SOURCES: Weisse, Todd, "A Sweet Deal: How Tasty Baking Co. Moved Its Data Center in 13 hours," *Computerworld*, December 17, 2009; "Tasty Baking Company Moves into New Corporate Headquarters at The Philadelphia Navy Yard," Tasty Baking Press Release, *www.tastykake.com/RelatedFiles/TSTY_HQ_Relocation_Release_Final.pdf*, April 20, 2009.

programs from old computers and transfer them to new ones. As mentioned in the section on environmental design, companies are disposing of old equipment in ways that minimize environmental damage.

Reasons for Maintenance

After a program is written, it will need ongoing maintenance. Experience shows that frequent, minor maintenance to a program, if properly done, can prevent major system failures later. Some of the reasons for program maintenance are the following:

- Changes in business processes
- New requests from stakeholders, users, and managers
- Bugs or errors in the program
- Technical and hardware problems
- Corporate mergers and acquisitions
- Government regulations
- Changes in the operating system or hardware on which the application runs
- Unexpected events, such as severe weather or terrorist attacks

Most companies modify their existing programs instead of developing new ones because existing software performs many important functions, and companies can have millions of dollars invested in their old legacy systems. So, as new systems needs are identified, the burden of fulfilling the needs most often falls on the existing system. Old programs are repeatedly modified to meet ever-changing needs. Yet, over time, repeated modifications tend to interfere with the system's overall structure, reducing its efficiency and making further modifications more burdensome.

Types of Maintenance

Software companies and many other organizations use four generally accepted categories to signify the amount of change involved in maintenance. A **slipstream upgrade** is a minor upgrade—typically a code adjustment or minor bug fix. Many companies don't announce to users that a slipstream upgrade has been made. A slipstream upgrade usually requires recompiling all the code, so it can create entirely new bugs. This maintenance practice can explain why the same computers sometimes work differently with what is supposedly the same software. A **patch** is a minor change to correct a problem or make a small enhancement. It is usually an addition to an existing program. That is, the programming code representing the system enhancement is usually "patched into," or added to, the existing code. Although slipstream upgrades and patches are minor changes, they can cause users and support personnel big problems if the programs do not run as before. Many patches come from off-the-shelf software vendors. A new **release** is a significant program change that often requires changes in the documentation of the software. Finally, a new **version** is a major program change, typically encompassing many new features.

The Request for Maintenance Form

Because of the amount of effort that can be spent on maintenance, many organizations require a **request for maintenance form** to authorize modification of programs. This form is usually signed by a business manager, who documents the need for the change and identifies the priority of the change relative to other work that has been requested. The IS group reviews the form and identifies the programs to be changed, determines the programmer who will be assigned to the project, estimates the expected completion date, and develops a technical description of the change. A cost/benefit analysis might be required if the change requires substantial resources.

slipstream upgrade
A minor upgrade—typically a code adjustment or minor bug fix—not worth announcing. It usually requires recompiling all the code and, in so doing, it can create entirely new bugs.

patch
A minor change to correct a problem or make a small enhancement. It is usually an addition to an existing program.

release
A significant program change that often requires changes in the documentation of the software.

version
A major program change, typically encompassing many new features.

request for maintenance form
A form authorizing modification of programs.

Performing Maintenance

Depending on organizational policies, the people who perform systems maintenance vary. In some cases, the team that designs and builds the system also performs maintenance. This ongoing responsibility gives the designers and programmers an incentive to build systems well from the outset: if problems occur, they will have to fix them. In other cases, organizations have a separate **maintenance team**. This team is responsible for modifying, fixing, and updating existing software.

A number of vendors have developed tools to ease the software maintenance burden. Modernization Workbench from Micro Focus is a collection of tools that help organizations analyze the inner workings of legacy applications that are written in older programming languages such as COBOL. After analyzing the programming code, companies can update, or modernize, the application so it is easier to maintain.[62]

maintenance team
A special IS team responsible for modifying, fixing, and updating existing software.

The Relationship Between Maintenance and Design

Programs are expensive to develop, but they are even more expensive to maintain. For older programs, the total cost of maintenance can be up to five times greater than the total cost of development. A determining factor in the decision to replace a system is the point at which it is costing more to fix than to replace. Programs that are well designed and documented to be efficient, structured, and flexible are less expensive to maintain in later years. Thus, there is a direct relationship between design and maintenance. More time spent on design up front can mean less time spent on maintenance later.

In most cases, it is worth the extra time and expense to design a good system. Consider a system that costs $250,000 to develop. Spending 10 percent more on design would cost an additional $25,000, bringing the total design cost to $275,000. Maintenance costs over the life of the program could be $1,000,000. If this additional design expense can reduce maintenance costs by 10 percent, the savings in maintenance costs would be $100,000. Over the life of the program, the net savings would be $75,000 ($100,000–$25,000). This relationship between investment in design and long-term maintenance savings is shown in Figure 13.12.

Figure 13.12

The Value of Investment in Design

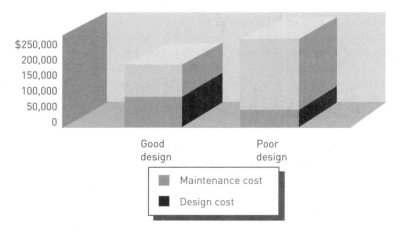

The need for good design goes beyond mere costs. Companies risk ignoring small system problems when they arise, but these small problems can become large in the future. As mentioned earlier, because maintenance programmers spend an estimated 50 percent or more of their time deciphering poorly written, undocumented program code, they have little time to spend on developing new, more effective systems. If put to good use, the tools and techniques discussed in this chapter will allow organizations to build longer-lasting, more reliable systems.

SYSTEMS REVIEW

Systems review, the final step of systems development, is the process of analyzing systems to make sure that they are operating as intended. The systems review process often compares the performance and benefits of the system as it was designed with the actual performance and benefits of the system in operation. In some cases, a formal audit of the application can be performed, using internal and external auditors.[63] Systems review can be performed during systems development, resulting in halting the new systems while they are being built because of problems.

Systems review can also be used to uncover potential problems and solve them before they occur. During a review of software developed for a national mortgage lender, a programmer discovered a computer virus that was inserted in an important program by a fired and vengeful employee.[64] If the review hadn't uncovered the malicious code, the result could have been lost data on about 4,000 computer servers.

Internal employees, external consultants, or both can perform systems review. When the problems or opportunities are industry-wide, people from several firms can get together. In some cases, they collaborate at an IS conference or in a private meeting involving several firms.

systems review
The final step of systems development, involving the analysis of systems to make sure that they are operating as intended.

Types of Review Procedures

The two types of review procedures are event-driven and time-driven. See Table 13.5. An **event-driven review** is triggered by a problem or opportunity such as an error, a corporate merger, a new market for products, or other causes.[65] In one case, a new cloud computing company suddenly told its clients that it was closing all operations.[66] This event-driven situation caused the companies using the cloud computing service to make other arrangements in a short amount of time. According to one of the cloud computing customers, "We'll be a little more wary with startups, as we realize the risk of going with one can be real." After an attack on its popular social-networking Internet site that resulted in hackers breaking into the accounts of about 30 celebrities and popular organizations, Twitter launched a full security review to analyze its defences against such attacks.[67]

event-driven review
A review triggered by a problem or opportunity such as an error, a corporate merger, or a new market for products.

Event Driven	Time Driven
Problem with an existing system	Monthly review
Merger	Yearly review
New accounting system	Review every few years
Executive decision that an upgraded Internet site is needed to stay competitive	Five-year review

Table 13.5

Examples of Review Types

A **time-driven review** is performed after a specified amount of time. Many application programs are reviewed every six months to one year. With this approach, an existing system is monitored on a schedule. If problems or opportunities are uncovered, a new systems development cycle can be initiated. A payroll application, for example, can be reviewed once a year to make sure that it is still operating as expected. If it is not, changes are made.

Many companies use both approaches. A billing application, for example, might be reviewed once a year for errors, inefficiencies, and opportunities to reduce operating costs. This is a time-driven approach. In addition, the billing application might be redone after a corporate merger, if one or more new managers require different information or reports, or if laws on bill collecting and privacy change. This is an event-driven approach.

time-driven review
Review performed after a specified amount of time.

System Performance Measurement

**system performance
measurement**
Monitoring the system—the
number of errors encountered,
the amount of memory required,
the amount of processing or CPU time
needed, and other problems.

Systems review often involves monitoring the system, called **system performance
measurement**. The number of errors encountered, the amount of memory required, the
amount of processing or CPU time needed, and other problems should be closely observed.
If a particular system is not performing as expected, it should be modified, or a new system
should be developed or acquired. Many companies use social media such as Twitter and
Facebook to get user feedback on the performance of its information systems and its operations. Some executives believe that using Twitter is like an "early-warning-system" that
alerts the company to potential problems before they become serious and hurt system
performance.

system performance products
Software that measures all
components of the computer-
based information system,
including hardware, software,
database, telecommunications,
and network systems.

System performance products have been developed to measure all components of the
information system, including hardware, software, database, telecommunications, and network systems. IBM Tivoli OMEGAMON can monitor system performance in real time.[68]
Precise Software Solutions has system performance products that provide around-the-clock
performance monitoring for ERP systems, Oracle database applications, and other programs.[69] HP also offers a software tool called Business Technology Optimization (BTO)
to help companies analyze the performance of their computer systems, diagnose potential
problems, and take corrective action if needed.[70] When properly used, system performance
products can quickly and efficiently locate actual or potential problems.

Measuring a system is, in effect, the final task of systems development. The results of
this process can bring the development team back to the beginning of the development life
cycle, where the process begins again.

SUMMARY

Principle:

Designing new systems or modifying existing ones should always help an organization achieve its goals.

The purpose of systems design is to prepare the detailed design needs for a new system or modifications to the existing system. Logical systems design refers to the way that the various components of an information system will work together. The logical design includes data requirements for output and input, processing, files and databases, telecommunications, procedures, personnel and job design, and controls and security design. Physical systems design refers to the specifications of the physical components. The physical design must specify characteristics for hardware and software design, database and telecommunications, and personnel and procedures design.

Logical and physical design can be accomplished using the traditional systems development life cycle or the object-oriented approach. Using the OO approach, analysts design key objects and classes of objects in the new or updated system. The sequence of events that a new or modified system requires is often called a scenario, which can be diagrammed in a sequence diagram.

A number of special design considerations should be taken into account during both logical and physical system design. Interface design and control relates to how users access and interact with the system. System security and control involves many aspects. Error prevention, detection, and correction should be part of the system design process. Causes of errors include human activities, natural phenomena, and technical problems. Designers should be alert to prevention of fraud and invasion of privacy.

Disaster recovery is an important aspect of systems design. Disaster planning is the process of anticipating and providing for disasters. A disaster can be an act of nature (a flood, fire, or earthquake) or a human act (terrorism, error, labour unrest, or erasure of an important file). The primary tools used in disaster planning and recovery are hardware, software, database, telecommunications, and personnel backup.

Security, fraud, and the invasion of privacy are also important design considerations. Most IS departments establish tight systems controls to maintain data security. Systems controls can help prevent computer misuse, crime, and fraud by employees and others. Systems controls include input, output, processing, database, telecommunications, and personnel controls.

Environmental design, also called green design, involves systems development efforts that slash power consumption, require less physical space, and result in systems that can be disposed of in a way that doesn't negatively affect the environment. A number of companies are developing products and services to help save energy. Environmental design also deals with how companies are developing systems to dispose of old equipment. Canada rates products with the Energy Star designation to help people select products that save energy and are friendly to the environment. Today, utility companies are providing their corporate and individual customers with "smart meters" and specialized software that can help them reduce their power consumption and electric bills.

Whether an individual is purchasing a personal computer or a large company is acquiring an expensive computer, the system could be obtained from one or more vendors. Some of the factors to consider in selecting a vendor are the vendor's reliability and financial stability, the type of service offered after the sale, the goods and services the vendor offers and keeps in stock, the vendor's willingness to demonstrate its products, the vendor's ability to repair hardware, the vendor's ability to modify its software, the availability of vendor-offered training of IS personnel and system users, and evaluations of the vendor by independent organizations.

If new hardware or software will be purchased from a vendor, a formal request for proposal (RFP) is sometimes needed. The RFP outlines the company's needs; in response, the vendor provides a written reply. In addition to responding to the company's stated needs, the vendor provides data on its operations. This data might include the vendor's reliability and stability, the type of postsale service offered, the vendor's ability to perform repairs and fix problems, the available vendor training, and the vendor's reputation. Financial options to consider include purchase, lease, and rent.

RFPs from various vendors are reviewed and narrowed down to the few most likely candidates. In the final evaluation, a variety of techniques—including group consensus, cost/benefit analysis, point evaluation, and benchmark tests—can be used. In group consensus, a decision-making group is appointed and given responsibility for making the final evaluation and selection. With cost/benefit analysis, all costs and benefits of the alternatives are expressed in monetary terms. Benchmarking involves comparing computer systems operating under the same conditions. Point evaluation assigns weights to evaluation factors, and each alternative is evaluated in terms of each factor and given a score from 0 to 100. After the vendor is chosen, contract negotiations can begin.

At the end of the systems design step, the final specifications are frozen and no changes are allowed so that implementation can proceed. One of the most important steps in systems design is to develop a good contract if new computer facilities are being acquired. A final design report is developed at the end of the systems design phase.

Principle:

The primary emphasis of systems implementation is to make sure that the right information is delivered to the right person in the right format at the right time.

The purpose of systems implementation is to install the system and make everything, including users, ready for its operation. Systems implementation includes hardware acquisition, software acquisition or development, user preparation, hiring and training of personnel, site and data preparation, installation, testing, start-up, and user acceptance. Hardware acquisition requires purchasing, leasing, or renting computer resources from an IS vendor. Hardware is typically obtained from a computer hardware vendor.

Software can be purchased from vendors or developed in-house—a decision termed the *make-or-buy decision*. Virtualization, first introduced in Chapter 3, has had a profound impact on many aspects of systems implementation. A purchased software package usually has a lower cost, less risk regarding the features and performance, and easy installation. The amount of development effort is also less when software is purchased. Software as a service (SaaS) is becoming a popular way to purchase software capabilities. Developing software can result in a system that more closely meets the business needs and has increased flexibility in customization and changes. Developing software also has greater potential for providing a competitive advantage. However, such software is usually more expensive than purchased software. More companies are using service providers to acquire software, Internet access, and other IS resources.

Cross-platform development and integrated development environments (IDEs) make software development easier and more thorough. CASE tools are often used to automate some of these techniques. Technical and user documentation is always important in developing in-house software.

Database and telecommunications software development involves acquiring the necessary databases, networks, telecommunications, and Internet facilities. Companies have a wide array of choices, including newer object-oriented database systems. Virtual databases and database as a service (DaaS) are popular ways to acquire database capabilities.

Implementation must address personnel requirements. User preparation involves readying managers, employees, and other users for the new system. New IS personnel might need to be hired, and users must be well trained in the system's functions. Preparation of the physical site of the system must be done, and any existing data to be used in the new system will require conversion to the new format. Hardware installation is done during the implementation step, as is testing. Testing includes program (unit) testing, systems testing, volume testing, integration testing, and acceptance testing.

Start-up begins with the final tested information system. When start-up is finished, the system is fully operational. There are a number of different start-up approaches. Direct conversion (also called plunge or direct cutover) involves stopping the old system and starting the new system on a given date. With the phase-in approach, sometimes called a piecemeal approach, components of the new system are slowly phased in while components of the old one are slowly phased out. When everyone is confident that the new system is performing as expected, the old system is completely phased out. Pilot start-up involves running the new system for one group of users rather than all users. Parallel start-up involves running both the old and new systems for a period of time. The output of the new system is compared closely with the output of the old system, and any differences are reconciled. When users are comfortable that the new system is working correctly, the old system is eliminated. Many IS vendors ask the user to sign a formal user acceptance document that releases the IS vendor from liability for problems that occur after the document is signed.

Principle:

Maintenance and review add to the useful life of a system but can consume large amounts of resources. These activities can benefit from the same rigorous methods and project management techniques applied to systems development.

Systems operation is the use of a new or modified system. Systems maintenance involves checking, changing, and enhancing the system to make it more useful in obtaining user and organizational goals. Maintenance is critical for the continued smooth operation of the system. The costs of performing maintenance can well exceed the original cost of acquiring the system. Some major causes of maintenance are new requests from stakeholders and managers, enhancement requests from users, bugs or errors, technical or hardware problems, newly added equipment, changes in organizational structure, and government regulations.

Maintenance can be as simple as a program patch to correct a small problem to the more complex upgrading of software with a new release from a vendor. For older programs, the total cost of maintenance can be greater than the total cost of development. Increased emphasis on design can reduce maintenance costs. Requests for maintenance should be documented with a request for maintenance form, a document that formally authorizes modification of programs. The development team or a specialized maintenance team can then make approved changes. Maintenance can be greatly simplified with the object-oriented approach.

Systems review is the process of analyzing and monitoring systems to make sure that they are operating as intended. The two types of review procedures are the event-driven review and the time-driven review. An event-driven review is triggered by a problem or opportunity. A time-driven review is started after a specified amount of time.

Systems review involves measuring how well the system is supporting the mission and goals of the organization. System performance measurement monitors the system for number of errors, amount of memory and processing time required, and so on.

CHAPTER 13: SELF-ASSESSMENT TEST

Designing new systems or modifying existing ones should always help an organization achieve its goals.

1. _____ details system outputs, inputs, and user interfaces; specifies hardware, software, databases, telecommunications, personnel, and procedures; and shows how these components are related.

2. Which of the following types of design deals with determining the hardware and software required for a new system?
   a. logical design
   b. physical design
   c. interactive design
   d. object-oriented design

3. Disaster planning is an important part of designing security and control systems. True or False?

4. _____ involves systems development efforts that slash power consumption and require less physical space.

5. Scenarios and sequence diagrams are used with which of the following?
   a. object-oriented design
   b. point evaluation
   c. incremental design
   d. nominal evaluation

6. A test that examines or compares computer systems operating under the same conditions is called _____ testing.

7. The design report is the final result of systems design that provides technical and detailed descriptions of the new system. True or False?

The primary emphasis of systems implementation is to make sure that the right information is delivered to the right person in the right format at the right time.

8. Software as a Service (SaaS) allows an organization to subscribe to Web-based applications and pay for the software and services actually used. True or False?

9. _____ software can make computers act like or simulate other computers, reducing costs and space requirements.

10. What type of documentation is used by computer operators, analysts, and programmers?
    a. unit documentation
    b. integrated documentation
    c. technical documentation
    d. user documentation

11. _____ testing involves testing the entire system of programs.

12. The phase-in approach to conversion involves running both the old system and the new system for three months or longer. True or False?

Maintenance and review add to the useful life of a system but can consume large amounts of resources. These activities can benefit from the same rigorous methods and project management techniques applied to systems development.

13. A(n) _____ is a minor change to correct a problem or make a small enhancement to a program or system.

14. Many organizations require a request for maintenance form to authorize modification of programs. True or False?

15. Which of the following is a systems review caused by a problem with an existing system?
    a. object review
    b. structured review
    c. event-driven review
    d. critical factors review

16. Corporate mergers and acquisitions can be reasons for systems maintenance. True or False?

17. Monitoring a system after it has been implemented is called _____.

CHAPTER 13: SELF-ASSESSMENT TEST ANSWERS

(1) *Systems design* (2) b (3) True (4) Environmental design (5) a (6) benchmark (7) True (8) True (9) Virtualization (10) c (11) *System* (12) False (13) patch (14) True (15) c (16) True (17) system performance measurement

REVIEW QUESTIONS

1. What is the purpose of systems design?
2. Describe the design of system security and controls.
3. How can the object-oriented approach be used during systems design?
4. What is the difference between logical and physical design?
5. What is environmental design?
6. What are the advantages and disadvantages of in-house developed software?
7. Identify specific controls that are used to maintain input integrity and security.
8. What is an RFP? What is typically included in one? How is it used?
9. What activities go on during the user preparation phase of systems implementation?

10. What is systems operation?
11. What are the major steps of systems implementation?
12. What are some tools and techniques for software development?
13. Give three examples of an IS vendor.
14. How can SaaS be used in software acquisition?
15. What are the steps involved in testing the information system?
16. What is the difference between an event-driven review and a time-driven review?
17. How is systems performance measurement related to the systems review?

DISCUSSION QUESTIONS

1. Describe the participants in the systems design stage. How do these participants compare with the participants of systems investigation?
2. Assume that you are the owner of a company that is about to start marketing and selling bicycles over the Internet. Describe what environmental design steps you could use to reduce power consumption with your information system.
3. Assume that you want to start a new video rental business for students at your college or university. Go through logical design for a new information system to help you keep track of the videos in your inventory.
4. You have been hired to design a computer system for a small business. Describe how you could use environmental design to reduce energy usage and the system's impact on the environment.
5. Identify some of the advantages and disadvantages of purchasing a database package instead of taking the DaaS approach.
6. Discuss the relationship between maintenance and systems design.
7. Is it equally important for all systems to have a disaster recovery plan? Why or why not?
8. Several approaches were discussed to evaluate a number of systems acquisition alternatives. No one approach is always the best. How would you decide which approach to use for evaluation when selecting a new personal computer and printer?
9. What are the advantages and disadvantages of the object-oriented approach to systems implementation?
10. You have been hired to oversee a major systems development effort to purchase a new accounting software package. Describe what is important to include in the contract with the software vendor.
11. You have been hired to purchase a new billing and accounting system for a medium-sized business. Describe how you would start up the new system and place it into operation.
12. Identify the various forms of testing. Why are there so many different types of tests?
13. What is the goal of conducting a systems review? What factors need to be considered during systems review?
14. Describe how you would select the best admissions software for your college or university. What features would be most important for school administrators? What features would be most important for students?
15. Assume that you have a personal computer that is several years old. Describe the steps you would use to perform systems review to determine whether you should acquire a new PC.

PROBLEM-SOLVING EXERCISES

1. You have been hired to develop a new student records and grade reporting system for your college or university. Describe how you would incorporate privacy and security measures into the design of the new system. Use a graphics program, such as PowerPoint, to develop a set of slides that shows how the different security and privacy measures will be included in the design. Write a brief report on the importance of including security and privacy concerns into your design.
2. A project team has estimated the costs associated with the development and maintenance of a new system. One approach requires a more complete design and will result in a slightly higher design and implementation cost but a lower maintenance cost over the life of the system. The second approach cuts the design effort, saving some dollars but with a likely increase in maintenance cost.
   a. Enter the following data in the spreadsheet. Print the result.

The Benefits of Good Design

	Good Design	Poor Design
Design costs	$14,000	$10,000
Implementation cost	$42,000	$35,000
Annual maintenance cost	$32,000	$40,000

   b. Create a stacked bar graph that shows the total cost, including the design, implementation, and maintenance costs. Be sure that the chart has a title and that the costs are labelled on the chart.
   c. Use your word processing software to write a paragraph that recommends an approach to take and why.
3. You have been hired to design a new sales ordering program. The program needs a database that contains a customer table containing important customer information, an inventory table that contains current inventory levels, and an order table that contains customer number, inventory number, and order quantity. Develop a database that shows the fields in each table. Include ten sample records in each table.

TEAM ACTIVITIES

1. Assume that your project team has been working for three months to complete the systems design of a new Web-based customer ordering system. Two possible options seem to meet all users' needs. The project team must make a final decision on which option to implement. The following table summarizes some of the key facts about each option.

Factor	Option 1	Option 2
Annual gross savings	$1.5 million	$3.0 million
Total development cost	$1.5 million	$2.2 million
Annual operating cost	$0.5 million	$1.0 million
Time required to implement	9 months	15 months
Risk associated with project (expressed in probabilities)		
Benefits will be 50% less than expected	20%	35%
Cost will be 50% greater than expected	25%	30%
Organization will not/cannot make changes necessary for system to operate as expected	20%	25%
Does system meet all mandatory requirements?	Yes	Yes

   a. What process would you follow to make this important decision?
   b. Who needs to be involved?
   c. What additional questions need to be answered to make a good decision?
   d. Based on the data, which option would you recommend and why?
   e. How would you account for project risk in your decision making?

2. Your team has been hired by the owner of a new restaurant to explore word processing, graphics, database, and spreadsheet capabilities. The new owner has heard about cloud computing, SaaS, and DaaS. Your team should prepare a report on the advantages and disadvantages of using a traditional office suite from a company such as Microsoft compared to other approaches.

3. Your team should perform a critical systems review of a computer application being used at your college or university. Include the strengths and weaknesses of the computer application and describe how it could be improved from a student perspective.

WEB EXERCISES

1. Use the Internet to find two different systems development projects that failed to meet cost or performance objectives. Summarize the problems and what should have been done. You might be asked to develop a report or send an e-mail message to your instructor about what you found.

2. Using the Web, search for information on the advantages and disadvantages of environmental design. Write a report on what you found.

CAREER EXERCISES

1. Describe what type of information system you would need in your chosen job. Your description should include logical and physical design. What specific steps would you include to be able to recover from a natural or man-made disaster, such as a flood or terrorist attack?

2. Research possible careers in developing applications for iPhones, other smartphones, and PDAs. Write a report that describes these opportunities. Include in your report applications that aren't currently available that you would find useful.

CASE STUDIES

Case One

Russian Sporting Goods Chain Scales Up Budgeting System

The Sportmaster Group is the largest sporting goods chain in Eastern Europe. It handles Sportlandia and Columbia brands and more than 200 other trademarks, including its own.

When Sportmaster was established, its CIO decided to build a budget planning system in-house. The system was built with Excel spreadsheets and was well suited for a young start-up business. But in recent years, with stores spread across Eastern Europe, the executives at Sportmaster Group wanted to gain better control of their budgets and use their financial information to make wise strategic decisions. Due to the large amount of data involved, using the current Excel-based system had become burdensome, and the information provided was too limited to support corporate needs.

In the process of system maintenance and review, Sportmaster realized that to progress to the next stage of growth, it needed to move to information systems used by large global corporations. In researching packages from a variety of vendors, the company settled on software from Cognos, an IBM company. To customize the Cognos software for its own needs, Sportmaster hired a company named IBS. Sportmaster chose IBS because it was a certified Cognos vendor and had experience working with Russian companies.

IBS consultants met with Sportmaster executives and information systems staff to discuss the expectations for the new budget analysis system. They worked on site so they could test prototypes on actual corporate data and have their progress reviewed by Sportmaster to confirm that they were on target.

The resulting system met the following goals defined by Sportmaster. According to the Cognos case study, the system could perform the following tasks:

- Create a basic gross profit budget
- Create budgets for investment activity, including opening new stores and capital investments
- Create an operating-expenses budget for all corporate divisions, including more than "500 centres of responsibility"
- Create specialized budgets, including a consolidated Revenue and Expenditure Budget, a Cash-Flow Budget, and a Balance Sheet of Payables and Receivables
- Create a Revenue and Expenditure Budget for the divisions
- Integrate with external accounting systems

Sportmaster used a parallel start-up method, introducing the new budget planning and accounting system, keeping the old system available as a back-up. After six months of successful use and a few tweaks to perfect the system, the company now fully depends on the new system and is enjoying its benefits. Sportmaster can access highly detailed budget reports that assist in making strategic decisions. The process for creating budget reports has been simplified, and the duration of the budget cycle is shortened. Operations that used to take days are now accomplished in near real time. Most important is that the reliability of the data is improved so that budget errors are minimized.

Discussion Questions

1. What motivated Sportmaster to start an IS project to build a new budget planning and accounting system?
2. What steps did the development team take to make sure that the project was completed in minimum time while meeting the company's needs?

Critical Thinking Questions

1. How can the level of detail of the information provided by a budget planning and accounting system affect a company's decision-making capability?
2. Why do you think Sportmaster decided to outsource the systems development project rather than work in house?

SOURCES: "Sportmaster Group," Cognos Case Study, www-01.ibm.com/software/success/cssdb.nsf/CS/ABRR-7WEBZ3?OpenDocument&Site=corp&cty=en_us, accessed March 3, 2010.

Case Two

Honeywell Building Next Gen UPS Device

UPS is recognized as a leader in digital innovation, and the DIAD is partially responsible for that reputation. The DIAD (delivery information acquisitions device) is the electronic pad carried by UPS delivery personnel to track shipping information and collect customer signatures. In 2003, the DIAD IV was released, providing wireless connections to UPS servers and reducing the need for paper-based signatures. UPS says that the DIAD has eliminated the use of 59 million sheets of paper a year. It also allows UPS to track its drivers using GPS technologies.

Although the DIAD IV was a cutting-edge device in 2003, by 2010 many new technologies emerged that the DIAD IV did not include. In the extended systems review phase of the DIAD, it was determined that a new DIAD, the DIAD V, should be considered. A UPS development team returned to the systems investigation stage to evaluate what changes were required for the DIAD system and if those changes were feasible.

UPS decided that it was indeed time for the DIAD V, and that the project was not only feasible, but also necessary if UPS was to maintain an advantage over its competition. One requirement of the new DIAD was to remain connected to the UPS network using any available cell phone network. The new DIAD should also use state-of-the-art mobile technologies and be virtually indestructible—both shockproof and waterproof. Although Motorola built the DIAD IV, UPS chose Honeywell for the DIAD V because of Honeywell's experience in designing cross-network devices with rugged designs. After selecting the manufacturer, UPS systems analysts collaborated with Honeywell engineers to determine what features the device could support.

Because electronic components shrink each time a new version is released, the DIAD V will be half the size of the DIAD IV and will easily slip into a holster or be held in one hand. The DIAD V will include automatic jumping between cellular networks to provide a high rate of connectivity. It will also include Wi-Fi support for much faster data transfer rates. The DIAD V will include a colour, autofocus flash camera making it easy for drivers to scan bar codes and capture signatures to verify delivery. The new DIAD will also include a much faster processor, increased storage, and a colour display that supports GPS navigation, and even allow drivers to stream and view training videos.

Honeywell planned to begin field-testing the DIAD V in late 2010, followed by a global deployment of 100,000 DIADs to more than 100 countries.

Discussion Questions

1. Why did UPS decide that it was time to develop the next generation DIAD?
2. What features will the DIAD V provide and how will they give UPS an advantage over the competition?

Critical Thinking Questions

1. Why does UPS want to design its own unique device rather than using an off-the-shelf product such as a BlackBerry?
2. How does a company in the shipping industry end up being a technology leader and innovator?

SOURCES: Hamblen, Matt, "Honeywell to Build Next-Gen Handhelds for UPS Drivers," *Computerworld*, www.computerworld.com, January 14, 2010; "The UPS Delivery Information Acquisition Device (DIAD IV)," UPS website, *www.pressroom. ups.com/Fact+Sheets/The+UPS+Delivery+Information+Acquisition+Device+ %28DIAD+IV%29*, accessed March 5, 2010.

Questions for Web Case

See the website for this book to read about the Altitude Online case for this chapter. Following are questions concerning this Web case.

Altitude Online: Systems Design, Implementation, Maintenance, and Review Considerations

Discussion Questions

1. How did Jon's team coordinate with the vendor in the implementation stage of the systems development project?
2. What did Jon's team do in advance of contacting SAP that made the design and implementation systems proceed as smoothly as possible?

Critical Thinking Questions

1. What risks were involved in the systems development project?
2. What benefits were gained from this systems development project? Was it worth the risks?

NOTES

Sources for the opening vignette: "Ryder Accelerates Close Rates and Increased Contract Renewals with SaaS CRM," CRM Management, October 19, 2009, *http://crm.enterpriseinnovation.net/content/ryder-accelerates-close-rates-and-increased-contract-renewals-saas-crm*; "Ryder's Supply Chain Solutions Division Nets Dramatic Improvements with Salesforce CRM," BNET, January 2009, *http://jobfunctions.bnet.com/abstract.aspx?docid=259797*; "Ryder—About Us," website, *www.ryder.com/aboutus_home.shtml*, accessed March 5, 2010.

1. Babcock, Charles, "Hybrid Clouds," *Information Week*, September 7, 2009, p. 15.
2. Hoover, Nicholas, "GE Puts the Cloud Model to the Test," *Information Week*, April 13, 2009, p. 32.
3. Wildstrom, Stephen, "What to Entrust to The Cloud," *BusinessWeek*, April 6, 2009, p. 89.
4. Greenberg, Andy, "No Phishing Zone," *Forbes*, April 27, 2009.
5. Healey, M., "Beat the Slow Commotion," *Information Week*, March 23, 2009, p. 40.
6. Patterson S., and Ng, S., "NYSE's Fast-Trade Hub," *Wall Street Journal*, July 30, 2009, p. C1.
7. Erickson, J., "Information Security," *Information Week*, June 22, 2009, p. 45.

8. Marew, T., et al., "Tactics Based Approach for Integrating Non-Functional Requirements in Object-Oriented Analysis and Design," *Journal of Systems and Software*, October 2009, p. 1642.
9. Lumpp, T., et al., "From Highly Availability and Disaster Recovery to Business Continuity Solutions," *IBM Systems Journal*, No. 4, 2008, p. 605.
10. Morrill, H., et al., "Achieving Continuous Availability of IBM Systems Infrastructures," *IBM Systems Journal*, No. 4, 2008, p. 493.
11. Rice, J., "Budget Ax Falls on Disaster Recovery," *Computerworld*, January 12, 2009, p. 28.
12. Babcock, Charles, "Virtual Beginning," *Information Week*, March 22, 2009, p. 22.
13. Marks, Howard, "When Failure Isn't an Option," *Information Week*, March 2, 2009, p. 43.
14. Babcock, Charles, "Virtualization Meets Automation," *Information Week*, June 22, 2009, p. 38.
15. Lawn, Greg, "How to Avoid an E-Discovery Disaster," *Computerworld*, October 5, 2009, p. 30.
16. Bustillo, Miguel, "Wal-Mart to Assign New Green Ratings," *Wall Street Journal*, July 16, 2009, p. B1.
17. Pratt, Mary, "Slow-Growing Green," *Computerworld*, January 1, 2009, p. 13.

18 Campbell, S., and Jeronimo, M., "Virtual Machines, Real Productivity," *Information Week*, January 26, 2009, p. 40.

19 Babcock, Charles, "Nissan Assembly Lines Roll with Fewer Servers," *Information Week*, July 6, 2009, p. 17.

20 Pratt, Mary, "Birth of an Energy Star," *Computerworld*, August 31, 2009, p. 24.

21 *www.Greenstarnetwork.com*, accessed October 18, 2010.

22 Badiga, L., "CIO Profiles," *Information Week*, March 2, 2009, p. 16.

23 Carlton, Jim, "The PC Goes on an Energy Diet," *Wall Street Journal*, September 8, 2009, p. R8.

24 Mies, Ginny, "Green Phones," *PC World*, September 2009, p. 28.

25 Voltaic Generator, *www.voltaicsystems.com/bag_generator.shtml*, accessed August 17, 2009.

26 Randall, David, "Be Green and Make a Buck," *Forbes*, March 2, 2009, p. 40.

27 Mossberg, Walter, "Where Old Gadgets Go to Breathe New Life," *Wall Street Journal*, August 13, 2009, p. D8.

28 Toronto Hydro, www.torontohydro.com/sites/electricsystem/residential/smartmeters/Pages/TOURates.aspx, accessed October 18, 2010.

29 Worthen, Ben, "Oracle Targets a New Rival: IBM," *Wall Street Journal*, October 15, 2009, p. B4.

30 Domeika, Max, "Evaluating the Performance of Multicore Processors," *Electronic Engineering Times*, September 28, 2009, p. 33.

31 Chen, Yaunyan, et al., "An Empirical Analysis of Contract Structures in IT Outsourcing," *Information Systems Research*, December 2009, p. 484.

32 "Citrix's Virtual Advantage," *Information Week*, April 20, 2009, p. 44.

33 Campbell and Jeronimo, "Virtual Machines, Real Productivity."

34 Babcock, Charles, "IBM Readies Tool to Contain VM Sprawl," *Information Week*, October 26, 2009, p. 14.

35 "The Infotech 100," *BusinessWeek*, June 1, 2009, p. 39.

36 Conry-Murray, A., "Engines of Innovation," *Information Week*, April 20, 2009, p. 30.

37 Poston, R., et al., "Managing the Vendor Set," *MIS Quarterly Executive*, June 2009, p. 45.

38 Hoover, Nicholas, "GE Puts the Cloud Model to the Test," *Information Week*, April 13, 2009, p. 32.

39 Babcock, Charles, "Red Hat to Certify Cloud-Ready Applications," *Information Week*, July 6, 2009, p. 14.

40 Hahn, J., et al., "Emergence of New Project Teams from Open Source Software Developer Networks," *Information Systems Research*, September 2008, p. 369.

41 "Printing Company Spreads the Word about Virtualization's Merits," *www.vmware.com/files/pdf/customers/VMW-81174-QuebecorWorld-Snapshot-09.pdf*, accessed October 18, 2010.

42 Crosman, Penny, "SaaS Gains Street Traction," *Wall Street & Technology*, September 1, 2008, p. 37.

43 Murphy, Chris, "UPS Works to Get Better One Step at a Time," *Information Week*, June 8, 2009, p. 36.

44 Erickson, J., "Programmer Productivity," *Information Week*, September 28, 2009, p. 51.

45 Bulkeley, William, "At IBM, New Uses for Old Software," *Wall Street Journal*, February 3, 2009, p. B4.

46 IT Redux website, *http://itredux.com/office-20/database/?family=Database*, accessed August 1, 2009.

47 Rackspace Hosting website, *www.rackspacecloud.com/who_uses_cloud_computing*, accessed October 20, 2010.

48 Weier, Mary, "Wal-Mart Change Hints at Data-Driven Marketing," *Information Week*, July 20, 2009, p. 10.

49 Foley, John, "Gold in the Clouds," *Information Week*, September 28, 2009, p. 24.

50 Babcock, Charles, "Platform as a Service," *Information Week*, October 5, 2009, p. 18.

51 "Apple Reveals top iPhone Apps of 2009," *www.canada.com/technology/Apple+reveals+iPhone+apps+2009/2326058/story.html*, accessed October 19, 2010.

52 Morrison, S., "A Second Chance for Second Life," *Wall Street Journal*, August 19, 2009, p. B5.

53 Hoover, N., "Tough Call," *Information Week*, February 23, 2009, p. 21.

54 Morrison, Scott, "Co-Op Field-Tests Software," *Wall Street Journal*, October 28, 2009, p. B5A.

55 Berkow, Jameson, "FP Tech Desk: HMV Canada Launches Online Music Store," *business.financialpost.com/2010/07/05/fp-tech-desk-hmv-canada-launches-online-music-store/*, July 5, 2010.

56 Capell, Kerry, "Vodafone: Embracing Open Source with Open Arms," *BusinessWeek*, April 20, 2009, p. 52.

57 Thompson, Herbert, "Secure Software Needs Careful Testing," *Information Week*, November 30, 2009, p. 37.

58 Hodgson, J., "Rethinking Software Support," *Wall Street Journal*, March 12, 2009, p. B8.

59 Weier, M., "Numbers Crunch," *Information Week*, January 26, 2009, p. 25.

60 Hoffman, Thomas, "Railroad Crossing," *Computerworld*, December 21, 2009, p. 22.

61 IBM website, *www.research.ibm.com/autonomic*, accessed June 26, 2011.

62 Microfocus website, *www.microfocus.com*, accessed April 2, 2010.

63 Kelly, C., "Getting an F and Turning It Into Fun," *Computerworld*, May 26, 2008, p. 32.

64 Gorman, S., "Virus Was Set to Destroy Fannie Mae Data," *Wall Street Journal*, February 1, 2009, p. 2.

65 "T-Mobile Data Gone," *Tampa Tribune*, October 13, 2009, p. 8.

66 Weier, M., "A Cautionary Tale, Brought to You by the Cloud," *Information Week*, March 2, 2009, p. 20.

67 Gaudin, Sharon, "Hack Forces Twitter into Full Security Review," *Computerworld*, January 12, 2009, p. 8.

68 IBM website, www-142.ibm.com/software/dre/eps/tivoli_epshome.wss, accessed June 26, 2011.

69 Precise website, *www.precise.com*, accessed June 26, 2011.

70 Hewlett Packard website, *https://h10078.www1.hp.com/cda/hpms/display/main/hpms_home.jsp?zn=bto&cp=1_4011_100__*, accessed August 1, 2009.

INTEGRATIVE CASE

Richard Ivey School of Business
The University of Western Ontario

IVEY | Ivey Publishing

Binnj on the Apple iPad

Ken Mark wrote this case under the supervision of Professor Derrick Neufeld solely to provide material for class discussion. The authors do not intend to illustrate either effective or ineffective handling of a managerial situation. The authors may have disguised certain names and other identifying information to protect confidentiality.

Richard Ivey School of Business Foundation prohibits any form of reproduction, storage or transmission without its written permission. Reproduction of this material is not covered under authorization by any reproduction rights organization. To order copies or request permission to reproduce materials, contact Ivey Publishing, Richard Ivey School of Business Foundation, The University of Western Ontario, London, Ontario, Canada, N6A 3K7; phone (519) 661-3208; fax (519) 661-3882; e-mail cases@ivey.uwo.ca.

Copyright © 2011, Richard Ivey School of Business Foundation Version: 2011-02-11

Introduction

"I think we can all agree that the meeting with the client went very well today. In fact, all three of our initial client sales meetings have drawn overwhelming responses," said Clay Hutcherson, founder, president and chief executive officer (CEO) of London, Ontario-based Binnj Inc.[1] "They love LiveMenu™," he declared, referring to the company's new product, a digital restaurant menu platform (see Exhibit 1 on the next page). "But the clients are almost too excited — everyone wants to participate in a pilot program, yet our product will not be ready for another two months. I'm afraid we may have let the genie out of the bottle too soon!"

Hutcherson stood up from his seat and walked to the door. It was 8:15 p.m. on August 2, 2010, and the Binnj team was having their weekly JAM session in the AdVendors boardroom (see Exhibit 2). The portable projector was heating the small room rapidly, forcing Hutcherson to swing the room door back and forth in an effort to draw cooler air into the space.

"Clay, we cannot wait another two months before starting the next sales calls!" protested James Hayes, Director, Sales and Marketing. Hayes was sitting straight up in his chair, his hands gesturing passionately. "Our first three client meetings were set up for us by friendly intermediaries — they were warm calls. The next ones will be cold calls. It's going to take us much longer to get through the gatekeepers. We might be facing a sales cycle of six to 12 months, or longer."

"But I think our only option is to wait," pushed back Nancy Philip, chief financial (CFO) and chief operating officer (COO). Philip was based in Ottawa and was joining in on the meeting via Skype. She continued: "What if our next sales meetings move forward just as quickly as the first three? There are good reasons why the restaurant chains we've approached thus far have been eager to jump on board. Yes, having introductions helped to create the marketing pitch opportunities, but it's really the promise of our product that is resonating with the industry. If customers decide to move fast, we cannot leave them waiting for a solution that works."

Hutcherson responded: "Okay. Customer reaction has exceeded our most optimistic expectations. My personal preference is to push as hard as possible, get a test going, and start building a sales funnel. Scott, how quickly can we have the product ready for beta testing?"

All eyes turned to Scott Corscadden, chief information officer (CIO). Corscadden had been typing an email on his iPhone, in preparation for a trip to Las Vegas where he was staffed on a software project for a medium-sized multinational firm. "Sorry, work stuff takes priority," he muttered, pocketing the phone before continuing. "We need more time. Look, we are designing something here that has never existed before in digital form, and there are many issues we need to resolve before it is ready. We need to figure out how to ensure the intellectual property is protected vis-à-vis cloud-based deployment. We need to establish that sensitive information can be properly encrypted before being transmitted. We need to pay attention to Canadian privacy regulations such as PIPEDA.[2] We need to continue developing the system with large-volume enterprise users in mind so that we can scale it later on."

Corscadden stopped for a breath, then continued. "Ideally, I'd want another three months to iron out all the bugs. However, if everything works out as planned with our developers, and the clients are able to provide us with the specifications on time, I'm optimistic that we can cut this down by a few weeks."

Jen Hosafros, Graphic Designer, spoke up: "Let's not forget, each client will want something different in terms of the look and feel of their menus, although we might be able to accelerate the design process by anticipating who our future clients will be. Also, we still need to agree on what our application icon should look like. If you guys want something more than a boring fork and spoon, I will need some time to come up with something that better conveys what our brand stands for."

"Assuming we know what our brand stands for," said Hutcherson, smiling as he scanned the faces of his team and sat down.

The team members felt a keen sense of mounting excitement as they saw that their efforts during the first 100 days had started to pay off. Still, many issues had not been addressed. For example, with the exception of Hutcherson, everyone on the team had full-time jobs. In addition, as Hutcherson had reminded everyone in a recent email, "We haven't raised any seed money yet, so now we are officially an unfunded startup."

---

[1] Pronounced "binge".

[2] Personal Information Protection and Electronic Documents Act *(PIPEDA). "Organizations covered by the Act must obtain an individual's consent when they collect, use or disclose the individual's personal information." Office of the Privacy Commissioner of Canada, www.priv.gc.ca/ information/guide_e.cfm, accessed September 11, 2010.*

Exhibit 1

Binnj LiveMenu™

(Source: Courtesy of Clay Hutcherson, Binnj.)

Without warning, a loud CRACK rang out, followed by a series of rapid gunshots. The room was suddenly pitched into complete darkness.

The Apple iPad Revolution

Eight months earlier, on January 27, 2010, Hutcherson had sat at the London airport waiting for a flight. He stared at his notebook computer, watching Apple CEO Steve Jobs unveil the company's latest device, the iPad. Hutcherson was spellbound as he watched Jobs, reclining in his leather chair, using the iPad to casually scroll through the *New York Times* with light finger swipes.

Hutcherson had seen many technology product announcements over the years, but he knew instinctively that this device was going to change things on a profound scale. He believed that the iPad was going to fundamentally change electronic content consumption forever with its light form factor, full-screen touch-based navigation system, wi-fi and 3G network connectivity, popular productivity and lifestyle applications, access to hundreds of thousands of additional applications from the iTunes App Store, and stable and highly popular software development kit. Over the next few weeks, industry pundits began to validate Hutcherson's initial suspicions. There was definitely an opportunity here. If only Hutcherson could figure out what it was.

Clay Hutcherson is the founder and CEO/President of Binnj. Prior to forming Binnj, Clay was a management consultant at Intellectual Ventures providing business, organizational and technical consulting to senior leadership in the Intellectual Property Licensing business unit. The patent and technology areas included digital imaging, mobile payments and global financial services. Intellectual Ventures is based in Seattle, WA, USA and is a world leader in IP and patent aggregation that manages a US $5B invention-capital fund. Clay was the SVP, CIO and member of the CEO's executive turnaround team at Interstate Brands in Kansas City, Kansas. His team developed and launched a modern technology roadmap that aligned with the strategic business plan contributing to successfully securing $400MM of needed financing, the emergence from Chapter 11 and the preservation of 29,000 US jobs. His teams stabilized the core SAP ERP implementation that, for a second time, threatened the existence of the organization while rescuing an SAP HR implementation for the companies $1B+ payroll. Interstate Brands owns iconic US brands such as Wonder, Hostess, Dolly Madison and Drakes. As CTO, Clay was a founding member of Filogix, (formerly Centric Systems) now acquired by Davis & Henderson, a TSX company. Filogix pioneered collaborative technology platforms for intermediary delivery of financial services products, including the first fully web-based real estate information portal in Canada. Today, this award winning Canadian technology originates in excess of 50 per cent of new consumer real estate credit products. Clay resides in London and holds an MBA from the Richard Ivey School of Business at the University of Western Ontario, Canada.

Nancy Philip is a Chartered Accountant and the CFO and COO of Binnj. Nancy was the Director of HR and CFO of CIRA in Ottawa, Ontario. Before joining CIRA, Nancy was Director of Finance at the Royal Canadian Mint for over five years. She was responsible for the day-to-day operations of the finance group as well as tax and statutory audits. Nancy previously held the position of Director of Finance with Spirent Communications, and with Doyle Salewski Inc. and a series of increasingly senior roles at ASI, Ameridata and Cognos. Nancy holds a Bachelor of Commerce degree from Carleton University and an MBA from the University of Western Ontario. She belongs to both the Ontario and Canadian Institutes of Chartered Accountants. Nancy resides in Ottawa.

Scott Corscadden is the CIO at Binnj. Prior to joining Binnj, he was the Director of Engineering at Joyent, helping the cloud-computing pioneer transform their highly successful public cloud software into private cloud turnkey solutions for enterprise clients. A former Director of Engineering for Comcast (in their wholly-owned TVWorks embedded software firm), as well as the CTO for Hostess Brands in Kansas City, Scott has spent his entire career in cutting edge technology and software development practices. He also led the Internet Application Group for FiLogix where he developed scalable mission-critical enterprise web applications for Canada's top banking institutions; many of which are still running today nearly 10 years later. Scott holds an honours B.E.Sc. from UWO in London, Ontario. Scott resides in London, Ontario with his wife and three children.

James Hayes is the Director, Sales and Marketing and leads the sales effort at Binnj. James has 15 years of enterprise account management and sales experience. Prior to joining Binnj James pioneered the successful Canadian Poker Exposition. The CPE is Canada's only poker centric consumer show for global leaders in the gaming industry. Prior to the CPE, James was a consultant to Tribute Resources Inc. a leading independent, market-based energy provider in Ontario. James worked with the team that developed a $35 million Tipperary Natural Gas storage project. The Tipperary storage pool is one of the first non-utility competitive storage facilities to be connected to the Union Gas lateral transmission system. James previously owned a regional printing operation in southern Ontario that he grew to be the largest agricultural sign supplier in Canada. He managed national accounts such as Monsanto, Pioneer Seeds, Syngenta, Pride Seeds and Dow Agro Sciences. James holds an MBA from the Richard Ivey School of Business at The University of Western Ontario. James resides in London, Ontario.

Jen Hosafros is Creative and User Experience Lead for Binnj. Jen is a freelance graphic design consultant and holds a provisional RGD. Jen has 10 years of digital creative experience and holds a BFA in visual arts and graphic design from Lake Superior State University in Michigan. Jen resides in London, Ontario.

Exhibit 2

Management Team

(Source: Courtesy of Clay Hutcherson, Binnj.)

Michael Kernahan is Senior Engineer at Binnj. He holds a Computer Engineering degree from the University of Alberta. Michael was previously an Engineering Manager at Comcast's TVWorks division. TVWorks developed set-top box and video distribution platforms for millions of consumers across North America. As a co-founder of Redshirt Labs, an indie mobile software company, Michael has experience designing, developing and releasing iPhone apps. Prior to management, Michael worked as a Software Developer at both TVWorks and the National Research Council (NRC) of Canada. The NRC is the government of Canada's premier organization for research and development, comprised of over 20 institutes and national programs. Michael resides just outside of London, Ontario.

Sam Maloney is Lead Software Engineer at Binnj. Sam has decades of experience in server-based web application technologies with a specialty in open source technologies and enterprise Java architectures. Sam is well known as a computer engineer that solves complex problems often abandon by others. Sam resides in London, Ontario.

Exhibit 2

Management Team (continued)

"As I casted about for a new venture, it became clear to me that the iPad would become an 'end point' for delivering content to each person," mused Hutcherson. "I saw four options: I could create content, purchase content, license content, or steal content. Regardless, I knew it would be about monetizing otherwise undervalued content." For weeks, he brainstormed situations in which people (including himself) consumed content frequently, and where there was an economic transaction involved. Ideas buzzed in the back of his mind, but nothing gelled.

A few weeks later, as Hutcherson was driving his son to a hockey practice, he began thinking about the ways that his kids accessed and consumed content. He later described his thinking: "My son was browsing his iPhone for a new motocross helmet for the upcoming race season. Here was a 12 year old, shopping in the car, wirelessly, with his finger. "Dad that one! Look at it. It's awesome! Look at the Monster logo on the back . . ." Coincidentally, I happened to be thinking about where to go out for dinner that evening. In an instant, a fresh idea struck: an iPad-based real-time electronic restaurant menu platform."

It had the basic elements Hutcherson had been searching for—a context where content was consumed frequently, and where an economic transaction was involved. Hutcherson spent the next six weeks analyzing the core idea, considering how it might work, and quite literally trying to "talk himself out of" the idea.

Lunch with Hosafros

On April 3, 2010, the iPad was finally released for sale in the United States, and Hutcherson decided it was time to get feedback about his idea from a few key people. He saw the iPad as a kind of "blank canvas," and so he reasoned, who better to "paint a picture" than an artist? He had previously worked with Jen Hosafros, a talented graphic designer, and so arranged to meet her for a lunch discussion at a local Mexican restaurant.

After the usual informal small talk, Hutcherson got down to business. "Jen, take a look at your menu. Is there anything wrong with it?" They were sitting beside the buffet table and it was 1 p.m. in the afternoon.

Hosafros hesitantly picked up the laminated menu and unfolded it. A moment of silence passed as she scanned the menu. "You know, it's interesting . . . even though I design restaurant menus, as a patron I don't really stop to think much about them from a design point of view. Maybe it's because I'm too hungry," she laughed.

Hutcherson was enthused: "Exactly my point! Restaurant menus haven't changed since their earliest handwritten days, and no one ever really stops to think about them. From breakfast diners, to high-end Michelin-starred restaurants, to hundred-location chains . . . everyone uses the same kind of traditional, printed, boring menus. And yet, the menu is the single most important selling opportunity for a restaurant. Why don't we pay more attention to it?"

Intrigued by Hutcherson's passionate proclamation, Hosafros was now studying her menu with a designer's eye. "The colours on this one have faded. And the graphics and typography could use some freshening. This page seems unbalanced—the box here could be a bit smaller. Pretty typical of restaurant menus actually." She continued paging through the menu. "And it would be nice to see some pictures of the food. I've never eaten here."

Hutcherson jumped in: "OK, so imagine that we can tear up this menu and start again from scratch. Imagine if we never knew that printed menus even existed, and now we have this iPad device." Hosafros had heard of the iPad, but she did not know much about it. Hutcherson spent a few minutes describing the basic iPad concept, and then continued: "Now, imagine having this iPad, this digital blank canvas with no rules or limitations. What would it be like to create a new kind of restaurant menu on this new blank canvas? Is it the kind of project you'd like to work on?"

Hosafros's mind was working. "So . . . rich colourful images, hyper-linked pages, video, maybe audio, all kinds of engaging content . . ." She had been staring at her paper menu, but finally looked up at Hutcherson. "Absolutely. I think any creative type would be thrilled to work on such a blue sky project," said Hosafros. Then, more cautiously, "But you know, I'm really just a graphic designer. I don't know anything about writing software."

Hutcherson reassured Hosafros: "Not a problem! In fact, I believe it's an opportunity. This project needs an artist who won't be constrained by preconceived notions about what the technology allows or doesn't allow. Too many projects involving technology become engineering-centric. This one must become design-centric."

"In that case, I'd love to help out," replied Hosafros enthusiastically. "When do we start?"

Assembling the Team

Returning to his Richmond Street office after lunch, Hutcherson scanned his email inbox and saw that Hosafros had already sent a follow up thank you note from her iPhone. He also had three new messages, each containing the word "Contract" in the subject line. Hutcherson had recently completed some major long-term consulting projects, one as the turnaround chief information officer (CIO) at a large U.S. bakery conglomerate, and another as a technology and market advisor for a global intellectual property bank. As soon as he left these projects, new consulting opportunities had begun to roll in, but Hutcherson found himself far more curious about the implications of this disruptive technology and the prospects of building a new company.

He deferred the emails, and instead composed three new messages.

> "Nancy, got an idea. Please let me know when you have time to chat."
> "James, let's meet asap—I have an idea I would like to bounce off you."
> "Scott, new tech idea brewing. When are you around London again?"

Skype Call with Philip

Late that night, as Hutcherson worked in his home office, a soft "ding-ding" came from his computer speakers and a message box indicated an incoming Skype call from Nancy Philip. Philip was a Chartered Accountant, a senior executive with an Ottawa-based technology company, and a former MBA classmate. Hutcherson clicked on the Skype icon and picked up the headphones.

"Hey Nancy," he said, "working late I see?"

"Yes actually, I just got home," she replied. "I saw your email and thought I'd give you a try. I'm surprised you're still up—it's after midnight. What's up?"

"What do you know about the Apple iPad?" Hutcherson briefly outlined his idea for recreating the restaurant menu experience, and then ended with a question. "What do you think?"

"Wow, interesting," offered Philip. "Sounds like it's right up your alley. But why would a restaurant want to switch from a traditional menu? Cost savings? How much do restaurants spend on printing menus now—and aren't iPads quite expensive?"

Hutcherson replied, "Great questions! I've done some initial research and talked with a restaurant industry contact who has enlightened me with a few facts. Printed menus are not cheap—a typical restaurant location spends about $12,500 per year to print a batch of menus, so a chain might spend several hundred thousand per year.

"But the cost of printed menus pales in comparison to the effects of making an error because of a bad assumption or an incorrect prediction, and you wouldn't believe the stilted processes that restaurant chains must go through to update their menus. Head office execs might meet once or twice a year to discuss the food lineup, develop new recipes and marketing materials, and arrange for menus to be printed, bound and distributed. They put a huge amount of effort into making sense of past trends, and anticipating what customers might want in the future. What raw materials will be available? How much will costs fluctuate? Which brands of wines and beers should be stocked? What's going to happen to labour costs? What about special promotions? The list of variables goes on and on, and everyone feels nervous. Because once the menu is printed, the restaurant is locked into fixed prices for extended periods of time. They have one shot at getting it right. Decisions often come down to educated guesses and gut feels, with little hard data to back them up."

Philip cut in. "OK, I think I'm getting it. An electronic menu will give the chain tighter control over their menu. And if changes can be made and updated at any time, costly mistakes can be avoided. This would drive down risk." She seemed to be talking out loud, so Hutcherson let her continue. "Anything could be adjusted at any time. New items could be added. Old items removed. Ingredients changed." Philip stopped for a moment, then asked quietly, "Clay, dynamic pricing?"

Hutcherson smiled. Within minutes, Philip was indeed getting it. "Absolutely. With traditional menus, chains have no way to enable zone pricing, or to offer temporary features or discounts on an item to manage inventory levels, or to take advantage of variable pricing based on demand. Why not charge a dollar or two more for a shrimp appie or steak entrée on the weekends? This incremental revenue would go directly to the bottom line. And all of the consumer level data would be captured and used for future decision-making. Think labour scheduling. Inventory management. Multi-language support. My intention is not to tell a restaurant how to make food or how much to charge customers, that's their business. But I can imagine a platform—let's call it LiveMenu™—that will give them a way to experiment, to learn, and to increase their profitability."

Hutcherson paused again, and noticed a wall clock ticking in the next room. He finally broke the silence, "Nancy?"

"It's dazzling. I haven't heard of an idea like this in a very long time. It looks like you've got a startup on your hands!" declared Philip.

"Not sure about that yet," breathed Hutcherson, leaning back in his chair. "I've seen too many startups with wild ideas crash and burn. I'm thinking of treating this more like a science experiment. A 100-day, carefully planned, team-based science experiment."

"So you're not going to raise money now?" Philip asked.

"Not yet. First we need to find out if the idea has any legs." Philip noted Hutcherson's use of the word "we." He continued: "Everyone I've talked to loves the idea, but then no one I've talked to has any stake in it. We need to get a quick prototype in front of a real client to see whether we're on to something. We also need to do the heavy lifting to learn about the restaurant business, so we can temper large assumptions with real data."

Hutcherson rubbed his eyes and glanced at his computer clock. He had a conference call scheduled with his colleagues in the United Kingdom at 4 a.m., just a few hours away. If he wanted to seriously explore the LiveMenu™ idea, he would have to put all of his consulting work on hold for now. "I want to assemble a team to explore this idea, quietly, with the understanding that each of us is putting in nothing but our *extra* time. At the end of the 100 days, we can figure out if we have something, and whether or not it's worth pursuing."

"Nice. No sense taking unnecessary risk," agreed Philip. "Who do you have in mind for this?"

Hutcherson responded immediately: "I need you to join in, obviously. I need your rational yet creative mind. If this thing takes off, we're going to need someone who has not only top-flight financial management credentials, but also expert capacity to effectively manage and control this kind of organization. What do you say?"

"It's been a few years since I've worked on a science experiment," smiled Philip. "It sounds like fun!"

Drinks with Hayes

Early the next morning, Hutcherson received a text message from James Hayes. "Clay, I'll buy you a beer this afternoon at the usual spot, say 4 pm?" Hutcherson responded affirmatively. The "usual spot" was a steakhouse chain, and potential customer brand, just on the east side of Richmond Street.

Hutcherson and Hayes were classmates from their MBA days five years earlier, and they had not seen each other for several months. Hutcherson found Hayes already sitting at a table when he arrived. "I heard from our friends that you've been living on an airplane," laughed Hayes. "How do you like the consulting life?"

Hutcherson shook his head and grinned. "It's really great . . . for now. Most of it is interesting work. But it sure takes a toll physically, and on the family."

"You have better ideas than globetrotting and making a few hundred bucks an hour?" Hayes cut to the chase. From the urgency in Hutcherson's message, Hayes sensed, correctly, that this meeting was not just a social call. Besides, Hayes was in the midst of organizing Canada's only poker consumer show in Toronto, and he had at least 20 different things to do.

"I do," said Hutcherson. "It's not yet a fully-formed idea—more the beginning of an idea. But as far as I can tell, and at the scale I am thinking, no one has jumped on it yet. It's about the next iteration of the restaurant menu." At that moment, a waiter arrived and handed them menus. Both men ordered a beer, and Hutcherson continued: "Look, you know as well as anyone how rapidly the online world has developed. The restaurant industry is no different. The Internet is loaded with restaurant advertisements and promotional campaigns. Online takeout and delivery systems have become commonplace. People use the Web to read and write independent restaurant reviews. Diners use smart phone apps to make reservations and upload restaurant-specific photos."

Hayes nodded as he listened, then offered: "Absolutely. Technology has had a huge impact on the restaurant industry, and really the entire entertainment sector. From a marketing perspective, the effectiveness of broadcast media—radio, television, newspapers, billboards and the like—is rapidly declining. This trend is driving advertisers away from broadcasting, and toward "narrowcasting"—focusing unique messages with ever-increasing precision and sophistication."

"Right, exactly," acknowledged Hutcherson. "James, you're a marketing guy. Would you agree that organizations generally prefer to have one-to-one relationships with their customers whenever possible?"

"Theoretically speaking, sure, absolutely," agreed Hayes. "Closer relationships allow organizations to serve their customers in the best possible ways, which in turn drives organizational value," Hayes stopped. "Clay, what does all this have to do with restaurant menus?"

"SoloCasting™," Hutcherson responded. He continued: "Imagine if restaurant owners had complete control to customize their restaurant menu? Imagine if a patron could be presented with up-selling and cross-selling recommendations, wine pairings, and specific promotions on a location-by-location basis, or by time of day? Imagine if a negative dining experience could be corrected as soon as it occurred? Imagine if a menu was instantly presented in a patron's first language? Imagine if a customer could pay when they wanted, rather than having to wait for the server?"

Hayes listened in fascination as Hutcherson went on to describe the LiveMenu™ idea. In less than two minutes, he was sold. "That, my friend, is one very cool idea." Hayes started to sip his beer as he collected his thoughts. The bar was filling up with patrons who had just finished work. "What about the cost of the iPad? Won't that be a sticking point for restaurant owners?"

Hutcherson replied: "Good question and I don't know. Depending on configuration options, an iPad cost $600 to $800, and we know that Apple doesn't do volume discounts. But we also know that the cost of the Apple iPhone has steadily dropped since its introduction, so we can probably anticipate something similar for the iPad. Worst case, we could simply rent the iPad hardware to restaurants for a dollar or two a day per device if necessary. Look, I don't have all the answers, but I don't believe the cost of the hardware needs to be a barrier.

"I could see this as a complete sales tool, just like the point-of-sale systems that so many other retailers are moving towards," said Hayes, then he paused. "To be honest though, I really don't know much about the restaurant industry, or even who the major players are."

Hutcherson chuckled: "Neither do I! But maybe that's not a bad thing. Maybe our lack of industry knowledge could actually be a kind of strength for us, because we won't be tied to traditional ideas? Kind of like, "we won't know what we can't do," if you know what I mean? Lack of knowledge is a great starting point for asking "stupid questions" and challenging conditioned behavior. Besides, as restaurant customers ourselves, we're ultimately the users. We understand the process implicitly."

"Do you have anyone looking at the sales side?" asked Hayes.

"That's why we're having this beer!" Hutcherson smiled at Hayes, "Are you up for some fun?"

Hayes smiled back. He looked at his BlackBerry and noticed that another dozen people had emailed him about the poker expo. Now instead of 20 items, he had 30 things to do. "My poker expo is next week," said Hayes. "I really can't commit to anything until a week after it's over. If the idea is still alive, can we talk after that?"

"Sure," said Hutcherson. "I am still in the early stages, but I want to get some forward momentum happening asap." Hutcherson finished his drink and set down the glass. "This round's on me."

Coffee with Corscadden

The next day, Hutcherson sat at a trendy coffee shop, playing with his new toy. iPads were not yet available for sale in Canada, but an American friend had special-ordered two of the devices, and Hutcherson had just returned from a quick drive over the border to pick them up. He was excited to show off the device to Scott Corscadden, a crackerjack software engineer with whom Hutcherson had worked on several past projects. When he saw Corscadden enter the coffee shop a few minutes later, Hutcherson slipped the iPad into his briefcase, and joined Corscadden in the lineup.

As the two shook hands, Hutcherson asked, "So Scott, I hear you're working in Vegas these days?"

"That's right," replied Corscadden, "though most of my time seems to be spent in the air, or stuck in an office!" The two chatted collegially about work and family. As they sat down, Corscadden got right to the point. "Tell me about the project."

Hutcherson quickly explained his LiveMenu™ ideas in terms of the business strategy and technology architecture, while Corscadden began sketching out flow diagrams on a napkin. Thirty minutes and three napkins later, Corscadden was sold on the concept. Suddenly Hutcherson pulled out the iPad.

"You dog!" exclaimed Corscadden. "How did you score one of these so quickly?"

Hutcherson smiled mysteriously, then turned serious: "Look, Scott, you know the drill. We need to develop this app, with supporting back-end enterprise infrastructure, very quickly. I'm developing a 100-day plan to prove or disprove this concept. At the end of that time, my intention is that we either walk away from this, or take a live, feasible business idea to the next level. Think you can assemble a part-time, unpaid development team?"

Corscadden was only half listening. As he scrolled around on the iPad, his mind was moving quickly. Hutcherson added, "By the way, I've got another one of those for you out in the car, if you're interested in burning a little weekend time."

Corscadden looked up. Hutcherson had his full attention. Corscadden nodded: "I'm ready. And I know two guys who will be perfect for this project. Sam Maloney is an expert at developing server-based web applications using open source technology, and Michael Kernahan is a gifted application developer. Both have developed successful iPhone apps in the past. They also have their own talent networks, so we'll be able to quickly grow the technology team if and when we need to."

Hutcherson grinned: "Perfect! I want to set this up so that each person on the team has complementary tasks. No one getting in anyone else's way. Management will set the direction and manage the various projects. Design will establish the desired look and feel of the user interface. Your tech team will translate the requirements into specific tasks for application development. Sales and marketing will test market assumptions and provide regular status updates as it interacts with potential clients."

Corscadden nodded once, and Hutcherson continued. "Of course, information technology will be instrumental to building the front-end interface, as well as the back-end database and infrastructure, for the LiveMenu™ product. How would you see this rolling out?"

"Let me guess," Corscadden replied, "we have no money yet, right? And you want a product with pretty much full functionality in 100 days . . .". Hutcherson just nodded. Corscadden continued: "OK. Well one thing is for sure—the waterfall method is out. Taking the time to map out all the detailed requirements in advance, around hardware, software, data structures, process flows, documentation and so on, will not allow us to get to the goal line in 100 days. Just assembling a complete set of customer requirements for an enterprise-class project like this would take months, and would have to happen before a single line of code was written. And I wonder, will customers even understand or be able to articulate what their 'requirements' are, for a disruptive product like LiveMenu™? The traditional approach would take 18 months, minimum, and then we'd probably just be in beta testing."

"Agreed," interjected Hutcherson.

Corscadden continued: "This project clearly calls for an agile development approach. Rather than spending a lot of time planning, we will jump directly to doing. We are talking about changing things and there is very little available in terms of a roadmap—I mean, the device has not even started shipping in Canada yet! The tech team will start with your initial ideas and assumptions, and we will immediately begin writing code. We will make a huge number of mistakes because we don't have a very accurate idea about the requirements. However, while my tech team is developing code, your management team can spend time learning about the industry and speaking with potential customers. As the project progresses, we will frequently sit down together. You will feed us with new information, and we will develop and build new solutions."

"Excellent, that is exactly how I see this happening," responded Hutcherson. "Specific thoughts about the technology platform?"

Corscadden replied: "It will probably make most sense for us to build on Apple's latest iOS 3.2 mobile operating system and Core Data persistence layer, a distributed SQL store called sqlite, and a cloud-based deployment model. Apple's own apps are built using these same technologies. This would keep everything maximally scalable and on-demand. As client specifications evolve, this kind of architecture will allow us to reconfigure and propagate LiveMenu™ in near real-time."

Hutcherson asked, "What do you think of Apple's latest developers tools and software development kit?"

Corscadden responded: "Apple's tools and SDK are pretty much bulletproof. They provide ready-to-use templates and code snippets—for example, related to networking, navigation, image management, and so on—that we can quickly customize and integrate. It's like building a complex art sculpture, where many of the parts are already pre-fabricated. Saves a ton of time, yet the result is still a masterpiece. And because the SDK is openly available to anyone who might want to create an app, it offers a brilliant reversal of Microsoft's closed, proprietary software development model."

"And changes in look, feel and function can be made easily?" asked Hutcherson.

Corscadden answered: "Absolutely. These software tools enable rapid creation, and rapid re-creation. To stick with the artwork analogy, instead of trying to change a sculpture that has been meticulously carved from a large chunk of stone, these software tools let us develop more of a 'Lego block' sculpture that can be easily reconfigured by adding, moving, or deleting blocks."

Hutcherson responded, "Sounds perfect for the front-end work. What about the back end? I'd like us to stay as technology-agnostic as possible."

Corscadden replied: "I agree one hundred percent. The cloud technologies will be completely hardware independent, and will run on any Linux/Unix derivative you can expect to find from cloud service vendors today. This will allow us to easily expand into other front-end platforms in the future, such as Android or RIM, as these platforms mature to the level we currently see in the iOS packages. We will stay prepared for sudden shifts in-flight. We can have a top-notch development server up and running on one of these turnkey platforms, overnight, for a couple of hundred dollars a month, and probably even less than that."

Hutcherson said: "Excellent—we are talking the same language. Now, as we develop the product itself, we must be sure to create an effective, collaborative, virtual working environment for the whole team. Everyone will be working from different places and at different times of day. We must avoid lengthy planning sessions and analysis, and instead focus pro-actively, on communication and output. No one should ever ask, "What's next?" Their task pipelines must always be full. Consistent and transparent communication tools will be essential to driving this project forward. Any thoughts?"

"I'm with you," nodded Corscadden. "We'll rely heavily on the agile 'scrum' process, so that as the project advances and requirements emerge, we can quickly respond to new features and changes as requested by all the different stakeholders."

Corscadden pulled out a fresh napkin, wrote the words "Users, Us, Customers," and began drawing boxes and lines (see Exhibit 3). "The product owner receives and prioritizes requests, and creates a Product Backlog. On a regular basis, say weekly, the backlog is reviewed and prioritized." Here Corscadden jotted the title "Weekly Sprint Backlog." As the development team comes to terms with each feature requested, they will plan and

---

Exhibit 3

Corscadden's Agile Development
Process Drawing

(Source: Company Records.)

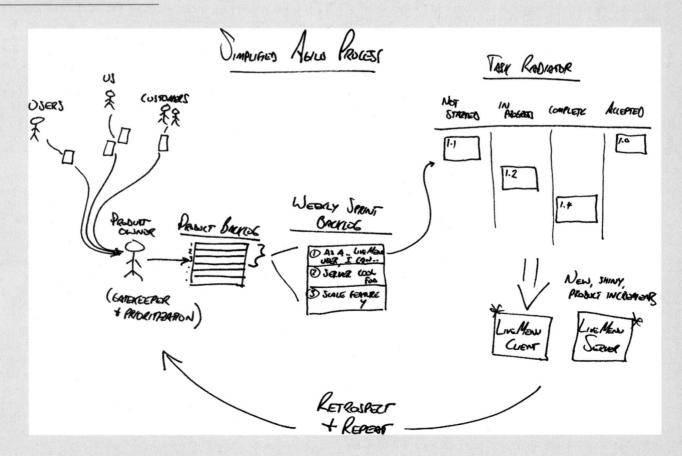

define the specific tasks required to deliver it." He paused to write down the term "Task Radiator." "By tracking our progress in completing individual tasks, we can monitor our overall progress. At the end of each sprint cycle, we have the next increment of the product, complete with new features that have been fully coded, tested, and incremented." Corscadden added the label "Retrospect and Repeat" to his diagram. "Finally, we return our attention to the backlog, which has in the meantime filled up again, and the process repeats."

"Superb. What if we need an immediate change in the middle of a sprint cycle?" asked Hutcherson.

Corscadden replied: "We can always respond to urgent needs, it will just require us to pause our sprint. We don't need to become slaves to any given development methodology. In general though, I think the agile approach should work nicely for this project."

"Agreed, it's the right process. What about specific software tools to help us keep ourselves organized?" asked Hutcherson.

Corscadden said: "We both know there are a ton of great open source apps available, such as Basecamp for overall project scheduling and task management, Redmine for feature, development tasks and bug tracking, SubVersioN for code management and DropBox for distributed file sharing. And of course, Skype is perfect for teleconferencing and videoconferencing. High volume enterprise versions are available if necessary (see Exhibit 4), but the basic versions should be robust for our needs

initially, and they are free. They will allow us to keep everyone connected, collaborating, and on track. We will centralize, virtually. Completely flexible, and more or less "in control" around the clock."

Hutcherson responded: "Beautiful. The main thing is that we select simple and effective tools, provide some basic training, and get everyone up and running immediately. We can't let those silly day jobs get in the way! We've got to break the three-horned dilemma of time, cost and scope on this one. To be successful, we've got to deliver all three."

Corscadden nodded, adding, "You know, we can have these tools up and running—from a development standpoint—immediately. It's all there and ready to go. Time, cost, scope, quality. We can do this."

Hutcherson replied: "I love it. Of course, putting the tools in place is only half the equation. We've got to make sure the team commits to using them. Built-in email notifications and reminders from Basecamp should help to drive everyone to constantly and meticulously review the evolving project plan. We don't have the luxury of working in the same building, at the same time. This will be the only way to create transparency, efficiency, and effectiveness."

"Sam and Michael already understand this. And I have a feeling they'll be ready to jump on this immediately." Corscadden stopped and looked at Hutcherson. "Of course, they're going to want a piece of this if it succeeds . . ."

Name	Description	How BINNJ Uses It
Apache SubVersioN	Revision control system allowing users to maintain current and historical versions of files such as source code, web pages and documentation 100% Open source software	Code repository and versioning system
Basecamp	Web-based project management tool and collaboration tool. Features include: wiki-style web-based text documents; to-do lists; milestone management; file-sharing; time tracking; messaging and alert system; calendaring	Track progress on the 100-day plan Post to-do lists for each function
DropBox	Uses cloud computing to enable online storing and sharing of files with collaborators Uses cross-platform P2P file synchronization iPhone/iPad integration for mobile document sharing, updates Web-based file hosting interface for browsers	Share large files that cannot be emailed or that need comments from various parties Central repository for key data Simple file browser interface
Redmine	Open source, web-based software project management and bug-tracking program Visual tools includes Calendar and Gantt chart functions Supports multiple projects and multi-stakeholders	Track progress on software development Team members post suggestions and bug fixes Tracks YTT lifecycle (yesterday, today, tomorrow)
Skype	Allows users to make voice calls over the Internet Free calls between Skype users, small fee for calls to landline telephones and mobile phones Supports instant messaging, file transfer and videoconferencing Operates without servers, utilizing background processing on computers running Skype software	Remote calling between management and technology team members Zero cost

Exhibit 4

Collaborative Tools

"Yeah, we'll have to write some equity checks eventually," Hutcherson waved a hand in the air. "But let's not get ahead of ourselves. Remember, right now it's just a quiet little science experiment. Let's set up a meeting for next week." Hutcherson made a mental note to contact his friend at the Ad Vendors office, to borrow a conference room for the first meeting.

Ad Vendors Boardroom with the Team

The lights snapped back on, and the Binnj team stared around the room, all eyes wide. The clap of thunder and torrent of gunshot-like hail had taken everyone by surprise. It was August 2, 2010, and the team was deeply engrossed in their weekly Jam session discussion.

Hayes restarted the conversation by describing his analysis of the restaurant market. "A few restaurant groups—let's call them Enterprise Restaurant Groups or ERGs—control the majority of the restaurant chain market. Each group has multiple locations ranging from a dozen to hundreds. There are 40 ERGs in Canada controlling 60 brands and 2,700 restaurants. In the U.S., there are 137 ERGs with about 37,000 locations. These groups are especially concerned with how to keep their offering consistent, while allowing for local variation. Inventory control is also key—managing your stock room, highlighting dishes to utilize excess ingredients, and so on. Ultimately, headquarters is looking to maintain visibility and control across its dispersed operations. Right now, with paper menus, there is little data, less control, and no real-time visibility. They don't know what they've sold until they look at the receipts, and they certainly don't know what they could have sold."

Hutcherson interjected, "So the ERGs are pivotal."

Hayes nodded: "Yes. Landing a single ERG could generate massive sales. The good news is that we've now talked to three of them, and all three seem enthusiastic about LiveMenu™. The bad news is that the ERGs tend to be rather large and bureaucratic, so it can be difficult to get face-to-face with the right person. Fortunately, there are also many smaller players—we'll call them Small & Medium Enterprise Restaurant Groups or SMERGs. There are about 1,000 SMERGs in Canada and each of these groups has between one and twelve restaurants. Because SMERGs are typically run by owner-operators, they might be a little more open to trying new ideas, especially if they can get a revenue boost. Control isn't that much of an issue for SMERGs, as the owners tend to spend time visiting their restaurants on a weekly basis."

Philip asked, "How much can we charge for LiveMenu™?"

"We don't really know," replied Hayes. "Actually, none of the three ERGs we've talked to so far have even asked us the price, despite the fact that after the product demos, all three have told us they want it!"

"What about competitors? Who could potentially beat us up?" asked Philip.

Hayes replied:"There are some major software players operating in the US restaurant space. "These guys provide a variety of reservation and social media ranking services, and earn fees from software rentals and diner placements. Incidentally, one of them IPO'd just over a year ago, and now has a market cap of $1.2 billion."

"But no one is focusing on the menu and operations, so far?" asked Philip.

Hayes paused thoughtfully: "These competitors might have the ability to quickly design something to digitize the menu. They already provide performance metrics so some bright manager or analyst might decide to extend their reach to the menu. But thus far, I have not found anything to suggest that anyone is seeking to re-design the menu experience at an enterprise scale.

"The initial search sounds very encouraging," added Corscadden. "There could be others in stealth mode, though. We won't really know for a few months."

Hayes turned to Corscadden. "Scott, I noticed a glitch on the first screen of the latest release. When will it be fixed?"

Corscadden asked: "Have you noted it in Redmine? Remember, Redmine shows all planned engineering activities for the next month. If there are any last minute priorities, or if you need us to reorder the list of projects, just let us know. Keep in mind though that we are trying to juggle several priorities at once so something moving up the list, will have to move something else down the list."

"So are you saying that the final application will be completed in a month?" asked Hayes hopefully. "We really have to get our sales engine going ..."

Corscadden interrupted: "Sorry, James, I think you're misunderstanding something. Rather than pushing towards a single, final, ideal version of the app, we're trying to focus our primary efforts on polishing up sections that can be demonstrated to clients. And we're trying to improve the product iteratively, as we go, one sprint at a time. When we decide to go live, we will have a refined product improvement process already underway. Of course . . . that's assuming we decide to make this science experiment into a business."

Hutcherson sat in the corner, staring at the now historical 100-day plan, lost in thought (see Exhibit 5).

Hayes responded, "I understand that we've been using an iterative development approach up to this point. But the market is heating up. It's time we finally 'give birth' and start selling this thing!"

All eyes turned to Hutcherson, who was now looking out a window. The hail had turned to rain, and a cool breeze was now circulating through the room. Hutcherson remained silent, and Philip spoke up. "James, we're all looking forward to arriving at Coors Light Island." This was the Binnj team's term for a saleable, deliverable software version that included all the wild ideas they had come up with. "But if we rush this, we'll blow it."

"And if we don't, someone else will get there first!" Hayes' growled. "We've already seen potential competitors surfacing. We are going to lose this market if we do not get out there, now."

Corscadden countered: "But we know the competitors you are talking about are not really competitors to us. They are single location restaurants that have attempted to digitize their menu. In most cases they are simply presenting a PDF image of a menu. They're not offering the same level of functionality or enterprise scale that we're talking about.

"Even so, they could be reaching out to the chains," said Hosafros. "It's a very small market. Maybe we should try sending out a two-page teaser brochure ourselves?" (See Exhibit 6 on page 578 for a preliminary brochure.)

binnj

		29-Mar	05-Apr	12-Apr	19-Apr	26-Apr	03-May	10-May	17-May	24-May	31-May	07-Jun	14-Jun	21-Jun	28-Jun	05-Jul	07-Jul	12-Jul
										56								
PLAN		Day 0				Day 30					Day 60			Day 90		Day 100		
	100 Day Goal					28-Apr					28-May			27-Jun		07-Jul		
	Funding Secured																	
	Contract, Major Chain (30+)					s												

Business

	FRD/SRD for POC																	
	Product Plan																	
	Prodcut RoadMap				v2.0													
	Market Anlaysis/Segmentation																	
	Competitor Analysis																	
	Technology Competitor																	
	Revenue / Cost Proforma																	
	Sales Plan			Pilot	Pilot				Stage 2									
	Legal Structure																	
	Draft Funding Deck																	
	Pilot Defined and Plan																	
	Draft Business Plan										Day 50 (first cut of number) << May 10 to PV							
	Review Plan																	
	Leadership Grant Submiission																	

Strategic Plan

	Strategic Focus					Strategic Plan Final												
	Business Plan Final																	
	Funding Deck Final																	
	Revenue/Financial Final																	
	Funding Calls										Funding Activities							
	Funding Pitch																	

Creative

	Logo/Brand	done																
	Cards		done															
	Website		in process		v1.0		v2.0											
	UI Graphics			McGinnis														
						BatonRouge												
								Moxies / Crabby Joes										
	Marketing Collateral																	

Pilot

McGinnis Landing

Meet																		
	Cold Call																	
1	Initial Contact																	
	Create UI Wireframe																	
2	Show and Tell																	
	Scorecard established																	
	binnj CRP																	
3	Pilot Table Team																	
4	Pilot - 1 week / 1 table																	
5	Scorecard results reviewed																	
	Changes / MODs / Roadmap																	
6	All Table Rollout																	

Moxies / Crabby Joes

	Cold Call																	
1	Initial Contact																	
	Create UI Wireframe																	
2	Show and Tell																	
	Scorecard established																	
	binnj CRP																	
3	Pilot Table Team																	
4	Pilot - 1 week / 1 table																	
5	Scorecard results reviewed																	
	Changes / MODs / Roadmap																	
6	All Table Rollout																	

PickelBarrel / Baton Rouge

	Cold Call																	
1	Initial Contact					27-Apr												
	Create UI Wireframe																	
2	Show and Tell																	
	Scorecard established																	
	binnj CRP																	
3	Pilot Table Team																	
4	Pilot - 1 week / 1 table																	
5	Scorecard results reviewed																	
	Changes / MODs / Roadmap																	
6	All Table Rollout																	

Sales

	Web Site																	
	Collateral Material																	
	Sales Cycle Design.Define																	
	Pricing Model																	
	Sales Pitch Design/Final							Selling Begins										
	Sales Activities / Calls																	
	Demos																	
	LOI/Close																	

Development/Technology — PRODUCT BUILD ROADMAP

	Foundation																	
	Server																	
	Client													PILOT				
	UI Creative					McGinnis												
								BatonRouge										

Exhibit 5

100-Day Plan

(Source: Courtesy of Clay Hutcherson, Binnj.)

 introducing .... LiveMenu.

LiveMenu is an enterprise class iPad digital menu platform for the full service enterprise restaurant market, globally.

Enterprise Class Solution
iPad and the Cloud

LiveMenu transforms traditional printed, static restaurant menu content into rich, real-time digital experiences for the at-table restaurant customer. LiveMenu is designed to support strong branding, self managed and flexible configuration with extremely rapid deployment for enterprise implementations.

LiveMenu Cloud manages and provisions enterprise menu assets through a scalable, secure, digital media content platform.

Hi Fidelity iPad Experience

LiveMenu has delivered the future of at-table menu presentation through the emotional impact of rich, digital media and the interactive engagement of an elegant software experience.

With realtime content control and distribution, the application responds to complex market environments that support enterprise marketing and operational agility enhancing the customer relationship inside and outside of the store.

Localization support is integral. Unlimited languages are supported with "in-place" language flip with one user touch.

Robust Core Functions, Digital Benefits.

The MENU

A highly engaging at-table menu experience providing digital dynamic product presentation including consistent brand delivery and pricing responsiveness. Wait staff selling support through dynamic rules based logic driving the suggested sell, cross-sell, up-sell and promotion programs. Rich imaging, and delicate animation to tantalize the palette. Defined searches for dietary restrictions with ingredient and nutritional details disclosure. Fine grain user behavior metrics for product, customer and selling performance. LiveMenu takes fragmented clumsy operational processes and consolidates them within a consistent experience to enhance the sales and service results. Customer experience metrics become transparent and discoverable. Menus are dynamic, supporting all variable content, branding, layout, user experience optimization and high value product placements.

CUSTOMER SURVEY & CRM
Customer surveys every time, every customer, instant alerts, analytics

PARTNER INTEGRATION
Sponsorship, Co-Branding and Advertising relationships

Bill 90 Compliance
Nutritional and Ingredient disclosure supporting Bill 90 and Canada Health Standards

PAYMENT
at table cheque payment including VISA/MC/DEBIT/AMEX/PayPal

Localization
N number of languages are supported and distributed in realtime. User language transitions are instantaneous.

MENU-tainment
access to iPad applications, content managed web, new, information and fun games for the kids, teens and big kids!

My ORDER & POS Integration
one-touch order preparation with custom item requirements support. Leading POS integration / wait staff integration.

binnj confidential - INTERNAL USE ONLY

300-717 Richmond Street, London, Ontario, Canada   519.851.4103

green solutions

Exhibit 6

Livemenu™ Brochure

(Source: Courtesy of Clay Hutcherson, Binnj.)

Architecture and Technology Stack

CLIENT: Built on the iPhone 3.2 SDK, the client application uses Core Data to ensure uninterrupted operability should the local in-restaurant network become unavailable.

Store-and-forward algorithms ensure that data is sent to the server once connectivity returns. All design is assuming the smallest (16GB) wifi-only device will provide the full feature set.

Advanced iPad features are used (Core Animation), yet in a minimal simple way to ease the diner through the experience.

SERVER: Optimized for cloud computing, 100% open-source frameworks are used in the creation of a completely stateless server (<u>REST</u>) using Apache frameworks (<u>CXF</u>, Commons, Maven), standard mid-tier application servers (<u>Tomcat</u>, <u>Jetty</u>) and ANSI-92 SQL backing store databases (<u>PostgreSQL</u>, <u>MySql</u>) that vend menu versions and content to client application. Infinitely customizable menus are provisioned to large groups of clients or differentiated down to the level of an individual device.

All communication is over HTTPS and further authenticated by an asymmetric embedded encrypted key in the client executable. Usage data is collected throughout the application's time in the restaurant to provide unparalleled, real-time access to business data.

Menu prices, items, descriptions, layout, languages, are all configurable at a moment's notice via the web and are pushed to target devices or groups as often as required supporting corporate consistency and local market variations as authorized. Enterprise organizational roles drive field level change and audit.

BETA v1.0 Feature Set

LiveMenu **Client**	LiveMenu **Cloud**
branded livemenu application	web based menu content management
standard and dynamic menu layout	enterprise class cloud computing infrastructure
unlimited menus and menu items	existing store pos integration (option)
unlimited product item images	business continuity; works without network
unlimited pricing changes and updates	device and data security
unlimited languages	sales, menu item, promo analytics, realtime, web
unlimited promotions	sponsorship revenue participation
unlimited customer surveys with manager alerts	at table payment (transaction based)
dietary information tags	real-time survey analytics
realtime pairings and suggested selling	Bill 90 "Healthy Eating Act..." compliance
realtime or staged menu updates by store/region	GREEN solution eliminating print process
customer order compilation with preferences	
nutritional and ingredient information	
customer menu-tainment apps and internet access	

binnj confidential - INTERNAL USE ONLY
300-717 Richmond Street, London, Ontario, Canada   519.851.4103

green solutions

Exhibit 6

Livemenu™ Brochure (continued)

Philip added: "What if we do send out a brochure, and they call our bluff? If a client wants to test LiveMenu™ in a pilot location, we'd have to put them off. And that might open an even more dangerous door for new competitors. At this point, our three potential clients are expecting the pilots to run at the end of September.

Philip paused to take a breath. "That's two months from now. Can we wait until then to formally announce our product?"

Hayes sighed heavily. No one spoke for a full sixty seconds. The rain tapped steadily against the glass.

Corscadden spoke cautiously: "It may not be the best time to bring this up, but I heard a CBC news report a few days ago discussing Ontario Private Members Bill 90, "Healthy Decisions for Healthy Eating Act." If the bill is passed into law, restaurants will be required to provide nutritional information on all menu items. Apparently the restaurant association is freaking out. Of course, with LiveMenu™, a restaurant could easily make the necessary nutritional information available, without requiring them to print new, more cumbersome menus.

Hutcherson turned his gaze back to the window. It seemed clear to everyone else in the room that the science experiment was over, and that Binnj had become a real business that could potentially create real value. However, to Hutcherson it felt like they were flying in the dark. Binnj had no product, no revenue,

and no customers. No one was certain what features customers would need, which customers would sign on, or how much customers would be willing to pay for the service. No one knew whether there were other competitors operating in stealth mode.

Hutcherson wondered what activities the team should focus on to continue building their high tech startup, and in what sequence.

Student Assignment Questions

1. What key enablers have allowed Binnj to engage in this "science experiment"?
2. Have you ever worked on, or led, a virtual team? What tools did you rely on, and what problems did you experience?
3. Binnj seems to have embraced the "agile" development approach. In what circumstances might a firm choose to use the slower, more traditional "waterfall" approach to developing a new system?
4. Since the start of the Binnj science experiment, a plethora of new tablets have been announced (e.g., from companies such as Research In Motion, Samsung and Hewlett Packard). Has Binnj chosen the right platform?
5. How should Binnj establish a price for the LiveMenu service?
6. What other revenue opportunities might Binnj create through LiveMenu, in addition to the digital menu?

GLOSSARY

acceptance testing Conducting any tests required by the user. (p. 550)

accounting MIS An information system that provides aggregate information on accounts payable, accounts receivable, payroll, and many other applications. (p. 417)

ad hoc DSS A DSS concerned with situations or decisions that come up only a few times during the life of the organization. (p. 421)

alpha testing Testing an incomplete or early version of the system. (p. 551)

antivirus program Software that runs in the background to protect your computer from dangers lurking on the Internet and other possible sources of infected files. (p. 69)

application flowcharts Diagrams that show relationships among applications or systems. (p. 516)

application program interface (API) An interface that allows applications to make use of the operating system. (p. 143)

application service provider (ASP) A company that provides software, support, and the computer hardware on which to run the software from the user's facilities over a network. (p. 158)

arithmetic/logic unit (ALU) The part of the CPU that performs mathematical calculations and makes logical comparisons. (p. 94)

ARPANET A project started by the U.S. Department of Defense (DoD) in 1969 as both an experiment in reliable networking and a means to link the DoD and military research contractors, including many universities doing military-funded research. (p. 276)

artificial intelligence (AI) A field in which the computer system takes on the characteristics of human intelligence. (p. 17)

artificial intelligence systems People, procedures, hardware, software, data, and knowledge needed to develop computer systems and machines that

demonstrate the characteristics of intelligence. (p. 446)

asking directly An approach to gather data that asks users, stakeholders, and other managers about what they want and expect from the new or modified system. (p. 518)

attribute A characteristic of an entity. (p. 190)

auditing Analyzing the financial condition of an organization and determining whether financial statements and reports produced by the financial MIS are accurate. (p. 408)

backbone One of the Internet's high-speed, long-distance communications links. (p. 277)

batch processing system A form of data processing whereby business transactions are accumulated over a period of time and prepared for processing as a single unit or batch. (p. 367)

benchmark test An examination that compares computer systems operating under the same conditions. (p. 543)

best practices The most efficient and effective ways to complete a business process. (p. 376)

beta testing Testing a complete and stable system. (p. 551)

blade server A server that houses many individual computer motherboards that include one or more processors, computer memory, computer storage, and computer network connections. (p. 124)

Bluetooth A wireless communications specification that describes how cell phones, computers, faxes, personal digital assistants, printers, and other electronic devices can be interconnected over distances of 1 to 10 metres at a rate of about 2 Mbps. (p. 238)

brainstorming A decision-making approach that consists of members offering ideas "off the top of their heads." (p. 426)

bridge A telecommunications device that connects two LANs using the same telecommunications protocol. (p. 253)

broadband communications A relative term but generally means a telecommunications system that can exchange data very quickly. (p. 234)

business intelligence (BI) The process of gathering enough of the right information in a timely manner and usable form and analyzing it to have a positive impact on business strategy, tactics, or operations. (p. 215)

business-to-business (B2B) e-commerce A subset of e-commerce in which all the participants are organizations. (p. 329)

business-to-consumer (B2C) e-commerce A form of e-commerce in which customers deal directly with an organization and avoid intermediaries. (p. 329)

byte (B) Eight bits that together represent a single character of data. (p. 98)

cache memory A type of high-speed memory that a processor can access more rapidly than main memory. (p. 99)

Cascading Style Sheet (CSS) A markup language for defining the visual design of a Web page or group of pages. (p. 286)

CASE repository A database of system descriptions, parameters, and objectives. (p. 517)

central processing unit (CPU) The part of the computer that consists of three associated elements: the arithmetic/logic unit, the control unit, and the register areas. (p. 94)

centralized processing An approach to processing wherein all processing occurs in a single location or facility. (p. 248)

certificate authority (CA) A trusted third-party organization or company that issues digital certificates. (p. 353)

change model A representation of change theories that identifies the phases of change and the best way to implement them. (p. 26)

channel bandwidth The rate at which data is exchanged, usually measured in bits per second (bps). (p. 234)

character A basic building block of most information, consisting of uppercase letters, lowercase letters, numeric digits, or special symbols. (p. 189)

chief knowledge officer (CKO) A top-level executive who helps the organization use a KMS to create, store, and use knowledge to achieve organizational goals. (p. 444)

chip-and-PIN card A type of card that employs a computer chip that communicates with a card reader using radio frequencies; it does not need to be swiped at a terminal. (p. 111)

choice stage The third stage of decision making, which requires selecting a course of action. (p. 398)

circuit switching network A network that sets up a circuit between the sender and receiver before any communications can occur; this circuit is maintained for the duration of the communication and cannot be used to support any other communications until the circuit is released and a new connection is set up. (p. 235)

click fraud A problem arising in a pay-per-click online advertising environment where additional clicks are generated beyond those that come from actual, legitimate users. (p. 346)

clickstream data The data gathered based on the websites you visit and the items you click. (p. 346)

client/server architecture An approach to computing wherein multiple computer platforms are dedicated to special functions, such as database management, printing, communications, and program execution. (p. 249)

clock speed A series of electronic pulses produced at a predetermined rate that affects machine cycle time. (p. 96)

cloud computing A computing environment where software and storage are provided as an Internet service and are accessed with a Web browser. (p. 281)

code of ethics A code that states the principles and core values that are essential to a set of people and that therefore govern their behaviour. (p. 81)

cold site A computer environment that includes rooms, electrical service, telecommunications links, data storage devices, and the like; also called a *shell*. (p. 536)

command-based user interface A user interface that requires you to give text commands to the computer to perform basic activities. (p. 142)

compact disk read-only memory (CD-ROM) A common form of optical disk on which data cannot be modified once it has been recorded. (p. 104)

competitive advantage A significant and ideally long-term benefit to a company over its competition. (p. 31)

competitive intelligence One aspect of business intelligence limited to information about competitors and the ways that knowledge affects strategy, tactics, and operations. (p. 215)

compiler A special software program that converts the programmer's source code into the machine-language instructions, which consist of binary digits. (p. 171)

computer network The communications media, devices, and software needed to connect two or more computer systems or devices. (p. 246)

computer programs Sequences of instructions for the computer. (p. 139)

computer-aided software engineering (CASE) Tools that automate many of the tasks required in a systems development effort and encourage adherence to the SDLC. (p. 507)

computer-assisted manufacturing (CAM) A system that directly controls manufacturing equipment. (p. 411)

computer-based information system (CBIS) A single set of hardware, software, databases, telecommunications, people, and procedures that are configured to collect, manipulate, store, and process data into information. (p. 12)

computer-integrated manufacturing (CIM) Using computers to link the components of the production process into an effective system. (p. 411)

concurrency control A method of dealing with a situation in which two or more users or applications need to access the same record at the same time. (p. 205)

consumer-to-consumer (C2C) e-commerce A subset of e-commerce that involves consumers selling directly to other consumers. (p. 330)

contactless card A card with an embedded chip that only needs to be held close to a terminal to transfer its data; no PIN number needs to be entered. (p. 111)

content streaming A method for transferring large media files over the Internet so that the data stream of voice and pictures plays more or less continuously as the file is being downloaded. (p. 306)

continuous improvement Constantly seeking ways to improve business processes to add value to products and services. (p. 28)

control unit The part of the CPU that sequentially accesses program instructions, decodes them, and coordinates the flow of data in and out of the ALU, the registers, the primary storage, and even secondary storage and various output devices. (p. 94)

coprocessor The part of the computer that speeds processing by executing specific types of instructions while the CPU works on another processing activity. (p. 100)

cost centre A division within a company that does not directly generate revenue. (p. 408)

cost/benefit analysis An approach that lists the costs and benefits of each proposed system. After they are expressed in monetary terms, all the costs are compared with all the benefits. (p. 542)

counterintelligence The steps an organization takes to protect information sought by "hostile" intelligence gatherers. (p. 215)

creative analysis The investigation of new approaches to existing problems. (p. 495)

criminal hacker (cracker) A computer-savvy person who attempts to gain unauthorized or illegal access to computer systems to steal passwords, corrupt files and programs, or even transfer money. (p. 60)

critical analysis The unbiased and careful questioning of whether system elements are related in the most effective ways. (p. 497)

critical path Activities that, if delayed, would delay the entire project. (p. 507)

critical success factors (CSFs) Factors that are essential to the success of a functional area of an organization. (p. 497)

cross-platform development A software development technique that allows programmers to develop programs that can run on computer systems having different hardware and operating systems, or platforms. (p. 548)

culture A set of major understandings and assumptions shared by a group. (p. 25)

customer relationship management (CRM) system A system that helps a company manage all aspects of customer encounters, including marketing and advertising, sales, customer service after the sale, and programs to retain loyal customers. (p. 383)

cybermall A single website that offers many products and services at one Internet location. (p. 338)

cyberterrorist Someone who intimidates or coerces a government or organization to advance his political or social objectives by launching computer-based attacks against computers, networks, and the information stored on them. (p. 58)

data Raw facts, such as an employee number, total hours worked in a week, inventory part numbers, or sales orders. (p. 6)

data administrator A nontechnical position responsible for defining and implementing consistent principles for a variety of data issues. (p. 208)

data analysis The manipulation of collected data so that the development team members who are participating in systems analysis can use the data. (p. 514)

data centre A climate-controlled building or set of buildings that house database servers and the systems that deliver mission-critical information and services. (p. 194)

data cleanup The process of looking for and fixing inconsistencies to ensure that data is accurate and complete. (p. 200)

data collection Capturing and gathering all data necessary to complete the processing of transactions. (p. 372)

data correction The process of reentering data that was not typed or scanned properly. (p. 373)

data definition language (DDL) A collection of instructions and commands used to define and describe data and relationships in a specific database. (p. 203)

data dictionary A detailed description of all the data used in the database. (p. 203)

data editing The process of checking data for validity and completeness. (p. 373)

data entry Converting human-readable data into a machine-readable form. (p. 108)

data input Transferring machine-readable data into the system. (p. 108)

data item The specific value of an attribute. (p. 190)

data loss prevention (DLP) Systems designed to lock down—to identify, monitor, and protect—data within an organization. (p. 215)

data manipulation The process of performing calculations and other data transformations related to business transactions. (p. 373)

data manipulation language (DML) A specific language, provided with a DBMS, which allows users to access and modify the data, to make queries, and to generate reports. (p. 205)

data mart A subset of a data warehouse, used by small and medium-size businesses and departments within large companies to support decision making. (p. 214)

data mining An information-analysis tool that involves the automated discovery of patterns and relationships in a data warehouse. (p. 214)

data model A diagram of data entities and their relationships. (p. 195)

data preparation, or data conversion Making sure all files and databases are ready to be used with new computer software and systems. (p. 550)

data storage The process of updating one or more databases with new transactions. (p. 373)

data store Representation of a storage location for data. (p. 516)

data warehouse A large database that collects business information from many sources in the enterprise, covering all aspects of the company's processes, products, and customers, in support of management decision making. (p. 212)

database An organized collection of facts and information. (p. 13)

database administrator (DBA) A skilled IS professional who directs all activities related to an organization's database. (p. 189)

database approach to data management An approach to data management whereby a pool of related data is shared by a variety of information systems. (p. 192)

database management system (DBMS) A group of programs that manipulate the database and provide an interface between the database and the user of the database and other application programs. (p. 189)

data-flow diagram (DFD) A model of objects, associations, and activities that describes how data can flow between and around various objects. (p. 515)

data-flow line Arrows that show the direction of data element movement. (p. 515)

decentralized processing An approach to processing wherein processing devices are placed at various remote locations. (p. 248)

decision room A room that supports decision making, with the decision makers in the same building, combining face-to-face verbal interaction with technology to make the meeting more effective and efficient. (p. 428)

decision support system (DSS) An organized collection of people, procedures, software, databases, and devices used to support problem-specific decision making. (p. 17)

decision-making phase The first part of problem solving, including three stages: intelligence, design, and choice. (p. 397)

delphi approach A decision-making approach in which group decision makers are geographically dispersed; this approach encourages diversity among group members and fosters creativity and original thinking in decision making. (p. 426)

demand report A report developed to give certain information at someone's request rather than on a schedule. (p. 404)

design report The primary result of systems design, reflecting the decisions made and preparing the way for systems implementation. (p. 544)

design stage The second stage of decision making, in which you develop alternative solutions to the problem and evaluate their feasibility. (p. 397)

desktop computer A relatively small, inexpensive, single-user computer that is highly versatile. (p. 122)

dialogue manager A user interface that allows decision makers to easily access and manipulate the DSS and to use common business terms and phrases. (p. 422)

digital audio player A device that can store, organize, and play digital music files. (p. 117)

digital camera An input device used with a PC to record and store images and video in digital form. (p. 109)

digital certificate An attachment to an e-mail message or data embedded in a website that verifies the identity of a sender or website. (p. 353)

digital rights management (DRM) Refers to the use of any of several technologies to enforce policies for controlling access to digital media such as movies, music, and software. (p. 345)

digital subscriber line (DSL) A telecommunications service that delivers high-speed Internet access to homes and small businesses over the existing phone lines of the local telephone network. (p. 257)

digital video disk (DVD) A storage medium used to store software, video games, and movies. (p. 104)

direct access A retrieval method in which data can be retrieved without the need to read and discard other data. (p. 102)

direct access storage device (DASD) A device used for direct access of secondary storage data. (p. 103)

direct conversion (also called *plunge* or *direct cutover*) Stopping the old system and starting the new system on a given date. (p. 551)

direct observation Directly observing the existing system in action by one or more members of the analysis team. (p. 513)

disaster recovery The implementation of the disaster plan. (p. 536)

disk mirroring A process of storing data that provides an exact copy that protects users fully in the event of data loss. (p. 103)

distributed database A database in which the data can be spread across several smaller databases connected via telecommunications devices. (p. 217)

distributed processing An approach to processing wherein processing devices are placed at remote locations but are connected to each other via a network. (p. 248)

document production The process of generating output records and reports. (p. 373)

documentation Text that describes a program's functions to help the user operate the computer system. (p. 139)

domain The allowable values for data attributes. (p. 197)

domain expert The person or group with the expertise or knowledge the expert system is trying to capture (domain). (p. 459)

downsizing Reducing the number of employees to cut costs. (p. 31)

drill-down report A report providing increasingly detailed data about a situation. (p. 405)

dumpster diving Going through the trash cans of an organization to find secret or confidential information, including information needed to access an information system or its data. (p. 57)

e-commerce Any business transaction executed electronically between companies (business-to-business, or B2B), companies and consumers (business-to-consumer, or B2C), consumers and other consumers (consumer-to-consumer, or C2C), business and the public sector, and consumers and the public sector. (p. 16)

economic feasibility The determination of whether the project makes financial sense and whether predicted benefits offset the cost and time needed to obtain them. (p. 510)

economic order quantity (EOQ) The quantity that should be reordered to minimize total inventory costs. (p. 410)

effectiveness A measure of the extent to which a system achieves its goals; it can be computed by dividing the goals actually achieved by the total of the stated goals. (p. 9)

efficiency A measure of what is produced divided by what is consumed. (p. 9)

e-Government The use of information and communications technology to simplify the sharing of information, speed formerly paper-based processes, and improve the relationship between citizens and government. (p. 330)

electronic business (e-business) Using information systems and the Internet to perform all business-related tasks and functions. (p. 16)

electronic cash An amount of money that is computerized, stored, and used as cash for e-commerce transactions. (p. 353)

electronic commerce Conducting business activities (e.g., distribution, buying, selling, marketing, and servicing of products or services) electronically over computer networks. (p. 328)

electronic document distribution A process that enables the sending and receiving of documents in a digital form without being printed (although printing is possible). (p. 258)

electronic exchange An electronic forum where manufacturers, suppliers, and competitors buy and sell goods, trade market information, and run back-office operations. (p. 339)

electronic retailing (e-tailing) The direct sale of products or services by businesses to consumers through electronic storefronts, typically designed around an electronic catalogue and shopping cart model. (p. 338)

empowerment Giving employees and their managers more responsibility and authority to make decisions, take certain actions, and have more control over their jobs. (p. 23)

encryption The process of converting an original message into a form that can be understood only by the intended receiver. (p. 254)

encryption key A variable value that is applied (using an algorithm) to a set of unencrypted text to produce encrypted text or to decrypt encrypted text. (p. 254)

end-user systems development Any systems development project in which the primary effort is undertaken by a combination of business managers and users. (p. 491)

enterprise data modelling Data modelling done at the level of the entire enterprise. (p. 195)

enterprise resource planning (ERP) system A set of integrated programs capable of managing a company's vital business operations for an entire organization. (p. 17)

enterprise sphere of influence The sphere of influence that serves the needs of the firm in its interaction with its environment. (p. 141)

enterprise system A system central to the organization that ensures information can be shared across all business functions and all levels of management to support the running and managing of a business. (p. 366)

entity A general class of people, places, or things for which data is collected, stored, and maintained. (p. 190)

entity symbol Representation of either a source or destination of a data element. (p. 516)

entity-relationship (ER) diagrams Data models that use basic graphical symbols to show the organization of and relationships between data. (p. 197)

environmental design Also called *green design*, it involves systems development efforts that slash power consumption, require less physical space, and result in systems that can be disposed of in a way that doesn't negatively affect the environment. (p. 538)

ergonomics The science of designing machines, products, and systems to maximize the safety, comfort, and efficiency of the people who use them. (p. 79)

event-driven review A review triggered by a problem or opportunity such as an error, a corporate merger, or a new market for products. (p. 557)

exception report A report automatically produced when a situation is unusual or requires management action. (p. 405)

execution time (E-time) The time it takes to execute an instruction and store the results. (p. 95)

executive support system (ESS) Specialized DSS that includes all hardware, software, data, procedures, and people used to assist senior-level executives within the organization. (p. 429)

expert system A system that gives a computer the ability to make suggestions and function like an expert in a particular field. (p. 17)

explanation facility Component of an expert system that allows a user or decision maker to understand how the expert system arrived at certain conclusions or results. (p. 458)

Extensible Markup Language (XML) The markup language designed to transport and store data on the Web. (p. 287)

external auditing Auditing performed by an outside company. (p. 408)

extranet A network based on Web technologies that allows selected outsiders, such as business partners and customers, to access authorized resources of a company's intranet. (pp. 14 and 315)

feasibility analysis Assessment of the technical, economic, legal, operational, and schedule feasibility of a project. (p. 510)

feedback Output that is used to make changes to input or processing activities. (p. 11)

field Typically a name, number, or combination of characters that describes an aspect of a business object or activity. (p. 189)

file A collection of related records. (p. 190)

File Transfer Protocol (FTP) A protocol that provides a file transfer process between a host and a remote computer and allows users to copy files from one computer to another. (p. 314)

final evaluation A detailed investigation of the proposals offered by the vendors remaining after the preliminary evaluation. (p. 541)

financial MIS An information system that provides financial information for executives and for a broader set of people who need to make better decisions on a daily basis. (p. 405)

five-forces model A widely accepted model that identifies five key factors that can lead to attainment of competitive advantage, including (1) the rivalry among existing competitors, (2) the threat of new entrants, (3) the threat of substitute products and services, (4) the bargaining power of buyers, and (5) the bargaining power of suppliers. (p. 33)

flat organizational structure An organizational structure with a reduced number of management layers. (p. 23)

flexible manufacturing system (FMS) An approach that allows manufacturing facilities to rapidly and efficiently change from making one product to making another. (p. 411)

forecasting Predicting future events to avoid problems. (p. 12)

front-end processors Special-purpose computers that manage communications to and from a large computer serving hundreds or even thousands of users. (p. 252)

full-duplex channel A communications channel that permits data transmission in both directions at the same time; a full-duplex channel is like two simplex channels. (p. 234)

game theory The use of information systems to develop competitive strategies for people, organizations, or even countries. (p. 470)

Gantt chart A graphical tool used for planning, monitoring, and coordinating projects. (p. 507)

gateway A telecommunications device that serves as an entrance to another network. (p. 254)

genetic algorithm An approach to solving large, complex problems in which many related operations or models change and evolve until the best one emerges. (p. 454)

geographic information system (GIS) A computer system capable of assembling, storing, manipulating, and displaying geographic information, that is, data identified according to its location. (p. 418)

gigahertz (GHz) Billions of cycles per second, a measure of clock speed. (p. 96)

Global System for Mobile Communications (GSM) A globally accepted standard for digital cellular communications. (p. 242)

graphical user interface (GUI) An interface that displays pictures (icons) and menus that people use to send commands to the computer system. (p. 143)

graphics processing unit (GPU) A specialized processor that offloads the tasks associated with 3D graphics rendering from the CPU. (p. 101)

green computing A program concerned with the efficient and environmentally responsible design, manufacture, operation, and disposal of IS related products. (p. 127)

grid chart A table that shows relationships among the various aspects of a systems development effort. (p. 517)

grid computing The use of a collection of computers, often owned by several individuals or organizations, to work in a coordinated manner to solve a common problem. (p. 101)

group consensus Decision making by a group that is appointed and given the responsibility of making the final evaluation and selection. (p. 541)

group consensus approach A decision-making approach that forces members in the group to reach a unanimous decision. (p. 426)

group support system (GSS) Software application that consists of most elements in a DSS, plus software to provide effective support in group decision making; also called *computerized collaborative work system*. (p. 424)

hacker A person who enjoys computer technology and spends time learning and using computer systems. (p. 60)

half-duplex channel A communications channel that can transmit data in either direction, but not simultaneously. (p. 234)

hand-held computer A single-user computer that provides ease of portability because of its small size. (p. 120)

hardware Computer equipment used to perform input, processing, and output activities. (p. 13)

heuristics "Rules of thumb," or commonly accepted guidelines or procedures that usually find a good solution. (p. 399)

hierarchy of data Bits, characters, fields, records, files, and databases. (p. 190)

highly structured problems Problems that are straightforward and require known facts and relationships. (p. 421)

hot site A duplicate, operational hardware system or immediate access to one through a specialized vendor. (p. 536)

HTML tags Codes that tell the Web browser how to format text—as a heading, as a list, or as body text—and whether images, sound, and other elements should be inserted. (p. 285)

human resource MIS (HRMIS) An information system that is concerned with activities related to previous, current, and potential employees of an organization, also called a personnel MIS. (p. 415)

hyperlink Highlighted text or graphics in a Web document, that, when clicked, opens a new Web page containing related content. (p. 284)

Hypertext Markup Language (HTML) The standard page description language for Web pages. (p. 284)

identity theft A crime in which an impostor obtains key pieces of personal identification information, such as Social Insurance Number or a driver's licence number, to impersonate someone else. (pp. 58 and 335)

IF-THEN statements Rules that suggest certain conclusions. (p. 456)

image log A separate file that contains only changes to applications. (p. 537)

implementation stage A stage of problem solving in which a solution is put into effect. (p. 398)

incremental backup A backup copy of all files changed during the last few days or the last week. (p. 537)

inference engine Part of the expert system that seeks information and relationships from the knowledge base and provides answers, predictions, and suggestions similar to the way a human expert would. (p. 457)

informatics A specialized system that combines traditional disciplines, such as science and medicine, with computer systems and technology. (p. 470)

information A collection of facts organized and processed so that they have additional value beyond the value of the individual facts. (p. 6)

information system (IS) A set of interrelated components that collect, manipulate, store, and disseminate data and information and provide a feedback mechanism to meet an objective. (p. 5)

information systems planning Translating strategic and organizational goals into systems development initiatives. (p. 494)

infrared transmission A form of communications that sends signals at a frequency of 300 GHz and above—higher than those of microwaves but lower than those of visible light. (p. 239)

input The activity of gathering and capturing raw data. (p. 11)

insider An employee, disgruntled or otherwise, working solo or in concert with outsiders to compromise corporate systems. (p. 60)

installation The process of physically placing the computer equipment on the site and making it operational. (p. 550)

instant messaging A method that allows two or more people to communicate online in real time using the Internet. (p. 301)

institutional DSS A DSS that handles situations or decisions that occur more than once, usually several times per year or more. An institutional DSS is used repeatedly and refined over the years. (p. 421)

instruction time (I-time) The time it takes to perform the fetch-instruction and decode-instruction steps of the instruction phase. (p. 95)

integrated development environments (IDEs) A development approach that combines the tools needed for programming with a programming language into one integrated package. (p. 548)

integration testing Testing all related systems together. (p. 550)

intellectual property Includes works of the mind such as books, films, music, processes, and software, which are unique and are owned or created by a single entity. (p. 345)

intelligence stage The first stage of decision making, in which you identify and define potential problems or opportunities. (p. 397)

intelligent agent Programs and a knowledge base used to perform a specific task for a person, a process, or another program; also called *intelligent robot* or *bot*. (p. 454)

intelligent behaviour The ability to learn from experiences and apply knowledge acquired from those experiences, handle complex situations, solve problems when important information is missing, determine what is important and to react quickly and correctly to a new situation, understand visual images, process and manipulate symbols, be creative and imaginative, and use heuristics. (p. 446)

internal auditing Auditing performed by individuals within the organization. (p. 408)

Internet The world's largest computer network, consisting of thousands of interconnected networks, all freely exchanging information. (p. 13)

Internet Protocol (IP) A communication standard that enables computers to route communications traffic from one network to another as needed. (p. 276)

Internet service provider (ISP) Any organization that provides Internet access to people. (p. 280)

intranet An internal network based on Web technologies that allows people within an organization to exchange information and work on projects. (p. 14)

intrusion detection system (IDS) Software that monitors system and network resources and notifies network security personnel when it senses a possible intrusion. (p. 67)

IP address A 64-bit number that identifies a computer on the Internet. (p. 278)

Java An object-oriented programming language from Sun Microsystems based on the C++ programming language, which allows applets to be embedded within an HTML document. (p. 287)

joining Manipulating data to combine two or more tables. (p. 198)

just-in-time (JIT) inventory An inventory management approach in which inventory and materials are delivered just before they are used in manufacturing a product. (p. 410)

kernel The heart of the operating system, which controls its most critical processes. (p. 142)

key A field or set of fields in a record that is used to identify the record. (p. 191)

key-indicator report A summary of the previous day's critical activities, typically available at the beginning of each workday. (p. 404)

keystroke loggers Software or hardware programmed to send a list of keystrokes typed by a user to a malicious person. (p. 62)

knowledge The awareness and understanding of a set of information and ways that information can be made useful to support a specific task or reach a decision. (p. 7)

knowledge acquisition facility Part of the expert system that provides a convenient and efficient means of capturing and storing all the components of the knowledge base. (p. 458)

knowledge base The collection of data, rules, procedures, and relationships that must be followed to achieve value or the proper outcome. (p. 456)

knowledge engineer A person who has training or experience in the design, development, implementation, and maintenance of an expert system. (p. 459)

knowledge user The person or group who uses and benefits from the expert system. (p. 459)

laptop computer A personal computer designed for use by mobile users; it is small and light enough to sit comfortably on a user's lap. (p. 120)

LCD display Flat display that uses liquid crystals—organic, oil-like material placed between two polarizers—to form characters and graphic images on a backlit screen. (p. 115)

learning systems A combination of software and hardware that allows the computer to change how it functions or reacts to situations based on feedback it receives. (p. 452)

legal feasibility The determination of whether laws or regulations may prevent or limit a systems development project. (p. 510)

linking Data manipulation that combines two or more tables using common data attributes to form a new table with only the unique data attributes. (p. 198)

local area network (LAN) A network that connects computer systems and devices within a small area, such as an office, home, or several floors in a building. (p. 246)

logical design A description of the functional requirements of a system. (p. 533)

machine cycle The instruction phase followed by the execution phase. (p. 95)

magnetic disk A direct-access storage device, with bits represented by magnetized areas. (p. 103)

magnetic stripe card A type of card that stores a limited amount of data by modifying the magnetism of tiny iron-based particles contained in a band on the card. (p. 111)

magnetic tape A type of sequential secondary storage medium, now used primarily for storing backups of critical organizational data in the event of a disaster. (p. 103)

mainframe computer A large, powerful computer often shared by hundreds of concurrent users connected to the machine via terminals. (p. 124)

maintenance team A special IS team responsible for modifying, fixing, and updating existing software. (p. 556)

make-or-buy decision The decision regarding whether to obtain the necessary software from internal or external sources. (p. 546)

management information system (MIS) An organized collection of people, procedures, software, databases, and devices that provides routine information to managers and decision makers. (p. 17)

market segmentation The identification of specific markets to target them with advertising messages. (p. 340)

marketing MIS An information system that supports managerial activities in product development, distribution, pricing decisions, promotional effectiveness, and sales forecasting. (p. 411)

massively parallel processing A form of multiprocessing that speeds processing by linking hundreds or thousands of processors to operate at the same time, or in parallel, with each processor having its own bus, memory, disks, copy of the operating system, and applications. (p. 101)

material requirements planning (MRP) A set of inventory-control techniques that help coordinate thousands of inventory items when the demand of one item is dependent on the demand for another. (p. 410)

megahertz (MHz) Millions of cycles per second, a measure of clock speed. (p. 96)

meta tag An HTML code, not visible on the displayed Web page, that contains keywords representing your site's content, which search engines use to build indexes pointing to your website. (p. 348)

metropolitan area network (MAN) A telecommunications network that connects users and their computers in a geographical area that spans a campus or city. (p. 247)

microcode Predefined, elementary circuits and logical operations that the processor performs when it executes an instruction. (p. 96)

middleware Software that allows various systems to communicate and exchange data. (p. 156)

MIPS Millions of instructions per second, a measure of machine cycle time. (p. 96)

mission-critical systems Systems that play a pivotal role in an organization's continued operations and goal attainment. (p. 497)

mobile commerce (m-commerce) The use of mobile, wireless devices to place orders and conduct business. (p. 16)

model base Part of a DSS that allows managers and decision makers to perform quantitative analysis on both internal and external data. (p. 423)

model management software (MMS) Software that coordinates the use of models in a DSS. (p. 424)

modem A telecommunications hardware device that converts (modulates and demodulates) communications signals so they can be transmitted over the communication media. (p. 252)

monitoring stage The final stage of the problem-solving process, in which decision makers evaluate the implementation. (p. 398)

Moore's Law A hypothesis stating that transistor densities on a single chip will double every two years. (p. 97)

MP3 A standard format for compressing a sound sequence into a small file. (p. 117)

multicore microprocessor A microprocessor that combines two or more independent processors into a single computer so they can share the workload and improve processing capacity. (p. 100)

multimedia Text, graphics, video, animation, audio, and other media that can be used to help an organization efficiently and effectively achieve its goals. (p. 462)

multiplexer A device that combines data from multiple data sources into a single output signal that carries multiple channels, thus reducing the number of communications links needed and lowering telecommunications costs. (p. 252)

multiprocessing The simultaneous execution of two or more instructions at the same time. (p. 100)

natural language processing Processing that allows the computer to understand and react to statements and commands made in a "natural" language, such as English. (p. 452)

Near Field Communication (NFC) A very short-range wireless connectivity technology designed for cell phones and credit cards. (p. 238)

netbook computer The smallest, lightest, least expensive member of the laptop computer family. (p. 121)

nettop computer An inexpensive desktop computer designed to be smaller, lighter, and consume much less power than a traditional desktop computer. (p. 122)

network operating system (NOS) Systems software that controls the computer systems and devices on a network and allows them to communicate with each other. (p. 254)

network-attached storage (NAS) Hard disk storage that is set up with its own network address rather than being attached to a computer. (p. 105)

networking protocol A set of rules, algorithms, messages, and other mechanisms that enable software and hardware in networked devices to communicate effectively. (p. 233)

network-management software Software that enables a manager on a networked desktop to monitor the use of individual computers and shared hardware (such as printers); scan for viruses; and ensure compliance with software licences. (p. 254)

networks Computers and equipment that are connected in a building, around the country, or around the world to enable electronic communications. (p. 13)

neural network A computer system that can act like or simulate the functioning of a human brain. (p. 453)

nominal group technique A decision-making approach that encourages feedback from individual group members, and the final decision is made by voting, similar to the way public officials are elected. (p. 426)

nonprogrammed decision A decision that deals with unusual or exceptional situations. (p. 399)

notebook computer Smaller than a laptop computer, an extremely lightweight computer that weighs less than 3 kilograms and can easily fit in a briefcase. (p. 120)

object-oriented database A database that stores both data and its processing instructions. (p. 218)

object-oriented database management system (OODBMS) A group of programs that manipulate an object-oriented database and provide a user interface and connections to other application programs. (p. 219)

object-oriented systems development (OOSD) An approach to systems development that combines the logic of the systems development life cycle with the power of object-oriented modeling and programming. (p. 509)

object-relational database management system (ORDBMS) A DBMS capable of manipulating audio, video, and graphical data. (p. 219)

off-the-shelf software Software mass-produced by software vendors to address needs that are common across businesses, organizations, or individuals. (p. 157)

on-demand computing Contracting for computer resources to rapidly respond to an organization's varying workflow. Also called on-demand business and utility computing. (p. 31)

online analytical processing (OLAP) Software that allows users to explore data from a number of perspectives. (p. 218)

online transaction processing (OLTP) A form of data processing where each transaction is processed immediately, without the delay of accumulating transactions into a batch. (p. 368)

open-source software Software that is distributed, typically for free, with the source code also available so that it can be studied, changed, and improved by its users. (p. 174)

operating system (OS) A set of computer programs that controls the computer hardware and acts as an interface with applications. (p. 141)

operational feasibility The measure of whether the project can be put into action or operation. (p. 510)

optical storage device A form of data storage that uses lasers to read and write data. (p. 104)

optimization model A process to find the best solution, usually the one that will best help the organization meet its goals. (p. 399)

organic light-emitting diode (OLED) display Flat display that uses a layer of organic material sandwiched between two conductors, which, in turn, are sandwiched between a glass top plate and a glass bottom plate so that when electric current is applied to the two conductors, a bright, electro-luminescent light is produced directly from the organic material. (p. 115)

organization A formal collection of people and other resources established to accomplish a set of goals. (p. 18)

organizational change How for-profit and nonprofit organizations plan for, implement, and handle change. (p. 26)

organizational culture The major understandings and assumptions for a business, corporation, or other organization. (p. 25)

organizational learning The adaptations to new conditions or alterations of organizational practices over time. (p. 27)

organizational structure Organizational subunits and the way they relate to the overall organization. (p. 21)

output Production of useful information, usually in the form of documents and reports. (p. 11)

outsourcing Contracting with outside professional services to meet specific business needs. (p. 31)

packet switching network A network in which no fixed path is created between the communicating devices and the data is broken into packets, with each packet transmitted individually and capable of taking various paths from sender to recipient. (p. 235)

parallel computing The simultaneous execution of the same task on many processors to obtain results faster. (p. 101)

parallel start-up Running both the old and new systems for a period of time and comparing the output of the new system closely with the output of the old system; any differences are reconciled. When users are comfortable that the new system is working correctly, the old system is eliminated. (p. 552)

password sniffer A small program hidden in a network or a computer system that records identification numbers and passwords. (p. 62)

patch A minor change to correct a problem or make a small enhancement. It is usually an addition to an existing program. (p. 555)

p-card (procurement card or purchasing card) A credit card used to streamline the traditional purchase order and invoice payment processes. (p. 355)

personal area network (PAN) A network that supports the interconnection of information technology within a range of 10 metres (33 feet) or so. (p. 246)

personal productivity software The software that enables users to improve their personal effectiveness, increasing the amount of work and quality of work they can do. (p. 140)

personal sphere of influence The sphere of influence that serves the needs of an individual user. (p. 140)

personalization The process of tailoring Web pages to specifically target individual consumers. (p. 349)

phase-in approach Slowly replacing components of the old system with those of the new one; this process is repeated for each application until the new system is running every application and performing as expected; also called a *piecemeal approach*. (p. 552)

phishing A practice that entails sending bogus messages purportedly from a legitimate institution to pry personal information from customers by convincing them to go to a "spoofed" website. (p. 345)

physical design The specification of the characteristics of the system components necessary to put the logical design into action. (p. 533)

pilot start-up Running the new system for one group of users rather than all users. (p. 552)

pipelining A form of CPU operation in which multiple execution phases are performed in a single machine cycle. (p. 95)

pixel A dot of colour on a photo image or a point of light on a display screen. (p. 115)

planned data redundancy A way of organizing data in which the logical database design is altered so that certain data entities are combined, summary totals are carried in the data records rather than calculated from elemental data, and some data attributes are repeated in more than one data entity to improve database performance. (p. 195)

plasma display A type of display using thousands of smart cells (pixels) consisting of electrodes and neon and xenon gases that are electrically turned into plasma (electrically charged atoms and negatively charged particles) to emit light. (p. 115)

Platform for Privacy Preferences (P3P) A screening technology in Web browsers that shields users from websites that don't provide the level of privacy protection they desire. (p. 73)

point evaluation system An evaluation process in which each evaluation factor is assigned a weight, in percentage points, based on importance. Then each proposed system is evaluated in terms of each factor and given a score ranging from 0 to 100. The scores are totalled, and the system with the greatest total score is selected. (p. 543)

point-of-sale (POS) device A terminal used to enter data into the computer system. (p. 111)

policy-based storage management Automation of storage using previously defined policies. (p. 107)

portable computer A computer small enough to carry easily. (p. 120)

predictive analysis A form of data mining that combines historical data with assumptions about future conditions to predict outcomes of events, such as future product sales or the probability that a customer will default on a loan. (p. 214)

preliminary evaluation An initial assessment whose purpose is to dismiss the unwanted proposals; begins after all proposals have been submitted. (p. 541)

primary key A field or set of fields that uniquely identifies the record. (p. 191)

primary storage (main memory; memory) The part of the computer that holds program instructions and data. (p. 94)

private branch exchange (PBX) A telephone switching exchange that serves a single organization. (p. 253)

problem solving A process that goes beyond decision making to include the implementation stage. (p. 398)

procedures The strategies, policies, methods, and rules for using a CBIS. (p. 13)

process A set of logically related tasks performed to achieve a defined outcome. (p. 7)

process symbol Representation of a function that is performed. (p. 516)

processing Converting or transforming data into useful outputs. (p. 11)

productivity A measure of the output achieved divided by the input required. (p. 37)

profit centre A department within an organization that focuses on generating profits. (p. 408)

Program Evaluation and Review Technique (PERT) A formalized approach for developing a project schedule. (p. 507)

programmed decision A decision made using a rule, procedure, or quantitative method. (p. 398)

programmer A specialist responsible for modifying or developing programs to satisfy user requirements. (p. 490)

programming languages Sets of keywords, commands, symbols, and a system of rules for constructing statements by which humans can communicate instructions to a computer. (p. 169)

project deadline The date the entire project is to be completed and operational. (p. 507)

project milestone A critical date for the completion of a major part of the project. (p. 507)

project organizational structure A structure centred on major products or services. (p. 24)

project schedule A detailed description of what is to be done. (p. 507)

projecting Manipulating data to eliminate columns in a table. (p. 198)

proprietary software One-of-a-kind software designed for a specific application and owned by the company, organization, or person that uses it. (p. 157)

prototyping An iterative approach to the systems development process in which at each iteration requirements and alternative solutions to a problem are identified and analyzed, new solutions are designed, and a portion of the system is implemented. (p. 500)

quality The ability of a product or service to meet or exceed customer expectations. (p. 30)

quality control A process that ensures that the finished product meets the customers' needs. (p. 411)

questionnaires A method of gathering data when the data sources are spread over a wide geographic area. (p. 513)

Radio Frequency Identification (RFID) A technology that employs a microchip with an antenna to broadcast its unique identifier and location to receivers. (p. 113)

random access memory (RAM) A form of memory in which instructions or data can be temporarily stored. (p. 98)

rapid application development (RAD) A systems development approach that employs tools, techniques, and methodologies designed to speed application development. (p. 502)

read-only memory (ROM) A nonvolatile form of memory. (p. 99)

record A collection of data fields all related to one object, activity, or individual. (p. 190)

redundant array of independent/inexpensive disks (RAID) A method of storing data that generates extra bits of data from existing data, allowing the system to create a "reconstruction map" so that if a hard drive fails, the system can rebuild lost data. (p. 103)

reengineering (process redesign) The radical redesign of business processes, organizational structures, information systems, and values of the organization to achieve a breakthrough in business results. (p. 27)

register A high-speed storage area in the CPU used to temporarily hold small units of program instructions and data immediately before, during, and after execution by the CPU. (p. 94)

relational model A database model that describes data in which all data elements are placed in two-dimensional tables, called *relations*, which are the logical equivalent of files. (p. 197)

release A significant program change that often requires changes in the documentation of the software. (p. 555)

reorder point (ROP) A critical inventory quantity level that calls for more inventory to be ordered for an item when the inventory level drops to the reorder point or critical level. (p. 410)

replicated database A database that holds a duplicate set of frequently used data. (p. 218)

report layout A technique that allows designers to diagram and format printed reports. (p. 519)

request for maintenance form A form authorizing modification of programs. (p. 555)

request for proposal (RFP) A document that specifies in detail required resources such as hardware and software. (p. 539)

requirements analysis The determination of user, stakeholder, and organizational needs. (p. 517)

return on investment (ROI) One measure of IS value that investigates the additional profits or benefits that are generated as a percentage of the investment in IS technology. (p. 38)

revenue centre A division within a company that generates sales or revenues. (p. 408)

reverse 911 service A communications solution that delivers emergency notifications to users in a selected geographical area. (p. 258)

rich Internet application (RIA) Software that has the functionality and complexity of traditional application software, but does not require local installation and runs in a Web browser. (p. 304)

robotics The development of mechanical or computer devices that perform tasks requiring a high degree of precision or that are tedious or hazardous for humans. (p. 449)

router A telecommunications device that forwards data packets across two or more distinct networks toward their destinations, through a process known as routing. (p. 253)

rule A conditional statement that links conditions to actions or outcomes. (p. 456)

satisficing model A model that will find a good—but not necessarily the best—solution to a problem. (p. 399)

scalability The ability to increase the processing capability of a computer system so that it can handle more users, more data, or more transactions in a given period. (p. 123)

schedule feasibility The determination of whether the project can be completed in a reasonable amount of time. (p. 511)

scheduled report A report produced periodically, such as daily, weekly, or monthly. (p. 404)

schema A description of the entire database. (p. 203)

screen layout A technique that allows a designer to quickly and efficiently design the features, layout, and format of a display screen. (p. 518)

script bunny A cracker with little technical savvy who downloads programs called scripts, which automate the job of breaking into computers. (p. 60)

search engine A valuable tool that enables you to find information on the Web by specifying words that are key to a topic of interest, known as keywords. (p. 295)

secondary storage Devices that store large amounts of data, instructions, and information more permanently than allowed with main memory. (p. 102)

Secure Sockets Layer (SSL) A communications protocol used to secure sensitive data during e-commerce. (p. 353)

security dashboard Software that provides a comprehensive display on a single computer screen of all the vital data related to an organization's security defences, including threats, exposures, policy compliance, and incident alerts. (p. 68)

selecting Manipulating data to eliminate rows according to certain criteria. (p. 198)

semistructured or unstructured problems More complex problems in which the relationships among the pieces of data are not always clear, the data might be in a variety of formats, and the data is often difficult to manipulate or obtain. (p. 421)

sequential access A retrieval method in which data must be accessed in the order in which it is stored. (p. 102)

sequential access storage device (SASD) A device used to sequentially access secondary storage data. (p. 103)

server A computer used by many users to perform a specific task, such as running network or Internet applications. (p. 123)

service-oriented architecture (SOA) A modular method of developing software and systems that allows users to interact with systems and systems to interact with each other. (p. 157)

simplex channel A communications channel that can transmit data in only one direction and is seldom used for business telecommunications. (p. 234)

single-user licence A software licence that permits only one person to use the software, typically on only one computer. (p. 174)

site preparation Preparation of the location of a new system. (p. 550)

slipstream upgrade A minor upgrade—typically a code adjustment or minor bug fix—not worth announcing. It usually requires recompiling all the code and, in so doing, it can create entirely new bugs. (p. 555)

smart card A credit card–sized device with an embedded microchip to provide electronic memory and processing capability. (p. 354)

smartphone A phone that combines the functionality of a mobile phone, personal digital assistant, camera, Web browser, e-mail tool, and other devices into a single hand-held device. (p. 120)

social engineering Using social skills to get computer users to provide information that allows a hacker to access an information system or its data. (p. 57)

software The computer programs that govern the operation of the computer. (p. 13)

Software as a Service (SaaS) A service that allows businesses to subscribe to Web-delivered business application software by paying a monthly service charge or a per-use fee. (p. 158)

software piracy The act of unauthorized copying or distribution of copyrighted software. (p. 64)

software suite A collection of single programs packaged together in a bundle. (p. 164)

source data automation Capturing and editing data where it is initially created and in a form that can be directly input to a computer, thus ensuring accuracy and timeliness. (p. 108)

speech-recognition technology Input devices that recognize human speech. (p. 109)

spyware Software that is installed on a personal computer to intercept or take partial control over the user's interaction with the computer without knowledge or permission of the user. (p. 62)

stakeholders People who, either themselves or through the organization they represent, ultimately benefit from the systems development project. (p. 489)

start-up The process of making the final tested information system fully operational. (p. 551)

statistical sampling Selecting a random sample of data and applying the characteristics of the sample to the whole group. (p. 514)

steering committee An advisory group consisting of senior management and users from the IS department and other functional areas. (p. 511)

storage area network (SAN) A special-purpose, high-speed network that provides high-speed connections among data-storage devices and computers over a network. (p. 105)

storage as a service Storage as a service is a data storage model where a data storage service provider rents space to individuals and organizations. (p. 107)

storefront broker A company that acts as an intermediary between your website and online merchants who have the products and retail expertise. (p. 348)

strategic alliance (or strategic partnership) An agreement between two or more companies that involves the joint production and distribution of goods and services. (p. 35)

strategic planning Determining long-term objectives by analyzing the strengths and weaknesses of the organization, predicting future trends, and projecting the development of new product lines. (p. 430)

structured interview An interview where the questions are written in advance. (p. 513)

supercomputers The most powerful computer systems with the fastest processing speeds. (p. 125)

supply chain management (SCM) A system that includes planning, executing, and controlling all activities involved in raw material sourcing and procurement, converting raw materials to finished products, and warehousing and delivering the finished product to customers. (p. 379)

switch A telecommunications device that uses the physical device address in each incoming message on the network to determine to which output port it should forward the message to reach another device on the same network. (p. 253)

syntax A set of rules associated with a programming language. (p. 169)

system A set of elements or components that interact to accomplish goals. (p. 9)

system performance measurement Monitoring the system—the number of errors encountered, the amount of memory required, the amount of processing or CPU time needed, and other problems. (p. 558)

system performance products Software that measures all components of the computer-based information system, including hardware, software, database, telecommunications, and network systems. (p. 558)

system performance standard A specific objective of the system. (p. 10)

system testing Testing the entire system of programs. (p. 550)

systems analysis The systems development phase involving the study of existing systems and work processes to identify strengths, weaknesses, and opportunities for improvement. (p. 500)

systems analyst A professional who specializes in analyzing and designing business systems. (p. 490)

systems controls Rules and procedures to maintain data security. (p. 537)

systems design The systems development phase that defines how the information system will do what it must do to obtain the solution. (pp. 500 and 532)

systems implementation The systems development phase involving the creation or acquisition of various system components detailed in the systems design, assembling them, and placing the new or modified system into operation. (pp. 500 and 544)

systems investigation The systems development phase during which problems and opportunities are identified and considered in light of the goals of the business. (p. 500)

systems investigation report A summary of the results of the systems investigation and the process of feasibility analysis and recommendation of a course of action. (p. 511)

systems maintenance A stage of systems development that involves checking, changing, and enhancing the system to make it more useful in achieving user and organizational goals. (p. 553)

systems maintenance and review The systems development phase that ensures the system operates and modifies the system so that it continues to meet changing business needs. (p. 500)

systems operation Use of a new or modified system. (p. 553)

systems request form A document filled out by someone who wants the IS department to initiate systems investigation. (p. 510)

systems review The final step of systems development, involving the analysis of systems to make sure that they are operating as intended. (p. 557)

tablet computer A portable, lightweight computer with no keyboard that allows you to roam the office, home, or factory floor carrying the device like a clipboard. (p. 121)

team organizational structure A structure centred on work teams or groups. (p. 24)

technical documentation Written details used by computer operators to execute the program and by analysts and programmers to solve problems or modify the program. (p. 548)

technical feasibility Assessment of whether the hardware, software, and other system components can be acquired or developed to solve the problem. (p. 510)

technology acceptance model (TAM) A model that describes the factors leading to higher levels of acceptance and usage of technology. (p. 29)

technology diffusion A measure of how widely technology is spread throughout the organization. (p. 29)

technology infrastructure All the hardware, software, databases, telecommunications, people, and procedures that are configured to collect, manipulate, store, and process data into information. (p. 12)

technology infusion The extent to which technology is deeply integrated into an area or department. (p. 29)

telecommunications The electronic transmission of signals for communications; enables organizations to carry out their processes and tasks through effective computer networks. (p. 13)

telecommunications medium Any material substance that carries an electronic signal to support communications between a sending and receiving device. (p. 233)

telecommuting The use of computing devices and networks so that employees can work effectively away from the office. (p. 259)

thin client A low-cost, centrally managed computer with essential but limited capabilities and no extra drives (such as CD or DVD drives) or expansion slots. (p. 122)

time-driven review Review performed after a specified amount of time. (p. 557)

total cost of ownership (TCO) The sum of all costs over the life of an information system, including the costs to acquire components such as the technology, technical support, administrative costs, and end-user operations. (p. 38)

traditional approach to data management An approach to data management whereby each distinct operational system used data files dedicated to that system. (p. 192)

traditional organizational structure An organizational structure in which the hierarchy of decision making and authority flows from the strategic management at the top down to operational management and nonmanagement employees. (p. 21)

transaction processing cycle The process of data collection, data editing, data correction, data manipulation, data storage, and document production. (p. 371)

transaction processing system (TPS) An organized collection of people, procedures, software, databases, and devices used to perform and record business transactions. (p. 17)

Transmission Control Protocol (TCP) The widely used Transport-layer protocol that most Internet applications use with IP. (p. 278)

tunnelling The process by which VPNs transfer information by encapsulating traffic in IP packets over the Internet. (p. 315)

ultra wideband (UWB) A form of short-range communications that employs extremely short electromagnetic pulses lasting just 50 to 1,000 picoseconds that are transmitted across a broad range of radio frequencies of several gigahertz. (p. 239)

Uniform Resource Locator (URL) A Web address that specifies the exact location of a Web page using letters and words that map to an IP address and a location on the host. (p. 278)

unit testing Testing of individual programs. (p. 550)

unstructured interview An interview where the questions are not written in advance. (p. 513)

user acceptance document A formal agreement signed by the user that states that a phase of the installation or the complete system is approved. (p. 552)

user documentation Written descriptions developed for people who use a program; shows how the program can and should be used, in easy to understand language. (p. 548)

user interface The element of the operating system that allows you to access and command the computer system. (p. 142)

user preparation The process of readying managers, decision makers, employees, other users, and stakeholders for new systems. (p. 549)

users People who will interact with the system regularly. (p. 489)

utility program Program that helps to perform maintenance or correct problems with a computer system. (p. 153)

value chain A series (chain) of activities that includes inbound logistics, warehouse and storage, production, finished product storage, outbound logistics, marketing and sales, and customer service. (p. 19)

version A major program change, typically encompassing many new features. (p. 555)

videoconferencing A set of interactive telecommunications technologies that enable people at various locations to communicate using simultaneous two-way video and audio transmissions. (p. 260)

virtual organizational structure A structure that uses individuals, groups, or complete business units in geographically dispersed areas; these groups can last for a few weeks or years, often requiring telecommunications and the Internet. (p. 24)

virtual private network (VPN) A private network that uses a public network (usually the Internet) to connect many remote locations. (p. 256)

virtual reality The simulation of a real or imagined environment that can be experienced visually in three dimensions. (p. 17)

virtual reality system A system that enables one or more users to move and react in a computer-simulated environment. (p. 465)

virtual tape A storage device for less frequently needed data so that it appears to be stored entirely on tape cartridges, although some parts of it might actually be located on faster hard disks. (p. 104)

virtual workgroups Teams of people located around the world working on common problems. (p. 429)

vision systems The hardware and software that permit computers to capture, store, and manipulate visual images. (p. 452)

voice mail Technology that enables users to send, receive, and store verbal messages to and from other people around the world. (p. 258)

voice mail-to-text service A service that captures voice mail messages, converts them to text, and sends them to an e-mail account. (p. 258)

volume testing Testing the application with a large amount of data. (p. 550)

Web Server and client software, the hypertext transfer protocol (http), standards, and mark-up languages that combine to deliver information and services over the Internet. (p. 284)

Web 2.0 The Web as a computing platform that supports software applications and the sharing of information among users. (p. 303)

Web application framework Web development software that provides the foundational code—or framework—for a professional, interactive website, allowing developers to customize the code to specific needs. (p. 289)

Web browser Web client software such as Internet Explorer, Firefox, Chrome, Safari, and Opera used to view Web pages. (p. 284)

Web log (blog) A website that people can create and use to write about their observations, experiences, and opinions on a wide range of topics. (p. 305)

Web portal A Web page that combines useful information and links and acts as an entry point to the Web—they typically include a search engine, a subject directory, daily headlines, and other items of interest. Many people choose a Web portal as their browser's home page (the first page you open when you begin browsing the Web). (p. 299)

wide area network (WAN) A telecommunications network that connects large geographic regions. (p. 247)

Wi-Fi A medium-range wireless telecommunications technology brand owned by the Wi-Fi Alliance. (p. 239)

wireless mesh A form of communication that uses many Wi-Fi access points to link a series of interconnected local area networks to form a wide area network capable of serving a large campus or entire city. (p. 242)

workgroup Two or more people who work together to achieve a common goal. (p. 140)

workgroup application software Software that supports teamwork, whether team members are in the same location or dispersed around the world. (p. 167)

workgroup sphere of influence The sphere of influence that serves the needs of a workgroup. (p. 140)

workstation A more powerful personal computer used for mathematical computing, computer-aided design, and other high-end processing, but still small enough to fit on a desktop. (p. 123)

Worldwide Interoperability for Microwave Access (WiMAX) The common name for a set of IEEE 802.16 wireless metropolitan area network standards that support various types of communications access. (p. 244)

ZigBee A form of wireless communications frequently used in security systems and heating and cooling control systems. (p. 239)

EMC, 107, 539
Empire Online, 309
EnCana, 322
ENMAX, 503, 504
Epson, 545
Equifax Canada, 76
Ericsson, 73, 336
Expedia, 199, 311, 347

F

Facebook, 13, 15, 25, 51–52, 73, 75, 78, 86, 137, 150, 166, 172, 214, 251, 273–274, 281, 282, 287, 299, 302, 303, 304, 312, 322, 346, 384, 396, 412, 425, 427, 476, 558
Fairfield, 3
FedEx, 6, 14, 333, 365, 367, 371, 404
Ford Motor Company, 173, 412, 415, 451, 469
Fujitsu, 64, 245
Future Shop, 545

G

GarageBand, 147
Gartner Group, 38
Gartner and Forrester, 531
Geek Squad, 553
Genalytics, 214
General Electric, 36, 454, 533, 546
General Motors, 261, 468
Gillette, 33
Gilt, 344
Goodmans LLP, 163
Google, 51, 62, 64, 87, 107, 133, 140, 141, 145, 150, 152, 155, 159, 160, 164, 165, 167–168, 172, 194, 196, 201, 209, 211, 232, 245, 251, 264, 281, 282, 283, 284, 287–288, 292, 294–296, 299, 300–305, 308, 311–312, 313, 317, 330, 342, 346, 387, 403, 409, 413, 418, 441, 452, 491, 548
Greenpeace, 126

H

Hayes, 252
HCL Technologies Ltd., 46
Heartland Payment Systems, 63, 208, 334
Hess Corporation, 496
Hewlett-Packard (HP), 64, 107, 117, 121, 122, 123, 128, 149, 151, 176, 194, 333, 402, 428, 481, 504, 539, 540, 545
Hitachi Data Systems Corporation, 107
Honda Motors, 212, 414, 448
Honeywell, 564–565
Hotwire, 527–528
HTC Corporation, 65, 251
Hulu, 307
Hyatt, 321, 339

I

IBM, 27, 64, 68, 74, 91, 96, 100, 101, 107, 124, 125, 137, 141, 145, 147, 149, 151, 155, 160, 167, 176, 195, 197, 202, 205, 209, 219, 221, 227, 294, 303, 343, 350, 360, 382, 402, 415, 422, 423, 427, 445, 451, 452, 456, 460, 471, 481, 487, 502, 503, 504, 507, 510, 544, 545, 548, 550, 553, 564
    IBM Cognos 8 Business Intelligence, 45
Identity Guard, 69
ID Watchdog, 69
i4i Inc., 65
Imperial Oil, 76
Indigo Books and Music, 17, 419
Infinium, 7
Infor Corporation, 22
ING DIRECT Canada, 14
Institute of Electrical and Electronics Engineers (IEEE), 233, 239, 244
Intel, 94, 96, 97, 98, 100, 121, 122, 147, 149, 245, 468, 545

International Telecommunication Union (ITU), 233, 242
Internet Content Rating Association (ICRA), 74
Internet Corporation for Assigned Names and Numbers (ICANN), 279, 336
Intuit, 32, 160, 168, 209, 371
Iomega, 117
Iridium Communication, 241–242
ISM Inc., 384

J

JasperSoft, 382
JD Edwards, 378, 395
JEA, 476
Johnson & Johnson, 330, 414

K

Kabbani Construction Group (KCG), 375
Kijiji, 330
Kiosk, 5, 112–113, 238, 464, 504, 525, 550
KnowledgeBase, 445
Knowledge Management Consortium International, 445
Knowledge Management Resource Centre, 445
Knowledge Management Solutions, Inc., 445
Knowledge Management Web Directory, 445
Kodak, 34, 38

L

Legato Systems, Inc., 107
LEGO, 487–488
Lenovo, 64, 66, 149, 245
LexisNexis, 298, 299, 445
Life Lock, 69
LinkedIn, 148, 302, 304, 427
Lions Gate Entertainment, 73, 414
Livent Inc., 408
Lloyd's of London Insurance, 12, 219
Loopt, 312, 413, 418
Lyons Bakeries, 168

M

MAFIABOY, 268
Magnify, 214
Mahalo, 296
Mantis Development Corporation, 466
Maple Leaf Foods, 30
Marketing Architects, 105
Marriott International Inc., 3, 340, 399, 414
Massachusetts Institute of Technology (MIT), 293, 468
MasterCard, 111, 353, 355
Mazda, 360
McAfee, 154, 553
McDonald's, 280
Megavolt Design, 371
Microcom, 252
Microsoft, 13, 64, 65, 73, 74, 79, 107, 109, 112, 133, 140, 141, 143, 145–147, 148, 150, 152–153, 154, 156, 158, 159, 160, 161–165, 167–168, 170, 172, 176, 194, 196, 201–202, 207, 209, 211, 214, 218, 231–232, 239, 251, 281, 282, 283, 288, 289–290, 294, 296, 300, 302, 304, 307, 309, 312, 341, 352, 375, 376, 378, 379, 382, 385, 387, 400, 402, 424, 427, 445, 462–463, 469, 493, 507, 508, 510, 531, 545, 548, 573
MicroStrategy, 218
MITRE Corporation, 475–476
Motorola, 30, 117, 133, 147, 245, 251, 252, 264, 336, 564
MSI, 121
MSN, 296, 299, 300
MWH Global, 444
MyOwnDB, 209
MySpace, 13, 15, 51, 73, 102, 166, 273, 302, 304, 337, 396, 425, 427

Note: Page numbers in bold refer to definitions.